ISBN 978-1-5282-5768-8
PIBN 10938638

English
Français
Deutsche
Italiano
Español
Português

www.forgottenbooks.com

Mythology Photography **Fiction**
Fishing Christianity **Art** Cooking
Essays Buddhism Freemasonry
Medicine **Biology** Music **Ancient
Egypt** Evolution Carpentry Physics
Dance Geology **Mathematics** Fitness
Shakespeare **Folklore** Yoga Marketing
Confidence Immortality Biographies
Poetry **Psychology** Witchcraft
Electronics Chemistry History **Law**
Accounting **Philosophy** Anthropology
Alchemy Drama Quantum Mechanics
Atheism Sexual Health **Ancient History**
Entrepreneurship Languages Sport
Paleontology Needlework Islam
Metaphysics Investment Archaeology
Parenting Statistics Criminology
Motivational

PUBLIC BUILDING NOW BEING CONSTRUCTED IN CHICAGO.

JANUARY 16, 1903.—Ordered to be printed.

Mr. MERCER, from the Committee on Public Buildings and Grounds, submitted the following

ADVERSE REPORT.

[To accompany H. Res. No. 344.]

The Committee on Public Buildings and Grounds, to whom was referred the resolution (H. Res. No. 344) requesting the Secretary of the Treasury, if not incompatible with public interests, to furnish the House of Representatives certain information with reference to the public building now in process of construction in the city of Chicago, Ill., having considered the same, submit the following report:

Resolution No. 344 was introduced in the House of Representatives by Representative Mann, of Illinois, and referred to your committee. Thereupon a copy of said resolution was referred to the Secretary of the Treasury for consideration. On January 12, 1903, the Secretary of the Treasury filed with your committee a full report responsive to said resolution No. 344, which report is herewith filed as a part of the report of your committee. The Secretary of the Treasury having anticipated formal action by your committee and the House of Representatives in the manner above set forth, no further action by your committee with reference to said resolution is necessary, wherefore your committee recommends that this report, including the report made to this committee by the Secretary of the Treasury, be printed as a House document, and that resolution No. 344 lie upon the table.

TREASURY DEPARTMENT, OFFICE OF THE SECRETARY,
Washington, January 12, 1903.

SIR: In response to your letter of December 11, 1902, in re resolution No. 344, I herewith inclose the following papers relating thereto, viz:

Copy of—

Report of board of award, interior finish and completion, bid and contract to John Pierce, New York.

Report of board of award, draining, plumbing, and gas fitting, bid and contract to Wells & Newton Company, New York.

H R—57-2—Vol 2——1

Report of board of award, heating system, bid and contract to Thomas & Smith, Chicago.

Report of board of award, electric system, bid and contract to Arthur Frantzen Company, Chicago.

Respectfully,

L. M. SHAW, *Secretary.*

Hon. DAVID H. MERCER.
Chairman Committee on Public Buildings and Grounds.

TREASURY DEPARTMENT, OFFICE CHICAGO BUILDING,
Washington, November 12, 1902.

Synopsis of bids for the interior finish and completion of the United States post-office, court-house, etc., Chicago, Ill., received under the advertisement of October 4, 1902, and opened on November 8, 1902, in the office of the architect of the building.

No.	Bidder.	Address	Date of completion.	Amount.
1	John Peirce	New York	Apr. 1, 1904	$997,500
2	Davidson Bros. Marble Co	Chicago	June 8, 1904	1,099,000
3	John Griffiths & Son	do	May 20, 1904	1,239,900
4	William Grace Co	do	Oct. 1, 1904	1,273,000

TREASURY DEPARTMENT, OFFICE ARCHITECT OF THE BUILDING,
Washington, D. C., November 12, 1902.

The above bids were opened in this office at 2 o'clock p. m. on the 8th day of November, 1902.

A certified check for $50,000 accompanied each bid.

HENRY IVES COBB,
Architect United States Government Building at Chicago.

TREASURY DEPARTMENT, OFFICE CHICAGO BUILDING,
Washington, D. C., November 12, 1902.

Respectfully submitted to the Secretary of the Treasury.

Four bids were received under the advertisement, and are inclosed.

We recommend that the bid of John Peirce, of New York, for $997,500 be accepted, he being the lowest bidder.

HENRY IVES COBB,
Architect United States Government Building,
J. K. TAYLOR,
Supervising Architect,
CHAS. E. KEMPER,
Chief Executive Officer,
JAMES C. PLANT,
Chief Computer,
Board of Award.

Approved November 17, 1902.

H. A. TAYLOR, *Acting Secretary.*

TREASURY DEPARTMENT, OFFICE CHICAGO BUILDING,
Washington, October 13, 1902.

Synopsis of bids for the drainage, plumbing, and gas fitting of the United States post-office, court-house, etc., Chicago, Ill., received under advertisement of September, 3, 1902, and opened on October 9, 1902, in the office of the architect of the building.

No.	Bidder.	Address.	Amount.	Time.
1	The Wells & Newton Co	New York	$53,700.00	100 and 60 days.
2	Henly-Casey Co	Chicago	62,283.58	150 and 120 days.
3	E. Baggot Co	do	65,792.00	160 and 90 days.
4	P. Nacey Co	do	68,091.00	150 and 150 days.
5	F. P. Gleason & Co	do	71,553.98	395 and 270 days.
6	Boyd & Co., Incorporated	do	74,460.00	120 and 100 days.
7	M. J. Corboy	do	82,000.00	120 and 90 days.
8	Edward Joy	Syracuse	105,000.00	450 and 120 days.

TREASURY DEPARTMENT, OFFICE ARCHITECT OF THE BUILDING,
Washington, D. C., October 13, 1902.

The above bids were opened in this office after 2 o'clock p. m: on the 9th day of October, 1902.

A certified check for $5,000 accompanied each bid

HENRY IVES COBB,
Architect United States Government Building at Chicago.

TREASURY DEPARTMENT, OFFICE CHICAGO BUILDING,
Washington, D. C., October 13, 1902.

Respectfully submitted to the Secretary of the Treasury.

Eight bids were received under the advertisement, and are inclosed with a copy of the specification. We recommend that the bid of the Wells & Newton Company, of New York, for $53,700, be accepted, they being the lowest bidders. We further recommend that the other items in their bid—tile drainage, $4,100; gas fitting, $970; fire protection, $3,270; temporary fixtures, $550 —be also accepted, making their contract $62,590.

HENRY IVES COBB,
Architect United States Government Building,
J. K. TAYLOR,
Supervising Architect,
CHAS. E. KEMPER,
Chief Executive Officer,
JAMES C. PLANT,
Chief Computer,
Board of Award.

Approved October 13, 1902.

L. M. SHAW, *Secretary.*

[Pierce, Richardson & Neifer (Incorporated), engineers.]

CHICAGO, *November 18, 1902.*

SIR: In accordance with your request of the 15th instant, we submit you herewith a report on Thomas & Smith, together with our recommendation covering the award of contract for heating system for the Chicago building.

The bid of Messrs. Thomas & Smith is in strict accord with the specifications. Their ability to carry out the contract is beyond question. They are backed financially by Graham & Sons, bankers, of this city, and their credit is good with the Crane Company, as well as with all Chicago manufacturers or others, for any material they will need in this work. Their guaranteed time of completing the work, viz, two hundred working days, is five months earlier than the date of completion of the next lowest bidder. The schedule which they have submitted in accordance with paragraph 29 of specifications provides for only the highest class of apparatus.

We recommend that the contract be awarded to Thomas & Smith and that it be awarded on the straight specifications, making a total of $144,802, and that no consideration be given to alternate proposals.

Respectfully submitted.

PIERCE, RICHARDSON & NEILER,
Per SAML. G. NEILER.

HENRY IVES COBB,
Architect Chicago Building, Treasury Department, Washington, D. C.

TREASURY DEPARTMENT, OFFICE CHICAGO BUILDING,
Washington, December 3, 1902.

Synopsis of bids for the heating system of the post-office, court-house, etc., Chicago, Ill., received under advertisement of October 4, 1902, and opened on November 8, 1902, in the office of the architect of the building.

No.	Bidder	Address.	Time.	Amount.
1	Thomas & Smith	Chicago	200 and 52 days	$99,346
2	S. Faith & Co	Philadelphia	350 and 60 days	99,700
3	C B. Kruse Heating Co	Milwaukee	360 and 50 days	101,590
4	Edward Joy	Syracuse	300 and 50 days	112,798
5	William A. Pope	Chicago	285 and 66 days	118,811
6	Robert Gordon	do	300 and 38 days	129,779
7	L. H. Prentice Co	do	150 and 120 days	130,100

TREASURY DEPARTMENT, OFFICE ARCHITECT OF THE BUILDING,
Washington, D. C., December 3, 1902.

The above bids were opened in this office at 2 o'clock p. m. on the 8th day of November, 1902. The board of award recommended that the bids be referred to Pierce, Richardson & Neiler, engineers, for their report and same was approved November 13, 1902.

The report of said engineers is hereto attached.

Respectfully,   HENRY IVES COBB,
Architect United States Government Building at Chicago.

TREASURY DEPARTMENT, OFFICE CHICAGO BUILDING,
Washington, D. C., December 3, 1902.

Respectfully submitted to the Secretary of the Treasury, with the report of the engineers thereon attached.

Seven bids were received under the advertisement, and are inclosed.

We recommend that the bid of Thomas & Smith, Chicago, Ill., for $99,346 be accepted, they being the lowest bidders.

HENRY IVES COBB,
Architect United States Government Building,

J. K. TAYLOR,
Supervising Architect,

CHAS. E. KEMPER,
Chief Executive Officer,

JAMES C. PLANT,
Chief Computer,
Board of Award.

Approved, December 4, 1902.

L. M. SHAW, *Secretary.*

[Pierce, Richardson & Neiler (Incorporated), engineers.]

CHICAGO, *November 19, 1902.*

SIR: We beg to acknowledge receipt of your letter of November 15, inclosing synopsis of bids for electrical switchboard, conduit, and wiring referred to us for recommendation.

In reply we have the honor to state that we recommend the acceptance of the proposition of Arthur Frantzen Company, of Chicago. We are familiar with the work and with the reputation of this firm and believe they are thoroughly competent to execute this work in a satisfactory manner.

In connection with this contract we would recommend that japanned lined piping be used throughout the building wherever iron conduit is specified. The last item in the schedule of unit prices states the amount to be added if japanned pipe is used throughout, viz, $3,750. We mention this item at this time in order that our position in regard to the iron conduit may be understood in case it is necessary to consider the point in the drawing up of the contract.

Yours, very respectfully,

PIERCE, RICHARDSON & NEILER,
Per R. H. PIERCE.

HENRY IVES COBB,
Architect Chicago Building, Treasury Department, Washington, D. C.

TREASURY DEPARTMENT, OFFICE CHICAGO BUILDING,
Washington, December 3, 1902.

Synopsis of bids for the electric switchboard, conduit, and wiring of the post-office, court-house, etc., Chicago, Ill., received under advertisement of October 4, 1902, and opened on November 8, 1902, in the office of the architect of the building.

No.	Bidder.	Address.	Time.	Amount.
1	Arthur Frantzen Co	Chicago	270 working days.	$69,838
2	F E Newbery Co	St Louis	180 working days.	77,134
3	McCay Engineering Co	Baltimore	......do	78,440
4	Cuthbert & Black	Chicago	325 working days.	87,476
5	Chicago Edison Co	......do	180 working days.	89,516
6	J F. Buchanan & Co	Philadelphia	200 working days.	104,000

TREASURY DEPARTMENT, OFFICE ARCHITECT OF THE BUILDING,
Washington, D. C., December 3, 1902.

The above bids were opened in this office at 2 o'clock p. m. on the 8th day of November, 1902.   The board of award recommended that the bids be referred to Pierce, Richardson & Neiler, engineers, for their report, and same was approved November 13, 1902.

The report of said engineers is hereto attached.

Respectfully,   HENRY IVES COBB,
Architect United States Government Building at Chicago.

TREASURY DEPARTMENT, OFFICE CHICAGO BUILDING,
Washington, D. C., December 3, 1902.

Respectfully submitted to the Secretary of the Treasury with the report of the engineers thereto attached.

Six bids were received under the advertisement and are inclosed.

We recommend that the bid of Arthur Frantzen Company, Chicago, $69,838, be accepted, said company being the lowest bidder.

HENRY IVES COBB,
Architect United States Government Building,

J. K. TAYLOR,
Supervising Architect,

CHAS. E. KEMPER,
Chief Executive Officer,

JAMES C. PLANT,
Chief Computer,
Board of Award.

Approved December 4, 1902.

L. M. SHAW, *Secretary.*

SPECIFICATION, PROPOSAL, CONTRACT, AND BOND FOR THE INTERIOR WORK AND COMPLETION OF THE UNITED STATES POST-OFFICE, COURT-HOUSE, ETC., AT CHICAGO, ILLINOIS.

PREAMBLE.

1. Bids are invited for the interior work and completion of the new United States post-office, court-house, etc., at Chicago, Ill., otherwise designated and referred to herein as the "Chicago building," that structure now under construction upon the block bounded by Adams, Clark, Jackson, and Dearborn streets, Chicago, Ill.

2. Besides the plans and these specifications for the contemplated work, bidders may also be furnished with a set of plans and specifications of the work now under way, in order that they may familiarize themselves with what has been done and what is necessary to be done to take the building in its present inclosed condition and fully complete it according to these new specifications.   It is further suggested that parties intending to bid visit the building and acquaint themselves with its magnitude, its complications, the difficulties there may be in handling the work, storing the material, getting it in place, the proximity to railway terminals, etc.

3. By "interior work and completion" is meant that the bidders will figure upon taking the building as it is left upon the termination of the existing contract and do all of the masonry work, granite curbing in driveway, granite face of the mailing platform, all of the brickwork, plain and ornamental, foundations for inner walls, all of the fireproofing in the shape of partitions, the fireproofing of the steelwork not covered by present contract; all of the structural steelwork in false ceilings, stairs, the dome, and wherever it is called for and necessary to finish the building and has not been done under the present contract; the decorative semistructural work of all kinds; the concreting, filling-in, cement and tiling of all floors; the plastering and stuccowork throughout, the marble and mosaic work, the scagliola and plastic work; the carpenter work; the joiner work and glazing of all kinds; the hardware in every detail; the painting and polishing; the cleaning up and leaving of all parts of the building finished to the architect's perfect satisfaction and ready in his judgment for immediate occupancy.   The bidders will find marginal notes giving a more complete index as to the items of work that will have to be performed, but, inversely, they are to understand and figure accordingly that this new contract is to include the doing of everything that has not been done under the present contract to completely finish the building, excepting *only* the drainage, plumbing, and gas-fitting;

the sidewalks, arches, and finish, curbing, prismatic lights, and framed openings; the electric calls, alarms, lights, fixtures, and wires; the steam-heating and ventilation pipes, ducts, and mechanism; the elevators, pumps, dynamos, and all engines and machines; all piping, conduits, and insulation of the same; the bronze or marble statuary, and the decorative pictorial painting of the walls and ceilings.

4. Bidders must deposit two hundred dollars ($200), in the form of a certified check made payable to the Treasurer of the United States, with the architect before securing plans and specifications, as the price thereof, which amount will be refunded them upon the return of all these papers in good order to the office of the architect at Washington on or before the time set for the opening of bids.

5. Bidders must also inclose with their bids a certified check for fifty thousand dollars ($50,000), drawn to the order of the Treasurer of the United States, as a guarantee that they will enter into a contract and furnish the required bond should their particular bid be accepted.

6. Should the successful bidder, for any reason whatsoever after the time set for opening of the bids, withdraw his bid or fail or refuse to execute the formal contract and bond within two weeks after the same are mailed to the address he gives with his bid, then his certified check may be declared forfeited and the acceptance of his bid revoked, and all obligations on the part of all persons acting for or in behalf of the United States in connection with the said matter will be released and annulled.

7. The certified check of the successful bidder will be returned to him as soon as he will have executed a formal bond and contract that, in sureties and all, are satisfactory to the Secretary of the Treasury and the same has been approved in writing by the Secretary of the Treasury.

8. The certified checks of the unsuccessful bidders will be returned to them within a reasonable time after the opening of the bids, although the Department reserves to itself the right to hold the three next lowest to the successful bidder until such time as the contract has been duly awarded. In receiving these checks from all the bidders and accepting them as a part of the proposal it is distinctly understood and agreed that the Government reserves the right to cash these checks only at such times as it deems it expedient so to do for its own interests, and holds itself in no way responsible for the fund represented in the case of a bank failure or any such contingency.

9. It is the intention of the Treasury Department to award the contract in bulk to one party if it deems it to its interest so to do, and it reserves the right to waive any informality in and even to reject any and all bids. Failure to comply with any of the conditions herein set forth, or to inclose the certified check above-mentioned, will jeopardize the bid's being considered; the awarding officers of the Treasury may arbitrarily decide whether they reject or accept such a bid even though it be the lowest or otherwise advantageous.

10. While this contract is in market for public competition it must be remembered that the Treasury Department will use judgment and discrimination in awarding it, and even in giving out the plans for figures. Parties who are unfamiliar with this class of work, who have never done large work, who it is well known have not the necessary plant or who have done work for the Government before but who have given unnecessary trouble to the Departments, or parties not known to be financially responsible, parties known to be unreliable, litigious, and who have been known to do poor work, all may as well save themselves the trouble of figuring on this work. Contractors who are personally unknown to the awarding officers of the Treasury Department must establish the fact to the architect's satisfaction that they are not to be classified in the foregoing category before plans and specifications are issued to them. Such issue of plans and specifications is absolutely at the discretion of the architect and does not obligate the Department to consider or accept the resultant bid.

11. Neither will bids be considered for portions of the work. Parties wishing to figure parts of the work must do so with the general contractors.

12. A bid must be made on the blank hereto attached. It must not be detached from this package to which it is bound, nor must any of the papers be detached therefrom; the entire package must be returned in good order and with all the blanks and items in the final bid filled out, but no marks or erasures made on the contract or any of the other papers.

13. A bid submitted by a firm must be signed by each member of the firm with his name in full or by one member having authority to sign each such name, and that submitted by a corporation must be signed with the name of the corporation and the full name of each of its executive officers or their properly authorized attorney, and it must bear the corporate seal in all due form.

14. Particular attention is called to the itemized schedule of prices, the alternative

bids, and the separate bids; all these are as important as the bulk sum itself.   There
are bound to be many changes in the work on so large and complicated a building as
this as it goes on; these changes will be paid for or deducted for according to that
schedule and items; much work, perforce, will be executed on the basis of that
itemization, the plans but tentatively show how many doors there will be ultimately,
or how many lineal feet there will be of partitions, or of tile flooring, etc., the quan-
titative element of the work will necessarily be most elastic, therefore is that schedule of the utmost importance.   So much so, that in weighing and comparing the
bids the differences in those items of cost will carry perhaps more weight than even
the bulk amounts.

15. Bidders must be prepared to submit samples of meterial called for herein should
the same be asked for by the architect before a contract is entered into.

16. Wherever "architect" is mentioned in these papers, the duly appointed architect of the Chicago building, an officer of the Treasury Department, is meant, and
wherever the contractor is spoken of it means the individual or company, or the
firm to whom will be awarded this contract.

17. Attention is also called to the fact that the question of time in which the work
may be completed is a consideration of great weight in the award.   Bidders will
state in the proper blank space the number of months in which they will agree to
complete the building from the time of the signing of the contract.   Although the
present contract is not yet entirely completed the work is in such condition that the
contractor for the interior work will be given access to the building, and he may be
getting his materials together, making the necessary shop drawings, and even working upon the premises at such places as may be designated by the architect during
the few remaining months between the time of signing of the new contract and the
time of completion of the present contract.   In this connection the bidder must
understand that at no time will he have exclusive possession of the premises.   His
rights will be clearly defined by the architect; any disputes arising on this point, or
any other point, for that matter, must be submitted to the architect, whose decision
in all matters will be final.   The contractor for this work must perform it in harmony
with not only the contractor who is completing the structural part, but also with the
different contractors for the heating, plumbing, etc.   Further instructions in this
connection will be found throughout these papers.

18. Bidders are requested to register their bids and to mail them sufficiently early
to reach this office before the hour named.   No telegraphic bids or modifications will
be considered at that time.   Properly addressed and franked envelopes will be found
with these papers for their return.

19. Bidders are invited to be present at the openings of the bids.   The attention
of bidders is called to the act of Congress approved August 1, 1892, limiting the
hours of labor employed upon public works of the United States to eight hours in
any one calendar day.

20. The architect has endeavored to make this specification perfectly clear and all-
covering, and the bidders are requested to refrain from asking for further information, particularly before reading it all over.   Unless very relevant no questions will
be answered by the architect.   The answering of all such questions entails considerable trouble, for, if the architect does answer them, both question and answer must
be sent to every bidder.

21. No member of Congress, or officer, inspector, or clerk of the Treasury Department shall be interested, either directly or indirectly, in this contract or the work
herein provided for, or in any subcontract, or be entitled to any benefit derived
therefrom; and any violation of the spirit or wording of this understanding shall
work a forfeiture of all moneys which may become due to the contractor for this
work.

22. The contractor must carry at his expense all the necessary policies of insurance
on the work and material supplied by him, as the same will be at his risk until the
final acceptance of the work.   Should any or all parts of his work in place be
destroyed by fire he and his bondsmen will be held to replace it all with new, and
again complete the work in its entirety before being released from their obligations
by the final acceptance of the architect.   Should there be a fire, from whatever cause,
during the execution of this work this contractor is alone responsible for his part of
the work that may be destroyed; hence the necessity to him of his keeping it well
insured.   The contractor will, however, be relieved of any risk for any portion of the
building that the Government may be permanently and formally occupying before
he has completed his entire contract.

23. In this connection it is further to be understood that the contractor will hold
himself ready to particularly expedite certain portions of the work, or parts of the
building, for which he will receive a special order from the architect.   It is not

intended to work any hardship upon the contractor, but contingencies may arise that will make it desirable for the Government to occupy some portions of the building before it is entirely ready.

24. In this case the contractor will not only have to hurry that particular part of the work above all others, but may have to proceed with it while the employees of the Government are moving in fixtures, desks, etc., and perhaps even carrying on the regular clerical work. The Government merely reserves this right.

25. This contractor must work not only in harmony with the best interests of the Government, but it must be remembered that there will be several other contracts going on at the same time as this—heating, plumbing, etc.; and this contractor must do everything that lies in his power, or that the architect can reasonably expect of him, to assist the other contractors in performing perfect work, each in his own line, and he must lay out his work, his apparatus, column furring, false ceilings, decorative beams, and all such details that will enable these other contractors to run their pipes, ducts, etc., through these various portions, at their proper angles and exact locations. The brunt of all this work necessarily must be on this contractor; his the task of laying out everything, providing the foundation, the supports, the exact location for everything that enters into the completion of this building. He must accommodate these other men by laying such framework or building such portions as they may need for the support or concealment of their piping, etc., and then leave that portion of the work free for them to operate in, resuming his plastering, finishing, etc., when their work is properly installed. These other contractors will be placed under proper restrictions by their contracts, and the architect will see that no injustice is done either party or advantage taken by any party, and to the architect must be submitted any dispute or controversy that may arise in this connection. While it is understood that this contractor is to leave the building completed and cleaned up ready for occupancy, it is not intended that he should suffer through the negligence of others. Therefore, should the other contractors, through neglect or for other reasons, not have their work properly installed in the various rooms before this contractor is ready to finish them, then he may ask of the architect and the latter may give him an order to complete his work in those particular places, and in this case the other or derelict contractor will have to cut this completed work to install his specialty, and replace it and finish it in perfect shape without any expense to this contractor. This is not intended, however, to relieve this contractor from the ordinary cutting and patching that is bound to occur in every building, and in this case, as in all others, the architect will be the arbiter as to the contractors' rights and claims.

26. This contractor is to do all the work necessary to the perfect completion of his contract. He is to furnish all the transportation, labor, materials, apparatus, scaffolding, and utensils necessary for the performing of his work in the best manner, to the satisfaction of the architect, according to the true intent and meaning of these specifications and the drawings which accompany them. He is to rectify any failure resulting from negligence or fault of material, and is to maintain secure and firm and in perfect shape the whole of his work, including any and all changes, should such be made by the architect.

27. All the work described in the specifications and shown on the drawings, or necessary to the carrying out of the true intent and spirit thereof, is to be executed in a thoroughly workmanlike manner. All materials are to be of the very best description, unless otherwise distinctly described; and in case the work done or materials provided should be unsatisfactory, even if they be permanently fixed in place, the contractor, upon being notified by the architect, must immediately remove such unsatisfactory work or materials and replace the same to the architect's satisfaction.

28. In this connection it is well to remember that the excuse that such and such material is "ordinary and usual" will not be accepted. This is not an ordinary building. It is a monumental building, and everything about it, unless otherwise specified, must be of the very highest quality and workmanship. It has not been attempted to show every item and iota of work on the plans. Sufficient has been shown, however, to convey an idea of what is wanted, and of the manner of assembling, and of the form of detail. Should a question arise as to the performance of some work not specifically shown on the plans, but evidently necessary to complete the building, the contractor is not the judge as to how it shall be done because he did it so and so somewhere else in some other building, but it must be carried out in perfect consonance with the remainer of the work, of the same high quality, and to the architect's perfect satisfaction.

29. The Department, acting for the United States, through its architect, reserves the right to suspend any portion of the work embraced in the contract whenever, in its opinion, it would be inexpedient to carry out said work.

30. Time, as has been stated, is one of the essential conditions of this contract.

Should the contractor fail to complete all the work herein specified or shown on the plans and deemed necessary to complete the work, he will be assessed one hundred dollars ($100) per day for every day's delay after the time he contracts to complete the building. Said fixed sum is computed, estimated, and agreed upon as the minimum amount of liquidated damages caused the United States by reason of continued expenses, rentals, salaries of the contingent force at the building, and other expenses entailed upon the Government by reason of such delay: Provided, however, that the collection of said sum may, at the discretion of the Secretary, be waived in whole or part, and that the contractor will be entitled to one day in addition to said stipulated time for each day's delay that may be caused him by the Government by reason of additional work ordered or other causes that may be deemed just reason for such concession by the architect.

31. The final inspection and acceptance of the work shown by the drawings and herein specified and forming a part of the contract shall not be binding or conclusive upon the United States if it shall subsequently appear that the contractor willfully, fraudulently, or through collusion with any representative of this Department, supplied inferior material or workmanship or has departed from the terms of his contract. In any such case the United States shall have the right, notwithstanding any such inspection and acceptance, to cause the work to be executed and satisfactory material supplied to such extent as in the opinion of the architect may be necessary to finish the work in due accordance with said drawings, specifications, and contract, at the cost and expense of the contractor and the sureties on his bond, and shall have the right to recover against the contractor and his sureties the cost of all such work, together with such other damages as the United States may suffer because of the defaults of said contractor in the premises, the same as though final acceptance and payment had not been made.

32. The drawings referred to in these specifications are Nos. 104, 105, 106, 107, 108, 109, 110, 111, 112, 113, 114, 115, 116, 117, 118, 119, 120, and 121. During the progress of the work other drawings and full-sized details may be made by the architect to further illustrate his idea as to how this work shall be performed.

33. The structural drawings of this building and the specifications for the contract under which the building is now being erected may likewise be furnished the bidder that he may see just in what condition the building will be turned over to him should he be awarded the contract, but he must not use the dimensions shown on the drawings or depend upon the condition of the work so specified without verifying the same at the building. The building is there substantially as it will be turned over to him—with the fireproof flooring laid between beams, the remainder of the structural work exposed, and some of the window openings closed with cotton and boarding—and in that condition will the contractor accept the building and put in his work so that it fits and covers and conforms in every part to this structural framework now in place. The failure of the contractor to visit the premises and verify the condition of everything there with the specifications for the structure will in no way relieve him of the necessity of furnishing all the materials and labor contemplated by these specifications and drawings made necessary by the structural condition of the building when turned over to this contractor.

34. The Department reserves the right to make any additions to, modifications, changes, or omissions from the work, as contemplated by these specifications and plans, without notice to the surety on the bond given to secure compliance with the terms of the contract. That contract is for a complete building; it is certain that many slight changes will become necessary as the work progresses; these will be ordered by the architect in writing and they will be as essential to the completion of the building as is any one of the items herein mentioned, and are therefore made, in advance, part and parcel of the contract, and the sureties on the bond become responsible for them as well as for the contract in the main. Such changes will always be paid for or deducted on the basis of the items herein enumerated and priced by the contractor, or in the absence of a specific item then such changes or omissions will be settled at market rates or upon the basis of a supplementary bid on this item that may be approved by the architect.

35. In connection with this matter of changes, it is hardly possible that changes will be made that may affect the time of the completion under this contract and bond. Chances are that any changes that may become necessary will be made well in advance of the time in which special material therefor may be needed, and few such changes can involve any question of time. However, when such changes may be ordered, if the contractor believes he is justified in asking for additional time on his contract, he is to make request immediately upon receipt of the order for such additional time.

36. Should the architect desire to make a change in the material or workmanship

in certain rooms or details, he is not to be confronted with the statement that such work has been ordered and partly executed. Until sufficient proof is shown him that the material has not only been ordered, but is actually worked into such shape that it can not then be changed, will he be at perfect liberty, and without cost, to make such change of form, etc., as he deems necessary; and none of this work is to be so cut or shaped, or set in place, without the shop working drawings therefor being first submitted to the architect for his approval.

37. No charge for material ordered will be approved by the architect for any change in the materials or workmanship that may have been ordered before the materials were supplied or the actual work done upon that portion of the building according to the original plans, nor will prospective profits ever be allowed for in such changes.

38. The plans show the general form and the detailed sheets are typical of the various branches of the work they show, but the contractor undertakes to make and submit for approval, full-sized, detailed, shop drawings for every item and portion of the work; likewise will he make suitable clay models of all ornamental work, and patterns for all metal work, and colored cartoons for all stained glass and glass and marble mosaic work. The architect shall, at his discretion, have these drawings, models, and patterns submitted to him at his office, at the building, or shall go to the various shops or contractors' premises to there inspect them, as he may deem best and expedient. And all such work, as well as samples of materials, must be submitted for inspection well in advance of the time that they will actually be required, in order to afford the architect ample opportunity to change the same, should he deem it necessary.

39. The contractor binds himself to have all these models, drawings, etc., made by the highest class of specialists and draftsmen and artists in the various lines.

40. Such men must not merely mechanically enlarge the small details already supplied by the architect, but must be of such caliber as to grasp his full meaning and to interpret in the very highest expression of his specialty the spirit of the architect's design. The contractor must submit the names of such specialists as will be intrusted with these various lines of work to the architect for his approval before he engages them.

41. Some of the drawings herein referred to were completed and printed some time ago, since when the architect has had occasion to change the nature of some of the work in a slight degree. The larger-scale details will, of course, take precedence over what may be shown on the small plans and scales, and the itemization of the work in these specifications—the last thing done before asking for bids—will necessarily take precedence, should there be any divergence, over what may be shown on the aforementioned general plans and small-scale drawings.

42. The contractor shall provide and maintain the necessary lights, guards, etc., for the proper protection of the public on the streets adjacent to the building. He must conform to all municipal ordinances, and procure and pay for all licenses, permits, etc., for his work, should the same be customary. He shall keep the doors and openings at the street level closed to the public and to all parties not having business in the building. He shall maintain certain openings open during business hours under the care of competent watchmen, who will not allow anyone to pass into the building unless provided with a written card or pass or number, issued by the contractor, or the architect, or the other contractors for their work upon the building. He is to maintain such openings as the architect shall think it requires to properly do the work, all during the time or life or this contract and from its very beginning. The contractors for the other work, plumbing, heating, etc., will have to have protection for their material and work in place; but the Government will not compel them to provide watchmen, doorkeepers, etc., but looks to this contractor to make the proper charge in this contract for the protection of all the work that may now be in place in the structure or may be put there by the other contractors. This is not to be a merely nominal watching and protecting, but must be efficient, and carried on night and day, to the perfect satisfaction of the architect.

43. By protection is meant that watchmen are to be provided to keep people out, and other guards provided to police the building by day and night, to protect against fire, disorder on the part of the workmen, to see that openings in the floors are guarded, that the men are not exposed to accident, etc. The entire work is placed in the keeping of this contractor, and to him and his bondsmen the Government looks for a proper stewardship thereof. He is likewise to sufficiently protect all the work all the time from all damages by the weather, storms, accidents, or by marring by anyone about the building. The architect will be the judge as to what sufficient protection means. He may also direct that when certain rooms or portions of building are completed, in their finish this contractor is to close off such parts with tem-

porary doors. He is the judge as to how much hose the contractor is to maintain for fire protection, when and how the fence surrounding the lot shall be taken down and where it shall be stored (it remains the property of the United States), etc.

44. If in the course of the execution of this work this contractor has to tear down or in any way disturb the work of the other contractors for plumbing, heating, ventilating, etc., he shall have the same properly replaced by the said contractors, but at his expense.

45. Wash sinks and water-closets, and a temporary water supply and pumps therefor, for general purposes of the building, will be provided by the plumbing contractor just as soon as possible. They will be for the use of all the men employed about the building, but shall be under this contractor's jurisdiction and protection. He shall see that closets, etc., are kept clean and in good condition. Until such time as these closets are installed at convenient points about the building he must see to it that all the men engaged upon the building use the closets now in place in the basement for the use of the men employed in the structural work. This contractor shall also pay for the operation of the temporary water-supply plant provided by the plumber. There will be convenient outlets about the various stories.

46. The hauling of heavy material shall be done through the main driveway, from thenceto the middle of the dome, and hoisted to the various stories through that dome until such time as the contractor for elevators shall have installed a temporary elevator service, which will be for the use of *all* the contractors upon the building. The Government will employ the necessary attendants to run the cars, but this contractor must agree with the contractor for the elevators as to whether the latter will put in boiler and engine, pump, etc., for the operation of these elevators, the actual (fuel and maintenance) expense of which shall be borne by this contractor alone, or whether said elevator constructor will install a temporary electric hoist with connections to the city power, to be paid for by this contractor. Until such time as some proper installation can be made, all the contractors may use the dome for hoisting purposes, and with such appliances—steam, electric, or hand power—as they may deem suitable and have approved by the architect, but the location of their hoisting machines must be subject to the instructions of the architect, and he, at any time, may order changes in said locations to be made, but in no case will a hoisting-engine boiler be allowed inside the building. The superintendent may grant permission to any of the contractors to set up an engine at some suitable point on the roofs of the main wings, or on the roofs of the two-story part, but in such place, however, that the smoke will not damage or soil any of the work now in place or that may be hereafter erected. Even as to the hoisting engines so erected on the roofs the superintendent will be the judge of the kind of coal that will be permitted to be used.

47. If lights are required about the building, properly protected temporary wires may be brought in from the city lighting companies' plants, and each contractor will pay for the light he uses in his work. This will be a subject for agreement between them, but no candles or other dangerous lights will be allowed about the premises. This will come under the proper policing of the building by this contractor, for which he will be accountable to the architect.

48. The contractor for the heating will install his direct-heating plant just as soon as possible, and he will provide sufficient radiation, in the opinion of the architect, to heat the building sufficiently to prevent damage by frost and to permit that the men may work conveniently all through the winter. The Government will operate the plant, but the cost of the fuel will be borne by this contractor.

In General.

49. One of the first things to be done by this contractor, before winter sets in, is to provide sufficient protection (if such does not now exist) at all openings against cold and the elements.

50. He is to insert the permanent sash as soon as building is in condition to receive them and will keep them in repair during progress of work.

51. When required, the contractor must furnish samples, in quantity and size wanted, of anything entering into this work that the architect may demand, and at all times the contractor shall afford every opportunity to the architect or his assistants to visit and inspect all plants, shops, or manufactories where any of the work is being done that will enter this building.

52. The contractor shall give his personal superintendence to the work. He is to keep a general superintendent, who is satisfactory to the architect, constantly upon the premises while the work is in progress; a responsible man and one having full authority to act for the contractor in his absence and to receive the instructions of

the architect or his deputies. The contractor shall also keep skilled foremen on the premises during the execution of each of the several branches of the work. The architect or his superintendent may at any time order the removal of any particular foreman, workman, or workmen from the building if in his judgment it will be for the best interests of the work that such individual or individuals should be removed.

53. All royalties for patents or damages for infringements thereof that may be involved in the prosecution of this work for the use thereof shall be included in the contract, and the contractor hereby assumes them to the absolute relief of the Government or any and all of its officers.

54. The contractor shall not make subcontracts with contractors not satisfactory to the architect. He shall obtain the approval of the architect before entering into such subcontracts, and while the architect, at his discretion, may instruct such subcontractor about his branch of the work, it is distinctly understood that even though such party should receive direct communication from the office of the architect, he is in no way to be recognized as a party to this contract or having any authority whatever in the premises. The Secretary of the Treasury and the architect will only recognize the party or parties who sign the contract, and under no circumstances will they recognize any subcontractor's claim for material, workmen's wages for men engaged upon the building or for any work embraced in this contract, or in any manner appertaining to the transaction of any business, or the adjustment of any accounts, or of any payments on account of the work.

55. The contractor, in equity and fair dealing, should advise each and every person with whom he may have any transaction for the supplying of materials or labor of the above notification, so that they may adopt such measures as they may deem proper to secure payment to them for such material and labor as they may supply this contractor in connection with the work and for which the architect, or the Secretary of the Treasury, will not in any way be responsible. The United States reserves the right to demand at any time before paying a certificate a properly executed affidavit from the contractor giving all claims and liabilities for labor and materials outstanding against him for this building.

56. No subcontractor or person furnishing material or work to the contractor will be recognized, as above stated, except as provided for by act of Congress approved August 13, 1894, which requires that before the commencement of the work the contractor shall execute a penal bond with good and sufficient surety providing that he shall promptly make payments to all persons supplying him with materials or labor for the prosecution of the work provided for in such contract.

57. By the terms of this contract, therefore, the contractor is to make prompt payment to all persons furnishing labor or materials used in the prosecution of the work. The Department, of course, can not be held responsible in any way for the claims of such persons; nevertheless, parties so furnishing materials or labor have a right of action on said bond, in the name of the United States, for their use.

58. The contractor, by entering into this agreement, accepts the building as it is; it is presumed that it is in accordance with the plans and specifications for the structure, copies of which are furnished him, but should there be any discrepancies in the levels, or other inaccuracies, this contractor will rectify them in order that his work shall conform, as stated before, to the spirit of these designs and specifications.

59. He is to furnish all the steel framing that is now shown on these drawings for the interior work, or that may be deemed necessary by the architect for the proper support and carrying of false ceilings, columns, and the other portions entering into this contract, and there are cases where he will receive orders from the architect to change some of the existing framing erected by the contractor for the structural work. There are places where stairs were intended in the original plans that are not now needed and there are places where stairs or elevators will now run that were not originally intended. These changes necessitate alterations in the existing framing. He will do all such work at a per pound ratio for the removal of structural steel (the actual steel to remain the property of the United States), and at a per pound ratio for the furnishing and erection of new steel framing where such structural changes are needed.

60. Should it become necessary to make changes in other portions of the structural work, the granite, the roof, etc., a reasonable price therefor will be awarded by the architect.

61. The contractor must exercise care in not overloading any portion of the structure with materials. This falls under his duty of policing the building, and he shall see that the other contractors do not overload the structure with their materials.

MASONRY, CONCRETE, FIREPROOF PARTITIONS, ETC., AND THE STEEL WORK IN CONNECTION THEREWITH.

62. In the driveway suitable footing stones, 12 inches thick by 3 feet wide, will be laid in a properly excavated trench, and upon this foundation will be laid a brick

wall with a granite facing, all properly bonded together, up to the top of the base course on the one side and to the buffer block on the other. In this wall and above it will be set the proper steel tees and channels for the door and window frames, and across them, or in places where there are no jambs of steel, in the brick walls themselves will be placed the proper door and window heads of tees, or other sections, with sufficient bearing and anchored in the walls or riveted together. And all such steelwork framing for the openings shall be thoroughly painted with two coats of red lead and oil before being placed in the wall, and then thoroughly slushed and embedded in the mortar of the wall when in place. On the engine-room side of the driveway, above this granite base, will be built a brick wall, faced with the highest grade American enameled cream-colored brick. This facing will be laid to a ¼-inch joint of cement mortar and will be bonded to the backing with galvanized-iron straps. On the post-office side, on the level of the mailing platform, will be another line of footing, and a similarly faced brick wall around the openings that will be framed in steel as above described. There will be a continuous wheel guard of granite each side of this driveway. There will be suitable wheel blocks at all the angles and guide ways off of this driveway. All this granite shall be from the same quarry, or similarly colored stone as is the structural work of the building. It will be 8-cut work and set with a ¼-inch cement joint.

63. When these driveway walls are completed and cleaned down, the joints both in the granite and the enameled brick will be raked out and then pointed with a nonstaining Portland cement mortar. The inner line of the brick backing in all these walls will be hollow brick, and the brick used for the backing will be the best quality of hard-burned common brick; no bats will be used and great care must be exercised in handling.

64. The foundations for the machinery, engines, etc., will be executed by the other contractors, but this contractor must provide suitable footing courses of stone or of concrete for all the basement walls and other foundations, not for machinery, that will be required in the basement, driveway, vaults, etc.

65. Where shown, brick walls in the basement must be built of a good, well-burned hollow brick.

66. The mortar used in all this brickwork will be composed of 3 parts clean sharp sand and 1 part American Portland cement. The brickwork will be laid with a flush struck joint and grouted at each course. Every fifth course will be a heading course and in warm weather the bricks must be thoroughly wetted. Proper care must be taken in bonding all those walls into the existing structure. The door and window frames of wood or of steel, whichever is directed, shall be properly set in these brick walls.

67. When the main hauling of material, etc., is done, the drainage all in place—in fact, just before the final completion of this general contract—the concreting of the basement shall be performed. Meanwhile, proper excavations shall be made, tamped, and prepared, and the earth so taken off may be used to level up portions that are below the established grade, or else entirely removed from the building.

68. Concrete composed of a high-grade American Portland cement, 1 part to 2 parts sand and 5 parts of broken or crushed stone, not over 1 inch in diameter, will then be laid and rammed in place to a thickness of 6 inches in the building part and 10 inches in the driveway from street to street. This concrete must be thoroughly and properly mixed before being used.

69. In such rooms of the basement where there will be no wood floor, this concrete will be topped off with a 1-inch coat of American Portland cement, 1 part cement to 3 parts sand, well troweled down to a smooth even finish.

70. Where wood flooring is to be laid, sleepers of beveled pine will be laid on top of 4 inches of concrete and then filled in between with thin gravel concrete instead of broken stone, and finished off with a smooth topping of American Portland cement. These strips will be 3 by 4's, beveled white pine, laid 16 inches on centers.

71. The driveway concrete will be covered with 4 inches thick of sharp, coarse sand, and a pavement will be laid thereon, to the proper pitch and grade, of asphalt concrete blocks of standard make and paving dimensions, true and smooth, and grouted full with best hot asphalt. The floors of the vaults under the sidewalk will be of finished concrete and concreted for wood floors same as above specified. The area ways will be concreted 6 inches deep and finished with a sheet asphalt paving the same as standard street paving. In all rooms, areas, etc., where there is a finished asphalt or cement floor, the same will be carried up in a quarter circle 2 inches high in all corners and angles. There will be no sharp angles at any junction of floor and wall or columns.

72. In laying this concrete flooring, care must be taken to properly cover and protect all plumbing, drains, ventilating, and electric-wire conduits. Proper connections will have to be made with all manholes and other openings into such pipes and runways, drainheads, etc.

73. When the other contractors have laid their conduits, ducts, etc., on the floors of the building, this contractor will proceed and build up a floor to the level of the tops of the beams, as follows: He will lay cross walls of 3-inch fireproof tile, forming squares about 15 inches either way to within 2 inches of the tops of the beams. These division tiles will be set in a good cement mortar and will be cut out to over-lap and protect all the pipes, conduits, ducts, etc.

74. Over these cross walls he will lay a 2-inch slab of fireproofing 18 inches square, also set in a cement mortar. In no case will this slab tile be supported by a pipe or duct, but must have a bearing arranged on the crisscross walls of tile. The lightest kind of porous terra cotta will be used for this leveling floor. The object in using it is to avoid the weight of solid concrete, which is usually used to fill up such space. Partitions of any height must rest upon a solid foundation of tile, not upon this built-up tile in false floors.

75. On top of this leveling floor, flush with the tops of the beams, will be laid 3 by 4 beveled strips of white pine, 16 inches on centers crossways of the beams, and clamped thereto with regular "holdfasts" nipped over the flanges of the beams in such rooms as will be floored with wood. Between these strips will be laid and rammed a 3-inch layer of grouting composed of 1 part American Portland or other equally good cement and 5 parts sand. (No cinders, clinkers, or any such partially carbonized material will be used anywhere about the building for concrete.) Smooth over with a 1-part-cement to 2-part-sand floating coat. This same form of grouting, and a floating coat (of nonstaining Portland cement), without the strips, will be laid on all floors that are to be tiled, marble or mosaic, and of such thick-ness as will allow of the proper laying of the finished floor. All this surface must be of such a nature as will withstand the rather rough usage it will meet with during the completion of the building, and must not crumble or crack.

76. It may be deemed inexpedient to lay the conduits for the electric wires before this leveling floor is set, in which case this contractor, upon the order of the archi-tect, will follow up the electrical contractor and lay the finishing strips and concrete in room after room as the other contractor completes his work. Under some circum-stances the architect will permit the electrical contractor to cut into the finished concrete and strips of certain rooms to make changes or even to lay these conduits. In such cases this contractor is to follow up such work and repair it properly before laying his finished floor, but in time enough for it to thoroughly dry before the wood is laid upon it.

77. The mailing platform in the basement will have a bed of 6-inch concrete, then 4 by 4 beveled strips, with the intervening spaces filled with concrete as specified above.

78. Except where otherwise specified, all the fireproof tiling, column covers, fur-ring, etc., will be of porous, hollow, "hard-burned" tile of the best quality and man-ufacture that the market affords, carefully molded, square and true, and *extra* deeply scored on the surface. Samples of this fireproofing must be approved by the archi-tect before the contractor will be permitted to place any in the building. It will be rigidly inspected, and in this connection the contractor is advised that with this and with all other materials it is cheaper and better for him to only bring to the building such grades as he knows will be accepted than it will be to have to haul away rejected material. In a general way this fireproofing must have about 40 per cent of its area void. It will all be laid and jointed in a mortar of 3 parts sharp sand and 1 part American Portland cement. (Wherever American Portland cement is specified it must be understood that the contractor may submit samples of other equally good cements that he desires to use, and if they meet with the approval of the architect, he may use them exclusively.) Joints shall not exceed ⅜ of an inch; no broken tile will be used and no shimming-up with other materials shall be permitted. Tiles specially made or accurately cut must be used for odd angles and shapes. All the work shall be properly anchored together and to the other parts with approved gal-vanized-iron strap anchors. The partitions shall be of the various thicknesses shown on the plans and details. Only those specifically called for will be 6 inches; all the others will be 4 inches. Particular attention is called to the scoring required. This scoring all to be not over an inch apart and at least ¼ of an inch deep, and very ragged.

79. Where there are openings left in the floors, where stairs were originally intended, etc., by contractor for structure, and these do not now conform with present plans, they are to be filled in as directed by this contractor.

80. Around all the columns in the basement, first and second stories, contractor will build a protecting furring of 4-inch tile. The corners will break joints and will be clamped down or bonded with galvanized-iron anchors. This furring will be set in a strong cement mortar, and care must be exercised that all air spaces are cleaned

and continuous from top to bottom. The sixteen main dome columns will also be furred to the eleventh story with 4-inch tile. All the other columns will be furred with 3-inch tile, all properly bonded, anchored, cemented, and cleaned. As this furring of the columns is carried up, a grouting of one part lime to four parts coarse sand will be run in between the steel and the furring; the purpose is to entirely and absolutely cover the steel work with this grouting, and thereby prevent the rusting that will even occur in spite of the painting already applied. This work will have to be very carefully done, and the architect will exact most rigid compliance with these instructions. From time to time he may order the fireproofing removed in part from some of these columns to see that this work has been well done. On the columns that have cover plates, some 500 in all, the space between the steel and the furring will permit of only a very little similar filling of this same grouting, but at the tops of these columns, under each floor and as high up as it can be done, this contractor shall drill an inch hole through the steel cover plate, through which, by a properly contrived funnel apparatus, he shall pour a similar grouting as thinly mixed as the architect will permit into the space between the Z bar and the cover plate. It shall be poured a little at a time, under the direction of the superintendent, and every care must be taken that the spaces are absolutely well filled up and protected. At all intersections of framing of floor beams into these columns where the fireproofing actually in place does not absolutely cover all the steel, properly slush around with cement grouting, and at all other places where the framework is at all exposed, before any decoration or steel is set in place, do such grouting so as to thoroughly protect the steel work at every point where it may be attacked by rust. This is of the most vital importance, and the contractor is requested to make such allowance in his figures for this work as will permit him to do this work conscientiously and well.

81. The partitions, whether of 6 or 4 inch tile, shall be carefully laid in cement mortar, well tied and anchored together with galvanized-iron anchors and clamps, and in all these partitions will be built in the steel or wood frames for the doors and windows or other openings. The lintels over double doors will be 2½-inch 2.9-pound tee irons, and 4 x ⅜ inch bar over all single doors, but in all cases, whether there be steel jambs or merely the partition built up to the frame, these lintels will extend into the wall at each side of the opening at least 18 inches bearing, and the tile walls that set above these lintels should be most carefully built, and with a thin joint, and extra anchored, to prevent the unsightly cracks that usually occur in such partitions over the door heads.

82. The I beam mullions in the corridor partitions, shown on sheet 119, will be dispensed with; a 4 x 4 inch pine mullion being used instead.

83. At many of the columns and in pretty nearly every room in the building there will be pipes and ducts running from floor to floor. All these pipes will have to be built into the partitions or furring; special tile may have to be used in cases to form a neat pilaster around all such projections into rooms. Where directed, these projections may be made up of angle bars and expanded metal, well bound together, instead of fireproof tile. The outer walls of several of the stories will have to be plugged and furred with 2-inch hollow tile, properly set in cement mortar and fastened to the plugs in the brick wall with long galvanized nails and washers every alternate course and about 2 feet apart. All these partition furring tiles are to be laid true and straight and vertical. They must be tried with a straightedge and brought to the proper line, so that in no case will there be more than ¾ inch to make up in the plastering for a true surface. Around the steam risers, water conductors, and the telephone or other runways on the tile walls this outside furring will be formed in pilasters extending, where possible, into the corners of the rooms, or, if in the center of the wall, then a pilaster equidistant from both windows will be formed. The object is to make all these projections symmetrical in a room. In some of the stories the details will show that the window sills and jamb project beyond the present line of the inside of the wall. All such projections shall be made up with furring tile.

84. In all this outside furring and in the partitions of such rooms as will be finished in wood there shall be inserted in the tile proper wooden blocks, to which may be nailed the baseboard, wainscoting, jambs, picture molding, etc.; and in all rooms cement finished or otherwise, blocks will be inserted for the reception of the picture molding.

85. Extra care will have to be taken in high stretches of fireproof walls, such as those inclosing the elevator shafts, stairs, etc., to get them exactly plumb and well anchored at every story and to the columns as they go up.

86. Wherever encountered, either in this fireproofing work of tile or in any false work of expanded metal, when once fastened to the structural framing the latter

must be properly inclosed and protected with other fireproofing slabs and a grouting of cement, so that, as above instructed, *all* the structural steel about the building will be absolutely incased in an impervious covering of cement.

87. Sheet 117 indicates in a general way the steel framing that will be required for the false ceilings and other work in the court rooms and the dome. This drawing is typical and is the guide to the style of all the work that will be required of the contractor all through the building in this connection. This framing must be securely fastened to the structural work, must be painted before it leaves the shops, and again when set in place, with good red lead and oil metal paint, and the last coat will have the addition of 38 per cent graphite, so as to make it of a different color than the first.

88. All the ceilings under the roofs, in the corridors under the ventilating ducts, and in many rooms through which ventilating ducts have to pass there will be suspended ceilings. These suspended ceilings in the corridors will be of 4-inch tees extending from the partition walls into the rooms, forming a duct along the ceiling of the latter and supported on channels and vertical eyebeams and other framing in the partitions and carried by ½-inch rods, with clamps, screw heads, and nuts and washers, from the floor beams. Elsewhere, where straight stretches of ceilings can be had, the tees may be 2 inches and set crossways of beams, and fastened thereto with ½-inch rods every 3 feet, and these tees may be 3 feet apart. Where the clamps, of approved pattern, nip into the floor beams the fireproofing will be chipped away so as to allow a proper grip to those clamps, but after the clamps are set a good cement mortar must be well packed into the broken place in the tile so as to thoroughly cover the exposed portions of the floor beam. A lot of projections, pilasters, etc., will be formed in the various rooms of tees and angles. These will be properly set in place and anchored and braced to the nearest structural portion of the building. All this steel framing, rods, etc., for suspended ceilings, columns, and other false work, wherever it is shown or may be required, and of whatever character it may be, will be painted two coats as aforementioned.

89. Then all the properly bound, and covered, and angled and molded, vaulted and straight surfaces of this false work will be roughly but truly formed of expanded metal, properly fastened to the framing with copper wire at every point of contact to secure a perfectly tight and sufficiently strong job; straight surfaces of No. 24 and cornices of No. 26 metal, of approved pattern.

90. This expanded metal must be properly formed up for all the cement finish in the rooms that are not wood trimmed. It must lap well over onto the brickwork or tile and be properly nailed to the door jambs of wood and wired to the door jambs of iron, then carried sufficiently over the partition, or furring, or brick wall, so that the plastering will have no chance to crack at the joining.

91. The inspection "lookout" runways in the two floors of the post-office and the ventilation ducts in these stories, as well as in the basement, will be built of suspension rods, tees, and angles of sufficient dimensions to carry the loads, cross tees for the flooring, and all the required bracing; on the outside of these ducts and runways will be similarly stretched expanded metal.

92. Tie-rods of sufficient size and floor beams of proper dimensions will be used to form two mezzanine floors in the first and second stories around the dome. The contractor may lay a tile floor between these beams, or angles and block tile floor, or a slab concrete floor with expanded metal formed around the steel beams for a plaster protection thereof.

93. All this false work and expanded metal will be left ready for the plasterer in good form and to the exact dimensions required. This work includes all the formation for decorative columns throughout the dome and court rooms, etc., and steel brackets, cantilever beams, and other stiff structural supports must be provided, thoroughly fastened into the structure of the building, all protected with fireproofing tile and cement. The columns themselves will be formed of tees or angles, as on the drawings may be indicated, latticed together, and an expanded metal circle well tied to them with copper wire. The floors of the inspection runways above mentioned will be formed of a fine concrete slab, built on a flat centering and incorporating the expanded metal above specified. The bottom of this concrete flooring will be properly scored to receive the finished plastering that will be applied to it and to all the ducts and other covers, and the floor inside will be a finished, smooth coat of "1 and 2" American Portland cement. A neat arrangement of eyeholes must be provided in these floors, small but radiating in diameter and with sufficient flanges to receive plastering and floor finish.

94. There will be a coved suspended ceiling formed of heavy tees and suspension rods and expanded metal over the inside of the dome. (See drawing No. 114.)

95. At the angles of all pilasters, projections, piers, edges of ducts—in fact, the outer

angle of everything vertical, so to speak—will be formed of extra-heavy galvanized-iron plastering angle piece. This will be set absolutely true to receive the plastering and will be of an approved pattern sufficiently cut out to give a good clinch to the plaster and a smooth, rounded corner of about ¼-inch circle. These angles will be nailed or wired tightly to the walls they protect, and wherever any nailing is done that will come in contact with the plaster such nails must be of galvanized iron.

96. In the post-office rooms, basement, first and second floors the metal corners' hereinbefore specified for the angles will be extra heavy, and in addition thereto, at all columns, on the mailing platform, between the doors on that mailing platform and over the plastering of the structural columns and other external angles in the first and second floor workrooms, there shall be bolted on 2-inch light steel angles. Holes may be made in the brickwork where it is difficult to bolt through. These may be plugged and the angles heavily screwed into the plugs. On the mailing platform, besides these angles, there will be a ₁₆-inch sheet-steel protection, properly screwed into the walls and reaching up to the line of enameled brick. All this protecting steel will be properly painted with one coat all around before being set in place.

97. All the ducts, runways, etc., as before mentioned will be protected with tees and expanded metal, excepting the vertical ones in the basement. These vertical ducts will be protected with 4-inch tiles (partition) built around them, but leaving an air space of two inches. The surface of these tiles, as well as that of all the furring, and, in fact, all the tile used about the building, will be extra heavily scored for plastering.

98. There will be heavy framing of channels and beams to form a ceiling for the alcoves both sides of all the main corridors on the first floor; these projections into the rooms will be used for storage purposes to carry 100 pounds per square foot.

99. There will be steel channels and beams framed as carriages for all the stairways, stiffly and strongly built to likewise sustain a load of 150 pounds per square foot. Between the beams for the carrying of the granite and marble steps in the vestibules and to the first floor there will be 8-inch brick arches sprung, the tops filled with concrete so as to make a continuous and solid bed for all such steps.

100. There will be framing for floors built into all false work where necessary, such as over the false dome; these floors to sustain a load of 50 pounds per square foot. These balconies or runways to be properly protected with 1-inch gas-pipe railing as may be approved by the architect, and reached by open-tread narrow iron stairs.

101. There will be a false work of angles, straps, and expanded metal in pretty nearly every room in the building. In the large court rooms this false work for the formation of the ceiling will be rather complicated and necessarily very carefully laid out. In the corridors, all about the dome and in the upper rooms, this strapwork, composed of ⅛-inch by 2-inch wide straps, well riveted or bolted, or otherwise properly fastened to the structural beams or into the fireproofing, will be set about 2 feet apart. It will all be properly painted before expanded metal is wired to it. Where marble is fastened to this strapwork, the straps will be ⅜ by 2 inches, properly punched, that the marble may be screwed up to it and fastened. Much of the ornamental finish, such as the alcoves in the first-floor corridors, etc., will have to be built upon the floors. In these alcoves, for instance, the framing for the ceiling will be carried from beam to beam and well fastened to the beams, but will be supported on channels, Z bars, and other sections of steel, used as door frames, struts, etc., running down to the floor. In every such case, where practicable, the footing for these supports must be upon a floor beam to which it will be bolted, or to an iron cross piece properly braced to beams.

102. In making the details, drawings, and these specifications for the interior and more decorative work, the architect has shown certain modes of assembling it together—constructing it. It is not to be understood, however, that he is arbitrarily determined upon the particular mode shown. His purpose is to attain the desired decorative appearance indicated by the simplest means possible and consistent with the stability and sound construction desired. He may change his ideas during the construction of the work, and in making the shop drawings for all this work the contractor may suggest other means of assembling the work that may be more economical to him while not affecting either its design or its stability, and the architect may approve the same if in his judgment it is adequate, but all such drawings or suggestions for departures from mode shown by plans must be made well in advance of the time when work is needed.

CARPENTER WORK.

103. The contractor will do all the carpentry work necessary about the building, centering for arches and other false work, frames for all doors and windows, flooring

strips, temporary stairs required by the architect for the proper superintendence of the work, etc., although such work may not be herein specifically referred to.

104. All door and window frames, wherever shown to be of wood, will be as detailed, and of clear, thoroughly kiln-dried pine lumber, free from sap, etc., with 1½-inch quarter-sawn pulley stiles and strips. All these frames will receive one good coat of white lead and oil paint before leaving the manufacturer's shop. These frames will be accurately set in place and made fast to the masonry or other surrounding bodies. They shall be anchored with suitable bolts and nuts and washers, etc. In places the heads of windows will have to be reenforced with steel braces, and in some cases, while the jambs of the doors and windows may be wooden, the heads will be of steel bars. In all such places, these will be thoroughly and securely bolted to the wood, the ironwork properly painted as hereinbefore specified. Around the outside frames there will be packed between them and the brick backing of the walls, well-picked mineral wool. Before putting on the outside staff beads, all gaps between stone and wood at the heads, jambs, and sills must be well calked with picked oakum. In places where deemed necessary the architect may direct that the back faces of the frames be coated with pitch before being set into place. The wood frames at the inside partitions will either be set into steel sections or will have tee pieces of wood nailed thereto and built into the broken flange of the fireproofing partition, or some other means of thoroughly binding the wood frame and the tile partition together. Unsparing use must be made of galvanized-iron straps, anchors, and bolts to secure everything perfectly tight and make it all homogeneous. There will be plastering grounds, of such sizes as may be directed, well anchored into walls, to which will be nailed the expanded metal for the plastering of the wood finish of the rooms. Sufficient of these grounds must be provided wherever the room is to be trimmed in wood to afford good and sufficient nailing for that trimming.

105. As before specified, the contractor will lay proper beveled 3 by 4 inch wood strips, properly clinched by approved means, to the floor beams in all rooms that will have finished wood floors.

106. The contractor will lay an under floor of dry first 6-inch fencing, tongued and grooved, surfaced one side, and laid with close joints to form all platforms, galleries, etc., wherever directed and where there is not provided fireproof floor arching or concrete slab floors.

PLASTERING.

107. The plastering throughout the building, in every room, corridor, closet, or other space, is to be—unless otherwise specifically directed herein—done with two coats of "Adamant," "King's Windsor," or other equally good patent plaster that meets with the approval of the architect. Assuming that "Adamant" is used, the following standard of work will obtain (in the event of other patent plasters being approved the manufacturer's specifications therefor, to secure like results to this, must be followed in every detail): All ceilings and walls of brick or terra cotta to be plastered with a coat of "No. 2 B Adamant" worked to grounds not exceeding ⅜ inch, and while this coat is still green a second finishing coat of the same mortar is to be well worked on. A true, carefully, and thoroughly worked "sand-finish" surface must be obtained. All the expanded-metal surfaces to be covered (and well clinched) with a heavy coat of "No. 2 Adamant," and when this coat is thoroughly dry, a second coat of "No. 2 B Adamant" will be worked on as above described. The walls and ceiling of all corridors, the dome and the ceilings of the five large court rooms, and the walls and ceilings of the subtreasury are to be plastered in a similar manner as to the first coat, but the second coat, laid on when the first is dry, is to be a "No. 1 XXX Adamant," gauged with ½ extra-fine lime putty. The lime to be equal to a "Thomastown" brand, sieved and mixed at least ten days before using.

108. All cornices and ceiling ornamentation and moldings or decorative work, unless otherwise specified, to be worked in a fine gypsum, calcined plaster, or plaster of paris and ½ lime putty finish, upon a base of the same material or of a "No. 1 XXX Adamant," these moldings to be very thoroughly worked to lines, true, sharp, and clear.

109. Bases in all rooms, except where otherwise specified, to be run in "No. 2 B Adamant," gauged with ½ American Portland cement.

110. Architraves at sides and over all corridor openings and about doors and windows of rooms of classes A and B, and wainscoting molds, to be run in a neat American Keene or other approved cement. Ornamental caps, consoles, etc., over the doors of rooms of these classes of finish (sheet 116) to be worked out in a similar plaster to that used for cornices as above described. (Read the specification carefully; it calls for less ornamentation than is shown on details.)

111. This plastering is to be applied, with all proper apparatus and means, cork-floating, grounds, floor and ceiling strips, etc., to secure perfect work, upon all fire-proofing, brick and expanded-metal surfaces, walls and ceilings, beams, pockets, shafts, pilasters, etc.

112. The mixing of all mortar must be done in tight boxes and restricted to certain rooms on each floor. The storing of this, as well as all other materials thus handled about the building, where it is to be mixed, etc., is all absolutely under the control of the architect. The architect will also establish such rules, from time to time, as he may see fit, about receiving all such materials in original packages and otherwise insuring the use of only the materials called for.

113. The contractor shall build proper scaffolding for the handling of *all* the work and its efficient inspection. Additional ladders and planking for its efficient inspection must be provided immediately they are ordered by the architect.

114. Care must be taken that rough coat is properly clinched to the fireproofing and the expanded metal, and where it is at all practicable the contractor will slush this mortar about and entirely cover the straps and anchors and other framing work supporting this plaster in place.

115. In such places as the architect may direct, or it is shown on the drawings that there will be but one coat of plaster, in the court rooms, for instance, in the spaces reserved for pictures painted on canvas, this coat is to be brought up to a sand finish, floated from proper top-ceiling strips, with good miters and angles, and forming a true and sufficiently adhesive background for the canvas.

116. The rough coating will be run down behind all wainscoting to level up any unevenness in the tile. In rooms where there are no cornices at the juncture of ceiling and wall, where the connection is perfectly plain, turn the angle in the rough coat, so that the finish will be a 3-inch radius, avoiding the sharp inner angle at all corners, projections, etc., and all so that the brown coating has a perfect clinch to the metal angle.

117. Moldings will be very carefully run, perfectly true and straight, or curved to the exact radii, and the ornaments cast in sharp, well-modeled molds and set in place to perfectly fit and match and miter. An extra-fine job of plastering will be exacted. There is a great deal of molded work throughout, sometimes of most intricate pattern, and in the dome, for instance, of the most elaborate design, calling for very fine modeling, casting by experts, and application by men thoroughly trained in that specialty. But very little of the ornamental molded work can be done by a plasterer accustomed to the ordinary run of cornice work in houses. Where shown some of the ornamental work will be of *papier-maché* or other approved porous material.

118. The fireproofing and brick walls and the brown coating must be properly prepared, dusted, and wetted before the application of each coat of plaster.

119. Models for all consoles, ornamental panels, enriched moldings and crestings must be first made in clay and submitted to the architect for his approval before any of the work is cast; cornice profiles will be cut in zinc and submitted for approval. Plaster cresting over the cornices and the dome, and other projecting members in plaster or cement, will be built up upon heavy wire frames with strap iron braces and expanded-metal forms, and every other precaution will be taken to secure the work in place.

120. After the ornamental metal and woodwork are completed, in fact just before the building is ready for occupancy, the contractor shall go over all this work and repair and neatly patch any portions that may have been broken.

121. The architect will exact the most approved and modern ways of doing all this plastering work.

JOINER WORK AND FLOORING.

122. All floors throughout, except where otherwise specifically mentioned, will be first and second selected white-maple flooring, tongued and grooved, 2¼ by 1 inch stuff, blind nailed to sleepers; and all trim and finish throughout, except, also, where otherwise specified, will be of quarter-sawn oak, as shown under "Note" by details for "Alternative" wood finish on sheet 119, and referred to herein as "Class E." The doors not otherwise described will be 2¼-inch oak-veneered pine-cored doors, all as detailed on sheet 119.

123. All the finished lumber for the trimming, the floors, etc., is to be of the very best purchasable, clear, thoroughly seasoned and kiln-dried, free from defects, and running even in color. Where oak is called for it will in every case mean a selected, clear oak, quarter-sawn, and neatly matched; mahogany will be a Cuban mahogany. Cherry and black walnut will be of a high grade, selected for color.

124. In no case will any of the finishing lumber be delivered at the building while masonry work or plastering is being done to any considerable extent. The finished lumber, doors, etc., will be kept just as dry as possible.

125. The backs of all window jambs, casings, etc., will be hollowed out to prevent warping and will receive one good coat of paint before being set in place. The architect may direct, if he deems it expedient, that a coat of filler be applied to all the hard wood at the factory. All the work shall be ploughed or rebated together in such a manner as to conceal any shrinkage. Glue and dowels will be used and wood blocks will be glued in the angles on the backs of the frames, etc., for stiffening; abutting joints to be framed or dowled where practicable, and no nailing will be permitted except where especially directed by the architect or his superintendent. The woodwork will be held in place, where practicable, by screws from the back and well concealed, all strongly put up. There shall be pine lookouts, blocks, furring strips, etc., to which all this finish will be fastened.

126. In this connection, relative to this wood finish, as well as to the putting together of *everything* else about the building, where specific instructions are not given herein or where they may be a trifle vague, the work shall be executed in accordance with instructions given by the architect, consistent, not with the "ordinary" practice, but with the very best methods known and generally used in the highest quality of similar work.

127. Paint the surfaces coming into contact with masonry or plastering with a good coat of priming before setting in place. Every precaution must be taken to prevent shrinkage and warping of this hard-wood work. Panels of any considerable size must be made up of reversed pieces glued and doweled together; and veneered panels, wherever practicable, will be glued to cores of narrow strips of white pine. Where this mode of coring can not be used the pine body of the panel should be cross-grained to the veneer.

128. Veneerings will be selected for their beauty and markings and will not be less than ¼ inch in oak and never less than $\frac{1}{16}$ of an inch thick in the expensive woods, and in one piece for each panel, unless the latter be of extraordinary size. Mahogany veneers for panels will be "crotch mahogany." Where there is but one face to a panel, hard-wood strips must be secured to the back with screws and washers, and these strips to be slotted to allow proper expansion and contraction. In no case may the panel be glued into the frame or moldings unless so shown; moldings must be glued to the splines, stiles, and rails, and the panels left free. The backs of all paneled wainscoting will be painted with three coats of paint, and paneled work will receive all but the last coat of finish before being set in place.

129. The doors will be made up of ⅞-inch pine strips veneered with ½-fnch on the edges and with at least ¼-inch veneer on the faces.

130. There will be a tongued and grooved backing to all mirrors.

131. All this interior wood finish must be of a very high grade of work, put together with the best skill of the joiner, the face free of nails and holding together in perfect shape without warp or twist, and equal in every respect to the very best work done in the highest grade of office building.

132. Wherever there are pine doors, such as in the basement, in the lookout runways, etc., they will be 1¾-inch doors. Where doors are covered with iron or tin, the core will be of pine, four rails with panels flush with the stiles and rails; so will be the big gates in the subtreasury storeroom in the basement that are covered with steel. These gates will have stiles, rails, and panels as detailed, and covered on the outside with a ¼-inch sheet-steel protection, ornamentally bolted through the door, the round heads of the bolts showing on the outside; additional similarly round-headed nails will be fastened on the plate to form a continuous line of supposed rivet heads. There will be many ornamental bronze doors throughout the building, all of which will have cores of pine. framed up to form a body to which may be fastened the bronze, and in some cases the insides of these doors will be heavily tinned.

133. Sash throughout the building must be most carefully made; wherever practicable in the double-hung sash, they shall be made with horns at the meeting rail. Some of this sash, in the first and second floors and in the dome, will be very large and must be extra strong: in some cases it will have to be reenforced with steel members.

134. All outside sash throughout the building will be pine, good, clear, well-seasoned, strictly clear lumber. The sash should receive one coat of oil before leaving the factory. Generally, all sash over 5 feet wide shall have 1¼-inch steel ties let into the meeting rails to stiffen the same, and all meeting rails shall be beveled. The sash in the windows of vaults under sidewalks will be swing hinged. All the corridor and inside sash will be quarter-sawn oak. Where rooms are in different woods, this oak sash will be veneered on the inside with the wood of that room. Pine frames will be provided for all outside windows and doors where required; and there will be iron frames to which will be bolted wood jambs for other windows.

135. The framing of the corridor partitions will be hard-wood jambs screwed to the iron or wood framing, and all the sash set thereto, hung, pivoted, or hinged, as the case may be, in a most thoroughly workmanlike manner.

136. There will be ceiling lights in a great many of the rooms and corridors; these will be made of pine, excepting where there are narrow sash bars, in which case these will be of oak for strength. Some of this sash, in ceilings and elsewhere, will be made to slide horizontally or to raise with pulleys and weights as traps.

137. The parting strips at all windows will be tightly fitted in the grooves, but never fastened. Where screws are used to fasten stops to the framing or elsewhere about these sash and doors they shall be round-headed bronze screws with bronze washers; where fastening into ironwork, these shall be tap screws. Washers for the outside windows, and elsewhere if directed, will have slotted eyelets.

138. The bidders are again urged to thoroughly inspect the building before figuring on this work, as otherwise they may find unexpected work to be performed, not only in the way of sashes, but other items of considerable importance that will have to be done to inclose and completely finish the structure. There are windows and doors to, perhaps, blind balconies, hidden stairways, etc., that are not of sufficient importance to warrant special drawings in this interior finish set and that they may overlook on the plans of the structure that are furnished them, but that are clearly apparent upon a minute inspection of the building as it stands. No excuses will be accepted that a contractor did not figure on such and such a piece of work; this contract is to all intents and purposes a blanket contract, and everything about the place that has to be done to finish the work is included herein, whether shown or specified or not; there may even be items that have escaped the architect's attention in writing these specifications. It is therefore suggested that the contractor make as liberal an allowance as he safely can for "contingencies," as there are bound to arise many such in a building of this magnitude.

139. Where the picture mold comes in connection with the wainscoting it shall be of the same wood as that room. Elsewhere the picture molding will be of oak.

140. The finished floors, where plain wood floors are called for in the offices throughout the building, will be a ⅞-inch thick by 2-inch face tongued-and-grooved and end-tongued white maple floor, toe-nailed into the flooring strips, and in no case less than 6 feet long. In the particularly fine rooms there will be laid a floor of 1¼ inches wide, clear quarter-sawn oak, tongued and grooved, blind nailed, and with a pattern border of similar oak and cherry and walnut strips.

141. The backside of all this flooring will be painted one coat before being set in place, and great care must be taken that none of this paint appears upon the face.

142. No floor will be laid until all the finish is in place; it must be in long pieces and fit snugly to the base with an oak shoe molding properly adjusted and nailed to the flooring. Carefully protect the surface of this floor from stains, grit, etc., and when ready to finish it have it thoroughly scraped and sandpapered down to a perfect surface. There will be cherry thresholds at all the doors except where otherwise specified. (The details show that all doors are to have bronze thresholds; cherry has been substituted therefor.)

143. All through this finish the contractor must use as long stuff as it is practicable to get. In no case will he be permitted to make up a casing or anything of that sort in two lengths. Mitered joints, splices in long wainscoting, and wherever a joint is permitted must be most carefully done—reenforced and blinded.

144. Around mirrors wherever shown the contractor will furnish and place a handsome narrow picture gilt frame of a pattern that may be selected by the architect.

145. Molded rails of mahogany to be properly fastened to all the stair and balcony metal handrails, the wood to be finished and polished as is specified for the other wood finish.

146. Mantels, wherever shown, to be as detailed, with the same trim as that for the door in that particular room. There will be a mantel shelf, as shown, supported by brackets carved from the solid piece, surmounted with a beveled mirror of French plate set in a picture gilt frame. The facing will be of marble, as specified in that room, two sidepieces, and a lintel (upon which carving is shown, but is to be omitted). There will be a bronze-plated back and sides, and casing mold to the opening. These may be selected from a handsome stock of mantel trimmings, and need not be specially made. There will be no grate, as later there will be provided by another contractor an electrical heating device in lieu of ordinary fires. The hearth will be the full width of the mantel in length and 2 feet in width and 1 inch thick, of the marble specified for the room, and set flush with the floor, with a piece of cherry mitered around it as a border.

147. Elsewhere than the mantel brackets, in this wood finish, the ornamental work will be a very high quality of wood composition stuck into place with strong glue, and after the first two coats of polish have been applied to the surrounding work. This composition will be cast from exceedingly sharply modeled dies, carved in wood that will leave the grain correspondingly marked in the casting. This

composition stuff will be properly stained before being applied and must be a perfect match to the wood to which it is applied. After having been most neatly set in place it will be finished as the rest is, with such parts polished as may be directed by the architect. Models for all this plastic decoration must be submitted to the architect and must be made by a well-known concern making the highest quality and grade of material in that line. The outlines to be sharp and decisive, high relief, and in every way a perfect imitation of the most artistic carving.

HARDWARE.

148. Every door and sash about the building must be properly hung and have attached all suitable fixtures necessary for its particular class. All skylights and ceiling lights must be provided with suitable lifts and mechanism to operate the same, and the contractor must suitably "trim" the entire building with its hardware to the entire satisfaction of the architect. Where hardware is not specifically described, the customary fastening bolts, butts, etc., to be set complete and of the same character as specified for other similar parts of the building. All hardware not otherwise specified is to be of extra heavy solid bronze.

149. As little hardware as possible must be placed about the work until the same has been finished and polished. All the hardware will be of liberal dimensions, handsome design, though comparatively plain, and of the very highest grade purchasable.

150. While insisting upon the very highest grade of material in this work, as well as in everything else, the architect does not specify any particular make of goods, but merely to facilitate his description he here states that the escutcheons and knobs of of the post-office workrooms and the other rooms, here and there, of lesser importance, will be equal to the Chicago Hardware Company's catalogue Nos. D 7563, and that the escutcheons and knobs of all the corridor and other important doors throughout will be of special design calling for about the same work as that catalogue indicates at D 7572.

151. The doors on main first-floor corridors will have trim specially designed, and to cost not less than $9 per knob and escutcheon, the rest of the hardware in connection therewith to be up to the standard here established for knobs and escutcheons.

152. All swinging doors in the offices, corridor and communicating, will be hung on three 5-knuckle, loose-pin, steel-bushed butts with tips. Butts for the 2¼-inch doors will be 5 inches high and weigh about 4½ pounds per pair, and for doors less than 1¾ inches thick, 4 inches and 3 pounds per pair, and all of sufficient width to allow the doors to swing clear of the finish.

153. Double-acting doors will hang with one pair double-acting spring hinges made of ample size to carry the door and allow it to act satisfactorily in every way. All locks and latches to be mortise, have antifriction attachments, bronze-metal faces and strike plates; the strike plates to be bent and of such size as to protect the finish. The tumblers of the locks must differ so that each lock can be only opened with the keys belonging to it, but the entire system of locks must be master-keyed for janitor purposes in such a system as will be approved by the architect. The locks for the interior doors opening from the corridors generally to be about 4½ by 3½ by ⅞ inch with cylinders, five tumblers, and three keys, so arranged that the outside knobs will be set by stop work on the face, or with a keyhole in the knob, all to be masterkeyed as above and in such a manner as to not lessen the security of the rooms. Locks for the jury rooms will be the same as specified above, excepting that there shall be a dead bolt to be opened by key only.

154. All corridor doors are to be fitted with an approved door check, finished and of a character similar to the other hardware about said doors.

155. The communicating doors will have latches, and, in addition, two dead bolts operated with thumb pieces on each side, independently of each other, the vertical axes of the thumb bolts and knobs to be the same. The doors from offices to toilet rooms to have knobs and plates on the faces and bolts on the toilet-room side only. There must be provision made that only the janitor may lock the public toilet-room doors.

156. The doors into the post-office proper from corridors or lobbies will be very handsomely trimmed, but the inside face, in the working rooms, and all doors in the working rooms, will be plainly though substantially finished as above described. Both sides of the basement doors and each leaf of all double doors in the workrooms to be provided with large ⅛-inch-thick bronze push and kick plates. The outsides of the doors on the mailing platform and all swing doors shall be provided with an approved device at the bottom for holding them in position when open.

157. The sliding doors will have large sunk handles in each leaf, and have approved sliding-door locks and pulls. Both leaves of double-acting doors to be trimmed.

False doors, as in court rooms, to be trimmed to match. All sliding doors to have approved overhead wrought-steel hangers, with antifriction bearings, necessary steel wires, guards, rails, stops, etc., and so hung as to work easily, and there will be bronze guides set into the threshold.

158. The box-frame windows shall have bronze-faced pulleys, with brass sheaves 2½-inch diameter on running face, steel axles, and antifriction bearings, the wheels turned to fit the metal sash chains. When necessary, special sash chains will be set diagonally from the center of the sash.

159. The sash in the box frames shall be hung on bronze composition cable chains having a tensile strength of at least 400 pounds and with weights to exactly balance the sash; many windows will require compressed-lead weights instead of iron, that may be generally used. The sliding sash shall have approved sash fasteners, two flush lifts in each lower sash, socket plates in upper sash, and rubber stops under sash horns. Furnish each room in the building with a sash-pull oak pole of sufficient length and approved pattern.

160. All horizontally hung sash, pivoted sash, and transoms to have bronze transom openers with no less than a ⅜-inch bronze plated or other finished rods or handles to come within easy reach. Outside trimmings to be fitted with spring ring catches, and where usual transom openers can not be used bronze composition stay chains at sides will be used instead. Suitable devices will have to be used for opening ceiling lights under the skylights. These devices to be operated from the most accessible point to these lights, of sufficiently heavy make and satisfactory pattern. Some sort of device will have to be arranged to open ventilators in the post-office skylights and in other skylights throughout the building. Where necessary, in outside doors, etc., sufficiently strong flush bolts will be provided at tops and bottoms of the doors, the top bolts to be within easy reach. There will be bronze-metal bumpers with rubber tips at all swinging doors, and neat wood and rubber devices to prevent all other doors from opening against and marring any finish.

161. The toilet-room hardware will be as selected by the architect, two double swing butts to each closet door, a thumb-piece flush bolt, fastening on the inside into a proper metal receptacle in the marble, a double-face clothes hook fitting over the partitions between the closets, three ornamental screw-cap holders at every joint of the marble divisions, and all in that line to make the toilet rooms complete in every respect (excepting paper holders and toilet hardware). All this toilet-room hardware to be of brass, properly polished and lacquered, likewise the regular door and window trim.

162. Provide a row of heavy bronze hat and coat hooks 8 inches apart in each closet or locker throughout the building.

GLASS.

163. All plate glass to be the best quality polished American plate. All sheet glass to be best quality selected, double strength (AA), and all other glass to be strictly in accordance with the specific requirements therefor and according to samples approved by the architect. All exterior glass throughout the building to be plate glass and prismatic glass, and all interior glass not otherwise specified to be double-thick sheet glass, as above.

164. The windows in the vaults under the sidewalks, the glass in the doors and sash in the inside walls all through the basement, that in the driveway and machinery rooms, will be double-strength sheet glass (AA). All the glass will be bedded in putty and back-puttied, sheet glass secured by glazier's points and putty, and the plate glass held in place with molding or glazing beads fastened to the sash or frame with screws in the finish of the hardware used in that room, these screws to be not over 8 inches apart and at least two to each side of the glass. The prismatic lights in the sidewalk and their cast-iron frames are matters for another contract. There will be prismatic glass in the basement windows and some dome windows, specified more in detail under items for those parts.

165. Wherever mirrors are required over the washbowls in all public and private toilet rooms, the same shall be of the best quality of American silvering plate, some, in the rooms of Class D, with beveled edges, and all with mercury backs, painted over with red lead and properly backed up with a thin backing of wood and felt cloth against the glass.

166. Wherever art glass is shown and not specifically described as different, the contractor will figure at the rate of $2 per superficial foot, including iron bars, rods, and labor necessary to complete the glass in the frames. The architect reserves the right to call for competitive designs for this glass from leading art glass makers, and the contractor agrees to accept and have executed the designs so selected by the architect.

167. The glass in outside doors, vestibule doors, and other points shown, or where directed, will be beveled polished plate, with a bevel of 1¼ inches. The glass in the corridor sash will be of approved pattern in crystalline plate. All the transoms will be clear plate. The door lights will also be crystalline plate, but with a handsome border of interlaced lines engraved around the edges. The lower parts of the post-office screens, where there are windows, will be of crystalline plate with 1½-inch beveled edges, and where necessary, words, names of divisions, etc., will be either engraved upon this glass or left clear in the crystallizing process.

168. Ceiling lights, where not of art glass, will be plain American plate; glass in the upper corridor ceiling lights will be crystalline glass, leaded in attractive patterns, but not coming under the heading of the art glass.

PAINTING.

169. All parts of the building usually painted (or wherever necessary that painting should be done to properly complete the building), and that are not specifically mentioned herein, will be painted three coats of white lead and oil of approved color, at such time and in such manner as the architect may direct.

170. All the framing, ironwork for false ceilings, cornice, etc., all straps, etc., will be properly painted as hereinbefore described. The exterior woodwork and metal work, where the latter is not plated, and all work usually painted about the outside of a building, shall be thoroughly cleaned and given three coats (in addition to a coat applied before being set in place to all frames, etc.) of pure white lead and linseed oil mixed with approved colors and well rubbed down.

171. The painting on the back of the woodwork will be yellow ocher and linseed oil. The inside of all inspectors' runways, their screens, etc., will be painted two coats of black paint. The inside of the sash will be stained and varnished the same color as the room finish.

172. All interior hard-wood finish will be carefully filled and stained, as may be directed, and given four coats of varnish equal to the highest grade of interior-work varnish made by the Chicago Varnish Company, the first coat to be sandpapered, the second and third coats to be rubbed down with pumice and oil, and the last coat rubbed down with pulverized rotten stone and water. Finish with a coat of bleached oil and polish. Wherever there is any exterior hard wood it will be filled and given four coats of outside varnish, an elastic coach varnish; the parting strips in windows shall receive three coats of linseed oil, not painted. The oak floors will be given a coat of hot linseed oil, then, after four days, a coat of approved wax, applied hot and properly polished; the maple floors, one coat linseed oil and two coats approved floor varnish.

173. Where directed in certain portions of bronze work or wood finish, such parts representing coats of arms or other figures will be painted and enameled in their respective colors, then varnished.

174. Wherever there may be any gilding or gold-tipping required on the bronze work or elsewhere, it will be done with the best quality of XX gold leaf. Each door opening from the corridors or lobbies into courts, offices, etc., will have a number of suitable size painted upon its glass panel. The number will be of XX gold leaf, backed and shaded in black.

175. All paints, varnishes, colors, and leads shall be of the very highest quality; white lead to contain no free carbonate and to have from 70 to 75 per cent of carbonate of lead and from 25 to 30 per cent of hydroxide; varnishes shall not contain less than 25 per cent of the best quality of imported vegetable gum, and all these materials are to be delivered in unbroken packages bearing brand and maker's name, and must be mixed on the premises, subject to inspection, and any rejected material must at once be removed from the premises.

176. All the bronze work, either solid or plated, will be properly polished and given a good coat of the best white French lacquer.

MARBLE AND TILING.

177. The marble finish of the different rooms and corridors will be as hereafter noted or shown on the drawings. Further details of the marble work may be supplied by the architect, or, as with all other work, he may direct that the shop drawings made by the contractor shall be tentatively submitted to him before completion. In any case the contractor shall employ only artists and experts to make these shop drawings and to execute marble work.

178. It is intended to use American marbles only, and the various marbles that may be specified are to be of the very best veins of their respective quarries, care-

fully selected as may be directed by the architect for particular effect, and must be put together showing as few joints as possible, concealing the ends of all slab work, and made up of various thicknesses as shown, but in no case will marble less than ⅛-inch be used.   Where a certain marble is specified, such for instance as a Tennessee Roseal, the "or other equally good and similarly colored marble" means that in texture, appearance, color, and every other particular, the alternative marble submitted by the contractor shall be absolutely equal to the standard that is established by the architect who, in specifying particular marbles or other materials, does not restrict contractor to their use, but wishes merely to indicate the scheme of design or color he desires and the relative quality of the material.

179. The marble work will all be set in the most approved manner known to the trade, by skilled mechanics and under expert foremen. It must be backed up with brick, or fireproof filling where large areas are covered in a most substantial manner, and shall be set and held in place with clamps, set screws, copper wire, and thoroughly steadied with plaster of paris. All this marble work must absolutely fit the structure and neatly join to all metal or woodwork with which it comes in contact.

180. All this marble work is to be set in an approved nonstaining Portland cement; even the grounding upon which the floor tile is set must be of this nonstaining cement, equal to the "Myers" or "La Farge."

181. By marble work is understood all the interior decoration that is not wood, plaster, or metal. It comprehends the granite for the walls and floors of the vestibules, granite steps, all the marble treatment of the walls, mosaic floors, and the artificial marble coming in connection with the real marble decoration, otherwise know as "scagliola," "Mycenian marble," etc., as well as any enameled tile or glass mosaic specified for wall or ceiling.

182. All this marble work, except where otherwise indicated, on the walls, and including the artificial marble, shall be polished to the highest possible gloss. All the marble in the floors, whether mosaic, or plain slab, or steps, shall be brought to a smooth-rubbed surface. The joints in the wall work will, of course, be plaster of paris, and as thin as can possibly be made, but those in the dark-colored marbles will be of similarly-colored plaster of paris. Floor slabs, tiles, etc., will be set in nonstaining cement, 1 part cement to 3 parts sand; ⅛-inch copper wire anchors about 12 inches apart will be generally used in all wall work, but heavy wainscoting caps and other heavy pieces of marble, where they can not be laid on a proper bearing bed, shall be held in place with a heavier wire let through drilled holes in the fireproofing partition, or otherwise most firmly fastened in place. The joints will all be true and square and close, and the marble generally to be in as long pieces as possible; caps of railings or marble in other places where it may receive hard usage shall be doweled with copper dowels at the joints. Contiguous slabs in wainscoting or in panels ought not to be from the same slab, though they must be of the same general tone and coloring, but it is not desired that two contiguous slabs shall be from the same block, reversed in veining, as is so often done. That effect is not sought in this building.

183. The granite steps in the vestibules shall have a wash at the back and sides as detailed; so will the first run of the dome stairs from the first floor to the first landing, but above that the marble steps shall be plain slabs with a nosing, but without any wash at the back or sides. In every case the treads and risers will be in pieces the full width of the stairs. The risers will be polished as is the marble wall; the treads a dull-rubbed surface.

184. In all toilet rooms, corridors, marble-finished rooms, vestibules, etc., wherever there is marble or granite finish there will be a properly-rounded wash block at the connection of floor and wall; this wash block will be a smooth-rubbed surface and of the thickness shown by the drawings and of the marble as hereafter directed for the several floors.

185. The corridor floors of the building (excepting that of the first floor) will be of marble tile, a border 12 inches wide and 1½ inches thick of dark Tennessee and with a filling between borders of marble tiles of gray Tennessee, laid brick-shape in about 10 by 16 inch sizes 1¼ inches thick; a variation of an inch, more or less, may be made in laying out these floor tiles in the different corridors, so as to finish them evenly against the border. This tile floor must be laid in the most skillful manner in nonstaining cement. The edges of all these tiles must be ground on a rubbing bed to an exact gauge, the joints must be very fine, and after the flooring is set they will be grouted with a neat Portland cement and rubbed down to an absolutely even surface.

186. In the toilet rooms there will be an 8-inch border of a selected white marble equal to Vermont "Sutherland Falls," and the floor space will be filled in with 8 or 10 inch tile of similar white marble. The joints in all these floors will be grouted and then the floor thoroughly rubbed down with heavy-weight emory or pumice stone and water to a smooth even finish and dull polish.

187. The designs of the mosaic flooring must be submitted to the architect and approved or changed by him, but in a general way, wherever they are specified, they are to conform to the rough sketch shown on dome detail No. 114.   There shall be no very large patches of mosaic; it is to be cut up by lines of marble tiling, borders, etc., so as to prevent the long and spreading cracks so common in large mosaic spaces. Where used, mosaic will be a Roman mosaic, and not over $\frac{3}{4}$-inch square, neatly fitted to form true lines in a pattern, and properly blended and shaded in the different colors; white will, of course, preponderate, with the patterns accentuated in greens and reds and blacks of various shades. The marble used in the mosaic must weigh on an average of 7 pounds to the foot.

188. Where shown there will be letters or figures of brass set into this mosaic; these will be about a quarter of an inch thick, rounded slightly on the surface so as to project a trifle above the mosaic and held in place with pins set into the concrete.

189. The floor of the outer vestibule will be of slabs of granite 2 inches thick, of the size shown on the drawings and brought to a coarsely tooled surface to prevent slipping; the walls of these vestibules will be of highly polished slabs of granite set up in ashlar form; the frieze, and other cut surfaces, bases, etc., will be very finely dressed, 12-cut, and the carving left in a most artistic finish.

190. All the carving in the marble work and all the ornamental work in the artificial marble work must be polished, some portions finished in a dull gloss and other portions highly polished.

191. Generally the molding and carved surfaces in this marble finish will be of scagliola, or artificial marble. In every case the latter is to perfectly resemble the marble with which it comes into contact, in color and veining and degree of polish as to its plain and molded surface.

192. This artificial marble must only be made by a concern of long standing and that thoroughly knows the business. The veinings must not only crudely resemble the marble it is to imitate, but must be done by a man who knows marble in its every detail. As a standard the architect will insist that this artificial marble shall be equal to the very best examples made by the Mycenian Marble Company of New York. The large columns, mostly, will be made of this artificial marble. They will be built of angles or tee irons and expanded metal, shaped to the proper form and finished with the hardest kind of Keene's cement, brought to the proper entasis and absolutely true and perfect in line. The slightest variation from this perfection in any column, whenever discovered, means the rejection and removal of that column. The coloring coat will be applied in a most artistic manner; burlap or other necessary binding material will be used for clinching purposes, and the surface must be left as if from a polishing lathe. The bases must be cast true and perfect; no irregular fitting or slight divergences will be tolerated in this material. All this artificial marble will be made of the very best American Keene cement and its backing must also be of Keene cement. A mere coating of coloring matter upon a body of another nature will not be permitted.

193. In submitting samples from the quarries and the names of the marbles that the contractor wishes to use instead of what is specified he must produce evidence that the quarry is opened, has the facilities for handling and cutting the material in due time, and has produced satisfactory work and material equivalent to that which is here specified.

194. Where indicated there will be set in the ceilings of the vestibules elaborate glass mosaic. This mosaic will be what is known as "Venetian, split American glass mosaic" of brilliant colors and small pieces. The contractor will figure on a basis of $2.40 per square foot of actual surface in these drawings of vaulted ceilings. The architect reserves the privilege of having competitive designs submitted for this and the other artistic work, and the contractor obliges himself to employ and pay the successful competitor for this work. Of course such a subcontractor will be selected as is competent and responsible. The work must be most carefully and artistically done. This item is under a separate bid.

195. The marble work for the toilet-room divisions, wainscoting, etc., shall be done by this contractor. The plumbing contractor will furnish and set in place the actual marble slabs for the tops and backs of his fixtures and the trays under washbowls and urinals, but the floor and divisions will be done by this contractor.

196. All the toilet rooms will be wainscoted in an American white marble of a clearer white in color but equal in texture and density to a "Hollister," 7 feet high, of $\frac{7}{8}$-inch stuff, without horizontal joints. On top of this 7-foot-high wainscoting will be a capping in long pieces 4 inches high, 2½ inches thick, rounded top and bottom. The water-closet divisions will be of the same marble of 1½-inch stock, the faces or door jambs also of 1½-inch stock 1 foot wide. All these divisions will be 15 inches from the floor, and shall line with the bottom of the wainscoting cap. The

faces will extend to floor, then all across tops of divisions and full length of fronts of closets the capping will be carried, forming a tie. All will be properly bedded and fastened and held together with ornamental brass fastenings, with brass ornamental screws and nuts. There will be three fastenings to each slat, one top and bottom, one in the middle, and one at intersection of caps. The faces will be securely fastened into a mop block forming bases therefor. Over all washbowls there will be plain mirrors, full length, and the tops extending to wainscoting cap, set in 4-inch-wide frames of marble mitering with caps and having a ½-inch gilt molding around glass and forming divisions where too long for one piece of mirror. This does not apply to working-room toilet ranges. All the edges of the marble will be dressed on a rubbing bed and the exposed edges brought to a high polish, and all external angles will be rounded and likewise polished. Proper polished brass double-spring butts and fasteners will be ornamentally bolted to this marble work to receive the swinging slat doors, and to it will also be bolted all the other water-closet fittings supplied by another contractor but put in place by this contractor.

197. The toilet rooms in the post-office working rooms and "swing" rooms will be wainscoted 3 feet 8 inches high with a gray Tennessee marble. On top of this there will be a 4 by 1½ inch capping of same marble, but it will not be carried over the divisions. The face pieces will extend to the floor and up 3 feet 8 inches high. From these will extend the divisions of same height, but 15 inches from the floor. The floor will be of 10 by 16 inch marble tiles, and all this toilet-room marble for such working rooms, etc., will be equal to a gray Tennessee. The urinal divisions and backs will also be of same marble.

198. These divisions are but shoulder high, so that the oak solid-panel doors in these closets will be but 2 feet 3 inches high and hung without locks or fastenings.

199. There will be mirrors 2 feet high by 6 feet long set over every three wash-bowls.

200. In entering into this contract the contractor guarantees to keep all the floor and wall marble work in repair (against ordinary wear, of course) for the term of three years after completion of building.

201. All the ornamental metal work throughout the building, outside and in, except where otherwise specified herein, is to be made up of wrought bars, cast ornaments, and hammered leaf work of steel and iron, artistically assembled, the means of assembling thoroughly concealed, and all most thoroughly plated with bronze to match the sample that may be approved by the architect. The recesses, and wherever else directed, to be oxidized a darker color, the high parts burnished and left a bright bronze, and the whole well coated with high-grade lacquer.

202. The details show all the entrance work to be of real bronze, also some other portions, elevator fronts, etc. This will be made a matter for an alternative bid, but in the main bid it is to be disregarded; *all* the ornamental metal work is to be figured upon the basis of plated work.

203. The entrance grills, their frames, sash, cornices, etc., the vestibule work, the grills in subtreasury, all the stair rails, balcony rails, elevator fronts, doors and frames and grills, well-hole facias, ramps, etc., will be of iron and steel so plated in bronze.

204. All this ironwork to be well cleaned from all defects, scales, etc., and then pickled, after which it will be plated in a strong cyanide solution of copper for twenty-two hours, then put in a solution of "statuary-bronze metal" plating, giving a "duplex" plate to all this ornamental metal work. All the lacquer will be the best French white lacquer, and all the work to be kept well greased until completion of the building. Exterior work must have a deposit upon it equal to 16-ounce copper.

205. All of the metal work will be thick enough in every case to give the proper structural strength to the part into which it is incorporated. Proper bracing and framework must be provided for it of such a character that will meet with the approval of the architect; such, in a general way, as is shown on the various details and framing sheets. The moldings must be true and perfectly finished and sharp lines. The butting of joints and fitting generally must be very closely adjusted. All the chasing and finishing required must be done by hand. All the metal work on the outside of the building must also be fitted and brazed in such a way as to absolutely prevent leaks. All the work must be most thoroughly anchored to the stone walls, the iron columns, or other structural parts near it, in order to secure perfect stability. The hardware for the main grilles and glass doors at the entrances will be particularly heavy. Besides four extra-heavy butts at each of these doors, there will be steel pivots set into steel sockets, provided with oil holes top and bottom. There

wifl be heavy extension bolts top and bottom and a suitable heavy lock operated from the inside, but neither handle, nor lock, nor escutcheon, nor other fastening device will appear from the outside.

206. The elevator fronts will be electro-bronzed iron on all floors. The design will be very handsome and elaborate and must be most carefully wrought out. The elevator doors must have the best antifriction adjustable sheaves, grooved thresholds, rubber bumpers, locking devices easily reached by the operator, and, in fact, equipped in every detail similar to the very best of office buildings.

207. At the place shown on plans there will be a letter chute of the usual pattern used for the best buildings. It must run straight and true, have beveled-glass face, brass-molded borders, handsome drops at each story, etc. This chute will begin at a point to serve the fifteenth story and will continue on down to the fourth floor, then will be curved into the post-office working room, terminating at the second-floor level. There will be no letter box.

208. The lamps shown on the drawings are no part of this contract.

209. In the dome decoration there are panels in the marble and other places shown where a bronzed molding is introduced. These bronzed moldings throughout the entire height of the dome will be cast or otherwise made up in long lengths and properly bolted into the marble with concealed bronze bolts.

210. There will be a heavy railing and posts set upon the coping around the areas on all four sides of the building, as shown in sketch on sheet 105. Cast posts and ornaments and wrought rail. The posts will be bronze doweled into the stone, securely set, and precautions taken against rusting the stone. This rail work will be painted four coats, well rubbed after each coat, the last coat mixed half and half with a good spar varnish.

211. All this fastening of the metal will be very thoroughly concealed, screw holes will be countersunk, and the screw heads perfectly flush and tight and, where possible, covered over with ornaments.

In Particular.

212. In general terms the architect has endeavored to give in what precedes this a description of the principal materials entering into the finish and decoration of this building. He has emphasized the fact that all these and all other materials would have to be of the highest grade, each of its class; they must be artistically assembled and all the work executed in as high a degree of perfection as may be expected in a piece of work that is not in any sense of the word "ordinary." While there will be no extravagance, or any attempt at wonderfully original effects anywhere in the building, the work and material must be of such character as will impart some beauty and commensurate dignity to the interior of this structure. Practically, it is a great office building and the contractor will be expected to finish his work in every detail in keeping with the character established by the finest office buildings in the country.

213. In what follows the architect wishes to give the contractor, now that the latter has a general idea of the material, a more intimate description of the building in its several parts and divisions.

214. The contractor may begin his work, and do such branches of it, in such order as may be most economical and advantageous to him, provided he has the consent of the architect to go along in that particular order; but, merely to facilitate this description, the architect starts with the eighth floor, taking story by story below that and story by story above, in the dome.

Note.—Since the plans have been printed it has been decided to add another class of room finish to those called A, B, C, and D, shown on sheet 116. It will be referred to as "Class E." Rooms of that class will be finished with a maple floor as specified throughout; walls and ceiling plastered as is the rest of the building; a cement base or mop block; no cornice or moldings or ornaments on ceiling or walls; plain 4-inch casings of quarter-sawn oak at all doors and windows and a one-molding cap across the same, all as shown as an alternative finish under heading of "Note" on sheet 119.

EIGHTH STORY (PLAN 112).

215. The interior of the dome, elevators, stairs, and as far into the four main corridors as the first pilasters, indicated on the eighth-floor plans, No. 112, by the letters A, B, will be described under another heading. The flooring of this portion, however, will be the same as that of the main corridors.

216. At the ends of skylight openings, over the four great court rooms, the contractor will put in the necessary steel and fireproofing for floors to carry 150 pounds per square foot of surface.

217. Lay a pine-plank flooring, not over 6 inches wide, in the attic or pipe loft over the eighth story.

218. Cut such openings as may be necessary to afford egress to the roofs from these attics, and said openings framed and filled with tin-covered pine doors. (Four in each wing.)

219. The corridor floors as far in the north wing as room 1, south wing to room 28, west wing to rooms 16 and 17, and east wing to room 31, will be as specified under the general clauses for corridor floors. Where projections are over 6 inches the border will form around such projections; where any less projection occurs in the corridor wall no notice will be taken of it in laying this border. The main toilet-room floor will be raised above the general level by two steps, about 13 inches; it will be built up with cross walls and slab tiles of fireproofing, the same as was specified for the general filling of the floor. Some of the private toilet rooms, those away from the main lines of structural columns, will also have to be raised about 8 inches. The others on the main lines of columns will be of the general level.

220. The floors of rooms Nos. 4 (marshal), 3, 5 (grand jury), G and D (district attorney) of 31 will be of selected quarter-sawn oak, perfectly clear, tongued and grooved, 1½ inches wide, and with a pattern border of oak, cherry, and walnut. Everywhere else but in the machinery room the flooring will be of first clear maple, as hereinbefore described. The machinery room will be of 4-inch wide tongued and grooved first common white pine. Rooms 4 and G D of 31 will have a high wainscoting of 8 feet 3 inches and door and window trim of selected quarter-sawn oak, as shown by sheet No. 116. Rooms 3, 5, 23, and 25 will have a low wainscoting of 4 feet, as shown at (mm) sheet No. 116.

221. In these rooms above the wainscoting, and in all the other rooms that are not wainscoted, the plastering will be as above described in the general terms.

222. The ceiling of this entire story to be a suspended ceiling of suitable framing and expanded metal.

223. There will be picture moldings at the ceiling juncture in every room excepting the machinery room; this picture molding will be of oak. Rooms 3, 4, 5, G, D 31, 19, 23, 25 will have plain plaster ceiling molds, as shown on sheet No. 121, but without the ornamentation there detailed.

224. All of the other ceilings will be plain.

225. The finish throughout the rooms, except as above specified for wainscoted rooms, will be that specified for rooms of Class E. The unassigned space No. 16 will be finished as one room.

226. The stairs from the eighth to the ninth floor will have the same rail, wainscoting, and marble finish as the main stairs.

227. The corridors to be as detailed on sheets 116, 119, 120, and 121. The base of the wainscoting will be a gray Tennessee marble, the body and cap of the wainscoting will be an American white marble, equal to Hollister in texture, but whiter in color, cement casings and cornice as shown on sheet 116, and oak doors and subtrim, all as detailed.

228. The description of the general toilet room will be found under another head. The private toilet rooms will have similar treatment and a wainscoting 4 feet high of American white marble with but a single ½-inch member capping it of the same marble, the usual plastering and plain oak trim, Class E.

229. In some of these private toilet-room doors the contractor may have to insert a register face that will be provided by another contractor.

230. The windows from the rooms into the large skylight space over the large court rooms will have fixed sash, excepting one in each of such rooms will be a pivoted sash properly fitted with all the necessary hardware.

231. The partitions around these light spaces under the skylights of the four courts will be plastered on the skylight side with the ordinary two-coat plaster, neatly fitted around the windows but without trim on the skylight side. These sash will be glazed with crystallized sheet glass.

232. Wherever there are steps into toilet rooms or raised spaces over the court rooms, these will be marble tread and riser, the same as the main stair.

233. The ceiling lights in this eighth floor will be neatly framed around in oak, with such subdivision and hinged sash as may be required, and glazed with sheet crystalline cut up into large but handsome patterns, with lead joints.

234. The detention room. No. E of No. 1, will have strong wire guards securely fastened outside of the windows, and on the inside of the door there will be no lock, latch, keyhole, or other means of fastening the door from that side or tampering with the lock. Provide suitable special bolts on the outside.

235. The vaults in the angles of façades (in the corner piers) must all be lined with 2-inch fireproof furring before plastering same; lining is shown by a heavy line on plans.

236. The ordinary fireproof vaults to be neatly plastered on the inside, floored in cement, and to have quarter-inch sheet-steel, single, stock, vault doors with suitable and customary reenforcement of angles, etc., but covered on the outside with a wood door, the same finish as the room door, properly bolted to the steel frame. The only conspicuous features about these doors will be the necessarily heavier butts and the high-grade combination lock and handle. The vaults on this floor are merely for the safe-keeping of books—fireproof vaults with moderate security against anyone tampering with them. The burglar-proof vaults occurring throughout the building will be specially noted and specified; they are indicated on plans by a heavy black line around inside of the space.

236. All the room partitions will be 4-inch tile. There will be many places around down spouts, beams in ceilings, steam risers, and other pipes and projections where furring of angles, tees, and expanded metal will have to be shaped for the finished plastering. There will probably be two or three such projections in nearly every room, and the contractor must take care of them all.

237. He must also look out for all the register faces provided by another contractor for the ventilation, neatly trimming around these, properly adjusting them, and assisting the other contractor to exactly locate them. He must also run his bases along the outside wall so as to cover and properly fit around the ducts provided for telephone wires, etc., leaving proper openings in them for threading.

238. He must be particularly careful that none of his men disturb any of the numerous wire and other ducts laid in the floors. These must not be walked upon, and a nail carelessly driven into them while laying the floor may do hundreds of dollars of damage to the lighting plant, and all such damage traced to this contractor's men will be assessed against him.

SEVENTH FLOOR (PLAN 111).

239. As above described for the eighth floor, the dome finish extending into beams AA, BB, CC, and DD will be hereafter specified.

240. The corridors extending on the north to room No. 1, south to No. 15, east to No. 21, west to No. 10 will be exactly as specified for the eighth-floor corridors as to flooring, wainscoting, sash, etc., the only difference being that the false ceiling of expanded metal and plaster to cover the ventilation ducts in these corridors is so low that there will be no plaster cornice at the intersection of wall and ceiling. The window casing will finish against the ceiling, but there will be an elaborate ceiling mold forming the panels as indicated by plans.

241. The general water-closet on this floor is elsewhere specified, together with all the other public toilet rooms. The clauses in the specification referring to the private toilet rooms of the eighth story hold good for those upon this story, as well as in all the stories below. So with the vaults and the clothes closets. All these accessories and conveniencies will be uniform in their finish throughout the building.

242. Shafts for the ventilating ducts will nowhere be plastered on the inside. The hose closets, marked "standpipe" on plans, will be plastered and finished, and floored with a plain maple floor.

243. The general terms describing the furred projections, vaults, care of ducts, etc., used in describing the eighth floor apply with equal force to this seventh story and all the others. In several places the columns will not only be fireproofed, but where ventilating ducts or plumbing pipes are brought down their faces the entire width of the column will be furred out with metal to inclose all such pipes. The false beams in the ceiling formed over all such columns will be symmetrically laid out and widened or narrowed to conform to such irregularities in the pilasters or columns. (Bidders who desire to accurately figure the amount of all this duct and pipe covering there will be to do may see the plans of the heating, electric, and other plants and piping at the offices of the consulting engineers, Messrs. Pierce, Richardson & Neiler, 1405 Manhattan Building, Chicago.)

244. Rooms 12, 13, 14, and A 15 (justices) will be floored with selected oak with a handsome border, all as described heretofore. All the other rooms, excepting 17 and 18, will be floored with plain first clear maple floor, laid in the usual manner.

245. The court of appeals, 17 and 18, will be specially described, along with the four other main courts, under a separate heading.

246. Communicating doors generally, upon this floor as well as throughout the building, will be solid doors; all corridor doors, unless specially called for, will be glazed.

247. Room 15 is shown on plans to be wainscoted and corniced; it has been changed, as far as finish is concerned, to a plain room of Class E. The beams and false ceiling remaining as shown, but not molded or ornamented.

248. Rooms 12, 13, 14, A 15 will be finished with a high oak wainscoting as shown by section kk 116. The communicating doors and the windows in these rooms will be cased and finished as shown, but all the doors into cupboards, toilet rooms, etc., will be part of the wainscoting. The hardware, however, will be the same as for all the other doors.

249. Rooms 8, 19, and A 10 will be finished in Class E except that there will be a plain molded cornice at ceiling. All the other rooms on this floor will be finished plainly Class E without cornices or ceiling molds.

250. The glazed partition in rooms 21 and 10 will be finished the same way as the room side of corridor partition—cement wainscoting and cap and wood trim.

251. Unassigned spaces 1, 3, 5, and 7 will be finished as one large room.

252. The stairs in rooms 9 and 4 will be marble tread and cast-iron riser, with rail as shown for the dome stairs on sheet 113. Marble treads 1¼ inches thick and the ironwork and rails to be electro-bronze.

SIXTH FLOOR (PLAN NO. 110).

253. The dome finish will in this case, as in the others, extend to AA, BB, CC, DD.

254. The courts will be taken care of elsewhere.

255. The corridors extending to the court rooms will be as hereinbefore described. Except that on this and the floors below, there will be a heavy molded and ornamented cornice as well as ceiling mold finishing the juncture betwixt wall and ceiling.

256. Rooms 3, 25, 12, and 20 (judges' private rooms) will be floored with selected clear oak and handsome border as above described for similar elaborate rooms.

257. Room 20 will be wainscoted 8 feet 4 inches high with heavy cornice trim over the corridor partition and over the communicating double doors, all as shown for Class D, sheet 116. This wainscoting and trim and doors will be veneered with specially selected handsome California white mahogany. The moldings and such portions as can not be veneered will be built up of the same wood, straight-grained. All this woodwork will be finished without stain and with white varnishes to preserve the natural color of the wood, and polished to a high gloss as to stiles and rails and moldings, but the panels to be left a dull, satin finish. The ceiling will be molded and ornamented as detailed. What projections may be necessary for pipes, etc., will be wainscoted around and formed into pilasters. The carved surfaces, panels, modillions, etc., in the woodwork will be, as heretofore described and detailed, of composition cleverly stained and made to perfectly imitate the wood; some of their members in high relief will be polished, but the carved surfaces will be left with a stained, filled, and a merely rubbed surface to simulate carved work as near as it is possible for a skilled craftsman to do.

258. Room 25 will be in every way finished the same as No. 20, excepting that all the woodwork will be a rich black walnut, the panels of dull beryl. The single doors in these rooms of Class D will be finished without casing, as part of the wainscoting.

259. Room 3 will be the same as these other two in every particular, save that the woodwork will be a rich oak, sixteenth-century finish, with panels of black walnut beryl finished very dark.

260. Room 12, the same in detail as the preceding, will be finished in Cuban mahogany unstained.

261. All the other rooms will have plain maple floors. Rooms 2, 7, 10, 11, 16, 19, 23, and 26, will be finished in quarter-sawed oak with a 4-foot wainscoting and molded trim around doors and windows, plaster cornices on the wall near the ceiling and cement door heads, all as shown on details for rooms of Class C, sheet 116. All other rooms to be finished in Class E.

262. The inside of all closets, where not otherwise specified, will be finished with a 4-inch plain oak trim around the doors, and hook boards. The toilet rooms will have a plain oak casing around the doors and the marble wainscoting will butt against this casing. The closets will have a cement base.

263. The witness rooms must be provided with a stout No. 10 wire window guard, 2-inch mesh, securely fastened outside the sash. These screens, wherever they occur throughout the building, will be locked and hinged to allow proper cleaning of the windows, and the screens will be painted three coats paint the same color as the sash.

FIFTH FLOOR (PLAN 109).

264. In a general way what was said above concerning the corridors, the termination of dome treatment, the fitting of vaults, water-closets, clothes closets, etc., applies with equal force to this floor.

265. The corridors extend in the north wing to rooms 48 and 52, the south wing to 22–28, east to 37, and west to 7.   The public space or corridor inside of main room No. 7 will have a marble tile floor the same as the outside corridor, and the door trim will be of Class B, in cement, with ornamental door heads and cornice around the walls, cement base, etc.

266. Attention is called to the fact that there will be suspended ceilings over many subcorridors, entrance ways, and rooms.   These are indicated on the plans.

267. Room F 7 (commanding general) is the only one on this floor that will be finished in Cuban mahogany, with high wainscoting, door caps and mantel (Utah onyx facing and hearth), as shown for Class D, sheet 116.   The floor of this room will be quarter-sawn oak, with a handsome border, as for similar rooms in the upper floors.

268. Rooms A 36, I 7, 46, 22, and 28 to be finished with cement casings, plaster caps and cornices, etc., all as shown for Class B, inclusive of plain maple flooring. All other rooms finished as herein specified for Class E.

269. The vaults in rooms 12, 14, 21, 25, 29, C 7, will be left unfinished inside. Another contractor will supply a steel and an electric-alarm lining therefor, but the general contractor will prepare the wood door fronts for these vaults so that the electrician may arrange similar protection on the inside of these doors.   The material will be the same, but a little more labor will be involved in arranging these doors in that way.   The lining of these wood doors to be ½-inch steel on suitable frames, and contractor must also provide and set inner vestibule doors ¼ inch thick with strong locks, etc.   The lock for the outside door will be a particularly high grade of combination lock with ample bolts and bars.   All other vaults are merely fireproof and finished as heretofore described for that class.

FOURTH FLOOR (PLAN 108).

270. General terms regarding dome treatment, corridor finish, etc., found above apply likewise to this story.

271. Notice that there will be a number of places where false ceilings and beams will have to be formed.

272. Rooms CD 9 (collector of customs), A 11 (collector internal-revenue), AB 2 (pension agent), will be finished in Cuban mahogany as above specified, high wainscoting, door caps, mantels, oak floor, etc., as shown for rooms of Class D, sheet 116.

273. Rooms 2, 4, A, and B 9 will also have oak floor and border, low wainscoting, wood trim of quarter-sawn oak, dark finish, cement casings, plaster head over doors, and ornamental plaster cornices, as shown for Class C, 116.

274. Rooms 9 and 11 will be finished with plain-molded cornices, ornamented caps to the piers, and paneled faces in the piers in cement and plaster, with plain molds on the ceilings, all as shown by section xx, sheet 116, except that the ornaments shown in cornices, etc., are to be omitted.

275. All the other rooms, including the unassigned space, room 1, will be plainly finished with the usual maple floor, plastered walls and ceiling, oak trim, without cornices or ornament (Class E).

276. The spaces inscribed within the lines of corridor columns, rooms A and E, and the ordinary vaults in the office of the collector of customs, will be floored the same as is the corridor, in marble tile.   There will be marble wainscoting, the same as in the corridors, inside the entrance to this room; also outside of the partition of the rooms A and E and the vaults, and a marble base around the structural columns. In other words, this space, so circumscribed (will ultimately be inclosed with counters), is a public space, and is to be treated the same as the corridors.   This also applies to the space and columns inside of room 11, between the columns, to the vaults.   There will be unornamented, molded, plaster cornices about these rooms, false beams, drop ceilings, and plain-paneled pilasters, but apart from that and the marble floors in public spaces they are essentially of Class E.

277. The private toilet rooms and clothes closets will be the same as for the upper floors.

278. The vaults, G of room 7, and CD of room 11, and F of 9, will be left rough inside for the electrical and steel lining, the clause referring to the arrangement of doors for such electrically protected vaults in the upper stories applies with equal force to these vaults.   All other vaults on this floor will be merely book vaults and finished with a steel-lined wood door, same as other vaults of this class throughout the building.

279. Throughout the building all unassigned spaces must be finished as one large room in each case.

THIRD FLOOR (PLAN 107).

280. The dome treatment will extend into AA, BB, CC, DD; beyond those points the corridor floor, as specified for the upper corridor, will extend in the south wing to rooms 1, 3, 4; in the corridor of the north wing this same floor will extend to rooms 42, 46, and 38; in the east wing this flooring will extend to 29, 21, 25, and in the west wing to room 51. The main corridor in the south wing will be treated exactly the same as the upper corridors, excepting there will be but few glazed partitions. All the doors opening from it will be glazed, but the walls will be plastered. The marble wainscoting will be continuous, excepting at the doors, and will turn into the two main branches to rooms 3 and 4. There will be false beams in the ceiling, decorated cornices, etc., the same as are shown for the fourth and fifth floors. The subcorridor off this main one, extending to rooms 13, 14, 12, and 6, will be tiled the same as the others, but will have no marble wainscoting. There will be a glazed partition the same as in the upper corridors, but the wainscoting, cap, etc., will be worked in cement. There will be a marble base, however, in these subcorridors; there will also be a plain molded cornice, with false beams, etc., as are indicated on the plans.

281. The corridors in the other three wings, being more or less private in nature, will have marble tile floors the same as the other and marble base around the walls, but no marble wainscoting. There will be a cement wainscoting cap run the same as in the marble, plain cement trim around the doors and windows, glazed doors and sash, the same as in the main corridor, and a plain molded cornice at the ceiling, with such false beams as are shown.

282. Note that in this story the ceiling between the main lines of structural columns, over all subcorridors, and over central vaults and storage rooms will all be suspended ceilings to afford ample opportunity for the concealing of ventilation pipes, ducts, etc.

283. The sills now in windows at each of the façades will be removed by this contractor, who will form a step only at the windows and fill these openings with swing sash instead of double hung, all properly hinged, etc., to open inward and give access to the balconies at front.

284. The main toilet rooms are taken care of in another part of this specification.

285. The floor in rooms No. 1, ABCDE 1 (postmaster), will be of extra selected oak, and with a handsome border forming around the rooms, projections, columns, etc., of oak, black walnut, and cherry similarly laid. Elsewhere in this story, excepting in the vault, the flooring will be first select white maple, laid in the ordinary manner, on the sleepers set in the concrete.

286. Room No. 1 will be finished with high wainscoting, wood cornices ornamented, veneered covering to the columns, pilasters, etc., all of Cuban mahogany finished quite dark, and according to the details of Class D. The double doors will have ornamental caps as shown, but all single doors will be part of the wainscoting. Room BC 1 will be as elaborately finished as Class D, with high wainscoting, mantel (with Mexican onyx facing and Utah onyx hearth), double doors with elaborate trim, all of California white mahogany. Room A 1 will be the same in finish as these, but of quarter-sawed oak. These rooms will have the false beams finished in the same wood as is used in the rooms, and also a wood cornice at juncture of wall and ceiling at both levels. In addition to this there will be the heavy ornamented plaster ceiling mold, forming the ceiling into panels ready for the painted decorations to be done under another contract.

287. Rooms D, E 1 and 2 will be trimmed in quarter-sawed oak, as for Class C, and with plaster cornices, ceiling mold, and caps over the doors.

288. Rooms 5, 13, 21, 25, 43, and 3 will be finished with cement trim, plaster caps, and plain molded cornice, etc., as for Class B.

289. All the other rooms on this floor will be plain finish, without plaster cornices, all as shown for Class E.

290. The private toilet rooms will be finished and fitted as specified for the upper stories.

291. The files and record rooms are but plain rooms of Class E, with ordinary solid doors. The vaults not otherwise described will be plainly finished, plastered inside, and with a cement floor, and a wood false-door covering and fastened to the vault door as specified for the other merely fireproof vaults throughout the building.

292. Vault A of the large room 12 will be left unfinished inside for the electrician to install his steel and protective lining. A one-half door of wood must also be provided in which the same electrician will install an electrical lining to cover the solid plate and vestibule doors furnished by this general contractor as specified for the burglar-proof vault.

293. There will be a marble and iron stair, the same as detailed for the dome, running from room 27 down to the second floor, practiced through the present structural framing. The contractor must remove fireproof flooring in this and all other openings that will be made through the floors, and provide such steel members as may be necessary to hold the remaining fireproofing adjacent to these openings in place, all as instructed by the architect. There will also be an elevator opening near room 3; the front of this elevator opening will be a solid partition with a double-faced door, the side in the corridor will be of the ordinary wood used elsewhere, but the elevator side will be a ⅞-inch pine door sheathed both sides with tin and properly blind-bolted to the wood door. In this door there will be a large panel of extra-heavy wired glass. The doors shall set in a properly tinned frame and run on suitable ways, etc., all most carefully arranged to prevent fire communicating from lower floors through this shaft. A similar door will be provided for the stairway near room 27.

294. In rooms 32, 30, 29, 16, and 12 the corners at the angles of the dome will be cut off; this partition will be fitted with fixed sash, so that the room will be lighted, but that there will be no way of tampering with the ventilating device. The floor in these triangular patches will be removed—that is, the fireproofing—to allow the ventilating engineer to introduce the fresh air through the opening provided in the outer wall. This general contractor will supply a heavy screen, as may be called for by the ventilating contractor, in lieu of sash for these outer openings, and there must be provision made below these windows at the mezzanine floor of the second story to catch and drain off all water that may come in through these screens.

295. The two cells B and A in room 26 will be built of the ordinary fireproofing. The floors will be the ordinary maple flooring, but the doors will be ⅞-inch bars, 2 inches apart, set in proper angle frame, stiffened with crosspieces, heavily hinged, and locked with a safety prison lock; in every sense a good prison door.

SECOND FLOOR (PLAN 106).

296. The limits of the dome finish are shown on this plan by the doorways entering into the post-office portion. Apart from that dome portion this entire story will be one large workroom, devoted to the mailing division of the post-office. The contractor will remove the beams at this floor level that at present cut off the head room of the dome stairs, as shown in the plans. The beams remain the property of the Government, and the contractor will not charge a pound rate for this removal; it is included in the contract.

297. This entire space will be finished as specified for Class E. There will be no cornices, but there will be neat trim or false beam formed around the openings of the skylights. There will be wood sash, pine frames, etc., for the ceiling lights under the smaller skylights. The glass in these will be wired crystalline, the woodwork painted three coats of an approved color. There will be ceiling sash (heavy wired crystalline glass) arranged under the large skylights; sash of pine, reenforced with iron and laid on iron angles and beams, strong enough to carry 50 pounds per foot, all arranged in panels, the sash and iron properly painted; also paint and finish the exposed steel work of skylights in enameled white.

298. Suitable arrangements will have to be attached to the louvres or other openings in the skylight and the hinged sash of the ceiling lights, that will be arranged for ventilation, to enable these to be opened and closed from convenient points; all such hardware will be iron electroplated in bronze. The hardware of the windows will be extra heavy, the chains and lead weights will be of suitable size to carry the very large sash.

299. The outside sash will have to be 2¾ inches thick; the sash will be circular on the outside, but will be paneled to a square head on the inside with triangular flush spandrel panels properly adjusted, all of pine stained the same as the room wood. These sash will run in a pocket formed over the window head and properly lined to a smooth finish with pine sheathing and covered over with expanded metal and plaster, expanded metal extending well over the solid work so as to insure that there will be no cracks in the plaster over these false heads at the windows. The finish will be square at top and of the same character as the plain rooms in the upper stories.

300. Where the floor is now jogged around the dome corners it will be filled out anglewise as shown on the plans. The necessary framing of beams, the fireproofing of the floors, etc., to fill out these spaces must be done by this contractor.

301. The railing around the skylight openings in the floors will be 3 feet 6 inches high, built up of 4-inch tile plastered both sides, with a cement base on the inside and a neat trimming at juncture of the false beam work at the line of the first-floor ceiling. The top of this railing will be formed of a 4-inch angle iron, framed into the structural column, to which the fireproofing will be doweled and on top of which

will be fastened a broad railing of oak quartersawn, 8 inches wide by 2 inches thick, properly shaped, in long pieces, and finished same as specified for all other hard wood.

302. The toilet rooms are specified elsewhere.

303. The contractor will build a mezzanine floor, supplying all the necessary framing, concreting, fireproofing, etc., around the dome in this second story. There will be 12-inch beams framed into the columns and tied at intervals with 3-inch angles to the third-floor beams above. Around the outer edge will be a tight partition of 3-inch fireproofing, plastered both sides, a cement base inside and a plain 3-inch oak casing around both sides of the openings. As this mezzanine is to serve for the purposes of a passage as well as for an air duct, these openings will be of glazed fixed sash 1¼ inches thick. All mezzanine floors will be made strong enough to carry 100 pounds per square foot.

304. Off from this mezzanine will be carried the post-office "lookout" passages (subject for a separate bid); these will be built of 2-inch tees in suspension from the ceiling beams, fastened to 4-inch angles at the bottom, across which will be fastened 3-inch tees, forming a floor. On the flanges of these tees will be built a floor of book tile or of corrugated iron and concrete 2 inches thick, or of "slab construction" with a finishing coat of neat cement that will serve as a floor. Around the outside and the bottom will be fastened expanded metal, over which will be the usual plaster finish of the walls and ceilings. The plastering will be brought to a neat finish at the metal angles on the bottom corners of this passageway; there will also be a neat iron finish around the peepholes in the floor and around the registers at the sides. The inside of these runways or passages will be similarly plastered and finished. These registers will be of cast iron, made in a very fine pattern with a member not over a quarter inch thick on the face, but an inch deep in the metal and beveled outward. These screens will be set at the proper angle, in suitable metal frames, and are to be "staggered" throughout the entire length of these passageways so that no two will be opposite each other. The screens will be painted black, three coats, and though shown differently on the drawing No. 118, need be not nearer together than 12 feet on centers. These screens are of different heights on the two sides of the passage owing to the fact that the ventilation ducts will be carried along the side of these passageways and must be covered by the contractor with expanded metal and plaster. The peep holes in the floor of the inspector's lookout passageway will be made of cast iron, painted black. The entire surface of walls and ceiling inside the passages will be painted two coats, black.

305. At the connection of these passageways with the mezzanine story around the dome there will be fixed patent revolving storm doors of the plainest design, of painted pine.

306. Where indicated on plans there will be a circular tower of fireproofing, or built of angles and expanded metal and plaster with a suitable cast-iron stairway inside, as a communication between the main second floor and these passageways; a plain oak door at the bottom will be the means of communication.

307. The stairways in the different portions of this floor leading up and down will be of cast risers and marble treads, 1⅜ inches thick, of gray Tennessee, with a pipe and bar railing and wood top, the iron electro-bronzed, all as shown for the dome stairs on sheet No. 113.

308. The elevator openings on this floor will be inclosed with solid partitions and tinned-wood finished doors and wire-glass panels as shown in some places, or with a plain angle and heavy wire screen and sliding door, all electro-bronzed.

309. The structural columns will be inclosed in 4 inches of fireproofing as specified generally and plastered, with a neat one-member cap worked around the top. The angles will be formed of a patent extra-heavy metal angle suitably rounded—that is, down to a point 4 feet above the floor. Below this point the columns will be covered with a ¼-inch steel plate and reenforced on the angles with a 2-inch light steel angle properly lag bolted into the fireproofing. The holes will be countersunk and all the screw and bolt heads flush. Similar angles will be attached to all projecting corners as a protection against trucks and heavy wear. This metal work will terminate at a suitable height above the floor, half an inch or so, that the usual wood base shoe may be fastened to form a trim.

310. There will be required for the post-office work a great deal of machinery, chutes, elevators, carriers, etc. All of this will be done under a separate contract, but if it is let during the life of this contract this contractor is to afford all the assistance that will be asked of him by the architect to properly lay out this other work in connection with his own, and he will make suitable arrangements that the two classes of work may be carried on together, and that when completed it will all have the appearance of uniformity. To that end he probably will have to do some cutting and

patching. At the present writing it is difficult to say just what that will be; it certainly will involve some labor, but hardly any material, and must be included under the general heading of contingencies; that, in a contract of this size, will be no mean item.

FIRST FLOOR (PLAN 105).

311. The dome finish, the outside of the main corridor finish, the vestibules, the subtreasury, the toilet rooms, will be taken care of elsewhere.

312. There will be built around the dome a mezzanine story as was specified for the second floor, excepting that instead of solid partition inclosing it there will be a suitable cast-iron standard and pipe rail marking its boundary. The plaster will be neatly finished around the edge beam, forming a fascia, curb, and soffit. The inside of the curb will be formed with a 2-inch angle properly fastened on. The pipe railing will be painted.

313. There will also be lookout passageways suspended from the ceiling, and essentially the same in construction as was specified for the second floor, excepting that instead of revolving storm doors at their connection with the mezzanine there will be ordinary oak doors as specified for the rest of the building.

314. Where the mezzanine floor (note that there is likewise a bridge crossing the Jackson street corridor) crosses the corridors the faces of this substory will, of course, be finished as is the main corridor; there will be panels and beveled plate glass and suitable sash of hard wood and art glass, as may be indicated in the different places, and the insides of these passageways will be furred and neatly plastered, so as to conceal all the breaks and angles of the outer arches, etc. There will also be a neat oak trim around these windows. This mezzanine story will be cut off from the money-order and registry divisions of post-office by a No. 10 painted wire guard, 2-inch mesh, from floor to ceiling, fastened to suitable angles, tees, etc.

315. Sheet No. 118 gives a hint in a general way of how the inside of these corridor partitions will be finished.

316. Wherever there is shown a lobby into the working room off of these main corridors such lobbies will be public spaces, treated much as is a banking room, necessarily handsomely and in keeping with the main corridor.

317. Where this corridor wall is the absolute line of demarcation between the public space and the working room of the post-office the inside finish will, of course, be exceedingly plain and in harmony with the general treatment of this big working room (Class E).

318. Detail sheets No. 118 and No. 120 give a general hint as to this treatment. Section MN No. 118 shows the platform over the alcove. This will be of ordinary pine sheathing, paper, and finished maple flooring laid on sleepers fastened to the beams, with the dust guard and base and plain trim around the circular sash of oak, with all the unevenness of the corridor framing concealed under an expanded metal and plaster covering; fireproofing partition wall below that platform, with a plain oak trim around that opening and a plain oak base at the floor. These alcove platforms will be built by this contractor. There is no framing in place at present. He will frame in suitable channels and beams to carry all this marble and ornamental work and also calculated to carry 100 pounds per square foot on the platforms. In the spaces marked "lobbies" there will be the same flooring as is specified for the general corridor. The teller's cages, counters, etc., forming the inner boundary of these lobbies will be furnished under a subsequent contract. The inside of the corridor partition and up to the line of the counter and screen work will be wainscoted to the counter height with a marble in color, market price, and quality equal to an Ellis pink Tennessee, with a cap and base of dark cedar Tennessee marble. Above this wainscoting the openings will have an architrave trim in cement the same pattern as the upper corridor trim.

319. The insides of the doors and all sashes will be of quarter-sawn oak.

320. The walls and ceilings in these lobby spaces will be same as specified in general; there will be a molded and ornamented cornice, the same as the third-story hallway around these lobbies, and a suspended false beam on the inner line to receive such cornice.

321. The different offices of the superintendents, etc., on this floor will be finished as directed for Class E.

322. The remainder of this floor will be substantially four great workrooms, and will be finished as to floor, walls, and ceiling as is specified for the second-story workroom. The columns will be similarly protected with steel. The elevators and stairs will be inclosed with fireproof partitions plastered both sides, with wood finish and tin-lined doors, glazed with wire glass. All the stairs will be marble treads, cast-iron risers, painted rails, etc., on steel carriages, the same as specified for second floor.

323. There will be circular and inclosed cast-iron stairs to the inspection lookouts where shown.

324. Some of the divisions in these rooms will be of wire. A No. 10 gauge steel wire, 2-inch mesh, suitably framed from floor to ceiling with angles, tees, etc., stoutly fastened thereto and all painted three coats of a white enamel.

325. Where there are glazed partitions between working spaces the same will be of 1¼-inch oak sash with suitable divisions and plain first-quality double-thick American sheet glass. These sash will have proper pockets, sash chain and weight for the lower half of the sash. Where these openings are near the skylights they shall extend to the ceiling in order to transmit all the light possible.

326. The office of the captain of the watch on the first floor will be finished as is shown for Class B, No. 116.

327. Some of the vaults will be double-decked vaults; these will have inner floors of suitable eyebeams, corrugated metal and concrete, or buckle plate. The walls of all these vaults will be of 6-inch fireproof tile, and will be lined with quarter-inch boiler plate around the sides, floor, and ceiling, properly fastened to angles, tees, etc., anchored to the walls. Where not shown as burglar-proof these vaults will have the usual first-class vault door and double vestibule door, combination locks, etc., but without the covering wood door.

328. Where they are burglar-proof there will be similar doors, but the contractor must also provide an oak-finished door to cover the electric protection that will be supplied by another contractor.

329. Where there are double-decked vaults there will be a stair such as is shown for the dome, painted rail, etc.

330. The general window trim will be the same as specified for the second story, except that there will be no pockets over the windows; the sash will be extra heavy and of first-quality pine stained and finished to represent oak.

331. Note that a great many of the columns will have to be furred out to inclose the ventilating ducts; there will be numberless heating and plumbing pipes carried up through this floor, and hundreds of feet of ventilating ducts, all of which must be inclosed by this contractor with expanded metal on iron framing and plaster.

332. There will also be ventilation ducts suspended from the ceiling, rising from the floor, and elsewhere that will all have to be inclosed with suitable angles, tees, expanded metal, and plastering, to make a neat-appearing and finished interior.

BASEMENT FLOOR (PLAN 104).

333. The driveway will be as hereinbefore specified, the side walls finished with granite and enameled brick, the ceiling of a good patent plaster, laid in sections to proper grounds to prevent cracking, and deeply V-lined with joints into squares of about 2 feet. There will be formed in this ceiling projections and false beams as indicated on plans, coves, and window lintels, etc., of plaster. The walls on the mailing platform, the structural columns, and the doors will be covered, as shown, with plate steel and angles for their protection. The floor of the driveway, extending to the street paving, will be of asphalt block, and that of the mailing platform will be of 2 by 6 inch tongued-and-grooved pine plank dressed and blind-nailed to the sleepers. There will be a 12 by 14 inch oak buffer block, in long lengths, fastened as directed to the edge of this mailing platform. In the inclines at ends of driveway will be inserted raised rough granite pieces, every 2 feet apart and 8 feet long, serving as clinches for the horses.

334. The doors into the engine room on the other side of the driveway will be of 2¼-inch solid oak, properly braced and framed and with iron suspension rods if necessary. The doors into the subtreasury and money-order department in the basement will be framed in pine and covered on the outside with steel plate, ornamentally bolted to the door. The inside of these doors will be stained to look like oak. The glass in all these basement doors and subdivisions and vaults will be first-quality double-thick American sheet glass. The glass in the outside windows and in the sixteen windows at the entrances to the driveway will be of an approved prismatic glass, equal in make and lighting qualities to the highest grade of "Luxfer prism."

335. The windows in the subtreasury and money-order parts of the building will have a 2-inch angle frame securely fastened into the granite and jambs and sills, in which will be arranged a grill of ¾-inch steel bars set in a suitable angle and 3 inches on centers, hung on extra-heavy strap hinges, and securely locked with two bolts into the frame top and bottom, locked from the inside with some suitable device. All the other windows on the outside of the basement and in the vaults will have similar frames of 1¼-inch angles fastened into the stonework, to which will be suspended with hinges a framed No. 10 wire 3-inch mesh screen, locked on the inside with

some suitable device. All of this outside metal work will be painted in three coats of some approved color.

336. Where shown on the plans, there will be brick-wall divisions of the thickness shown; the remainder of the partitions will be 6-inch tile.

337. It will be noticed that each of the larger spaces in the basement has an opening on the driveway and at some windows on the outside wall. Most of these places will be used as rough working rooms or storage rooms, where there is danger from fire. The partitions between these spaces, therefore, will be solid as far as possible, but wherever there are openings, doors, or borrowed lights the glass in them will be wire glass set in metal sash or wood sash, tinned, and the doors will be framed of pine, but tinned both sides.

338. All the elevators, stairs, and inclosures that communicate with the first floor (some 60 or more, about 4 feet square) shall also be inclosed with 6-inch tile partition and tinned doors. All of the ducts leading from floor to ceiling will be incased with 4-inch fireproofing, and extra precautions will have to be taken with the horizontal runs of ventilating ducts on the ceiling to protect them extra well with asbestos covering, expanded metal, and plaster, because these basement rooms are the most likely places where fire may originate, and every possibility of its communicating with the upper stories or marring them with smoke must be most carefully guarded against.

339. The engine-room floor will be of marble tile, same as corridor floors. The boiler-room floor and the subtreasury space floor, and the repair room H will be concrete, cement finish floor. The space under the dome will also be a concrete, cement finish floor, and the floors elsewhere in the basement will be of second select hard maple not over 4 inches wide and in long pieces, tongued and grooved.

340. The finish of all the rooms in the basement is to be of Class E. There must be a suspended ceiling over boiler room. All the columns will be plastered, rounded angles, and a neat molding at ceiling and have an extra-heavy metal angle in the plaster, and those in the boiler room, in the bag-repair room, in the finance workroom, and in the spaces directly adjacent to the mailing platform will be protected with plate steel and steel angles, all as specified for the platform, and all the angles projecting into these rooms will likewise be protected with steel angles 4 feet high.

341. The flooring in the vaults under sidewalk will be of maple, same as the rest of the basement, and in the coal room it will be a concrete and cement floor. The walls in all these vault spaces under the sidewalk will be first carefully pointed up with cement to prevent leakages, then a 4-inch tile wall built 2 inches away from it and plastered the same as all the inside basement walls.

342. There will be one coat of plastering for the ceiling on the under finished side of sidewalk.

343. Where shown, there will be cast-iron open-riser steps with pipe rails from the sidewalk to the basement level, all painted and properly adjusted. Doors leading from the area to the basement will be 2½-inch solid oak doors, glazed panels, plate glass and heavy wire screens over the same.

344. The engineer's private office in the engine room will be finished as Class E. His public office will be inclosed with a glazed partition, a cement wainscoting mold, oak sash, crystalline glass, substantially the same as the corridor partitions above.

345. In the depressions under the main entrances the contractor will face up the difference in levels with plaster on fireproofing, cement base, and oak capping, on top of which will be an electro-bronze rail, with wood top, same as the dome stairs, and steps connecting the two levels of marble treads and risers.

346. As stated before, there must be arranged for, under a subsequent contract, many post-office mechanical devices, elevators, conveyors, etc. There will be very much of all this in the basement. The work may be begun before the completion of this contract, and this contractor must so accommodate the other and arrange his work, trim, etc., that when completed there will be reasonable harmony in the two branches of the work.

347. The subtreasury vault will be erected under another contract, but this contractor must afford every facility for that work's execution, and when it is completed he will build the partitions around it, plaster the same, and finish its outer surface in harmony with the rest of the work and the rooms through which it passes. The partition on the boiler room side of this vault will be of brick.

FINISHED STORIES OF THE DOME (PLAN 114).

348. The dome stories will be finished substantially as is the rest of the building. The floors will be filled up with fireproof blocking, concrete, and wood strips where there are wood floors. The finished floor of all the galleries and public space on the

ninth story and the tenth story, the public spaces by the elevator and stairways in the other stories, hallways, etc., and in all the toilet rooms, will be the same as is specified for the toilet rooms elsewhere. The finish of the toilet rooms will be the same as in the others, but the finish of the public spaces referred to will be as is described for Class E.

349. The large window openings at the angles of the ninth floor will be filled with iron frames and "Luxfer" or other prismatic glass, all set flush with the granite face of wall.

350. At the eleventh-floor line there will be a cast-iron painted transom of suitable but plain design to finish those large dome windows that will extend 2 feet above the floor finish and 10 inches below the ceiling finish, paneled and suitably painted and sanded to imitate the granite outside.

351. The elevator inclosures will be of angles and stout wire of small mesh with some slight ornamentation, all electro-bronzed and in keeping with the stair and gallery rail shown on sheet No. 113.

352. The stairs will be cast-iron risers and marble equal to Ellis gray for the tread. All the metal work will be electro-bronzed. The windows throughout will be of pine sash properly hung, swung, or hinged, as the case may be, with all the necessary hardware as is provided for the other windows throughout the building. The glazing will be of second American plate. Doors and sash inside will be of oak, the same as detailed for the rest of the building. Glazing of inside sash will be plain crystalline.

353. The floors of all these rooms will be of first select white maple, the same as specified for lower floors.

354. The civil-service rooms, the large examination room on the thirteenth story, the exhibition lobby, the office of the professor in charge, and the observer in charge of the weather bureau on the fourteenth story will be finished according to Class F, except that there will be a plain molded 4-member plaster cornice about them. All the other rooms throughout dome will be straight Class E.

355. The main girders will be inclosed with 3-inch partitions each side of their members. On the twelfth and fifteenth stories openings will be left and neatly finished in the upper half of these spandrels, finished with an oak sill. On the eleventh and fourteenth stories the lower portions of these spandrels will be open arched or otherwise formed for sufficient headroom for passage.

356. The fifteenth story, though unassigned, will be finished as one large room; so will the sixteenth. The exposed ribs and girders, etc., in the ceilings of these rooms must be covered with expanded metal and plaster. The entire ceiling or underside of the dome in the sixteenth story will likewise be covered, either each separate girder plastered on both sides or a false ceiling arranged under the bottom chords of the minor girders and projecting down as beams below the heavier girders. In other words, the entire framing and fireproofing of the dome roof must be thoroughly protected with expanded metal and plaster.

357. The structural columns everywhere in this dome will be thoroughly built in after being grouted, and plastered, and with rounded metal angles, a neat molding at the ceiling, and a cement base at the floor.

358. The stairs from the sixteenth floor to the observer's platform on top of the dome will be of cast-iron treads and risers with a plain pipe rail, painted. These stairs will be arranged in easy runs and landings; suitable weather-proof door will be arranged at the top and a wood-slat platform laid on the two levels of the corona. The ventilation ducts, heating pipes, electric wires, plumbing pipes, etc., wherever they occur in these stories, must be covered with angles, expanded metal, and plaster. A neat, trim job throughout.

TOILET ROOMS.

359. For the marble work, the floors, the divisions, etc., in these rooms see general clauses under head of "Marble work."

360. The casings for the doors and windows above this marble wainscoting will be of cement, molded as is detailed for Class A, No. 116

361. The walls and ceilings will be plastered with a patent plaster equal to an "Adamant No. 1 XXX," gauged with ¼ lime-putty and worked up to clear white, highly-polished surface. There will be no cornices in any of these rooms, public or private.

362. The hardware for these toilet rooms, the entrance doors, water-closet doors, windows, etc., will be polished brass finish. Contractor must work in harmony with the plumbing contractor so that these rooms will be handsomely finished. Plumbing contractor will only furnish the actual backs of the wash basins and slabs and trays

of marble and the toilet hardware; everything else in marble or hardware about the room will be supplied by this contractor.

363. The floors will be raised two steps high; these steps will be marble risers and treads of the same marble as the corridor finish.

364. The doors into the little passageways back of the fixtures will be solid doors; the doors to the water-closets will be the usual height, except the low ones for the work-room toilets; 1¼-inch, four-paneled solid or slat doors as the architect may direct, all of quarter-sawn selected oak, handsomely finished, light in color.

COURT ROOMS (DRAWING NO. 115).

365. This drawing more fully illustrates the scheme of decoration of the four main court rooms on the sixth story and the court of appeals on the seventh story.

366. There will be an elaborate system of ventilation introduced in these floors, so that this contractor must exercise special care in laying the fireproof blocking, or false floors about and over these pipes.   Nowhere must the tile be supported by the pipes, and where they pass up through the floor he will properly and neatly finish around the nozzles.

367. Fitting snugly up to the black marble base around all these rooms, and omitting the marble mop block shown on plans, there will be laid a 4-inch wide tongued and grooved first common pine flooring over the entire space inclosed in each room. (The interlocking tile shown on plans will not be in this contract.)

368. The seat platform of the court of appeals will be made up of pine sleepers and rough pine flooring, upon which will be laid a finished floor of the regular narrow white maple; around the edge of this platform will be a molded cast-iron nosing electro-bronzed.   At the edge of this platform will be set handsome bronzed standards and a bronzed rail with a mahogany hand piece similar in design to the main stairway railing.

369. The wainscoting of this court of appeals will be of especially selected marble equal to a Georgia verd antique. It will be made up of sections 1 inch thick and about 2 feet 6 inches wide, most carefully jointed, with a V joint and every way arranged to conceal the fact that the circle of the room is made up of straight slabs of marble, a polygonic figure.   In every case there must be a joint in this wainscoting behind the detached columns.   The necking of this wainscoting will be cut to the same angle as these faces.   The plain piece above the necking, the frieze of this wainscoting, will be cut in pieces of the same width as the wainscoting, but to a true circle.

370. The high base at the back of the room will be of black marble equal to a Glens Falls.   The wainscoting paneling will be in two shades of green, equal to a Georgia verd antique and Champlain green.   The pilasters, bases and caps, and the two columns back of the bench will be marble equal to the dark cedar Tennessee. The pilaster treatment forming the sort of proscenium will be of this same dark cedar marble.

371. The architrave and plain frieze over the doors will also be dark cedar marble.

372. The wainscoting cap will be molded and ornamented, as detailed on sheet No. 120, in artificial marble to perfectly imitate the green wainscoting below.   The entablature of the back screen, the archivolts over its three openings, the arched heads, capitals, and niches in the proscenium treatment will all be of this artificial marble (in the several colors required); so will the molded heads over the doors (the clock and bronze ornaments shown will be no part of this contract).   All this artificial marble, excepting that portion in the proscenium face, will be made to perfectly imitate dark cedar marble; that in the proscenium to imitate the green.   The isolated columns in this court of appeals will be made up of steel angles, expanded metal, and a neat Keene cement basis, to which must be applied, in the highest perfection of the art, the finishing coat of artificial marble to represent beautiful examples of "old Convent Sienna" marble, or other rare marble the architect may select.   All this artificial marble must be equal to the very best examples found abroad; threads must be introduced to form the veinings, and the work performed in every detail by skillful craftsmen.   These columns must be perfect as to entasis, form, and color.

373. All the ceiling work, false beams, groins, vaulting, etc., must be done in plaster as heretofore specified, built upon expanded metal properly formed over suitable steel framing of the same general character as is shown on sheet No. 117.   All this expanded metal work must be so thoroughly lapped, interlaced with copper wire, and other precautions taken that there will not be the slightest possibility of settlement or crack.   The capitals, corbels, and other such work will be cast, from particularly clear models, according to sheet No. 120, in plaster, polished, as will be

directed by the architect, and left in its natural color for decorations under another contract. The moldings forming the cornice and architrave, etc., will be run in perfectly true lines.

374. All the ornaments in these cornices and friezes will be applied after the cornices have been run; they must be properly stuck on to make a good and permanent job, and will be cast in papier-maché, or some other material of that character that will fulfill the purpose for which this is intended, i. e., to offer as much porous, nonresonant, nonresilient surface as possible to counteract the acoustical fault so much marble in a room of this size is liable to create. The walls above the wainscoting will be trued-up with one coat of well-clinching brown mortar, simply to afford an even surface, to which will be fastened the painted decorations on canvas supplied by another contractor.

375. The judge's bench and other furnishing of this room will be executed under another contract.

376. The insides of the doors facing into this room will be of mahogany richly and darkly finished. The glass will be beveled crystalline plate, with the name of the court blown or engraved on this crystalline.

377. The art glass in the three openings back of the judge's bench, in the nine panels of the ceiling, and in the dome central light will be of a high grade and handsome in design, set in thin lead joints and properly fastened to steel bars and angles to make a strong and perfect job. All this glass will be opened to competitive design, if the architect so desires, and the successful competitor will supply the glass to this contractor. That in the flat portions will be more or less conventional in design—a field of clear glass with foliation or geometric designs worked in rich opalescent glass, worth $2 per square foot of surface for the glass alone without framing. That in the dome part will be pictorial in character, but with large fields of clear crystal. For the purposes of this contract it may be figured as worth $6 a square foot of surface for the glass alone without the framing.

378. The four main courts in the sixth story will be floored as is specified for the court of appeals.

379. The bases around these rooms will be of Glens Falls black marble. There will be no mop block. The top member forming the plinth of the columns, and the window sills will also be of black marble. The wainscoting will be of marble, with a marble necking, cap molding at the windows and paneled pilasters between the windows, marble jambs and caps at the windows, and an artificial marble capping, all as shown on sheets No. 115 and No. 120. The wainscoting will be made up of very large slabs of inch stuff, and heavier, if needed, with rounded corners, set true and perfect, and most highly polished.

380. In the south court the base molding on top of the plinth will be Georgia verd antique. The wainscoting proper will be marble equal in color, texture, and cost to Champlain green. The west court will be equal to a Champlain mahogany marble. The east and north courts will be equal in color, texture, and price to a Blount Tennessee.

381. The wainscoting cap, the archivolt, architrave, and soffit, the architraves around the clear-story windows, the cornice, capitals, the treatment over the doors (clock and bronze work not in this contract) will all be in artificial marble exactly matching the wainscoting marble, properly jointed, etc. The columns and bases each side of the doors and the architrave around the doors will all be of the wainscoting marble. The pilasters and columns in the green court room will be of artificial marble, perfectly made in every respect and imitating the finest foreign yellow jasper. The bases will be in imitation of the green.

382. In the mahogany red room the pilasters and colums will perfectly imitate a fine example of dark old convent sienna, with large fields of cream white running through it, and as translucent as overlaying opaque bodies can be made. The north court will have pilasters and columns imitating a warm Pavonnazza with the minimum of black. The east court room will be imitation of St. Baum. These pilasters and columns in every case are to be made to represent monoliths.

383. The ceiling will be properly framed, as shown on drawing No. 117, with suspended angles, bars, etc., over which will be carefully formed and tied expanded metal, over which, again, will be run the moldings in plaster, perfect and true.

384. The niches will have shell ornaments, etc., of artificial marble, the same as the wainscoting. The high-relief eagles under the circular windows will be cast in plaster and left for decoration. The panel and inlaid work over the first row of windows will be done in artificial marble, likewise the panels over the niches.

385. The capitals throughout these court rooms will be sharply cast in plaster and left for painted decoration.

386. All the applied decorations, ornaments, etc., in these friezes, cornices, soffits, panels, modillions, etc., will be of papier-maché or some such substance, and for the same reason given for making them so in the court of appeals.

387. The divisions, paneled and ornamented, in the ceiling lights in these rooms will be worked in plaster on stable iron frames, but the ornamentation thereon will be in plaster, not papier-maché. The wooden sash in the flat ceiling light will be of pine, painted, and left for the ceiling decoration.

388. The domed portion will be worked up in cast and wrought iron frames, well braced but light in construction, and with stiffening bars, to which will be fastened the leaded glass.

389. These domed ceiling lights will be formed of very thin ribs, umbrella fashion, of steel, bent to form, to which will be attached similar thin bars horizontally, affording ample opportunity to fasten the stained glass thereto, and yet casting but little shadow on the same. All the steel work will be properly painted in white.

390. The leaded glass in the wood inner sash in the upper story of windows and the glass in the flat sash of the ceiling lights will be handsomely leaded clear fields with opalescent, conventionalized ornamentation, worth $2 per foot, and opened to competition as before described, if the architect so desires. The glass in the four spandrels of the dome, the pendatives, and the dome portion in each of these four court rooms will be very handsome leaded glass, pictorial subjects upon clear crystal fields, and worth, for the leaded glass alone, $6 per surface foot.

391. In one case the arch over the main entrance to the large court room will be filled in with leaded glass the same as specified for the other wall openings.

392. The bottom of some of the niches in these rooms, and in some cases the coved-top ornament of the niche, will be of cast iron of elaborate design open work, serving as register faces for ventilating appliances. Similar registers will be fixed in the bases in the pilasters in the ends of the rooms, all of which will be properly bronze-plated.

393. In some panels of the ceiling beams and spaces there will be deeply sunken ornaments, in which will be fixed electric lights by another contractor. All this work where such arrangements have to be made, pockets behind cornices, openings in the dome portions, etc., this contractor must provide for and afford every facility for the introduction of lights and ventilation into these rooms in an artistic as well as an effective manner.

394. In the niches will be placed, as shown on sheet No. 113, handsome molded pedestals of the same marble as the wainscoting, for the ultimate reception of statuary.

395. The wall space above the wainscoting will be trued-up with one coat of strong brown mortar, forming base for pictorial canvases.

396. The passageways between the court of appeals, and other spaces adjacent to these court rooms and possibly not covered in other parts of the specification, will be plainly finished, plastered, and trimmed, but in no case will there be any unfinished corners left.

397. The doors to the large court rooms will be as specified for the court of appeals, mahogany in two cases and black walnut and oak in the other two.

398. The doors to the court of appeals will be built on curves to conform to the shape of the room.

399. The piers forming the proscenium in the court of appeals will serve as ducts for ventilating flues. These must be built up strongly of steel members and expanded metal, to which will be fastened the blocks and marble finishing these piers, and behind which a good grouting will be backed up into the expanded metal. Wherever there are any steps in the court rooms, such as the entrances to the court of appeals, these will be marble risers and treads.

400. The wood inner sash in the upper windows of the court room will be hung so that they will slide clear up into a pocket between the walls and the finish, in order that the outer sash may be gotten at. Some of the windows in these court rooms will be condemned, that is, the marble and other finish will cover them. In these cases the sash will be so made that the glass will be set in from the outside, and reached, in case of breakage, from the outside; over these sash on the inside will be tightly nailed a covering of heavy canvas of a color to be selected by the architect, and then the marble and other finish of the room will be built up independently from these windows and kept away from any contact with them.

THE DOME (DRAWING NO. 114.)

401. The framing of steel beams, channels, angles, straps, bars, tees, etc., shown on this sheet, the various plans, and on sheet No. 117 will sufficiently indicate the rather

complicated nature of the provision that will have to be made to carry the marble and other decorations of this dome portion, its galleries, and parts of corridors pertaining thereto. Where possible build up solidly for piers, etc., with brickwork set in cement, first making sure of the proper supports therefor in the structural portions.

402. In the Architect's Office in the Treasury Department, Washington, D. C., may be seen some colored drawings, pictures showing portions of this dome and the court rooms. An inspection of these drawings may give the contractors bidding on this work some additional light as to its character and the perfection of execution that is expected.

403. The floors of the galleries at the various levels will be the same as is specified for the corridors of the respective stories. The floor of the main portion of dome and the first landing at the stairways will be a mosaic floor—a Roman mosaic. No piece will be over $\frac{3}{4}$ inch square and must be nearly that deep; in other words, there must be at least 7 pounds of marble to the square foot of mosaic. The panels will be formed of gray Tennessee slabs. The field of the mosaic will be white, the patterns made up of verd antique, mahogany, Ellis pink, and Glens Falls black in some suitable design, equal in cost to that shown on sheet No. 114. In the middle of the dome floor will be the names of the streets in brass inlaid letters.

404. The first run of the stairs to the landings will be made of gray Tennessee treads and risers cut with washes at backs and sides as shown on sheet No. 120, set on cast-iron brackets framed to the carriage beams that will be spaced not over 3 feet apart. These treads and risers to be of one slab each, the full length the width of the stairs.

405. Above the first landings all the stairways will be built up on similar carriages but without washes to the steps, and of 1½-inch treads ⅞-inch risers of this same gray Tennessee marble. This marble work will be lag-screwed in from the back and most thoroughly fastened.

406. The main piers of the dome, all the way up, the dies of the pedestals, the friezes of the cornices, the spandrel panels of the arches, the wainscoting up the stairways, the wainscoting around the galleries (the same height as in the corridors), and the starting of the corridors, the pilasters in this starting of the corridors and around the walls of the dome and back of the main piers will all be of a marble equal in color and texture to an American Lyonaise (Swanton).

407. The bases on the first floor and along the gallery side of all the upper floors will be Glens Falls black and a dark Tennessee.

408. The cornices, or such portions of them as are detailed to be of marble (see sheets No. 114 and No. 120), the bases and caps of the pedestals, the pilaster-cap moldings, the voussoirs of the archivolts, and all other molded work in the dome that is shown to be of marble will be of a rich pink Knoxville marble, or the equal thereto, uniform in color and suitable in every way for this molded work.

409. The isolated columns at the angles of the dome will be built of Z bars, angles, expanded metal, and Keene's cement, with a finishing coat of the highest grade of artificial marble, made to perfectly represent a rich, warm, light Sienna. These columns are to be perfectly formed, with entasis, all true and in strict conformity with the architect's instructions, and are to be graduated in colors lighter and lighter as they go up. The capitals of these columns, the corbels under the galleries, most of the moldings, and all the decorations of the cornices, the balusters, will all be of artificial marble of high grade and perfectly matching the molded marble work.

410. All these portions of marble or artificial marble will be in long lengths, true in alignment and brought to a high perfection of polish, excepting in such portions of ornamented work, capitals, etc., as may be directed by the architect to be left unpolished.

411. The contractor will state in the proper blank of bid the reduction he will make in his figures if all of this work that is specified to be of these dark marbles is changed to the finest and hardest white American marble equal in texture, color, and market price to a high grade of white Italian.

412. The contractor will also state the reduction he will make in his bid if, instead of marble and artificial marble as specified for this dome, the galleries, the stairways (except steps), and the starting of the corridors, he is ordered to make a substitution of terra cotta.

413. (This terra cotta, if the substitution is ordered, will be made equal to the very finest product of the best terra-cotta plant in the country, of a high-grade clay, skillfully burned in large pieces, and long lengths, sharp in outline, straight of molding, and perfectly glazed and overlaid to a polished-marble surface rather than the glassy surface usual in terra cotta. In color this terra cotta will be made, without attempting to imitate the veinings of a special marble, of the general tone and harmonious blending of the enamels and glazes to come as close to the foreign Jaspers,

St. Baums, and Siennas, in tone and richness, as it is possible to do in a terra cotta. This in no way affects the specification for the isolated columns at the angles, which in every case of substitution will remain of artificial marble, or the steps, that will also remain of marble.   In general the molded work in such terra cotta will be of a more or less uniform color, with but little veining or blend, but the plain surfaces should be artistic richness itself in diversity of blending and warmth of color and veining.   All this terra cotta would be built up and fastened to the framing in the best manner known to the trade.)

414. Above the plinth at the seventh-floor level all the ceiling of the dome will be of plaster in the plain surfaces and in the molded and decorative portions, as set forth under the respective headings of "Plastering." The moldings will be bold and sharp, and all the ornamented surfaces, the eagles in relief, the frieze ornaments, the keys, the arches, corbels, crestings, etc., will be bold in outline and effective in composition, but not over-detailed in execution. The stiles forming the panels in this dome portion will be corrugated surfaces, but the plain surfaces, spandrels of arches, etc., will be of perfectly smooth finish well worked-up plaster.

415. Around the marble panels in the piers, pilasters, etc., in the cornices wherever else shown on details there will be a bronzed beading and egg and dark moldings of suitable sizes, buushed and lacquered and set in place in long lengths without breaks in the panel.

416. The sides of the stairs, the fascias and rails at the balcony fronts, with the frame for a clock in one bay at the second story, will all be of iron and steel electro-bronzed, and made, finished, and fastened as shown on details and elsewhere described.   Sheets No. 114 and No. 119 show this work in detail.

417. The elevator fronts upon the various floor levels, the balcony railings, and all the other metal work about the dome must be daintily, strongly, and artistically made, assembled, and plated in electro-bronze, all as described under "ornamental metal work."

418. The clock itself, the lamps shown at the first floor, at the seventh floor, and the register indicators in the elevator fronts will be no part of this contract.

419. This contractor must provide smooth pockets back of cornices, spaces in decorative rosettes, hinged flaps in the corona cornice of dome shown on sheet No. 121, etc., for the fittings of lights, as indicated by the drawings, by another contractor, or for the introduction of ventilation.

420. The elevator shafts to be plastered in a white finish, highly worked and jointed with a deep V joint to represent large slabs of marble.

421. Contractor must provide wood platforms, runways, hand rails, etc., around the several portions at the top of this dome, also a cast-iron stairway from the ninth floor to the corona. The flat portion outside of the regular gallery railing will be neatly finished in cement, strongly enough built up to carry 50 pounds to the square foot, and the back of the dome proper will be covered with expanded metal and two coats of ordinary plaster, nicely trued up and smoothed with a neat molding around all openings.

422. In the large circular and curved openings in the dome there will be a grill work of cast iron rigidly fastened and secured to suitable frame. The whole will be most stoutly made, but thin on edge, to offer as little obstruction as possible to the light. These grilles will be made up in sections, fastened separately into a main frame made up of steel members and finally painted with two coats of white enamel and left for decoration along with the rest of the dome.

423. Special attention is called to the fact that the plaster crestings in the dome are in exposed places and will have to be made up on heavy iron and rigidly fastened; they must be gauged with $\frac{1}{2}$ cement.

424. As shown on sheet No. 114, there will be a false ceiling suspended from the eleventh floor. It will be made up of rods, angles, keys, and expanded metal, all of sufficient stability to carry 40 pounds to the square foot.   This will be plastered over on top with a fair cement that will do to walk on, and the under surface perfectly trued up with plaster.   This surface is intended for a grand historical painting on the plaster, and it must be prepared therefor.

425. The ceilings of all these dome galleries and the abutting corridors will be of two-coat plaster, as specified for all the rest of the work, with cornices, ornaments, capitals, brackets, etc., as are indicated on the various details.   The only difference between those portions and the regular corridors will be that the dome part will be slightly more elaborate and of a different marble from that specified for the corridors. These will be so arranged as to not make the point of juncture conspicuous, and will be a subject for special orders from the architect.

CORRIDORS, LOBBIES, SUBTREASURY ON FIRST FLOOR.

426. The main vestibule floors will be of granite tile set in concrete, with a granite slab border of a different color, the slabs full size of the door openings forming the floors between the grilles and the wood doors. The vestibule steps will be of granite, cut in one piece, with washes at the back and sides. The floor of the inner vestibules will have a granite slab border and the central portion floored with a gray Tennessee 10 by 16 inch tiling, properly set on a finished cement base.

427. From this inner-vestibule line to the last bay of the corridor the flooring between the lines of structural columns will be a 12-inch border of dark Tennessee marble, with a main body of gray Tennessee tiling 10 by 16 inches. Back of these structural column lines, in the spaces formed into alcoves and circular bays outside of the corridor partitions, the floor will be made up with panels of dark and gray Tennessee borders and mosaic marble centers, the mosaic to be the same quality and character as that specified for the dome floor.

428. Inside the lobbies off of these corridors the flooring will be dark Tennessee marble tile borders 12 inches wide and gray Tennessee 10 by 16 inch tiling.

429. At the doors in these corridor partitions there will be thresholds formed of gray Tennessee marble; at the entrance door these thresholds will be of solid bronze, arranged for proper drainage.

430. The walls of the main vestibule will be finished with slab granite, molded cornices and bases, and surfaces polished and unpolished, as shown by sheets No. 118 and No. 120. This granite will be a fine white or a richly colored native granite. It must be of fine texture, however, and of a color that will receive the architect's approval.

431. The walls wherever shown in ashlar work will be a selected, variegated, and richly colored pink Tennessee. The large panels, such as is shown for the inscription on section ST No. 118, will be of Utah or California onyx. The bases, the counter tops, and sills, the pilasters and their paneled surfaces, the friezes and architraves, and all such portions of these corridors will be of dark cedar Tennessee marble, or something like it.

432. The mop block around these corridor walls will be of the same marble as the floor border. The base block throughout will be of Glens Falls black. The base will be of dark cedar Tennessee, or, as understood for all other marbles that may be specified, something of equal color, and texture that may be approved by the architect.

433. The isolated columns in these corridors will be perfectly turned and polished monoliths of "Swanton Oriental" or Lyonaise marble, or, if they can be procured, a finely selected California or Utah onyx, or of special cast, polished, richly colored art glass.

434. The archivolts to these corridor windows and their soffits, all the capitals, the cornices, the column bases, and whatever else may be shown so by the details will be of artificial marble of the same color as the portion it is intended to complete.

435. The bronze door grilles, frames, transoms, cornices, post-office screen openings, such as at QR No. 118 and KL, are detailed to be of solid bronze. Regardless of this, however, all of the ornamental metal work throughout is to be electro-bronze plated, or painted, or otherwise finished, but in no case of solid bronze. The ceiling light ribs and other metal work in ceilings will also be electroplated in bronze.

436. Sash will be of wood and iron painted with the decoration and retaining in place the beveled plate glass, plain plate, crystalline bevel, and art glass as may be severally indicated.

437. The glass mosaic ceilings of the outer and inner vestibules will be Venetian mosaic of split American glass set in cement and all as hereinbefore described.

438. The art glass will also be as before described.

439. The lamp fixtures are not in this contract.

440. The plastering, coving, cornices, ornaments, etc., will all be plaster as before specified, run true and smooth and brought to a high finish, the ornaments perfectly modeled, the ceilings cut off into panels with interlacing ribs where so shown, etc. The groining in the ceiling will be brought to a slightly rounded edge, not a bead, but formed by a patent metal angle.

441. This contractor must provide openings, pockets, and troughs in cornices, etc., that may be required for lights and ventilation.

442. Where clusters of lights are shown in the ceiling, this contractor will form a sinkage therefor, and run a one-member molding in plaster the exact size that will be required for the glass globe and bronze fittings furnished by another contractor.

443. The marble counter shelf in post-office screen will be built under this contract and suitably supported in its full width, but the fitting of drawers underneath it on the room sides will all be done under another contract.

444. The doors and their frames will be of mahogany on the corridor and vestibule sides and oak on the room sides.

445. The additional doors at the Clark street entrance will be of metal and glass the same as the main doors, with an inner swing door of wood, also, the same as at the main entrance. Similar swing doors with beveled plate-glass panels will cut off the main vestibule from the subtreasury. These outer vestibule doors will all be of mahogany.

446. There will be a metal and glass grille between the vestibule and subtreasury.

447. The walls of the subtreasury vestibule will be equal to a "Swanton mosaic" marble.

448. The piers, counter fronts, wainscoting, etc., in the public part of the subtreasury and in the assistant treasurer's private room will be of a pink Tennessee marble. The bank front cornices and grilles, facing of doors and the gates, will all be electro-bronze, in bars, straps, plates, and applied cast ornaments. The cornices and the doors will be built up upon iron forms.

449. The floor of the public part will be of marble mosaic with marble-slab borders same as in the main corridors. The floor in the assistant treasurer's private room will also be of marble mosaic. The floor in the banking portion of the subtreasury and the floor in the back portion or workroom will be first select maple floor laid on strips.

450. The walls and ceilings, all through, above the wainscoting in the public portion and to the floor in the other portions will all be the usual plaster finish. The subtreasury vestibule and the main office ceiling will be groined, corniced, beamed, and ornamented as detailed, all supported on good and sufficient framing and expanded metal. The ceiling of the workroom will be plain and with a two-member cornice at juncture of ceiling and wall and under the drop beams formed for the ventilating ducts.

451. This subtreasury room will have to have extra precautions taken in its construction to make it doubly secure against fire and robbery. Extra bolts and bars must be provided for doors. The outside windows will be protected by steel bars an inch in diameter set 4 inches on centers in a suitable frame and with a strengthening bar across the middle and with cast ornaments at the connections, all electro-bronzed and set in a suitable outer frame heavily bolted and locked from the inside and with sufficient doweled fasteners into the stone.

452. The division between this room and the post-office will have a heavy steel wire bedded into the plaster; the partition will be a 6-inch fireproof tile, and the sash will be stoutly built of angles and Z bars and made up of a heavy wired glass in 6 by 12 inch panes set in a suitable cast-iron frame. These sash will be permanently fixed. The doors leading to the basement, elevators, etc., will be steel plated and extra strongly bolted.

453. In other words, this room will be the repository of considerable money and must be in every sense a "strong room."

454. The vault will be built by another contractor, but the outside finishing of the walls, the cast-iron stairway leading to the second deck, the gallery, electro-bronzed railings, the wood-finished doors covering the electrical protection, etc., will all be done by this contractor.

455. It is possible that some portions of the building or rooms may not have been specifically and individually described herein. Contractors figuring on this work must understand, as has been before stated, that this contract is to *entirely* finish the building in every particular (except herein specifically omitted or made subject for additional or alternative bid in the blank form) ready for the furnishing and occupancy. Where a room or a portion of the finish has not been specifically covered in the above general description, such work must be performed nevertheless, and the architect will be the judge as to its character, and his decision will be based upon what he would naturally expect such a room or portion of the work to be, judging by contiguous portions, or what he may have specified for similar rooms and work in other parts of the building. In every case all of this work is to be of the highest quality in material and workmanship, and the bidder's attention is again called to the importance of amply providing for contingencies that are so sure to arise.

456. As the work progresses, when some portions are ready for occupancy, or when the work generally is finished, or whenever the architect may order it, the contractor will wash all windows, patch every bit of broken plaster, remove any broken marble, replacing it with new, properly fill and varnish or wax all wood floors, leaving them all smooth, clean, and polished. He will wash all mosaic and tile floors and thoroughly clean the building from top to bottom, removing all débris from the place and turning over the keys of a perfectly finished, appointed, completed, and in every way satisfactory building to the architect.

457. The accompanying bid must be made out in every particular as heretofore described, all its blanks must be properly filled, and, just as it is, attached to this specification and other papers.   It must be forwarded to the architect, preferably in the accompanying franked envelope, so as to be opened at the time set forth in the advertisement for bids.

458. Furthermore, some of the materials and work shown on plans and even described herein are (for good and sufficient reasons that have arisen since plans were printed) specifically omitted in this blank bid, and made subjects for additional or alternative bids.   Hence is it the most important paper to the bidders, for upon its basis (without interlineations or erasures) will be awarded the final contract.

PROPOSAL FOR THE INTERIOR WORK AND COMPLETION OF THE UNITED STATES POST-OFFICE, COURT-HOUSE, ETC., AT CHICAGO, ILL.

NOVEMBER 7, 1902.

HENRY IVES COBB,
   Architect U. S. Government Building at Chicago, Ill.,
          Treasury Department, Washington, D. C.

SIR: I hereby propose to furnish all the labor and materials required for the interior work and completion of the United States post-office, court-house, etc., at Chicago, Ill., all in strict accordance with the true intent and spirit of the specifications hereto attached and the plans mentioned therein, excepting only such labor and materials as the following omissions from or amendments to the specifications cover:

A. The main vestibule described in article 426 as having granite wainscoting, etc., to have a first base of plain Glens Falls black marble 12 inches high; all above that base to be of the same design shown, but finished in the patent plaster specified for wall finish, and the lime plaster specified for the molded cornice and ceiling regular work.

B. The granite steps in vestibules to be replaced with marble of quality and design called for for the main stairs above the first run, and that first run of the main stairs to be the same as specified for the remainder of the main stairs.

C. All the main entrance doors and the vestibule screens now shown to be bronze plated to be replaced with frames of similar general design executed in quarter-sawed oak, and solid 6-paneled doors 3 inches thick, also of quarter-sawed oak, all finished as specified under general clauses of joiner and painter work.

D. All the corridors and vestibules of first floor now shown and specified to be finished in real and artificial marbles, mosaic ceilings, etc., to be replaced with patent plaster walls and columns and pilasters, etc., and lime plaster moldings, capitals, ceilings, etc., above the cornice line all of the same design as now shown; the mahogany doors to be replaced with quartered oak; a plain Glens Falls black marble base 10 inches high the only marble work; the counter fronts of patent plaster with tops and molded edges of quartered oak, and all of the glass and screen work, P. O. grilles, etc., now shown at Q. R. and K. L. sheet 118, to be omitted, also the ceiling-light ribs and art glass shown at Q. R. 118.

E. The finish of the subtreasury described under article 448, etc., to be amended omitting the circular ended counter front of marble and all the ornamental iron grilles above it and above the divisions in the room.   The vestibule and room proper to be finished as designed, but with patent plaster walls and lime plaster cornices and ceilings where marble walls and mosaic ceilings are now shown.

F. The steel bars, specified under article 451 for the protection of the subtreasury windows, to be omitted; also, all the other outside window protection specified under article 335 to be omitted.

G. All the granite tile, marble tile, and mosaic floors now specified for corridors, dome, vestibules, toilet rooms, etc., throughout the building, to be replaced with "terrazzo" floors of ¾-inch wearing surface of equal parts Portland cement and white marble chips.   The finished floor to be troweled and rubbed to a true, smooth, well-finished surface.

H. The corridor marble wainscoting, the toilet room wainscoting and mirrors and the stair wainscoting, throughout the entire building, to be omitted and replaced with a plain 10-inch base of Glens Falls black marble, and the walls and wainscot molding to be run in patent plaster, as specified for the general work.

I. All the work in the dome now shown and specified to be executed in marble and artificial marble to be replaced with plaster of the same design as now shown.   The walls, the columns, the bases, and pilasters to be of patent plaster worked over the metal forms, brick walls, etc., and all cornice work, capitals, etc., to be run or cast in plain lime plaster. There will be a 10-inch Glens Falls, or other black marble, plain base around every story wall, along the stairs, and around the first story piers. The ornamental bronze moldings shown in the panels to be replaced with plaster.

(The general design to remain absolutely as shown, but the work, instead of being executed in marbles, scagliola, and bronze-plated metal, will be done in plaster and painted metal.

J. All the elevator screens now shown on drawings and referred to under articles 206 and 417 to be replaced with plain tile and plaster partition, the screen doors with an 8-inch molded frame and the threshold to remain as at present shown, of cast and wrought iron, but painted four coats of paint of approved color instead of bronze-plated.

K. All the ornamental ironwork now shown to be bronze-plated to be changed to cast and wrought iron, just as specified, but painted one coat of red lead at the shop and three coats of approved colors when erected.

L. The four main court rooms and the court of appeals described under articles 365, 366, etc., to be changed in that there will be a black marble, plain ¼-inch thick base, 10 inches high, about all these rooms, pedestals, etc., but no other marble or artificial marble work whatever. The design to remain unchanged, but all the wainscoting, the pilasters, the columns and pedestals, etc., to be of patent plaster, and all the wainscoting caps, the door ornaments, the capitals, and other decorative work to be run, molded, or cast in plain lime plaster.

M. Omit all art glass in ceilings and domes in court rooms, etc., and omit all the plate crystalline, bordered, beveled and engraved, in the corridor sash throughout the building, replacing it all with plain double-strength sheet crystalline glass.

N. Omit all oak floors throughout, replacing them with plain maple floors, as specified for the general flooring.

O. All the rooms specified to be finished in classes A, B, C, D, shown on sheet 116, in cement trim, mahogany, walnut, or other woods, to be changed to plain finish of quartered oak without cornices or other elaboration than is shown and called for in the finish of rooms of Class E.

P. Omit all mantels and fireplaces throughout, replacing with the finish called for for each particular room.

Q. Omit the mail chutes under article 207.

R. Omit the post-office "lookout" runways shown for the inspection of first and second stories.

all for the sum of $997,500, and complete the same to your entire satisfaction on or before April 1, 1904.

I am familiar with all the requirements of this specification, contract, and bond, the site and condition of the work so far performed upon the structure, and what will be required of the contractor for this new work. Further, I propose to accept the following figures as a basis for settlement for all additions to or deductions from the work, or any and all changes ordered in the work.

Should any or all of the foregoing omissions or changes in the work not be made, or, in other words, if I am ordered to proceed with any or all such work exactly as specified, then I agree that each of the items may be so restored for the additional payment as follows:

For item A of ommissions, restored as specified, add......................... $26, 395
For item B of ommissions, restored as specified, add......................... 6, 368
For item C of ommissions, restored as specified, add......................... 39, 446
For item D of ommissions, restored as specified, add......................... 109, 044
For item E of ommissions, restored as specified, add......................... 27, 883
For item F of ommissions, restored as specified, add......................... 6, 487
For item G of ommissions, restored as specified, add......................... 40, 523
For item H of ommissions, restored as specified, add......................... 39, 865
For item I of ommissions, restored as specified, add......................... 182, 883
For item J of ommissions, restored as specified, add......................... 40, 471
For item K of ommissions, restored as specified, add......................... 9, 900
For item L of ommissions, restored as specified, add......................... 81, 713
For item M of ommissions, restored as specified, add......................... 41, 488
For item N of ommissions, restored as specified, add......................... 2, 844
For item O of ommissions, restored as specified, add......................... 39, 053
For item P of ommissions, restored as specified, add......................... 2, 287
For item Q of ommissions, restored as specified, add......................... 13, 530
For item R of ommissions, restored as specified, add......................... 20, 465

If ordered to restore all of these items as specified, I propose to complete the entire work on or before April 1, 1905.

As a basis for any further change, addition, or deduction, I propose the following prices:

Per square foot of fire proof 4-inch partition tile......................	$0.14
Per square foot of 2-inch furring tile, in place	.10
Per square foot of surface of expanded metal and average cornice framing	.19
Per square foot of framing, expanded metal and plaster for duct and pipe covering, etc	.17
Per square yard of two-coat patent plaster (name make figured on)...	.44
Per single doorway for cement casing, Class A	24.00
Per single doorway for cement casing, head, consoles, etc., Class B ...	33.00
Per single doorway for wood casing and finish, Class E	16.50
Per running foot of cornice in rooms, Class B.........................	1.50
Per square foot of oak flooring, including border, all in place, waxed, etc	.36
Per square foot of the usual maple flooring, in place, finished	.08
Per square foot of herringbone maple flooring, set in cement, dovetailed, etc..	.50
Per single door, communicating, of upper floors, oak, framed, hung, hardware, etc., finished in place...................................	44.60
Per double door finish trim (exclusive of doors proper) pilasters, head, etc., in oak shown for Class D....................................	339.90
Per mantle, including hearth, mirror, etc., in place, Class D, oak.....	414.00
Per mantle, including hearth, mirror, etc., in place, Class D, Cuban mahogany	500.00
Per running foot of finished oak wainscoting, in place, Class C........	2.50
Per running foot finished oak wainscoting, in place, Class D..........	5.00
Per running foot of finished Cuban mahogany wainscoting, in place, Class D	10.70
Per door for all hardware trimmings, Class D.........................	8.25
Per square foot for the upper corridor floors of marble tile, set in place.	.80
Per linear foot for the upper corridor marble wainscoting, set in place.	6.66
Per square foot mosaic floor in dome.................................	2.80
Per stall, water-closet marble work, back, division, etc., all in place...	78.00
Per stall for marble work in workroom toilet room....................	39.00
Per linear foot, cap and all, of marble wainscoting north court sixth floor...	25.20
Per linear foot of wainscoting, cap and all, in first floor inner vestibule.	29.40
Per square foot marble flooring in toilet room	.87
Per story for all the dome electro-bronze elevator inclosures..........	2,429.00
Per tread of marble and iron stairs, as for upper dome stairs, rail and all, 3 x 6 feet wide for additional stairs	26.31
Per running foot sixth floor corridor partition, doors, marble, plaster, glass, etc...	21.50
Per running foot of outside railing around building if of solid bronze..	20.25
For one flap of electro-bronze doors, glazed, and its part of frame at main entrances..	880.50
Price of room No. 8, sixth floor, including floor, wainscoting, plaster, and hardware, and all about it complete, if finished in Class D:	
In Cuban mahogony..	3,000.00
In California mahogany...	3,000.00
In black walnut..	2,261.50
In oak..	2,046.00
Price of same room finished in Class C, oak	1,019.00
Price of same room finished in Class B, oak	800.00
Price of same room finished in Class A, oak	549.00
Price of same room finished in Class E, oak	438.00
Per ordinary single wood-covered fireproof vault door, finished.......	117.50
Per double fireproof vault door and vestibuled door for post-office vault.	179.50
Price per pound for the removal of present structural steel work, necessitated by any future changes made in arrangement.................	.05½
Per pound for substitution of new framing steel work where same is not provided for specifically herein....................................	.06

If all the ornamental metal work of the first story, front doors, grilles, elevator fronts, post-office screens, etc., is changed to a solid bronze instead of electroplated work, there will be added to the bid for the plated work the sum of $156,860.00

If all the decoration in the wood trim be made of real wood carving instead of composition, there will be added............................ 14,300.00

If all the work rooms, toilet rooms, and the public and private toilet rooms are tiled with a fine American enameled white tile above the marble wainscoting, there will be added the sum of.................. 20,000.00

If the four main court rooms on sixth floor and the court of appeals are floored with an interlocking hard-rubber tile, as shown on plans instead of the pine floor specified, there will be added the sum of.... 21,532.58

If a fine white marble is substituted for the specified colored marble finish of dome, there will be deducted from the price for that dome marble work as specified the sum of—no change in price.

If a fine terra cotta is substituted for the colored marble finish of dome, there will be deducted from the price for that dome work as specified the sum of.. 50,000.00

JOHN PEIRCE,
277 Broadway, New York City.

Opened November 8, 1902.

HENRY IVES COBB,
Architect U. S. Govt. Bldg., Chicago.
J. K. TAYLOR,
Supervising Architect.
C. E. KEMPER,
Chief Executive Officer.
H. D. GREEN,
Accountant.

TREASURY DEPARTMENT, OFFICE OF THE SECRETARY,
Washington, November 17, 1902.

JOHN PEIRCE, Esq., 277 Broadway, New York.

SIR: Your proposal, dated November 7, 1902, the lowest bid received under advertisement dated October 4, 1902, and opened on November 8, 1902, to furnish labor and materials required for the interior work and completion of the new post-office, court-house, etc., at Chicago, Ill., for the sum of nine hundred and ninety-seven thousand five hundred dollars ($997,500), and to be finished and completed on or before the 1st day of April, 1904, is hereby accepted.

The Department reserves the right to order you to proceed with any or all the items A, B, C, D, E, F, G, H, I, J, K, L, M, N, O, P, Q, R, etc., excepted under your proposal, and at the prices stated in said proposal, on or before the 1st day of April, 1903.

As understood and agreed, you are required to execute a formal contract, with bond in the sum of three hundred thousand dollars ($300,000), as a guaranty for the faithful performance of the work embraced in your proposal (a form for which will be sent you for execution and return to this Department for examination, approval, and file); and it is understood and agreed also that the said contract, with bond, must be executed and returned within five days from date of the receipt by you of the said form.

The certified check which accompanied your proposal will be retained at this Department until the approval of your formal bond by the Secretary of the Treasury. Promptly acknowledge the receipt of this letter.

Respectfully,

H. A. TAYLOR, Acting Secretary.

Contract between the United States of America and John Peirce.

Whereas by advertisement duly made and published according to law, proposals were asked for the interior work and completion of the United States post-office, court-house, etc., at Chicago, Ill.; and

Whereas the proposal of John Peirce furnished in response thereto was duly accepted on the 17th day of November, 1902, on condition that he execute a contract in accordance with the terms of his bid:

Now, therefore, this agreement, made and entered into by and between Horace A. Taylor, Acting Secretary of the Treasury, for and in behalf of the United States of America, of the first part, and John Peirce, of the city of New York, of the second part.

Witnesseth that the party of the second part, for the consideration hereinafter mentioned, covenants and agrees to and with the party of the first part to furnish all of the labor and materials, and do and perform all the work required for the interior finish and completion of the United States post-office, court-house, etc., at Chicago, Ill., in the fullest sense of the word *completion*, according to the specification hereto attached and the drawings therein referred to, and signed by said second party and the architect of the United States Government building at Chicago, Ill., in strict and full accordance with the requirements of all such drawings and such other detail drawings as may be furnished to the party of the second part by the architect of the United States Government building at Chicago, Ill., or any written orders issued by said architect; the advertisement for proposals, dated October 4, 1902; the general instructions and specifications for the work, and the proposal dated November 7, 1902, addressed to the said architect by the said party of the second part, and the letter dated November 17, 1902, addressed to the said party of the second part by H. A. Taylor, Secretary of the Treasury, accepting said proposal. A true and correct copy of each of said papers is hereto attached and forms a part of and is this contract, and which said drawings, bearing the signature of the said architect and the signature of the said party of the second part, and numbered 104 to 121, both inclusive, are on file in the office of the architect of the United States Government building at Chicago, Ill., and are hereby also made a part of this contract.

And the said party of the second part further covenants and agrees that all the materials used shall be of the very best quality; that all of the work performed shall be executed in the most skillful and workmanlike manner; and that both the materials used and the work performed shall be to the entire and complete satisfaction of the said architect.

It is further covenanted and agreed that the entire work shall be completed by the first day of April, nineteen hundred and four (1904); that any particular portion of the work herein provided for shall be completed within such reasonable time as may be hereafter specified by the architect, representing the party of the first part, in written notice to the party of the second part, and should the said party of the second part fail to complete the entire work or any particular portion of the work within the time so specified, then the party of the second part shall forfeit to the party of the first part one hundred dollars ($100) per day as liquidated damages for each and every day thereafter until the completion of the same: *Provided*, That if through any fault of the party of the first part, the party of the second part is delayed in the execution of the work included in this contract, the party of the second part shall be allowed one day additional to the time above stated for each and every day of such delay so caused, the same to be ascertained and awarded by the said architect: *Provided further*, That no claim shall be made or allowed for damages which may arise out of any delay caused by the party of the first part.

The party of the second part further covenants and agrees to promptly pay for all labor and materials used in and about the building and to hold and save the United States harmless from and against all and every demand, or demands, of any nature whatsoever, and, too, on account of the use of any patent invention, article, or appliance included in the materials or workmanship hereby agreed to be furnished under this contract.

It is further covenanted and agreed by the parties hereto that the said party of the second part will at his own expense comply with all municipal building ordinances and regulations in so far as the same are binding upon or usually observed by the United States, and obtain all required licenses and permits, and be responsible for all damages to persons or property which may occur in the prosecution of this work; that all the work made necessary by the drawings and specifications, though every item may not be particularly shown on the first or mentioned in the second, or in either, but judged necessary by the architect, shall be executed and performed in accordance with the true spirit and intent of said plans and specifications, just as though such work were particularly shown in each, respectively, unless otherwise specifically provided; that all materials and work furnished shall be subject to the approval of the said architect, and that the said party of the second part shall be responsible for the proper care and protection of all materials delivered and work performed by him until the completion and final acceptance in writing of the same by the architect for the party of the first part. It is further agreed that the architect, or his duly appointed representatives, shall control the location of the storing of materials, the mode of progress of the work, that is, where the plastering shall be mixed, what rooms will be first required, etc., although the party of the second part may appeal in writing from the order and decision of the said architect's representatives to the architect direct, who, in all these matters, as in all else pertaining to this building, will be the arbiter and judge.

In this connection it must also be thoroughly understood that all the transactions between the architect, representing the party of the first part, and the party of the second part must be in writing; that no instructions or orders allegedly given verbally by the architect or his representative will be considered in the final or any other adjustment of accounts.

It is further covenanted and agreed by and between the parties hereto that the said party of the second part will make any omissions from, or additions to, or changes in the work or materials herein provided for, whenever required by the said architect, acting for the said party of the first part; the valuation of all such omissions or additions or changes in work or material, in so far as this contract may be affected, will be determined on the basis of the contract unit value of material and work referred to; or, in the absence of such unit of value, then on prevailing market rates at the time of such change, which market rates, in case of dispute, are to be determined by the said architect, whose decision in reference thereto shall be binding upon both parties, and that no claim for damages on account of such changes or for anticipated profits shall be made or allowed. In cases where there is no basis of valuation upon which to determine the adjustment of such omission or addition the architect may ask the party of the second part to submit a bid therefor, which the said architect may accept if he deem it just, or he may order the work to proceed, first notifying the party of the second part, however, of the settlement or arrangement he deems to be just. The party of the second part may then file a protest against such award in writing with said architect and go on with the work. Said protest will receive due consideration at the time of final adjustment.

It is further covenanted and agreed that no addition to or omission from this work herein provided for shall be construed to extend the time fixed herein for the final completion of the work, unless an extension be deemed just and granted in writing by the party of the first part at the time the order is given by the architect for the change.

It is further covenanted and agreed that no addition to or omission from the work herein specifically provided for shall make void or affect the other provisions or covenants of this contract and bond, but merely the difference in the cost thereby occasioned, as the case may be, shall be added to or deducted from the total amount of the contract. It would be manifestly unfair to consider the amount of this contract, protected by its bond, as an absolutely fixed quantity, as conditions are bound to arise that will compel considerable portions of the work to be performed according to the schedule prices of the bid. There are sure to be changes in the location of certain officers' rooms in the building and in other such details that, while hardly affecting the final total cost of the building to any material degree, yet will affect the manner in which that total will be reached.

It is further covenanted and agreed by the parties hereto that all materials furnished and work done under this contract shall at all times and places be subject to the inspection and direction of the said architect and his representative, the superintendent of the building, and of other inspectors appointed by the said party of the first part, with the right to reject any and all work or material not in strict accordance with the spirit of these requirements; and the decision of the said architect as to quantity and quality shall be final and binding. And it is further covenanted and agreed by and between the parties hereto that the said party of the second part will at his expense, within a reasonable time, to be specified by the said architect, remedy or remove any defective or unsatisfactory material or work; and that, in the event of his failure immediately to proceed and faithfully so to do, the said party of the first part may have the same done and charge the cost thereof to the account of the said party of the second part.

It is further covenanted and agreed by and between the parties hereto that until final inspection and acceptance of, and payment for, all of the material and work provided for under this contract, and the final acceptance of the completed work by the architect of the building for the party of the first part, no prior inspection, payment, or other act is to be construed as a waiver of the right of the party of the first part to reject any defective work or material, or to require the fulfillment of any of the terms of the contract, which, of course, also means the specifications and all drawings referred to therein or yet to be made in their true spirit and intent.

It is further covenanted and agreed by and between the parties hereto that if the said party of the second part shall fail to complete the work herein contracted for, or any part thereof, in accordance with this agreement, within the time provided for, or shall fail to prosecute said work with such diligence as in the judgment of the architect will insure the completion of the said work within the time provided, the said party of the first part may withhold all payments for work in place until final completion and acceptance of the same, and is authorized and empowered, after eight days' notice thereof in writing, served personally upon or left at the shop, office, or usual place of abode of the said party of the second part, or with his agent, and the said party of the second part having failed to take such action within the said eight days as will, in the judgment of the architect, remedy the default for which said notice was given, to take possession of the said work, in whole or in part, and of all machinery and tools employed thereon, and all materials belonging to the said party of the second part delivered on the site, and, at the expense of the said party of the second part, to complete or have completed the said work, and to supply or have supplied the labor, materials, and tools, of whatever character, necessary to be purchased or supplied by reason of the default of the said party of the second part; in which event the said party of the second part shall be further liable for any damage incurred through such default, and the indemnity above referred to for delay and for all or any other breaches of this contract.

And the said party of the first part, acting for and in behalf of the United States, covenants and agrees to pay, or cause to be paid, unto the said party of the second part, or to his heirs, executors, or administrators or bondsmen, in the case of his failure to fulfill this contract and of their completing it in his place, in lawful money of the United States, in consideration of the herein-recited covenants and agreements made by the party of the second part, the sum of $397,500.$\frac{00}{100}$.

And the party of the first part covenants and agrees that payments will be made in the following manner, to wit: Ninety per cent (nine-tenths) of the value of the work executed and actually in place, to the satisfaction of the architect, will be paid from time to time as the work progresses (the said value to be ascertained by any means the architect may deem just and effective), and ten per cent (one-tenth) of the value of said work in place will be retained until the completion of the entire work, and the approval and acceptance of the same by the architect for the party of the first part, which amount shall be forfeited by the said party of the second part in the event of the nonfulfillment of this contract, it being expressly covenanted and agreed that said forfeiture shall not relieve the said party of the second part from liability to the party of the first part for any and all damages sustained by reason of any breach of this contract.   But in certifying to these payments the architect, regardless of this ninety per cent payment and ten per cent retained clause, may at all times hold back a sufficient sum, in his estimation, to complete the uncompleted portions of this contract at the then prevailing market rates for material and labor should the contractor fail to so complete his work.

It is an express condition of this contract that no member of Congress, officer, or employee of the Treasury Department or other person whose name is not at this time disclosed, shall be admitted to any share of this contract or any benefit to arise therefrom as a subcontractor or otherwise; and it is further covenanted and agreed that this contract shall not be assigned.

In witness whereof the parties have hereunto subscribed their names this 17th day of November, A. D. 1902.

[All erasures, additions, and interlineations in the body of the contract to be noted here before execution of document.]

It is further expressly understood and agreed by the parties hereto that the said party of the first part shall have the right at any time before April 1, 1903, to order the performance of any or all of the items "A" to "R," inclusive, mentioned herein, to be done in strict, full, and exact compliance with the specification requirements at the increased prices named therefor in said proposal; and further, that the units of value mentioned on pages 29 and 30 of said proposal "as a basis for any further change, addition, or deduction" shall remain in force during the entire continuance of this contract, regardless of whether the above option is or is not exercised.

                                                H. A. TAYLOR,
                                    Acting Secretary of the Treasury.

We hereby certify that this contract and bond have been correctly prepared and compared.

HENRY IVES COBB,
    Architect of the U. S. Gov't Building at Chicago, Ill.

                                        JOHN PEIRCE, *Contractor.*

Witnesses to the signature of the contractor:

H. S. LAMPHER.
EMIL DIEBITSCH.

No. 1391A.   Contract of John Peirce, of New York, for interior work and completion of the U. S. post-office, court-house, etc., at Chicago, Ill.   Dated November 17th, 1902.   Amount, $997,500.   Time to complete, April 1, 1904.   Penalty for each day's delay, $100.   Bond dated December 1, 1902.   Amount of bond, $300,000.

The following instructions must be particularly observed and complied with, viz:

1st.   The Christian names must be written in the body of the bond in full, and so signed to the bond.

2d.   A seal of wax or wafer must be attached to each signature on the bond.   No seals required for signatures to contract except corporate seals.

3d.   Each signature must be made in the presence of two persons, who must sign their names as witnesses.

4th.   Each surety must make and sign an affidavit of the amount he is worth after paying his just debts and deducting all exemptions by the laws of the State in which he resides, and liabilities of whatever nature, as per form herewith.

5th.   A district judge or attorney of the United States, or clerk of a United States court, must certify that the sureties are sufficient to pay the penalty of the bond.

6th.   The affidavits of the sureties must be taken and signed before an officer authorized to administer oaths generally.   The officer must certify that he administered the oaths.   If the magistrate is not a judge of the United States court, his authority to administer oaths must be certified by the clerk of a court of record having official knowledge of that fact.

7th.   Bond must be dated.

8th.   Residence of principal and sureties must be distinctly stated.

9th.   The sureties must justify in amounts the aggregate of which will be equal to twice the penal sum of the bond.

10th.   When the contracting party is a partnership concern, the contract must be signed with the firm name without seal, and the bond must be signed by each member of the firm with seal to each signature; when a corporate body, there should be attached to the contract duly authenticated evidence that the officer or officers executing the contract and bond have authority to do so, and the corporate seal must be affixed to each instrument.

TREASURY DEPARTMENT,
OFFICE OF THE ARCHITECT OF THE
U. S. GOVERNMENT BUILDING AT CHICAGO, ILL.,
December 18, 1902.

Respectfully referred to the Solicitor of the Treasury for examination and indorsement.

HENRY IVES COBB,
Architect of the U. S. Government Building at Chicago, Ill.

DEPARTMENT OF JUSTICE,
OFFICE OF THE SOLICITOR OF THE TREASURY,
Dec. 19, 1902.

I have examined the within contract and bond as to form and execution, and in these respects they are approved when the contract is duly executed on behalf of the United States.

F. A. REEVES,
Assistant Solicitor of the Treasury.

TREASURY DEPARTMENT, OFFICE OF THE SECRETARY,
December 20, 1902.

The within bond is hereby approved.

O. L. SPAULDING,
Acting Secretary.

SPECIFICATION, PROPOSAL, CONTRACT, AND BOND FOR THE DRAINAGE, PLUMBING, AND GAS FITTING FOR THE UNITED STATES POST-OFFICE COURT-HOUSE, ETC., AT CHICAGO, ILLINOIS.

1.   Bids are invited for the drainage, plumbing, and gas fitting for the new United States post-office, court-house, etc., at Chicago, Illinois, now being erected on the block bounded by Adams, Clark, Jackson, and Dearborn streets, in Chicago, Illinois. The building is now inclosed, with rough floors only in place.

2.   The Treasury Department reserves the right to accept any part or parts of the bid made and at the prices stipulated in same; also to waive any informalities in and to reject any and all bids.

3. Should the successful bidder, for any reason whatsoever after the time set for the opening of the bids, withdraw from the competition, or fail or refuse to execute the formal bond or contract within two weeks after the same are sent to him, his certified check may be declared forfeited and the acceptance of his bid revoked, and all obligations on the part of all persons acting for and in behalf of the United States in connection therewith will be released and annulled.

4. A bidder must submit with his bid a certified check of five thousand dollars ($5,000), drawn to the order of the Treasurer of the United States, as a guarantee that he will fully and faithfully comply with the terms of his bid should the same be accepted, and that, within two weeks after the form is sent to him, he will execute the bond and contract in accordance therewith; the sureties on the bond to be approved by the Secretary of the Treasury.

5. The certified check of the successful bidder will be retained until the execution of a formal bond and contract, and the approval of the same by the Secretary of the Treasury.

6. The certified checks of the unsuccessful bidders will be returned immediately after the bid of the successful bidder shall have been accepted and the contract executed, and all plans and specifications have been returned to the architect.

7. Wherever the word "architect" is used herein it shall be held to mean the Architect of the United States Government building at Chicago, Illinois.

8. Wherever the word "bidder" is used it shall be held to mean any individual or firm of individuals, or any member of a firm or any corporation signing a bid submitted, and the word "contractor" shall mean the successful bidder to whom this contract will be awarded.

9. The original drawings named herein will be retained at the office of the architect; copies of the same will be prepared for the use of the bidders. Parties obtaining copies of the drawings must return them to the office of the architect on or before the time set for receiving bids, and no bid will be considered unless said drawings are returned as set forth. Bidders must make a deposit of a certified check for one hundred dollars ($100), drawn to the order of the Treasurer of the United States, before being given the plans; which sum will revert to the United States if the plans and these papers are not promptly returned. Before submitting their bids, contractors should make a careful examination of the site, the drawings, and specifications, to be fully informed as to the condition of the work, the quality of the material, and the character of the workmanship required, and make a careful examination of the place where the materials are to be delivered and the work performed, and all the conditions governing the fulfillment of the contract; for when a bid is accepted no consideration will be given for any error in the bid resulting from failure or oversight to do so.

10. In referring to the drawings and specifications it must be understood that figures always take the precedence before what a drawing may scale; that the large-scale drawings rank ahead of the small-scale ones, and that the specifications or written notes on plans precede all else. It must also be understood that the architect reserves the right to make any changes in the construction arrangement, or details before the work is actually executed, and such changes or alterations will only entitle the contractor to an extra or deduction, according to the schedule, such as may be proven by measurement of the difference in the work as first shown, and as amended; and until such material or work is delivered or executed in place no allowance for time or other damages claimed for such changes will be considered.

11. Bidders are warned that a bid which is deficient in any of the requirements set forth herein may be rejected as informal.

12. A bid submitted for this work by parties whom the architect may have reason to believe are not experienced or regularly engaged in this line and class of work, or not having the proper facilities and financial standing to properly and promptly execute the same as herein required, will not receive consideration, and contractors contemplating bidding on this work must show that they have such experience and standing before obtaining plans.

13. A bid must be made upon the blank hereto attached.

14. A bid must not be detached from this package in which it is bound, nor must any of the accompanying papers be detached herefrom; but the entire package must be unbroken and in good order when the bid is delivered to the architect.

15. A bidder must state in writing in his bid and in figures (without interlineations, alterations, or erasures) the sum of money for which he will supply the materials and perform the work required by the drawings and specifications, and in accordance with the conditions of the contract and bond, etc., as herein set forth, should his bid be accepted.

16. A bid must state the price per unit of quantity for all work bid upon, and which unit price shall be used for any additions to or omissions from the work in each class or kind of work shown on the drawings, and required by the specifications; said prices to be the basis of computation for any change that may be desired, and made by order of the architect, and the bidder must also state the amount included in his bid for each class or kind of work as per schedule herein set forth.

17. A bid submitted by a firm must be signed with the firm name and by the member of the firm duly authorized to sign for that firm.

18. A bid submitted by a corporation must be signed with the name of the corporation and the full name of each officer of the corporation and have the official corporate seal attached.

19. Bidders must also give in their bids the names of three prominent buildings in which they have done the plumbing.

20. A bidder must be prepared to submit, at his expense, samples of all the materials which he proposes to use, before a contract is signed; the samples to have the name of the bidder and the title and location of the building plainly marked thereon. Each sample of material must be delivered at this office prior to the time the contract is to be signed, and be approved in writing by the architect before said contract is signed. The samples submitted will be retained, and whenever required the contractor must furnish duplicates of the samples at his expense.

21. Sealed bids must be delivered in the office of Henry Ives Cobb, architect of the Chicago building, Treasury Department, Washington, D. C., on or before 2 p.m. —— ——, 1902. Envelopes must bear the name of the bidders and the words "Bid for plumbing, etc., Chicago building." Franked envelopes have been furnished with these papers for their return.

22. Bidders who send their bids to this office through the mails are requested to register the same, and to place the name, address, and title of bid on the ouside of the envelope for identification, and to mail such bid sufficiently early to reach its destination by the time required, as it is a frequent and vexing occurrence that bids reach this office after the hour named. A bid received after the time stated in the advertisement will be returned unopened to the bidder if the proper name and address be known. If the name and address are not known, then the bid will necessarily be opened to ascertain the same.

23. Bidders are hereby notified that the certified checks required with their bids must be drawn to the order of the Treasurer of the United States; a check drawn to the bidder's own order, or to the order of any other person than the Treasurer of the United States, although indorsed by the party to whose order it is drawn, and although certified or accepted by the bank on which it is so drawn, will not be accepted as a certified check, such as is required under these regulations.

NOTE.—The Government frank sent to intending bidders is to be used for the return of drawings and specifications and for no other purpose.

GENERAL CONDITIONS.

24. NOTICE TO SURETIES.—The attention of sureties is particularly directed to the following conditions:

The final inspection and acceptance of work called for by the drawings and specifications forming a part of the contract shall not be binding or conclusive upon the United States if it shall subsequently appear that the contractor has willfully or fraudulently, or through collusion with any of the representatives of the Department in charge of the work, supplied inferior material or workmanship, or has departed from the terms of his contract. In any such case, the United States shall have the right, notwithstanding such final acceptance and payment, to cause the work to be properly performed and satisfactory materials supplied to such extent as in the opinion of the architect may be necessary to finish the work in accordance with the drawings and specifications thereof, at the cost and expense of the contractor and the sureties on his bond, and shall have the right to recover against the contractor and his sureties the cost of such work, together with such other damages as the United States may suffer because of the default of the contractor in the premises, the same as though such acceptance and final payment had not been made. The contractor must at all times keep his work insured for his own protection in case of fire, as the Government assumes none of the responsibility therefor, even though it pays for portions of the work in place. In case of damage by fire this contractor must renew all such work, as final acceptance will only be made and paid for upon the turning over of a perfect, whole, and complete job.

25. PAYMENTS.—Payments will be made monthly on account of the work satisfactorily in place in the building, based on the estimated value thereof, as ascertained by the architect, less 10 per cent of such estimate, which will be retained until the final inspection of all materials and labor embraced in the contract and the acceptance of the work, after which the final payment of the balance due will be made. Provided further, however, that the architect will at all times, regardless of this 10 per cent clause, retain a sufficient sum to complete the uncompleted work at market rates.

26. PROPOSALS.—Proposals as hereinbefore called for must be based on plumbing drawings 122 to 138, inclusive, and this specification, and must include everything necessary and requisite to place the work complete in every detail.

27. The drawings and specifications are to be interpreted together, and all work included in either, though not in both, must be included in the proposal.

28. INSPECT THE BUILDING.—Bidders must visit the building, compare the drawings and specifications, examine the work in place, inform themselves as to all conditions, include in their proposals all items of labor and material mentioned, shown, or necessarily implied, that may be required in the full completion of the work in accordance with the true intent and meaning of the drawings and specifications, whether each item be specifically mentioned or not, and all such items must conform to the class to which they belong or are attached.

29. KIND AND QUALITY OF MATERIAL.—The required materials and fixtures in each case must be of the best of their respective kinds and grades found in the market, and the bidders are to name on the proposal sheet the kind of materials and fixtures they desire to use. In the event any of the submitted materials and fixtures are not considered first-class and satisfactory the architect will select the materials or fixtures, and the selection shall be final and binding upon the successful bidder.

30. The acceptance by the architect of any materials or fixtures named on the proposal sheet is to be understood as an acceptance of the same only upon its conforming with the requirements of the specifications in relation thereto, and not as an absolute acceptance of the article without respect to the requirements of the specifications.

PATENT RIGHTS.—If any part of the material or fixtures proposed to be furnished by the bidder is covered by the claims or patents of whatsoever nature of any other parties, the contractor proposing to use such appliances will be required to pay all royalties therefor. The Government will not recognize any demand brought by anyone on account of claims for infringement of patents, but will hold the contractor and his bondsmen strictly responsible for any delay or any cost resulting from his failure to fully protect the Government against delays, etc., growing out of such use of patented materials.

32. VISIT THE DEPARTMENT.—The architect reserves the right to require the contractor or his authorized representative to visit this office without expense to the Government, if at any time it is considered to be in the interest of the Government that a conference is necessary for an early adjustment of any complicated or unsatisfactory conditions that may have developed in connection with his contract, but the result of such conference shall not be binding until formally approved.

33. DETAIL DRAWINGS.—The successful bidder upon request of the architect will be required to submit for approval of the architect detail drawings of any portion of the work, these drawings to be furnished in triplicate and to be approved before the execution of such portion of work. The approval of the architect of any drawings submitted by the contractor, as hereinbefore required, must be understood to be the approval of the general arrangement only, as the architect assumes no responsibility for details of construction, dimensions, performance, etc.

34. TIME OF COMPLETION.—The work is to commence immediately upon official notice from the architect that the building is ready to have the work under this contract installed, and the bidders must state in what time from said notice they will complete the work, except placing the plumbing fixtures and putting on pipe covering. The excepted work must be commenced immediately upon receipt of a second notice from the architect that the building is ready for such work.

35. Bidders must also state in what time they will complete this part of the work from the date of said second notice, which must include the completion of the entire work. And the successful bidder, hereafter called the contractor, undertakes to complete any special portion of the work he may be ordered to by the architect ahead of all else.

36. Temporary light wires may be brought into the building by this contractor for use in connection with his work, but he must not use candles and other dangerous lighting devices about the premises.

37. In this and in all else properly coming under "policing" of the building he must submit to such rules as may be established by the general contractor, who is held responsible by the Government for the proper care of the building during completion.

38. GUARANTEE.—Each bidder must also understand that if his proposal is accepted, his contract and bond will guarantee the entire work under this contract, and each and every part thereof, and the contractor will be required to remedy all defects at his expense which may develop by reason of the use of any inferior or defective material or workmanship until the acceptance of the entire work, and final payment therefor, subject, however, to the additional requirements expressed in paragraph (24) and entitled "notice to sureties," and subject to any time-limit guarantee on any particular portion of work hereafter mentioned in specifications.

39. All questions as to the satisfactory completion of the work and the defects necessary to be remedied are to be determined by the architect or his authorized representatives.

40. GENERAL REQUIREMENTS.—This contractor is to perform his work expeditiously in such manner and at such times as will avoid interference with the execution of other contracts. Contractor to employ, continually, a sufficiently large force of men to carry on his work properly and finish same in specified time. In failure so to do the architect may direct said contractor to increase his force.

41. Contractor to keep a foreman, satisfactory to the architect, constantly on the ground to receive instructions from the architect, and any employee of this contractor, about the building, must be removed from the premises if the architect so directs.

42. Contractor to supply his own light for the performance of all the work. He may introduce wires, etc., under instructions of the architect, but he will not be permitted to use candles and other dangerous means of lighting.

43. The dimensions and scaled proportions given on the drawings are in accordance with the general plans, but as variations therefrom may occur in construction, the contractor must make his own measurements at the building, and he will be held responsible for the proper fitting of his work. He must check and verify all drawings, and will be held responsible for any errors which could have been avoided by such checking.

44. The contractor will lay out all his work in conjunction with the general contractor, so that all parts of the different work come together in good shape and that there will be no marring of decorations, changes made necessary, or other troubles.

45. STORAGE OF STOCK.—Contractor to store stock where directed by architect, and to remove the same at his own expense when so directed by architect.

46. PERMITS.—Contractor to take out at his own expense all necessary permits for carrying on his work and for connecting with the sewer, water, and gas supply, etc.

47. GENERAL DESCRIPTION OF WORK.—This contractor shall furnish all labor and material and build and construct, in a good substantial manner, in place in and around building, the drains, sewers, and all their appurtenances, and all piping for gas, water supply, wastes, ventilation of wastes, and the plumbing fixtures and all their appurtenances, and furnish and set all tanks in connection with the water supply, making the entire system of water supply, use and waste, complete and ready for service.

48. All sewage and waste above the first floor is to be run direct to street sewers. The first floor and basement sewage and waste is to be run to ejector, hereinafter specified, and thence forced to street sewer.

49. The down spouts from roofs and balconies to be connected at basement ceiling and thence run to sewer. The underground drainage of building is to be conducted to catch basins and thence pumped to sewer. The cold-water supply for basement and first-floor plumbing fixtures and for all sill cocks and hose connections is to be supplied by one system of pipes.

50. The plumbing fixtures on second to eighth floors, inclusive, to be supplied from a second system of pipes, and all fixtures in dome above ninth floor to be supplied by a third system of pipes. There will be one hot-water system of pipes to supply all fixtures below ninth floor and another system of pipes to supply all fixtures above ninth floor.

51. WORK NOT INCLUDED IN THIS CONTRACT.—The house pumps and cooling-water machinery and pumps are not included in this contract, but this contractor is to make all water connections to and from same. The down spouts from roof are to be brought down to basement ceiling by another contractor, this contractor to connect same at this point.

52. When so ordered by the architect, this contractor will run two temporary supply cocks and the necessary 1½-inch piping and waste to serve each floor of main

building, at such points as the architect may determine; also one cock at the twelfth and one at the fifteenth floors of dome.   Contractor will, if necessary, attach an electric pump or other suitable appliance to this temporary service, to raise the water the necessary height, but the general contractor, for whose use the water is chiefly intended, will pay for the operation of said pump.

53. MATERIAL.—All material used in this work shall be the best of its kind.

54. All pipe and fittings shall be of the inside diameter designated.   Cast-iron pipe, when used for sewers, shall be extra-heavy soil pipe, each pipe marked and bearing the maker's name, of equal thickness throughout, and of proper weight, to be coated inside and outside while hot, with coal-tar varnish.

55. Fittings for cast-iron soil pipe shall be especially made drainage fittings, of equal thickness and weight, and of the same class and inside diameter and coated the same as pipe with which they are used.   Cast-iron pipe, when used for water connections, shall be standard water pipe and fittings shall be of same grade.

56. Wrought-iron pipe shall be standard, and all sizes of greater diameter than 1½-inch shall be lap-welded.   When used for soil or waste, it shall be coated inside and outside while hot with coal-tar varnish.   When used for vent or water supply, shall be galvanized pipe.   Fittings for wrought-iron pipe for soil, waste, or ventilating pipes shall be long-turn cast-iron recessed drainage fittings of same inside diameter and coated the same as the pipe with which they are used, and those supporting risers shall have a proper shoe cast on them.   Graded fittings shall have the grade cast in them.   Fittings for water pipe shall be of malleable iron, galvanized, and all changes in the direction of the water pipe and connections to pipe shall be made with long-sweep water elbows and water tees.   All wrought-iron pipe and fittings shall be cut with full threads, and when used for waste and ventilating pipe, cut to a gauge.   Fittings for junctions of cast-iron and wrought-iron pipe shall be cut at one end with full threads.   Lead pipe for water-supply connections shall be strong pipe weighing as follows: ½-inch pipe, 1 pound 12 ounces per linear foot; ⅝-inch pipe, 2 pounds 8 ounces per linear foot; ¾-inch pipe, 3 pounds per linear foot.

57. For waste and ventilating connections light lead pipe shall be used, weighing as follows: 1¼-inch pipe, 3 pounds per linear foot; 1½-inch pipe, 4 pounds per linear foot; 2-inch pipe, 5 pounds per lenear foot.   All exposed pipe or fittfngs for connection in toilet rooms, except basement toilet rooms, shall be of polished brass, nickel plated.

58. The brass pipe for hot and cold water connections to be seamless drawn tubing of same size and thickness as standard wrought-iron pipe.   Brass flush pipes to be of seamless drawn tubing not less than No. 18 B. W. G.   Fittings for brass pipe to be heavy pattern cast brass.

59. Sheet lead for safing and flashing shall weigh 3 pounds per square foot.

60. All brackets, clamps, pipe hooks, or hangers shall be of wrought iron and constructed to the satisfaction of the architect.

61. Drain tile shall be hard-burned vitrified tile.

62. Brick shall be hard-burned sewer brick, free from lime, and shall be thoroughly wet before laying.

63. Broken stone shall be limestone, free from dust and not larger than will pass through a 2-inch ring.   Sand shall be clean and sharp.

64. American Portland cement shall be of brand approved by the architect.

65. Mortar for brickwork shall be made of 1 part Portland cement and 3 parts sand.

66. The cement and sand shall be thoroughly mixed dry and wet with as little water as will make mortar of proper consistency when well worked.   All mortar which shall have set or become hard in the box shall be thrown out and not used in the work.

67. Lead shall be soft pig.   Gaskin shall be picked oakum.

68. EXCAVATION.—The contractor shall do all excavation necessary in the laying of the work included in this specification, and shall furnish all necessary sheeting and bracing and use the same for protection of walls and foundations wherever necessary or when ordered by the architect, and shall keep the trenches free from water during the progress of the work by pumping or bailing.

69. A line shall be used to mark out sewer trenches and there shall be no variations from the plans except on order of the architect.

70. For water pipe the trenches outside of building shall not be less than 6 feet below street grade.

71. EJECTOR PLANT.—Where shown on plans, this contractor shall furnish and set a duplicate set of hydropneumatic ejectors, complete with ejector chamber and all apparatus for operating ejectors.   This set of ejectors is to receive the discharge of all sewage from basement and first floor.

72. STEEL EJECTOR CHAMBER.—Where shown, this contractor shall furnish and set a steel tank of form and dimensions shown on plan, and provided with all flanged openings for pipe connections to ejectors. This contractor shall do all excavation necessary to install said chamber and shall first sink a 3-inch oak or cypress tank without bottom, of diameter 12 inches greater than steel tank. The bottom of this wood tank to be filled in with concrete 1 foot thick and then the steel tank lowered in position, and the space between tanks filled in with concrete. All concrete to be made in the proportions of 1 part Portland cement, 3 parts sand, and 5 parts broken stone; stone to be not larger than will pass through a 1-inch ring. All concrete to be tamped solid. The bottom of steel tank will also be filled with concrete to level shown, and finished with a 1-inch coat of cement mortar made of 1 part cement to 2 parts sand, and troweled smooth. The dished bottom of the tank to be made of one piece, and the sides as two sections. The tank is to be riveted and caulked perfectly tight and to be painted two coats of best asphaltum varnish. The tank will be covered at top with I beams and brick arches, as shown, and provided with an iron manhole cover with perforated top. The tank shall also be provided with a wrought-iron ladder attached to walls of pit, and extending from top to bottom of tank.

73. EJECTORS.—This contractor shall furnish and set two hydropneumatic ejectors in the ejector chamber as hereinbefore specified, each of 200 gallons capacity; said ejectors shall be capable of allowing sewage to flow into them and automatically ejecting their contents when filled, and they shall be fitted with all appliances necessary for this purpose, together with flanged openings for the air and sewage connections.

74. This contractor shall connect the ejector to the sewage inlet and discharge pipes hereinafter specified.

75. AIR COMPRESSORS.—This contractor shall furnish two direct-connected air compressors and shall erect them upon foundations to be supplied by him. Foundations to be Portland cement foundations, faced with best wide enameled brick, and to extend 18 inches above the floor line. The compressors shall be capable of supplying air in sufficient quantity and of the required density to maintain, with the specified ejectors, a discharge of 400 gallons per minute continuously against an actual head of 15 feet.

76. MOTORS AND AUTOMATIC CONTROLLING APPARATUS.—This contractor shall furnish and set on similar foundations as specified for air compressors, two compound-wound electric motors with sliding bases and self-oiling bearings of suitable power to operate the air compressors at the capacity specified. Motors to have pinions which will mesh with the gear wheels on compressor and to be equipped with two sets of automatic air-pressure regulating apparatus mounted on a white marble footboard with iron frame attached to wall. This apparatus is to be capable of operating within a range of 5 pounds per square inch air pressure, to be cross-connected and fitted with all necessary switches and fuses complete, and to be so arranged as to cut the motors out of circuit at any time if current fails.

77. Other contractors are to bring the main wires to switch board, but this contractor to run wires from board to motors, said wiring to be done in accordance with the wiring specifications of building.

78. AIR RECEIVER.—This contractor shall set where directed, on proper foundation, or securely supported, one receiver for the compressed air of capacity sufficient to operate the ejectors. Receivers shall be built of the best quality flanged steel, outside painted with two coats of black asphaltum varnish, properly stayed and tested to withstand a pressure of 100 pounds per square inch above atmosphere. This receiver shall be fitted with pop safety valve, hand-hole, and blowoff cock.

79. CONNECTING PIPE AND APPURTENANCES.—This contractor shall furnish the necessary material and connect the air compressor to receiver; the receiver to the ejectors and to a pressure gauge and the automatic apparatus on switch board; the ejectors to a ventilating shaft, vapor pipe, or flue from boilers, as may be directed. In case the exhaust from ejectors is connected to vapor pipe, a suitable 2½-inch fitting shall be provided in this pipe by another contractor. The ejectors, compressors, motors, automatic apparatus, and receiver shall be complete with all pipes, valves, fittings, and appurtenances necessary for the continuous and convenient operation of the plant.

80. OPERATION.—When set and connected as specified this apparatus shall be automatic in its action, the ejectors shall operate each its own discharge when filled, and the motors and compressors shall start automatically when the pressure is released in the receiver. This intermittent operation engaging one or both of the ejectors and one or both sides of the air-compressor apparatus, as may be necessary, shall continue and discharge all sewage flowing to the ejectors up to the specified quantity of 400 United States gallons per minute day by day, failure from accident or ordinary wear and tear excepted.

81. TEST.—When the apparatus is complete and ready for service, this contractor shall give notice to the architect and shall, if so desired, make a test trial of the plant in his presence. Taking the sewage and such additional water as may be necessary, the whole apparatus shall run at its full capacity of 400 gallons per minute for thirty minutes, and if any defect shall show in the apparatus this contractor shall make the same good and repeat the test, and said contractor shall not be entitled to demand or receive money on this portion of his work until the same is in satisfactory running order.

82. GUARANTEE.—This contractor guarantees the ejector plant as specified and the continual operation of the same in this building for a term of one year from the date of final certificate of acceptance, and shall at his own cost and expense make good, repair, or replace any part of this apparatus which may show defects during the time, provided the architect deems said defect is due to imperfection in material or workmanship as specified.

83. SURFACE DRAIN EJECTORS.—Where shown on plan or directed by architect, this contractor shall furnish, set, and connect electric bilge pumps to receive surface drainage. Pumps to have a safe working capacity of 60 gallons per minute against a head of 15 feet.

84. CAST-IRON CHAMBERS.—Contractor to furnish and set cast-iron catch basins of sufficient diameter to work the centrifugal pump with inlet connections for drainage pipes. Basin to be at least 2 feet deeper than lowest inlet pipe; to be made perfectly tight and fitted with an air-tight iron cover, provided with suitable manhole and stuffing boxes for float rod and pump shaft.

85. PUMPS.—Pumps to consist of a vertical motor mounted on the cast-iron cover for basin and direct connected to the shaft of a vertical submerged centrifugal pump, this pump to be constructed with suitable thrust bearings and sleeve bearings so as to run without lubrication and without danger of binding when not submerged. Pumps to have enlarged passages and solid volute. No gaskets to be employed.

86. Motor armature to rotate on ball bearings with sight-feed lubrication. Motor to be compound-wound, entirely inclosed. Pump and motor to be so mounted as to be entirely self-contained and held in perfect alignment, regardless of floor level. Float to be copper, running on brass guides and attached to brass rod, which shall actuate float switch. Float switch to be of the double-pole gravity type, polished brass, mounted on basin cover, with knife switches and fuses complete. Pumps to operate automatically on any desired water level in the catch-basins and to be entirely noiseless. Contractor to connect the discharge pipe to iron sewer pipe with 2½-inch pipe with swing check valve inserted above the floor line. All fittings on pipe to be long-sweep fittings.

87. DRAINS.—Where shown on plans, this contractor shall lay in tile drains. Drains shall conform to the grades given as shown by the sections and have a uniform grade between sections.

88. The tile shall be laid in wooden boxes made of 1-inch boards, the boxes being 2 inches higher and 4 inches wider than the tile laid therein, each box being dovetailed into the preceding and following box so as to make one continuous box. Tile shall be laid in box in a true line, with close joints. Broken stone shall then be placed in and around tile, filling up all the box and trench, and shall be continued up to the bottom of the concrete basement floor.

89. Where shown, this contractor shall build brick catch-basins in connection with the drainage tile, basins to have 8-inch walls, resting on two flat courses on bottom, to be laid up with cement mortar; to be 24 inches inside diameter and 4 inches deeper than the outlet drain; to be drawn in to 18 inches at top and covered with an approved iron ring and flush cover 18 inches in diameter, set flush with top of basement floor. Covers to have drop lift, recessed handles, and diagonal channelled surfaces.

90. CAST-IRON SEWERS.—All sewers laid in ground through and inside of building shall be of cast iron. Commencing at street sewer, where shown, this contractor shall connect therewith and lay in cast-iron sewers and connect to building sewer system. He shall also run the sewers in ground inside of building as shown. The pipe shall be imbedded its entire length in dry earth or sand with a proper bell hole at each joint. All pipe shall be laid truly in line and grade with a grade of ¼-inch to 1-foot of length, unless otherwise directed by the architect. Any change in line or grade shall be made with proper curve fitting, and any junction shall be made with a Y branch. Hand-hole fittings shall be used where shown, and each hand-hole shall be fitted with a brass trap screw leaded and calked as specified for joints.

91. Fittings receiving risers shall be firmly supported. All joints shall be tightly calked with hemp gasket, leaving not less than 1½ inches depth of lead room, and then thoroughly filled with molten lead and calked tight. Care shall be taken that

the joint is left perfectly smooth inside. All openings for connections shall be closed with plugs until used, and all hand-holes shall be closed at once and the sewer shall be kept clean. Any dirt which shall get in shall be removed by the contractor. The trenches in street shall be at once refilled in layers of 12 inches and thoroughly tamped and the pavement replaced to the satisfaction of the city street department and the South Park commissioners. Dry dirt shall be rammed in place at the sides of the pipe laid inside of building, leaving the joints and top exposed until tested as hereinafter specified. After testing, the trenches shall be filled in layers not more than 9 inches deep, each thoroughly rammed.

92. MANHOLES.—Where shown, the contractor shall build brick manholes. Those for end clean-outs to be 24 inches in diameter, drawn in to 18 inches at top, and those for clean-outs on run to be 18 by 30 inches. The bottom of basins to be of concrete 6 inches thick and the walls to be 8-inch brick walls laid up in cement mortar, built to the proper height to receive the iron frames and covers. The tops of frames and covers to be set flush with the basement floor line. Covers and frames to be reset by this contractor after the finished floor is laid when necessary to bring them flush with the floor. Covers to have drop lift, recessed handles, and diagonal channelled surfaces. The bottom and inside faces of wall to be plastered with a coat of mortar ½ inch thick, troweled smooth.

93. CATCH-BASIN.—Where shown in engine room and in machinery room on plan, this contractor shall furnish, set, and connect sectional iron catch-basins. Basins to be 30 inches in diameter and 30 inches deep below outlet and made perfectly tight. Inlets of basin to be connected to drips of tanks, pumps, etc., and outlet of basins to sewer.

94. DRIVEWAY CATCHDRAINS.—At ends of driveway, where shown, this contractor shall furnish, set, and connect to sewer an iron graded gutter, as shown on detail sheet, extending clear across driveway, with grated iron cover set flush with top of floor to allow ingress of rain water. Gutter to be connected into standard iron bell trap made specially for said gutter, with cover same as gutter. The bell trap to be connected to an iron combination backwater and clean-out trap with manhole connection brought up to surface of driveway floor and covered with an iron cover set flush with basement floor.

95. FLOOR WASHES.—In basement driveway, in engine room, and in machinery room under dome, and at two other undetermined points in basement, this contractor shall set and connect, where shown or directed by architect, iron floor drains with 4-inch outlets, 10-inch diameter brass top with brass perforated hinged covers set flush with top of finished floor. Floor drains to have deep seal traps with backwater gate on sewer side of trap.

96. REMOVAL OF EARTH.—Contractor shall remove from the building all surplus earth resulting from his work and dispose of the same at his own expense wherever so directed by architect.

97. SUSPENDED SEWERS.—All suspended sewers shall be of wrought-iron pipe suspended from ceiling of basement as near the ceiling as possible, rising ¼ inch to 1 inch of length unless otherwise directed by the architect or superintendent. The pipes shall be firmly secured to beams with wrought-iron hangers not more than 12 feet from center to center, and each fitting for riser shall be seated upon a bracket or hanger bolted or clamped securely to wall or beam.

98. All junctions shall be made with Y branches and proper curve fittings. Hand-hole fittings shall be provided where shown, each hand-hole being closed with a brass trap screw.

99. DOWN SPOUTS.—Down spouts will be brought down to the basement ceiling by the other contractors. This contractor shall connect the same at bottom and run a waste pipe along basement ceiling to curb wall and then to sewer, providing a deep running trap with hand-hole just inside of curb wall on connection to sewer. A side outlet or hand-hole not less than 2 inches diameter shall be placed in pipe at foot of each down-spout riser, said outlet to be closed with an iron or brass screw plug

100. HANGERS AND HOOKS.—Pipes run on ceiling to be supported every 12 feet with approved adjustable wrought-iron hangers; vertical pipes to have heavy wrought-iron collars for support securely fastened to I beams at every second floor. All hangers and collars must be in proportion to the size and weight of the pipe and will be subject to the approval of the architect. Nickel-plated brass pipes to be supported with neat nickel-plated brass bands.

101. FLOOR AND CEILING PLATES.—Where pipes pass through floors, ceilings, or walls of finished rooms, they are to be fitted with approved plates secured in place.

102. Plates for iron piping to be cast iron, japanned, and for nickel-plated brass piping to be finished cast brass, nickel-plated.

103. Joints.—Joints in and to cast-iron pipe and fittings shall be made with calked lead, as specified for sewers. Joints in and to wrought-iron fittings shall be made with threads fully coated with red lead and oil and screwed perfectly tight. Joints in lead pipe or of lead pipe with brass fittings shall be made of solder neatly wiped. Joints of lead pipe to wrought-iron or cast-iron pipe shall be made with a brass ferrule. All joints must be finished smooth inside.

104. Cutting and Fitting.—This contractor shall do all cutting, fitting, and patching necessary in securing his pipe and all carpenter work in connection with the troughs, gutters, and safes hereinafter specified, and all necessary for supports in setting the fixtures and marble included in this specification. All this work must be done under the direction of the architect and subject to his approval. This contractor shall be held responsible for and be required to make good at his own expense any and all damage done other work. All cutting through the floors will be done by drilling upward, not by breaking through the fireproofing from above.

105. Waste and Ventilating Risers and Branches.—All risers and concealed branches for soil, waste, safe waste, or trap ventilation shall be of wrought-iron pipe. The trap ventilation risers to be galvanized wrought-iron pipe.

106. All connections through which water is to pass shall be made with Y branches. hese Y's used to change from vertical to horizontal runs, or to receive water-closets, shall be cut to the proper grade of horizontal pipe. Junctions or soil and waste risers with horizontal soil pipes in basements to be made with Y branches and eighth bends. Branches to water-closets and slop sinks to be run in floor, finishing at floor level with flange proper to receive the fixtures set level and true. At foot of each soil-pipe stack near where connection is made to horizontal drain, a hand-hole fitting is to be placed with brass clean-out plugs.

107. All vertical stacks of soils and waste-pipe to be extended up into attic and there run directly out through roof or collected into groups as indicated on plans and extended through roof in some symmetrical manner as to groups of outlets to be approved by architect.

108. Vent risers from traps of fixtures shall be connected into soil or waste risers where shown on riser diagrams. Safe-waste risers shall be located as shown and at bottom shall be connected together by pipe run on basement ceiling and discharging over nearest sink with end closed with a safe-waste valve of brass loosely hung.

109. Branches for ventilation of traps shall be run at such height as to give continuous rise to the connection from crown of trap. Where a branch crosses room or corridor on any floor, it shall be run to the floor above and dropped to fixture. In all cases, whether waste or vent pipe, the iron shall go through the floor or plaster, leaving the opening at finished floor or plaster line ready for connection

110. All branches from soil or waste pipes shall rise ¼ inch to 1 foot in length, unless otherwise directed by the architect.

111. All risers shall be set so as to be conveniently encased.

112. Flashing.—All pipes passing through roof shall be flashed at roof line with a piece of sheet lead not less than 18 inches in diameter larger than the pipe, and a piece of lead soil pipe run from sheet lead to top of pipe and turned over inside of pipe 1 inch. The sheet lead and pipe shall be joined with a wiped joint, and contractor will carefully cement around pipe and thoroughly fill holes he may have made in roof, which holes shall be drilled, not broken through.

113. Water supply.—The system of supply shall furnish both hot and cold water for all wash basins, bath tubs, shower baths, and sinks, and cold water only to all urinals, water-closets, and hose connections, and a separate and distinct cold water supply for drinking fountains. In addition to this, there shall be a special fire-protection service. This contractor shall also furnish, set, and connect all hot-water tanks, house tanks, and surge tank, in connection with the water-supply system.

114. The drinking-water refrigerating apparatus and the pumps for house-supply service and fire protection will be furnished and set by other contractors, but this contractor shall make all water connections to the flange openings on same.

115. The water supply for the building will be taken from two sources, viz, from the city mains and from artesian well in basement. The supply from artesian well to be supplied to surge tank by other contractors.

116. This contractor to supply surge tank with all flanged openings ready for such supply.

117. Street connections.—This contractor shall connect to the city water mains in Dearborn street and in Clark street, as shown, and take off a 4-inch branch from each, and run same inside of curb wall and there connect to meter, each branch having a separate meter. All of this work shall be done in compliance with the rules and regulations of the water department of the city of Chicago, providing all

necessary corporation valves with cast-iron boxes and covers as required; contractor shall pay for all permits for making the connections with the water mains in the street and shall replace all pavements as required by the city street department.

118. METERS.—This contractor shall set and connect, where shown or directed, two 4-inch water meters of make approved by the architect, providing said water meters with suitable foundation.

119. COLD-WATER DRUMS.—Where shown on plans, this contractor shall set and connect cold-water drums, one drum being located over one of the hot-water tanks in basement under dome and firmly suspended to ceiling of basement by wrought-iron hangers, the other drum to be located in engine room, where shown or directed by the architect, and suspended in the same manner from the basement ceiling. These drums are to be cast iron, ¾ inch thick, 10 inches inside diameter, and are to be cast with bosses, 8 inches on centers and of thickness so as to have not less than 1¼ inches of metal for all pipe connections.

120. Each cold-water drum shall be of sufficient length to provide connections for all pipes shown, and in addition each drum will have four extra outlets 2½ inches in diameter threaded and plugged with brass plugs, with square-headed nut tops for future connections. The ends of drums are to have screwed cast-iron caps. Drums to be painted with two coats of asphaltum paint.

121. HOT-WATER TANKS.—Where shown in machinery room in basement, this contractor shall furnish, set, and connect three hot-water tanks, the tanks to be 3 feet 6 inches in diameter and 8 feet long over the dished heads, and are to be set at such height and in such relative position to each other as shown on plan.

122. The tanks to be constructed of the best quality "homogeneous" steel; shell to be ¾ inch thick and heads to be ⅝ inch thick, properly riveted together with ¾-inch diameter rivets spaced 2 inches on centers; longitudinal seams to be riveted staggered; rivets for same to be 3¼ inches on centers; the heads of tanks to be properly dished. Each tank to be fitted with brass steam coil; dimensions of coil to be such as to raise the temperature of 300 gallons of water every twenty minutes from a temperature of 40° F. to 180° F. Steam to be furnished from the steam-heating main at atmospheric pressure.

123. The connection to steam coil and return from same shall be made by another contractor, but this contractor shall provide flanged openings in boilers to receive such connection.

124. Each tank is to be provided with flanged inlet and outlet openings as shown, the outlet openings to be located at top of boiler and the inlet at opposite end of boiler and at the bottom, each tank to be provided with suitable hand-hole and manhole with plate, yoke, bolts, and gaskets complete. Tanks are to be set in cast-iron saddles; one saddle to be placed near each end of tank; saddles to be securely bolted to brick or concrete piers, built by this contractor, piers to be faced with white enameled brick; the tanks to be so installed that the ends from which the drip connection is taken will be at least 1 inch lower than the opposite end. Care must be taken to provide a proper drainage of the steam coil. Each tank is to be provided with a thermometer attached so as to indicate the true temperature of the water in the tank.

125. The regulating device for automatically regulating steam supply will be furnished and set by steam contracter. The hot-water tanks are to be tested to a hydrostatic pressure of 200 pounds to the square inch.

126. SURGE TANK.—Where shown, this contractor shall furnish, set, and connect an open vertical tank to receive artesian-well water supply. Tank to be made of ¼-inch best tank steel, securely riveted throughout, with flanged bottom stiffened with angles. Tank to be 6 feet in diameter and 8 feet high, to be set on a suitable and acceptable I-beam foundation, approved by architect, set on brick or concrete piers, faced with white enameled brick, to be furnished by this contractor. Tank to be set in an iron safe pan made of ₁₆-inch iron, 7 feet in diameter and turned up at edges 3 inches. Tank shall be provided with flanged openings for intake from well pump and outlet to house pumps and boiler-feed pump of size required by pump connections and with special 2-inch drip pipe with valve connected to nearest drain.

127. HOUSE TANKS.—Contractor to furnish and set the house tanks on ninth and fifteenth floors. Tanks on ninth floor to be set on suitable and acceptable I-beam foundation. Beams to be 8-inch I set not less than 2 feet on centers and of length required by architect. Tank to be 8 feet in diameter and 7 feet high, made of ¼-inch best tank steel securely riveted and properly stayed and braced. To have flanged bottom stiffened with angles and made perfectly tight and secure in all respects. Tanks to be set in safe pans to be furnished by this contractor, made of ₁₆-inch iron turned up at edges 3 inches, and to be 9 feet in diameter. Tanks to be covered with wood covers made of double thickness of finished inch boards, painted two coats of approved paint.

128. The fifteenth-floor tanks to be 6 feet in diameter and 3 feet high, constructed the same as those on the ninth floor, and provided with acceptable hangers to suspend them from floor beams of fifteenth floor.

129. Tanks to have safe pans and covers same as before specified; pans hung a little below the tanks, in a manner approved by architect, and to be 1 foot greater in diameter than the tank.

130. All tanks to be provided with flanged openings for all piping connections. The flanged openings to be made where directed by architect. Tanks shall also be provided with 2-inch drain pipe, with valve on drain.

131. METER CONNECTIONS.—Contractor to connect the 4-inch street supply to each meter and from meters run a 4-inch supply on basement ceiling, as shown.

132. The meters are to have wheel-handled shut-off valves on inlet and outlet sides to meter and the outlet from meters shall also be provided with check valve. All valves to be full area of pipe.

133. COLD-WATER DRUM CONNECTIONS.—Contractors to connect the 4-inch supply from meters to each cold-water drum with 4-inch pipe with shut-off valve on connection to drum. Also cross-connect the cold-water supply from ninth floor tanks to hot-water boilers, to cold-water drum in machinery room with shut-off valve on connection to drum. From each drum, contractor shall take off the main supply pipes as shown, running around on basement ceiling with galvanized wrought-iron pipe to supply the various branches, risers, and fixtures.

134. All supplies run from drums are to be provided with shut-off valves at drums and with separate drip pipes and valves so that each main from drum can be shut off and drained without interfering with the rest of the system. Drips are to be connected to nearest catch-basin or sewer.

135. Underneath each drum suspend a copper trough made of No. 30 planished copper 6 inches wide and connected at one end with special drip pipe and valve to drain connection.

136. HOT-WATER TANK CONNECTIONS.—Contractor to make all connections to the hot-water tanks in the basement. One of these tanks will be used for the main-building service, including basement to eighth floor inclusive; one for tower service, and one to serve as an auxiliary tank to be used in either service.

137. The tower service hot-water tank shall be connected at bottom with a cold-water supply from tower-house tank and with a return hot-water circulating pipe from tower hot-water risers, both of these pipes to be provided with shut-off valves and drain connection with valves so that each pipe may be shut off and drained separately.

138. The return hot-water circulating pipe shall also be provided with a check valve to prevent back flow of cold water. From the top of tank and at opposite end from inlet shall be taken the hot-water supply for tower fixtures, with gate valve on connection to same and fitted with drip pipe and valve so that it may be drained. The tank shall also be provided with 2-inch drainpipe and valve, drains to be connected to catch-basin.

139. The main-building service hot-water tank to be connected at bottom with the cold-water supply from ninth-floor house tanks and with return hot-water circulating header, as shown on plans.

140. The connection to tank shall be provided with a straightway gate valve to shut-off tank and the connection to return hot-water circulating header shall have a check valve to prevent back flow of cold water. The supply from house tank to be provided with shut-off valves and drip pipe connections as shown.

141. From the top of tank and at opposite end from inlet shall be taken the hot-water supply and connected into a 6-inch crosshead set above boiler with shut-off valve on connection to same. From this header shall be taken off the hot-water supply mains as shown on plans, running around on basement ceiling, with galvanized wrought-iron pipe to supply the various raisers and branches.

142. The hot-water returns shall be run on basement ceiling and connected to return hot-water header. All these supplies and returns shall be supplied with separate shut-off valves at headers and also with drip connections as shown, so that any pipe can be shut off and drained without interfering with the working of the rest of the system.

143. Contractor shall connect the auxiliary hot-water tank, as shown, with the tower tank and main-building-service tank, with stop valves on connections so that it can be used in either service.

144. PUMP CONNECTIONS.—Contractor shall connect the 4-inch suction of the two house pumps in basement to a 4-inch supply from cold-water drum and to a 4-inch supply from surge tank with valve on connection to each pump and on each supply, so that either pump may be operated separately or together, and water supply may

be taken from surge tank or cold-water drum as desired. From pumps run supply to house tanks on ninth floor with valve on connection to each pump and check valve on supply pipe near pump. The supply from pumps shall be branched just beyond check valve and mains run to connect the two separate risers to house tanks with shut-off valves and drip-pipe connections on each, so that either riser can be shut off or drained.

145. This contractor shall connect the suction of house pump on ninth floor to mains on ninth floor, as shown with valve on connections to pump, and from pump shall take a 2-inch riser and run same to house tanks on fifteenth floor with shut-off valves and check valve on connections to pump. This riser shall have a drip connection at bottom connected into nearest soil pipe with valve on drip. In case two pumps are installed on ninth floor, this contractor shall provide all necessary valves and connections so that either or both pumps can be used in the service.

146. This contractor shall connect the 4-inch supply from meters into 12-inch tee near location of fire pump, and from 12-inch tee take off supply to suction of fire pump with shut-off valve on connection to pump. From pump run supply in ground and connect to the fire-protection system with shut-off valve and check valve on connection to pump.

147. HOUSE-TANK CONNECTIONS.—Contractor shall connect the supply from house pumps in basement to the house tanks on ninth floor with shut-off valve on connections to tanks. From tanks this contractor shall run mains around on the ninth floor with shut-off valve on connection to tanks. From these mains branches shall be taken off and run into each wing of building to supply the various risers.

148. Connect the 4-inch overflow pipe of tanks to the nearest down spout. Also connect 2-inch drain from bottom of tank into same overflow pipe, with shut-off valve on drainpipe. Also connect the drip from safe pans under tanks to nearest safe waste.

149. Connect the supply from ninth-floor house pump to tower-house tanks with shut-off valve on connection to each tank. From tower tanks take off supply to supply the tower fixtures. Supply pipes to be provided with shut-off valves at connection to tank. Also provide each tank with 3-inch overflow pipe, connect the overflow of tanks into one pipe, and run same down to and connect with supply main on ninth floor. Also connect the 2-inch drain of each tank to nearest soil pipe with shut-off valve at tank.

150. Also connect one of the tanks to the fire riser which extends into tower by a 1½-inch pipe with valve on connection to riser. Also connect the drip pans under tanks to overflow pipe.

151. SURGE-TANK CONNECTIONS.—The connection of surge tank to well will be made by other contractors. From surge tank this contractor shall take off a 4-inch connection with shut-off valve on connection to tank, and run a 4-inch supply and make connections to the house pumps, cooling water apparatus, and supply for boiler feed pumps. This supply for boiler feed pump to be taken to engine room where directed by the architect and there provided with shut-off valve and couplings ready for connections.

152. COOLING-APPARATUS CONNECTIONS.—This contractor shall connect the cooling apparatus for drinking water to the surge-tank supply and to the city supply, and suitably valve the same so that either source of supply can be used. Also connect the cooling-water apparatus to the supply and return circulating pipes of drinking-water system with shut-off valves on connection to same, and in addition provide a check valve on supply. Also provide drain connections to cooling apparatus with valve on same, so that the system can be drained.

153. BRASS TAGS.—The contractor shall provide and attach brass tags to all supplies and returns to hot-water boilers, cold-water drums, and house tanks, these tags having plainly engraved upon them the destination of supply.

154. SUPPLY RISERS AND BRANCHES.—All risers shall be galvanized wrought-iron pipe securely clamped to walls or beams at every second floor. Each riser shall be provided with wheel-handled shut-off valve at bottom, and each descending riser from ninth floor and from tower shall be provided with a shut-off valve at top.

155. Each hot-water riser shall be made with offsets or other satisfactory manner so that expansion at fixtures shall not exceed ⅛ inch. The hot-water risers from ninth floor shall be connected at basement and returned to hot-water tank. The hot-water return riser from tower shall be returned to tower hot-water tank.

156. All branches shall be of galvanized wrought iron carried through the floor or outside plaster line, exposed branches in toilet rooms, except in basement toilet rooms, to be nickel-plated brass pipes. All branches from risers and from main supplies in basement, ninth floor, and sixteenth floor to be provided with shut-off valves at connection to same easily accessible so that any portion of the work may be shut off.

157. All horizontal pipes or branches shall be laid to drain. The hot-water supply mains in basement shall have uniform rise from header at hot-water tank to farthest riser. The hot-water returns shall have a corresponding fall from the farthest riser to hot-water tank.

158. The cold-water mains run from cold-water drums to drain toward drum. From the top of each of the hot-water supply mains to ninth floor and the hot-water supply to tower, an air pipe shall be taken and run up to and discharge into house tank above overflow line of tank.

159. All risers shall be set so as to be conveniently encased.

160. All connections to fixtures shall be of galvanized iron or nickel-plated brass, as specified. Connections shall be of the following sizes: To each wash basin, water-closet, cistern, urinal cistern, drinking fountain, and bath tub, $\frac{1}{2}$ inch; to sinks, $\frac{3}{4}$ inch; to shower baths, $\frac{3}{4}$ inch; to street washes, $\frac{3}{4}$ inch; to hose connections, $\frac{3}{4}$ inch.

161. VALVES.—All stop valves on main and supply branches of the cold and hot water supply, drips, etc., unless otherwise specified, to be wheel-handled, heavy-weight, double-seat gate valves of the best make, approved by architect. All stop valves 2 inches and under to be of best quality brass; larger valves to have iron bodies, be brass mounted, and flanged. Valves on nickel-plated pipe to be brass, nickel-plated all over. The valves on supplies to single fixtures to be key-handled stops. Check valves to be of first-class approved manufacture. All 2 inches and under to be of best quality brass; larger to have iron bodies brass mounted and flanged.

162. SAFING.—All horizontal supplies run on ninth floor shall be safed. The contractor shall provide neat, smooth-finish wood boxes lined with sheet lead neatly formed and turned over the edge of boxes and securely nailed with copper nails. The safe-waste boxes to be of sufficient size to carry away the water in case of burst and shall be connected to safe-waste risers with 1½-inch lead pipe with funnel-shaped connections to box. Boxes shall be fitted with covers of No. 26 galvanized iron, soldered at joints and turned down over the edges of the box 1 inch on each side. Boxes to be painted two coats of paint of color directed by the architect.

163. STREET WASHES AND HOSE CONNECTIONS.—At point indicated on plans this contractor shall set and connect $\frac{3}{4}$-inch brass hose sill cocks with loose key. These cocks will be connected to wrought-iron supply pipe run around on basement ceiling, as shown.

164. HOSE CONNECTIONS.—This contractor shall provide two hose connections in driveway; one in coal room and one in engine room where directed by architect. The supply pipe for these connections to be taken from the overhead mains and carried down wall to within 4 feet of bottom and provided with a key-handled $\frac{3}{4}$-inch brass hose cock.

165. FIRE PROTECTION.—The 8-inch discharge from fire pump shall be connected to a 6-inch main laid in basement floor as shown, which main shall connect to the foot of all fire risers and also extend to both ends of driveway and there end in a standard Siamese connection with shut-off valves so as to permit of connections with the fire-protection steamers of the city of Chicago. For the protection of the building there will be four risers run direct to roof, one in each wing of building, and two additional risers run in pipe shaft, where shown, one of these in pipe shaft extending to eighth floor and the other extending to sixteenth floor.

166. The four risers run to roof shall be provided with a standard city of Chicago outlet just above the roof line. The valves for these risers shall be located in attic above eighth floor, and each riser shall be provided with drainpipe and valve, so that the part above valve can be drained into nearest soil or waste riser.

167. The two risers run in pipe shaft shall be provided with regulation city of Chicago hose nozzles at each floor, and in addition shall have a 1½-inch hose valve at each floor for house-hose connection. The two risers just described shall also be provided with an approved hose rack or reel and 175 feet of 1½-inch Underwriter's rubber-lined hose, with approved Underwriter's brass nozzle at each floor. Hose to be made in two or three pieces, with brass couplings.

168. The fire system shall be provided at floor of each story with safing and a drainpipe, with valve and valve box complete, said drainpipe to connect to nearest sewer. Near top of the riser extending into tower shall be connected a 1½-inch pipe, with valve on same, said pipe being connected into the top of the house tank.

169. PAINTING.—The tanks on the ninth floor and sixteenth floor, and the hot-water tanks and surge tank in the basement are to be thoroughly cleaned with a wire brush and painted one coat of antirust paint, equal to "Harrison's Antoxide F" paint, both inside and out, and a second coat applied equal to "Harrison's Antoxide D" paint.

170. All hangers and clamps, and all exposed wrought-iron piping not galvanized, shall be cleaned and painted one coat of approved asphaltum paint.

171. PIPE AND TANK COVERINGS.—This contractor shall cover the hot-water tanks with a plastic covering consisting of galvanized-iron netting, with raised ribs 9 inches apart, so as to hold netting about ½ inch from tank. On this the plastic asbestus covering to be applied in three layers, each layer to be thoroughly dried out before the second is applied. Over this plastic covering a 7-ounce canvas hall be stretched and securely fastened and painted with two coats of white antiflame paint.

172. After all piping has been tested as hereinafter specified this contractor shall cover the hot-water pipes, the drinking-water pipes, and the cold-water mains run on basement ceiling with a 1-inch covering of wool felt lined with tar paper, seams and joints to be thoroughly sealed with pitch. Covering to have a canvas 7-ounce jacket, secured with lacquered tin bands and thoroughly coated with pitch and painted same as covering for hot-water boilers.

173. TESTING.—All supply pipes shall be stopped off at outlet and filled with cold water. All soil, drain, waste, and vent pipes to be tested by filling with cold water before connecting to fixtures. Said test to continue for a period of six hours when, if proved tight, they may be emptied and fixtures connected. All gutters shall be stopped off and filled with water. All of the foregoing shall be carefully examined, and if any are found to leak they shall be made tight and the test repeated.

174. After fixture connections are made the smoke test or peppermint test shall be made. The cost of all tests and the making good of all defects to be borne by the contractor. Testing and proving of all work to be to the perfect satisfaction of the architect.

175. The hot-water boilers in basement shall be tested to a hydrostatic pressure of 200 pounds to the square inch. The water piping and risers for fire service to be tested to a hydrostatic pressure of 200 pounds to the square inch.

176. GAS PIPING.—Gas outlets shall be provided where shown in basement and first and second floors only. In basement there will be tee connections on gas mains adjacent to every column near which mains run. These tees to be plugged with screw plugs, so that connections can be made with them if required. Risers shall also be taken off from these mains for the first and second floors, these risers being run in columns, with capped outlets brought through the face of column on each floor at such height from floor as the architect shall direct.

177. METER.—This contractor shall provide a gas meter and suitably support the same on inside of curb wall on Clark street side of building where shown, and shall connect meter to street gas main with shut-off valve on connection to meter. The size of meter and connection to street main to be such as approved by the Chicago Gas Light and Coke Company. In case the gas company makes this street connection, this contractor shall pay all fees and charges for bringing this supply into building.

178. PIPING.—From meter this contractor shall run the gas mains securely suspended in iron hangers to basement ceiling, and from mains shall take off ½-inch risers for first and second floors, leaving the plugged connections on mains for basement supply as before specified. All of this piping, including the risers, shall be of standard-guage black wrought iron, and all fittings shall be malleable-iron fittings. All joints shall be made with red lead.

179. This contractor shall provide a stopcock on connection of main to meter, and also stop cocks on main branches run in basement and at the foot of all risers. Contractor shall also provide all necessary alcoholic cocks. All work of pipe laying and connections shall be done in compliance with the rules of the Chicago Gas Light and Coke Company, and this contractor shall present a certificate from it certifying that the work has been tested and approved by it before the final acceptance of the architect.

180. TEMPORARY FIXTURES.—This contractor to provide temporary fixtures for use of workmen in the building and to make all connections and provide all necessary pumps, tanks, etc., necessary to operate fixtures within ten days after notification from the architect that the same are wanted. Fixtures to consist of a three-seat, painted iron wash-out closet range, with perforated wash-down pipe on front and back, cast-iron flush pipe, ash seat and hinges, siphon automatic tank, all complete.

181. One painted iron roll-edge urinal 30 inches long, with back, strainer, coupling and tailpiece, flush pipe, and automatic siphon tank, all complete.

182. One 18 by 30 inch painted iron sink set on proper support, provided with two ¾-inch brass hose bibbs.

183. Contractor to provide a set of these fixtures just described on every second floor on some permanent line of fixtures where directed by the architect, at such times as directed by the architect, and to provide temporary wooden stalls surrounding fixtures so as to conceal them from public view.

184. Contractor shall remove all or any portion of the fixtures when ordered to do so by the architect, and shall reset the same on other floors or in any other positions when so ordered by architect.

185. The pumps for supplying water to temporary fixtures and hose outlets hereinafter specified shall be either electric-motor or steam pumps, at the discretion of the architect, and in case electric-motor pumps are used this contractor shall furnish them and make the connections between pumps and city power wires, but another contractor will pay the cost of operating them.

186. Contractor shall also provide two hose outlets on each floor and six hose outlets in basement, together with the necessary 1½-inch piping, for the use of all contractors about the building.

187. PERMANENT FIXTURES.—All fixtures included in this specification are to be set without casing, and the contractor shall set the same and the connections thereto in a neat finished and uniform manner.

188. All earthenware closets and urinals to be vitreous ware of the best grade, each piece to be unwarped and perfect in all respects. All porcelain lavatories and sinks to be of the best porcelain, unwarped and substantial in all respects. All enameled-iron ware to be of the best grade white enamel.

189. WATER-CLOSETS.—Where shown on plans, in all places, except basement and the first and second floor post-office workrooms, this contractor shall set and connect siphon-jet water-closets. Closets to be of vitreous porcelain ware with plain white finish outside, to have large bowl, trap, pedestal, and flushing rim of one piece of porcelain. Closet to be equal to the "Lupus" closet, made by the L. Wolff Manufacturing Company. Closets shall be set on brass floor flanges, joint packed with a rubber ring, and closet bolted to flange with brass bolts with nickel-plated heads. Each closet is to be vented by a 2-inch vent connection made in iron bend below floor and connected to vent riser. Where single closets are provided for private toilet rooms, they shall be provided with mahogany seats and covers attached directly to bowl with nickel-plated brass hinges. These closets to be flushed by an approved 18-ounce, planished, copper-lined, mahogany, round-cornered, cabinet-finished siphon tank, set on nickel-plated brass brackets, provided with approved nickel-plated brass guide, chain, and pull, and connected to closet bowl with nickel-plated heavy 1½-inch brass flush pipe with clips and seat protector. Tanks connected to water supply with ½-inch nickel-plated brass supply pipe from wall or floor, as the case may require, with key-handled, nickel-plated brass stop on supply.

190. Closets set in stalls of large toilet rooms, with the exception of those on the floors hereinbefore mentioned, shall be provided with plain wood, 18-ounce, planished, copper-lined siphon tanks of size specified, set behind backs of stalls and suitably supported on wooden frames and connected to bowl with 1½-inch galvanized-iron flush pipe with nickel-plated extension and with nickel-plated brass wall plate where it passes through back. The tank will be connected to supply with ½-inch galvanized-iron pipe with key-handled stop on supply, and will be operated by nickel-plated brass pull passing through nickel-plated brass face plate at back and operating chain to tank concealed behind back of stall. The closets will all be fitted with mahogany seats only and with nickel-plated brass hinges attached directly to bowl. Closets vented same as single closets.

191. In large toilet rooms at post-office working rooms, first and second floors, contractor to furnish extra-heavy siphon-jet closets of vitreous ware with full opening equal to the "Oceanic" siphon-jet closet made by J. B. Clow & Sons, and trimmed, connected, flushed, and operated same as the siphon-jet closets set in stalls before specified, and with hard-wood seats cut out to special pattern.

192. In basement, where shown, this contractor shall set and connect enamel-iron front washout water-closets. Closets to have bowl, trap, and flushing rim in one piece, to be enameled inside and outside, to be fitted with hard-wood seat, with opening cut out to a special pattern, and connected directly to bowl. Closets set in stalls to have plain wood 18-ounce planished copper-lined siphon tanks set behind backs, operated by nickel-plated brass pulls, as before specified. Closets to be set on iron flange, joint packed with a rubber ring, and closets bolted to flange with brass bolts. Each closet to be vented with a 2-inch vent to riser. Closets connected to bowl with 1½-inch galvanized-iron flush pipe, with brass extension through back of stall to closet, and provided with nickel-plated brass wall plate. Tanks not concealed behind back are to be cabinet finished and provided with bronzed-iron brackets, chain, and pull.

193. ENAMELED-IRON WASH BASINS.—In basement toilet rooms, and in post-office working rooms, first and second floors, this contractor shall set and connect white enameled-iron sectional wash basins with enameled-iron backs 10½ inches high, and

enameled-iron brackets equal to those shown in F 1459 of the Wolff catalogue. Single basins to be of the same kind, with enameled-iron backs and rounded corners, set on approved enameled-iron brackets.

194. The slab, bowl, and overflow of all basins to be in one piece. Each section to be 24 by 18 inches, with 12 by 15 inch oval basins, and to have soap cup molded in slab of basin. Each basin to be provided with overflow strainer, nickel-plated chain, snap stopper, and waste plug and coupling.

195. Each group of basins to have enameled connecting plate to make close fit between basins. Each basin to be fitted with two approved self-closing nickel-plated brass faucets connected to cold and hot water by supply pipes with pipe air chambers 12 inches long. The supplies of each single basin and each group of basins to have key-handled stops. Each single basin shall be provided with nonsiphon trap with 1¼-inch waste and vent connections. Each group of basins shall have an extended waste pipe connected to nonsiphon trap. The waste pipe and trap to be 1½ inches for a maximum of four basins and to be 2 inches for more than four basins.

196. The supplies and air chambers of basins in basement to be of galvanized iron; those of basins in first and second floors to be of nickel-plated brass. The waste connections and traps of the basement fixtures to be of rough brass, painted three coats of zinc-white enamel paint. The waste connections and traps of the fixtures on first and second floors to be nickel-plated brass.

197. In all the private single toilet rooms in connection with the private offices of the executive chiefs of each department—the justices' private rooms, the commanding general, the collectors of customs and internal revenue, the pension agent, district attorney, postmaster, etc., to the number of eighteen in all—this contractor shall set and connect porcelain lavatories, Class B, 30 by 22 inches, with large oval bowl and roll rim on all sides of lavatory. Lavatories to be set 3 inches away from the wall; to be fitted with nickel-plated brass self-closing faucets, nickel-plated brass combined waste and overflow connections, equal to the Wolff "Ideal" waste, with porcelain handle. Basins connected to waste through 1½-inch nickel-plated brass waste pipe connected to nickel-plated brass nonsiphon trap with nickel-plated brass vent connection. Faucets connected by nickel-plated brass supplies to floor or wall, as the case may be, with bulb air chambers. Supplies to have nickel-plated brass key-handle stop.

198. MARBLE LAVATORIES.—Elsewhere where shown in building, this contractor shall set and connect in marble slabs 14 by 19 inch single D-shaped basins with combination nickel-plated brass overflow and waste connections. Basins to be fitted with approved nickel-plated brass self-closing basin faucets. Faucets connected to hot and cold water with nickel-plated brass supply pipes with air chambers and key-handle stops.

199. Single bowls to have 1¼-inch nickel-plated waste pipe and nonsiphon nickel-plated brass traps, with nickel-plated brass vent connection. Groups of basins to have extended nickel-plated brass 1½-inch waste pipe connected to nickel-plated brass nonsiphon trap with vent connection. In places where basins are in rooms not adjacent to vent risers, vent connections to trap shall be omitted. Basins shall be set in marble slabs and have marble backs and aprons of dimensions hereinafter specified, and shall be supported on approved enameled-iron legs on free ends and enameled-iron apron supports at wall.

200. URINALS.—Where shown on plans, this contractor shall set and connect siphon-jet lip urinals. Urinals to be constructed so as to hold a large body of water in bowl. Backs of urinals to be ground so as to fit perfectly against the marble backs of stalls. Exposed inlet and waste connections to be of nickel-plated brass and all clamps to be of porcelain or nickle-plated brass. Each urinal or set of urinals to be provided with an approved 18-ounce planished, hard-wood, round-cornered, automatic siphon flushing tank set on approved enameled-iron brackets The exposed flushing pipe from tank and the supply pipe to tank, except in basement, to be nickel-plated brass. Supply pipe to tank to have key-handled stop.

201. One tank shall not supply more than four urinals. In case there are five urinals in groups, one tank shall be provided for two and one for three. Tanks shall be of such sizes as to supply two gallons for each urinal which they flush. In basement the exposed flush connections from tank shall be of rough brass, painted with three coats of zinc-white enamel paint.

202. BATH TUBS.—Where shown on plans, except for engineer's bath tub, this contractor shall set and connect enameled bath tubs, finished zinc-white outside with 3 inches under rolled enameled rim. Tubs to be 6 feet over rim, 19 inches deep inside, and 3 feet wide over all.

203. Tubs in gymnasium, eleventh floor, to have nickel-plated brass special "Fuller" double faucet and rough brass connected overflow and waste connections, rubber stopper, nickel-plated chain, and nickel-plated brass supplies with key stops.

204. In private rooms, where shown, bath tubs are to be fitted with polished nickel-plated all-over compression supply fittings; nickel-plated all-over "Ideal" bath wastes and nickel-plated brass supply pipes with key stops.

205. Bath tub in engineer's room to be white enameled-iron bath tub with 1½-inch enameled rolled rim. Tub to be 6 feet long and to be provided with No. 1 nickel-plated "Fuller" bath faucet, rough brass connected overflow and waste connections, rubber stopper, and chain. Supplies to be ¾-inch galvanized iron with key stops.

206. The waste of all tubs to be connected to 4-inch drum trap with nickel-plated brass trap screw set at floor level; trap to be vented with a 1½-inch vent pipe to vent riser.

207. SHOWER BATHS.—Where shown on eleventh floor, this contractor shall set and connect in marble stalls nickel-plated brass showers, to consist of overhead shower and perforating ring shower with upper self-closing valves, 12-inch mixing chamber with thermometer, and supply pipes with wheel-handled valves connected to overhead supplies. Diameter of ring to be 20 inches. Diameter of shower, 8½ inches. Each shower to have a 5-inch brass waste strainer, 2-inch outlet coupling, and tailpiece connected to waste pipe run in floor. Waste pipe shall be connected to 3-inch running trap just before connection to soil riser. Running trap vented to vent riser. Also connect four rubber-tube hand sprays where directed.

208. SLOP SINKS.—Where shown on plans, this contractor shall set and connect roll rim porcelain slop sinks 24 by 20 by 12 inches with enameled-iron trap standard; nickel-plated brass vent connection. Sinks to have nickel-plated brass strainer and nickel-plated "Fuller" double faucet with long spout, in case supplies are taken from wall. If supplies are taken from floor, sinks shall be fitted with nickel-plated double compression faucets with ¾-inch nickel-plated supply pipes to floor with pipe air chambers 12 inches long. Supplies to have key-handle stops.

209. ENAMELED-IRON SINKS.—Where shown, this contractor shall set and connect enameled-iron roll-rim sinks 18 by 30 inches with 24-inch ash drip board. Sinks to have enameled-iron back and end 15 inches high. Backs to be full length of sink and drip board. The sinks to be supported on enameled-iron brackets with enameled-iron leg on free end. Backs to have air chambers and to be fitted with two nickel-plated improved "Fuller" faucets with flange for iron pipe. Sinks to have metal plugs and stopper and improved overflows, and to be connected to wastes by 2-inch nickel-plated brass waste pipe and nonsiphon trap with 1½-inch nickel-plated brass vent connection. The waste connection to trap and vent connection from trap of sink in engineer's room to be of rough brass or galvanized iron.

210. DRINKING FOUNTAINS.—Where shown on plans, this contractor shall set and connect porcelain drinking fountains with ornamental exterior, equal to those shown in F 1929 of the "Wolff" catalogue. The fountain discharge is to be in the shape of a bronze dolphin with spout. Fountain to be operated by a push button coming through back. Fountain to be provided with a nickel-plated brass cup holder and chain and approved silver-plated cup. Waste of fountain to be connected to 1½-inch nonsiphon trap concealed behind back with vent connection to vent riser. Fountain to be provided with a marble back and bronzed-iron frame, as shown.

211. TOILET ARTICLES.—Contractor to furnish and set approved nickel-plated brass coat hook in each of the marble water-closet stalls, and a nickel-plated brass approved toilet paper holder, holder to be of design to discharge detached sheets of toilet paper and to have key lock on cover.

212. Also furnish and set a nickel-plated brass cigar holder in each of the water-closet stalls for men. In large toilet room and small public toilet room, this contractor shall provide approved roller towel racks, the roller to be of hard wood, brackets to be of nickel-plated brass.

213. There will be two of these towel racks provided for each large toilet room, except for toilet room off of men's swing room in basement and ladies' toilet room, third floor, which rooms shall have four each.

214. Bath tubs to be furnished with an approved nickel-plated brass soap cup to fit on rim of tub. Shower baths to be fitted with approved nickel-plated brass soap and sponge holder. Lavatories, or private toilet rooms, to have approved nickel-plated brass towel rack, soap holder with porcelain dish, and comb and brush holder. Water-closets in private toilet rooms to be provided with approved nickel-plated brass toilet paper holders.

215. The private bath rooms shall also be provided with nickel-plated brass coat hooks.

216. All of these toilet articles to be set where directed by architect, and where secured to marble or tile wainscoting or to marble stalls to be fastened securely with nickel-plated brass bolts.

217. MARBLE WORK.—Contractor shall furnish and set the marble backs, sides, slabs, and aprons necessary for all wash basins; the marble bases for all shower baths and urinals, and the marble for all drinking fountains and slop sinks.

218. The marble to be best quality selected American marble, same as the rest of the marble work in each particular room; the floor pieces, above the second story, to be equal to a Vermont "Sutherland Falls" white marble; those on and below second story will be equal to a "gray Tennessee" marble; the fixture marble above second story will be of a clearer white than "Hollister," but equal to it in density and texture; the fixture marble below second story will be equal to a "gray Tennessee;" the floor slabs to have smooth rub finish. All other marble to be highly polished on all exposed surfaces and edges. The exposed edges of marble work to be molded stop chamfered or finished square, as desired by the architect.

219. Marble for basin slabs shall be as follows: Single basins to be 32 by 22 by 1¼ inches; two-hole slabs, 60 by 22 by 1¼ inches. Slabs containing more than two basins shall be of such length as to allow 2 feet 6 inches, center to center of basin, and shall be 1¼ inches thick. Corner slabs to be made octagonal and to be 24 by 24 inches on edges against wall. In case slabs are shown on plans to fit into recess space, they shall be of the length shown.

220. All basin slabs shall be countersunk ⅜ inch and shall have neatly molded edges. The backs and ends to be ⅞ inch thick and 16 inches high and apron ⅞ inch thick and 5 inches wide. All backs to be beveled and properly stopped off.

221. The marble bases for shower baths shall be 2 inches thick and countersunk ½ inch around edges and beveled so as to drain to center.

222. Marble bases for urinals shall be 1½ inches thick, of size required, and shall be countersunk ¼ inch at front, grading to ½ inch at back.

223. The marble backs for slop sinks, where slop sinks are not set in wainscoted rooms, shall be 24 inches wide, 4 feet 6 inches high, and ⅞ inch thick. All marble coming against wall shall be fastened to wall with concealed fastenings and set plumb and true.

224. The bases for urinals and shower baths shall be securely bedded in nonstaining cement.

225. SHOWER-BATH CURTAINS.—The front of each shower bath is to be provided with a white rubber curtain of sufficient width to inclose stall and to extend to the floor. The curtain to be hung to nickel-plated brass rod at front of stalls. Brass rod to be supplied with rings for holding curtain. Contractor shall also provide hook or clasp in each stall to hold back curtain when stall is not occupied.

226. SHOWER-BATH FLOOR.—This contractor shall provide a copper safe pan made of 18-ounce copper under the marble floor slabs of shower baths; this safe pan to be of the outside diminsions of the floor slabs, to turn up at edges, and to be built and bedded in a manner satisfactory to the architect.

227. The architect may order that all the finished, exposed piping, fixtures, collars, etc., now specified to be nickel-plated shall be finished and polished brass. Contractor will indicate in the proper blank of bid the amount he will deduct from his bid if such order be given.

228. The contractor before ordering any fixtures, pumps, or machines shall consult with the architect and make out his list in accordance with the latter's directions and selections, and have the same approved by the architect.

229. Bidders' attention is called to the FORM of the accompanying blank bid; no deviation from it will be considered; the exceptions, items, and divisions of that bid are important. The contract may be considerably more or less than the bulk sum filled in the bid, and these items and general form of bid must perforce be the only means of reaching the equitable adjustment of that contract amount.

PROPOSAL FOR THE DRAINAGE, PLUMBING, AND GAS FITTING FOR THE UNITED STATES POST-OFFICE BUILDING AT CHICAGO, ILL.

To the ARCHITECT OF THE CHICAGO POST-OFFICE BUILDING,
    Treasury Department, Washington, D. C.

SIR: We hereby propose to furnish all the labor and materials required to place complete the drainage, plumbing, and gas fitting for the United States post-office building at Chicago, Ill., in strict accordance with the true intent and spirit of the drawings and this specification, for the sum of fifty-three thousand seven hundred dollars ($53,700).

This figure does not include the tile drainage, the temporary fixtures and water supply, the gas fitting, or the necessary piping, etc., for the fire protection.

We agree to do all the tile drainage as described on page 5 and shown on plans for the additional sum of forty-one hundred dollars ($4,100).

We agree to likewise do all the gas fitting as described in specification and shown on plans for the additional sum of nine hundred and seventy dollars ($970); and further agree to do all the work specified and shown for fire protection for the additional sum of thirty-two hundred and seventy dollars ($3,270).

We agree to install the temporary fixtures required during the prosecution of the work, according to specification, and the temporary water supply and pumps for the sum of five hundred and fifty dollars ($550).

Opened at office of the architect of the U. S. Gov't. bldg. at Chicago, Ill. Treasury Dept., Washington, D. C., Oct. 9, 1902.

> F. W. FITZPATRICK, *Acting Architect.*
> C. E. KEMPER, *Acting Supervising Architect.*
> JAS. A. WETMORE, *Acting Chief Ex. Officer.*
> H. D. GREEN, *Accountant.*

Bidders are also required to name a price which will be the basis of all settlements for work that may be added to or deducted from contract price for the following materials, the fixtures in every case to be set in place, connected and complete in all respects:

Price to be deducted for each ninth-floor house tank omitted............	$325.00
Price for each private room siphon-jet closet and cabinet tank...........	58.00
Price for each heavy siphon-jet closet and plain wood tank..............	53.00
Price for each private-room bath tub, complete.........................	73.00
Price for each urinal, complete.......................................	56.00
Price for each slop sink, complete....................................	57.00
Price for each drinking fountain......................................	78.00
Price for each enameled-iron closet and cistern, complete	43.00
Price for each enameled-iron lavatory, complete........................	57.00
Price for each porcelain lavatory, complete	71.00
Price for each marble lavatory, complete	63.00
Price per foot of draintile, wood box, etc.............................	.75
Price for cold-water drums..	250.00
Price for total ejector plant...	7,100.00
Price for pump and motor...	425.00
Price per foot of sewer piping, excavation of similar size to that just inside of building line...	2.50
Price per foot of ½-inch gas piping, hung and connected	.25
Price for 2-inch valve on supply pipes.................................	5.00
Price per foot of fire-protection risers	.75
Price per foot of ½-inch supply pipe...................................	.28
Price per foot of ¾-inch supply pipe...................................	.30
Price for temporary water-closets on second floor......................	75.00
Price per additional story for such temporary water-closets...............	75.00
Price per foot of water-closet soil pipe................................	1.26
Price per water-closet for all toilet hardware specified..................	6.00
Price per washbowl for all toilet hardware specified.....................	4.50
Price per bath for all toilet hardware specified.........................	1.50
Price included for all of the hot-water supply, piping, tanks, etc..........	3,200.00
Price included for all of the "roughing-in" of all plumbing work.........	24,000.00
Price included for all of the fixtures set in place throughout.............	18,000.00

If all of the exposed plumbing fixtures and piping are directed by the architect to be made of finished polished brass instead of finished nickel-plating, as herein specified, we agree to make the change for the deduction of two hundred dollars....................................... 200.00

We propose to complete all the work, except connecting fixtures, covering pipes, etc., in one hundred (100) working days and to complete remainder of work in sixty (60) days after being ordered to proceed with said completion.

> THE WELLS & NEWTON Co.,
> By J. LELAND WELLS, *Presdt.,*
> *539 East 17th St., New York, N. Y.*

Oct. 7, 1902.   539 E. 17th St.; 292-298 Ave. B.

Names of individual members of firm:

J. Leland Wells, *Presdt.*
Chas. P. Newton, *V.-Pres.*
Wilson G. Cornell, *Sec.*
Morris S. King, *Dept. Treasurer.*

Name of corporation, The Wells & Newton Co.
Name of president, J. Leland Wells.
Name of secretary, Wilson G. Cornell.
Under what law corporation is organized, New Jersey.
[Corporate seal.]

October 22, 1902.

The Wells and Newton Company,
    539 East Seventeenth street, New York, N. Y.

Sirs: Your proposal, dated October 7, 1902, addressed to Henry Ives Cobb, architect of the Chicago building, Treasury Department, Washington, D. C., the lowest received under advertisement dated September 3, 1902, to furnish all labor and materials required to place complete the drainage, plumbing, and gas fitting, including all the work for fire protection, and install the necessary temporary fixtures and water supply, as specified, for the United States post-office, court-house, etc., at Chicago, Illinois, in strict accordance with the true intent and spirit of the drawings and specifications, for the sum of sixty-two thousand five hundred and ninety dollars ($62,590) for the entire work, as per plans and specifications therefor, is hereby accepted.

It is further understood and agreed that all of the work will be completed, except connecting fixtures, covering pipes, etc., in one hundred (100) working days from the approval of the bond, and the remainder of the work will be completed within sixty days (60) after being ordered to proceed with said completion.

It is further understood and agreed that you are to execute a formal contract, with bond, in the sum of thirty thousand dollars ($30,000), as a guarantee for the faithful performance of the work embraced in your proposal, a form of which will be sent you for execution and return to this Department for examination, approval, and file; and it is understood and agreed also that the said contract, with bond, must be executed and returned within five days (5) from date of receipt by you of said form.

Payment of said work will be made from the appropriation for the post-office, court-house, etc., Chicago, Illinois, on filing of proper vouchers duly signed and approved.

The certified check which accompanied your proposal will be retained at this Department until approval of your formal bond by the Secretary of the Treasury.

Promptly acknowledge receipt of this letter.

Respectfully, yours,

O. L. Spaulding,
Acting Secretary.

Contract between the United States of America and The Wells & Newton Company.

Whereas by advertisement duly made and published according to law, proposals were asked for the drainage, plumbing, and gas fitting for the United States post-office, court-house, etc., at Chicago, Illinois; and

Whereas the proposal of The Wells & Newton Company, of the city of New York, furnished in response thereto, was duly accepted on the 22 day of October, 1902, on condition that it execute a contract in accordance with the terms of their bid.

Now, therefore, this agreement, made and entered into by and between O. L. Spaulding, Acting Secretary of the Treasury, for and in behalf of the United States of America, of the first part, and The Wells & Newton Company, a corporation organized under the laws of the State of New Jersey, and having executive offices in New York, New York, of the second part,

Witnesseth, that the party of the second part, for the consideration hereinafter mentioned, covenants and agrees to and with the party of the first part to furnish all of the labor and materials, and do and perform all the work required for the drainage, plumbing, and gas fitting for the United States post-office, court-house, etc., at Chicago, Illinois, according to the specifications hereto attached and the drawings herein referred to, and signed by said second party and the architect of the United States Government building at Chicago, Illinois, in strict and full accordance with the requirements of drawings numbered one hundred twenty-two to one hundred thirty-eight, inclusive (122 to 138), and such other detail drawings as may be furnished to the party of the second part by the architect of the United States Government building at Chicago, Illinois; the advertisement for proposals, dated September 3rd, 1902; "General instructions and information;" the specification for the work; the proposal dated October 7th, 1902, addressed to the said architect by the said party of the second part; and letter dated October 22nd, 1902, addressed to the said party of the second part by O. L. Spaulding, Acting Secretary of the Treasury, accepting said proposal; a true and correct copy of each of which said papers is hereto attached and forms a part of this contract; and which said numbered drawings, bearing the signature of the said architect and the signature of the said party of the second part, are on file in the office of the architect of the United States Government building at Chicago, Illinois, and are hereby made a part of this contract.

And the said party of the second part further covenants and agrees that all of the materials used shall be of the very best quality; that all of the work performed shall be executed in the most skillful and workmanlike manner; and that both the materials used and the work performed shall be to the entire and complete satisfaction of the said architect.

It is further covenanted and agreed that the entire work shall be completed, except connecting fixtures, covering pipes, etc., in one hundred working days, and to complete remainder of work in sixty days after being ordered to proceed with completion; that any particular portion of the work herein pro ded for shall be completed within such reasonable time as may be hereafter definitely specified by the said architect in written notice to the said party of the second part; and that should the said party of the second part fail to complete the entire work or any particular portion of the work within the time so specified, then the said party of the second part shall forfeit to the said party of the first part fifty dollars per diem as liquidated damages for each and every day thereafter until the completion of the same: *Provided,* That if through any fault of the party of the first part the party of the second part is delayed in the execution of the work included in this contract, the party of the second part shall be allowed one day additional to the time above stated for each and every day of such delay so caused, the same to be ascertained and decided by the said architect: *Provided further,* That no claim shall be made or allowed for damages which may arise out of any delay caused by the party of the first part.

The party of the second part further covenants and agrees to promptly pay for all labor and materials used in and about the building and to hold and save the United States harmless from and against all and every demand or demands of any nature or kind and for or on account of the use of any patented invention, article, or appliance included in the materials hereby agreed to be furnished under this contract.

It is further covenanted and agreed by and between the parties hereto that the said party of the second part will, at its own expense, comply with all municipal ordinances and regulations in so far as the same are binding upon the United States, and obtain all required licenses and permits, and be responsible for all damages to person or property which may occur in connection with the prosecution of the work; that all work called for by the drawings and specifications, though every item may not be particularly shown on the first or mentioned in the second, or in either, but that is judged necessary by the architect to complete the contract, shall be executed and performed as though such work were particularly shown and mentioned in each, respectively, and both, unless otherwise specifically provided; that all materials and work furnished shall be subject to the approval of the said architect, and that said party of the second part shall be responsible for the proper care and protection of all materials delivered and work performed by it until the completion and final acceptance in writing of same by the party of the first part.

It is further covenanted and agreed by and between the parties hereto that the said party of the second part will make any omissions from or additions to the work or materials herein provided for, whenever required by said architect for the party of the first part; the valuation of such work and materials to be determined on the basis of the contract unit of value of material and work referred to; or, in the absence of such unit of value, then on prevailing market rates, which market rates, in case of dispute, are to be determined by the said architect, whose decision in reference thereto shall be binding upon both parties, and that no claim for damages on account of such changes or for anticipated profits shall be made or allowed.

It is further covenanted and agreed that no claim for compensation for any extra materials for the work is to be made or allowed, unless the same be specifically agreed upon in writing, or directed in writing by the architect; and that no addition to, or omission from the work herein specifically provided for shall make void or affect the other provisions or covenants of this contract; but the difference in the cost thereby occasioned, as the case may be, shall be added to or deducted from the amount of the contract, and in the absence of any express agreement or provision to the contrary, no addition to or omission from the work herein specifically provided for shall be construed to extend the time fixed herein for the final completion of the work.

It is further covenanted and agreed by and between the parties hereto that all materials furnished and work done under this contract shall be subject to the inspection of the said architect, or his duly accredited representatives, and of other inspectors appointed by the said party of the first part, at any and all times, with the right to reject any and all work or material not in accordance with these requirements; and the decision of said architect as to quality and quantity shall be final. And it is further covenanted and agreed by and between the parties hereto that said party of the second part will, at its expense, within a reasonable time to be specified by the said architect, remedy or remove any defective or unsatisfactory material or work; and that, in the event of its failure immediately to proceed and faithfully continue so to do, said party of the first part may have the same done and charge the cost thereof to the account of said party of the second part.

It is further covenanted and agreed by and between the parties hereto that until final inspection and acceptance of and payment for all of the material and work herein provided for, and the approval thereof by the Secretary of the Treasury, no prior inspection, payment, or act is to be construed as waiver of the right of the party of the first part to reject any defective work or material, or to require the fulfillment of any of the terms of the contract and the guaranties referred to in specification, said right also to continue, to recover against party of second party even after acceptance for said guaranties, or should it appear that the party of the second part did poor work or supplied inferior materials knowingly or fraudulently.

It is further covenanted and agreed by and between the parties hereto that if the said party of the second part shall fail to complete the work herein contracted for or any part thereof, in accordance with this agreement, within the time herein provided for, or shall fail to prosecute said work with such diligence as in the judgment of the party of the first part will insure the completion of the said work within the time hereinbefore provided, the said party of the first part may withhold all payments for work in place until final completion and acceptance of same, and is authorized and empowered, after eight days' notice thereof in writing, served personally upon or left at the shop, office, or usual place of abode of the said party of the second part, or with its agent, and the said party of the second part having failed to take such action within the said eight days as will, in the judgment of the said party of the first part, remedy the default for which said notice was given, to take possession of the said work, in whole or in part, and of all machinery and tools employed thereon, and all materials belonging to the said party of the second part delivered on the site, and, at the expense of the said party of the second part, to complete or have completed the said work, and to supply or have supplied the labor, materials, and tools of whatever character necessary to be purchased or supplied by reason of the default of the said party of the second part, in which event the said party of the second part shall be further liable for any damage incurred through such default and any and all other breaches of this contract.

And the said party of the first part, acting for and in behalf of the United States, covenants and agrees to pay, or cause to be paid, unto the said party of the second part, or to its successors, in lawful money of the United States, in consideration of the herein-recited covenants and agreements made by the party of the second part, the sum of sixty-two thousand five hundred ninety dollars ($62,590).

And the party of the first part covenants and agrees that payments will be made in the following manner, viz: Ninety per cent (nine-tenths) of the value of the work executed and actually in place, to the satisfaction of the party of the first part, will be paid from time to time as the work progresses (the said value to be ascertained by the party of the first part), and ten per cent (one-tenth) thereof will be retained until the completition of the entire work, and the approval and acceptance of the same by the party of the first part, which amount shall be forfeited by said party of the second part in the event of the nonfulfillment of this contract, it being expressly covenanted and agreed that said forfeiture shall not relieve the party of the second part from liability to the party of the first part for any and all damages sustained by reason of any breach of this contract. It is further agreed, however, that regardless of this ten per cent clause the architect shall at all times retain a sufficient amount to complete the work at market rates, should the party of second part fail to so complete it satisfactorily.

It is an express condition of this contract that no member of Congress, officer or clerk or other employee of the Treasury Department, or other person whose name is not at this time disclosed shall be admitted to any share in this contract, or to any benefit to arise therefrom; and it is further covenanted and agreed that this contract shall not be assigned.

In witness whereof the parties have hereunto subscribed their names this 22nd day of October, A. D. 1902.

[All erasures, alterations, and interlineations to be noted here before execution.]

Page 16 (first page of this contract) the following words have been erased, "by the —— day of ——, nineteen hundred and ——," and the following words interlined, "except connecting fixtures, covering pipes, etc., in one hundred working days, and to complete remainder in sixty days after being ordered to proceed with completion;" also, same page, the word "eight" is inserted after the word "thirty" and before the word "inclusive."

O. L. SPAULDING,
Secretary of the Treasury.

We hereby certify that this contract and bond have been correctly prepared and compared:

HENRY IVES COBB,
Architect of the U. S. Gov't Building of Chicago, Ill.
J. K. TAYLOR,
Supervising Architect of the Treasury Department.

[SEAL, 1892.]   THE WELLS & NEWTON CO.,
Contractor.
By J. LELAND WELLS,
President.

Witnesses to the signature of the contractor:
HENRY W. ARCHIBALD.
GEO. K. ROSE.

BOND.

Know all men by these presents, that we, The Wells & Newton Company, a corporation organized under the laws of the State of New Jersey, and having executive offices in the city of New York, county of and State of New York, principal, and Fidelity and Deposit Company of Maryland, a corporation organized under the laws of the State of Maryland, of the city of Baltimore, county of Baltimore and State of Maryland, suret   , are held and firmly bound unto the United States of America in the sum of thirty thousand dollars ($30,000), lawful money of the United States, for the payment of which, well and truly to be made to the United States, we bind ourselves, our heirs, executors, administrators, successors, and assigns, jointly and severally, firmly by these presents.

Sealed with our seals and dated this 25th day of October, A. D. 1902.

The condition of the above obligation is such that whereas the said The Wells & Newton Company has entered into a certain contract, hereto attached, with O. L. Spaulding, Acting Secretary of the Treasury, acting for and in behalf of the United States, bearing date the 22nd day of October, A. D. 1902: <i>Now,</i> if the said The Wells & Newton Company shall well and truly fulfill all the covenants and conditions of said contract, and shall perform all the undertakings therein stipulated by it to be performed, and shall well and truly comply with and fulfill the conditions of and perform all of the work and furnish all the labor and materials required by any and all changes in or additions to said contract which may hereafter be made, and shall perform all the undertakings stipulated by it to be performed in any and all such changes in or additions thereto, notice thereof to the said suret   being hereby waived, and shall promptly make payment to all persons supplying labor or materials in the prosecution of the work contemplated by said contract, then this obligation to be void; otherwise to remain in full force and virtue.

In testimony whereof the said The Wells & Newton Company, principal, and Fidelity and Deposit Company of Maryland, suret   , have hereunto subscribed their hands and affixed their seals the day first above written.

[SEAL, 1892.]   THE WELLS & NEWTON CO.,
By J. LELAND WELLS, <i>President.</i></div>

Signed, sealed, and delivered in presence of—
HENRY W. ARCHIBALD.
GEO. K. ROSE.

[SEAL, 1890.]   .   FIDELITY AND DEPOSIT COMPANY OF MARYLAND.
By HUGH M. ATTWOOD, <i>Attorney in Fact.</i></div>

FRANK ECKHOFT.
ERNEST L. HICKS.

Attest:
JAMES R. KINGSLEY, <i>Attorney in Fact.</i>

No. 1381 A. Contract of the Wells and Newton Co., of New York, N. Y., for drainage, plumbing, and gas fitting for U. S. post-office, court-house, etc., at Chicago, Ill., dated October 22nd, 1902.   Amount, $62,590.   Time to complete, 100 and 60 days. Penalty for each day's delay, $50.   Bond dated October 25th, 1902.   Amount of bond, $30,000.

The following instructions must be particularly observed and complied with, viz:

1st. The Christian names must be written in the body of the bond in full, and so signed to the bond.

2d. A seal of wax or wafer must be attached to each signature on the bond.   No seals required for signatures to contract except corporate seals.

3d. Each signature must be made in the presence of two persons, who must sign their names as witnesses.

4th. Each surety must make and sign an affidavit of the amount he is worth after paying his just debts, and deducting all exemptions by the laws of the State in which he resides, and liabilities of whatever nature, as per form herewith.

5th. A district judge or attorney of the United States, or clerk of a United States court, must certify that the sureties are sufficient to pay the penalty of the bond.

6th. The affidavits of the sureties must be taken and signed before an officer authorized to administer oaths generally. The officer must certify that he administered the oaths. If the magistrate is not a judge of the United States court, his authority to administer oaths must be certified by the clerk of a court of record having official knowledge of that fact.

7th. Bond must be dated.

8th. Residence of principal and sureties must be distinctly stated.

9th. The sureties must justify in amounts, the aggregate of which will be equal to twice the penal sum of the bond.

10th. When the contracting party is a partnership concern, the contract must be signed with the firm name without seal, and the bond must be signed by each member of the firm with seal to each signature; when a corporate body, there should be attached to the contract duly authenticated evidence that the officer or officers executing the contract and bond have authority to do so, and the corporate seal must be affixed to each instrument.

TREASURY DEPARTMENT,
OFFICE OF THE ARCHITECT OF THE
U. S. GOVERNMENT BUILDING AT CHICAGO, ILL.,
Oct. 22nd, 1902.

Respectfully referred to the Solicitor of the Treasury for examination and indorsement.

HENRY IVES COBB,
Architect of the U. S. Government Building at Chicago, Ill.

DEPARTMENT OF JUSTICE,
OFFICE OF THE SOLICITOR OF THE TREASURY,
October 31, 1902.

I have examined the within contract and bond as to form and execution, and in these respects they are approved when the contract is duly executed on behalf of the United States.

F. A. REEVES,
Acting Solicitor of the Treasury.

TREASURY DEPARTMENT, OFFICE OF THE SECRETARY,
October 31, 1902.

The within bond is hereby approved.

H. A. TAYLOR, *Acting Secretary.*

SPECIFICATION, PROPOSAL, CONTRACT, AND BOND FOR HEATING SYSTEM OF THE UNITED STATES POST-OFFICE, COURT-HOUSE, ETC., AT CHICAGO, ILLINOIS.

1. Bids are invited for the heating system of the new United States post-office, courthouse, etc., situated on the block bounded by Adams, Clark, Jackson, and Dearborn streets, in the city of Chicago, Ill.   The bid is to include all labor and materials called for in the following and set forth upon the drawings herein referred to.

2. The Treasury Department reserves the right to waive any informalities in and to reject any and all bids.

3. A bidder must submit with his bid a certified check for five thousand dollars ($5,000), drawn to the order of the Treasurer of the United States, as a guarantee

that he will fully and faithfully comply with the terms of his bid should the same be accepted, and that within two weeks after the form is sent to him he will execute bond and contract in accordance therewith, the sureties on the bond to be approved by the Secretary of the Treasury.

4. Should the successful bidder, for any reason whatsoever after the time set for the opening of the bids, withdraw from the competition or fail or refuse to execute the formal bond or contract within two weeks after the same are sent to him, his certified check may be declared forfeited, and the letter of acceptance of his bid may be revoked, and all obligations on the part of all persons acting for and in behalf of the United States in connection therewith will be released and annulled.

5. The certified check of the successful bidder will be retained until the execution of a formal bond and contract and the approval of the same by the Secretary of the Treasury. The certified checks of the unsuccessful bidders will be returned immediately after the bid of the successful bidder shall have been accepted and the contract executed.

6. Wherever the word "architect" is used herein it shall be held to mean the architect of the United States Government building at Chicago, Ill.

7. Wherever the word "bidder" is used herein it shall be held to mean any individual or firm of individuals, or any member of a firm, or any corporation signing a bid submitted, and "contractor" means the successful bidder to whom the contract is finally awarded.

8. The checks for $100 filed with the architect for these plans and specifications will be returned to the bidders upon their sending back all plans, etc., in good shape to the architect; otherwise that sum will be retained as the price of said plans.

9. Before submitting a bid, make a careful examination of the building, the drawings and specifications, to be fully informed as to the condition of the work, the quality of the material, and the character of the workmanship required, and make a careful examination of the place where the materials are to be delivered and the work performed, and all the conditions governing the fulfillment of the contract, as, should a bid be accepted, no consideration will be given for any error in the bid resulting from failure to do so.

10. Bidders are warned that a bid which is deficient in any of the requirements set forth herein may be rejected as informal.

11. A bid submitted for this work by parties not experienced or regularly engaged in this line and class of work, or not having the proper facilities and financial standing to properly and promptly execute the same as herein required, will not receive consideration.

12. A bid must be made upon the blank hereto attached, and have every blank and item properly filled in.

13. A bid must not be detached from the package in which it is bound, nor must any of the accompanying papers be detached therefrom; but the entire package must be unbroken and in good order when the bid is delivered to the architect.

14. A bidder must state in his bid in writing and in figures (without interlineations, alterations, or erasures) the sum of money for which he will supply the materials and perform the work required by the drawings and specifiations, and in accordance with the conditions of the contract and bond, etc., as herein set forth, should his bid be accepted.

15. A bid must state the price per unit of quantity for all work bid upon, and which unit price shall be used for any additions to or omissions from the work in each class or kind of work shown on the drawings, and required by the specifications, said prices to be the basis of computation for any changes that may be desired, and made by order of the architect; and the bidder must also state the amount included in his bid for each class or kind of work as per schedule, all as herein set forth.

16. A bid submitted by a firm must be signed with the firm name and each member of the firm with the name in full.

17. A bid submitted by a corporation must be signed with the name of the corporation and the full name of each officer of the corporation, with official corporate seal thereto. A bid must contain the address of the bidder.

18. A bidder must be prepared to submit, at his expense, samples of any of the specialties, radiation, valves, etc., which he proposes to use before a contract is signed, the samples to have the name of the bidder and the name, use, and location of the apparatus plainly marked thereon. Each sample must be delivered at this office prior to the time the contract is signed, or at such times as called for by the architect, and none of the material is to be used until accepted or approved by the architect in writing. The samples submitted will be retained, and when required the contractor must furnish duplicates of the samples at his expense.

19. A bid must be delivered in a sealed envelope addressed: Henry Ives Cobb, architect, Treasury Department, Washington, D. C. "Bid for heating system of

Chicago building," from—(name of bidder)—(address of bidder)—and delivered at this office in the Treasury Department on or before 2 p. m. on the day mentioned in the advertisement.

20. Bidders who send their bids to this office through the mails are requested to register same, and to place their name, address, and title of bid on the outside of the envelope for identification, and to mail such bid sufficiently early to reach its destination by the time required, as it is a frequent occurrence that bids reach this office after the hour required. A bid received after the time stated in the advertisement will be returned unopened to the bidder if the proper name and address be known. If the name and address are not known, then the bid will be opened to ascertain the same. It is suggested that bidders use the franked envelopes found inclosed with this specification.

21. Bidders are hereby notified that the certified check required with their bid must be drawn to the order of the Treasurer of the United States; a check drawn to the bidder's own order or to order of any other person than the Treasurer of the United States, although indorsed by the party to whose order it is drawn, and although certified or accepted by the bank on which it is so drawn, may not be accepted as a certified check such as is required under this invitation.

GENERAL CONDITIONS.

22. NOTICE TO SURETIES.—The attention of sureties is particularly directed to the following conditions: The final inspection and acceptance of the work shown by the drawings and specifications, forming a part of the contract, shall not be binding or conclusive upon the United States if it shall subsequently appear that the contractor has willfully or fraudulently, or through collusion with the representatives of the Department in charge of the work, supplied inferior material or workmanship, or has departed from the terms of his contract. In any such case the United States shall have the right, notwithstanding such final acceptance and payment, to cause the work to be properly performed and satisfactory materials supplied to such an extent as, in the opinion of the architect, may be necessary to finish the work in accordance with the drawings and specifications thereof, at the cost and expense of the contractor and the sureties on his bond, and shall have the right to recover against the contractor and his sureties the cost of such work, together with such other damages as the United States may suffer because of the default of the contractor in the premises, the same as though such acceptance and final payment had not been made.

23. PAYMENTS.—Payments will be made monthly, on account of the work satisfactorily in place in the building, based on the estimated value thereof, as ascertained by the architect, less 10 per cent of such estimate, which will be retained until the final inspection of all such materials and labor embraced in the contract and the acceptance of the work, after which the final payment of the balance due may be made.

24. PROPOSALS.—Proposals as hereinbefore called for must be based on drawings 159, 162 to 173, inclusive, except 171, and the specifications, and must include everything necessary and requisite to place the work completed in every detail.

25. The drawings and specifications are to be interpreted together, and all work included in either, though not in both, must be included in the proposal.

26. INSPECT THE BUILDING.—Bidders must visit the building, compare the drawings and specifications, examine the work in place, inform themselves as to all conditions, and include in their proposals all items of labor and material mentioned, shown, or necessarily implied that may be required in the full completion of the work in accordance with the true intent and meaning of the drawings and specifications, whether each item be specifically mentioned or not.

27. TIME TO COMPLETE WORK.—The bidders must state in their proposals the number of working days after the approval of bond by the Secretary of the Treasury in which they will complete the work, and the work is to be commenced immediately upon notification after such approval. Should the condition of the building not permit of the commencement of the work at the time stipulated, or should the execution or condition of other contracts require the stoppage of all work on this contract, allowance for such delays will be made in accordance with provisions as made in the general conditions accompanying this specification. No claim by the contractors for damage on account of such delays will be recognized by the Government.

28. Notice is hereby given that under otherwise equal conditions favorable consideration will be given to the proposal of such bidder as guarantees to have work completed at the earliest date.

29. KIND AND QUALITY OF MATERIAL.—The material supplied must in each case be of the best class and grade found in the market, and, before the contract is awarded, any bidder, when requested by the architect, will be required to submit a schedule of the kind of material, appliances, etc., which he desires to use.   In the event of any of the submitted machinery, appliances, material, etc., not being satisfactory, the architect will select the machinery, appliances, or material of such types and capacities as ma   be satisfactory, which selection shall be final and binding upon the successful biddey.

30. The acceptance by the architect of any machinery, appliances, or material named is to be understood as an acceptance only upon its conforming with the requirements of the specifications in relation thereto, and not as an absolute acceptance of the article without respect to the requirements of the specifications.

31. PATENT RIGHTS.—If any part of the machinery, material, or appliances purposed to be furnished by the bidders is covered by the claims or patents, of whatsoever nature, of any other parties, the contractor purposing to use such appliances will be required to pay all royalties therefor.   The Government will not recognize any demand brought by anyone on account of claims for infringement of patents, but will hold the contractor and his bondsmen strictly responsible for any delay from any cause resulting from his failure to fully protect the Government against all patent rights.

32. VISIT THE DEPARTMENT.—The architect reserves the right to require the contractor, or his authorized representative, to visit this office, without expense to the Government, if at any time it is considered to be in the interest of the Government that a conference is necessary for an early adjustment of any complicated or unsatisfactory conditions that may have developed in connection with his contract, but the result of such conference shall not be binding until formally approved.

33. GUARANTEE.—The bidder must also understand that if his proposal is accepted his contract and bond will guarantee the entire work under this contract, and each and every part thereof, and the contractor will be required to remedy all defects at his expense which may develop by reason of the use of any inferior or defective material or workmanship until the acceptance of the entire work and final payment therefor, subject, however, to the additional requirements expressed in paragraph entitled "Notice to sureties," and subject to any time-limit guarantee on any particular portion of work hereafter mentioned in specification.

34. All questions as to the satisfactory completion of the work and the defects necessary to be remedied are to be determined by the architect or his authorized representative.

35. GENERAL REQUIREMENTS.—This contractor is to perform his work expeditiously in such manner and at such times as will avoid interference with the execution of other contracts.   Contractor to employ continually a sufficiently large force of men to carry on his work properly and finish same in specified time.   In failure so to do, the architect may direct said contractor to increase his force.

36. Contractor to keep a responsible foreman constantly on the ground to receive instructions from the architect, one who is satisfactory to the architect.

37. The dimensions and scaled proportions given on the drawings are in accordance with the general plans, but, as variations therefrom may occur in construction, the contractor must make his own measurements at the building, and he will be held responsible for the proper fitting of the work.   He must check and verify all drawings, and will be held responsible for any errors which could have been avoided by such checking.

38. STORAGE OF MATERIAL.—Any material that the contractor may deliver on the premises will be located or stored at such points and in such manner as may be directed by the architect.   The contractor will be required to remove at his own expense such apparatus or material upon notice from the architect within twenty-four hours after receipt of such order.

SPECIFICATIONS.

39. GENERAL.—The following specifications are designed to govern the furnishing, installing, and delivering of the entire apparatus required for the heating of the building as hereinafter set forth, complete and ready for service.

40. It is the intention of these specifications to provide for the installation of a complete and comprehensive system of steam heating, including all apparatus for such service as hereinafter provided, and, in addition, to provide for temporary heating, this temporary work being installed to provide heat during the completion of the interior work upon the building.

41. DETAILED DRAWINGS.—The drawings and specifications are intended to cooperate and to provide for and comprise everything necessary for the proper and complete finishing of the work, but any work shown on the drawings, and not particularly described in the specifications, or called for in the specifications but omitted on the drawings, and any work reasonably implied and evidently necessary for the complete finishing of the work, although omitted from both, is to be done by the contractor without extra charge, the same as if it were both shown and specified, unless such omissions are expressly mentioned in these specifications.

42. Immediately after the awarding of the contract, the successful bidder will prepare such detailed drawings of piping, arrangements, and connections as may be called for by the architect; these to be submitted for approval.

43. The contractor shall furnish such dimensions, drawings, and specifications for all machinery and apparatus as the architect may from time to time call for. He shall also furnish the architect with duplicates of all drawings and specifications furnished by him to his subcontractors and intended for use in any portion of the work.

44. The contractor will be required to make such detailed working drawings of any or all portions of the work as the architect may call for. The drawings accompanying the specifications show approximately what is required and are made to assist the bidder in preparing his estimates and such detailed drawings as he may be called upon to furnish. Scale of drawings may vary, but all sheets must be of same dimensions as those accompanying this specification.

45. The approval by the architect of any drawings submitted by the contractor, as hereinbefore required, must be understood to be the approval of the general arrangement only, as the architect assumes no responsibility for details of construction, dimensions, etc.

46. MEASUREMENTS.—The contractor must make all his own measurements at the building, and shall check and verify all drawings, details, etc., as he will be held responsible for the proper fitting and connections of his work.

47. In making his own measurements, as herein provided, contractor must understand that he is to do all of his own laying out of every portion of the work included in this specification.

48. The contractor, before the completion and acceptance of his work, shall furnish the architect with the original cloth tracings of the piping drawings, so as to show the work complete in all particulars as finally installed. Drawings to be purely assembly drawings, showing pipe lines diagrammatically. All drawings to be made to the same scale and made on sheets of same dimensions as those accompanying this specification.

49. In all drawings made by the contractor, as provided in this specification, the execution must be in all respect equal to those sent out by the architect.

50. LOCATION.—The approximate location of all apparatus and machinery is shown or indicated on drawings.

51. The arrangement is only shown to assist the bidder in estimating, and is subject to change dependent on the class or design of apparatus selected. The arrangement and approximate length of runs of all high-pressure steam piping are shown so as to indicate the manner of making such connections, but the exact location of connections will depend upon the design and arrangement of engines, pumps, etc.

52. The drawings show the approximate location of steam-actuated apparatus as provided by other contractors and to which this contractor will make steam and exhaust connections.

53. Drawings also show location of all direct radiation which this contractor furnishes and installs, making all connections thereto. The location of all heating coils to be used in connection with the ventilating fans, and which heating coils are to be furnished by the ventilating contractor, is shown on the various drawings. These fans are located in the machinery room in the basement underneath the dome, on the eighth floor in the wings immediately above the four court rooms, and on the ninth floor.

54. OTHER CONTRACTORS.—For the purpose of facilitating the progress of the work and to avoid making of any changes after any of the work has once been done, this contractor will place himself in touch with other contractors on the building whose work may in any way interfere, be part of, or in proximity to his work. He will particularly familiarize himself with the temperature regulating requirements of the ventilating system.

GENERAL DESCRIPTION OF PLANT.

55. Under this specification the contractor will provide, all complete and ready for service, water-tube boilers, special furnaces, feed-water heater, boiler-feed pumps,

induced-draft fan, economizer, smoke connections, etc., coal charging cars and track, all water piping and all high-pressure steam piping connections throughout the entire plant, all exhaust connections, all low-pressure steam heating mains, piping, and all radiation other than the fan coils.   All as herein set forth and described in connection with the drawings.

56. The complete system as contemplated shall also include the furnishing and installing of an approved system of automatic heat regulation, including all piping valves and accessories going to make a comprehensive system covering all the work as outlined hereinafter under the heading "Temperature regulation."

57. The boiler plant to be installed complete in all particulars, all connections of every kind and description being made with the plant, and, as a whole, made complete and ready for operation.

58. The smokeless furnaces to be set with the boilers. These to be of an approved type and so proportioned and set as to prevent, as far as possible, the generation of smoke.

59. The economizer, induced-draft fan, and breeching connections will be so designed and installed as to provide for the escaping gases to pass directly from boilers to chimneys or to fan or to pass through economizer flue to chimneys or to fan; the fan discharging into the chimneys as may be desired. Damper regulator to be furnished and installed as provided hereafter.

60. Arrangements to be made for delivering coal from the storage space to the firing floor in front of boiler batteries. The ashes to be dumped into a bucket hoist so arranged as to deliver ashes from the ash-storage room to wagons in the driveway.

61. Contractor to provide everything in the way of foundations and supports of every kind, such as may be required for piping or any apparatus included in this specification.

62. It is contemplated to install single-column, direct radiation practically under each set of double windows on all stories from the third to the eighth inclusive. The basement, first and second stories, as well as the dome proper, will contain radiation of two or three column pattern distributed under or near the windows, substantially as shown on the drawings.

63. The amount of radiation will be only that as required to make up for the building loss, plus a reasonable margin, and will be as given on the drawings or called for herein.

64. It is proposed to utilize the exhaust steam from the several engines, pumps, and other steam-actuated apparatus as distributed throughout the premises, supplementing the system, when required, by live steam from the boilers fed into the system through pressure-reducing valves.

65. Work to include all the high-pressure boiler piping and connections to engines, pumps, compressor, auxiliary steam-actuated apparatus, and miscellaneous connections as described; to include all exhaust-steam connections from all apparatus; all water-supply piping; overflow, blow-off, and drip piping; steam and oil separators; traps and miscellaneous appurtenances incident to a plant such as proposed.

66. The piping system for the steam heating to be arranged on what is known as a two-pipe vacuum system. The contractor running all mains, risers, supply and return pipes, and providing all apparatus, valves, and fittings as required to make a complete and comprehensive system throughout.

67. The entire plant, as well as each individual part thereof, shall be arranged and installed in a manner dictated by the latest approved practice, but shall be subject to such modifications as the conditions and design of building demand.   Every portion of the plant to embody all improvements and corrections of design and construction as experience and observation of recent installations of like character may have shown to be advisable or necessary.

68. The arrangement of any apparatus or any part of the work as covered by these specifications, so far as details are concerned, is susceptible to change or modification and may be so changed or modified by the architect at any time before work has been begun on the installation of such particular portion of the plant in which a change may be desired to be made, and any changes, deviations, or additions which may be so made, with a view to the betterment of the arrangement or operation of the plant, and when made, as herein stipulated, shall not be the basis of an extra charge.

69. Should any improvements be made in any of the apparatus, in part or in whole, included in this contract, after the execution of latter but prior to its completion, the Government shall derive the benefit of such approved apparatus and the contractor to furnish and install same without extra cost. The architect to determine whether or not it is desirable to make use of such improvements, etc.

70. The contractor to furnish, deliver, and erect complete, with inclosing brick-work, six water-tube boilers. There will be two batteries of two boilers each, and two boilers set singly, all arranged substantially as shown on the drawings.

71. The boilers will be of the type known as vertical header type; to be 16 tubes wide and 9 tubes high, headers being of cast iron and serpentine in form. The tubes to be seamless cold-drawn steel tubes, 4 inches in diameter and 18 feet long.

72. Each boiler shall have at least 3,000 square feet of heating surface; heating surface, as measured, to include only outside of tubes between headers, rear connection tubes, and one-half the shell of each drum; no account to be taken of any other surface whatever in estimating the surface of boiler proposed.

73. Boilers to be designed to sustain a constant working pressure of 150 pounds by gauge.

74. Boilers to be complete with wrought-iron supporting frames.

75. Each boiler to have two 42-inch drums; all horizontal seams of drums to be triple-riveted double-strap butt joints; these joints all to be made above the center line of drums.

76. The cross pipes for safety valves to be so arranged that valves may be placed on their sides, the openings being taken out in the rear ends of the drums; the cross or balance pipe connecting the steam drums to be extra heavy and provided with side opening, 8 inches pointing toward the rear and 4 inches toward the front.

77. The upper half cast-iron fronts of the boilers only to be furnished with the boilers proper. The lower half fronts with supporting construction will be omitted, and the arrangement of the boiler supports made to fit the special furnace as hereinafter provided; all fronts and cleaning doors to be furnished complete, and all to be tight fitting.

78. Each boiler shall be provided with the latest and most modern improvements and appliances, all necessary mountings and trimmings complete, including water column and all requisite valves, gauges, and piping, together with nickel-seated lockup, pop safety valve, equal to the "Consolidated;" one 4-inch diameter lever safety valve of approved construction; bronze combined feed and check valves and bronze-mounted blow-off valves; these latter to be similar and equal to the "Cadman;" all valves, gauges, fittings, etc., to be acceptable to the architect.

79. All connections for boiler feed and blow-offs to be made with brass pipe and fittings. All angles to be made with crosses and tees for cleaning, the spare openings being closed with square-headed brass plugs.

80. All pipe, unless otherwise specified, to be standard full weight wrought iron. Flanges to be extra heavy, straight faced. Valves to be extra heavy and flanged for 2½ inches and above. Feed piping to be arranged as directed.

81. There will be furnished with the boilers three complete sets of fire and cleaning tools, each set including steel wrench for hand-hole nuts, tube cleaner equal to the "Niagara" pattern, poker, slice bar and hoe, together with one set of best steam hose and a cleaning pipe for blowing dust and soot from exterior of tubes.

82. Across the rear of the boilers and immediately above the doors there shall be riveted a heavy 4-inch angle, upon which will rest the cast tees supporting breeching.

83. An iron ladder to be furnished with each of the two batteries; these to be placed at some convenient point as may be designated. Also provide iron platform between batteries and from battery to each single setting.

84. The contractor must furnish suitable foundations of a very permanent and substantial character, all as may be approved by the architect.

85. These foundations to be built of concrete in a manner as provided under the subheading "Foundations."

86. The front faces of not only the boiler setting, but front and sides of the extension furnaces to be of white enamel brick laid up in white mortar. The side walls of the entire boiler settings to be faced with pressed red brick laid up in red cement mortar. All brick to be laid up with close joints, all outside joints to be pointed.

87. The boilers in all respects to be set in accordance with the best accepted practice.

88. Boilers to be set with vertical flame passes, to be complete with all necessary tile as required. Sides of boiler setting to be lined with first quality fire brick back to the bridge wall and first flame plate, and from underside of lowest grates of special furnace up to the underside of drums. Second quality fire brick to be used for all other inside walls. Bridge wall to be of first quality. First quality fire brick to be equal to that known as "Franklin Crown." All fire brick to be laid and rubbed into place with fire-clay cement. All other than fire brick to be selected first quality hard-burned brick, laid up in best lime mortar with close joints.

89. All boiler clean-out doors to be set flush with the outside walls of setting.

90. The ash pits under furnace grates to be paved with vitrified paving block "seconds" laid up on edge upon a bedding of concrete 8 inches in thickness.

91. When boilers are set complete with furnaces and smoke connections, the contractor shall thoroughly dry out the brickwork by keeping slow wood fires in each furnace continuously for a period of at least ten days.

92. The contractor shall arrange to install the boiler plant and prepare same for service previous to the completion of any other portion of his work, with the exception of placing temporary radiation, as it is essential to have this part in service in advance of most of his work as well as that of other contractors on the building.

FURNACES.

93. The special furnaces with which every boiler furnished under this contract is to be equipped shall be the latest and most approved pattern specially designed to prevent the generation of smoke. Furnaces to be installed with all special tile, attachments, pipe connections, and fronts complete and ready for service; to be of a down-draft type and set as extension furnaces.

94. The grates to be water tubes set in double rows and staggered. The top of furnaces to be water tubes, over which shall be laid special fire tile. Below the water grates shall be arranged a set of plain grates of the "herringbone" or other acceptable pattern.

95. The entire design and construction of these furnaces to be such as to make them suitable for economically burning Illinois slack bituminous coal.

96. The contractor guarantees that by the use of these furnaces the capacity of the boilers to which they are attached will be increased at least 20 per cent; that by their use the life of the boilers will in no way be impaired, and that their design will be such as to rather facilitate firing than otherwise. He further guarantees to prevent at least 90 per cent of the smoke as determined by chart measurements in a manner as prescribed by the code adopted by the American Society of Mechanical Engineers.

97. In submitting proposition, the bidders must be prepared to submit a complete drawing of the type and design of furnace proposed.

FEED-WATER HEATER.

98. Contractor will furnish complete in all details, and install upon suitable and substantial brick or concrete foundation, an open type combined exhaust steam feed-water heater and receiving tank, as may be acceptable to the architect. This heater to be of cast iron and rectangular in section. The heater may be arranged to "draw" its supply, or arranged so as to pass exhaust steam through the heater. Heater to have a nominal rated capacity of 1,500 horsepower.

99. Heater will be provided with an automatic intake valve, and will be furnished with suitable and approved water gauge.

100. On the water inlet and on the pump suction shall be placed first-class thermometers, these to have brass cases fitted with slide for protection of glass. Heater to be furnished with air relief valves, brass safety valve, and inside automatic overflow valve to prevent blowing out of water seal. Connections to be arranged and valved to permit of reversing the current of water through the filtering chamber for the purpose of cleaning out. The pans of heater to be made of heavy perforated copper.

101. The heater as furnished is to be used as a receiving tank in connection with the steam-heating system, and at no time will be subjected to a pressure exceeding 3 pounds by gauge.

102. There will be furnished and made part of the heater an efficient oil separator. Provision to be made for flanged pipe connections for discharge from vacuum pumps and for traps draining high-pressure piping. The heater to be installed with all connections, valves, flanged fittings, and all appurtenances complete and ready for service.

103. Before the contract is awarded, any bidder, upon the request of the architect, will furnish a complete specification of the heater he proposes; this to be made on regular specification blank form, as is usual and customary. He must give the dimensions of heater, size and number of pans, cubic feet of steam space, cubic feet of water space exclusive of filtering chamber, and the total cubic space.

BOILER FEED PUMPS.

104. For boiler feeding there will be furnished and installed on substantial and acceptable concrete foundations two pumps, each to be a duplicate of the other. Pumps to be of the vertical piston-packed pattern, known as the "Admiralty" type; to be duplex and compounded.

105. Each pump to run noncondensing and to be of size to deliver 125 gallons per minute against a pressure of 150 pounds by gauge. The speed of pump when performing maximum required duty not to exceed 48 strokes per minute for *both* sides of pump or 24 strokes for any one plunger.

106. Pumps to be so designed that each will rest on cast-iron base or feet set on foundation top, the water pistons being removable from the top. Pumps to have brass rods and be composition fitted throughout on water ends; the water pistons to be packed with ⅝-inch square canvas and white rubber insertion packing rings, sufficient in number to prevent slippage; pumps to be complete with all compression relief and drain valves.

107. Each pump to be furnished with a complete set of nickel-plated heavy brass sight-feed oil cups of the adjustable spring-snap pattern. Furnish and connect a quadruple feed half-gallon, single-compartment, nickel-plated lubricating pump, fitted with approved and acceptable sight-feed attachments, the pump in all particulars to be equal to that known as the "Hills-McCanna."

INDUCED-DRAFT APPARATUS.

108. The arrangement of fan, breeching, economizer flue and chimney connections will be substantially as shown on the drawings. The arrangement will be such that the fan may take its suction from the smoke breeching or from the economizer flue as may be desired, delivering into the chimneys. The contractor will provide all dampers as may be required to accomplish the purpose as herein described.

109. The fan will be a full housing angular discharge and arranged for direct connection to vertical inclosed type steam engine, which the contractor will furnish complete in all particulars as hereinafter described. All substantially as shown on the drawings.

110. Fan to be capable of handling the gases from boilers in which will be burned 4½ tons of coal per hour as a maximum. The total square feet of grate surface to be such as may be acceptable with the special design of furnace herein provided. The temperature of escaping gases to be 550° maximum.

111. Fan wheel to be not less than 10 feet in diameter by approximately 50 inches wide at tips of blades.

112. Fan at a speed not exceeding 165 revolutions per minute to provide a draft equivalent to at least 1.5 inches water column at the fan inlet.

113. The fan to be complete with water-cooled bearings. Fan housing to be built of No. 10 steel. All seams and angles will be reenforced with angle and tee irons.

114. Contractor will furnish and make all connections of every sort and description to the smoke breeching and to the economizer flue, and will furnish and provide all discharge connections to the chimneys. All of these connections, unless otherwise shown on the drawings, to be made of No. 10 steel, suitably stiffened and reenforced with angles and tee irons.

115. The shaft of the fan will be so arranged as to permit of bearings being located outside of suction chamber.

116. With the fan, contractor will furnish complete, with all connections, one vertical pattern inclosed type engine as may be best suited, in the opinion of the architect, for the limited space available. Engine to be of ample capacity for driving the fan when performing its maximum duty, as called for in these specifications. The engine to develop the required horsepower at one-quarter cut-off when running at a maximum speed of 200 revolutions per minute. Steam to be furnished at a pressure of from 140 to 150 pounds by gauge.

117. With the engine will be furnished approved throttle governor; a full and complete set of heavy sight-feed snap oil cups; a one-quart sight-feed cylinder lubricator, and a full set of wrenches to fit all bolts.

118. In connection with this induced-draft apparatus the contractor will make an entire drawing of the arrangement as described herein and as shown approximately on the drawings, submitting same for the approval of the architect.

119. With the complete apparatus, contractor will furnish a full set of foundation bolts and plates and necessary wrenches to fit all nuts. He will provide all foundations of every sort and description, and will build flues and do all masonry work and cutting as may be required, or as hereinafter described.

FUEL ECONOMIZER.

120. DESIGN.—The contractor to furnish, deliver, and erect complete in position, as shown on the drawings, one fuel economizer of construction and design as may be approved by the architect.

121. The economizer to be composed of 28 sections, and each section to contain 10 tubes 4⅛ inches external diameter and 11 feet 3 inches long, connected at the top and bottom by headers. The ends of tubes to be turned and pressed by hydraulic machinery into the sockets of the top and bottom headers, joints to be iron to iron. The top headers to be planed along the edges so that when they come together they form a tight joint, and to be provided with turned hand-hole lids opposite the vertical tubes to allow access for cleaning and scraping internally, and, if required, the drawing out of tubes through such hand-hole lids.

122. The outlet and inlet branch pipes at top and bottom to be planed and faced and fitted with access lids for cleaning out the bottom headers.

123. The sections to be securely mounted on brick walls, this contractor to provide all such walls inclosing the soot pit and providing such soot pit, all as shown on the drawings. In the supporting walls all necessary cast-iron soot manhole frames and doors will be provided, these to be faced and made air-tight.

124. INCLOSURE.—Contractor shall provide all front brick inclosing wall, as shown, and in addition shall inclose the entire front next to the driveway with a removable cover, this to be made of No. 10 sheet steel and protected with at least 2 inches of block nonconducting material, all as may be approved by the architect. The economizer will be provided with single side dampers or baffle plates, all erected complete in position as shown.

125. FLUE CONNECTIONS.—Contractor to provide in connection with the economizer setting all connections between the breeching and economizer flue, and provide substantial and acceptable "Louvre" dampers so as to permit of economizer being used as provided in this specification under the general description of plant.

126. SCRAPERS.—The economizer is to be provided with an approved scraper, to be complete with self-acting triple beveled-edge scrapers, with lifting bars, guards, rods, chains, and improved scraper gear with positive reversing lever.

127. SAFETY VALVE.—The economizer to be furnished with safety valve 3 inches in diameter and set to blow off at 165 pounds pressure; blow-off valve 3 inches in diameter and with all necessary bolts for fitting up.

128. CONSTRUCTION.—The whole economizer to be of the best material, of perfect construction and workmanship throughout, and to be tested at a pressure of 350 pounds per square inch before leaving the works of the manufacturer.

129. GUARANTEE.—The manufacturer guarantees to replace and make good any part of this economizer which may pro e defective due to faulty workmanship or material within five years from the datevof the final acceptance of the plant without cost to the United States, economizer during this period being given proper care and attention. This guarantee to be part of the bond attached.

SMOKE CONNECTIONS.

130. The boiler breeching to be located and made of such dimensions with all connections from boilers as shown on the drawings.

131. The bottom of the entire breeching will be on a level and immediately above the rear sheet-iron access doors at back of each boiler. The wrought tees on bottom of breeching to rest on a 13-inch brick wall which this contractor shall build on the east or driveway side, reparating the economizers from space at rear of boilers. The other end to rest on angle irons riveted to rear door frames and boiler column, this angle iron being provided for under specifications for "Boilers."

132. The side wall of the economizer flue to be built of hard-burned brick laid up in cement mortar in the same manner as provided for boiler settings. This wall will be lined on economizer side with second-quality fire brick acceptable to the architect; fire brick to be laid in fire-clay cement. All joints to be struck.

133. Between the boiler settings there will be carried a 4-inch I beam, this beam to be set either in the brick wall or be properly bolted to the rear supporting boiler columns. Breeching to be made throughout of ⅛-inch black iron suitably stiffened with tees and angle irons, contractor providing for all supports of whatever nature that may be required to hold this breeching in place, such as brick walls and I beams as herein called for.

134. Where breeching is carried along by the economizer, a secure and tight joint will be made so as to prevent any possible infiltration into the economizer flue between the brick division wall and the iron breeching.

135. Along the top of breeching will be run 2 by 2 inch angles, the sides and top to be stiffened by riveting a suitable number of 2 by 2 inch angles, the bottom by tees as provided.

136. Provide for connections to be made to the heavy cast damper frames. Provide for connecting necks from boiler dampers to breeching. All necks to be connected to respective boiler openings, being bolted thereto.

137. The breeching to be thoroughly riveted throughout, all joints to be **tight**. The entire breeching when complete will be painted with a heavy coating of **best** asphaltum paint.

138. DAMPERS.—Provide cast-iron vertical "Louvre" dampers with **ball-bearing** trunnions, and with heavy damper frames at all points, as shown on the **drawings**, so as to permit of the gases passing from boilers directly to chimney, **directly to** economizer flue, directly to fan intake or from economizer flue to fan intake, **or from** economizer flue to chimneys, all as outlined under "General description of **plant."** Breeching to be provided with cast-iron doors and frames, placed where required, to permit of convenient and thorough cleaning of breeching. The doors to be **planed,** to be tight fitting, and provided with the necessary hasps and catches. **In the** entire breeching all joints to be thoroughly tight, and all brickwork to be laid **up in** such a manner as to prevent any infiltration of air.

DAMPER REGULATOR.

139. The contractor shall furnish complete in all particulars, and install **with all** connections ready for service, an acceptable damper regulator, which must be **so** designed that it will make a partial stroke and stand at any intermediate **point** between wide-open and closed position. Regulator to be complete in every **essential** particular, and installed in position in the engine or boiler room as directed, **all as** may be approved by the architect.

140. In connection with the regulator, contractor shall furnish a substantial **and** acceptable "Louvre" damper complete, with heavy cast-iron damper frame, **with** all levers and accessories, and locate same in the main breeching at the point **designated** on the drawings, all to be connected and put in operating condition.

141. The regulator, when located as directed, shall be inclosed in a finished **casing** made of quarter-sawed white oak and provided with glass door fitted **with** finished brass hinges, catch, and Yale lock.

142. All piping connections to the regulator to be made with brass pipe; pipe **to be** polished where exposed in engine room, in case damper regulator is so placed.

INDUSTRIAL RAILWAY.

143. GENERAL.—The contractor shall furnish and install complete, ready for **service**, two systems of industrial railway, one for the handling of coal which is **to be** delivered from the coal-storage space to the firing floor in front of boilers, the other to provide for the removing of ashes from front of boilers to ash hoist which this contractor furnishes and installs in connection with this coal and ash handling system.

144. The tracks and turntables to be arranged substantially as shown on the drawings.

145. TRACKS AND TURNTABLES.—For the coal cars the gauge of track to be 20 inches; rails to be 12-pound tee rails, 2½ inches high, securely bolted to cup-shaped steel cross-ties spaced not to exceed 24 inches center to center; the ties of this track to be laid on a bed of concrete as shown. Concrete will be laid by others. The turntables to be at least 68 inches in diameter and designed to turn on rings of hardened steel balls running in accurately machined ball race, the arrangement being such that the ball bearings will entirely prevent tilting of the table platforms and will work perfectly and be tight fitting, so as to keep out dust and dirt. Turntables to be provided with an approved locking device. The tops to be set flush with the finished floor and grooved to receive the flanges of car wheels, the remaining surface of the tables to be checkered in a manner so as not to wear smooth or slippery. The turntable frames to be laid on and properly bedded in concrete, this concrete being laid by others, but all necessary excavating to be done by this contractor.

146. The top of all coal-car rails to be set flush with the finished floor line. Between these rails contractor shall provide a grouting of finely crushed granite and cement, all to be set substantially as shown in detail on the drawings.

147. For the ash-car tracks running along immediately in front of the boilers furnish and lay on concrete bed (furnished by others) cast-plate track joined up with cast-plate tile. The construction of this track and tile must be such that it will not buckle or warp, the checkering to be such as not to wear smooth or slippery. The cast-plate tile to be at least 13 inches wide on side of track next to coal room, and on east side to be carried over to front line of boilers along the entire length at south end to continue on to the curve and then follow track as a 13-inch tile plate to extreme end at ash-storage room. Plates to be neatly and closely fitted to furnace or boiler fronts and to track. The gauge of this track to be 20 inches, same as that for coal-car tracks, so as to permit of cars being used on either of the set of tracks should occasion require.

148. The curves in this ash-car track to be so arranged that the outside wheel will run on its flange while the inside wheel will run on its tread.

149. CARS.—With this entire equipment contractor shall furnish five V-shaped self-balanced double-tip cars built with swing trucks; cars to be so built that the bed will hang low between the wheels, thereby permitting of a large capacity car in smaller space. Capacity of cars to be 18 cubic feet. Length of car to be approximately 6 feet, with maximum height of 36 inches above the rails, with width of car not to exceed 50 inches.

150. These cars as furnished to be suitable in every way for carrying coal and ashes on the tracks as herein provided. The wheels of car to be cast iron, 12 inches in diameter. Cars to be properly painted and delivered in perfect running order, all as may be acceptable to the architect.

151. As other contractors lay the concrete floor in the boiler and coal rooms it is essential that this contractor place himself in touch with them, and he shall so arrange his work as to lay all tracks and cast-plate flooring and to set turntables that all may be thoroughly embedded and properly set in the concrete work.

152. ASH HOIST.—In connection with industrial railway outfit, herein provided, the contractor shall furnish and install an ash hoist, this to be used for hoisting ashes from the ash-storage room and delivering same through spout into wagons in the driveway.

153. Elevator to have vertical lift as shown on the drawings, and to be composed of two strands of heavy steel thimble roller chain having 3-inch-diameter rollers with 12 by 6 by 6 inch malleable-iron buckets with renewable steel band, these buckets to be placed approximately every 12 inches. Elevator leg to be made of $\frac{1}{4}$-inch steel plates, with 2 by 2 inch steel corner angles placed at various points on front and back of elevator leg, to be arranged so that they can be readily removed in order to facilitate repairs. The steel boot and flaring spout to be made with $\frac{1}{4}$-inch sides and $\frac{1}{2}$-inch bottom plates, and to be equipped with adjustable bearings to take up slack in chain.

154. The steel hood at the top to be $\frac{1}{8}$-inch metal, and provided with hinged spout, arranged so as to deliver ashes into wagons in the driveway, and when not in service to drop into recess, closing opening and being flush with face of wall. To be entirely operated from ash-storage room.

155. Contractor shall do all excavating that may be necessary for the proper installation of his apparatus, furnish proper substantial supports, and do all cutting as provided in the body of these specifications.

156. The floor of the ash room will be built by this contractor, and arranged to pitch toward the hopper, which he will set below the lowest point of the floor line so that ashes dumped into the storage room will gravitate to the hopper.

157. The entire apparatus to be complete in all particulars and installed with slow-speed electric motor of such type and design as may be acceptable to the architect, motor to be wound for 220-volt circuit and to be complete with a universal type starting box. The motor to be mounted on brackets, or in some other acceptable manner, the contractor furnishing all necessary shafts, sprocket wheels, and special high-speed noiseless sprocket chains.

158. The entire apparatus to be completed and ready for service with all meter wiring.

COAL SCALES.

159. Contractor to furnish and install an approved floor scale with pillar beam outfit, suitable for weighing coal in the hopper cars, this to be furnished and installed in a position substantially as shown on drawings. The platform of scales to be arranged with grooved track. The entire arrangement to be acceptable and complete in every particular ready for service.

TEMPORARY CONNECTIONS.

160. It must be understood and agreed by the contractor that he includes in his contract amount all labor and the material necessary for making such temporary connections as may be required during the construction of the system and before its completion; such connections to cover all the heating surface, valves, pipes, fittings, and accessories that may be required for temporarily furnishing heat in such portions of the building as may be desired, and at such times and to such extent as may be called for from time to time by the architect; and in submitting his proposal the contractor does so with the understanding that at such time as may be required the architect will be allowed the free use of the apparatus for temporary purposes; the contractor to furnish the necessary men to look after and operate the same during

the temporary usage thereof; and he shall further furnish under this contract a man to superintend the work who shall have the complete installation under his charge, it being understood and agreed that in the event of any damage resulting through mismanagement, or other circumstances, the United States is not to be held responsible for same, and that the contractor is to make good to the United States, or to other contractors, any damage due to such neglect, the architect to determine the extent of the injury in all cases.

161. Whatever arrangements this contractor is called upon to make they must be complete, and all condensation must be returned to the boilers. He will be allowed the free use of one or more of the new boilers, as may be required for furnishing steam for temporary heating purposes, provided he has such boilers installed. The United States will furnish all fuel and pay for all water used for this purpose. This contractor, however, will be required to furnish the competent firemen necessary to keep up a continuous steam supply.

162. The contractor will be held responsible for the boilers used in this temporary service, and same will not be accepted by the United States until they are thoroughly cleaned and put in condition as good as before service, less ordinary wear and tear.

163. Provided the permanent boilers are neither wholly or partly installed, or boiler feed pumps in position when request is made for temporary heating, the contractor will, within ten days after receipt of written notice, provide temporary boiler, or boilers, and such pumps as may be necessary or required by the architect.

164. The contractor will be required, after the main temporary heating pipes are run, to install radiation as may be called for, and to place the same, complete with all connections, within three days after receipt of written notice from the superintendent of the building requesting such radiation.

165. Upon written notice from the architect such radiation, pipes, valves, fittings, etc., as may have been used in any manner for temporary purposes will be removed, transposed, or redisposed, as he may direct.

166. When, in the opinion of the architect, the permanent heating system has so far progressed as to permit of the removal of the temporary apparatus, either in whole or in part, the contractor will be required, upon receipt of instructions from the architect, to immediately remove such portions, or all, as may be designated.

167. In addition to the labor and material to be provided for the temporary heating of the building, the contractor shall make all connections of a temporary nature, as may be necessary or called for by the architect, for operating or making ready for service any of the steam-actuated apparatus furnished and installed under this contract or by others, in case it is required to start any such machinery or make ready for operation previous to the completion of the steam piping which is provided in this specification. The provision herein made for attendants and fuel, etc., to apply to this work also. Other contractors, however, to furnish their own men to operate any machinery or appliances which they may install, and to which temporary connections are made.

168. The steam pressure to be carried for temporary heating purposes will be only that necessary to supply sufficient steam to the surface as installed. The piping must be of capacity sufficient for the surface with a maximum pressure of 20 pounds by gauge.

169. The temporary boilers, if necessary to install same, shall be such as may be safely operated under a constant working pressure of 100 pounds by gauge, and be inspected and passed upon by a reputable boiler inspection and insurance company, acceptable to the architect, who shall be provided with the certificate issued by such company. This pressure will be carried in case any of the machinery installed by others, as above mentioned, is to be tested or operated.

170. As it is essential to provide temporary heat for the building during the winter of 1902-'03, the time of completing connections ready for temporary heating will be an important factor in awarding the contract.

TEMPERATURE REGULATION.

171. GENERAL.—The contractor under this specification will furnish and install in connection with the steam heating and ventilating systems an apparatus for the regulation and control of the temperature throughout the building. He will furnish and install a complete and perfect system of automatic heat regulation, including all piping, thermostats, diaphragm valves, air compressors and tanks, together with all other accessories going to make a comprehensive system covering all work as outlined herein. The system of temperature regulation shall be simply pneumatic and such that it will be completely operated with an air pressure of 10 pounds per square inch.

172. All portions of the system are to be provided with thermostatic means for their control and regulation; all direct radiators individually or by groups as provided hereinafter; all by-pass dampers, tempering and heating coils of ventilating system, and all hot-water tanks heated by steam. Thermostats to be furnished in sufficient number to perform the required duty as herein provided.

173. One thermostat to be provided for each room, but in any unfinished or undivided spaces where the floor area exceeds 2,500 square feet one thermostat shall be furnished for each additional 1,800 square feet or fraction thereof, as may be directed by the architect.

174. The intention is to maintain a constant temperature of 70° F. in all the rooms, corridors, etc., to be controlled and to maintain a constant predetermined temperature in each of the three hot-water tanks. The thermostats will be so designed as to operate in each case the controlling device within a variation in temperature of 1° above or below this point.

175. There will be furnished and installed thermostats for controlling by-pass dampers and steam-supply valves of the hot-blast ventilating apparatus.

176. In the basement thermostats will be placed in the most advantageous location and, in a number of cases, be arranged to operate special diaphragm valves placed in heating mains or branches leading to certain sections, thus controlling groups of radiators rather than individual units. The manner of dividing basement into these sections to be substantially that as shown on the drawings.

177. The thermostats are to be placed in each and every room. In all rooms the thermostats will operate the radiator diaphragm valves furnished by the contractor and attached to each radiator as required.

178. Thermostats as provided will be placed in the intakes, and the discharges of all supply ventilating fans as located in basement, eighth floor above court rooms and on ninth floor. In each instance, the one placed in the fresh-air intake shall operate the valve in feed to each row of tempering coils; the others to be placed in the discharge of the fan, one to operate by-pass damper provided by others; the remaining thermostats each to operate its respective valve in main steam supply to each row of heater coils, all to be so adjusted that by-pass damper will be brought into operation first, then in case the temperature in the discharge duct continues to rise, the main heater coils will be successively cut out. The thermostats in the intake will be so adjusted that when the outside air reaches a temperature of approximately 68° F., the valves in the supply to tempering coils will be closed one after the other with by-pass damper wide open.

179. All thermostats controlling valves in steam supply pipes to hot-blast heater or to tempering coils to operate positively or with graduated motion and in conjunction with the thermostat controlling the by-pass dampers; all to be so adjusted as to maintain a constant temperature in the discharge duct. The thermostats controlling by-pass dampers shall operate so as to provide for a graduated movement of such dampers.

180. Contractor to make all connections of every sort and description to the coils of the hot-water tanks, the devices being so arranged as to automatically maintain the temperature of the water in each of the tanks at 185° F. The valves to be operated by air pressure same as all radiator valves provided under this contract.

181. DAMPERS.—This contractor shall furnish and install in each of the foul-air outlets from fans exhausting to atmosphere suitable and acceptable dampers made of heavy black iron, properly stayed or ribbed, and provided with brass trunnions. The frames of these dampers are to be of heavy cast or wrought iron, dependent on their size, and provided with brass boxes to fit trunnions. These dampers to be so constructed as to remain closed normally, and so as not to appreciably reduce the cross section of area of ducts or hinder the free movement of air when held open by the motor valve. Connect to each individual damper an air motor valve, making all connections thereto. Each of these dampers to be so connected as to allow of an individual control, a separate pipe being carried from each one down to the engine room, where arrangement will be made in such a manner that by opening a suitably arranged valve or valves in the engine room, the foul-air dampers may be individually or collectively held open. Air pipes, where brought into the engine room, to be connected to one header which in turn is connected with air tank. A valve shall be placed in this main pipe in addition to valves in each independent lead.

182. There will be twelve of these dampers in all. Two will be installed in the basement of the dome, four in the eighth story, and four in the ninth story. In addition, there will also be placed one in each of the discharges of the pair of exhaust fans located in the basement of the subtreasury. The pair of dampers from subtreasury exhaust fans may be operated by one motor valve.

183. LOCATION OF THERMOSTATS.—The location of all thermostats placed in the rooms or elsewhere will be determined by the contractor, but it is understood that the architect reserves the right to change the location of any or all of such, provided the same does not affect the operation of the system and is changed before this portion of the work has commenced, and that any change so made shall not constitute the basis of an extra charge. The contractor will run no pipes and place no thermostats until such location has been appoved by the architect.

184. DESIGN OF THERMOSTATS.—The thermostats provided, as herein specified for the automatic operation of the various diaphragm valves or dampers, must be entirely metallic, excepting as to necessary diaphragms, and the thermostatic action to be that as caused by the relative contraction and expansion of two metals firmly brazed together. All the operative mechanism shall, when the protecting case or front is removed, be expos d to view, and this mechanism must be of such construction that the valves and their seats may be removed or exchanged without removing the thermostat from the wall. Each thermostat controlling radiator steam-supply valves must be supplied with a device whereby an instantaneous movement may be obtained in such a manner that full air pressure will be supplied to or released from the diaphragm valves at once, with the possible exception of those controlling hot-blast coils.

185. All thermostats controlling direct radiator valves must be designed to operate completely on a change of temperature of not less than 1° above or below a predetermined point as herein provided. All others to operate as called for.

186. DIAPHRAGM VALVES.—The diaphragm steam valves which contractor will furnish for each steam radiator, feed pipe, or for hot-blast supply to coils must be positive or graduated in their action. Valves in all cases will be of size as given in the tabulation under "Radiator tapping," or as shown on drawings. The design and style to be suitable for the location. The bodies of all valves to be made of the best steam metal and of extra heavy pattern, being fitted with composition disks and nipple connections. The rubber diaphragms used with these valves must be of pure gum with not less than two layers of fine cotton. All to be acceptable to the architect.

187. FINISH.—The finish of all thermostats placed in rooms or corridors to be what is known as "Bower Barff" or other finish as may be selected by the architect. All diaphragm valves for direct radiators to be rough body, nickel plated all over. The diaphragm to be finished in dead black or otherwise to correspond with the thermostats. The rims to be nickel plated and finished. For all other diaphragm valves, finish and style to conform to the particular location in which they are placed. The design of all thermostat-protecting cases to be such as may be approved by the architect.

188. AIR COMPRESSOR.—The air compressor and the tank for providing the necessary air for the operation of the valves, dampers, etc., to be furnished by this contractor and installed at some convenient point in the engine room. Air compressors to be installed in duplicate, each to be of such capacity as the system demands; to be steam driven, water jacketed, and of approved design; in connection with each compressor provide an automatic pneumatic governor to stop and start compressor at any desired variation of air pressure in the tank.

189. These air compressors to be cross-connected so that either may be used independently or in connection with the other.

190. Air pumps of temperature-control system to be set together on one foundation 12 inches above the floor and built of concrete faced with white enamel tile; foundation to be finished on top with a cast-iron plate made with lip all around and with flange extending below to hold tile securely in position.

191. The tank or air reservoir to be of such capacity as the system demands, and to be guaranteed to be absolutely air-tight under a pressure of 50 pounds. At the tank provide suitable and acceptable valves and fittings, so that sections of the air mains may be shut off if desired. Furnish an approved and acceptable accurate pressure gauge for the air system, this to be attached to the tank. In addition provide a pressure gauge, 6¾-inch dial, gauge to be provided with deep nickel-plated case, and to be mounted with and marked in manner provided for other gauges on the gauge board in the engine room, the exact location of which will be determined later. The air reservoir to be located as may be directed in close proximity to the duplicate air compressors.

192. PIPING.—The air piping to be used in connection with the system of temperature regulation shall be of either iron or steel pipe thoroughly galvanized inside and outside, the exception to this to be made where pipes are carried in partition walls, and safely concealed, in which case pipe may be a composition of lead and tin acceptably armored. All runs of pipe must be suitably proportioned and of sufficient size to furnish an ample supply of air for the entire system.

193. From the air tank there will be carried four main runs of pipe, these to run in the basement to the four corners of the dome. At such points risers will be placed connecting in such a manner that each of the main wings will be an independent system. The capacity of any one of these four mains to be sufficient for the entire system, likewise the four risers. The four main leads will in the engine room be connected to one header, which in turn will be connected to the tank. In each of these separate pipes valves will be placed, also place one in main connection from tank. Valves will also be placed at the base of each riser. On each floor of each wing piping will be so arranged that it may be cut out without interfering with any other portion of the system. Pipes will also be led from the air tank to other sections of the building as may be necessary or required to make a flexible arrangement. The four dome risers to be cross-connected on the ninth story and valved so each may be cut off if necessary. From this loop run pipe to dome above ninth story. All piping to be guaranteed to be absolutely air-tight under an air pressure of 20 pounds.

194. The piping for the intake to the compressors must be taken from some suitable point outside of the building as free from dust and moisture as possible, this intake to be furnished with adequate and acceptable air filters, which shall be so constructed as to be readily accessible for cleaning purposes.

195. Raceways have been provided in nearly all instances on each floor of the four wings, in which all main air pipes may be carried for each story. These channels or raceways are carried along the floor line back of the baseboard. In these main pipes contractor shall provide connections to all thermostats, and in addition to such connections he shall provide tees in the main pipes placed approximately every 16 feet, in any case these plugged tees to come opposite hand-hole plates provided by others.

196. At suitable positions in various rooms, or other locations, where thermostats are to be placed, the pipes will terminate with a permanent metallic disk or plate securely fastened in position. To this plate the thermostat provided will be attached in a manner that it may be readily removed in case of necessity for inspection or repairs.

197. CONTROL OF HUMIDITY.—The contractor shall provide, in connection with the temperature regulating and the ventilating system, for the automatic regulation and control of atmospheric humidity. The device to be so constructed that all air delivered by fans to such portions of the building as hereinafter stated, and which is to be used for heating or ventilating purposes, will be artificially humidified according to the varying conditions of temperature and natural moisture.

198. Humidistats will be placed, one in each of the four main court rooms on the sixth floor and one in each of the four spaces of the first floor devoted to post-office proper. The exact location of these humidistats to be designated by consultation and agreement with the architect.

199. Each humidistat must be attached to the wall and piped in a manner identical with the thermostats used for controlling dampers, diaphragm valves, etc., and must operate in conjunction with such thermostats. The design of the humidistat must be of the same general character as provided herein for thermostats, excepting in so far that a member subject to change of moisture is to be substituted in place of the thermally actuated metallic strip of the thermostat. All humidistats shall be susceptible of an adjustment that will maintain a certain predetermined percentage of humidity within 5 per cent of that for which they may be set.

200. All piping used in connection with the humidistats is to conform in all respects to that as provided herein, to be used in connection with the temperature-regulating system.

201. The humidifiers to be installed in connection with the humidistats shall be placed in each general air supply to each of the fans delivering air to rooms in which humidistats are to be installed. Humidifiers to consist of grids of galvanized-iron pipe properly perforated. These must be arranged so as to be noiseless in operation and to have sufficient capacity to raise the humidity of the incoming air to such a point as to render possible 70 per cent saturation in air as delivered to room or rooms, if desired.

202. These humidifiers are to be properly hung with iron straps and braces and to be provided with an acceptable hand valve on the steam supply. Each humidifier will also be supplied with an automatic diaphragm valve to conform in all respects with those as furnished with the temperature-regulating system.

203. Carry all high-pressure steam-supply pipes to each humidifier, these pipes to be collected in the basement and connected to the main high-pressure pipe; each separate individual branch as well as the main connection to the high-pressure system of steam-piping to be provided with an independent hand valve so that steam may be

cut off from all or any individual pipe leading to a humidifier; these valves to be placed in the basement as directed and to be in addition to those as called for to be furnished at each fan.

204. OPERATING BOARD.—Furnish and install as directed highly polished Vermont marble board supported on heavy angle-iron frame with acceptable legs.   Attach to board nickel-plated indicating valves connected to individual pipe leads to motor valves operating foul-air outlet dampers; to each individual main air riser in dome; to main outlet from air receiver, and to air pipe controlling steam valve in compressor supplies.

HEATING SYSTEM.

205. GENERAL.—The building shall be warmed throughout by exaust steam from the several engines, pumps, and other steam-actuated apparatus in the power plant, supplementing the system when required by live steam from the boilers fed to the system through pressure-reducing valves and supplied to radiation distributed substantially as shown on the drawings.   The class of radiation to be used shall be direct.   The ventilation will be accomplished by mechanical means and sufficient heated air will be supplied to all rooms, corridors, etc., to maintain with the direct radiation the desired temperature in the building.

206. The piping system, supplying all radiation, to be arranged on what is known as a two-pipe vacuum system, the contractor furnishing and installing all special valves as may be required, together with duplicate equipment of pumps and all the necessary apparatus, regulators, piping, and accessories incident to the convenient and successful operation of such a system as is proposed.   The system to be what is known as a vacuum system of steam heating, in which the air and the water of condensation are together removed from the radiator by connection made at the base and at the opposite end to that of the steam supply.   At each and every outlet shall be attached a polished nickel-plated motor valve specially designed for a system of this character.   This vacuum system to be attached to the steam coils of hot water heating tanks and to the heating coils furnished in connection with the ventilating fans.   All to be arranged throughout so as to prevent short circuiting of any heating surface; to cause an even and continued supply of steam to each individual radiator as installed; to properly and effectively drain all piping and all heating surface, and to entirely relieve engines, pumps, etc., from back pressure.

207. Temperature regulation will be provided as herein specified and be made part of the completed systems of heating and ventilation, all as described.   This contractor must confer with the ventilating contractor on all points where systems overlap and make all arrangements for facilitating the advancement of the work as provided under heading "Other contractors."

208. If the contractor has any special arrangements or any devices for attaching to the complete system of heating or of temperature control as herein provided, by the use of which the arrangement or details as described will in any way be changed, consideration will be given to such, provided in the opinion of the architect such change will benefit and not in any manner impair or otherwise affect the results to be attained or the efficiency of the apparatus or system, in whole or in part, as covered by this specification.

209. HEATING SURFACE.—Building is to be heated throughout from the basement to the sixteenth story, inclusive, and the minimum amount of superficial radiating surface shall be 39,000 square feet, exclusive of all mains and risers, and this amount is deemed sufficient to provide for the building loss from the various stories in the coldest weather, and not less than this amount will be accepted.   The square feet of surface of radiators furnished must be based on the actual heating surface contained in each section.

210. The ventilating contractor installs in connection with the ventilating fans heater coils, tabulation of which is given in this specification, the total square feet of radiating surface in these heaters being 16,600.

211. All radiators for direct service to be either single-column or multiple-column radiation as may be called for on the drawings; to be plain cast iron, steam loops, exclusive of ornamentation, except in certain cases; all as may be approved by the architect.   The height and approximate location of all radiators will be as given on the drawings, and they must be placed as close to walls as piping will permit.

212. The radiating surface will be distributed throughout substantially as shown on the drawings, but it is understood that the architect shall have the right to determine the exact location of any and all mains, risers, or radiators, and that any changes in position shall be made before the work has been installed and are not to be the basis of an extra charge.

213. The bidder must state what kind and make of radiators he proposes to furnish, as quality and style of radiators will be considered in awarding the contract.

214. RADIATOR VALVES.—Wherever radiators are not provided with diaphragm valves furnished in connection with the temperature-regulating system, contractor will furnish heavy brass-bodied "Globe" or "Angle" valves, which shall be rough-bodied, nickel-plated all over. All valves will be provided with wood wheel; "differential" stems; the disks to be renewable and to be either made of asbestus or a special composition similar and equal to the "Jenkins." All motor valves to be brass-bodied, nickel-plated, and polished.

215. The contractor shall furnish the above specified valves for only such radiators as are not controlled by a thermostatic valve, but will attach these latter valves to his radiators. In the basement, where groups of radiators are controlled by diaphragm valves placed in supply mains, each individual radiator shall have its own hand valve for separate control.

216. The following to govern the minimum size of valves allowable for radiators: 1 inch to supply a maximum of 79 square feet; 1¼-inch to supply from 80 to 149 square feet; 1½-inch to supply 150 up to 250 square feet.

217. SUPPLY AND RETURN MAINS.—The drawings in a general way show the distribution of the heating mains in the basement of the building, but their exact location relative to walls and ceilings is not figured, the contractor being required to determine such location so as to admit of draining and expansion, as called for herein, and also to avoid interference with any other work.

218. The riser pipes will be connected to the top of the steam supply mains in the basement and carried to the floor as indicated in the riser diagram; all connections to be made by offsets to allow for expansion. All risers to be located approximately in the positions shown on the drawings, the exact location to be given by the architect in case of any interference with work already in place, or to be placed by others.

219. Each and every riser pipe, whether radiator supply or feed to upper-floor systems, to be provided with a straightway valve placed where connection is made to basement-heating mains. Beyond each valve place a ½-inch brass plug drip cock for draining in addition to the connection to the vacuum return piping.

220. Wherever it is necessary to change the position of these vertical risers on account of varying thickness of wall, or for any other purpose, such as clearing beams, etc., all the offsets must be made by 45-degree angles, the pipes, however, in all cases, being carried as near the walls as practicable.

221. The return or vacuum pipes to be carried back of the radiator in each instance and to drop to basement with the riser pipes, where they shall be collected and run to a main-pump suction header, to which the vacuum pumps are connected.

222. It is the intention to conceal all riser pipes, whether steam or vacuum returns, especially above the second story, and in running these pipes the contractor must keep this point in view, and so arrange pipes as to come within the space allowed. Wherever it is necessary to do any cutting in floors or walls contractor must obtain permission from architect and follow his directions how it shall be done, and in every case the building, in all its parts, is to be left in a condition satisfactory to the architect.

223. All pipes to be so arranged as to admit of a full and free circulation of steam in all radiation throughout the entire building, with a vacuum at the pumps not to exceed 8 inches by gauge.

224. The sizes of all pipes are given on the drawings, and contractor will understand that no pipes of smaller diameter than those specified will be allowed.

225. Suitable provision to be made for the proper draining of all heating mains, branches, and risers. Sediment pockets to be placed at base of all risers and wherever motor valves are installed, the pockets to be arranged so as to permit of easy cleaning.

226. Wherever radiators are called for, the connections for the same throughout to be made above the floor level in raceways, unless otherwise specifically called for herein or shown on the drawings.

227. All radiators to be connected to the risers on the double-pipe system, as required by the special vacuum system herein called for. Should the length of any of these steam-supply pipes to radiator exceed 10 feet, then a pipe one size larger than that as called for by radiator-valve schedule shall be put in.

228. The contractor, in connection with other piping, will be required to furnish all piping, valves, and fittings and make connections to fan coils as furnished by the ventilating contractor, these being located as shown on the drawings. There will be 56 fan coils, each containing 96 1-inch pipes, 6 feet 6 inches high; 12 fan coils, each containing 96 pipes 5 feet high; 8 fan coils, each containing 126 pipes 6 feet 6 inches high; 4 fan coils, each containing 126 pipes, 5 feet high.

229. The pressure-reducing connections, as well as supply-pipe connections to the heating mains, are described under heading of "Power-plant piping."

230. CONNECTION TO HOT-WATER TANKS.—The contractor to make all connections from the steam-heating mains to the steam coil of each of the three hot-water heating tanks, as provided by the plumbing contractor.

231. In each separate steam-supply pipe to tank there will be properly connected an automatic temperature-regulating valve, as provided under "Temperature regulation."

232. Return from each coil in each tank to be carried to a special trap or motor valve provided with a vacuum system of steam heating as called for to be furnished.

POWER-PLANT PIPING.

233. GENERAL.—The steam piping to comprise all high-pressure steam-piping connections through the entire plant; exhaust connections from all steam-actuated apparatus, together with all exhaust connections to low-pressure steam heating mains; all heating mains, risers, returns, and piping connections to direct radiation and to hot-water tanks, and connections to headers of the hot-blast heating coils. It is also to include all valves, fittings, and accessories necessarily involved for the proper and complete finishing and convenient operation of the entire system.

234. This contractor shall furnish all piping, valves, and fittings, and make all connections complete to each and every individual piece of apparatus, whether installed under this contract or provided and installed by others.

235. The system of high-pressure piping is such that the two batteries and two single boilers are connected through extra heavy wrought-iron pipes, bends, and valves, all substantially as shown on the drawings or as described herein.

236. It is contemplated to install three engines in the plant, these being furnished by others and installed on foundations complete with all fittings and attachments, including vertical steam separators; the specifications provide for these engines to be horizontal, cross-compound, noncondensing.

237. A high-pressure hydraulic elevator system is contemplated. With this there will be furnished and installed complete by the elevator contractor a high-duty compound noncondensing three-cylinder pump, together with two auxiliary duplex compound pumps, besides which he installs an air pump. All of the drips from these pumps are provided in elevator contract. This contractor, however, shall make all steam connections and all exhaust connections complete.

238. Contractor shall provide all drip, blow-off, and overflow pipes in connection with the dynamo engines and any and all apparatus as installed by him or to which he may connect, with the exception of the elevator machinery. In this particular piping will be included the connections to the 3-inch water-relief valves attached to each end of each cylinder of the dynamo engines, valves being furnished with the engines; also make connections to air compressors provided under this specification in connection with the temperature regulation. Make connections to boiler feed and to vacuum pumps for both steam and exhaust. Cross-connect steam supply to boiler feed pumps, so that either one or both of the pumps can be used as occasion may require; likewise cross-connect vacuum pumps.

239. HIGH-PRESSURE CONNECTIONS.—Contractor shall connect each of the main 8-inch boiler outlets to the header or headers as shown on the drawings. At each outlet a by-pass gate valve will be placed, and where pipes are connected to the headers an acceptable automatic stop and check valve of the globe pattern shall be placed. All tees used in this work to be double sweep.

240. VALVE AUXILIARY STEAM CONNECTION.—Connections from boilers to headers and from steam outlets to auxiliary header to be made by wrought-iron pipe bends, all substantially as shown on the drawings and as the limited space available will permit.

241. Auxiliary header to be 6 inches diameter. To this connect all steam-supply pipes to boiler-feed pumps, draft-fan engine, and to air compressors of temperature-control system; also cross-connect to 6-inch steam lead to elevator and vacuum pumps, and make connections to 3-inch pressure regulator, as provided under heading "Pressure-reducing connections."

242. Carry this 6-inch steam pipe from boiler header across driveway and over to machinery room in basement of dome for supplying steam to elevator and vacuum pump, and from this main take branches to humidifiers in dome basement and continue as 2-inch pipe to dome, as provided under heading "Miscellaneous connections." This 2-inch pipe to be connected to dome heating supply pipe on the ninth story, through a pressure-reducing valve, as specified herein. Main in boiler room to be cross-connected to auxiliary header.

243. Valve each pipe where leaving boiler room or at header connection, as directed.

244. Connections will be made from the main header to corrugated-copper expansion joint provided with reenforcing rings, and pipe be carried overhead into the engine room, where connection will be made to each of the three direct-connected cross-compound engines by pipes of such size as the engines demand. All of these engine connections to be taken out of the top of the main supply header, led over and down through extra heavy wrought-iron bends, and connect with the flanges of the vertical steam separators as furnished and attached to the automatic stop valves by the engine contractor; these separators are provided with companion flanges. Place valve in main where entering engine room.

245. EXHAUST MAINS.—Provide valve in each exhaust from direct-connected engines. These to be complete, with polished valve stands, as provided under subheading "Valves." These connections all to be made with single-sweep tees to the main exhaust header.

246. The main exhaust pipe to be carried below the engine-room floor line, in trench built by this contractor, out into the boiler room, where pipe will turn west and continue in trench, then run north across the boiler room and make connection to the feed-water heater. This heater to be arranged and suitably valved so as to permit of its being by-passed to atmosphere; use long-sweep ells and double-sweep tees in this piping. Where exhaust is carried along west side of boiler room carry in trench made in elevated portion of room, all as shown.

247. In the atmospheric connection from the heater place double-seated, semi-balanced, horizontal back-pressure valve. This valve to be specially designed for use in connection with the vacuum system of steam heating as herein proposed. This valve to be perfect in operation.

248. CONNECTIONS TO HEATING SYSTEM.—Out of the main engine exhaust header running through the boiler room, make, by double-sweep tees, two 12-inch connections; make expansion connections, valve with globe angles or straightway valves, and carry overhead across the driveway into the main portion of the basement of the building, where connections will be made to the system of piping for heating distribution, all substantially as shown on the drawings or described herein, and as may be approved by the architect.

249. The basement piping for heating system proper is arranged so that the basement first and second stories are supplied from one system of loops. Each wing has its own independent loop, from which risers are run to supply all stories above the second. All court rooms are on separable leads taken from the wing loops, all substantially as shown on the drawings.

250. Each main, submain, and branch to be valved so as to permit of any single loop or branch to be cut out of service if required. The main risers to court rooms to be valved in eighth story, near fan coils, in addition to basement valve, as will also the main running to the ninth-story machinery room.

251. The riser diagram clearly shows the size, number, and location of each individual riser pipe in the building.

252. The hot-blast heater coils to be fed from the mains in the basement of dome. Connections to be taken out of bottom of pipe, if headroom permits, and carried over and down to connection with headers of coils, which headers are provided ready for attaching by the ventilating contractor. Each row of coils to be provided with special trap or motor valve to permit of thorough and positive draining; these valves or traps to be connected to and be part of the vacuum system.

253. Run riser to ninth story for supplying fan heater coils of ventilating system. Make same connections to these coils as herein provided for other similar heaters, and extend risers, as shown, for supplying steam to all radiation placed in dome stories.

254. ATMOSPHERIC EXHAUST.—Atmospheric exhaust to be carried from boiler room up to and above roof and fitted with exhaust head hereinafter provided. Pipe to be flanged, spiral-riveted, galvanized iron of proper gauge; to be supported at bottom and arranged for free upward expansion, being supported at intervals by bands loosely clamped around pipe below 2 by 2 inch angles which are to be riveted to the pipe.

255. WATER CONNECTIONS.—Contractor shall furnish and install all water piping in connection with the heater and boiler feed pumps. These pumps to be cross-connected on their 5-inch suctions, connections being so made that either pump or both may take supply from header provided by plumbing contractor and installed in the boiler or engine room, being arranged so that this contractor may make his connections thereto. In addition, connection will be made to the 4-inch deep-well water-supply pipe, which another contractor brings from the surge tank into the engine or boiler room. Connection to be made to the outlet of the feed-water heater, all

arranged so as to permit of water being furnished to either or both of the pumps from any of these three sources, independently of the other.

256. Horizontal swing check valves to be placed in each pump suction, as well as in each of the pipes from the three sources of supply.

257. The 6-inch boiler feed-pump discharges to be cross-connected so that either one or both pumps may be used as may be desired, horizontal swing check valves being placed in each pump discharge, as well as in the main feed line to the boilers. This feed header to run along the top of the boilers toward the front end and be connected through individual check and valve to the brass piping furnished with the boilers. These connections to be made at the top of boilers, all as may be directed, the valves being furnished with extension stems, so as to permit of being operated from the floor level.

258. Connect to the city main a 1½-inch pipe, which will be carried along the entire length of the boiler room above and toward the front of the boiler. Make three connections to this piping, one between each of the boiler settings, this pipe in each case to be carried down to within approximately 3 feet from the floor line and there fitted with a ¾-inch gate-valve hose bib fitted with tee handle.

259. Make all required suction and discharge connections for vacuum pumps.

260. Connect city pressure main to the automatic intake valve of feed-water heater with pipe of size as called for by heater valve.

261. BLOW-OFFS AND DRIPS.—The blow-offs from the boilers will be run as called for herein and as shown on the drawings, the main blow-off pipe being carried in a trench at the rear of the boilers over to and connecting with the catch basin located in the boiler room. Use long sweep fittings for all of this piping.

262. The overflow from the feed-water heater will be carried to the catch basin in the boiler room, pipe to run in trench as elsewhere provided.

263. All drips from the two boiler feed pumps to be collected and carried to the catch-basin in the boiler room.

264. From the three engines and from the air compressors of temperature-regulating system, drips to be collected and run to the catch-basin located in the engine room.

265. Drips from the three vertical steam separators furnished by the engine contractor and attached to engine throttles to be run to and connected, in each instance, with "differential" traps, as hereinafter provided, the discharge of each trap to be connected into a main 1½-inch pipe, which will be carried back to and connected with the top of the feed-water heater and to a 1¼-inch pipe leading directly to sewer. This 1½-inch heater connection also being by-passed to the catch basin in the boiler room. Connect up in similar manner the drips from the steam separators furnished by the engine contractor for reheater-coil connections; these drips to be carried in each instance to and connected with the drips from throttle steam separators with by-pass to 1½-inch sewer main.

266. Provide similar drips to all other steam separators throughout plant, these to be connected in like manner to same style of traps and arranged to discharge back to feed-water heater and by-passed to the nearest catch basin.

267. Connect up "differential" traps furnished by engine contractor, one for reheater coil and one for receiver of each engine. Those for receiver to be arranged to discharge directly into the sewer; those for reheating coil to discharge into main pipe leading to heater and also to 1½-inch sewer main.

268. Drips from all oil separators to be run to and connected, in each instance, with a pot trap, these traps discharging directly to the nearest catch basin. In drip to these traps place tee between check and separator for connection to small vacuum pump hereinafter provided.

269. If necessary to prevent dripping, contractor will tap automatic stop and check valves in the high-pressure boiler piping in such a manner as to permit of their being properly drained. All to be suitably valved.

270. In each and every individual drip and in all individual discharges from the traps to heater or sewer mains contractor shall place horizontal swing check valves, and in all of the piping provide suitable straightway valves.

271. In each drip from steam separators place a tee between the drip connection and the check; to this tee make connection to the gravity return system. All to be suitably valved and arranged so as to permit of traps caring for separators or for the gravity system to take drips, as desired.

272. On each engine engine contractor will provide special 3-inch automatic water-relief valves. This contractor connects these from each cylinder and carries same to a 6-inch pipe running in trench to the nearest catch basin, as elsewhere provided.

273. The main high-pressure header to be dripped at each end in the boiler room by 1¼-inch pipes which connect with a 1¼-inch header carried beneath the main header. At each boiler make connection to 1¼-inch drip header and carry 1¼-inch pipe back to and connect with mud drum of boiler; in each connection to mud drum place check and hand valves. No other valves to be connected to any of this header drip piping.

274. MISCELLANEOUS CONNECTIONS.—Contractors shall connect all gauges, water columns, and other boiler appliances which he provides. He will also make connection to auxiliary header as required for steam-piping connections to soot blower; pipe to be brought down in each case between each of the boiler settings. Provide hose connection and suitable valve.

275. The pop safety-valve outlets to be connected to a header with area 100 per cent in excess of area of valve outlets on four of the boilers. This pipe to be run over and connected into the main atmospheric exhaust pipe by a single-sweep tee placed above the back-pressure valve. In this main relief pipe there will be connected a safety valve opening directly into the boiler room, this valve having an area equal to twice the area of any one pop valve and will be set so as to open up wide should the pressure in the atmospheric pipe equal or exceed 5 pounds.

276. For admitting steam to down spouts to prevent freezing of same, the contractor shall tap into ells of each and every down spout in the basement for a 1-inch pipe. Where pipe connection is made into down spout, there will be provided a set-up nut with rainbow packing. After entering ell, the pipe will extend up vertically at least 18 inches.

277. There are sixteen down spouts from the main roofs of the building, these being 8-inch wrought-iron pipes. In addition there will also be four at each of the skylights above the second-story portions, these down spouts being 6 inches in diameter. There will also be one 4-inch down spout at each entrance, making a total of 36.

278. Carry a 2-inch high-pressure steam pipe from main in basement of dome to the ninth story, leave tee for connection to humidifiers for dome and for courtroom fans. At ninth floor run 1¼-inch pipes to each wing, carrying same in attic spaces above eighth story. These branches to extend to the farthest point of skylight and there, as well as at inner end of skylight, branch each way and carry through to outside of building, where ends will be fitted with ¾-inch hose-bib connections. Place valve on ninth story in each of the four pipes and one in each of the branches to outside of building. From this 2-inch riser make connection at ceiling of second story and run to each of the four skylights over the two-story postoffice portions, and at each point carry up pipes at north and south ends and run outside of skylights; valve each main leading to the four points and also valve each pipe leading to outside of building; outside ends of pipes to be fitted with ¾-inch hose-bib connections. Make all valves in all of this piping readily accessible by hand or provide with extension stems where necessary.

279. Make all connections to air tank furnished with the oiling system carrying a 1¼-inch galvanized-iron pipe into the main engine room and making connections on the west wall to points opposite each generator. Also carry 1¼-inch galvanized-iron pipe over to machinery room in the basement of the dome, where pipe will branch to outlets on north and south sides. At all of these points pipes to be fitted with ¾-inch hose bibs of the same type as hereinbefore provided.

280. Make all connections to reheater coils in receivers of all engines and to main elevator pumping engine.

281. Tap feed-water heater or make such connection as may be necessary to receive the discharge from steam traps, draining steam separators. Also tap feed-water heater for return of discharge from vacuum pumps of the heating system.

282. Contractor shall furnish and install one acceptable 2-inch steam siphon, this to be complete with all piping connections, valves, fittings, etc., and to be placed in the bilge-pump catch-basin to boiler room, the discharge being carried to sewer as may be directed.

283. The drip from the main exhaust head to be carried down and connected to sewer at the nearest point in the boiler room.

284. Make steam and exhaust connections to draft-fan engine.

285. Connect discharge from vacuum pumps to heater in boiler room. Also connect vacuum suction to heater through motor valve.

286. For positive draining of oil separators provide small vacuum pump of same make as furnished with the heating system and connect pump suction to the drip of each oil separator between outlet and check. Place this pump in engine room in location as directed. Arrange for discharge to be carried directly to nearest catch-

basin. The steam and exhaust connections to this pump to be properly made with exhaust made common with that from air pumps of temperature-control system.

287. Place in main boiler feed, as directed, a 6-inch water relief valve similar and equal to the "Crosby."

288. The sizes of all pipes where possible, especially in connection with heating-system supplies, are given on the drawings, and the contractor will understand that no pipes of smaller diameter than those as specified will be allowed. Where sizes are not given and where connection is made to apparatus, etc., furnished by other contractors, all piping to be of such size as called for by the type and design of apparatus selected by the architect. Return piping to be proportioned by the contractor, who shall submit a schedule to the architect for approval before work is begun.

289. All heating mains, branches, risers, etc., to be so arranged as to permit of a full and free circulation of steam throughout the entire building, so that in the entire system a complete, uniform, continuous, and noiseless circulation of steam will be established throughout the mains, branches, etc., to each and every radiator, stack, or coil, with steam at atmospheric pressure, and that at such pressure such radiation will be thoroughly heated in all its parts. The circulation must be completed fully and freely, without any parts of the piping or apparatus filling with water, and without hammering or surging.

290. All piping throughout the entire plant to be arranged to permit of free expansion without straining joints or fittings, and to be put up so as to be free from any undue vibration.

291. GRAVITY RETURN SYSTEM.—For draining certain portions of the system of piping and insuring the return of condensation to the boilers, contractor shall provide a gravity return system similar to that known as the "Holly." One system to be installed to drain the high-pressure headers and supply piping, as well as the steam separators provided in this contract or as furnished and installed by others. This system to be complete in every essential particular, and installed with all piping, valves, fittings, and accessories incident to its convenient and successful operation.

292. PIPE.—All high-pressure steam piping, and all water piping in connection with the boilers, throughout the entire plant, to be "standard," full-weight, wrought-iron, lap-welded pipe.

293. All exhaust piping, excepting that below engine and boiler room floors, and all heating mains, risers, and radiator connections, together with all drips, blow-offs, etc., to be "standard," full-weight, wrought-iron, lap-welded pipe.

294. All pipe furnished throughout to be round, straight, and true to size, free from weld flaws and all other defects; to be full weight, a variation of not over 2 per cent being allowed in any of this pipe. All wrought-iron pipe to be taper-threaded in accordance with dimensions and proportions as formally adopted by the manufacturers of wrought-iron pipe and boiler tubes. All of these threads to be neatly, cleanly, and evenly cut.

295. All pipe work throughout the entire plant 3 inches and over to be flanged. All other to be screwed, providing, however, in such screwed piping a sufficient number of flanged unions, especially next to valves, to permit of taking down piping without disturbing long runs.

296. The cast-iron exhaust connections from dynamo engines and the main 24-inch exhaust under floor and running over to heater to be of standard dimensions for 50 pounds' pressure, as adopted by the United States Cast-Iron Pipe and Foundry Company.

297. All piping used for returns in connection with the vacuum system to be made with graphite joints. All of the pipe used in this vacuum system to be carefully reamed. All to be perfectly air-tight throughout the entire system.

298. FITTINGS.—All flanges, elbows, tees, and special fittings of any sort used on any of the high-pressure piping, steam or water, throughout the entire plant to be "extra heavy." These same fittings, where used on any other piping throughout the plant, whether for exhaust, steam mains or risers, or for water piping, to be what are known as "standard" fittings. All fittings of every sort and description to be drilled in accordance with the following:

299. For extra heavy, unless otherwise called for by flanges on apparatus furnished by others, drilling to be in accordance with the "Manufacturers' standard" adopted July 25, 1901. Drilling for standard flanges to be in accordance with "Crane" drilling, May, 1901.

300. All flanged fittings to be straight-faced.

301. All flanges on all the high-pressure steam piping, or water piping in connection with the boilers, and in boiler blow-off piping, up to the second blow-off valve,

to be screwed into the pipe so as to have an absolutely tight joint, hen the pipe, in every such instance, to be placed in a lathe and flanges and pipe end faced off.   For all exhaust piping, steam-heating mains, and supply pipes no lathe work will be required; flanges, however, to be faced and ends of pipe to come flush in all instances with the flange; in no case to project.

302. In all flanged work square-headed bolts will be used.   Bolts, but not heads, to be finished and furnished with hexagonal nuts.

303. Throughout the entire work contractor shall avoid the use of all fittings or connections which will admit of any lodgment of water, using eccentric fittings, especially in the heating mains wherever the sizes of horizontal pipes are decreased.

304. VALVES.—All valves of every sort and description used on high-pressure steam work or in boiler-feed piping, as well as in boiler blow-off piping, to be "extra heavy" pattern.   With the exception of the automatic stop and check valves in boiler connections to headers, all valves above 2½ inches to be bronze-mounted gate valves, to be outside yoke, rising-stem pattern.

305. All valves up to and including 2½ inches to be bronze-bodied gate valves, with the exception of boiler blow-off valves, which will be bronze-mounted plug valves, similar and equal to those known as the "Cadman."

306. All valves 6 inches and over to be by-passed, with the exception of those used with the pressure-reducing valves.

307. Globe valves will be allowed on steam supply pipes to air compressors of temperature-regulating and oiling systems; to steam siphon and to all small steam-actuated apparatus.   These valves to be of a very heavy pattern and to be equal to those called for in connection with radiators.

308. Valves used in exhaust piping to be standard gate valves of the rising-stem pattern.   Valves in each of the dynamo engine exhausts to be provided with polished floor stands of neat design; these stands to be securely fastened in position.

309. All valves throughout the steam-heating system, unless otherwise specifically stated to the contrary, to be double-gate valves.   Angle globe valves will be considered where connections are made to hot-blast coils if the limited space available will not permit of the use of gates.

310. Provide back-pressure and pressure-reducing valves as called for under heading "Pressure-reducing connections."

311. All check valves used to be brass-bodied horizontal swing checks up to and including 2½ inches; above this size bodies of valves to be iron.

312. Only the best valves of any style called for herein will be considered, and all must be acceptable to the architect.

313. PRESSURE-REDUCING CONNECTIONS.—From the main high-pressure header in the boiler room carry 6-inch pipe to a 6 by 12 inch special vacuum pressure-regulating valve, connecting the 12-inch outlet to the two 12-inch supply pipes leading from the boiler room to the system of heating mains in the basement of the building.   Connect the 6-inch auxiliary header by 3-inch pipe to a 3 by 6 inch pressure-reducing valve, the outlet of which will be connected in like manner to the two 12-inch heating supply mains.

314. Also connect a second 3 by 6 inch pressure-reducing valve to the main steam supply pipe carried over for furnishing steam to the elevator pumps in the machinery room in the basement of the dome.   The outlet of this valve to be connected to the inner loop or that portion from which supplies are led to hot-blast heating coils.

315. Connect to the 2-inch high-pressure main provided under "Miscellaneous connections," to be run to the ninth story, a 2 by 4 inch reducing valve; to 4-inch outlet of this valve, connect the system of heating mains on the ninth story, from which supplies are taken for all dome floors above.

316. On either side of pressure-regulating valves, herein called for, will be placed straightway valves.   Regulators will also be by-passed as follows: 2-inch regulators, 1½-inch pipe; 3-inch regulators, 2-inch pipe; 6-inch regulators, 3-inch pipe.

317. In each by-pass place straightway valve.

318. These pressure-reducing valves to be special vacuum pressure-regulating valves constructed especially to meet the requirements of the heating system, and to have the sensitiveness necessary to respond to the slightest fluctuation in pressure, and to be provided with an independent diaphragm to which is connected the actuating pressure; the pressure governing the operation of each valve to be taken from the low-pressure heating main at some distance from the valve itself and at any suitable point desired.

319. THIMBLES AND PIPE SLEEVES.—All places where any of the heating pipes or vacuum returns pass through floors, ceilings, or walls, same shall be fitted with approved cast-iron insulating thimbles.   These thimbles to have a diameter ½ inch greater than the pipe so as to leave a ¼-inch space all around.   Where any of the

risers or radiator supplies, including all returns, pass through floors, ceilings, or walls, they shall be provided with plates secured in place. These plates to be nickel-plated and polished.

320. All of these thimbles to be independent of and free from pipe, so as to admit of free contraction and expansion in the steam pipe without injury to the plaster or other finish. Where any other pipes pass through floors, ceilings, partitions, walls, or masonry work of any sort or description, suitable and acceptable pipe sleeves will be provided and installed, these to be made of standard wrought-iron pipe or split castings, as the finish of the building may call for.

FILTER.

321. Contractor shall furnish and install complete one 6-inch filter, similar and equal in all respects to that known as the "Ross;" filter to be complete with gauges, one spare internal chamber, and four linen cylinders. Filter to be tested under a pressure of 500 pounds before shipment.

322. Filter to be set upon substantial supporting legs. To be connected on the discharge side of the boiler feed pumps and arranged to be by-passed so that either pump may discharge through the filter or that one may discharge in this manner and the other direct to the boilers, should occasion require.

VACUUM PUMPS.

323. There shall be three main vacuum pumps furnished in connection with the system of steam heating herein called for. All of the pumps to be of the same size. Two of the pumps to be of ample capacity to care for the entire amount of radiation as installed throughout the building. The third pump to be used as a relay. Pumps to be single-cylinder, double-acting pattern, provided with balanced piston type valves, valves being actuated directly by the steam pressure, and not through any intermediate valve gear. Pumps to have large water spaces and valve areas; water ends to be bronze-fitted throughout with composition piston rods. Pumps to be able to care for water of condensation and to maintain the required vacuum when running at a speed not to exceed 100 feet per minute. Pumps to be complete with strainers, automatic governors, and condenser heads.

324. All pumps to be connected to one main vacuum return header, into which are brought all of the returns from the vacuum system.

325. The foundations for vacuum pumps in basement of dome to be concrete, and to be raised above the floor line 12 inches. Finish with a coating of neat cement.

326. HANGERS AND SUPPORTS.—All piping throughout the plant to be substantially supported either by pipe hangers or floor stands or, in case of pipes carried in trenches, on acceptable roller bearings.

327. The high-pressure steam header in the boiler room, together with all connections, auxiliary header, cross connections, and heating mains, to be supported with adjustable ball and socket pipe hangers of approved make. This also applies to all other pipes carried across the boiler room and to the boiler feed piping; expansion pipe hangers being sufficient in number and so disposed as to relieve the strain on any joints in any portion of this piping.

328. The main steam supply pipe in the engine room to be supported in a manner similar to the main steam header in the boiler room.

329. All pipes, whether live steam or exhaust, carried across the driveway will hug the ceiling of driveway as closely as possible, allowing only sufficient room for covering; the hangers on these pipes to be placed near the ends so as not to, in any case, take up more of the small available headroom than absolutely required.

330. Where these pipes enter basement of building to the east of driveway, they will be supported in a similar manner to piping in boiler room, as will also all of the heating and distributing mains throughout the entire basement of the building.

331. All pipes carried in trenches, either in the engine room, boiler room, or basement of the main building, to be supported on acceptable roller bearings, such bearings being spaced to suit, but not over 8 feet center to center, dependent upon the size of pipes to be supported.

332. Where the main exhaust pipe rises in the engine room at the northwest corner and connection is made to the heater, pipe will be supported with a rigid adjustable pipe stand with semicircular yoke, all to be of type acceptable to the architect.

333. These same stands will be used for supporting a considerable portion of the piping in the machinery room in the basement of the dome, especially the two systems of loops for the heating system and the high-pressure steam connections, feeding elevator pumps. Similar pipe stands will also be installed at the base of bracketed ell supporting main exhaust pipe leading to atmosphere, also at base of all pipes

whether live steam or heating mains that are carried from the basement to court-room heating plants or to ninth floor in dome; all of these pipes being fitted at the base with bracketed elbows. Also place such stands at any other points where it is necessary or deemed advisable by the architect.

334. All other steam, water, air, or oil piping in any portion of the engine or boiler rooms, in the basement of building, or in any of the floors above to be supported by adjustable expansion pipe hangers of design as herein called for.

335. All pipe hangers, where possible, to be clamped to the floor I beams, but wherever pipes are supported in this manner there will be placed between pipe and the hanger some suitable and acceptable incombustible material for the purpose of avoiding, as far as possible, the transmission of sound from pipes to structure.

336. All riser pipes for heating system to be supported and firmly anchored in position at some point in the basement, and, if necessary, to be supported near the middle of their length so as to prevent, as far as possible, any vibration, and at the same time allow a free vertical expansion from the point of support. Allowance for expansion of all vertical pipes must be made in connections leading to radiators, while that for basement mains shall be made where connected to risers.

337. Piping will be anchored at such points as may be deemed necessary by the architect.

338. Any water pipes or small steam pipes, where carried along the walls, may be held in position by acceptable pipe hooks.

339. All supports of whatever kind to present a neat and finished appearance when in position.

340. Contractor will arrange all pipe hangers, supports, and anchorages so as to prevent any vibration in the system of piping as designed, this specification providing for the furnishing and installing of pipe bends, expansion joints, and expansion connections so as to prevent any undue strains being thrown upon any of the piping or joints throughout the entire system.

341. ADJUSTMENT OF VALVES.—After the completion of his work the contractor will be required to adjust all automatic valves of every description that may be furnished under this contract. He shall pack all stems in valves throughout the entire plant and leave this entire work in complete adjustment in every particular ready for service.

342. Contractor shall thoroughly clean, from time to time, all valves, traps, or accessories used in connection with the vacuum system of steam heating, and keep these clean from dirt and grit. After the system is thoroughly cleaned, all of these valves will be properly adjusted.

343. Every valve on pipes leaving boiler or engine rooms, together with all valves in the basement of the building, which are placed in distributing mains, branches, and in independent risers leading to heating apparatus on the eighth story and on the ninth story, as well as such pipes as leave ninth story high-pressure main, to be tagged. These tags to be made of heavy brass, at least 2 inches in diameter. Each tag to be attached to its respective valve in an acceptable manner and stamped to sufficiently indicate what portion of the system is controlled by such valve.

TRAPS, SEPARATORS, FILTERS, ETC.

344. STEAM TRAPS.—All differential steam traps provided for in this specification to be of the "differential" pattern similar and equal in all respects to those known as the "Flinn." These to be provided with gauge glass, to be suitable for a pressure of 150 pounds, and each to be of capacity sufficient for draining 7,000 lineal feet of 1-inch pipe. The pot traps called for herein to be similar and equal to the "Acme," each to be of sufficient size to drain 7,000 lineal feet of 1-inch pipe.

345. Each discharge of each separate trap to be fitted with a horizontal swing check valve, and each individual trap to be by-passed so as to discharge directly to the sewer.

346. OIL FILTER.—Contractor shall furnish and install on suitable and substantial I-beam supports one rectangular oil filter of approved design. Filter to have three sections, with five filtering beds and two steam coils; to have a capacity of filtering 75 gallons of oil in twenty-four hours. Filter to be complete with thermometer, gauge glasses, draw-off cocks, and all connections complete. All piping connections to be made and filter arranged to drain into one of the small tanks used in connection with the pressure oiling system; location of filter to be determined upon when all apparatus is selected and contracts awarded.

347. All of this piping to be complete with horizontal swing check valves. All piping to be suitably valved to permit of connections to oiling system described hereafter.

348. EXHAUST HEAD.—Furnish and install exhaust head in the main atmospheric exhaust. Head to be of size as called for on the drawings, to be placed above the roof in location as shown, and to be of design acceptable to the architect.

349. STEAM AND OIL SEPARATORS.—The contractor shall furnish and install complete, in location as indicated on the drawings, or as determined by the architect, during the progress of the work, steam and oil separators, as follows:

350. Vertical pattern steam separator arranged for bolting directly to the chronometer valve flange on high-duty elevator pump.

351. Horizontal type steam separators, one in each of the main exhausts from engine units; one in main exhaust from boiler feed pumps; one in exhaust of main elevator pumping engine, and one in the exhaust of elevator auxiliary pumps.

352. These separators each to be provided with automatic self-closing water-gauge cocks.

353. Steam separators to be fitted with "extra heavy" wedge gate, brass angle valves; oil separators with standard brass-bodied straightway valves.

354. Steam separator flanges and rims to be polished.

355. All separators to be in every essential particular similar and equal to those known as "zigzag."

356. The engine contractor furnishes steam separators bolted to engine throttles. He also furnishes steam separator in the supply pipe to each reheating coil. All of these separators being complete with companion flanges.

357. DRAFT GAUGE.—Contractor to furnish and install upon slate back, as a permanent fixture, an approved differential draft gauge, similar and equal to that known as the "Eames 1900 model." Gauge to be mounted in boiler room as may be directed, and all piping connections made by individual ⅜-inch pipes from a header to the breeching at connection of each boiler and to each boiler ash pit; to suction chamber of draft fan, and to each chimney base. Each of these separate pipes to be valved at header with nickel-plated cock. The pipe header to be nickel-plated and mounted on same slate back as the gauge.

OIL AND WASTE CANS.

358. Contractor to furnish two acceptable oil-storage cans, one for cylinder oil and the other for engine oil. Furnish two hand pumps with these cans.

359. Also provide four acceptable galvanized-iron cans for waste. Two to be placed in main engine room and two in machinery room in basement of dome.

OILING SYSTEM.

360. The engine contractor provides with his engines "pressure" oil cups in addition to the cylinder lubricators.

361. This contractor will furnish and connect to these cups the complete system of piping for a pressure oiling system in connection with the engines.

362. All piping to be run in trenches, and to be standard black iron, but where carried above the floor line all piping about the engines to be polished brass. All connections to the pressure oil cups to be made with ⅜-inch polished brass tubing. All of this piping to be run as may be directed by the engine company's superintendent in charge of erecting the engines, but subject to the approval of the architect.

363. The system to be complete in all particulars; contractor furnishing tanks, as provided herein, with all pipe connections, checks, valves, and fittings. System to be complete in every essential detail, ready for operation.

364. In connection with the oiling system, provide and install complete in all particulars standard pattern air pump, complete with gauge and governor. With this pump will be furnished one tank 24 inches in diameter and 5 feet long. Also two smaller tanks 18 inches in diameter and 3 feet long. These tanks for air and oil, respectively. To tanks will be connected a complete system of air piping and the oil piping to and connecting with the pressure oil cups on engines, as provided herein. Also provide small tank into which drip engine oil reservoirs and connect to system as directed.

365. The contractor will make all steam and exhaust connections to the air pump, and will so adjust governor as to maintain a pressure of approximately 20 pounds air pressure in the large receiver.

GAUGE BOARD AND GAUGES.

366. In addition to all of the material, apparatus, and fittings as provided in this specification, contractor shall furnish and install a highly polished gray Vermont-

marble gauge board, upon which will be mounted and connected the following gauges, all provided with nickel-plated deep cases and back connections.

367. The board to be rectangular, with beveled edges, and to be of such size as not to crowd the instruments, which will be arranged so as to permit of a wide border around the entire tablet. The board to be placed in the engine room, either in the chief engineer's office or at some convenient point to be determined upon later.

368. Contractor shall furnish and attach to this board, complete with all connections, drips, valves, etc., ready for service, the following gauges of the best quality and highest standard of the manufacturer, and of make acceptable to the architect.

One 300-pound pressure recorder and gauge, 6¾-inch dial, connected in the main high-pressure steam header in the boiler room; with this recorder a complete set of charts to be furnished.

Two combined pressure and vacuum gauges, 6¾-inch dial; these to be connected respectively to the main return header of the vacuum system, from which vacuum pumps take their suction, and to exhaust header in the engine room.

Three 60-pound low-pressure gauges, 6¾-inch dial; these to be connected respectively to each engine receiver.

One draft recorder to be connected to the draft-fan suction chamber; with this recorder a complete set of charts to be furnished.

One 40-pound low-pressure gauge for indicating air pressure on oiling system.

369. All gauges to be so connected that they may indicate the true pressure unaffected by any water column.

370. Connect also to this board the extra gauge as provided to be furnished with the air receiver of temperature-regulating system.

371. Furnish and attach three special nickel-plated sight-feed attachments, of same design as provided with the engine-cylinder lubricating pump. One of these to be connected in series with the piping from pump to head end of each high-pressure cylinder. This contractor to make all piping connections between engines and board. Below each sight feed attach to tablet nickel-plated name plate, with engine number stamped thereon.

372. The exact arrangement of gauges upon the tablets will be made by the architect before the work is commenced, the contractor, however, to submit a dimensioned drawing of the gauge board with gauges, etc., located thereon.

373. In mounting the tablet same will be bolted with polished nickel-plated acorn nuts to iron brackets, which will hold the board approximately 10 inches from the wall. The design of these brackets to be acceptable to the architect.

374. Furnish and mount on polished gray Vermont-marble tablet the gauges to be provided with the vacuum system. This board to be mounted on angle-iron frame with supporting legs, or attached to column or wall in close proximity to the vacuum pumps, as may be directed. Gauges to have nickel-plated cases and back connections. All gauges furnished for any portion of the plant, with exception of boiler gauge, to have black face with white figures, and to be engraved to indicate to what portion of the system attached. Also engrave name of building as directed by the architect.

CABINET FOR TOOLS.

375. This contractor shall furnish and install in suitable location in engine or boiler room, as may be determined upon by the architect, a properly constructed cabinet made of finished quarter-sawed white oak. This cabinet to be complete with paneled doors, hinges, lock, and keys. This cabinet to be arranged with suitable hooks, brackets, or holders for holding all wrenches furnished with the boilers, engines, economizer, and other wrenches or tools of any sort or description furnished under this contract or needed in the proper and convenient operation of the plant.

376. In the upper portion of the cabinet will be a shelf suitably arranged for indicator boxes, reducing motions, etc.

FOUNDATIONS, SCAFFOLDING, TRENCHES, ETC.

377. FOUNDATIONS.—Contractor will furnish all foundations for the reception of all of his apparatus. He will do all excavating and refilling and remove from the premises all surplus material and débris, such as may have accumulated on account of this foundation work or any other work caused by his contract. He will be required to remove earth and débris at such times and in such a manner as may be directed by the architect.

378. All concrete to be made of 1 part American Portland cement, 3 parts clean, sharp, torpedo sand, and five parts good crushed limestone or broken cobblestones,

the largest sized stone being such as will pass through a 2-inch ring; the smallest being that which will pass through a ½-inch ring. All to be clean and free from loam or dust.

379. All concrete foundations above the floor line to be finished with a coating of neat cement. All brick piers or foundations as called for to be built above the floor level to be of hard-burned brick laid in American Portland cement mortar; to be faced with red pressed brick laid up in red cement mortar, unless provided in the body of the specifications to be faced with white enameled tile or brick, all as may be acceptable to the architect.

380. SCAFFOLDING.—In addition to foundation work, the contractor will be required to provide all scaffolding necessary in the execution of all parts of his work; he shall maintain scaffolding and all requisite guards for the protection of his work and the safety of the premises, and remove same upon completion of the work for which they were used, when so instructed by the architect. Scaffolding must be arranged so as not to interfere with work of other contractors.

381. TRENCHES.—Contractor to build all trenches for such pipes as are to be run below the floor line, these to be of dimensions shown on the drawings, and where no dimensions are given to be made of suitable size, the width approximately twice the diameter of pipe, and depth 25 per cent greater than width.

382. In the main engine room the engine exhaust pipes, as well as all of the trap discharges and drip pipes from engines and other apparatus, to be carried below the floor.

383. In the boiler room the blow-off pipes will be carried in trenches at the rear of the boilers, substantially as shown on the drawings. The overflow and blow-off from heater, also drips from boiler-feed pumps and drips or drains from other apparatus, to be below the floor line.

384. Provide in machinery room in basement of dome portion of the building trenches for carrying exhaust pipes from the main high-duty elevator pumping engine.

385. Wherever throughout the entire basement of the building it is necessary or required to run vacuum returns below the floor line, provide trenches as called for herein.

386. Contractor to do all excavating, refilling, and remove all surplus material. Trench walls to be built of 8 inches of concrete with 6-inch bottoms. The bottom to be V-shaped, and each trench to be pitched toward one point and there properly connected to the sewer.

387. Provide trench along portion of west side of boiler room for carrying main exhaust pipe; this to be in the ledge or raised portion, substantially as shown on the drawings.

388. For all trenches provide angle-iron edges arranged for carrying or holding covers; these angles to be securely anchored into the concrete flooring.

389. TRENCH COVERS AND FLOOR PLATES.—Contractor shall provide all trenches in the engine room and in the boiler room for carrying exhaust pipes, drips, trap discharges, sewer connections, boiler blow-offs, etc., all as provided for herein. All trenches and in all spaces of engine room between cylinders of each engine and about the receivers contractor shall cover with ⅜-inch wrought-iron "Diamond Pattern" floor plates. Provide same type covers for all trenches in which pipes are carried in the machinery room in the basement of the dome.

ALTERNATE BIDS FOR STOKERS.

390. Alternate propositions will be received for automatic stoking devices in lieu of furnaces as herein provided for the boiler plant. In making his proposition the bidder will understand these are to replace the special furnaces as called for in the body of these specifications, his proposition to include the furnishing and delivering of stokers complete in every essential particular with all fittings, attachments, and accessories incident to the convenient and successful operation of the same. The whole to be installed complete and ready for firing.

391. If such devices are selected by the Department the contractor will be required to make all steam and exhaust connections, such as may be necessary for driving engines, connections to be made as required by the architect.

392. If traveling grates are proposed, arches must be 48 inches deep. The rails must be properly arranged and fitted where running through cast-tile floor and crossing cast-plate ash-car track. The concrete ash pits extending in front of boilers to be at least 24 inches deep, walls 12 inches, bottom 8 inches, and be covered with acceptable cast plates or stamped steel, made up in sections and arranged for convenient handling.

393. In submitting his proposition on automatic stokers the bidder will hold himself ready to submit full and complete specifications and drawings of his device.

394. In the bidder's proposition he guarantees that neither the output or efficiency of the boiler of type as called for herein, to which his device is attached, will in any wise be decreased, and that the device will not interfere with the accessibility of any part of the boiler; that by the use of the device, as proposed, the life of the boilers will not be endangered, and that its use will rather facilitate firing than otherwise.

395. It is further understood that the bidder, in making his proposition, guarantees to prevent at least 90 per cent of the smoke, as determined by chart measurements in a manner as prescribed by the code adopted by the American Society of Mechanical Engineers, when the boilers are operated under normal working conditions of 300 centennial horsepower each, or with output of 375 horsepower; and that when devices are in operation the apparatus will demand no special attention from the fireman or engineer; that they will be entirely automatic after once being adjusted, and, further, that no adjustment will be necessary or required should the demands on boiler or boilers be varied from one-half rating up to 25 per cent overrating, excepting such changes as may be made in the speed of the feeding mechanism.

396. The contractor further guarantees that the workmanship and material throughout shall be of the best of its respective kind that can be obtained, and he guarantees to replace and to make good any part of the entire apparatus which may prove defective within two years from date of final acceptance of the work by the architect.

397. The unit price to be given on schedule sheets to include the complete apparatus with all masonry work, concrete ash pits, special tile, tile arches, duplicate driving-engine equipment, shafting, etc.

ALTERNATE BIDS FOR HOT-WATER HEATING.

398. Alternate propositions will be considered for the heating of the entire building with a forced circulation of hot water.

399. Bidders desiring to make proposals covering such a system will provide for increasing the entire amount of radiation throughout the building to an extent of 50 per cent in excess of that provided in the body of these specifications. They shall also include duplicate pumping plant, together with all appurtenances of every sort and description that may be required or deemed necessary by the architect for the proper and convenient operation and control of their system.

400. In making his proposition the bidder must include the furnishing and installing, complete in every essential particular, all the hot-blast heating coils to be used in connection with the ventilating system. Provision is now made for the furnishing of these coils by the ventilating contractor, who also furnishes the necessary steel-plate casings for same. The size of casing will require to be increased to accommodate the added amount of radiating surface incident to the hot-water system, and the bidder must include not only sufficient radiating surface in hot-blast coils to give equivalent results to those called for, but will also provide for the increased amount of casing and any other labor or material that may be involved in this portion of the work.

401. The bidder's attention is called to the present arrangement of steam mains, whereby divisions are made providing for several separate and distinct circulating systems, and in laying out his plans for the hot-water circulation this arrangement must be adhered to, although the bidder may amplify same to any extent he may desire as long as system of piping is not complicated and meets with the approval of the architect.

402. Complete detailed drawings of all piping, accessories, connections, etc., to be submitted complete in all details before a contract is signed.

403. The type of radiation and arrangement, as shown on the drawings or as called for in the specifications, shall not be altered or modified, excepting in so far as to change from steam loops to water loops.

TESTING.

404. The entire apparatus, as installed under this specification, to be tested to determine if it complies with the specification; this contractor furnishing at his own expense all instruments and a sufficient force of men of proper qualification to conduct such tests as architect may require; the tests as herein contemplated being only such as are, in the opinion of the architect, necessary to determine whether all of the apparatus, etc., has been furnished and installed in accordance with the specification.

405. The entire plant shall be operated under the direction of an expert furnished by the contractor at his own expense; said expert to attend to all adjustments or corrections necessary in any portion of the system. Dating from the starting of the plant, the expert to remain for a period of one month, or until such time thereafter as may be necessary to put all apparatus, piping, valves, fittings, etc., in acceptable and successful working conditition. The expert to instruct the Government employees or engineer as to the proper method of operating and adjusting valves, pumps, heating-system accessories, or any other apparatus which he may furnish under this specification.

406. It is expressly understood that the temperature-regulating apparatus will not be accepted until the weather is sufficiently cold to have it in working order for a period of one month after completion. The contractor's expert shall be present and with his own men conduct such tests in connection with this system as may be required by the architect.

GUARANTEES.

407. The contractor guarantees by the acceptance of this specification, in the signing of the contract, that every part going to make up the complete power plant and heating system, as herein provided, shall be of the best of its respective kind that can be obtained, and shall be erected in a most thorough and substantial manner by none but experienced labor.

408. He guarantees that in the entire heating system a complete, uniform, continuous, and noiseless circulation of steam will be established throughout the mains to each and every radiator or coil, with steam at atmospheric pressure, and that the circulation shall be completed fully and freely, all as herein provided, and that not over 8 inches of vacuum will be required at the pumps to keep the entire system clear of all air and water of condensation and allow a free, unobstructed circulation of steam uniformly throughout the system.

409. He further guarantees the entire operation of the temperature-controlling system, and that a temperature varying 1° either above or below 70° will be maintained in all the rooms to be be controlled, provided the supply of steam to the radiators is maintained.

410. The contractor further guarantees to hold himself responsible for any defects which may develop in any part of his entire system, including apparatus, pipe, valves, or fittings, as installed under this specification, due to faulty workmanship or material of any sort or description whatsoever, and to replace and make good any such faulty parts during a period of two years from the date of final acceptance of his work without cost to the United States.

NONCONDUCTING INSULATING COVERING.

411. When the different portions of the piping provided in this specification have been completed and subjected to tests, as provided or as called for by the architect, all piping will be covered with a nonconducting covering, as called for herein.

412. The vacuum returns from the heating system will not be covered. Neither will any vacuum returns which are carried under the basement floor be required to be covered. No covering for heater overflow, boiler blow-offs, engine and pump cylinder drips, or the sewer discharges from traps.

413. PIPE COVERING.—All high-pressure steam piping, including the valves, fittings, and steam separators throughout the entire plant, together with all boiler feed piping, exhaust piping, and heating mains, with the exception of the main cast-iron engine exhaust header, shall be thoroughly covered with an asbestus, felted, sectional pipe covering, this to consist of pure carded asbestus fiber, finely divided, not pulped or molded; coil in laminations on a form to the desired thickness of 1 inch. There will be 60 laminations to the inch, with weight not to exceed 40 ounces per superficial square foot. Insulation to be finished with a covering of canvas, the insulation being first covered with a coating of silicate; canvas to be standard 8-ounce; the covering to be furnished in regular sections of approximately 3 feet in length.

414. All of this felted covering to be carefully put in place, using lacquered tin bands throughout the engine and boiler rooms, basement of main building, and in all machinery rooms of the eighth and ninth stories, three bands to every section. Black bands to be used in all places where lacquered tin bands are not provided. All seams to be perfectly air-tight.

415. The sections in all riser pipes of heating system, in addition to coating beneath canvas, to be coated with silicate on the ends to an extent sufficient to entirely close up the end. When two ends are so coated, they are to be put together and the silicate allowed to harden in this position

416. All of the covering to be painted with at least two coats of paint. For all covering, except that in the boiler room, the first coat to be white lead and oil; the second coat to be a white antiflame paint. In boiler room and in riser shafts use an air-tight paint, drab in color, for both coats. This color also applies to the feed-water heater, which shall be painted in the same manner as the pipe covering.

417. CAST-IRON EXHAUST-PIPE COVERING.—Cover all cast-iron exhaust piping, valves, and fittings, where same are carried in trenches in engine and boiler rooms. To be covered with acceptable plastic asbestus, nonconducting covering; the pipe to be wrapped with iron-wire netting, ½-inch mesh, with separators spaced every 9 inches. These separators so arranged as to hold the netting at least ½ inch away from the pipe. The covering in all instances to be applied in three coats; the second coat not to be applied until the first coat is thoroughly dry; likewise the third coat. Covering to be at least 2 inches in thickness. Over this covering there will be tightly stretched a heavy 8-ounce canvas.

418. HEATER, EXHAUST AND RECEIVER COVERING.—The feed-water heater will be covered in a manner similar to that provided for the cast-iron exhaust piping; also cover the main atmospheric exhaust pipe in a manner similar to that as provided for feed-water heater and engine exhaust. Cover in like manner the receiver on elevator pumping engine.

419. All of this plastic covering to be carefully put in place and to present a neat and finished appearance when completed. All to be painted with three coats of best asphaltum as directed.

420. COVERING FOR BREECHING, ECONOMIZER, ETC.—Contractor shall cover the exposed portions of the boiler drums, the entire breeching, induced-draft fan housing and economizer flues with a first-class nonconducting fireproof sectional block covering. Blocks to be securely held in position in an approved manner. All joints to be thoroughly cemented and in every case the surface to be finished hard and smooth. All of this covering to be 2 inches in thickness and applied in a first-class, acceptable manner, and painted as directed.

421. PAINTING.—All heaters, pumps, radiators, appliances, and piping throughout the entire plant to be thoroughly cleaned of all rust, and all iron cuttings to be removed from interior of pipes and apparatus. The radiators, pumps, and special valves and appliances not required under this specification to be covered shall be thoroughly painted with enamel or metallic bronzes, as may be directed by the architect, the color used for all radiators and radiator supply pipes to suit the color of the room in which they are installed. All painting, bronzing, gilding, or other finish for direct radiators to be applied in the most approved manner, all as may be acceptable to the architect.

422. All exposed pipes in the boiler and engine rooms and in the machinery rooms in the basement and in the dome, eighth floor over court rooms, and on the ninth floor, not required to be covered in this specification, will be thoroughly painted with two coats of a maroon japan, or such other color as the architect may select.

CONCLUSION.

423. After the pipe work is completed and before connections are made to apparatus other than to the boilers, contractor shall blow out all piping, so as to thoroughly clean same.

424. After all connections are made, all joints in steam piping must be tight and free from leaks, as hereinbefore provided.

425. All vacuum returns shall be tested by the contractor in the presence of a representative of the architect, and under such test the vacuum returns must be absolutely air-tight with valves in supply pipes to system closed. The operation and result of this test to be to the satisfaction of the architect.

426. The bidder's proposition includes *all* labor and material for the proposed work as called for in the entire specification, and any of this work not fully described shall not be a warrant for the installation of poor workmanship or poor material, nor for the omission of any apparatus, valves, fittings, or auxiliaries incident to the complete and successful operation of the plant as a whole, that a complete and perfectly working system may be had ready for operation.

RISK.

427. All work and materials embraced in his contract shall remain at the risk of the contractor until the final completion and acceptance of the same, and the contractor must, at his own expense, take out all necessary policies of insurance for his own protection and be responsible for the work until same is finished and accepted.

PROPOSAL FOR THE HEATING SYSTEM OF THE UNITED STATES POST-OFFICE, COURT-HOUSE, ETC., AT CHICAGO, ILLINOIS.

HENRY IVES COBB,
Architect of the U. S. Government Building at Chicago, Illinois,
Treasury Department, Washington, D. C.

SIR: We hereby propose to furnish all the labor and materials required for the complete heating plant for the United States post-office, court-house, etc., at Chicago, Illinois, strictly in accordance with the plans and specifications therefor, excepting only the temporary heating, furnaces, draft apparatus, economizer, temperature regulation, industrial railway, feed-water filter, oiling system, nonconducting covering, brickwork, and connections required or called for in connection with the installing of each of the above excepted items, for the sum of $99,346.00.

Should we be ordered to proceed with any of the above excepted items, we hereby propose to furnish and install each or all, without asking for any additional time, and for the following prices for such items, with foundations, connections, etc., complete and in strict accordance with the plans and specifications:

Price for temporary heating, as per specification......................... $4,570.00
Price for furnace, as specified 2,090.00
Price for induced-draft apparatus, with connections complete 1,765.00
Price for fuel economizer 4,363.00
Price for temperature regulation, complete, as specified 17,850.00
Price for complete industrial railway 4,263.00
Price for feed-water filter 484.00
Price for oiling system.. 805.00
Price for nonconducting insulating covering............................. 9,266.00

In case of additions or deductions being ordered in connection with this branch of the work, we propose the following schedule of prices to obtain in the settlement of such changes:

Price per boiler, with single setting..................................... $4,650.00
Price for feed-water heater.. 915.00
Price per boiler feed pump... 1,449.00
Price of damper regulator, with damper complete 402.50
Price deducted from price given for temporary heating if temporary boilers are not required 1,970.00
Price per loop for 26-inch single-column radiation, installed 0.79
Price per loop for 32-inch single-column radiation, installed 1.24
Price per loop for 32-inch two-column radiation, installed 1.05
Price per loop for 38-inch two-column radiation, installed 1.20
Price per loop for 44-inch two-column radiation, installed 1.42
Price per loop for 45-inch two-column radiation, installed 1.42

And as alternate bids we propose to furnish and supply stokers, as per specification, if ordered, for the sum of $1,648.00 and a hot-water system, in lieu of the steam system now specified, guaranteeing such hot-water system to perform all that is called for under the steam specifications, complete and perfect, for the additional sum of $110,054.00 over and above the first figure mentioned above for the complete steam system.

If awarded the contract, we agree to complete all of the work contemplated by specification in 200 working days after the approval of the bond; and furthermore agree to complete the installation sufficient for temporary heating, as specified, in 52 working days after notification from the architect to proceed with that work.

(Bidder to give below the location and date of performance by him of work of similar character to that herein called for.)

U. S. post-offices: Little Rock, Ark., Ft. Worth, Texas; Rock Island, Ills.; U. S. Marine Hospital, Chicago, Ills.

THOMAS & SMITH,
16 North Canal Street, Chicago, Ills.

November 6th, 1902.
Members of firm: Richard H. Thomas, Henry F. Smith.

HENRY IVES COBB,
Archt. U. S. Govt. Bldg., Chicago.
J. K. TAYLOR,
Supr. Archt., Treasury Department.
C. E. KEMPER,
Chief Executive Officer, Supv. Archt.'s Office.
H. D. GREEN,
Accountant.

WASHINGTON, D. C., *December 5, 1902.*

Messrs. THOMAS & SMITH,
    16 North Carroll Street, Chicago, Illinois.

SIRS: Your proposal, dated November 6, 1902, addressed to Mr. Henry Ives Cobb, architect of the U. S. Government building at Chicago, Illinois, Treasury Department, Washington, D. C., the lowest received under advertisement dated October 4, 1902, to furnish all the labor and materials required for the complete heating plant for the U. S. post-office, court-house, etc., at Chicago, Illinois, strictly in accordance with the p ans and specifications therefor, excepting only the temporary heating, furnaces, draft apparatus, economizers, temperature regulation, industrial railway, feed-water filter, oiling system, nonconducting covering, brickwork, and connections required or called for in connection with the installing of each of the above excepted items, for the sum of ninety-nine thousand three hundred forty-six dollars ($99,346), is hereby accepted.

It is further understood and agreed that the entire work embraced in this acceptance is to be completed within two hundred (200) working days from the date of the approval of your bond by the Secretary of the Treasury, of which you will be duly advised.

It is further understood and agreed that should you be ordered, on or before April 1, 1903, to proceed with any of the above excepted items you will furnish and install each or all without asking for or being granted any additional time, and for the prices for such items, with foundations, connections, etc., complete and in strict accordance with the plans and specifications, as set forth opposite said items in your bid.

It is further understood and agreed that should you be ordered, on or before April 1, 1903, to supply stokers, as per specifications, for the additional sum of one thousand six hundred forty-eight dollars ($1,648) each, per furnace, you will do the same subject to the same conditions set forth in the above clause.

It is further understood and agreed that as far as the temporary heating is concerned you are to make no arrangements or preparation therefor in any way until notified by the architect of the building that such heating will be required.

It is further understood and agreed that wherever it is necessary to do any cutting of any description whatsoever through floors, ceilings, or walls for the proper running of pipes, or for other work in connection with this heating installation, same will be done by the contractor, and before such cutting is done the contractor must have the permission of the architect of the building. In every case, after completion of such work, the building is to be left in a condition satisfactory to the said architect.

It is further understood and agreed that in case it is deemed advisable by the architect of the building, duplicate reducing valves will be furnished where same reduce from high pressure to that carried in the heating system mains and thus afford the reduction in pressure to be made by two stages from approximately 150 pounds down to that pressure carried in the heating system. This to be included in the contract price as herein stated.

It is further understood and agreed that you are to execute a formal contract, with bond, in the sum of fifty thousand dollars ($50,000), as a guarantee for the faithful performance of the work embraced in your proposal, a form of which will be sent you for execution and return to this Department for examination, approval, and file; and it is understood and agreed also that the said contract, with bond, must be executed and returned within five days from the date of receipt by you of said form.

Payment of said work will be made from the appropriation for the post-office, court-house, etc., Chicago, Ill., on filing of proper vouchers duly signed and approved.

The certified check which accompanied your proposal will be retained at this Department until approval of your formal bond by the Secretary of the Treasury.

Kindly acknowledge receipt of this letter.

Respectfully, yours,

L. M SHAW, *Secretary.*

Contract between the United States of America and Thomas and Smith.

Whereas, by advertisement duly made and published according to law, proposals were asked for furnishing all of the labor and materials for the heating system of the United States post-office, court-house, etc., at Chicago, Illinois; and

Whereas the proposal of Thomas and Smith, of Chicago, Illinois, furnished in response thereto, was duly accepted on the fifth day of December, 1902, on condition that they execute a contract in accordance with the terms of said bid:

Now, therefore, this agreement, made and entered into by and between Leslie M. Shaw, Secretary of the Treasury, for and in behalf of the United States of America, of the first part, and Thomas and Smith, a partnership composed of Richard H. Thomas and Henry F. Smith, of the second part:

Witnesseth that the party of the second part, for the consideration hereinafter mentioned, covenants and agrees to and with the party of the first part to furnish all of the labor and materials, and do and perform all the work required for the heating system, etc., of the United States post-office, court-house, etc., at Chicago, Illinois, in strict and full accordance with the requirements of drawings numbered 159 and 162 to 173 inclusive, excepting No. 171, and such other detail drawings as may be furnished to the party of the second part by the architect of the United States Government building at Chicago, Illinois; the advertisement for proposals, dated October 4th, 1902; the specification for the work; the proposal dated November 6th, 1902, addressed to the said architect by the said party of the second part; and letter dated December 5th, 1902, addressed to the said part of the second part by Leslie M. Shaw, Secretary of the Treasury, accepting said proposal; a true and correct copy of each of which said papers is attached hereto and forms a part of this contract; and which said numbered drawings, bearing the signature of the said architect and the signature of the said party of the second part, are on file in the office of the said architect and are hereby made part of this contract.

And the said party of the second part further covenants and agrees that the work herein agreed to be performed shall be commenced promptly upon receipt of notice of the approval of the bond hereto attached, and will carry on the same in such order and at such times and seasons as shall from time to time be directed or prescribed by the said architect or his representative, and will complete the same in all its parts within 200 working days from the date of the approval of said bond hereto attached; that all materials used shall be of the very best quality of their respective kinds; that all the work performed shall be executed in the most skillful and workmanlike manner, and that both the materials used and the work performed shall be in every respect to the entire and complete satisfaction of the said architect.

And the said party of the second part expressly covenant and agree that they will well and truly perform and fulfill the stipulations of the third and fourth paragraphs of said letter of acceptance whenever required so to do.

It is expressly covenanted and agreed by and between the parties hereto that time is and shall be considered as of the essence of the contract on the part of the party of the second part, and in the event that the said party of the second part shall fail in the due performance of the entire work to be performed under this contract, by and at the time herein mentioned or referred to, the said party of the second part shall pay unto the party of the first part, as and for liquidated damages and not as a penalty, the sum of fifty dollars for each and every day the said party of the second part shall be in default, which said sum of fifty dollars per day in view of the difficulty of estimating such damages with exactness, is hereby expressly fixed, estimated, computed, determined, and agreed upon as the damages which will be suffered by the party of the first part by reason of such default, and it is understood and agreed by the parties to this contract that the liquidated damages hereinbefore mentioned are in lieu of the actual damages arising from such breach of this contract; which said sum the said party of the first part shall have the right to deduct from any moneys in its hands otherwise due, or to become due, to the said party of the second part, or to sue for and recover compensation or damages for the nonperformance of this contract at the time or times herein stipulated or provided for.

The party of the second part further covenants and agrees to hold and save the United States, its officers, agents, servants, and employees, harmless from and against all and every demand, or demands, of any nature or kind, for, or on account of, the use of any patented invention, article, or appliance, included in the materials hereby agreed to be furnished under this contract.

It is further covenanted and agreed by and between the parties hereto that the said party of the second part will, without expense to the United States, comply with all the municipal building ordinances and regulations, in so far as the same are binding upon the United States, and obtain all required licenses and permits, and be responsible for all damages to person or property which may occur in connection with the prosecution of the work; that all work called for by the drawings and specifications, though every item be not particularly shown on the first or mentioned in the second, shall be executed and performed as though such work were particularly shown and mentioned in each, respectively, unless otherwise specifically provided; that all materials and work furnished shall be subject to the approval of the said architect; and that said party of the second part shall be responsible for the proper care and protection of all materials delivered and work performed by them until the completion and final acceptance of same.

It is further covenanted and agreed by and between the parties hereto that the said party of the second part will make any omissions from, additions to, or changes in the work or materials herein provided for whenever required by said party of the first part, the valuation of such work and materials to be determined on the basis of the contract unit of value of material and work referred to, or, in the absence of such unit of value, on prevailing market rates, which market rates, in case of dispute, are to be determined by the said architect, whose decision with reference thereto shall be binding upon both parties, and that no claim for damages on account of such changes or for anticipated profits shall be made or allowed.

It is further covenanted and agreed that no claim for compensation for any extra materials or work is to be made or allowed unless the same be specifically agreed upon in writing or directed in writing by the said architect, and that no addition to, omission from, or changes in the work or materials herein specifically provided for shall make void or affect the other provisions or covenants of this contract, but the difference in the cost thereby occasioned, as the case may be, shall be added to or deducted from the amount of the contract; and in the absence of an express agreement or provision to the contrary no addition to, or omission from, or changes in the work or materials herein specifically provided for shall be construed to extend the time fixed herein for the final completion of the work.

It is further covenanted and agreed by and between the parties hereto that all materials furnished and work done under this contract shall be subject to the inspection of the said architect, the superintendent of the building, and of other inspectors appointed by the said party of the first part, with the right to reject any and all work or material not in accordance with this contract; and the decision of said architect as to quality and quantity shall be final.   And it is further covenanted and agreed by and between the parties hereto that said party of the second part will, without expense to the United States, within a reasonable time to be specified by the said architect, remedy or remove any defective or unsatisfactory material or work; and that in the event of the failure of the party of the second part immediately to proceed and faithfully continue so to do said party of the first part may have the same done and charge the cost thereof to the account of said party of the second part.

It is further covenanted and agreed by and between the parties hereto that until final inspection and acceptance of, and payment for, all of the material and work herein provided for, no prior inspection, payment, or act is to be construed as a waiver of the right of the party of the first part to reject any defective work or material or to require the fulfillment of any of the terms of the contract.   And, further, that the party of the second part guarantees all and the various portions of the work for the time and according to the various clauses set forth in the specification, notably paragraphs 407, 408, 409, and 410.   And, further, that this clause in no way invalidates or weakens the force of paragraph 22 of specification, "Notice to sureties," but is in consonance with it and makes it, as all else of the specification, an integral part of this contract.

It is further covenanted and agreed that the party of the first part shall have the right to require that any particular portion of the work herein provided for shall be completed within such time as may be hereafter definitely specified by the said party of the first part in written notice to the said party of the second part; and that should the said party of the second part fail to complete such particular portion of the work within the time so specified, or fail to complete the entire work contemplated by this contract within the time or times herein stipulated or provided for, or fail to prosecute said work with such diligence as in the judgment of the party of the first part will insure the completion of the said work within the time hereinbefore provided, the said party of the first part may withhold all payments for work in place until final completion and acceptance of same, and is authorized and empowered, after eight days' due notice thereof in writing, served personally upon or left at the shop, office, or usual place of abode, or with the agent of the said party of the second part, and the said party of the second part having failed to take such action within the said eight days as will, in the judgment of the said party of the first part, remedy the default for which said notice was given, to take possession of the said work in whole or in part and of all machinery and tools employed thereon and all materials belonging to the said party of the second part delivered on the site, and, at the expense of said party of the second part, to complete or have completed the said work, and to supply or have supplied the labor, materials, and tools, of whatever character necessary to be purchased or supplied by reason of the default of the said party of the second part, in which event the said party of the second part shall be further liable for any damage incurred through such default and any and all other breaches of this contract.

It is further covenanted and agreed that the said party of the first part shall have the right of suspending the whole or any part of the work herein contracted to be done, whenever, in the opinion of the said architect, it may be necessary for the purposes or advantage of the work, and upon such occasion or occasions the said party of the second part shall, without expense to the United States, properly cover over, secure, and protect such of the work as may be liable to sustain injury from the weather or otherwise; provided, that for all such suspensions and other delays caused by the said party of the first part, the party of the second part shall be allowed one day additional to the time herein stated, for each and every day of such delay so caused, in the completion of the contract, the same to be ascertained by the said architect; provided, that no claim shall be made or allowed to the said party of the second part for any damages which may arise out of any delay caused by the said party of the first part.

And the said party of the first part, acting for and in behalf of the United States, covenants and agrees to pay, or cause to be paid, unto the said party of the second part, or to their heirs, executors, administrators, or successors, in lawful money of the United States, in consideration of the herein recited covenants and agreements made by the party of the second part, the sum of $99,346.

And the party of the first part covenants and agrees that payments will be made in the following manner, viz: Ninety per cent of the value of the work executed and actually in place, to the satisfaction of the said architect, will be paid from time to time as the work progresses (the said value to be ascertained by the said architect), and ten per cent thereof will be retained until the completion of the entire work, and the approval and acceptance of the same by the party of the first part, which amount shall be forfeited by said party of the second part in the event of the non-fulfillment of this contract, it being expressly covenanted and agreed that said forfeiture shall not relieve the party of the second part from liability to the party of the first part for any and all damages sustained by reason of any breach of this contract; provided, however, that no payment hereunder shall be due to the said party of the second part until every part of the work to the point of advancement reached—on account of which payment is claimed—shall be found to be satisfactorily supplied and executed in every particular and any and all defects therein remedied to the entire satisfaction of the said party of the first part.

It is an express condition of this contract that no member of Congress, or other person whose name is not at this time disclosed, shall be admitted to any share in this contract or to any benefit to arise therefrom; and it is further covenanted and agreed that this contract shall not be assigned.

In witness whereof the parties hereto have hereunto subscribed their names this fifth day of December, 1902.

L. M. SHAW,
Secretary of the Treasury.

I hereby certify that this contract and bond have been correctly prepared and compared.

HENRY IVES COBB,
Architect of the U. S. Govt. Building at Chicago, Ill.
THOMAS & SMITH,
Contractors.

[Bond executed. Not yet approved. January 12, 1903.]

No. 1395A. Contract of Thomas and Smith, of Chicago, Ills., for heating system of the U. S. post-office, court-house, etc., at Chicago, Ill., dated December 5th, 1902. Amount, $99,346. Time to complete, 200 working days. Penalty for each day's delay, $50. Bond approved, ——— ——, 1902. Amount of bond, $50,000.

The following instructions must be particularly observed and complied with, viz:

1st. The Christian names must be written in the body of the bond in full, and so signed to the bond.

2d. A seal of wax or wafer must be attached to each signature on the bond. No seals required for signatures to contract, except corporate seals.

3d. Each signature must be made in the presence of two persons, who must sign their names as witnesses.

4th. Each surety must make and sign an affidavit of the amount he is worth after paying his just debts and deducting all exemptions by the laws of the State in which he resides and liabilities of whatever nature, as per form herewith.

5th. A district judge or attorney of the United States or clerk of a United States court must certify that the sureties are sufficient to pay the penalty of the bond.

6th. The affidavits of the sureties must be taken and signed before an officer authorized to administer oaths generally. The officer must certify that he administered the oaths. If the magistrate is not a judge of the United States court, his authority to administer oaths must be certified by the clerk of a court of record having official knowledge of that fact.

7th. Bond must be dated.

8th. Residence of principal and sureties must be distinctly stated.

9th. The sureties must justify in amounts the aggregate of which will be equal to twice the penal sum of the bond.

10th. When the contracting party is a partnership concern, the contract must be signed with the firm name without seal, and the bond must be signed by each member of the firm, with seal to each signature. When a corporate body, there should be attached to the contract duly authenticated evidence that the officer or officers executing the contract and bond have authority to do so, and the corporate seal must be affixed to each instrument.

TREASURY DEPARTMENT,
OFFICE OF THE ARCHITECT OF THE
U. S. GOVERNMENT BUILDING AT CHICAGO, ILL.,
—— ——, 1902.

Respectfully referred to the Solicitor of the Treasury for examination and indorsement.

HENRY IVES COBB,
Architect of the U. S. Government Building at Chicago, Ill.

TREASURY DEPARTMENT,
OFFICE OF THE ARCHITECT OF THE
U. S. GOVERNMENT BUILDING AT CHICAGO, ILL.,
December 5, 1902.

I hereby certify that the within papers are true and correct copies of the originals on file in this office.

HENRY IVES COBB,
Architect of the U. S. Government Building at Chicago, Ill.

SPECIFICATION, PROPOSAL, CONTRACT, AND BOND FOR ELECTRIC SWITCH BOARD, CONDUIT, AND WIRING OF THE UNITED STATES POST-OFFICE, COURT-HOUSE, ETC., AT CHICAGO, ILLINOIS.

1. Bids are invited for the electric switch board, conduit, and wiring of the new United States post-office, court-house, etc., situated on the block bounded by Adams, Clark, Jackson, and Dearborn streets, in the city of Chicago, Ill. The bids are to include underground ducts, conduit, wiring, switch board, outlet boxes, cut-out cabinets, switches, and all labor and materials called for in the following, and set forth upon the drawings and judged necessary by the architect to complete the work.

2. The Treasury Department reserves the right to waive any informalities in and to reject any and all bids.

3. Should the successful bidder, for any reason whatsoever, after the time set for the opening of the bids, withdraw from the competition or fail or refuse to execute the formal bond or contract within two weeks after the same are sent to him, his certified check may be declared forfeited, and the letter of acceptance of his bid may be revoked, and all obligations on the part of all persons acting for and in behalf of the United States in connection therewith will be released and annulled.

4. Bidders must deposit a certified check for $100 with the architect, as the price of these plans and specifications, which sum will be repaid them upon the return of all the papers in good shape.

5. A bidder must submit with his bid a certified check for $4,000, drawn to the order of the Treasurer of the United States, as a guarantee that he will fully and faithfully comply with the terms of his bid should the same be accepted, and that, within two weeks after the form is sent to him, he will execute bond and contract in accordance therewith, the sureties on the bond to be approved by the Secretary of the Treasury.

6. The certified check of the successful bidder will be retained until the execution of a formal bond and contract and the approval of the same by the Secretary of the Treasury. The certified checks of the unsuccessful bidders will be returned immediately after the bid of the successful bidder shall have been accepted and the contract executed.

7. Wherever the word "architect" is used herein it shall be held to mean the architect of the United States Government building at Chicago, Ill.

8. Wherever the word "bidder" is used herein it shall be held to mean any individual or firm of individuals, or any member of a firm, or any corporation signing a bid submitted, and where "contractor" is mentioned it means the successful bidder to whom the contract is awarded.

9. Before submitting a bid, make a careful examination of the building, the drawings, and specifications, to be fully informed as to the condition of the work, the quality of the material, and the character of the workmanship required, and make a careful examination of the place where the materials are to be delivered and the work performed, and all the conditions governing the fulfillment of the contract, as should a bid be accepted no consideration will be given for any error in the bid resulting from failure to do so.

10. Bidders are warned that a bid which is deficient in any of the requirements set forth herein may be rejected as informal.

11. A bid submitted for this work by parties not experienced or regularly engaged in this line and class of work, or not known to have the proper facilities and financial standing to properly and promptly execute the same as herein required, will not receive consideration.

12. A bid must be made upon the blank hereto attached.

13. A bid must not be detached from the package in which it is bound, nor must any of the accompanying papers be detached therefrom; but the entire package must be unbroken and in good order when the bid is delivered to the architect.

14. A bidder must state in his bid in writing and in figures (without interlineations, alterations, or erasures) the sum of money for which he will supply the materials and perform the work required by the drawings and specifications, and in accordance with the conditions of the contract and bond, etc., herein set forth, should his bid be accepted.

15. A bid must state the price per unit of quantity for all work bid upon, and which unit price shall be used for any additions to or omissions from the work in each class or kind of work shown on the drawings and required by the specifications, said prices to be the basis of computation for any changes that may be desired and made by order of the architect, and the bidder must also state the amount included in his bid for each class or kind of work as per schedule herein set forth, or as an alternative proposal.

16. A bid submitted by a firm must be signed with the firm name and each member of the firm with the name in full.

17. A bid submitted by a corporation must be signed with the name of the corporation and the full name of each officer of the corporation, with official corporate seal attached. A bid must contain the address of the bidder.

18. A bidder must be prepared to submit, at his expense, samples of the materials which he proposes to use before a contract is signed, the samples to have the name of the bidder and the title and location of the building plainly marked thereon. Each sample of material must be delivered at this office prior to the time the contract is signed and be approved in writing by the architect before the contract is signed. The samples submitted will be retained, and, when required, the contractor must furnish duplicates of the samples at his expense.

19. A bid must be delivered in a sealed envelope addressed Henry Ives Cobb, architect, Treasury Department, Washington, D. C. "Bid for electric switch board, conduit, and wiring, etc., for Chicago building," from—(name of bidder) (address of bidder)—and delivered at this office in the Treasury Department on or before 2 p. m. on the day named in the advertisement to bidders.

20. Bidders who send their bids to this office through the mails are requested to register same, and to place their name, address, and title of bid on the outside of the envelope for identification, and to mail such bid sufficiently early to reach its destination by the time required, as it is a frequent occurrence that bids reach this office after the hour required. A bid received after the time stated in the advertisement will be returned unopened to the bidder if the proper name and address be known. If the name and address are not known, then the bid will be opened to ascertain the same.

21. Bidders are hereby notified that the certified check required with their bid must be drawn to the order of the Treasurer of the United States. A check drawn to the bidder's own order or to order of any other person than the Treasurer of the United States, although indorsed by the party to whose order it is drawn, and although certified or accepted by the bank on which it is so drawn, will not be accepted as a certified check such as is required under this clause.

22. NOTICE TO SURETIES.—The attention of sureties is particularly directed to the following conditions:

The final inspection and acceptance of the work shown by the drawings and specifications, forming a part of the contract, shall not be binding or conclusive upon the United States if it shall subsequently appear that the contractor has willfully or fraudulently, or through collusion with the representatives of the Department in charge of the work, supplied inferior material or workmanship, or has departed from the terms of his contract.   In any such case, the United States shall have the right, notwithstanding such final acceptance and payment, to cause the work to be properly performed and satisfactory materials supplied, to such an extent as in the opinion of the architect may be necessary to finish the work in accordance with the drawings and specifications thereof, at the cost and expense of the contractor and the sureties on his bond, and shall have the right to recover against the contractor and his sureties the cost of such work, together with such other damages as the United States may suffer because of the default of contractor in the premises, the same as though such acceptance and final payment had not been made.

23. PAYMENTS.—Payments will be made monthly on account of the work satisfactorily in place in the building, based on the estimated value thereof as ascertained by the architect, less 10 per cent of such estimate, which will be retained until the final inspection of all such materials and labor embraced in the contract and the acceptance of the work, after which the final payment of the balance due will be made.

24. PROPOSALS.—Proposals as hereinbefore called for must be based on drawings Nos. 144 to 156, inclusive, and 159 and 160, and the specifications, and must include everything necessary and requisite to place the work complete in every detail.

25. The drawings and specifications are to be interpreted together, and all work included in either, though not in both, must be included in the proposal.

26. INSPECT THE BUILDING.—Bidders must visit the building, compare the drawings and specifications, examine the work in place, inform themselves as to all conditions, and include in their proposals all items of labor and material mentioned, shown, or necessarily implied, that may be required in the full completion of the work in accordance with the intent and meaning of the drawings and specifications, whether each item be specifically mentioned or not.

27. TIME TO COMPLETE WORK.—The bidders must state in their proposals the number of working days after the approval of bond by the Secretary of the Treasury in which they will complete the work, and the work is to be commenced immediately after such approval. Should the condition of the building not permit of the commencement of the work at the time stipulated, or should the execution or condition of other contracts require the stoppage of all work on this contract, allowance for such delays will be made in accordance with provisions as made in the general conditions accompanying this specification. No claim by the contractors for damage on account of such delays will be recognized by the Government.

28. Notice is hereby given that under otherwise equal conditions, favorable consideration will be given to the proposal of such bidder as guarantees to have work completed at the earliest date.

29. KIND AND QUALITY OF MATERIAL.—The material supplied must in each case be of the best class and grade found in the market, and before a contract is let any bidder may be required to make out a schedule of the kind of material, appliances, etc., which he desires to use. In the event of any of the submitted machinery, appliances, materials, etc., not being satisfactory, the architect will select the machinery, appliances, or material of such types and capacities as he deems satisfactory, which selection shall be final and binding upon the successful bidder.

30. The acceptance by the architect of any machinery, appliances, or material named on the proposal sheet is to be understood as an acceptance only upon its conforming with the requirements of the specifications in relation thereto and not as an absolute acceptance of the article regardless of the requirements of the specifications.

31. PATENT RIGHTS.—If any part of the machinery, material, or appliances proposed to be furnished by the bidders is covered by the claims or patents of whatsoever nature of any other parties, the contractor proposing to use such appliances will be required to pay all royalties therefor. The Government will not recognize any demand brought by anyone on account of claims for infringement of patents, but will hold the contractor and his bondsman strictly responsible for any delay from any cause resulting from his failure to fully protect the Government against all patent rights.

32. VISIT THE DEPARTMENT.—The architect reserves the right to require the contractor or his authorized representative to visit this office without expense to the Government, if at any time it is considered to be in the interest of the Government that a conference is necessary for an early adjustment of any complicated or unsatisfactory conditions that may have developed in connection with his contract, but the result of such conference shall not be binding until formally approved.

33. GUARANTEE.—The bidder must also understand that if his proposal is accepted, his contract and bond will guarantee the entire work under this contract, and each and every part thereof, and the contractor will be required to remedy all defects, at his expense, which may develop by reason of the use of any inferior or defective

material or workmanship until the acceptance of the entire work and final payment therefor, subject, however, to the additional requirements expressed in paragraph entitled "Notice to sureties," and subject to any time limit guarantee on any particular portion of work hereafter mentioned in specification.

34. All questions as to the satisfactory completion of the work and the defects necessary to be remedied are to be determined by the architect or his authorized representative.

35. .GENERAL REQUIREMENTS.—This contractor is to perform his work expeditiously in such manner and at such times as will avoid interference with the execution of other contracts. Contractor is to employ continually a sufficiently large force of men to carry on his work properly and finish same in specified time.   In failure so to do, the architect may direct said contractor to increase his force.

36. Contractor is to keep a responsible foreman constantly on the ground—one satisfactory to the architect—to receive instructions from the architect, who also reserves the right to order and keep from the building any unsatisfactory workmen or employees of this contractor's.

37. The dimensions and scaled proportions given on the drawings are in accordance with the general plans, but as variations therefrom may occur in construction, the contractor must make his own measurements at the building, and he will be held responsible for the proper fitting of his work.   He must check and verify all drawings and will be held responsible for any errors which could have been avoided by such checking or inspection.

38. STORAGE OF MATERIAL.—Any material that the contractor may deliver on the premises will be located or stored at such points and in such a manner as may be directed by the architect.   The contractor will be required to remove at his own expense such apparatus or material upon request of the architect within twenty-four hours after the receipt of such request.

SWITCH BOARD, CONDUIT, AND WIRING.

39. IN GENERAL.—This specification contemplates the erection complete in place and ready for operation of an electric light and power switch board; also a complete system of conduit for carrying all conductors for lighting, power, telephone, and burglar alarm service.

40. Also all necessary conductors for electric light and power service complete from street-service connection to engine-room switch board and from engine-room switch board to outlets, including all main and distributing cut-out cabinets, cut-outs, and switches.

41. The generators and motors are made the subject of other specifications, but this specification includes the furnishing of all motor leads, and the connecting of the motors to the wiring system.

42. CAPACITY OF PLANT.—The electric plant comprises switch board, conduit, and wiring for
    6,550 light outlets.
    174 switch outlets.
    19,200 16-candlepower lamps or their equivalent in ampere capacity.
    433 horsepower of motors.

43. DESCRIPTION OF BUILDING.—The building is of first-class fireproof construction in process of erection, and bidders should visit same in order to obtain information relative to work in place and difficulties to be met with in connection with their work.

44. CONDUIT AND WIRING.—The building is to be wired on the three-wire system, all lamps to be operated at 110 volts and motors at 220 volts.

45. The leads to switch board to be of paper and lead covered cables run beneath the floor in vitrified-tile ducts.

46. Switch board to be equipped with all necessary conductors and controlling and indicating devices for feeders for light and power as hereinafter enumerated.

47. Switch board to have double-bus system, arranged so that each feeder can be connected to either one of two separate sources of supply.

48. The main feeders from the switch board to be three-wire feeders for lighting and two-wire feeders for power.

49. The positive, neutral, and negative wires of each lighting feeder to have the same sectional area.

50. The light and power feeders to be of paper and lead covered cable from the switch board to the vertical runways, and to be run in vitrified-tile conduit below the basement floor.

51. The principal vertical mains and feeders to be carried in four runways. These runway conductors to have insulation of the kind known as "slow-burning water-proof," and to be run upon porcelain insulators of type such as is commonly used for central-station construction.

52. On each floor there will be main cut-out cabinets at each vertical runway for controlling all circuits in adjacent portions of building.

53. At central points in each wing there will be distributing cabinets containing switches and cut-outs for all main and tap circuits. The subfeeders, connecting mains and distributing cabinets, to be of rubber-covered and braided wire run in steel pipe or steel interior conduit.

SWITCH BOARD.

54. GENERAL DESCRIPTION.—It is the intent of this specification to provide for the furnishing complete and connected up in place ready for operation of a switch board for controlling the current for furnishing all the electric light and power in the building.

55. The switch board to consist of thirteen feeder panels and one totalizing panel, to be equipped as hereinafter specified.

56. This specification also includes conduit and cables from the street service to the totalizing panel.

57. LOCATION.—The switch board to be located in the engine room of the building, the front of the board to be 4 feet from the wall. The probable location is shown on drawing No. 159, but the exact location to be determined by the architect before construction commences.

58. DRAWINGS.—Before work on same commences, the contractor shall furnish the architect with a working drawing on a scale of not less than ¾ of an inch to the foot, showing the front, back, and side elevations of the board complete with all instruments, switches, conductors, and connections; this drawing to be subject to the approval of the architect, and any changes which the architect may require before the construction commences, either to make the board conform to the letter and spirit of these specifications or to improve the arrangement thereof, shall be made by the contractor, and such changes shall not become the basis of an extra charge.

59. GENERAL DIMENSIONS.—The marble for each panel to be 62 inches in height, 2 inches in thickness; each panel to be equipped with a base of the same width and 28 inches in height, 2 inches in thickness. All front edges to have a ¼-inch bevel.

60. FRAMING.—The vertical sides of each panel, except at ends of board, shall be supported by steel 2½ by 3 inch 7.2-pound tee uprights. The outer sides of end panels to be supported by 2½ by 2 by ⅜ inch angle uprights. For holding the angles to the frame ½-inch bolts having coppered acorn heads shall be used, and at least six for each panel and four for the base. There shall be copper washers under these heads. Between the marble and frame at each bolt there shall be a rubber washer 1 inch in diameter and at least $\frac{1}{32}$ inch thick. The bottoms of uprights shall be secured in place by suitable bolts. (See Drawing No. 155.)

61. The front of board to be 4 feet from wall of building and to be held rigidly in place at bottom by above-mentioned bolts, and at top by suitable iron braces at each upright extending horizontally from the board to the wall. The steel work to be given three coats of durable metallic paint, or of a dead-steel color, at least one coat to be applied before marble is attached. The whole framework and board to be erected in a rigid and stable manner; the face of the board to be truly vertical and the top horizontal. The bottom of bases of panels to come to the floor.

62. GENERAL CONSTRUCTION.—The construction of board, location of wires, connectors, and instruments on the same, also the construction of instruments, including the fittings, switches, meters, etc., to conform to the latest rules and requirements of the National Board of Fire Underwriters, except as herein otherwise specified or otherwise permitted by the architect.

63. MAKES OF INSTRUMENTS.—Before the contract is awarded him, the selected bidder is to furnish the architect with the names and makes of instruments, switches, meters, etc., which he proposes to use, together with cuts and general description of same, and he shall also state the guarantees of accuracy, workmanship, and reliability which he may receive from the makers of such instruments, and such guaranty, or guaranties, are to form a part and parcel of his contract.

64. MARBLE.—Board to be constructed of selected blue Vermont or white Italian marble, free from metallic veins or any flaws or imperfections. Marble to be 2 inches in thickness. Each panel to be made of two slabs, one 62 inches in height and the other 28 inches in height, of width as hereinabove specified. The front of each panel, including bevels, to be highly polished. Sample of marble to be sub-

mitted subject to approval of architect. In drilling holes for all studs or connections of instruments, fittings, etc., care shall be taken that the drill does not break through, but that the hole shall be clean on both sides of marble.

65. NAME PLATES.—Above and near each switch handle, on every panel, shall be a copper card holder suitable for holding a card 1½ by 3 inches, to be provided with a transparent celluloid piece 1½ by 3 inches to protect the face of the card. The holder to be fastened securely to the marble.

66. BUS BARS.—All bus bars and connections on the back of the board to have a sectional area of not less than 1 square inch for every 800 amperes of their rated load. All bus bars to be built of drawn copper, bar having conductivity of not less than 98 per cent of that of pure copper.

67. CONNECTORS AND LUGS.—All connectors and lugs to be of copper of a cross section equivalent to at least 1 square inch of 98 per cent conductivity copper to every 800 amperes of current of the rated load of the circuit of which they form a part.

68. CONNECTIONS.—All instruments to have connections made on the back of the board. All back connections of knife switches, circuit breakers, and fuse terminals to be threaded copper studs, equipped with flat copper hexagonal nuts.

69. FINISH.—All metal parts of trimmings, etc., on the face of the board to be of polished copper, excepting instruments, which may be of Bauer Barff finish. Wherever switches or other apparatus on back of board are fastened to the marble, the ends of bolts projecting through front of board shall have ornamental acorn coppered heads, or nuts, under which shall be copper washers.

70. AMMETERS.—All ammeters to be shunt ammeters, equipped with necessary shunts. They shall be dead beat and shall not be affected by external currents or magnetism, and for one year from installation shall show a precision of at least 1 per cent.

71. VOLTMETERS.—All voltmeters to be of illuminated-dial type, to be dead beat and so designed as not to be affected by external currents of magnetism, and for one year from installation snall show a precision of at least 1 per cent.

72. GROUND DETECTORS.—The voltmeter on the totalizing panel shall be used as a ground detector, and shall be connected up to points provided for this purpose on the voltmeter switch.

73. TYPE OF INSTRUMENTS.—Where illuminated-dial voltmeters and ammeters are used, they shall be similar and equal to the Weston Type B illuminated-dial voltmeters and ammeters.

74. Wherever round-pattern ammeters are specified, they shall be similar and equal to the round-pattern Type F Weston ammeters.

75. VOLTMETER SWITCHES.—The voltmeter switches to be of type having connections mounted on back of board and operated by polished copper wheel on front of board, equipped with plate and pointer to show position of switch. The points of switch to be marked on plate by letters to indicate circuits. All contacts to be rubbing contacts of ample capacity and pressure to insure a permanent connection of such low resistance that no error will be thereby introduced into the reading of the instruments.

76. INSTRUMENT LEADS, ETC.—All instrument leads and other insulated wires upon the rear of the switch board to be rubber covered, and to be held in place to the switch board by hard rubber, fiber, or porcelain cleats screwed to lead plugs in board by brass screws.

77. SWITCHES.—All knife switches to be constructed with blades and contacts of pure drawn copper of conductivity not less than 98 per cent of that of pure copper and having a cross section of not less than 1 square inch for every 800 amperes and a contact surface of not less than 1 square inch for every 50 amperes of rated load. All connections and studs to be of cast copper of conductivity at least equal to that of the blades. To have hard-rubber handles and spade handles to be used for all double or triple pole switches.

78. Construction and dimension of switches also to be equal to those required by the rules and regulations of the National Board of Fire Underwriters, except where otherwise specified or permitted by architect.

79. All switches having rated capacity of over 2,000 amperes to be single pole, of a type and make equal, in the opinion of the architect, to the toggle-joint type leaf switches of the General Electric Company and equipped with auxiliary contracts for breaking arc.

80. FUSES AND FUSE HOLDERS.—All fuses to be mounted on the back of the board. Fuse holders to be attached to copper studs. All fuses to be of inclosed type, where rated capacity of circuit is less than 600 amperes, but to be open fuses of pure copper where the circuit carries 600 amperes or more.

81. All neutral fuses to have double the capacity of positive and negative fuses on same circuit.

82. CIRCUIT BREAKERS.—All circuit breakers to be of carbon break laminated type and make equal to the type C, form D, circuit breaker manufactured by the General Electric Company.

83. EQUIPMENT OF PANELS.—Switch board shall comprise fourteen panels equipped in the following manner:

84. LIGHTING FEEDER PANELS.—There will be eleven panels. Each lighting feeder to be equipped with one triple-pole, double-throw knife switch of capacity shown on drawing No. 156, entitled "Diagram of circuits." Switches to be equipped with fuse holders and fuses mounted on back of board.

85. Also two round-pattern shunt ammeters on each feeder, except feeder for patrol lighting. All corridor lighting to be on one pair of ammeters. ·

86. POWER FEEDER PANELS.—There will be two panels, each feeder to be equipped with:

One double-pole, double-throw knife switch of capacity as stated in schedule entitled "Diagram of circuits."
Two fuses mounted on rear of board.
One single-pole circuit breaker.
One round-pattern ammeter.

87. TOTALIZING PANEL.—There will be a totalizing panel to be equipped with:
Two totalizing shunt, illuminated dial, 7,000-ampere ammeters.
Two illuminated dial, 150-volt voltmeters, reading from 96 to 130 volts.
Two 3-circuit voltmeter switches for reading on the illuminated voltmeters the voltage of each bus and pressure line.
One 6-circuit voltmeter switch for reading on portable voltmeter the voltage on positive, negative, and neutral buses, and voltage between each bus and the ground.

88. The totalizing pane also to be equipped with a portable direct-reading voltmeter, reading from 0 to 250 volts. This instrument to be similar and equal to the portable voltmeter, type No. 2, manufactured by the Weston Electrical Instrument Company. Voltmeter to rest upon shelf of marble of same kind as panel, and to be equipped with flexible leads and plugs for connecting to receptacles sunk in face of panel; these receptacles to be connected to the 6-circuit voltmeter switch hereinabove specified.

89. ARRANGEMENT OF BUSES.—Switch board will be arranged on a three-wire double-bus system, so as to provide for taking current from two independent sources of supply.

90. LIGHTING OF BOARD.—All instruments on switch board which are not of the illuminated-dial type are to be lighted by means of concealed lamps. For this purpose there shall be installed over each instrument a polished copper bracket equipped with polished copper key socket and opaque shade of half-round shape, of Bauer Barff finish.

91. CLOCK.—A first-class eight-day clock, of marine or locomotive type, to be securely mounted on top of switch board in copper-plated cast-iron frame or ornamental design acceptable to the architect.

92. SHOP INSPECTION.—Upon the completion of the switch board in all its details the contractor must give the architect fifteen days' notice of his readiness for a shop inspection, which must take place where board is built.

93. SWITCH-BOARD PANELS, CONDUITS, AND CONDUCTORS FOR GENERATOR PLANT.—The bidder shall also state in his proposition the amount which will be added to the contract provided he furnishes generator panels, conduit, and conductors for connecting the generators to the switch board, and for equalizers; also, pedestals complete with equalizer switches, all erected in place ready for erection.

94. CONSTRUCTION OF PANELS.—The construction of the switch-board panels to be the same in every respect as for the feeder panels hereinabove specified, excepting that the equipment shall be as follows:

95. GENERATOR PANELS.—Each generator panel to be equipped in the following manner:

One double-pole, single-throw, 3,000-ampere switch, complete with fuse holders and fuses.
One 3,600-ampere illuminated-dial ammeter.
One 150-volt, round-pattern voltmeter.
One dynamo field rheostat (mounting only).

96. RHEOSTATS.—Rheostats will be installed in the back of the board, operated by handwheel on the front of the board, these to be furnished by the dynamo contractor and to be installed and connected up in place by this contractor.

97. PEDESTALS.—With each generator panel there is also to be provided one cast-iron pedestal equipped with single-pole, 3,600-ampere switch for equalizer connection; pedestal to be located near dynamo and constructed as herein specified.

98. DYNAMO LEADS.—Dynamo leads to be of paper and lead covered cables as hereinabove specified, each lead to consist of four 1,000,000 circular mil cables for two-wire generators of 300 kilowatts capacity, or three-wire generators of 600 kilowatts capacity.

99. Five 1,000,000 circular mil cables for two-wire generators of 750 kilowatts capacity, or three-wire generators of 350 kilowatts capacity.

100. EQUALIZER LEADS.—Equalizer leads to run from generator to generator, each conductor to consist of two 1,000,000 circular mils paper and lead covered cables. Equalizers to run to switch pedestals hereinabove specified.

101. CONNECTIONS.—All dynamo leads and equalizer cables to be furnished and connected up in place, equipped with lugs and terminals, the same as hereinbefore spec;fied.

102· CONDUIT.—Dynamo leads and equalizer cables to be run in vitrified-tile conduit same as specified for feeders below the basement floor and street-service conductors.

· 103. ARRANGEMENT OF BUSES.—If generators are installed, the generator panels are to be equipped with a bus having a capacity equivalent to 1 square inch of copper for every 800 amperes of rated load; these buses to be connected to instruments on totalizing panel and to the upper feeder bus. The lower feeder bus in this connection to be connected with street-service cable through switch on totalizing panel.

104. Positive, negative, and neutral conductors to be of the same size. Bus bars to be held rigidly in place and, where necessary, to be supported by suitable brackets.

105. ALTERNATE PROPOSITIONS ON GENERATOR PANELS, ETC.—Bidder shall also state in his proposition the additional price for furnishing generator panels, conduits, generator leads, equalizer cable, and pedestals for each arrangement of the following installation of generators:

Six 300-kilowatt, 125-volt, two-wire generators.
Four 300-kilowatt, 125-volt, two-wire generators.
Six 375-kilowatt, 125-volt, two-wire generators.
Four 375-kilowatt, 125-volt, two-wire generators.
Three 600-kilowatt, 250-volt, three-wire generators.
Two 600-kilowatt, 250-volt, three-wire generators.
Three 750-kilowatt, 250-volt, three-wire generators.
Two 750-kilowatt, 250-volt, three-wire generators.

CONDUIT FOR LIGHT AND POWER CIRCUITS.

106. IRON CONDUIT.—All conduits, except below the floor and basement, will be of steel pipe, of standard gas-pipe thickness. All pipes to be thoroughly plugged and carefully reamed, so as to be free from all fins and burrs; allowance in thickness will be made for amount necessary for plugging.

107. KIND OF IRON CONDUIT.—The bulk sum of bid includes plain iron-pipe conduit. The itemized schedule calls also for a price per foot of conduit having an interior covering of japan. If japan-lined, japanning must be so applied that it will not crack when pipe is bent to a radius of 6 inches in any temperature above zero.

108. SIZE OF CONDUIT.—Size of conduit to be not less than that shown on drawing entitled "Diagram of circuits." In any event the pipes furnished must be large enough to admit of the easy drawing and withdrawing of any of the sizes and kinds of conductors herein specified.

109. METHOD OF FASTENING CONDUITS.—Conduits to be securely fastened in place by pipe hooks of approved design.

110. CONTINUITY OF CONDUITS.—Conduits must be continuous from outlet to outlet and from outlet to tablet or junction box, and not more than four quarter-turn elbows or bends are to be used in any run between outlets and boxes.

111. SUPPORTING CONDUIT.—Wherever it is necessary to prevent sag in horizontal runs of conduit, the conduit shall be securely supported by blocking or tile.

112. BENDS IN CONDUIT.—All elbows must be smooth inside and out and free from kinks. No bends sharper than a 6-inch standard elbow will be allowed. Where possible sweeps of large radius must be used.

113. TERMINALS OF CONDUITS.—Terminals of all conduits to be supplied with capping or bushing fitted so as to protect the wire from abrasion; bushing to be of material and design approved by the National Board of Fire Underwriters.

114. Wherever conduits enter outlet boxes they shall be rigidly clamped to the box between bushings and check nuts.

115. PROTECTION OF CONDUIT.—Conduits for all main lateral runs and for all tap circuits, except in rooms having decorative treatment, to be run as far as possible under the finished floor in spaces left above iron beams by 3-inch furring strips. This pipe will be embedded in concrete. Wherever pipe is not to be embedded in

concrete it shall be painted, after being installed, with two coats of elastic protecting paint, acceptable to the architect. Wherever pipe is concealed, last coat of paint to be applied just before it is concealed. Or in such places pipes electro-galvanized outside may be used instead of the painted pipe.

116. JOINTS IN CONDUIT.—The joints of all tubes are to be smooth-faced, reamed, and laid butt to butt, and in order to insure positive continuity one end of every section of tubing, whether for feeder or distribution purposes, shall be provided with a long or running thread without taper, so that the ends of tubes may be placed butt to butt before running coupling to make necessary connection.

117. Joints are to be made with lead and oil in same manner as for water pipes. All joints at floor outlet boxes or junction boxes are to be made water-tight.

118. TIME OF RUNNING CONDUIT.—Conduit system to be installed complete before pulling of wire, and wire to be pulled in after the building is plastered, except where it is desired to omit floor plates of floor boxes, in which case the wire shall be drawn in before the finished floor is laid.

119. CEILING OUTLETS.—Wherever location of floor outlet boxes comes over partitions, pipes, or any other part of the building construction or equipment, so it is not desirable in the opinion of the architect to have ceiling outlet located directly under such boxes, then the location of the floor boxes to be changed to avoid this obstruction, or the floor boxes shall be connected to ceiling outlet by a sweep, so that the ceiling outlet comes in location acceptable to architect. The architect to determine in such case which method of construction is to be used.

120. FLOOR OUTLET BOXES.—Wherever floor outlet boxes are shown on plans, these shall be cast-iron waterproof boxes, having circular brass covers easily removable and adjustable for height. Connection to conduit to be made by water-tight joints. Boxes to be not less than $3\frac{3}{4}$ inches deep inside and to be not less than $4\frac{3}{4}$ inches in diameter inside where conduit enters box, and not less than $3\frac{3}{4}$ inches in diameter inside at any point. Box to be $\frac{1}{4}$ inch thick. Where box is directly over ceiling outlet, it is to be equipped with $\frac{1}{4}$-inch iron conduit screwed into bottom, which shall serve both as a conduit for ceiling outlet and a support for fixture.

121. Contractor to submit for approval of architect working drawings showing complete box with all connections to conduit.

122. All floor outlet boxes on first and second floors to be equipped with special receptacles suitable for receiving plug of dimensions and type shown on drawing No. 155. Design of receptacle to be subject to approval of architect.

123. All floor outlets above second floor to be equipped with porcelain receptacle sockets. Both receptacle and socket to be so supported in box as not to interfere with wires where two sets of conductors are installed in one box and to be connected to circuit without cutting of wires.

124. Bidder shall state in his proposition the additional price which will be charged per box for floor outlet boxes where the cover is equipped with two outlets.

125. SWITCH OUTLET BOXES.—Wherever snap switches are to be provided, the conduit outlets are to be equipped with steel or cast-iron outlet boxes of thickness equal to that of other ceiling and wall boxes, these to be of suitable size for receiving pushbutton switches of make acceptable to the architect.

126. STREET CONNECTIONS.—There shall be a conduit of not less than twelve ducts from the point below and where the street-service switch enters the building to a point beyond the panel where connection for this circuit is made to the switch board. This is to be of same material and construction as that for feeders from engine room to center of building.

127. DUCTS.—All conduits to be vitrified clay, of a type equal to that known as "multiple-duct conduit." Conduit to be thoroughly vitrified, and to have an internal diameter of approximately 4 inches. All ducts to be uniform, straight, smooth, and thoroughly vitrified.

128. TRENCH.—To be of ample width to permit of the convenient laying of the ducts to such depth as may be directed by the architect. All excavation made below the bottom lines of conduit to be filled with good material and solidly rammed in place.

129. MANNER OF LAYING CONDUIT.—Lay on foundation of concrete for a thickness of at least 3 inches. All space between ducts to be filled with cement. A layer of concrete 3 inches in thickness to be applied at top of concrete throughout its entire length; also at sides opposite joints. Concrete to be made of 1 part cement, 3 parts sand, and 5 parts gravel or broken stone, the cement and sand to be first thoroughly mixed dry, then a sufficient quantity of water added to form a rather soft mortar; the stone to be afterwards added and thoroughly mixed with it. Broken stone not

to exceed 1 inch in its greatest diameter.   All material in any way larger to be thrown out.   The materials to be cleaned from dust or dirt before being used.

130. All spaces between ducts to be filled with cement mortar.   This mortar to be mixed in the proportion of 1 part cement, 2 parts sand.

131. The work to be so conducted that the ducts shall not be disturbed while the mortar is setting and the free ends of all ducts in the trenches to be firmly stopped with wooden stoppers when the work is left at night, or other times, care being taken to leave the inside of the pipes free from all obstructions.

132. The ends of all conduits to be butted securely together.   Ducts to be held in position by steel dowels.

133. When conduit is laid, the joints to be surrounded with muslin to prevent the cement from entering the ducts.

134. The construction of duct and manner of laying shall be such as to leave the conduit perfectly smooth on the interior when completed.   After conduit is in place each and every place in its interior shall be large enough so that a rod 3½ inches in diameter and 30 inches long can be drawn through it with ease.

135. CONDUITS SHALL BE STRAIGHT.—All runs of conduit to be as nearly as possible straight between outlets, except that conduits will pitch toward outlets sufficiently so there will be no opportunity for collection of water in same.

136. MATERIALS.—All the materials furnished for the work to be of first quality of their kinds and to be subject to the inspection of the architect.   All cement furnished for the work to be of the best quality of American Portland hydraulic cement or make acceptable to the architect, fresh made and fine ground, and to be tested before use in a manner satisfactory to the architect; to be protected from the weather when stored and to be in unimpaired condition when used.   Any material that may be rejected to be at once removed from the work.

137. CONSTRUCTION OF MANHOLE.—There will be manholes located at points indicated on drawing No. 144.   These manholes, unless otherwise required by the architect, will be 5 feet square and 6 feet deep in the clear.

138. The manholes shall be built of such form and dimensions as the architect may, from time to time, direct.   The foundation will consist of a layer, 6 inches thick, of cement concrete mixed in the proportions of 1 part cement, 3 parts sand, and 5 parts of broken stone; the cement and sand to be first thoroughly mixed dry,. then a sufficient quantity of water to be added to form a rather soft mortar; stone to be afterwards added and thoroughly mixed with it.   The broken stone not to exceed 2½ inches in its greatest diameter; all material in any way larger to be thrown out. The walls of the manholes are to be of good hard brick, laid in and well plastered on the outside with cement mortar.   The mortar to be mixed in the proportion of 1 part of hydraulic cement and 2 parts of good, clean, sharp sand.   They are, in general, to be 8 inches in thickness, but when, in the judgment of the architect, they require to be built stronger, they shall be built of such thickness as may be directed.

139. The top of manhole to be constructed of brick similar to that used in the construction of the manhole.   This brick to be laid between pieces of tee iron, having section of at least 3 by 3 by ½ inch, and of length sufficient to extend to the outside end of the brickwork.   Brickwork and iron to be covered with ½ inch of mortar, same as above specified, and the tee iron to be arranged to support manhole cover.

140. MANHOLE COVERS.—Manholes to be equipped with cast-iron covers of design acceptable to the architect.   Contractor to submit drawing of covers to the architect for approval.

141. IRON PIPE.—The conductors will be led from the manholes to the points where the paper and lead covered cables end in 3-inch iron pipe.   These pipes to be securely cemented in the top of the manhole and to be so arranged that the cables of such size and number as herein specified can be readily drawn in.   Pipes to be held in place in a manner directed by the architect.

142. TRENCH.—At rear of switch board there will be a trench the full length of switch board, extending from switch board to wall, and of sufficient depth to accommodate all vitrified ducts.   Top of ducts to be not less than 12 inches below the finished floor; the trench to be constructed in the same manner as manhole; inside of trench to be plastered throughout with Portland cement mortar, same as herein elsewhere specified.   The edge of the trench next to the switch board to be equipped, its entire length, with 4-inch 5.25-pound channel iron, this channel iron to form a support for the switch board and cables.

143. LOCATION OF CONDUIT.—All conduits to switch boards and between switch boards and risers to be of 4-inch vitrified duct laid beneath the floor, and all other conduit to be iron conduit as hereinafter specified.

144. All the vertical iron conduits shall be run, for the most part, in runways, location of which is shown on plans Nos. 144 to 153, inclusive, horizontal runs to be

made above the tiling beneath the finished floor.   In cutting through floors do so with a sharp drill from *below*.   Location of all conduits to be approved by the architect before work commences.

145. The contractor shall furnish complete plans showing the location, sizes, and radius of bends of all conduits; also location and description of all outlet boxes. These plans to be subject to approval of architect before construction commences, and any changes required in these plans before construction commences shall not be the basis of an extra charge.   The original tracings of all these drawings for installation shall be corrected as work proceeds or is changed, so that upon completion they are perfectly correct, when they must be filed with the architect.

146. LOCATION OF OUTLETS.—The exact locations of outlets are to be determined by the architect, and no allowances will be made the contractor for any changes in conduit work, wiring, etc., made necessary by his neglect to have all locations approved by the architect.

147. FASTENING OF OUTLET BOXES.—All outlet boxes shall be securely fastened in place.   All ceiling and wall outlet boxes, unless otherwise permitted by architect, to be set level or plumb, as the case may be, and as nearly as possible so that the top will come flush with the finished surface of the plaster; in any event not to extend more than ¼ inch beyond finished surface.   All conduits at outlets to be so supported that outlet boxes will be securely held in place.   All floor outlets to be set perfectly level and securely supported in this position by suitable blocking and to be set at such a height that top of uncovered boxes will not be more than ½ inch nor less than ¼ inch below the bottom of the finished floor.

148. OMISSION OF OUTLET BOXES.—Where outlets come in marble work, cornices, or moldings, the box may be omitted at the discretion of the architect, and the tubes firmly secured in position.

149. OUTLET BOXES.—All wall and ceiling outlets, except where otherwise specified or permitted by architect, shall be equipped with outlet boxes of wrought steel or cast iron, not less than $\frac{1}{16}$ inch thick; if of steel they shall be protected inside and out with a coating of elastic protecting paint.

150. BOXES FOR PLUG SWITCHES AND RECEPTACLES.—Wherever vault plug switches are indicated on plans, suitable steel or cast-iron boxes must be set, which will contain both the plug and its connections.

151. Wherever ceiling outlets and floor outlets are provided from the same floor outlet boxes in the floor of the first and second floors, separate circuits are to be run for ceiling and for floor outlets, circuits being run from distributing boxes on the same floor as the outlet.   To accomplish this without the use of an unnecessary amount of conduit and wire, the conduits for tap circuits are to be cross-connected wherever necessary in pairs, so that each pair will have one conduit running to distributing cabinet on the same floor as the outlet box, and one conduit to distributing cabinet on the same floor as the ceiling outlets.   This arrangement is shown in a general way by diagram on drawing No. 155.

152. SAMPLES.—Contractor must submit to architect for approval, as required, samples of conduit, outlet boxes, wire, bushings, distributing tablets, etc., which he intends to install, and all material and appliances furnished must be equal to samples submitted as well as according to specifications.

153. TELEPHONE CONDUIT.—This contractor shall provide a system of conduits for carrying the cables and wires for telephone service, the main cables to be carried from a point where they enter the building to a point below vertical runway II in vitrified duct.   From this point the cables will be run exposed to the switch-board room on the eighth floor.   From this room cables will be run in ducts to each of the four closets containing the main cut-out cabinets, and from these closets the cables will then run up and down exposed in the same runway with lighting cables, and on each floor will be carried in iron pi es from the vertical runways to the space behind the baseboard on the outside wall of the building.   Following is a description of the conduit system, which is a part of the specifications:

154. At a point as near as possible where the cables enter the building, also at a point as near as possible directly under the vertical runway II, there shall be installed a small manhole, these manholes to have concrete bottoms and 8-inch brick walls. Construction and material to correspond to that specified for electric-light and power cables.   Manhole to be equipped with iron covers acceptable to the architect.   The exact location of these manholes to be determined by the architect.   Before construction commences, contractor shall submit to the architect detailed drawings of these manholes for approval.   These manholes to be connected to one another by conduit of four 4-inch vitrified tile ducts.   Construction of this duct to correspond in every particular to that specified for electric-light cables.

155. Conduit to be as near as possible straight, and whenever it is necessary to make turns which, in the opinion of the architect, are too sharp for the drawing in of a 300-pair telephone cable, then, at such turns, there shall be installed an extra manhole, these manholes to correspond to the same specifications as those above mentioned, but, in any event, to be not less than 2 feet square on the inside.

156. The route and depth of the ducts to be determined by the architect. It is assumed that the top of the ducts will be 18 inches below the finished floor of the basement, but the exact depth as well as route of the ducts to be determined by the architect.

157. IRON CONDUIT.—On the eighth floor there shall be run two 1½-inch iron conduits to each of the closets located on vertical runways I, III, and IV. On each floor of the building above the basement and from each vertical runway a 1-inch iron conduit shall be run to the hollow space behind baseboard on the outside wall of building. In general, the conduits to enter this space at a point as near as possible to runway, but the exact location to be determined by architect.

158. On each floor above the second floor there shall be run from the space behind the baseboard on the outside wall a ½-inch iron conduit to the floor-outlet boxes the outside wall.

159. The iron conduit to conform in every particular to the specifications for iron nearest conduit for electric-light circuits.

160. CONDUIT FOR BURGLAR ALARM.—There shall also be installed a complete system of iron piping for the cables for burglar-alarm system. This conduit to be installed complete and continuous from watchman's room on the first floor to vaults and between vaults as shown on drawings Nos. 144 to 149, inclusive. The exact location of ends of all conduits to be determined by the architect.

161. Conduits running from the vaults to the different alarms should be of 1-inch pipe, and where they connect one vault with another and the run is short, may be of ½-inch pipe. All turns and bends in the conduits should be made with a wide arc and a continuous No. 12 galvanized-iron fish wire installed, to use in pulling in the cables. Special care should be taken in installing these conduits to have no burrs or rough edges inside which may injure the cable while being pulled through.

162. This conduit and its installation to conform in every respect to the specifications for conduit for electric lighting, except that short bends will not be permitted.

WIRING.

163. ARRANGEMENT OF CIRCUITS.—All circuits are designated by letters and numbers, which are the same as shown on drawing No. 156, these numbers designating the location of switch boards, cabinets, etc., between which the circuits run.

Lighting circuits:

Feeder S I (1)
    S II (1) } These to feed all lights in basement and first and second
    S III (1) } floors, excepting in corridor and dome.
    S IV (1) }

Feeder S I (3)
    S II (3) } This to feed all lights above the second floor, except in
    S III (3) } corridors and dome.
    S IV (3) }

Feeder S-ss I.—All corridor lights except patrol lighting.
    S II.—All patrol lights.
    S-ss II.—All lights in dome.
    S. E.—All lights in engine room and boiler room.

Power circuits:
    Feeder S. B.—For all motors in basement except engine and boiler room.
    Feeder S. II (9).—For all motors on and above eighth floor.

164. LIGHTING CIRCUITS FOR BASEMENT AND FIRST AND SECOND FLOORS.—From main cut-out cabinets on first floor at points I, II, III, and IV, run subfeeders to each of the distributing cabinets on basement and first and second floors designated on drawings Nos 144, 145, and 146 by Nos. D 1, D 2, D 3, D 4, D 5, D 6, D 7, D 8 on each floor.

165. All of these circuits to be three-wire.

166. From distributing cabinets run two-wire taps of No. 12 B. & S. gauge wire to tap outlets, these outlets being arranged so there shall be not more than twelve lights on any tap circuit except as otherwise herein specified. The number of lamps marked at outlets on plans being the basis of arrangement.

167. CIRCUITS FOR LIGHTING ABOVE SECOND FLOOR.—From main cut-out cabinets at I (3), II (3), III (3), and IV (3) runs vertical mains—

    I (3) to I (8).
    II (3) to II (16).
    III (3) to III (8).
    IV (3) to IV (16).

168. These mains furnish current to main cut-out cabinets located at runways on each floor. Each main cabinet on floors 3 to 8, inclusive, to be connected to distributing cabinets in corresponding wing of building, these cabinets being shown on plans Nos. 147 to 152, inclusive, and designated by the following numbers on each floor: D 1, D 2, D 3, D 4.

169. On floors 9 to 16, inclusive, the main cabinets to be also used as distributing cabinets and contain fuses and switches for tap circuits on these floors.

170. From all distributing cabinets run two-wire tap circuits to outlets same as specified on lower floor.

171. DOME LIGHTING.—All dome lighting to be taken from feeder S-ss II. This feeder to be continued to ss IV (1) and from s II and ss IV (1). Vertical mains to be run to cut-out cabinets II (8) and IV (8); each of these vertical mains to supply one-half of all the lights in the dome from the nearest main cut-out cabinet to which it runs, all tap circuits being run from main distributing box, tap, fuses, and switches being located in same.

172. One-half of dome lighting to be on each of the two risers above specified, the wiring to be so arranged that each riser will be connected to every other outlet on each level.

173. All tap circuits for dome lighting to be of such size that a maximum drop in voltage on any tap, at full load, shall not exceed two volts.

174. The bracket lights on rear of columns in dome are a part of the corridor lighting.

175. CORRIDOR LIGHTING.—From ss II continue the circuit S-s II (1) to cut-out boxes I (1) and II (1), III (1) and IV (1), and from these points run vertical risers to I (8), II (8), III (8), and IV (8). From main cabinets on each floor run three-wire laterals to distributing cabinets on that floor. These laterals to have cut-out and switch in main cut-out cabinet, and to connect at distributing cabinet with the tap circuits for corridor lighting. These tap circuits to be independent of other circuits in same cabinet.

176. PATROL LIGHTING.—From main switch board run circuit to cabinet II (1), and from II (1) to III (1), IV (1), and V (1). From these points run risers to I (8), II (8), III (8), and IV (8). From main cabinets on each floor run tap circuits to certain corridor and room outlets designated as patrol lights on plans Nos. 147 to 153, inclusive.

177. PRESSURE LINE.—From II (1) run a No. 14 B. and S. three-wire rubber and lead covered cable to totalizing panel on main switch board.

178. This cable may be run in same duct with a neutral feeder.

179. ENGINE AND BOILER ROOM CIRCUIT.—From triple-pole double-throw switch on switch board run a three-wire circuit to cut-out cabinet in engine room for controlling all lights in boiler and engine room.

180. LIGHTING INSPECTOR'S RUNWAYS.—In inspector's runways there shall be run eight tap circuits, each circuit to have 20 one-light outlets. Wires to be No. 12 B. and S. guage, and to be run in upon conduit work on the ceiling of the runways.

181. The outlet boxes to be equipped with keyless receptacle sockets of approved design, connected up in place. These circuits to be connected to the nearest cut-out box.

182. TAP CIRCUITS.—All distributing or tap circuits for lights to be of No. 12 B. & S. gauge, duplex rubber-covered and braided wire, except as herein otherwise specified.

183. ELEVATOR LIGHTS.—There shall be a five-light outlet equipped with an approved outlet block in each elevator shaft midway between limits of run.

184. SPECIAL LIGHTING.—There will be special arrangements of lighting the court rooms, corridors, subtreasury department, and dome. The location and arrangement of these lights is shown on detailed plans, which may be consulted at the office of the architect, Treasury Department, Washington, or at the office of the consulting electrical and mechanical engineers, Nos. 1409-10 Manhattan Building, Chicago.

185. The plans accompanying specifications show only the number of lights and outlets in these locations. The lights above referred to are for the most part arranged for concealed lighting. Contractor must arrange conduit and wiring so as to carry out the details of lighting shown on plans above referred to, and he shall, if required, furnish the Architect for approval detailed drawings of wiring, conduits, and outlets for this portion of the work, and his work must be made to conform to the details of the construction and decoration furnished by other contractors.

186. VAULT LIGHTING.—All vaults which have burglar protection to have permanent conduit and wiring inside the vaults, this wiring to be connected to the wiring ouside the vault by means of a plug receptacle located inside the vault door and a plug receptacle located outside near the vault door, these two being connected by flexible cord equipped at each end with an attaching plug. Other vaults to have permanent conduit and wiring.

187. POWER CONNECTIONS.—The end of power feeder B to be connected to switch board located at point B, said switch board to comprise a regulating and controlling device for each motor located in central basement.

188. End of power feeder S II (9) to be attached to switch board comprising all regulating and controlling devices for each motor on the ninth floor, which is located so that it and the switch board can be seen at the same time. Switch board to also be equipped with knife switches and fuses for circuits to each of the other motors on the ninth floor, and to each court-room motor on the eighth floor. Switches to be double pole, of ample capacity, and to be equipped with inclosed fuses.

189. The contractor shall also run circuits of the size shown on attached schedule and drawing No. 156 from this switch board to the motor starters, located at points near motors. Another contractor will furnish motor and motor starters, but this contractor shall furnish wire, conduit, and terminals for making all connections to and between the motor starters and motors.

190. WIRING AND CONDUIT FOR MOTORS.—This contractor shall furnish a complete system of conduits and conductors for electric motors according to the following schedule of motors. The motors and controlling devices shall be furnished by another contractor, but this contractor shall connect up to the motors and controlling devices.

191. SCHEDULE OF MOTORS: H. P.

Basement of dome portion, eight 20-horsepower	160
Basement of dome portion, two 14½-horsepower	29
For running centrifugal pump, one 10-horsepower	10
Running fans in engine room and subtreasury, two 3-horsepower	6
One 20-horsepower motor on ninth floor	20
Four 14½-horsepower motor on ninth floor	58
One 20-horsepower for water-closet fan on ninth floor	20
For north, east, and west court rooms, two 5-horsepower in eighth story over courts	30
For south court rooms, two 10-horsepower in eighth story over courts	20
Total horsepower for motors for ventilating system	353

192. In addition to the above there will be three 15-horsepower motors installed in the basement of the dome. One of these will be used in connection with the elevator system. The other two motors will operate house pumps, also in boiler room a 3-horsepower motor for bilge pump.

193. On the ninth floor will be placed a 5-horsepower motor operating pump for elevating water to the fifteenth story.

194. In the basement part under dome there will also be one 5-horsepower motor for the ice-water system, one 15-horsepower motor for the refrigerating machine, and one 10-horse power motor for the deep-well plant.

195. STREET CONNECTION.—The connection from the street service to the totalizing panel to be installed as follows:

196. A three-wire circuit, the positive, negative, and neutral conductors, each consisting of four 1,000,000 circular mil cables from the street service to the triple-pole single-throw switch on totalizing panel.

197. SYSTEM OF WIRING.—Wiring to be done in three-wire system for all feeders, subfeeders, and mains, and two-wire system for all tap or distributing circuits.

198. SIZE AND ARRANGEMENT OF CONDUCTORS.—The arrangement of all circuits, together with sizes of conductors, as shown on circuit diagram No. 156.

199. The size, insulation, and estimated maximum load of all conductors is shown on attached schedule designated "Schedule of conductors." In any event, conductors to have carrying capacity required by the Rules and Regulations of the National Board of Fire Underwriters.

200. ARRANGEMENT OF TAP CIRCUITS.—All tap circuits for lights to be run to distributing cabinets located upon the same floor as the lights. The outlets to be so arranged to be not more than twelve lights upon any tap circuit, unless otherwise permitted by architect.

201. The tap circuits for the ceiling outlets in the basement and floor outlets of first floor to be run in the same set of conduits, and same construction to be used for

ceiling outlets of first floor and floor outlets of second floor, the conduit being cross-connected as herein elsewhere stated.

202. On floors above the second floor, the conductors for floor outlets to be provided only at such points as are shown upon drawings Nos. 147-152, inclusive.

203. Wherever such floor outlets are shown, the floor outlet boxes shall be equipped with porcelain keyless receptacle sockets, so designed and installed as not to interfere with the wires of the circuits for ceiling outlets.

204. Where ceiling outlets are not on snap switches, the floor outlets at the same boxes shall be fed from the same wires as the ceiling outlets.

205. When ceiling outlets are on snap switches, then the floor outlets at the same floor outlet boxes shall be on a separate branch tap circuit of No. 14 wire, which shall be connected to the same wiring as ceiling outlets, but between the snap switch and the cut-out cabinet.

206. SNAP SWITCHES.—Wherever switches are shown on plans, except switches on the switch board and in cabinets, these shall be single-pole push-button snap switches, similar and equal to the type known as the "Thompson flush push-button switch," manufactured by the Perkins Electric Switch Manufacturing Company.

207. PLUG SWITCHES AND RECEPTACLES.—Wherever plug switches and receptacles are required they shall be equal and similar to the "Chapman" receptacle and plug manufactured by the Bryant Electrical Company.

208. All floor outlet boxes on the first and second floors shall be equipped with plug receptacles of suitable size and designed to receive plug shown on drawing No. 155, these receptacles to be connected to the wires for the floor outlets; to be so designed that they can be readily fastened to same after the wires are drawn into the boxes and without cutting the wires.

209. CONDUIT AND WIRING PLANS.—The location of all cut-out cabinets and all lights and switch outlets is shown approximately on drawings Nos. 144 to 153, inclusive. Before construction commences the contractor shall submit for approval of the architect conduit and wiring plans showing arrangement of all conduits and circuits and size of all pipes and conductors. No wiring or conduits to be installed until the general arrangement is approved by the architect, and no work to be done on any section of the work until complete conduit and wiring plans of that portion of the work have been approved by the architect.

210. LEAD AND PAPER COVERED CABLES.—The paper and lead covered cable herein mentioned shall be constructed as follows:

211. Conductor cable to be of soft-drawn stranded copper having conductivity of not less than 98 per cent of that of ure copper, no strand to be larger than No. 8 B. & S. gauge, insulation to consist of paper saturated with moisture-proof compound and having a minimum thickness of $\frac{1}{4}$ inch. Protecting covering to consist of pure lead having minimum thickness of $\frac{1}{8}$ inch.

212. There will be no joints in cable between outlets. If in any case joints in cable are absolutely necessary, they shall be so insulated as to have insulation resistance and dielectric strength equal to that of the cable. The joints in the lead to be protected with lead sleeve equal in thickness to the lead covering of the cable, and connected to same by wipe joints.

213. The ends of all cables to be equipped with hard-rubber terminals not less than 6 inches long, the hard rubber to be not less than $\frac{3}{16}$-inch in thickness. These terminals to be filled with compound which will not soften and run at a temperature of 120° F., terminals to be equipped with hard-rubber caps.

214. RUBBER-COVERED CONDUCTORS.—All wire throughout the building, except as otherwise specified for use in tile ducts and in vertical runways, to be rubber covered and braided. The rubber-covered wire to have an insulation of quality and thickness required for voltage between zero and 600 volts by the Rules and Regulations of the National Board of Fire Underwriters. Measures of insulating wall to be made at the thinnest point of the dielectric.

215. All wires which are run in iron conduit to be double braided, and all No. 12 B. & S. gauge wire to be duplex wire with one braiding over each conductor and a second braiding over both.

216. SLOW-BURNING WEATHERPROOF CONDUCTORS.—Slow-burning weatherproof wire to be used only for cables to be run upon insulation of porcelain or glass, in vertical runways, as herein specified. Where this wire is used, the insulation to be of the kind and thickness required by the Rules and Regulations of the National Board of Fire Underwriters.

217. Connection to all stranded wire to be made with copper terminals securely soldered to same.

218. JOINTS AND CONDUCTORS.—There will be no joints in any conductors between outlets.

219. Wherever joints are necessary they shall be Western Union twist joints for wires of No. 10 B. & S. or smaller, and for larger conductors they shall be made with copper sleeves of conductivity equal to that of the wire.

220. All joints are to be well soldered. The joints to be covered first by an approved rubber tape and protected by an external wrapping of friction tape which will adhere firmly at any temperature to which it is liable to be exposed. The whole to be painted with an insulating paint similar and equal to what is known as P. & B. paint.

221. ENDS OF CONDUCTORS AT OUTLETS.—At all tap outlets wire shall be brought out with a loop at least 8 inches in length, unless otherwise permitted by architect, and at all motor outlets ends of circuit wire shall be left of such length as directed by the architect.

222. LUGS.—The ends of all cables shall be soldered to copper lugs of design acceptable to the architect. These lugs to have a conductivity at least equal to that of the cable to which they are connected.

223. All contact surfaces shall be carefully finished and fitted so as to have a bearing at every point, contact surface to be not less than 1 square inch for every 200 amperes of rated current which they will be required to carry under this specification and schedule.

224. SUPPORTS OF RISERS.—All cables in vertical raceways to be supported upon porcelain insulators of design acceptable to the architect, these insulators to be designed so as to hold the cables without tie wires; insulators to be securely bolted to steel bars, which in turn shall be fastened by bolts or screws to the steel work of the building.

225. Wherever the cables pass through floors they shall be equipped with glass or porcelain floor insulators of approved design, and wherever cables come in close proximity to one another or to conducting material they shall be surrounded by tubes of glass, porcelain, or vitrified clay, or any acceptable insulating material which, when broken or submerged one hundred hours in pure water at 70° F., will not absorb over one-half of 1 per cent of its weight.

226. All conductors which are not run in conduit to be supported and insulated in the same manner as if they were bare wire.

227. MARKING OF WIRE.—All wires and cables delivered at the building shall be marked with the maximum voltage at which the wire is designed to be used, the words "National Electrical Code Standard," the name of the manufacturing company, and the trade name of the wire, and the month and year when manufactured.

228. SAMPLES OF WIRE FOR TESTS.—The Department will select for test purposes samples not less than 1 foot long of any or all wire intended for use from the material delivered at the building.

229. All wire shall conform to the specifications contained in the Rules and Requirements of the National Board of Fire Underwriters, and all test samples shall stand the insulation and break-down tests specified therein.

230. Wherever samples shall fail to meet these requirements the wire of which they are a part will be rejected.

231. SUB SWITCH BOARDS.—There will be provided four sub switch boards, two for lighting, located in the spaces below stairways on the first floor, one for power located in the basement of dome, and one for power located on the ninth floor. Location of these switch boards is shown on Plans Nos. 145 and 153.

232. The lighting switch board shall be equipped with the necessary bus bars and connections for the system of conductors herein described. It shall also be equipped with knife switches of suitable capacity for controlling the dome and corridor lighting circuits; switches to be equipped with inclosed fuses. Boards to be made of marble and to have framing similar to that used for main switch board.

233. Switch board to rest upon floor and to be supported upon and substantially fastened to the floor and wall.

234. The power switch boards to be built up of marble slabs, carrying regulating and controlling devices. These slabs and controlling devices to be furnished by another contractor, but this contractor shall assemble the same in place, furnish the necessary steel supports similar to those used for main switch board, and equip the switch boards with the necessary bus bars and connections.

235. He shall also furnish the knife switches and fuses for the subswitch board on the ninth floor, these to be mounted upon marble slabs to correspond in size and finish to the rest of the switch board.

236. Material and construction to be subject to the same conditions as for the main switch board.

237. DISTRIBUTING CABINETS AND CUT-OUT BOXES.—All distributing cabinets and all cut-out boxes to be constructed of No. 10 sheet steel. These to be equipped with doors and hinges complete. All cut-out cabinets and boxes to be equipped with two

plain iron doors provided with suitable and acceptable claps. The doors to be reenforced with angles to give them the necessary stiffness.

238. Wherever, in the opinion of the architect, it is desirable to omit the iron doors, then this contractor shall line the interior of whatever type of door is provided with slate not less than ½ inch in thickness.

239. All doors throughout to be of such design as will conform to the interior finish and to be such as will be acceptable to the architect.

240. The large main distributing cabinets in the basement, first and second stories, will be built against columns in the central portions of the room, and will be provided with marble doors and sides with hinges, catches, and Yale locks of a finish as selected by the architect.

241. The main distributing cabinets on the third and to the eighth story, inclusive, will be built into the walls of the corridors, and will be provided with marble doors with hinges, catches, and Yale locks of a finish as selected by the architect.

242. The small cut-out boxes in the corridors of the building from the first to the eighth story, inclusive, which control corridor lights, will also be provided with marble doors similar to the large cabinets.

243. The distributing boxes from the ninth to the sixteenth story, inclusive, will be provided with ornamental iron fronts. The hardware, including Yale locks, to be of a finish which may be acceptable to the architect.

244. Detailed drawings of all doors to be furnished by the contractor will be required and to be subject to the approval of the architect.

245. TYPE OF CABINETS.—The general type of cut-out cabinet which will be acceptable is shown on drawing No. 154. This is not intended as a working drawing, but is intended as a guide to the bidder in making his estimate, and to the contractor in preparing his working drawings.

246. All copper work is to be of pure forged or rolled metal, milled to the proper shape and carefully polished and lacquered. All marble or slate must be of selected quality and free from mineral veins. Switch handles to be of vulcanized rubber, polished.

247. LOCATION OF CABINETS.—The location of all cut-out cabinets to be substantially as shown on drawings 144 to 153, inclusive, exact location and space available to be determined by architect.

248. DRAWINGS OF CABINETS, ETC.—Before construction commences contractor shall submit to architect for approval working drawings of all main and distributing cut-out cabinets showing buses, fuses, switches, connections, and method of installing and connecting up of same, and any changes in dimension or arrangement required by the architect shall be made by the contractor without extra charge, and construction shall not proceed until such drawings are approved.

249. DESIGNATION OF SWITCHES AND TAP CIRCUITS.—Each tap switch and circuit it controls must be designated by a number clearly marked between the blades of the switch, each cut-out cabinet to be designated by letters and numbers hereafter to be provided, these to be marked between the blades of the main switch controlling the cabinet.

250. SCHEDULE OF CIRCUITS.—The contractor shall furnish for each distribution tablet a neat schedule of the circuits controlled by that tablet. Schedules to be in ink on white cardboard, or on paper mounted on cardboard, covered with glass and in a neat frame, and should show number of lamps, size of wire, and numbers of rooms for each tap circuit. Cards to be mounted under direction of architect.

251. All cut-out and switch tablets to be inspected before installation.

252. GRADE OF WORK AND MATERIALS.—Unless otherwise herein specified or allowed by the architect, all workmanship and material shall conform to the requirements of the National Board of Fire Underwriters, and all fittings shall be equal to those included in its list of electrical fittings, dated April, 1902.

253. INSULATION RESISTANCE.—After the installation is completed, all wiring in the building must test free from ground.

254. The complete installation must have an insulation resistance between conductors and between all conductors and the ground of not less than 10,000 ohms, each circuit of 5 amperes to show an insulation resistance of 4,000,000 ohms, and circuits of greater capacity to show a corresponding insulation resistance, allowing the insulation resistance to vary inversely with the maximum load in amperes of current; that is to say, the insulation shall be 2 megohms for 10 amperes and at least 200,000 for a 100-ampere circuit.

255. NOTE TO CONTRACTORS.—All contractors for mechanical work must lay out all curves, piping, etc., in connection with contract for the general finish.

256. UNIT PRICES.—Bidders must fill out and include in their proposals the list of prices for units of material and labor, which prices shall serve as a basis of settlement for additions to or omissions from the work done under this contract.

257. ALTERNATE PROPOSITIONS.—In the event that it is decided to use electric elevators, the capacity of the system will be increased 25 per cent; a corresponding increase must be made in the capacity of all leads, panels, bus bars, instruments, and conductors on totalizing panel. Two additional panels to be equipped the same as other feeder panels, each to have a capacity of 800 amperes at 230 volts. In the event of such change, contractor will also provide four additional tile ducts from trench in rear of switch to manhole, designated on Drawing No. 144. Contractor shall state in his proposition the addition which will be made to his contract price for furnishing the increased capacity of switch boards, conduits, and conductors.

258. SAMPLES.—Upon request, the contractor shall submit to the architect for his approval samples of any material, fitting, or appliance herein specified, and all material, fittings, or appliances furnished shall be of kind and workmanship equal to that of samples submitted.

259. OTHER CONTRACTORS.—For the purpose of facilitating the progress of the work and to avoid making of any changes after any of the work has once been done, this contractor will place himself in touch with other contractors on the building whose work may in any way interfere, be a part of, or in proximity to his work. He will particularly familiarize himself with the interior finish and decoration.

260. RISK.—All work and materials embraced in this contract shall remain at the risk of the contractor until the final completion and acceptance of the same, and the contractor must, at his own expense, take out all necessary policies and insurance for his own protection.

PROPOSAL FOR THE ELECTRIC SWITCH BOARD, CONDUIT, AND WIRING FOR THE UNITED STATES POST-OFFICE, COURT-HOUSE, ETC., AT CHICAGO, ILLINOIS.

HENRY IVES COBB,

Architect of the U. S. Government Building at Chicago, Illinois,

Treasury Department, Washington, D. C.

SIR: We hereby propose to furnish all the labor and materials required for the electric switch board, conduit, and wiring for the United States post-office, court-house, etc., at Chicago, Illinois, including all underground ducts, conduit, wiring, switch-board outlet boxes, cut-out cabinets, switches, and all other work and materials mentioned in this specification for the sum of sixty-nine thousand eight hundred and thirty-eight dollars ($69,838.00) and agree to the following schedule of prices as a basis for all additions and deductions should we be awarded the contract:

(The following unit prices are for appliances installed complete.)

½-inch enameled conduit	per foot..	$0.12
¾-inch enameled conduit	per foot..	.14
1-inch enameled conduit	per foot..	.17
1¼-inch enameled conduit	per foot..	.20
1½-inch enameled conduit	per foot..	.25
2-inch enameled conduit	per foot..	.45
½-inch plain iron pipe	per foot..	.11
¾-inch plain iron pipe	per foot..	.13
1-inch plain iron pipe	per foot..	.16
1¼-inch plain iron pipe	per foot..	.19
1½-inch plain iron pipe	per foot..	.24
2-inch plain iron pipe	per foot..	.43
Per circuit for switch and fuse on tablet		2.00
Snap switch with outlet box		2.25
Plug receptacle		2.40
Plug receptacle socket		2.54
Floor outlet box with receptacle		8.00
Floor outlet box without receptacle		6.60
Per additional outlet in floor outlet box		2.00
Per ceiling fixture outlet box		1.50
Per side fixture outlet box		1.20
No. 14 rubber-covered wire	per foot, $0.03; weatherproof..	.01½
No. 12 rubber-covered wire	per foot, .04; weatherproof..	.02
No. 10 rubber-covered wire	per foot, .06; weatherproof..	.02½
No. 8 rubber-covered wire	per foot, .07; weatherproof..	.03
No. 6 rubber-covered wire	per foot, .09; weatherproof..	.04
No. 5 rubber-covered wire	per foot, .11; weatherproof..	.05
No. 4 rubber-covered wire	per foot, .13; weatherproof..	.06
No. 3 rubber-covered wire	per foot, .14; weatherproof..	.07
No. 2 rubber-covered wire	per foot, .16, weatherproof..	.09

No. 1 rubber-covered wire.................per foot, $0.18; weatherproof.. $0.11
No. 0 rubber-covered wire.................per foot, .20; weatherproof.. .13
No. 00 rubber-covered wire...............per foot, .23; weatherproof.. .15
No. 000 rubber-covered wire...... ......per foot, .26; weatherproof.. .17
No. 0000 rubber-covered wire.............per foot, .30; weatherproof.. .20
200,000 circular mil, weatherproof...........................per foot.. .20
300,000 circular mil, weatherproof...........................per foot.. .24
400,000 circular mil, weatherproof.......................,....per foot.. .32
500,000 circular mil, weatherproof...........................per foot.. .40
600,000 circular mil, weatherproof.........................+...per foot.. .50
700,000 circular mil, weatherproof...........................per foot.. .60
800,000 circular mil, weatherproof...........................per foot.. .70
900,000 circular mil, weatherproof...........................per foot.. .80
1,000,000 circular mil, weatherproof...........................per foot.. .90
200,000 circular mil paper and lead covered cable ....per foot.. .35
300,000 circular mil paper and lead covered cable ....per foot.. .45
400,000 circular mil paper and lead-covered cable ....per foot.. .55
500,000 circular mil paper and lead-covered cable ....per foot.. .65
600,000 circular mil paper and lead-covered cable ....per foot.. .75
700,000 circular mil paper and lead-covered cable ....per foot.. .85
800,000 circular mil paper and lead-covered cable ....per foot.. .95
900,000 circular mil paper and lead-covered cable ....per foot.. 1.00
1,000,000 circular mil paper and lead-covered cable.... ......per foot.. 1.20
1,100,000 circular mil paper and lead-covered cable ....per foot.. 1.30
1,200,000 circular mil paper and 'ead-covered cable ....per foot.. 1.40
1,300,000 circular mil paper and lead-covered cable ....per foot.. 1.50
1,400,000 circular mil paper and lead-covered cable ....per foot.. 1.60
1,500,000 circular mil paper and lead-covered cable ....per foot.. 1.70
1,600,000 circular mil paper and lead-covered cable ....per foot.. 1.80
1,700,000 circular mil paper and lead-covered cable ....per foot.. 1.90
1,800,000 circular mil paper and lead-covered cable ....per foot.. 2.00
1,900,000 circular mil paper and lead-covered cable ....per foot.. 2.20
2,000,000 circular mil paper and lead-covered cable ....per foot.. 2.60
Two vitrified-tile ducts ....per running foot.. .65
Four vitrified-tile ducts..............................per running foot.. .90
Six vitrified-tile ducts...............................per running foot.. 1.30
Eight vitrified-tile ducts..............................per running foot.. 1.50
Ten vitrified-tile ducts ....per running foot.. 1.75
Twelve vitrified-tile ducts ....per running foot.. 2.10
Eleven feeder panels 2,650.00
Two power-feeder panels... 550.00
One totalizing panel 948.00
Two subswitch boards for corridor and power lighting................... 500.00
Two additional feeder panels for electric elevators 600.00
Six lighting feeder panels with two feeders per panel.................... 2,200.00

ALTERNATE PROPOSITION ON GENERATOR PANELS, ETC.

The following unit prices are for complete installation and equipment of generator panels, conduits, generator leads, equalizing cable and pedestals for each arrangement of the following installation of generators:

Six 300-kilowatt, 125-volt, two-wire generators $6,733.00
Four 300-kilowatt, 125-volt, two-wire generators 4,709.00
Six 375-kilowatt, 125-volt, two-wire generators 6,835.00
Four 375-kilowatt, 125-volt, two-wire generators......................... 4,952.00
Three 600-kilowatt, 250-volt, three-wire generators 6,733.00
Two 600-kilowatt, 250-volt, three-wire generators........................ 3,824.00
Three 750-kilowatt, 250-volt, three-wire generators 5,761.00
Two 750-kilowatt, 250-volt, three-wire generators........................ 4,099.00

The following are unit prices per marble door complete with hardware as specified for the cut-out boxes and cabinets to be deducted if doors are provided by the general contractor:

Price per door complete on basement cabinet $20.00
Price per door complete on first-floor cabinet............................. 23.00
Price per door complete on second-floor cabinet 23.00

Price per door as provided for distributing cabinets on third to eighth
  floors, inclusive $20.00
Price per door as provided for distributing cabinets on the dome floors.... 12.00
Price per door as rovided for cut-out boxes for corridor lights 12.00
Additional price fpr furnishing the 25 per cent increased capacity of switch
  boards, conduits, conductors, and the furnishing of two additional
  panels; all as provided under paragraph 257 of specification 2,000.00
Additional price if all the iron conduit work is changed to a japanued-
  lined piping 3,750.00

If awarded the contract we agree to complete all work herein called for within
270 working days from the time of notification to proceed with the work.
(Bidder to give below the location and date of performance by him of work of
similar character to that herein called for.)

  Bush Temple of Music, Chicago, 3,000 lts., July, 1902.
  Gayisa Hotel, Memphis, Tenn., 2,600 lts., Apr., 1902.
  James Hobart Moore, Lake Geneva, May, 1901.
  Iowa Hospital for Insane, Cherokee, Ia., Aug., 1902.
  Board of Assessors and Plymouth bldg's, Chicago, 1899.
  Univ. of Chicago: Green Hall, School of Education, Press bldg., Gymnasium
bldg., 1901–1902.

ARTHUR FRANTZEN COMPANY,
ARTHUR FRANTZEN, <i>Secy. and Treas.,</i>
Rms. 12–14, 225 Dearborn St., Chicago, Ill.

November 5th, 1902.
Members of firm: Wm. H. Rattenbury, pres.; Rees D. Jones, v. pres.; Arthur
Frantzen, sec. and treas.
Nov. 8, 1902.

HENRY IVES COBB,
Architect U. S. Govt. Bldg., Chicago.
J. K. TAYLOR,
Supervising Architect, Treas. Dept.
CHAS. E. KEMPER,
Chief Executive Officer, Supv. Archt.'s Office.
H. D. GREEN,
Accountant.

TREASURY DEPARTMENT, OFFICE OF THE SECRETARY,
Washington, D. C., December 5, 1902.

ARTHUR FRANTZEN COMPANY,
  225 Dearborn Street, Chicago, Illinois.

SIRS: Your proposal dated November 5, 1902, addressed to Mr. Henry Ives Cobb,
architect of the U. S. Government building at Chicago, Illinois, Treasury Department,
Washington, D. C., the lowest received under advertisement dated October 4, 1902,
to furnish all the labor and materials required for the electric switch board, conduit,
and wiring for the United States post-office, court-house, etc., at Chicago, Illinois,
including all underground ducts, conduit, wiring, switch-board outlet boxes, cut-out
cabinets, switches, and all other work and materials mentioned in the specifications,
for the sum of sixty-nine thousand eight hundred thirty-eight dollars ($69,838), is
hereby accepted.

It is further understood and agreed that the entire work embraced in this acceptance is to be completed within two hundred and seventy (270) working days from
the approval of your bond by the Secretary of the Treasury, of which you will be
duly advised.

It is further understood and agreed that the Department reserves the right to order
on or before April 1, 1903, and that you will furnish a twenty-five (25) per cent
increase in capacity of switch-board, conduit, conductors, and furnish the additional
panels, all as provided under paragraph 257 of the specifications, for the additional
sum of two thousand dollars ($2,000); and further, that the Department may order.
and you will furnish japan-lined piping throughout, as per your bid, for the additional
sum of thirty-seven hundred and fifty dollars ($3,750) without asking for or being
granted any additional time.

It is further understood and agreed that you will execute a formal contract, with
bond in the sum of twenty thousand dollars ($20,000) as a guarantee for the faith-
ful performance of the work embraced in your proposal, a form of which will be sent
you for execution and return to this Department for examination, approval, and file;

and it is understood and agreed also, that the said contract, with bond, must be executed and returned within five days from the date of receipt by you of said form.

Payment of said work will be made from the appropriation for the post-office, court-house, etc., Chicago, Illinois, on filing of proper vouchers duly signed and approved.

The certified check which accompanied your proposal will be retained at this Department until approval of your formal bond by the Secretary of the Treasury.

Kindly acknowledge receipt of this letter.

Respectfully,

                                                L. M. SHAW, *Secretary*

Contract between the United States of America and Arthur Frautzen Company.

Whereas by advertisement duly made and published according to law, proposals were asked for furnishing all the labor and materials for the electric switch board, conduits, and wiring of the United States post-office, court-house, etc., at Chicago, Illinois; and

Whereas the proposal of Arthur Frautzen Company, of Chicago, Ill., furnished in response thereto, was duly accepted on the fifth day of December, 1902, on condition that —— execute a contract in accordance with the terms of said bid.

Now, therefore, this agreement, made and entered into by and between Leslie M. Shaw, Secretary of the Treasury, for and in behalf of the United States of America, of the first part, and Arthur Frautzen Company, a corporation organized under the laws of the State of Illinois and having executive offices in Chicago, Illinois, of the second part,

Witnesseth, that the party of the second part, for the consideration hereinafter mentioned, covenants and agrees to and with the party of the first part to furnish all of the labor and materials, and do and perform all the work required for the electric switch board, conduits, and wiring of the United States post-office, court-house, etc., at Chicago, Illinois, in strict and full accordance with the requirements of drawings numbered 144 to 160, inclusive, and such other detail drawings as may be furnished to the party of the second part by the architect of the United States Government building at Chicago, Illinois; the advertisement for proposals, dated October fourth, 1902; the specification for the work; the proposal dated November 5th, 1902, addressed to the said architect by the said party of the second part; and letter dated December 5th, 1902, addressed to the said party of the second part by Leslie M. Shaw, Secretary of the Treasury, accepting said proposal, a true and correct copy of each of which said papers is attached hereto and forms a part of this contract; and which said numbered drawings, bearing the signature of the said architect and the signature of the said party of the second part, are on file in the office of the said architect and are hereby made part of this contract.

And the said party of the second part further covenants and agrees that the work herein agreed to be performed shall be commenced promptly upon receipt of notice of the approval of the bond hereto attached, and will carry on the same in such order and at such times and seasons and with such force as shall from time to time be directed or prescribed by the said architect or his representative, and will complete the same in all its parts within 270 working days from the date of the approval of said bond hereto attached; that all materials used shall be of the very best quality of their respective kinds; that all the work performed shall be executed in the most skillful and workmanlike manner; and that both the materials used and the work performed shall be in every respect to the entire and complete satisfaction of the said architect.

And the party of the second part expressly convenants and agrees that he will well and truly perform and fulfill the stipulations of the third paragraph of said letter of acceptance whenever required so to do.

It is expressly covenanted and agreed by and between the parties hereto that time is and shall be considered as of the essence of the contract on the part of the party of the second part, and in the event that the said party of the second part shall fail in the due performance of the entire work to be performed under this contract, by and at the time herein mentioned or referred to, the said party of the second part shall pay unto the party of the first part, as and for liquidated damages, and not as a penalty, the sum of fifty dollars for each and every day the said party of the second part shall be in default, which said sum of fifty dollars per day, in view of the difficulty of estimating such damages with exactness, is hereby expressly fixed, estimated, computed, determined, and agreed upon as the damages which will be suffered by the party of the first part by reason of such default, and it is understood and agreed by the parties to this contract that the liquidated damages hereinbefore mentioned are in lieu of the actual damages arising from such breach of this contract; which said sum the said party of the first part shall have the right to deduct from any moneys in its hands otherwise due, or to become due, to the said party of the second part, or to sue for and recover compensation or damages for the nonperformance of this contract at the time or times herein stipulated or provided for.

The party of the second part further covenants and agrees to hold and save the United States, its officers, agents, servants, and employees, harmless from and against all and every demand or demands, of any nature or kind, for or on account of the use of any patented invention, article, or appliance included in the materials hereby agreed to be furnished under this contract.

It is further covenanted and agreed by and between the parties hereto that the said party of the second part will, without expense to the United States, comply with all the municipal building ordinances and regulations, in so far as the same are binding upon the United States, and obtain all required licenses and permits, and be responsible for all damages to person or property which may occur in connection with the prosecution of the work; that all work called for by the drawings and specifications, though every item be not particularly shown on the first or mentioned in the second, shall be executed and performed as though such work were particularly shown and mentioned in each, respectively, unless otherwise specifically provided; that all materials and work furnished shall be subject to the approval of the said architect, and that said part of the second part shall be responsible for the proper care and protection of all materials delivered and work performed by it until the completion and final acceptance of same.

If is further covenanted and agreed by and between the parties hereto that the said party of the second part will make any omissions from, additions to, or changes in, the work or materials herein provided for whenever required by said party of the first part; the valuation of such work and materials to be determined on the basis of the contract unit of value of material and work referred to; or, in the absence of such unit of value, on prevailing market rates; which market rates, in case of dispute, are to be determined by the said architect, whose decision with reference thereto shall be binding upon both parties; and that no claim for damages, on account of such changes or for anticipated profits, shall be made or allowed.

It is further covenanted and agreed that no claim for compensation for any extra materials or work is to be made or allowed, unless the same be specifically agreed upon in writing or directed in writing by the said architect; and that no addition to, omission from, or changes in the work or materials herein specifically provided for shall make void or affect the other provisions or covenants of this contract, but the difference in the cost thereby occasioned, as the case may be, shall be added to or deducted from the amount of the contract; and, in the absence of an express agreement or provision to the contrary, no addition to, or omission from, or changes in the work or upon materials herein specifically provided for shall be construed to extend the time fixed herein for the final completion of the work.

It is further covenanted and agreed by and between the parties hereto that all materials furnished and work done under this contract shall be subject to the inspection of the said architect, the superintendent of the building, and of other inspectors appointed by the said party of the first part, with the right to reject any and all work or material not in accordance with this contract; and the decision of said architect as to quality and quantity shall be final. And it is further covenanted and agreed by and between the parties hereto that said party of the second part will, without expense to the United States, within a reasonable time to be specified by the said architect, remedy or remove any defective or unsatisfactory material or work; and that, in the event of the failure of the party of the second part immediately to proceed and faithfully continue so to do, said party of the first part may have the same done and charge the cost thereof to the account of said party of the second part.

It is further covenanted and agreed by and between the parties hereto that until final inspection and acceptance of, and payment for, all of the material and work herein provided for, no prior inspection, payment, or act is to be construed as a waiver of the right of the party of the first part to reject any defective work or material or to require the fulfillment of any of the terms of the contract.

It is further covenanted and agreed that the party of the first part shall have the right to require that any particular portion of the work herein provided for shall be completed within such time as may be hereafter definitely specified by the said party of the first part in written notice to the said party of the second part; and that should the said party of the second part fail to complete such particular portion of the work within the time so specified, or fail to complete the entire work contemplated by this contract within the time or times herein stipulated or provided for; or fail to prosecute said work with such diligence as in the judgment of the party of the first part will insure the completion of the said work within the time hereinbefore provided, the said party of the first part may withhold all payments for work in place until final completion and acceptance of same, and is authorized and empowered, after eight days' due notice thereof in writing, served personally upon or left at the shop, office, or usual place of abode, or with the agent of the said party of the second part, and the said party of the second part having failed to take such action within the said eight days as will, in the judgment of the said party of the first part, remedy the default for which said notice was given, to take possession of the said work in whole or in part and of all machinery and tools employed thereon, and all materials belonging to the said party of the second part delivered on the site, and, at the expense of said party of the second part, to complete or have completed the said work, and to supply or have supplied the labor, materials, and tools, of whatever character necessary to be purchased or supplied by reason of the default of the said party of the second part; in which event the said party of the second part shall be further liable for any damage incurred through such default and any and all other breaches of this contract.

It is further covenanted and agreed that the said party of the first part shall have the right of suspending the whole or any part of the work herein contracted to be done whenever, in the opinion of the said architect, it may be necessary for the purposes or advantage of the work, and upon such occasion or occasions the said party of the second part shall, without expense to the United States, properly cover over, secure, and protect such of the work as may be liable to sustain injury from the weather, or otherwise; provided that for all such suspensions and other delays caused by the said party of the first part the party of the second part shall be allowed one day additional to the time herein stated for each and every day of such delay so caused in the completion of the contract, the same to be ascertained by the said architect; provided, that no claim shall be made or allowed to the said party of the second part for any damages which may arise out of any delay caused by the said party of the first part.

And the said party of the first part, acting for and in behalf of the United States, covenants and agrees to pay, or cause to be paid, unto the said party of the second part, or to its heirs, excutors, administrators, or successors, in lawful money of the United States, in consideration of the herein-recited covenants and agreements made by the party of the second part, the sum of sixty-nine thousand eight hundred and thirty-eight dollars ($69,838.00).

And the party of the first part covenants and agrees that payments will be made in the following manner, viz: Ninety per cent of the value of the work executed and actually in place, to the satisfaction of the said architect, will be paid from time to time as the work progresses (the said value to be ascertained by the said architect), and ten per cent thereof will be retained until the completion of the entire work and the approval and acceptance of the same by the party of the first part, which amount shall be forfeited by said party of the second part in the event of the nonfulfillment of this contract; it being expressly covenanted and agreed that said forfeiture shall not relieve the party of the second part from liability to the party of the first part for any and all damages sustained by reason of any breach of this contract; provided, however, that no payment hereunder shall be due to the said party of the second part until every part of the work to the point of advancement reached—on account of which payment is claimed—shall be found to be satisfactorily supplied and executed in every particular and any and all defects therein remedied to the entire satisfaction of the said party of the second part.

It is an express condition of this contract that no member of Congress or other person whose name is not at this time disclosed shall be admitted to any share in this contract or to any benefit to arise therefrom; and it is further covenanted and agreed that this contract shall not be assigned.

In witness whereof the parties hereto have hereunto subscribed their names this fifth day of December, 1902.

[Bond executed.   Not yet approved.   January 12, 1903.]

No. 1396 A.   Contract of Arthur Frantzen Company, of Chicago, Ill., for electric switch board, conduit, and wiring of the U. S. post-office, court-house, etc., at Chicago, Ill., dated December 5th, 1902.   Amount, $69,838.00.   Time to complete, 270 working-days.   Penalty for each day's delay, $50.   Bond approved, ——— ——, 1902.   Amount of bond, $20,000.

The following instructions must be particularly observed and complied with, viz: 1st. The Christian names must be written in the body of the bond in full, and so signed to the bond.

2d. A seal of wax or wafer must be attached to each signature on the bond.   No seals required for signatures to contract except corporate seals.

3d. Each signature must be made in the presence of two persons, who must sign their names as witnesses.

4th. Each surety must make and sign an affidavit of the amount he is worth after paying his just debts and deducting all exemptions by the laws of the State in which he resides, and liabilities of whatever nature, as per form herewith.

5th. A district judge or attorney of the United States, or clerk of a United States court, must certify that the sureties are sufficient to pay the penalty of the bond.

6th. The affidavit of the sureties must be taken and signed before an officer authorized to administer oaths generally. The officer must certify that he administered the oaths. If the magistrate is not a judge of the United States court, his authority to administer oaths must be certified by the clerk of a court of record having official knowledge of that fact.

7th. Bond must be dated.

8th. Residence of principal and sureties must be distinctly stated.

9th. The sureties must justify in amounts the aggregate of which will be equal to twice the penal sum of the bond.

10th. When the contracting party is a partnership concern, the contract must be signed with the firm name without seal, and the bond must be signed by each member of the firm with seal to each signature; when a corporate body there should be attached to the contract duly authenticated evidence that the officer or officers executing the contract and bond have authority to do so, and the corporate seal must be affixed to each instrument.

O

SALARIES OF CERTAIN JUDGES OF THE UNITED STATES.

JANUARY 16, 1903.—Committed to the Committee of the Whole House on the state
of the Union and ordered to be printed.

Mr. WARNER, from the Committee on the Judiciary, submitted the
following

REPORT.

[To accompany S. 3287.]

The Committee on the Judiciary, to which was referred the bill
(S. 3287) to fix the salaries of certain judges of the United States,
respectfully reports that it has carefully considered the same and
recommends that it be amended as follows, viz:

(1) Strike out the words "five hundred" in line 11 on page 1.

(2) Strike out the words "two hundred and fifty" in line 13 on page 1.

(3) Strike out the word "one" in line 15 on page 1 and insert in
lieu thereof the word "five."

(4) Strike out the words "and twenty-five" in line 15 on page 1.

(5) Strike out the words "associate justices" in line 1 on page 2
and insert in lieu thereof the words "other judges."

(6) Strike out the word "five" in line 1 on page 2 and insert in lieu
thereof the word "six."

(7) Strike out the words "six hundred and twenty-five" in line 2
on page 2.

(8) Strike out the word "eight" in line 4 on page 2 and insert in
lieu thereof the word "six."

(9) Insert immediately after the word "thousand" in line 4 on page
2 the words "five hundred."

(10) Strike out the word "seven" in line 5 on page 2 and insert in
lieu thereof the word "six."

(11) Strike out the words "five hundred" in line 6 on page 2.

(12) After the words "Chief Justice" in line 7 on page 2 insert the
words "and to each associate justice."

(13) Strike out all of line 8 after the word "Columbia," and all of
line 9 on page 2.

(14) Strike out the words "two hundred and fifty" in line 10 on
page 2.

(15) Strike out the word "judges" in line 17 on page 2 and insert in lieu thereof the words "the Chief Justice and to the associate justices."

(16) Strike out the word "judges" in line 18 on page 2 and insert in lieu thereof the words "the Chief Justice and to the associate justices."

And that when so amended it be passed.

Your committee is of opinion that, in view of the increased amount of business coming before and being considered by the justices and judges mentioned in the bill, the increased amount of work such business compels them to perform, the increase in the cost of living, and the increase in the amounts men qualified for such positions are able to earn by the practice of their professions, the salaries fixed by the bill as amended are justified, if not demanded.

It will hardly be doubted that a lawyer with the legal knowledge and ability that should be possessed by a Federal judge can, without any great labor, earn more each year by his practice than the highest salary fixed by the bill.

While it is true that a Federal judge may retire on full pay at any time after he has served ten years on the bench and arrived at the age of 70 years, it is also true that while he is so serving he can not with propriety, and in fact seldom does, engage in any private business, and, as a rule, his entire salary is consumed by his personal and family expenses, and if he should retire when authorized by law, he would then be too old to practice his profession or engage in any business. It is seldom that a Federal judge avails himself of the statute and retires before he has been convinced that his faculties have become so far impaired that he is incapacitated for further work.

The Federal judges give the best years of their lives to their country, and your committee is of opinion that their salaries should be such that qualified persons may accept the positions and give them their undivided time and attention, without too great pecuniary sacrifices, and that they may be able to save something out of their salaries for their widows and children, when they are gone.

O

SALARIES OF CERTAIN JUDGES OF THE UNITED STATES.

JANUARY 19, 1903.—Committed to the Committee of the Whole House on the state of the Union and ordered to be printed.

Mr. SMITH, of Kentucky, from the Committee on the Judiciary, submitted the following as the

VIEWS OF THE MINORITY.

[To accompany S. 3287.]

The undersigned, members of the Judiciary Committee, are of the opinion that this bill (S. 3287) ought not to pass, with or without the amendments proposed by the Committee.

The salaries which will be increased by it, if enacted into a statute, were in most instances fixed at dates when the cost of both the necessities and luxuries of life was as great as it is now, and upon a thorough consideration of the facts that are pertinent they are certainly as liberal as those paid to any other class of civil officers of the United States, and much higher than the average paid corresponding judicial officers by the States.

These offices are also held for life or during good behavior, with the privilege to him who has served in any one of them for a period of ten years and arrived at 70 years of age of retiring with full pay for the remainder of his life—a very valuable privilege not accorded to any other class of civil officers in this country. With the compensation as now fixed by law they are, and long have been, universally conceded to be the most desirable offices under the Federal Government. Nor do we believe that the salaries proposed in this bill for the different classes of judicial officers therein named bear the proper and just relation to each other required by the relative service, dignity, and importance of such classes.

For these, among many reasons that could be stated, we think the bill should be defeated.

D. H. SMITH.
H. D. CLAYTON.
D. A. DE ARMOND.
R. L. HENRY.

O

DISTRICT OF COLUMBIA APPROPRIATION BILL.

JANUARY 17, 1903.—Committed to the Committee of the Whole House on the state of the Union and ordered to be printed.

Mr. McCLEARY, from the Committee on Appropriations, submitted the following

REPORT.

[To accompany H. R. 16842.]

The Committee on Appropriations, in presenting the bill making appropriations for the support of the government of the District of Columbia for the fiscal year ending June 30, 1904, submit the following in explanation thereof:

The estimates of the Commissioners of the District of Columbia, upon which the bill is based, will be found on pages 339 to 383 of the Book of Estimates, and, exclusive of the water department, aggregate $10,872,372, one-half of which amount, exclusive of expenses under the highway act, or of such sum as Congress may appropriate, is required to be drawn from the revenues of the General Government and the remaining one-half to be levied upon the taxable property and privileges in the District of Columbia other than the property of the United States and the District of Columbia, pursuant to section 3 of the act approved June 11, 1878, entitled "An act providing a permanent form of government for the District of Columbia." (Stat. L., vol. 20, p. 102.)

The total amount recommended to be appropriated for the general expenses of the District of Columbia for the fiscal year 1904 in the bill submitted herewith is, exclusive of the water department, $7,618,449, of which sum the General Government is required to pay $3,807,974.50, that being one-half of the whole, exclusive of the amount ($2,500) recommended for expenses under the highway act. The first-named sum is $3,253,923 less than the estimate submitted by the Commissioners.

The amount appropriated for the general expenses of the District of Columbia for the current fiscal year (1903) is $8,462,923.97, or $844,474.97 more than is recommended in the accompanying bill for 1904.

The amount recommended for the water department, all of which is payable from the water revenues, is $132,206, being an increase of $9,040 over the appropriations for the water department for the current fiscal year.

It is estimated that the water revenues available for the fiscal year 1904 will amount to $402,000; but it is provided in the accompanying bill, as it was in the acts for the current and eleven preceding fiscal years, that any surplus of these revenues over the appropriations made specifically therefrom shall be applied to the work of extending the high-service system of water distribution. Under these indefinite appropriations of the surplus water revenues there has been expended to date, for extending the high-service system of water distribution, about $1,500,000. The estimated ultimate cost is $3,844,786.47.

The total general revenues of the District of Columbia for the fiscal year 1904, it is estimated, will amount to $5,400,000.

The appropriations recommended in the accompanying bill and payable from the revenues of the District amount to $3,810,474.50.

In addition to the foregoing sum, appropriations have already been passed by the House in the legislative, executive, and judicial act, and are estimated under the sundry civil bill, chargeable next year to the revenues of the District, aggregating $90,043.

Under the provisions of section 3 of the last District of Columbia appropriation act, authorizing advances from the Treasury of the United States for the support of the government of the District of Columbia, it is estimated by the Secretary of the Treasury that advances will have been made by June 30, 1903, amounting to $1,901,726.15, which advances, it is required, shall be reimbursed to the Treasury "from time to time, out of the surplus revenues of the District of Columbia, beginning July 1, 1903, together with interest thereon at the rate of 2 per cent per annum until so reimbursed, which reimbursement shall be made within three years from said last-named date." Assuming that at least one-third of the sum estimated—$1,901,726.15—together with 2 per cent per annum interest on the whole debt, will be paid out of the revenues of the District during the fiscal year 1904, the sum of $671,943.23 will be required.

By section 12 of the act of February 12, 1901, as amended by the last District of Columbia appropriation act a highway bridge is required to be constructed within four years from said date across the Potomac River, above the site of the present Long Bridge, at an authorized cost of $996,000, of which sum $568,000 has been appropriated, payable one-half out of the revenues of the District of Columbia. Proposals are about to be invited and contracts will soon be entered into for this work, requiring the payment, probably, of all of the whole sum which has been appropriated, or $284,000 out of the District revenues, before the close of the fiscal year 1904.

The act to provide for a union railroad station in the District of Columbia, now pending in conference, as amended by the House provides for expenditures aggregating at least $3,770,000, payable one-half, or $1,855,000, out of the revenues of the District, of which latter sum $100,000 is in terms appropriated for each of the five years beginning July 1, 1903, and the whole amount it is proposed shall be payable within the ensuing five fiscal years, thus requiring provision, if not actual payment therefor, by equal annual reservations out of the District revenues, amounting to $371,000.

For the municipal building, authorized at the last session of Congress, there yet remains to be appropriated equally from the Treasury and the District revenues the sum of $900,000, at least $300,000 of which, or $150,000 out of the District revenues, will be required during the fiscal year 1904, if the work of constructing the building is to be pressed with proper vigor and dispatch.

It will thus be seen that obligations fixed by law, proposed in regular appropriation bills other than the accompanying one, and in other pending legislation practically sure of enactment during this session against the revenues of the District to be met or provided for during the fiscal year 1904, aggregate $1,566,986.23, which sum added to the amount payable out of District revenues by the terms of the accompanying bill amounts to $5,377,460.73, or well within the total revenues of the District, estimated at $5,400,000.

GENERAL SUMMARY.

The following general summary indicates the appropriations for 1903 that have been omitted, the appropriations for 1903 that have been reduced, and the new items or increases proposed over the appropriations for 1904.

Appropriations for 1903 omitted.

Contingent items, such as office furnishings, etc	$9,650.00
Special street-paving items	37,300.00
Condemnation of streets	1,000.00
Hay scales for Center Market	450.00
Massachusetts avenue bridge completion	10,000.00
Aqueduct avenue bridge repairs	65,000.00
Anacostia River survey	5,000.00
Electrical department, special items	15,250.00
Aqueduct tunnel, completion	67,240.00
Extension high-service water system	200,000.00
Total, omitted	410,890.00

Appropriations for 1903 reduced.

Salaries and contingencies of executive offices, net	$2,440.00
Public Library, new books, from $40,000 to $5,000	35,000.00
Paving city streets, from $150,000 to $50,000	100,000.00
County roads and streets, improving, from $151,000 to $54,500	96,800.00
Public pumps, from $5,000 to $4,000	1,000.00
New school buildings, from $234,944 to $155,000	79,944.00
Metropolitan police, net	560.00
Interest and sinking fund	238,539.97
Charities and corrections, net	70.00
Militia, from $59,145 to $58,820	325.00
Total reductions	554,678.97
Total, omitted and reduced	965,568.97

New items and increases.

Reconstructing cement warehouse	$3,000.00
Opening alleys	10,000.00
For sewers, from $634,000 to $647,000	13,000.00
Bathing beach	1,000.00
Electrical department, underground wires, rebuilding police-patrol circuits and fire-alarm transmitters	22,700.00
Public schools, general expenses, net	48,494.00
Health department	5,000.00
Police court building improvements	4,000.00

Fire department, net $12,790. 00
Opinions court of appeals 110. 00
Support of prisoners 1,000. 00

Total increases 121,094. 00

Net reduction 844,474. 97

LIMITATIONS.

Limitations with reference to appropriations made in the bill not heretofore imposed, or changes in existing limitations, are recommended as follows:

On page 8 the following:

Hereafter the inspector of gas and meters and assistant inspector of gas and meters of the District of Columbia shall be appointed by the Commissioners of the District of Columbia.

On page 12 the limitation with reference to horses, etc., enacted last year is repeated, modified to read as follows:

No part of the money appropriated by this act shall be used for the purchase, livery, or maintenance of horses or for the purchase, maintenance, or repair of buggies or carriages and harness except as provided for in the appropriation for contingent and miscellaneous expenses or unless the appropriation from which the same is proposed to be paid shall specifically authorize such purchase, livery, maintenance, and repair, and except also as hereinbefore authorized.

No part of the money appropriated by this act shall be used for the payment of premiums or other cost of fire insurance.

On page 14 the "property owned by foreign governments for legation purposes" is exempted from assessments for improvements.

On page 15, under the appropriation for paving streets and avenues named in schedules referred to in the bill, it is provided that—

Streets and avenues named in said schedules already paved with Belgian block or granite shall not be paved or otherwise improved under this appropriation.

On page 16 the prices for the two classes of asphalt street paving are reduced from $1.80 to $1.70 and from $2 to $1.80, respectively.

On page 18 the following:

That in order to more fully carry out the intent of the provision in the appropriation act approved July first, nineteen hundred and two, providing for the expenses of the government of the District of Columbia, authorizing the readjustment of the lines of the streets on the east side of the Zoological Park, the Commissioners of the District of Columbia be, and they are hereby, authorized to use as a highway so much of the Zoological Park as lies within a proposed street on the east side of said Zoological Park, between Kenyon street and Klingle road, the bounds of said street being located as follows: The east building line to be distant fifteen feet from the present improved thirty-foot roadway, and the west line to be distant forty-five feet from the present improved thirty-foot roadway.

On page 25 the following:

And during the fiscal year nineteen hundred and three and annually thereafter the price per annum prescribed by Congress for lighting each street lamp in the District of Columbia with gas or oil shall be construed to include the cost of the illuminating material used, lighting and extin-

quishing lamps, repairing, painting, cleaning, purchasing, and expense of erecting and maintaining lamp-posts, street designations, lanterns, and fixtures.

On page 39 the following:

Provided, That hereafter the disbursing officer of the District of Columbia is authorized to advance to the major and superintendent of the Metropolitan police, upon requisitions previously approved by the auditor of the District of Columbia, sums of money, not exceeding three hundred dollars at one time, to be used only for the prevention and detection of crime, and to be accounted for monthly on itemized vouchers to the accounting officers of the District of Columbia.

On page 40 it is required that the chief engineer of the fire department shall be a person *who shall have had at least five years' actual experience as a member of some organized municipal fire department.*

On page 47, in connection with the appropriation for interest and sinking fund on the funded debt, the following:

Any excess of said sum or of sums hereafter appropriated for this purpose over and above the amount required for the payment of the interest on the funded debt of the District of Columbia shall be applied by the Treasury of the United States to the purchase and redemption of the bonds of the District of Columbia: Provided, That should the Treasurer of the United States at any time be unable to secure bonds of the District of Columbia at a price which he may deem advantageous, he is hereby authorized to invest the amount available for the said sinking fund in bonds of the United States, the bonds so purchased to be registered in the name of the Treasurer of the United States, trustees for the sinking fund of the District of Columbia, and it shall be the duty of the Treasurer of the United States to collect the interest, when due, on the bonds so held, and to invest the same for account of said sinking fund: Provided further, That the Treasurer of the United States is hereby authorized, by exchange or by sale and reinvestment, to substitute bonds of the District of Columbia for the bonds of the United States, so held, when he shall deem it to be to the interest of the said sinking fund to do so.

COMPARATIVE STATEMENT.

The following comparative statement shows in detail the amounts appropriated for the current fiscal year, the amounts estimated for 1904, and the amounts recommended in the accompanying bill:

DISTRICT OF COLUMBIA APPROPRIATION BILL, 1904.

Comparative statement, showing the appropriations for 1903, the estimates for 1904, and the amounts recommended in the accompanying bill for 1904.

OBJECT.	Appropriations for 1903.		Estimates for 1904.		Recommended for 1904.	
	Amounts.	Number of salaries.	Amounts.	Number of salaries.	Amounts.	Number of salaries.
Salaries:						
Executive office	$69,224.00	67	$102,444.00	91	$70,664.00	68
Assessor's office	43,600.00	29	42,800.00	30	42,100.00	30
Excise board	5,500.00		5,500.00		4,800.00	3
Personal tax board	18,000.00	7	19,200.00	8	15,200.00	8
Collector's office	19,400.00	13	19,200.00	13	19,400.00	13
Preparation of tax-sale certificates	800.00		800.00		800.00	
Auditor's office	22,850.00	14	24,050.00	15	22,850.00	14
City solicitor's office	12,720.00	7	12,720.00	7	12,720.00	7
Sinking-fund office	2,500.00	2	2,700.00	2	2,500.00	2
Coroner's office	1,800.00	1	2,700.00	2	1,800.00	1
Market masters	4,980.00	3	4,980.00	3	4,980.00	3
Sealer of weights and measures	5,980.00	5	6,080.00	5	6,080.00	5
Engineer's office	67,012.00	57	70,840.00	58	67,012.00	57
Special assessment office	11,900.00	10	11,900.00	10	11,900.00	10
Street-sweeping office	25,100.00	22	40,840.00	38	25,100.00	22
Board of Examiners, Steam Engineers	900.00	3	900.00	3	900.00	3
Department of Insurance	5,600.00	8	10,400.00	9	5,600.00	3
Surveyor's office	17,800.00	2	21,484.00	21	17,800.00	2
Free public library (including $1,620 for 1903 in deficiency act)	17,420.00	29	25,560.00	48	18,440.00	32
Total, salaries	353,086.00	274	425,498.00	381	360,646.00	288

Contingent and miscellaneous:			
Free public library (including $40,000 for 1903 in deficiency act)	52,000.00	29,000.00	17,000.00
Executive office	30,000.00	30,000.00	30,000.00
Engineer department, stables, etc.	5,000.00	5,000.00	5,000.00
Rent of District offices	9,600.00	10,000.00	9,000.00
Rent of old record vault	600.00	600.00	600.00
Rent, office for Department of Insurance	540.00	840.00	540.00
Rent of property yards	300.00	300.00	300.00
Rent of storeroom	300.00	300.00	300.00
Collecting overdue personal taxes	1,500.00	1,500.00	1,500.00
Judicial expenses	1,000.00	2,000.00	1,000.00
Coroner's office, livery, expenses, etc.	1,200.00	2,460.00	1,200.00
Advertising, general	3,000.00	3,000.00	3,000.00
Advertising, notice of taxes in arrears	3,000.00	3,000.00	3,000.00
Market houses, repairs	2,250.00	2,250.00	
Enforcement of game and fish laws	500.00	500.00	500.00
File cases, office of Register of Wills	2,000.00	2,500.00	
Restoration of records, office of Register of Wills	2,000.00		
Card index, Register of Wills	600.00		
Enlargement of fireproof file case, Surveyor's office	300.00		
Photolithographing maps	2,000.00		
Resurvey of Beatty and Hawkins addition, Georgetown		1,500.00	
Resurvey of District boundary line		7,500.00	
Purchase of Latimer field		500.00	
Printing, permit clerk's office fees			
Reconstructing cement storehouse	3,000.00	3,000.00	3,000.00
Total, contingent and miscellaneous	117,590.00	105,750.00	75,940.00
Permanent system of highways (payable wholly out of District revenues)	2,500.00	2,500.00	2,500.00
Improvements and repairs:			
Assessment and permit work	145,000.00	175,000.00	145,000.00
Paving roadways under permit system	10,000.00	10,000.00	10,000.00
Work on streets and avenues	150,000.00	200,000.00	50,000.00
Work on certain specified streets	37,300.00	44,500.00	
Grading streets, roads, and alleys	8,000.00	10,000.00	8,000.00

District of Columbia appropriation bill, 1904—Continued.

OBJECT.	Appropriations for 1903. Amounts.	Number of salaries.	Estimates for 1904. Amounts.	Number of salaries.	Recommended for 1904. Amounts.	Number of salaries.
Improvements and repairs—Continued.						
Condemnation of streets, roads, and alleys	$1,000.00		$1,000.00			
Plats of subdivisions outside of Washington	2,000.00		2,000.00		$2,000.00	
Opening alleys			25,000.00		10,000.00	
??ity ??ds, construction	151,300.00		200,000.00		54,500.00	
Repairs of streets, avenues, and alleys, including re-surfacing	200,000.00		200,000.00		200,000.00	
Sidewalks and curbs, public reservations	10,000.00		10,000.00		10,000.00	
Repairs, county roads	80,000.00		100,000.00		80,000.00	
Bridges—						
Care of	4,000.00		4,000.00		4,000.00	
Construction and repairs	15,000.00		15,000.00		15,000.00	
Rock ??ek, ??chusetts avenue	10,000.00					
??t Bridge, ???	65,000.00					
Rock ??k, Connecticut ? ??e.			100,000.00			
??ia Bridge, reconstruction			100,000.00			
Total, improvements and repairs	888,600.00		1,196,500.00		588,500.00	
Anacostia River flats, survey	6,000.00					
Sewers:						
Cleaning and repairing sewers and basins	58,000.00		58,000.00		58,000.00	
Main and pipe sewers and receiving basins	50,000.00		50,000.00		50,000.00	
Suburban sewers	50,000.00		50,000.00		50,000.00	
Rights of way	1,000.00		1,000.00		1,000.00	
Automatic flushing tanks	1,000.00		1,000.00		1,000.00	
Construction east side intercepting sewer between Twenty-second and A streets NE. and Twelfth street SE	52,000.00					

Construction B street and New Jersey avenue trunk sewer	50,000.00	400,000.00	400,000.00
Construction Arizona avenue sewer		75,000.00	
Extension of boundary sewer to Twenty-second and A streets NE	40,000.00	40,000.00	40,000.00
Construction Ivy City trunk sewer		40,000.00	
Construction outlet sewer, Takoma Park		50,000.00	
Draining Takoma Park		150.00	
		100.00	
Construction trunk sewer, Georgetown	20,000.00	22,000.00	22,000.00
Sewage-disposal system pumping station	250,000.00	125,000.00	25,000.00
Low-area trunk sewer	60,000.00		
Fencing James Creek Canal	2,000.00		
Total, sewers	684,000.00	872,250.00	647,000.00
Streets:			
Sprinkling, sweeping, and cleaning	190,000.00	205,000.00	190,000.00
Removal of snow and ice from cross walks	1,000.00	5,000.00	1,000.00
Collection and disposal of garbage, ashes, and refuse from private houses	115,000.00	102,460.00	115,000.00
Collection and disposal of ashes and miscellaneous refuse from business establishments	25,000.00	35,000.00	
Parking Commission		40,000.00	25,000.00
Improving grounds around municipal buildings		1,000.00	
Harbor and river front	3,000.00	8,480.00	3,000.00
Bathing beach	6,500.00	4,000.00	7,500.00
Public scales	200.00	200.00	200.00
Hay scale for Center Market	450.00		
Public pumps	5,000.00	4,000.00	4,000.00
Total, streets	346,150.00 [19]	405,140.00 [37]	345,700.00 [19]
Electrical department:			
For salaries	16,220.00	31,270.00	16,220.00
General supplies and repairs	14,060.00	11,400.00	14,000.00
Placing wires underground	9,000.00	18,950.00	18,950.00
Extension of fire-alarm telegraph	6,250.00		
Purchase of poles and fittings	5,000.00		
Repairs to fire-alarm headquarters	4,000.00		

District of Columbia appropriation bill, 1904—Continued.

OBJECT.	Appropriations for 1903.		Estimates for 1904.		Recommended for 1904.	
	Amounts.	Number of salaries.	Amounts.	Number of salaries.	Amounts.	Number of salaries.
Electrical department—Continued.						
Extension of patrol system	$5,000.00		$5,000.00		$5,000.00	
Rebuilding police-patrol circuits			20,000.00		7,500.00	
Manual transmitter, fire-alarm system			5,250.00		5,250.00	
Lighting, gas or oil	200,000.00		219,700.00		200,000.00	
Lighting, electric arc	76,000.00		77,400.00		76,000.00	
Total, Electrical Department	335,470.00	19	388,970.00	37	342,920.00	19
Washington Aqueduct:						
Operation and maintenance	33,000.00		33,000.00		33,000.00	
Building storehouse and stable, Great Falls			3,000.00			
Preliminary surveys, additional conduit, Great Falls			8,000.00			
Filtration plant	600,000.00		1,468,405.00		600,000.00	
Total, Washington Aqueduct	633,000.00		1,512,405.00		633,000.00	
Increasing water supply: Completing aqueduct tunnel and Howard University reservoir	67,240.00					
Rock Creek Park	2,500.00		100,000.00		2,500.00	
Public schools:						
For officers	18,620.00	15	20,920.00	16	18,620.00	15
For teachers	918,175.00	1,301	968,975.00	1,346	951,775.00	1,346
Night schools and kindergarten instruction	36,500.00		51,000.00		41,500.00	
For janitors and care of buildings	82,196.00		90,800.00		85,256.00	
Contingent expenses	85,000.00	125	45,000.00	127	85,000.00	127

Item						
Rent of buildings	$17,000.00		$17,000.00		$15,684.00	
Repairs and improvements to buildings and grounds	55,000.00		75,000.00		55,000.00	
Plumbing	25,000.00		25,000.00		25,000.00	
Repairs to ... and ventilating apparatus	12,000.00		3,500.00		3,500.00	
Improving ...			5,000.00			
Manual training, tools, and material	15,000.00		20,000.00		15,000.00	
Fuel	45,000.00		45,000.00		45,500.00	
Furniture for new buildings			12,250.00		12,250.00	
Pianos	2,500.00		2,500.00		2,500.00	
Replacing and repairing furniture	3,000.00		3,000.00			
Text-books and supplies	52,500.00		52,500.00		52,500.00	
Flags	1,000.00		1,000.00		1,000.00	
...			2,000.00			
Pblic playground			7,028.00	11		
Medical ...			5,500.00			
Fire extinguishers and ...			2,400.00		2,400.00	
Extending the ...			5,000.00		5,000.00	
New buildings	234,944.00		515,233.00		155,000.00	
Col ... his Institution for ... af and Dumb	10,500.00		10,500.00		10,500.00	
Total, public schools		1,441	1,986,106.00	1,500	1,532,485.00	1,488
Metropolitan police:						
For salaries	713,260.00	724	800,220.00	792	743,100.00	761
Miscellaneous expenses	71,285.00		77,905.00	15	41,385.00	
House of Detention	8,000.00		11,840.00		8,000.00	
Total, Metropolitan police	793,045.00	724	889,965.00	807	792,485.00	761
Fire Department:						
For salaries	247,280.00	288	275,360.00	310	264,320.00	308
Miscellaneous expenses	65,860.00		80,360.00		65,860.00	
Increase of department	43,50.00		68,500.00		39,500.00	
Total, Fire Department	356,890.00	288	422,220.00	310	369,680.00	308
Health Department:						
For salaries	46,900.00	37	54,520.00	41	46,900.00	37
Rent	120.00		120.00		120.00	

District of Columbia appropriation bill, 1904—Continued.

OBJECT.	Appropriations for 1903. Amounts.	Number of salaries.	Estimates for 1904. Amounts.	Number of salaries.	Recommended for 1904. Amounts.	Number of salaries.
Health Department—Continued						
Prevention of scarlet fever and diphtheria	$20,000.00		$30,000.00		$25,000.00	
Maintaining ...ing service	5,000.00		5,000.00		5,000.00	
Removal of weeds			5, 0.00			
Emergency ...nl. drainage of lots	2,500.00		2,500.00		2,500.00	
Expenses of sanitary and food inspectors	1,000.00		1,500.00		1,000.00	
Regulating sale of milk	1,000.00		1,000.00		1,000.00	
Pound and stable, site			10,000.00			
Erection and equipment			15,000.00			
Stable for smallpox hospital			1,000.00			
Isolating wards, Garfield and Providence hospitals	8,000.00		8,000.00		8,000.00	
...g adulteration of drugs and foods	100.00		100.00		100.00	
Total, Health Department	84,620.00	37	133,740.00	41	89,620.00	37
Courts:						
For salaries, police court	20,990.00	16	23,240.00	16	20,990.00	16
For salaries, justices of the peace	22,500.00	10	32,500.00	10	22,500.00	10
Miscellaneous expenses	13,700.00		17,700.00		17,700.00	
Opinions of court of appeals, District of Columbia			110.00		110.00	
Defending suits in Court of Claims	3,000.00		3,000.00		3,000.00	
Writs of lunacy	1,500.00		5,000.00		1,500.00	
Total, Courts	61,690.00	26	81,550.00	26	65,800.00	26
Interest and sinking fund	1,213,947.97		975,408.00		975,408.00	
General emergency fund	8,000.00		8,000.00		8,000.00	

Courts and Prisons:						
Support of convicts	45,000.00	19	45,000.00	19	45,000.00	19
Salaries, court-house employees	12,960.00	1	12,960.00	1	12,960.00	1
Warden of jail	2,000.00		2,000.00		2,000.00	
Support of prisoners	45,000.00		46,000.00		46,000.00	
Total, Courts and Prisons	104,960.00	20	105,960.00	20	105,960.00	20
Charities and Corrections:						
Board of Charities	7,160.00	6	14,360.00	11	10,400.00	11
Reformatories and correctional institutions—						
Washington Asylum, salaries	25,478.00	68	30,563.00	76	27,618.00	70
Miscellaneous expenses	58,000.00		163,700.00		60,200.00	
Mail the, site, plans, etc			125,000.00			
ary building for thiosis patients			10,000.00			
Reform School, salaries	16,452.00	30	17,252.00	30	16,452.00	30
Support of rues	26,000.00		26,000.00		26,000.00	
New family building and furniture			26,500.00			
Repairs	1,500.00		2,000.00		1,500.00	
Reform School for Girls	16,385.00	14	22,765.00	14	16,765.00	14
Transportation of prisoners	2,000.00		2,000.00		2,000.00	
Medical charities—						
Freedmen's Hospital and Asylum	54,000.00	10	54,000.00	10	54,000.00	10
spital and Lying-in Asylum	26,000.00		22,500.00		22,500.00	
Garfield Hospital			19,000.00			
re Hospital			19,000.00			
Children's Hospital	10,000.00		12,000.00		10,000.00	
National Homeopathic Hospital	8,500.00		8,500.00		8,500.00	
Central ry and Emergency Hospital	16,458.00		16,000.00		15,000.00	
Eastern Dispensary	2,000.00		2,000.00		2,000.00	
Women's clinic	1,000.00		1,000.00		1,000.00	
Washington Home for Incurables	2,000.00		2,000.00		2,000.00	
Municipal Hospital			250,000.00			
Child-caring institutions—						
Board of Children's Guardians	66,600.00		60,900.00	7	54,600.00	
Industrial Home School	21,702.00		15,550.00		15,550.00	
National Association for Colored Women and Children	9,900.00		9,900.00		9,900.00	
Newsboys and Children's Aid Society	1,000.00				1,000.00	
Washington Hospital for Foundlings	6,000.00		5,000.00		6,000.00	

District of Columbia appropriation bill, 1904—Continued.

OBJECT.	Appropriations for 1903.		Estimates for 1904.		Recommended for 1904.	
	Amounts.	Number of salaries.	Amounts.	Number of salaries.	Amounts.	Number of salaries.
Charities and Corrections—Continued.						
Child-caring institutions—Continued.						
St. Ann's Infant Asylum	$5,400.00		$5,000.00		$5,400.00	
German Orphan Asylum	1,800.00		1,800.00		1,800.00	
Temporary homes—						
Municipal Lodging House	4,000.00		4,000.00		4,000.00	
Temporary Home for ex-Union Soldiers and Sailors	4,000.00		4,000.00		4,000.00	
Women's Christian Association	4,000.00		2,000.00		4,000.00	
Young Women's Christian Home	1,000.00				1,000.00	
Hope and Help Mission	2,000.00		1,000.00		2,000.00	
Miscellaneous—						
Hospital for the Insane	215,220.00		229,300.00		229,300.00	
Deportation of nonresident insane	1,000.00		2,000.00		2,000.00	
Relief of the poor	13,000.00		13,000.00		13,000.00	
Transportation of paupers	2,000.00		2,000.00		2,000.00	
Total, Charities and Corrections	631,555.00	128	1,201,590.00	148	631,485.00	135
Militia	59,14.00	2	58,820.00	2	58,820.00	2
Continuing extension of high-service water system	200,000.00					
Grand total, District of Columbia, exclusive of Water Department	8,462,923.97	2,959	10,872,372.00	3,252	7,618,449.00	3,079
Amount payable from District revenues	4,282,711.98		5,437,486.00		3,810,474.50	
Amount payable from United States Treasury	4,230,211.98		5,434,936.00		3,807,974.50	

Water Department:					
Salaries	$30,666.00	29	$30,266.00	27	$29,706.00	27
Contingent expenses	2,500.00	......	3,000.00	......	2,500.00	......
Fuel and repairs to machinery	90,000.00	......	100,000.00	......	100,000.00	......
Total, Water Department	123,166.00	29	133,256.00	27	132,206.00	27
Grand total, including Water Department	8,586,089.97	2,988	11,005,628.00	3,279	7,750,655.00	3,108

O

FORT HALL INDIAN RESERVATION.

JANUARY 17, 1903.—Committed to the Committee of the Whole House on the state
of the Union and ordered to be printed.

Mr. MARTIN, from the Committee on the Public Lands, submitted the
following

REPORT.

[To accompany S. 6502.]

The Committee on the Public Lands, to whom was referred Senate
bill 6502, submit the following report:

On June 6, 1900, Congress passed an act providing for the settlement and disposal of a portion of the Fort Hall Indian Reservation in
the State of Idaho. The city of Pocatello is situated within the area
of the land affected by the act referred to. Section 5 of the act provided for the entry of a large portion of the lands referred to under
the homestead, town site, stone and timber, and mining laws of the
United States; but also provided that all lands within 5 miles of the
boundary line of the town of Pocatello should be sold at public auction,
but for not less than $10 per acre. Pursuant to this legislation, the
honorable Commissioner of the General Land Office proceeded to offer
the lands within the 5-mile limit referred to for sale to the highest
bidder at public auction. As to most of these lands it was found that
the minimum price of $10 per acre fixed in the statute was considerably
in excess of the real value of the land.

The lands embraced within the 5-mile limit comprised a total area
of practically 60,000 acres. As a result of the efforts of the honorable
Commissioner to sell these lands at public auction, only 2,758.67 acres
have been sold. The honorable Commissioner reports that the remaining lands within the 5-mile limit of Pocatello are practically of no
greater value than the remaining portion of the reservation opened to
entry by the act of June 6, 1900, and recommends that these lands
should be subject to entry under the same provisions governing the
other lands opened to settlement by the act. The bill now under consideration has been prepared for the purpose of carrying out this suggestion of the honorable Commissioner of the General Land Office.

In his report to the honorable Secretary of the Interior of December 13, 1902, the Commissioner states:

DEPARTMENT OF THE INTERIOR, GENERAL LAND OFFICE,
Washington, D. C., December 13, 1902.

SIR: I have the honor to acknowledge receipt, by reference from the Commissioner of Indian Affairs, of a bill (S. 6502) entitled "A bill relating to ceded lands on the Fort Hall Indian Reservation."

I would respectfully suggest that the following be added as a proviso to the bill, to be inserted after line 15, on page 1, to wit:

"*Provided*, That the improvements made by certain Indians upon the following-described lands, namely, lot four of section one, the southeast quarter of the northeast quarter of section eighteen, the southeast quarter of the northwest quarter and the northwest quarter of the southwest quarter of section eight, township seven south, range thirty-five east, and the east half of the southeast quarter of section twenty-one, township six south, range thirty-four east, and which have heretofore been appraised, shall be paid for at the said appraised value at the time of and by the person making entry of the respective tracts upon which such improvements are situated."

As thus amended, I would recommend the passage of the bill.

Under the act of Congress of June 6, 1900 (31 Stats., 672), an effort was made to sell the lands within the 5-mile limit of the boundary line of the town of Pocatello, Idaho, at public auction at not less than $10 per acre. The lands embraced within this boundary consisted of 1,505 40-acre tracts, comprising a total area of practically 60,000 acres. Of this land, 69 tracts, amounting to 2,758.67 acres, were sold for the sum of $42,337.80, and no bid was received upon any other tract, although each one was separately offered for sale.

Although great publicity had been given through the newspapers and also by the railroad companies running through that part of the country to the fact that this land was to be offered for sale, it attracted very little attention, and very few people attended the sale, except those living in the immediate vicinity of the land.

The land was not sold, for the reason that it is not worth the minimum price fixed upon it by the act, nor, in my opinion, is its value any greater than that of the remaining portion of the reservation opened to entry by the same act. In my judgment, not a sufficient quantity of this land could be sold at public auction at any price greater than that named in the proposed bill to warrant the expenses incident to another offering. Under existing conditions no disposition whatever can be made of this land, and, deeming it advisable that the land should not be longer kept in a state of reservation, I am of opinion that the best disposition that can be made of it is to make it subject to entry under the same provisions as govern the remaining portions of the reservation, except as to those tracts upon which there are Indian improvements, which is what the bill contemplates.

Very respectfully,

W. A. RICHARDS,
Assistant Commissioner.

The SECRETARY OF THE INTERIOR.

Your committee considers that it is for the best interest not only of the local section where these lands are situated, but also for the entire country, that these lands should be opened to settlement and appropriation under the general laws of the United States. The bill in question will accomplish this, and we recommend its favorable consideration and passage.

O

CLERKS OF CIRCUIT AND DISTRICT COURTS OF THE UNITED STATES.

JANUARY 17, 1903.—Committed to the Committee of the Whole House on the state of the Union and ordered to be printed.

Mr. POWERS, of Massachusetts, from the Committee on the Judiciary, submitted the following

REPORT.

[To accompany H. R. 14047.]

The Committee on the Judiciary, to whom was referred the bill (H. R. 14047) for the relief of the clerks of circuit and district courts of the United States, have carefully considered the same and report the same back with a favorable recommendation.

Prior to 1893 the Attorney-General issued a circular letter requiring all clerks of the circuit and district courts to report all earnings and fees of whatsoever kind received by them. In pursuance of said request certain clerks reported and turned in all fees so received, covering the fees from 1893 to 1900, inclusive. The fees so turned over were in excess of the maximum compensation allowed said clerks by law, and a portion of the fees turned over were not fees to which the Government was entitled. For instance, the money received from attorneys on admission to practice and money paid to the clerks for services in naturalization papers were held by the Comptroller of the Treasury, in decision of July 29, 1901, to be not official emoluments within the meaning of section 833, Revised Statutes, and that the clerks of courts were not required to include in their half-yearly returns such fees collected by them. United States v. Hill, 120 U. S., 169, and 40 Federal Reporter, 441, were the decisions upon which the Comptroller based his decision.

The great majority of clerks declined to comply with the order above referred to, and did not turn over the fees received, which under the decisions properly belonged to them. The clerks who did turn over such fees were permitted under a restatement of the accounts by the officers of the Treasury to receive back the fees so turned over within six years prior to the decision of the Comptroller of the Treasury, which was on July 29, 1901, but were not permitted to receive back the fees which they were legally entitled to during the years 1893 and

1894, the officers of the Treasury claiming they were barred by the statute of limitations.

This bill authorizes or directs the accounting officers of the Treasury to reopen and restate the emolument accounts of the clerks for the years 1891 to 1900 inclusive, but as a matter of fact there are but two or, at most, three years to which such accounting will apply under the provisions of this bill, and the amount which is involved is not a large amount.   This legislation appears to be fully justified for the reason that it simply turns over to these clerks money which the Government has unjustly withheld for many years and which was turned over to the Government in compliance with orders made upon the clerks by the proper officers, which orders have since been held to have been erroneous and invalid.

O

TERMS OF UNITED STATES COURTS AT SUPERIOR, WIS.

JANUARY 17, 1903.—Committed to the Committee of the Whole House on the state of the Union and ordered to be printed.

Mr. KAHN, from the Committee on the Judiciary, submitted the following

REPORT.

[To accompany H. R. 16599.]

The Committee on the Judiciary, to whom was referred the bill (H. R. 16599) "amending chapter five hundred and ninety-one of the United States Statutes at Large, Fifty-sixth Congress, approved May twenty-sixth, nineteen hundred, entitled 'An act to provide for the holding of a term of the circuit and district courts of the United States at Superior, Wisconsin,'" has considered the same and report it back with a recommendation that it pass.

Under the foregoing statute only one term of court is held annually at Superior, Wis. The present bill provides that two terms shall be held there annually, one term beginning on the first Tuesday in May and another beginning on the third Tuesday in October. Under existing conditions litigants, attorneys, witnesses, etc., are frequently compelled to go to Madison, Wis., distant 337 miles from Superior, to attend court. It is contended that the enactment of this bill into law will mean the saving of large sums to litigants in the matter of railroad fares and mileage for witnesses, and that it will also avoid considerable delay in procuring and executing processes. The citizens of

Superior, and also the members of the bar of Douglas County, Wis., have petitioned for the proposed change, and as the reasons therefor are fully set forth in said petitions they are hereto annexed.

At a meeting of the Superior Commercial Club and mass meeting of citizens, held on Wednesday, January 7, which was called for the purpose of listening to addresses on matters of interest relating to the city, and which was addressed by J. Adam Bede, member of Congress from the Duluth district, the following resolution was introduced and unanimously adopted:

"Whereas the bar of Superior has prepared an amendment to the bill establishing a United States court at Superior and has recommended the passage of said bill; and

"Whereas it is important and for the best interests of this city and the head of the lakes that said amendment should be enacted into a law for the reasons set forth in the petition accompanying said proposed amendment: Now, therefore, be it

"*Resolved*, That our Senators and Representatives in Congress from Wisconsin are hereby respectfully requested to enact said proposed bill into a law."

We do hereby certify that the above resolution was duly passed at the above-mentioned meeting, held on January 7, 1903, and that said meeting was attended by nearly all of the business men of the city of Superior.

J. B. NOYES, *President.*
E. A. LE CLAIR, *Secretary.*

To the honorable the United States Senators and Members of the House of Representatives in Congress from Wisconsin:

The undersigned, members of the Douglas County, Wis., bar, do respectfully represent and petition as follows:

We petition for the enactment into law the bill hereto annexed, amending chapter 591 General Statutes United States, Fifty-sixth Congress, approved May 26, 1900, entitled "An act to provide for the holding of a term of the circuit and district courts of the United States at Superior, Wisconsin;" which bill, hereto attached, shall provide for holding two terms of said courts at Superior each year; for the appointment of a clerk, who shall be clerk of both the circuit and district courts of said western district of Wisconsin, perform the duties pertaining to his office, receive such fees and compensation for services performed as are fixed and limited for clerks by law, and who shall keep in his office all records, files, papers, and documents relating to causes and proceedings commenced and pending in said courts at Superior; which shall provide that all summonses, writs, and processes, civil and criminal, issued from said courts at Superior or by the clerk thereof at Superior, shall be returnable at the office of the clerk at Superior; which shall provide that all causes triable in either of said courts shall be triable at Superior and tried at Superior whenever said summonses, writs, warrants, and processes shall be returnable at Superior, unless by consent of parties or for other legal cause said causes may be removed for trial to some other county in said western district of Wisconsin; which shall provide for summoning grand and petit juries for each of said terms; which shall provide for the appointment of a deputy marshal, who shall reside and keep his office at Superior, and in the absence of the marshal shall serve all summons, writs, warrants, and processes issued from said courts at Superior or by the clerk thereof.

We respectfully urge the enactment into law of the bill hereto attached, embracing the provisions above set forth, and we give the following reasons therefor:

That Lake Superior is the only large body of water forming a part of and connected with the chain of Great Lakes bordering upon the western district of Wisconsin, and all of the shore line of Lake Superior within the limits of the State of Wisconsin is within the western district of Wisconsin, and said Lake Superior forms the northern boundary of said western district of Wisconsin for a distance eastward from Superior about 80 miles by direct line; that all of the ports, bays, harbors, and Federal waters of Lake Superior bordering upon the State of Wisconsin are within said western district of Wisconsin and within a distance of 80 miles from the city of Superior; that the city of Superior is easily reached both by rail and water (during season of navigation) from all of said harbors, ports, bays, and the cities and villages situated thereat; that much litigation, both civil and criminal, arising from violations of the laws of Congress respecting ports, bays, harbors, Government channels, harbor improvements, Federal waters, and also from violations of the laws of Congress respecting the regulation of lake commerce, originates at said ports, bays, harbors, Federal waters, and at the cities and villages situated thereat, and all such prosecutions and litigations could be heard, tried, and disposed of at Superior at a greatly reduced expense to the Government of the United States, and with greater convenience and less expense to parties and litigants concerned therein.

That the Indian reservations within the western district of Wisconsin, where violations of laws of Congress are committed in furnishing intoxicating liquors to the wards of the Government, are in the northern part of said western district, and not far distant from Superior, and the mileage of officers and witnesses in these prosecutions would be greatly reduced were they tried and disposed of at Superior; that fully five-sixths of the entire area of the western district of Wisconsin lies north of Madison, the present seat of the court in said district; that the entire population of said western district, according to the census of 1900, is 993,691, of which 732,591 live north of the city of Madison and Dane County, being 73 per cent of the population of said district; that there are 42 counties in the western district of Wisconsin, of which 35 counties lie north of the city of Madison and Dane County, being 83 per cent of all of the counties of said district.

Said act (chapter 591, General Statutes United States, Fifty-sixth Congress) gives no relief to litigants, attorneys, witnesses, and the general public for the following reasons:

That litigants and attorneys are greatly hampered and put to great inconvenience because no records, papers, files, and documents of causes and proceedings commenced and emanating from said courts at Superior are kept at Superior, but, on the contrary, all such records, papers, files, and documents are sent to and kept at the city of Madison, Wis., in said district; that the appointment of a clerk of said courts for said district, who shall reside at Superior and who shall have the custody of all such records, papers, files, and documents and keep the same in his office at Superior, is necessary and indispensable to carry out the provisions of the bill hereto attached and to establish such a court at Superior as the public now demands.

That the distance by nearest railroad to the city of Madison, Wis., is 337 miles, and because of such great distance litigants, attorneys, witnesses, and the general public residing in this part of said district are put to great and unreasonable expense in having to attend court at the city of Madison in the trial of their causes, as they are now and have been compelled to do.

That the marshal of said district and all of his deputies now have their official residence and hold their offices in the city of Madison, and by reason of their great distance from Superior the cost for mileage of the marshal in serving summonses, writs, warrants, and processes on parties in this part of said district is large, unreasonable, and prohibitory.

That by reason of such great distance and large expense for mileage for serving summonses, writs, warrants, and processes, and by reason of the lack of all necessary facilities for transacting business in said courts at Superior, a large part of the litigation in this part of said district is now brought in the State courts, which could, so far as Federal jurisdiction is concerned, and otherwise would be brought in the Federal courts in the western district of Wisconsin.

That by reason of such great distance and large expense for mileage of said marshal for serving summonses, writs, warrants, and processes on parties in this part of said district, causes have been and will continue to be commenced in the Federal courts of Minnesota at Duluth, where the costs for mileage of the marshal is reduced to the minimum.

That by reason of there being no marshal or deputy marshal at or near Superior, parties and litigants in admiralty cases emanating from Superior and vicinity are compelled to lose their remedy and are without relief; this is particularly true and very common in admiralty causes relating to seamen's wages, as vessels in the harbor at Superior have ample time to get beyond the jurisdiction of the court before the marshal can arrive from Madison.

That although said chapter 591 has been enacted since May, 1900, only one term of said courts has been held at Superior by virtue of said act, notwithstanding that a large amount of the Federal court business in said western district of Wisconsin emanates from the city of Superior and its immediate vicinity; and it is the opinion of your petitioners that at least one-half of all of the Federal court business in said western district of Wisconsin emanates from Superior and vicinity, or in which the city of Superior and her commercial interests are directly interested.

FRANK A. ROSS, West Superior.
J. A. MURPHY, West Superior.
SOLON L. PERRIN, West Superior.
H. H. GRACE, West Superior.
HOWARD D. BAILEY.
ALBERT C. TITUS, West Superior.
GEO. C. COOPER, West Superior.
WEBER McHUGH, West Superior.
L. S. LARSEN, West Superior.
G. E. DIETRICH, West Superior.
F. S. PARKER, West Superior.
ARCHD. McKAY, West Superior.
CARL M. WILSON, West Superior.
GEO. P. KNOWLES, West Superior, Wis.
EDWIN C. F. KNOWLES, West Superior, Wis.
H. B. ARNOLD, West Superior, Wis.
L. K. LUSE.
LYMAN T. POWELL, West Superior.
PHIL. H. PERKINS, Superior, Wis.
JOHN B. ARNOLD, West Superior, Wis.
ERNEST A. ARNOLD, West Superior, Wis.
H. W. DIETRICH, West Superior, Wis.
HENRY W. GILBERT.
G. D. AMBOR, West Superior.
A. T. ROCK, West Superior.
J. M. REED, West Superior.
I. L. LEMOOT, West Superior.
W. M. STEELE, West Superior.
W. R. FOLEY.
LOUIS HANITCH, West Superior.
JOHN BRENNAN, West Superior.
T. M. SHORSON, West Superior.
GEO. B. HUDNALL, West Superior.
V. LIRLEY, West Superior.
JAMES R. HILE, West Superior.
H. V. GARD, West Superior.
F. H. DE GOOT, West Superior.
C. S. CRAWNHART, West Superior.
H. E. TICKNOR, West Superior.
MYRON REED, West Superior.
A. B. ROSS, West Superior.
H. L. SMITH.
HENRY C. WILSON, West Superior.
T. L. McINTOSH, West Superior, Wis.
JOHN H. VAUGHN, West Superior, Wis.
W. P. CRAWFORD, West Superior, Wis.
W. E. HAILY, West Superior, Wis.
S. V. DICKINSON, West Superior, Wis.
C. R. DUDLEY, West Superior, Wis.
R. I. TIPTON, West Superior, Wis.
D. E. ROBERTS, West Superior, Wis.
W. E. PICKERING.
HIRAM HAYES, Superior, Wis.
E. B. MANWARING, Superior, Wis.
W. D. DWYER, West Superior, Wis.
E. F. McCAUSLAND, West Superior, Wis.

A BILL for an act amending chapter 591 of the United States Statutes at Large, Fifty-sixth Congress, approved May 26, 1900, entitled "An act to provide for the holding of a term of the circuit and district courts of the United States at Superior, Wis."

Be it enacted by the Senate and House of Representatives of the United States of America in Congress assembled, That chapter five hundred and nineteen of the United States Statutes at Large, approved May twenty-sixth, nineteen hundred, be, and is hereby, amended so as to read as follows:

"SECTION 1. That two terms of the circuit and district courts of the United States for the western district of Wisconsin shall be held annually at the city of Superior, one term beginning on the first Tuesday in May and another term beginning on the third Tuesday in October.

"SEC. 2. That the circuit and district judges of the western district of Wisconsin shall appoint a clerk who shall be clerk both of the circuit and district courts of the western district of Wisconsin, who shall reside and keep his office at Superior, Wisconsin, and who shall receive such fees and compensation for services performed by him as are now fixed for clerks and limited by law; and one or more deputies of the clerk of the circuit and district courts may be appointed by the judges of said courts on the application of the clerk, and may be removed at the pleasure of the judges authorized to make the appointments. In case of the death of the clerk, his deputy or deputies shall, unless removed, continue in office and perform the duties of the clerk in his name until a clerk is appointed and qualified.

"SEC. 3. That all summonses, writs, warrants, and processes issued by the said courts or the clerk thereof at Superior shall be made returnable at Superior, and the clerk shall keep in his office the original records of all actions, prosecutions, and special proceedings commenced and pending therein.

"SEC. 4. That all causes triable in either of said courts when the summonses, writs, warrants, or processes shall be issued from the said court at Superior shall be tried at Superior, unless by consent of parties, or on other legal grounds, the causes may be removed for trial to some other county in said western district of Wisconsin where said courts are held.

"SEC. 5. That a grand and petit jury shall be summoned for each term of said court, which petit jury shall be competent to sit and act as such jury in either or both of said circuit and district courts at said terms: *Provided,* That the judge of the district court may, in his discretion, dispense with the summoning or impaneling of a grand jury at either or both of said terms.

"SEC. 6. That the marshal of said western district of Wisconsin shall appoint a deputy marshal, who shall reside and keep his office at Superior, Wisconsin, whose compensation shall be fixed as provided by section ten, chapter two hundred and fifty-two of the General Statutes of the United States, approved May twenty-eighth, eighteen hundred and ninety-six.

"SEC. 7. That this act shall take effect and be in force from and after its passage and publication."

O

ABATEMENT OF NUISANCES IN THE DISTRICT OF COLUMBIA.

JANUARY 17, 1903.—Referred to the House Calendar and ordered to be printed.

Mr. PEARRE, from the Committee on the District of Columbia, submitted the following

REPORT.

[To accompany H. R. 13630.]

The Committee on the District of Columbia. to whom was referred the bill (H. R. 13630) to provide for the abatement of nuisances in the District of Columbia by the Commissioners of said District, and for other purposes, respectfully report as follows:

This bill was introduced at the instance of the health officer of the District of Columbia, and has his approval and that of the Commissioners of the District. Its principal purpose is to add some provisions to the existing law for the abatement of nuisances, which will facilitate the collection of such expenses as the District may incur in the abatement thereof.

The existing law upon this subject may be found at pages 303 to 305, volume 1 of the Supplement of the Revised Statutes of the United States, and consists of a joint resolution legalizing the health ordinances and regulations for the District. These ordinances define the various nuisances and provide fines against those who shall commit, create, or maintain them.

Section 26 of said ordinances provides further that the health officer of the District may, after notice to parties committing, creating, and maintaining them to abate them within twenty-four hours, or such reasonable time as may be determined by the board, and on failure of the person or persons so notified to abate the same within the time prescribed in the notice to remove, cause to be removed said nuisances, and that the costs and expenses for such removal shall be paid by the person or persons committing, creating, keeping, or maintaining the same, and that said costs and expenses, if not paid within ten days thereafter, shall be collected from the person or persons maintaining the same, by suit at law.

It will be observed that the principal change made in the present law by the pending bill is, that in addition to the remedies provided in existing law, the Commissioners shall have the right to assess the cost of correcting such condition and all expenses incident thereto (including the cost of publication, if any) as a tax against the property on which such condition existed or from which such condition arose.

The committee recommend that said bill do pass.

The following letters of the Commissioners and the health officer of the District of Columbia are incorporated as a part of this report:

OFFICE COMMISSIONERS OF THE DISTRICT OF COLUMBIA,
Washington, April 14, 1902.

DEAR SIR: The Commissioners of the District of Columbia have the honor to transmit herewith a draft of a bill "To provide for the abatement of nuisances in the District of Columbia by the Commissioners of said District, and for other purposes," and recommend its early enactment.

The object of this bill, which was prepared by the health officer and approved by the city solicitor, is to enable the Commissioners to provide for the summary correction of conditions of real property inimical to the public interest, and existing in violation of laws, or regulations made in pursuance of law, in cases where owners of property are practically inaccessible for criminal prosecution by reason of residence outside of the jurisdiction, physical disability, or otherwise, and to collect the cost involved by an assessment against the property on which such work shall be done. A copy of the health officer's letter submitting the draft of the bill is herewith transmitted.

Very respectfully,   HENRY B. F. MACFARLAND,
President Board of Commissioners District of Columbia.

Hon. J. W. BABCOCK,
    Chairman Committee on District of Columbia, House of Representatives.

HEALTH DEPARTMENT, DISTRICT OF COLUMBIA,
Washington, March 14, 1902.

GENTLEMEN: In view of the frequency with which the District government has been unable to secure compliance with laws and regulations requiring the maintenance of real property in certain specified conditions—such ordinarily as relate to the health or safety of the occupants, of persons living in the vicinity, or of the public generally—because of ownership by nonresidents or by persons too aged or infirm to be within the reach of criminal prosecution, and for similar reasons, I have prepared and submit herewith the draft of a law designed to enable the Commissioners to cause unlawful conditions existing in connection with or arising from real property to be corrected, and to recover the cost of correction by assessment against the property improved.

This proposed law makes nothing illegal which is not so now, but provides merely for carrying into effect laws and regulations now in force, and such as may be made hereafter, in cases in which it is impossible or inexpedient to employ ordinary criminal process to accomplish that end.

I respectfully recommend that this proposed law be submitted to the city solicitor, and, if approved by him, or with such reasonable modifications as he may suggest, be forwarded to Congress with a request for its early enactment.

Respectfully,

WM. C. WOODWARD, M. D., ·
Health Officer.

The COMMISSIONERS OF THE DISTRICT OF COLUMBIA.

O

WIDOWS ISLAND, MAINE.

JANUARY 17, 1903.—Committed to the Committee of the Whole House on the State of
the Union and ordered to be printed.

Mr. WHEELER, from the Committee on Naval Affairs, submitted the
following

REPORT.

[To accompany H. R. 3100.]

. The Committee on Naval Affairs, to whom was referred the bill
(H. R. 3100) providing for the conveyance of Widows Island, Maine,
to the State of Maine, beg leave to submit the following report:

Widows Island, which is authorized to be conveyed by this bill to
the State of Maine, is situated on the coast of Maine. It was purchased
by the Light-House Board in 1857, of private individuals, for the sum
of $500. In 1887 a naval hospital was constructed thereon, at an
expense of $50,000, for the purposes and under the circumstances set
forth in the letter of the Secretary of the Navy, containing the report
of the bureau of medicine and surgery approving the bill, which is
now quoted:

NAVY DEPARTMENT, *Washington, January 16, 1901.*

SIR: Referring to bill H. R. 12001, providing for the conveyance of Widows Island,
Maine, to the State of Maine, and to your request of the 11th instant for an expression of the Department's views in regard thereto, I have the honor to state that the
bureau of medicine and surgery, which has charge of the property in question,
reports as follows:

The naval hospital on Widows Island, Maine, was built in 1887. It is a two-story
building, 50 by 69 feet. It will accommodate about 30 patients. It was intended
principally as an administration building, and a majority of the patients were to be
accommodated in outside pavilions.

The hospital was built to meet an emergency which no longer exists. The Navy
Department had a small yellow-fever hospital on Woods Island, near Portsmouth,
but local influences necessitated its abandonment, and it became immediately necessary to provide other accommodations for possible yellow-fever cases that could not
then be cared for elsewhere.

In consequence of wise and effective sanitary precautions the vessels of the Navy
cruising in the West Indies have been free from yellow fever for several years.
Meanwhile, the health authorities of the State of New York have established in the
lower bay, inside of Sandy Hook, very extensive and very complete contagious-
disease hospitals, where every attention can be given to the officers and crews of
infected vessels and the vessels thoroughly disinfected. In the event of yellow fever

appearing on any vessel of the Navy it would be immediately sent to the New York quarantine station, which is now thoroughly well equipped for service.

This renders the Widows Island Hospital unnecessary as a yellow-fever hospital, for which it was built, and it is not required for a general hospital. There is a naval hospital at Portsmouth, N. H., which meets all requirements of the station.

The Widows Island Hospital has been a source of expense to the Bureau of Medicine and Surgery for many years, as it was necessary to keep it in repair and have it properly guarded. It was not needed during the war with Spain, and it is altogether improbable that it would ever be needed by the Navy or be anything else than a continued expense. The Bureau, therefore, entirely approves of H. R. 1201 and recommends its approval by the Department.

This property having ceased to be of service to the Navy, so far as this Department is concerned, no objection is perceived to the passage of the measure above mentioned ceding it to the State of Maine.

Very respectfully,   JOHN D. LONG,
                                                              Secretary.

Hon. GEORGE EDMUND FOSS,
   Chairman Committee on Naval Affairs, House of Representatives.

Since this hospital was built in 1887, for the reasons, presumably, indicated in the letter of the Secretary of the Navy, it has never been occupied by a single patient. Its only occupant has been the keeper, who has had charge of the property for the Government, without having been of any use to the Government. Since its erection it has been a constant source of expense, the items for the last four years being as follows:

1897—Keeper	$720.00
Miscellaneous expenses	207.99
Total	927.99
1898—Keeper	720.00
Miscellaneous expenses	65.00
Total	785.00
1899—Keeper	720.00
Miscellaneous expenses	72.33
Repairs to roof	30.00
Total	822.33
1900—Keeper	720.00
Miscellaneous expenses	183.75
Wharf	650.00
Total	1,553.75

We are of the opinion that there is no reasonable probability of its use by the Government, and if it is to be kept by the Government and kept in proper condition, it will involve an annual outlay of from $720 to $1,000 or more. Under the circumstances we recommend the passage of the bill.

O

ADDITIONAL JUDGE FOR THE SOUTHERN DISTRICT OF NEW YORK.

JANUARY 19, 1903.—Committed to the Committee of the Whole House on the state of the Union and ordered to be printed.

Mr. ALEXANDER, from the Committee on the Judiciary, submitted the following

REPORT.

[To accompany H. R. 16724.]

The Committee on the Judiciary, to whom was referred House bill 16724, has carefully considered the same and reports as follows:

Hon. George B. Adams, the present judge of the United States district court for the southern district of New York, writing of the necessity of an additional district judge for that district, says:

The amount of work which the district judge of this court is called upon to perform is too great a tax upon the power of any single judge, no matter what his capacity may be. There has always been enough in this district with the general business of the court, principally admiralty, to fully occupy the judge, and when the present bankruptcy bill came into effect it cast a burden upon him which in 1901 drove Judge Brown out of office. while still in the height of his powers and usefulness. I have now been striving for about sixteen months to cope with the work, and find that it will be impossible for me to continue to perform the exacting duties which have been cast upon me, even to the extent that I have hitherto been able to. The work has run behind, notwithstanding I have used every available resource to save my time, even to the extent of requiring, practically, all testimony to be taken out of my presence, which is very unsatisfactory to the bar and litigants, especially in admiralty cases. Such a method deprives me of the opportunity of seeing and hearing the witnesses whose credibility I have to pass upon, which makes it much more difficult to determine what is the truth between conflicting testimony.

Some idea of the volume of work which I am required to perform may be judged from the following statement, showing, in a general way, the business of the court since September 4, 1901:

ADMIRALTY.

Cases pending September 4, 1901 (approximate)	166
Cases commenced since	386
Cases heard and decided	71
Cases submitted and awaiting decision	16
Cases partially tried and awaiting submission of further testimony	10

Cases otherwise disposed of:
By settlement, etc 124
By final decrees in default 46
_____
170
Cases pending, these excluding all dead cases (approximate)................ 285

BANKRUPTCY.

Petitions filed;
Voluntary 1,037
Involuntary.. 396
_____
1,433
Adjudications.. 1,291
Discharges.. 1,033
General orders entered 6,256
Receiverships running from small amounts up to $400,000................. 332
Motions decided, most of them after hearing argument or submission on briefs. 1,282
Proceedings pending, these excluding all dead matters (approximate)....... 1,600

MISCELLANEOUS.

Cases brought by the United States.. 51

SPECIAL PROCEEDINGS.

Consisting of proceedings for remission, habeas corpus proceedings, suits
against the United States, etc... 31
Number of persons naturalized... 4,561
Number of persons admitted to the bar 255

This only gives, however, an outline and leaves unmentioned many things which have consumed a great deal of time. It will be remarked that in bankruptcy I am called upon to supervise the work of 20 referees, and that while in admiralty I pass in the first instance upon the testimony relating to the merits of the main issues, the questions of the extent of damages are the subjects of references which I also have to review. Some admiralty cases are very important and involve the expenditure of a great deal of time. For example, the fire in Hoboken, which burned the wharves of the North German Lloyd Steamship Company and threatened the destruction of several very valuable steamers, caused salvage actions in this court, some parts of which were disposed of by Judge Brown. At least a month of my time was consumed last year in disposing of the remainder, which resulted in awards of $82,480. This is only one of a large number of important cases decided in which full opinions have been written. I find that in admiralty, I have written about forty unabbreviated opinions, most of which will be found in the Federal Reporter, and in bankruptcy over twenty, most of which will be found in the same publication and in the Bankruptcy Reports. In addition to these, I have written about one hundred and eighty memoranda opinions, many of them of importance, but lack of time and the necessity of deciding the cases promptly prevented full opinions. The number of additional cases decided, without opinions or by a simple indorsement on the papers, has been very large. The motions decided by me in bankruptcy alone amount to about 1,282. These covered a great variety of legal questions and include motions for confirmation of the referees' reports, which involved, as well, the review of questions of fact, decided upon a mass of testimony and exhibits. And many of the other motions presented complicated questions, requiring close attention and study, which do not show in the record because it was impossible, except in a few cases, to do more than give the result of the work in bare decisions. It is a matter of absolute necessity that provision be made immediately for an additional judge.

In view of the foregoing statement it is unnecessary to add further reason why relief should be given to the southern district of New York by the appointment of an additional district judge.

The Judiciary Committee is in receipt of resolutions from the Manufacturers' Association of New York and other organizations urging upon Congress the great necessity for an additional judge.

The committee therefore report the same back with the recommendation that the same be passed when amended as follows:

Strike out all of section 2 and make section 3 section 2.

O

JURISDICTION OVER CERTAIN LANDS FORMERLY IN FORT SMITH RESERVATION, ARK

JANUARY 19, 1903.—Committed to the Committee of the Whole House on the state of the Union and ordered to be printed.

Mr. FLEMING, from the Committee on the Judiciary, submitted the following

REPORT.

[To accompany H. R. 15595.]

The Committee on the Judiciary, to whom was referred House bill 15595, have had the same under consideration and beg to submit the following report:

The bill as originally drawn covers only those portions of the reservation that were ceded under the act of 1897 (29 Stat. L., p. 596). But in 1884 there were similar cessions of other lands in the same reservation (23 Stat. L., p. 19).

As a matter of law the committee are of the opinion that the United States did not retain any jurisdiction over any of the lands aliened in any one of these acts, but inasmuch as some dispute over that issue has arisen the committee think best to remove all doubt by legislative action.

In order to cover the subject-matter with more precision and accuracy, the committee recommend that the bill pass by substitute as follows:

That jurisdiction is hereby confirmed and ceded to the State of Arkansas over all those portions of the Fort Smith Reservation which have heretofore been aliened by the United States either to the city of Fort Smith in trust or otherwise or to other parties; and complete Federal jurisdiction is hereby asserted and retained over all portions of the said reservation that have not been specially aliened.

The committee further recommend that the title of the bill be amended so as to read as follows:

A bill confirming and ceding jurisdiction to the State of Arkansas over certain lands formerly in the Fort Smith Reservation in said State and asserting and retaining Federal jurisdiction over certain other lands in said reservation.

O

TERM OF THE UNITED STATES DISTRICT COURT IN ADDISON, W. VA.

JANUARY 19, 1903.—Referred to the House Calendar and ordered to be printed.

Mr. OVERSTREET, from the Committee on the Judiciary, submitted the following

REPORT.

[To accompany S. 5914.]

The Committee on the Judiciary have carefully considered Senate bill 5914, establishing a regular term of United States district court in Addison, W. Va.

This bill passed the Senate, and is favorably recommended by the gentlemen representing that territory in the House. Your committee therefore respectfully recommend the passage of the Senate bill.

O

TIMES, ETC., OF HOLDING UNITED STATES COURTS IN WESTERN DISTRICT OF VIRGINIA.

JANUARY 19, 1903.—Committed to the Committee of the Whole House on the state of the Union and ordered to be printed.

Mr. SMITH, of Kentucky, from the Committee on the Judiciary, submitted the following

REPORT.

[To accompany H. R. 16202.]

The Committee on the Judiciary, to whom was referred the bill (H. R. 16202) fixing the times and places for holding regular terms of the United States circuit and district courts in the western district of Virginia, and for other purposes, having considered same make the following report:

The purpose and effect of this bill if it shall be enacted into law are to provide for two terms of both the circuit and district courts of the United States each year at Roanoke and Charlottesville, Va., instead of one as now, and to provide for the appointment of a clerk for said courts at Charlottesville by the judges thereof instead of a deputy at that place appointed under existing law by the clerk at Lynchburg. The prompt disposition of the business in said courts at the points above mentioned seems to require the additional terms, and the members representing the districts in which these cities are located concur in the statement that the changes made by this bill are greatly needed.

The committee recommend that the bill do pass.

O

CREDITORS OF THE DEPOSIT SAVINGS ASSOCIATION OF MOBILE, ALA.

JANUARY 19, 1903.—Committed to the Committee of the Whole House and ordered to be printed.

Mr. REID, from the Committee on Claims, submitted the following

REPORT.

[To accompany H. R. 13520.]

The Committee on Claims, to whom was referred the bill (H. R. 13520) for the relief of the creditors of the Deposit Savings Association of Mobile, Ala., submit the following report:

The facts relating to this claim are clearly set forth in a report upon a former bill for the same purpose by Hon. G. W. Ray, at that time of the Committee on Claims. Upon a consideration of the same it is recommended that the bill pass. The above-mentioned report is appended hereto and made a part hereof, as follows:

The Deposit Savings Association of Mobile was chartered by the general assembly of Alabama. It was authorized to issue to depositors vouchers or certificates of deposit in such form as might be agreed upon between it and its depositors. It had issued vouchers or certificates of deposit amounting to about $20,000, which are still outstanding, at the time hereinafter mentioned. The question arose whether or not the association was liable, under section 6, act of March 3, 1865, as amended by section 9, act of July 13, 1866, to a tax of 10 per cent upon the amount of its own issue of certificates or circulating notes. That question was submitted to the Commissioner of Internal Revenue by the president of the association. The Commissioner decided on the 29th day of October, 1869, that it was not subject to said tax.

The same question was again submitted to the Commissioner, and the Acting Commissioner, on the 13th day of September, 1870, rendered a similar decision.

The question was, for the third time, decided in the same way by Hon. A. Pleasanton on the 3d day of March, 1871.

Acting upon these repeated decisions the association issued its certificates of deposit to the amount above stated, which were outstanding, when, in the assessment list of the Commissioner of Internal Revenue for November, 1873, the association was assessed at $40,000, being an assessment of 10 per cent of the amount of the certificates of said association ($400,000), which the Commissioner assumed had been issued by the association between the 11th day of October, 1873, and the 30th day of November, 1873.

The collector of internal revenue at Mobile issued his warrant to seize the assets of said association for the payment of this assessment, and under it seized and sold and conveyed to the United States its bank building in Mobile at a bid of $5,500. The collector also seized the sum of $7,394.73 in money, the property of the association, which he deposited in the Treasury of the United States. The seizure was made about June, 1864. The deed under which the land was conveyed to the United States is dated August 25, 1875. The said property was afterwards sold by the United States, and title made thereto on the 12th day of September, 1881, for $5,100, and can not, therefore, be returned in kind.

It appears that as soon as the change of ruling by the Commissioner of Internal Revenue was brought to the attention of the board of directors of the association, the board at once directed the discontinuance of the issuing of certificates of deposit.

The association is insolvent. A receiver has been appointed by the chancery court at Mobile, who asks that the money realized by the United States by the sale of the bank building and the money seized by the collector of internal revenue and paid into the Treasury be refunded for the benefit of the creditors of the association.

The case, in the opinion of your committee, is one of peculiar hardships. The repeated rulings of the Commissioners of Internal Revenue, that the association was not liable to the tax of 10 per cent of its circulation, were certainly sufficient to justify the belief on the part of the association that it would never be subjected to the tax. The amount of the assessment, being of itself probably about double the amount of the certificates of deposit in circulation, is a matter of astonishment, to say the least.

The association applied for relief under the act of Congress approved March 3, 1875, entitled "An act to authorize the Secretary of the Treasury to adjust and remit certain taxes and penalties claimed to be due from mining and other corporations, and for other purposes," but the Commissioner of Internal Revenue, Hon. D. D. Pratt, ruled that as the money had been covered into the Treasury, and a deed of the land to the United States had been made, the case was no longer "pending" in the sense of that act. Since then the association has been making its appeal to Congress.

It is not the policy of the Government to impose impressive burdens, in the way of taxes, upon its citizens. It would amount to confiscation to retain the sum exacted of this association in view of the facts. The class of certificates or notes in question have ceased to exist as a part of the currency of the country. No injury can result in that direction, therefore, by granting the relief sought, but justice to the creditors of the association will be done by it, for they, in fact, are the innocent sufferers by the seizure of the association's property.

The committee report the bill back with the recommendation that it do pass.

O

COURTS AT DUNCAN AND MARIETTA, IND. T.

JANUARY 19, 1903.—Referred to the House Calendar and ordered to be printed.

Mr. HENRY, of Texas, from the Committee on the Judiciary, submitted the following

REPORT.

[To accompany H. R. 16775.]

The Committee on the Judiciary, to whom was referred the bill (H. R.16775) establishing courts at Duncan and Marietta, Ind. T., beg leave to report and recommend the passage of the bill with the following amendment:

After the word "Marietta," at the end of line 5, add the following words: "and Comanche, and the court held at Ryan, in said Territory, is hereby discontinued and the records thereof transferred to the town of Comanche."

The necessity for the passage of this bill arises from the fact there has been a great increase of inhabitants and litigation in and around the towns of Duncan, Marietta, and Comanche, and their distance from the towns now having courts make it necessary for the creation of the new courts now provided by this bill.

O

LABORATORY FOR THE STUDY OF THE CRIMINAL, PAUPER, AND DEFECTIVE CLASSES.

JANUARY 19, 1903.—Committed to the Committee of the Whole House on the state of the Union and ordered to be printed.

Mr. DE ARMOND, from the Committee on the Judiciary, submitted the following

REPORT.

[To accompany H. R. 14798.]

The Committee on the Judiciary having carefully considered the bill (H. R. 14798) to establish a laboratory for the study of the criminal, pauper, and defective classes, report the same back to the House with the recommendation that it do pass with the amendment herewith submitted.

The committee has received a large number of communications from all over the country, from individuals, organizations, and associations of high rank, strongly urging the enactment of a law such as we here recommend.

We believe much good, at a comparatively small cost, may be secured by the passage of the bill with the amendment proposed, and we are convinced that investigations provided for in and by it may be most properly made under the Department of Justice.

O

CANCELING CERTAIN TAXES ON THE KALL TRACT IN THE DISTRICT OF COLUMBIA.

JANUARY 19, 1903.—Referred to the House Calendar and ordered to be printed.

Mr. BABCOCK, from the Committee on the District of Columbia, submitted the following

REPORT.

[To accompany H. R. 16099.]

The Committee on the District of Columbia, to whom was referred the bill (H. R. 16099) to cancel certain taxes assessed against the Kall tract in the District of Columbia, report the bill back to the House with the recommendation that it do pass.

In the year 1899 the owners of the Kall tract donated some 77,000 feet of land for the opening of S, Decatur, and Twenty-second streets NW., in order to make a passage between Connecticut avenue and Massachusetts avenue extended.

This land was worth not less than $80,000 but, in spite of this large donation, the jury which condemned the remainder of the land necessary to perfect these streets through the property of a party who refused to donate a foot of ground, assessed as benefits $14,000 against the owners of the Kall tract.

It is to relieve this inequitable assessment that the bill provides, and it is fully explained in the report of the Commissioners of the District of Columbia, hereto appended, who recommend the passage of the bill.

OFFICE COMMISSIONERS OF THE DISTRICT OF COLUMBIA,
Washington, January 15, 1903.

DEAR SIR: The Commissioners of the District of Columbia beg to acknowledge receipt of H. R. bill 16099, entitled "A bill to cancel certain taxes against the Kall tract," and to submit the following views thereon:

In the spring of 1899 the owners of the Kall tract, certain ground adjoining Kalorama Heights and supposed to embrace 9 acres, but afterwards found to contain only 7 acres, generously dedicated 77,925 square feet of ground for public use as streets, or two-sevenths of the entire tract. The owner of the adjoining tract, however, declined to contribute any of his ground for such purpose, and 33,428 feet were condemned. The jury found the value of the land taken from him to be $52,000, and they awarded him that sum in bulk, which is at the rate, on the average, of a little over $1.54 per square foot. Against this sum they levied benefits to the amount of

$10,000, leaving the net sum of $42,000 actually paid to him as the result of the condemnation proceedings.

The owners the of Kall tract, on the other hand, were assessed $14,000 in benefits. They could not, of course, be allowed compensation for the land which they had contributed, and so they found themselves in the position of donating over 77,000 square feet of ground, worth at least $80,000, and of being asked to pay $14,000 in addition, or a total of $94,000 in all; while the owner of the property adjoining, who gave nothing, received $42,000 in cash.

The Commissioners submit that the owners of the Kall tract are acting within the bounds of equity in asking the cancellation of the assessment for benefits, and therefore recommend the passage of the bill.

Very respectfully,

HENRY B. F. MACFARLAND,
President of the Board of Commissioners of the District of Columbia.

Hon. J. W. BABCOCK,
Chairman Committee on the District of Columbia,
House of Representatives.

O

ELLEN JOHNSON.

JANUARY 20, 1903.—Committed to the Committee of the Whole House and ordered to be printed.

Mr. KLEBERG, from the Committee on Invalid Pensions, submitted the following

REPORT.

[To accompany H. R. 16697.]

The Committee on Invalid Pensions, to whom was referred the bill (H. R. 16697) granting a pension to Ellen Johnson, submit the following report:

This bill proposes to pension Ellen Johnson, widow of Edmond Johnson, late of Company B, Fifty-second Indiana Infantry, at $12 per month.

Edmond Johnson, the soldier named in this bill, served as a private in Company B, Fifty-second Indiana Volunteers, from September 9, 1862, to June 3, 1865, when honorably discharged. He was a pensioner under the general law on account of a disease of the urinary organs of accepted service origin. He died February 22, 1900.

Ellen Johnson, the beneficiary named in this bill, and now 64 years of age, is shown to have entered into a ceremonial marriage with the soldier on July 15, 1867, to have lived with him as his wife until his death, and to be without means of support, having no property except several lots valued at about $600.

Her claim to pension under the act of June 27, 1890, was rejected by the Pension Bureau in August, 1902, upon the ground that the beneficiary was not the legal widow of the soldier, as she had a lawful husband living and undivorced at the date of her marriage to the soldier: that her union with the soldier was illegal and void, and that there was never any change in such relationship.

It appears that the beneficiary was divorced from her first husband, Thomas Harper, upon her own application, on September 5, 1867, some eight weeks subsequent to her marriage to the soldier.

It was held by the Pension Bureau, in view of the deposition made by the beneficiary before a special examiner, that she represented to the soldier that she had been divorced from her former husband, and that he married her relying upon her representation of the fact of such divorce, that a common-law marriage could not have arisen after the impediment had been removed.

The records of the circuit court of Shelby County, Tenn., show that proceedings for divorce were instituted by the beneficiary against her first husband on August 20, 1866, and that depositions were taken on July 29 and August 12, 1867.

The beneficiary testified before the special examiner that she was advised by her attorney, whom she employed in the divorce proceedings long prior to her marriage to the soldier, that the divorce had been granted, and that he would deliver the decree to her as soon as she paid his fee, and that she never knew until making her application for pension that the decree of divorce was not entered until September 5, 1867.

The fact, however, remains that the beneficiary for nearly thirty-three years was known and recognized as the wife of the soldier, and that she lived and cohabited with him as such.

Under these circumstances the relief sought for in the bill should be granted; hence the bill is reported back with the recommendation that it pass.

O

CHARLES S. WAINWRIGHT.

JANUARY 20, 1903.—Committed to the Committee of the Whole House and ordered
to be printed.

Mr. SULLOWAY, from the Committee on Invalid Pensions, submitted
the following

REPORT.

[To accompany H. R. 16499.]

The Committee on Invalid Pensions, to whom was referred the bill
(H. R. 16499) granting an increase of pension to Charles S. Wain-
wright, submit the following report:

This bill proposes to increase the pension of the officer named
therein from $12 to $72 per month.

This officer, now 77 years of age, served as major, lieutenant-colonel,
and colonel of the First New York Light Artillery from October 17,
1861, to June 21, 1865, when mustered out. He was appointed
brigadier-general by brevet to rank from August 1, 1864.

He was on leave of absence by reason of sickness—great debility
consequent upon intermittent fever—from June 11, 1862, to some time
after July 18, 1862.

He is pensioned under the act of June 27, 1890, at $12 per month.

He was examined December 8, 1902, by a board of pension examining surgeons in this city and found to be suffering from chronic
glaucoma of both eyes, able to distinguish light from darkness only
with left eye, debility from age, and tremor of hands.

The case of this aged and practically blind officer, who rendered gallant services during the civil war, comes within the action of the House
taken on June 16, 1902, for which reason an increase of his pension
from $12 to $30 per month is recommended and the bill is reported
back with the recommendation that it pass after the same shall have
been amended as follows:

In line 6, after the word "late," insert the words "colonel First Regiment New York Volunteer Light Artillery and brevet."

In line 8 strike out the word "seventy-two" and insert in lieu
thereof the word "thirty."

O

CYRUS V. GORRELL.

JANUARY 20, 1903.—Committed to the Committee of the Whole House and ordered to be printed.

Mr. DEEMER, from the Committee on Invalid Pensions, submitted the following

REPORT.

[To accompany H. R. 5511.]

The Committee on Invalid Pensions, to whom was referred the bill (H. R. 5511) granting an increase of pension to Cyrus V. Gorrell, submit the following report:

This bill proposes to increase the pension of the beneficiary named therein from $17 to $30 per month.

The soldier named in this bill, now 59 years of age, who served as private in Company K, Seventy-fifth Indiana Infantry, from July 25, 1862, to June 8, 1865, when honorably discharged, is now a pensioner under the general law at $17 per month on account of the loss of the sight of the right eye and impaired sight of left eye, indigestion, and nervous debility.

A claim for increase of pension, filed June 3, 1899, in which the soldier alleged disease of heart as a result of the pensioned causes, was rejected on May 4, 1901, upon the ground that the rating of $17 per month was fully commensurate with the degree of disability arising from the pensioned causes, and that the alleged disease of heart could not be accepted as a result of the same.

This rejection was affirmed by Assistant Secretary Campbell under date of May 31, 1901, upon the ground that the disease of heart from which the soldier was suffering and which undoubtedly contributed to his degree of disability, had no connection with the disabilities for which he had been pensioned.

When last examined on April 10, 1901, the board of surgeons rated the soldier $8 for indigestion, $4 for piles, $2 for nervous debility, and $8 for disease of the heart.

The board of surgeons then stated that he was very nervous and restless; that they believed that the nervousness was purely functional and to be due, with his heart trouble, to his indigestion.

There have been filed with your committee the affidavits of three physicians to the effect that the beneficiary's nervous and enfeebled condition had resulted in an irregular action of the heart; that on account of the same, indigestion, nervous debility, loss of sight of one eye and impaired vision of the other, he was unable to perform manual labor or to attend to the work of his profession, that of a physician and surgeon; that the only property owned by him consisted of two vacant lots in Payne, Ohio, worth together about $235, a horse and buggy, a cow and a calf; that he has no means of support other than the pension, and was wholly disabled.

It seems to your committee that the disease of heart from which this soldier is suffering must have some connection with the nervous debility of accepted service origin, and, inasmuch as the soldier is also shown to have lost the sight of one eye and to be suffering from impaired vision of the other, an increase of his pension to $24 per month seems justified under the circumstances, hence the bill is reported back with the recommendation that it pass after the same shall have been amended as follows:

Strike out all after the enacting clause and insert in lieu thereof the following: •

That the Secretary of the Interior be, and he is hereby, authorized and directed to place on the pension roll, subject to the provisions and limitations of the pension laws, the name of Cyrus V. Gorrell, late of Company K, Seventy-fifth Regiment Indiana Volunteer Infantry, and pay him a pension at the rate of twenty-four dollars per month in lieu of that he is now receiving.

O

JOHN SNODGRASS.

January 20, 1903.—Committed to the Committee of the Whole House and ordered
to be printed.

Mr. Deemer, from the Committee on Invalid Pensions, submitted the
following

REPORT.

[To accompany H. R. 15358.]

The Committee on Invalid Pensions, to whom was referred the bill
(H. R. 15358) granting a pension to John Snodgrass, submit the following report:

This bill proposes to increase the pension of John Snodgrass, late
lieutenant-colonel One hundred and thirty-ninth Pennsylvania Infantry, from $12 to $50 per month.

The files of the Pension Bureau show that this officer, now 70 years
of age, served as second lieutenant and captain of Company F, One
hundred and thirty-ninth Pennsylvania Infantry, from August 12,
1862, to June 21, 1865, when honorably discharged; that he never
applied for pension under the general law, but is now a pensioner
under the act of June 27, 1890, at $12 per month, the maximum rating
for total inability to earn a support by manual labor, the result of
rheumatism and resulting disease of heart and debility.

This allowance was based upon a certificate of medical examination
made on November 4, 1891, which showed him to be suffering from
rheumatism of the shoulders, knees, and hips, disease of heart, and
general debility.

The affidavits of Drs. Theodore Diller and R. L. McGrew, of Pittsburg, Pa., filed with your committee, set forth that the soldier had
been treated in the Alleghany General Hospital in 1901 for hemiplegia
with contractures due to a stroke of apoplexy, and that he was in
November, 1901, paralyzed on the right side.

Other statements filed with your committee show that since the
stroke of apoplexy the officer has required the attendance of another
person.

The case of this paralyzed officer who rendered nearly three years'
service and who requires the aid and attendance of another person
comes within the action of the House taken on June 16, 1902, hence

an increase of his pension from $12 to $30 per month is warranted, and the bill is reported back with the recommendation that it pass after the same shall have been amended as follows:

Strike out all of lines 6, 7, and 8 and insert in lieu thereof the following:

of John Snodgrass, late captain Company F, One hundred and thirty-ninth Regiment Pennsylvania Volunteer Infantry, and pay him a pension at the rate of thirty ·dollars per month in lieu of that he is now receiving.

Amend title so as to read: "A bill granting an increase of pension to John Snodgrass."

O

WILLIAM KEITH.

JANUARY 20, 1903.—Committed to the Committee of the Whole House and ordered
to be printed.

Mr. APLIN, from the Committee on Invalid Pensions, submitted the
following

REPORT.

[To accompany H. R. 15617.]

The Committee on Invalid Pensions, to whom was referred the bill
(H. R. 15617) granting an increase of pension to William Keith, submit the following report:

This bill proposes to increase the pension of this soldier from $12
to $30 per month.

The beneficiary named in this bill, now 70 years of age, served as
second and first lieutenant in Company F, Fifth Michigan Cavalry,
from August 28, 1862, to March 4, 1864, when his resignation, based
upon a medical certificate showing him to be suffering from eruptions
over his entire person of a scorbutic character, was accepted.

The medical records of the War Department show that he was under
treatment in November and December, 1863, for the results of malarial
toxemia.

His claim under the general law, filed in August, 1899, and based
upon scurvy, was rejected in 1900, upon the ground that a disability
from that cause had not existed since the filing of the claim.

He is now a pensioner under the act of June 27, 1890, at $12 per
month, for inability to earn a support by manual labor, the result of
senility and disease of heart and rectum.

This last allowance was based upon a certificate of medical examination of December 10, 1902, which described his disability as follows:

Is somewhat debilitated. The arteries are sclerosed. Movements slow.

Has a harsh aortic murmur, some cyanosis, heart beats slow and feeble.

Has two internal piles one-half by one-half inch, sensitive. Rectal vessels congested.

Has no teeth. Tongue is much coated and creased. Has an eczematous rash
back of the ears and on chest. Alleges it is worse at times.

Stomach tympanitic and tender.

Medical testimony filed in the Pension Bureau in January, 1901, sets
forth that the beneficiary has been under treatment for the last

twenty-five years for the results of scurvy contracted during the service, rectal troubles, and enlargement of the heart; that by reason of said disabilities he is wholly disabled for the performance of manual labor, and that there is no probability of his recovering.

It is evident that the results of scurvy, for which this officer has been treated for the last twenty-five years, are the results of the erup tions of scorbutic character from which the officer suffered at the time when his resignation was accepted, and as he is now totally disabled from the performance of all manual labor, your committee believes, following precedents, that an increase of his pension is justified, hence the bill is reported back with the recommendation that it pass after the same shall have been amended as follows:

In line 6, before the word "Company," strike out the word "of" and in insert in lieu thereof the words "first lieutenant."

In same line, after the word "Regiment," strike out the word "of."

In line 8 strike out the word "thirty" and insert in lieu thereof the word "twenty-four."

O

LUCINDA LAWRENCE.

JANUARY 20, 1903.—Committed to the Committee of the Whole House and ordered
to be printed.

Mr. SULLOWAY, from the Committee on Invalid Pensions, submitted
the following

REPORT.

[To accompany H. R. 16344.]

The Committee on Invalid Pensions, to whom was referred the bill
(H. R. 16344) for the relief of Lucinda Lawrence, submit the following report:

This bill proposes to pension Lucinda Lawrence, helpless child of
Albert A. Lawrence, late of Company M, First Michigan Engineers,
at $15 per month.

Albert A. Lawrence, the soldier named in this bill, served as a
private and fifer in Company M, First Michigan Volunteer Engineers
and Mechanics, from July 20, 1863, to September 22, 1865, when honorably discharged, and was treated at different hospitals in November
and December, 1863, for pneumonia and diarrhea.

He never applied for pension under the general law, but was pensioned in 1901 under the act of June 27, 1890, at $6 per month, for
partial inability to earn a support by manual labor, the result of loss
of the sight of the left eye.

It appears from papers on file in the Pension Bureau that the soldier
died August 29, 1902.

From proof filed with your committee it appears that the beneficiary
named in the bill is a child of the soldier, 26 years of age (having
been born March 15, 1876); that from birth she has suffered with
a deformity of the left hip, with 2 inches of shortening of the
left leg and a resulting compensating curvature of the spine; that she
also suffers from a weak and irregular heart action, has frequent
periods of unconsciousness, is pale and anæmic, and absolutely and
totally unfit for any form of labor, and that she has been entirely
dependent upon her father for maintenance and support; that she has
now no one to help her along except a sister about 22 years of age,
who is small and frail and can hardly provide for herself, and that she
is likely to become a charge upon the county.

Her post-office address is 87 Welker street, Buffalo, N. Y.

From a statement filed with your committee it appears that the beneficiary is a son by the first marriage, that his mother is dead, that the soldier remarried about six years ago, and that his present widow has abandoned the support of the girl.

Following precedents this helpless and dependent daughter of the soldier is entitled to relief to the extent of a pension of $12 per month.

The bill is therefore reported back with the recommendation that it pass after the same shall have been amended as follows:

Strike out all after the enacting clause and insert in lieu thereof the following:

That the Secretary of the Interior be, and he is hereby, authorized and directed to place on the pension roll, subject to the provisions and limitations of the pension laws, the name of Lucinda Lawrence, helpless and dependent daughter of Albert A. Lawrence, late of Company M, First Regiment Michigan Volunteer Engineers and Mechanics, and pay her a pension at the rate of twelve dollars per month.

Amend the title so as to read: "A bill granting a pension to Lucinda Lawrence."

O

DOLLIE COSENS.

JANUARY 20, 1903.—Committed to the Committee of the Whole House and ordered
to be printed.

Mr. MIERS, from the Committee on Invalid Pensions, submitted the
following

REPORT.

[To accompany S. 5280.]

The Committee on Invalid Pensions, to whom was referred the bill
(S. 5280) granting a pension to Dollie Cosens, have examined the same
and adopt the Senate report thereon and recommend that the bill
do pass.

[Senate Report No. 2318, Fifty-seventh Congress, second session.]

The Committee on Pensions, to whom was referred the bill (S. 5280) granting a
pension to Dollie Cosens, have examined the same and report.

Dollie Cosens, whose post-office address is Jefferson, Mont., is the daughter of
Henry Clay Cosens, who served in Company E, First Regiment Iowa Volunteer
Infantry, from May 7, 1861, to August 20, 1861, and in Company C, Thirtieth Regiment Iowa Volunteer Infantry, from August 2, 1862, to June 5, 1865. She was born
December 17, 1877. Her father died July 13, 1893, and her mother died January 8,
1878. At the time of his death her father was receiving a pension of $4 per month
for gunshot wound of right leg received in battle. He never remarried after the
death of claimant's mother, and there is no one now receiving any pension on
account of his service and death.

On November 21, 1900, claimant made claim under the general law, which was
rejected June 20, 1902, for the reason that she was unable to prove that soldier's death
from cardiac asthma was the result of his military service. She has made no claim
under the act of June 27, 1890, and can obtain no pension under that law, being now
over 16 years of age.

It appears from evidence filed with the bill that claimant has been totally blind
since she was 15 months old. This, of course, has made her permanently helpless.
It is also shown that she is destitute, her sole possession being one cow of the value
of $35. She has no income whatever.

Claimant having been blind for a period prior to 16 years of age and being now also
destitute, her case comes within rule 5 of this committee, which is as follows:

"Bills proposing to pension sons or daughters of soldiers will not be entertained
except in cases where it is shown by satisfactory evidence that the proposed beneficiary has been idiotic, deformed, or otherwise permanently helpless from a period
antedating the age of 16 years, and then only in case of destitution. In such cases
the rate allowed shall not exceed $12 per month."

Your committee report the bill back favorably with a recommendation that it pass.

O

WILLIAM H. MAXWELL.

JANUARY 20, 1903.—Committed to the Committee of the Whole House and ordered
to be printed.

Mr. SULLOWAY, from the Committee on Invalid Pensions, submitted
the following

REPORT.

[To accompany S. 5244.]

The Committee on Invalid Pensions, to whom was referred the bill
(S. 5244) granting an increase of pension to William H. Maxwell,
have examined the same and adopt the Senate report thereon and
recommend that the bill do pass.

[Senate Report No. 2146, Fifty-seventh Congress, second session.]

The Committee on Pensions, to whom was referred the bill (S. 5244) granting an
increase of pension to William H. Maxwell, have examined the same and report.

This bill proposes to increase from $12 to $30 per month the pension of William
H. Maxwell, late captain Company D, Third Regiment New Hampshire Volunteer
Infantry.

The military records show that William H. Maxwell served in Company I, Tenth
U. S. Infantry, from June 8, 1855, to March 31, 1860. He was mustered in as first
lieutenant Company H, Third New Hampshire Infantry, August 20, 1861; promoted
captain Company D of same regiment June 22, 1862, and honorably discharged
December 14, 1864.

Captain Maxwell was wounded in left hip in battle at Hatchers, Va., June 16,
1864 and for this wound he was pensioned under the general law in September, 1866,
at $5 per month from discharge, which was increased to $10 per month October 14,
1885. March 10, 1902, he was pensioned under the act of June 27, 1890, at $12 per
month for total disability, resulting from gunshot wound of left hip, disease of lungs
and heart, right inguinal hernia, and senile debility.

Captain Maxwell is 72 years of age, and the certificate of medical examination
upon which he was granted his pension of $12 per month showed that he was totally
disabled for manual labor by reason of gunshot wound, hernia, and disease of heart
and lungs, and evidence filed with the bill shows that his condition is such that he
requires the aid and attendance of another person a large portion of the time. It is
also shown that he is very poor and has no income except his pension for the support
of himself and an invalid daughter.

Captain Maxwell served his country faithfully for eight years, and in the light of
numerous precedents for increasing the pensions of the aged, destitute, and totally
disabled veterans your committee report the bill back favorably with a recommendation that it pass.

O

LEVI H. PEDDYCOARD.

JANUARY 20, 1903.—Committed to the Committee of the Whole House and ordered
to be printed.

Mr. MIERS, from the Committee on Invalid Pensions, submitted the
following

REPORT.

[To accompany S. 252.]

The Committee on Invalid Pensions, to whom was referred the bill
(S. 252) granting an increase of pension to Levi H. Peddycoard, have
examined the same and adopt the Senate report thereon and recommend that the bill do pass.

[Senate Report No. 2233, Fifty-seventh Congress, second session.]

The Committee on Pensions, to whom was referred the bill (S. 252) granting an
increase of pension to Levi H. Peddycoard, have examined the same and report.

This bill proposes to increase from $8 to $30 per month the pension of Levi H.
Peddycoard, late of Company I, Thirtieth Regiment Indiana Volunteer Infantry.

Levi H. Peddycoard enlisted September 24, 1861, in Company I, Thirtieth Indiana Infantry, and was honorably discharged December 2, 1865, for gunshot wounds
of right foot and left hand, the former received in battle at Shiloh, Tenn., May 7,
1862, and the latter received in battle at Resaca, Ga., May 14, 1864. He was wounded
and taken prisoner in battle at Stone River, Tennessee, December 31, 1862, confined
in Richmond, Va., and paroled January 26, 1863. The hospital records show that
he was treated for chronic diarrhea and gunshot wound of left hand.

Claimant, who is now 62 years of age, filed and established a claim under the general law, and was pensioned July 20, 1886, for gunshot wound of left thigh, received
at Stone River, Tenn., December 31, 1862; gunshot wound of left hand, received at
Resaca, Ga., May 14, 1864, and chronic diarrhea contracted during his service, at $6 per
month from discharge and $8 per month from April 28, 1886. Several claims for
increase were rejected on the ground that his present rate was adequate for the pensioned disabilities. His last claim for increase was made November 3, 1898, and it
was rejected April 3, 1900.

Claimant has also made claim under the general law for additional disabilities—
rheumatism, disease of heart, and gunshot wound of left knee—but he has never succeeded in establishing the service origin of these disabilities, although the evidence
on file indicates that the rheumatism and wound of left knee were incurred while he
was in the Army.

A medical examination made April 28, 1897, rated claimant $5 for gunshot wound
of left hand; $10 for gunshot wound of left thigh; $7 for gunshot wound of left knee;
$10 for disease of heart; $9 for chronic diarrhea; $7 for rheumatism; $4 for gunshot

wound of right foot, and $8 for loss of teeth and scurvied gums. A medical exami-
nation made March 29, 1899, rated him $6 for gunshot wound of left thigh; $2 for
gunshot wound of left hand; $4 for diarrhea and results; $4 for rheumatism and
disease of heart; $2 for gunshot wound of left knee. His last medical examination,
made April 22, 1902, shows him to be disabled by gunshot wounds of left knee, left
thigh, loss of teeth, and a serious disease of the heart.

Claimant's petition is as follows:

A PETITION.

To the Committee on Pensions, United States Congress, Washington, D. C.

GENTLEMEN: In support of my private pension claim, as per bill formally introduced by the honorable Senator A. G. Foster, I most respectfully petition, and set
forth for your consideration the following facts:

I enlisted July 8, 1861, at Warsaw, Ind., in Company I, Thirtieth Indiana Infantry. I was discharged December 2, 1865, at Indianapolis, Ind., having served my
country four years and five months.

I was wounded at the battle of Shiloh and was also shot in the foot at the battle
of Corinth, but for neither of these wounds did I go to the hospital, although they
were very painful.

After hard marches and severe exposure I was taken to the hospital at Tuscumbia,
suffering from dropsy and chronic diarrhea caused by exposure and lack of proper
food.

After leaving the hospital I joined my company at Stevenson, Ala. I was there
for five or six weeks, at which time I rested up, and we were then ordered to follow
General Bragg back to Louisville. On this entire march we were fighting each day
and watching at night.

At the battle of Murfreesboro, Tenn., I was struck between the shoulders (while
my company was retreating from a position we had taken) by a piece of shell with
such force that the blood came from my ears, nose, and mouth, and caused me to
temporarily lose consciousness, and I was taken prisoner; but being so badly injured
that I could not walk, the rebels put me on a horse and allowed me to ride about
a mile and then compelled me to dismount and walk, although suffering terrible
pain. I was taken to Richmond and placed in Libby Prison on January 18, 1863,
and was there until June 22, 1863, on which date I, with others, was exchanged.

To show you that the treatment we received at this horrible place was killing on
us, I will say that a few days before I was captured I weighed 189 pounds, and a few
days after being exchanged I weighed 90 pounds, losing nearly 100 pounds. At this
prison I contracted scurvy in its worst form, caused by improper food, and I have
been a great sufferer from it ever since. The treatment we received in this place was
beyond description, and after spending about six months there it put me in such
shape that I have felt its effects all through life.

After being exchanged I rejoined my regiment in September of 1863, and in the
battle near Tullahoma, Tenn., was shot in the left knee and was sent to the hospital.
After leaving the hospital I again joined my regiment and was wounded in the left
leg, and was in the field hospital for about twelve days.

At the battle of Resaca, in the Atlanta campaign, I was shot through the left hand.
I was sent to the hospital at Nashville and was there about three weeks. This
wound has bothered me more or less ever since, and has caused me at many times to
be unable to do any work for the support of my family.

Ever since my discharge from the Army I have been a great sufferer from the
wounds received and from the diseases contracted in the Army, namely, chronic
diarrhea, scurvy, and heart and stomach trouble. These things have made life
miserable for me, and for days and days I have been unable to do any kind of work
on account of the misery.

At the present time and for years I have been unable to do any kind of labor to
speak of, and have no means of support for myself and family except the small
pension I now receive, and what little help my children can give me.

No, gentlemen, I have set forth my record as near as I can from memory, but no
one can put in cold letters the su..ering that was endured by us in the line of duty,
the many nights we were compelled to endure suffering and privation, roll into our
blankets without a bite to eat, and the many hardships we had to undergo when on
the march. These matters can not all be explained on paper, but I think that my
record will show that I served my country to the best of my ability during the entire
time I was out, nearly four and one-half years. Also that I was a strong, healthy
young man when I joined the Army at the age of 21, that I have never seen a well
day since, and that I gave the best part of my life to the Government.

This being my condition, because of my service in the Army, I feel that I am entitled to thoughtful consideration on the part of the committee, and after reading my petition and looking up my record in the Pension Office, I hope and pray your honorable body will consider my bill favorably, and your petitioner will ever pray.

LEVI H. PEDDYCOARD.

STATE OF WASHINGTON, *County of Whitman, ss:*

Levi H. Peddycoard, being first duly sworn, on oath deposes and says that the above and foregoing facts as fully set forth are true and correct to the best of his knowledge and belief.

LEVI H. PEDDYCOARD.

Subscribed and sworn to before me this 21st day of December, A. D. 1901.
[SEAL.]   W. H. LICHTY,
                                  Notary Public, Palouse, Wash.

Accompanying the bill is the following evidence of claimant's poverty and disability:

STATE OF WASHINGTON, *County of Whitman, ss:*

Chas. E. Isenberger, being first duly sworn, on oath deposes and says that he is and has been for the past six years personally and well acquainted with Levi H. Peddycoard; that during this time his health has been very poor, and at times he is a very great sufferer from heart trouble, dropsy, and chronic diarrhea, caused, as I believe, from exposures in the Army; that within the past two years he is almost wholly incapacitated for work in making a living, and all caused, as I verily believe, from exposure and ailments contracted while in the Army. From my personal knowledge of his condition I am satisfied that he is justly entitled to the relief for which he is asking.

C. E. ISENBERGER.

Subscribed and sworn to before me this 1st day of November, 1902.
[SEAL.]   W. H. LICHTY,
                                  Notary Public, Palouse, Wash.

MONROE, WASH., *October 15, 1902.*

DEAR SIR: We, the undersigned, have known L. H. Peddycoard for the past two years, and know that he is not able to do any hard work of any kind, and that he has to be kept, financially, by his children. We also know that he has the piles and heart disease.

Yours, truly,   ELI J. ALTIZER.
                                          J. E. DOLLOFF.

Hon. A. G. FOSTER, *Tacoma, Wash.*

Pesonally appeared before me this 15th day of October, 1902, Eli J. Altizer and J. E. Dolloff, to me known to be the individuals who signed the above affidavit, and upon oath depose and say that the statements above made are true.

Subscribed and sworn to before me this 15th day of October, 1902.

In witness whereof I have hereunto affixed my hand and official seal.
[SEAL.]   R. J. FAUSSETT,
                                  Notary Public, Monroe, Wash.

In view of his faithful service of over four years, his wounds received in battle and other disabilities incurred in service, his great poverty and almost total incapacity to earn a support, your committee are of opinion that he is worthy of an increase of his pension.

The bill is therefore reported back favorably with a recommendation that it pass.

O

WILLIAM MARKLE.

JANUARY 20, 1903.—Committed to the Committee of the Whole House and ordered
to be printed.

Mr. MIERS, from the Committee on Invalid Pensions, submitted the
following

REPORT

[To accompany S. 6155.]

The Committee on Invalid Pensions, to whom was referred the bill
(S. 6155) granting an increase of pension to William Markle, have
examined the same and adopt the Senate report thereon and recommend that the bill do pass.

[Senate Report No. 2166, Fifty-seventh Congress, second session.]

The Committee on Pensions, to whom was referred the bill (S. 6155) granting an
increase of pension to William Markle, have examined the same and report:
This bill proposes to increase from $12 to $24 per month the pension of William
Markle, late of Company F, Twenty-ninth Regiment Wisconsin Volunteer Infantry.
Soldier enlisted August 27, 1864, and was discharged June 22, 1865. He is now
receiving a pension of $12 per month under the act of June 27, 1890, for total inability
to earn a support by manual labor due to disease of heart, injury to left ankle, and
senile debility. He was formerly pensioned under the general law at $6 per month
for injury to left ankle incurred in the service. He also claimed under the general
law for injury to right leg, catarrh, neuralgia, and heart disease.
The first-named disability was rejected on the ground that he had not been disabled thereby since date of discharge, and the other disabilities were rejected on the
ground of no record or other evidence of service origin.
Claimant, who resides at 527 Twenty-third avenue, Seattle, Wash., is now 76 years
of age. His last medical examination, made May 8, 1895, shows that he was totally
incapacitated for manual labor by reason of feebleness of heart's action, old age, and
weakness of left ankle. Other evidence on file in the Bureau shows that he is
totally disabled for earning a living for himself and family.
Accompanying the bill is the claimant's petition, in which he states that he is
wholly unable to earn a support by manual labor by reason of disabilities incurred
in the service; that he has no real estate and no personal property except household
goods and clothing, and that his only means of support is his pension.
In view of his extreme old age, his poverty and total disability, and faithful service,
and in line with numerous precedents, your committee report the bill back favorably,
with a recommendation that it pass.

O

EMMA DEAN POWELL.

JANUARY 20, 1903.—Committed to the Committee of the Whole House and ordered
to be printed.

Mr. SULLOWAY, from the Committee on Invalid Pensions, submitted
the following

REPORT.

[To accompany S. 6361.]

The Committee on Invalid Pensions, to whom was referred the bill
(S. 6361) granting a pension to Emma Dean Powell, have examined
the same and adopt the Senate report thereon and recommend that
the bill do pass after the same shall have been amended as follows:

In line 8 strike out the letter "a" and insert in lieu thereof the
word "per."

[Senate Report No. 2802, Fifty-seventh Congress, second session.]

The Committee on Pensions, to whom was referred the bill (S. 6361) granting a
pension to Emma Dean Powell, have examined the same and report:

Emma Dean Powell, whose post-office address is Washington, D. C., is the widow
of John Wesley Powell, who was major of the Second Illinois Light Artillery, and
who after the war organized and conducted as its director the Bureau of Geological
Survey, and who died at Haven, Me., at the age of 68 years, after a lifetime spent in
the military and civil service of the Government.

Major Powell entered the military service May 8, 1861, as a private soldier in the
Twentieth Illinois Infantry, and upon the reorganization of the regiment, May 14,
1861, was made sergeant-major. He was promoted second lieutenant June 13, 1861,
and captain Company F, Second Illinois Light Artillery, December 11, 1861. He
was promoted major May 28, 1864, and in that capacity served with great distinction
until January 4, 1865, when he was honorably discharged on account of wounds
received in battle.

Major Powell participated in the earlier campaigns in Missouri and mounted the
heavy guns at Cape Girardeau, Mo., in 1861. He took part in the battle of Shiloh,
in April, 1862, where he lost his right arm from gunshot wound. He afterwards
participated with his battery in the battles of Corinth, Iuka, Black River, Champion
Hill, Raymond, and the siege of Vicksburg, occupying at that place the important
position of chief of artillery of General McPherson's Seventeenth Army Corps.

Notwithstanding the loss of his arm at Shiloh early in 1862, Major Powell soon
returned to active service in the field, and for nearly three years thereafter served
effectually with the Army of the Tennessee, the stump of his arm being a frequent
source of severe trouble for lack of proper attention.

Upon his return to civil life Major Powell was given the duty of organizing and advancing the Bureau of Geological Survey.

After explorations in the far West, especially that of the Grand Canyon of the Colorado from 1869 to 1879, unexcelled in personal danger and far-reaching scientific and beneficial results, he rapidly developed the surveys of that region, prognosticating with great forethought the necessity of providing for adequate irrigation of the vast areas of land west of the Missouri and Red rivers and east of the Sierra Nevada ranges, as well as in southern California. He organized the ethnological and anthropological departments of his bureau and lived to see realized many of the results he had foreseen and labored to secure for his country.

Mrs. Powell, who is now well advanced in years, was married to the officer November 28, 1861. During most of his military service she kept near him, and it is due to a large extent to her loving care and intelligent nursing that Major Powell was able so soon after the amputation of his right arm to rejoin his command in the field and render valuable and conspicuous service to his country in his campaigns during the nearly three years of his army life which followed. At the siege of Vicksburg she not only ministered to her husband's wants, but also gave her best services in the hospitals at Vicksburg to other wounded officers, being retained within the lines by special direction of General Grant.

Mrs. Powell is left with but little for her support, and needs the pension proposed in this bill to supplement what she has for an adequate sustenance in her declining years. She has endeavored to obtain relief at the Bureau, but is unable, on account of the lapse of years since the war, to obtain the evidence to show that her husband's fatal disease was of army origin.

In view of the eminent and distinguished services of her husband, her own valuable services during the war and her present needs, it seems but just and proper that a grateful country should accord to her a measure of relief for her remaining years.

Your committee therefore report the bill back favorably with a recommendation that it pass.

O

JAMES MATTINGLY.

JANUARY 20, 1903.—Committed to the Committee of the Whole House and ordered
to be printed.

Mr. SULLOWAY, from the Committee on Invalid Pensions, submitted
the following

REPORT.

[To accompany H. R. 16591.]

The Committee on Invalid Pensions, to whom was referred the bill
(H. R. 16591) granting an increase of pension to James Mattingly,
submit the following report:

This bill proposes to increase the pension of the soldier named
therein from $12 to $17 per month.

This soldier, who is now 56 years of age, served as a private in
Company D, Forty-sixth Illinois Infantry, from January 5, 1864, to
January 20, 1866, when honorably discharged.

The medical records of the War Department show that he was under
treatment for intermittent fever in December, 1865, and January,
1866.

He is now drawing a pension of $12 per month under the act of
June 27, 1890, for total inability to earn a support by manual labor,
the result of an injury of left foot.

A claim to pension under the general law, filed on July 10, 1888, and
based upon chills and fever and a sprain of the left foot, contracted
in July, 1865, by being caught in a root while on detail to accompany
a wagon train on a foraging expedition, was rejected by the Pension
Bureau in February, 1900, upon the ground that a pensionable disability from chills and fever had not existed since the filing of the
claim, and that there was no record in the War Department of treatment for the sprain of the foot, and no other satisfactory evidence
showing the origin in the service and existence of the same at
discharge, etc.

The soldier alleged, as stated above, that he sprained his ankle by
being caught in a root; that but two or three members of his company
were with him on the detail; that after he incurred the injury he rode
back to camp in a wagon; that his ankle swelled up; that he was under
the treatment of the regimental surgeon; that he performed no service

thereafter, and was always lame, using a cane; that his lameness continued after discharge; that in 1872 he had a most serious time, the ankle swelling and becoming painful; that in 1875 it again swelled more than usual, and that an ulcer first appeared in 1875; that it kept up for about three months and broke out again in 1876, and that two years thereafter his foot was in its worst state; that he was compelled to go on crutches to get about, and that he was finally operated on and a part of the diseased bone taken out, and that a second operation became necessary.

The testimony obtained upon special examination of the case indicates that the claimant was lame in the service at about the time he alleged he injured his foot, but none of the deponents seemed to have any personal knowledge of the incurrence of the injury.

The surgeon of the regiment testified in 1889 that the beneficiary sprained his foot during the summer of 1865 while on detail, which troubled him thereafter to such an extent that he was unfit for duty at times, and that he still suffered from that sprain at the time of his discharge.

This witness, however, could not recollect the beneficiary's case when a special examiner called upon him in 1899, but stated that his affidavit given in 1889 must be correct.

The allegations of the beneficiary that he was lame in his ankle at the time of his return from the Army, and that the ankle became worse in 1872; that an ulcer appeared in 1875, etc., are fairly corroborated by testimony of parties who knew him and knew of his condition since his discharge.

When last examined, in 1897, the board of surgeons rated him $17 for the injury of left foot, and the board of surgeons then stated that the claimant would be better off if his foot was amputated, as he was totally unfit for labor and the foot and leg were very painful.

The statement of the beneficiary filed with your committee sets forth that he has no means of support except his pension of $12 per month and what little he could earn in his crippled condition, and this statement is corroborated by a number of citizens of Waterloo, Iowa.

It is the opinion of your committee that the injury to left foot from which this soldier is now suffering is traceable to his army service and that he is therefore entitled to the relief sought for in the bill; hence the same is reported back with the recommendation that it pass.

O

BENJAMIN W. WALKER.

JANUARY 20, 1903.—Committed to the Committee of the Whole House and ordered to be printed.

Mr. SULLOWAY, from the Committee on Invalid Pensions, submitted the following

REPORT.

[To accompany H. R. 16358.]

The Committee on Invalid Pensions, to whom was referred the bill (H. R. 16358) granting an increase of pension to Benjamin W. Walker, submit the following report:

This bill proposes to increase the pension of the soldier named therein from $12 to $30 per month.

This soldier, now 64 years of age, served as a private in companies A and B, First Rhode Island Light Artillery, from August 15, 1862, to June 12, 1865, when honorably discharged.

He was a prisoner of war from August 25 to October 8, 1864, and was under treatment at various dates for fever, diarrhea, dyspepsia, erysipelas, and chronic rheumatism.

He never applied for pension under the general law.

He is now drawing a pension of $12 per month under the act of June 27, 1890, being totally disabled from earning a support by manual labor by reason of rheumatism, dyspepsia, disease of throat and rectum, and paralysis of left side.

The soldier's medical examination of June 14, 1897, after describing the disability from rheumatism and piles, stated that he had paralysis of the left half of body; that he could not use the left hand or arm, leg or thigh; that when examined he was in an invalid chair, and that he had a young man attending him whenever he went any place.

Under the action of the House on June 16, 1902, the relief sought for in the bill is justified, the soldier having served nearly three years and being now paralyzed and requiring the aid and attendance of another person.

The passage of the bill is recommended after the same shall have been amended as follows:

In line 5 strike out the words "of the."

In line 6 strike out the words "United States."

In line 7, after the word "First," insert the word "Regiment."

In line 8, after the word "pension," insert the words "at the rate."

In line 9 strike out the words "the amount" and insert in lieu thereof the word "that."

JOHN DINNEEN, NOW KNOWN AS JOHN J. DAVIDSON.

JANUARY 20, 1903.—Committed to the Committee of the Whole House and ordered
to be printed.

Mr. KLEBERG, from the Committee on Invalid Pensions, submitted
the following

REPORT.

[To accompany H. R. 16512.]

The Committee on Invalid Pensions, to whom was referred the bill
(H. R. 16512) granting an increase of pension to John Dinneen, alias
John J. Davidson, submit the following report:

This bill proposes to increase the pension of the soldier named
therein from $12 to $16 per month.

The files of the Pension Bureau show that John Dinneen, now known
as John J. Davidson, and now 58 years of age, served under the name
of John Dinneen as a private in Company G, Thirty-third Massachusetts Infantry, from June 25, 1862, to June 11, 1865, when honorably
discharged. He never applied for pension under the general law, but
was pensioned in October, 1902, at $12 per month, the maximum rating
under the act of June 27, 1890, from September 15, 1900, for total
inability to earn a support by manual labor, the result of loss of a part
of the right foot and disease of lungs.

It appears that the beneficiary lost a part of his right foot in 1881
while attempting to mount a tramway engine in Georgia.

When last examined, on November 7, 1900, upon which certificate of
examination the pension of $12 per month was allowed in the Pension
Bureau, the beneficiary was found to be suffering from loss of a part
of the right foot (Chopart's amputation) and disease of the right lung.

The statement of the beneficiary filed with your committee sets
forth that he is unable to do any labor; that his health is very poor;
that he has to buy a great deal of medicine, being consumptive, and
that the pension of $12 per month which he is receiving is insufficient
to support him, etc.

A petition signed by a number of prominent citizens of Pearly, Ga.,
asking for Congressional relief for the beneficiary, has also been filed
with your committee.

An increase of the soldier's pension from $12 to $16 per month, as
sought for in the bill, appears warranted, it being shown that he ren-

dered three years of service, has lost part of his right foot, and is suffering from consumption.

The bill is reported back with the recommendation that it pass after the same shall have been amended as follows:

In line 6 strike out the word "alias" and insert in lieu thereof the words "now known as."

In line 7, before the word "Thirty-third" insert the letter "G."

Amend the title so as to read: "A bill granting an increase of pension to John Dinneen, now known as John J. Davidson."

O

THOMAS E. PEABODY.

JANUARY 20, 1903.—Committed to the Committee of the Whole House and ordered to be printed.

Mr. SULLOWAY, from the Committee on Invalid Pensions, submitted the following

REPORT.

[To accompany H. R. 15438.]

The Committee on Invalid Pensions, to whom was referred the bill (H. R. 15438) granting an increase of pension to Thomas E. Peabody, submit the following report:

This bill proposes to increase the pension of the soldier named therein from $12 to $30 per month.

The soldier named in this bill, now 59 years of age, served as a private in Company A, First New Hampshire Cavalry, from March 24, 1864, to June 22, 1865, when honorably discharged, and was captured on June 30, 1864, and paroled at Aikens Landing August 13, 1864.

The records of the War Department also show that he was absent in hospital from February 26, 1865, as wounded.

He is now a pensioner under the act of June 27, 1890, at the maximum rating on account of disease of spine and gunshot wound of the left hand.

When last examined, on February 11, 1891, the board of surgeons rated him $30 for the condition due to disease of spine, and stated that he could not stand or walk with his eyes closed, had muscular tremor of tongue, and that he described sensations as though blocks of wood were attached to his feet; that he has pain over the middle dorsal region and describes the constriction around the body over the stomach, and that he failed to recognize the point of the divider at either foot, or so far as the knee of either leg.

The board also found and rated him $8 for the wound of the hand and found total deafness of one ear.

Medical testimony filed with your committee sets forth that he had been under treatment for the last ten months for malaria, which at times renders him unconscious for seven or eight hours at a time; that he is very hard of hearing; that his eyesight is very bad, and his left leg so badly damaged that he had almost lost the use of it; that the knee was badly swollen, caused by water around the joint; that he is obliged to wear a steel brace in order to keep his leg in place, otherwise the leg would be comparatively useless; that he has loco-motor ataxia, is badly ruptured, and that he has to have an attendant to help dress and undress him.

Other testimony filed shows that he has no means of support except his pension, and that he is supported by his wife, who works in a factory.

The case of this soldier comes within the action of the House on June 16, 1902, increasing the pension of those who require the aid and attendance of another person from $12 to $30 per month, and such relief is recommended and the bill is reported back with the recommendation that it pass.

O

SOLOMON S. SHANER.

JANUARY 20, 1903.—Committed to the Committee of the Whole House and ordered
to be printed.

Mr. DEEMER, from the Committee on Invalid Pensions, submitted the
following

REPORT.

[To accompany H. R. 15585.]

The Committee on Invalid Pensions, to whom was referred the bill
(H. R. 15585) granting an increase of pension to Solomon S. Shaner,
submit the following report:

This bill proposes to increase the pension of the soldier named therein
from $17 to $36 per month.

This soldier, now 60 years of age, served as a private in Company
D, Third Pennsylvania Reserves, from June 4, 1861, to June 17, 1862,
when honorably discharged, and is shown by the medical records of
the War Department to have been under treatment for a contusion of
the leg by a shell received in action at Fredericksburg in December,
1862, and for intermittent fever and debility.

He is now pensioned under the general law at $17 per month on
account of chronic diarrhea and resulting disease of the rectum.

A claim for increase of pension, filed in May, 1898, was rejected on
February 1, 1900, upon the ground that the disability from chronic
diarrhea and resulting disease of the rectum did not warrant a rating
in excess of $17 per month, and that the rheumatism and lumbago alleged
as resulting from the pensioned causes had no pathological connection
therewith.

When last examined, on December 28, 1898, the board of surgeons
described his condition as follows:

We find that the claimant has a violent chronic diseased condition of his rectum,
in all probability a secondary result of the previously existing diarrhea. He has
both external and internal piles, which are congested and freely bleed at times
owing to the presence of numerous ulcers. His rectum is covered with numerous
small ulcers, which exude a copious mucopurulent discharge, and a number of
small fissures are also present, which we have no doubt substantiate his statements
when he says that he suffers continual torture, especially on defecation. This continuous pain and numerous hemorrhages with which he suffers cause him to be
markedly debilitated and weak, rendering him absolutely unable to do any manual
labor. Rate. $16.

He also has rheumatism, affecting principally the muscles of the back and of the thighs, while all the large joints are crepitant and limited somewhat in their motion. The lumbar muscles are extremely painful, as are also the musc es of both the inner and posterior portion of the thighs, both on pressure and motion.

He has a slightly disturbed condition of liver, which in all probability is due to his general debilitated condition.

As to his alleged insomnia we have but his statement as to such a condition, and we are of the opinion that such a condition might be produced as a result of his foregoing disabilities.

The affidavits of Drs. Davis and Porter, of Pottstown, Pa., filed with your committee, set forth that they have attended the soldier for many years for chronic rheumatism and chronic diarrhea and a spinal affection; that his case is incurable, and that by reason of his diseases he is unable to perform work of any kind.

The testimony of several neighbors, also filed with your committee, corroborates the soldier's physical condition as described by the physicians named above.

In the opinion of your committee the description of the soldier's disabilities by the board of examining surgeons warrants an increase of his pension from $17 to $24 per month by reason of the disabilities of accepted service origin; hence relief to that extent is recommended and the bill reported back with the recommendation that it pass after the same shall have been amended as follows:

In line 6, after the word "Third," insert the word "Regiment."

In line 7 strike out the word "Reserves" and insert in lieu thereof the words "Reserve Volunteer Infantry."

In lines 7 and 8 strike out the word "thirty-six" and insert in lieu thereof the word "twenty-four."

O

JOHN CORBETT.

JANUARY 20, 1903.—Committed to the Committee of the Whole House and ordered
to be printed.

Mr. MIERS, from the Committee on Invalid Pensions, submitted the
following

REPORT.

[To accompany H. R. 16058.]

The Committee on Invalid Pensions, to whom was referred the bill
(H. R. 16058) granting a pension to John Corbett, minor heir of John
Corbett, submit the following report:

This bill proposes to pension John Corbett, minor heir of John Corbett, late of Company H, One hundred and eightieth Ohio Infantry,
at $30 per month.

John Corbett, the soldier named in this bill, served as a private in
Company H, One hundred and eightieth Ohio Infantry, from October
3, 1864, to March 15, 1865, when honorably discharged, and was a
pensioner under the general law on account of disease of lungs, varicose veins of both legs, rheumatism, and disease of heart.

The files of the Pension Bureau show that his name was dropped
from the rolls in August, 1898, upon information furnished by the
postmaster at Columbus, Ohio, that he died April 3, 1898.

No one has applied in the Pension Bureau on account of the service
and death of this soldier.

From medical and other testimony filed with your committee it
appears that the beneficiary named in the bill is a son of the soldier,
born in May, 1864; that he resides at Marion, Ind., and that by reason
of a defective mental development he has been entirely unable to earn
a livelihood or to provide for himself and has been entirely dependent
upon his father, and since his father's death upon a brother.

Following precedents. a pension to the extent of $12 per month is
warranted for this helpless and dependent son of the soldier, hence the
bill is reported back with the recommendation that it pass after the
same shall have been amended as follows:

In line 6 strike out the words 'minor heir" and insert in lieu
thereof the words "helpless and dependent son.".

In line 8 strike out the word "thirty" and insert in lieu thereof the
word "twelve."

Amend the title so as to read: "A bill granting a pension to John
Corbett."

O

CALEB C. VAN SICKELL.

JANUARY 20, 1903.—Committed to the Committee of the Whole House and ordered
to be printed.

Mr. DEEMER, from the Committee on Invalid Pensions, submitted the
following

REPORT.

[To accompany H. R. 16522.]

The Committee on Invalid Pensions, to whom was referred the bill
(H. R. 16522) for the relief of Caleb C. Van Sickell, submit the following report:

This bill proposes to increase the pension of the soldier named
therein from $17 to $72 per month.

This officer, now 80 years of age, served as first sergeant and
second and first lieutenant in Company I, Fourth New Jersey Volunteers, from August 13, 1861, to September 14, 1864, when honorably
discharged.

He was a prisoner of war from June 27 to August 12, 1862, and also
received a gunshot wound of the right groin at the battle of the
Wilderness, May 6, 1864.

He has been drawing a pension on account of this wound ever since
his discharge and is now drawing one of $17 per month.

When last examined, in March, 1900, the board of surgeons rated
him $17 for the wound, $6 for rheumatism, and $2 for varicose veins.

Medical and other proof filed with your committee shows that the
officer since March, 1902, has suffered from blood poisoning from a
spider bite, causing abcesses and running sores of both feet, rendering
him unable to walk and requiring the aid and attendance of another
person; that he is too old for surgical interference; that his wife, also
aged, is suffering from blindness; that he has no property except a
life interest in the house in which he lives, valued at $800, and no
means of support other than his pension.

An increase of this officer's pension from $17 to $30 per month is
warranted under the action of the House on June 16, 1902, it being
shown that the soldier requires the aid and attendance of an another
person.

The bill is therefore reported back with the recommendation that it pass after the same shall have been amended as follows:

In line 7 strike out the word " Volunteers" and insert in lieu thereof the words " Volunteer Infantry, and pay him a pension."

In line 8 strike out the word " seventy-two " and insert in lieu thereof the word "thirty."

In same line, after the word "month," insert the words "in lieu of that he is now receiving."

Amend the title so as to read: "A bill granting an increase of pension to Caleb C. Van Sickell."

O

SARAH A. GERRY.

JANUARY 20, 1903.—Committed to the Committee of the Whole House and ordered to be printed.

Mr. SULLOWAY, from the Committee on Invalid Pensions, submitted the following

REPORT.

[To accompany H. R. 15437.]

The Committee on Invalid Pensions, to whom was referred the bill (H. R. 15437) granting an increase of pension to Sarah A. Gerry, submit the following report:

This bill proposes to increase the pension of the beneficiary named therein from $8 to $12 per month.

The soldier named in this bill served as a musician in Captain Chandler's company, New Hampshire Militia, from April 27 to July 27, 1864, when honorably discharged with his company, and again as a private and musician in Company C, First New Hampshire Heavy Artillery, from August 16, 1864, to July 15, 1865, when honorably discharged.

He died March 7, 1899, of disease of the heart.

His widow, the beneficiary named in the bill, now 58 years of age, who married him on July 21, 1866, was pensioned under the act of June 27, 1890, at $8 per month.

Medical and other testimony filed with your committee sets forth that the beneficiary is afflicted with valvular heart disease and chronic arthritis of the joints of the fingers, both secondary to rheumatism; that she is unable to take any exercise with safety, and is wholly incapacitated from earning her living; that she can not walk any distance on account of swollen and affected joints, and at times requires the periodical aid and attendance of another person, and that she has no property or means of support except the pension of $8 per month.

In view of the helpless condition of the beneficiary the relief sought for in the bill, an increase of her pension from $8 to $12 per month, is believed to be justified, hence the bill is reported back with the recommendation that it pass.

O

WILSON G. GRAY.

JANUARY 20, 1903.—Committed to the Committee of the Whole House and ordered to be printed.

Mr. KLEBERG, from the Committee on Invalid Pensions, submitted the following

REPORT.

[To accompany H. R. 16492.]

The Committee on Invalid Pensions, to whom was referred the bill (H. R. 16492) granting a pension to Wilson G. Gray, submit the following report:

This bill proposes to increase the pension of the beneficiary named therein from $30 to $50 per month.

This soldier, now 65 years of age, served as a private in Company K, Third Arkansas Cavalry, from February 1, 1863, to June 30, 1865, when honorably discharged.

He is now pensioned under the general law at $30 per month on account of caries of left tibia and varicose veins of the left leg.

Claims for increase of pension, filed in 1891, 1892, and 1897, in which the soldier alleged varicose veins of the right leg and feet, ulceration of the same, etc., as results of the pensioned causes, and which he claimed were of such a nature as to require the aid and attendance of another person, were rejected by the Pension Bureau, the last one on June 30, 1900, upon the ground that the alleged ulcers and varicose veins of the right leg could not be accepted as results of that of the left leg, and that by reason of the pensioned causes he was not entitled to a rating in excess of $30 per month.

He filed in the Pension Bureau medical and lay testimony showing that in the opinion of the physicians who treated him his left leg was a useless and painful limb; that the right leg is but little better, as it has been compelled to do duty for twenty years for both, and that the disability of the right leg was due to overwork as a result of the disability of the left leg; that he requires aid and attendance to help him up when down and dress him; that when walking he always uses two crutches and carries his left foot clear off the ground or floor; that his left leg is suppurating, etc.

When last examined, on March 15, 1899, the board of surgeons described his condition as follows:

Caries of left tibia and varicose veins of the left leg and foot. Measurement of left calf of leg, 12¾ inches; right leg, 17½ inches. Skin of left leg from 4 inches below the knee to toes indurated and infiltrated and of a dark purple copper color. There are three ulcers on the inner aspect of the leg above the inner malleolus 1¾ inches in diameter and one on the outer aspect above the malleolus three-fourths by 2½ inches, all sloughing. Left ankle is completely anchylosed. Muscles of leg atrophied and tendo-achilles contracted so as to raise the left heel 4 inches above the floor. Claimant can not use the leg or foot at all in walking. He uses two crutches all the time when walking.

Right leg: We find superficial veins below the knee and ankle of the leg varicosed, indurated, and of a dark purple copper color down to toes, same as the left leg. Motion of right ankle joint limited to one-fourth. Both legs above the induration up to kneejoints are œdematous and pit on pressure.

General debility: Very marked; due to continued drain of ulcers and inability to take exercise.

This claimant is so disabled from necrosis and its consequences as to require the frequent and periodical aid and attendance of another person, and is entitled to $50 per month.

The affidavits of Drs. Brown and Westerfield, of Conway, Ark., filed with your committee, set forth that they made an examination of the soldier's legs on December 1, 1902, and found a large, deep ulcer on the inner side of the left ankle, discharging a very foul pus; that the left leg is much swollen and the tissues all about the ankle are apparently in a constant state of inflammation; that the skin up the leg toward the knee shows evidences of inflammation and ulceration that are now healed over with an ill health of skin; that his right leg is impaired by reason of the old trouble, and that the left is worse than useless; that his condition is such as to render him wholly unable to do any manual labor, and that he must, for a greater part of the time, require the attention of another person to take care of him and provide for his wants and comfort.

In the opinion of your committee the relief sought for in the bill is fully warranted in view of the medical evidence filed in the Pension Bureau, and the findings of the examining surgeons and the affidavits of Drs. Brown and Westerfield filed with your committee.

The bill is therefore reported back with the recommendation that it pass after the same shall have been amended as follows:

In line 6 strike out the word "Arkansas."

In line 7, before the word "Volunteer," insert the word "Arkansas."

Amend the title so as to read: "A bill granting an increase of pension to Wilson G. Gray."

O

ANNIE W. COIT.

JANUARY 20, 1903.—Committed to the Committee of the Whole House and ordered to be printed.

Mr. APLIN, from the Committee on Invalid Pensions, submitted the following

REPORT.

[To accompany H. R. 16269.]

The Committee on Invalid Pensions, to whom was referred the bill (H. R. 16269) granting a pension to Annie W. Coit, submit the following report:

This bill proposes to increase the pension of the beneficiary named therein from $8 to $25 per month.

James B. Coit, the husband of the beneficiary named in the bill, served as private and sergeant-major in Company B, Second Connecticut Infantry, from April 22 to July 25, 1861, when honorably discharged, and again as first lieutenant of Company K, Fourteenth Connecticut Infantry, and as captain and major of said regiment from May 26, 1862, to September 6, 1864, when his resignation, based upon debility arising from wounds and injuries received in action at Antietam, Gettysburg, and Morton's Ford. and from a compound fracture of the right forearm, caused by a bullet received in action at the battle of the Wilderness, was accepted.

He was a pensioner under the general law, on account of gunshot wounds of right thigh, shell wound of face, and gunshot wound of right forearm, at $25 per month from the date of his discharge.

He died December 8, 1894, of disease of the heart.

The beneficiary named in the bill, now 54 years of age, who was married to the officer on October 26, 1869, is now and has been since September 3, 1896, a pensioner under the act of June 27, 1890, at $8 per month, upon proof that she was without other means of support than her daily labor, etc.

Her claim under the general law was rejected in March, 1896, upon the ground that the disease of heart of which her husband died had no connection with the wounds for which he had been pensioned and was not otherwise shown to be due to his military service.

This claim was specially examined and the beneficiary then testified during such special examination that her husband from the time of his

return from the Army had trouble with his heart and swelling of the
feet and ankles; and other testimony obtained upon such special
examination shows that while the officer was home on furlough he
complained of his heart, was very weak, and had shortness of breath;
that after his return from the Army he still complained of heart trouble,
but tried to keep the fact of said disease from his father and mother;
was short of breath, and that this condition seemed to grow worse
until his death.

The chaplain of his regiment testified that in July, 1863, after the
battle of Gettysburg, the officer received a violent blow from a horse
running against him, and that in the fall of 1863 he was very sick with
malarial fever and its complications, and that the great shock to his
system resulting from the blow, together with the subsequent fever,
was, in affiant's opinion, sufficient to cause a derangement of the heart.

Dr. A. W. Nelson, of New London, Conn., whose deposition was
taken by the special examiner of the Pension Bureau in September,
1895, testified that he had been acquainted with the officer for twenty
years prior to his death; that from the knowledge he had of the soldier and his wounds he believed that his disease of heart was caused
as a result of the wounds received in the service; that he had several
hemorrhages from the femoral artery, as he understood, producing
anæmia and suppuration of the wounds, resulting in bad health, and
that these wounds together were, in his opinion, the direct cause of
the disease of heart, inasmuch as the walls of the heart were thereby
weakened.

The husband of the beneficiary at the close of the war was brevetted
lieutenant-colonel for gallant and meritorious services at Antietam,
colonel for gallant and meritorious services at Gettysburg, and brigadier-general for gallant and meritorious services in the Wilderness.

In view of the gallant and meritorious services rendered by the
officer during the civil war and the probabilities that not only the
many wounds received by him during such service and in line of duty
were factors in his death cause, but that his disease of heart, which
caused his death, was due to the shortness of breath, etc., shown in
the testimony, your committee believes that the relief sought for in
the bill is warranted.

The husband of this beneficiary rendered conspicuous services during the civil war, having been brevetted brigadier-general for gallant
and meritorious services in several battles, and the evidence in the
case tends to show that the heart disease from which he died was a
result of the exposure of his service of more than three years.

In view of this your committee believes that the beneficiary should
be entitled to the rate provided by the general law for the widow of a
major, namely, $25 per month, and the bill is reported back with the
recommendation that it pass after the same shall have been amended
as follows:

In line 6 strike out the word "as."

In line 7 strike out the word "Volunteers" and insert in lieu thereof
the words "Volunteer Infantry."

In lines 8 and 9 strike out the words "from and after the passage
of this act" and insert in lieu thereof the words "in lieu of that she
is now receiving."

Amend the title so as to read: "A bill granting an increase of pension to Annie W. Coit."

O

EUDORA WELLS.

JANUARY 20, 1903.—Committed to the Committee of the Whole House and ordered
to be printed.

Mr. CROWLEY, from the Committee on Invalid Pensions, submitted
the following

REPORT.

[To accompany H. R. 15443.]

The Committee on Invalid Pensions, to whom was referred the bill
(H. R. 15443) granting a pension to Eudora Wells, submit the following report:

This bill proposes to pension Eudora Wells, helpless und dependent
daughter of Isaac M. Wells, late of Company E, Twenty-first Wisconsin Infantry, at $12 per month.

The beneficiary named in the bill, and now 43 years of age, is the
daughter of Isaac M. Wells, who served as a private in Company E,
Twenty-first Wisconsin Volunteers, from August 13, 1862, to March
3, 1864, when honorably discharged, and was a pensioner under the
general law on account of rheumatism and resulting disease of heart,
and whose name was dropped from the rolls in March, 1900, by reason
of his death.

He left no widow surviving him, and no one has been drawing any
pension on account of his services and death.

The claim of the beneficiary as helpless child was rejected by the
Pension Bureau upon the ground that inasmuch as she was over sixteen years of age at the date of her father's death title to pension
under the general pension laws could not obtain.

Proof on file with your committee shows that the beneficiary when
about six months old had an inflammatory affection of the spine, and
that she is now a hunchbacked dwarf by reason of that affliction; that
she has no means of support and is unable by reason of her helpless
and crippled condition to earn a living for herself.

Under the rules of the House and the Senate the relief sought for in
the bill for this helpless and dependent child is fully warranted; hence
the bill is reported back with the recommendation that it pass.

O

LUCINDA J. PRATT.

JANUARY 20, 1903.—Committed to the Committee of the Whole House and ordered
to be printed.

Mr. SAMUEL W. SMITH, from the Committee on Invalid Pensions, submitted the following

REPORT.

[To accompany H. R. 15483.]

The Committee on Invalid Pensions, to whom was referred the bill (H. R. 15483) granting a pension to Lucinda J. Pratt, submit the following report:

This bill proposes to pension Lucinda J. Pratt, former widow of Joseph Letcher, late of Company G, Ninth Michigan Infantry, at $12 per month.

It appears from the records of the War Department that Joseph Letcher, the soldier named in this bill, was drafted and assigned as a private of Company G, Ninth Michigan Infantry, on September 27, 1864, and that he died October 21, 1864, of acute dysentery.

The records of the War Department further show that the soldier was received at the draft rendezvous on October 5, 1864, and that he was assigned and forwarded to the Ninth Michigan Infantry on October 12, 1864, taken up on the rolls of Company G, but never joined that company, and that he was under treatment from October 16, 1864, to the date of his death for jaundice and acute dysentery.

The claim of his widow, Lucinda Jane Letcher, for pension under the general law was rejected by the Pension Bureau on March 19, 1867, upon the ground that the disease from which her husband died existed prior to his enlistment.

Congress on July 27, 1868, passed an act granting a pension to the beneficiary as the widow of the soldier from the date of his death.

The report upon which this special act was based reads as follows:

The claim of the beneficiary was rejected at the Pension Bureau on the ground that the disease of which her husband died was not contracted in the service. It appears in evidence that the man had for some time been suffering from what the physician called chronic diarrhea, and this evidence he presented to the examining surgeon (Letcher being a drafted man), but notwithstanding this, he was forced in the service, and from overexposure his disease was made worse and he soon died. Your committee believes his widow entitled to a pension, and report the accompanying bill granting her a pension.

The beneficiary remarried one Marshall T. Pratt on December 15, 1868.

Notwithstanding the fact that the Pension Bureau rejecteu the widow's claim under the general law and that the special act was for the benefit of the widow only, the Pension Bureau in June, 1869, pensioned under the general law the minor children of the soldier from the date of the remarriage of the widow until April 19, 1881, when the youngest child became 16 years of age.

The beneficiary was married to the soldier on February 12, 1862, and therefore was his wife both before and during his service.

Her claim for restoration to the roll under the provisions of the act of March 3, 1901, was rejected by the Pension Bureau in May, 1901, upon the ground that inasmuch as the beneficiary had never been pensioned under the general law, title under the act named above could not obtain, her husband's death not having been due to his military service.

Proof filed in the Pension Bureau shows that the second husband of the beneficiary died May 22, 1891, and that the beneficiary has not remarried since his death.

Congress having held that the soldier died of disease contracted in the service, and having pensioned his widow by special act, it is believed that her case comes within the spirit of the act of March 3, 1901, her second husband having died, and the relief sought for in the bill is therefore recommended and the bill is reported back with the recommendation that it pass after the same shall have been amended as follows:

Strike out all after the enacting clause and insert in lieu thereof the following:

That the Secretary of the Interior be, and he is hereby, authorized and directed to place on the pension roll, subject to the provisions and limitations of the pension laws, the name of Lucinda J. Pratt, former widow of Joseph Letcher, late of Company G, Ninth Regiment Michigan Volunteer Infantry, and pay her a pension at the rate of $12 per month.

O

GUSTAVUS W. PEABODY.

JANUARY 20, 1903.—Committed to the Committee of the Whole House and ordered
to be printed.

Mr. SULLOWAY, from the Committee on Invalid Pensions, submitted the
following

REPORT.

[To accompany H. R. 16271.]

The Committee on Invalid Pensions, to whom was referred the bill
(H. R. 16271) granting an increase of pension to Gustavus W. Peabody,
submit the following report:
This bill proposes to increase the pension of the beneficiary named
therein from $12 to $30 per month.
This soldier, now 62 years of age, served as a private in Company I,
Tenth Massachusetts Infantry, from June 21, 1861, to July 21, 1864,
when honorably discharged as of the One hundred and fourteenth Com-
pany, Second Battalion, Veteran Reserve Corps, to which transferred.
The medical records of the War Department show that the soldier
received a wound of the right arm at the battle of Chancellorsville on
May 3, 1863, and that he was under treatment for said wound.
The soldier has been a pensioner under the general law on account
of this gunshot wound of the right shoulder and resulting neuralgia at
$4 per month from discharge, at $6 from December 16, 1885, at $8 from
December 22, 1886, and at $12 from May 28, 1890.
A claim for increase of pension, filed in March, 1897, was rejected
in November, 1897, upon the ground that the disability from the gunshot wound of the right shoulder and resulting neuralgia did not warrant a rating in excess of $12 per month.
A claim on account of additional disabilities under the general law,
based upon disease of liver, heart, stomach, and jaundice, filed January 14, 1898, was rejected on June 18, 1900, upon the ground of no
record of treatment for said disabilities in the service or at the date of
discharge and the best obtainable evidence failing to establish the
origin and continuance of said disabilities.
In support of that claim the beneficiary filed proof of some comrades tending to show that while in the service he suffered from what
was supposed to be jaundice for the reason that he looked very yellow,

so that he was called a Chinaman; also medical testimony as to treatment for liver affection from 1864 to 1866, and from 1869 to 1874 for chronic inflammation or enlargement of the liver, with disturbances of the stomach, heart, and kidneys, and lay testimony as to the existence of these disabilities ever since discharge.

When last examined before the board of surgeons at Norwich, Conn., on November 9, 1898, the board of surgeons rated him $12 for the gunshot wound of shoulder and neuralgia, $10 for disease of stomach, and $6 for disease of heart.

In the opinion of your committee this soldier has clearly established his claim on account of disease of stomach, medical testimony filed with your committee showing that he was treated for that disability from shortly after his discharge to 1866, and again from 1869 to 1874, and lay testimony having been filed as to the existence of the same ever since discharge.

Under these circumstances an increase of his pension to $24 per month is justified and the bill is reported back with the recommendation that it pass after the same shall have been amended as follows:

In line 6, after the word "Tenth," insert the word "Regiment."

In line 7 strike out the word "Volunteers" and insert in lieu thereof the words "Volunteer Infantry."

In line 8 strike out the word "thirty" and insert in lieu thereof the word "twenty-four."

O

MARTIN G. COLE.

JANUARY 20, 1903.—Committed to the Committee of the Whole House and ordered
to be printed.

Mr. CROWLEY, from the Committee on Invalid Pensions, submitted
the following

REPORT.

[To accompany H. R. 15733.]

The Committee on Invalid Pensions, to whom was referred the bill
(H. R. 15733) granting an increase of pension to M. G. Cole, submit
the following report:

This bill proposes to increase the pension of the beneficiary named
therein from $12 to $30 per month.

Martin G. Cole, the soldier named in this bill, now 61 years of age,
served as a corporal in Company G, First Wisconsin Cavalry, from
September 21, 1861, to October 31, 1864, when honorably discharged.

He was under treatment while in the service for typhoid fever and
intermittent fever.

He is now a pensioner under the general law at $12 per month on
account of disease of lungs and rheumatism.

Claims for increase of pension, in which disease of stomach and mind
and disease of heart were alleged as results of the pensioned causes,
were rejected in February, 1901, and July, 1902, upon the ground
that neither disease of heart, stomach, nor the disease of mind could be
accepted as results of the disease of lungs and rheumatism.

Proof was filed in the Pension Bureau showing that the beneficiary
was confined in the Hospital for the Insane at Independence, Iowa, in
1899, for several months; that his malady there was diagnosed as softening of the brain, and that he was returned to his home as incurable.

Medical testimony filed in support of the claims for increase of pension in the Pension Bureau sets forth that the disease of heart from
which the beneficiary has been suffering for some time was a result of
the rheumatism; that he has required an attendant for several years;
that he is failing quite rapidly, and that he has no property of any
kind except a little home worth a few hundred dollars, and that his
family has been dependent upon the county fund for indigent soldiers
and their families.

A medical examination of the soldier on July 18, 1900, revealed rheumatism and hypertrophy of the heart and also disease of lungs, and the board of surgeons then also found his mental condition almost a blank, stating that he was unable to carry on a rational conversation on any subject, unable to feed, dress, or undress himself without assistance, etc.

The last medical examination of the soldier, made on April 8, 1902, found pleuritic adhesions, the result of pneumonia, heart's action feeble and slow with dilitation, frequent attacks of dyspnœa and fainting spells, and the surgeon who then examined him at his home further stated:

This man is also suffering from chronic dementia. He has attacks of vertigo, is tremulous and unsteady on his feet, with marked incoordination, tongue and all muscles very tremulous, can not connect his words to form a sentence or answer a question, talks incoherently, can not attend to calls of nature without help, depends constantly on an attendant. I believe this man is suffering from arterio sclerosis.

In view of the action of the House on June 16, 1902, an increase of this soldier's pension from $12 to $30 per month is justified, it being shown that by reason of softening of the brain he requires the aid and attendance of another person, etc.

The bill is therefore reported back with the recommendation that it pass after the same shall have been amended as follows:

In line 6 strike out the letter " M " and insert in lieu thereof the word " Martin. "

Amend the title so as to read: " A bill granting an increase of pension to Martin G. Cole."

O

DAVID E. LAWTON.

JANUARY 20, 1903.—Committed to the Committee of the Whole House and ordered to be printed.

Mr. CROWLEY, from the Committee on Invalid Pensions, submitted the following

REPORT.

[To accompany H. R. 14475.]

The Committee on Invalid Pensions, to whom was referred the bill (H. R. 14475) granting an increase of pension to David E. Lawton, submit the following report:

This bill proposes to increase the pension of this soldier from $12 to $36 per month.

This soldier, now 70 years of age, who served as a private in Company G, Thirty-fifth Wisconsin Infantry, from February 1, 1864, to January 25, 1866, when honorably discharged, and who was under treatment at various dates during his service for diarrhea and remittent fever, is now and has been since July 26, 1890, a pensioner under the act of June 27, 1890, at the maximum rating, namely, $12 per month, for total inability to ear a support by manual labor, the result of disease of eyes and lungs.

His claim to pension under the general law, filed in 1878, and based upon disease of eyes alleged to have been contracted at Port Hudson, La., in May, 1864, was rejected by the Pension Bureau in 1886, after a special examination of the case, upon the ground that that disability was shown to have existed prior to the soldier's enlistment, and a claim for disease of lungs was rejected at the same time upon the ground that the evidence furnished by the soldier was considered incompetent to prove that his disability originated in the service and line of duty.

Subsequent to that rejection the soldier filed a mass of testimony tending to show that his eyes were sound at enlistment and that he suffered from disease of eyes while in the service and ever since. The Pension Bureau, however, held that this testimony did not outweigh that obtained upon special examination showing that the soldier had suffered from sore eyes prior to his enlistment.

DAVID E. LAWTON.

The last medical examination of the soldier, made on April 3, 1901, showed him to be practically blind, and also to be suffering from disease of lungs and heart and enlarged prostate gland to such an extent that he required the aid and attendance of another person.

The case of this soldier comes within the action of the House on June 16, 1902, increasing from $12 to $30 per month the pension of those who are blind, paralyzed, etc., and require the aid and attendance of another person.

The bill is therefore reported back with the recommendation that it pass after the same shall have been amended as follows:

In line 8 strike out the word "thirty-six" and insert in lieu thereof the word "thirty."

O

HERCULES H. PRICE.

JANUARY 20, 1903.—Committed to the Committee of the Whole House and ordered
to be printed.

Mr. SULLOWAY, from the Committee on Invalid Pensions, submitted
the following

REPORT.

[To accompany H. R. 6670.]

The Committee on Invalid Pensions, to whom was referred the bill
(H. R. 6670) granting a pension to Hercules H. Price, submit the
following report:

This bill proposes to pension the beneficiary named therein at $17
per month.

Hercules H. Price, the beneficiary named in this bill, filed a claim
to pension under the act of June 27, 1890, on April 6, 1895, alleging
that he served as second and first lieutenant of Company B, Fifth
(colored) Cavalry, from July 3, 1865, to March 16, 1866, when honorably discharged, and that he also rendered services in the Fifth U. S.
Cavalry, Company G, from August, 1868, to August, 1873, and also
in the general-service detachment, headquarters military division of
the Pacific, and that he incurred a rupture of both sides at Helena,
Ark., on February 22, 1866.

In an affidavit, filed on July 29, 1895, the claimant set forth that he
served in a civil capacity, but not as an enlisted man or as a commissioned officer prior to July 3, 1865; that he was attached to and did
service with what was known as "Stoneman's independent brigade
of cavalry;" that he joined that organization at Paris, Ky., at which
place he was a clerk in the post commissary, in the year 1864; that the
command was making a flying train into Florida; that he was issued a
horse, carbine, revolver, etc.; that some days after joining, when on
the march, he was taken sick with scurvy, was left at a post at the
South Fork of the Cumberland River, thinks the name of the place was
Burnside Point, where he remained under medical treatment for about
one month, when informally discharged; that he was never formally
enlisted nor formally discharged, but had the status of "recruit
joined," as he presumed; that he was subsequently arrested at Somer-
set, Ky., as a deserter from the Eleventh Kentucky Cavalry, and

during part of his imprisonment was ordered on several mounted scouts with other paroled prisoners, and that he was eventually discharged from imprisonment at Camp Nelson, Kentucky, the date of which he does not remember and can not give, having lost all his memoranda.

His claim was rejected on June 17, 1895, upon the ground that inasmuch as he did not render services during the war of the rebellion title to pension under the act of June 27, 1890, could not obtain.

The War Department advised the Pension Bureau that the beneficiary named in the bill served as second and first lieutenant of Company B, Fifth U. S. Colored Cavalry, from July 3, 1865, to March 16, 1866, when honorably discharged; that he again served as corporal and private of Company G, Fifth U. S. Cavalry, from August 7, 1868, to August 7, 1873, when honorably discharged; that he again enlisted January 22, 1874, and was assigned to the general service detachment at headquarters of the military division of the Pacific, and was discharged January 22, 1879; that he reenlisted January 23, 1879, in the same detachment and was discharged January 22, 1884; reenlisted in the same detachment January 23, 1884, and was discharged July 1, 1886, to date June 30, 1886, under General Orders, No. 43, of the Adjutant-General's Office, 1886, reducing the number of general service clerks and messengers.

The War Department further advised the Pension Bureau that the beneficiary is shown by the medical records of that department to have been under treatment in 1865 for bronchitis, in 1866 for hepatitis, in 1869 for rheumatism, in 1870 for acute indigestion and rheumatism, and in 1871 and 1872 for catarrh, colic, etc.

The War Department further advised the Pension Bureau that it did not appear from the records of that Department that such an organization as "Stoneman's independent brigade of cavalry" was in the military service of the United States during the civil war; that General Stoneman commanded the cavalry division of the army of the Ohio, and on July 27, 1864, started with his command on a raid around Atlanta, Ga.; that it was, however, clear from Mr. Price's statements that he was not legally in the military service of the United States at any time during the period embraced by his allegations.

The beneficiary never applied for pension under the general law.

He appealed from the action of rejection of his claim under the act of June 27, 1890, but the action of the Pension Bureau was affirmed by Assistant Secretary Webster Davis, under date of July 20, 1897, upon the ground that in view of the well-known fact that all active organized antagonism of the rebellion ceased immediately or soon after General Lee's surrender; that where service was rendered subsequent to July 5, 1865, it would be presumed to have not been war service, and that claimants would have the burden of proving affirmatively that their service subsequent to July 5, 1865, was rendered in some connection with the rebellion.

There has been filed with your committee a lengthy statement of the beneficiary, setting forth his alleged service with the independent brigade, etc.; that about two weeks before being mustered out as lieutenant of the Fifth U. S. Colored Cavalry he was slightly ruptured, but that he thought nothing of it at the time; that subsequently he wore a truss a short time, and that the rupture seemed to disappear, but that it afterwards reappeared, etc.; that if he could have proven that he was ruptured before being mustered out from the colored cavalry he would have been entitled to $17 per month for the same, but that he was too young and thoughtless; that he now suffers from double rupture, hemorrhoids, varicose veins, indigestion, etc.

The beneficiary having rendered service in a colored volunteer organization until March, 1866, it should, in the opinion of your committee, be held that the service by him in that organization was during the war of the rebellion, and inasmuch as he is shown to have rendered over twenty years of service to the Government and to have been under treatment for various disabilities, your committee believes that relief to the extent of granting him a pension of $12 per month is warranted, hence the bill is reported back with the recommendation that it pass after the same shall have been amended as follows:

Strike out all of lines 6, 7, and 8 and insert in lieu thereof the following:

of Hercules H. Price, late first lieutenant Company B, Fifth Regiment United States Colored Volunteer Cavalry, and pay him a pension at the rate of twelve dollars per month.

O

JOSEPH BART.

JANUARY 20, 1903.—Committed to the Committee of the Whole House and ordered to be printed.

Mr. DARRAGH, from the Committee on Invalid Pensions, submitted the following

REPORT.

[To accompany H. R. 12411.]

The Committee on Invalid Pensions, to whom was referred the bill (H. R. 12411) granting an increase of pension to Joseph Bart, submit the following report:

This bill proposes to increase the pension of the soldier named therein from $17 to $30 per month.

This soldier, now 71 years of age, served as a private in Company E, Twenty-first Wisconsin Infantry, from August 11, 1862, to December 3, 1862, when discharged on surgeon's certificate of disability by reason of—

a gunshot wound received in the chest. The ball entered the right side about 3 or 4 inches below the axilla, penetrating the cavity. Had no exit.

This wound was received by the soldier in action at Perryville, Ky., October 8, 1862.

He first applied for pension in December, 1862, on account of this wound, which the soldier then claimed was a wound of the right side involving the shoulder and arm, and he was pensioned on account of this gunshot wound of the right side involving the shoulder and arm at $8 per month from discharge, at $10 from July, 1876, at $18 from July, 1877, and at $20 from March 3, 1883.

When first examined by a board of surgeons, on March 24, 1863, that board of surgeons described the wound as follows:

A minie or other ball entered the right side between the sixth and seventh ribs, directly below the axilla, and seems to have taken an upward and forward direction and lodged in the wall of the chest under the pectoralis muscles. The history of the case indicates that the pleura was opened. There is great soreness and lameness about the wound. The wound and the lancet opening are both discharging pus. Respiration is impeded by the soreness of the wound.

In March, 1886, the soldier's pension was reduced to $12 per month, the Pension Bureau having held that the disability from the wound

did not warrant a rating in excess of that amount, and this rating was
again increased to $16 per month from November 3, 1897, and to $17
per month from August 2, 1899.

In May, 1875, the soldier alleged that he received two gunshot
wounds at the battle of Perryville, Ky., namely, the one for which
now pensioned and the one of the face, the ball lodging in the vicinity
of the right shoulder, and he filed some ex parte proof tending to show
the receipt of two wounds while at the battle of Perryville, but upon
special examination of the case all the witnesses, with the exception of
a brother of the beneficiary, who served in the same company and regiment with him, were unable to testify definitely and positively that the
beneficiary received two wounds on the same day; hence that claim was
rejected in October, 1895, upon the ground of no record of treatment
for a wound other than that for which pensioned, and claimant's inability, aided by a special examination, to furnish satisfactory evidence
of the origin of another wound in the service.

The ball causing the wound for which pensioned was extracted by
Dr. La Count in 1864.

The soldier alleged sciatic rheumatism in the right shoulder and
right side and numbness of the right limb below the knee as results of
the wound of the right side involving shoulder and arm, but the Pension Bureau declined to accept that condition as results of the wound.

The last medical examination of the soldier, made in November,
1900, shows that by reason of the gunshot wound of right side, making
his right arm practically useless, rheumatism, disease of heart, lungs,
varicose veins, impaired sight, and deafness, the soldier required the
periodical aid and attendance of another person, and that senility was
evident to a greater or less degree.

The affidavit of the beneficiary filed with your committee sets forth
that he was twice wounded at the battle of Perryville, first in the
right shoulder, resulting in total loss of the use of his right arm, with
partial loss of the use of his left arm; that the other wound penetrated
his back a little above the loin, to the right of the spine, lodged in his
breast, and was extracted from a spot near the right nipple; that he
is unable to perform any kind of labor, and at times can neither feed
nor dress himself without aid; that he has no income aside from his
pension and no property except a house and lot, which he occupies as
a home.

While your committee can not admit that the proof is sufficient to
show that the soldier received two wounds while in the service, it
believes, however, that the disability from the wound of accepted
service origin is such as to warrant an increase of his rating from $17
to $24 per month.

The bill is therefore reported back with the recommendation that it
pass after the same shall have been amended as follows:

In line 8 strike out the word " thirty " and insert in lieu thereof the
word "twenty-four."

O

BENJAMIN F. OLCOTT.

JANUARY 20, 1903.—Committed to the Committee of the Whole House and ordered to be printed.

Mr. CROWLEY, from the Committee on Invalid Pensions, submitted the following

REPORT.

[To accompany H. R. 13316.]

The Committee on Invalid Pensions, to whom was referred the bill (H. R. 13316) granting an increase of pension to Benjamin F. Olcott, submit the following report:

This bill proposes to increase the pension of the soldier named therein from $10 to $30 per month.

The records of the War Department show that this soldier, who is now 57 years of age, served as a private in Company I, Tenth Michigan Infantry, from March 28, 1864, to July 19, 1865, when honorably discharged, and that he was under treatment at various dates between May 12, 1864, and August 12, 1864, for dysentery and intermittent fever.

He is now a pensioner under the general law at $10 per month on account of disease of the back and kidneys of accepted service origin.

Claims for increase of pension, filed November 30, 1891, and July 30, 1897, were rejected, the last one on January 8, 1898, upon the ground that the rating of $10 per month was fully commensurate with the degree of disability arising from the pensioned causes, and that disease of eyes, rheumatism, and constipation, alleged as results of the pensioned causes, could not be so accepted.

The soldier's claim to pension under the general law was filed on January 31, 1887, and was allowed in 1888 at $8 per month from the date of the filing of the claim, and was increased to $10 per month from October 1, 1890.

This increased rating was based upon a certificate of medical examination of October 1, 1890, which rated the soldier $17 for disease of the spine and back and $10 for disease of the kidneys, and the board of surgeons then stated that there was tenderness of the whole spinal column on pressure, aggravated by jar or palpation, worse in the lumbar region; that there was slight œdema, with sluggish capillary circulation, œdema of ankles and feet, and some abdominal dropsy; that when stooping or sitting down he had to catch something to hold himself, and that there was considerable mental incapacity, and it was very difficult to get him to tell his story without confusion of ideas, etc.

A certificate of medical examination of January 27, 1892, rated him $17 for rheumatism and results, $12 for disease of heart, $4 for catarrh, and $4 for disease of eyes.

The last certificate of medical examination, made October 6, 1897, upon which the rejection of the claim for increase on January 8, 1898, was based, described his condition as follows:

Claimant is quite corpulent. Tongue coated white. A slight catarrhal inflammation of the throat exists. There is no marked tenderness over stomach and bowels. We believe claimant's bowels are very inactive, with digestive and assimilative powers deranged as a result.

There is some atrophy of muscles in the lumbar region of the spine, and claimant claims tenderness on percussion along the whole length of spine. We believe claimant suffers from chronic lumbago and general rheumatism, due to faulty secretion as a result of long-continued and obstinate constipation. There is no enlargement of joints or marked contraction of tendons. The joints appear quite stiff. We should judge from his walk that his joints are limited in motion one-eighth. Heart is weak; pulsations over apex very faint; pulsations soft and regular; pulse, standing, 90; after exercise, walking the office floor slowly, 99. Claimant uses a cane continuously when he walks. No albumen; no sugar, but some excess of uric acid found.

Claimant's flesh is not good, and it is the opinion of the board that probably some fatty degeneration of the heart exists.

Rate, $17 for constipation, impaired digestion, and resulting rheumatism, and heart trouble. No rating for catarrh or kidney disease.

The claimant appealed from the action of rejection of his claim for increase of pension. This action, however, was affirmed by Secretary Bliss under date of October 20, 1898, upon the ground that after a careful examination of the evidence presented and the certificate of examination of October 6, 1897, the action of the Pension Bureau rejecting the claim on the grounds stated was proper.

There has been filed with your committee the statement of Dr. J. B. Hare, of McCook, Nebr., setting forth that the beneficiary had been under affiant's medical care for the three months prior to February 15, 1902, and was wholly incapacitated from physical labor on account of spinal injuries alleged by him to have been received during the war of the rebellion.

A petition signed by a large number of residents of McCook, Nebr., has also been filed with your committee, setting forth that for the last five years the beneficiary had been totally disabled from performing any kind of manual labor on account of spinal and kidney trouble, the result of his army service, and that since October, 1901, he had not been able to leave his house but twice; that he has no means of support other than his pension of $10 per month, out of which he must support himself and wife and pay house rent.

In the opinion of your committee the several certificates of medical examination, as well as the medical testimony filed with your committee, warrant an increase of this soldier's pension from $10 to $24 per month.

Relief to that extent is recommended, and the bill is reported back with the recommendation that it pass after the same shall have been amended as follows:

In line 7, after the word "pension," insert the words "at the rate."

In line 8 strike out the word "thirty" and insert in lieu thereof the word "twenty-four."

O

GUSTAVUS S. PERKINS.

JANUARY 20, 1903.—Committed to the Committee of the Whole House and ordered
to be printed.

Mr. LINDSAY, from the Committee on Invalid Pensions, submitted the
following

REPORT.

[To accompany H. R. 12991.]

The Committee on Invalid Pensions, to whom was referred the bill
(H. R. 12991) granting a pension to Gustavus S. Perkins, submit the
following report:

This bill proposes to increase the pension of the officer named therein
from $12 to $50 per month.

Gustavus S. Perkins, the officer named in this bill, and now 69 years
of age, served as acting second and first assistant engineer in the Navy
from September 20, 1862, to September 27, 1865, when honorably
discharged.

He never applied for pension under the general law, but is now a
pensioner under the act of June 27, 1890, at the maximum rating,
namely, $12 per month, for total inability to earn a support by manual
labor, the result of senile debility and disease of kidneys.

This allowance was based upon a certificate of medical examination
of the officer made by the board of surgeons at Hartford, Conn., on
February 26, 1902, which described his condition as follows:

Claimant is well fed, but appears about seven years older than his age. On slight
exercise a tremor agitans shakes his hands, and on moderate standing his legs and
body tremble. The grasp is fair, but the hands show no familiarity with work. The
gait is unsteady. The movements are slow and awkward. The memory is impaired
only as is usual with aged persons.

Urine: Specific gravity, 1.024; clear, amber, acid; no albumin, but a demonstrable
amount of sugar.

There has been filed with your committee the statement of the beneficiary setting forth that he took part in the capture and destruction
of Fort Fisher; that in December, 1864, his ship towed a powder boat
from Newport, N. C., to Fort Fisher, beached the boat under the walls
of the fort, and blew her up; that by the explosion he was stunned and
practically buried in the sand; that the permanent injuries received at
that time had constantly aggravated his trouble since; that about that

time he was possessed of an excellent memory, but since that time his memory had been badly impaired; that he has had a ringing in his ears by day and by night; that he also contracted chills and fever in the service in an aggravated form and had been a constant sufferer therefrom up to 1876, since which time he had suffered from the same at frequent intervals.

Petitions filed with your committee and signed by a large number of prominent citizens of Hartford, Conn., set forth that the beneficiary is a man of irreproachable character, habits, and industry, and is deserving of an increase of pension by act of Congress.

This officer, who rendered three years of service, is now wholly disabled from senile debility, disease of the kidneys, and paralysis agitans.

Following precedents, an increase of his pension from $12 to $24 per month is justified under the circumstances, and the bill is therefore reported back with the recommendation that it pass after the same shall have been amended as follows:

In line 8 strike out the word "fifty" and insert in lieu thereof the word "twenty-four."

In same line, after the word "month," insert the words "in lieu of that he is now receiving."

Amend the title so as to read: "A bill granting an increase of pension to Gustavus S. Perkins."

MARY E. WINTERBOTTOM.

JANUARY 20, 1903.—Committed to the Committee of the Whole House and ordered
to be printed.

Mr. GIBSON, from the Committee on Invalid Pensions, submitted the
following

REPORT.

[To accompany H. R. 11682.]

The Committee on Invalid Pensions, to whom was referred the bill
(H. R. 11682) granting a pension to Mary E. Winterbottom, submit
the following report:

This bill proposes to pension the beneficiary at $18 per month.

The beneficiary named in this bill, now 69 years of age, was pensioned in 1895 under the provisions of the act of June 27, 1890, at $8
per month, as the widow of Harrison T. Winterbottom, upon a report
of the War Department made in 1894, showing that said Harrison T.
Winterbottom served as first sergeant of Company A, First Eastern
Shore Maryland Infantry, from September 11, 1861, to August 16,
1862, when honorably discharged, and upon proof that she was married
to the soldier on November 27, 1850; that he died July 14, 1880; that
she had not remarried since his death and that she was dependent upon
her daily labor for support.

In January, 1902, the name of the beneficiary was dropped from the
roll upon the ground that, according to a new report of the War
Department, dated March 3, 1900, the soldier had not been honorably
discharged from the service; that the company in which the husband
of the beneficiary served was mustered out of service in accordance
with special instructions of Major-General Wool of August 6 and 12,
1862, for refusing to obey orders, and that on January 4, 1896, it was
decided by the War Department that members of the company mustered out of service with the company were to be regarded by that
Department as having been discharged without honor.

A good many members of Company A of the First Eastern Shore
Maryland Infantry and their widows were pensioned under the provisions of the act of June 27, 1890, upon reports furnished by the War
Department to the Pension Bureau, showing that these men were honorably discharged the service.

As stated above, in 1896 the War Deeartment advised the Pension
Bureau that they regarded the men of that company mustered out with
it as having been discharged without honor upon the ground that they
refused to obey orders.

The writer's recollection is that some of the officers of that regiment
desired to enter the Confederate service and that the refusal to obey
orders by the men was wholly due to the actions of the officers and
that the men were in no wise to blame for this refusal to obey orders.

Under these circumstances your committee believe that the name of
the beneficiary should be restored to the pension roll at the rate of $8
per month.

The bill is therefore reported back with the recommendation that it
pass after the same shall have been amended as follows:

In line 7 strike out the words "a private in the Union Army during
the civil war" and all of line 8 and insert in lieu thereof the following:

late of Company A, First Regiment Eastern Shore Maryland Volunteer Infantry, and
pay her a pension at the rate of eight dollars per month.

O

PATRICK MAHAN.

JANUARY 20, 1903.—Committed to the Committee of the Whole House and ordered
to be printed.

Mr. SAMUEL W. SMITH, from the Committee on Invalid Pensions, submitted the following

REPORT.

[To accompany H. R. 5281.]

The Committee on Invalid Pensions, to whom was referred the bill
(H. R. 5281) granting a pension to P. H. Mahan, submit the following
report:

The purpose of this bill is to increase the pension of the soldier
named therein from $10 to $30 per month.

It appears from the records of the War Department that Patrick
Mahan, the soldier named in this bill, and now 56 years of age, served
as a private in Company B, One hundred and twenty-fourth Ohio
Infantry, from August 14, 1862, to September 2, 1863, when discharged
on surgeon's certificate of disability on account of disease of the heart
and an inguinal hernia of very large size, and the medical records of
that Department further show that he was treated for chronic diarrhea
from February 11, 1863, to March 12, 1863.

He is now a pensioner under the general law at $10 per month on
account of the hernia of the right side.

His claim for increase of pension and for additional disabilities,
namely, hernia of the left side as a result of that of the right side,
varicose veins of the left foot and leg, and disease of the rectum, were
rejected in July, 1896, upon the ground that the disability from the
hernia of the right side did not warrant a rating in excess of $10 per
month; that the hernia of the left side could not be accepted as a
result, and that the claimant with the aid of a special examination had
been unable to prove the origin in the service of varicose veins of the
left leg and disease of the rectum by satisfactory evidence.

The hernia of the right side for which this soldier is now pensioned
was incurred by him from injuries received at Elizabethtown, Ky., in
January, 1863, while building stockades, when he was hurt by a log
which threw him on his back, and the soldier alleged that the hernia
of the left side was a result of that same injury, although he admits

that the hernia of the left side did not come down until after he came home from the service; that the injury produced a bad sore on his left leg; that he had diarrhea while in the service and at times since his discharge, and that he suffered either from constipation or piles ever since his discharge.

The records of the War Department, as stated above, show that the soldier was under treatment for quite a while for chronic diarrhea while in the service, and proof obtained upon special examination shows that upon his return from the service the soldier complained of bowel trouble and disease of the rectum and piles, and existence of disease of the rectum and piles since about 1870 or 1873 is amply shown by medical testimony.

The varicose veins, however, were not established as having been due to the soldier's military service.

A medical examination of the soldier in May, 1890, rated him $12 for the double hernia, $4 for disease of the rectum, $4·for varicose veins, and $4 for atrophy of the right testicle.

The last certificate of medical examination in the case, made January 31, 1894, after describing the double hernia, both passing through the external ring, stated that there was evidence of rectal disease and evidence of operation for fistula; that there were five external hemorrhoids about the size of peas and ten internal hemorrhoids about the size of peas, and that there were varicose veins of the left foot and leg, the veins being enlarged eight or ten times their natural condition, with tendency to ulceration; and the board of surgeons then stated that the left hernia probably resulted from the right.

Medical testimony filed in the Pension Bureau in October, 1897, shows that the beneficiary was then suffering from piles and a double inguinal hernia; that each hernia passes through the external ring down into the scrotum; that each tumor is 1½ inches in diameter; that the right hernia was the original hernia and that the left was secondary, and, in the opinion of the physicians, resulted from the right.

In view of the opinion of the physicians that the hernia of the left side resulted from that of the right, and the further fact that the disease of rectum from which the soldier is now suffering is traceable to his military service, an increase of his pension to $24 per month appears justified; hence the bill is reported back with the recommendation that it pass after the same shall have been amended as follows:

Strike out all after the enacting clause and insert in lieu thereof the following:

That the Secretary of the Interior be, and he is hereby, authorized and directed to place on the pension roll, subject to the provisions and limitations of the pension laws, the name of Patrick Mahan, late of Company B, One hundred and twenty-fourth Regiment Ohio Volunteer Infantry, and pay him a pension at the rate of twenty-four dollars per month in lieu of that he is now receiving.

Amend the title so as to read: "A bill granting an increase of pension to Patrick Mahan."

O

CALLIE WEST.

JANUARY 20, 1903.—Committed to the Committee of the Whole House and ordered
to be printed.

Mr. KLEBERG, from the Committee on Invalid Pensions, submitted
the following

REPORT.

[To accompany H. R. 12492.]

The Committee on Invalid Pensions, to whom was referred the bill
(H. R. 12492) granting an increase of pension to Callie West, submit
the following report:

This bill proposes to increase the pension of the beneficiary named
therein from $8 to $20 per month.

Burris C. West, the soldier named in this bill, served as sergeant in
Company G, Sixty-sixth Illinois Infantry, from October 31, 1861, to
September 2, 1864, when honorably discharged.

He never applied for pension and died December 27, 1884, from
malignant ulceration of the rectum.

The beneficiary, now 55 years of age, who was married to him on
October 10, 1867, is now and has been since July 18, 1890, a pensioner
under the act of June 27, 1890, at $8 per month upon proof that she
was his legal widow at the time of his death, that she has not remarried,
and that she was without other means of support than her daily labor.

Her claim under the general law was rejected in 1902 upon the
ground that the evidence filed failed to show that her husband's death
from malignant ulceration of the rectum was due to his military
service; that there was no record of treatment for said disability in
the service or other satisfactory evidence of service origin of the same,
and that claimant had declared her inability to furnish the evidence
necessary to establish the claim.

The beneficiary filed some testimony of comrades tending to show
that her husband while in the service complained a great deal of what
some affiants thought to be diarrhea and some thought to be piles; also
testimony of neighbors tending to show that upon his return from the
Army he took medicine for piles, that he was very weak, and medical
testimony as to treatment since 1880 for ulceration of the rectum and
a tumor in the rectum, and that he finally died January 14, 1883, of
malignant ulceration of the rectum.

Proof filed with your committee shows that the beneficiary has no property of any kind except a one-half interest in 40 acres of poor farm land, worth not exceeding $1.50 per acre, and that she is absolutely dependent and helpless, without any support from any source save the pension of $8 per month.

Inasmuch as the evidence tends to show that the beneficiary's husband suffered from diarrhea and piles in the service, and that the ulceration of the rectum, from which he died, was due to those diseases, an increase of the beneficiary's pension to that allowed by law to the widow of an enlisted man, namely, $12 per month, is justified; hence the bill is reported back with the recommendation that it pass after the same shall have been amended as follows:

Strike out all after the enacting clause and insert in lieu thereof the following:

That the Secretary of the Interior be, and he is hereby, authorized and directed to place on the pension roll, subject to the provisions and limitations of the pension laws, the name of Callie West, widow of Burris C. West, late of Company G, Sixty-sixth Regiment Illinois Volunteer Infantry, and pay her a pension at the rate of twelve dollars per month in lieu of that she is now receiving.

O

ISAAC HARRIS.

JANUARY 20, 1903.—Committed to the Committee of the Whole House and ordered
to be printed.

Mr. HOLLIDAY, from the Committee on Invalid Pensions, submitted the
following

REPORT.

[To accompany H. R. 11616.]

The Committee on Invalid Pensions, to whom was referred the bill
(H. R. 11616) granting an increase of pension to Isaac Harris, submit
the following report:

The bill proposes to increase the pension of the beneficiary named
therein from $10 to $50 per month.

This soldier, who is now 65 years of age, served as a private in Company F, Second New Jersey Infantry, from May 28, 1861, to February
2, 1863, when promoted to second lieutenant, and was honorably discharged April 15, 1863, upon tender of resignation based upon a
surgeon's certificate showing him to be suffering from epileptic convulsions.

He again served as first sergeant of Company C, Thirty-ninth New
Jersey Infantry, from September 16, 1864, to June 17, 1865, and as
first lieutenant of Company A, Seventh U. S. Veteran Volunteers,
from August 29, 1865, to April 2, 1866, when honorably discharged.

According to the files of the Pension Bureau he established a claim
under the general law on account of epilepsy contracted by him while
holding the rank of private in Company F, Second New Jersey Volunteers, and was pensioned on account of said disability at $2 per
month from the date of his discharge from that organization on April
16, 1863 (deducting his subsequent service), but pension was made to
cease June 4, 1891, upon the ground that the disability had ceased to
exist.

He filed a claim to pension under the act of June 27, 1890, on July
8, 1890, alleging inability to earn a support by manual labor by reason
of impaired sight and general debility.

This claim was rejected by the Pension Bureau in August, 1893,
upon the ground that he had not been ratably disabled under the act
quoted.

He again filed a claim under said act on September 30, 1893. which was admitted from that date at $8 per month for partial inability to earn a support by manual labor, the result of epilepsy, rheumatism, and disease of heart.

This rating was increased to $10 per month from May 3, 1902, under an application for increase filed July 6, 1901, and he is now in receipt of that pension.

In July, 1898, he filed a claim for reissue under the act of March 6, 1896, alleging that he was entitled to a pension under the act of June 27, 1890, from the date of the filing of the original claim on July 8, 1890. The Pension Bureau, however, rejected that claim on June 6, 1899, and this action of the Pension Bureau was affirmed by Assistant Secretary Campbell, under date of January 28, 1902, upon the ground that while the beneficiary filed a joint affidavit of two of his neighbors tending to show that he was materially and substantially disabled for the performance of manual labor at and from the date of the filing of his original claim in July, 1890, the report of the medical examination under the claim made December 23, 1892, however, showed no disability from any cause whatever, and recommended no rating, and that the last preceding examination, made on June 4, 1891, was to the same effect.

The last certificate of medical examination of the beneficiary, made on May 3, 1902, upon which his pension under the act of June 27, 1890, was increased from $8 to $10 per month, described his condition as follows:

Spare and delicate looking. Muscles of palms soft.

Epilepsy: He describes attacks occurring twice a week beginning with the aura. Is entirely unconscious and must remain in bed during the day. No scars on the tongue. Scar on vertex from a fall. Mental condition good. Special senses normal. No paresis or paralysis.

Rheumatism: No evidence of rheumatism in any of his joints, muscles, or tendons.

Heart: Dullness increased to the left border of sternum. Pulse accentuated with clear systolic murmur transmitted to axilla. No œdema. Lips are cyanotic. Marked dyspnœa.

Dyspepsia: Loss of nearly all his teeth. Liver dullness extends 2 inches below costal margin. Abdomen tympanitic.

Loss of right index finger: There is no injury to either index finger, but there is atrophy of distal phalanx of right middle finger and anchylosis of distal joint, the result of a felon.

General debility is well marked.

We find the aggregate permanent disability from performance of manual labor is due to epilepsy, enlarged prostate, injury to finger and right knee, and entitles to $12 per month.

The beneficiary filed in the Pension Bureau medical and lay testimony setting forth that he is taken with epileptic seizures while walking in the street, at his employment, and in various ways, places, and under different circumstances; that he has been continuously affected by these seizures, and that his life on many occasions has been in danger by reason of the same; that the worst feature in connection with his case is that he has been obliged to leave one occupation after another because of the fact that fellow-employees are afraid to work with him; that he is totally and permanently disabled from following any occupation, and requires the constant protection and attendance of another person in order to prevent him doing harm to himself or others; that in character and in habits he is a most worthy and exemplary gentleman, etc.

In the opinion of your committee the evidence filed and mentioned above shows that the officer, by reason of attacks of epilepsy of accepted service origin, is so disabled as to warrant an increase of his pension to $17 per month, the committee not being satisfied that the case falls within the action of the House of June 16, 1902, for the reason that the attendance, if any, in this case is only necessary for a short time following an epileptic seizure.

The bill is therefore reported back with the recommendation that it pass after the same shall have been amended as follows:

In line 7 strike out the words "and pay him a pension at the," and all of line 8, and insert in lieu thereof the following:

and Company A, Seventh Regiment United States Veteran Volunteer Infantry, and pay him a pension at the rate of seventeen dollars per month in lieu of that he is now receiving.

O

HENRY STAFF.

JANUARY 20, 1903.—Committed to the Committee of the Whole House and ordered
to be printed.

Mr. MIERS, from the Committee on Invalid Pensions, submitted the
following

REPORT.

[To accompany H. R. 8812.]

The Committee on Invalid Pensions, to whom was referred the bill
(H. R. 8812) granting an increase of pension to Henry Staff, submit
the following report:

This bill proposes to increase the pension of the beneficiary named
therein from $30 to $72 per month.

Henry Staff, now 60 years of age, served as a private in Company
F, Twentieth Indiana Infantry, from July 22, 1861, to June 10, 1865,
when honorably discharged.

Records of the War Department show that he received a gunshot
wound of the upper third of both thighs, passing through the muscles
and out to the femur, at Coal Harbor, May 20, 1864, and that he was
also under treatment for catarrh, costiveness, and diarrhea.

He is now a pensioner under the general law at $30 per month, on
account of gunshot wound of left thigh, scrotum, and right thigh, and
resulting injury to nerves.

Numerous applications for increase of pension, filed since November
23, 1888, have been rejected, the last one on November 26, 1901, upon
the ground that the disabilities of accepted service origin did not warrant a rating in excess of $30 per month.

In some of these applications for increase of pension the soldier
alleged paralysis as a result of the wounds.

The Pension Bureau, however, held that no paralysis was shown in
the soldier's case except that caused by injury to the nerves, and that
the existing disease of heart, also alleged as a result, could not be so
accepted.

When the last claim for increase of pension was rejected, the Pension
Bureau held that the alleged paralysis was not shown, and if shown,
could not be accepted as a result of the wounds.

Medical testimony filed in the Pension Bureau in 1901 shows that
the soldier was partially paralyzed in his lower limbs; that he gets
about most of the time with great difficulty; uses a cane, and has sciatic neuralgia as result of the wounds, and that he has attacks which
confine him to his bed for several days at a time, when hypodermic
injections have to be resorted to.

The certificate of medical examination of the soldier made by the Greenfield (Ind.) board of surgeons, on January 12, 1898, described his condition as follows:

General appearance very feeble; walks with slow, hesitating gait, with use of cane, or help of another person. Hands and head are in constant tremor. Voice husky and jerky; stutters considerably, etc.

Claimant appears accompanied by an attendant.

Gunshot wound of the anterior aspect of left thigh, about 5 inches below Poupart's ligament; wound depressed and very tender. The ball ranged inward and slightly downward, passing through the muscles of the left thigh, passing through scrotum, injuring left testicle, entering right thigh, and passing out on the anterior aspect about one-half inch below the point of entrance and 6½ inches below the center of Poupart's ligament. The track of the missile is apparently same. Scar is depressed and very tender. The left testicle is atrophied as a result of wound and exceedingly tender.

There is evident loss of power in left arm and leg. Leg frequently gives away under him, causing him to fall. Left hand about one-half as strong as right. Can not get around after night. Has sensation as though walking into a hole. When walking, has to walk with his eyes on his steps. Complains of sense of constriction about the chest. Spine very tender to pressure over its whole extent. Complains of constant pain in spine and back of head. There is great difficulty in articulation, causing him to stutter and hesitate in his speech. Voice is very husky and slow. Complains of difficulty in swallowing and occasionally of incontinence of urine. These difficulties have come on recently and are increasing.

There is no cystitis. The movements are feeble. Easily fatigued. Can scarcely walk at all with eyes closed. On turning around quickly would fall if not caught. Constant tremor of hands and head.

This claimant is suffering from a progressive spinal disease, probably posterior sclerosis. It may have had its origin in the irritation caused by injury to testicle.

We rate him for gunshot wound and results $30.

Chest at rest, 45½. Inspiration, 46. Expiration, 43.

Lungs normal. Heart normal in position and sounds. Complains of pain about the heart, and sensation of smothering. Heart action rapid but regular. (Angina.)

This claimant requires aid in dressing and undressing, and occasionally aid in getting about.

This claimant is so disabled from gunshot wound and results as to require frequent and periodical, though not the constant and personal, aid and attendance of another person, and is entitled to $50 per month.

The last medical examination of the soldier, made on June 19, 1901, revealed no hemiplegia, paraplegia, or paresis, but, like the previous certificate, found a disease of the spinal cord and organic disease of the heart, and the board of surgeons then stated that—

This claimant is so disabled from gunshot wound and cardiac and respiratory enfeeblement as to be incapacitated for performing manual labor, and doubtless requires the frequent aid and assistance of another person, if not constant supervision. His hands and muscles indicate nonuse, and in our opinion he is entitled to $30 per month.

Your committee believes that relief to the extent of increasing his pension from $30 to $40 per month is justified for the reason that no doubt part of his present disability resulted from the wounds received in the service.

The bill is therefore reported back with the recommendation that it pass after the same shall have been amended as follows:

Strike out all after the enacting clause and insert in lieu thereof the following:

That the Secretary of the Interior be, and he is hereby, authorized and directed to place on the pension roll, subject to the provisions and limitations of the pension laws, the name of Henry Staff, late of Company F, Twentieth Regiment Indiana Volunteer Infantry, and pay him a pension at the rate of forty dollars per month in lieu of that he is now receiving.

O

MARY R. BAYLY, FORMERLY MARY S. REDICK.

JANUARY 20, 1903.—Committed to the Committee of the Whole House and ordered to be printed.

Mr. CROWLEY, from the Committee on Invalid Pensions, submitted the following

REPORT.

[To accompany H. R. 10175.]

The Committee on Invalid Pensions, to whom was referred the bill (H. R. 10175) granting a pension to Mary R. Bagley, submit the following report:

This bill proposes to pension Mary R. Bagley, late an army nurse, at $12 per month.

Mary Redick Bayly, the beneficiary named in this bill, now 75 years of age, applied for pension as an army nurse under the provisions of the act of August 5, 1892, on June 11, 1893, alleging that she served as army nurse under the name of Mary S. Redick in General Hospital No. 4, ward No. 2, New Albany, Ind., from March 20, 1863, to September 21, 1863, and that she was now unable to support herself, etc.

Her claim was rejected on December 26, 1896, upon the ground of no title, she not having been properly employed and paid as a nurse of the Medical Department, etc.

Neither the War Department nor the Treasury Department has any record of the employment of the beneficiary as a nurse, but she filed in support of her claim the testimony of Dr. Moses E. Elrod, whom the records of the War Department show to have been an acting assistant surgeon, U. S. Army, on duty at No. 4 General Hospital at New Albany, Ind., from February to October, 1863, to the effect that the beneficiary on March 20, 1863, came to said hospital and remained with her brother, who was an inmate of said hospital from February until September 21, 1863, and did service as a nurse from March 20 until September 21, 1863; that she not only took care of said brother but cared for and administered to the wants of all the patients in the ward where her brother was confined; that he recollected the circumstances in this case because the beneficiary's brother was suffering from hospital gangrene, and was the first patient in said hospital whom affiant treated for gangrene with pure bromide, according to the instructions of Surg. Middleton Goldsmith, of Louisville, Ky.; that the beneficiary was not formally employed as a nurse, nor was she ever paid by the United States as such, but did voluntary work as a nurse during the whole of the period stated.

The fact of the beneficiary's services as nurse for the period of six months as above stated in said hospital is further shown by the testimony of a member of Company E, of the Ninety-eighth Ohio Infantry, who was detailed as nurse in said hospital, and whom the records of the War Department show to have been in said hospital from February to October, 1863.

Other proof filed in the Pension Bureau shows that the beneficiary is not physically able to follow her profession of teacher by reason of age and infirmities.

The case of the beneficiary comes clearly within the spirit, if not the letter, of the army nurse act, and the relief sought for in the bill should therefore be granted.

The bill is therefore reported back with the recommendation that it pass after the same shall have been amended as follows:

Strike out all of lines 6 and 7 and insert in lieu thereof the following:

of Mary R. Bayly, formerly Mary S. Redick, late nurse, Medical Department, United States Volunteers, and pay her a pension at the rate of twelve dollars per month.

Amend title so as to read: "A bill granting a pension to Mary R. Bayly, formerly Mary S. Redick."

O

SARAH BOWEN.

JANUARY 20, 1903.—Committed to the Committee of the Whole House and ordered to be printed.

Mr. APLIN, from the Committee on Invalid Pensions, submitted the following

REPORT.

[To accompany H. R. 7895.]

The Committee on Invalid Pensions, to whom was referred the bill (H. R. 7895) granting an increase of pension to Sarah Bowen, submit the following report:

This bill proposes to increase the pension of the beneficiary named therein from $8 to $20 per month.

Henry Bowen, the officer named in this bill, served as captain in Company H, Eleventh Michigan Cavalry, from November 24, 1863, to September 22, 1865, when honorably discharged as of Company B of the Eighth Michigan Cavalry, to which transferred.

Medical records of the War Department show that he was under treatment on March 27, 1864 (no diagnosis).

The beneficiary named in the bill, now 70 years of age, who was married to the officer on January 9, 1856, is now and has been since June 12, 1895, a pensioner under the act of June 27, 1890, at $8 per month upon proof that her husband died March 4, 1895; that she was his legal widow, and was dependent upon her daily labor for support.

The officer died of disease of the heart.

Her claim under the general law was rejected in August, 1898, upon the ground that there was no record of treatment for the disease of which the officer died or for any other disability liable to produce disease of heart; that there was no medical testimony as to treatment of the officer in the service or thereafter, save during his last illness, and that the evidence obtained upon special examination and that presented by the beneficiary was insufficient to establish the officer's death as being due to his military service.

Testimony obtained upon special examination shows that while in the service the officer complained of a pain in his left side and of shortness of breath; that this condition continued to exist after his discharge, and that he finally died in March, 1895, of disease of the heart.

There has been filed with your committee testimony showing that the beneficiary is deaf and can hardly hear anything; that she is old and feeble, not able to work to earn any money, and that she is without property, means, or anything, except the pension of $8 per month.

The probabilities in this case are that the disease of heart of which the husband of the beneficiary died was a result of his condition as described in the testimony mentioned above.

At any rate, your committee believe that the doubts in the case should be resolved in favor of the beneficiary, and that she should be granted the pension allowed under the general law to the widow of a captain, namely, $20 per month.

The bill is therefore reported back with the recommendation that it pass after the same shall have been amended as follows:

Strike out all of lines 6, 7, 8, and 9 and insert in lieu thereof the following:

of Sarah Bowen, widow of Henry Bowen, late captain Company H, Eleventh Regiment, and Company B, Eighth Regiment, Michigan Volunteer Cavalry, and pay her a pension at the rate of twenty dollars per month in lieu of that she is now receiving.

O

WILLIAM P. RHODES.

JANUARY 20, 1903.—Committed to the Committee of the Whole House and ordered to be printed.

Mr. MIERS, from the Committee on Invalid Pensions, submitted the following

REPORT.

[To accompany H. R. 4632.]

The Committee on Invalid Pensions, to whom was referred the bill (H. R. 4632) granting an increase of pension to William P. Rhodes, submit the following report:

This bill proposes to increase the pension of the officer named therein from $12 to $50 per month.

It appears from the records of the War Department that William P. Rhodes, now 70 years of age, served as captain of Company K, One hundred and thirty-fifth Indiana Infantry, from April 30, 1864, to September 21, 1864, when honorably discharged, and that he was under treatment at various dates during his period of service for dysentery, diarrhea, intermittent fever, and typhoid fever.

He is now a pensioner under the act of June 27, 1890, at $12 per month for total inability to earn a support by manual labor, the result of a double inguinal hernia and migraine.

His claim under the general law, filed on February 6, 1901, and based upon a double rupture alleged to have been incurred at Bridgeport, Ala., in July, 1864, was rejected on April 24, 1902, upon the ground of no record of treatment for said disability in the service and claimant's declared inability to furnish the necessary evidence to establish the claim.

The beneficiary stated in an affidavit filed in the Pension Bureau in March, 1902, that it was absolutely impossible for him to furnish the testimony of persons who had personal knowledge of the incurrence of his double rupture in the service, etc.; that it was his misfortune, he supposes, that at the time the disability occurred it was so slight as not to cause him any serious alarm, and as his term of enlistment was so short he did not deem it necessary to take treatment or make it public; that there was no one who knew anything about it; that in order to have a short rest he procured a ten days' furlough and was

in officers' hospital at Nashville, Tenn.; that he did not then understand the dangers and inconveniences of a hernia as he has learned them
since, and did not realize the importance of prompt treatment, and
that he could furnish no other testimony to support his own statement.

When last examined, on October 10, 1894, the board of surgeons
found a double hernia, both passing through the external rings, and
that he was suffering from migraine and a weak heart, and that he
was totally disabled for the performance of any manual labor.

There has been filed with your committee the statement of Hon.
E. J. Crumpacker, the member who introduced this bill, setting forth
that he had known the beneficiary personally and quite intimately for
a number of years; that two or three years ago he was stricken with
paralysis; that he is now absolutely unable to do anything, even to
take care of himself; that he can not walk a step, and can hardly feed
himself, and that he has no means of support except the pittance of
$12 per month, and no property except a house and lot in which he
lives, and that he requires a good share of his wife's time to take care
of him.

Relief to the extent of increasing this officer's pension from $12 to
$30 per month is warranted under the action of the House on June 16,
1902, it being shown that the officer requires the aid and attendance of
another person by reason of paralysis.

The bill is therefore reported back with the recommendation that it
pass after the same shall have been amended as follows:

In line 6, before the word "Company," strike out the word "of"
and insert in lieu thereof the word "captain."

In line 8 strike out the word "fifty" and insert in lieu thereof the
word "thirty."

O

ALONZO PENDLAND.

JANUARY 20, 1903.—Committed to the Committee of the Whole House and ordered
to be printed.

Mr. SULLOWAY, from the Committee on Invalid Pensions, submitted
the following

REPORT.

[To accompany H. R. 7844.]

The Committee on Invalid Pensions, to whom was referred the bill
(H. R. 7844) granting a pension to Alonzo Pendland, submit the following report:

This bill proposes to pension Alonzo Pendland, the soldier named
therein, at $72 per month.

Alonzo Pendland, now 56 years of age, is shown by the records of
the War Department to have been an unassigned recruit for the
Thirty-third Indiana Volunteers; to have been enrolled February 22,
1865; to have been mustered out May 10, 1865, and to have been
under treatment from March 25 to April 27, 1865, for diarrhea.

His claim to pension under the act of June 27, 1890, filed on April
10, 1891, was rejected upon the ground that title to pension under said
law could not obtain for the reason that he did not serve ninety days
during the war of the rebellion.

His claim to pension under the general law, filed July 7, 1890, and
based upon measles and resulting disease of eyes, and disease of the
respiratory organs, was also rejected in 1892 upon the ground that the
alleged disease of eyes existed prior to enlistment and that there had
been no ratable disability from disease of the respiratory organs since
the filing of the claim.

Appeal was taken from this decision of the Pension Bureau, and so far
as it related to the rejection of the claim on account of disease of the
respiratory organs to the Secretary of the Interior, and under date of
May 19, 1894, the action of the Pension Bureau was affirmed by
Assistant Secretary Reynolds upon the ground that the evidence did
not show a pensionable degree of disability from that disease.

Proof obtained upon special examination shows that the soldier had
measles while in the service, but also shows that he was nearsighted
prior to his enlistment, and that two of his brothers also had weak

eyes before the war and that they, like the soldier, had become nearly blind.

There is also some proof tending to show that since his discharge from the service the soldier complained of some bronchial trouble.

The only certificate of medical examination in the case, made January 28, 1891, found the nasal passages, throat, and lungs healthy, but did find disease of eyes, for which the board of surgeons rated him at $30; and the special examiner who investigated the case in 1892 then stated that the disability from impaired sight was then almost total.

There has been filed with your committee the affidavit of Dr. Gochenaur, of San Diego, Cal., setting forth that he has known the beneficiary for the last two years, and that he has been totally blind during said period; also other testimony showing that aside from the total blindness he suffers from disease of the respiratory organs; that, of course, he is unable to do the least thing for his support; that he is a poor man; that he has no children to depend upon; that his wife takes in washing for their support, and that the case is a most urgent and worthy one in every way.

Statements of the postmaster and the collector of customs of San Diego, Cal., also filed with your committee, set forth that the case of this soldier is one deserving of the consideration of Congress by reason of his total blindness and destitution.

In view of the soldier's helpless condition from blindness, your committee believe that the requirements of the act of June 27, 1890, as to the length of service may well be waived in this case and that he be granted the maximum pension under said act, namely, $12 per month.

The bill is therefore reported back with the recommendation that it pass after the same shall have been amended as follows:

In line 6 strike out the word "private."

In line 8 strike out the words "seventy-two" and insert in lieu thereof the word "twelve."

O

REUBEN F. CARTER.

JANUARY 20, 1903.—Committed to the Committee of the Whole House and ordered to
be printed.

Mr. SULLOWAY, from the Committee on Invalid Pensions, submitted
the following

REPORT.

[To accompany H. R. 5898.]

The Committee on Invalid Pensions, to whom was referred the bill
(H. R. 5898) granting an increase of pension to Reuben F. Carter,
submit the following report:

This bill proposes to increase the pension of the soldier named therein
from $17 to $50 per month.

This soldier, now 63 years of age, is shown by the records of the War
Department to have served as a private in Company G, Second U. S.
Sharpshooters, from October 22, 1861, to July 11, 1865, when he was
discharged as of Company H, Fifth New Hampshire Infantry, to which
transferred.

He received a wound of the chest at Antietam, another through the
face at Petersburg, and one through the right forearm at Hatchers Run.

He is now a pensioner under the general law on account of these
wounds and varicose veins of the left leg at $17 per month.

A claim for increase of pension, filed in May, 1898, was rejected in
December, 1899, upon the ground that the disability from the causes
of accepted service origin did not warrant a rating in excess of $17 per
month, and that the loss of his right hand, due to a recent accident,
could not be accepted as a result of the pensioned causes.

It appears that the soldier had his right arm amputated 4½ inches
below the elbow as a result of a circular-saw wound through the hand
and wrist in the spring of 1898.

When last examined, in October, 1898, the board of surgeons rated
him $4 for varicose veins, $10 for the gunshot wound of the face, $6
for the gunshot wound of chest, $30 for the loss of the right hand,
and $12 for loss of the sight of the right eye.

There has been filed with your committee the statement of Drs.
Mitchell and Stockwell, of Lancaster, N. H., setting forth that the
beneficiary since his army service lost the sight of one eye and his

right forearm by accident, and that it was reasonable to infer that the disabled condition of the right hand contributed to the accident which resulted in the loss of his arm.

It is shown that the only property owned by the beneficiary is a small farm worth about from $1,000 to $1,200, encumbered by $300, and that he has no means of support except the pension which he is now receiving.

This soldier, who rendered nearly four years of service, and who was three times wounded during his service, has now lost the sight of one eye and the right forearm by accident, and hence is wholly incapacitated for the performance of any manual labor.

In view of his services and his present condition, your committee believe that an increase of his pension from $17 to $24 per month is justified.

The bill is therefore reported back with the recommendation that it pass after the same shall have been amended as follows:

In line 8, before the word "Sharpshooters," insert the word "Volunteer."

In line 9 strike out the word "fifty" and insert in lieu thereof the word "twenty-four."

O

JAMES W. PACE.

JANUARY 20, 1903.—Committed to the Committee of the Whole House and ordered
to be printed.

Mr. SULLOWAY, from the Committee on Invalid Pensions, submitted
the following

REPORT.

[To accompany H. R. 5010.]

The Committee on Invalid Pensions, to whom was referred the bill
(H. R. 5010) granting an increase of pension to James W. Pace, submit the following report:

This bill proposes to increase the pension of the soldier named
therein from $14 to $24 per month.

Mr. Pace, now 61 years of age, served as a private in Company G,
Third Iowa Cavalry, from August 13, 1861, to August 9, 1865, when
honorably discharged.

In August, 1863, he incurred a sunstroke at or near Brownsville,
Ark., and disease of heart and asthma resulted from the same.

For these disabilities he was pensioned under the general law at $14
per month.

A claim for increase of pension, filed in 1898, was rejected upon the
ground that the disabilities of accepted service origin did not warrant
a rating in excess of $14 per month, and a claim on account of addi-
tional disabilities—namely, chronic diarrhea and piles—was rejected
upon the ground that a pensionable disability from these causes had not
existed since the filing of the claim, and a claim on account of rupture
was also rejected upon the ground that according to the claimant's
own statement it was impossible for him to prove the origin of such
rupture in the service for the reason that he did not know himself
that he was ruptured until about 1889.

When last examined, on September 21, 1898, upon which examination
the claim for increase of pension was rejected, the board of surgeons
described his disability as follows:

Some asthmatic sounds over both lungs. He has frequent attacks of asthma, often
having to sit up one-half to two-thirds the night. Exercise induces asthmatic breathing. He can not walk in the dark or with his eyes shut without staggering. Has a
feeling of constriction around the chest; feet swell at times; cushion feeling under
feet; memory is impaired; does not sleep well. Has a right direct inguinal hernia,
tumor descends into the scrotum; also has two small pile tumors, but no ulceration
and no bleeding or prolapsus.

In 1892 the board of surgeons rated him $17 for the degree of disability arising from the pensioned causes.

From papers filed with your committee it appears that the beneficiary had to give up employment as janitor; that he is unable to secure any work; that his case is a pitiable one, and that he is dependent upon his pension for support.

In the opinion of your committee this soldier, who rendered four years of service, according to the description of his disabilities by the board of examining surgeons in 1898, from causes of accepted service origin, is entitled to an increase of his pension from $14 to $20 per month, and the bill is reported back with the recommendation that it pass after the same shall have been amended as follows:

In line 8 strike out the word "twenty-four" and insert in lieu thereof the word "twenty."

O

JOSEPH A. BUCKHOLZ.

JANUARY 20, 1903.—Committed to the Committee of the Whole House and ordered
to be printed.

Mr. SAMUEL W. SMITH, from the Committee on Invalid Pensions, submitted the following

REPORT.

[To accompany H. R. 3569.]

The Committee on Invalid Pensions, to whom was referred the bill (H. R. 3569) granting an increase of pension to Joseph A. Buckholz, submit the following report:

This bill proposes to increase the pension of the soldier named therein from $12 to $30 per month.

It appears from the records of the War Department that this soldier, who is now 55 years of age, served as a private in Companies H and I, One hundred and eighth Ohio Infantry, from December 8, 1863, to July 22, 1865, when honorably discharged; and again as private in Troop M, Second U. S. Cavalry, from September 7, 1865, to September 7, 1868, when honorably discharged; and the medical records of that Department show that he was under treatment in January, 1864, for acute bronchitis and in March and April, 1865, for wound of the right shoulder, received at Bentonville March 19, 1865, and in April and May, 1865, for remittent fever.

He first applied for pension under the provisions of the act of June 27, 1890, on July 7, 1890, and was pensioned in 1891 at the maximum rating, namely, $12 per month, from the date of the filing of his application, for total inability to earn a support by manual labor, the result of disease of the left ankle and general debility.

On December 30, 1897, he filed a claim under the general law alleging that in January, 1865, while stationed in Nebraska, he was badly frozen, and that as a result of the same he was suffering from locomotor ataxia and muscular neuralgia.

The beneficiary stated in an affidavit filed in the Pension Bureau on September 29, 1900, that the locomotor ataxia and muscular neuralgia did not manifest themselves while in the service nor for several years subsequent to his final discharge.

From proof filed in the Pension Bureau it appears that the beneficiary, with his company, participated in an expedition against hostile

2 JOSEPH A. BUCKHOLZ.

Indians in January, 1867, during a severe snowstorm, and that 27 of
the men were badly frozen as a result of the exposure, and that the
beneficiary was one of the men so afflicted. Medical testimony filed in
the Pension Bureau shows that since 1884 the beneficiary had been suf
feriṅg from attacks of gastritis and with cramps in the lower limbs
and eet.

This claim was rejected in November, 1900, upon the ground of
claimant's declared inability to connect the locomotor ataxia and muscular neuralgia with his military service as the result of freezing or
otherwise.

When first examined, on January 28, 1891, the board of surgeons
rated the beneficiary $24 for general debility and $6 for a fracture of
the leg.

The last medical examination, made on September 30, 1898, found
him to be suffering from disease of the left ankle, general debility,
muscular neuralgia, constipation, disease of stomach, and locomotor
ataxia, and rated him $30 for that condition.

Proof filed in the Pension Bureau shows that the beneficiary is not
able to walk or even take a single step.

Relief to the extent of increasing the soldier's pension to the amount
sought for in the bill is warranted in view of the fact that he is suffering from locomotor ataxia and totally helpless.

The bill is therefore reported back with the recommendation that it
pass after the same shall have been amended as follows:

In line 6, after the word "Company," insert the words "I, One hundred and eighth Regiment Ohio Volunteer Infantry, and Troop."

O

JOHN SULLIVAN.

JANUARY 20, 1903.—Committed to the Committee of the Whole House and ordered
to be printed.

Mr. SULLOWAY, from the Committee on Invalid Pensions, submitted
the following

REPORT.

[To accompany H. R. 2614.]

The Committee on Invalid Pensions, to whom was referred the bill
(H. R. 2614) granting a pension to John Sullivan, submit the following report:

This bill proposes to pension the beneficiary named therein subject
to the provisions and limitations of the pension laws.

John Sullivan, now 63 years of age, served as a private in Company
E, Second New Hampshire Infantry, from May 17 to October 5, 1861,
when honorably discharged, and as assistant surgeon of the Thirteenth
New Hampshire Volunteers from September 26, 1862, to August 16,
1864, when his resignation, tendered upon a report of a medical examining board, which found him to be suffering from chronic diarrhea,
to be much debilitated, and to have a phthisical diathesis, was accepted.

He served subsequently as contract surgeon, U. S. Army, from September 16, 1864, to June 15, 1865.

His claim to pension under the general law, filed in June, 1897, and
based upon rheumatism and malaria, was rejected in the Pension Bureau
in 1899, upon the ground of claimant's stated inability to furnish medical or other satisfactory evidence of the continuance of the alleged
disability from the date of his discharge in 1862 to 1870.

The beneficiary stated that he was unable to furnish further proof
as to his condition from 1864 to 1870, by reason of the fact that he was
not in any one place long enough to make acquaintances who knew him
well enough to now describe his condition at that time, and could find
no living person who could give the desired testimony.

It will be seen from the rejection of his case that the Pension Bureau
accepted the fact that the officer contracted rheumatism and malaria in
the service while assistant surgeon of the Thirteenth New Hampshire
Volunteers, and that these disabilities continued to exist ever since 1870.

When last examined, on November 5, 1897, the board of surgeons found him to be so disabled from rheumatism as to be totally incapacitated for the performance of any manual labor, and rated him $30 for that condition.

No disability from malarial poisoning was found upon that examination.

Relief by Congress is fully warranted in the opinion of your committee, there being no question that the rheumatism from which this officer is shown to have suffered since 1870 was the same disability shown to have originated and existed during his military service.

The bill is therefore reported back with the recommendation that it pass after the same shall have been amended as follows:

In line 6, after the word "Thirteenth," insert the word " Regiment."

In line 7, after the word "Infantry," insert the words ".and pay him a pension at the rate of thirty dollars per month."

O

LANGSTON P. BRYANT.

JANUARY 20, 1903.—Committed to the Committee of the Whole House and ordered
to be printed.

Mr. GIBSON, from the Committee on Invalid Pensions, submitted the
following

REPORT.

[To accompany H. R. 1644.]

The Committee on Invalid Pensions, to whom was referred the bill
(H. R. 1644) granting an increase of pension to L. P. Bryant, submit
the following report:

This bill proposes to increase the pension of this soldier from $12
to $30 per month.

Records of the War Department show that Langston P. Bryant, the
officer named in this bill, who is now 67 years of age, served as first
lieutenant in Company I, Twenty-first Kentucky Volunteers, from
January 2, 1862, to November 29, 1862, when his resignation, based
upon a surgeon's certificate showing him to be suffering from anasarca,
was accepted.

He is now and has been since July 28, 1890, a pensioner under the
act of June 27, 1890, at the maximum rating, namely, $12 per month,
for total inability to earn a support by manual labor, the result of
disease of lungs, heart, chronic diarrhea, piles, and rheumatism.

His claim to pension under the general law, filed on May 8, 1889,
and based upon rheumatism, bronchitis, diarrhea, and scurvy, was
rejected in September, 1899, upon the ground of no record in the
War Department of the existence of said disabilities, and the evidence
taken on special examination being insufficient to show that said disabilities originated in the service and line of duty, and the claim on
account of anasarca (dropsy) was rejected at the same time upon the
ground of no proof showing the continuance of said disability from
the date of the officer's discharge and the claimant waiving his claim
for the same.

The surgeon of the soldier's regiment testified that the beneficiary
suffered from anasarca, as shown by the records of the War Department, while in the service; that his condition was a critical one,
that he did not remember, however, the cause of the disability, and

several comrades testified that the beneficiary complained of rheumatism in his legs, or that he was deficient in one leg and could hardly use it while in the service, and another one testified that the beneficiary had diarrhea and dropsy while in the service, and a cough.

Other proof filed and obtained upon special examination shows that upon his return home from the Army he was in bad shape, his legs and feet swollen; that he complained of his stomach, bowels, back, and legs, and of rheumatism affecting his knees and of an affection of the breast; that in 1866 or 1867 he had a bad cough and bronchitis; that in 1874 he looked like a man going into consumption, and that he limped considerably for years—in fact, that he complained of a rheumatic affection ever since his discharge, and that he was laid up between 1870 and 1875 on account of the same, and medical evidence obtained upon special examination shows that the officer had been under treatment since 1879 for rheumatic and liver trouble and since 1898 for a bronchial affection.

The first medical examination in the case, made in August, 1889, recommended a rating of $4 for diarrhea, $6 for rheumatism, and $4 for disease of lungs.

The last examination, made on August 17, 1898, rated him $6 for chronic tuberculosis, $8 for disease of stomach, and $6 for rheumatism.

There has been filed with your committee the affidavit of Dr. B. L. Bruner, of Hardyville, Ky., setting forth that he had been the family physician of the beneficiary since August 22, 1899; that during that period the beneficiary had been wholly disabled for manual labor, and had required most of the time an attendant to nurse him, his trouble being bronchitis, functional disease of heart, and chronic diarrhea.

Other testimony filed with your committee shows that the beneficiary had been totally disabled for the performance of any kind of labor, confined to his room at times, and that his income from his farm does not amount to $200 per year.

In the opinion of your committee the evidence in the case shows fairly well that the soldier's present disabilities are due to his military service.

An increase of his pension from $12 to $20 per month is therefore justified and the bill is reported back with the recommendation that it pass after the same shall have been amended as follows:

Strike out all after the enacting clause and insert in lieu thereof the following:

That the Secretary of the Interior be, and he is hereby, authorized and directed to place on the pension roll, subject to the provisions and limitations of the pension laws, the name of Langston P. Bryant, late first lieutenant Company I, Twenty-first Regiment Kentucky Volunteer Infantry, and pay him a pension at the rate of twenty dollars per month in lieu of that he is now receiving.

Amend the title so as to read: "A bill granting an increase of pension to Langston P. Bryant."

O

JAMES R. WARD.

JANUARY 20, 1903.—Committed to the Committee of the Whole House and ordered
to be printed.

Mr. GIBSON, from the Committee on Invalid Pensions, submitted the
following

REPORT.

[To accompany H. R. 1024.]

The Committee on Invalid Pensions, to whom was referred the bill
(H. R. 1024) granting a pension to James R. Ward, submit the following report:

This bill proposes to pension the soldier named therein at $12 per
month.

This soldier, now 62 years of age, while a prisoner of war in the
hands of the Federal authorities, having been captured July 5, 1864,
while a member of the Thirty-ninth Georgia Infantry, Confederate
States army, enlisted in Company F, Fifth Regiment United States
Volunteers, at Camp Douglass, Ill., on April 1, 1865, and was mustered
out with his company on October 15, 1866.

The medical records of the War Department show that the beneficiary, while a prisoner of war at Camp Douglass, was under treatment
for smallpox, and in August, 1865, while in the Federal service, for
scurvy.

His claim to pension under the act of June 27, 1890, was rejected in
September, 1894, upon the ground that title under that act could not
obtain for the reason that he had rendered voluntary service in the
Confederate army.

His claim to pension under the general law, filed June 15, 1887, and
based upon disease of lungs alleged to have been contracted at Fort
Halleck, Dak., in January, 1866, was rejected in February, 1900, upon
the ground that the evidence as to the origin of that disease in the
service was unsatisfactory and of questionable competency, and that
there appeared to be no probability that the requisite evidence could
be furnished to establish the claim for disease of lungs of which there
was no record in the War Department.

The case has been specially examined and proof obtained during the
special examination, and that filed by the beneficiary tends to show that

the soldier was free from disease of the lungs at the time of his enlistment in the Union Army, that he had a cold while in that army which appeared to settle on his lungs, and that he appeared to suffer from disease of lungs at or soon after his discharge and continuously thereafter to the present time.

The last medical examination of the soldier, made on April 5, 1899, rated him $12 for disease of lungs and described his condition as follows:

Chest measures on forced expiration 36, at rest 36½, and on full inspiration 37½ inches. Right side, forced expiration 17½, forced inspiration 18 inches. Dullness on percussion over apex of right lung. Clavicle and spleen sunken. Find crepitant râles heard on auscultation. Left lung is free from abnormal changes.

It is admitted that the proof filed in the case is hardly such as to have warranted the Pension Bureau in admitting the claim under the general law, yet it would seem that the doubts in the case should be resolved in favor of the beneficiary.

The bill is therefore reported back with the recommendation that it pass after the same shall have been amended as follows:

Strike out all after the enacting clause and insert in lieu thereof the following:

That the Secretary of the Interior be, and he is hereby, authorized and directed to place on the pension roll, subject to the provisions and limitations of the pension laws, the name of James R. Ward, late of Company F, Fifth Regiment United States Volunteer Infantry, and pay him a pension at the rate of twelve dollars per month.

O

JAMES BILLINGSLEY.

JANUARY 20, 1903.—Committed to the Committee of the Whole House and ordered to be printed.

Mr. HOLLIDAY, from the Committee on Invalid Pensions, submitted the following

REPORT.

[To accompany H. R. 2473.]

The Committee on Invalid Pensions, to whom was referred the bill (H. R. 2473) granting an increase of pension to James Billingsley, submit the following report:

This bill proposes to increase the pension of this soldier from $12 to $25 per month.

It appears from the files of the Pension Bureau that James Billingsley, the soldier named in this bill, and now 63 years of age, and who served as private in Company B, First West Virginia Infantry, from February 25, 1862, to March 1, 1865, when honorably discharged, and who was a prisoner of war from September 11, 1863, to March 15, 1864, and who was under treatment in the service for remittent fever, diarrhea, and catarrh, is now a pensioner under the general law at $12 per month on account of chronic diarrhea and piles, and that the Pension Bureau held that such rating included every disability from malarial poisoning, from which the soldier was suffering.

Claims for increase of pension filed in 1892 and 1897 were rejected, the last one September 6, 1900, upon the ground that the degree of disability arising from the pensioned causes did not warrant a rating in excess of $12 per month, and a claim on account of scurvy and resulting loss of teeth was also rejected on August 30, 1900, upon the ground of no record, and no medical evidence of existence of said disability in the service or at discharge, and claimant's disability to furnish satisfactory evidence of the service origin of the same.

The soldier alleged that the scurvy was contracted by him while held as prisoner of war, and in support of that claim he filed the testimony of two comrades, showing that upon his return from rebel prison he was afflicted with scurvy, and that he had lost his teeth, and that after the return from the service his mouth was diseased and his teeth all came out, and that he had been under treatment for such scurvy from about 1890.

When last examined, on July 13, 1898, the board of surgeons rated him $4 for diarrhea, $6 for piles, $4 for malarial poisoning, $4 for disease of heart, and $3 for disease of mouth, the result of scurvy.

No reason is apparent why the testimony of this soldier's comrades to the effect that after his return from rebel prison where he was held for five months he was afflicted with scurvy affecting the mouth, etc., should have been set aside by the Pension Bureau, it being a well-known fact that nearly all soldiers who had been imprisoned for any length of time suffered from that disease when paroled.

It being shown that the soldier is now suffering from the effects of scurvy an increase of his pension from $12 to $17 per month is therefore justified, and the bill is reported back with the recommendation that it pass after the same shall have been amended as follows:

In line 8 strike out the word "twenty-five" and insert in lieu thereof the word "seventeen."

O

JULIA A. COOK.

JANUARY 20, 1903.—Committed to the Committee of the Whole House and ordered
to be printed.

Mr. SULLOWAY, from the Committee on Invalid Pensions, submitted
the following

REPORT.

[To accompany H. R. 4059.]

The Committee on Invalid Pensions, to whom was referred the bill
(H. R. 4059) granting an increase of pension to Julia A. Cook, submit the following report:

This bill proposes to increase the pension of the beneficiary named
therein from $12 to $30 per month by reason of the fact that she was
not only the widow of a soldier who died of disease contracted in the
service, but also served as an army nurse, and lost her only son, who
also served during the entire civil war.

The files of the Pension Bureau show that the beneficiary named in
the bill, and now 79 years of age, is the widow of Enos Cook, who
served as a private in Company I, One hundred and forty-third New
York Volunteers, from August 20, 1862, to December 18, 1863, when
he died, while in the service, of diarrhea, and that she has been a
pensioner under the general law since the soldier's death at $8 per
month, and at $12 from March 19, 1886, upon proof that she was mar-
ried to the soldier February 21, 1842, etc.

On April 17, 1893, she applied for pension under the army-nurse
act of August 5, 1892, alleging that she served as nurse in Judiciary
Square Hospital from June 7, 1864, to ———, and in that declaration
she also alleged that her son, James H. Cook, who was a private in
Company A, Tenth New York Cavalry, died January 6, 1888.

This claim was rejected on June 3, 1893, upon the ground that even
if it were shown that the claimant served as a nurse for six months, as
required by the act of August 5, 1892, she would have no title to additional pension, by reason of the fact that section 4715 of the Revised
Statutes provides that no person shall draw more than one pension
covering the same period of time.

The records of the War Department, however, do not show that the
claimant served as nurse for a period of six months, but do show that she

was employed as nurse in Judiciary Square Hospital from June 17 to June 30, 1864, only.

From a letter of the claimant filed in the Pension Bureau September 3, 1891, it appears that she came to Washington under the call of Miss Dix, reported at her headquarters, and next day was sent to Columbia College; that after staying there a few days Miss Dix sent her to Judiciary Square Hospital; that she was taken sick there and removed from the hospital to a house on Capitol Hill, where she was kindly cared for until able to come home.

Nothing has been filed with your committee as to the service of the son of the beneficiary, and the Pension Bureau reports that no claim had been filed by anyone on account of the services or alleged death of that son.

There has been filed with your committee the affidavit of the beneficiary, setting forth that for the past three years she has been totally blind so far as to be unable to distinguish objects, her only power of sight for the past two years being to realize a faint glimmer of shade and light at times, so that for a great part of the daytime as well as the night she is compelled to keep to her bed and has become very feeble and emaciated; that her condition is such that she requires the constant attendance of a nurse, and that the pension of $12 per month was insufficient to provide her with the necessaries of life.

The fact that the beneficiary is practically blind and requires the aid and attendance of another person, and that she is in destitute circumstances, is shown by the testimony of the supervisor of the town of Dryden, N. Y., and the president and postmaster of that place, a member of the assembly of Tompkins County, N. Y., and Dr. Allen, a practicing physician of Dryden, N. Y.

In view of the services of the beneficiary as a nurse, her great age, and her blindness, your committee believes that she should not be permitted to suffer want, and recommend an increase of her pension from $12 to $20 per month.

The bill is therefore reported back with the recommendation that it pass after the same shall have been amended as follows:

Strike out the preamble and all after the enacting clause and insert in lieu thereof the following:

That the Secretary of the Interior be, and he is hereby, authorized and directed to place on the pension roll, subject to the provisions and limitations of the pension laws, the name of Julia A. Cook, widow of Enos Cook, late of Company I, One hundred and forty-third Regiment New York Volunteer Infantry, and pay her a pension at the rate of twenty dollars per month in lieu of that she is now receiving.

O

ALFRED O. BLOOD.

JANUARY 20, 1903.—Committed to the Committee of the Whole House and ordered
to be printed.

Mr. CROWLEY, from the Committee on Invalid Pensions, submitted the
following

REPORT.

[To accompany S. 4515.]

The Committee on Invalid Pensions, to whom was referred the bill
(S. 4515) granting an increase of pension to Alfred O. Blood, have
examined the same and adopt the Senate report thereon and recommend that the bill do pass.

[Senate Report No. 1551, Fifty-seventh Congress, first session.]

The Committee on Pensions, to whom was referred the bill (S. 4515) granting an
increase of pension to Alfred O. Blood, have examined the same and report:

This bill proposes to increase from $12 to $30 per month the pension of Alfred O.
Blood, late of Company I, Twenty-fourth Regiment Massachusetts Volunteer Infantry.

Soldier enlisted September 23, 1861, and was discharged September 24, 1864. He
has no hospital record. November 24, 1890, he was pensioned under the act of June
27, 1890, at the rate of $12 per month, for diarrhea and nervous prostration and
amputation of right arm. On August 10, 1889, he made claim under the general
law, alleging that in April, 1862, he contracted chronic diarrhea, causing nervous
prostration. He has never been able to file any testimony in support of this claim
and has long since abandoned its prosecution.

According to his medical examination, claimant is wholly incapacitated for manual
labor. He suffers from chronic diarrhea, extreme nervous prostration, and also has
had his right arm amputated between the wrist and elbow. The loss of this arm
was due to an accident from a circular saw, occurring in 1868.

According to his petition, claimant is in dependent circumstances and has no property of any kind. He has a wife who is practically an invalid, and also a daughter
who looks to him for support, and his only income is the small pension he now
receives.

While there is no evidence showing that his diarrhea and nervous prostration are
the results of his military service, it is very probable that such is the case. He
served faithfully for three years, and is now crippled and destitute, and your committee are of opinion that his case is one in which the bounty of the Government
may very properly be bestowed. The bill is therefore reported back with the
recommendation that it pass.

O

SAMUEL E. EWING.

JANUARY 20, 1903.—Committed to the Committee of the Whole House and ordered
to be printed.

Mr. CROWLEY, from the Committee on Invalid Pensions, submitted
the following

REPORT.

[To accompany S. 2084.]

The Committee on Invalid Pensions, to whom was referred the bill
(S. 2084) granting an increase of pension to Samuel E. Ewing, have
examined the same, and adopt the Senate report thereon, and recommend that the bill do pass.

[Senate Report No. 1199, Fifty-seventh Congress, first session.]

The Committee on Pensions, to whom was referred the bill (S. 2084) granting an
increase of pension to Samuel E. Ewing, have examined the same and report:
This bill proposes to increase from $12 to $30 per month the pension of Samuel E.
Ewing, late of Company I, Third Regiment Iowa Volunteer Cavalry, who served from
August 21, 1861, to August 9, 1865.
Mr. Ewing is now receiving a pension of $12 per month, under the act of June 27,
1890, for total inability to earn a support by manual labor. His disability is paralysis
of the right side. His medical examination shows that he is totally disabled from
paralysis, which has also affected his mind. He can not walk at all alone and has to
have some one to support him. The examining surgeons state his mind is a blank
and that there is absolutely no motion or sensation in right arm and hand and but
little in leg. His condition is the result of a cerebral hemorrhage.
Mr. Ewing has a faithful and dutiful wife, who cares for him as much as she
possibly can. They have, however, no means of support. He was a dentist by profession and depended on his occupation for a living, but for some time he has been
helpless and unable to earn anything. His service lasted nearly four years, extending beyond the close of the war; he was faithful in all respects and is now helpless
and in need, and your committee are of opinion that he is entitled to the bounty
which a grateful Government bestows on its defenders in the days of their adversity.
The bill is therefore reported back favorably with the recommendation that it pass.

O

WINFIELD S. PIETY.

JANUARY 20, 1903.—Committed to the Committee of the Whole House and ordered
to be printed.

Mr. CROWLEY, from the Committee on Invalid Pensions, submitted
the following

REPORT.

[To accompany S. 3250.]

The Committee on Invalid Pensions, to whom was referred the bill
(S. 3250) granting an increase of pension to Winfield S. Piety, have
examined the same and adopt the Senate report thereon and recommend that the bill do pass.

[Senate Report No. 1251, Fifty-seventh Congress, first session.]

The Committee on Pensions, to whom was referred the bill (S. 3250) granting an
increase of pension to Winfield S. Piety, have examined the same and report:

This bill as amended proposes to increase from $12 to $30 per month the pension
of Winfield S. Piety, late of Company F, Sixth Regiment Indiana Volunteer Cavalry,
who served from February 3, 1863, to September 15, 1865, when he was honorably
discharged.

Mr. Piety is now receiving a pension of $12 per month under the act of June 27,
1890, for total inability to earn a support by manual labor. His disabilities are disease of heart, lungs, and rectum. He has never made claim under the general law,
and made no claim under the act of June 27, 1890, until he became broken down by
disease and incapacitated for earning a support. His medical examination at Colorado Springs, Colo., June 22, 1898, shows he is totally disabled by disease of heart,
lungs, and rectum. The examining surgeons state he is unable to work on account
of general weakness.

Mr. Piety comes of a patriotic family. His father lost his life in the war of the
rebellion, and he has a son who served in the Philippine trouble. He has no property and no income but his pension. He is confined to his bed a great deal of the
time now and his wife has to go out and work and earn what she can for the support
of the family. The soldier himself always earned a good living until his health
failed; it was only then that he asked help from the Government. He is now living
in a two-roomed shack, dependent on his pension and the earnings of his wife.

In view of his poverty and total disability, and of his faithful service for over two
years, your committee are of opinion that an increase of his pension would be just
and proper. The bill is therefore reported back favorably, with the recommendation
that it pass.

O

WILLIAM A. KIMBALL.

JANUARY 20, 1903.—Committed to the Committee of the Whole House and ordered to be printed.

Mr. CROWLEY, from the Committee on Invalid Pensions, submitted the following

REPORT.

[To accompany S. 3298.]

The Committee on Invalid Pensions, to whom was referred the bill (S. 3298) granting an increase of pension to William A. Kimball, have examined the same and adopt the Senate report thereon and recommend that the bill do pass.

[Senate Report No. 1111, Fifty-Seventh Congress, first session.]

The Committee on Pensions, to whom was referred the bill (S. 3298) granting an increase of pension to William A. Kimball, have examined the same and report:

This bill proposes to increase from $12 to $30 per month the pension of William A. Kimball, late of Company H, Fifty-first Regiment Massachusetts Volunteer Infantry, and Company A, Second Regiment Massachusetts Volunteer Heavy Artillery.

The military records show that William A. Kimball served in Company H, Fifty-first Massachusetts Infantry, from September 30, 1862, to July 27, 1863, and in Company A, Second Massachusetts Heavy Artillery, from December 15, 1863, to September 3, 1865. He is now receiving a pension of $12 per month under the act of June 27, 1890, for total inability to earn a support by manual labor, due to disease of lungs, impaired vision, and general debility. He was formerly pensioned under the general law for disease of lungs, of service origin, at the rate of $8 per month, and several claims for increase under this law were rejected on the ground that $8 per month was a proper rate for his service disability.

It appears that Mr. Kimball is now almost totally blind. His last medical examination, March 14, 1901, shows that he has no vision in left eye and that the vision in right eye is very much impaired and almost gone. He can distinguish forms about the street, can tell men from horses, and that is all. He is also suffering from indigestion, weak heart, and general debility; it is impossible for him to perform any kind of labor.

Evidence filed in the Bureau and also with the bill shows that Mr. Kimball has no estate, property, income, or means of support except his pension, which is wholly insufficient to supply the unavoidable wants of one in his condition. In view of his great poverty, his almost total blindness, and his faithful service of over two and one-half years, your committee report the bill back favorably with a recommendation that it pass.

O

FREDERICK KROPF.

JANUARY 20, 1903.—Committed to the Committee of the Whole House and ordered to be printed.

Mr. CROWLEY, from the Committee on Invalid Pensions, submitted the following

REPORT.

[To accompany S. 4401.]

The Committee on Invalid Pensions, to whom was referred the bill (S. 4401) granting an increase of pension to Frederick Kropf, have examined the same and adopt the Senate report thereon and recommend that the bill do pass.

[Senate Report No. 1569, Fifty-seventh Congress, first session.]

The Committee on Pensions, to whom was referred the bill (S. 4401) granting an increase of pension to Frederick Kropf, have examined the same and report:

This bill as amended proposes to increase from $12 to $30 per month the pension of Frederick Kropf, late of Company B, Eleventh Regiment Wisconsin Volunteer Infantry.

The soldier enlisted October 21, 1861, and was discharged September 4, 1865. He is now receiving a pension of $12 per month under the act of June 27, 1890, for total inability to earn a support by manual labor, due to disease of spine. On December 16, 1889, he made claim under the general law, alleging that he was overcome by the heat in July, 1863, which resulted in loss of use of legs, or paralysis. This claim was rejected April 29, 1898, on the ground that paralysis was not due to service, having first appeared about 1884.

It appears from evidence on file in the Bureau that claimant is totally helpless from paralysis. He is confined to a chair, and his wife has to take the same care of him that she would of a child. This condition has existed for a period of seven or eight years. His last medical examination, November 4, 1896, showed that his case was one of aggravated locomotor ataxia and rated him $72 per month, his disability being equal to the loss of use of both legs.

Claimant's financial condition is such that he can not afford to employ anyone to take care of him, and he is compelled to rely on his wife, who is growing old and who can not help him much longer. He lives at Schuyler, Nebr., where he has a home, which is a shelter only and produces no income, and also about $2,500 worth of other property. He needs continual medical care, which in the past has cost him from $25 to $40 per month.

In view of his faithful service of nearly four years, his helplessness and straitened circumstances, and the probability that his health suffered in consequence of the hardships and exposure of army life, your committee are of opinion that an increase of his pension would be both just and proper.

The bill is therefore reported back favorably with a recommendation that it pass.

O

JONAS OLMSTEAD.

JANUARY 20, 1903.—Committed to the Committee of the Whole House and ordered
to be printed.

Mr. CROWLEY, from the Committee on Invalid Pensions, submitted
the following

REPORT.

[To accompany S. 3730.]

The Committee on Invalid Pensions, to whom was referred the bill
(S. 3730) granting an increase of pension to Jonas Olmstead, have
examined the same and adopt the Senate report thereon and recommend that the bill do pass.

[Senate Report No. 1217, Fifty-seventh Congress, first session.]

The Committee on Pensions, to whom was referred the bill (S. 3730) granting an
increase of pension to Jonas Olmstead, have examined the same and report:

This bill as amended proposes to increase from $12 to $30 per month the pension of
Jonas Olmstead, late second lieutenant Company G, Third Regiment Missouri Volunteer Cavalry, who served from October 15, 1861, to October 19, 1862, when he was
honorably discharged.

Mr. Olmstead resides at Los Angeles, Cal. He is 83 years of age. He is now
receiving a pension of $12 per month under the act of June 27, 1890, for total deafness
of right ear, slight deafness of left ear, sciatica, and injury of right hand. He was
formerly pensioned under the general law for rheumatism of service origin at the rate
of $8 per month. His last claim for increase under the general law was rejected
August 25, 1897.

The evidence on file in the Pension Bureau shows that Mr. Olmstead, by reason
of his great age and its attendant infirmities, is wholly disabled for manual labor.
He suffers from rheumatism, heart trouble, deafness, and enlarged prostate gland.
His last medical examination, made over five years ago, rated him $30.

Evidence on file in the Bureau also shows that Mr. Olmstead is without any means
of support except his pension, and it is reliably stated that for some years he has
been aided to a large extent by the charitable contributions of his associates and his
friends.

In the natural order of things Mr. Olmstead will not long enjoy his pension, and
that his few remaining days may be attended with a measure of comfort your committee are of opinion that an increase of his pension may very properly be allowed
him.

The bill is therefore reported back favorably with a recommendation that it pass.

O

HAMLINE B. WILLIAMS.

JANUARY 20, 1903.—Committed to the Committee of the Whole House and ordered
to be printed.

Mr. CROWLEY, from the Committee on Invalid Pensions, submitted
the following

REPORT.

[To accompany S. 1903.]

The Committee on Invalid Pensions, to whom was referred the bill
(S. 1903) granting an increase of pension to Hamline B. Williams,
have examined the same and adopt the Senate report thereon and recommend that the bill do pass.

[Senate Report No. 1120, Fifty-seventh Congress, first session.]

The Committee on Pensions to whom was referred the bill (S. 1903) granting an
increase of pension to Hamline B. Williams, have examined the same and report:

This bill as amended proposes to increase from $24 to $30 per month the pension
of Hamline B. Williams, of Whatcom, Wash., late of Company D, Twenty-first
Regiment Wisconsin-Volunteer Infantry.

The military records show that Hamline B. Williams served from August 15, 1862,
to December 9, 1862, when he was discharged for disability due to gunshot wound
through left lung received in battle at Perryville, Ky., October 8, 1862.

Mr. Williams, who is 60 years of age, is pensioned on account of disease of the
heart resulting from gunshot wound of chest. His pension was originally granted in
1868 at the rate of $8 per month from December 10, 1862. His pension was increased
to $15 per month August 12, 1868; to $18 per month June 4, 1872; it was reduced to
$16 per month April 4, 1883, and increased to $24 per month April 27, 1887. Subsequently the reduction of his pension was corrected, and he was allowed $24 per month
from March 3, 1883.

Accompanying the bill is the following medical affidavit of Dr. H. E. Henderson,
of Whatcom, Wash., dated March 24, 1902:

"I have this day made a careful and thorough examination of his (claimant's)
physical condition, with the following result, to wit: A gunshot wound of left side;
ball entered at lower edge of left nipple and made its exit in sixth intercostal space
about 2 inches from spine on left side, having passed directly through chest; the
results of extensive pleuritic adhesions and inflammatory condition of lung tissue are
easily discernible. He has had violent heart lesions, which are now partly compensated. There is a decided hypertrophy of left heart, with both mitral and aortic
murmur; pulse is irregular and he suffers much pain in heart. His eyesight is rapidly failing, arcus senilis marked; has only six teeth left. He has two senile ulcers

on left knee which fail to respond to treatment. He is, in my opinion, totally incapacitated by said disabilities for the performance of any manual labor whatever, even the lightest. His disabilities are undoubtedly, in my opinion, permanent in character, and instead of being rated as equivalent to the loss of a hand or a foot should be rated as equivalent to the loss of hand and a foot."

The general-law rate for total incapacity for manual labor is $30 per month, and it is evident the claimant is disabled in that degree by reason of his army wound and resulting heart disease. Your committee therefore recommend an increase of his pension to the rate provided by the general law for total incapacity for manual labor.

The bill is reported back favorably, with a recommendation that it pass.

O

NELSON W. CARLTON.

JANUARY 20, 1903.—Committed to the Committee of the Whole House and ordered
to be printed.

Mr. CROWLEY, from the Committee on Invalid Pensions, submitted
the following

REPORT.

[To accompany S. 1614.]

The Committee on Invalid Pensions, to whom was referred the bill
(S. 1614) granting an increase of pension to Nelson W. Carlton, have
examined the same and adopt the Senate report thereon and recommend that the bill do pass.

[Senate Report No. 1311, Fifty-seventh Congress, first session.]

The Committee on Pensions, to whom was referred the bill (S. 1614) granting an
increase of pension to Nelson W. Carlton, have examined the same and report:

This bill proposes to increase from $12 to $30 per month the pension of Nelson W.
Carlton, late of Company K, Second Regiment Minnesota Volunteer Cavalry.

Nelson W. Carlton served from December 14, 1863, to January 31, 1865. He was
discharged on surgeon's certificate of disability in consequence of asthma, contracted
prior to enlistment. He is now receiving a pension of $12 per month, under the act
of June 27, 1890, for disease of lungs. His original claim under the general law, filed
February 14, 1879, alleged chronic pneumonia as having been contracted in the service,
and that claim was rejected March 6, 1880, upon the ground that his disability existed
prior to enlistment. On October 9, 1895, he made another claim under the general
law, alleging catarrh of head and resulting loss of sense of smell. This claim was
rejected August 2, 1898, on the ground of no record or other satisfactory evidence of
service origin and continuance of the alleged disability. This action was affirmed on
appeal by Assistant Secretary F. L. Campbell, under date of July 31, 1901.

The only evidence on file as to service origin is that of a few comrades to the effect
that claimant suffered from a cold and cough and water discharges from the eyes
and nose while in the service. There is no evidence of continuance, however, and
the claim under the general law is not established.

Mr. Carlton is now wholly disabled by disease of lungs. His last medical examination, January 17, 1896, is as follows:

"Circumference of chest at repose, 40 inches; full expiration, 39 inches; full inspiration, 41½. Both lungs involved; crepitant and subcrepitant rales over entire region;
breathing difficult, audible across room, labored in character, especially after least
exercise. Has had asthma since entrance to hospital; condition at present fast
developing into phthisis.

"Turbinated bones almost entirely destroyed by catarrh, mucous membrane of nostrils, posterior, nasal, and throat highly injected, purulent discharge. Heart action quick, nervous in character, almost a wiry pulse; intermits one to three times per minute, sometimes losing but one beat, again two or three; an indistinct, perhaps unfounded, mitral regurgitation."

Dr. J. M. Woodburn, of Rexburg, Idaho, where the claimant lives, who made the foregoing examination, testified July 13, 1901, that he, claimant, is in destitute circumstances, unable to stand the slightest exertion, and his early demise is certainly imminent, and that his condition is one of augmentation of symptoms described in that examination.

Accompanying the bill is a certificate of Dr. Woodburn to the effect that the claimant is in a deplorable condition, incapable of the slightest exertion, and that his disability is total. There is also other evidence showing that the claimant is in destitute circumstances.

It would appear that Mr. Carlton is in the last stages of consumption. He can not long survive and he is destitute, and your committee are of opinion that favorable action in his case would be eminently proper, and therefore report the bill back favorably, with a recommendation that it pass.

O

MARY ELIZABETH FALES.

JANUARY 20, 1903.—Committed to the Committee of the Whole House and ordered
to be printed.

Mr. CROWLEY, from the Committee on Invalid Pensions, submitted
the following

REPORT.

[To accompany S. 3970.]

The Committee on Invalid Pensions, to whom was referred the bill
(S. 3970) granting an increase of pension to Mary Elizabeth Fales,
have examined the same and adopt the Senate report thereon and
recommend that the bill do pass.

[Senate Report No. 2058, Fifty-seventh Congress, first session.]

The Committee on Pensions, to whom was referred the bill (S. 3970) granting an
increase of pension to Mary Elizabeth Fales, have examined the same and report:

Mary Elizabeth Fales is the widow of William R. Fales, alias William Webb, late
of the United States Navy.

It appears from the files of the Pension Bureau that William R. Fales served several enlistments in the United States Navy under the name of William Webb, the
last one beginning April 25, 1878, and terminating with his death, October 9, 1879,
from disease of lungs, contracted in line of duty in the service.

Mary Elizabeth Fales is now receiving the pension of $12 per month provided by
the general law. She is upward of 63 years of age, and was married to the sailor
January 3, 1856. Her post-office address is 801 New Jersey avenue NW., Washington, D. C., and her petition accompanying the bill shows that she owns no real
estate and that she is dependent on her pension for her support.

It appears also from evidence in the Bureau that claimant's health was very much
impaired in an explosion which occurred in the Washington Arsenal, where she was
employed some years ago. Her nervous system was shattered to the degree that she
can not obtain any regular employment, and she has to eke out a livelihood by such
small jobs as she can get and the charity of friends.

There are numerous precedents for increasing pension in cases of this character,
in view of which your committee report the bill back favorably with a recommendation that it pass.

O

MILTON FRAZIER.

JANUARY 20, 1903.—Committed to the Committee of the Whole House and ordered
to be printed.

Mr. CROWLEY, from the Committee on Invalid Pensions, submitted
the following

REPORT.

[To accompany S. 5976.]

The Committee on Invalid Pensions, to whom was referred the bill
(S. 5976) granting an increase of pension to Milton Frazier, have
examined the same and adopt the Senate report thereon and recommend that the bill do pass.

[Senate Report No. 1958, Fifty-seventh Congress, first session.]

The Committee on Pensions, to whom was referred the bill (S. 5976) granting an
increase of pension to Milton Frazier, have examined the same and report:

This bill proposes to increase from $12 to $30 per month the pension of Milton
Frazier, late of Company A, First Regiment Missouri Volunteer Engineers.

Soldier enlisted July 28, 1861, and was discharged July 22, 1865. He was pensioned August 12, 1891, under the act of June 27, 1890, at $12 per month for lumbago
and senility. The medical examination on which his claim was allowed was made
March 4, 1891, and showed that he was totally disabled for manual labor by reason
of chronic lumbago, diarrhea, and general enfeeblement of age.

Claimant has made no claim under the general law. His post-office address is
Parkersburg, Ill. He is 79 years of age and totally helpless. In April, 1901, he was
stricken with paralysis, and since then has required the constant attention of a nurse
day and night. He is as poor as poverty, without property or income or means of
support except his pension. These facts are substantiated by medical and other evidence filed with the bill.

In view of the soldier's faithful service of four years, his great age, poverty, and
total helplessness, your committee report the bill back favorably with a recommendation that it pass.

O

JOHN A. SMITH.

JANUARY 20, 1903.—Committed to the Committee of the Whole House and ordered
to be printed.

Mr. MIERS, from the Committee on Invalid Pensions, submitted the
following

REPORT.

[To accompany H. R. 1482.]

The Committee on Invalid Pensions, to whom was referred the bill
(H. R. 1482) granting an increase of pension to John A. Smith, submit
the following report:

This bill proposes to increase the pension of the beneficiary named
therein from $12 to $30 per month.

John A. Smith, now 58 years of age, who served as a private in
Company G, Fourth Provisional Regiment Enrolled Missouri Militia
from May 16 to October 1, 1863, is now and has been since August 21,
1890, a pensioner under the act of June 27, 1890, at the maximum
rating, namely, $12 per month, for total inability to earn a support
by manual labor, the result of disease of eyes, heart, and respiratory
and digestive organs.

A claim under the general law, filed on May 5, 1890, and based upon
measles and resulting disease of the eyes, lungs, heart, kidneys, bladder, and diabetes, was rejected in June, 1895, upon the ground of no
record of treatment for said diseases in the War Department, and
inability of the claimant, after a full special examination, to furnish
satisfactory evidence to show the origin of said disabilities in service
and line of duty, and this rejection was affirmed by Assistant Secretary Webster Davis under date of January 30, 1899, upon the ground
that the evidence filed and that obtained upon special examination
failed to show that any of the soldier's alleged disabilities originated
in line of duty and while in the service.

According to the statement of the beneficiary, he served as second
lieutenant of Company L of the Sixty-sixth Enrolled Missouri Militia
from September 5 to December 30, 1864, which service was rendered
to the State of Missouri and not to the United States.

He claimed in his application for pension under the general law that
in the summer of 1863 he took sick and that the measles broke out a
few days thereafter; that his chest and lungs hurt him before the

attack of measles, and that his eyes became sore and weak when the
measles broke out; that his back also began to hurt him, and that he
is afflicted with heart trouble and urinary disease.

The evidence obtained upon special examination is quite conflicting.

That the beneficiary was taken with measles in the service can not
be questioned, the proof being ample as to that disease, but as to any
resulting disease or diseases the proof is conflicting, some of the witnesses who testified ex parte repudiating their affidavits before the
special examiner as to certain diseases, and the testimony of the other
witnesses not being from personal knowledge, but based upon complaints made by the soldier.

The evidence, however, shows that the soldier has been a sickly man
from soon after his discharge from the United States service, and that
he was under medical treatment in 1866 or 1867 for liver and eye
trouble, and from 1870 to 1883 for fever, piles, and liver trouble.

When last examined, in March, 1892, the board of surgeons rated
him $4 for disease of the rectum, $2 for constipation, $4 for lung
trouble, $6 for disease of heart, $2 for disease of eyes, and $6 for
rheumatism.

There is no doubt that part of the soldier's present disabilities, if
not all, are traceable to his military service; hence an increase of his
pension from $12 to $20 per month appears justified.

The bill is therefore reported back with the recommendation that it
pass after the same shall have been amended as follows:

In line 6 strike out the words "a private in" and insert in lieu
thereof the word "of."

In line 8 strike out the word "thirty" and insert in lieu thereof the
word "twenty."

O

JOHN E. PICKARD.

JANUARY 20, 1903.—Committed to the Committee of the Whole House and ordered to be printed.

Mr. CROWLEY, from the Committee on Invalid Pensions, submitted the following

REPORT.

[To accompany H. R. 3752.]

The Committee on Invalid Pensions, to whom was referred the bill (H. R. 3752) granting a pension to John E. Pichard, submit the following report:

This bill proposes to increase the pension of the beneficiary named therein from $14 to $36 per month.

John E. Pickard, now 62 years of age, is shown by the records of the War Department to have served as a private in Company G, Eighth Kansas Infantry, from October 21, 1861, to September 5, 1864, when discharged on surgeon's certificate of disability by reason of—

Gunshot wound of right arm received at the battle of Chattanooga, Tenn., November 25, 1863; also granulated inflammation of eyelids contracted since last enlistment.

The medical records of the War Department show that the beneficiary was wounded severely at the battle of Mission Ridge, November 25, 1863; that the ball entered the lower third of the humerus and emerged on the opposite side, fracturing the humerus, etc.

The files of the Pension Bureau show that the beneficiary is now in receipt of a pension of $14 per month under the general law on account of the disability from the gunshot wound of the right arm and disease of eyes, and that claims for increase of pension were rejected in May, 1900, and October, 1901, upon the ground that the disabilities of accepted service origin did not warrant a rating in excess of $14 per month, and that the refractive error and senile cataract were not due to the disease of eyes of accepted service origin.

When last examined, on May 8, 1901, the board of surgeons at Winfield, Kans., described his physical condition as follows:

There is a smooth, depressed, and adherent cicatrix on the outer portion of the surface of the right arm 4 inches above the elbow, and a depressed, adherent cicatrix on the posterior surface of the right arm. There is evidence that a portion of the humerus has been removed.

There is also a smooth, nondepressed, nonadherent cicatrix one-half inch long at the junction of the anterior and outer surfaces of the right arm one-half inch above the elbow joint, where the claimant says a part of the ball was extracted in 1869.   Flexion is impaired one-fourth.   There is overextension.   The distance between the point of entrance and exit is 3 inches, ball having shattered the bone.   The usefulness of arm for manual labor is impaired three-fourths.   Rating, $17.

There is chronic conjunctivitis of both eyes, sight of left eye twenty two-hundredths, of right eye twenty-fiftieths, sight of both eyes twenty-fiftieths.   Rating, $4.

Statements of physicians of Winfield, Kans., filed with your committee set forth that the soldier's right arm had been badly mangled between the elbow and the shoulder, and in consequence it is practically useless, so far as the performance of manual labor is concerned; that, in fact, it would probably be better if it had been amputated at the shoulder, which would have freed him from the constant pain that he is now suffering; that he is pale and anæmic, probably caused by the absorption of the diseased matter from the shattered bone in his arm; that he is totally unfit to perform labor of any kind, etc.

Other testimony filed with your committee shows that the beneficiary is also suffering greatly with rheumatism and that part of the time he is unable to walk without the aid of a cane and part of the time is confined to his room, not being able to walk at all.

The degree of disability from the wound received by this soldier at the battle of Mission Ridge no doubt is such, as stated by his attending physician, that it totally disables him for the performance of any manual labor.

In view of this and the further fact that the soldier is also suffering from impaired sight of accepted service origin, an increase of his pension to $30 per month is justified; hence the bill is reported back with the recommendation that it pass after the same shall have been amended as follows:

In line 6 strike out the word "Pichard," and insert in lieu thereof the word "Pickard."

In line 8 strike out the word "thirty-six" and insert in lieu thereof the word "thirty."

In same line strike out the words "any pension" and insert in lieu thereof the word "that."

Amend the title so as to read: "A bill granting an increase of pension to John E. Pickard."

O

JOHN H. KEHN.

JANUARY 20, 1903.—Committed to the Committee of the Whole House and ordered
to be printed.

Mr. MIERS, from the Committee on Invalid Pensions, submitted the
following

REPORT.

[To accompany H. R. 3353.]

The Committee on Invalid Pensions, to whom was referred the bill
(H. R. 3353) granting an increase of pension to John Kehn, submit
the following report:

This bill proposes to increase the pension of the officer named therein
from $25 to $50 per month.

John H. Kehn, the beneficiary, now 72 years of age, served as a
sergeant in Company K, Twenty-fifth Ohio Volunteers, from June
24, 1861, to May 25, 1864, when he was promoted to first lieutenant of
Company I of the same regiment, and was honorably discharged July
8, 1865, on tender of resignation, accompanied by a medical certificate
showing him to be suffering from eczema of the scrotum.

Medical records of the War Department show that he was under
treatment at different dates for dysentery, diarrhea, contusion, and
remittent fever.

He is now pensioned under the general law at $25 per month on
account of total deafness of the left ear and severe deafness of right
ear and injury to testicles.

Claims on account of rheumatism and disease of lungs and the effects
of sunstroke were rejected upon the ground that a pensionable disability from these causes had not existed since the filing of the claim;
and a claim on account of disease of eyes was rejected in July, 1900,
upon the ground of no record of treatment in the War Department
and claimant's inability to show the origin of the same in service, etc.

The officer alleged that he received a sunstroke in July, 1864, and
that in 1891 his eyes' began to fail, and that he had been totally blind
since April, 1894, and medical examinations beginning in July, 1895,
show that he has been totally blind since that time by reason of atrophy
of the optic nerve and operation for cataract, and that by reason of
such blindness he requires the personal aid and attendance of another
person.

2

JOHN H. KEHN.JOHN H. KEHN.

The affidavit of the beneficiary filed with your committee sets forth that he received a sunstroke; that his sight became defective; that with the aid of glasses, however, he was able to see moderately well; that in 1894 he became totally blind, since which time he had required the attendance of another person; that all the property he owns is a cottage of four rooms, valued at about $500 and encumbered for $132, and personal property amounting to about $75; that he has no income aside from the pension of $25 per month, which is insufficient for his and his wife's support in his present helpless condition, etc.

The beneficiary's allegations as to his present physical and financial condition are corroborated by the affidavits of two persons, also filed with the committee.

Following precedents, it being shown that the officer is totally blind and requires the aid and attendance of another person and that he is in destitute circumstances, an increase of his pension from $25 to $40 per month is justified.

The bill is therefore reported back with the recommendation that it pass after the same shall have been amended as follows:

Strike out all of lines 6, 7, and 8 and insert in lieu thereof the following:

of John H. Kehn, late of Company K, and first lieutenant Company I, Twenty-fifth Regiment Ohio Volunteer Infantry, and pay him a pension at the rate of forty dollars per month in lieu of that he is now receiving.

Amend the title so as to read: "A bill granting an increase of pension to John H. Kehn."

O

CHARLES S. F. HILTON.

JANUARY 20, 1903.—Committed to the Committee of the Whole House and ordered
to be printed.

Mr. DARRAGH, from the Committee on Invalid Pensions, submitted the
following

REPORT.

[To accompany H. R. 1016.]

The Committee on Invalid Pensions, to whom was referred the bill
(H. R. 1016) granting a pension to Charles S. F. Hilton, submit the
following report:

This bill proposes to pension Charles S. F. Hilton, foster father of
John Hilton, late of the U. S. gunboat *Tahoma*, at $12 per month.

It appears from the records of the Navy Department that John
Hilton, the sailor named in this bill, enlisted at Boston, Mass., in the
U. S. Navy on November 13, 1861; that he served on board the
Tahoma, was captured at Tampa Bay, Florida, October 11, 1863, con-
fined at Andersonville, and died at that place of acute diarrhea June
20, 1864.

No claim for pension has been filed in the Pension Bureau on account
of the services and death of the sailor, and the beneficiary named in
the bill would have no title to pension under the general pension laws
by reason of the fact that he was not the natural father of the soldier.

From proof filed with your committee it appears that in 1844,
while the beneficiary was master of the schooner *Tasso*, a fishing vessel, and while cruising at Nova Scotia, he met an old friend named
McGuire, who had a boy 6 years of age whose parents had both died
and who was without other relatives; that McGuire wanted the beneficiary to take the lad, and the beneficiary having recently lost a son
about that age, and the boy being bright and attractive, took him and
adopted him in the place of the son he had lost; that he came home
with the beneficiary in the vessel and lived with him as his son, and
was named and known in the neighborhood as John Hilton; that being
an unusually bright boy he was sent by the beneficiary to Georgetown
and Lewiston for extra schooling, and that afterwards he gave the
beneficiary his earnings when he went fishing.

He died as stated above. He left no widow surviving him, having
never been married.

The beneficiary named in the bill, now 77 years of age, is shown to be feeble and unable to work, and his financial standing is of the poorest, he having only a mortgaged place valued at $950, and mortgaged at $450. His foster son, on whom the beneficiary relied for support in his old age, would have faithfully supported the beneficiary had he been spared.

The beneficiary's post-office address is Boothbay, Me.

Under these circumstances the relief sought for in the bill is fully warranted, there being many precedents for the pensioning of foster fathers.

The bill is therefore reported back with the recommendation that it pass after the same shall have been amended as follows:

Strike out all of lines 7 and 8 and insert in lieu thereof the following:

the United States steamship *Tahoma*, United States Navy, and pay him a pension at the rate of twelve dollars per month.

O

FRANKLIN T. MILLER.

JANUARY 20, 1903.—Committed to the Committee of the Whole House and ordered to be printed.

Mr. APLIN, from the Committee on Invalid Pensions, submitted the following

REPORT.

[To accompany H. R. 12052.]

The Committee on Invalid Pensions, to whom was referred the bill (H. R. 12052) granting an increase of pension to Franklin T. Miller, submit the following report:

This bill proposes to increase the pension of the soldier named therein from $36 to $50 per month.

Franklin T. Miller, the soldier named in this bill, and now 67 years of age, who served as private and corporal in Company A, Ninety-third Pennsylvania Infantry, from September 11, 1861, to September 22, 1864, when honorably discharged, and who received a gunshot wound of the right shoulder in action at Mary's Heights, May 3, 1863, is now a pensioner under the general law on account of this gunshot wound of right shoulder, and resulting total disability of right arm, at $36 per month.

This last allowance was based upon a claim for increase of pension, filed June 15, 1898, upon which the beneficiary was examined January 4, 1899, and was made to commence from the date of his certificate of that examination.

The certificate of medical examination of January 4, 1899, upon which the rating of $36 per month was based, described the disability from the wound of the shoulder, etc., as follows:

Scar of entrance of missile about 3½ inches to the right of spinal column and 3½ inches below the shoulder joint. Scar of exit is on the right side of neck, 3½ inches below the ear, and almost on direct line with the ear. The missile took an upward and forward course, disabling the right arm totally. The right arm is swollen and measures around the biceps muscles 1½ inches larger than the left arm. The arm is perfectly useless, having no motion whatever in it, hangs to his side, and he can neither raise nor lower it. He can not even use his fingers. There is total disability of the right arm, and by virtue of it he is entitled to $36 per month.

He is unable to move his right shoulder at all; unable to flex or extend his right elbow at all. He can move the wrist to a small degree—about 10 degrees; can move the fingers and thumb of the right hand a very little, the motion in the little, ring, and middle fingers being about 50 degrees, in the index finger 20 degree, and in the thumb 10 degrees. He is unable to grasp any object with the fingers or thumb of the right hand. He is unable to use his right hand or his right arm in feeding, dressing, or undressing himself.

He has almost total loss of power of the right arm and hand, and uses his left hand to place his right arm or hand in the position he wants it.

There has been filed the affidavit of Dr. Weiss, of Lebanon, Pa., setting forth that the beneficiary while following his vocation, in which he was greatly hampered by reason of the wound of the right shoulder, had a splinter enter his left hand, which was followed by a general cellulitis of the left hand and forearm, resulting in adhesion of the tendons to their sheaths, which caused total and permanent disability of the left hand.

An affidavit signed by a dozen residents of Lebanon Pa., also filed with your committee, sets forth that by reason of the injury to the left hand, the beneficiary is so crippled that he is unable to do any labor of any kind whatever, not being able even to put on a portion of his clothing without assistance.

The soldier is shown to require the aid and attendance of another person in dressing, etc., by reason of the total disability of the right arm, due to the service, and the injury to his left hand received since discharge.

Under these circumstances your committee believe that an increase of his pension from $36 to $50 per month is warranted; hence the bill is reported back with the recommendation that it pass.

O

WILLIAM M. WILSON.

JANUARY 20, 1903.—Committed to the Committee of the Whole House and ordered to be printed.

Mr. APLIN, from the Committee on Invalid Pensions, submitted the following

REPORT.

[To accompany H. R. 13881.]

The Committee on Invalid Pensions, to whom was referred the bill (H. R. 13881) granting a pension to W. M. Wilson, submit the following report:

This bill proposes to pension W. M. Wilson as the dependent father of Thomas Wilson, late of Company C, Fourth Vermont Volunteers, at $24 per month.

Thomas Wilson, the soldier named in the bill, served as a private in Company C, Fourth Vermont Infantry, from September 21, 1861, to December 27, 1862, when honorably discharged, and was a pensioner under the general law on account of injury of spine and resulting disease of lungs.

He died of pulmonary consumption on January 28, 1870.

His widow, who married him on July 4, 1863, was pensioned under the general law up to the date of her remarriage in February, 1871, and thereafter his two minor children were pensioned up to June 29, 1883, when the youngest child became 16 years of age, since which time no one has been drawing any pension on account of the services and death of the soldier.

William M. Wilson, the beneficiary named in the bill, and now 85 years of age, applied for pension as the dependent father of the soldier, but his claim was rejected in January, 1898, upon the ground that inasmuch as the soldier left a widow and minor children surviving him, title to pension as dependent father could not obtain under the pension laws.

The beneficiary alleged in his declaration for pension, and proof filed in 1897 shows, that he was then supported by the town of Mount Holly, Vt.

Proof on file in the Pension Bureau shows that the soldier was a son of the beneficiary named in the bill.

The statement of Hon. D. J. Foster filed with your committee sets forth that the beneficiary is absolutely without means of support and is a town charge on the town of Mount Holly, Vt.

In the opinion of your committee this beneficiary should not be made to suffer want at his great age and be a town charge, he having furnished to his country a son who died of disease contracted in the service and upon whom, were he alive, he would now rely for support.

Under these circumstances relief to the extent of granting to the beneficiary a pension of $12 per month is warranted, and the bill is reported back with the recommendation that it pass after the same shall have been amended as follows:

In line 6 strike out the letter "W" and insert in lieu thereof the word "William."

In line 7, before the word "Vermont," insert the word "Regiment."

In the same line strike out the word "Volunteers" and insert in lieu thereof the words "Volunteer Infantry."

In line 8 strike out the word "twenty-four" and insert in lieu thereof the word "twelve."

Amend the title so as to read: "A bill granting a pension to William M. Wilson."

O

HIRAM D. DEMING.

JANUARY 20, 1903.—Committed to the Committee of the Whole House and ordered to be printed.

Mr. DEEMER, from the Committee on Invalid Pensions, submitted the following

REPORT.

[To accompany H. R. 13088.]

The Committee on Invalid Pensions, to whom was referred the bill (H. R. 13088) granting an increase of pension to Hiram D. Deming, submit the following report:

This bill proposes to increase the pension of this soldier from $12 to $25 per month.

This soldier, now 75 years of age, served in Company A, One hundred and seventy-first Pennsylvania Infantry, from October 16, 1862, to August 8, 1863, when honorably discharged, and again as a private in Company G, Forty-fifth Pennsylvania Infantry, from February 25, 1864, to July 17, 1865, when mustered out with the field and staff of that regiment.

He never applied for pension under the general law, but is now and has been since July 8, 1890, a pensioner under the act of June 27, 1890, at the maximum rating, namely, $12 per month, for total inability to earn a support by manual labor, due to disease of heart and urinary organs, and injury to right shoulder.

This allowance was based upon a certificate of medical examination made on January 17, 1891, the only one in the case, which rated him $2 for cystitis, $6 for disease of heart, and $6 for dislocation of right arm.

From proof filed with your committee it appears that the beneficiary is a sufferer from catarrh of the kidneys and bladder; that he has a son living with him who is between 35 and 40 years old, and whose mind is affected; that the son seldom ever leaves the room and requires constant watching.

In view of the great age of the soldier, his total inability to perform manual labor, and the fact that he has an insane son dependent upon him for support, an increase of his pension to $24 per month appears

warranted, and the bill is therefore reported back with the recommendation that it pass, after the same shall have been amended as
follows:

Strike out all of lines 6, 7, 8, 9, and 10 and insert in lieu thereof the
following:

of Hiram D. Deming, late of Company G, Forty-fifth Regiment Pennsylvania Volunteer Infantry, and pay him a pension at the rate of twenty-four dollars a month
in lieu of that he is now receiving.

O

CHARLES A. RITTENHOUSE.

JANUARY 20, 1903.—Committed to the Committee of the Whole House and ordered to be printed.

Mr. DEEMER, from the Committee on Invalid Pensions, submitted the following

REPORT.

[To accompany H. R. 2987.]

The Committee on Invalid Pensions, to whom was referred the bill (H. R. 2987) granting an increase of pension to Charles A. Rittenhouse, submit the following report:

This bill proposes to increase the pension of the beneficiary named therein from $12 to $30 per month.

This officer, now 74 years of age, served as chaplain of the Seventh Pennsylvania Cavalry from March 4, 1864, to July 25, 1865, when honorably discharged on account of physical disability due to chronic diarrhea, dyspepsia, and nervous debility.

He is now a pensioner under the act of June 27, 1890, at $12 per month for total inability to earn a support by manual labor, the result of hydrocele, rheumatism, and general debility.

His claim under the general law, filed in 1892 and based upon chronic diarrhea resulting in nervous debility, was rejected in February, 1899, upon the ground of claimant's declared inability to furnish satisfactory evidence of the continuance of said disabilities since discharge.

A prior claim based upon hæmoptitis from injury, hernia, and hydrocele was rejected in 1876 upon the ground of no record of the alleged disabilities and claimant's inability to furnish the necessary testimony.

The beneficiary stated that owing to the decease of his father-in-law, mother-in-law, his father, step-mother, and sister he was unable to furnish evidence as to the continuance of diarrhea since discharge.

He did, however, furnish the affidavit of one person to the effect that he suffered from chronic diarrhea and nervous debility ever since discharge, and medical testimony as to treatment since 1889 for nervousness, insomnia, and general debility, and for chronic diarrhea.

When last examined on October 5, 1898, the board of surgeons rated him $15 for paralysis agitans, $10 for rheumatism, $4 for hydrocele, and $8 for diarrhea and disease of the rectum.

Medical and other testimony filed with your committee shows that the beneficiary is now a great sufferer from chronic rheumatism of an incurable type; that he requires assistance in dressing, is wholly disabled from following any occupation or calling, and a man of unblemished character and reputation, and highly respected in the county in which he resides.

This officer, who is suffering from paralysis agitans, is, in view of numerous precedents, entitled to an increase of his pension from $12 to $24 per month, and relief to that extent is recommended, and the bill is reported back with the recommendation that it pass after the same shall have been amended as follows:

In line 6 strike out the words "of the."

In line 8 strike out the word "thirty" and insert in lieu thereof the word "twenty-four."

O

LAWRENCE H. ROSSEAU.

JANUARY 20, 1903.—Committed to the Committee of the Whole House and ordered
to be printed.

Mr. GIBSON, from the Committee on Invalid Pensions, submitted the
following

REPORT.

[To accompany H. R. 2136.]

The Committee on Invalid Pensions, to whom was referred the bill
(H. R. 2136) for the relief of Lawrence H. Rousseau, submit the following report:

This bill proposes to increase the pension of this officer from $15 to
$30 per month.

The records of the War Department show that Lawrence H. Rousseau,
now 73 years of age, served as a private in Company H, Fourth Kentucky Volunteers, war with Mexico, from October 3, 1847, to July 25,
1848, when he was honorably discharged, and that he also served as
captain of Company C, Twelfth Kentucky Volunteers, and as lieutenant-
colonel of same regiment from January 31, 1862, to July 11, 1865, when
honorably discharged; that he was under treatment in March, 1865, for
intermittent fever.

He was pensioned from the date of his discharge on account of
nasal catarrh at $7.50 per month and at $15 per month from January
14, 1882; and he is now in receipt of such pension, the same being
one-half of total of lieutenant-colonel's pension.

In a declaration filed March 25, 1880, the officer alleged, among other
things, that while his regiment was about to reenlist as veteran volunteers the men were granted veteran furloughs; that he obtained leave
of absence from the 1st to the 29th of March, 1864, and returned to
his home, and while there was vaccinated with impure virus, from the
effects of which he became disabled.

This claim was first rejected upon the ground that a disability contracted by a soldier or officer while on leave of absence or veteran
furlough was not considered as having been incurred in the line of
duty, and such action was affirmed by Assistant Secretary Hawkins in
January, 1888, and a motion for reconsideration was overruled by the
same Assistant Secretary in June, 1888.

Upon another appeal, filed in 1891, Assistant Secretary Bussey held that the beneficiary was in the line of duty on leave of absence, but that the evidence submitted was not sufficient to show a disability from the alleged impure vaccination virus; and that while the testimony showed that he was nervous and that his general health was not good, it failed to show that he was suffering from the effects of vaccination after his return from furlough, and that none of the officers whose testimony was taken before the special examiner appeared to have known or heard of his vaccination at all.

On August 31, 1898, Assistant Secretary Webster Davis also held that inasmuch as the decision made by Assistant Secretary Bussey had long been overruled and set aside, the opinion of Assistant Secretary Hawkins to the effect that the beneficiary was not in line of duty while home on leave of absence was reaffirmed.

A claim for increase of pension for disease of lungs and heart was rejected July 24, 1897, upon the ground that a disability arising from nasal catarrh did not warrant a rate in excess of $15 per month; that disease of lungs was not shown in a pensionable degree, and that disease of heart, according to claimant's own admission, was not of service origin, he having stated that he only knew of it some years ago.

The last certificate of medical examination in the case, made April 15, 1896, described the officer's condition as follows:

He has post nasal catarrh, with discharge from post nasal space abundant and purulent; he has no disease of the lungs; he has an irregular heart, sometimes tumultuous in action. He shows evidence of impaired general health; he has a lot of scars over arms and back, which have the appearance of rupia, the one where vaccination was introduced very large. Has atrophy of right testicle; has also two large external piles, one-half inch in diameter. Rate, one-half for nasal catarrh, $10 for disease of heart, $4 for general debility, $3 for piles, and $4 for diseased testicle.

He is without means of support, and financially destitute, and very feeble both from age and disabilities.

Following precedents an increase of his pension to $30 per month is therefore justified, and the bill is reported back with the recommendation that it pass after the same shall have been amended as follows:

Strike out all after the enacting clause and insert in lieu thereof the following:

That the Secretary of the Interior be, and he is hereby, authorized and directed to place on the pension roll, subject to the provisions and limitations of the pension laws, the name of Lawrence H. Rosseau, late lieutenant-colonel Twelfth Regiment Kentucky Volunteer Infantry, and pay him a pension at the rate of thirty dollars per month in lieu of that he is now receiving.

Amend the title so as to read: "A bill granting an increase of pension to Lawrence H. Rosseau."

O

WINFIELD PIERCE.

JANUARY 20, 1903.—Committed to the Committee of the Whole House and ordered to be printed.

Mr. MIERS, from the Committee on Invalid Pensions, submitted the following

REPORT.

[To accompany H. R. 659.]

The Committee on Invalid Pensions, to whom was referred the bill (H. R. 659) increasing the pension of Winfield Pierce, submit the following report:

This bill proposes to increase the pension of the soldier named therein from $14 to $30 per month.

The soldier named in this bill, now 55 years of age, served as a private in Company A, Seventh Indiana Cavalry, from July 21, 1863, to February 18, 1866, when honorably discharged.

He has been a pensioner under the general law ever since his discharge at $4 per month for disease of eyes; at $6 per month from September 17, 1879; at $8 from January 18, 1888; at $10 from March 25, 1891, and at $14 from July 13, 1892.

Claims for increase of pension have been rejected upon the ground that the disability from disease of eyes of accepted service origin did not warrant a rating in excess of $14 per month, and that all disability due to myopic astigmatism was not dependent upon the disease of service origin.

In other words, the Pension Bureau held that a part of his difficulty was nearsightedness, and that this was congenital and not the result of army service, and therefore separated that disability from that accepted to be due to the service.

The beneficiary proved by a number of witnesses that before he went into the Army he was able-bodied and that his sight was perfect, and that he worked on a farm and could mark out corn rows, driving to a stake 80 rods away.

Dr. Starky, an eye specialist, who examined him, testified that his whole disability was the result of exposure and inflammation; that is, that the myopia and myopic astigmatism now existing were due to long-continued corneal inflammation, and not to the original shape of the eye.

The board of pension examining surgeons, one of whom was also a specialist in diseases of the eye, found the same myopia and myopic astigmatism, but the Pension Bureau held that this disease was usually congenital or hereditary; that a slight degree of myopia undoubtedly existed during the claimant's boyhood, but was then not sufficient to prevent him marking out corn ground, etc., as stated by him; that want of proper attention to the refractive error and his continued use of the eyes increased the trouble and constantly impaired the sight, and that the present structural changes were entirely independent of his service disability.

When last examined, vision in right eye was six two-hundredths; vision in left eye only light in most directions. In certain position he could see two two-hundredths.

Hon. E. D. Crumpacker, who introduced this bill, has filed with your committee his statement that he has known the beneficiary for more than twenty-five years; that in view of the evidence on file in the Pension Bureau and the testimony of Dr. Starky he was satisfied that there was but little doubt that the beneficiary's entire disability was chargeable to his military service; that he knows his financial condition, and that all he has is a little property worth perhaps $800 and the pension of $14 per month.

In view of the testimony of Dr. Starky, the eye specialist, your committee believe that the doubts in the case as to whether the serious condition of the soldier's eyes from myopic astigmatism is due to the disease of eyes of accepted service origin should be resolved in claimant's favor, and he be allowed an increase of his pension from $12 to $24 per month.

The bill is therefore reported back with the recommendation that it pass after the same shall have been amended as follows:

In line 7, before the word "Cavalry," insert the word "Volunteer."

In same line, after the word "pension," insert the words "at the rate."

In same line strike out the word "thirty" and insert in lieu thereof the word "twenty-four."

In same line strike out the word "a" and insert in lieu thereof the word "per."

Amend the title so as to read: "A bill granting an increase of pension to Winfield Pierce."

O

WILLIAM W. SMITHSON.

JANUARY 20, 1903.—Committed to the Committee of the Whole House and ordered
to be printed.

Mr. APLIN, from the Committee on Invalid Pensions, submitted the
following

REPORT.

[To accompany H. R. 10355.]

The Committee on Invalid Pensions, to whom was referred the bill
(H. R. 10355) granting an increase of pension to William W. Smithson,
submit the following report:

This bill proposes to increase the pension of the officer named therein
from $17 to $30 per month.

William W. Smithson, the beneficiary named in this bill, is shown
by the records of the War Department to have served as a private in
Company I, Thirteenth New York Heavy Artillery, from May 28 to
September 12, 1862, when honorably discharged, and to have again
served as sergeant, first sergeant, first lieutenant, and captain in Companies K, C, G, and H of the One hundred and seventy-sixth New York
Infantry, from November 7, 1862, to April 27, 1866, when honorably
discharged.

He first applied for pension in August, 1889, on account of a gunshot wound of the left shoulder received at La Fourche, La., June 20,
1863, and on account of an injury to and resulting varicose veins of the
right leg received at the battle of Cedar Creek, Virginia, in October,
1864, the wound having been received while he held the rank of
sergeant and the injury while first lieutenant.

He was pensioned in 1893 on account of this wound of the shoulder
and injury and varicose veins of the right leg at $17 per month from
the date of the filing of his claim, on August 20, 1889.

Claims for increase of pension filed in 1897 and 1900, in which the
officer alleged partial paralysis of the left arm, spinal disease, loss of
the sight of the left eye, and partial loss of hearing of the left ear as
results of the pensioned causes, were rejected, the last one on June
26, 1901, upon the ground that the degree of disability arising from
the pensioned causes did not warrant a rating in excess of $17 per
month, and that the disabilities alleged as results had no pathological
connection with the same.

In support of those claims the beneficiary filed the affidavits of several physicians who gave it as their opinion that the wound of the left shoulder injured the nerves and the blood vessels of the arm and impaired it in such a manner as to impede the circulation of the blood and nerve forces so as to produce paralysis; that the ball also affected the upper portion of the spinal column so as to leave the spine permanently tender and painful, and that the loss of hearing of left ear was also caused by the same gunshot wound.

When last examined, on December 5, 1900, the board of surgeons at Hot Springs, S. Dak., described the officer's physical condition as follows:

Gunshot wound of left shoulder: There is a gunshot wound of left shoulder. Ball entered the anterior part of shoulder just above middle of the clavicle, passing through the trapezius muscle, with exit on the posterior part of the shoulder 4 inches above the acromion process of scapula. Scars of entrance and exit are both adherent, sore, and tender, with limitation of motion of left shoulder and arm three-fourths.

Varicose veins and injury to right leg: There are varicose veins of the right leg extending from the knee to the ankle and over the whole surface of the leg. Size of each vein about three-fourths inch. There is tendency to rupture.

Paralysis of left arm: The left arm is paralyzed; motion limited three-fourths; muscles atrophied; arm measures 2 inches less than the right at middle third of the humerus and radius, due, in our opinion, to the gunshot wound of shoulder.

Spinal disease: The fourth, fifth, sixth, and seventh cervical and the first, second, third, and fourth vertebræ are tender and sore on pressure. There is pain in the neck, back, and shoulders, and a sense of constriction about the thorax and abdomen, and partial paralysis of the left arm, left leg, bowels, and bladder, with a sense of cushion beneath the feet. Movements feeble and easily fatigued; coordination of movements are impaired in walking or when eyes are closed.

Eyes: Left eye is virtually blind.

Ears: There is nearly total deafness of left ear and slight deafness of right ear.

Rate, $12 for gunshot wound of the shoulder; $8 for injury to and varicose veins of right leg; $6 for partial paralysis of left arm and right leg; $8 for spinal disease; $12 for loss of the sight of left eye, and $15 for impaired hearing.

The affidavit of the beneficiary filed with your committee sets forth that the board of surgeons as well as other physicians had testified that his spinal trouble was the result of his wound; that his disabilities totally disabled him for the performance of manual labor; that he does not own any property and has no income except the pension of $17 per month.

As stated by the physicians whose testimony the beneficiary filed in the Pension Bureau, the probabilities are that the paralysis from which this officer is now suffering had some connection with the gunshot wound of the left shoulder, and inasmuch as the beneficiary is now shown to be totally disabled from the wound of shoulder and varicose veins of right leg of accepted service origin, paralysis of the left arm, spinal disease, and blindness of the left eye, the relief sought for in the bill is justified, hence the bill is reported back with the recommendation that it pass after the same shall have been amended as follows:

Strike out all after the enacting clause and insert in lieu thereof the following:

That the Secretary of the Interior be, and he is hereby, authorized and directed to place on the pension roll, subject to the provisions and limitations of the pension laws, the name of William W. Smithson, late sergeant and first lieutenant, Companies K and C, One hundred and seventy-sixth Regiment New York Volunteer Infantry, and pay him a pension at the rate of thirty dollars per month in lieu of that he is now receiving.

SABINA LALLY.

JANUARY 20, 1903.—Committed to the Committee of the Whole House and ordered
to be printed.

Mr. DARRAGH, from the Committee on Invalid Pensions, submitted
the following

REPORT.

[To accompany H. R. 8617.]

The Committee on Invalid Pensions, to whom was referred the bill
(H. R. 8617) granting a pension to Sabina Lally, submit the following
report:

This bill proposes to pension Sabina Lally, mother of Patrick Lally,
late of Company B, Seventh Wisconsin Infantry, at $24 per month.

Patrick Lally, the soldier named in this bill, served as a private in
Company B, Seventeenth Wisconsin Infantry, from October 18, 1864,
to July 14, 1865, when honorably discharged, and is shown by the
medical records of the War Department to have been under treatment
in March and April, 1865, for acute diarrhea and bronchitis. He never
applied for pension.

Sabina Lally, the beneficiary named in this bill, and now 77 years
of age, applied for pension as the dependent mother of the soldier on
July 21, 1890, alleging that the soldier, her son, died unmarried on
August 22, 1885, of disease contracted in the service; that the father
of the soldier died in 1855, and that she was dependent upon the soldier
for support.

She filed in support of her claim a transcript from the records of the
register of deeds of Portage County, Wis., showing that the soldier
died August 22, 1885, of inflammation of the stomach; also proof that
he was never married; that the beneficiary lived with and was supported by the soldier, her son, up to his death, the beneficiary not
being possessed of any property or income; that at and prior to his
enlistment the soldier was a man of good, sound physical health; that
upon his return from the service he was in poor health, complaining
of disease of the stomach, and that he continued so to complain until
his death in 1885.

The beneficiary declared her inability to furnish proof as to the
origin of the soldier's fatal disease in the service by comrades, etc.;

hence her claim was rejected by the Pension Bureau on March 31, 1902, upon the gound of her inability to show by competent and satisfactory evidence that her son's death, on August 22, 1885, from inflammation of the stomach was due to his military service.

Your committee do not believe that this beneficiary should suffer want at her great age, and inasmuch as it is shown that her son was under treatment in the service for diarrhea, and the probabilities being that the inflammation of the stomach from which he died in 1885 was dependent upon the same, relief to the extent of granting her a pension of $12 per month appears justified; hence the bill is reported back with the recommendation that it pass after the same shall have been amended as follows:

Strike out all of lines 6, 7, and 8 and insert in lieu thereof the following:

of Sabina Lalley, dependent mother of Patrick Lalley, late of Company B, Seventeenth Regiment Wisconsin Volunteer Infantry, and pay her a pension at the rate of $12 per month.

Amend the title so as to read: "A bill granting a pension to Sabina Lalley."

O

GEORGE W. STEFFEY.

JANUARY 20, 1903.—Committed to the Committee of the Whole House and ordered
to be printed.

Mr. DARRAGH, from the Committee on Invalid Pensions, submitted
the following

REPORT.

[To accompany H. R. 9072.]

The Committee on Invalid Pensions, to whom was referred the bill
(H. R. 9072) granting an increase of pension to George W. Steffey,
submit the following report:

This bill proposes to increase the pension of the soldier named
therein from $8 to $24 per month.

This soldier, now 61 years of age, served as a private in Company
F, One hundred and forty-eighth Pennsylvania Infantry, from August
21, 1862, to June 1, 1865, when honorably discharged.

Records of the War Department show that he received a gunshot
wound of the right side of the chest at Spottsylvania in May, 1864,
and that he was under treatment for the same.

He is now a pensioner under the general law on account of this
wound at $8 per month.

Claims for increase of pension, in which the soldier alleged disease
of lungs and spine as results of the gunshot wound of the right side,
were rejected in 1897 and 1902, respectively, upon the ground that the
disability from the wound did not warrant a rating in excess of $8 per
month, and that the condition of his right lung and the alleged disease
of spine could not be accepted as results of the wound.

On January 6, 1902, he filed a claim on account of additional disabilities on account of saber wound of the right arm alleged to have
been received at Sailors Creek after the evacuation of Petersburg, and
on account of rupture of the right side by heavy lifting while making corduroy roads between Culpeper Court-House and Brandy
Station, Va.

He alleged his inability to furnish the testimony of any comrade as
to the origin of these disabilities and filed no proof whatever in support of said claim except the affidavit of a doctor who testified that he
examined him in January, 1902, and found a hernia of the right side.

Certificates of medical examination described the wound of the right side as a cicatrix 1⅓ inches above the right nipple, 1 by 1⅓ inches in diameter, quite tender on pressure and somewhat dragging, with marked dullness over the lower second third of the right lung, with nearly entire absence of the vesicular murmur and moist rales over the upper portion of the right lung.

The certificate of medical examination of January 30, 1901, also found him suffering from disease of the heart, for which he was rated $12, and from a right inguinal hernia, for which rated $10.

When last examined, on June 1, 1902, the board of surgeons rated him $8 for the gunshot wound, $2 for the saber wound, and $10 for the hernia.

There has been filed with your committee the affidavit of two persons setting forth that for the last six years the beneficiary had suffered from lung trouble; that one day he was taken with hemorrhage; that his son helped him to affiant's house; that they are satisfied that he is not getting any better; that he also complained of having a rupture and a saber cut of the right arm, and that they consider him totally unable to perform any manual labor.

The supervisor of the township in which the beneficiary resides also testified that the only property owned by the beneficiary is 15 acres of land, assessed at $125, and that he has no personal property.

In the opinion of your committee not only the disease of lungs but also the disease of heart must be a result of the gunshot wound of the right side of chest, and inasmuch as the soldier is shown to be totally disabled from these causes the relief sought for in the bill appears justified; hence the bill is reported back with the recommendation that it pass.

O

MICHAEL K. STRAYER.

JANUARY 20, 1903.—Committed to the Committee of the Whole House and ordered
to be printed.

Mr. DARRAGH, from the Committee on Invalid Pensions, submitted
the following

REPORT.

[To accompany H. R. 10869.]

The Committee on Invalid Pensions, to whom was referred the bill
(H. R. 10869) granting an increase of pension to Michael K. Strayer,
submit the following report:

This bill proposes to increase the pension of the soldier named
therein from $12 to $24 per month.

Mr. Strayer, now 78 years of age, served as a private in Company
C, Eighth Michigan Volunteers, from August 20, 1861, to September
22, 1864, when honorably discharged.

He was under treatment while in the service in August and October,
1863; diagnosis not stated.

He is now pensioned under the act of June 27, 1890, at $12 per
month for total inability to earn a support by manual labor by reason
of disease of heart and varicose veins of left leg.

He was formerly pensioned under the general law at $2 per month
for chronic diarrhea from the date of his discharge to July 12, 1882,
when pension was made to terminate, upon the ground that the disability had ceased to exist.

A claim on account of chills and fever, fever sore or erysipelas,
and varicose veins and ulcers, also filed under the general law, was
rejected in September, 1884, and April, 1889, upon the ground of no
record of treatment in the War Department and claimant's inability
to furnish testimony of a definite and explicit character to connect said
disabilities with his service or to overcome his conflicting statements
as to the origin of varicose veins.

According to one of claimant's statements, he first noticed the existence of varicose veins soon after he came home; that he used to look
at them and wondered whatever caused them. In another statement
made to the board of examining surgeons he stated that twenty months
after his return from the Army he had erysipelas of the right hand,
and that six years after his discharge erysipelas of the left leg set in

and had continued ever since; and still later he claimèd origin in the
service in January, 1862.

In view of these conflicting statements of the claimant, the Pension
Bureau declined to accept the testimony filed by the claimant from
several of his comrades as to the existence of a disease of the left leg
(varix and pimples) in the service and of a swollen left leg, with resulting ulcer, since discharge as sufficient to warrant allowance of the claim.

All certificates of soldier's medical examinations, beginning in 1882,
have shown him to be a sufferer from varicose veins and ulcers of the
left leg, with veins enlarged four to eight times, nodulated and broken,
and the leg swollen, very red, indurated, and ulcerated with three open
ulcers varying in size fron 1 to 2¼ inches in diameter, and that he walks
very lame.

Medical evidence filed with your committee sets forth that in December, 1902, the beneficiary was suffering from a large varicose ulcer of
the left leg about 6 inches in length and from one-half to 2¼ inches in
width; that the bone is necrosed the full length of the sore; that he
is now wholly incapacitated to perform manual labor, and is a total
nervous wreck as a result of the limb.

Other proof filed with your committee shows that the beneficiary is
assessed for real estate at $600.

A petition signed by a large number of residents of Gratiot County,
Mich., also filed with your committee, sets forth that the beneficiary
has been suffering from varicose veins and ulceration of the left leg
below the knee ever since his return from the service, and that he
was unable to furnish all the evidence called for by the Pension Bureau
to establish such claim.

In view of claimant's present deplorable condition, his great age,
his services of over three years, and the probability that the serious
ulcer of the leg was due to this army service, the relief sought for in
the bill seems justified, and the passage of the bill is therefore
recommended.

O

CHESTER W. ABBOTT.

JANUARY 20, 1903.—Committed to the Committee of the Whole House and ordered
to be printed.

Mr. DEEMER, from the Committee on Invalid Pensions, submitted the
following

REPORT.

[To accompany H. R. 15889.]

The Committee on Invalid Pensions, to whom was referred the bill
(H. R. 15889) granting an increase of pension to Chester A. Abbott,
submit the following report:

The bill proposes to increase the pension of the soldier named therein
from $12 to $50 per month.

The files of the Pension Bureau show that Chester W. Abbott, the
beneficiary named in the bill, who is now 65 years of age, served as a
private in Company I, One hundred and third Ohio Infantry, from
August 11, 1862, to June 12, 1865, when honorably discharged; that
he was under treatment in December, 1862, for remittent fever; in
April, 1863, for rheumatism; in March, 1864, for diarrhea and dysentery, and in April, 1864, for diarrhea, and that he is now a pensioner
under the general law at $12 per month on account of chronic diarrhea
and piles of accepted service origin, and that a claim for increase of
pension was rejected on April 21, 1902, upon the ground that the disability did not warrant a rating in excess of $12 per month.

His claim for an additional disability, filed on August 7, 1901, and based
upon partial blindness alleged to be due to sore eyes contracted in the
service, was rejected on April 10, 1902, upon the ground of no record
of treatment for said disability in the service and claimant's declared
inability to prove the origin of said disability in the service and line
of duty by reason of his inability to find any comrades who were
cognizant of the origin of his eye trouble in the service, etc.

The beneficiary filed some proof in the Pension Bureau tending to
show that his eyesight had been affected since about 1884, and that he
had been under treatment for the same; and medical testimony as to
his condition in February, 1902, also filed in the Pension Bureau, shows
that he was then suffering from a cataractous condition of the lenses,

an atrophied condition of the cilliary processes, that he would gradually become worse, and that no treatment would be of benefit to him.

The last medical examination of the soldier, made on December 31, 1901, rated him $12 for the disabilities of accepted service origin and $12 for disease of eyes, which disease is described in the certificate as chronic choroditis and retinitis, $8 for disease of heart, and $2 for rheumatism.

There has been filed with your committee the affidavit of the beneficiary, setting forth that he is practically blind in his right eye; that he is owner of 80 acres of land, valued at $3,200, encumbered at $1,250, and that his whole income from all sources, including his pension, amounts to $319 per year.

A petition signed by a large number of residents of Seville, Ohio, filed with your committee, sets forth that the beneficiary is incapacitated for manual labor by reason of blindness, and that in their opinion the same is a result of his military service of three years.

The probabilities in this case are that the soldier's blindness of the right eye is a result of his service of three years, in view of which, under precedents, an increase of his pension from $12 to $24 per month is warranted.

The bill is therefore reported back with the recommendation that it pass after the same shall have been amended as follows:

In line 6 strike out the letter "A" and insert in lieu thereof the letter "W."

In line 8 strike out the word "fifty" and insert in lieu thereof the word "twenty-four."

Amend the title so as to read: "A bill granting an increase of pension to Chester W. Abbott."

O

JOSEPH M. RICHARDSON.

JANUARY 20, 1903.—Committed to the Committee of the Whole House and ordered to be printed.

Mr. KLEBERG, from the Committee on Invalid Pensions, submitted the following

REPORT.

[To accompany H. R. 15670.]

The Committee on Invalid Pensions, to whom was referred the bill (H. R. 15670) granting an increase of pension to Joseph M. Richardson, submit the following report:

This bill proposes to increase the pension of the soldier named therein from $12 to $40 per month.

Joseph M. Richardson, now 57 years of age, served as a private in Company I, Fifteenth New York Cavalry, from September 5, 1863, to January 8, 1866, when honorably discharged.

He filed a claim to pension under the general law in February, 1879, alleging that at Hallstown, Va., in December, 1864, while going to water the horses, the horse he rode became frightened at something in the road and reared and fell back, rupturing him in the right scrotum, and upon the testimony of three comrades as to the origin of right hernia in the service and under the circumstances set forth by the beneficiary, his claim was allowed in August, 1881, at $4 per month from the date of his discharge, after the case had been specially examined by a special examiner of the Pension Bureau.

Subsequently another special examination of the case was had, and upon such special examination his name was dropped from the rolls in May, 1882, upon the ground that the original testimony was false and fraudulent, and that there was no proof to show the incurrence in the service and line of duty of the hernia.

In 1891, the name of the soldier was placed upon the rolls under the act of June 27, 1890, at $12 per month for total inability to earn a support by manual labor, the result of rheumatism, disease of heart and nervous system, and right hernia.

The last medical examination of the soldier, made on September 12, 1895, found him to be suffering from locomotor ataxia and resulting partial paralysis of both legs.

The testimony of Drs. Masterson and Schaffhirt, of this city, filed with your committee, sets forth that the beneficiary is now a wreck, emaciated to the last degree, and utterly helpless, suffering from locomotor ataxia, with no use of his legs; that some ten years ago he propelled himself on a tricycle, but was compelled to discontinue its use, owing to weakness of his legs.

Other testimony filed with your committee sets forth that the beneficiary is partially paralyzed below the hips, suffering from a general breaking down and wasting away; that of late he has hardly been able to be about without assistance of other persons; that he is totally unfit for manual labor; that he is not the possessor of any property, and that if relief does not come soon he will not live to see it.

The case of this soldier comes within the action of the House, taken on June 16, 1902, in Senate bill 4850, increasing from $12 to $30 per month the pension of those who require the aid and attendance of another person.

The bill is therefore reported back with the recommendation that it pass after the same shall have been amended as follows:

Strike out all of lines 6, 7, 8, 9, and 10 and insert in lieu thereof the following:

of Joseph M. Richardson, late of Company I, Fifteenth Regiment New York Volunteer Cavalry, and pay him a pension at the rate of $30 per month in lieu of that he is now receiving.

O

LOTT VAN NORDSTRAND.

JANUARY 20, 1903.—Committed to the Committee of the Whole House and ordered to be printed.

Mr. MIERS, from the Committee on Invalid Pensions, submitted the following

REPORT.

[To accompany H. R. 15387.]

The Committee on Invalid Pensions, to whom was referred the bill (H. R. 15387) granting an increase of pension to Lot Van Nordstrand, submit the following report:

This bill proposes to increase the pension of the beneficiary named therein from $12 to $17 per month.

Lott Van Nordstrand, the beneficiary named in this bill, and now 70 years of age, is shown by the records of the War Department to have served as a private and wagoner in Battery M, First New York Light Artillery, from March 28, 1864, to June 23, 1865, when honorably discharged, and to have been under treatment from October 15, to 18, 1864 (no diagnosis).

He never applied for pension under the general law, but is now a pensioner under the provisions of the act of June 27, 1890, at $12 per month for total inability to earn a support by manual labor, the result of rheumatism, disease of heart, and senile debility.

When last examined, on June 4, 1902, by the board of surgeons at Rockyford, Colo., they found him totally disabled for either mental or manual labor by reason of chronic diarrhea, piles, rheumatism, and disease of the heart, and the board of surgeons further stated that he was also suffering from impaired hearing of both ears and that there was staggering or unsteady gait and that he was unable to walk in a straight line.

There has been filed with your committee the affidavit of the beneficiary setting forth that he was suffering from failure of eyesight; that he was almost deaf, and was seriously troubled with asthma, heart trouble, rheumatism, and injury to right leg; that he was so blind that he could not recognize his own people at all times, and so deaf that he could not hear well enough to converse with the people around him; that he has no means of support except the pension, and that he is dependent, with his wife, upon a daughter, who is the wife of a poor man.

The testimony of Dr. J. O. Hardy, of Las Animas, Colo., also filed with your committee, sets forth that the beneficiary in November, 1892, was suffering from total blindness of the right eye, and nearly total blindness of the left eye due to senile cataract; that he was deaf, and also suffering from chronic rheumatism affecting the arms, shoulders, back, hips, and legs, and from dilatation of the heart; that he is totally unable to perform any kind of labor, and has asthma all the time with frequent attacks of bronchitis.

The case of this soldier comes within the action of the House taken on June 16, 1902, it being shown that the beneficiary is virtually blind besides suffering from other serious disabilities, etc.

The passage of the bill is therefore recommended after the same shall have been amended as follows:

In line 6 strike out the word "Lot" and insert in lieu thereof the word "Lott."

In the same line strike out the words "teamster in" and insert in lieu thereof the word "of."

In line 7 strike out the word "Infantry" and insert in lieu thereof the word "Artillery."

In line 8 strike out the word "seventeen" and insert in lieu thereof the word "thirty."

Amend the title so as to read: "A bill granting an increase of pension to Lott Van Nordstrand."

O

MARY A. TALBOTT.

JANUARY 20, 1903.—Committed to the Committee of the Whole House and ordered to be printed.

Mr. KLEBERG, from the Committee on Invalid Pensions, submitted the following

REPORT.

[To accompany H. R. 14758.]

The Committee on Invalid Pensions, to whom was referred the bill (H. R. 14758) granting an increase of pension to Mary A. Talbott, submit the following report:

This bill proposes to increase the pension of the beneficiary named therein from $8 to $15 per month.

The officer named in this bill served as second lieutenant of Company H, Fifth Maryland Infantry, from October 24, 1861, to November 21, 1862, when he tendered his resignation from the service on account of family affairs.

He was a pensioner under the general law at $15 per month on account of an injury to both hands received during the battle of Antietam while tearing down a rail fence during said battle.

He died March 25, 1892, from cerebral apoplexy.

The beneficiary named in this bill, now 71 years of age, who married the officer on June 2, 1862, is now a pensioner under the act of June 27, 1890, at $8 per month, upon proof that she was the legal widow of the officer, had not remarried, and was dependent upon her daily labor.

Her claim under the general law was rejected in April, 1895, upon the ground that the cerebral apoplexy which caused her husband's death had no connection with the injury of both hands for which he had been pensioned and was not otherwise shown to be due to his military service.

Since the rejection of the beneficiary's claim under the general law she has contended that her husband's death was due to an injury to the head received while in the Army, but no evidence was filed tending to show that her husband received an injury while in the service other than the wound to his hands, except that testimony was filed, consisting of indefinite and meager statements imputed to the officer long since his discharge, that he received an injury to his head while in the service.

Some proof was filed by the beneficiary tending to show that upon her husband's return from the Army he complained of a great deal of suffering from trouble with his head, that he had dizzy or fainting spells, and that he continued to complain of these troubles until November, 1891, when he had a stroke of apoplexy or paralysis.

Proof filed in the Pension Bureau shows that the beneficiary is in destitute circumstances, dependent entirely upon her own daily labor and upon the small earnings of her son.

The doubts in this case your committee believes should be resolved in favor of the beneficiary, evidence having been filed by her tending to show that her husband did suffer from some trouble with his head and that he had dizzy and fainting spells ever since his return from the service.

Had the Pension Bureau accepted the officer's death cause to be due to his service, the widow, under the general pension laws, would have been entitled to the relief sought for in the bill, and that is now recommended, and the bill is reported back with the recommendation that it pass after the same shall have been amended as follows:

In line 7, after the word "Fifth," insert the word "Regiment."

In same line strike out the word "Volunteers" and insert in lieu thereof the words "Volunteer Infantry."

In line 8, after the word "pension," insert the words "at the rate."

In same line strike out the word "which."

O

WILLIAM H. KNEPPLE.

JANUARY 20, 1903.—Committed to the Committee of the Whole House and ordered to be printed.

Mr. MIERS, from the Committee on Invalid Pensions, submitted the following

REPORT.

[To accompany H. R. 16465.]

The Committee on Invalid Pensions, to whom was referred the bill (H. R. 16465) granting an increase of pension to William H. Knepple, submit the following report:

This bill proposes to increase the pension of the soldier named therein from $12 to $40 per month.

The soldier is 73 years of age and served as a private and sergeant in Company B, One hundred and ninety-fifth Ohio Volunteers, from February 27 to December 14, 1865, when honorably discharged. He was under treatment at various dates in August, 1865, for diarrhea and intermittent fever. He is pensioned under the act of June 27, 1890, at the maximum rating, $12 per month, on account of paralysis.

His claim under the general law, filed in March, 1892, and based upon a sunstroke alleged to have been incurred at Stevenson Station, W. Va., in May, 1865, and resulting general debility and paralysis of left side, was rejected by the Pension Bureau in June, 1900, upon the ground of no record of treatment for said disability in the service and claimant's declared inability to show by sufficient evidence that the alleged sunstroke and resulting paralysis were incurred in the service.

The testimony in the case tends to show that the beneficiary was overcome by heat while on review; that thereafter while in the service he was sickly, unable to march unless his comrades carried his knapsack and gun; that his health after the war was poor, and that in May, 1885, he suffered a stroke of paralysis, since which time he had been totally disabled.

He filed no medical evidence as to treatment prior to 1874 for the reason that, having been a physician, he treated himself.

When last examined, in June, 1898, the board of surgeons found paralysis of motion and sensation of the left side, and incoordination of motion in walking, blindness of left eye, and nearly total deafness of left ear.

The board further stated that he had all the characteristic symptons of the sequelæ of sunstroke, etc.

While it is admitted by your committee that the proof filed by the beneficiary was not sufficient to give him title to pension at the Pension Bureau under the general law, your committee believe, however, that the evidence filed by him is sufficient to give him some relief by Congress, it being shown that the officer is suffering from paralysis of the left side, blindness of the left eye, etc.

An increase of his pension from $12 to $20 per month is therefore recommended, and the bill is reported back with the recommendation that it pass after the same shall have been amended as follows:

In line 6 strike out the words "a private."

In line 8 strike out the word "forty" and insert in lieu thereof the word "twenty."

O

ENOCH DODD.

JANUARY 20, 1903.—Committed to the Committee of the Whole House and ordered to be printed.

Mr. APLIN, from the Committee on Invalid Pensions, submitted the following

REPORT.

[To accompany H. R. 16272.]

The Committee on Invalid Pensions, to whom was referred the bill (H. R. 16272) granting an increase of pension to Enoch Dodd, submit the following report: .

This bill proposes to increase the pension of the beneficiary named therein from $12 to $30 per month.

Records of the War Department show that this soldier, now 69 years of age, served as a private in Company H, Seventh Connecticut Infantry, from September 5, 1861, to July 20, 1865, when honorably discharged.

He never applied for pension under the general law, but is now a pensioner under the act of June 27, 1890, at the maximum rating, namely, $12 per month, for total inability to earn a support by manual labor, the result of rheumatism and resulting disease of the heart.

When last examined, in April, 1891, the board of surgeons rated him $17 for heart disease and $8 for chronic rheumatism.

There has been filed with your committee the affidavit of Dr. E. H. Marsh, setting forth that he had been the family physician of the beneficiary for more than twelve years; that the beneficiary is now 71 years old; that he had been for years afflicted with chronic rheumatism and cardiac trouble; that the rheumatism produced so much soreness and stiffness of the muscles and other tissues of the shoulders that he has only a partial use of these joints; that he also has sciatica of both legs so that he can not stoop over, and can only raise the right foot just enough to clear the ground or floor, and that he is totally incapacitated for the performance of any manual labor or to do anything to earn a living.

Like testimony by Dr. Isaac B. Gallup has been filed with your committee.

Following precedents, this soldier having rendered nearly four years of service and now suffering from permanent disabilities of an extreme

nature, an increase of his pension from $12 to $24 per month is justified; hence the bill is reported back with the recommendation that it
pass after the same shall have been amended as follows:

In line 6 strike out the word "the" and insert in lieu thereof the
words "Company H."

In same line, before the word "Connecticut," insert the word "Regiment."

In line 7 strike out the word "thirty" and insert in lieu thereof the
word "twenty-four."

In line 8 strike out the words "under certificate" and all of lines 9
and 10.

O

JAMES H. DURHAM.

JANUARY 20, 1903.—Committed to the Committee of the Whole House and ordered
to be printed.

Mr. SULLOWAY, from the Committee on Invalid Pensions, submitted
the following

REPORT.

[To accompany H. R. 16534.]

The Committee on Invalid Pensions, to whom was referred the bill
(H. R. 16534) granting an increase of pension to James H. Durham,
submit the following report:

This bill proposes to increase Mr. Durham's pension from $12 to
$24 per month.

Mr. Durham is 81 years of age, and served as a private in the Twenty-
second Battery Indiana Light Artillery from November 14, 1863, to
May 28, 1865.

He is pensioned under the act of June 27, 1890, at $12 for total ina-
bility to earn a support by manual labor, the result of disease of heart
and spine and senile debility.

He never applied under the general law.

In his application for pension the soldier alleged that he rendered
two terms of service before his enlistment in the Twenty-second Indiana
Light Artillery, namely, as musician in Company B, Ninth Indiana
Volunteers, from April 19 to July 29, 1861, and as first lieutenant and
adjutant of the Thirty-third Indiana Volunteers from September 15,
1861, to October 14, 1862, when he resigned.

The soldier alleged in his statements filed with your committee that,
although severely wounded several times during the civil war, when
the wounds healed he was as good as ever and could not swear hard
enough to get a pension under the general law; that during the three
months' campaign in West Virginia in 1861 he performed secret and
extra hazardous duties as scout, etc.

He filed with the committee a statement of Gen. Morris Burnett as
to his acts as scout during the campaign in the early days of 1861, going
into the enemy's lines and reporting upon matters of importance; that
he exhibited tact, courage, and industry not unattended with great
hazard, from which he never flinched, and General Burnett further states

that he ought to be properly recognized for this service to the Government to which he was so loyal and brave.

When last examined, in November, 1891, the board of surgeons found his heart's action increased in force and frequency, pulse 104 when standing, three of the lower cervical vertebræ, with the first dorsal vertebra, inflamed, swollen, and exceedingly tender, a cicatrix of a saber wound of the left foot and a severe bayonet wound of the left leg, with a gunshot wound of the left foot, just above the instep, and the board of surgeons then rated him $6 for disease of heart, $6 for disease of spine, and $6 for the wounds.

In view of the beneficiary's great age, 81 years, and his service as testified to by General Burnett, your committee believes that the relief sought for in the bill might well be granted, and the bill is therefore reported back with the recommendation that it pass after the same shall have been amended as follows:

Strike out all of lines 6, 7, 8, and 9 and insert in lieu thereof the following:

of James H. Durham, late of Twenty-second Battery Indiana Volunteer Light Artillery, and pay him a pension at the rate of twenty-four dollars per month in lieu of that he is now receiving.

O

ISAAC J. NICHOLS.

JANUARY 20, 1903.—Committed to the Committee of the Whole House and ordered
to be printed.

Mr. HOLLIDAY, from the Committee on Invalid Pensions, submitted
the following

REPORT.

[To accompany H. R. 15186.]

The Committee on Invalid Pensions, to whom was referred the bill
(H. R. 15186) granting an increase of pension to Isaac J. Nichols, submit the following report:

This bill proposes to increase the pension of the officer named therein
from $12 to $30 per month.

Isaac J. Nichols, now 63 years of age, is shown by the records of
the War Department to have served as a private in Company F,
Ninety-seventh Pennsylvania Infantry, from September 23, 1861, to
March 28, 1865, when discharged by reason of promotion to first lieutenant of the same company and regiment, and that he served as such
first lieutenant until August 28, 1865, when honorably mustered out.

The records of the War Department further show that the beneficiary received a gunshot wound of the leg in battle at Bermuda
Hundred, Va., in May, 1864.

He is now a pensioner under the act of June 27, 1890, at $12 per
month, for total inability to earn a support by manual labor, the result
of rheumatism and disease of lungs.

When last examined, on April 12, 1899, the board of surgeons described
his condition as follows:

A pale, feeble man, much emaciated and showing the effects of serious illness to a
marked extent, with a severe cough. On examination we find dullness on percussion
from the apex to the base of left lung, with increased percussion resonance over the
middle of lung.

Auscultation reveals diminished respiratory murmur over the upper and lower
portion of left lung, blowing murmur over center, showing cavity size of an orange.
The claimant is so disabled from disease of lungs as to be incapacitated from doing
any manual labor, and is entitled to a rating of $30 per month.

The claimant also suffers from atrophy of muscles in both arms, with partial anchylosis of the left shoulder joint; unable to raise it to the level of shoulder, and restric-
tion of motion in right arm, with heart rapid and feeble; rate, $12.

This aged officer, who rendered nearly four years' service and who was wounded in battle, is now suffering from phthisis pulmonalis to such an extent that he is wholly disabled for any labor, besides being otherwise seriously disabled.

Following precedents, your committee believe that an increase of his pension to $24 per month is justified; hence the bill is reported back with the recommendation that it pass after the same shall have been amended as follows:

In line 6, before the word "Company," strike out the word "of" and insert in lieu thereof the words "first lieutenant."

In line 8 strike out the word "thirty" and insert in lieu thereof the word "twenty-four."

O

ORIN T. FALL.

JANUARY 20, 1903.—Committed to the Committee of the Whole House and ordered to be printed.

Mr. SULLOWAY, from the Committee on Invalid Pensions, submitted the following

REPORT.

[To accompany S. 6526.]

The Committee on Invalid Pensions, to whom was referred the bill (S. 6526) granting an increase of pension to Orin T. Fall, have examined the same and adopt the Senate report thereon and recommend that the bill do pass.

[Senate Report No. 2261, Fifty-seventh Congress, second session.]

The Committee on Pensions, to whom was referred the bill (S. 6526) granting an increase of pension to Orin T. Fall, have examined the same and report:

It is proposed by this bill to increase from $12 to $24 per month the pension of Orin T. Fall, of Farmington, N. H., late of Company D, First Regiment New Hampshire Volunteer Heavy Artillery, who served from August 29, 1864, to June 15, 1865, when he was honorably discharged.

Claimant is now receiving a pension of $12 per month under the act of June 27, 1890, for total disability, due to disease of liver, heart, and rectum and chronic rheumatism. He is now about 74 years of age and very badly broken down; in fact, almost helpless. He is more or less crippled by rheumatism, and suffers from paralysis, heart disease, nervous prostration, and impaired sight, the left eye being entirely blind. He is in such a feeble and debilitated condition that he stands greatly in need of the aid and attendance of another person, but having no means with which to employ such help is obliged to do without it. He lives alone in a small house worth about $200, which is his only possession. His only means of support is the pension he is now receiving. These facts are all substantiated by evidence filed with the bill.

Claimant's medical examination, made April 22, 1891, over eleven years ago, rated him $12 for rheumatism and resulting disease of heart, $8 for disease of rectum, and $10 for loss of right index finger and resulting affection of right hand and nervous system.

He is shown to be an intelligent and highly respected citizen of exemplary habits. Considering his faithful service, his advanced age, and deplorable condition and great poverty, your committee report the bill back favorably with a recommendation that it pass.

O

GRACE A. NEGLEY.

JANUARY 20, 1903.—Committed to the Committee of the Whole House and ordered
to be printed.

Mr. DEEMER, from the Committee on Invalid Pensions, submitted the
following

REPORT.

[To accompany H. R. 3504.]

The Committee on Invalid Pensions, to whom was referred the bill
(H. R. 3504) granting a pension to Grace Ashton Negley, submit the
following report:

This bill proposes to increase the pension of the beneficiary named
therein from $8 per month to $2,000 per annum.

It appears from the records of the War Department that James S.
Negley, the officer named in this bill, served as a sergeant in Company K,
First Pennsylvania Infantry, from December 8, 1846, to July 25, 1848,
when honorably discharged (war with Mexico); that he was appointed
brigadier-general of volunteers October 1, 1861, and accepted the
appointment March 4, 1862; that he was appointed major-general of
volunteers November 29, 1862, and accepted the appointment April 15,
1863, and that he was discharged the service upon tender of resignation on January 19, 1865.

Medical records of the War Department show that the officer was
granted leave of absence of thirty days in October, 1863, upon a surgeon's certificate showing him to be suffering severely from diarrhea.

He was a pensioner as a Mexican war survivor, at $8 per month,
from December 26, 1888. He died August 7, 1901, of diabetes and
carbuncle.

Grace A. Negley, the beneficiary named in this bill and now 55 years
of age, who married the officer on May 18, 1869, is now a pensioner
under the act of June 27, 1890, at $8 per month, upon proof that she
was the legal widow of this officer and that she was not in possession of
an actual net income exceeding $250, as provided in the act of May 9,
1900, the proof filed showing that she was only the owner of a house
and lots situated in Plainfield, N. J., of the value of $15,000, and
encumbered by mortgages to the amount of $13,338; that she had no
interest in any other property, either personal or real, except furniture

in said house of the value of about $1,000, and no income from any source.

From papers filed with your committee it appears that General Negley rendered conspicuous services during the civil war; that in 1868 he was elected as a Representative from the Twenty-second Congressional district of Pennsylvania; that he was again elected to the Forty-second Congress, reelected to the Forty-fourth, and again to the Forty-ninth Congress; that during the period of fifteen years he was one of the managers of the National Home for Volunteers, and was instrumental in establishing two of these Homes, etc.

The services of the husband of this beneficiary during the civil war are so well known that no special reference need be made thereto; so are his services while he was a member of this body.

In recognition of his gallant services to his country in two wars and in view of the destitute circumstances of his widow, your committee recommend that her pension be increased from $8 to $50 per month, and therefore report the bill back with the recommendation that it pass after the same shall have been amended as follows:

Strike out all of lines 6 and 7 and insert in lieu thereof the following:

of Grace A. Negley, widow of James S. Negley, late major-general, United States Volunteers, and pay her a pension at the rate of fifty dollars per month in lieu of that she is now receiving.

Amend the title so as to read: "A bill granting an increase of pension to Grace A. Negley."

O

NICHOLAS SMITH.

JANUARY 20, 1903.—Committed to the Committee of the Whole House and ordered to be printed.

Mr. HOLLIDAY, from the Committee on Invalid Pensions, submitted the following

REPORT.

[To accompany S. 5642.]

The Committee on Invalid Pensions, to whom was referred the bill (S. 5642) granting an increase of pension to Nicholas Smith, have examined the same and adopt the Senate report thereon and recommend that the bill do pass.

[Senate Report No. 2169, Fifty-seventh Congress, second session.]

The Committee on Pensions, to whom was referred the bill (S. 5642) granting an increase of pension to Nicholas Smith, have examined the same and report:

Nicholas Smith enlisted August 18, 1862, at Shullsburg, Wis., in Company H, Thirty-third Regiment Wisconsin Volunteer Infantry. He was promoted second lieutenant October 6, 1862; first lieutenant, May 11, 1863; captain, August 8, 1863, and was honorably discharged on tender of resignation, January 10, 1865. He is now receiving a pension of $12 per month under the act of June 27, 1890, for disease of digestive organs and debility.

Captain Smith never made claim for pension under the general law, but it appears from the evidence that he was twice sunstruck during the summer of 1864, which so seriously affected his health that he is unable to do manual labor. A medical examination made April 2, 1891, showed him to be suffering from headache, vertigo, indigestion, and impaired circulation, all results of sunstroke. A second medical examination, made July 15, 1891, rated him $12 for nervous prostration and results and $12 for indigestion, dyspepsia, and headaches.

Captain Smith is now 65 years of age. His present condition, physical and financial, has reached a point where he is comparatively helpless, and he can never expect again to enter upon the activities of life. Dr. Walter Kempster, of Milwaukee, Wis., his family physician, states that his disabilities are of such a nature as to unfit him for any labor, and he requires the services of some one to attend him during his attacks of pain, when he is confined to his bed, and that these attacks are becoming more frequent and less amenable to treatment, and he will never recover.

It is shown that Captain Smith is a man of unblemished reputation and high character and standing. Although he has refrained from making a claim under the general law, yet it would seem that his disabilities are of service origin. Considering his long and faithful service, his great poverty, and total disability, your committee report the bill back favorably with a recommendation that it pass.

O

ELIZA C. DEERY.

JANUARY 20, 1903.—Committed to the Committee of the Whole House and ordered to be printed.

Mr. DARRAGH, from the Committee on Invalid Pensions, submitted the following

REPORT.

[To accompany S. 3940.]

The Committee on Invalid Pensions, to whom was referred the bill (S. 3940) granting an increase of pension to Eliza C. Deery, have examined the same and adopt the Senate report thereon and recommend that the bill do pass.

[Senate Report No. 2379, Fifty-seventh Congress, second session.]

The Committee on Pensions, to whom was referred the bill (S. 3940) granting an increase of pension to Eliza C. Deery, have examined the same and report:

Eliza C. Deery, whose post-office address is Rice Lake, Wis., is the widow of James Deery, late first lieutenant Company K, Fifth Regiment Wisconsin Volunteer Infantry.

The military records show that James Deery enlisted July 26, 1861, as private in Company B, Sixth Wisconsin Infantry. He was appointed sergeant and transferred to Company K, Fifth Wisconsin Infantry, in January or February, 1862; promoted first lieutenant October 25, 1862, and honorably resigned March 12, 1863.

He died April 20, 1888, the cause of his death being chronic diarrhea. At the time of his death he was receiving a pension of $8 per month for chronic diarrhea and gunshot wound of left leg.

Eliza C. Deery is now receiving a pension under the general law of $12 per month, it having been determined that soldier's fatal disease was contracted when he held the rank of sergeant. Mrs. Deery is 75 years of age. She is an invalid and crippled and is wholly unable to perform any manual labor, and is wholly without property or means of support except her pension. These facts are substantiated by evidence filed with the bill. She was married to the soldier May 10, 1864. Her claim was made special at the Bureau on account of her destitution.

The pension which the claimant is receiving is the pension which the general law provides for the widow of a private or noncommissioned officer. Soldier was subsequently promoted first lieutenant and held that rank until his discharge. Considering claimant's great age, her crippled condition, and absolute poverty, your committee are of opinion that her pension should be increased to the rate which the general law provides for the widow of a first lieutenant.

The bill is therefore reported back favorably with the recommendation that it pass.

O

LEROY ROBERTS.

JANUARY 20, 1903.—Committed to the Committee of the Whole House and ordered to be printed.

Mr. MIERS, from the Committee on Invalid Pensions, submitted the following

REPORT.

[To accompany S. 3773.]

The Committee on Invalid Pensions, to whom was referred the bill (S. 3773) granting an increase of pension to Leroy Roberts, have examined the same and adopt the Senate report thereon and recommend that the bill do pass.

[Senate Report No. 2250, Fifty-seventh Congress, second session.]

The Committee on Pensions, to whom was referred the bill (S. 3773) granting an increase of pension to Leroy Roberts, have examined the same and report:

This bill proposes to increase from $6 to $17 per month the pension of Leroy Roberts, late of Company F, Thirty-seventh Regiment Indiana Volunteer Infantry.

Soldier enlisted September 18, 1861, and was discharged October 27, 1864. The hospital record shows that he was treated from November 22 to 27, 1861, for catarrh. He was pensioned under the general law January 5, 1892, for catarrh, at $4 per month from September 22, 1890, which was increased to $6 per month under the act of March 2, 1895. He made claim for increase April 9, 1898, which was rejected May 18, 1901, on the ground that his rate was adequate for his pensioned disability.

On September 22, 1890, he made claim for additional disabilities, alleging that he contracted rheumatism about January, 1863, and chronic diarrhea, resulting in disease of rectum, stomach, liver, and spleen, in January, 1862. This claim was rejected April 26, 1901, because of his inability after special examination to furnish satisfactory evidence of existence at discharge and continuance. The evidence on file shows that claimant contracted rheumatism and chronic diarrhea and results in the service. Upon this point the evidence of several comrades and of the hospital steward who assisted in his treatment is conclusive.

No objection to this evidence is made by the Pension Bureau, and, as a fact, the service origin of rheumatism and chronic diarrhea and results is conceded as established. The Bureau, however, holds that the evidence is insufficient to satisfactorily show existence at discharge and continuance, but it is the best the claimant can furnish, and, giving it fair and sympathetic consideration, its weight is altogether in favor of the claimant. There is some little medical evidence of treatment within a few years after discharge, and several neighbors testified that he has always complained of rheumatism, chronic diarrhea, piles, and stomach and liver trouble. In more recent years the existence of his disabilities is shown by medical evidence.

Claimant has always been an active, energetic, and ambitious man, and would keep going whether able or not. Some of the physicians who gave him treatment during the years since discharge are dead. Up to within a few years ago he was prosperous in business and did not think about a pension and did not seek to make his disabilities generally known. He has met with reverses and has now no occupation and is in much need of assistance.

Claimant is 58 years of age, and a special examiner of the Bureau reported that he had the appearance of a man in poor health. His last medical examination, made at Osgood, Ind., March 15, 1899, rated him $12 for catarrh and disease of lungs, $6 for rheumatism, and $4 for piles.

After careful consideration of all the evidence your committee are of opinion that it should be accepted as sufficient to show that claimant's disabilities are the result of his military service, and therefore report the bill back favorably with a recommendation that it pass.

O

GEORGE A. KING.

JANUARY 20, 1903.—Committed to the Committee of the Whole House and ordered
to be printed.

Mr. DARRAGH, from the Committee on Invalid Pensions, submitted
the following

REPORT.

[To accompany S. 5355.]

The Committee on Invalid Pensions, to whom was referred the bill
(S. 5355) granting an increase of pension to George A. King, have
examined the same and adopt the Senate report thereon and recommend that the bill do pass.

[Senate Report No. 2155, Fifty-seventh Congress, second session.]

The Committee on Pensions, to whom was referred the bill (S. 5355) granting an
increase of pension to George A. King, have examined the same and report:

This bill proposes to increase from $12 to $24 per month the pension of George A.
King, of Steele, N. Dak., late of the Eighteenth Independent Battery, Ohio Volunteer Light Artillery.

Soldier enlisted July 31, 1862, and was honorably discharged June 29, 1865. He
is now receiving a pension of $12 per month, under the act of June 27, 1890, for total
inability to earn a support by manual labor, due to rheumatism, disease of heart, and
chronic diarrhea. On April 20, 1882, he made claim under the general law, alleging
that he contracted measles about January, 1863, resulting in bronchitis and disease
of lungs. Said claim was rejected July 31, 1883, on the ground that he was not
ratably disabled by causes alleged.

Claimant is 58 years of age. A medical examination made September 7, 1898,
rated him $12 for disease of heart, $16 for chronic diarrhea, and $12 for general
debility. The examining surgeons stated:

"He looks at least 70; his face is very full; his eyes red; his hair scant and white;
his hand trembles and his general appearance that of an old man. His hands show
no sign of recent manual labor."

His last medical examination, made November 9, 1901, is as follows:

"Rheumatism: There is nothing apparent on examination; there is no enlargement of joints and no wasting of muscles. Claimant can not properly elevate his
arms above his head, otherwise there is no limitation of motion.

"Heart—boundaries: Upper border of fourth rib one-half inch to left of left nipple
line, midsternal line. Apex beat is not visible nor palpable. Upon auscultation a
slight systolic murmur is heard over the apex. There is slight cyanosis and marked
dyspnœa on exertion; no œdema.

"Chronic diarrhea: Claimant states that he is not troubled with diarrhea since last
summer, when he suffered from appendicitis; no sign of it on examination.

"General debility: Claimant is much stooped, hair perfectly white, and looks to be 75 years old. Skin flabby, and hands show no signs of manual labor. Catarrh of throat present. Teeth are in bad condition, many having been lost. Arcus senilis appearing on both eyes."

Evidence filed with the bill shows that claimant has a small house of the value of $400, which is a shelter and nothing more. His income is practically nothing but his pension.

In view of his faithful service of three years, his total disability, and great poverty, your committee report the bill back favorably, with a recommendation that it pass.

O

AGRICULTURAL APPROPRIATION BILL.

January 20, 1903.—Committed to the Committee of the Whole House on the state of the Union and ordered to be printed.

Mr. Wadsworth, from the Committee on Agriculture, submitted the following

REPORT.

[To accompany H. R. 16910.]

The Committee on Agriculture, having had under consideration the estimates of appropriations required for the Department of Agriculture for the fiscal year ending June 30, 1904, respectfully submit the accompanying bill (H. R. 16910) and report as follows:

The total amount appropriated by this bill for the Department of Agriculture is $5,238,860, and the amount carried by the bill for the current fiscal year is $5,208,960, showing a net increase of $29,900.

Though the amount hereby appropriated is about $400,000 less than the estimates, your committee, taking into consideration the very ample and generous increases allowed for the current year, deem the sums appropriated herein ample to carry on successfully and progressively the work of the Department.

The appropriation for the Department of Agriculture in 1897–98 was $3,182,902. The amount carried by this bill, as stated above, is $5,238,860, an increase (in six years) of $2,055,958.

The following table shows the appropriations made for the current fiscal year and also those made by this bill for the coming fiscal year for the bureaus, divisions, and sections of the Department of Agriculture and indicates specifically the increases and decreases contemplated by this bill.

Bureau or division.	Appropriations for current fiscal year.	Appropriations by this bill (1903–4).	Increase.	Decrease.
Office of Secretary	$74,410	$74,410	....	$200
Weather Bureau	1,248,760	1,248,560	....	
Animal Industry	1,247,180	1,287,380	$40,200	....
Plant Industry	612,730	612,730	....	....
Forestry	291,860	291,860	....	....
Chemistry	75,700	85,300	11,600	....
Soils	169,680	172,480	2,800	....
Entomology	57,450	77,450	a20,000	....

a An apparent increase of $20,000, but $10,000 of this was carried last year as a separate item for silk investigations. The actual increase for entomology is, therefore, only $10,000.

Bureau or division.	Appropriations for current fiscal year.	Appropriations by this bill (1903–4).	Increase.	Decrease.
Biology	$45,850	$45,850		
Accounts	24,100	24,100		
Publications	228,820	229,820	$500	
Statistics	141,160	141,160		
Foreign Markets	15,000	15,000		
Library	18,000	18,000		
Museum	2,260	2,260		
Contingent	87,000	87,000		
Experiment Stations	796,000	801,000	5,000	
Nutrition	20,000	20,000		
Irrigation	65,000	25,000		$40,000
Public Roads	80,000	80,000		
Silk	10,000	(a)		10,000
Total	5,208,960	5,288,860	80.100	50,200

a Transferred to entomology; see above.

Total net increase, $29,900.

Two increases in salaries have been allowed, $200 to the assistant chief of the Biochemic division of the Bureau of Animal Industry and $500 to the chief of the Division of Publications. Both of these cases were carefully looked into by the committee and were considered only fair and just on account of long and efficient service.

Two additional places have been provided for, viz: An assistant chief of Weather Bureau, and a chief clerk, at $1,600, for the Bureau of Chemistry.

The creation of the office of assistant chief of Weather Bureau does not increase the salary list of that Bureau; in fact, the salary list shows a reduction of $200. It must be remembered that the weather service covers an area of 3,000 miles in every direction. It now comprises 190 observatories, with a flood-warning service and a marine-warning service, besides the daily forecast and climate work. It has 1,400 employees, and its work continues every day in the year; and it is a physical impossibility for one man to remain constantly on duty.

A chief clerk is allowed to the Bureau of Chemistry because of the increase of the work of that Bureau, and particularly of its correspondence. A large part of the clerical work of the Bureau has heretofore been performed personally by the head of the Bureau and his scientific aids; which work, the committee believes, could be more economically and advantageously performed by a competent chief clerk.

In the rearrangement of the paragraphs covering the lump sums appropriated for the Weather Bureau no new powers whatever have been delegated to the Secretary of Agriculture or the chief of that Bureau. The old paragraphs were somewhat in the nature of "patchwork," and the new arrangement simplifies and makes them briefer. The apparent increase in the salary roll of the Weather Bureau is caused by the transfer from the different lump-sum appropriations of all labor employed in the District of Columbia (except the employees of the printing establishment), and causes no increase in the net total appropriation for the Weather Bureau.

An increase of $40,000 has been allowed to the Bureau of Animal Industry, partially to enable the Secretary to enlarge the quarantine station at Athenia, N. J., and to purchase land adjacent to the harbor for a quarantine station at Boston, and to carry out the provisions of the oleomargarine act in so far as it relates to process, renovated, and adulterated butter.

The increase of $10,000 allowed the Bureau of Chemistry is recommended by the committee to enable that Bureau to make further experiments and researches into the manufacture of table sirup from cane.

The increase of $10,000 allowed to the Division of Entomology is recommended to enable the Department to make further and more extended investigations into the cotton-boll weevil and worm, with a view to ascertaining the best methods for their extermination. The rapid spread of this pest threatens to destroy the cotton-raising industry of Texas and all contiguous States, and should it once cross the Mississippi River the loss to the great cotton industry of the South will be incalculable.

Five hundred dollars has been added to the appropriation for "Agricultural experiment stations" to enable the Secretary of Agriculture to report upon the organization and progress of farmer's institutes in the several States and Territories and upon similar organizations in foreign countries, with the view of making more effective the dissemination of the results of the work of the Department of Agriculture and of the agricultural experiment stations.

The amount appropriated by this bill for "Irrigation investigations" is $25,000, as against $65,000 carried in the appropriation for the current fiscal year.

Upon full and careful consideration your committee reached the conclusion that the appropriation heretofore made for this specific purpose might be reduced without detriment to the public interest, and has therefore recommended the sum of $25,000 for the ensuing year.

In recommending this reduction the committee does not wish to be understood as questioning the value of the work that has heretofore been done by the Department along these lines. On the contrary, the committee is of the opinion that this work has been so thoroughly and well done as to render unnecessary a continuation of the large appropriation heretofore made for its prosecution.

The view of your committee is that the full duty of the Federal Government will be performed if it maintains a small staff of trained experts on irrigation, who shall keep abreast of all the developments relating to this subject, compile and publish from time to time such information as they may acquire and the interests of the people may demand, and offer suggestions and advice in response to individual requests. It would seem that $25,000 annually should be ample for this purpose, and that amount is accordingly recommended.

O

CONSIDERATION OF H. R. 15520.

JANUARY 20, 1903.—Ordered to be printed.

Mr. DALZELL, from the Committee on Rules, submitted the following

REPORT.

[To accompany H. Res. No. 393.]

The Committee on Rules, to whom was referred the resolution of the House No. 393, have had the same under consideration and report the same herewith, with an amendment inserting, in line 5, after the words "and, after," the words "not more than," and with the recommendation that as amended the resolution be agreed to.

O

WEDEN O'NEAL.

January 21, 1903.—Committed to the Committee of the Whole House and ordered
to be printed.

Mr. Gibson, from the Committee on Invalid Pensions, submitted the
following

REPORT.

[To accompany H. R. 12316.]

The Committee on Invalid Pensions, to whom was referred the bill
(H. R. 12316) granting an increase of pension to Weden O'Neal, submit the following report:

This bill proposes to increase the pension of the officer named therein
from $8 to $75 per month.

This officer, now 64 years of age, served as lieutenant-colonel and
colonel of the Fifty-fifth Kentucky Volunteers from December 27,
1864, to September 19, 1865, when honorably discharged.

He is now pensioned under the act of June 27, 1890, at $8 per month
on account of disability arising from disease of rectum, lumbago, disease of heart, and senile debility.

He filed a claim to pension under the general law, basing the same
upon fistula in ano, rheumatism, and neuralgia, and filed the testimony
of the second lieutenant of Company F of his regiment to the effect
that some time in April or May, 1865, he became afflicted with fistula
or piles, he having been compelled to perform great service on horse-
back, being in the saddle a greater portion of the time, undergoing
great hardships in the effort to capture the guerrilla bands that infested
the counties of northern Kentucky at the time; that in consequence of
that disease he was compelled to use extra blanket pads on his saddle
and suffered great pain therefrom, and that it was a fact well known
among the members of several companies of the regiment that he had
become diseased with fistula from this continuous and hard riding;
also testimony showing that he suffered from fistula or piles since his
discharge from the service.

Medical testimony also filed by the beneficiary shows that he is now,
and has been for the last four years, suffering from paralysis agitans
and softening of the brain; that he is even unable to dress himself
without the assistance of others; that his malady grows steadily worse,

and that there is no prospect that he will ever be able to perform labor, and that he is wholly destitute.

When last examined, on July 25, 1900, the board of surgeons stated as follows:

This claimant is very feeble from old age. He is as old at 61 as a man of 85.

His claim under the general law was rejected in January, 1903, upon the ground of no record of treatment for the disabilities in the service or medical evidence of treatment in the service or at discharge, and claimant's apparent inability to furnish satisfactory competent evidence to show the origin of his disabilities in the service and ever since.

Your committee is fully satisfied that the officer incurred a fistula in ano while in the service, as shown by the testimony filed in the Pension Bureau, and inasmuch as he is shown by medical testimony filed in the Pension Bureau to be suffering from softening of the brain and paralysis agitans to such an extent as to require the periodical aid and attendance of another person, an increase of his pension to $30 per month is warranted under the action taken by the House on June 16, 1902, and the bill is therefore reported back with the recommendation that it pass after the same shall have been amended as follows:

In line 8 strike out the word "seventy-five" and insert in lieu thereof the word "thirty."

O

WESLEY S. POTTER.

JANUARY 21, 1908.—Committed to the Committee of the Whole House and ordered
to be printed.

Mr. SULLOWAY, from the Committee on Invalid Pensions, submitted
the following

REPORT.

[To accompany S. 1978.]

The Committee on Invalid Pensions, to whom was referred the bill
(S. 1978) granting an increase of pension to Wesley S. Potter, have
examined the same and adopt the Senate report thereon and recommend that the bill do pass.

[Senate Report No. 2154, Fifty-seventh Congress, second session.]

The Committee on Pensions, to whom was referred the bill (S.1978) granting a
pension to Wesley S. Potter, have examined the same and report:

This bill proposes to increase from $17 to $30 per month the pension of Wesley S.
Potter, late captain Company D, Thirty-sixth Regiment Wisconsin Volunteer
Infantry.

The military records show that Wesley S. Potter enlisted in the First Wisconsin
Cavalry January 4, 1864, and was honorably discharged April 10, 1864, to accept
promotion as first lieutenant Company D, Thirty-sixth Wisconsin Infantry. He was
mustered in as first lieutenant Company D, Thirty-sixth Wisconsin Infantry, April
12, 1864; was promoted captain December 20, 1864, and honorably discharged May
25, 1865.

Captain Potter was pensioned under the general law August 30, 1890, for disease
of back and right hip (rheumatism) at $5 per month from discharge and $9 per
month from April 16, 1890, which was increased to $17 per month September 16,
1891, for disease of back and right hip (rheumatism) and resulting disease of heart.

He made claim for increase May 11, 1900, alleging pensioned disabilities and also
that on account of lameness from rheumatism he slipped and fell on the floor of the
United States court-house at Sioux Falls, S. Dak., October 20, 1898, and sustained a
fracture of the left hip. This claim was rejected June 25, 1901, as noted on the
official records, as follows:

"Disease of back and right hip (rheumatism) and resulting disease of heart,
seventeen-eighteenths, no increase. Condition partly due to other than causes for
which pensioned."

Captain Potter is 68 years of age. His last medical examination, made January 2,
1901, shows him to be totally disabled for manual labor by reason of rheumatism
and resulting disease of heart and hip and impaired vision and entitled to $30 per

month. The examining board give it as their opinion that the fall that injured claimant's hip was likely due to lameness and clumsiness caused by rheumatism. One of the members of the board saw claimant professionally at the time, and was cognizant of the circumstances. He states that claimant was walking along the smooth tiled floor of the court-house in Sioux Falls, when he slipped and fell, fracturing the thigh bone.

Evidence filed with this committee shows that Captain Potter is now so debilitated that he seldom leaves his house, and when he walks a block or two with the aid of a cane is completely used up, and that he is very lame and helpless and has to be helped very often in dressing and undressing. It is also shown that his sole means of support is the pension he is now receiving.

It seems only reasonable to attribute claimant's total disability to the diseases he contracted in service and line of duty. Your committee are inclined to this view of his case and are of opinion that he is entitled to the general-law rate for total incapacity for manual labor.

The bill is therefore reported back favorably with a recommendation that it pass.

O

JOHN J. REES.

JANUARY 21, 1903.—Committed to the Committee of the Whole House and ordered
to be printed.

Mr. SULLOWAY, from the Committee on Invalid Pensions, submitted
the following

REPORT.

[To accompany S. 4412.]

The Committee on Invalid Pensions, to whom was referred the bill
(S. 4412) granting an increase of pension to John J. Rees, have examined
the same and adopt the Senate report thereon and recommend that the
bill do pass.

[Senate Report No. 2156, Fifty-seventh Congress, second session.]

The Committee on Pensions, to whom was referred the bill (S. 4412) granting an
increase of pension to John J. Rees, have examined the same and report:

This bill proposes to increase from $17 to $24 per month the pension of John J.
Rees, of Powell, S. Dak., late of Company F, Seventh Regiment Ohio Volunteer
Infantry.

Soldier enlisted April 24, 1861, and was discharged March 4, 1863, for hæmoptysis
(hemorrhage from lungs). He was pensioned under the general law March 23, 1891,
for disease of liver of service origin, at $4 per month from September 4, 1889, which
was increased to $12 per month April 19, 1893, and to $17 per month September 15,
1897.

Claimant is 63 years of age, and the evidence on file indicates that he is wholly
incapacitated for manual labor. He made claim for increase April 21, 1900, which
was rejected March 22, 1901, on the ground that his rate was commensurate with the
degree of disability from pensioned cause.

Claimant's last medical examination, made September 26, 1900, rates him $30 for
disease of liver. A prior medical examination, made September 15, 1897, showed
that he was totally disabled for manual labor, and rated him $17 for disease of liver,
$8 for disease of heart, and $10 for deafness.

Another medical examination, made November 10, 1893, reported him as totally
and permanently incapacitated for manual labor by reason of disease of liver and
results.

Claimant owns no real estate and but little personal property. His income is
limited to the pension he is now receiving. His evidence and medical examinations
fairly show him to be entitled to an increase of his pension, and your committee
recommend the passage of the bill, which will give him the next higher rate provided by the general law.

O

HENRY E. SPRING.

JANUARY 21, 1903.—Committed to the Committee of the Whole House and ordered to be printed.

Mr. NORTON, from the committee on Invalid Pensions, submitted the following

REPORT.

[To accompany S. 5412.]

The Committee on Invalid Pensions, to whom was referred the bill (S. 5412) granting an increase of pension to Henry E. Spring, have examined the same and adopt the Senate report thereon and recommend that the bill do pass.

[Senate Report No. 2330, Fifty-seventh Congress, second session.]

The Committee on Pensions, to whom was referred the bill (S. 5412) granting an increase of pension to Henry E. Spring, have examined the same and report:

This bill proposes to increase from $17 to $30 per month the pension of Henry E. Spring, late of Company K, Eighth Regiment Ohio Volunteer Infantry.

Soldier enlisted in Company K, Eighth Ohio Infantry, April 27, 1861, and was discharged July 13, 1864. He again enlisted April 13, 1865, in Company B, One hundred and ninety-eighth Ohio Infantry, and was discharged May 8, 1865. He was wounded in left leg or ankle in battle at Gettysburg, Pa., July 3, 1863, and was again wounded in left hand in battle at the Wilderness, Virginia, May 6, 1864. The hospital records show that he was treated for gunshot wound of left leg, gunshot wound of left hand, intermittent fever, and neuralgia.

Claimant is now pensioned at $17 per month for prolapsus ani, result of piles, and gunshot wound of left ankle. His former rates were $2 from discharge; $8 from February 12, 1881; $12 from September 3, 1884, and $16 from May 24, 1890. His present rate of $17 dates from November 13, 1895. He also claims under the general law for additional disabilities—rheumatism, chronic diarrhea, neuralgia, and double rupture.

His claim for rheumatism and chronic diarrhea was rejected May 29, 1900, on the ground of no record or other satisfactory evidence of service origin and continuance; his claim for neuralgia was rejected on the ground that a ratable disability from that cause was not shown to exist, and his claim for double rupture was rejected on the ground that his own statements show that that disability did not originate in service, but occurred after his discharge.

Claimant, who is 62 years of age, lives in Paulding, Ohio. He has lived there since 1868, and the evidence of his neighbors shows that during this period he has suffered from rheumatism, at first not so marked, but increasing in severity with

2 HENRY E. SPRING.

succeeding years until he is now badly crippled and deformed and totally incapacitated for manual labor. His captain and one comrade testified that he was sick at
Romney, W. Va., in the winter of 1861 and 1862, and that his trouble was rheumatism.

Their evidence is somewhat lacking in positiveness, but it seems to indicate that
claimant's rheumatism dates from that time and was due to the hardships and
exposure which the command then underwent. There is also evidence of members
of his family that he complained of rheumatism when he returned home after his
discharge.

A few comrades testified that claimant contracted chronic diarrhea in service, but
there is no good evidence of the continuance of this disability.

Claimant's last medical examination, made April 12, 1899, shows that he is totally
disabled for manual labor by reason of prolapsus ani, gunshot wound of left ankle,
chronic diarrhea, rheumatism, and resulting disease of heart and curvature of spine.
He was rated $8 for prolapsus ani, $4 for gunshot wound of left ankle, $6 for chronic
diarrhea, and $30 for rheumatism and disease of heart and curvature of spine.

The examining surgeons describe claimant as a very much bowed and bent man,
his head and neck projecting almost at right angle with trunk, all muscles small and
soft, and cervical and dorsal vertebræ arched forward until the body is shortened
7 inches, as shown by actual measurement. They also state that the curvature of
spine is probably due to rheumatism and was superinduced by his position when
suffering.

Accompanying the bill is much evidence showing that claimant is totally disabled
for manual labor and is to a large extent physically dependent on his wife. It is
also shown that his resources are very limited; that what little property he has is
heavily encumbered with mortgages, and that his income is practically his pension
alone.

The evidence in the case tends strongly to show that claimant's deplorable condition is the result of his military service, and considering his excellent army record
of over three years, his great disability and need, your committee are of opinion that
he should be given the benefit of all doubts in his case, and therefore report the bill
back favorably with a recommendation that it pass.

O

DAVID C. MORGAN.

JANUARY 21, 1903.—Committed to the Committee of the Whole House and ordered
to be printed.

Mr. SULLOWAY, from the Committee on Invalid Pensions, submitted
the following

REPORT.

[To accompany S. 6543.]

The Committee on Invalid Pensions, to whom was referred the bill
(S. 6543) granting an increase of pension to David C. Morgan, have
examined the same and adopt the Senate report thereon and recommend that the bill do pass.

[Senate Report No. 2271, Fifty-seventh Congress, second session.]

The Committee on Pensions, to whom was referred the bill (S. 6543) granting an
increase of pension to David C. Morgan, have examined the same and report:

This bill proposes to increase from $12 to $30 per month the pension of David C.
Morgan, late of Company C, Second Regiment Minnesota Volunteer Infantry.

The military records show that David C. Morgan enlisted June 29, 1861, and was
honorably discharged June 28, 1864. The files of the Pension Bureau show that he
is now pensioned at $12 per month under the act of June 27, 1890, for total disability,
due to gunshot wound of left leg and disease of lungs and eyes. He was formerly
pensioned under the general law at $8 per month for disease of lungs and gunshot
wound of left leg received in battle at Chickamauga, Ga., September 20, 1863.

The evidence on file shows that claimant is now in a hopeless and helpless condition. He is totally blind, and suffers from various ills, such as disease of lungs, rheumatism, and disease of mastoid bones, and requires the regular aid and attendance of
one or more persons constantly. He is continuously confined to his bed, and is in
every respect totally helpless. These facts are substantiated by his medical examination and by the evidence of his attending physician.

It is also shown that claimant is desperately poor. He has no property and no
means of support except his pension, and has been compelled to accept charitable
contributions from his neighbors.

Claimant served honorably for three years. He was a good soldier, and in his
dire distress he appeals to Congress for relief, and your committee, impressed with
his sufferings and great need, are of opinion that he is worthy of an increase of his
pension.

The bill is reported back favorably with a recommendation that it pass.

O

SYDDA B. ARNOLD.

JANUARY 21, 1903.—Committed to the Committee of the Whole House and ordered
to be printed.

Mr. LOUDENSLAGER, from the Committee on Pensions, submitted the
following

REPORT.

[To accompany S. 1131.]

The Committee on Pensions, to whom was referred the bill (S. 1131)
granting an increase of pension to Sydda B. Arnold, have considered
the same and respectfully report as follows:

The bill is accompanied by Senate Report 2220, this session, and
from the same the following statement of facts is taken:

This bill proposes to increase from $30 to $50 per month the pension of Sydda
B. Arnold, widow of Abraham K. Arnold, late brigadier-general, U. S. Volunteers.

A statement of this officer's service, furnished by the War Department, is as follows:

WAR DEPARTMENT, ADJUTANT-GENERAL'S OFFICE,
Washington, December 3, 1902.

*Statement of the military service of the late Abraham K. Arnold, of the U. S. Army,
compiled from the records of this office.*

He was appointed cadet at the U. S. Military Academy July 1, 1854; appointed
brevet second lieutenant, Second Cavalry, July 1, 1859; appointed second lieutenant
June 28, 1860; promoted to be first lieutenant, Fifth Cavalry, April 6, 1861; promoted
to be captain, Fifth Cavalry, July 17, 1862; promoted to be major, Sixth Cavalry,
June 22, 1869; promoted to be lieutenant-colonel First Cavalry June 11, 1866; promoted to be colonel Eighth Cavalry February 7, 1891; transferred to First Cavalry
April 22, 1891; transferred to Eighth Cavalry February 23, 1891; retired (under act
of June 30, 1882, 64 years old) March 24, 1901; accepted appointment as brigadier-
general of volunteers May 11, 1898; honorably discharged as brigadier-general of
volunteers only May 12, 1899; died November 23, 1901.

Service.—He was on duty at Carlisle Barracks, Pa., from September, 30, 1859, to
October 30, 1860; with regiment in Texas to April, 1861; in the Shenandoah Valley,
Virginia, to August, 1861; in the defense of Washington to March 10, 1862; in the
field in Virginia in the Army of the Potomac to June 27, 1862; absent sick on account
of wounds to September 19, 1862; on recruiting service to September, 1863; commanding regiment in the Army of the Potomac to August 13, 1864; on duty at the
Military Academy as an instructor from August 23, 1864, to August 28, 1869; on leave
to February, 1870; with regiment on frontier duty in Texas to April, 1871, and in
Kansas to September, 1872; on disbursing duty in the Bureau of Refugees, Freedmen,
and Abandoned Lands, and settling his accounts to November 5, 1878; on leave to

March 5, 1879; with regiment in Arizona to November 29, 1880; acting inspector-general, Department of Arizona, to August 15, 1884, and acting assistant adjutant-general of troops in the field operating against hostile Indians from September 6 to November 10, 1881; with regiment in New Mexico to May 16, 1885; on leave to July 15, 1885; on duty at the Infantry and Cavalry School and senior instructor of military arts at the same school to August 29, 1887; with regiment in Montana to October 7, 1889; on leave to January 8, 1890; with regiment in Montana to April 20, 1892; in Arizona (on leave June 1 to September 24, 1892) to May, 1895; at Fort Riley, Kans. (on sick leave September 8 to 29, 1896), to April, 1898; Jacksonville, Fla., to October, 1898; at Huntsville, Ala., to January, 1899; at Habana, Cuba, to April, 1899; commanding regiment at Fort Meade, S. Dak., to August, 1900; sick in quarters July 24 to August 7, 1900, and on sick leave from August 8 to October 7, 1900; on leave October 8, 1900, to February 7, 1901; awaiting retirement to March 24, 1901. He died November 23, 1901, at Cold Spring on the Hudson, N. Y., and the cause of death is reported to have been "heart failure, due to chronic catarrhal gastritis, with chronic diffuse nephritis existing as a complication."

H. C. CORBIN,
Adjutant-General, Major-General, U. S. Army.

The CHAIRMAN OF THE COMMITTEE ON PENSIONS,
United States Senate.

Mrs. Arnold is now receiving a general-law pension of $30 per month, it having been established that her husband's death was due to diseases contracted while he was serving as brigadier-general, U. S. Volunteers. She is about 56 years of age, and was married to the officer October 16, 1866. She is in dependent circumstances, having no means of support except her pension.

General Arnold served in the U. S. Army for forty-seven years. He participated in the war of the rebellion as well as in the war with Spain, and also took part in several expeditions against hostile Indians in the West.

Mrs. Arnold has lived most of her life on the Indian frontier and is a good specimen of the rifle-loading woman who helped her husband in his many campaigns. In the light of numerous precedents for increasing pension in cases of this character, your committee report the bill back favorably with a recommendation that it pass.

In view of the above statement of facts your committee concur in the belief that a substantial increase of the pension is fully justified, and the bill is therefore returned with the recommendation that it be passed.

O

OLIVER P. HELTON.

JANUARY 21, 1903.—Committed to the Committee of the Whole House and ordered to be printed.

Mr. LOUDENSLAGER, from the Committee on Pensions, submitted the following

REPORT.

[To accompany S. 3607.]

The Committee on Pensions, to whom was referred the bill (S. 3607) granting an increase of pension to Oliver P. Helton, have considered the same and respectfully report as follows:

The bill is accompanied by Senate Report No. 2196, this session, and the same fully setting forth the facts is adopted by your committee as their report, and the bill is returned with a favorable recommendation. The Senate report on the bill is as follows:

Oliver P. Helton served during the war with Mexico from May 4, 1847, to October 17, 1848, in Company G, First Regiment Illinois Volunteer Infantry. He is now receiving a pension of $12 per month under the general laws for injury to breast and back and resulting disease of lungs and kidneys. He made claim for increase August 4, 1898, which was rejected December 13, 1898, on the ground that his rate was commensurate with the disability from pensioned causes.

Claimant is 76 years of age. It is shown in evidence that he is greatly disabled by injury of breast and back and chronic rheumatism and that he is almost totally blind, the sight of left eye being completely lost and the sight of right eye very much impaired. He is so disabled by rheumatism as to be compelled to walk with crutches. It is further shown that he is in destitute circumstances, without property or income, except his pension, and with an aged and helpless wife to support.

There are numerous precedents for increasing the pension of the aged, destitute, and helpless veterans of the Mexican war, and the facts stated above bring this case fully within such precedents.

O

MARY B. HEDDLESON.

JANUARY 21, 1903.—Committed to the Committee of the Whole House and ordered
to be printed.

Mr. LOUDENSLAGER, from the Committee on Pensions, submitted the
following

REPORT.

[To accompany S. 4332.]

The Committee on Pensions, to whom was referred the bill (S. 4332)
granting an increase of pension to Mary B. Heddleson, beg leave to
submit the following report and recommend that said bill do pass
without amendment.

Said bill is accompanied by Senate Report No. 2347, this session, and
the same setting forth all the facts is adopted by your committee as
their report, as follows:

Mary B. Heddleson is the widow of John M. Heddleson, who served in the war
with Mexico from September 28, 1847, to February 12, 1848, as second lieutenant
Company B, Third Regiment Kentucky Volunteer Infantry.

Soldier died August 26, 1897, and his widow, the claimant under this bill, is now
receiving the pension of $8 per month provided by the Mexican war service act of
January 29, 1887.

Mrs. Heddleson is over 77 years of age, and it appears in evidence that she is
almost blind and very much crippled from rheumatism, depriving her of her power
of locomotion and necessitating the constant attention of another person. It also
appears that she is destitute and without property or income except her pension.

There are numerous precedents for increasing pension in cases of this character, in
view of which your committee report the bill back favorably with a recommendation that it pass.

O

JOEL C. SHEPHERD.

JANUARY 21, 1903.—Committed to the Committee of the Whole House and ordered to be printed.

Mr. LOUDENSLAGER, from the Committee on Pensions, submitted the following

REPORT.

[To accompany S. 5835.]

The Committee on Pensions, to whom was referred the bill (S. 5835) granting an increase of pension to Joel C. Shepherd, have considered the same and respectfully report as follows:

Said bill is accompanied by Senate Report No. 2183, this session, and from the same the following facts are taken:

Joel C. Shepherd, whose post-office address is Windsor, Mo., served during the Mexican war in Company D, Sixth Regiment United States Infantry, from March 1, 1848, to July 18, 1848. He is now receiving the pension of $12 per month provided by the acts of January 29, 1887, and January 5, 1893, for the totally disabled and destitute survivors of the Mexican war.

Claimant is 83 years of age, and evidence on file shows that he is totally disabled by reason of rheumatism and the infirmities of old age. He has a little property worth less than $500, but he is dependent on his pension for the support of himself and his aged wife, who is unable to render him any assistance.

In view of the foregoing your committee believe that the case is a proper one for the allowance of some measure of relief by private act, but the bill comes within the precedents for a rating of $16 per month, and the passage of the bill is therefore recommended when amended so as to fix that rating.

O

WILLIAM FLINN.

JANUARY 21, 1903.—Committed to the Committee of the Whole House and ordered
to be printed.

Mr. LOUDENSLAGER, from the Committee on Pensions, submitted the
following

REPORT.

[To accompany S. 5352.]

The Committee on Pensions, to whom was referred the bill (S. 5352)
granting an increase of pension to William Flinn, have considered the
same and respectfully report as follows:

Said bill is accompanied by Senate Report No. 2311, this session, and
the same fully setting forth the facts is adopted by your committee as
their report and the bill returned with a favorable recommendation.

The report of the Senate committee on the bill is as follows:

William Flinn, whose post-office address is Tiger, N. C., served during the Cherokee Indian war from May 16, 1838, to July 5, 1838, in Captain Dickerson's company,
North Carolina Volunteers. He is now receiving the pension of $8 per month pro-
vided by the Indian war service act of July 27, 1892.

Claimant is 87 years of age, and it appears in evidence that he is totally unable to
work and is so feeble as to be frequently confined to his bed. He suffers from rupture, rheumatism, impaired sight, and the general infirmities of age.

He is much in need of relief, and, in the light of numerous precedents for increasing the pensions of the aged and destitute survivors of the Indian wars, your committee report the bill back favorably, with a recommendation that it pass.

O

MARY MANES.

JANUARY 21, 1903.—Committed to the Committee of the Whole House and ordered to be printed.

Mr. LOUDENSLAGER, from the Committee on Pensions, submitted the following

REPORT.

[To accompany S. 6071.]

The Committee on Pensions, to whom was referred the bill (S. 6071) granting an increase of pension to Mary Manes, have considered the same and respectfully report as follows:

The bill is accompanied by Senate Report No. 2339, this session, and the same fully setting forth the facts is adopted by your committee as their report and the bill is returned with a favorable recommendation.

The report of the Senate committee on the bill is as follows:

Mary Manes, whose post-office address is Deer, Newton County, Ark., is the widow of Pleasant R. Manes, who served during the Cherokee Indian disturbance from November 1, 1837, to May 9, 1838, as a corporal in Captain Elliott's company, Tennessee Mounted Infantry.

She is now receiving the pension of $8 per month provided by the Indian war service act of July 27, 1892. Soldier died June 29, 1869. Claimant was married to him in 1852.

Mrs. Manes is 77 years of age, and evidence filed with the bill shows that she is in feeble health and unable to do even her housework, and is without means of support other than her small pension.

O

LILA L. EGBERT.

JANUARY 21, 1903.—Committed to the Committee of the Whole House and ordered to be printed.

Mr. LOUDENSLAGER, from the Committee on Pensions, submitted the following

REPORT.

[To accompany S. 6182.]

The Committee on Pensions, to whom was referred the bill (S. 6182) granting an increase of pension to Lila L. Egbert, have considered the same and respectfully report as follows:

The bill is accompanied by Senate report No. 2184, this session, and the same setting forth the facts is adopted by your committee as their report, and the bill is returned with a favorable recommendation. The report of the Senate on the bill is as follows:

This bill proposes to increase from $20 to $30 per month the pension of Lila L. Egbert, widow of Augustus R. Egbert, late captain, Second Regiment U. S. Infantry.

A statement of this officer's service, as it appears on the official record, is as follows:

"Augustus R. Egbert accepted appointment as surgeon, U. S. Volunteers, November 15, 1861, and was honorably mustered out of service October 7, 1865.

"He accepted appointment as second lieutenant, Twenty-first U. S. Infantry, January 4, 1867; became unassigned April 19, 1869; assigned to Eighth Infantry July 14, 1869; was transferred to Second Infantry May 26, 1870; promoted first lieutenant December 18, 1873, and captain May 27, 1889.

"He was on duty as attending surgeon, San Francisco, Cal., from January to March, 1862; at Humboldt, Cal., to February, 1863; at San Francisco, Cal., to July, 1864, and at Fort Vancouver, Wash., to October 7, 1865.

"He was granted delay from January to June, 1867; with regiment and on regimental and other duties pertaining to his rank to January 14, 1873; on sick leave to January 14, 1874; on ordinary leave to February 14, 1874; with regiment and performing other military duties to June 2, 1884; on ordinary leave to November 11, 1884; with regiment in Oregon and Nebraska to May, 1890; on ordinary leave to June 30, 1890; with regiment at Omaha, Nebr., to September 25, 1890, on which date he died of paralysis incurred in service and line of duty."

Mrs. Egbert is now receiving a general-law pension of $20 per month. Her post-office address is No. 5825 Florence boulevard, Omaha, Nebr. She is 59 years of age, and was married to the officer February 11, 1859.

Evidence filed with the bill shows that Mrs. Egbert is in very straitened circumstances, her annual income being about $300, and this it appears includes her present pension.

Captain Egbert, during nearly thirty years of service, commencing in 1861, earned a most honorable record by his faithful and efficient performance of varied military duties in both the staff and line of the Army. He was a thoroughly educated physician and filled highly responsible positions in the Medical Department while serving on the Pacific coast. He was brevetted lieutenant-colonel October 6, 1865, and engaged in an expedition against hostile Nez Percé Indians in Washington and Idaho Territories in 1877.

( )

MARY B. KELLER.

JANUARY 21, 1903.—Committed to the Committee of the Whole House and ordered to be printed.

Mr. LOUDENSLAGER, from the Committee on Pensions, submitted the following

REPORT.

[To accompany S. 6257.]

The Committee on Pensions, to whom was referred the bill (S. 6257) granting an increase of pension to Mary B. Keller, have considered the same and respectfully report as follows:

Said bill is accompanied by Senate Report No. 2159, this session, and the same, fully setting forth the facts, is adopted by your committee as their report and the bill is returned with a favorable recommendation. The report of the Senate on the bill is as follows:

This bill proposes to increase from $30 to $40 per month the pension of Mary B. Keller, widow of Charles Keller, late colonel Twenty-third Regiment U. S. Infantry.

A statement of this officer's service, furnished by the War Department, is as follows:

WAR DEPARTMENT, ADJUTANT-GENERAL'S OFFICE,
Washington, September 5, 1902.

Statement of the military service of the late Charles Keller, of the U. S. Army, compiled from the records of this office.

Served as a cadet at the U. S. Military Academy from July 1, 1861, to June 23, 1865; appointed second lieutenant, Sixteenth Infantry, June 23, 1865; promoted to be first lieutenant, Sixteenth Infantry, June 23, 1865; transferred to Second Infantry, April 17, 1869; promoted to be captain, Second Infantry, July 20, 1875; promoted to be major, Eighteenth Infantry, August 8, 1897; promoted to be lieutenant-colonel Twenty-fourth Infantry, April 25, 1899; transferred to Twenty-second Infantry, August 7, 1900; promoted to be colonel Twenty-third Infantry, February 28, 1901; died April 22, 1901.

Service: He joined his regiment September 30, 1865, and served with it at Madison Barracks, N. Y., to October, 1865; on regimental recruiting service to April, 1866; on general recruiting service to September, 1866; with regiment at Nashville, Tenn., to December, 1866; at Savannah, Ga., to April, 1867; at Pulaski, Ga., to May, 1867; on duty at headquarters, district of Georgia, to August, 1867; with regiment at Savannah, Ga., to November, 1867, and continued on duty in the State of Georgia to April, 1869; at Huntsville, Ala., to November, 1869; at Charleston and Corinth, Miss., to February, 1870; at Summerville, Ga., to August, 1870; at Huntsville, Ala., to February 1,

1871; on general recruiting service to February 1, 1873; on delay to March 3, 1873; with regiment at Spartanburg, S. C., to June, 1873; at Atlanta, Ga., to September 1, 1873; at Mount Vernon Barracks, Ala., to December, 1873; at Atlanta, Ga., to July 1, 1874; at Mount Vernon Barracks, Ala., to September, 1876; at Atlanta, Ga., Edgefield, S. C., and Tallahassee, Fla., to December, 1876; at Columbia, S. C., to February, 1877; at Atlanta, Ga., to July, 1877; at Lewiston and Fort Lapwai, Idaho, to April, 1878; at Fort Coeur d'Alene, Idaho, to November, 1882; at Fort Spokane, Wash. (on leave February 11 to September 10, 1885), to July, 1886; at Fort Niobrara, Nebr., to November, 1886; at Fort Omaha, Nebr. (at Pine Ridge Agency, S. Dak., November 25, 1890, to January 27, 1891), to June 29, 1896; at Fort Yates, N. Dak., to August 18, 1897; on leave to November 18, 1897; with regiment at Fort Sam Houston, Tex., to April 18, 1898; at New Orleans, La., to May 24, 1898; at San Francisco, Cal., to June 27, 1898; en route to and in Philippines (sick in hospital at Manila, P. I., from December 24, 1900, to January 8, 1901) to January 8, 1901; en route to the United States to February 6, 1901; sick in hospital at Presidio of San Francisco, Cal., February 6 to 13, 1901; on sick leave at Fort Sam Houston, Tex., to April 22, 1901, when he died, the cause of death being reported as chronic nephritis, contracted in the Philippines.

W. P. HALL,
Assistant Adjutant-General, U. S. Army.

Mrs. Keller is now receiving a general law pension of $30 per month, with an additional $2 per month for one child under the age of 16 years. She is 54 years of age, and was married to the officer January 19, 1876. Her post-office address is Fort Sam Houston, Tex.

Evidence filed with the bill shows that Mrs. Keller has no property and no means of support aside from her pension. She has two children, one of whom, a daughter, has recently passed the age of 16 years.

Colonel Keller's military record covers a period of nearly forty years, and his death was the result of service in the Philippine Islands. There are numerous precedents for increasing pensions in cases of this character, in view of which your committee report the bill back favorably with a recommendation that it pass.

O

SARAH E. ROPES.

JANUARY 21, 1903.—Committed to the Committee of the Whole House and ordered
to be printed.

Mr. LOUDENSLAGER, from the Committee on Pensions, submitted the
following

REPORT.

[To accompany S. 6467.]

The Committee on Pensions, to whom was referred the bill (S. 6467)
granting an increase of pension to Sarah E. Ropes, have considered
the same and respectfully report as follows:

The bill is accompanied by Senate Report 2216, this session, and
from the same the following statement of facts is taken:

Sarah E. Ropes, whose post-office address is Salem, Mass., is the widow of James
M. Ropes, who served as first lieutenant and captain Company F, Second Regiment
California Volunteer Cavalry, and also as first lieutenant and captain, Eighth Regi-
ment U. S. Cavalry.

A statement of Captain Ropes's service in the Regular Army furnished by the War
Department is as follows:

WAR DEPARTMENT, ADJUTANT-GENERAL'S OFFICE,
Washington, May 23, 1901.

*Statement of the military service of the late James M. Ropes, of the U. S. Army, compiled
from the records of this office.*

Second lieutenant, Eighth Cavalry, June 18, 1867; first lieutenant December 28,
1868; regimental adjutant March 17, 1881, to October 9, 1882; captain October 9,
1882; retired February 20, 1891; died June 4, 1897.

SERVICE.

He joined his regiment January 19, 1868, and served with it at Vancouver Bar-
racks, Wash., to May, 1868; at Camp Harney, Oreg., to July, 1868; at Camp McGarry,
Nev., to September, 1868; at Camp Winfield Scott, Nev., to November, 1868; at Drum
Barracks, Cal., to February, 1869, and at Camp McDermit, Nev., to April 21, 1870;
on leave to July 24, 1870; with regiment in the field, Colorado, to October, 1870; at
Fort Garland, Colo., to June 12, 1872; at camp on the Canadian, New Mexico, to
July 12, 1872, and at Fort Union, N. Mex., to December 18, 1872; on recruiting
service to October 3, 1874; with regiment at Fort Union, N. Mex., to January 26,
1875; in the field, New Mexico, to April 6, 1875, and at Fort Union, N. Mex., to
January, 1876; en route to and at Fort Clark, Tex., to April 17, 1876; at Fort Ringgold, Tex., to November 20, 1876; at Edinburg, Tex., to January, 1877; at Fort

Brown, Tex., to February 27, 1878, and at Fort Clark, Tex., to March 8, 1878; on leave to August 30, 1878; conducting recruits en route to and with regiment at Fort Clark, Tex., to March 31, 1880; at San Felipe, Tex., to March, 1881, and at Fort Clark, Tex., to April 23, 1882; on leave to September 9, 1882; awaiting orders and conducting recruits to Texas to December 27, 1882; with regiment at Fort Ringgold, Tex. (sick November 10 to December 19, 1883), to July 24, 1884; on leave to September 22, 1884; with regiment at Fort Ringgold, Tex., to November, 1885; at Fort Brown, Tex. (sick February to March, 1887, sprained ankle), to July 28, 1887· on leave to September 8, 1887; on recruiting service to October 8, 1889; on leave January–February, 1890, and on sick leave until retired February 20, 1891.
     Died June 4, 1897, at Salem, Mass.

JOHN A. JOHNSTON,
Assistant Adjutant-General.

     Captain Ropes also served during the war of the rebellion. He assisted in organizing the Second California Volunteer Cavalry and was commissioned first lieutenant of Company F of that regiment August 29, 1861; was promoted captain Company G January 31, 1863; was brevetted major March 13, 1865, for meritorious services, and after the close of the war was honorably mustered out of service February 1, 1866.
     Captain Ropes died of heart disease, the result of rheumatism contracted while he was first lieutenant in the Eighth United States Cavalry. His widow is now receiving the pension of $17 per month provided by the general law for the widow of a first lieutenant. Mrs. Ropes, at the age of 62 years, is a chronic invalid. She is a sufferer from neurasthenia, and very recently sustained a serious fall, the results of which compel her to use crutches. Her circumstances are limited, and she is unable to earn anything toward her own support. Her petition, filed with the bill, is as follows:

The honorable Senate and House of Representatives of the Congress of the United States of America:

     Your petitioner, Sarah E. Ropes, of Salem, in the county of Essex and Commonwealth of Massachusetts, respectfully represents that she is the widow of James M. Ropes, who was formerly a captain in the Eighth Cavalry of the U. S. Army; that she was born September 17, 1840, and was married to said James M. Ropes September 4, 1867; that the said James M. Ropes was second lieutenant in said cavalry June 18, 1867, and rose to position of captain October 9, 1882; he was retired February 20, 1891, and died at said Salem June 4, 1897.
     Your petitioner further deposes that her property consists of a house and land in said Salem, taxed at $2,600, upon which there is a mortgage of $1,600; that she has the interest on $575 in the savings bank, at 3½ per cent, and the interest on $500, at 6 per cent, and has an annuity policy of $260 during life; that she is receiving a pension of $17 per month, being rated as a lieutenant's widow. Her total income is therefore only about $500, out of which must be deducted interest on the mortgage debt, taxes, and insurance, which leaves a very limited income, upon which your petitioner must depend for her subsistence. Considering the fact that her husband was for over twenty-eight years in the active service of his country, and in very truth gave his life to her service (for it was from disease contracted in the service that he died), it would not seem unreasonable that your petitioner should ask through your honorable bodies for such favorable legislation as will relieve her from her present urgent need. Your petitioner further declares that she had a severe illness about twenty-six years ago, from which she has never fully recovered, and a few months since sustained a serious fall, which compels her to use crutches.
     In consideration of the facts herein alleged, that her income is limited; that she has absolutely no other sources of income other than those stated; that she is incapacitated from sickness and infirmity from putting forth more than ordinary efforts to earn a livelihood; that the services of her husband to his country were long and meritorious, your petitioner therefore respectfully urges that you give careful consideration to this petition, believing that it merits your favorable action, and that you grant such relief as under the circumstances you may regard as just.

SARAH E. ROPES.

COMMONWEALTH OF MASSACHUSETTS, *County of Essex, ss:*

NOVEMBER 26, 1902.

     Personally appeared the above-named Sarah E. Ropes, and made oath that the above statements by her subscribed are in her belief true.
     And I certify that I have no interest in the prosecution of this claim.
     Before me,

EZRA L. WOODBURY,
Justice of the Peace.

COMMONWEALTH OF MASSACHUSETTS, *Essex, ss:*

To all people to whom these presents shall come.

Be it known that I, E. B. George, clerk of the superior court for the county of Essex, aforesaid, the same being a court of record, having by law a seal, do hereby certify that Ezra L. Woodbury, esq., by whom the accompanying affidavit was taken, was at the date thereof a justice of the peace within and for said county and residing in said county, duly commissioned and sworn and authorized by the laws of said Commonwealth to administer oaths and take and certify the acknowledgments and proofs of deeds or conveyances for lands, tenements, or hereditaments in said Commonwealth, and other instruments in writing to be recorded in said Commonwealth; that I am well acquainted with the handwriting of said justice of the peace, and verily believe that his signature to the foregoing certificate is genuine.

In testimony whereof I hereunto set my hand and affix the seal of said court, at Salem, in said county, on this 26th day of November, in the year of our Lord 1902.

E. B. GEORGE, *Clerk.*

There are many precedents for increasing the pensions of widows of officers of the Army, and in view of the facts set forth above your committee recommend the passage of the bill when amended, however, as follows:

In line 8 strike out "thirty" and insert in lieu thereof "twenty-five," said rating of $25 per month being the precedent established by your committee in recommending increases for widows pensioned with rank of first lieutenant in the Army.

O

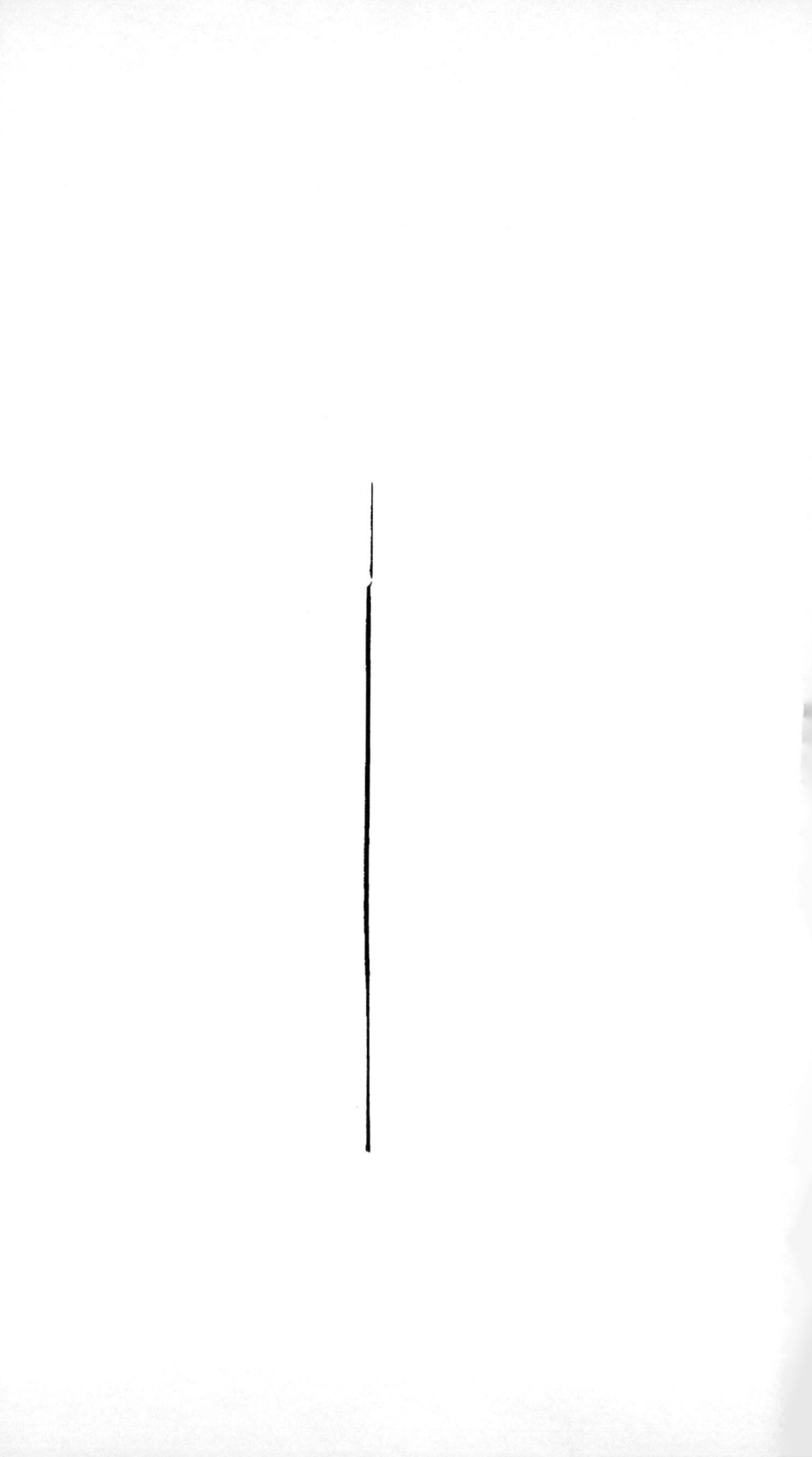

STEPHEN J. HOUSTON.

JANUARY 21, 1903.—Committed to the Committee of the Whole House and ordered
to be printed.

Mr. LOUDENSLAGER, from the Committee on Pensions, submitted the
following

REPORT.

[To accompany S. 6514.]

The Committee on Pensions, to whom was referred the bill (S. 6514)
granting an increase of pension to Stephen J. Houston, have considered the same and respectfully report as follows:

Said bill is accompanied by Senate Report No. 2282, this session, and
your committee adopt the same as their report and return the bill with
a favorable recommendation.

The report of the Senate is as follows:

Stephen J. Houston, whose post-office address is Lloyd, Fla., served during the
Seminole Indian war from December 12, 1835, to January 12, 1836, as a private in
Capt. J. D. Parish's company, Florida Volunteers. He also served during the same
war as a sergeant in Captain Hollman's company, from March 3, 1836, to June 3,
1836, and in Capt. Arthur Burney's company, Florida Volunteers, from February 25,
1840, to November 24, 1840.

He is now receiving the pension of $8 per month provided by the Indian war service
act of July 27, 1892. He is 86 years of age, blind, and helpless, unable to walk or help
himself or to earn anything whatever. He has no property, except a very poor piece
of pine land that is practically valueless, and has no means of support for himself and his
old and crippled wife, except his pension of $8 per month. These facts are all sub-
stantiated by evidence filed with the bill.

In the light of numerous precedents for increasing the pensions of aged, disabled,
and destitute veterans of the Indian wars, your committee report the bill back favorably with a recommendation that it pass.

O

BERTHA R. KOOPS.

JANUARY 21, 1903.—Committed to the Committee of the Whole House and ordered
to be printed.

Mr. LOUDENSLAGER, from the Committee on Pensions, submitted the
following

REPORT.

[To accompany S. 6614.]

The Committee on Pensions, to whom was referred the bill (S. 6614)
granting an increase of pension to Bertha R. Koops, have considered
the same and respectfully report as follows:

Said bill is accompanied by Senate report 2366, this session, and the
same, fully setting forth the facts, is adopted by your committee as
their report, and the bill is returned with a favorable recommendation.

The report of the Senate on the bill is as follows:

Bertha R. Koops, whose post-office address is No. 31 Lilac street, Buffalo, N. Y.,
is the widow of Carl Koops, late first lieutenant, Tenth Regiment, U. S. Infantry.

A statement of this officer's service furnished by the War Department is as follows:

WAR DEPARTMENT, ADJUTANT-GENERAL'S OFFICE,
Washington, October 14, 1902.

*Statement of the military service of Carl Koops, of the U. S. Army, compiled from the
records of this office.*

Born August 21, 1858, in Germany, and appointed from Illinois.

Private, corporal, and sergeant, C, Second Cavalry, November 17, 1881, to October
22, 1886; second lieutenant, Thirteenth Infantry, October 22, 1886; first lieutenant,
Fourteenth Infantry, March 1, 1894; transferred to Tenth Infantry, May 5, 1894.

SERVICE.

With his regiment at Fort Stanton, N. Mex., November, 1886, to August, 1887;
student officer at U. S. Infantry and Cavalry School at Fort Leavenworth, Kans., to
August, 1889; with regiment at Little Rock, Ark., to September, 1890; Fort Supply,
Ind. T., to July, 1891; professor of military science and tactics at Austin College,
Sherman, Tex., to July, 1894; Fort Reno, Okla., to October, 1897; Fort Sill, Okla.,
to April, 1898; Tampa, Fla., to June 14, 1898; Santiago campaign to August 6, 1898,
where he died of yellow fever, near Santiago, Cuba.

Lieutenant Koops was wounded in action at San Juan, Cuba, July 1, 1898, and
Col. Philip Reade, acting inspector-general, in his report, says that after Lieutenant

Koops had been badly wounded in the head he made a map and sent it to General Kent; was recommended by Capt. J. T. Kirkman, Col. E. P. Pearson, and Gen. Jacob F. Kent for brevet for personal gallantry in battle and siege of Santiago and for iron fortitude throughout the siege.

HENRY P. McCAIN,
Assistant Adjutant-General.

Mrs. Koops is now receiving a general-law pension of $17 per month, with an additional allowance of $2 per month for each of her three minor children under the age of 16 years. She was married to the officer July 25, 1893. Evidence filed with the bill shows that she has an income of only $200 per year in addition to her pension for the support of herself and her three children. She is unable to support herself and her children upon this income, and she is largely dependent on relatives and friends for aid.

At the outbreak of the war with Spain Lieutenant Koops was commissary of subsistence at Fort Sill, Ind. T., and was relieved from that duty at his own urgent request in order to be with his regiment in the expedition to Santiago, Cuba. He was wounded in the head in the battle of San Juan, July 2, 1898, and was sent to hospital, but declined to stay there, and insisted upon returning to his regiment, which he did on the following day, and took command of his company. Just before his regiment was ordered back to the United States he was taken sick and died in a few days of yellow fever.

He was a zealous and patriotic officer, who rose from the ranks by force of his own energy and great ability. His widow is in urgent need of relief, and in the light of numerous precedents your committee report the bill back favorably, with a recommendation that it pass.

O

MARY J. IVEY.

JANUARY 21, 1903.—Committed to the Committee of the Whole House and ordered
to be printed.

Mr. LOUDENSLAGER, from the Committee on Pensions, submitted the
following

REPORT.

[To accompany S. 6693.]

The Committee on Pensions, to whom was referred the bill (S. 6693)
granting a pension to Mary J. Ivey, have considered the same and
respectfully report as follows:

The bill is accompanied by Senate Report No. 2361, this session,
and from the same the following facts are taken:

Mary J. Ivey, whose post-office address is O'Brien, Fla., is the widow of Robert
L. Ivey, who served during the Seminole Indian war in Capt. J. A. Newman's company, Georgia Volunteers, and in Capt. John C. Pelott's company, Florida Volunteers.

Mrs. Ivey made claim at the Bureau, under the Indian war service act of July 27,
1892, and her claim was rejected on the ground that the organizations in which her
husband served were not in the United States service.

It appears from the official records that Robert L. Ivey served twenty-nine days
during June, July, and August, 1836, in Capt. J. A. Newman's company, Georgia
Volunteers, and from April 6, 1838, to July 22, 1838, in Capt. John C. Pelott's company, Florida Volunteers, Seminole Indian war. The former company was among
the militia organizations called out by the governor of the State of Georgia for local
protection against Indian hostilities. It was engaged in battle at Brushy Creek,
Lowndes County, Ga., July 15, 1836, and also in battle, at a date not mentioned, in
Chickasawhatchee Swamp. This company was paid by the State of Georgia, which
was reimbursed by the United States under an act of Congress approved August 11,
1842.

Captain Pelott's company, Florida Militia, was ordered into the service of the Territory of Florida by Governor R. K. Call. It was paid by the United States under
an act of Congress approved March 3, 1845.

Robert L. Ivey was pensioned at $8 per month under the Indian war service act
of July 27, 1892. He was receiving this pension at the time of his death, which
occurred June 7, 1900. He also received a bounty land warrant for 160 acres on
account of his service.

Mrs. Ivey is 68 years of age. She was married to the soldier July 17, 1851. Evidence on file shows that she is poor and in needy circumstances.

The service rendered by this soldier was the same as that rendered by organizations the members of which were mustered in and mustered out by United States
officers. Congress recognized this in its enactment of the laws providing indirectly

for the payment of the members of soldier's commands. He was pensioned during his lifetime, and your committee are of opinion that his widow also should be pensioned.

In view of the foregoing your committee believe that the claimant should be granted a pension, but as the general law rating is $8 in these cases, it is believed that that allowance would be just and equitable, and the passage of the bill is therefore recommended with an amendment fixing the rate of pension at $8 per month.

O

BRIDGET AGNES TRIDEL.

JANUARY 21, 1903.—Committed to the Committee of the Whole House and ordered to be printed.

Mr. WILEY, from the Committee on Pensions, submitted the following

REPORT.

[To accompany H. R. 1377.]

The Committee on Pensions, to whom was referred the bill (H. R. 1377) granting an increase of pension to Bridget Agnes Tridel, have considered the same and respectfully report as follows:

Bridget Agnes Tridel, of Burkes Station, Fairfax County, Va., is the widow of John T. Tridel, who served from December 1, 1846, to August 1, 1848, as a private in Company B, First Regiment, Virginia Volunteers, in the war with Mexico, and she now receives a pension of $8 per month under the general law.

The claimant was married to the soldier in 1860, and he died January 14, 1899. Papers accompanying the bill show that she is 60 years old and in poor health. Her property consists of a small farm and cow, the whole valued at not over $520. Her dependence was accepted by the Pension Bureau and her claim there was allowed on that account, she not having reached the age qualification, viz, 62 years.

In the light of the foregoing facts and circumstances your committee believe that a small increase in the pension is justified, and the passage of the bill is therefore recommended when amended as follows: Strike out all after the enacting clause and insert in lieu thereof the following:

That the Secretary of the Interior be, and he is hereby, authorized and directed to place on the pension roll, subject to the provisions and limitations of the pension laws, the name of Bridget Agnes Tridel, widow of John T. Tridel, late of Company B, First Regiment Virginia Volunteers, war with Mexico, and pay her a pension at the rate of twelve dollars per month in lieu of that she is now receiving.

O

SUSAN KENT.

JANUARY 21, 1903.—Committed to the Committee of the Whole House and ordered
to be printed.

Mr. LOUDENSLAGER, from the Committee on Pensions, submitted the
following

REPORT.

[To accompany H. R. 2812.]

The Committee on Pensions, to whom was referred the bill (H. R.
2812) granting a pension to Susan Kent, have considered the same
and respectfully report as follows:

Susan Kent, of Marianna, Jackson County, Fla., is the widow of
John Kent, who enlisted November 1, 1842, as a private in Captain
Daniels's company of Florida Volunteers, and was honorably discharged
November 26, 1842. The claimant filed an application for pension
September 30, 1892, under the Indian war service pension act of July
27, 1892, declaring that her husband served in Captain Hentz's company of Georgia Volunteers in 1836 and was discharged in 1837, after
service in the Indian wars. The records fail to show the soldier's name
on the roll of Captain Hentz's company, and subsequently the widow
declared that the service was rendered in a company commanded by
Captain Daniels, and upon an examination of the records the name of
John Kent was found on the muster roll of Capt. Stephen Daniels's
company of Florida Volunteers, with dates of enrollment and discharge
as above set forth. The claim was rejected by the Bureau January
26, 1895, on the ground that the service was rendered subsequent to
the close of the Florida war.

This ruling may be technically correct, and it appears also that the
period of service was a few days short of that required under the general law, but it seems reasonable to suppose that the claimant would
not have been enlisted and mustered into the United States service in
November, 1842, if there had been no emergency calling for the employment of troops. Active hostilities may have ended in August, as
appears in the record, but the claimant enlisted apparently for service
against the Indians, and no doubt many others who rendered no more
service than he did have been recognized by the granting of pension.
Claimant is now about 68 years old, and the papers show that she is

wholly dependent upon the charity of others not legally bound to her support.

She married the deceased soldier March 4, 1840, and he died August 5, 1888. In the light of the facts above set forth, the passage of the bill is recommended when amended as follows:

Strike out all after the enacting clause and substitute in lieu thereof the following:

That the Secretary of the Interior be, and he is hereby, authorized and directed to place on the pension roll, subject to the provisions and limitations of the pension laws, the name of Susan Kent, widow of John Kent, late of Captain Daniels's company, Florida Volunteers, Florida Indian war, and pay her a pension at the rate of eight dollars per month.

Amend the title so as to read: "A bill granting a pension to Susan Kent."

O

CATHERINE P. McLORINEN.

JANUARY 21, 1903.—Committed to the Committee of the Whole House and ordered to be printed.

Mr. WILEY, from the Committee on Pensions, submitted the following

REPORT.

[To accompany H. R. 6127.]

The Committee on Pensions, to whom was referred the bill (H. R. 6127) granting an increase of pension to Mrs. Catherine P. McLorinan, have considered the same and respectfully report as follows:

Catherine P. McLorinen, of 331 Royal street, New Orleans, La., is the widow of William H. McLorinen, who was a private in Company H, Fourth Regiment, U. S. Artillery, and served from September 14, 1841, to September 13, 1846. A part of this service was rendered in the war with Mexico, and the claimant is now receiving the pension of $8 per month allowed by law to widows of soldiers of said war.

In addition to the above service the soldier also served as captain of Company D, Eighty-sixth Regiment U. S. Colored Troops, from October 29, 1863, to April 10, 1866, in the civil war. He died March 1, 1882, and his widow, who married him in 1849, is now 70 years old and without property or income aside from her pension.

The passage of the bill is recommended when amended as follows: Strike out all in the bill after the words "name of," in lines 5 and 6, and insert in lieu thereof the following:

Catherine P. McLorinen, widow of William H. McLorinen, late of Company H, Fourth Regiment, United States Artillery, war with Mexico, and captain Company B, Eighty-sixth Regiment, United States Colored Infantry, and pay her a pension at the rate of $12 per month in lieu of that she is now receiving.

Amend the title so as to read: "A bill granting an increase of pension to Catherine P. McLorinen."

O

JOHN WALLACE.

JANUARY 21, 1903.—Committed to the Committee of the Whole House and ordered
to be printed.

Mr. SHELDEN, from the Committee on Pensions, submitted the
following

REPORT.

[To accompany H. R. 9237.]

The Committee on Pensions, to whom was referred the bill (H. R.
9237) granting a pension to John Wallace, have considered the same
and respectfully report as follows:

John Wallace, of 220 Wisner street, Saginaw, Mich., enlisted June
13, 1870, in the general mounted service, U. S. Army, at Rochester,
N. Y., and was discharged at Fort Union, N. Mex., June 13, 1875.
He reenlisted July 12, 1875, in the Fifth U. S. Cavalry and joined
Troop K of that regiment in September, 1875. He was discharged at
Fort Laramie, Wyo., July 11, 1880. He filed a claim for pension
January 8, 1894, alleging that in the summer of 1876, near Fort Lar-
amie, he incurred injury of eyes by being struck by the limb of a tree
while riding at night.

The hospital records show claimant was treated during service as
follows: April 10 to 18, 1871, catarrh; January to July, 1874, intermittent fever; August 4, 1876, incised wound; January 3 to 8, 1877,
acute diarrhea; February 12 to 14, 1878, contusion of right hand;
August, 1878, headache; September, 1878, punctured wound; October,
1878, headache; March, 1879, rheumatism, and in November, 1879, and
February, 1880, for catarrh.

Claimant's allegation as to injury of eyes was corroborated under
oath by a comrade, and a history of an affection of the eyes from discharge is set forth in the papers, but claimant could not furnish a
second comrade's testimony, and the claim was thereupon rejected. He
is now about 76 years old and clearly in dependent circumstances.
Medical examinations held in connection with his claim show him to be
much disabled by eye difficulty.

Under all the circumstances your committee believe that a pension
graded according to the degree of disability now existing from affec-

tion of eyes can properly be allowed, and the passage of the bill is therefore recommended when amended as follows:

In line 6 strike out "Companies A and" and substitute therefor the word "Company."

In line 7 strike out "Volunteer;" and in lines 7 and 8 strike out "and pay him a pension at the rate of $24 dollars per month."

O

MARY WILLIAMS.

.

JANUARY 21, 1903.—Committed to the Committee of the Whole House and ordered
to be printed.

Mr. SHELDEN, from the Committee on Pensions, submitted the
following

REPORT.

[To accompany H. R. 9814.]

The Committee on Pensions, to whom was referred the bill (H. R.
9814) granting an increase of pension to Mary Williams, have considered the same and respectfully report as follows:

Mary Williams, of Monroe, Mich., is the widow of Francis C. Williams, late of Company H, Ninth U. S. Infantry, war with Mexico,
and she is now receiving the pension of $8 per month allowed under
the act of January 29, 1887.

Mrs. Williams is 74 years old. She married the soldier in 1859, and
he died December 24, 1900. Medical evidence on file shows that
claimant is totally disabled by age and disease of heart, and it is shown
that she is without property or income and that she has no relatives to
care for her.

There are many precedents for the proposed legislation, and the
passage of the bill is recommended when amended as follows:

In lines 6 and 7 strike out "a member."

In line 7, after the word "Ninth," insert "Regiment," and in the
same line, after the word "Infantry," insert "war with Mexico."

Amend the title so as to read: "A bill granting an increase of pension to Mary Williams."

O

WILLIAM KENNY.

JANUARY 21, 1903.—Committed to the Committee of the Whole House and ordered to be printed.

Mr. BOREING, from the Committee on Pensions, submitted the following

REPORT.

[To accompany H. R. 12771.]

The Committee on Pensions, to whom was referred the bill (H. R. 12771) granting a pension to William Kenny, beg leave to submit the following report, and recommend that said bill do pass with amendments.

William Kenny, of 712 Hoag avenue, Minneapolis, Minn., enlisted October 17, 1870, as a musician in Company B, Twenty-second U. S. Infantry, and served a term of five years, being discharged October 17, 1875. In an application for pension, filed March 24, 1898, claimant alleges that on an expedition in North Dakota and Montana, in spring and summer of 1873, he contracted rheumatism and piles, also that he contracted partial deafness in the service, but whether from blowing his bugle or catarrh, or some other cause, he can not say. This claim was supported by the hospital record of treatment for catarrh and repeatedly for acute diarrhea, diseases which not infrequently result in piles and deafness, and also by the testimony of several of his comrades, and although the claimant is unable to furnish medical evidence, the examiner having the case in charge submitted it for admission, and it was approved for allowance by the reviewer so far as the piles and impaired hearing of both ears were concerned, but on objection by the re-reviewer the case was sent to the field for special examination.

In this examination the witnesses in the main corroborated their former testimony, and the reviewer, as the result of the investigation, again approved for admission, for piles and impaired hearing, but upon an objection by the re-reviewer the case was rejected. In the absence of anything in the record indicating rheumatism, and there being no medical evidence supporting that part of the claim, a rejection of the rheumatism was probably correct, but the evidence seems to reasonably show that piles and impaired hearing, which upon medical examination are rated together at $8 per month, had their origin · in the service.

The passage of the bill is recommended with the following amendments:

In line 6 change the spelling of the claimant's surname to "Kenny," and in the same line, after the word "Twenty-second," insert "Regiment;"

In line 8 strike out "twelve" and insert "eight."

Amend the title so as to read: "A bill granting a pension to William Kenny."

O

ELIZABETH A. WILDER.

JANUARY 21, 1903.—Committed to the Committee of the Whole House and ordered
to be printed.

Mr. DRAPER, from the Committee on Pensions, submitted the following

REPORT.

[To accompany H. R. 13358.]

The Committee on Pensions, to whom was referred the bill (H. R. 13358) granting a pension to Elizabeth A. Wilder, have considered the same and respectfully report as follows:

Elizabeth A. Wilder, of 1312 South Salina street, Syracuse, N. Y., is the widow of Titus Wilder, who enlisted February 7, 1845, as an armorer, U. S. Navy, and was honorably discharged September 14, 1846. The soldier in his lifetime made application for a pension under the act of January 29, 1887, allowing pensions on account of Mexican war service, and the same was allowed at $8 per month. He had previously applied for a disability pension based upon total blindness, but the same was rejected in 1883 on the ground of his inability to supply satisfactory evidence of origin in service and line of duty. By an act of Congress approved July 2, 1888, he was allowed a pension of $72 per month on account of blindness, and this rate he was drawing when he died, August 12, 1901.

After the soldier's death this beneficiary applied for pension under the act of January 29, 1887, but the same was rejected on the ground that the ship on which her husband served was not in Mexican waters sixty days during the war. The war officially began April 24, 1846, and it is shown by the records that the vessel on which the sailor was serving was in Mexican waters from April 29 to June 16, 1846, a period of forty-nine days.

The claimant is now 76 years old and in needy and dependent circumstances. She married the sailor July 8, 1847. There are many precedents for the allowance of a pension in cases of this kind. The sailor's service was recognized by the allowance of a pension under the general law, and your committee recognize the justice of the widow's application to be placed upon the roll.

The passage of the bill is therefore recommended when amended as follows:

Strike out all in the bill after the words "Titus Wilder," in line 6, and substitute therefor the following:

"late armorer, United States Navy, war with Mexico, and pay her a pension at the rate of eight dollars per month."

O

MARY L. PURINGTON.

JANUARY 21, 1903.—Committed to the Committee of the Whole House and ordered
to be printed.

Mr. BROMWELL, from the Committee on Pensions, submitted the
following

REPORT.

[To accompany H. R. 14254.]

The Committee on Pensions, to whom was referred the bill (H. R.
14254) granting a pension to Mary L. Purington, have fully considered the same and respectfully report as follows:

Mary L. Purington, of Fort Sill, Okla., is the widow of George A.
Purington, who served as first sergeant Company G, Nineteenth Ohio
Infantry, from April 22 to August 26, 1861; as captain, Second Ohio
Cavalry, from August 27, 1861; major from September 10, 1861, and
lieutenant-colonel from July 10, 1863, to November 1, 1864, when honorably mustered out. He accepted appointment as captain, Ninth
U. S. Cavalry, January 21, 1867, promoted major, Third Cavalry,
October 25, 1883, and lieutenant-colonel, October 20, 1892. He was
retired as lieutenant-colonel, U. S. Army, July 17, 1895, and died May
31, 1896, at Metropolis, Ill., of diabetes, incurred while ranking as
major.

Mrs. Purington, who married the deceased officer March 21, 1864, is
now receiving a pension of $25 per month allowed under the general
law. She is 62 years old, and her property consists of a farm in New
Mexico of little value, from which she receives no income, and it is
shown that her entire income, aside from her pension, is about $120
per annum.

There are many precedents for the allowance of an increase of
pension in a case of this character. The deceased officer's death arose
from causes incurred while ranking as major, and the maximum rating
recommended by your committee in cases of that rank is $35 per month.
This rating your committee believe the widow should have, and the
passage of the bill is recommended when amended as follows:

In line 7 strike out "lieutenant-colonel" and substitute therefor "major;" and in the same line, after the word "Third," insert "Regiment;" and in the same line strike out the word "to."

In line 8 strike out "fifty" and insert "thirty-five."

Strike out all in line 9 and insert in lieu thereof the words "that she is now receiving."

Amend the title so as to read: "A bill granting an increase of pension to Mary L. Purington."

O

ALMEDIA J. ROBISON.

JANUARY 21, 1903.—Committed to the Committee of the Whole House and ordered to
. be printed.

Mr. BROMWELL, from the Committee on Pensions, submitted the
following

REPORT.

[To accompany H. R. 14811.]

The Committee on Pensions, to whom was referred the bill (H. R.
14811) granting a pension to Almedia J. Robinson, have considered the
same and respectfully report as follows:

Almedia J. Robison is the widow of Marion S. Robison, who served
as second lieutenant Company H, Eighth Regiment Ohio Volunteer
Infantry, from April 25, 1898, to November 21, 1898, in the war with
Spain. During his lifetime, viz, on January 28, 1899, the soldier
filed an application for pension, declaring that in August, 1898, at
Santiago de Cuba, he incurred malarial fever, causing heart trouble,
eczema, and general debility. He died April 3, 1899, before the settlement of his claim. However, this was subsequently allowed at
$7.50 per month for malarial poisoning, and payment was made to the
widow upon proof of her legal widowhood. Mrs. Robison filed a
claim in her own right in May, 1899, declaring that soldier's death was
due to exposure to typhoid infection in the service. As stated above,
malarial poisoning by soldier in service and the claimant's widowhood
were both accepted by the Bureau as established, but the medical
division held that the soldier's death was due to typhoid fever not the
outgrowth of the malarial poisoning for which he was pensioned, and
the widow's claim was rejected.

The claim was specially examined, and in a general way a history of
malarial poisoning and general physical breakdown in the soldier's case
was adduced, and it further appeared that in order to identify the
bodies of some of the soldiers of his command who had died in Cuba
the soldier went to Cuba in January, 1899, and that the typhoid fever,
which caused his death, supervened after his return. The claimant,
now about 48 years old, married the deceased soldier in December,
1881, and it is shown that she has no property and no means of support aside from the proceeds of her daily labor. There are no children.

From the history of this case your committee believe that the soldier's health was seriously impaired in the service, and it is reasonable to presume that the disease of service origin was at least a factor in the death cause.

The passage of the bill is therefore recommended when amended as follows:

Strike out all after the enacting clause and substitute therefor the following:

That the Secretary of the Interior be, and he is hereby, authorized and directed to place on the pension roll, subject to the provisions and limitations of the pension laws, the name of Almedia J. Robison, widow of Marion S. Robison, late second lieutenant Company H, Eighth Regiment Ohio Volunteer Infantry, war with Sprin, and pay her a pension at the rate of fifteen dollars per month.

Amend the title so as to read: "A bill granting a pension to Almedia J. Robison."

O

MARGARET SNYDER.

JANUARY 21, 1903.—Committed to the Committee of the Whole House and ordered to be printed.

Mr. BROMWELL, from the Committee on Pensions, submitted the following

REPORT.

[To accompany H. R. 14845.]

The Committee on Pensions, to whom was referred the bill (H. R. 14845) granting a pension to Margaret Snyder, have considered the same and respectfully report as follows:

Margaret Snyder, of Wooster, Ohio, is the mother of John Snyder, who served honorably from October 1, 1863, to November 14, 1865, in Company A, Twelfth Ohio Volunteer Cavalry, civil war, and from November 29, 1866, to June 30, 1871, as a private in Troop G, Seventh U. S. Cavalry.

On August 31, 1866 (between his two terms of service), the soldier made application for pension on account of rheumatism alleged to have been incurred at Saltville, Va., about December 30, 1863; on this application he was examined in 1866 and found to be suffering from sciatica; but a few months later he enlisted in the Regular Army and his claim was abandoned and the Bureau never heard anything further from him. The claimant filed an application for pension July 9, 1890, as the mother of the soldier, alleging that he disappeared in the summer of 1871, immediately following his discharge from the Regular Army, and has never since been heard from, and that he is presumed to be dead. Her claim was rejected on the ground of her inability to show date or cause of death or that his service caused death. From this action appeal was taken to the Secretary of the Interior, who sustained the action of rejection, but in his decision the Secretary says that the fact of soldier's death may be conceded.

The relationship of claimant to soldier, his celibacy, and the fact that she is a widow 78 years old and very poor and dependent mainly upon charity, are all shown in the papers, as is also the fact that two sons were in the country's service during the civil war.

The hospital records show that the soldier was treated during the term of his second service for incised wound and incontinence of urine, and on the chance that his death, the fact of which is now conceded, was due to his service, your committee believe that his poor and aged mother is justly entitled to a pension.   The passage of the bill is therefore recommended when amended as follows:

Strike out all in the bill after the word "place," in line 4, and substitute in lieu thereof the following:

on the pension roll, subject to the provisions and limitations of the pension laws, the name of Margaret Snyder, mother of John Snyder, late of Company A, Twelfth Regiment Ohio Volunteer Cavalry, and Troop G, Seventh Regiment United States Cavalry, and pay her a pension at the rate of twelve dollars per month.

O

WILLIAM E. SHARP.

JANUARY 21, 1903.—Committed to the Committee of the Whole House and ordered
to be printed.

Mr. BOREING, from the Committee on Pensions, submitted the
following

REPORT.

[To accompany H. R. 14961.]

The Committee on Pensions, to whom was referred the bill (H. R.
14961) granting a pension to W. E. Sharp, have considered the same
and respectfully report as follows:

William E. Sharp, of Lancing, Morgan County, Tenn., is the foster
father of Walter F. Sharp, who is shown by the official records to have
enlisted March 4, 1901, at Helenwood, Tenn., as a private in Company
M, Seventh Regiment U. S. Infantry, and died July 8, 1901, in the
Philippine Islands, of measles contracted in line of duty.

The testimony accompanying the bill shows that the soldier was the
natural son of claimant's daughter and that the mother died when soldier
was a child but 2 years old; and further that the claimant raised and
cared for soldier until he attained his majority, at which time soldier
frequently acknowledged his obligation to his grandfather and aided
in the latter's support.

It is further shown that soldier left no widow or child surviving, and
that claimant, now 70 years old, is wholly incapacitated for manual
labor and without property or income.

Your committee believe the case to be an equitable one, and the
passage of the bill is recommended when amended as follows:

In line 6 change the initial "W." to "William."

Amend the title so as to read: "A bill granting a pension to William
E. Sharp."

O

GRACE HARRINGTON.

JANUARY 21, 1903.—Committed to the Committee of the Whole House and ordered
to be printed.

Mr. DRAPER, from the Committee on Pensions, submitted the following

REPORT.

[To accompany H. R. 15362.]

The Committee on Pensions, to whom was referred the bill (H. R. 15362) granting an increase of pension to Grace C. Harrington, have considered the same and respectfully report as follows:

Grace Harrington, of Albany, N. Y.,-is the widow of Henry M. Harrington, late second lieutenant Company C, Second Regiment U. S. Cavalry, who entered the service by graduation from the Military Academy June 14, 1872, and was killed in action with Sioux Indians June 25, 1876, at Little Big Horn River, Montana Territory. On December 1, 1876, Grace Harrington filed an application for pension, and the same was allowed at $15 per month; but subsequently she failed to draw her pension, and it was supposed that she was dead, her whereabouts being unknown for a long time and diligent search and inquiry for her not having resulted in success. Thereupon Congress granted her two children a pension of $15 per month each, to end upon their reaching the age of 16 years. The claimant afterwards reappeared, and she is now in receipt of the general-law pension of $15 per month, the same having been restored to her. The children are now over age and no pension is drawn on their account.

Mrs. Harrington married the deceased officer November 15, 1872, and she is now 53 years of age, and she swears that she has no property of any kind or character, either real or personal. There are several precedents for granting increase of pension to the widows of officers who were killed in the battle of the Little Big Horn with Custer, and in view of the widow's necessities the passage of the bill is recommended when amended as follows:

In line 6 strike out the Christian name "Gerard."

In line 7, after the word "Regiment," insert "United States;" and in lines 7 and 8 strike out "United States Army."

In line 8 strike out "fifty" and insert "twenty-five."

Amend the title so as to read: "A bill granting an increase of pension to Grace Harrington."

O

DELITHA A. COOK.

JANUARY 21, 1903.—Committed to the Committee of the Whole House and ordered to be printed.

Mr. RICHARDSON, of Alabama, from the Committee on Pensions, submitted the following

REPORT.

[To accompany H. R. 15693.]

The Committee on Pensions, to whom was referred the bill (H. R. 15693) granting an increase of pension to Deletha Cook, have considered the same and respectfully report as follows:

Delitha A. Cook, of Annemanie, Wilcox County, Ala., is the widow of Zoroaster Selman Cook, who served from November 10, 1847, to June 27, 1848, as a sergeant in Company B, Seibel's battalion, Alabama Volunteers, in the war with Mexico, and she is now receiving the pension of $8 per month allowed by law to the widows of the soldiers of that war. The testimony before your committee shows that the parties were married October 25, 1849, and that the soldier died January 26, 1893. The claimant is now 70 years of age and the possessor of 100 acres of poor hill land upon which she lives, and another tract of 40 acres in the same county, all of the value of about $600.

There are many precedents for the proposed legislation, and the passage of the bill is recommended when amended as follows:

Change the spelling of the claimant's Christian name in the body of the bill to "Delitha."

After the words "widow of," in line 6, insert "Zoroaster."

In lines 7 and 8 strike out "in the Mexican war" and substitute "war with Mexico."

In line 8, after "pension," insert "at the rate," and in the same line strike out "sixteen" and insert "twelve."

Amend the title so as to read: "A bill granting an increase of pension to Delitha A. Cook."

O

BESSIE LEDYARD.

JANUARY 21, 1903.—Committed to the Committee of the Whole House and ordered
to be printed.

Mr. RICHARDSON, of Alabama, from the Committee on Pensions, submitted the following

REPORT.

[To accompany H. R. 15694.]

The Committee on Pensions, to whom was reported the bill (H. R. 15694) granting a pension to Bessie Ledyard, respectfully report as follows:

Bessie Ledyard, of Montgomery, Ala., is the widow of John B. Ledyard, who enlisted June 13, 1898, as a private in Company M, Fifth U. S. Volunteer Infantry, and was honorably discharged May 31, 1899. The soldier died February 9, 1901, and the claimant filed an application for pension, declaring that his death cause was congestion of stomach, due to yellow fever contracted at Santiago de Cuba. The hospital records show that soldier was treated on numerous occasions for malarial fever, acute diarrhea, and hemorrhoids, contracted in line of duty. He was also under treatment for acute alcoholism from February 27 to March 11, 1899, and also for alcoholic gastritis from May 4 to May 8, 1899. At the time of his muster out claimant stated that he had then no disabilities, but the examining surgeon certified that he found slight external hemorrhoids. Col. A. A. Wiley, of his regiment, swore that the soldier was a good man and did his duty, and, further, that he contracted a malignant fever in Cuba which shattered his health and which ultimately caused his death.

The claim was specially examined to determine death cause, and Dr. R. F. Michael, the family physician, swore that at the time of his return home soldier was suffering from gastro-intestinal trouble, which, from the history of the case, likely grew out of fever incurred in Cuba. His liver was very much enlarged and the spleen slightly engorged. The doctor was sick at the time of the soldier's fatal illness, and was not in attendance upon him at that time, but from his knowledge of the case believes that the immediate cause of death was disease of stomach and bowels, and that alcoholism was not a factor in death cause.

Dr. John M. Sadler, who was called in, in the absence of Dr. Michael, the day before claimant died, swears that claimant was perfectly conscious, and with no evidence of delirium; soldier showed evidence of having had malaria; his liver or spleen being very much enlarged, probably both. The doctor diagnosed the trouble as acute gastritis, and while the disease might have been caused by alcoholism he did not have any of the brain symptoms, and if it was alcoholism, the case was a different one from any the doctor had ever seen. It was shown by other testimony that the claimant was more or less of a drinking man, but by no means a common drunkard. The Pension Bureau holds that death was due to alcoholic gastritis, and hence not occasioned by disease arising in service and line of duty.

Claimant married soldier February 8, 1891, and she is now 30 years of age. There are three little children under the age of 16 years depending upon her for support.   •

Your committee has given this case careful consideration and believe it to be reasonably well established that the malarial fever which the soldier undoubtedly had in a severe form in Cuba was an important and probably the controlling factor in his death cause, and, further, that his widow is justly entitled to a pension. The passage of the bill is therefore recommended when amended as follows:

In line 5 strike out "otherwise."

In line 7 strike out "a private in" and substitute therefor "late of."

In lines 8 and 9 strike out "during the Spanish-American war" and insert "war with Spain."

In line 9 strike out "twenty" and insert "twelve."

Add to the end of the bill the words: "and two dollars per month additional on account of each of the minor children of said John B. Ledyard until they reach the age of sixteen years."

O·

FRANCES C. BROGGAN.

JANUARY 21, 1903.—Committed to the Committee of the Whole House and ordered
to be printed.

Mr. BOREING, from the Committee on Pensions, submitted the following

REPORT.

[To accompany H. R. 15757.]

The Committee on Pensions, to whom was referred the bill (H. R.
15757) granting a pension to Frances C. Broggan, have considered the
same and respectfully report as follows:

The claimant, Frances C. Broggan, is the helpless and dependent
daughter of Francis Broggan. The soldier died from disease originating in service and line of duty, and his widow, Mary Broggan, now
dead, was granted a pension under the general law at $12 per month
and $2 additional on account of two minor children (one of them being
the beneficiary under the pending bill) until they became 16 years of
age. This pension to Mary Broggan was increased to $14 per month
by private act of the Fifty-fifth Congress because of the fact that this
child, Frances C., was in a permanently helpless condition and dependent upon her (Mary Broggan) for support.

The report of the committee on the bill granting the increase of
pension to the widow contained the following statement of facts
pertinent to this bill:

The claimant is the widow of Francis Broggan, late a corporal in the Ordnance
Corps, U. S. Army, and who died May 5, 1888, from chronic bronchitis incurred in
the line of his duty during his service, which covered the period from November 27,
1869, to March 19, 1887.

Mrs. Broggan was granted a pension in 1888 at $12 per month, with $2 additional
for each of two minor children. Both of these children are now over the age of 16
years, and the increased allowance on their account has ceased. It is alleged, however, that the child, Frances Caroline, whose pensionable minority ended January
25, 1895, is in such a condition of permanent helplessness that the increased allowance
on her account should continue under the letter and spirit of the act of June 27, 1890,
but the claimant's application for same at the Pension Bureau has been disallowed
by the medical referee, notwithstanding the fact that the examiner in charge of the
case submitted it for admission.

The testimony on file at the Pension Bureau and additional proof accompanying
the bill show that the child in question is under the care of the claimant; that she
is a sufferer from chorea, or St. Vitus dance, and from paralysis of left leg, arising in
infancy, and causing such atrophy and weakness of the leg as to necessitate the use
of steel rods from the shoe to the knee.

It further appears that the mother of the child (this beneficiary) is about 57 years old, blind in one eye, and dependent almost entirely upon her small pension for the support of herself and helpless daughter.

In addition to the service described above, the deceased soldier rendered two terms of honorable volunteer service in the civil war, and then in the infantry arm of the Regular Army from 1866 to 1869.

This claimant, now nearly 24 years old, is shown by the papers accompanying the bill to have continued in a condition of helplessness noted in the foregoing report on her mother's bill; and it is further shown that she has now no relative to care for her other than her brother, a quartermaster-sergeant of the Twenty-sixth Infantry, serving in the Philippine Islands. It is further shown that at the time of her death Mary Broggan, the mother, left a very little property, which she gave equally to the two children. The facts are shown by a numerously signed petition by reputable citizens of Vancouver, Wash. In view of the long and honorable service of the soldier and the fact that he died from causes arising in the line of his duty in such service, and the further fact that the beneficiary is now helpless and dependent, and there being no existing law under which she can be pensioned, the passage of the bill is respectfully recommended.

O

JOHN DA SILVA.

JANUARY 21, 1903.—Committed to the Committee of the Whole House and ordered
to be printed.

Mr. DRAPER, from the Committee on Pensions, submitted the following

REPORT.

[To accompany H. R. 15841.]

The Committee on Pensions, to whom was referred the bill (H. R. 15841) granting an increase of pension to John Da Silva, have considered the same and respectfully report as follows:

John Da Silva, of 346 Keap street, Brooklyn, N. Y., was an ordinary seaman aboard the *Savannah*, U. S. Navy, from February 20, 1844, to September 23, 1847, and while so serving participated in the war with Mexico. He also served from January 16, 1862, to July 22, 1862, as a musician in the Seventieth New York Infantry, in the civil war.

Mr. Da Silva is now in receipt of the pension of $12 per month allowed by law to the totally disabled and dependent survivors of the war with Mexico. He is now about 78 years old, and the evidence, including the affidavit of his physician, is to the effect that he is totally disabled by age and a complication of ailments, and that his pension constitutes his sole income, he having no property of any kind, either real or personal.

In view of the claimant's service in two wars and in the light of his great age and necessities your committee recommend the passage of the bill when amended as follows:

In line 6 strike out "of the" and insert in lieu thereof "ordinary seaman."

In lines 7 and 8 strike out "Volunteers" and substitute "Volunteer Infantry."

In line 8 strike out "war of 1861."

In line 9 strike out "thirty" and insert in lieu thereof "twenty."

O

JOHN H. WHEELER.

JANUARY 21, 1903.—Committed to the Committee of the Whole House and ordered
to be printed.

Mr. BROMWELL, from the Committee on Pensions, submitted the
following

REPORT.

[To accompany H. R. 15735.]

The Committee on Pensions, to whom was referred the bill (H. R.
15735) granting an increase of pension to John H. Wheeler, have
considered the same and respectfully report as follows:

John H. Wheeler, of No. 1208 Morton avenue, Louisville, Ky., was
a private in Company H, First Regiment Kentucky Foot Volunteers,
and served from May 19, 1846, to June 9, 1847, in the war with Mexico, and he now receives the pension of $12 per month allowed by law
to the totally disabled and dependent survivors of said war.

The papers accompanying the bill show that claimant is now 76
years old, wholly disabled by paralysis and the infirmities of age, and
without property or income aside from his pension. In view of the
foregoing facts, your committee recommend the passage of the bill when
amended as follows:

In line 7, strike out " Volunteer Infantry " and substitute therefor
the words " Foot Volunteers;" and in the same line strike out "in the
Mexican war " and insert " war with Mexico."

In line 8 strike out " fifty " and insert " twenty."

O

GEORGE W. CHOATE.

JANUARY 21, 1903.—Committed to the Committee of the Whole House and ordered to be printed.

Mr. DRAPER, from the Committee on Pensions, submitted the following

REPORT.

[To accompany H. R. 16153.]

The Committee on Pensions, to whom was referred the bill (H. R. 16153) granting a pension to George W. Choate, have considered the same and respectfully report as follows:

George W. Choate, of Auburn, N. Y., was a private in Company M, Third Regiment New York Volunteer Infantry, and served from May 1, 1898, to November 30, 1898, in the war with Spain. On April 28, 1899, he filed an application for pension, declaring that at Auburn, N. Y., in September, 1898, he incurred typho-malarial fever, resulting in heart trouble and general debility. The medical records show that he was treated during his service as follows: From June 4 to 5, 1898, for dermatitis, result of rhustox, in line of duty; July 19 to 20, for malaria tertian in line of duty; later (in September, 1898) he is shown to have been sick in city hospital, Auburn, N. Y., but the nature of his sickness there is not a matter of record. Upon medical examination preliminary to muster out, claimant declared that he was then suffering from fever sore on left leg, weakness of back, and kidney trouble, all incurred in September, 1898.

The medical officer making the examination at muster out certified that claimant had an abscess of left thigh, result of probable cellulitis, healing bed sore, backache, dysuria (retention of urine), great emaciation and weakness, the result of malarial and typhoid fever. He was found to be convalescing at that time, but still entirely disabled for manual labor. Upon medical examination in connection with his application for pension claimant was found to be suffering from disease of heart, but the claim was rejected in January, 1901, on the ground that he was not disabled by typho-malarial fever and that the disease of heart could not be accepted as a result. Thereupon, viz, in June, 1902, he filed a new claim, alleging weakened lungs and general debility, and a necessity for an operation for removal of enlarged lymphatic cervical glands from the right cervical region, causing a partial loss of use of right arm and deafness of right ear, all the result of typho-malarial fever, as claimed in original application; also chronic diarrhea contracted at Camp Alger in summer of 1898.

A medical examination held January 15, 1902, at Syracuse, N. Y., revealed tuberculosis, and this was confirmed November 5, 1902, by the Seneca Falls (N. Y.) board, who rated him ten-eighteenths for results of typho-malarial fever, twelve-eighteenths for diarrhea, probably tubercular, and seventeen-eighteenths for disease of lungs, and the board adds:

We are of the opinion that his tuberculosis is a result of typho-malarial fever. This claimant is so disabled from the above-mentioned disabilities as to be incapacitated for performing any manual labor, and is entitled to $30 per month.

There is a history of extreme disability and emaciation from date of discharge, and, on special examination, it was developed that claimant had a gland lanced before enlistment, and the special examiner who conducted the investigation thought that this should be accepted as evidence of the existence of tubercles before enlistment, but admits that diarrhea and typho-malarial fever in service did much to develop the disease.

The claimant's second application was also rejected by the Pension Bureau, and the rejection was sustained by the Secretary on appeal.

From the history of this case your committee is thoroughly convinced that the soldier's military service is responsible for his present serious physical condition and that there is no question but that he should be granted the pension recommended by the examining surgeons, viz, $30 per month. The passage of the bill is therefore recommended when amended as follows:

In line 7, after the word "Infantry," insert "war with Spain."

O

FRANCIS A. TRADEWELL.

JANUARY 21, 1903.—Committed to the Committee of the Whole House and ordered to be printed.

Mr. RICHARDSON, of Alabama, from the Committee on Pensions, submitted the following

REPORT.

[To accompany H. R. 16161.]

The Committee on Pensions, to whom was referred the bill (H. R. 16161) granting an increase of pension to Francis A. Tradewell, have considered the same and respectfully report as follows:

Francis A. Tradewell, of Sumter, S. C., was a private in Captain Ellmore's company of South Carolina Volunteers, and served from February 15 to May 12, 1836, in the Florida Indian war.

Mr. Tradewell is now receiving the pension of $8 per month allowed by act of July 27, 1892, to the survivors of the old Indian wars.

In his sworn petition accompanying the bill claimant swears he is 86 years old and wholly incapacitated by age and complication of ailments from earning a support, and, further, that aside from one small cottage at Sumter, S. C., renting for $10 per month, from which taxes, repairs, and insurance must be paid, he has no property or income, but is dependent upon his pension.

In view of the facts above related and in the light of numerous precedents, the passage of the bill is recommended when amended as follows:

In line 6, after the word "Tradewell," insert "late."

In the same line, after the word "Ellmore's," insert "company."

In line 7, after the word "Volunteers," insert "Florida."

O

JULIA E. JONES.

JANUARY 21, 1903.—Committed to the Committee of the Whole House and ordered
to be printed.

Mr. BOREING, from the Committee on Pensions, submitted the
following

REPORT.

[To accompany H. R. 16217.]

The Committee on Pensions, to whom was referred the bill (H. R.
16217) granting an increase of pension to Julia E. Jones, have considered the same and respectfully report as follows:

Julia E. Jones, of Pulaski, Giles County, Tenn., is the widow of
James L. Jones, who served from October 7, 1847, to July 23, 1848,
as second lieutenant of Company C, Third Regiment Tennessee Volunteers, in the Mexican war. The soldier died December 26, 1890, and
his widow, then about 48 years old, was, upon proof of disability and
dependency, allowed the pension of $8 per month provided to Mexican
war widows under the act of January 29, 1887. The testimony
accompanying the bill shows that claimant is now 59 years old, in
feeble health, and mainly dependent upon her own exertions for support. She has a home valued at $1,100, against which there is a mort-
gage and other debts amounting to $500. Aside from this she has no
property, and her pension is her only source of income. Her children
are all married and are not in financial condition to render her any
assistance.

In view of the foregoing facts your committee recommend the passage of the bill when amended as follows:

In line 8 strike out the words "in the."

O

LABAN McGAHAN.

JANUARY 21, 1903.—Committed to the Committee of the Whole House and ordered
to be printed.

Mr. BOREING, from the Committee on Pensions, submitted the
following

REPORT.

[To accompany H. R. 16291.]

The Committee on Pensions, to whom was referred the bill (H. R.
16291) granting a pension to Laban McGahan, have considered the
same and respectfully report as follows:

Laban McGahan, of Vinnie, Ky., enlisted April 11, 1848, in the
Fourth Kentucky Volunteers, for service in the war with Mexico, and
was discharged July 5, 1848, at Newport Barracks, Ky. After the
passage of the act of January 29, 1887, granting pensions to survivors
of the Mexican war, he made application under the act, and was granted
$8 per month. Subsequently he filed a claim for increase under the
act of January 5, 1893, but instead of receiving an allowance his name
was stricken from the roll on the ground that his service did not begin
until a less time than sixty days prior to the official ending of the war,
and that he therefore did not render sufficient service in the war to give
him title to the pension.

It is further shown that he is 74 years old and very poor.

This soldier enlisted in good faith for the war with Mexico, and the
service has once been recognized as sufficient to entitle him to a pension.

Under the circumstances your committee believe that his name should
again be placed on the roll, and the passage of the bill is therefore
recommended when amended as follows:

In line 6 strike out "of company" and substitute "of the."

In line 7 strike out "Mexican war" and substitute "war with
Mexico."

O

ELLA F. SHANDREW.

JANUARY 21, 1903.—Committed to the Committee of the Whole House and ordered
to be printed.

Mr. BOREING, from the Committee on Pensions, submitted the following

REPORT.

[To accompany H. R. 16391.]

The Committee on Pensions, to whom was referred the bill (H. R.
16391) granting a pension to Ella F. Shandrew, have considered the
same and respectfully report as follows:

Ella F. Shandrew is the widow of John C. Shandrew, who entered
the service of the United States July 2, 1898, as colonel of the Fifteenth Regiment Minnesota Volunteer Infantry, and served until
August 16, 1898, in the war with Spain.

The medical records show that Colonel Shandrew was admitted to
regimental hospital July 29, 1898, with aphasia (speechlessness, usually resulting from congestion of brain or apoplexy) incurred in line
of duty, and he resigned August 14, 1898, on account of sickness. In
December, 1898 (four months after discharge), he filed a claim for
pension, alleging aphasia, and this claim was pending and unsettled
when he died, July 21, 1899.

Mrs. Shandrew filed a claim for pension January 8, 1900, but the
same was rejected March 17, 1902, on the ground that soldier's death
was due to disease of kidneys existing prior to enlistment; at the same
time the deceased officer's claim was rejected on the ground that the
alleged aphasia was the outgrowth of disease of kidneys existing prior
to enlistment. The testimony presented in this case shows that the
deceased soldier was a most efficient officer of the Minnesota National
Guard for seventeen years, ending a few months before the beginning
of the Spanish war, and that soon after war was declared he offered
his services to the governor, and, being appointed colonel of the Fifteenth Regiment, immediately went to work in hot weather to organize his regiment, which was largely composed of raw and undisciplined
men, and that while in the active duties of camp he was stricken with
paralysis, accompanied temporarily by total loss of speech.

Dr. Henderson, who treated soldier at the time of being stricken,
swears that in his opinion the attack was due to severe physical and

mental strain in the performance of his duties, and Dr. C. E. Riggs testified practically to the same effect.

In the widow's case Dr. Henderson made affidavit that he was the soldier's personal and family physician, and that prior to the beginning of his fatal illness the soldier was treated for more or less trifling complaints from time to time, such as headaches from catarrh, an occasional slight disturbance of stomach and bowels, and such urinary disturbances as are produced by a more or less lithamic (excess of uric acid) condition, but that at time of enlistment soldier was in strong and vigorous physical condition.

Before a special examiner Mrs. Shandrew testified that aside from rheumatism, for which he went to some springs for treatment, and erysipelas soldier never had any ailment before enlistment. None of the physicians who testify in the case appear to have any knowledge that claimant's husband had disease of kidneys before the fatal attack, but it seems that Bright's disease was present after that attack. One or two lay witnesses swear, however, that soldier complained of his kidneys before enlistment, and was obliged to diet on account of the same. The evidence on this point is conflicting, however, and the weight of the evidence is apparently on the side of his freedom from any serious ailment until stricken in active service.

Mrs. Shandrew married the soldier April 5, 1870, and she is now about 50 years old. There are no children now under 16 years of age.

Representative Stevens, who introduced the bill in the House, makes the following statement pertinent to the case:

COMMITTEE ON MILITARY AFFAIRS, HOUSE OF REPRESENTATIVES,
Washington, D. C., January 6, 1903.

DEAR SIR: In matter of bill introduced by me for a pension to Mrs. Ella F. Shandrew, widow of the late Col. J. C. Shandrew, colonel of the Fifteenth Minnesota Volunteer Infantry, I desire to state that I very well knew the late Colonel Shandrew, since he and his family, composed of his wife, Ella F. Shandrew, and daughter, Hazel Shandrew, age about 16 years, lived opposite my house at St. Paul, Minn., for about ten years previous to the death of Colonel Shandrew. I was intimately acquainted with him in a social, business, and political way, and knew his circumstances and conditions, physically and financially.

I knew him well while he was colonel of one of the regiments of the National Guard of our State, which regiment subsequently during the Spanish war became enrolled as the Fifteenth Minnesota Volunteer Infantry. I knew him at that time as a man of apparently splendid physique and of great mental and physical force, and when he was mustered into the service of the United States he seemed to be in the best of health and spirits and with no ailments which would be the cause of his death. I was at my residence the day he was brought home suffering from a stroke of apoplexy, caused by excessive labors with his regiment during the hot days of July, 1898, and I saw him nearly every day at his home until the time of his death, in November. I personally knew that his health and strength failed on account of that stroke, and that his death apparently occurred by reason of that cause, and was certainly much hastened by it.

I well know the financial condition of the widow and child since the death of Colonel Shandrew. They did not own their own home and were compelled to move to a small and cheap house, where they now reside. Colonel Shandrew left no property. He was engaged in the insurance business for many years and at his death the widow realized from it a few hundred dollars. He had a small life insurance, not exceeding $1,500, which has been used up in living expenses and paying the large expense caused by the illness and death of Colonel Shandrew. The widow has no property or income for the support of herself and daughter. She works out by the day sewing at the houses in that vicinity, and also assists in preparing for entertainments, and work of that kind.

I know this of my own personal knowledge, and that by this labor Mrs. Shandrew has provided for herself and kept her daughter at school.

It would be an act of justice that a pension be granted to Mrs. Shandrew for the same amount that would be granted to a widow of an officer of the same rank of Colonel Shandrew at the time of his death.

Very truly,

F. C. STEVENS.

Hon. H. C. LOUDENSLAGER,
 Chairman Committee on Pensions, Washington, D. C.

After taking all the facts and circumstances into consideration, your committee believe that the claimant is justly entitled to a pension, and the passage of the bill is recommended when amended as follows:

In line 6 strike out the word "Colonel."

In line 7 strike out "of the Fifteenth Minnesota Volunteer Infantry" and insert in lieu thereof "colonel Fifteenth Regiment Minnesota Volunteer Infantry, war with Spain."

O

JAMES HUNTER.

JANUARY 21, 1903.—Committed to the Committee of the Whole House and ordered to be printed.

Mr. RICHARDSON, of Alabama, from the Committee on Pensions, submitted the following

REPORT.

[To accompany H. R. 16564.]

The Committee on Pensions, to whom was referred the bill (H. R. 16564) granting an increase of pension to James Hunter, have considered the same and respectfully report as follows:

James Hunter, of O'Neals Mills, Troup County, Ga., was a private in Captain Hardin's company, Georgia Volunteers, and served from June 5, 1836, to July 16, 1836, in the Creek Indian war, and he is now receiving the pension of $8 per month allowed by law for such service. In his sworn petition accompanying the bill claimant sets forth that he is 93 years old, as helpless as a child from age and infirmity, and without property or means of support whatever except his small pension.

This case appears to be an especially deserving one, and the passage of the bill is recommended when amended as follows:

In line 7 strike out the word "Regiment" and change the word "Volunteer" to "Volunteers," and in the same line strike out the word "Infantry" and substitute therefor "Creek Indian war."

In line 8 strike out "twenty-five" and insert "sixteen."

O

ANN GILBERT.

JANUARY 21, 1903.—Committed to the Committee of the Whole House and ordered
to be printed.

Mr. LOUDENSLAGER, from the Committee on Pensions, submitted the
following

REPORT.

[To accompany H. R. 16711.]

The Committee on Pensions, to whom was referred the bill (H. R.
16711) granting a pension to Ann Gilbert, have considered the same
and respectfully report as follows:

Ann Gilbert, of New Haven, Conn., is the widow of Amos Gilbert,
late seaman, U. S. Navy, who entered the service June 28, 1839, and
was honorably discharged July 13, 1842.

By private act of the Fifty-first Congress the sailor was granted a
pension at the rate of $25 per month on account of disabilities incurred
in the service. He died February 2, 1901, aged 86 years. His death
was caused by cerebral thrombosis and senility, and the widow can not,
of course, under the circumstances, make the proof necessary to show
that his death was due to service. Claimant, now 76 years old, married the sailor in 1857, and it is stated by the gentleman who introduced the bill that she is very poor and unable to earn a support by
daily labor.

Under all the circumstances your committee believe that the claimant should be granted a pension, and the passage of the bill is respectfully recommended when amended as follows:

In lines 6 and 7 strike out "of the United States steamship
Brandywine" and substitute therefor "seaman, United States Navy."

O

JAMES L. DAVENPORT, ALIAS DEXTER DAVIS.

JANUARY 21, 1903.—Committed to the Committee of the Whole House and ordered
to be printed.

Mr. APLIN, from the Committee on Invalid Pensions, submitted the
following

REPORT.

[To accompany H. R. 16313.]

The Committee on Invalid Pensions, to whom was referred the bill
(H. R. 16313) granting an increase of pension to James L. Davenport,
submit the following report:

This bill proposes to increase the pension of the soldier named
therein from $12 to $24 per month.

The files of the Pension Bureau show that James L. Davenport,
who served under the name of Dexter Davis as an unassigned recruit
of the Twenty-fourth Michigan Infantry from March 30 to June 28,
1865, when honorably discharged, is now a pensioner under the act of
June 27, 1890, at $12 per month, the maximum rating, for total inabil-
ity to earn a support by manual labor, the result of an injury to right
leg and senile debility.

The injury to right leg was sustained in May, 1890, while the beneficiary was loading a stationary engine on his dray at the Michigan
Central depot at West Bay City, Mich.

The beneficiary is now 80 years of age.

The certificate of medical examination of March 16, 1898, upon
which his pension of $12 per month was allowed under the act of June
27, 1890, described his condition as follows:

Is unable to do manual labor; is 75 years old; is much stiffened as the result of
rheumatism and old age; both shoulders are grating, stiff, and tender, motion limited
one-half in each.

Right elbow stiff; flexion limited one-third; left elbow stiff, flexion limited one-
fourth. Both hips stiff, tender, and painful, and motion limited one-half in each.
Left knee stiff, flexion limited one-third.

Applicant has a large and oblique fracture of the femur 2 inches above the knee-
joint. There is much callous around the seat of the fracture and extending into the
joint. Flexion in right knee is limited three-fourths. There is shortening of 1½
inches and the right leg is three-fourths inch lower than its fellow.

Heart's action weak, irregular, and intermittent. In fact, the action of this applicant's heart is so very weak and irregular that we are unable to get a correct count
of his pulse, nor can we exercise him on account of his crippled condition. Probable origin, rheumatism.

There has been filed with your committee the statement of the member who introduced the bill, setting forth that he had been personally acquainted with the beneficiary for the last thirty-five years; that he was severely injured on the Michigan Central Railroad, since which time he had been a great sufferer and a hopeless cripple, and that he has a wife 75 years of age dependent upon him for support; that said wife has been an invalid for the past thirty-five or forty years, not able to take care of herself, and that he has no income or property except a little home where he lives worth from four to five hundred dollars.

It being shown that this aged beneficiary is suffering from disabilities of an extreme nature, your committee, following precedents, recommend that his pension be increased from $12 to $20 per month, and report the bill back with the recommendation that it pass after the same shall have been amended as follows:

Strike out all of lines 6, 7, and 8 and insert in lieu thereof the following:

of James L. Davenport, alias Dexter Davis, late unassigned Twenty-fourth Regiment Michigan Volunteer Infantry, and pay him a pension at the rate of twenty dollars per month in lieu of that he is now receiving.

Amend the title so as to read: "A bill granting an increase of pension to James L. Davenport, alias Dexter Davis."

O

WILLIAM DUGDALE.

JANUARY 21, 1903.—Committed to the Committee of the Whole House and ordered
to be printed.

Mr. BOUTELL, from the Committee of the Post-Office and Post-
Roads, submitted the following

REPORT.

[To accompany H. R. 948.]

The Committee on the Post-Office and Post-Roads, to whom was
referred the bill (H. R. 948) for the relief of William Dugdale, postmaster at Noroton Heights, Conn., respectfully report that they have
examined the same and recommend its passage.

The facts of the case are as follows:

In January, 1894, one Leroy Harris, who had been for several years
in the postal service, came to Noroton Heights, Conn., and represented
himself as a post-office inspector, with instructions from the Department at Washington to examine the smaller money-order offices, and
where the business was not sufficient to justify the continuance of the
system to discontinue the money-order branch and substitute therefor
the transmission of money by postal notes. As his papers were in
form the examination was permitted, and upon its completion Harris
ordered the funds of the Noroton office sent to Washington, and took
up the money-order blanks, giving receipt therefor. On communication by Dugdale with the Department on the following day it appeared
that Harris was a fraud and his papers a forgery.

Harris filled out the orders which he had obtained, mailed them to
post-offices in Ohio and Indiana, and procuring them there raised
money on them to the amount of $3,100. He was arrested, tried, and
convicted, and is now in prison at Joliet, Ill., under a sentence of six
years.

The sum of $1,010 was found upon his person.

Later one Joseph Hyland, of New York, was arrested as a confederate and was also tried and convicted and is now serving his sentence.

The sum secured by them was		$3,100.00
Fees charged for issuing orders		13.95
Total loss		3,113.95
Collected from Leroy Harris	$1,010.00	
Commission allowed	1.08	
		1,011.08
Balance due United States		2,102.87

This sum of $2,102.87 is now—after eight years have expired, both of the guilty parties now serving their sentences in prison—disallowed in the accounts of the postmaster at Noroton Heights, Conn. The facts are not disputed, but the disallowance is based upon the rule that the money-order books must be kept "under lock and key, in some place of security, to which unauthorized persons can not have access."

Your committee are of the opinion that this case does not come within the rule, and that the postmaster, acting in good faith and in pursuance of orders which a duly authorized inspector would have a right to give, and in accordance with authority and instructions which had every appearance of genuineness, should not in equity be held for the loss incurred. Your committee can see no difference between this case and that of a bank teller who accepts a counterfeit bill or pays a forged check. The bank, and not the employee, would suffer the loss, and in this case your committee are of the opinion that the fraud was upon the Department, and that the amount should not be disallowed in the accounts of the postmaster.

They therefore recommend the passage of the bill and the allowance of the accounts which are now being held by the Post-Office Department awaiting the action of Congress, as per letter and memorandum herewith annexed.

TREASURY DEPARTMENT,
OFFICE AUDITOR FOR POST-OFFICE DEPARTMENT,
Washington, December 19, 1899.

DEAR SIR: Since my personal interview with you a few days ago I have looked up the case of the postmaster at Noroton Heights, Conn., and inclose herein a memorandum of the facts therein. After full consideration I am satisfied that it is not a proper case for the interference of this Bureau to relieve the postmaster from legal obligation incurred. As I stated to you, committees of Congress can, and frequently do, take into consideration indirect mitigating circumstances which we have no legal right to consider.

If you decide to press a bill for the relief of Mr. Dugdale, we will suspend all proceedings for any reasonable time pending the consideration of the measure.

Very respectfully, yours,

HENRY A. CASTLE, *Auditor.*

Hon. E. J. HILL,
House of Representatives, Washington, D. C.

MEMORANDUM.

In January, 1894, a person representing himself to be a post-office inspector, and believed to be one Leroy Harris, visited the post-office at Noroton Heights, Conn., and obtained from William Dugdale, the postmaster, thirty-one blank money-order forms, Nos. 170 to 200, inclusive. These were subsequently cashed in Ohio, Indiana, and Illinois for $100 each.

The money orders, as soon as received at this office by the postmasters paying them, were furnished the chief post-office inspector for investigation and use as evidence.

They were not charged to the money-order account of the postmaster at that time, for the reason that it had not then been determined upon whom the responsibility for the loss sustained by the surrender of the forms rested. The orders were only recently returned to this office by the inspector in charge at Chicago, Ill. They were at once charged to the money-order account of the postmaster at Noroton Heights, and he was notified under date of September 27, 1899. The amounts and fees, less commissions, was $3,112.87. His account was credited with $1,010, found upon the person of Leroy Harris when arrested, which, by order of the court, was turned over to the United States, leaving a balance of $2,102.87 due the United States.

()

PERSONAL REPRESENTATIVES OF JOHN McCABE AND PATRICK McCABE, DECEASED.

JANUARY 21, 1903.—Committed to the Committee of the Whole House and ordered
to be printed.

Mr. MAHON, from the Committee on War Claims, submitted the
following

REPORT.

[To accompany H. Res. No. 402.]

The Committee on War Claims, to whom was referred the claim for
the relief of the personal representatives of John McCabe and Patrick
McCabe, deceased, submit the following report:

The evidence offered in support of this claim is in the form of ex
parte affidavits, and your committee have no opportunity of subjecting
the witnesses to cross-examination, and are therefore of the opinion
that this claim should be referred to the Court of Claims, where depositions can be taken in the usual manner prescribed by law, counsel
for the Government and for the claimant having the right to cross-
examine the witnesses making such depositions, and when the facts
shall have been determined by the court upon the legal testimony thus
taken and submitted, said facts to be reported to Congress for its
consideration; and report herewith a resolution to that effect and
recommend its adoption.

O

REORGANIZATION OF THE CONSULAR SERVICE.

JANUARY 21, 1903.—Committed to the Committee of the Whole House on the state
of the Union and ordered to be printed.

Mr. ADAMS, from the Committee on Foreign Affairs, submitted the
following

REPORT.

[To accompany H. R. 16023.]

The Committee on Foreign Affairs on April 2, 1902, reported the
bill (H. R. 84) to increase the efficiency of the foreign service of the
United States and to provide for the reorganization of the consular
service. To meet certain defects and objections advanced against said
H. R. 84, the committee reports H. R. 16023, with amendments, to
the favorable consideration of the House and recommend the passage
of the same.

The report on H. R. 84 is hereby appended, as the reasons apply
equally to the present bill.

H R—57-2—Vol 2——28

House Report No. 1313, Fifty-seventh Congress, first session.

Mr. ADAMS, from the Committee on Foreign Affairs, submitted the
following

REPORT.

[To accompany H. R. 84.]

The Committee on Foreign Affairs, to whom was referred the bills
(H. R. 84 and 7482) for the reorganization of the consular service,
reports back the bill H. R. 84 with amendments. As this bill provides for a commission to reorganize the consular service, it is a
declaration of the lines upon which it is to be done rather than a
description of details.

The fact that for the first hundred years of its existence our country
was engaged in developing its internal resources for the supply of the
home markets is the explanation of the apparent lack of interest on
the part of Congress and the country at large to this important business branch of our Government, whose purpose was to develop our
commerce abroad. The service was instituted by the acts of July 1,
1790, and April 14, 1792. Even at its inception, Washington called
attention to the purpose and importance of this branch of the service.
A half a century elapsed before Congress showed any further interest
in our consular service, when the act of 1856 was passed, which slightly
enlarged the service and created certain abuses therein by closer supervision of the fees. The shipping statute of 1883 swept away the whole
schedule of fees for services to American vessels, which up to that time
had been a lucrative emolument to the consuls, and little or nothing
has since been given to them in compensation for their loss.

Such changes in condition show the necessity for the careful revision
of the salaries throughout the service, as at present some receive enormous compensation, as at London and Paris, for their services while
others only a salary of $1,000 or $1,500 a year. To illustrate: The
consul at Montevideo has a salary of $3,000, with official fees of $922,
showing the amount of business done at the office, while the consul at
Stettin, Germany, has a salary of $1,500, with fees of $1,192, showing a much larger business transacted there. So also at Demarara,
British Guiana, the consul has a salary of $3,000, though the official

fees amount to only $637, while at Leipzig, where the official fees amount to $5,118, the salary was only $2,000. The consul at Nuremberg, Germany, a city of 160,000 inhabitants, has a salary of $3,000, while the consul at Munich, the capital of Bavaria, with 450,000 inhabitants, has a salary of only $2,000. The recital of these facts assuredly shows the need of a revision of our consular service, and they could be amplified in every portion of the globe to which that service is extended.

The advantage of a reorganization of our consular service has been called to the attention of Congress from time to time by those who saw the growing necessity for some legislation in that regard. The Department of State has long recognized the inadequacy of the consular service to the growing needs of the country and to the proper protection of the business and property of our citizens residing abroad, either for business or the pleasure of travel.

Secretary of State Livingston, in 1833, and Secretary of State Buchanan, in 1846, called attention to the evils existing in the service, but it was not until 1884, when Secretary of State Frelinghuysen discussed the subject in his admirable and exhaustive report, transmitted to Congress by President Arthur March 20 of that year, that the strong necessity for action was made apparent. In it he said:

Until recently the demands of Europe, which consumed the greater portion of our exports, and the condition of the producing countries were such as to give us control in the supply of certain products, such as breadstuffs, provisions, cotton, and petroleum, etc. The demands of Europe for all these products and of the other continents for petroleum especially were so positive, and our producing conditions so favorable, as to give us practically a monopoly for their supply.

These conditions of international demand and supply are undergoing radical changes, which the near future will intensify.

The efforts which have been made and which are being made by Europe to enlarge the field of supply in the above-mentioned products, aided by the ambition which prevails in all countries for the development of natural and artificial resources to meet their own wants and to supply the wants of others, have resulted in awakening competition for the supply even of those products which we have heretofore controlled. It is true that thus far this competition has not effected our trade to any appreciable extent, but the desire for development which is now abroad and the ambition which prevails to increase the production (outside of the United States) of the foregoing articles render consular supervision of absolute importance. *The complex commercial relations and industrial interests which now prevail in Europe have originated hostility to American products in many countries and afford additional reasons for the enlargement and perfection of the consular service.*

The same necessity has been pressed upon the Government at home by our representatives in the service abroad. In 1864 John Bigelow, consul at Paris, wrote:

The practical results of our system, which in this respect has no parallel under any other Government, are—

(1) That we are obliged to select for consular posts men without the proper training and qualifications.

(2) We are obliged to select men who have no intention of making a career in the consular service. Consequently they have no great inducement to qualify themselves properly for a post which they can hope to hold only for a brief term by the acquisition of knowledge of little or no use to them in any other profession.

(3) The fact that our consuls are so transitory deprives them of their proper influence in the consular body, as well as in most political and social circles where it is the interest of the Government that they should circulate.

(4) Such frequent changes prevent anything like uniformity or regularity in the conduct of consular business, which results in a serious prejudice to commerce and a grave inconvenience to the Department.

(5) With each change of Administration the Government is exposed to lose the benefit of whatever knowledge and influence its agents have acquired during their

terms of service, and thus most of the time is served by raw and, therefore, to a considerable extent, by incompetent officers.

There is no other country in the world where the tenure of the consular office is dependent upon the permanence of the home Administration. Nor can the practice be defended by any consideration whatever which looks to its usefulness and efficiency.

Surely no stronger evidence could be adduced coming from one of experience in the consular service.

The Hon. Robert Adams, jr., when United States minister to Brazil in 1889, wrote in the North American Review:

The method by which the men are chosen for the positions necessarily brings forth poor candidates, while the short tenure of office, which is generally limited to the Presidential term, almost certainly so if a change of party takes place, and the meager salaries paid—in some posts hardly sufficient to support life in a respectable manner—deters competent men from entering the service. It should also be remembered that there is no promotion for efficient service; that a consul can not hope for a change of climate from a trying to a more healthful and genial one after a given period of service, and that there is always the prospect of returning to the United States broken down in health, unfitted to resume private business, and without prospect of further employment at the hands of the Government.

His excellency the Chinese minister, in a recent address before the University of Pennsylvania, says:

Most European governments send young men to the East to learn the language and study the customs of the country. After a residence of two or three years, when they have proved themselves proficient, after passing a strict examination, they are then placed in responsible positions as student interpreters, consular assistants, etc. Merit is awarded by promotion. Thus those governments have competent men specially fitted for service in the Orient. It might not be unwise for your Government to adopt a similar system.

Assistant Secretary Rockhill, in an article in the Forum for the month of February, 1897, sums up the evils of our consular system as follows:

(1) Imperfect mode of selection of consular officers.
(2) No permanency of tenure.
(3) Inadequate compensation, resulting in (a) the exaction of excessive fees and (b) the creation of consular agencies to increase salaries.
(4) Excessive number of fee consulates and commercial agencies.
(5) Imperfect enforcement of regulations, especially as regards amounts of fees and their collection.

This judgment from the late Assistant Secretary of State, who had especial charge of the consular service, is certainly deserving of great weight upon this subject.

The President in his message to Congress at its present session impressed upon it the necessity of legislation on this subject. He said:

The consular service is now organized under the provisions of a law passed in 1856, which is entirely inadequate to existing conditions. The interest shown by so many commercial bodies throughout the country in the reorganization of the service is heartily commended to your attention. Several bills providing for a new consular service have in recent years been submitted to Congress. They are based upon the just principle that appointments to the service should be made only after a practical test of the applicant's fitness, that promotion should be governed by trustworthiness, adaptability, and zeal in the performance of duty, and that the tenure of office should be unaffected by partisan considerations.

The guardianship and fostering of our rapidly expanding foreign commerce, the protection of American citizens resorting to foreign countries in lawful pursuit of their affairs, and the maintenance of the dignity of the nation abroad combine to make it essential that our consuls should be men of character, knowledge, and enterprise. It is true that the service is now, in the main, efficient, but a standard of excellence can not be permanently maintained until the principles set forth in the bills heretofore submitted to the Congress on this subject are enacted into law.

For further information on the necessity of legislation on this subject reference is hereby made to the report of the Hon. John T. Morgan, made to the Senate of the United States on February 6, 1895, which is appended to this report as Exhibit C.

This bill proposes that all grades of consuls shall be citizens of the United States and shall be placed under a salary; does away with consular or commercial agencies, and provides that all fees of all kinds must be accounted for and covered into the United States Treasury. Of the advantages of this system over the present one abundant evidence is presented by those most conversant with the needs of the service. In 1871 Inspector Keim reported:

> The act of 1856 was doubtless designed to correct the most conspicuous of the abuses which prevailed. * * * The evils prior to that date may have been mitigated or may have suffered temporary abatement. * * * They were certainly not eradicated; and these abuses * * * have been perpetuated in most cases by each succeeding officer.

Again, in 1879, Gen. Julius Stahel, then consul at Hiogo, Japan, wrote to the Department of State:

> The permission granted to consular officers of receiving unofficial fees for notarial acts, etc., is liable to abuse, and is the root of many evils and irregularities. * * * I suggest that the permission to charge unofficial fees be withdrawn, and that all fees received by consular officers, for whatsoever service rendered, be considered as official, and so accounted for. * * * In this way one of the greatest evils of our service would be remedied and dignity added to the representation of the United States in foreign countries.

Secretary Frelinghuysen, in his report of 1884 on the consular service, said:

> In the opinion of the Department, the present system of compensation by fees, either official or unofficial, should be abolished. Whatever money comes into the consul's hands should be turned into the Treasury of the United States, and he should depend for his support entirely upon the salary allowed by Congress.

In 1885, writing on the same subject to the Department, Gen. John S. Mosby, consul at Hongkong, expressed himself even more emphatically:

> Consular fees should, in my opinion, be altogether abolished. * * * The best way to secure honesty in the public service is to make it impossible for officers to be dishonest. I can see no sound reason for sending consuls abroad to collect revenue for the Government. You might as well send the Navy to do it.

Your committee calls the attention of members of Congress to the changed conditions which have arisen during the past two years, which emphasize the necessity that our merchants should be furnished with the most accurate and recent information by the consular service. The recent acquisitions of territory to our domain, the later diplomatic victory which has assured to us an open door to the trade of China, thereby securing the markets of four hundred millions of people sufficiently civilized to require our manufactured textiles, railroad supplies, electrical equipments, and all forms of products of iron, make it absolutely essential that our merchants and exporters should receive information and statistics gathered by men competent, in the full sense of the word, to give reliable information. The wonderful increase in our export trade, reaching a billion dollars within the past year, is an evidence of what can be done by American energy and enterprise; and with an efficient consular corps, which is the business branch of our foreign service, furnishing reliable information, these exports can be largely increased. Some of our merchants are so alive to the value of this information that they are sending special agents to examine and report the resources and necessities of these new fields. With a proper consular service this would not be necessary.

That the business and commercial members of the community are fully alive to the importance of this question is evident by the resolution of the National Board of Trade, as follows:

Resolved, That Congress be urged to authorize the President to appoint a commission, to be composed of members of the Senate, of the House of Representatives, and of the State and Treasury Departments, and, perhaps, one or two citizens of experience and fitness, which shall by inspection and inquiry make a complete examination of our entire consular system and laws, to the end that any further legislation by Congress shall be based upon such ample information and observation and meet the demands of the expanding commerce of the country.

and by communications received from the National Association of Manufacturers and from nearly every board of trade, chamber of commerce, and similar association throughout our country urging that our consular service be put upon a permanent and businesslike basis.

Attention is called to Exhibit A, attached to this report.

These opinions represent the judgment of men best informed as to the needs of the consular service by the practical experience of our representatives abroad, and those having the supervision of the service at home, and of those who have the most material interest at stake.

No stronger argument could be offered for the necessity of a reform in the consular service than the war with Spain. Our naval authorities had a right to look to the consuls to keep them informed on all matters of interest appertaining to the movements of the enemy's vessels of war, whether separately or in squadrons; of the movements of war supplies, whether of munitions or fuel; with the measures taken by the Government for the prosecution of the war, whether of a legislative or military character. How could men, however patriotic they may have felt, be competent to furnish such information when many of them had been inducted into office for less than a year, most of whom could neither read nor speak the language of the country to which they had been accredited, thus making it impossible for them, of their own knowledge, to gather information from the people, or even the newspapers thereof, without the aid of interpreters who may be false in their service to them? It is practical facts like these which emphasize the business character of our consular service and illustrate the necessity of conducting it on business principles.

So great has been the necessity for reliable information of the needs and requirements of foreign countries as well as of the articles, whether natural or manufactured, they have for export, that it has been found necessary for the merchants to establish a commercial museum at Philadelphia to supply this information. So useful has this institution proved itself to be that Congress, by a two-thirds vote, made an appropriation of $350,000 to promote this object and to hold a commercial export exposition. This institution, in conjunction with an efficient and well-trained consular service, would supply our manufacturers and merchants with reliable information with which to expand our growing export trade. These changed conditions, both at home and abroad, press this subject upon the attention of Congress to a greater degree than ever before.

The importance of our consular service being recognized, as well as the useful part it may be made to play in the hoped-for extension of the foreign trade, the question naturally arises, "How can it be improved?" Two great obstacles appear at the first step in that direction: First, the ignorance of the majority of the people of the importance of the consular service as affecting their individual interests; and, second, the reward for political service that has engrafted itself on our political parties. Let the people understand this question and they will soon insist that proper rules shall be applied to this branch of the Government service.

Our consuls should be trained for their positions and pass an examination on such subjects as the laws regulating shipping, the commercial treaties existing between their own and other countries, the laws relating to intestates, on the consular regulations of the United States, and on such other subjects as relate to their duties. They should also be required to have a practical knowledge of French or of the language of the country to which they are to be sent. It will be demanded, "Where will such a specially educated class come from?" Once it is understood that the service is a permanent one, young men will prepare for it the same as they do for other professions, and in sufficient numbers to arouse competition. That this was not a matter of conjecture was fully established by the experience in Great Britain when the examination for the civil service was thrown open to all, the number of applicants having increased the first year from 5,000 to 15,000, and the character and ability of the applicants having proved as high, if not better than that of the selected applicants had been before.

To insure this, however, the salaries must be raised. How can a man be expected to live at Para, in Brazil, under an equatorial sun, exposed to malarial and yellow fevers, and deprived almost entirely of all social intercourse, for $2,000 a year, or, even worse, at Santos, where the town was decimated by yellow fever, the victims including the United States vice-consul? Yet the importance of these positions to our country can best be stated by the value of the exports to the United States, which amount annually to about twelve and a half million dollars. These cases could be amplified, but they are sufficient to illustrate the present state of affairs.

Nowhere is the adage "The best is the cheapest" more forcibly illustrated than in the consular service. Had it been composed of the proper material, no necessity could have arisen for the establishment of the South American Bureau, or of sending special commissioners to the foreign governments to make arrangements for the exhibits at the Columbian Exposition.

For these reasons your committee submit this bill to the favorable consideration of the House, and recommend the passage of the same.

APPENDIX A.

The Committee on Foreign Affairs of the House of Representatives present the communications and statements made before the committee from time to time during the consideration of the bill to reorganize the consular service, as follows:

STATEMENT OF WILLIAM R. CORWINE, OF THE MERCHANTS' ASSOCIATION OF NEW YORK CITY.

Whereas the commercial interests of the United States are suffering from the competition of foreign nations and by reason of a lack of foreign markets for our surplus manufacturing and agricultural products; and

Whereas it is believed that our foreign commerce may be promoted and new markets opened by a change in the methods of our consular service; and

Whereas a bill has been introduced in the House of Representatives by Mr. Adams to increase the efficiency of the foreign service of the United States and to provide for the reorganization of the consular service, being House of Representatives bill No. 4334:

Resolved, If the Senate concur, that our Senators and Representatives in Congress are hereby requested to support such measure or some measure of a similar character, and if possible secure its enactment into law.

THE BOARD OF TRADE OF THE CITY OF BALTIMORE,
Baltimore, January 16, 1899.

THE MERCHANTS' ASSOCIATION OF NEW YORK,
New York.

GENTLEMEN: I am in receipt of your much valued favor of 10th instant inclosing copy of House bill No. 10524, known generally as a bill to increase the efficiency of the foreign service of the United States and to provide for the reorganization of the consular service; also inclosing copy of the report of the Committee on Foreign Affairs, known as Report No. 1260.

This board has taken action long ago, and again within the last week upon this subject, and is alive to the importance of the matter. I inclose you copy of report adopted and sent to the members of the United States Senate and House of Representatives.

Yours, very truly, etc.,

HENRY C. LANDIS, *Secretary.*

P. S.—I shall be pleased to confer with Mr. Corwine.

ROOMS OF THE BOARD OF TRADE OF THE CITY OF BALTIMORE,
RIALTO BUILDING,
Baltimore, January 9, 1899.

DEAR SIR: I have the honor to invite your attention and beg your consideration of the following report and resolution unanimously adopted by this board at meeting held this day.

Very respectfully,

HENRY C. LANDIS, *Secretary.*

A BILL TO INCREASE THE EFFICIENCY OF THE FOREIGN SERVICE OF THE UNITED STATES AND TO PROVIDE FOR THE REORGANIZATION OF THE CONSULAR SERVICE.

The committee on foreign commerce, to whom was referred a communication from the Merchants' Association of New York, dated December 27, 1898, calling attention to a bill now pending before Congress entitled "A bill to increase the efficiency of the foreign service of the United States and to provide for the reorganization of the consular service," beg to submit the following report:

The subject of improving the consular service of the United States has in former years been under consideration by this board, and resolutions were adopted by it on March 4, 1895, in favor of a bill then pending in the Senate, introduced by Senator Lodge, having this object in view.

The large yearly increase in the foreign trade of the United States, and especially the great expansion that is now taking place, makes it more than ever important that our consular service should be placed on a footing of efficiency that will compare favorably with other countries, and notably with our chief competitors, Great Britain and Germany.

The bill now pending in Congress, known as House bill No. 2524, and which has been favorably reported by the Committee on Foreign Affairs, is designed to place the consular service on a better footing than that upon which it now stands: Therefore, be it

Resolved, That the Board of Trade of Baltimore is heartily in favor of such measures being adopted by Congress as will secure efficient and creditable service, and would urge the passage of House bill No. 2524 at the earliest practical date.

Resolved, That copies of these resolutions be sent to the members of the United States Senate and House of Representatives, and that the Senators and Representatives from Maryland be requested to do all in their power to secure passage of the bill.

THE CHAMBER OF COMMERCE OF SAN FRANCISCO,
San Francisco, January 24, 1899.

Hon. DAVID B. HENDERSON,
House of Representatives, Washington, D. C.

DEAR SIR: Realizing with other commercial bodies the great need of a radical improvement in the system under which our consular service is operated, and also being firmly impressed by the great importance of having this department of our Government in as efficient condition as possible, particularly as we are now as a nation engaged more than ever in a great commercial struggle to place our products in the markets of the world, and as a means of accomplishing this end we consider the aid which can be rendered by a properly organized corps of consuls of immense benefit, we therefore respectfully urge that you will take such steps as will bring up for the earliest possible consideration in the House of Representatives the bill known as House bill No. 10524, as a means of effecting the desired improvement in that branch of the service.

Trusting that this will meet with your approval and hearty support, we have the honor to subscribe ourselves,

Your obedient servants,

THE CHAMBER OF COMMERCE OF SAN FRANCISCO.
CHARLES NELSON, *President.*
E. SCOTT, *Secretary.*

THE CHAMBER OF COMMERCE OF SAN FRANCISCO,
San Francisco, January 25, 1899.

MERCHANTS' ASSOCIATION OF NEW YORK,
New York Life Building, New York City.

DEAR SIRS: I beg to acknowledge receipt of your favors of the 9th and 10th of January in regard to a bill introduced by Congressman Adams, namely, H. R. 10524, for the improvement of the consular service. This is a matter in which we are in full and hearty accord with you, and have the pleasure of inclosing you a copy of a letter sent to Hon. David B. Henderson, one of the members of the House Committee on Rules. We have sent a similar letter to each of the members of that committee, also practically the same to Hon. John A. Barham, Hon. James G. Maguire, Hon. Eugene F. Loud, and Hon. Samuel G. Hilborn, of the California delegation in the House, with the slight addition of a request to urge upon the House committee the necessity and urgency of this matter.

Joining with you in the hope that the bill will meet with an early approval, I beg to remain,

Yours, very respectfully, E. SCOTT, *Secretary.*

CHAMBER OF COMMERCE AND MERCHANTS' EXCHANGE,
Cincinnati, January 9, 1899.

Mr. WILLIAM F. KING,
President The Merchants' Association of New York,
New York Life Building, New York City.

DEAR SIR: Referring to your communication under date December 27, in regard to consular service, I have the honor of inclosing copy of action upon the same by our board of directors.

Truly, yours, C. B. MURRAY, *Superintendent.*

CINCINNATI CHAMBER OF COMMERCE.

The Cincinnati Chamber of Commerce, recognizing the importance of effective service in the consular offices representing our Government in its influence for the promotion of the industrial interests of our country, joins in commending the passage of the measure pending in Congress known as H. R. bill No. 2524, Report No. 1480, entitled "A bill to increase the efficiency of the foreign service of the United States and to provide for the reorganization of the consular service," it being believed that such measure would be promotive of improvement in result of each service.

LITTLE ROCK BOARD OF TRADE,
Little Rock, Ark., January 12, 1899.

MERCHANTS' ASSOCIATION,
New York City, N. Y.

GENTLEMEN: Herewith please find copy of resolutions adopted by our board of directors.

Whenever we can be of service, please command us.

Respectfully, etc.,

LITTLE ROCK BOARD OF TRADE,
By GEO. R. BROWN, *Secretary.*

LITTLE ROCK BOARD OF TRADE, LITTLE ROCK, ARK.

Resolved by the Little Rock Board of Trade, That we heartily concur in the memorial of the Merchants' Association of New York City favoring the passage by Congress of the bill entitled "A bill to increase the efficiency of the foreign service of the United States and to provide for the reorganization of the consular service."

Resolved, That the consular service should be made as efficient as possible and placed on a par with the service of Germany and Great Britain, and under the civil-service rules.

MEMPHIS MERCHANTS' EXCHANGE,
Memphis, Tenn., February 21, 1899.

Mr. WILLIAM F. KING,
President Merchants' Association, New York, N. Y.

DEAR SIR: I have the honor of transmitting to you herewith resolution adopted at a general meeting of this exchange, held this morning, upon the subject of the reorganization and improvement of the consular service of the United States.

Very truly, yours,

N. S. GRAVES, *Secretary.*

MEMPHIS MERCHANTS' ASSOCIATION, MEMPHIS, TENN.

Resolutions adopted at a general meeting of the Memphis Merchants' Exchange, February 21, 1899.]

Whereas an effort is now being made to secure such legislation by the Congress of the United States as will insure a thorough reorganization of the consular service of the United States and increase its efficiency by establishing a classified service, with permanency of tenure and with appointments and promotions based on examinations as to experience and fitness for positions: Be it

Resolved, That the Memphis Merchants' Exchange, in the interest of American commerce and the life and property of American citizens in foreign countries, ask the earnest consideration of our Senators and Representatives to the organization and improvement of the consular service, and invoke their prompt and hearty cooperation in securing the early consideration of the bill recently introduced in the House of Representatives by the Hon. Robert J. Adams, of Pennsylvania, known as H. R. 10524, Report No. 1460; and further be it

Resolved, That we urge the adoption of said bill No. 10524 or such other measure as will substantially carry into effect its provisions.

Resolved also, That a copy of these resolutions be sent to each of the Senators from this State and to the Representatives in Congress from this particular district, as also the adjoining districts of the States of Mississippi and Arkansas, with the request that they interest themselves in securing the proposed legislation.

[OFFICIAL SEAL.]   N. S. GRAVES, *Secretary.*

WASHINGTON, D. C., *March 1, 1899.*

Mr. N. S. GRAVES,
Secretary Memphis Merchants' Exchange, Memphis, Tenn.

DEAR SIR: I send you herewith a copy of bill and accompanying report on the reorganization of the consular service, concerning which I received some days ago a petition or memorial from the merchants' exchange, which I presented to the House.

I send you a number of copies of the bill and report, so that you can place them with those who you think will take an interest in the matter. This is a matter in which I have taken a good deal of interest for some time, and I hope the exchange and the individual members of it will become actively interested in the subject.

I wrote a number of editorials on this line when I was editor of the Commercial-Appeal, and have published several interviews since. I am heartily in favor of the general principle of the Adams bill, and am preparing to discuss that measure when it can be got up for consideration in the House.

The rapid and steady increase of our foreign trade for the last few years has directed public thought to the possibilities in that direction. The one thing we lack is an intelligent and efficient system, by means of which our export trade can be kept in sympathetic touch with the varying needs and conditions of foreign markets. I believe this can be largely accomplished by a reorganization of our consular service and placing it upon the basis of merit.

I have taken the liberty of writing you thus somewhat at length on the subject because I think it of very great importance.   .

Very truly, yours,   E. W. CARMACK.

NATIONAL ASSOCIATION OF MANUFACTURERS
OF THE UNITED STATES OF AMERICA,
Philadelphia, Pa., January 31, 1900.

Hon. ROBERT R. HITT,
    Chairman Committee on Foreign Affairs,
        House of Representatives, Washington, D. C.

SIR: As it is not possible for me to appear in person before your committee and thus convey an expression of opinion from members of the National Association of Manufacturers relative to the pending bills for the reorganization of the consular service, I beg leave to submit herewith some suggestions on behalf of the 1,100 manufacturers embraced in the membership of this association.

Upon many occasions this association' has placed itself on record as desiring most earnestly the reorganization of our consular service in such manner as will increase its efficiency and eradicate many of the evils which now exist as the result of the present system.

Perhaps the position of this association is most concisely and most clearly expressed in the following recommendations which were transmitted to the President under date of April 5, 1897:

That the changes in the consular service shall be as few as possible.

That removals shall be made only because of demonstrated incapacity.

That vacancies shall be filled as far as possible by promotions or transfers.

That appointments shall be made solely upon the basis of proper qualification for the position and without regard to political service.

That only American citizens shall be appointed to any consular offices.

I can only repeat the recommendations to express the present position of this association, and I believe that they will equally well express the opinion of every thoughtful business man who has any familiarity with the needs and requirements of our consular service and with its present condition.

I am not one of those who pronounce sweeping condemnation of our consular service; for a somewhat intimate acquaintance with many of our consular officers and a careful investigation of the records of a large number of them have shown me that the service contains many men of marked ability, and also a large number of men who are both unqualified for and unworthy of the positions they hold. That we have any efficient men in the service is not due to the system under which the service is organized and maintained; the efficient men are there in spite of the system rather than because of it. It is in accord with the sound principles which have governed every business enterprise, and which as well should be applied to the conduct of the business functions of our Government, that this branch of the governmental service should be organized and conducted upon such a basis as shall insure the appointment of competent men rather than make their presence in the service merely the result of accident. I take this to be the principle which has actuated those who have formulated the bills looking to the improvement of the consular service that have been introduced into Congress and are now pending.

With particular reference to H. R. 1026, which I have examined with much care, I beg to offer the suggestion that while this measure seems to provide a very efficient manner for placing the consular service upon a much better business basis, it is lacking in one or two points, the provision of which would make the meaning and purposes of the bill clearer and stronger. For example, while the wording of several paragraphs very clearly implies that vacancies in each grade shall be filled by promotions from the next lower grade, this fact is not stated in specific terms, and to place this method of procedure beyond question, I beg leave to suggest that the wording of the bill should be made more specific on this particular point.

Furthermore, there seems to be in this bill no provision touching the manner of making removals from the consular service, a matter of quite as much importance as the making of appointments or promotions.

I take the liberty of suggesting that the wording of the bill should be made very clear and specific on this point, to provide that removals shall not be made except for cause, and that the causes and the manner in which removals therefor should be made should also be very distinctly expressed.

With the general purposes of this bill I am in hearty accord, and I know that the ends it seeks to accomplish command the most earnest approval of the business men of the United States as a whole. The astonishing increase in our foreign trade during the past three or four years, I regard as only the beginning of our conquest of the world's markets, and the consular service of the United States is a most essential and vital factor in the growth of this business. It is this that gives to the manufacturers of the United States such deep interest in everything that tends to improve the efficiency of our consular representation.

Respectfully yours,

THEODORE C. SEARCH,
President National Association of Manufacturers.

RESOLUTIONS ON IMPROVEMENT OF CONSULAR SERVICE OFFERED BY H. R. WHITMORE, OF MISSOURI.

Whereas the functions of our consular service are almost exclusively confined to matters pertaining to our foreign commerce, which should therefore be regarded as a branch of a great business enterprise and administered strictly on business principles; and

Whereas the rapid growth and increasing importance of our foreign commerce specially demand men of the best business qualifications and unsullied reputations, who will command alike the confidence and respect of all who have business with them: Therefore,

Resolved, That the Trans-Mississippi Commercial Congress earnestly urges such thorough organization of our consular service as to secure the most efficient service to our business interests, and it believes that this can be best accomplished by basing appointments on experience, ability, and character, unbiased by any political consideration, thus assuring that efficiency which is only attained by extended experience. With this end in view it urges upon its Representatives in Congress the passage of bill No. 1026, now pending in the House of Representatives.

To the Committee on Foreign Affairs of the House of Representatives.

GENTLEMEN: Representing the National Business League, and at the suggestion of the executive committee of that league, I ask your indulgence while I make a brief statement of our reasons for believing that a reorganization of the United States consular service is necessary and urgent. I have no expectation of saying anything new on the matter concerning which this committee is undoubtedly fully informed, and in the reform of which some of your members have been notably active for several years. Our principal object is to assure you that the evils for which we ask a remedy have been constantly growing until the burden has become almost unbearable, and that the increasing demands of our commerce require that there be no further delay.

Our consular system—if it can be called a system—is substantially the same as it was a hundred years ago, notwithstanding repeated efforts at reform. In no other civilized country are the commercial agents in foreign countries selected on the basis of political services rendered to the party in power, and without regard to their fitness to perform the duties of their position. The results of this practice are plainly apparent. Our public commercial statistics will not stand comparison with those of the other countries. The necessity for trained men as consuls is greater than in positions of similar grade in the civil service. Among the duties of consuls is that of verifying invoices of merchandise exported to this country; of detecting frauds on the customs, undervaluations, etc.; investigating and reporting on the products, industries, etc., of the country, and on all subjects which will assist the merchant and manufacturer of this country in his search for new markets and in keeping him informed of the requirements of the foreign market.

There are over fifty subjects which the United States consul is required to investigate, including "technical and industrial education," and kindred matters requiring special training and a knowledge of the language of the country. In seaports they are required to settle disputes involving legal questions, and in oriental countries they have judicial powers, both civil and criminal. No one has spoken more strongly or intelligently of the worse than absurdity of selecting men for such positions at the behest of the political boss under the "spoils system" than Mr. Adams, of this committee.

While France is the model in the matter of the consular system, England is not far behind. All applicants in England have to pass an examination, and while the examinations are not competitive, except for service in oriental countries, the requirements are quite strict. The act of Parliament of 1825 provided that the civil service commissioners should conduct the examinations, and that among the requirements shall be proficiency in the French language and in the language of the country to which the candidate is to be accredited, knowledge of English mercantile law and arithmetic.

The higher grades are mostly filled by promotions according to merit, and removals are rare. Consuls to oriental countries must pass a competitive examination. They must study the oriental languages, and pass further examinations at intervals. They are first appointed as assistants, then vice-consuls, and consuls, as vacancies occur.

The French system is excellent. The examinations are competitive, and entry is into the lowest grade, with promotion according to merit. In order to compete, the applicant must first serve a probationary period of from one to three years.

I am aware that members of this committee have been diligent for many years in their efforts to put some system into this service. It is true also that Presidents and the State Department have made attempts in that direction, always abortive. Nearly forty years ago Secretary Seward made a regulation that applicants for consularships should be submitted to examination and should be required to know the French language and the language of the country to which they should be sent. The regulation was not enforced.

In 1866 and twice in 1872 similar orders were made by the State Department with like fruitless results. In 1895 President Cleveland made an order that applicants for consulates where the salaries were between $1,000 and $2,500 should be examined in that Department, and whatever effect may have been given to that order at first it has now become ineffective. In fact "passed examinations" like those contemplated in the orders mentioned have now been found to be of very little if any value. They are easily manipulated for "spoils" purposes when desired. Competitive examinations are the only real and effective examination.

In view of these failures to accomplish anything by departmental orders or without legislation by Congress, it seems imperative that Congress should act explicitly and promptly.

That the time has come when legislation is urgent there can be no question. This league has been in correspondence for several months with organizations of business men all over the country, and a demand is unanimous for the reform. The league has cooperated with representatives of the Chamber of Commerce of Cleveland, Ohio, and the Chamber of Commerce of New York in the examination of this matter, and is in accord with them in asking your favorable consideration and recommendation for passage of the bill which has resulted from such examination and which will be presented at this hearing, and which, in our opinion, formulates a plan upon which the consular service can be reorganized, as far as now practicable, on the lines I have indicated.

The question of the constitutionality of a law which requires the appointments of consuls to be only made from persons who have passed an examination—in view of the fact that the Constitution puts the appointment of consuls into the hands of the President, with the approval of the Senate—has, I know, been raised at various times.

Upon the examination of this question we believe that even if a bill should be so framed it would not be held unconstitutional. The question has not been raised in the Supreme Court of the United States, but there are decisions of State supreme courts that requirements of the same character in civil-service laws which direct that the appointment shall be made of one out of three applicants found to be fit by examination do not take the power of appointment away from the appointing officer, but are merely regulations for ascertaining qualifications, and are constitutional.

The same principle seems to have been acted upon by Congress in its legislation on consular matters, for in 1855, and later, it has prescribed where consuls shall be sent and their rank and salaries. But no President could refuse to be governed by a requirement of this nature when public opinion so plainly demands that it be obeyed, and therefore the question of its constitutionality would not be raised. In any event, this bill is not subject to such an objection.

The constitutional requirement that these appointments must be approved by the Senate is no objection to the plan we propose. They would be submitted to the Senate for its approval just the same. If the Senate did not approve, then new names, taken from the fittest as determined by the examination, would be submitted, as the President now has to submit new names when the first ones are not approved, and so in the end the fittest would be appointed, or the position remain vacant, in which case the fault would be with the Senate.

Respectfully submitted.

JOHN W. ELA,
General Counsel National Business League.

The National Board of Trade, at its thirty-second annual meeting, held in Washington in January, 1902, resolved—

"That the National Board of Trade strongly urges Congress to pass, at an early day, such legislation as is necessary to reorganize our consular service on the lines of the bills now before it, which demand greater efficiency, permanency of tenure, with compensation sufficient to attract agents of such technical and commercial education as is absolutely essential to the maintenance and growth of our vast commercial interests."

Recommendations and resolutions considered by the National Board of Trade at its meeting in Washington, January, 1902.

WILMINGTON BOARD OF TRADE.

To make the principles of commercial reciprocity a success, thereby establishing more intimate commercial relations with the United States and other nations.

BALTIMORE CHAMBER OF COMMERCE.

Resolved, That the National Board of Trade renews its efforts in favor of reform in our consular service, and urges upon Congress the passage of the carefully prepared bills now before each House.

BOSTON CHAMBER OF COMMERCE.

Resolved, That the National Board of Trade earnestly urges upon Congress the necessity for early action looking to the reorganization of our consular service and its establishment upon a purely business basis.

BOSTON MERCHANTS' ASSOCIATION.

Resolved, That the National Board of Trade continue its agitation of the question of the improvement of the consular service to the end that our great business interests in all quarters of the globe be finally intrusted to men of integrity and experience in business affairs and without reference to their political standing or political ability.

NEW YORK BOARD OF TRADE AND TRANSPORTATION

Resolved, That the reform of our consular service is required, if not imperative, for the permanent extension of our foreign commerce.

MERCHANTS' EXCHANGE OF ST. LOUIS.

That the reorganization of the consular service, in the interest of the constantly expanding foreign commerce of the country, should have early and earnest consideration by Congress, and all appointments should be based upon business qualifications and not on political preferment.

APPENDIX B.

STATEMENT OF HON. JAMES T. DU BOIS BEFORE THE HOUSE COMMITTEE ON FOREIGN AFFAIRS, FEBRUARY 20, 1902.

To every intelligent consular officer who has spent sufficient time in the service to become conversant with its faults and strong points, it must be apparent that a reorganization of the service on broad lines has become necessary in order to obtain the best results.

There are two features necessary to any bill aiming at a proper reorganization of the present system which may receive some earnest opposition. One is the increase of salaries; the other a civil-service feature, something like that contained in both bills now before the committee, which should be on the most practical possible basis.

The increase in salaries proposed by the Burton bill is just, adequate, and urgent. By this increase you will do away with the unofficial fee system, which has a pernicious influence on a correct administration of consular affairs, and place the 288 principal consular offices proposed on a salaried basis that will not only help the Government to secure first-class consular talent, but will enable capable men of limited means to occupy these positions. The present consular salaries will not permit this in 70 per cent of the places, although I know that there are plenty of men willing to try. The Government can not afford to have cheap men in a service where there is so much important work to perform.

The civil-service feature of both bills will have opponents. Men will oppose it who are fearful that it may create and protect a so-called "dry rot" in the consular corps. I am not in favor of a cut-and-dried civil service, but one based upon the merit of the man more than the merit of the mind, for the latter would give us a corps of educated and gentlemanly theorists as little capable of discharging the practical duties of a consul as they would be of charging up San Juan Hill on the gossamer wings of a butterfly. There should be firm opposition to any system that will put indifferent men in the service and help to keep them there. What we need is a civil service for the consular corps that will obtain useful work and clean records from the incumbents. Where this result is not obtained, the law should make it easy to remove the derelict and put a well-disciplined soldier of commerce in his place.

The consular officers of all the great powers, especially of England, Germany, and the United States, are the soldiers of commerce, stationed as outposts and scouts, and in the irrepressible conflict for the mastery of the marts of trade will in the future have increasing and important duties to perform. In this respect the American consular corps has already won high commendation, but those who know by real experience know well that there is room for great improvement. For this reason there is no department of the Government where a common-sense civil service would operate to a better advantage and tend to more useful results than in the consular branch of our foreign affairs. The chambers of commerce and boards of trade, made up of practical business men who have their hands constantly upon the pulse of foreign trade, are conscious of this fact and are earnestly urging our legislators to make it possible to get the best men in the service and protect them against partisan removal, which comes in the change of every administration, and disorganizes the service and paralyzes its usefulness to a degree that is but little understood. All intelligent and successful consuls of my acquaintance who are now in or have been in the service are in favor of a permanent tenure, based on useful administration of office. Equal sympathy and interest by your honorable committee will make almost certain a successful issue of this cause.

If your committee are not disposed to reorganize the consular system with a civil-service clause attached, there is another course, not as safe nor as just, but a course which will be one long step forward. If your committee will so frame a law as to unmake the pernicious unofficial fee system, give the consuls adequate salaries, put Americans in the 567 vice-consulships, consular agencies, and clerkships now occupied by foreigners, most of whom have no sympathy with our foreign or domestic policies, but who stand as a Chinese wall against our advancing commerce, a great result will have been accomplished. But in doing this you should not forget the most important thing of all, and that is to so frame the law that every consul who makes a useful record will be shielded against the common practice of being removed like an outcast upon the change of an administration. Gentlemen, these men render the State a real service. The State knows it, and the State ought not, in the mad rush for place, to forget it. If there be an unworthy "in" who ought to be out, and a worthy "out" who ought to be in, frame a law which will help to dispose of the incapables and take care of the capables. It is easy to separate the consular drones from the consular bees. The records of the consulates, the files of the department, and the inspections of courageous and able consuls-general will readily determine these facts. When once determined, make it imperative that they be promptly acted on for the good of the service.

Objections will be made to an increase of salaries. To those who object I respectfully submit that one consul in one year helps to save enough to pay the total expense of the consular service for one year.

In 1899 the total expense was $1,073,531.73. In the same year the saving to the revenue on St. Gall embroideries, laces, handkerchiefs, curtains, and ramsch goods by the consul-general, sustained by the appraising department in New York, was over $1,000,000, which I will prove to the committee at any time I have the honor of being requested to do so. The following letter bearing the date of June 27, 1899, from the Secretary of the Treasury to the Secretary of State, in a measure sustains the above statement:

"SIR: I have the honor to acknowledge the receipt of your letter of the 21st instant, transmitting an extract from a report, dated the 31st ultimo, from the United States consul-general at St. Gall, Switzerland, relating to the invoicing of embroideries and the diminution in the undervaluations of that commodity shipped to this country.

"The Department has received a report, dated the 19th instant, from Special Agent G. F. Cross, of New York, stating that the increased and additional duties collected at the port of New York on embroideries from St. Gall since the investigation of the subject was instituted about a year ago amounted to $144,667.63. The increase in the revenue on this class of merchandise is estimated by the appraiser at New York to amount to more than $800,000 a year. This result is very largely due to the most efficient cooperation of the consul-general at St. Gall, and I shall be pleased if you will send to him a copy of this communication."

I beg the indulgence and pardon of the committee in referring to my work at St. Gall, but the result of this work demonstrates that if the consul is careful, industrious, and intelligent in the administration of his office, especially if the post is an important one like St. Gall, he may not only increase the revenue enough to help pay a good portion of the total consular expenditures, but he may render a valuable service to trade by compelling honest competition. There are ten United States consulates which, combined, can help save to the revenue every year enough to meet the total expenditures of the diplomatic and consular service and leave some money for necessary improvements. Two consulates, St. Gall and Coburg, have accomplished this result.

I took charge of the consulate-general at St. Gall, Switzerland, January 1, 1898. Shortly afterwards I informed the Department of State that undervaluations existed at St. Gall on a large scale, and for the sake of honest trade and fair competition in our markets, it ought to be stopped. Owing to the invoice-as-you-please plan existing, and which had existed for years, the Government was losing large amounts in revenue and honest exporters and importers were being seriously injured; for if one man is allowed to land his goods in New York at 30 per cent lower than a competitor who gives honest market value in his invoice, he will eventually drive his honest competitor out of our markets and possibly out of business. It was apparent to me that every man interested in getting goods to our markets from foreign countries should be treated exactly alike at the custom-house and in the consulate. Convinced of the evils existing, I urged the establishment of an expert bureau at my office, and upon investigation, Special Agent George W. Whitehead recommended such a course. By the aid of this expert and the support of the appraiser and Board of General Appraisers at the port of New York, a reform was quickly instituted which brought about the most beneficial results, not only to the revenue but to trade. From July 15, 1898, to May 25, 1899, I forwarded to the appraiser at the port of New York, and to appraisers at other ports in the United States, 551 expert reports, covering 1,200 pages, on invoices of embroideries, laces, curtains, handkerchiefs, ramsch goods, etc.

Out of the first 500 invoices examined, 364 were undervalued from 4 per cent to 118 per cent—that is, advances had to be made on these invoices up to these amounts in order to make market value on the day of shipment, which the law requires. In the first 25 reports only one invoice gave honest market value. In the last 25 reports out of the first 500—made nearly a year after the fight for honest invoice values was begun—19 were correct and 6 were undervalued from 4 per cent to 35 per cent. It took ten months of persistent and careful work to obtain this change in the invoice-as-you-please system at St. Gall. From July 1, 1898, to July 1, 1899, about 40,000,000 francs ($8,000,000) worth of the St. Gall product was shipped to our markets. The records of the consulate will show that considerably over $1,000,000 was saved to the Government during this period of one year, and all honest shippers at St. Gall rejoiced at the change, for honest trade and fair competition were made possible, and the men who were giving actual market value in their invoices were saved from being driven to the wall by the undervaluation system of their competitors. If a vigilant and fair control at St. Gall and New York is maintained, this large and just increase in the revenue will continue from year to year.

This shows the great usefulness of consular officers at posts where trading is large with the United States, and it demonstrates that one consular officer can help to save revenue enough in one year to more than cover all of the extra expense which the reorganization of the service on a fair and proper basis may require.

The actual savings made to the revenue at St. Gall during the past four years aggregate fully $4,000,000. The actual expenditures made for the consular service during the same period (1898–1901) amount to $4,466,867 83, or an excess over the actual savings made at St. Gall during this period of $466,867.83, or a yearly average of $116,714.45. As under either bill the unofficial fees are to be turned into the Treasury, the amount from this source would cover this excess and leave a handsome sum as a surplus. The saving to the revenue obtained by the consular corps from year to year makes, by this item alone, the consular service self-supporting. Add this important statement to the other important fact, that the expenditures for the service in 1901 exceeded the receipts in official fees by only $147,040.16, and that the unofficial fees under both bills are to go into the Treasury, the receipts of the service will—exclusive of the revenue saved by active consuls—nearly or quite meet the total expenditures; at least the excess of expenditures over receipts will not be as much as they are under the present system. Under these circumstances the increase in salaries proposed ought not to stand in the way of reorganization, for these salaries are just, reasonable, and necessary.

The Burton bill proposes two consuls-general at $10,000 per annum, eight at $8,000, thirteen at $6,000, and thirteen at $5,500, making a total expenditure of $233,500. For consuls provisions are made for thirty-seven at $5,000, thirty-five at $4,000, sixty at $3,000, forty at $2,500, thirty at $2,000, and fifty at $1,800, making a total expenditure of $755,000, plus salaries of consuls-general makes $988,500 total amount of salaries for principal officers. The additional expense for transit, contingent, and other items would be, under this bill, approximately, $400,000, making a total of $1,388,500. There were $1,004,824 collected in official fees during the fiscal year ended June 30, 1901, and turned into the Treasury. There were during the same period $145,238 in unofficial fees reported collected, but retained by the consular officers, making a total of $1,150,062, which is only $1,802 less than the total expenditure under the present system last year and only $238,440 less than the approximate expenditures would be under the Burton bill. This sum would be considerably reduced under the Adams bill.

Both bills require all fees to be turned into the Treasury. This will include a great many thousands of dollars which are, under the present system, never reported, such as taking depositions, preparing different documents, and settling estates, all of which would materially increase the total receipts of the Treasury. By a careful adjustment of the details of expenditure the actual receipts under either bill would leave the excess of expenditures not as much as they are under the present system. If with these facts you take the large savings to the revenue that are possible if consular officers do their whole duty at important trading centers and are sustained by the appraising department of the Government, it seems to me that all reasonable opposition to the salary increase proposed by these bills ought to be overcome.

REFORMS RESPECTFULLY SUGGESTED IN DETAIL.

On March 1, 1855, Congress passed a law, section 9 of which reads as follows (vol. 10, p. 623):

"That the President shall appoint no other than citizens of the United States who are residents thereof, or who shall be abroad in the employment of the Government at the time of their appointment, as envoys extraordinary and ministers plenipotentiary, commissioners, secretaries of legation, dragomans, interpreters, consuls, or commercial agents, nor shall other than citizens of the United States be employed either as vice-consuls or consular agents, or as clerks in the offices of either, and have access to the archives therein deposited."

Every position in the United States service abroad should be filled, whenever possible, by an American citizen, self-respecting, high minded, intelligent, and industrious. Our country is full of them, and they can be had if properly paid for their services, especially if they know that a good record will secure to them a reasonable tenure of office.

Seventy per cent of all of our subordinate consular offices abroad are now filled by foreigners. Some of them are able, distinguished, and wealthy men, but not 5 per cent of them have the least interest in the American foreign trade, and if they had they would suppress their interest for fear of the criticism and ostracism of their fellow-countrymen, which never fails. But few of them have any real sympathy in this direction, and many of them are an actual hindrance, not even a passive force. Some of them can not speak our language. But few of them have any idea of our policies, foreign or domestic, and many of them are enemies of our policy of American commercial expansion.

One hundred and fifty foreigners fill the important positions of United States vice-consuls, where they have free access to the secrets of trade movements as far as the consulate holds them, as well as access to all of the trade secrets contained in the invoices of their neighbors. This is unjust to the honest exporter.

Two hundred and ninety foreigners occupy our consular agencies out of a total of 395, and 120 foreigners out of a total of 180 are receiving over $60,000 annually as clerks to the various consulates. Besides this, there are foreigners occupying a few of our principal offices. Seventy-five per cent of all these foreign gentlemen filling our consular offices are in social and commercial positions that naturally prohibit their taking an energetic and active part in the extension of our trade, no matter how conversant they may be with the American trade aims and methods, which is rarely the case. In Germany, out of 40 vice and deputy consuls, 60 per cent are of foreign citizenship. In the British Empire there are 114 United States vice and deputy consuls, of which 83 are foreigners of different nationalities.

A real improvement would obtain if, at each consulate—especially consulates where shipments to the United States are of any importance—an American citizen were appointed vice-consul, who should act as clerk to the consulate, and at offices where there are more than one clerk he should be the chief clerk. These men should be paid salaries according to the grade of the consulates where they serve, ranging from $1,000 to $1,500, and, where any one of them makes a good and useful record, he should, in due time, become consul of the sixth grade proposed in the Burton bill. For the amount mentioned, young Americans of good character and ability could be secured, and these positions would be the best possible school in which to train them for the duties of a principal officer.

Foreign vice-consuls are not qualified for these places, not only owing to characteristics already mentioned, but their control of affairs in the absence of the consul is simply nominal, as the clerk, owing to the vice-consul's want of knowledge of affairs of the office, is practically in charge of the place. Besides this, shippers criticise and resent the fact that a fellow-countryman, perhaps a neighbor, knows the secret contents of his invoices, for they are conscious that great injury can inure to them if the contents of their invoices are known to their competitors. These things happen and they ought to be stopped. Americanize the American consular service and keep it Americanized. This will be a long step forward in the scheme of reform.

CONSULAR AGENCIES.

There are 395 consular agencies of the United States scattered throughout the world. Two hundred and ninety of these are in the hands of foreigners. In the earlier days many of these agencies were created through political influence to give to the consul an additional revenue. Some were created by consuls to gratify the vanity of wealthy foreigners who were anxious for a consular title, a consular shield over their business houses, and the right to fly our flag; others were established for the so-called convenience of shippers. Both bills by the adjustment of salaries do away with the necessity of these agencies as a source of private revenue for the consul. The foreign incumbents would lose the title, the shield, and the flag, but the United States Treasury would gain the fees, amounting to over $60,000, which go into the pockets of these gentlemen, whose real service is usually limited to signing a few invoices which could more properly be sent to the principal office through the mails, signed by the manufacturer, and promptly returned.

This system would be far more convenient to the shipper. The money in fees retained by the 395 agencies, 38 feed consulates, and 16 commercial agencies, amounting, approximately, to $220,000, could be turned into the Treasury, and only the important and necessary places retained and changed to vice-consulates, with Americans in charge. These offices should be under the supervision of the consul in whose district they are located, and the salaries should be from $1,000 to $1,500, or more, according to the importance of the post. These places would also be excellent preparatory schools from which the most useful and successful men could be selected, from time to time, for advanced positions.

With 36 consuls-general and 252 consuls, called for by the Burton bill, and about 350 vice-consuls which the foregoing plan would create, all men of character and intelligence and having a love for consular work, the United States Government would have in a short time an army of disciplined soldiers of commerce scattered through the centers of foreign trade and on the outskirts of civilization, and these men, under the lead of able consuls-general and guided by wise instructions from the home Government, would shield American interests, protect the revenue, and help capture the foreign markets with a success that would satisfy Congress that every dollar appropriated for the service had been profitably and wisely invested.

THE UNOFFICIAL FEE SYSTEM.

Both bills require that all fees, official and unofficial, shall be turned into the Treasury. Reorganization or no reorganization, this feature ought to be adopted at once, but every consulate affected by this change should be fully reimbursed for the losses sustained, except in cases where the salary and the unofficial fees make the income larger than at other consulates of the same grade.

The strongest barrier to an improvement of the service is the unofficial fee system. It tempts to extortion; it creates friction among consuls; it often wrongs the American citizen at home and abroad, and it is sometimes an unjust burden to the foreigner. An instance: An ex-consul was appointed vice-consul. He had an American estate to settle in which foreigners were interested. This work came to his office while he was still consul. The final settlement occurred after he became vice-consul and before he had received his exequatur. He told me that the sum in his hands was 10,000 francs, and that he intended to keep 5,000 francs as his compensation. I told him that if he did such a high-handed act of legacy looting I would report him to the Department of State. He dropped in price, but the final settlement was modified extortion, nevertheless. He is now out of the service.

The unofficial fee system has always created contentions among consular officers, each claiming that the others have no right to unofficial fees other than those coming from within their prescribed districts. In case of depositions there is no regulation fee, and different consuls charge various prices, ranging from $10 to $50 per day for their services.

Any bill looking to reforms in the consular service ought to abolish the unofficial fee system and make it a cause for removal for any consul to charge more than schedule fees, which schedule should be carefully prepared and enforced, and if any consul fails to return to the Treasury all fees received for consular work, official or unofficial, that act should also be a cause for removal, and the removal ought not to be delayed. If such a provision is adopted there will be no disposition to demand unreasonable fees and no temptation great enough to keep the fees from being promptly returned to the Treasury. It is believed by some that such a provision can not be successfully enforced. It can if the punishment is removal and the punishment is applied when a violation of the provision is discovered.

Another evil of the consular agency system is the manipulation of fees. Where the normal receipts of an office are only $200 or $300 they have been increased as high as $2,000, the limit amount which the law allows a consul to divide with his agent. Illustration: An agency was established at a small town 9 miles from the consulate. The normal amount of fees was not over $500. In one year the receipts of that office increased to over $2,000. Some time afterwards this agency was made a salaried place, and the fees soon fell back to the normal $500, or about that sum. When the office was entitled to the fees many invoices belonging to the consulate were forced into the agency. When a salary was allowed the invoices went to the principal office, where they belonged.

Another illustration: An agency was established 10 miles from the consulate. The normal income of the agency was about $300. A duplicate seal of the agency was made and used at the principal office on invoices enough to raise the income of the agency up to the $2,000 which the law permits the consul to divide with his agent in case of a natural but not forced revenue. Both agencies are now abolished. Neither had any just cause for existence.

These incidents are only two of many. They are object lessons and warnings. There are established throughout the world over 400 United States commercial and consular agencies, most of them occupied by foreigners, who collect annually over $200,000 in official and unofficial fees. If such irregularities as I have described can happen in two of them, is it not possible that in others the public revenue may be sacrificed to private gain and practices prevail which must depress the moral tone of the service?

The best way to secure honesty in public office is to limit the temptations to dishonesty. Do away with the agencies and the unofficial fees and much will have been accomplished toward a reform of the consular service.

SYSTEM OF APPOINTMENTS.

If good men could be appointed simply to the service, and not to a particular place, great good would be accomplished from the fact that the proper authority could send this man to any post where his training and experience would be the most effective. It is a fact that a man well equipped to fill a consular position in a woolen district has been sent to a beet-sugar region; a man acquainted with laces to a toy district; a man well versed in the china and porcelain trade to a pin and needle district; a silk-ribbon man to a fur district, and a political striker to perform consular functions at a fashionable resort. This condition is unavoidable under the present system of appointment. By appointing men simply to the service they could be located by the Government where their experience and ability would be of real service, not only to our trade but to the customs revenue. Under the present system, if a man is assigned to a place where he is best equipped to administer the affairs or his office it is usually by mere accident.

INSPECTION OF CONSULATES.

Under the Burton bill there are to be 36 consuls-general. These men will have certain jurisdiction over a number of consulates. If they are industrious, capable, and thorough, they will best know the needs of the service within their prescribed jurisdiction. A careful inspection of the consular offices two or three times a year by these officers would result in small traveling expense to the Government, but the effect of the inspections, if properly and courageously done, would be of great benefit, as every active consul-general would have natural pride in securing the best possible record from men within his jurisdiction. The consul-general who has had experience in the service will be the best-equipped man for the work, because he understands the conditions of trade in his district and is conversant with the requirements necessary for useful results in consular work.

THE TRANSIT QUESTION.

The present arrangement for transit to consular posts does injustice to many officers, especially of lower grades. They are allowed their salary during transit, and the time of transit to the different posts is limited to a certain number of days. Illustration: The time allowed for Liege, Belgium, is twenty days. The monthly salary is $125, or $4.16 per day. For twenty days it would amount to $83.20. A first-class ticket to Southampton would be at least $90, and extra transportation from starting point in the United States to destination would be at least $30 more, making a total of $120. If the officer has a family consisting of wife and two adults, the transportation would cost him $480, which is nearly one-third of his salary for a year.

The consul at Patras, Greece, receives $83 per month. He is allowed salary rate for thirty-five days for transit, which, at $2.76 per day, would amount to $96.60. His transportation expenses for self, wife, and two adults would not be less than $600. This would leave him $503.40, upon which, if he has no private income, he must, with his family, live for one year. There are many other instances where the present transit arrangements are unjust, and a reform in this direction would have a wholesome effect and cause no large outlay to the Government.

THE RENT QUESTION.

At present principal consular officers are supposed to be allowed 20 per cent of their salaries for rent. One hardship of the rent system now in force is, if the consular office is connected with the residence and the rent comes within the allotted amount of 20 per cent of the consul's salary, the Government usually allows two-thirds of the cost. If the rent is above the 20 per cent, sometimes the Government allows the full 20 per cent, but if it is impossible for the consul to obtain quarters large enough and properly located for office and residence combined, and he is compelled to rent separately, and the rent of the consulate only costs one-third of the 20 per cent of his salary, he is only allowed the actual amount paid for the consulate and nothing for the residence. This system causes annoyance to both Department and consul, and is often very unjust to the latter. The whole question would be simplified by allowing the consul 20 per cent of his salary where his rent amounts to that or above it, whether the consulate and residence are combined or not. But if the consul pays less than that sum, for both residence and office, then he should be allowed only the amount actually paid.

THIRTY DAYS FOR INSTRUCTIONS.

Consuls are allowed thirty days for instructions after they have taken oath of office, during which time their salaries are allowed them. Every consul who is appointed to an important trade center where exports to the United States are large should during this instruction period spend at least one week at the appraiser's stores in New York, where, with the help of the examiners of the imports from his district, he could gain much information that would be of real value to him in the invoice work of his office.

SUMMARY.

A reorganization of the consular system on broad lines, retaining its present virtues and abolishing its present vices, is a pressing necessity, apparent to everyone who has had experience in the service.

With 36 consuls-general and 252 consuls, and the vice-consular force suggested in the foregoing statement, the United States Government would have a sufficient corps to handle successfully the business of the service, provided the men are experienced, able, and industrious.

If Congress is not ready to pass a reorganization bill with civil-service features in it, a bill containing the features mentioned in this statement, exclusive of the civil-service idea, would be a long and wise step in the right direction.

All reasonable objections against the increase of salaries ought to be overcome when it is considered that they are only just and fair, and that one consular officer saves to the revenue in one year enough to pay the total expense of the service for the same period.

Five hundred and sixty-seven foreigners are holding positions in our consular service, who are keeping at least $200,000 from reaching the Treasury. Eighty per cent of these incumbents are not in sympathy with our institutions and policies, and 70 per cent, from a natural condition of things, are a hindrance instead of a help to the extension of American trade. They are mostly our commissary soldiers of commerce in our struggle for the trade of the world.

The pernicious unofficial fee system ought to be abolished, reorganization or no reorganization; but consular salaries should be advanced at least sufficient to meet this loss.

Of the 395 agencies, 290 are occupied by foreigners. Many of these agencies are unnecessary, and those that are necessary should be changed either to consulates of the lowest grade or to vice-consulates, with salaries ranging from $1,000 to $1,500 or more, and in all cases where it is possible Americans should be appointed. Plenty of young Americans of ability and character stand ready to enter these places as stepping-stones to something better in the service if their work merits it and a reasonably permanent tenure of office is assured.

The clerks at the consulates should be in all cases Americans, and they should also hold the position of vice-consul. The salaries should range from $1,000 to $1,500 or more, according to grade of the consulate. There will be no difficulty in securing the right young men for these places.

The increase in salaries proposed will leave the excess of expenditures over receipts less than they were last year, provided the unofficial fees of all kinds are turned into the Treasury and the total revenue of two-thirds of the agencies, as suggested, reach the same destination.

The natural inspector of consular offices is the consul-general credited to the country where the offices are located. He knows, or ought to know, the condition of each consular district and the character and work of every member of the corps within his jurisdiction. If reforms are needed, it is easy for him to ascertain that fact. If the consular officers are not doing their best for the service, there is no reason why he should not find it out and use, in a tactful and consistent way, corrective measures that would promptly correct. The expense of this system of inspection would be nominal, the system itself would be natural, and the results practical and of importance to the service.

The Burton bill provides that when a man is appointed to the service and assigned to a consulate in a country where the United States has extraterritorial jurisdiction he must pass an examination in the fundamental principles of the common law, the rules of evidence, and the trial of civil and criminal cases. There is, I understand, not a lawyer stationed as United States consul in any country of the Orient where this Government has extraterritorial jurisdiction.

It is important that a new man appointed to the service should speak the language of the country to which he is sent, but it is not absolutely necessary. While the English language is the tongue of commerce and is now spoken in every trade center on earth by many of the business men, yet where two men of equal ability and character apply for a place in the service and one can and the other can not speak the language of the country to which he is to be accredited, the one speaking the language will prove the most valuable officer. If two candidates appear for examination and one can speak the English language only, but is a high-minded, experienced, and progressive business man, while the other can speak six languages, but knows no more about dissecting the contents of an invoice than an East Indian—who dresses in a turban and a pocket handkerchief—knows about socks, the former should be recommended for the place. It is easy for a keen and practical board of examiners to separate the sheep from the goats.

The foregoing statement contains my personal views concerning some of the needs and defects of our consular system which have come to my notice during ten years of experience in the service. The defects pointed out can be remedied. That they ought to be remedied at once no one who has intimate knowledge of the true conditions existing will deny. If you remedy these defects, even without establishing a reasonable permanent tenure of office, you will have accomplished a much-needed work. If you remedy these defects and give to the mighty commercial forces in the United States the aid of an experienced and well-disciplined corps of consuls, protected by a reasonable permanent tenure of office, you will have rendered a service which will be lasting and benificent in its effect upon our trade and other interests throughout the world.

APPENDIX C.

The following report was made by Mr. Morgan on February 6, 1895, to accompany a similar bill when it was reported to the Senate at that time. It covers many of the essential points in regard to the proposed reorganization:

The consular service of the United States, like that of other nations, developed gradually out of the necessities of commerce and the willingness of merchants in foreign countries to represent other governments than their own and to discharge certain fiscal and other duties for the sake of the fees to be collected for such services. While the other great commercial nations of the world have at intervals down to recent times been active in the improvement of their consular service, in order to meet satisfactorily the exigencies of a steadily increasing competition in international trade, the consular system of the United States has remained practically unchanged since the time it was called into existence on a small scale by the acts of July 1, 1790, and of April 14, 1792, and kept alive by a number of subsequent unimportant acts.

The act "to remodel the diplomatic and consular system" of March 1, 1855, is entitled to be regarded as an improvement only so far as it slightly enlarged the service and corrected certain abuses therein by a closer supervision of the fees. It in no way, however, effected a change in the principle of consular representation or in the system of appointment. Apart, therefore, from the act of June 20, 1864, which provided for the establishment of a small body of thirteen consular clerks with a permanent tenure of office, a measure which at its inception was intended to form the nucleus of an entire reform of the service on that basis, this institution, so important to our foreign trade, has suffered the oversight and indifference of Congress.

This neglect is the more striking and the less excusable when our foreign trade of half a century ago is contrasted with that of to-day. In 1850 the combined value of our imports and domestic exports amounted to $308,409,759; in 1893 it reached the figure of $1,697,431,707. But notwithstanding these present vastly increased and far more intricate commercial relations indicated by these figures, no step whatever to increase the efficiency of the consular service, to which the direction and fostering of these relations are intrusted, has been taken. That this has entailed a great loss annually to our foreign trade can not be questioned; that there is also an urgent necessity to correct this want of efficiency is equally apparent.

Even more applicable to the industrial and commercial conditions of to-day, but with reference to those of a decade ago, Secretary Frelinghuysen said in 1884:

"Until recently the demands of Europe, which consumed the greater portion of our exports, and the condition of the producing countries, were such as to give us control in the supply of certain products, such as breadstuffs, provisions, cotton, petroleum, etc. The demands of Europe for all these products, and of the other continents for petroleum especially, were so positive, and our producing conditions so favorable, as to give us practically a monopoly for their supply.

"These conditions of international demand and supply are undergoing radical changes, which the near future will intensify.

"The efforts which have been made and which are being made by Europe to enlarge the field of supply in the above-mentioned products, aided by the ambition which prevails in all countries for the development of natural and artificial resources to meet their own wants and to supply the wants of others, have resulted in awakening competition for the supply even of those products which we have heretofore controlled. It is true that thus far this competition has not affected our trade to any appreciable extent, but the desire for development which is now abroad, and the ambition which prevails to increase the production (outside of the United States) of the foregoing articles, render consular supervision of absolute importance. *The complex commercial relations and industrial interests which now prevail in Europe have originated hostility to American products in many countries, and afford additional reasons for the enlargement and perfection of the consular service.*" *

In 1888 Mr. Cleveland, in his message to Congress, expresses himself to the same effect when he says: "The reorganization of the consular service is a matter of serious importance to our national interests," and in 1893 he again refers to the subject as follows:

"During my former administration I took occasion to recommend a recast of the laws relating to the consular service, in order that it might become a more efficient agency in the promotion of the interests it was intended to subserve. The duties and powers of consuls have been expanded with the growing requirements of our foreign trade. Discharging important duties affecting our commerce and American citizens abroad, and in certain countries exercising judicial functions, these officers should be men of character, intelligence, and ability."

In addition to these expressions from a high official source, the necessity of a reform has been recognized by men of letters, eminent statesmen, journalists, and important boards of trade of this country.

It must be admitted that the present management of our foreign service is burdened with many drawbacks to its efficacy by considerations that relate to domestic politics. Partisan policy, when strictly carried out in making appointments in our foreign service, has no other meaning than that the consular offices are primarily regarded as rewards for political services. The real capacity and usefulness of a consul is too often a secondary consideration.

This important and indispensable part of the machinery by which our foreign intercourse is conducted is often employed to pension political favorites. That to subserve the interests of the service ought to be the sole end in view in the selection of incumbents can not be disputed. To consider the offices merely as sources from which these partisan officeholders may derive four years of maintenance is as absurd as it would be to construct a navy to defend the country and to intrust its command to landsmen without experience for whom we might desire to provide a living and comfortable quarters.

Such a purpose, or one not more gratifying, has often been put into practice in our diplomatic and consular service. To protect and promote in time of peace our varied foreign interests through the agency of a trained personnel is not a less important subject for legislative consideration and provision than in time of war to defend them by the most efficient means at our command.

The object of this act is to provide a system by which persons shall be trained for the duties of the consular service, so that they shall be able to perform them in the best possible way at a reasonable expense to the Government. That this can not be obtained without removing the selection of persons for this service from the control of party politics is shown by our experience, if any proof were required to establish a conclusion so entirely true and indisputable.

Fitness of the candidate, permanency of tenure during good behavior, and an impartial method of selection and to govern promotion as reward for efficiency are the principles on which a useful consular service can alone be based, with an expectation of the best results.

Under our present system a consular or diplomatic officer has no sooner familiarized himself with the duties of his office and begun to acquire a knowledge of its business and fitness for his duties than he is removed to make room for another novice, who is likewise superseded as soon as his experience begins to enable him to discharge the duties of his office to the satisfaction of himself and others. Thus, in one generation the same post is frequently filled by a number of men, who are successively displaced as soon as they have learned to transact the business of their offices with something of professional knowledge and skill.

This system is not only unjust to the people, but it is equally unjust to the agents, who are thrown back upon their own resources just at the time when a three or four

---

* Communication of the Secretary of State to the President, March 20, 1884.

years' preparation has fitted them to devote their energies and capacity with advantage to the foreign service.

To compete successfully with the agents of foreign powers, and to conduct advantageously the political and commercial affairs of our own country, the appointees to this service should be familiar not only with the laws, customs, industries, manufactures, and natural products of our own land, but they should be instructed in the laws, pursuits, language, the contributions to commerce, and the character of the people to whom they are accredited. To this should be added a competent knowledge of the law of nations and of commercial law. As long as these officers are transferred from pursuits and associations which have no connection with commerce or the foreign service, however able and skillful they may be in other things, they can not possess the special knowledge and skill which will render their labors either useful or creditable to the consular service.

The foreign service of European governments for many years has been the object of careful solicitude on their part. An outline statement of them will better enable us to understand the disadvantage we suffer from a defective system.

The French consular service is composed of—

40 consuls-general, at a salary each	$3,600
50 consuls of the first class, each	2,800
80 consuls of the second class, each	2,000
100 vice-consuls	1,400
24 pupil consuls	800

The conditions for admission to the diplomatic and consular service of France are prescribed in a decree of October 15, 1892, and, to show how important France considers its foreign service, attention is called to the fact that over thirty decrees have been issued since 1880 tending to perfect the system.

The pupil consuls are appointed by the minister of foreign affairs. They can only be drawn from the body of attachés on probation who have passed a competitive examination for admission into the service and who have served not less than one year in the home office.

Before being assigned to a diplomatic or consular post they are required to spend at least one year at one of the principal chambers of commerce, where they are to acquire a thorough knowledge of the methods and needs of commerce, and whence they must send the minister periodical reports on the trade of the district. After three years of service, half of which time must be rendered abroad, the pupil consul becomes eligible for vice-consul, and after a service of three years in each subsequent grade he becomes eligible for promotion to a higher one.

Candidates for admission in the French diplomatic and consular service must be under 27 years of age and must have taken a collegiate degree in law, science, or letters, or must have passed certain other examinations, or be the holders of commissions in the army or navy.

The examination for entrance into the service is either written or oral, as may be required.

The written test consists of a composition on public and private international law and a translation into French from English and German, which is dictated. Those candidates who aspire to the diplomatic career are to write also a composition on a subject of diplomatic history that occurred since 1648; those destined for the consular service must write a composition on a subject of political economy or of political and commercial geography.

Those whose papers are sufficiently creditable in the opinion of the examiners to warrant their going any further are then subjected to a public oral examination on public and private international law, political and commercial geography, political economy, and a conversation in English and German. Candidates for the diplomatic career are further examined orally in diplomatic history since 1648, and candidates for the consular service are examined on maritime and customs laws.

The French foreign service is under very strict discipline, and for misconduct or inefficiency there are the following penalties:

(1) Reprimand.

(2) Withholding a part of the salary, not exceeding one-half thereof and not for a longer period than two months.

(3) Suspension from the service without salary for two or more years.

(4) Dismissal.

The last three penalties are imposed by the minister of foreign affairs, with the consent of the council of directors, and after a written or oral hearing of the party under censure.

In addition to their regular salaries, the French consular officers are entitled to traveling expenses and allowances for house and office rent, and for entertaining where it is necessary.

Such a course of training and discipline must produce thorough efficiency; and the generous rewards given for faithful and profitable service must encourage a good class of men to adopt such employment as a profession to which all their energies and abilities are industriously devoted. The permanency of employment, during good behavior, gives confidence to the officer and constantly increasing benefit to the Government.

The British system of regulations for the admission of applicants to the consular service are as follows:

·"Persons selected for the consular service, whenever the circumstance of their being resident in England, on their first appointment, or of their passing through England on their way to take up such first appointment, may admit of their being subject to examination, will be expected to satisfy the civil service commissioners—

"(1) That they have a correct knowledge of the English language, so as to be able to express themselves clearly and correctly in writing.

"(2) That they can write and speak French correctly and fluently.

"(3) That they have a sufficient knowledge of the current language, as far as commerce is concerned, of the port at which they are appointed to reside, to enable them to communicate directly with the authorities and natives of the place; a knowledge of the German language, being taken to meet this requirement for ports in northern Europe; of the Spanish or Portuguese language, as may be determined by the secretary of state, for ports in Spain, Portugal, Morocco, and South or Central America; and of the Italian language for ports in Italy, Greece, Turkey, Egypt, and on the Black Sea or Mediterranean, except those in Morocco or Spain.

"(4) A sufficient knowledge of British mercantile and commercial law to enable them to deal with questions arising between British shipowners, shipmasters, and seamen. As regards this head of examination, candidates must be prepared to be examined in Smith's Compendium of Mercantile Law.

"(5) A sufficient knowledge of arithmetic for the nature of the duties which consuls are required to perform in drawing up commercial tables and reports. As regards this head of examination, candidates must be prepared to be examined in Bishop Colenso's Arithmetic.

"Moreover, all persons on their first nomination to consulships, and after having passed their examination before the civil-service commissioners, will be required, as far as practicable, to attend for at least three months in the foreign office, in order that they may become acquainted with the forms of business as carried on there.

"Limit of age for candidates, 25 and 50, both years inclusive. (Fee for examination, £1 to £6.)"

Mr. Henry White, formerly secretary of legation at London, in an article contributed to the North American Review, makes the following instructive statements concerning the British consular service:

"The British service was established in its present form by act of Parliament in 1825 (6 Geo. IV, cap. 87). Up to that time its members had been appointed, on no regular system, by the King, and were paid from his civil list. This act placed the service under the foreign office, and provided for its payment out of funds to be voted by Parliament. Since then it has been the subject of periodical investigation by royal commissions and parliamentary committees, with a view to the improvement of its efficiency. The evidence taken on these occasions is published in voluminous blue books, the perusal of which I recommend to those interested in the reform in our service.

"Appointments are made by the secretary of state for foreign affairs. Candidates must be recommended by some one known to him, and their names and qualifications are thereupon entered on a list, from which he selects a name when a vacancy occurs. The candidate selected, whose age must be between 25 and 50, is then required to pass an examination before the civil-service commissioners.

"The salaries of British consular officers are fixed, under the act of Parliament of July 21, 1891 (54 and 55 Vict., cap. 36), by the secretary of state, with the approval of the treasury, and no increase can be made in any salary without the approval of the latter. They average about £600 ($3,000) a year, but, of course, some of the important posts are much more highly paid, the salary of the consul-general at New York being £2,000 (nearly $10,000), with an office allowance besides of £1,660, and a staff consisting of a consul at £600 and two vice-consuls at £400 and £250, respectively; that of the consul at San Francisco, £1,200 (nearly $6,000), with an office allowance of £600 besides.

"British consular officials are retired at the age of 70 with a pension.

"There is also an unpaid branch of the service, consisting chiefly of vice-consuls, appointed at places which are not of sufficient importance to merit a paid official. They are usually British merchants, but may be foreigners. They are not subjected to an examination, and are rarely promoted to a paid appointment.

"Consular clerks are required to pass an examination in handwriting and orthography, arithmetic, and one foreign language (speaking, translating, and copying)."

Mr. White through a series of years was our secretary of legation at London, and is thoroughly informed on the subject of consular duties and the acquirements that are essential to an efficient and respectable service. His approval of the plan adopted in this bill for the reformation of our consular system and service is a strong recommendation of its future advantages.

In Germany persons are appointed to the office of consular chancellor who have passed their examinations as "referendary," a title which requires graduation at a German university and requires a thorough knowledge of law, political science, statistics, etc. The chancellor of the consulate is promoted gradually until he reaches the rank of consul-general.

As a rule, the personnel of our consular establishment is not in unfavorable contrast with that of the leading European States as to intelligence and sagacity; but our consuls have not usually the liberal education characteristic of the consular representatives of the great European States, nor are they so well informed as to commerce and its great variety of contributory pursuits, or with the exact business methods employed in conducting the commerce of the leading nations. This seems to be our point of most serious deficiency.

It is proper, and may be necessary, that the laws should designate the places at which consulates are established, but discretion should be given to the President to send consuls to other places, at least temporarily, to meet the demands of trade and intercourse that may arise in new and unexpected quarters. Especially is this necessary in cases where other countries are engaged in war and a sudden emergency calls for the protection of our citizens in places which are not designated by law as the location of consular establishments.

But the laws should not designate the individual who is to be the consul at any particular locality. That matter should be left to the discretion of the President so that he can at all times have the right man at the right place, to meet any demand of trade, or to secure the adequate protection of the persons and property of our citizens in any emergency, or for any public reason.

The arrangement of the fixed residences of consuls of the several classes is not attempted in this bill. The laws and the practice of the Department of State are, for the present at least, a sufficient guide in that matter.

The President should, however, be left free in his authority to send a consul of any class to any consulate when he may consider that the demands of the public service require such transfers.

The reasons for such a provision of law are many and cogent, and they are so obvious as not to require any elaboration in this report. They relate as well to the fitness of consular officers for the particular duties of the occasion as to their usefulness because of their experience as to the condition of the people, the trade, and the language of the particular locality where their services are required.

The consular establishments thus mobilized would soon show a great growth in useful knowledge of the affairs of various parts of foreign countries, and our trade with many foreign countries would be greatly increased and rendered more secure.

The following statements, showing the present condition of our consular service, will show that the change in the organization of the system will add materially to the revenue derived from that source, without a material increase of the expenditures:

Expenditures for salaries of consular officers and amount of compensation in fees, where the officer has no salary, for the year 1894.

26 consuls-general (not including those also commissioned ministers resident)	$98,000.00	
188 salaried consuls	371,500.00	
11 salaried commercial agents	22,000.00	
13 salaried consular clerks	15,000.00	
62 feed consuls (personal perquisites in official fees)	36,152.85	
33 feed commercial agents (personal perquisites in official fees)	36,505.53	
Notarial and unofficial fees retained by consular officers as personal perquisites (lowest estimate)	250,000.00	
333 Total	829,158.38	

Officers of the diplomatic service embraced in this bill.

6 secretarys of embassy		$15,875.00
17 secretarys of legation		31,975.00
23	Total	45,850.00

According to the Annual Report of the Fifth Auditor of the Treasury for the year ended June 30, 1894—

The expenses for last year of the consular service were	$1,055,417.43
The consular fees received for official services were	758,410.81
Excess of expenditures over receipts	297,006.62

This excess of expenses is larger than it has been for ten years. In 1893 it only amounted to $96,042. The difference is not due to an increase of expenditures, but, no doubt, may be found to a great extent in the changes of our tariff laws. This excess, though larger than customary, is, after all, a small sum when considered with reference to the important purposes for which it is disbursed, and, with the payment into the Treasury of the unofficial fees, as proposed under this bill, it is likely to be greatly reduced, if not changed into a balance in favor of the income from that source.

The entire excess of expenditures for salaries in the Department of State and in the diplomatic and consular service over the receipts amounts to only $615,909.19, the smallest amount expended by any of the great powers of the world. The expenditures of the foreign service of Great Britain, Russia, Germany, Italy, and Spain exceed this amount by very considerable figures, and the report of the ministry of foreign affairs of France for the year 1893 shows only $240,000 receipts and $3,266,960 expenditures, a sum almost double that expended by the United States, including even the incidental and contigent expenses of the consular and diplomatic service of the latter country.

This bill adopts the principle of permanent official tenure, so far as the laws can control that subject, but permanent only as it is of benefit to the service. It leaves the power of removal from office to the discretion of the President. The position of each employee of the service is protected against the uncertain and demoralizing effects of changes for merely political reasons in the administration of the Government as far as Congress can control the subject. But this protection is as necessary in practice for efficient work as it is just in theory, and if the plan is adopted of appointing consuls after they are found to be qualified for the respective classifications of the consular service they will seldom, if ever, be dropped from the service for the purpose of supplying their places with political favorites.

The required examination for appointment and promotion creates an impediment in the way of those who may demand office as a reward for political partisanship, without having adequate knowledge of the duties of this peculiar branch of the public service.

Each consul must, on frequent occasions, be the judge of his proper line of action without aid or direction from the minister to whom he is required to report or from the Department of State. In such cases it is requisite to the honor and security of the Government that the consul should be well informed as to his duties.

The right of the President to select from the whole body of consuls any man for any place he may prefer, and to assign him to such place for duty, and to transfer him at pleasure to another place, is the full equivalent of the power of appointment to a particular office.

These functions are to be exercised in foreign countries, for the most part distant from the United States, and disconnect the incumbents from participation in our home politics.

In so far as they may be given as awards for party services, they are a sort of pension system for men who have not been successful in getting offices at home or who have failed of success in the usual channels of business.

The consular system should be based upon the plan of personal qualification for its important and peculiar duties, ascertained by the examination and experience of those employed in it, rather than upon the plan of selecting those for this service who have failed in other pursuits, or those who desire to go abroad for purposes of travel, recreation, or amusement.

This is the only branch of the public service that has been used, to any great extent, for the gratification of the incumbents, without regard to their capacity to render efficient service to the country, and it is time that our policy in respect of these offices was changed.

Taken in the aggregate, there is no class of representatives of our Government who can so seriously affect our commerce with other countries, in their actual and direct conduct and dealings, as our consuls and commercial agents.

We should encourage our best classes of people to qualify themselves for this important service by giving them just compensation for their work and by securing them in these offices during good behavior.

They have much to do with the dignity of our Government, its credit in foreign lands, the honor of its flag, and the safety of its citizens.

VIEWS OF THE MINORITY.

The undersigned members of the Committee on Foreign Affairs are unable to agree with the majority of the committee in favorably reporting the accompanying House bill No. 16023.

We concur in the opinion that the system of notarial fees now obtaining should be abolished and that consular officers should receive their only compensation in stated salaries. The principal object of the bill, however, is to take from the President of the United States the freedom of selection which he now has and restrict appointments to the consular service to such persons as may be certified for appointment by a board of examiners provided for in the bill, and to establish a permanent consular civil list. To that we are unalterably opposed. It is undeniable that under the present system occasionally undesirable persons are appointed, but this evil would not be corrected by the remedy proposed. On the contrary, we believe that if it is adopted the personnel of the service will decline in its vigor, its efficiency, and usefulness. It is un-American and to us wholly objectionable.

Our service is, in our opinion, as good as any in the world. Observation has shown that our officers are usually capable, competent, and self-reliant. These qualities have been acquired under the inspiration of American institutions, from contact with Americans and American ideas. We find it undesirable to change their relations with their Government and people, and turn them over to the stagnation and decay of a permanent civil service.

HUGH A. DINSMORE.
CHAMP CLARK.
WM. M. HOWARD.
A. S. BURLESON.
CHAS. E. HOOKER.

29

O

NATIONAL BANKS HOLDING UNITED STATES DEPOSITS.

JANUARY 21, 1903.—Referred to the House Calendar and ordered to be printed.

Mr. FOWLER, from the Committee on Banking and Currency, submitted the following

REPORT.

[To accompany H. Res. No. 395.]

The Committee on Banking and Currency, to whom was referred House resolution No. 395, report it favorably to the House, amended by striking out the words beginning in line 10 with the word "together" and concluding with the word "years," in line 13.

O

APPROPRIATION FOR MILITARY ACADEMY.

JANUARY 21, 1903.—Committed to the Committee of the Whole House on the state of
the Union and ordered to be printed.

Mr. HULL, from the Committee on Military Affairs, submitted the
following

REPORT.

[To accompany H. R. 16970.]

The Committee on Military Affairs, to whom was referred the estimates for the support of the Military Academy for the fiscal year ending
June 30, 1904, submit the accompanying bill (H. R. 16970) therefor,
and recommend the passage of the same.

The estimates are contained in the Book of Estimates, pages 148 to
152 and 255 to 261.

A detail of the estimates and amounts appropriated in this bill are as
follows:

	Asked for in estimates.	Appropriated by this bill.	Decrease from estimates.	Increase from estimates.
Permanent establishment	$288,600.00	$278,100.00	$10,500.00	
Extra pay of officers	26,084.25	25,884.25	200.00	
Band and general army service	91,780.37	92,884.42	280.00	$1,384.05
Pay of civilians	39,780.00	38,180.00	2,200.00	600.00
Current and ordinary expenses	92,813.00	92,478.00	335.00	
Miscellaneous	86,071.00	33,190.00	3,100.00	219.00
Buildings and grounds	121,430.20	83,657.00	37,773.20	
Total	696,458.82	644,273.67	54,388.20	2,203.05

It will be seen by the foregoing table that the amount carried in
this bill is $644,273.67, while the estimates called for $696,458.82,
being $52,185.15 reduction from the estimates.

In a few instances the appropriation is slightly increased over the
estimates on the earnest solicitation of Colonel Mills, Superintendent
of the Academy, who was before the committee and stated that he
was by the Secretary of War authorized to ask for these increases.

On page 6 an item occurs for "interest on deposits due enlisted
men, one hundred dollars" and an item for "traveling allowances to
enlisted men on discharge, six hundred dollars." These items, the

committee were informed by Colonel Mills, were left out of the estimates and were necessary.

On page 7 is an item—

For extra pay of two enlisted men employed as clerks in the office of the adjutant,
United States Military Academy, at fifty cents each per day, three hundred and
sixty-five dollars.

In this case only one was asked for in the estimates, but at Colonel
Mills's request the item was included in the bill for two.

On page 9 an item occurs as follows:

For extra pay of four enlisted men as assistants and attendants at the library, at
fifty cents each per day, six hundred and eighty-four dollars.

In this case two were asked in the estimates and it was increased to
four at the request of Colonel Mills.

Also on same page (9) occurs the following item.

For extra pay of two enlisted men as messengers in the office of the adjutant,
United States Military Academy, at thirty-five cents per day, two hundred and nineteen dollars and ten cents.

In this case only one was asked by the estimates, but Colonel Mills
assured the committee of the needs of two.

On page 12 appears the item:

For one stenographer and typewriter in the adjutant's office, to be selected and
appointed by the Superintendent, six hundred dollars.

This was not in the estimates, but was asked by Colonel Mills and
seems to be a necessity. On page 23 is the following item:

For purchase of one boiler for the cadet laundry, to be added to the appropriation
of one thousand four hundred and ninety-eight dollars in the act approved June
twenty-eigl. h, nineteen hundred and two, "For replacing, by exchange, one old
boiler in cadet laundry by one one hundred and twenty-five horsepower Fitzgibbon
boiler, delivered and installed," which is hereby made available for part payment
of the purchase of the boiler called for in this estimate, the total appropriation to be
immediately available and to be expended without advertising, two hundred and
nineteen dollars.

This item was not in the regular estimates, but was presented by
Colonel Mills with the following note:

NOTE.—The estimate of $1,498 in last year's bill has proved to be too low. Cost
of raw material and labor has advanced so much that the manufacturers declined to
furnish even a smaller boiler for the amount appropriated. Owing to the improvements soon to be made in the plant of the Military Academy, a new laundry building
will be constructed which will necessitate the removal of the boiler plant to the new
site, or the purchase of a new plant. For this reason it is now deemed advisable to
ask for only sufficient money to procure a boiler of 65 horsepower, the duplicate of
the one now in use, which is in good condition, but much too small. This new boiler
together with the old one will furnish ample power for immediate needs, and will be
much less costly to install than the 125-horsepower boiler originally estimated for,
besides which the two will furnish more power. This duplicate plant will be used
for running the engine, while the other is used at lower pressure for furnishing steam
and hot water throughout the laundry. Thus in case of accident or necessary repairs
to boilers it will not be necessary to shut down the laundry as is the case at present
or would be with one large boiler.

On page 29 the following:

That twenty thousand dollars of the appropriation made by act of June twenty-
eighth, nineteen hundred and two, entitled "An act making appropriations for the
support of the Military Academy for the fiscal year ending June thirtieth, nineteen
hundred and three, and for other purposes," under the head of the item "To
increase the efficiency of the United States Military Academy at West Point, New
York," is hereby made available for the purchase of the "Dassouri" tract of land,
containing two hundred and twenty acres, more or less, adjoining the military
eservation at West Point, New York.

This is strongly recommended by the Honorable Secretary of War, who has had a board convened for the purpose of investigating this matter, as well as giving it personal examination.

The last item in the bill is—

That the unexpended balance of the appropriation of ten thousand eight hundred and ninety-four dollars contained in the act approved June twenty-eighth, nineteen hundred and two, "For increasing the section room and lavatory facilities of the Academy building and furnish same, to be immediately available," is hereby made available until expended and applicable for such changes in and improvements to the building in addition to those specified at the time that the appropriation was made as may now be found necessary.

This was presented by Colonel Mills, with the following explanatory note:

NOTE.—Since this appropriation was made the appropriation for the enlargement of the Academy has become available, and the new conditions which have arisen, due to this last appropriation, will make it desirable to do work in the Academy building in addition to that indicated at the time the appropriation was asked for.

O

TENTS FOR USE OF KNIGHTS OF PYTHIAS.

JANUARY 22, 1903.—Committed to the Committee of the Whole House on the state of the Union and ordered to be printed.

Mr. HULL, from the Committee on Military Affairs, submitted the following

REPORT.

[To accompany H. J. Res. 252.]

The Committee on Military Affairs, to whom was referred House Joint Resolution 252, report the same back to the House with the recommendation that it do pass with the following amendment:

Insert after the word "War" in line 3, page 1, the words "in his discretion."

O

SERENUS KILBOURNE.

JANUARY 22, 1903.—Committed to the Committee of the Whole House and ordered
to be printed.

Mr. BRICK, from the Committee on Military Affairs, submitted the following

REPORT.

[To accompany H. R. 15132.]

The Committee on Military Affairs, to whom was referred the bill (H. R. 15132) for the relief of Serenus Kilbourne, report the same back to the House with the recommendation that it do pass with the following amendment:

Strike out all after the enacting clause and insert in lieu thereof the following:

That Serenus Kilbourne, of Battery L, First United States Artillery, shall be held not to have deserted on July thirty-first, eighteen hundred and sixty-five, but shall be held to have been discharged as of that date, and that the Secretary of War is hereby authorized to issue to him an honorable discharge in accordance herewith: *Provided*, That no pay, bounty, or other emoluments shall become due or payable by virtue of the passage of this act.

The records of the War Department show that this soldier served faithfully in Company I, Seventh Vermont Infantry Volunteers, from March 8, 1862, when mustered in, to November 16, 1862, when he was discharged by reason of reenlistment in Company L, First U. S. Artillery. He is further shown to have served faithfully in Battery L, First U. S. Artillery, from November 17, 1862, to July 31, 1865, when he is reported to have deserted at Winchester, Va.

The evidence presented to the committee is sufficient to convince your committee that no willful desertion existed and recommend that the bill as amended do pass.

The evidence presented is hereto attached and made a part of this report.

STATE OF VIRGINIA, *County of Rockingham, to wit:*

This day, before the undersigned, a notary public in and for the county and State aforesaid, personally appeared Serenus Kilbourne, who, after being first duly sworn, on oath doth say:

That I, Serenus Kilbourne, enlisted on the 7th day of February, 1862, in Rutland, Vt., in Company I, Seventh Regiment Volunteer Infantry; I was discharged in Pensacola, Fla., on the 17th day of November, 1862, and enlisted at once in Battery L, U. S. Artillery, as a blacksmith; I remained in said last-named command until taken sick at Winchester, Va., in the month of June, 1865, the early part of June, the exact date I am unable to recall; I was wounded at Pleasant Hill, La., and served faithfully from the date of my first enlistment, in Vermont, until I was taken sick at Winchester; I came with my company, under Capt. ——— Clauston, belonging to the Nineteenth Corps, which joined Sheridan in the valley of Virginia in 1864.

I was taken sick, as stated, in 1865, of typhoid fever, or swamp fever, during which time my company left Winchester and I did not know where they were, and I could not write and was afraid to ask anyone, so I staid in Winchester, as the war was then over. Since that time I could not get satisfaction of my claims, having no one to represent me. I have never been discharged from the said United States battery, or been paid for my services; I was promoted to artificer about a month before I was taken sick; I never deserted from my company, or thought of deserting, but was left, on account of my sickness, at Winchester when my company moved away from that place in 1865. The war being ended, I went to work at my trade as blacksmith and resided in Frederick County from that time until my removal to Rockingham County, as above stated.

Given under my hand this 18th day of June, 1902.

SERENUS (his x mark) KILBOURNE.

Witness:
A. U. LEWIS.

Subscribed and sworn to before me this 18th day of June, 1902.

A. U. LEWIS, *Notary Public.*

———

STATE OF VIRGINIA, *Frederick County, to wit:*

This date, before the undersigned, a notary public in and for the county aforesaid in the State of Virginia, personally appeared Dr. Golf Miller, to me personally known, and after being first duly sworn, on his oath doth say:

That I am well acquainted with Serenus Kilbourne, and attended him through an attack of malaria or swamp fever in the year 1865, I believe, beginning in June, 1865; that I was appointed by United States officials, but the command of which Serenus Kilbourne was a member having left the city of Winchester before his recovery, I did not have anyone to whom to report his case. After the close of the war said Kilbourne remained at Winchester, or in the county of Frederick, following his trade as a blacksmith. I believe him to be honest, industrious, and truthful. Said Kilbourne married in this county, and is the head of a large family.

Given under my hand this —— day of June, 1902.   GOLF MILLER.

Subscribed and sworn to before me in my said county this 17th day of June, 1902.

JUSTIN RODGERS, *Notary Public.*

———

STATE OF VIRGINIA, *County of Frederick, to wit:*

This is to certify that we have known comrade Serenus Kilbourne, and that he was left here in 1865 by his company, near the close of the war, while he was sick of a fever. He is a man of little or no education and we do not believe he was able to write his name at that time. Since the establishment of a post, Grand Army of the Republic, in this city, we, the comrades of Mulligan Post, No. 30, Winchester, Va., have ever recognized Mr. Kilbourne as a worthy comrade, and that he was not a deserter, but was left here sick, as above stated, and at the close of the war he married and settled in this Winchester, and that he has resided in this county ever since the close of the war, until his removal to Rockingham County, in 1898. We, the comrades of this post, know the physician who attended him and the nurses who administered to him during his illness, under the circumstances as above stated; that he, said Kilbourne, is a truthful and honest man. He is now growing blind, and we wish and pray that the unjust charge of desertion may be removed and he be granted an honorable discharge, to which we feel satisfied he is justly entitled.

Given under our hands this 17th day of June, 1902.

H. G. HOUSTON,
Commander of Mulligan Post, No. 30, G. A. R.

Dr. JAMES BROWN,
Quartermaster of Mulligan Post, No. 30.

JOSEPH BEAN,
Adjutant of Mulligan Post, No. 30.

JESSIE SOWERS,
Secretary of Mulligan Post, No. 30.

Subscribed and sworn to before me this 17th day of June, 1902.

N. C. JARVIS, *Notary Public.*

O

RIGHT OF WAY THROUGH THE SAN FRANCISCO MOUNTAINS FOREST RESERVE.

JANUARY 22, 1903.—Committed to the Committee of the Whole House on the state of the Union and ordered to be printed.

Mr. LACEY, from the Committee on the Public Lands, submitted the following

REPORT.

[To accompany H. R. 16760.]

The Committee on the Public Lands, to whom was referred the bill (H. R. 16760) granting the Central Arizona Railway Company a right of way through the San Francisco Mountains Forest Reserve, in the Territory of Arizona, beg leave to submit the following report, and recommend that said bill do pass without amendment.

A bill similar in its terms was reported in the present Congress by your committee and passed both houses of Congress, but was vetoed by the President. At the time of the executive veto the San Francisco Mountains Forest Reserve consisted of alternate sections only, and since that time, by an Executive order, the "checkerboard" reserve has been so modified as to include the other sections.

Therefore the original bill would not, if passed by a two-thirds vote, be adequate to meet the present conditions in the modified reserve. The committee have therefore considered a new bill granting the right of way. In the present bill the objections of the President in his veto message, we think, have been obviated.

As to the granting of a right of way by the Secretary of the Interior under the general law, the parties who are expected to furnish the funds to build the railway, it is said, have declined to accept the bonds of the company secured by a mortgage upon the right of way under the general statute, on the ground that "there is no granting clause under that statute, and because the right of way under that act and the regulations of the Department of the Interior is a mere license, revocable at the will of the Department."

Your committee think there is sufficient reason for the apprehension expressed by those proposing to furnish the capital, and that the right of way for this proposed railway should be made irrevocable by a special grant.

The forest reserve is adequately protected by the provisions of this bill and we recommend its passage.

O

CLOSING PORTION OF ALLEY IN SQUARE 189, WASHINGTON, D. C.

JANUARY 22, 1903.—Referred to the House Calendar and ordered to be printed.

Mr. COWHERD, from the Committee on the District of Columbia, submitted the following

REPORT.

[To accompany S. 4221.]

The Committee on the District of Columbia, to whom was referred the bill (S. 4221) authorizing the Commissioners of the District of Columbia to extinguish a portion of an alley in square 189, report the same back to the House with the recommendation that it do pass with the following amendment:

Page 2, in lines 6 to 14, inclusive, strike out the following:

And any and all right, title, interest, and demand that the United States of America or the District of Columbia may have in and to the above-described portion of said alley shall revert to the original dedicator, his heirs and assigns, provided he pays to the collector of taxes for the District of Columbia an amount equal to the sum that would have been assessed against the land embraced within the above-described area of the said alley from the time it was laid out to the time this act takes effect as law.

The purpose of the bill, as will be seen by reference to the map hereto attached, is to vacate a small portion of an alley no longer needed for public use. The committee thought it was not within the province of Congress to say to whom the title to this piece of land should revert, and therefore recommend striking out that portion of the bill.

This bill has the approval of the Commissioners of the District of Columbia in the following communication:

OFFICE COMMISSIONERS OF THE DISTRICT OF COLUMBIA,
Washington, December 12, 1902.

DEAR SIR: The Commissioners of the District of Columbia have the honor to acknowledge the receipt of your letter of December 3 inclosing copy of Senate bill 4221, Fifty-seventh Congress, first session, "Authorizing the Commissioners of the District of Columbia to extinguish a portion of an alley in square 189," as amended in the Senate, and requesting to be informed when this portion of alley was opened for public use; what, if any, consideration was paid to the owners of the property at the time it was opened; if the vacation of this portion of the alley will affect any interests outside of lot 54 in square 189, and if the original dedicator still owns lot 54, and any further information which the Commissioners have regarding the matter.

In reply the Commissioners have the honor to state that the portion of alley in question was dedicated for public use on June 14, 1889, by Ethan Allen; that no consideration was paid to the owners of the property by the District at the time the alley was opened; that the vacation of the portion of the alley in question would reduce the frontage of lot 53, square 189, on the alley, but not materially, as, if the portion in question were closed as proposed in the bill, this lot would still have ample alley facilities; and that lot 54, square 189, is assessed in the name of Lewis Tillman, trustee, who was not the original dedicator.

The Commissioners inclose a blue print showing the portion of alley proposed to be closed.

Very respectfully,

HENRY B. F. MACFARLAND,
President Board of Commissioners, District of Columbia.

Hon. J. W. BABCOCK,
Chairman Committee on the District of Columbia, House of Representatives.

The letter of the Commissioner to Senator McMillan and the map prepared to show the portion of the alley to be extinguished are hereby made a part of this report.

OFFICE COMMISSIONERS OF THE DISTRICT OF COLUMBIA,
Washington, March 13, 1902.

SENATOR: The Commissioners have the honor to return herewith Senate bill 4221, Fifty-seventh Congress, first session, authorizing them to extinguish a portion of an alley in square 189 in the city of Washington, which you referred to them for report, with the statement that they see no objection to the action proposed by the bill. They would invite attention, however, to lines 7 and 8 on page 2 of the bill, which state that the title to the land in the alley proposed to be closed shall revert to the owner of lot 54, Lewis Tillman. They are advised by the city solicitor that as they have merely an easement in the land for alley purposes, their abandonment of the alley under the provisions of the bill would cause the land to revert to the original dedicator by operation of law, and they understand that Lewis Tillman was not the original dedicator.

Very respectfully,

HENRY B. F. MACFARLAND,
President Board of Commissioners, District of Columbia.

Hon. JAMES MCMILLAN,
Chairman Committee on the District of Columbia, Senate.

O

.189

The portion (

113.40

45.42

20

65.42

54

15TH STREET, WEST.

18.34

19.33

19.33

19.33

19.33

18.34

65.42

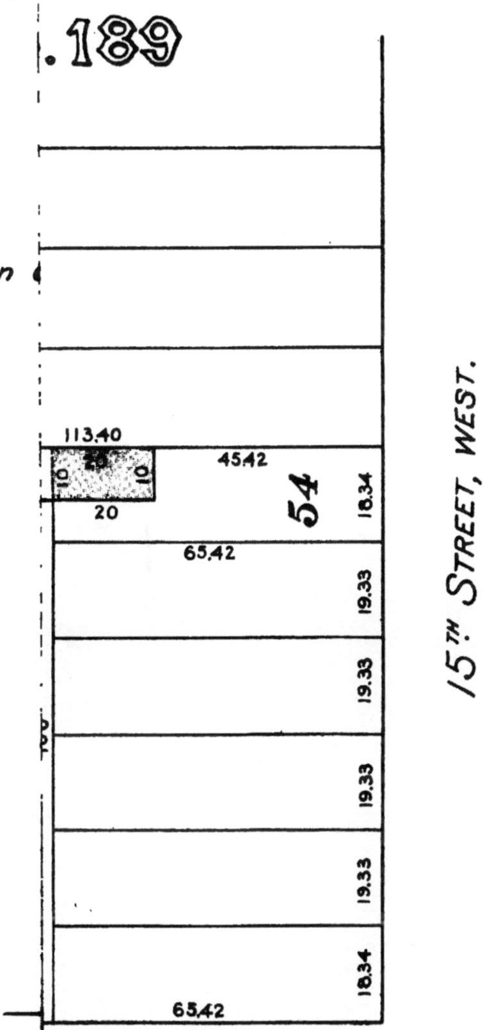

H Rep 3311 57 2

SEWARD SQUARE.

JANUARY 22, 1903.—Referred to the House Calendar and ordered to be printed.

Mr. BABCOCK, from the Committee on the District of Columbia, submitted the following

REPORT.

[To accompany H. R. 15799.]

The Committee on the District of Columbia, to whom was referred the bill (H. R. 15799) to confirm the name of Seward place for the space formed by the intersection of C street south and Pennsylvania and North Carolina avenues, District of Columbia, report the same back to the House with the recommendation that it do pass with the following amendments:

Amend the title so that it will read as follows:

To confirm the name of Seward Square for the space formed by the intersection of C street south and Pennsylvania and North Carolina avenues, District of Columbia.

Line 8, strike out the word "place" and insert in lieu thereof the word "Square."

This bill has the approval of the Commissioners of the District of Columbia in the following communication:

OFFICE COMMISSIONERS OF THE DISTRICT OF COLUMBIA,
Washington, December 19, 1902.

SIR: The Commissioners of the District of Columbia have the honor to submit the following upon House of Representatives bill No. 15799, Fifty-seventh Congress, second session, "To confirm the name of Seward place for the space formed by the intersection of C street south and Pennsylvania and North Carolina avenues, District of Columbia," which you referred to them for report:

A map, showing the location of the proposed Seward place in red, is inclosed. This map also shows a similarly situated space in the northeastern section of the city, which is designated as "Stanton Square."

The Commissioners are informed that Stanton Square received its designation by an act of the old corporation of Washington approved April 12, 1870, and that at the time it was so designated it was the intention to designate the space formed by the intersection of C street south, Pennsylvania and North Carolina avenues as Seward Square, the former being named in honor of Edwin M. Stanton, Secretary of War, and the latter name being intended to be in honor of William H. Seward, Secretary of State in the Cabinet of President Lincoln. The latter intention, however, was not carried out. The Commissioners are informed, however, that the space has popularly been called Seward place or square. The Commissioners are in receipt of a resolution of the East Washington Citizens' Association recommending favorable action on the bill.

The name seems to be a very proper one and the Commissioners favor it. They would recommend, however, that the bill be amended so as to designate the space as "Seward square," instead of "Seward Place," as the word "place" is generally used in the District of Columbia to designate short streets.

Very respectfully,   HENRY B. F. MACFARLAND,
                          President Board of Commissioners, District of Columbia.

Hon. J. W. BABCOCK,
    Chairman Committee on the District of Columbia,
                              United States House of Representatives.

A communication from the East Washington Citizens' Association is also incorporated as a part of this report:

THE EAST WASHINGTON CITIZENS' ASSOCIATION, .
                    Washington, D. C., December 6, 1902.

GENTLEMEN: By direction of the East Washington Citizens' Association, expressed in a motion adopted by unanimous vote of the association at its regular meeting on the 4th instant, I have the honor to inclose herewith the draft of a bill to officially confirm the name of Seward place, and to request action favorable to its enactment.

Yours, respectfully,

A. F. SPERRY, *Secretary.*
The COMMITTEE ON THE DISTRICT OF COLUMBIA,
                    House of Representatives.

O

CERTAIN OUTSTANDING CERTIFICATES OF THE DISTRICT OF COLUMBIA.

JANUARY 22, 1903.—Committed to the Committee of the Whole House and ordered to be printed.

Mr. SAMUEL W. SMITH, from the Committee on the District of Columbia, submitted the following

REPORT.

[To accompany S. 3243.]

The Committee on the District of Columbia, to whom was referred the bill (S. 3243) to redeem certain outstanding certificates of the board of audit of the District of Columbia, report the same back to the House with the recommendation that it do pass with the following amendments:

Amend the title so that it will read: "A bill to redeem certain outstanding certificates of the board of audit, the board of public works, and the Commissioners of the District of Columbia."

Page 2, line 2, after the word "cents," insert the following:

numbered forty-six hundred and sixty-five, for the sum of twenty dollars and ninety cents; numbered forty-six hundred and sixty-six, for the sum of twenty dollars and ninety cents; numbered forty-six hundred and sixty-seven, for the sum of sixty-eight dollars and twenty cents; numbered fourteen thousand seven hundred and eighty, for the sum of sixty-four dollars and twenty-five cents; numbered sixteen thousand four hundred and fifty-four, for the sum of forty-three dollars and twenty-two cents; numbered sixteen thousand four hundred and fifty-five, for the sum of thirteen dollars and nineteen cents; numbered sixteen thousand four hundred and fifty-six, for the sum of thirteen dollars and nineteen cents.

Page 2, line 3, after the word "Columbia," insert the following:

sewer certificate numbered seven hundred and ninety-two, for the sum of fifty dollars, issued by the board of public works of the District of Columbia.

Page 2, line 8, after the word "eighty," insert the following:

and to pay to the holders the amount due on drawback certificates numbered, respectively, forty-two hundred and fifty-nine, forty-six hundred and sixteen, seventy-six hundred and thirty-seven, seventy-six hundred and thirty-nine, ninety-five hundred and seventy, ninety-five hundred and seventy-one, ninety-five hundred and seventy-two, twelve thousand eight hundred and sixty-nine, fifteen thousand nine hundred and seventy-four, sixteen thousand six hundred and eleven, and sixteen thousand seven hundred and seventy-four, amounting in the aggregate to three hundred and twenty-seven dollars and fifty cents; and to redeem tax-lien certificates numbered two hundred and fifty-one, for the sum of nine dollars and ninety-seven cents; numbered three hundred and forty-nine, for the sum of nine dollars and thirty-five cents; numbered twelve hundred and fifty-two, for the sum of ninety-three dollars and thirty-seven cents; and numbered fifty-four hundred and fourteen, for the sum of seventeen dollars and ten cents; and to pay to the holder of tax-sale certificate on lot three, square numbered nine hundred and forty-seven, the sum of one hundred and twelve dollars and ninety cents, with interest at six per centum per annum for two years from its date.

The Senate bill carried the sum of $150.42 principal and a small amount of interest, to be expended in the redemption of five certain certificates of the old board of audit of the District of Columbia, and at the instance of the Commissioners of the District and the auditor your committee have amended the Senate bill by including all certificates of a like character which have been presented to the Commissioners for redemption.

Your committee have added seven additional certificates of indebtedness of the board of audit, amounting to $243.85; one sewer certificate, amounting to $50; eleven drawback certificates, amounting to $327.50; four tax-lien certificates, amounting to $129.79; and one tax-sale certificate, amounting to $112.90, making the bill as reported by your committee carry in the aggregate $1,014.56 and a small amount of interest.

The Government is not bound by law to pay these certificates, but they were issued and accepted in good faith for value received by the District of Columbia, and the holders have an indisputable claim in equity for their redemption. In the Fifty-fifth Congress a bill was drawn by the Commissioners covering all certificates of this character which had been presented to them for redemption up to that time, and Congress enacted the measure into law, it being Public, No. 226, approved March 3, 1899.

The following explains the character of the certificates provided for redemption in the amended bill:

CERTIFICATES OF INDEBTEDNESS.

These certificates of indebtedness were issued by the board of audit created by the act of June 20, 1874, and were designed to provide for obligations incurred by the board of public works in the prosecution of the work of improvement, and which remained unpaid when the latter board was abolished by the said act of June 20, 1874. They were fundable in 3.65 bonds if presented before December 16, 1880, after which date they were barred by the statute. They are, therefore, not legal, but entirely equitable, claims against the District of Columbia.

SEWER CERTIFICATE.

This sewer certificate is one of a class of indebtedness issued by the board of public works under the act of the legislative assembly of June 26, 1873, providing for drainage and sewerage of the District of Columbia, and was receivable in payment of special assessments levied for this purpose against private property. It should have been funded in 3.65 bonds not later than June 16, 1880.

DRAWBACK CERTIFICATES.

These drawback certificates were issued by the Commissioners under the act of Congress of June 29, 1879, to reimburse property owners who had paid special assessments in excess of the actual cost thereof. They were receivable only for general taxes prior to July 1, 1877. As taxes for this period are no longer collectible, there is no method by which these certificates can be redeemed. No interest is allowed on them.

TAX-LIEN CERTIFICATES.

These tax-lien certificates were provided for by the act of the legislative assembly of June 25, 1873, which authorized the governor to anticipate the payment of the arrears of taxes for 1872 and 1873. About $400,000 of the tax arrearages were unpaid at this time and certificates to this amount were issued as liens against the property upon which the taxes in arrears were due. They were used by the District government in payment of obligations for labor and materials. Their redemption was contingent upon the sale of the property against which they were issued. This penalty from various causes was found in many cases to be impracticable of enforcement. This form of indebtedness is therefore legal in its character, but no means are available for redemption.

TAX-SALE CERTIFICATE.

This tax-sale certificate represents the amount for which a piece of property was sold for arrears of taxes, subject to redemption by the owner in two years, with interest at 15 per cent per annum from date of sale to date of redemption. At the end of two years, if not redeemed, a deed to be issued to the purchaser. Some error was discovered which invalidated the sale, and as the holder has no recourse to the property owner, he is entitled to receive back his purchase money, with interest at 6 per cent for the redemption period of two years.

The report made in the Senate by Mr. Martin is in part as follows:

The bill involves the sum of $150.42 principal and a small amount of interest to be expended in the redemption of certain certificates issued by the old board of audit of the District of Columbia, which certificates were not presented within the time set for such representation by Congress, namely, January 16, 1880.

While there is no legal obligation on the part of the Government to pay them, they are equitable claims against the District, and in the last Congress these claims were recognized by the passage of a similar measure.

There are still outstanding a small number of these certificates, and the books of the auditor's office contain a complete record of the issues.

The bill was submitted to the Commissioners of the District of Columbia, who report as follows:

OFFICE COMMISSIONERS OF THE DISTRICT OF COLUMBIA,
Washington, January 13, 1900.

DEAR SIR: The Commissioners have the honor to recommend favorable action upon Senate bill 851, "To redeem certain outstanding certificates of the board of audit of the District of Columbia," which was referred to them at your instance for their views thereon.

While the certificates mentioned in the bill are no longer legal obligations of the District of Columbia, for the reason that they were not presented for settlement within six months from the passage of the act of June 16, 1880, as required by said act, the claim for their redemption has an equitable basis.

A copy of the bill, amended as suggested, is herewith transmitted.

Very respectfully,

JOHN B. WIGHT,
President Board of Commissioners District of Columbia.

Senator JAMES MCMILLAN,
Chairman Committee on District of Columbia, United States Senate.

The following letters from the Commissioners and the auditor of the District of Columbia on the subject of this proposed legislation are made a part of this report:

OFFICE COMMISSIONERS OF THE DISTRICT OF COLUMBIA,
Washington, March 14, 1902.

DEAR SIR: The Commissioners have the honor to recommend, with reference to H. R. bill 10388, "To redeem certain outstanding certificates of the board of audit of the District of Columbia," which was referred to them at your instance for their exmination and report, that it be amended as follows and receive favorable action:

Amend the title by inserting after the word "audit" the words "the board of public works and the Commissioners."

Page 1, line 14, after the word "cents" insert the words: "numbered four thousand six hundred and sixty-five, for the sum of twenty dollars and ninety cents; numbered four thousand six hundred and sixty-six, for the sum of twenty dollars and ninety cents; numbered four thousand six hundred and sixty-seven, for the sum of sixty-eight dollars and twenty cents; numbered sixteen thousand four hundred and fifty-four, for the sum of forty-three dollars and twenty-two cents; numbered sixteen thousand four hundred and fifty-five, for the sum of thirteen dollars and nineteen cents; numbered sixteen thousand four hundred and fifty-six, for the sum of thirteen dollars and nineteen cents."

Page 2, line 1, insert after the word "Columbia" the words "sewer certificate numbered seven hundred and ninety-two, for the sum of fifty dollars."

Page 2, line 6, after the word "eighty," insert "and to pay to the holders the amount due on drawback certificates numbered, respectively, four thousand two hundred and fifty-nine, four thousand six hundred and sixteen, seven thousand six hundred and thirty-seven, seven thousand six hundred and thirty-nine, nine thousand five hundred and seventy, nine thousand five hundred and seventy-one, nine thousand five hundred and seventy-two, twelve thousand eight hundred and sixty-nine, fifteen thousand nine hundred and seventy-four, sixteen thousand six hundred and eleven, and sixteen thousand seven hundred and seventy-four, amounting in the aggregate to three hundred and twenty-seven dollars and fifty cents; and to redeem tax-lien certificate numbered twelve hundred and fifty-two, for the sum of ninety-three dollars and thirty cents."

A copy of the bill modified as herein proposed is herewith submitted, with a report of the auditor for the District on the subject of the bill.

Very respectfully,

HENRY B. F. MACFARLAND,
President of the Board of Commissioners of the District of Columbia.

Hon. J. W. BABCOCK,
Chairman of Committee on District of Columbia, House of Representatives.

OFFICE OF THE AUDITOR OF THE DISTRICT OF COLUMBIA,
Washington, March 13, 1902.

GENTLEMEN: I have the honor to return herewith bill H. R. 10388, Fifty-seventh Congress, first session, "to redeem certain outstanding certificates of the board of audit of the District of Columbia," referred to me, with the following report:

These certificates were issued under the act of June 20, 1874, in payment of indebtedness of the District of Columbia, and were fundable in 3.65 bonds. Not having been redeemed under the act of June 20, 1874, they should have been presented for settlement under the act of June 16, 1880, but, failing this presentation, they ceased at the end of six months after the passage of the latter act, or on the 16th of December, 1880, to be legal obligations of the District of Columbia.

While the Government is not bound in law to pay these certificates, they were issued and accepted in good faith for value received by the District of Columbia, and the holders have an indisputable claim in equity for their redemption. The bill provides for their payment and allows interest from the date of issue to that upon which they should have been funded at the rate which they would have received had they been presented in accordance with the terms of the act of June 16, 1880.

I would suggest the addition of certain amendments, designed to include other certificates on file of a similar character which can not now be redeemed, but which are also equitable claims against the District, for which provision should be made.

The amendments proposed are as follows:

After the word "audit" in the title, insert the words: "the board of public works and the Commissioners."

After the word "cents," in line 14, page 1, insert the words: "numbered four thousand six hundred and sixty-five, for the sum of twenty dollars and ninety cents; numbered four thousand six hundred and sixty-six, for the sum of twenty dollars and ninety cents; numbered four thousand six hundred and sixty-seven, for the sum of sixty-eight dollars and twenty cents; numbered sixteen thousand four hundred and fifty-four, for the sum of forty-three dollars and twenty-two cents; numbered sixteen thousand four hundred and fifty-five, for the sum of thirteen dollars and nineteen cents; numbered sixteen thousand four hundred and fifty-six, for the sum of thirteen dollars and nineteen cents."

After the word "Columbia," in line 1, page 2, insert: "sewer certificate numbered seven hundred and ninety-two, for the sum of fifty dollars."

After the word "eighty," in line 6, page 2, insert the words "and to pay to the holders the amount due on drawback certificates numbered, respectively, four thousand two hundred and fifty-nine, four thousand six hundred and sixteen, seven thousand six hundred and thirty-seven, seven thousand six hundred and thirty-nine, nine thousand five hundred and seventy, nine thousand five hundred and seventy-one, nine thousand five hundred and seventy-two, twelve thousand eight hundred and sixty-nine, fifteen thousand nine hundred and seventy-four, sixteen thousand six hundred and eleven, and sixteen thousand seven hundred and seventy-four, amounting in the aggregate to three hundred and twenty-seven dollars and fifty cents, and to redeem tax-lien certificate numbered twelve hundred and fifty-two, for the sum of ninety-three dollars and thirty cents."

With these amendments I have the honor to recommend that the bill be returned to Congress with the approval of the Commissioners.

Respectfully,

J. T. PETTY,
Auditor District of Columbia.

The COMMISSIONERS OF THE DISTRICT OF COLUMBIA.

———

OFFICE COMMISSIONERS OF DISTRICT OF COLUMBIA,
Washington, May 8, 1902.

DEAR SIR: The Commissioners have the honor to recommend favorable action upon H. R. bill 13837, "authorizing the Commissioners of the District of Columbia to receive and audit certificate of indebtedness No. 14,780," and to transmit herewith a report made to them by the auditor for the District on the subject.

Very respectfully,

HENRY B. F. MACFARLAND,
President Board of Commissioners District of Columbia.

Hon. J. W. BABCOCK,
Chairman of Committee on District of Columbia,
House of Representatives.

———

OFFICE OF THE AUDITOR OF THE DISTRICT OF COLUMBIA,
Washington, May 1, 1902.

GENTLEMEN: The certificate of the board of audit, for the redemption of which provision is made in bill H. R. 13837, Fifty-seventh Congress, first session, herewith, is of the same character as those to which reference was made in my report of March 13, 1902, on bill H. R. 10388, Fifty-seventh Congress, first session, an extract from which follows:

"These certificates were issued under the act of June 20, 1874, in payment of indebtedness of the District of Columbia, and were fundable in 3.65 bonds. Not having been redeemed under the act of June 20, 1874, they should have been presented for settlement under the act of June 16, 1880, but failing this presentation, they ceased at the end of six months after the passage of the latter act, or on the 16th of December, 1880, to be legal obligations of the District of Columbia.

"While the Government is not bound in law to pay these certificates, they were issued and accepted in good faith for value received by the District of Columbia, and the holders have an indisputable claim in equity for their redemption. The bill provides for their payment and allows interest from the date of issue to that upon which they should have been funded at the rate which they would have received had they presented them in accordance with the terms of the act of June 16, 1880.''.

As the certificate under consideration is, like those described in the aforesaid report, an equitable claim against the District of Columbia, I have the honor to recommend that bill H. R. 13837 be returned to the Committee on the District of Columbia with a request for favorable action.

Respectfully,   J. T. PETTY,
                                        Auditor District of Columbia.

The COMMISSIONERS OF THE DISTRICT OF COLUMBIA.

O

POST-OFFICE APPROPRIATION BILL.

JANUARY 23, 1903.—Committed to the Committee of the Whole House on the state of the Union and ordered to be printed.

Mr. LOUD, from the Committee on the Post-Office and Post-Roads, submitted the following

REPORT.

[To accompany H. R. 16990.]

In presenting the bill making appropriations for the service of the Post-Office Department for the fiscal year ending June 30, 1904, the Committee on the Post-Office and Post-Roads submit the following in explanation thereof:

The bill is based upon estimates found on pages 273, 274, 275, 276, and 277 of the Book of Estimates, amounting to $153,010,520. The bill recommends an appropriation of $153,420,049.75, or $419,529.75 more than the estimates. The sum recommended by the committee is $15,013,451 more than the appropriation for the current year, which amounted to $138,416,598.75.

The committee recommend an appropriation of $19,801,900 for clerk hire in post-offices, or $2,662,100 more than the appropriation for the current fiscal year, this amount being that estimated by the Department. While this very large increase appears to be excessive, your committee do not feel warranted in reducing the amount. The large increases made in this item during the last three years have been for the purpose of increasing the salaries of clerks, shortening their hours, and providing for the large increase in business. It was believed that the promotions provided for last year, and the amount allowed for lessening the hours of work in large offices, would not make it necessary to appropriate so large a sum for the next fiscal year, but the Department represent a necessity for this apparent abnormal increase, and the committee have allowed it. The average salary of the post-office clerk is now about $900.

The Department estimated $300,000 for rental and purchase of canceling machines, an increase of $110,000 above the appropriation for the current year. Your committee have allowed $210,000, an increase of $20,000. The large increase in amount of money asked for was for the purpose of placing canceling machines in all second-class offices, and possibly some third-class offices. Your committee do not believe that such action would be of any particular advantage to offices of that size, and have allowed an amount in accordance with such views.

The estimated amount for rural free-delivery service was $12,655,-800. The committee have recommended the sum of $12,619,300, or $36,500 less than the estimate. Ten special agents in charge of divisions were asked for, an increase of three above the present number; and an increase of salary was recommended by the Department for such officials of $100 per year—from $2,400 to $2,500. Your committee do not allow the additional agents asked for of three, nor do they believe it necessary to increase the salaries of those serving at this time above that fixed by law.

Your committee have also disallowed the four special agents estimated for to receive a salary of $1,800 per year, not believing it necessary to create such class at this time, and have reduced the estimated number of special agents to receive $1,600 from 30 to 25, the latter number being 10 more than at present employed. An increased number of 10 route inspectors are provided for by the committee above the estimates, and the per diem allowance for such inspectors is placed at the amount they now receive, $3 instead of $4, that estimated for. The number of clerks allowed at division headquarters is 46, or 4 less than the estimate, and, no doubt, amply sufficient for the coming year; and the new grade for clerks of $1,300 is not recommended, the present limit of $1,200 being deemed sufficient.

Your committee recommend an appropriation of $12,148,301 for Railway Mail Service, which is $16,301 more than the estimate and $865,761 more than the appropriation for the current year. A new grade of railway mail clerks, class 6, is established, with a salary of $1,500 per annum, it being the intention to promote to this grade next year 225 clerks from class 5 who are in charge of two or more cars. Your committee deemed it advisable to recognize the responsibility attached to such clerks and advance their compensation $100 per year. An increase of salary of $300 per year is also allowed for division superintendents of Railway Mail Service, namely, from $2,700 to $3,000. These superintendents have direct administrative charge of more than 1,000 men, and their salary has been placed at a figure adjudged commensurate with their responsibilities.

The estimate of the Department for mail depredations and post-office inspectors was $600,000, which was afterwards revised to $629,000. A more complete segregation of post-office inspectors and clerks at division headquarters has been made with a view of conforming to that of other departments of the service, and to carry into effect this change in the arrangement an additional sum of $29,000 is allowed.

We have recommended a provision permitting the Postmaster-General to contract for the marine service at Detroit for a period of ten years, it being felt that more perfect service and advantageous terms can be secured under such arrangement.

The amounts at present paid for special mail facilities from Washington to New Orleans, and Kansas City to Newton, Kans., are recommended.

The Postmaster-General submitted provisions for $5,000 to print and bind the opinions of the Assistant Attorney-General for the Post-Office Department, and $5,000 to defray expenses of delegates to the International Postal Congress at Rome, Italy, both of which have been allowed, the amount for the latter service being increased to $7,500, if such increased sum of $2,500 should be needed.

Legislative provisions have been introduced in the bill as follows:

Section 2 removes the limitation formerly placed upon special-delivery messengers to earn no more than $30 per month, it being felt that the interests of the service would be subserved by such amendment.

Section 3 brings the penalties applicable to violations of the present law in cases of malicious destruction, injury, or defacement of mail boxes or mail matter along rural routes, to include star routes and other mail routes; and section 3 brings within the protection of existing statutes special-delivery messengers when engaged in carrying or delivering letters or other mail matter.

Section 4 is a provision submitted by the Postmaster-General permitting the Department to more thoroughly regulate the system of collection of revenue for third and fourth class matter when such matter is accepted for transmission in large quantities. At present, precanceled stamps have been issued for large mailings of identical pieces of third and fourth class matter, but the Department believe that abuses have grown up under the system that may be corrected, and the service greatly improved, both within the Department and to the public, by the adoption of the legislation recommended.

Your committee, after an investigation, are of the same opinion, and recommend the legislation.

Advertising in the office of the Postmaster-General.—The estimate is $7,000. The sum recommended is $7,000. The sum appropriated for 1902 was the same.

Miscellaneous items, office Postmaster-General.—The amount in the Book of Estimates is $1,000, but afterwards revised to $6,000, which your committee recommend.

The expenditures have been for a series of years—

1898	$483.84
1899	818.91
1900	393.99
1901	167.02
1902	215.98

For printing and binding opinions of the Assistant Attorney-General for the Post-Office Department, $5,000.—This was submitted by the Department subsequent to the regular estimates, and your committee have allowed it.

OFFICE FIRST ASSISTANT POSTMASTER-GENERAL.

Compensation of postmasters.—The amount of the estimate is $21,500,000. This bill provides for $21,750,000, which is $250,000 more than the estimate, and $750,000 more than the appropriation for the current year.

The expenditures for a series of years have been—

1897	$16,914,728.19
1898	17,453,433.58
1899	18,223,506.81
1900	19,112,096.99
1901	19,949,514.79
1902	20,783,919.00

For a series of years the appropriations have been—

1897	$16,250,000.00
1898	16,750,000.00
1899	16,750,000.00
1900	17,000,000.00
1901	18,000,000.00
1902	20,000,000.00
1903	21,000,000.00

For a series of years the deficiencies have been—

1897	$664,728.19
1898	703,433.58
1899	1,473,506.81
1900	2,112,096.99
1901	1,970,728.93
1902	796,868.78

Compensation to assistant postmasters in first and second class offices.—
The amount of the estimate is $1,894,100, and your committee recommend the sum of $1,893,600, or $500 less than the estimate. The amount appropriated for the current year was $1,701,500.

Compensation to clerks in post-offices.—The amount of the estimate is $19,801,900. The amount appropriated is the same, which is $2,662,100 more than the appropriation for the current year.

The appropriations for previous years have been as follows:

1897	$10,400,000.00
1898	10,600,000.00
1899	11,000,000.00
1900	12,398,900.00
1901	12,829,700.00
1902	14,363,700.00
1903	17,139,800.00

. The expenditures have been—

1897	$10,374,568.39
1898	10,589,069.23
1899	11,095,554.31
1900	12,400,393.93
1901	12,840,738.60
1902	14,434,047.50

The unexpended balances have been—

1897	$25,431.61
1898	10,930.77
1899	12,545.69
1900	18,468.26
1901	25,175.54
1902	....

For rent, light, and fuel in first, second, and third class post-offices.—
The amount estimated is $2,500,000, afterwards increased to $2,550,-
000, and the amount recommended is the latter sum. The expenditures
have been, for 1898, $1,581,649.80; 1899, $1,695,586.73; 1900, $1,801,-
994.81; 1901, $1,942,692.76, and 1902, $2,122,299.29.

For necessary miscellaneous and incidental items directly connected
with first and second class post-offices, $250,000, which is the same as
the appropriation for the current year.

The appropriations for a series of years have been—

1897	$150,000.00
1898	150,000.00
1899	175,000.00
1900	200,000.00
1901	225,000.00
1902	250,000.00
1903	250,000.00

The expenditures have been—

1897	$149,631.39
1898	146,531.69
1899	175,131.26
1900	196,109.13
1901	221,709.55
1902	250,477.10

The unexpended balances have been—

1897	$368.61
1898	3,468.31
1899	a 131.26
1900	8,890.87
1901	3,290.45
1902	250.00

For advertising and purchase of newspapers containing official advertisements, etc., at first and second class post-offices, $25,000.—The amount appropriated for 1901 was $22,500, for 1902 $25,000, and for 1903 $25,000.

For rental or purchase of canceling machines and motors, and power therefor.—The amount of the estimate is $300,000. Your committee recommend $210,000. The amount appropriated for the current year is $190,000.

For seven assistant superintendents, salary and allowance division.—The estimate is $14,000. Your committee allow this amount, which is the same as for the current year.

For per diem allowance for seven assistant superintendents, salary and allowance division, $10,220, which is the amount of the estimate.

Free-delivery service.—For pay of letter carriers in offices already established, etc., the amount of the estimate is $19,028,800, and the amount recommended is the same, being $1,598,350 more than the appropriation for the current year.

For pay of letter carriers in new offices entitled to free-delivery service under the present law the estimate is $100,000, and we recommend the same. The appropriation for the current fiscal year is $90,000.

For horse-hire allowance the estimate is $750,000, and we recommend the same, which is $100,000 more than the appropriation for the current fiscal year.

For car fare and bicycle allowance the estimate is $300,000, and we recommend the same, being $25,000 more than the appropriation for the current fiscal year.

For pay of twenty-two mechanics employed exclusively in painting, repairing, and erecting street letter boxes, the estimate is $19,800, and the amount allowed the same.

For marine postal service, Detroit, Mich., $4,500, which is the amount estimated.

---

a Expended in excess of appropriation.

For pay of four assistant superintendents, city delivery service, $8,000, which is the amount of the estimate.

For per diem allowance of four assistant superintendents, city delivery service, $5,200, the amount estimated.

For other incidental expenses, including letter boxes, package boxes, posts, etc., $300,000, the amount estimated.

For car fare and bicycle allowance for special-delivery messengers in emergency cases, $12,000, which is the amount of the estimate.

For fees to special-delivery messengers, $800,000. The amount estimated is the same. The amount expended in 1902 was $621,014.85.

The appropriations for the support of the free-delivery service for a series of years have been—

1897	$12, 857, 201. 45
1898	13, 387, 000. 00
1899	13, 800, 400. 00
1900	14, 512, 200. 00
1901	14, 787, 600. 00
1902	17, 140, 900. 00
1903	19, 505, 450. 00

The expenditures have been—

1897	$12, 842, 678. 99
1898	13, 386, 593. 69
1899	13, 800, 000. 00
1900	14, 512, 190. 04
1901	15, 752, 600. 00
1902	17, 123, 310. 90

The unexpended balances have been—

1897	$14, 522, 46
1898	406. 31
1899	None.
1900	9. 66
1901	None.
1902	17, 589. 10

Rural free-delivery service.—The original estimate submitted by the Department for this service is $12,655,800. The sum allowed is $12,619,300, or $36,500 less than the estimate. The amount appropriated for the current year was $7,529,400.

The following items constituting the rural free-delivery service have been specifically appropriated for as follows:

For pay of special agents in charge of divisions, $16,800.

For pay of clerks at division headquarters, $46,800.

For pay of special agents, $103,000.

For per diem allowance for special agents, $84,000.

For pay of route inspectors, $81,600.

For per diem allowance of route inspectors, $62,100.

For incidental expenses of special agents in charge of divisions, special agents, route inspectors, and livery hire, etc., $25,000.

For incidental expenses, including letter boxes, furniture, satchels, straps, etc., $200,000.

For pay of letter carriers and clerks in charge of substations, $12,000,000.

The appropriations for this service since its inauguration experimentally have been—

1892	$10,000.00
1893	10,000.00
1894	10,000.00
1895	20,000,00
1896	Indefinite.
1897	10,000.00
1898	50,000.00
1899	150,000.00
1900	300,000.00
1901	1,750,000.00
1902	3,500,000.00
1903	7,529,400.00

Supply division.—For stationery for postal service $75,000, the amount of the estimate.

For a series of years the appropriations, including deficiencies, have been—

1897	$50,000.00
1898	55,000.00
1899	55,000.00
1900	55,000.00
1901	55,000.00
1902	70,000.00
1903	70,000.00

The expenditures have been—

1897	49,887.05
1898	54,915.21
1899	54,881.57
1900	64,991.03
1901	69,695.05
1902	69,439.97

Wrapping twine.—The estimate was $135,000, which amount is recommended.

For a series of years the appropriations, including deficiencies, have been—

1897	$80,000.00
1898	85,000.00
1899	90,000.00
1900	90,000.00
1901	100,000.00
1902	165,000.00
1903	125,000.00

The expenditures have been—

1897	$79,971.63
1898	84,990.72
1899	89,999.95
1900	100,000.00
1901	159,662.72
1902	116,707.38

Wrapping paper.—The estimate is $45,000. The amount recommended is the same, which is $5,000 more than the amount appropriated for the current year.

For a series of years the appropriations, including deficiencies, have been—

1898	$50,000.00
1899	45,000.00
1900	30,000.00
1901	30,000.00
1902	30,000.00
1903	40,000.00

For a series of years the expenditures have been—

1897	$49,940.00
1898	28,638.60
1899	33,353.43
1900	36,330.48
1901	34,906.71
1902	29,970.32

The unexpended balances have been—

1897	$60.00
1898	21,361.40
1899	11,646.57
1900	a 6,330.48
1901	3.29
1902	29.68

Letter balances, etc.—The estimate is $15,000. The sum recommended is the same.

For a series of years the appropriations have been—

1897	$10,000.00
1898	10,000.00
1899	7,500.00
1900	10,000.00
1901	10,000.00
1902	12,500.00
1903	15,000.00

The expenditures have been—

1897	$6,679.13
1898	9,986.78
1899	7,414.43
1900	9,747.48
1901	9,964.73
1902	12,465.57

Postmarking and rating stamps, repairs, etc.—The amount of estimate is $45,000, which sum is recommended, being the same as the appropriation for the current year.

The appropriations for a series of years have been—

1897	$30,000.00
1898	45,000.00
1899	27,000.00
1900	40,000.00
1901	30,000.00
1902	37,500.00
1903	45,000.00

The expenditures have been—

1897	$29,971.32
1898	44,965.40
1899	26,974.98
1900	39,965.73
1901	32,986.75
1902	37,446.44

---

a Deficiency.

The unexpended balances have been—

1897	$28.68
1898	34.60
1899	25.02
1900	34.27
1901	13.25
1902	53.56

Rubber stamps, type, etc.—The estimate is $5,000, which sum your committee recommend.

Packing boxes, etc.—The estimate is $2,000. The sum recommended is the same.

The appropriations for a series of years have been—

1897	$1,500.00
1898	1,500.00
1899	1,000.00
1900	1,000.00
1901	1,000.00
1902	1,250.00
1903	2,000.00

The expenditures have been—

1897	$753.05
1898	1,351.21
1899	998.84
1900	999.92
1901	999.72
1902	1,230.30

The unexpended balances have been—

1897	$746.95
1898	146.79
1899	1.16
1900	.08
1901	.28
1902	19.70

Printing facing slips, etc., and manifold books for the registry service.—The amount of estimate is $30,000, and the amount recommended is the latter sum, being $20,000 less than the appropriation for the current year.

The appropriations for a series of years have been—

1897	$15,000.00
1898	20,000.00
1899	20,000.00
1900	20,000.00
1901	20,000.00
1902	30,000.00
1903	50,000.00

The expenditures have been—

1897	$14,419.14
1898	16,368.27
1899	19,795.81
1900	19,936.18
1901	16,998.40
1902	26,584.03

The unexpended balances have been—

1897	$580.86
1898	3,631.73
1899	204.19
1900	63.82
1901	3,001.60
1902	3,415.97

Blanks, blank books, printed matter, metal advertising, etc., for the Money-Order Service.—The amount of the estimate is $125,000 and the appropriation recommended the same. The amount appropriated for the current fiscal year was $115,000.

Rubber and metal stamps and repairs thereto for the Money-Order Service.—The amount of the estimate is $8,000, which sum is recommended, being the same as the amount for the current year.

Copying presses, typewriting machines, etc. (Money-Order Service).— The amount of the estimate is $20,000. This amount is recommended, which is the same as the amount for the current year.

Exchange on drafts, stationery, and miscellaneous incidental expenses of the Money-Order Service.—The estimate is $15,000. The amount recommended is the same. The appropriation for the current year is $15,000.

Miscellaneous items.—The estimate is $1,000, afterwards revised to $2,000, which we recommend.

OFFICE OF THE SECOND ASSISTANT POSTMASTER-GENERAL.

Inland mail transportation by star routes.—The estimate is $6,960,000, which is the sum recommended, being $245,000 more than the appropriation for the current year.

The appropriations for a series of years have been—

1897	$5,354,000.00
1898	5,450,000.00
1899	5,095,000.00
1900	5,025,000.00
1901	5,240,000.00
1902	5,580,000.00
1903	6,715,000.00

The expenditures have been—

1897	$5,324,681.53
1898	5,286,614.87
1899	4,999,280.88
1900	5,041,338.85
1901	5,143,211.11
1902	5,725,531.00

The unexpended balances have been—

1897	$29,318.47
1898	163,385.13
1899	95,719.12
1900	a 16,338.85
1901	96,788.89
1902	14,469.00

Inland mail transportation by steamboat routes.—The estimate is $693,000, which sum we recommend.

The appropriations for a series of years have been—

1897	$402,515.32
1898	434,000.00
1899	450,000.00
1900	515,000.00
1901	545,000.00
1902	586,000.00
1903	641,000.00

a Deficiency.

The expenditures have been—

1897 .... $402,505.91
1898 .... 418,635.14
1899 .... 434,200.98
1900 .... 497,938.04
1901 .... 508,444.48
1902 .... 563,062.75

The unexpended balances have been—

1897 .... $9.41
1898 .... 15,346.86
1899 .... 30,799.02
1900 .... 17,061.96
1901 .... 36,555.52
1902 .... 35,937.25

Mail messenger service.—The amount asked for is $1,160,000. The sum recommended is the same.

The appropriations for a series of years have been as follows:

1897 .... $1,130,000.00
1898 .... 1,000,000.00
1899 .... 950,000.00
1900 .... 950,000.00
1901 .... 950,000.00
1902 .... 1,038,000.00
1903 .... 1,083,000.00

The expenditures have been—

1897 .... $950,886.63
1898 .... 987,163.91
1899 .... 907,668.25
1900 .... 915,186.10
1901 .... 973,471.98
1902 .... 1,025,245.50

The unexpended balances have been—

1897 .... $179,113.37
1898 .... 12,836.09
1899 .... 42,331.75
1900 .... 34,813.90
1901 .... 11,528.02
1902 .... 12,754.50

Pneumatic-tube service, $800,000.—Amount of the estimate.

For regulation screen or other wagon service.—The estimate is $990,000. The amount recommended is the same. The amount appropriated for the current fiscal year is $875,000.

Mail bags, cord fasteners, etc.—The estimate is $280,000, afterwards revised to $300,000, which your committee recommend.

For a series of years the appropriations have been—

1898 .... $320,000.00
1899 .... 275,000.00
1900 .... 275,000.00
1901 .... 275,000.00
1902 .... 275,000.00
1903 .... 275,000.00

The expenditures have been—

1897 .... $341,965.16
1898 .... 314,867.33
1899 .... 274,624.42
1900 .... 268,224.12
1901 .... 265,077.86
1902 .... 273,844.02

The unexpended balances have been—

1897	$3,034.84
1898	5,130.67
1899	375.58
1900	6,775.88
1901	9,922.14
1902	1,155.98

Mail locks and keys, etc.—The estimated amount is $45,000. The sum recommended is the same.

The appropriations for a series of years have been—

1897	$45,000.00
1898	45,000.00
1899	48,000.00
1900	43,000.00
1901	43,000.00
1902	43,000.00
1903	43,000.00

The expenditures have been—

1897	$44,663.46
1898	38,128.02
1899	42,395.89
1900	42,277.34
1901	40,560.97
1902	42,150.44

The unexpended balances have been—

1897	$336.54
1898	6,871.98
1899	5,604.11
1900	722.66
1901	2,439.03
1902	849.56

Rent of building for mail-bag repair shop, etc.—The estimate is $9,200. The sum recommended is $9,200.

The appropriations for a series of years have been—

1897	$8,500.00
1898	8,500.00
1899	8,500.00
1900	8,500.00
1901	8,500.00
1902	8,500.00
1903	8,500.00

The expenditures for a series of years have been—

1897	$7,749.24
1898	8,450.46
1899	8,073.87
1900	8,251.48
1901	8,263.86
1902	8,449.67

Inland transportation by railroad routes.—The amount asked for is $38,242,000. The sum recommended by the committee is the same, being $1,982,000 more than the appropriation for 1903.

The appropriations for a series of years have been—

1897	$28,000,000.00
1898	29,000,000.00
1899	30,500,000.00
1900	33,275,000.00
1901	33,870,000.00
1902	34,700,000.00
1903	36,260,000.00

The deficiency appropriations have been—

1897	$1,013,688.45
1898	1,450,000.00
1899	42,486.12
1900	a 334,205.52
1901	a 347,955.08
1902	None.

Railway post-office car service.—The estimate is $5,411,000. The sum recommended is the same, being $307,040 more than the appropriation for the current year.

The appropriations for a series of years have been—

1898	$3,600,000.00
1899	4,000,000.00
1900	4,204,500.00
1901	4,561,000.00
1902	4,816,000.00
1903	5,104,960.00

The expenditures have been—

1898	$3,753,416.64
1899	3,960,953.86
1900	4,182,482.79
1901	4,408,639.00
1902	4,657,368.57

Railway Mail Service.—The estimate is $12,132,000. Your committee recommend $12,148,301, which is $16,301 more than the estimate and $865,761 more than the appropriation for the current year.

The appropriations for a series of years have been—

1898	$8,100,000.00
1899	8,425,000.00
1900	8,765,000.00
1901	9,863,900.00
1902	10,374,700.00
1903	11,089,540.00

The expenditures have been—

1897	$7,730,394.59
1898	8,066,602.54
1899	8,429,980.00
1900	8,838,993.92
1901	9,675,436.50
1902	10,264,588.38

For inland transportation of mail by electric and cable cars.—The amount of the estimate is $510,000. The sum recommended is the same, being $60,000 more than the appropriation for the current year.

For necessary and special facilities on trunk lines, $167,728.75.

The appropriations have been for a series of years—

1897	$196,614.22
1898	171,238.75
1899	{ 171,238.75 / 25,000.00
1900	{ 171,238.75 / 25,000.00
1901	196,238.75
1902	196,238.75
1903	167,728.75

a Unexpended balance.

The expenditures have been—

1897	$159, 120. 64
1898	175, 973. 00
1899	176, 903. 95
1900	181, 154. 70
1901	167, 010. 40
1902	150, 319. 13

For miscellaneous items.—The amount asked for is $1,000. The amount recommended is $1,000.

The appropriations for a series of years have been—

1898	$1, 000. 00
1899	1, 000. 00
1900	1, 000. 00
1901	1, 000. 00
1902	1, 000. 00
1903	1, 000. 00

The expenditures have been—

1898	$914. 17
1899	999. 41
1900	998. 70
1901	969. 63
1902	997. 65

For transportation of foreign mails.—The estimate is, including amount to Oceanic Steamship Company and for transferring foreign mails at New York and San Francisco, $2,566,000. The amount recommended is the same.

The appropriations for a series of years have been—

1899	$1, 850, 000. 00
1900	2, 154, 000. 00
1901	2, 248, 000. 00
1902	2, 549, 000. 00
1903	2, 587, 000. 00

The expenditures have been—

1898	$1, 620, 282. 71
1899	1, 629, 749. 83
1900	1, 956, 701. 87
1901	2, 004, 249. 60
1902	2, 268, 690. 75

For balances due foreign countries.—The estimate is $165,000. The sum recommended is the same.

The appropriations for a series of years have been—

1899	$142, 000. 00
1900	145, 000. 00
1901	145, 000. 00
1902	155, 000. 00
1903	160, 000. 00

The expenditures have been—

1898	$139, 808. 42
1899	140, 101. 15
1900	143, 563. 95
1901	144, 385. 03
1902	141, 782. 07

For expenses of United States delegates to the Universal Postal Congress, at Rome, Italy.—The estimate is $5,000. Your committee have allowed $7,500.

Manufacture of adhesive postage and special-delivery stamps.—The estimate is $376,000, and the sum recommended is the same.
The appropriation for a series of years have been—

1899	$178,000.00
1900	199,000.00
1901	223,000.00
1902	287,000.00
1903	280,000.00

The expenditures have been—

1899	$178,000.00
1900	199,969.42
1901	253,000.00
1902	281,922.80

Pay of agent and assistants to distribute stamps, and expenses of agency.—The amount estimated is $12,000. The sum recommended is $12,000.
The appropriations for a series of years have been—

1899	$12,000.00
1900	12,000.00
1901	12,000.00
1902	12,000.00
1903	12,000.00

The expenditures have been—

1898	$10,211.80
1899	11,090.31
1900	11,688.27
1901	11,902.03
1902	11,887.78

Manufacture of stamped envelopes and newspaper wrappers.—The estimate is $795,000, and the amount recommended is the same, being $79,000 more than for the current year.
The appropriations for a series of years have been—

1899	$800,000.00
1900	694,000.00
1901	603,000.00
1902	648,000.00
1903	716,000.00

The expenditures have been—

1897	$719,194.79
1898	751,045.09
1899	536,155.79
1900	506,875.12
1901	570,441.86
1902	621,327.30

Pay of agent and assistants to distribute stamped envelopes, etc., and expenses of agency.—The estimate is $20,000, which sum we recommend, being the same as for the current year.
The appropriations for a series of years have been—

1900	$17,800.00
1901	17,800.00
1902	20,000.00
1903	20,000.00

The expenditures have been—

1899	$17,584.09
1900	17,765.58
1901	17,465.57
1902	17,429.05

Manufacture of postal cards.—The estimate is $189,000. **The sum** recommended is the same.

The appropriations for a series of years have been—

1900	$149,000.00
1901	158,000.00
1902	165,000.00
1903	177,000.00

The expenditures have been—

1899	$142,786.40
1900	148,504.11
1901	156,702.37
1902	111,670.56

Postal-card agency; pay of agents and assistants to distribute.—The estimate is $18,000. The sum recommended is the same.

For a series of years the appropriations have been—

1900	$7,000.00
1901	7,800.00
1902	7,800.00
1903	18,000.00

The expenditures have been—

1899	$6,075.38
1900	6,917.18
1901	7,694.30
1902	7,558.30

Registered-package, etc., and dead-letter envelopes.—The estimate is $163,000. The sum recommended is the same, being $17,000 greater than the appropriation for the current year.

The appropriations for a series of years have been—

1900	$97,000.00
1901	101,000.00
1902	128,000.00
1903	146,000.00

The expenditures have been—

1899	$86,108.24
1900	96,987.52
1901	128,000.00
1902	126,649.85

Ship, steamboat, and way letters.—The estimate is $1,000. The sum recommended is $1,000.

The appropriations for a series of years have been—

1899	$1,000.00
1900	1,000.00
1901	1,000.00
1902	1,000.00
1903	1,000.00

The expenditures have been—

1898	$716.28
1899	554.72
1900	333.62
1901	319.34
1902	279.56

For payment of limited indemnity for loss of first-class registered matter, the amount of the estimate is $12,000, which is recommended.

For blanks, books, and printed matter of urgent or special character, etc.—The estimate is $20,000, which sum your committee recommend.

For miscellaneous items.—The sum recommended is the same as the estimate, $1,000.

The appropriations for a series of years have been—

1898	$500.00
1899	500.00
1900	500.00
1901	500.00
1902	1,000.00
1903	1,000.00

The expenditures have been—

1896	$377.60
1897	000.00
1898	16.00
1899	121.75
1900	493.86
1901	495.11
1902	631.00

OFFICE OF THE FOURTH ASSISTANT POSTMASTER-GENERAL.

Mail depredations and post-office inspectors.—The amount estimated is $600,000, afterwards revised to $629,000, which amount your committee recommend, being $29,000 more than the appropriation for the current year.

For a series of years the appropriations have been—

1898	$400,000.00
1899	430,000.00
1900	450,000.00
1901	550,000.00
1902	550,000.00
1903	600,000.00

The expenditures have been—

1898	$361,744.57
1899	406,772.89
1900	421,672.22
1901	492,859.27
1902	529,096.21

For payment of rewards for the detection, arrest, and conviction of post-office burglars, robbers, and highway mail robbers, $25,000, which is the amount of the estimate and that appropriated for the current fiscal year.

For miscellaneous items, $1,000, which is the amount recommended.

EXPENDITURES IN DETAIL.

The expenditures of the postal service for the fiscal year 1902 are shown, by items, in the following statement:

Transportation of mails on railroads	$34,700,000.00
Compensation to postmasters	20,783,919.97
Free-delivery service	17,123,310.90
Compensation of clerks in post-offices	14,434,047.70
Railway Mail Service	10,264,588.38

H. Rep. 3314——2

Transportation of the mails on star routes	$5, 725, 531. 00
Railway post-office car service	4, 657, 368. 57
Experimental rural free delivery	3, 993, 706. 51
Transportation of foreign mails	2, 268, 690. 75
Rent, light, and fuel for first, second, and third class post-offices	2, 122, 299. 29
Compensation to assistant postmasters at first and second class post-offices	1, 479, 674. 05
Mail-messenger service	1, 025, 245. 50
Transportation of mails—regulation, screen, or other wagon service	788, 423. 59
Special-delivery service	621, 645. 85
Manufacture of stamped envelopes	621, 327. 30
Transportation of mails on steamboats	563, 062. 75
Mail depredations and post-office inspectors	529, 096. 21
Transportation of the mails, electric and cable cars	389, 987. 61
Manufacture of postage stamps	281, 922. 29
Mail bags and catchers	273, 844. 02
Miscellaneous items at first and second class offices	250, 477. 10
Canceling machines	195, 418. 25
Transportation of the mails, special facilities	150, 319. 13
Balances due foreign countries	141, 782. 07
Payment of money orders more than one year old	130, 365. 11
Registered-package, tag, official, and dead-letter envelopes	126, 649. 85
Blanks, blank books, etc., for money-order ser. 3	120, 752. 65
Wrapping twine	116, 707. 38
Manufacture of postal cards	111, 670. 56
Stationery for postal service	69, 439. 97
New territory and military postal service	49, 637. 09
Mail locks and keys	42, 150. 44
Postmarking and rating stamps	37, 446. 44
Wrapping paper	29, 970. 32
Printing facing slips, slide labels, etc	26, 584. 03
	124, 247, 062. 63
Expenditures under twenty smaller items of appropriation	145, 409. 39
Total expenditures for the year	124, 392, 472. 02
Add expenditures during the year on account of previous years	393, 225. 05
Total expenditures during the year	124, 785, 697. 07

THOMAS J. McGINNIS.

JANUARY 24, 1903.—Committed to the Committee of the Whole House and ordered
to be printed.

Mr. GRAFF, from the Committee on Claims, submitted the following

REPORT.

[To accompany S. 3779.]

The Committee on Claims, to whom was referred the bill (S. 3779)
for the relief of Thomas J. McGinnis, beg leave to submit the following report:

The evidence in this case is that the Bourse substation is the most important one at Philadelphia, its receipts being fully 25 per cent of the said office, the sale of stamps amounting to nearly $800,000 in 1900, and the greater portion of this amount was handled and sold by Judson F. Vodges, the clerk from whom the stamps were stolen. Mr. Vodges sold at the time of the theft an average of $2,000 worth of stamps per day, and was obliged to keep sufficient quantities conveniently at hand in order to facilitate business.

On the day in question, November 29, Clerk Vodges entered his cage at 12.30 p. m. About 1 o'clock he had a call for 50 stamped envelopes of a variety seldom sold. He stooped to examine his stock of envelopes and, not finding the kind wanted, called back in the office to Superintendent McGinnis for them, who procured the envelopes from the adjoining cage while Vodges stood waiting. In this way his mind must have been off the window at least two minutes, perhaps double that time. The waiting customer, identity unknown, received his envelopes and departed. Clerk Vodges made two more sales, and then, turning, he suddenly discovered the loss of the stamps.

There is no reason to doubt that this was a genuine depredation from the outside, without collusion or criminal complicity on the part of any employee.

The committee recommend that all after the enacting clause of the bill be stricken out and the following inserted:

That the Secretary of the Treasury be directed to pay, out of any money in the Treasury not otherwise appropriated, to Thomas J. McGinnis, superintendent of the Bourse substation of the post-office at Philadelphia, Pennsylvania, the sum of eight hundred and nineteen dollars and seventy-eight cents, being on account of the loss of eight hundred and nineteen dollars and seventy-eight cents in postage stamps by robbery of said station on the twenty-ninth day of November, eighteen hundred and ninety-nine.

And the committee recommend that the bill so amended do pass.

O

MARCUS L. VERMILLION.

JANUARY 28, 1903.—Committed to the Committee of the Whole House and ordered
to be printed.

Mr. MIERS, from the Committee on Invalid Pensions, submitted the
following

REPORT.

[To accompany H. R. 13772.]

The Committee on Invalid Pensions, to whom was referred the bill
(H. R. 13772) granting an increase of pension to Marcus L. Vermillion,
submit the following report:

This bill proposes to increase the pension of the soldier named
therein from $12 to $30 per month.

The records of the War Department show that Marcus L. Vermillion, the soldier named in this bill, and now 58 years of age,
served as a private in Company G, Eighteenth Missouri Volunteers,
from February 1, 1862, to February 1, 1865, when honorably discharged, and the medical records of that Department show that he was
under treatment in regimental hospital in June, 1864, for dysentery.

His claim to pension, filed September 30, 1879, and based upon an
enlargement of the throat and neck, alleged to have been caused by
the strap of his cartridge box, catarrh of the head, and on account of
disease of the neck and throat as a result of a sunstroke, was allowed in
1890 so far as it related to disease of throat at $2 per month from dis-
charge, at $4 from June 16, 1881, and at $8 from June 11, 1890.

The claim on account of catarrh was rejected in April, 1901, upon
the ground of no record of treatment in the War Department and
inability of the claimant to establish the origin of the same in the
service.

On August 28, 1890, his name was placed upon the roll under the
act of June 27, 1890, at the maximum rating, namely, $12 per month,
for total inability to earn a support by manual labor, the result of
nasopharyngeal catarrh and goiter.

The claimant alleged that in April, 1862, he had a high fever, with
resulting loss of sense of smell, followed by headache and bleeding
from the nose; that in July, 1864, he was overcome by heat during
the march to Atlanta; that he was unconscious for about three hours,

was sent to Marietta hospital, and while under treatment there had a
pain in the neck, something like a crick, and he attributes the goiter
to the sunstroke and the carrying of straps of accouterments around
his neck. He admits that he did not know what catarrh was until
several years after his discharge, but that the symptoms which manifested themselves in the service, namely, loss of smell, headache, and
sore throat, were those of catarrh. He further states that the goiter
developed before discharge in the shape of a slight enlargement on the
right side; that it gradually became worse, and that he noticed the
greatest change in the neck about 1888 and 1899, and that about 1876
the hearing of his right ear became first impaired.

He filed the testimony of a number of comrades who recollected and
testified to his having bleeding from the nose with fever and headache
during the service; that he became exhausted from heat during the Atlanta campaign and
wore a handkerchief around his neck, claiming he had a stiff neck; that
these severe frontal headaches, loss of sense of smell, and pains and
cramps of the right side of the neck continued to exist ever since his
discharge, and that they first noticed the presence of a goiter about a
year after his discharge.

He also filed medical testimony that he was examined for catarrh
and enlargement of the thyroid gland in 1889; that since that time the
enlargement of his gland had extended from the right to the left side,
forming across his windpipe, thereby producing shortness of breath,
which, together with the throat trouble and catarrh of the head, incapacitated him from the performance of manual labor; that he has not
performed any manual labor of any kind for some time, is not possessed of any property, and is entirely dependent upon his pension.

When last examined, on July 20, 1898, the board of surgeons found
the mucous membrane of the nose and throat inflamed and hypertrophied and covered by a mucopurulent discharge, and rated him $10
for that condition. They also found an immense goiter measuring
about 10 inches by 5 inches, the neck over the goiter measuring 21
inches in circumference, and that this tumer was more or less lobu-
lated and was distributed rather evenly in front and on each side;
that his pulse after brisk exercise was 140 and the respiration 36, and
rated him $15 for that condition.

A perusal of the testimony in this soldier's case leads your committee
to the belief that the immense goiter as well as the catarrh from which
he is shown to be suffering are traceable to his military service, and
that therefore relief to the extent of increasing the soldier's pension to
$24 per month is warranted.

The bill is therefore reported back with the recommendation that it
pass after the same shall have been amended as follows:

In line 6 strike out the word "Nineteenth" and insert in lieu thereof
the word "Eighteenth."

In line 8 strike out the word "thirty" and insert in lieu thereof the
word "twenty-four."

O

JAMES M. CARTMILL.

JANUARY 26, 1903.—Committed to the Committee of the Whole House and ordered
to be printed.

Mr. MIERS, from the Committee on Invalid Pensions, submitted the
following

REPORT.

[To accompany H. R. 14448.]

The Committee on Invalid Pensions, to whom was referred the bill
(H. R. 14448) granting a pension to James M. Cartmill, submit the
following report:

This bill proposes to increase the pension of the beneficiary named
therein from $12 to $30 per month.

It appears from the records of the War Department that James
M. Cartmill, the soldier named in this bill, and now 70 years of age,
served in Company B of the Pike County Regiment of Missouri
Home Guards from July 5 to September 2, 1861, and that he was
allowed by the Hawkins Taylor Commission pay for one month of
actual military service rendered to the United States while serving
with that organization, and that he again served in Companies E and
I of the First Provisional Enrolled Missouri Militia from March 17
to November 14, 1863, when relieved, and the files of the Pension
Bureau show that he is now and has been since August 1, 1892, a pensioner under the act of June 27, 1890, at the maximum rating, namely,
$12 per month, for total inability to earn a support by manual labor,
the result of asthma, disease of heart, and rheumatism.

He never applied for pension under the general law, but alleged in
one of the affidavits filed by him in support of his claim under the
act of June 27, 1890, that while a member of Company E of the First
Provisional Enrolled Missouri Militia, while on a scout in and around
Bloomfield, Mo., he was shot across the breast by unknown parties,
supposed to have been bushwhackers, on or about the last day of
July, 1863, and he filed in the Pension Bureau testimony of comrades
tending to show that he was wounded at the time and place and under
the circumstances alleged by him.

The only certificate of medical examination in this case, made on
October 5, 1892, upon which the Pension Bureau allowed his claim

under the act of June 27, 1890, at $12 per month, rated him $2 for the wound of the breast, $8 for asthma, $4 for disease of heart, and $4 for rheumatism.

Testimony filed in the Pension Bureau shows that the beneficiary for the past fifteen years has been an invalid, unable to get about a great part of the time, and confined to his house and bed, and that he is dependent in a great measure upon the labors of his wife and the sympathy of the citizens of his town.

Medical testimony also filed in the Pension Bureau shows that he has been a great sufferer from asthma, heart and stomach trouble, that both of his lungs are involved, that his rest is broken at night, and that he is greatly emaciated.

It being shown that the beneficiary is suffering from disabilities of an extreme nature, and in destitute circumstances, your committee, following precedents, recommend that his pension be increased to $24 per month, and report the bill back with the recommendation that it pass after the same shall have been amended as follows:

In line 6 strike out the words "I and E" and insert in lieu thereof the words "E and I."

In line 8 strike out the word "thirty" and insert in lieu thereof the word "twenty-four."

In same line, after the word "month," insert the words "in lieu of that he is now receiving."

Amend the title so as to read: "A bill granting an increase of pension to James M. Cartmill."

O

JESSIE V. CLUXTON.

JANUARY 26, 1903.—Committed to the Committee of the Whole House and ordered
to be printed.

Mr. SAMUEL W. SMITH, from the Committee on Invalid Pensions, submitted the following

REPORT.

[To accompany H. R. 9274.]

The Committee on Invalid Pensions, to whom was referred the bill
(H. R. 9274) granting a pension to Jessie V. Cluxton, submit the fol-
lowing report:
This bill proposes to pension Jessie V. Cluxton, daughter of John
V. Cluxton, late first lieutenant Company F, Eighty-eighth Ohio
Infantry, at $30 per month.
John V. Cluxton, the soldier named in this bill, served as sergeant
in Company F, Eighty-fifth Ohio Infantry, from June 9, 1862, to Sep-
tember 23, 1862, when honorably discharged with his company, and
again as sergeant of Company B, Eighty-eighth Ohio Infantry, from
September 24, 1862, to July 20, 1863, when he was promoted to first
lieutenant of Company F, of said regiment, serving as such until July
3, 1865, when honorably discharged.
He died March 17, 1890.
His widow, Belle Cluxton, who married him on April 18, 1865, was
pensioned in 1892 under the provisions of the act of June 27, 1890, at
$8 per month from August 6, 1890, and was allowed an additional sum
of $2 per month on account of three minor children, the youngest of
whom became sixteen years of age on August 23, 1895.
The name of the widow was dropped from the rolls by reason of her
death on December 9, 1900.
From proof filed with your committee it appears that the beneficiary
is the daughter of the officer; that she was born February 4, 1866,
being now 36 years of age; that she had suffered from epilepsy since
she was 5 years old, having been a marked imbecile since that time,
wholly incapacitated for the performance of any domestic labor whatever, and that she is entirely dependent upon her brothers and sisters
for support.

Dr. George W. Osborn, who has known the beneficiary since February, 1879, testifies that the beneficiary has been a sufferer from epilepsy and consequent imbecility of the mind during the period of his acquaintance with her; that she has been incapable of taking care of herself and really needs the constant care and attendance of another person, and that by reason of the death from tuberculosis of several sisters and one brother the family has become so financially embarrassed as to render the care and maintenance of the beneficiary a charge to them which is well-nigh impossible to bear.

It being shown that the beneficiary is helpless by reason of epilepsy and imbecility, and in destitute circumstances, your committee, following precedents, recommend that she be granted a pension at the rate of $12 per month, and report the bill back with the recommendation that it pass after the same shall have been amended as follows:

In line 6, before the word "daughter," insert the words "helpless and dependent."

In line 7, before the word "Company," strike out the word "of."

In line 9 strike out the word "thirty" and insert in lieu thereof the word "twelve."

O

FRANKLIN PEALE.

JANUARY 26, 1903.—Committed to the Committee of the Whole House and ordered
to be printed.

Mr. CROWLEY, from the Committee on Invalid Pensions, submitted
the following

REPORT.

[To accompany H. R. 14439.]

The Committee on Invalid Pensions, to whom was referred the bill
(H. R. 14439) granting an increase of pension to Franklin Peale,
submit the following report:

This bill proposes to increase the pension of the beneficiary named
therein from $14 to $30 per month.

Mr. Peale, now 66 years of age, served as a private in Company G,
One hundred and eighteenth Pennsylvania Infantry, from August 4,
1862, to July 21, 1865, when he was discharged as of Company K of
the Sixteenth Veteran Reserve Corps, to which transferred.

He received a gunshot wound at Shepherdstown Heights on September 20, 1862, the ball entering the inside of the left thigh at about
the upper third, passing inward and upward and making its exit on
the opposite side a few inches above the point of entrance.

He is now a pensioner under the general law at $14 per month on
account of this wound of the left thigh.

A claim on account of blindness, filed in January, 1899, was rejected
by the Pension Bureau on April 18, 1902, upon the ground that the
same did not exist in the service, as shown by the claimant's own affidavit, in which he stated that he had more or less pain in his head in
the service; that his eyes became more or less weak since he was
wounded; that he did not wear glasses, however, until he was 45 years
of age; that his left eye started to go blind in January, 1897, and
became blind in December, 1897; that in January, 1898, his right eye
commenced to go, and that now he could only distinguish darkness
from light.

When last examined, on June 6, 1900, the board of surgeons, aside
from the gunshot wound of left thigh, found him to be totally blind
in the left eye, and that while he could see to walk with the other eye
the sight was failing very fast; that he was extremely nervous, with

trembling of the extremities; and the board of surgeons then stated that by reason of the gunshot wound, the blindness, and the nervous debility he required the periodical aid and attendance of another person.

Medical and other testimony filed with your committee shows that the beneficiary is now totally blind; that he is quite lame from the effects of the gunshot wound of the leg, and can only get around with the aid of a cane; that he has no property except what is mortgaged for more than it is worth, and no source of income except his pension, and that he has a wife dependent upon him for support.

The relief sought for in this bill is fully warranted under the action of the House on June 16, 1902, it being shown that the beneficiary, by reason of blindness and disease of the nervous system, requires the periodical aid and attendance of another person.

The passage of the bill is therefore recommended after the same shall have been amended as follows:

In line 7, before the word "Pennsylvania," insert the word "Regiment."

O

WILLIAM F. RITCHIE.

JANUARY 26, 1903.—Committed to the Committee of the Whole House and ordered
to be printed.

Mr. APLIN, from the Committee on Invalid Pensions, submitted the
following

REPORT.

[To accompany H. R. 16353.]

The Committee on Invalid Pensions, to whom was referred the bill
(H. R. 16353) granting an increase of pension to William F. Ritchie,
submit the following report:

This bill proposes to increase the pension of the soldier named
therein from $12 to $24 per month.

The records of the War Department show that William H. Ritchie,
the soldier named in this bill, served as a private in Company F,
Eighty-third Illinois Infantry, from August 15, 1862, to June 26, 1865,
when honorably discharged, and that he was under treatment in April,
1864, for cholera morbus.

He is now pensioned under the act of June 27, 1890, at $12 per
month, for total inability to earn a support by manual labor, the result
of disease of the heart and epilepsy.

He was formerly pensioned under the general law on account of
disease of the chest at $4 per month from discharge, and at $8 per
month from June 1, 1887.

Medical evidence filed in the Pension Bureau shows that the beneficiary has epileptic seizures almost daily and nightly for a week or two
and then slacking up for a week or two; that he is almost helpless and
requires the attention of some one to care for him, as he is liable to
fall over; that his mind is giving away, and that he is totally unable
to do manual labor.

When last examined on June 6, 1900, the board of surgeons stated
that they were satisfied that he was suffering from epilepsy; that the
spells were liable to come on at any time, and that he would fall and
be unconscious from thirty to sixty minutes.

Testimony filed with your committee sets forth that it is not safe
for the soldier to be left alone at any time, as he is liable to fall any
moment in an epileptic seizure; that he needs constant care and watch-

ing and is a constant care on his family and others; that he is not able to do manual labor of any kind, etc.

It being shown that the beneficiary suffers from a disability of an extreme nature (epilepsy), and that he has to be constantly watched and cared for, an increase of his pension to $24 per month is warranted under numerous precedents.

The bill is therefore reported back with the recommendation that it pass.

O

WILLIAM T. MOORE.

JANUARY 26, 1903.—Committed to the Committee of the Whole House and ordered
to be printed.

Mr. CROWLEY, from the Committee on Invalid Pensions, submitted the
following

REPORT.

[To accompany H. R. 8187.]

The Committee on Invalid Pensions, to whom was referred the bill
(H. R. 8187) granting a pension to William T. Moore, submit the following report:

This bill proposes to increase the pension of this soldier from $12
to $50 per month.

This soldier, now 63 years of age, served as private in Company H,
Eighty-first Illinois Volunteers, from August 12, 1862, to August 5,
1865, when honorably discharged, and medical records of the War
Department show that he was under treatment at different times during
his period of service for intermittent fever, cholera morbus, and
diarrhea.

He has been a pensioner under the general law ever since his discharge at $6 per month, and at $12 per month from June 18, 1884, on
account of rheumatism and disease of kidneys of accepted service origin.

Claim for additional disability filed in September, 1889, and based
upon varicose veins of both legs, was rejected in September, 1897, upon
the ground of no record of treatment for same in the War Department
and claimant's inability, after having been aided by a special examination, to prove the origin of the same in the service and line of duty.

Claims for increase of pension were rejected, the last one on September 24, 1900, upon the ground that the disability from causes of accepted
service origin did not warrant a rating in excess of $12 per month.

But one witness of fair reputation was found by the special examiner who testified to the origin of varicose veins in the service, and a
number of other comrades testified that they did not know that the
soldier suffered from any disability at the time of his return home
from the Army. One witness, however, testified that he saw the soldier's varicose veins within a few months after his discharge; another
that he saw them about a year after discharge, and other testimony to the

effect that he complained of trouble with his legs since about one year after discharge.

When last examined on December 6, 1899, the board of surgeons recommended a rating of $12 per month for rheumatism, $2 for hydrocele, and $3 for varicose veins, and that board then stated:

There is much roughness in shoulder, elbow, knee, and ankle joints. There is a tenderness on freely moving these joints. Joints of fingers are a little enlarged, and we find tenderness of lumbar muscle.

This applicant has a chronic form of rheumatism, affecting him more or less all over the body, and, we think, rather severe at times.

No evidence of disease of the kidneys.

We find applicant has a large hydrocele on the left side—tumor is 11 inches in circumference and 5 inches long.

Has varicose veins of legs. They are one-fourth to three-fourths inch in diameter. Skin looks healthy, and there is no tendency to rupture.

From lay testimony filed in the Pension Bureau on December 1, 1899, it would appear that the beneficiary was then unable to perform any manual labor by reason of general debility, resulting from rheumatism and disease of kidneys; that he is a physical wreck, and has disabilities equal to the loss of a hand or foot, and that he often needs the assistance of another person to help him dress and move about the house.

The probabilities in this case are that the varicose veins from which this soldier is shown to be suffering are the result of his military service of three years, and the beneficiary is therefore entitled to an increase of his pension on account of said disability.

An increase of his pension from $12 to $17 per month is therefore recommended and the bill reported back with the recommendation that it pass after the same shall have been amended as follows:

In line 8 strike out the word "fifty" and insert in lieu thereof the word "seventeen."

In the same line, after the word " month," insert the words " in lieu of that he is now receiving."

And the title so as to read: "A bill granting an increase of pension to William T. Moore."

O

JOHN BROWN.

JANUARY 26, 1903.—Committed to the Committee of the Whole House and ordered
to be printed.

Mr. MIERS, from the Committee on Invalid Pensions, submitted the
following

REPORT.

[To accompany H. R. 16756.]

The Committee on Invalid Pensions, to whom was referred the bill
(H. R. 16756) granting an increase of pension to John Brown, submit
the following report:

The soldier named in this bill, and now 58 years of age, served as a
private in Company G, Fourth Maryland Infantry, from September
16, 1862, to May 31, 1865,.when honorably discharged.

He never applied for pension under the general law, but is now and
has been since January 5, 1901, a pensioner under the act of June 27,
1890, for total inability to earn a support by manual labor, by reason
of the loss of sight, injury of head, and loss of left arm.

It is shown that on December 18, 1900, the beneficiary while
employed at a limestone quarry in Maryland, and engaged in loading
a hole about 6 feet deep with dynamite, the dynamite exploded, throw-
ing him into the air. Pieces of rock hit him on the left arm, mash-
ing it so that the same had to be amputated, fracturing his skull,
knocking out his right eye and injuring the .other, making the eyes
entirely sightless.

When last examined on February 19, 1901, the board of surgeons
stated that he was horribly mutilated and crippled for life; that his
eyes are entirely sightless, and that he will be totally blind for the
balance of his life; that he received a fracture of the outer table of the
skull, and had the left arm amputated as a result of the accident; and
that he required the constant aid and attendance of another person.

Following the action of the House, taken on June 16, 1902, in Senate
bill 4850, increasing from $12 to $30 per month the pension of those
who require the aid and attendance of another person, your committee
recommend a like increase in this case, and report the bill back with
the recommendation that it pass after the same shall have been amended
as follows:

In line 8 strike out the word "forty" and insert in lieu thereof the
word "thirty."

O

GEORGE M. DUFFY.

JANUARY 26, 1903.—Committed to the Committee of the Whole House and ordered
to be printed.

Mr. MIERS, from the Committee on Invalid Pensions, submitted the
following

REPORT.

[To accompany H. R. 304.]

The Committee on Invalid Pensions, to whom was referred the bill
(H. R. 304) granting an increase of pension to George M. Duffy, submit the following report:

This bill proposes to increase the pension of the soldier named
therein from $12 to $24 per month.

This soldier, now 63 years of age, served as a corporal in Company
K, Eleventh West Virginia Infantry, from August 14, 1862, to May
22, 1865, when honorably discharged.

He received a gunshot wound of the right side in action at Hatches
Run, Virginia, March 31, 1865, and was treated for this wound and also
for intermittent fever, chronic rheumatism, and inflammation of the
lungs while in the service.

He was pensioned under the general law on account of the gunshot
wound of the right side at $2 per month from discharge and at $8 per
month from January 22, 1890, until December 15, 1891, when he was
pensioned under the act of June 27, 1890, at $12 per month for total
inability to earn a support by manual labor, the result of disease of
the nervous system and this gunshot wound.

Claims under the general law, based upon rheumatism, sunstroke and
resulting dizziness, partial paralysis, and blindness, and on account of
disease of lungs, were rejected in May, 1890, upon the ground that
there had been no pensionable degree of disability from these causes.

Subsequently the claim was reopened and that part which was based
upon sunstroke was rejected in 1896 upon the ground that no results
of sunstroke were found and that the paralysis and blindness alleged
as results were due to other causes not connected with the military
service.

The claimant alleged that he incurred a sunstroke on the retreat
from Lynchburg, becoming unconscious and remained so for some
hours; that in July he was sent to the hospital, where he remained

until October, when he rejoined his regiment; that the effects of sun-stroke disappeared before he left the hospital and that he observed no further difficulty with his eye or ear and that his limbs appeared to be in a normal state, but in 1877 the same symptoms appeared again and that he became partially deaf and blind and had numbness of the legs and arms, and that the paralysis gradually came on and had grown slowly and gradually worse.

He filed the testimony of four comrades as to the origin of sunstroke and that thereafter he complained of his head and eyes, but only one of these comrades was present at the time he incurred the alleged sun-stroke and his testimony is in conflict with the record as to the nature of the disease on account of which applicant was sent to the hospital, the medical records showing that soon after the date of the alleged sunstroke the claimant was sent to the hospital for treatment for chronic rheumatism.

When last examined in September, 1892, the board of surgeons found the soldier to be suffering from advanced paralysis; that the lesion was of cerebral origin; that there was nearly total loss of power in the lower limbs, with loss of power of the right shoulder, arm, forearm, and hand; that he was totally unable to dress himself and had to be lifted by straps and pulleys from his bed to a reclining chair, and that it was apparently one of the not uncommon cases of paralysis following sunstroke.

The board of surgeons then rated him $72 for the paralysis and $4 for the gunshot wound of right side.

It being shown that this soldier who rendered nearly three years' service is now suffering from advanced paralysis to such a degree as to require the aid and attendance of another person, your committee, following the action of the House on June 16, 1902, recommend an increase of his pension from $12 to $30 per month, and report the bill back with the recommendation that it pass after the same shall have been amended as follows:

In line 8 strike out the word "twenty-four" and insert in lieu thereof the word "thirty."

O

ELIZA WENDE.

JANUARY 26, 1903.—Committed to the Committee of the Whole House and ordered
to be printed.

Mr. APLIN, from the Committee on Invalid Pensions, submitted the
following

REPORT.

[To accompany H. R. 4155.]

The Committee on Invalid Pensions, to whom was referred the bill
(H. R. 4155) granting an increase of pension to Eliza Wende, submit
the following report:
This bill proposes to increase the pension of the beneficiary named
therein from $8 to $17 per month.
Richard Wende, the soldier named in this bill, served as a bugler in
Company B, Third United States Artillery, from September 9, 1861, to
June 1, 1866, when, honorably discharged.
He was a pensioner under the general law on account of chronic
diarrhea and resulting piles and disease of rectum and liver at $2 per
month from June 22, 1881; at $6 from July 6, 1887; at $10 from March
6, 1889; at $12 from February 18, 1891, and at $24 from April 3, 1895.
In February, 1895, the soldier claimed that his then existing disease
of the lungs was a result of the pensioned causes, but the Pension
Bureau declined to accept the same as such.
He died December 2, 1895, of disease of the lungs.
His widow, Eliza Wende, now 56 years of age, who married him on
December 11, 1872, is now a pensioner under the act of June 27, 1890,
at $8 per month.
Her claim under the general law was rejected in December, 1896,
upon the ground that her husband's fatal disease of lungs had no connection with the chronic diarrhea and resulting piles and disease of
rectum and liver, for which he had been pensioned.
In support of her claim the beneficiary filed the affidavit of Dr.
George F. Heath, setting forth that he was the soldier's medical attendant for about twelve years prior to his death, in 1895; that early in
his acquaintance he was often called to prescribe for him for chronic
diarrhea and rectal trouble; that the soldier, being a veterinary surgeon and hence more or less conversant with medical subjects,

continued the prescribed treatment himself; that in 1889, or about
seven years prior to his death, he began to have hemorrhage from the
lungs and tubercular trouble following; that bowel trouble was the
cause of the disease of the lungs primarily, the fact being recognized
by the best medical authorities that there was often a metastasis or
changing of the seat of tubercular disease from bowels to lungs, or
vice versa; that in this instance affiant had no doubt but that such a
metastasis took place, and that while tubercular disease was the immediate cause of death, a primary tubercular condition of the bowels
existed previously and was the original cause of the disease which
extended to the lungs.

Proof filed with your committee shows that the beneficiary's husband
died leaving her no means of support; that the beneficiary herself is
under medical treatment and unable to do hard work, and that she has
no property except a small house which she occupies as a home.

Your committee is satisfied from the above that the soldier's death
was the result of the causes for which he had been pensioned and which
were contracted by him during his service of nearly five years during
the civil war, and that his widow is therefore entitled to an increase of
her pension from $8 to $12 per month.

The bill is therefore reported back with the recommendation that it
pass after the same shall have been amended as follows:

In line 6 strike out the word "Company" and insert in lieu thereof
the word "Battery."

In line 8 strike out the word "seventeen" and insert in lieu thereof
the word "twelve."

O

ELIAS G. RUTHERFORD.

JANUARY 26, 1903.—Committed to the Committee of the Whole House and ordered
to be printed.

Mr. CROWLEY, from the Committee on Invalid Pensions, submitted
the following

REPORT.

[To accompany H. R. 16789.]

The Committee on Invalid Pensions, to whom was referred the bill
(H. R. 16789) granting an increase of pension to E. G. Rutherford,
submit the following report:

This bill proposes to increase the pension of the soldier named
therein from $12 to $30 per month.

Elias R. Retherford, the soldier named in this bill and now 58 years
of age, served as a corporal in Company H, One hundred and fifty-
second Illinois Infantry, from February 11, 1865, to September 11, 1865,
when honorably discharged.

He was under treatment at various dates during his period of service
for hepatitis and intermittent fever.

He is now a pensioner under the general law at $12 per month on
account of disease of lungs and rheumatism.

A claim for increase was rejected in 1893 upon the ground that the
rating of $12 per month covered all disability from the causes of
accepted service origin.

A claim on account of additional disabilities, based upon diarrhea
and resulting piles, filed on February 7, 1898, was rejected on May 14,
1900, upon the ground of no record of treatment for said disabilities in
the service and claimant's inability to show by medical or other satisfactory evidence that these disabilities were incurred in the service
and line of duty.

He filed the testimony of several of his comrades to the effect that
in the spring of 1865, while at Tullahoma, Tenn., he was taken with
constipation so that for days he had no evacuation of the bowels;
that this condition continued during the balance of his service and
resulted in piles; and that this condition continued to exist ever since
his discharge. And he also filed medical testimony as to treatment for
these disabilities since 1881.

Certificates of medical examination beginning in June, 1888; show the existence of piles, and the last certificate of medical examination, made on March 1, 1899, rated him $16 for rheumatism and resulting disease of heart, found two external and three internal piles, with atrophy of liver, and rated him $10 for diarrhea, constipation, and resulting disease of the rectum and liver.

The proof in this case tends to show that the diarrhea and piles, etc., for which the board of surgeons rated the soldier $10 in their certificate of medical examination of March, 1899, are due to his military service and that the beneficiary, in view of the recommendation of that board of surgeons, is therefore entitled to a rating of $24 per month for the disease of lungs and rheumatism of accepted service origin and the diarrhea and piles, and relief to that extent is recommended, and the bill is reported back with the recommendation that it pass after the same shall have been amended as follows:

In line 6 strike out the letter "E" and insert in lieu thereof the word "Elias."

In line 8 strike out the word "thirty" and insert in lieu thereof the word "twenty-four."

Amend the title so as to read: "A bill granting an increase of pension to Elias G. Rutherford."

O.

WILLIAM W. DOWNS.

JANUARY 26, 1903.—Committed to the Committee of the Whole House and ordered
to be printed.

Mr. CROWLEY, from the Committee on Invalid Pensions, submitted
the following

REPORT.

[To accompany H. R. 16538.]

The Committee on Invalid Pensions, to whom was referred the bill
(H. R. 16538) granting an increase of pension to William Downs, submit the following report:

This bill proposes to increase the pension of the soldier named
therein from $12 to $40 per month.

William W. Downs, the soldier named in this bill, and now 65 years
of age, served as a private in Company A, Twelfth Ohio Infantry,
from August 15, 1861, to August 7, 1865, when honorably discharged
as of Company C, Twenty-third Ohio Infantry, to which transferred.

He is now in receipt of a pension under the act of June 27, 1890, at
the maximum rating, namely, $12 per month, for total inability to
earn a support by manual labor, the result of chronic diarrhea, disease
of the stomach and liver, and resulting piles.

His claim to pension under the general law, filed in November, 1884,
and based upon diarrhea and piles alleged to have been contracted in
November, 1862, was rejected in January, 1888, upon the ground of
his failure after a reasonable time and due notification to furnish the
necessary evidence to establish the claim.

In support of the last-named claim he filed the testimony of neighbors and acquaintances tending to show that upon his return from the
Army he had chronic diarrhea, complained of his back, and was
slightly deaf, and that he continued to complain thereafter in each
year since.

When last examined, in June, 1896, the board of surgeons rated him
$6 for chronic diarrhea and resulting hemorrhoids, $2 for disease of
kidneys, and $2 for rheumatism.

There has been filed with your committee the affidavit of Dr. L. A.
Buck, of Peabody, Kans., setting forth that the beneficiary had been
under his professional care suffering from paralysis agitans since

2 WILLIAM W. DOWNS.

November 2, 1901; that he was now entirely helpless, requiring the assistance of a nurse to dress and feed him and care for his daily wants; also a petition signed by a number of residents of his home to the effect that he has no other means of support except his pension; that he owns a residence property valued at $250, etc.; also the statement of Hon. J. M. Miller, who introduced the bill, to the effect that for more than a year past he had been unable to either dress or feed himself and required the constant care of an attendant; that he is as helpless as a babe, and that during the last year the county of Marion, in which he resides, had to contribute to his support, etc.

It being shown that this soldier, who rendered four years of service, is now suffering from paralysis agitans to such a degree that he is as helpless as a babe and requires the aid and attendance of another person, your committee, following the action of the House on June 16, 1902, recommend that his pension be increased to $30 per month, and therefore report the bill back with the recommendation that it pass after the same shall have been amended as follows:

In line 6, after the word "William," insert the letter "W."

In line 9 strike out the word "forty" and insert in lieu thereof the word "thirty,"

Amend the title so as to read: "A bill granting an increase of pension to William W. Downs."

O

DANIEL VAN WIE.

JANUARY 26, 1903.—Committed to the Committee of the Whole House and ordered
to be printed.

Mr. SULLOWAY, from the Committee on Invalid Pensions, submitted
the following

REPORT.

[To accompany H. R. 10691.]

The committee on Invalid Pensions, to whom was referred the bill
(H. R. 10691) granting an increase of pension to Daniel Van Wie,
submit the following report:

This bill proposes to increase the pension of the soldier named
therein from $14 to $50 per month.

The soldier named in this bill, now 60 years of age, served as a private in Company E, Seventy-sixth New York Infantry, from July 16,
1863, to December 31, 1864, when he was discharged on surgeon's certificate of disability as of Company H of that regiment by reason of gunshot fracture of the femur received in battle at Spottsylvania May 12,
1864.

He has been pensioned under the general law on account of this
gunshot wound of the left hip at $2 per month from discharge, at $6
from August 7, 1868, at $8 from March 19, 1884, at $12 from April
30, 1890, and at $14 from May 29, 1891.

In August, 1898, he alleged cramps in the left hip joint and rheumatism as results of the gunshot wound of left hip. The Pension
Bureau, however, held that these alleged cramps of the left hip joint
were not the results of the wound, but of a rheumatic character.

Medical evidence filed in the Pension Bureau shows that in March
and April, 1901, the beneficiary was confined to his bed, that he suffered from inflammation of the veins of the right leg, chronic diarrhea,
muscular rheumatism, etc.

When last examined, on May 29, 1901, before a member of the board
of surgeons at Cloversville, N. Y., that surgeon described his disabilities as follows:

Gunshot wound of left hip: Scar of entrance located 5½ inches below the crest of
the ilium and 1½ inches posterior to the great trochanter. Size of scar 1 by three-fourths inch; scar tender, depressed, adherent, dragging, and attended by muscular

atrophy of the gluteus hip. Scar of exit is located at the coccyx; size of scar 1 by one-half inch, adherent to the bone and causing adhesion of the surrounding tissues; scar of second entrance located nearly continuous with scar of exit on right buttock. This scar is one-half by three-fourths inch in size, also adherent. Scar of exit 2 inches to the right of scar of entrance. This scar is about three-fourths inch in diameter and is adherent and dragging. In my opinion these scars were the result of one missile having emerged and reentered the hip through the gluteii muscles of both sides and doing osseous injury to the coccyx. The result of this injury is to produce swelling of the left leg, so that it is 2 inches larger than the right leg. This I believe to be due to the retracted return flow. The pain which is alleged is probably due to an injury either to the sciatic nerve itself or to the tissues adjacent to it.

The injury to the coccyx producing necrosis has produced considerable subacute inflammation of the nerves and other tissues in that vicinity, so that it is extremely painful and tender. In my opinion, impairment of the use of the left leg is one-half. Rate, $17.

Rheumatism: Movements of joints of shoulders and right knee partially limited, due to the claimant being in bed. It was impossible to elicit any further evidence of this alleged condition. Rate, $2.

Chronic diarrhea: There is stomach distended with gas. Liver and spleen normal in size and abdomen protruding. Rectum fissured and congested, and a pile tumor on the right side one-half inch in diameter. Claimant emaciated and debilitated. Rate, $10.

There has been filed with your committee the affidavit of Dr. Frank E. Simmons, dated January 28, 1902, setting forth that he had been the family physician of the beneficiary since March, 1879; that he had seen him almost weekly since that time, and found his physical condition at that time as follows:

Severe pain in the left thigh, extending up the left hip and into the back; that these pains were caused by gunshot wound in the left hip, the ball passing through the left hip, entering near the great trochanter and coming out on the middle of the right gluteus maximus muscle, injuring the left hip bone and the various muscles and ligaments of the left hip; that this condition had continued since 1879; that he was not wholly incapacitated from the performance of manual labor of any kind, and that the left limb had continued to become gradually worse until the same was now swollen and very painful.

In the opinion of your committee the disability arising from the gunshot wound of left hip entitles this soldier to an increase of his pension to $24 per month, the disability being equivalent to the loss of a hand or foot.

For these reasons the bill is reported back with the recommendation that it pass after the same shall have been amended as follows:

In line 8 strike out the word "fifty" and insert in lieu thereof the word "twenty-four."

O

JOSEPH FELDHAUSEN.

· JANUARY 26, 1903.—Committed to the Committee of the Whole House and ordered to be printed.

Mr. DARRAGH, from the Committee on Invalid Pensions, submitted the following

REPORT. ·

[To accompany H. R. 10922.]

The Committee on Invalid Pensions, to whom was referred the bill (H. R. 10922) granting an increase of pension to Joseph Feldhausen, submit the following report:

This bill proposes to increase the pension of the soldier named therein from $17 to $30 per month.

This soldier, who is now 62 years of age, served as a private in Company H, Fourth Wisconsin Cavalry, from July 21, 1861, to December 18, 1865, when honorably discharged.

The medical records of the War Department show that he was under treatment in 1862 at various dates for intermittent fever.

He is now a pensioner under the general law at $17 per month, on account of piles (disease of rectum), rheumatism, and resulting disease of heart.

Claims for increase of pension were rejected, the last one on June 15, 1901, upon the ground that the rating of $17 per month was fully commensurate with the degree of disability arising from the pensioned causes.

When last examined, on December 5, 1900, the board of surgeons recommended a rating of $12 for piles, $4 for disease of heart, $6 for lame back, and $8 for general debility, and the board of surgeons then described his disability as follows:

Piles: Appears to be one mass of tumors on anterior portion, which is markedly ulcerated and bleeds profusely. The posterior portion is the size of walnut, livid and very congested and angry looking. The mucous membrane of the rectum is congested and covered with liquid fæces.

Heart: Apex beat is detected on palpitation two inches below and one-half inch to the side of left nipple. The second sound is accentuated.

Lame back: There is marked left curvature in the dorsal region of the spine, in consequence of which the right shoulder is lower than the left. There is wasting of the rhomboid muscles of the left side.

General debility: Teeth are all gone, tongue coated, marked scar on the phalanx, hands show no signs of manual labor. Claimant appears older than he is by ten years.

The claimant in a declaration filed March 28, 1882, alleged that while out scouting, in February, 1864, near Baton Rogue, La., he was thrown from his horse and injured in his back.

This claim was rejected after special examination in October, 1891, upon the ground of no record of treatment in the War Department, and claimant's inability, with the aid of a special examination, to show the origin of that injury in the service and line of duty.

The special examiner was unable to obtain any testimony as to the origin of the injury of back. Testimony, however, was obtained tending to show that ever since his return from the service the soldier suffered from a lame back.

From the affidavit of the beneficiary filed with your committee it appears that he has no means of support except the pension of $17 per month, and no property except a small house and lot valued at $500 and encumbered to the extent of $100.

As stated above, the soldier is now pensioned under the general law on account of disease of rectum, rheumatism, and resulting disease of heart, and the last certificate of medical examination, made in 1900, has rated him for the disabilities in excess of the $17 per month which he is now receiving; in view of which your committee believe that the degree of his disabilities of accepted service origin warrants an increase of his pension from $17 to $24 per month, and relief to that extent is recommended, and the bill reported back with the recommendation that it pass after the same shall have been amended as follows:

In line 8 strike out the word "thirty" and insert in lieu thereof the word "twenty-four."

O

FLORENCE M. STOUT.

JANUARY 26, 1903.—Committed to the Committee of the Whole House and ordered
to be printed.

Mr. CROWLEY, from the Committee on Invalid Pensions, submitted
the following

REPORT.

[To accompany H. R. 16859.]

The Committee on Invalid Pensions, to whom was referred the bill
(H. R. 16859) granting a pension to Florence M. Stout, submit the
following report:

This bill proposes to pension the beneficiary named therein as the
widow of William H. B. Stout, late of Company B, First Battalion
Nebraska Cavalry, at $24 per month.

The soldier named in this bill served as a sergeant in Company B,
Second Nebraska Cavalry, from October 14, 1862, to September 14,
1863, when honorably discharged, and as second lieutenant and first
lieutenant of Company B, First Battalion Nebraska Veteran Cavalry,
from May 6, 1864, to July 1, 1866, when honorably discharged.

The medical records of the War Department show that during his
period of service he was suffering from hemorrhoids and an umbilical
hernia.

He was pensioned under the general law on account of hemorrhoids
and ventral hernia, and at the time of his death was drawing a pension
of $15 per month by reason of the same. He died January 1, 1902,
of disease of heart.

The claim of the beneficiary, who is now 48 years of age, and who
was married to the officer on November 24, 1892, which claim was filed
under the general law, was rejected on July 3, 1902, upon the ground
that her husband's fatal disease had no connection with the hemorrhoids
and ventral hernia for which he had been pensioned under the general
law.

A claim under the act of June 27, 1890, was not filed by the beneficiary for the reason that she did not marry the officer prior to June
27, 1890, and hence had no title under that law.

The beneficiary alleged that her husband's death from heart disease
was a result of the stomach trouble which produced the hemorrhoids

for which he had been pensioned, and the testimony of a physician filed during the prosecution of his claim under the general law shows that while in the service he was a sufferer from bloody flux, that hemorrhoids followed as a result, that after the war he suffered from hemorrhoids and ulceration of the rectum, also from malaria, and medical examinations as early as 1892 revealed disease of heart.

Medical testimony filed by the beneficiary in the Pension Office during the prosecution of her claim under the general law shows that during his last illness her husband was suffering from acute stomach trouble and indigestion, that he died from heart failure as a result, and that he also had chronic valvular disease of the heart.

The hemorrhoids for which the officer had been pensioned under the general law were contracted by him while he held the rank of second lieutenant.

Your committee believes that the doubts in this case as to whether the soldier's fatal disease of heart was a result of the disability for which he had been pensioned under the general law should be resolved in favor of the beneficiary and that she should be granted the pension allowed under the general law to the widow of a second lieutenant, namely, $15 per month.

The bill is therefore reported back with the recommendation that it pass after the same shall have been amended as follows:

In line 6, after the word "late," strike out the word "of" and insert in lieu thereof the words "second lieutenant."

In line 7, before the word "Cavalry," insert the words "Veteran Volunteer."

In line 8 strike out the word "twenty-four" and insert in lieu thereof the word "fifteen."

O

ALBERT W. THOMPSON.

JANUARY 26, 1903.—Committed to the Committee of the Whole House and ordered
to be printed.

Mr. SULLOWAY, from the Committee on Invalid Pensions, submitted
the following

REPORT.

[To accompany H. R. 16717.]

The Committee on Invalid Pensions, to whom was referred the bill
(H. R. 16717) granting an increase of pension to Albert W. Thompson,
submit the following report:

This bill proposes to increase the pension of the soldier named
therein from $12 to $24 per month.

The medical records of the War Department show that this soldier,
now 58 years of age, served as a private in Company G, One hundred
and forty-seventh New York Volunteers, from August 23, 1863, to
June 28, 1865, when honorably discharged on surgeon's certificate of
disability by reason of gunshot wound of the great toe of the left foot,
impairing motion of the foot, received at Petersburg, Va., June 18,
1864.

He has been a pensioner under the general law on account of this
wound ever since his discharge, and is now pensioned at $12 per month
for the same.

A claim for increase of pension was rejected in August, 1902, upon
the ground that the disability from the wound did not warrant a rating
in excess of $12 per month, and a claim for additional disabilities,
namely, injury to left eye and deafness of left ear, claimed for on
November 20, 1890, was rejected in June, 1894, upon the ground of
no record of treatment for said disabilities in the service, and claimant's declared inability to furnish the necessary evidence showing the
origin of the same in the service.

The soldier alleged that the injury to his eye was caused by gravel
thrown by a solid shot striking the ground in front of him, striking
him in the left eye, and that he also contracted deafness at the battle
of Cold Harbor, Va., in June, 1864.

He declared his inability to furnish proof as to the origin of said
disabilities in the service.

He filed the testimony of one person to the effect that he had been a sufferer from impaired sight of the left eye and deafness of the left ear since 1866, and medical testimony as to treatment for said disabilities since November, 1890.

When last examined, on March 12, 1902, the board of surgeons rated him $12 for the wound of left foot and $12 for blindness of the left eye.

Medical testimony filed with your committee shows that upon an examination of the soldier on January 15, 1903, he was found to be suffering from gunshot wound of the left foot; that said wound had not healed and does not heal; that he was totally blind in the left eye and nearly blind in the right; that he was also suffering from rheumatism and heart disease, and was unable to perform any manual labor.

A petition of D. T. Vickers Post, No. 297, Grand Army of the Republic, of Randolph, N. Y., also filed with your committee, asks Congressional relief for the beneficiary; and other papers filed with the committee show that the beneficiary formerly owned a house and lot, but that he had in recent years been compelled to sell the house to procure means of subsistence.

There are many precedents for increasing the pension of those who are suffering from disabilities of an extreme nature, and the facts stated bring this case fully within such precedents, in view of which an increase of the soldier's pension from $12 to $20 per month is recommended, and the bill is reported back with the recommendation that it pass after the same shall have been amended as follows:

In line 3 strike out the word "is," and in same line, before the word "hereby," insert the word "is."

In line 8 strike out the word "twenty-four" and insert in lieu thereof the word "twenty."

O

JOHN BURKE.

JANUARY 26, 1903.—Committed to the Committee of the Whole House and ordered
to be printed.

Mr. CROWLEY, from the Committee on Invalid Pensions, submitted the
following

REPORT.

[To accompany H. R. 16856.]

The Committee on Invalid Pensions, to whom was referredt he bill
(H. R. 16856) granting a pension to John Burke, submit the following report:

This bill proposes to increase the pension of the soldier named
therein from $12 to $30 per month.

This soldier, now 78 years of age, served as a private in Company E,
Twenty-seventh Iowa Infantry, from January 16, 1864, to August 3,
1865, when honorably discharged as of the Veteran Reserve Corps, to
which organization he was transferred by reason of gunshot wound
of the left leg received while in the service and line of duty on August
17, 1864.

He is now pensioned under the general law at $12 for this gunshot
wound of the left leg.

A claim for increase of pension, filed in August, 1900, in which the
soldier alleged resulting loss of the use of said leg, was rejected on
July 9, 1901, upon the ground that the loss of the use of the leg was not
shown and that the degree of disability arising from the wound of the
leg did not warrant a rating in excess of $12 per month.

When last examined on March 25, 1901, the board of surgeons
described his disabilities as follows:

Gunshot wound of left leg. The bullet entered the leg at the inner margin of the
left tibia, partially fracturing the head of the same; then passing between the tibia
and fibula, partially fracturing the fibula; also making its exit on the external aspect
of the leg about 7½ inches below the head of the fibula. The scar is very tender,
adherent, and dragging. Left leg measures 7½ inches around the ankle and 11 inches
around the calf, the right measuring 7½ around the ankle and 11¾ around the calf.
There is very marked lameness. He is confined to the house almost constantly on
account of the injury.

From the disabilities of this man from the gunshot wound of left leg and from his
disability from age he is so disabled as to be incapacitated for the performance of
any manual labor, and is entitled to a pension of $30 per month.

While it is admitted that the soldier's great age is a factor in his present disability, your committee believes, however, that the degree of disability from the wound of the left leg of accepted service origin is such as to be equivalent to the loss of a hand or a foot, and that the beneficiary is therefore entitled to a pension for that degree of disability; namely, $24 per month.

The bill is therefore reported back with the recommendation that it pass after the same shall have been amended as follows:

In line 6 strike out the letter "C" and insert in lieu thereof the letter "E."

In line 7, before the word "Infantry," insert the word "Volunteer."

In same line strike out the word "thirty" and insert in lieu thereof the word "twenty-four."

Amend the title so as to read: "A bill granting an increase of pension to John Burke."

O

REUBEN VERMILLION.

JANUARY 26, 1903.—Committed to the Committee of the Whole House and ordered
to be printed.

Mr. KLEBERG, from the Committee on Invalid Pensions, submitted
the following

REPORT.

[To accompany H. R. 14378.]

The Committee on Invalid Pensions, to whom was referred the bill
(H. R. 14378) granting a pension to Reuben Vermillion, submit the
following report:

This bill proposes to pension the soldier named therein as late of
Company D, Seventy-fourth Enrolled Missouri Militia, at $20 per
month.

This soldier, now 71 years of age, filed a claim to pension in December, 1886, under the general law, basing the same upon hemorrhage
of the lungs, alleged to have been contracted in line of duty at Marsh-
field, Mo., in August, 1863.

His claim was rejected in June, 1894, upon the ground that he was
never enrolled or mustered into the United States service.

A claim under the act of June 27, 1890, in which the soldier alleged
service in Company A of the Webster County Battalion Missouri
Home Guards was also rejected in November, 1902, upon the ground
that he did not render ninety days' service during the civil war, as
shown by the records of the War Department.

The records of the War Department do show that the beneficiary
rendered one month's actual military service to the United States
between July 4 and September 5, 1861, as a member of Company A,
of the Webster County Battalion, Missouri Home Guards.

He testified before a special examiner of the Pension Bureau that
in the spring of 1863 he took the place of one John Wilkerson in the
ranks of Company D, of the Sixth Provisional Enrolled Missouri
Militia, and remained with that company, although nominally transferred to Company M, until August 7, 1864; that the command was
mustered into the United States service as the Sixteenth Missouri
Cavalry; that his captain then told him he could go, and he went; that
he received no discharge certificate and did not claim to have been

sworn into the United States service; that inasmuch, however, as the regiment was mustered in to date back a number of months covering the period he did duty as John Wilkerson's substitute, he believed he was entitled to a pension on that account.

The soldier also alleged that he rendered service in Company D, of the Seventy-fourth Enrolled Missouri Militia from August, 1862, to the spring of 1863, when that organization became the Sixth Provisional Enrolled Missouri Militia.

The Seventy-fourth Enrolled Missouri Militia, however, was also a State organization until it became the Sixth Provisional Regiment of Enrolled Missouri Militia, and the Sixth Provisional Missouri Militia was a State organization until the summer of 1864, when it wa smustered into the service of the United States to serve twenty months from November 1, 1863.

As stated above, the claimant alleged that he served as a substitute for John Wilkerson in the Sixth Provisional Militia, and the name of John Wilkerson is borne on the rolls of the Sixth Provisional and the Sixteenth Missouri Cavalry, but it appears from testimony obtained that Wilkerson's son, William H., took his father's place as a substitute in that organization and was sworn into Company M of the Sixteenth under his father's name and served therein until discharged, and the widow of John Wilkerson or William H. Wilkerson is now pensioned on account of the service in Company M of the Sixteenth Missouri.

Some proof was filed tending to show that the claimant served in the Sixth Provisional Militia as a substitute for a substitute, but for whom the proof does not show.

A medical examination of the soldier in 1891 shows that he was then suffering from catarrh, rheumatism, and fracture of the right patella.

In view of the claimant's service in the Webster County Battalion Missouri Home Guards, which organization was recognized by the Hawkins Taylor commission as having been in the military service of the United States, and in view of his age and present infirmities, your committee believes that relief to the extent of granting the beneficiary a pension of $12 per month is justified, for which reason the bill is reported back with the recommendation that it pass after the same shall have been amended as follows:

Strike out all after the enacting clause and insert in lieu thereof the following:

That the Secretary of the Interior be, and he is hereby, authorized and directed to place on the pension roll, subject to the provisions and limitations of the pension laws, the name of Reuben Vermillion, late of Company A, Webster County, Missouri, Home Guards, and pay him a pension at the rate of twelve dollars per month.

O

THOMAS B. FAUGHT.

JANUARY 26, 1903.—Committed to the Committee of the Whole House and ordered to be printed.

Mr. DARRAGH, from the Committee on Invalid Pensions, submitted the following

REPORT.

[To accompany H. R. 6876.]

The Committee on Invalid Pensions, to whom was referred the bill (H. R. 6876) granting an increase of pension to Thomas B. Faught, submit the following report:

This bill proposes to increase the pension of this soldier from $30 to $50 per month.

It appears from the files of the Pension Bureau that this soldier, now 60 years of age, who served as a private in Company G, Fourth Illinois Cavalry, from August 14, 1861, to May 29, 1866, when honorably discharged, has been a pensioner on account of gunshot wound of right heel, injury to left hip, and gunshot wound of the left leg at $8 per month from his discharge, at $15 from June 6, 1866, at $18 from June 4, 1872, at $24 from March 3, 1883, and at $30 from February 12, 1896, and that a claim for increase of pension filed in 1900 was rejected June 5, 1901, upon the ground that the disabilities of accepted service origin did not warrant the next higher rating under the law, namely, $50 per month.

This action was based upon a certificate of medical examination of October 17, 1900, made by a board of examining surgeons in this city, that there was no pensionable disability from the wound of the heel nor from the wound of left leg; that the claimant, however, was suffering from the injury to left hip, the head of the femur having been dislocated upward and backward, and that by reason of the same he was unable to perform any manual labor and was entitled to a $30 rating; that he did not require any assistance; that he could dress and undress and attend to the calls of nature unaided, and could feed himself.

In his application for increase of pension he stated that he believed himself entitled to an increase on account of the increase of his disabilities as a result of advancing age, and filed in support of his claim lay testimony showing that he had been constantly seeking relief through medicines; that he had been confined to his room for some time suffering from kidney trouble and the wounds, but such proof does not set forth that he requires the aid and attendance of another person.

There has been filed with your committee the affidavit of the beneficiary, setting forth that he was totally disabled for the performance of manual labor by reason of his pensioned disabilities; that he owns no property and has no income except the pension of $30 per month.

There has also been filed with your committee the affidavit of Laura A. Faught, the wife of the beneficiary, setting forth that for more than a year her husband has been a constant sufferer from rheumatism, making constant care and attendance necessary; that many times his heart has been attacked so severely that his life was in danger; that he is now unable to perform any kind of manual labor, and that it is unsafe for him to be left without an attendant at any time; also other testimony showing that in March last the beneficiary's rheumatism became so severe that he was for several days confined to his bed, unable to stand and scarcely able to move, suffering intense pains in left hip and knee, and that he required an attendant to wait on him and nurse him through his many attacks of kidney trouble and rheumatism, and that such attendance was furnished by Mrs. Cecelia Fegan, in whose house he lived.

Other testimony filed with your committee sets forth that it is difficult for the beneficiary to walk, even for a short distance, and that he complains of a numbness of his feet, legs, and spine, and that by reason of the dislocation of the left hip the left leg was 4 inches shorter, rendering an artificial shoe support necessary in walking.

The only question that arises in this case is as to whether there is total disability of the left leg by reason of the injury to hip and wound of said leg.

Your committee, from an examination of the evidence, is led to believe that there is such total disability within the meaning of the pension laws, and therefore recommend the rating allowed by law for that degree of disability, namely, $36 per month, and report the bill back with the recommendation that it pass after the same shall have been amended as follows:

Strike out all after the enacting clause and insert in lieu thereof the following:

That the Secretary of the Interior be, and he is hereby, authorized and directed to place on the pension roll, subject to the provisions and limitations of the pension laws, the name of Thomas B. Faught, late of Company G, Fourth Regiment Illinois Volunteer Cavalry, and pay him a pension at the rate of thirty-six dollars per month in lieu of that he is now receiving.

O

ANTON SAUTHOFF.

JANUARY 26, 1903.—Committed to the Committee of the Whole House and ordered to be printed.

Mr. HOLLIDAY, from the Committee on Invalid Pensions submitted the following

REPORT.

[To accompany H. R. 16752.]

The Committee on Invalid Pensions, to whom was referred the bill (H. R. 16752) granting a pension to Anton Sauthoff, submit the following report:

This bill proposes to pension this soldier at $12 per month.

Mr. Sauthoff is 77 years of age, and was a member of Company D, Cape Girardeau Battalion, Missouri Home Guards, which battalion was organized June 27, 1861, and discharged September 29, 1861.

The Hawkins-Taylor commission, appointed under the joint resolution of Congress of July 12, 1862, and February 16, 1863, determined in this soldier's case that he rendered to the United States one month of actual military service during the period between June 27 and September 29, 1861.

His claim to pension under the act of June 27, 1890, was rejected in March, 1894, upon the ground of insufficient service, and his claim under the general law, filed in June, 1890, and based upon double rupture, rheumatism, and diseased eyes, was rejected in 1895, upon the ground of no record of treatment in the War Department and claimant's failure, aided by special examination, to furnish competent proof connecting said diabilities with his service.

The claimant in his declaration alleged incurrence of these disabilities during his one month's service in Cape Girardeau.

In February, 1891, however, he told the board of surgeons who examined him that the hernia of the right side came on soon after the war; a year later that of the left side appeared; that he had rheumatism for several years, and that he had sore eyes several years prior to 1891.

He filed the ex parte affidavits of three of his comrades as to the origin of his disabilities in the service, but during the special examination two of these comrades whose depositions were taken testified that they knew nothing of the origin of his diseases in the service.

The third comrade was not interviewed.

Since the rejection of the claim he filed the testimony of the first lieutenant of his company, to the effect that he complained of pain in his limbs and joints and that his eyes were watery in the service; that he, however, had no knowledge of any rupture.

He also filed proof of several members of his organization that after the disbandment of the same, in the fall of 1861, he complained of severe rheumatic pains in his muscles and joints and had a stiffness of the limbs when he walked about, and that he also had sore and diseased eyes, and that he continued to suffer therefrom ever since.

The soldier alleges that the physicians who treated him before 1876 are dead.

Medical testimony as to treatment since 1877 for attacks of chronic rheumatism, disease of eyes, deafness, and double rupture was filed by him.

The certificate of medical examination of March, 1894, shows a complete right hernia, an indirect left hernia, rheumatism, disease of eyes, piles and heart disease.

In view of the great age of the beneficiary and the probability that some of his disabilities are traceable to his military service in the Missouri Home Guards, your committee believe that the relief sought for in the bill is warranted, and therefore report the same back with the recommendation that it pass after the same shall have been amended as follows:

In line 6, after the word "Girardeau," insert the word "Battalion."

O

REBECCA RANDOLPH.

JANUARY 26, 1903.—Committed to the Committee of the Whole House and ordered to be printed.

Mr. DARRAGH, from the Committee on Invalid Pensions, submitted the following

REPORT.

[To accompany H. R. 13713.]

The Committee on Invalid Pensions, to whom was referred the bill (H. R. 13713), granting an increase of pension to Rebecca Randolph, submit the following report:

This bill proposes to increase the pension of the beneficiary named therein from $8 to $20 per month.

Alonzo T. Randolph, the soldier named in this bill, served as a private in Company A, Thirty-third New York Volunteers, from May 22, 1861, to June 2, 1863, when honorably discharged, and again as a private of Company H, One hundred and forty-eighth New York Volunteers, from December 16, 1863, to August 28, 1865, when honorably discharged as of Company K, One hundredth New York Volunteers, to which transferred.

Medical records of the War Department show that he was under treatment in October and November, 1864, for diarrhea; and a medical certificate of July 12, 1865, shows him to be suffering at that time from cutaneous affection and that he had a fever and diarrhea.

He filed a claim to pension under the general law of July 28, 1880, basing the same upon a rupture alleged to have been incurred in June, 1864, while unloading commissary stores, and on account of disease of kidneys, and filed in support of the same the testimony of the colonel of his regiment as to the incurrence of the rupture at the time and place alleged by him, but this witness failed to reply to the Bureau letters addressed to him relative to his knowledge of the matter; also the testimony of a comrade to the effect that he was sick while in the service and that affiant assisted him into an ambulance to take him to the hospital.

The testimony of neighbors, etc., was also filed by him tending to show that upon his return from the Army he was covered with sores from scurvy; complained of a rupture, and had trouble with his kidneys, and that he had been under treatment since the spring of 1881 for kidney trouble and a right hernia.

This claim is still pending in the Pension Bureau.

The soldier was pensioned under the act of June 27, 1890, at $12 per month from July 17, 1890, for total inability to earn a support by manual labor, the result of a right hernia and hypertrophy of the prostate gland.

The soldier died November 27, 1894, from cancer of the liver.

The beneficiary named in the bill, now 78 years of age, who married the soldier on January 23, 1847, is now pensioned under the act of June 27, 1890, at $8 per month, upon proof that she was the legal widow of the soldier at the time of his death, had not remarried, and was dependent upon her daily labor.

Proof filed in the Pension Bureau shows that the beneficiary is a poor old lady, crippled up, and hardly able to dress herself.

The beneficiary never applied for pension under the general law.

There has been filed with your committee the affidavit of Dr. G. McAllister, of Stanwood, Mich., setting forth that the beneficiary's joints and wrists of both hands are badly deformed; that the right elbow joint has become immovable as a result of rheumatism; that the toes of the right and left feet are also deformed, as well as the right knee joint, on account of rheumatic deposits; that the general health is exceedingly poor, and that she is practically a helpless invalid, being unable to dress herself or even walk about the house without the aid of some other person.

The statement of the supervisor of Austin township, also filed with your committee, sets forth that the beneficiary has no property and is very poor, and a petition signed by a number of prominent citizens of the beneficiary's home sets forth her helpless condition from rheumatism and her destitution.

Your committee believes that Congress should come to the relief of this very aged widow, who is a helpless invalid and whose husband rendered over three and a half years of service.

An increase of her pension from $8 to $12 per month seems therefore justified, and the bill is reported back with the recommendation that it pass after the same shall have been amended as follows:

In line 7, before the word "New York," insert the word "Regiment."

In line 8, before the word "New York," insert the word "Regiment."

In line 9 strike out the words "of twenty" and insert in lieu thereof the words "at the rate of twelve."

In line 10 strike out the words "the pension" and insert in lieu thereof the word "that."

O

ELLEN A. PLUMLEY.

JANUARY 26, 1903.—Committed to the Committee of the Whole House and ordered
to be printed.

Mr. CROWLEY, from the Committee on Invalid Pensions, submitted the
following

REPORT.

[To accompany H. R. 12871.]

The Committee on Invalid Pensions, to whom was referred the bill
(H. R. 12871) granting a pension to Ellen A. Plumley, submit the
following report:

This bill proposes to pension the beneficiary named therein as the
widow of Samuel I. Plumley, late of Company G, First Indiana Heavy
Artillery, at $20 per month.

A similar bill granting the beneficiary a pension of $8 per month
was favorably reported by your committee in the second session of
the Fifty-sixth Congress, and the report of that committee is herewith.

For the reasons set forth in that report the passage of the bill is
again recommended after the same shall have been amended as follows:
In line 8 strike out the word "twenty" and insert in lieu thereof
the word "eight."

[House Report No. 2872, Fifty-sixth Congress, second session.]

The Committee on Invalid Pensions, to whom was referred the bill (H. R. 13466)
granting a pension to Ellen A. Plumley, submit the following report:

This bill proposes to pension Ellen A. Plumley as the late widow of Samuel T.
Plumley, late of Company G, First Indiana Heavy Artillery, at $24 per month.

The soldier named in the bill served as private in Company G, First Indiana
Heavy Artillery, from October 5, 1864, to October 4, 1865, when honorably discharged, and never applied for pension.

On August 7, 1899, Ellen A. Plumley, now 56 years of age, applied for pension
under the act of June 27, 1890, as the widow of the soldier, alleging that he died
August 6, 1893, and that she was married to him February 27, 1864, and filed proof
of such marriage and also a transcript from the records of the district court for
Kossuth County, Iowa, showing that she brought proceedings in divorce against
the soldier (cause not set forth in papers filed), and that she was granted a divorce
from him December 12, 1888, and that as alimony in lieu of dower she was decreed
a lot with buildings and furniture, a cow, and $150 in cash.

There was also filed some ex parte proof tending to show that one Beulah Dickinson alienated the soldier's affections from his wife; that through intimidation she consented to be divorced; that she always appeared to be very fond of her husband; that it was her wish to be with the soldier during his sickness, but that Miss Dickinson prevented her coming there; and that after the divorce she did the soldier's washing, and he visited her house often; that he bought meat and carried it to her house; that when taken sick he desired to have the beneficiary take care of him, etc.

She also filed proof that she was not assessed for any property, and has not remarried since her divorce from soldier.

The claim was rejected by the Pension Bureau February 26, 1900, upon the ground that she was not the widow of the soldier, she having been divorced from him in 1888.

There has been filed with your committee the statement of the Hon. Mr. Conner, a member of this House, to the effect that he has investigated as to whether the soldier, after the beneficiary had been divorced from him, married again, and found that he never resumed marital relations.

It would seem evident from the above that while the beneficiary was not the wife in law of the soldier at the time of his death, he nevertheless had due regard for her; that it may be said that she was his wife in fact, it being shown that he had assisted her in various ways; and under these circumstances the committee reports the bill back with the recommendation that it pass at the rate provided by law for widows under the act of June 27, 1890, namely, $8 per month.

O

WILLIAM J. JUBB.

JANUARY 26, 1903.—Committed to the Committee of the Whole House and ordered
to be printed.

Mr. APLIN, from the Committee on Invalid Pensions, submitted the
following

REPORT.

[To accompany II. R. 15768.]

The Committee on Invalid Pensions, to whom was referred the bill
(H. R. 15768) granting an increase to William J. Jubb, submit the following report:

This bill proposes to increase the pension of the soldier named
therein from $10 to $24 per month.

The soldier named in this bill, now 68 years of age, served as a
private in Company A, Third Michigan Infantry, from June 10, 1861,
to September 4, 1863, when discharged on surgeon's certificate of disability by reason of "confirmed tuberculosis, hernia, loss of left thumb,
all contracted since enlistment."

The records of the War Department further show that the beneficiary was captured at Chancellorsville, Va., May 2, 1863, and paroled
at United States Fort, Virginia, May 15, 1863; that he was admitted
to corps hospital with continued fever, and that he was under treatment
in June, August, and September, 1863, for rheumatism and bronchitis,
and from August 1 to 8, 1863, for incised wound.

He has been pensioned under the general law since his discharge on
account of a rupture of the right side, and is now in receipt of a pension
of $10 per month on account of the same.

A claim on account of the loss of the left thumb, alleged to have
been incurred in November or December, 1862, at Falmouth, Va., by
a cut from an axe while making a temporary boottree for the purpose
of straightening a boot heel, was rejected by the Pension Bureau in
January, 1901, upon the ground of claimant's inability to prove the
origin of such injury in line of duty.

The soldier alleged that while making a stick about 2 feet long to
put into the boot ring for the purpose of straightening the heel of the
boot, which was turned in sideways and which interfered with his left
ankle, and while chopping the end of the stick off square with an axe,
he slipped and fell and cut his thumb on the side, that he caught cold

in the cut and the thumb had to be amputated, and that this accident
happened while he was about 12 feet from his tent.

None of the comrades of the soldier who were interviewed by the
special examiner had any personal knowledge of the injury causing
the loss of the thumb, their testimony all being based upon hearsay,
and one comrade testified that there was some talk at the time or
shortly afterwards to the effect that it was an act of cowardice, that
he, however, never believed that the beneficiary purposely cut his
thumb off, for the reason that he was a good soldier and never shirked
his duty.

When last examined, on April 16, 1902, the board of surgeons rate
the beneficiary $8 for the hernia, $2 for loss of left thumb, and $2
for rheumatism.

There has been filed with your committee the statement of Dr.
W. H. Marshall, of Gaylord, Mich., setting forth that he examined the
beneficiary on December 5, 1902, and found him suffering from a right
inguinal hernia, loss of left thumb at second phalangeal joint, dilitation and fatty degeneration of the heart, indigestion, and muscular
rheumatism.

The statement of Dr. L. A. Harris, of Gaylord, Mich., also filed with
your committee, sets forth that he examined the beneficiary on January
20, 1903, and found him suffering from a right inguinal hernia, muscular
rheumatism, chronic bronchitis, and hemorrhoids and considered him
unable to perform manual labor of any kind.

The affidavit of the beneficiary, also filed with your committee, sets
forth that he has no property and no means of support aside from his
pension; and a number of prominent citizens of the beneficiary's town
also state that he had not been able to perform any manual labor for the
past eight years.

The physical condition of this soldier, who is now quite aged and who
rendered two years of service, is such as to bring him within the
numerous precedents of special pension legislation, hence the bill is
reported back with the recommendation that it pass.

O

MARY H. TALCOTT.

January 26, 1903.—Committed to the Committee of the Whole House and ordered
to be printed.

Mr. Sulloway, from the Committee on Invalid Pensions, submitted
the following

REPORT.

[To accompany H. R. 15842.]

The Committee on Invalid Pensions, to whom was referred the bill
(H. R. 15842) granting a pension to Mary M. Talcott, submit the
following report:

This bill proposes to pension Mary M. Talcott, the former wife of
Col. George Nelson Macy, of the Twentieth Massachusetts Volunteers,
at $30 per month.

George N. Macy, the officer named in this bill, served as lieutenant-
colonel of the Twentieth Massachusetts from May 1, 1863, to July 22,
1865, when honorably discharged.

He received a gunshot wound of the left hand at the battle of Gettysburg, July 3, 1863, causing amputation of the left arm, and also
received wounds in the right leg and left leg at the battle of the Wilderness, in May, 1864.

He was a pensioner under the general law at $30 per month on
account of the amputation of the left arm from gunshot wound.

He died February 13, 1875.

The pension which accrued between the date of his last quarterly
payment of pension and his death was paid to Mary H. Macy, his
wife, who married him in February, 1863.

The beneficiary named in the bill never applied for pension.

From proof filed with your committee it appears that the beneficiary
on November 8, 1877, remarried one Willam Henry Talcott; that said
Talcott died on July 28, 1897; that the officer's death was the result
of accidentally shooting himself while going upstairs; that the benfi-
ciary is now wholly dependent upon her labor for support, and that
she is 63 years of age, and that the only property owned by her is an
undivided one-half in a small lot of land at Nantucket, Mass., worth
perhaps five or six hundred dollars, and from which no income is
derived.

There has been filed with your committee the testimony of a party who was a servant in the officer's house, setting forth that after the officer's hand was amputated he was in the habit of carrying a small firearm, usually a small Colt pistol, in his vest pocket, for the sole reason of protection to himself, he having but one hand; that after his return from the service he was practically broken in health and his formerly strong and vigorous constitution was undermined from exposure, wounds, and the amputation of the hand; that he had rheumatism of the heart and was a great sufferer, and was subject to not infrequent attacks of vertigo; that it was apparently during one of these attacks of vertigo that he fell while he was going upstairs at his home in Boston; that the pistol which he carried was discharged, and the ball from said pistol entered his body, and as a result he died from said wound; that affiant fully believed that the accident which caused his death would never have occurred had it not been for his crippled condition and shattered and undermined health, due to his unfaltering bravery and his splendid military service.

The testimony of another party who had also been intimately acquainted with the officer and often visited at his home was also filed corroborating the statements of the previous witness, and also setting forth that the beneficiary was wholly dependent upon others for her support, being possessed of no property and having no income whatever.

It is admitted that the beneficiary would have no title to pension under the general pension laws, for the reason that her husband's death was not directly due to the amputation of the left arm and the wounds of the left leg and right leg received while in the service.

Inasmuch, however, as it is probable that the officer's rheumatism and heart trouble (vertigo) were the results of his military service, and that his death was directly due to a fall while suffering from vertigo, your committee believes that the beneficiary, as the former widow of the officer, should be held to have shown that her husband's death was due to his military service and that consequently she should be granted relief under the provisions of the act of March 3, 1901, relating to remarried widows.

The passage of the bill is therefore recommended after the same shall have been amended as follows:

Strike out all of lines 6, 7, and 8 and insert in lieu thereof the following:

of Mary H. Talcott, former widow of George N. Macy, late lieutenant-colonel Twentieth Regiment Massachusetts Volunteer Infantry, and pay her a pension at the rate of $30 per month.

Amend the title so as to read: "A bill granting a pension to Mary H. Talcott."

O

FRANKLIN CHASE.

JANUARY 26, 1903.—Committed to the Committee of the Whole House and ordered
to be printed.

Mr. SULLOWAY, from the Committee on Invalid Pensions, submitted the
following

REPORT.

[To accompany S. 699.]

The Committee on Invalid Pensions, to whom was referred the bill
(S. 699) granting an increase of pension to Franklin Chase, have
examined the same and adopt the Senate report thereon and recommend that the bill do pass.

[Senate Report No. 2139, Fifty-seventh Congress, second session.]

The Committee on Pensions, to whom was referred the bill (S. 699) granting an
increase of pension to Franklin Chase, have examined the same and report:
This bill proposes to increase from $30 to $50 per month the pension of Franklin
Chase, late of Company E, First Regiment Massachusetts Volunteer Cavalry.
The military records show that Franklin Chase enlisted September 7, 1861, and
was discharged November 7, 1864. During service he bore the rank of private. He
was taken prisoner at Culpeper, Va., September 13, 1863; was confined at Richmond,
Va., and paroled December 28, 1863. The hospital records show that he was treated
after his release from prison for anæmia, intermittent fever, and heart disease.
Claimant was first pensioned under the general law May 18, 1889, for right inguinal
hernia, saber wound of left hand, and gunshot wound of neck, at $8 per month from
August 25, 1884, which was increased
to $14 per month December 24, 1888, for right inguinal hernia, saber wound of left
hand, gunshot wound of neck, and disease of heart, all of service origin. It was
increased to $16 per month April 23, 1890; to $17 per month December 4, 1891; to
$24 per month June 21, 1895, and to $30 per month February 24, 1899.
In addition to the disabilities for which he is pensioned claimant is also troubled
with left inguinal hernia, and for all purposes is totally blind. These disabilities, it
seems, originated some years subsequent to his discharge from the Army. His last
medical examination was made February 24, 1899, and the examining surgeon rated
him $72 for loss of sight of both eyes, $14 for double hernia, $2 for saber wound of
left hand, $4 for gunshot wound of neck, and stated that by reason of double inguinal
hernia and heart disease he was totally disqualified for manual labor.
Claimant has completely lost the sight of right eye and with left eye he can see
only a little light. It also appears that because of the general feebleness of his condition, due principally to heart disease, he can only walk with the aid of crutches.
Evidence on file shows that claimant has a wife and four small children depend-

ent on him, and that his only means of support is his pension. For some years he received State and military aid from the town of Chicopee, Mass., where he formerly resided.   His present address is 98 Cedar street, Fitchburg, Mass.

Although entitled to a pension, claimant did not make claim in time to obtain arrears, whereby he might take care of himself in his misfortunes of later years, and in that way he saved to the Government some hundreds of dollars.   While it is_not shown that his greatest affliction is the result of his military service, yet it may be that it is due to the constitutional changes produced by the hardships and exposures of his service and prison life.   .

Aside from this, the disability resulting from his pensioned troubles would seem to entitle him to increase of pension, and, in view of his faithful and honorable service of over three years and his deplorable condition, your committee report the bill back favorably with a recommendation that it pass.

O

HARRIET HATCH.

JANUARY 26, 1903.—Committed to the Committee of the Whole House and ordered to be printed.

Mr. SULLOWAY, from the Committee on Invalid Pensions, submitted the following

REPORT.

[To accompany S. 1043.]

The Committee on Invalid Pensions, to whom was referred the bill (S. 1043) granting an increase of pension to Harriet Hatch, have examined the same and adopt the Senate report thereon and recommend that the bill do pass.

[Senate Report No. 2144, Fifty-seventh Congress, second session.]

The Committee on Pensions, to whom was referred the bill (S. 1043) granting an increase of pension to Harriet Hatch, have examined the same and report:

This bill proposes to increase from $8 to $20 per month the pension of Harriet Hatch, of Washburn, Me., widow of Albion L. Hatch, late of Company F, Twenty-fourth Regiment Maine Volunteer Infantry.

Soldier enlisted September 10, 1862, and was honorably discharged August 25, 1863. He died from paralysis September 23, 1896, being a pensioner at time of his death at the rate of $8 per month, for disease of urinary organs incurred during his military service.

Harriet Hatch, the claimant under this bill, is 66 years of age and was married to the soldier January 28, 1865. She is now receiving the pension of $8 per month provided by the act of June 27, 1890. She is in poor health and has no means of support except her pension of $8 per month. Her property consists of a small house valued at $150, which is simply a shelter and yields no income.

Cassie R. Hatch, daughter of the soldier, is with her mother, Harriet Hatch, and is wholly under her care and maintenance. She is totally blind and has been so from her infancy, and needs her mother's care and attention all the time. This child was born February 8, 1871, and being over 16 years of age has no title to pension under existing laws.

The military records show that the soldier, Albion L. Hatch, rendered faithful and honorable service. His widow, now advanced in years and in poor health and dependent circumstances, is burdened with the care of a blind child. The case comes within rule 5 of your committee, which is as follows:

"Bills proposing to pension sons and daughters of soldiers will not be entertained except in cases where it is shown by satisfactory evidence that the proposed beneficiary has been idiotic, deformed, or otherwise permanently helpless from a period antedating the age of 16 years, and then only in case of destitution. In such cases the rate allowed shall not exceed $12 per month."

Your committee are of the opinion that the widow's pension should be increased to aid her in the support of her afflicted child.

The passage of the bill is recommended.

O

CHARLES W. COLBY.

JANUARY 26, 1903.—Committed to the Committee of the Whole House and ordered
to be printed.

Mr. SULLOWAY, from the Committee on Invalid Pensions, submitted
the following

REPORT.

[To accompany S. 1166.]

The Committee on Invalid Pensions, to whom was referred the bill
(S. 1166) granting an increase of pension to Charles W. Colby, have
examined the same and adopt the Senate report thereon and recommend that the bill do pass.

[Senate Report No. 2145, Fifty-seventh Congress, second session.]

The Committee on Pensions, to whom was referred the bill (S. 1166) granting an
increase of pension to Charles W. Colby, have examined the same and report:
This bill proposes to increase from $12 to $24 per month the pension of Charles W.
Colby, of East Weare, N. H., late of Company G, First Regiment New Hampshire
Volunteer Cavalry, who served from August 11, 1864, to July 15, 1865, when he was
honorably discharged.
Claimant is 71 years of age. He was first pensioned in November, 1897, under the
act of June 27, 1890, at $6 per month from July 1, 1892, which was increased to $8
per month February 21, 1900; to $10 per month October 17, 1900, and to $12 per
month June 18, 1902. The disabilities for which he is receiving pension under the
act of June 27, 1890, are loss of sight of left eye, disease of heart, and senile debility.
On December 17, 1883, claimant made claim under the general law, alleging injury
to head and shoulder, incurred about June 1, 1865, by being thrown from his horse;
partial sunstroke, incurred in the summer of 1865, and injury to left eye, incurred in
December, 1864. This claim was rejected October 12, 1899—so much thereof as is
based on sunstroke and injury to left eye—on the ground of no record or other satisfactory evidence of service origin, and claimant, with the aid of a special examination, was unable to furnish same, and so much thereof as relates to injury to head
and shoulder on the ground of no pensionable degree of disability therefrom since
date of filing claim.
There is no evidence to show that claimant received injury to head and shoulder
in service, and the several reports of examining surgeons do not show that any disability from such injury now exists. There is some evidence to show that claimant
was overcome by the heat while in the service, though none of his comrades have
any personal knowledge of this fact. This is explained by the fact that he was alone
when he incurred this disability. He was the mail carrier for his command and was
carrying dispatches to Washington at the time he was overcome by heat, and none
of his comrades nor anyone else was with him at the time.

Prior to the war, and when quite young, claimant was hit in the left eye with a pebble, and it bothered him for some time, and he could not see quite as well thereafter with that eye as with the other. At enlistment, however, he was told by the examining surgeon that there was nothing about the eye which would prevent him being a soldier, and a couple of his comrades testify that during service claimant was injured in the left eye by being struck with a twig or a limb of a tree, as he alleges, and that thereafter he complained of this trouble.

After his discharge his complaints about his eye continued, until finally the sight was altogether lost; and it also appears in the evidence that after his return from the Army he complained of dizziness, vertigo, headaches, and other characteristic symptoms of the result of overheat. It seems highly probable that claimant did receive a partial sunstroke in the service and suffered with his head thereafter in consequence, and also that the eye trouble existing prior to enlistment was aggravated very much by an injury received in the service.

Claimant's last medical examination, made at Manchester, N. H., June 18, 1902, shows that he is totally disabled for manual labor by reason of injury to left eye, disease of heart and kidneys, and general debility, the result of age.

Evidence filed with this committee shows that claimant is totally incapacitated for manual labor and is not capable of earning his own living; that he has no real estate, and that his annual income, including his pension, is less than $300.

While the action of the Bureau in rejecting claimant's general-law claim was technically correct, yet the evidence seems to indicate very strongly that his disabilities are due to his military service. However this may be, he served faithfully, and is now aged, poor, and unable to labor, and your committee are of the opinion that he is worthy of an increase of his pension.

The bill is therefore reported back favorably with a recommendation that it pass.

O

THOMAS J. GEORGE.

JANUARY 26, 1903.—Committed to the Committee of the Whole House and ordered
to be printed.

Mr. DARRAGH, from the Committee on Invalid Pensions, submitted the
following

REPORT.

[To accompany S. 1194.]

The Committee on Invalid Pensions, to whom was referred the bill
(S. 1194) granting an increase of pension to Thomas J. George, have
examined the same and adopt the Senate report thereon and recommend that the bill do pass.

[Senate Report No. 2170, Fifty-seventh Congress, second session.]

The Committee on Pensions, to whom was referred the bill (S. 1194) granting an
increase of pension to Thomas J. George, have examined the same and report:

Thomas J. George served in Company D, Fourth Regiment Wisconsin Volunteer
Infantry, from May 8, 1861, to April 11, 1862, and he also served during the war
with Spain as major, Third Regiment Wisconsin Volunteer Infantry from April 28, 1898,
to January 11, 1899. He filed and established a claim under the general law and
was pensioned June 12, 1886, for disease of legs and nearly total deafness of right
ear, results of typhoid fever, at $3 per month from discharge and $4 per month from
April 3, 1884. March 9, 1887, his pension was increased to $6 per month from May
27, 1884, and $8 per month from October 27, 1886, for disease of legs and nearly
total deafness of right ear, results of typhoid fever and rheumatism, and it was later
increased to $10 per month from November 15, 1887, and to $16 per month from
August 27, 1888.

Major George continued to receive pension at the rate of $16 per month until the
breaking out of the war with Spain, when by reason of reenlistment it was made to
cease. After his discharge from his Spanish war service his pension for his former
disabilities, disease of legs and nearly total deafness of right ear, results of typhoid
fever and rheumatism, was renewed at $12 per month, at which rate he is now
pensioned.

Major George's discharge from service in April, 1862, was based on disability
caused by loss of use of both legs succeeding an attack of typhoid fever in October
and November, 1861. His captain stated that prior to his illness with fever he was
an industrious, honest, and faithful soldier. The hospital records show that he was
under treatment at various dates during this service for measles, cholera morbus,
mumps, sprained ankle, diarrhea, remittent fever, rheumatism, and debility.

During the war with Spain soldier participated in the campaign in Porto Rico, and
the evidence of his regimental surgeon shows that he was at times under treatment
for slight attacks of diarrhea and malaria. During the winter of 1898–99, while on

waiting orders preliminary to his discharge from the service, he had an attack of la grippe, following which he began to experience severe pains in his head. About a month after his return from the service he broke down completely, mentally and physically, and for a time it was thought he was suffering from softening of the brain. Though now improved somewhat, he is wholly unable to do any kind of work, and at his age, being now 60 years old, it is almost certain he never will be fit to earn a livelihood.

Claimant was last examined at his home in Menomonie, Wis., November 15, 1899, being unable to appear before the board for examination. He was then found to be badly nourished, emaciated, feeble in mind and body, memory poor, and suffering from disease of heart, disease of legs, impaired hearing, disease of nervous system, including brain degeneration, chronic malarial poisoning, and piles. For these disabilities ratings aggregating $38 per month were recommended.

Major George has endeavored to obtain further relief at the Bureau, but has been unable to do so, it being held there that his present totally disabled condition is not shown to be due to his military service. While in camp at Chickamauga his home with all its contents was destroyed by fire, and his sole earthly possession now is a little house which affords him a shelter and yields no income.

His present means of support for himself and family, which consists of a wife and four small children, is his pension and contributions of comrades and friends. In view of his faithful service in two wars, his great poverty, and total disability, your committee are of opinion that an increase of his pension is eminently just and proper.

The bill is therefore reported back favorably, with a recommendation that it pass.

O

HILAS D. DAVIS.

JANUARY 26, 1903.—Committed to the Committee of the Whole House and ordered
to be printed.

Mr. SULLOWAY, from the Committee on Invalid Pensions, submitted
the following

REPORT.

[To accompany S. 1873.]

The Committee on Invalid Pensions, to whom was referred the bill
(S. 1873) granting an increase of pension to Hilas D. Davis, have
examined the same and adopt the Senate report thereon and recommend that the bill do pass.

[Senate Report No. 2293, Fifty-seventh Congress, second session.]

The Committee on Pensions, to whom was referred the bill (S. 1873) granting an
increase of pension to Hilas D. Davis, have examined the same and report:

This bill proposes to increase from $14 to $24 per month the pension of Hilas D.
Davis, late of Company K, Fifth Regiment New Hampshire Volunteer Infantry.

The military records show that Hilas D. Davis enlisted August 29, 1862, and was
discharged December 24, 1864, for gunshot wounds in right arm, one in arm and
one in forearm. The hospital records show that he was treated for remittent fever
and for gunshot wound of thumb received in battle at Fredericksburg, Va., December
13, 1862, and for gunshot wounds of right arm received in battle at Gettysburg, Pa.,
July 2, 1863.

Claimant was first pensioned May 6, 1865, for gunshot wounds of right arm at $2⅔
per month from discharge, which was increased to $6 per month September 26, 1867,
to $8 per month October 6, 1873, and to $12 per month June 15, 1887. On November
21, 1887, his pension was rerated at $8 per month from discharge and $12 per month
from June 15, 1887, and it was increased to $14 per month May 20, 1889, for gunshot
wounds of right arm and gunshot wound of right thumb.

On September 24, 1898, claimant made claim for increase, alleging pensioned disabilities and resulting nervous prostration and disease of stomach, which claim was
rejected August 22, 1900, on the ground of no increase in pensioned causes and no
results accepted. October 10, 1899, he made claim for additional disability (rheumatism), which he alleged he contracted at Fredericksburg, Va., in 1863. This claim
was rejected August 20, 1900, on the ground of no record or medical evidence in
service or at discharge, and no evidence of continuance from 1864 to 1868.

Claimant is 63 years of age, and his post-office address is South Newbury, Vt. He
was last examined March 15, 1899, and rated $12 for gunshot wounds of right arm,
$2 for gunshot wound of right thumb, and $10 for rheumatism and resulting disease
of heart. The examining surgeons stated that the sum of his disabilities incapacitated

2 HILAS D. DAVIS.

him in a degree equivalent to the loss of a hand or foot for purposes of manual labor and entitled him to $24 per month.

In support of his claim for rheumatism, claimant filed the evidence of his lieutenant-colonel, who testified that that disability was incurred in 1863 and was induced by cold and exposure to wet weather, and also the evidence of his second lieutenant, who testified that he remembered claimant's stiffness and lameness in service and was of the impression his trouble was rheumatism.

George F. Talbot, druggist, of Lawrence, Mass., testified that he filled prescriptions and gave claimant liniments and medicines for rheumatism and other troubles from 1868 to 1878, and neighbors and physicians testified to existence of rheumatism in recent years, or since 1890.

Claimant states that his regimental surgeons are dead, for which reason he is unable to furnish their evidence. His means are exhausted, and he is now practically dependent upon his pension.

It would seem from the evidence on file that his rheumatism, as well as his several wounds, were incurred in service, and your committee are of opinion that he is entitled to an increase of pension at the rate recommended by the examining surgeons

The bill is therefore reported back favorably with a recommendation that it pass

O

SARAH B. BARGER.

JANUARY 26, 1903.—Committed to the Committee of the Whole House and ordered
to be printed.

Mr. SAMUEL W. SMITH, from the Committee on Invalid Pensions, submitted the following

REPORT.

[To accompany S. 2114.]

The Committee on Invalid Pensions, to whom was referred the bill
(S. 2114) granting an increase of pension to Sarah B. Barger, have
examined the same and adopt the Senate report thereon and recommend that the bill do pass.

[Senate Report No. 2251, Fifty-seventh Congress, second session.]

The Committee on Pensions, to whom was referred the bill (S. 2114) granting an
increase of pension to Sarah B. Barger, have examined the same and report:
This bill proposes to increase from $8 to $25 per month the pension of Sarah B.
Barger, widow of Benjamin F. Barger, late major Thirty-third Regiment Ohio Volunteer Infantry.
The military records show that Benjamin F. Barger was mustered into service
January 19, 1864, as major Thirty-third Ohio Infantry. He was severely wounded
in the left thigh in battle near Atlanta, Ga., August 7, 1864, and was honorably discharged on account of physical disability March 17, 1865. He died June 12, 1894,
from "paralysis, cerebral"—that is, paralysis due to a cerebral lesion. At the time
of his death he was receiving a pension of $25 per month for gunshot wound of left
thigh.
Sarah B. Barger, the widow of this officer, is now receiving the pension of $8 per
month provided by the act of June 27, 1890. She was married to him August 13,
1874. On August 11, 1894, she made claim, under the general law, alleging that the
officer died from the direct result of gunshot wound received in service. Her claim
was rejected January 12, 1895, on the ground that the officer's fatal disease could
not be accepted as a result of the gunshot wound of left thigh, for which he was
pensioned.
The officer's attending physician was Dr. James E. Welliver, of Dayton, Ohio.
He testified July 30, 1894:
"That in September, 1893, he opened an abscess on the soldier's left thigh, midway
between hip and knee; that the limb finally healed, but the soldier never regained
his full strength; that in January, 1894, he again prescribed for the limb, fearing a
return of the abscess; that in May, 1894, he made a diagnosis of cerebral thrombosis, or embolism; that partial paralysis of left side set in slightly about the 1st of May
and gradually deepened until complete of left side, and three or four days before

death the right side also became paralyzed; that the soldier died in a comatose condition; that the abscess formed at the seat of the old wound; that affiant believes that either from absorption or poisoned condition of blood the artery became plugged as a result of an embolus produced as result of abscess and produced the paralysis by causing softening of the brain."

Dr. Welliver again testified February 21, 1895, making a more detailed statement of his views as to the connection between the gunshot wound for which the soldier was pensioned and the disease of brain from which he died. He expresses the opinion that either a metastatic abscess developed in the officer's brain which produced softening and resulted in paralysis, coma, and death, or that from his septicæmic condition from the seat of the injury a thrombosis of the cerebral sinuses developed which gave rise to the subsequent symptoms and death. He also says that "all emboli do not come from a diseased heart. He died from an embolism of cerebral artery, or thrombosis of sinus, caused from condition of blood produced by the abscess and condition of bone in old wound of left thigh."

Dr. Benjamin F. Miller, late surgeon Second Ohio Infantry, who dressed the officer's left thigh when he was wounded in 1864, testified to that fact, and also that he saw Major Barger in 1866, at which time he was called to attend him for a threatened abscess on posterior surface of left thigh; that upon examining a sinus in the groin at the same time he found the ball (minie) lying over the femoral artery, and removed it; that he never treated the officer thereafter, but from his history since that date as to recurrences of abscesses in the left thigh and the drain on the nervous system from time to time he has no doubt that the paralysis that ultimately developed had its origin in the gunshot wound of 1864.

Dr. H. B. Wright, of San Francisco, Cal., who was the officer's family physician from 1870 to 1881, expresses the opinion that "there is no doubt that such a severe wound which caused so much severe distress and nervous prostration would cause paralysis in many cases."

Dr. A. G Hart, of Cleveland, Ohio, late surgeon Forty-first Ohio Infantry, who treated the officer while in the service for wound of left thigh, testified to that fact and further states:

"From my experience with and observation of old soldiers since the war, I am convinced that in many cases, where such a great drain was made for so long a time upon the circulatory system and the intense strain upon the nervous system was maintained by months of wasting and suffering, all the vital organs were impaired; and in my judgment, even after thirty years, the occurrence of cerebral paralysis in the case of this officer may fairly be referred to the profound shock to the system, due to his severe wound and his prolonged and painful convalescence."

The consensus of medical opinion is that the officer's death is chargeable to the exhausting effects of the gunshot wound he received in battle, and great weight should be accorded the evidence of these surgeons and physicians, who are cognizant of the officer's condition during his service and since his discharge up to the date of his death.

The claimant is poor, as is evidenced by the fact that she is pensioned under the act of June 27. 1890. She has one child under the age of 16 years to support.

Your committee recommend the passage of the bill.

O

SARAH J. WARREN.

JANUARY 26, 1903.—Committed to the Committee of the Whole House and ordered
to be printed. ·

Mr. SAMUEL W. SMITH, from the Committee on Invalid Pensions, submitted the following

REPORT.

[To accompany S. 2270.]

The Committee on Invalid Pensions, to whom was referred the bill
(S. 2270) granting an increase of pension to Sarah J. Warren, have
examined the same and adopt the Senate report thereon and recommend that the bill do pass.

[Senate Report No. 2334, Fifty-seventh Congress, second session.]

The Committee on Pensions, to whom was referred the bill (S. 2270) granting an
increase of pension to Sarah J. Warren, have examined the same and report:
Sarah J. Warren, whose post-office address is East Berlin, Pa., is the widow of
Thaddeus S. Warren, who served in Company E, Second Regiment Pennsylvania
Volunteer Infantry, from April 20, 1861, to July 26, 1861, when he was honorably
discharged. She is totally blind and very poor, and is now receiving the pension of
$8 per month provided by the act of June 27, 1890. She is 63 years of age and was
married to the soldier March 13, 1864.
Soldier died of consumption April 19, 1868, less than nine years after his discharge.
Mrs. Warren made claim at the Bureau under the general law, alleging that the
soldier's fatal disease was due to chronic diarrhea contracted in the service. She was
not able to establish this claim, however, the death of comrades and neighbors making it impossible for her to supply evidence of service origin or of continuance for
several years after discharge.
One comrade testified that soldier complained during service and was not well.
One neighbor testified that soldier was suffering from chronic diarrhea when he
returned home at discharge. Dr. N. S. Lincoln, now dead, a highly reputable physician of this city, testified that soldier was under his care from about 1865 until his
death, April 18, 1868, on account of chronic diarrhea, which was finally complicated
with pulmonary consumption; that soldier was suffering from chronic diarrhea when
he, witness, was first called to see him, and that soldier then attributed the origin of
his disease to exposure while serving in the Army. Dr. Lincoln gives it as his own
opinion that the chronic diarrhea and consumption were caused by exposure and
hardship of the service.
Your committee concur in the opinion given by Dr. Lincoln, and believe that the
evidence is sufficient to show that soldier's death was the result of his military service.
Claimant is blind, unable to help herself, and in great need, and the bill is reported
back favorably with a recommendation that it pass.

O

JOHN T. DEWEESE.

JANUARY 26, 1903.—Committed to the Committee of the Whole House and ordered to be printed.

Mr. DARRAGH, from the Committee on Invalid Pensions, submitted the following

REPORT.

[To accompany S. 3912.]

The Committee on Invalid Pensions, to whom was referred the bill (S. 3912) granting an increase of pension to John T. Deweese, have examined the same and adopt the Senate report thereon and recommend that the bill do pass.

[Senate Report No. 2172, Fifty-seventh Congress, second session.]

The Committee on Pensions, to whom was referred the bill (S. 3912) granting an increase of pension to John T. Deweese, have examined the same and report:

This bill proposes to increase from $12 to $30 per month the pension of John T. Deweese, late lieutenant-colonel Fourth Regiment Indiana Volunteer Cavalry.

Colonel Deweese at the outbreak of the war was a resident of Pike County, Ind. He entered the Army July 6, 1861, as second lieutenant with Company E, Twenty-fourth Indiana Infantry, and served with that command until February, 15, 1862, when he honorably resigned. He was mustered in as captain, Company F, Fourth Indiana Cavalry, August 8, 1862; was promoted major February 12, 1863, and lieutenant-colonel May 17, 1863. He was also promoted colonel, but his regiment being reduced in numbers below the minimum strength allowable by law, he was never mustered in as of that rank, and was honorably discharged March 11, 1864.

Upon the reorganization of the Army Colonel Deweese was appointed second lieutenant, Eighth United States Infantry, July 24, 1866, and resigned therefrom August 14, 1867, when he was elected to Congress.

Colonel Deweese has made no claim for pension under the general law. He is now receiving the maximum pension of $12 per month provided by the act of June 27, 1890, for total inability to earn a support by manual labor, due to disease of the heart, paralysis agitans, and senile debility.

Colonel Deweese is now 67 years of age, but is very much older in appearance. His medical examination, made June 18, 1902, shows him to be totally unable to perform manual labor, and also unable to move about the streets with safety. The examining surgeon reports that he "has well-marked paralysis agitans, sways with both feet together and eyes closed; constant tremor of hands; reflexes exaggerated; some anæsthesia of hands and arms; walks with difficulty with aid of cane."

"Is well nourished, but feeble; muscles flabby; pupils not equal in size and respond feebly to light. Has crepitus in large joints, which are tender on manipulation; suffers from indigestion; is active in mind but feeble in body; is prematurely old in appearance; is unable to perform any manual labor."

Evidence on file in the Pension Bureau shows that Colonel Deweese is without means and is wholly dependent on his small pension for his support. He declares that his paralysis was contracted during the performance of his duties as a soldier in the Army, and it may be that this is so, although no proof of the same is on file.

In view of his highly honorable service, his total disability, and great poverty, your committee report the bill back favorably with a recommendation that it pass.

O

ALMAN J. HOUSTON.

JANUARY 26, 1903.—Committed to the Committee of the Whole House and ordered
to be printed.

Mr. SAMUEL W. SMITH, from the Committee on Invalid Pensions,
submitted the following

REPORT.

[To accompany S. 4023.]

The Committee on Invalid Pensions, to whom was referred the bill
(S. 4023) granting an increase of pension to Alman J. Houston, have
examined the same and adopt the Senate report thereon and recom
mend that the bill do pass.

[Senate Report No. 2189, Fifty-seventh Congress, second session.]

The Committee on Pensions, to whom was referred the bill (S. 4023) granting an
increase of Pension to Alman J. Houston, have examined the same and report:
This bill proposes to increase from $12 to $30 per month the pension of Alman J.
Houston, late of Company D, Twenty-fourth Regiment Michigan Volunteer Infantry.
Soldier enlisted August 2, 1862. He was taken prisoner at the battle of Gettysburg, July 1, 1863, and confined at Belle Isle, Va., and Andersonville and Millen, Ga.,
and was paroled November 19, 1864. He was honorably discharged July 30, 1865.
Claimant is now receiving a pension of $12 per month under the act of June 27,
1890, for chronic diarrhea, loss of sight of left eye, right inguinal hernia, disease of
gums and loss of teeth, and loss of two toes of right foot. He was formerly pensioned under the general law at $4 per month for chronic diarrhea and gunshot
wound of right groin received in battle at Gettysburg, July 1, 1863. He also made
claim under the general law for rupture as a result of gunshot wound of right groin
and for deafness, impaired sight, and results of scurvy contracted while in prison at
Andersonville, Ga. His claim was rejected March 10, 1900, on the ground that the
evidence did not show that his present condition was the result of his military
service.
Claimant was confined in Confederate prisons for nearly seventeen months, suffering all the unusual hardships and exposures of those places. He returned home from
his long confinement starved and emaciated and in every sense a physical wreck. It
is in evidence that while in prison he suffered from scurvy, diarrhea, and general
debility. It also appears that his hearing and sight became affected, and, in fact,
some of his comrades say he had everything he could have and live.
Since his discharge his health and constitution have been greatly impaired, sometimes better and sometimes worse, but at no time has he been able to perform manual
labor. During this period he has suffered from rupture, from impaired sight and hearing, from chronic diarrhea, from results of scurvy, and from an extremely debilitated

condition generally. Of late years he has been quite often in hospital, and has paid out large sums for various operations, and it has taken all he could earn to pay his doctors' bills.

Since 1865 claimant has made 24 affidavits, some of them of late years more or less conflicting, and he has also filed 32 affidavits from witnesses in support of his claims. He is at times so afflicted that he can hardly remember anything, and again his memory is clearer, and undoubedly the inconsistencies and contradictions in his various statements made from time to time are the result of a disordered mind due to disease. Two of his witnesses were fellow-prisoners in Andersonville, and are men of excellent standing, but their memories are nearly as bad as that of the claimant, and all attribute this defect to prison life.

Claimant's last medical examination, made October 24, 1900, rates him $30 for chronic diarrhea, loss of eyesight, right inguinal hernia, loss of toes, and weak heart. The loss of toes, it is stated by the surgeon who amputated them, was due to necrosis of bones, for which he could find no other cause than scurvy.

Claimant has no property. He is attempting to fill the position of mail carrier at the Detroit post-office, but is unable to be on duty over two days a week. He is in a pitiable condition at times, and has been given the easiest position on the carrier's force because of his disabilities, and even this he can not fill except in a most unsatisfactory manner, and it is only his war record that keeps him in his place.

While the proof on file may not be technically such as meets the requirements of the Pension Bureau, yet your committee, from a careful examination thereof, are satisfied that the soldier's present totally disabled condition is the result of his long confinement and the exposure and hardships of prison life, and therefore report the bill back favorably with a recommendation that it pass.

O

JAMES O'NEIL.

JANUARY 26, 1903.—Committed to the Committee of the Whole House and ordered
to be printed.

Mr. SULLOWAY, from the Committee on Invalid Pensions, submitted ·
the following

REPORT.

[To accompany S. 4140.]

The Committee on Invalid Pensions, to whom was referred the bill
(S. 4140) granting an increase of pension to James O'Neil, have examined the same and adopt the Senate report thereon and recommend
that the bill do pass.

[Senate Report No. 2295, Fifty-seventh Congress, second session.]

The Committee on Pensions, to whom was referred the bill (S. 4140) granting an
increase of pension to James O'Neil, have examined the same and report:

This bill as amended proposes to increase from $12 to $30 per month the pension
of James O'Neil, late second lieutenant Company E, Twenty-fifth Regiment Massachusetts Volunteer Infantry.

It is shown by the military records that James O'Neil was enrolled September 10,
1861, at Worcester, Mass., as a corporal in Company E, Twenty-fifth Massachusetts
Infantry. He was promoted second lieutenant May 1, 1863, and was honorably discharged August 25, 1864, upon tender of resignation because of debility, consequent
on chronic diarrhea and intermittent fever.

Mr. O'Neil is now receiving a pension of $12 per month under the act of June 27,
1890, for total inability to earn a support by manual labor, his disability under this
law being impairment of sight. On February 15, 1888, he made claim under the
general law, alleging that at Petersburg, Va., in June, 1864, he contracted chronic
diarrhea and malarial poisoning, and this claim was rejected August 1, 1894, on the
ground that a ratable disability from causes alleged was not shown to exist.

According to his medical examinations claimant is now almost totally blind, with
every prospect that his disability will result in complete loss of sight in a short
while. In the summer of 1901 his left eye was removed because of glaucoma, and
the vision in his right eye was then reduced to six one-hundredths. So far as manual
labor is concerned, his disability is total. It is shown that he is without means of
support other than his pension, which, under the circumstances, is wholly inadequate
for his necessary wants, and that he is much in need of relief.

Claimant is 63 years of age, and resides at No. 40 Ballard street, Worcester, Mass.
He is the last one of five brothers who enlisted for the service of their country.
In view of his faithful and honorable service of three years, his great poverty, and
total disability, your committee report the bill back favorably with a recommendation
that it pass.

O

OSCAR H. PRINK.

JANUARY 26, 1903.—Committed to the Committee of the Whole House and ordered to be printed.

Mr. DARRAGH, from the Committee on Invalid Pensions, submitted the following

REPORT.

[To accompany S. 4239.]

The Committee on Invalid Pensions, to whom was referred the bill (S. 4239), granting an increase of pension to Oscar H. Prink, have examined the same and adopt the Senate report thereon and recommend that the bill do pass.

[Senate Report No. 2370, Fifty-seventh Congress, second session.]

The Committee on Pensions, to whom was referred the bill (S. 4239) granting an increase of pension to Oscar H. Prink, have examined the same and report:

This bill proposes to increase from $14 to $24 per month the pension of Oscar H. Prink, of Sioux Falls, S. Dak., late of Company E, First Regiment Wisconsin Volunteer Cavalry.

Soldier enlisted September 15, 1861, and was honorably discharged October 31, 1864. During service he bore the rank of corporal and sergeant. He received a gunshot wound of left thigh in a skirmish at L'Anguelle Ferry, Arkansas, August 3, 1862, and was taken prisoner at the same time and held in confinement until October 21, 1862, when he was released. The hospital records show that he was treated for chronic diarrhea from October 28, 1863, to October 10, 1864.

Claimant was pensioned under the general law December 13, 1882, for gunshot wound of left thigh and injury of right side at $4 per month, from discharge, which was increased to $10 per month September 4, 1889, and to $14 per month November 5, 1890. He made claim for increase July 17, 1899, alleging pensioned disabilities and resulting neuralgia and varicose veins. This claim was rejected August 29, 1900, on the ground of no increase in disability from pensioned causes and no results accepted.

Claimant is 63 years of age. His medical examination, dated January 3, 1900, shows that he is totally disabled for manual labor by reason of gunshot wound of left thigh, varicose veins of right leg, injury of chest, heart disease, piles, enlarged prostate, and injury to right hand, and entitled to $30 per month. A prior medical examination, dated February 2, 1898, also showed total disability for manual labor. He declares that all of his disabilities are the result of his service, but owing to the death of his comrades and the surgeon who attended him he can not make proof to that effect.

Evidence filed with the bill shows that claimant is without property or means of support except his pension. In view of his honorable service of over three years, his total disability, and great poverty, your committee are of opinion that an increase of his pension would be eminently just and proper.

The bill is therefore reported back favorably with a recommendation that it pass.

DANIEL G. TOWLE.

JANUARY 26, 1903.—Committed to the Committee of the Whole House and ordered
to be printed.

Mr. SULLOWAY, from the Committee on Invalid Pensions, submitted
the following

REPORT.

[To accompany S. 4305.]

The Committee on Invalid Pensions, to whom was referred the bill
(S. 4305) granting an increase of pension to Daniel G. Towle, have
examined the same and adopt the Senate report thereon and recommend that the bill do pass.

[Senate Report No. 2141, Fifty-seventh Congress, second session.]

The Committee on Pensions, to whom was referred the bill (S. 4305) granting an
increase of pension to Daniel G. Towle, have examined the same and report:
This bill proposes to increase from $20 to $30 per month the pension of Daniel G.
Towle, of Monmouth, Me., late captain Company E, Fourth Regiment Minnesota
Volunteer Infantry.
The military records show that Daniel G. Towle enlisted October 1, 1861, as
sergeant, Company E, Fourth Minnesota Infantry. He was promoted second lieutenant April 18, 1863; first lieutenant November 7, 1863, and captain January 29, 1864,
and was honorably discharged on account of physical disability April 5, 1865. He
was severely wounded in right side and right arm in battle at Allatoona, Ga., October
5, 1864, and for such wounds he was pensioned, April 3, 1867, at $20 per month from
discharge.
On December 7, 1900, claimant made claim for increase, which claim was rejected
December 26, 1901, on the ground that his pension was commensurate with the
degree of disability from his pensioned wounds.
Claimant is about 87 years of age. His medical examination made July 23, 1901,
shows him to be a feeble, tottering old man, so disabled that he requires the frequent
and periodical aid and attendance of another person. The examining surgeon says
he is toothless, almost blind, and a constant care; that he is just able to go staggering
around, and unless constantly watched will fall down and injure himself. It is also
shown that he has no property and no means of support except his pension.
Claimant's course of life is well-nigh run, and he can not long enjoy the bounty
which the Government has provided. He gave his services fully and freely to his
country in the time of its need, and it is meet and proper that relief should be
extended to so good a soldier in the days of his extremity. In view of his faithful
and honorable service of over three years, his advanced age, and total disability and
destitution, your committee report the bill back favorably with a recommendation
that it pass.

()

ORLANDO S. OSBORN.

JANUARY 26, 1903.—Committed to the Committee of the Whole House and ordered
to be printed.

Mr. SULLOWAY, from the Committee on Invalid Pensions, submitted
the following

REPORT.

[To accompany S. 4656.]

The Committee on Invalid Pensions, to whom was referred the bill
(S. 4656) granting an increase of pension to Orlando S. Osborn, have
examined the same and adopt the Senate report thereon and recommend that the bill do pass.

[Senate Report No. 2219, Fifty-seventh Congress, second session.] .

The Committee on Pensions, to whom was referred the bill (S. 4656) granting an
increase of pension to Orlando S. Osborn, have examined the same and report:

This bill proposes to increase from $12 to $24 per month the pension of Orlando S.
Osborn, of Weston, Vt., late of Company C, Sixteenth Regiment Vermont Volunteer
Infantry, who served from August 29, 1862, to August 10, 1863, when he was honor-
ably discharged.

Claimant is now receiving a pension of $12 per month under the act of June 27,
1890, for piles and loss of sight of both eyes. He was formerly pensioned under the
general law at $10 per month for piles incurred during his military service. In Octo-
ber, 1899, he became totally and permanently blind, caused by the rupture of a blood
vessel in the brain. His last medical examination, dated June 6, 1900, rates him $10
for piles and $72 for total blindness.

Claimant has no means of support except his pension, and, being totally blind, is
unable to earn anything whatever. He has an interest in a small house, which is
heavily mortgaged, and the value of his real and personal property is about $500.
His house affords him a shelter and nothing more, and produces no income. Accompanying the bill is a numerously signed petition from his neighbors praying for his
relief.

In view of his faithful service, his total blindness, and great poverty, your committee report the bill back favorably with a recommendation that it pass.

O

EPHRAIM CUNNINGHAM.

JANUARY 26, 1903.—Committed to the Committee of the Whole House and ordered
to be printed.

Mr. SULLOWAY, from the Committee on Invalid Pensions, submitted
the following

REPORT.

[To accompany S. 4702.]

The Committee on Invalid Pensions, to whom was referred the bill
(S. 4702) granting an increase of pension to Ephraim Cunningham,
have examined the same and adopt the Senate report thereon and
recommend that the bill do pass.

[Senate Report No. 2138, Fifty-seventh Congress, second session.]

The Committee on Pensions, to whom was referred the bill (S. 4702) granting an
increase of pension to Ephraim Cunningham, have examined the same and report:
This bill proposes to increase from $17 to $30 per month the pension ot Ephraim
Cunningham, of Bangor, Me., late of Company F, Fourteenth Regiment Maine Volunteer Infantry.
The military records show that Ephraim Cunningham enlisted Octoberr 22, 1861,
and was discharged March 20, 1865, for exhaustion and debility caused by two years'
service in the Department of the Gulf. He is now receiving a pension of $17 per
month under the general law for injury to left side, rheumatism and resulting disease
of heart, and piles. He made claim for increase May 31, 1901, which was rejected
June 30, 1902, on the ground that his rating was adequate for his pensioned disabilities.
Claimant is now 61 years of age. His last medical examination, made October 2,
1901, shows that he was suffering from injury of left side, rheumatism, and disease
of the heart. He was rated $2 for injury of left side, $6 for rheumatism, and $12 for
disease of heart.
The following certificate of his family physician shows that claimant is practically
disabled for all manual labor by reason of rheumatism and disease of heart:

"This certifies that I have known Mr. Ephraim Cunningham, of Bangor, Me., for
many years, and at different times have prescribed for him—generally for rheumatism. Since my acquaintance with him he has never done any heavy, laborious
work, and now by reason of a diseased heart (probably of rheumatic origin), occa-
sioning pain and shortness of breath, there are times when he is hardly able to do
his household chores.
"I have no personal interest in this case, but as his family physician I have been
somewhat familiar with his condition.

"H. L. JEWELL, M. D.

"BANGOR, October 4, 1902."

The following petition from prominent ex-soldiers of Maine, including Gen. Joseph S. Smith and Adjt. Gen. Aug. B. Farnham, shows claimant's total disability and his extreme need for relief:

"We, the undersigned citizens of Bangor, in the county of Penobscot and State of Maine, are well acquainted with Ephraim Cunningham, formerly a soldier in Company F, Fourteenth Maine Volunteers, and recommend that his pension be increased to $30 per month. The soldier is now totally disabled for the performance of manual labor on account of a bad heart trouble, rheumatism, and severe injury to left side. He is without other means of support than his present pension, which is inadequate for the support of himself and his wife, who is a chronic invalid. We request that his case may be made special and that the same be given immediate attention.

"JOSEPH S. SMITH.
"AUG. B. FARNHAM.
"FRANK D. PULLEN.
"HUGH MITCHELL.
"CHAS. HAMLIN.
"JOHN M. OAK."

Claimant's inability to perform manual labor is caused entirely by diseases contracted while he was in the Army and for which he is pensioned. He was a good soldier, having rendered faithful service for nearly three and one-half years, and your committee are of opinion that he is eminently entitled to an increase of his pension.

The bill is therefore reported back favorably with a recommendation that it pass.

O

CASSIUS B. FISHER.

JANUARY 26, 1903.—Committed to the Committee of the Whole House and ordered
to be printed.

Mr. SULLOWAY, from the Committee on Invalid Pensions, submitted
the following

REPORT.

[To accompany S. 4854.]

The Committee on Invalid Pensions, to whom was referred the bill
(S. 4854) granting an increase of pension to Cassius B. Fisher, have
examined the same and adopt the Senate report thereon and recommend that the bill do pass.

[Senate Report No. 2296, Fifty-seventh Congress, second session.]

The Committee on Pensions, to whom was referred the bill (S. 4854) granting an
increase of pension to Cassius B. Fisher, have examined the same and report:
This bill proposes to increase from $17 to $30 per month the pension of Cassius B.
Fisher, of Auburn, Me., late of Company K, Third Regiment Vermont Volunteer
Infantry.
Soldier enlisted August 23, 1862, and was discharged June 19, 1865. He received
a gunshot wound of back in battle of the Wilderness, Virginia, May 5, 1864. He was
pensioned under the general law July 12, 1866, for gunshot wound of spine, at $5.33⅓
per month from discharge, which was increased to $8 per month June 16, 1875; to
$10 per month September 21, 1887, and to $17 per month March 31, 1897.
Claimant made claim for increase July 22, 1898, which was rejected April 10, 1900,
on the ground that his rate was commensurate with the disability from pensioned
cause. He was last examined February 1, 1899, and the report thereof is as follows:
"He has sustained a gunshot wound, the ball entering upon the right side of spine
and emerging just over the vertebræ in the upper lumbar region. There are also
scars upon the left side of spine, which he says are the result of abscesses following
the wound. The scar of entrance is the size of a silver dollar and that of exit about
an inch in length; the others are about an inch in diameter.
"The scar tissue is thin and the scars are depressed and adherent. He complains
of pain when pressure is made upon the region of the injury, especially over the
spinous processes. He stoops with difficulty, and he says it makes his back feel as if
it was pulling his back apart. He walks in a stiff, hesitating manner, and says that
any jar hurts his back. Plantar and patellæ reflexes normal. Sensation in legs
apparently normal. He states that he has headache at times. No evidence of head
trouble except his statement. We rate his disability from gunshot wound and
results at seventeen-eighteenths."
A prior medical examination, made March 31, 1897, rated him $24 for gunshot
wound of back.

H R—57-2—Vol 2——37

The following letter addressed to Senator Frye, who introduced the bill in claimant's behalf, shows his present disabled condition and also his needy circumstances:

"DECEMBER 1, 1902.

"DEAR SIR: I am writing this letter in behalf of Cassius B. Fisher, a pensioner, who lives at 111 Pleasant street, Auburn, Me. Mr. Fisher is now receiving a pension of $17 per month. He applied for an increase in 1899, but the application was not allowed. A bill, numbered S. 4854, was introduced into the Senate March 31, 1902, to pay him a pension at the rate of $30 per month in lieu of what he is now receiving. The number of his pension certificate at present is 67946.

"Some of the reasons why I think this special bill should be passed are the following: Mr. Fisher is a constant sufferer from a gunshot wound in the spine, and has not been able to labor since March, 1890. He is about 70 years of age, but looks very much older than he is. I am intimately acquainted with him, and know that he is not able to earn anything whatever, and a very small amount of exertion, like taking off a screen door, or something of that kind, often puts him under the doctor's care. He and his wife live near me, in a house which he purchased, but which is mortgaged in the sum of $1,900, pretty nearly all its value.

"He tries to help himself a little by letting a part of this house as a rent, and living in the other part. He is under some physician's care a very large part of the time, and has to practice constant self-denial as well as economy. Mr. Fisher is a thoroughly good man, without a bad habit, with an excellent reputation, and is thoroughly reliable. He was a good soldier and has always been a loyal citizen, and is now a prematurely old man, who creeps along with his cane whenever he goes out of doors and impresses one as being a constant sufferer. I believe he is not only worthy, but entitled to the pension which the special bill proposes to give him.

"Respectfully,

"C. S. CUMMINGS,
"Chaplain First Infantry, National Guard.

"Hon. WILLIAM P. FRYE,
"United States Senate, Washington, D. C."

This is one of those cases in which the full extent of disability can not be determined by a physical examination. The amount of labor the claimant can and does perform is a question of fact to be determined by proof rather than by medical opinion. That the claimant was severely wounded in battle is a matter of record, and the evidence goes to show that he is now practically totally disabled for manual labor by reason of his wound. Considering all the circumstances, your committee are of opinion that he is worthy of an increase of pension.

The bill is therefore reported back favorably with a recommendation that it pass.

O

GEORGE J. CHENEY.

JANUARY 26, 1903.—Committed to the Committee of the Whole House and ordered to be printed.

Mr. SAMUEL W. SMITH, from the Committee on Invalid Pensions, submitted the following

REPORT.

[To accompany S. 5508.]

The Committee on Invalid Pensions, to whom was referred the bill (S. 5508) granting an increase of pension to George J. Cheney, have examined the same and adopt the Senate report thereon and recommend that the bill do pass.

[Senate Report No. 2188, Fifty-seventh Congress, second session.]

The Committee on Pensions, to whom was referred the bill (S. 5508) granting an increase of pension to George J. Cheney, have examined the same and report:

This bill proposes to increase from $16 to $24 per month the pension of George J. Cheney, of Lansing, Mich., late of Company A, Twentieth Regiment Michigan Volunteer Infantry.

Soldier enlisted August 9, 1862, and was discharged May 30, 1865. He was pensioned under the general law January 31, 1889, for rheumatism, at $4, from April 5, 1888, which was increased to $10 February 5, 1890, and to $16 December 1, 1890, for rheumatism and chronic diarrhea.

Claimant made claim for increase May 11, 1900, which was rejected April 30, 1901, on the ground that his pension was commensurate with the degree of his disability from pensioned causes. In support of this claim he filed the evidence of his family physician, and also of two neighbors, showing that he was almost totally disabled for manual labor by reason of rheumatism and chronic diarrhea.

Claimant is 68 years of age. He was last examined November 14, 1900, and rated $16 for rheumatism, $10 for chronic diarrhea, and $4 for heart disease. The objective conditions found on examination are as follows:

"Rheumatism: There is general muscular tenderness, severe of muscles of back. He can raise the right arm about 45 degrees above a horizontal, the left about 15 degrees above; motion is restricted by tenderness and rigidity of muscles. Muscles generally are considerably stiffened. No comparative muscular atrophy. There is tenderness of all the joints of upper and lower extremities, severe of shoulders, elbows, and hips. All his joints are somewhat stiffened. He can extend fingers; he can not flex them. No crepitus, swelling, or enlargement of joints. No other indications of rheumatism.

"Chronic diarrhea: Abdominal walls are thin and tense. Belly is bloated, tympanitic over colon, quite tender all over. Stomach is slightly tympanitic, extremely

2

GEORGE J. CHENEY.

tender, not distended. No disease of liver or spleen. No piles, ulcers, fissures, stricture, or fistula. Hemorrhoidal veins are not engorged. Mucous membrane of rectum is thin, irritable, dark red.

"Heart trouble: Apex impulse of heart can be seen and felt in fifth space a little to left of nipple; not diffused. Heart's action is irregular, not violent; sounds are normal; volume and tension of pulse are good. At times the heart intermits frequently. After exercise the heart beats violently, pulse is full and hard, breathing is somewhat labored. No œdema or cyanosis."

It appears from claimant's petition filed with the bill that in addition to his pensioned disabilities he is also afflicted with great loss of sight, being almost blind; that he has no property, and that his only means of support is his pension.

It would seem from the report of his medical examination that claimant is not properly rated for the disabilities contracted in the service. In view of his good military record, his poverty, and great disability, your committee report the bill back favorably with a recommendation that it pass.

O

JOSEPH TWYCROSS.

JANUARY 26, 1903.—Committed to the Committee of the Whole House and ordered
to be printed.

Mr. DARRAGH, from the Committee on Invalid Pensions, submitted
the following

REPORT.

[To accompany S. 5610.]

The Committee on Invalid Pensions, to whom was referred the bill
(S. 5610) granting an increase of pension to Joseph Twycross, have
examined the same and adopt the Senate report thereon and recommend that the bill do pass.

[Senate Report No. 2240, Fifty-seventh Congress, second session.]

The Committee on Pensions, to whom was referred the bill (S. 5610) granting an
increase of pension to Joseph Twycross, have examined the same and report:
   This bill proposes to increase from $12 to $30 per month the pension of Joseph
Twycross, late of Company G, Second Regiment Wisconsin Volunteer Infantry.
   Soldier enlisted April 19, 1861, and was honorably discharged June 30, 1864.
During service he held the rank of private and sergeant. He was wounded in mouth
and right shoulder in battle at South Mountain, Maryland, September 14, 1862, and
for such wounds he was pensioned October 2, 1889, under the general law, at $6 per
month, which was increased to $12 per month July 7, 1890. On February 11, 1901,
he made claim for increase, which was rejected April 2, 1902, on the ground that his
present pension was adequate for the disability resulting from pensioned causes.
   Claimant's present condition is one of helplessness. For a dozen years or more he
has been a paralytic, requiring the aid and attendance of another person. His last
medical examination, made October 12, 1901, reports that he is so disabled from
paralysis as to require the frequent and periodical aid and attendance of another
person, and is entitled to $50 per month. Claimant contends that his present condition is due to his gunshot wound of shoulder. The proof, however, does not
establish this point.
   Claimant is declared by his officers and comrades to have been a very good soldier,
always ready for duty. It is in evidence that he is wholly dependent, without property or income, or means of support, except his pension.
   In view of his faithful service of over three years, his helplessness and destitution,
your committee report the bill back with a recommendation that it pass.

O

JULIA A. JORDAN.

JANUARY 26, 1903.—Committed to the Commmittee of the Whole House and ordered to be printed.

Mr. SAMUEL W. SMITH, from the Committee on Invalid Pensions, submitted the following

REPORT.

[To accompany S. 5786.]

The Committee on Invalid Pensions, to whom was referred the bill (S. 5786) granting a pension to Julia A. Jordan, have examined the same and adopt the Senate report thereon and recommend that the bill do pass.

[Senate Report No. 2333, Fifty-seventh Congress, second session.]

The Committee on Pensions, to whom was referred the bill (S. 5786) granting a pension to Julia A. Jordan, have examined the same and report:

Julia A. Jordan, whose post-office address is Ocean Grove, N. J., is the mother of Frank H. Jordan, who served as sergeant, second lieutenant, and captain Company E Ninety-first Regiment Illinois Volunteer Infantry.

The military records show that Frank H. Jordan enlisted July 18, 1862, as sergeant, Company E, Ninety-first Illinois Infantry. He was promoted second lieutenant April 24, 1863, and captain November 4, 1863, and was honorably discharged July 12, 1865.

Mrs. Jordan made claim for pension at the Bureau, and the same was rejected on the ground that the soldier left a widow surviving him. The soldier died of softening of the brain June 19, 1887. He was married, but had no children, and his widow, Amelia Jordan, survived him about three years, dying in New York City May 13, 1890. Neither the soldier nor his widow ever made claim for pension, and no one has ever received any pension on account of his service and death.

It is declared by witnesses that Captain Jordan entered the service a man of unusual health and physical vigor; that after his discharge he suffered from the effects of malaria contracted, as was supposed and believed, while he was in the Army and that this malaria manifested itself variously in the form of jaundice, chills and fever, headaches, mental depression and derangement, and finally and fatally in softening of the brain, from the effects of which, after about four years of increasing helplessness, he died.

Mrs. Jordan is upward of 80 years of age. She has been a widow since 1856, and was dependent on her son, the soldier, for support. Since his death she has maintained herself by keeping boarders. She is now without property or income, and is so far advanced in years as to be unable to earn a support.

The soldier served faithfully at the front for three years, and no doubt his health suffered in consequence. It seems altogether probable that his death was attributable in a measure to his service.

His dependent mother is now very old and poverty stricken, and your committee are of opinion that her case is a worthy one for relief.

The bill is therefore reported back favorably with a recommendation that it pass.

O

JOHN A. BARCUS.

JANUARY 26, 1903.—Committed to the Committee of the Whole House and ordered
to be printed.

Mr. SAMUEL W. SMITH, from the Committee on Invalid Pensions, submitted the following

REPORT.

[To accompany S. 5841.]

The Committee on Invalid Pensions, to whom was referred the bill
(S. 5841) granting an increase of pension to John A. Barcus, have
examined the same and adopt the Senate report thereon and recommend that the bill do pass.

[Senate Report No. 2161, Fifty-seventh Congress, second session.]

The Committee on Pensions, to whom was referred the bill (S. 5841) granting an
increase of pension to John A. Barcus, have examined the same and report:
This bill proposes to increase from $12 to $24 per month the pension of John A.
Barcus, late of Company A, One hundred and eighty-sixth Regiment Pennsylvania
Volunteer Infantry.
Soldier enlisted January 25, 1864, and was discharged August 15, 1865. He is now
receiving a pension of $12 per month under the act of June 27, 1890, for total inability
to earn a support by manual labor, due to rheumatism and locomotor ataxia. He
has never made claim under the general law, although he declares he has suffered
from rheumatism from the time he was discharged from the Army.
Claimant is 55 years of age and resides at No. 2143 North Park avenue, Philadelphia,
Pa. His last medical examination, made September 2, 1899, shows that he is totally
incapacitated for manual labor. The examining surgeons describe his condition as
"stooped, slow moving, staggers in walking; countenance distressed; marked muscular
atrophy; is debilitated and weak; a remarkable muscular atrophy of hands both in
contractors and extensors; palms are entirely flat and bony, with loss of sensation
and two-thirds loss of grip; atrophy of leg and thigh muscles; he can not walk
straight with eyes open, and falls at once on attempt to walk with eyes closed; marked
evidence of paresis."
Evidence filed with the bill shows that claimant is totally disabled and requires
help in dressing and undressing, and that he is without property or resources and is
dependent on his pension.
In view of his faithful service, his total disability, and destitution, your committee
report the bill back favorably, with a recommendation that it pass.

O

HENRY L. DAVENPORT.

JANUARY 26, 1903.—Committed to the Committee of the Whole House and ordered
to be printed.

Mr. SAMUEL W. SMITH, from the Committee on Invalid Pensions, submitted the following

REPORT.

[To accompany S. 5952.]

The Committee on Invalid Pensions, to whom was referred the bill
(S. 5952) granting an increase of pension to Henry L. Davenport, have
examined the same and adopt the Senate report thereon and recommend that the bill do pass.

[Senate Report No. 2377, Fifty-seventh Congress, second session.]

The Committee on Pensions, to whom was referred the bill (S. 5952) granting an
increase of pension to Henry L. Davenport, have examined the same and report:
This bill proposes to increase from $12 to $24 per month the pension of Henry L.
Davenport, of Detroit, Mich., late of Company A, Sixteenth Regiment Michigan
Volunteer Infantry.
The military records show that Henry L. Davenport enlisted August 2, 1861, and
was discharged July 8, 1865. He was taken prisoner June 1, 1863, and released
August 29, 1863, and he was again taken prisoner December 9, 1864, and released
February 15, 1865. During his captivity he was confined at Richmond, Va.
Claimant is now receiving a pension of $12 per month under the act of June 27,
1890, for total disability due to gunshot wound of right hand and right leg and disease of eyes and stomach. He was pensioned under the general law at $6 per month
from February 13, 1890, to July 16, 1890, for gunshot wound of right hand, received
in battle at Bull Run, Virginia.
He made claim under the general law February 13, 1890, for gunshot wound of
right leg, which he alleged he received at Bull Run, Virginia, August 30, 1862, and
also for disease of eyes, rheumatism, and dyspepsia, which he alleged he incurred in
Libby and Bell Isle prisons, Richmond, Va. This claim was rejected August 14,
1902, on the ground of no record or other satisfactory evidence of service origin of
rheumatism, disease of eyes, and dyspepsia, and on the ground of no ratable disability from gunshot wound of right leg.
There is some evidence on file to show that claimant complained of rheumatism
and eye trouble during service, but it is of a very vague and general character.
There is also some very indefinite evidence of the continuance of these troubles
since discharge. While this evidence indicates that claimant's disabilities are
probably the result of the exposure and hardships of prison life, yet it is not sufficient to have justified the Bureau in allowing the claim.

Claimant is about 75 years of age. A medical examination made December 5, 1894, reported him as so disabled as to be incapable of performing manual labor. His last medical examination, made June 1, 1898, rated him $8 for gunshot wound of right hand, $3 for shell wound of right leg, $6 for disease of eyes, $17 for rheumatism, and $10 for hernia, a total of $44.

Evidence on file in the Bureau shows that claimant is a poor man and that he would be an object of charity if it were not for the aid he receives from relatives.

The action of the Bureau in rejecting claimant's general-law claim was undoubtedly correct. But he is old and poverty stricken and totally disabled; he served faithfully for four years and was four months in prison, and your committee are of opinion that he is worthy of an increase of his pension to relieve the want of his declining years.

The bill is reported back favorably with a recommendation that it pass.

O

ELIZA LITTLE.

JANUARY 26, 1903.—Committed to the Committee of the Whole House and ordered
to be printed.

Mr. SULLOWAY, from the Committee on Invalid Pensions, submitted the
following

REPORT.

[To accompany S. 6026.]

The Committee on Invalid Pensions, to whom was referred the bill
(S. 6026) granting an increase of pension to Eliza Little, have examined
the same and adopt the Senate report thereon and recommend that
the bill do pass.

[Senate Report No. 2143, Fifty-seventh Congress, second session.]

The Committee on Pensions, to whom was referred the bill (S. 6026) granting an
increase of pension to Eliza Little, have examined the same and report:

It is proposed by this bill to increase from $8 to $20 per month the pension of Eliza
Little, widow of Edward H. Little, late captain Company H, Sixty-fifth Regiment
New York Volunteer Infantry.

The military records show that Edward H. Little served as sergeant, Company D,
Seventh New York State Militia, from April 17, 1861, to June 3, 1861. He was commissioned first lieutenant Company C, Sixty-fifth New York Infantry, July 11, 1861;
promoted captain Company H, same regiment, June 1, 1862; promoted major, One
hundred and twenty-seventh New York Infantry, September 1, 1862, lieutenant-
colonel March 5, 1865, and honorably discharged June 30, 1865.

Colonel Little died of chronic myelitis December 26, 1898, being a pensioner at the
time of his death at $12 per month under the act of June 27, 1890, for total disability,
due to disease of nervous system.

Eliza Little, the claimant under the bill, is now receiving the pension of $8 per
month provided by the act of June 27, 1890. She is 58 years of age, and was married to the officer June 9, 1861, and was his wife during nearly the whole period of
his service. On March 19, 1900, she made claim under the general law, which was
rejected November 22, 1901, on the ground that the evidence fails to satisfactorily
show that her husband's death was the result of his military service.

It is claimed that Colonel Little died from myelitis, resulting from an injury to
head from the falling limb of a tree during a severe storm at Harrisons Landing,
Virginia, in August, 1862. The hospital records show that he was treated August 12,
1862, for "injured by fall," and his regimental surgeon gave him a certificate for leave
of absence, dated August 23, 1862, because he was then suffering from severe pain in
the head from fall of tree thereon during a gale of wind on the 12th of that month.

It appears that subsequently during his service soldier complained frequently of

pains in the back of his neck and at the base of brain, and, while they did not inca-
pacitate him from duty, they caused him much suffering. This condition continued
after his discharge, but steadily grew worse from year to year. He had several
strokes of paralysis, the first being in 1873, and for several years before his death he
was a hopeless and helpless invalid, a pensioner on the bounty of his former
employers.

Colonel Little himself always laid his physical decline to the injury of head received
in the service. He made claim to that effect at the Bureau, but was unable to furnish sufficient evidence to establish his claim. The witnesses in the case are men of the
very highest repute and standing. Gen. Stewart L. Woodford, of New York, served
with Colonel Little from the fall of 1862, and he states that there is no question in
his mind but what soldier's death was the direct result of the ailment or pain in the
head with which he suffered in service and since and of which he, the witness, had
personal knowledge.

Dr. Wm. E. Griffiths, of New York City, eminent in his profession, treated soldier
from 1871. He says:

"There is no question in my mind but that this soldier when he came under my
professional care in 1871 was suffering from incipient spinal derangement, due to
shock from previous injury, said degeneration progressing from year to year and
finally culminating in a well-marked case of myelitis of the cord, which was the chief
cause of his death."

There is much other evidence of similar import on file, and it seems to be fairly
proved that the soldier's death was the result of his military service. He has an
exceptionally good military record, and his widow is now without means of support
except her small pension of $8 per month and what little she can earn by her daily
labor.

Your committee are of opinion that Mrs. Little is entitled to a pension at the rate
provided by the general law for the widow of a captain, and therefore report the bill
back favorably with a recommendation that it pass.

O

CHARLES H. BARNES.

JANUARY 26, 1903.—Committed to the Committee of the Whole House and ordered
to be printed.

Mr. SULLOWAY, from the Committee on Invalid Pensions, submitted the
following

REPORT.

[To accompany S. 6050.]

The Committee on Invalid Pensions, to whom was referred the bill
(S. 6050) granting an increase of pension to Charles H. Barnes, have
examined the same and adopt the Senate report thereon and recommend that the bill do pass.

[Senate Report No. 2147, Fifty-seventh Congress, second session.]

The Committee on Pensions, to whom was referred the bill (S. 6050) granting an
increase of pension to Charles H. Barnes, have examined the same and report:
This bill proposes to increase from $12 to $30 per month the pension of Charles H.
Barnes, late of Company F, Fifty-seventh Regiment Massachusetts Volunteer Infantry.
The military records show that Charles H. Barnes enlisted January 26, 1864, and
was discharged July 7, 1865. He is now receiving a pension of $12 per month under
the act of June 27, 1890, for total disability, due to chronic diarrhea and injury to
spine. He was formerly pensioned under the general law for chronic diarrhea of
service origin at $4 per month.
It appears from the evidence on file that claimant received an injury to spine by
falling from a building in 1867, since which date he has been paralyzed and helpless
and unable to go about except in a rolling chair. During all these years he has
required the aid and attendance of another person. His last medical examination,
at Worcester, Mass., November 25, 1891, rated him $8 for chronic diarrhea, $4 for
disease of heart, $4 for disease of liver and spleen, and $72 for injury to spine and
resulting helplessness.
The following letter, addressed to Senator Hoar, who introduced the bill in the
claimant's behalf, shows all the facts in his case and the grounds for an increase of
his pension:

WORCESTER, MASS., May 31, 1902.

DEAR SIR: Herewith hand you a bill and other papers, seeking to secure an increase
of pension for Charles H. Barnes, who served with me in the Fifty-seventh Massachusetts Infantry.
Barnes joined us in February, 1864, and was finally discharged July, 1865. The
record shows that four out of every five of the 1,052 men enrolled in the Fifty-seventh
were, in July, 1865, dead or suffering from wounds received in action. Barnes was
one of the few men who was not seriously disabled in service.

As will be seen by the testimony of Dr. Myron H. Davis, which accompanies these papers, Barnes was disabled after his discharge. For thirty-five years he has been a physical wreck, disabled to such an extent that had his infirmities been incurred in service and line of duty he would for the past thirty-five years have been a first-grade pensioner instead of a small pensioner prior to the act of June 27, 1890; under that act he receives the maximum rating. Under existing laws he can secure no further aid at the Pension Bureau.

This bill and accompanying papers have been prepared complying, as far as possible, with the rules of the Senate Committee on Pensions, and by reason of which I have advised the asking for a rating of $50 per month instead of the first-grade rate, $72, hoping that your good judgment would prompt you to present a bill asking for the first-grade rate.

Charles H. Barnes for more than a third of a century has been so helpless as to require and have the regular personal aid and attendance of another person. During this long period of terrible suffering and misfortune he has been noted for his patience; his cheerfulness has been the envy of his comrades. He is a very worthy man. Having followed for many years the yearly increasing tide of special-pension legislation, having read in full all debates and reports of committees as they have appeared in the Congressional Record during the past twelve or more years, I can truthfully say that I have yet to find a more pitiable or worthy case than that of Barnes, as disclosed by the accompanying picture and papers.

The statements of his comrades of Post No. 179, of Barre, including the post commander, who is also postmaster, and 22 others, as well as the statement of one of the selectmen, the three assessors, tax collector, postmaster, and four others of New Braintree, tell the story of the helplessness of Barnes better than I can. Those statements also leave upon one's mind an abiding conviction that beyond a doubt Barnes has no property, no income, and no means of support except a pension of $12 per month.

Having made a very exhaustive special examination of this case, I fully indorse the petition, and, contrary to my custom, I come to you asking you, as I know you will, to urge its favorable consideration. I can truthfully write that the statements submitted utterly fail to present even an imperfect pen picture of the condition and sufferings of Barnes. I know him and of him so well that I know that he is in every way worthy and deserves the recognition he and his comrades are seeking.

Very sincerely, yours,

J. BRAINERD HOLT,
Formerly of Company B, Fifty-seventh Massachusetts Infantry.

Hon. GEORGE F. HOAR,
Washington, D. C.

Evidence accompanying the bill shows that the claimant is without property or means of support except his pension. In view of his faithful service, his helplessness, and destitution your committee report the bill back favorably with a recommendation that it pass.

O

HATTIE CONNELL.

JANUARY 26, 1903.—Committed to the Committee of the Whole House and ordered
to be printed.

Mr. SULLOWAY, from the Committee on Invalid Pensions, submitted
the following

REPORT.

[To accompany S. 6107.]

The Committee on Invalid Pensions, to whom was referred the bill
(S. 6107) granting an increase of pension to Hattie Connell, have
examined the same and adopt the Senate report thereon and recommend that the bill do pass.

[Senate Report No. 2142, Fifty-seventh Congress, second session.]

The Committee on Pensions, to whom was referred the bill (S. 6107) granting an
increase of pension to Hattie Connell, have examined the same and report:
This bill proposes to increase from $12 to $15 per month the pension of Hattie
Connell, widow of John P. Connell, late second lieutenant Company G, Sixth Regiment Connecticut Volunteer Infantry.
The official records show that John P. Connell served as coal heaver in the U. S.
Navy from October 6, 1858, to June 4, 1859. He enlisted April 23, 1861, as private,
Company G, First Connecticut Infantry, and served as such until July 31, 1861, when
he was honorably discharged. He again enlisted August 26, 1861, as corporal, Company G, Sixth Connecticut Infantry; was promoted second lieutenant January 3, 1865;
captain Company E, February 2, 1865, and honorably mustered out with his command August 21, 1865. He received a gunshot wound of right knee in battle at
Deep Bottom, Virginia, August 16, 1864, and was treated in hospital for such wound
until December 25, 1865.
Captain Connell was pensioned under the general law for gunshot wound of right
knee and rheumatism and resulting disease of heart, and at the time of his death,
which occurred August 26, 1901, he was receiving $30 per month. The cause of his
death was disease of heart.
Hattie Connell, the widow of this officer and the claimant under this bill, is now
receiving the pension of $12 per month provided by the general law for the widow
of a noncommissioned officer. She is 50 years of age, and was married to the officer
April 28, 1875.
The evidence on file shows that soldier incurred his fatal disease in August, 1864,
at which time the official military records show he bore the rank of sergeant. It
appears, however, that he was commissioned second lieutenant by the governor of Connecticut to date June 1, 1864; but owing to the absence of the mustering officer and
also because of his sickness in hospital from wounds received in battle he was not

mustered in as a commissioned officer until January, 1865. The War Department does not recognize him as second lieutenant prior to January 3, 1865, and the Bureau refuses to grant claimant a pension as the widow of a commissioned officer.

It appears in evidence that Mrs. Connell is in straitened circumstances. She has no property, and her income is less than $250 per year.

The action of the Bureau in granting claimant a pension of $12 per month only was undoubtedly correct. In view of all the circumstances of the case, however, your committee are of opinion that it would be eminently just to increase her pension to the rate provided by the general law for the widow of a second lieutenant, to which rank it appears her husband was commissioned by the governor of his State prior to the incurrence of his fatal disease.

The bill is therefore reported back favorably with a recommendation that it pass.

O

NANNIE CUSHMAN.

JANUARY 26, 1903.—Committed to the Committee of the Whole House and ordered
to be printed.

Mr. SULLOWAY, from the Committee on Invalid Pensions, submitted
the following

REPORT.

[To accompany S. 6219.]

The Committee on Invalid Pensions, to whom was referred the bill
(S. 6219) granting an increase of pension to Nannie Cushman, have
examined the same and adopt the Senate report thereon and recommend
that the bill do pass.

[Senate report No. 2300, Fifty-seventh Congress, second session.]

The Committee on Pensions, to whom was referred the bill (S. 6219) granting an
increase of pension to Mrs. Charles H. Cushman, have examined the same and report:
Nannie Cushman is the widow of Charles H. Cushman, late commander, U. S.
Navy. She is now receiving a general-law pension of $30 per month, it having been
shown that the officer died November 11, 1883, of pulmonary tuberculosis, due to
exposure while holding the rank of lieutenant-commander.
The official records show that Charles H. Cushman served in the Navy from March
29, 1849, to April 28, 1877, when he was placed on the retired list as a commander,
to which grade he was promoted July 25, 1866. During his long and faithful services he performed much duty on shipboard and distinguished himself for bravery
on several occasions, in particular on the ironclad *Montauk*, at Charleston, S. C., and
in the charge of Fort Fisher.
Mrs. Cushman was married to the officer June 14, 1855, and was his wife during
the period of the war. She is 70 years of age and in poor health, and the pension
which she is now receiving is insufficient to properly care for her.
Commander Cushman's reputation in the service was that of a highly efficient,
zealous, brave, and patriotic officer, and it is but meet and fitting that some provision should be made for his aged and failing widow to insure to her a measure of
comfort for her last days.
The bill is therefore reported back favorably with a recommendation that it pass
when amended as follows:
Strike out all after the enacting clause and insert:
"That the Secretary of the Interior be, and he is hereby, authorized and directed
to place on the pension roll, subject to the provisions and limitations of the pension
laws, the name of Nannie Cushman, widow of Charles H. Cushman, late commander, United States Navy, and pay her a pension at the rate of forty dollars per
month in lieu of that she is now receiving."
Amend the title so as to read: "A bill granting an increase of pension to Nannie
Cushman."

H R—57-2—Vol 2——38   O

CHARLES C. CHESLEY.

JANUARY 26, 1903.—Committed to the Committee of the Whole House and ordered
to be printed.

Mr. SULLOWAY, from the Committee on Invalid Pensions, submitted
the following

REPORT.

[To accompany S. 6262.]

The Committee on Invalid Pensions, to whom was referred the bill
(S. 6262) granting an increase of pension to Charles C. Chesley, have
examined the same and adopt the Senate report thereon and recommend that the bill do pass.

[Senate Report No. 2135, Fifty-seventh Congress, second session.]

The Committee on Pensions, to whom was referred the bill (S. 6262) granting an
increase of pension to Charles C. Chesley, have examined the same and report:
Charles C. Chesley enlisted October 21, 1861, as a private in Company I, Sixth
Regiment New Hampshire Volunteer Infantry. He was promoted second lieutenant
Company F, June 28, 1865, and was honorably discharged July 17, 1865. At the
battle of Fredericksburg, Va., December 13, 1862, he received a gunshot wound of
the right shoulder, and was treated in hospital for such wound until about June 1,
1863. He was also treated in hospital December 12 and 13, 1864, for acute rheumatism.
Claimant, who is now 57 years of age, was pensioned December 26, 1866, for gunshot wound of right shoulder at $2 per month, which was increased to $4 per month
October 6, 1880, and to $6 per month December 5, 1888. He has since made three
claims for increase, all of which were rejected on the ground that his pension was
commensurate with the degree of disability from pensioned cause. In his last claim
for increase, filed January 26, 1895, he alleges that his wound had produced rheumatism. This claim was rejected February 10, 1898, rheumatism not being accepted as
a result.
On January 25, 1892, claimant made claim under the act of June 27, 1890, which
was rejected September 19, 1894, on the ground that he was not ratably disabled
under this law in such a degree as to entitle him to an allowance in excess of that
which he was receiving under the general law.
Claimant was last medically examined April 28, 1897, and the report thereof is as
follows:
Skin dark, body well nourished, muscles firm, conjunctivæ normal, arcus senilis
present, tongue broad, pale, not coated. Heart not enlarged; apex beat 1½ inches below
and three-fourths inch inside nipple, by auscultation and palpation; sounds weak,
but no murmurs; pulse standing 96, after exercise 104; complains of pain just under

short ribs, in left mammary line, after exertion. Lungs, liver, and spleen normal. Abdomen flat, not tender, not tympanitic. Gunshot wound of right shoulder: Wound of entrance, scar over 1¼ by ⅝ inches, situated just over outer side of head of humerus; scar slightly adherent, but not tender. Wound of exit, oval, 1¼ by ¾ inches, situated on outer border of posterior aspect of arm and 6 inches below wound of entrance; scar not adherent, not tender. Claims can not raise right arm above head to lift or to do overhead carpenter work. No evidence of rheumatism in any joint. Piles: One large external pile on left margin of anus, 1¼ by ¾ inches, inflamed and ulcerated; says it bleeds freely each time bowels move. No internal piles; sphincter not relaxed. No evidence of vicious habits; no other disabilities. Rating for gunshot wound of right shoulder, six-eighteenths; piles, four-eighteenths; neuralgia of heart, six-eighteenths.

It will be observed that this soldier had a service extending over a period of almost four years. The wound he received at Fredericksburg kept him in hospital almost six months; consequently it must have been a very severe one. It will also be noticed that soldier was in hospital suffering from rheumatism. He is vouched for by the officers and leading members of the New Hampshire Department, G. A. R., as a man of honor and integrity. His last rating by a board was $16, and your committee are of opinion that he is justly entitled to at least that amount, which is the rate named in the bill.

The passage of the bill is recommended.

O

RACHEL E. BULLARD.

JANUARY 26, 1903.—Committed to the Committee of the Whole House and ordered to be printed.

Mr. SULLOWAY, from the Committee on Invalid Pensions, submitted the following

REPORT.

[To accompany S. 6263.]

The Committee on Invalid Pensions, to whom was referred the bill (S. 6263) granting a pension to Rachel E. Bullard, have examined the same and adopt the Senate report thereon and recommend that the bill do pass.

[Senate Report No. 2136, Fifty-seventh Congress, second session.]

The Committee on Pensions, to whom was referred the bill (S. 6263) granting a pension to Rachel E. Bullard, have examined the same and report:

Rachel E. Bullard is the widow of Edmund E. Bullard, alias Charles Howard, who served in Company A, First Regiment, New Hampshire Volunteer Light Artillery, and Company C, Eleventh Regiment Vermont Volunteer Infantry. She made claim at the Bureau under the act of June 27, 1890, but the same was rejected on the ground that soldier was not honorably discharged from all rebellion service.

It appears that soldier enlisted August 20, 1862, in Company A, First New Hampshire Light Artillery, and, having had some trouble with one of his officers, shortly after the battle of Fredericksburg left his command and returned home. He was marked as deserted December 26, 1862. He subsequently, however, on December 3, 1863, enlisted under the name of Charles Howard in Company C, Eleventh Vermont Infantry, and served until the close of the war, having been honorably discharged to date from July 26, 1865.

Soldier applied for and obtained a pension under the general law for a gunshot wound of left forearm and hand which he received in battle at Cold Harbor, Virginia, June 4, 1864. At the time of his death he was receiving $6 per month. He died August 6, 1901, of ulcers of stomach.

Claimant is well advanced in years, being now 69 years of age. She has a little property, but is clearly dependent under the law. She was married to the soldier November 1, 1863, and was his wife during the period of his second service and shared in all the trials and anxieties which his absence at the front occasioned. While the ill-advised act of the soldier in leaving his first command is of itself a matter of condemnation, yet it would seem that his offense was fully condoned and expiated by his subsequent enlistment and faithful service to the close of the war. His being wounded in battle shows pretty well that he was of the stuff of which soldiers are made, and bears ample testimony to his patriotism and love of country.

Under the circumstances it would seem to be a great hardship to deprive his widow of a pension in the days of her advanced age and great need. She is in every way worthy of relief, and your committee report the bill back favorably with a recommendation that it pass.

O

LUTHER D. GODDARD.

JANUARY 26, 1903.—Committed to the Committee of the Whole House and ordered
to be printed.

Mr. SULLOWAY, from the Committee on Invalid Pensions, submitted
the following

REPORT.

[To accompany S. 6326.]

The Committee on Invalid Pensions, to whom was referred the bill
(S. 6326) granting an increase of pension to Luther D. Goddard, have
examined the same and adopt the Senate report thereon and recommend that the bill do pass.

[Senate Report No. 2301, Fifty-seventh Congress, second session.]

The Committee on Pensions, to whom was referred the bill (S. 6326) granting an
increase of pension to Luther D. Goddard, have examined the same and report:

This bill proposes to increase from $12 to $24 per month the pension of Luther D.
Goddard, late of Company D, Fifteenth Regiment Massachusetts Volunteer Infantry.

The soldier's petition is as follows:

"*To the honorable the Senate and House of Representatives, Washington, D. C.:*

"The undersigned, your petitioner, Luther D. Goddard, a resident of Worcester,
Mass., late a sergeant of Company D, Fifteenth Regiment Massachusetts Infantry
Volunteers, inscribed on the pension roll of Boston, Mass., certificate No. 869102,
draws $12 per month for disease of nervous system and left inguinal hernia and
paralysis of right side and arm and senility, being 77 years of age, said pension being
under act of June 27, 1890.

" I applied for pension under the general law February 25, 1882, which claim was
rejected July 11, 1898, on the ground that there was no record in the War Department of the incurrence of said disabilities. That I was a prisoner of war some four
months, and the hardships I underwent while in said prison broke down my constitution. That I was wounded at the battle of Balls Bluff, October 21, 1861, and while
in said prison became paralyzed in my right side and arm. The rupture was also of
army origin, but as said troubles were incurred in battle and in prison it was impossible to furnish eyewitnesses to said incurrence of the disabilities, and that they were
incurred in line of duty. That all of said troubles were the result of my army life,
and for two years after my discharge I was totally disabled for all labor, and ever
since said discharge I have not been able to do what would be called 'manual
labor.'

"The sight of my right eye is all gone and I am deaf in my right ear, and I now most respectfully ask that a special act may be passed giving me what pension I am entitled to; that all of said troubles were contracted in the United States service and in line of duty.

    "Yours, respectfully,   "L. D. GODDARD."

The military records show that soldier served from July 12, 1861, to June 20, 1862. He was taken prisoner at the battle of Balls Bluff, Virginia, October 21, 1861, confined at Richmond, and paroled February 20, 1862.

His last medical examination, made October 10, 1900, shows that he is suffering from hernia, paralysis agitans, loss of sight of right eye, and disease of heart, and is totally disabled for earning a support by manual labor. Evidence on file in the Pension Bureau shows that he has no means of support for himself and wife save his small pension.

It is probable that some of soldier's disabilities are the result of his service and prison life, though he seems to be unable to furnish proof to establish that fact. However that may be, he is extremely aged and in great need, and, considering all the facts in his case, your committee are of opinion that he is worthy of an increase of his pension.

The bill is therefore reported back favorably with a recommendation that it pass.

O

MARY A. NOYES.

JANUARY 26, 1903.—Committed to the Committee of the Whole House and ordered
to be printed.

Mr. SULLOWAY, from the Committee on Invalid Pensions, submitted
the following

REPORT.

[To accompany S. 6329.]

The Committee on Invalid Pensions, to whom was referred the bill
(S. 6329) granting an increase of pension to Mary A. Noyes, have
examined the same and adopt the Senate report thereon and recommend that the bill do pass.

[Senate Report No. 2134, Fifty-seventh Congress, second session.]

The Committee on Pensions, to whom was referred the bill (S. 6329) granting an
increase of pension to Mary A. Noyes, have examined the same and report:

Mary A. Noyes is the widow of Edward Noyes, who served in Company C,
Eleventh Regiment Maine Volunteer Infantry.

Soldier enlisted July 23, 1862, and was discharged January 26, 1865, for loss of
right arm above elbow from gunshot wound received in battle at Deep Run, Virginia,
August 16, 1864. He was pensioned April 20, 1865, for loss of right arm, at $8 from
discharge, which was increased to $15 June 6, 1866; to $18 June 4, 1872; to $24 June
4, 1874; to $30 March 3, 1883, and to $45 August 4, 1886. He died August 25, 1899,
and the cause of his death, as shown by the public records, was angina pectoris.

Mary A. Noyes is now receiving the pension of $8 per month provided by the act
of June 27, 1890. She is 55 years of age, and was married to the soldier March 31,
1867. On April 9, 1900, she made claim under the general law, which was rejected
March 16, 1901, on the ground that the soldier's fatal disease was not the result of
the disability for which he was pensioned and was not otherwise shown to have
resulted from his military service.

Dr. Charles C. Larrabee, of Prospect Harbor, Me., testified March 26, 1900, as
follows:

"The claimant at times complained of trouble with left side, which I attributed to
the use of left arm for all purposes, causing weakness of the left side. My first treatment to him I find, by memorandum of account, to be August 23, 24, 25, 1899, when
he was suffering from angina pectoris, which I consider, to the best of my knowledge and belief, to be aggravated or caused from severe loss of blood at the time of
the amputation of arm, and use of left arm, causing severe muscular strain."

Dr. Fred. W. Bridgham, of Sullivan, Me., testified March 13, 1900, as follows:

"I saw said Noyes a few hours before death, and diagnosed his disease as neuralgia
of the heart. It was impossible at that time to make a thorough examination of the
heart. but from the history of the case I have no doubt his disease was aggravated

by excessive strain of the left side, as his right arm had been amputated a few inches below the shoulder joint. From the description at the time of the amputation I have no doubt that the excessive loss of blood at the time of operation and by secondary hemorrhage directly induced the condition of the heart from which he always suffered. I have often heard him complain of shortness of breath on exertion, and of numbness and swelling of the left arm and hand. Being a great worker, and lifting much with the left arm, I have no doubt but that his heart trouble, originating in excessive loss of blood, was aggravated by great muscular strain and vascular tension, eventually resulting in his death."

Mrs. Noyes resides at No. 16 Nonquit street, Dorchester, Mass. Evidence on file shows that she has no property and that her means of support are limited to her pension and what she can earn by her daily labor.

From the evidence of the attending physicians it seems reasonably certain that soldier's death was indirectly, at least, attributable to the loss of right arm, for which he was pensioned. It is well known that a very large proportion of men who suffer amputations likewise suffer from heart trouble, induced, no doubt, by the interruption of the circulation and the consequent overworking of the heart. Your committee are of opinion that the relation of cause and effect should be accepted in this case and that the widow is entitled to a pension at the rate provided by the general law.

The bill is therefore reported back favorably, with a recommendation that it pass.

O

ANN A. HERSUM.

JANUARY 26, 1903.—Committed to the Committee of the Whole House and ordered
to be printed.

Mr. SULLOWAY, from the Committee on Invalid Pensions, submitted
the following

REPORT.

[To accompany S. 6422.]

The Committee on Invalid Pensions, to whom was referred the bill
(S. 6422) granting an increase of pension to Ann A. Hersum, have
examined the same and adopt the Senate report thereon and recommend that the bill do pass.

[Senate Report No. 2187, Fifty-seventh Congress, second session.]

The Committee on Pensions, to whom was referred the bill (S. 6422) granting an
increase of pension to Ann A. Hersum, have examined the same and report:
   Ann A. Hersum, whose post-office address is Milton, N. H., is the widow of George
L. Hersum, who served in Company A, Fifth Regiment New Hampshire Volunteer
Infantry.
   Soldier enlisted September 28, 1861; he was promoted second lieutenant October
28, 1863, and was honorably discharged October 12, 1864. The hospital records
show him under treatment on several dates in 1862 and 1864 for malaria and rheumatism. He died February 7, 1890, and the cause of his death, as shown by the
public record, was malaria and organic heart disease.
   Ann A. Hersum, who is about 60 years of age, was married to the soldier November 25, 1871. She is now receiving the pension of $8 per month provided by the act
of June 27, 1890. She has no property and is wholly dependent on her small pension and what little she can earn by her own labor.
   April 10, 1890, claimant made claim under the general law, which claim was
rejected May 3, 1900, on the ground of her inability to prove that the soldier's fatal
disease of heart had its origin in the military service.
   It appears in evidence that soldier incurred chills and fever or malarial poisoning
and diarrhea during the campaign on the Peninsula in the summer of 1862. There is
also some evidence indicating that he was overcome by heat before Petersburg in
August, 1864. The evidence as to his condition for some years after his discharge is
somewhat vague and indefinite. It seems, however, that he suffered at intervals
from malaria, and in later years rheumatism manifested itself, culminating in the
heart disease of which he died. He is highly spoken of as a man of great energy and
much will power, who would not give up, and who continued to work when wholly

unfit to do so. He complained but little, and it is probably because of this that his neighbors and associates know comparatively nothing of his ailments.

Upon the evidence as a whole the action of the Pension Bureau was technically correct. It is highly probable, however, that the soldier's fatal disease was largely contributed to by the disabilities incurred during his service. He has a good military record, and his widow is now very poor and much in need of help, and your committee recommend the passage of the bill which grants her the same rate of pension she would have received had the Bureau accepted the death cause as of service origin.

O

S. JOSIE HILL.

JANUARY 26, 1903.—Committed to the Committee of the Whole House and ordered to be printed.

Mr. SULLOWAY, from the Committee on Invalid Pensions, submitted the following

REPORT.

[To accompany S. 6452.]

The Committee on Invalid Pensions, to whom was referred the bill (S. 6452) granting a pension to S. Josie Hill, have examined the same and adopt the Senate report thereon and recommend that the bill do pass.

[Senate Report No. 2218, Fifty-seventh Congress, second session.]

The Committee on Pensions, to whom was referred the bill (S. 6452) granting a pension to S. Josie Hill, have examined the same and report:

A similar bill was introduced in the Senate during the Fifty-sixth Congress, reported favorably with an amendment reducing the rate to $20, and passed the Senate.

The report was as follows:

"S. Josie Hill is the widow of David Hill, who served as first lieutenant and captain Company F, One hundred and fifty-second Regiment New York Volunteer Infantry.

"The official military records show that this officer was enrolled September 22, 1862, promoted captain January 3, 1863, and was discharged October 29, 1864, for disability, gunshot resection of right wrist received in battle at Spottsylvania, Va., May 12, 1864. The hospital records show him treated in December, 1863, and January, 1864, for rheumatism; in February, 1864, for typhoid fever; in March, 1864, for rheumatism; and from May, 1864, to date of discharge, for gunshot fracture of right hand. A medical certificate dated July 25, 1863, shows him suffering from a bilious attack and diarrhea; a medical certificate dated December 10, 1863, shows him suffering from typhoid fever, and a medical certificate for extension of furlough, dated July 22, 1864, shows him suffering from gunshot wound of right hand, attended with erysipelas and inflammation.

"Captain Hill was pensioned April 22, 1865, for gunshot wound of right wrist, at the rate of $20 per month, and this pension was increased to $24 per month March 3, 1883, and to $30 per month August 4, 1886. July 1, 1898, he made claim for increase, alleging resulting nervous prostration necessitating the aid and attendance of another person. This claim was rejected May 19, 1899, on the ground that the alleged nervous prostration was due to apoplexy and was not accepted as a result of pensioned wound.

"Captain Hill died January 9, 1900, and the cause of his death as given in the public records was 'progressive paralysis terminating with heart failure; duration of sickness, about thirty-five years.'

"Mrs. Hill resides at Easthampton, Mass. She is about 49 years of age and was married to this officer June 7, 1880. She has two children under the age of 16 years and one who a few months ago attained his sixteenth year.

"January 27, 1900, she made claim under the general law, alleging that her husband died of progressive paralysis, caused by gunshot wound of right wrist, for which he was receiving a pension. This claim was rejected May 28, 1900, on the ground that the fatal disease was not a result of gunshot wound and not otherwise shown to have been due to his military service.

"The physician in attendance at the officer's death was Dr. Oliver W. Cobb, of Easthampton, Mass., who stated that he had no doubt that Captain Hill's disability and death were the direct result of his injury received in the service of the United States.

" Captain Hill was free from any and all forms of vicious habits, and was a strong temperance man. After the war he worked his way through Amherst College, taught four years in Williston Seminary, Easthampton, Mass., studied law, was admitted and practiced at the Hampshire County bar, and was a public speaker of considerable note.

" There is evidence on file to the effect that this officer, at the the time of his being wounded, received a shock to his nervous system from which he never recovered; and that he suffered from frequent and very violent neuralgic headaches, and in later years developed disease of brain and spine, believed to be a result of his wound.

" While it is not proved conclusively that the soldier's death was a result of his military service, yet your committee believe that the severe wound which he received in service, and the several diseases from which he suffered while in the Army, as shown by the hospital records, contributed largely to his fatal disease, and recommend the passage of the bill.

O

ALONZO GILBERT.

JANUARY 26, 1903.—Committed to the Committee of the Whole House and ordered
to be printed.

Mr. SULLOWAY, from the Committee on Invalid Pensions, submitted
the following

REPORT.

[To accompany S. 6465.]

The Committee on Invalid Pensions, to whom was referred the bill
(S. 6465) granting an increase of pension to Alonzo Gilbert, have
examined the same and adopt the Senate report thereon and recommend that the bill do pass.

[Senate Report No. 2214, Fifty-seventh Congress, second session.]

The Committee on Pensions, to whom was referred the bill (S. 6465) granting an
increase of pension to Alonzo Gilbert, have examined the same and report:

It is proposed by this bill to increase from $12 to $24 per month the pension of
Alonzo Gilbert, late of Company K, One hundred and tenth Regiment New York
Volunteer Infantry, who served from August 8, 1862, to August 28, 1865, when he
was honorably discharged.

Soldier is now receiving the maximum pension of $12 per month, provided by the
act of June 27, 1890, for total disability due to rheumatism and disease of heart.
He resides at Suncook, N. H. He is 63 years of age and his medical examination
rated him $24 for rheumatism and resulting heart disease and $4 for disease of
prostate gland.

Claimant is a much afflicted man. He is now suffering from chronic rheumatism,
heart disease, stomach trouble, catarrh, and disease of kidneys and bladder. He is
totally unable to work and is without means of support, except his small pension and
the help of relatives. He has made no claim under the general law, but declares that
his rheumatism, which is so great a part of his present disability, was contracted in
the service, but this he is unable to prove. It may be that his rheumatism is due to
his army life, and in view of his good record and his faithful service of over three
years, his total disability and great poverty, your committee report the bill back
favorably with a recommendation that it pass.

O

WILLARD A. JACKSON.

JANUARY 26, 1903.—Committed to the Committee of the Whole House and ordered
to be printed.

Mr. SULLOWAY, from the Committee on Invalid Pensions, submitted
the following

REPORT.

[To accompany S. 6466.]

The Committee on Invalid Pensions, to whom was referred the bill
(S. 6466) granting an increase of pension to Willard A. Jackson, have
examined the same and adopt the Senate report thereon and recommend that the bill do pass.

[Senate Report No. 2215. Fifty-seventh Congress, second session.]

The Committee on Pensions, to whom was referred the bill (S. 6466) granting an
increase of pension to Willard A. Jackson, have examined the same and report:
This bill proposes to increase from $12 to $24 per month the pension of Willard A.
Jackson, of Nashua, N. H., late of Company A, Seventeenth Regiment New Hampshire Volunteer Infantry.
Soldier enlisted November 19, 1862, and was discharged May 16, 1863, for disabled
joint of right arm. He is now receiving a pension of $12 per month under the act
of June 27, 1890, for right inguinal hernia and injury to right elbow.
May 31, 1879, claimant made claim under the general law, alleging strain of muscles
of right arm from drilling with a heavy gun in the winter of 1862-63, and by reason
of which he was discharged from service. This claim was rejected December 15,
1880, and again November 11, 1882, on the ground that his disability of right arm
existed prior to his enlistment.
It appears from the evidence on file that claimant when a boy had some trouble
with his arm by which it was bent or partially drawn up. Surg. James D. Folsom,
who was a competent man, examined him at enlistment and passed him as a sound
man, and he was accepted into the service as such. Several witnesses testified that
claimant was apparently sound before enlistment, able to do full work at his trade of
shoemaker, and that they knew of no disability at that time. In the early spring of
1864 claimant was put on light duty, in charge of the officers' horses, and continued
on such duty until discharged.
Claimant is now totally disabled for manual labor. His medical examination,
made October 29, 1890, shows that he is suffering from right inguinal hernia and
injury to right elbow. His arm disability is described as follows:
"The right arm shows a previous fracture of the radius and a dislocation of head
of the radius behind the external condyle, which was never reduced and at present

prevents extension for about one-half its normal extent. The right forearm is also fixed at full pronation and can not be supined at all. Flexion of the arm from the fixed right angle position is also slightly impeded and he can not quite raise the hand to the back of head. The hand is quite weak and the right arm is almost worthless for any hard manual labor.''

Evidence filed with bill shows that claimant is not able to do work, on account of a withered right arm, hernia, hemorrhoids, and cancer of face, which has lately been operated upon, but is liable to return. His pension of $12 per month is all he has for his support, and he has been compelled to call on his county authorities for help.

It would seem that the Government, by its properly constituted authorities, having examined claimant at enlistment and accepted him as sound and fit for service, should now be estopped from setting up the claim of prior unsoundness in order to deprive him of the benefits of the general pension laws.

It may be that there was a predisposition to disability before service; but this would not, under the law, operate to defeat his title to pension. If he had any disability at enlistment it was undoubtedly aggravated in service, and considering all the circumstances of the case, your committee are of opinion that he is entitled to an increase of his pension.

The bill is therefore reported back favorably with a recommendation that it pass.

O

CAROLINE W. BIXBY.

JANUARY 26, 1903.—Committed to the Committee of the Whole House and ordered
to be printed.

Mr. SULLOWAY, from the Committee on Invalid Pensions, submitted
the following

REPORT.

[To accompany S. 6500.]

The Committee on Invalid Pensions, to whom was referred the bill
(S. 6500) granting an increase of pension to Caroline W. Bixby, have
examined the same and adopt the Senate report thereon and recommend that the bill do pass.

[Senate Report No. 2217, Fifty-seventh Congress, second session.]

The Committee on Pensions, to whom was referred the bill (S. 6500) granting an
increase of pension to Caroline W. Bixby, have examined the same and report:

Caroline W. Bixby is the widow of Daniel P. Bixby, who served in Company L,
First Regiment New Hampshire Volunteer Cavalry, from December 27, 1861, to July
15, 1865, when he was honorably discharged.

Soldier died May 21, 1897, the cause of his death being heart disease. At the
time of his death he was receiving a pension of $12 per month, under the act of June
27, 1890, for complete left inguinal hernia and injury of both wrists.

Caroline W Bixby is now receiving the pension of $8 per month provided by the
act of June 27, 1890. She is 65 years of age and was married to the soldier January
18, 1862. Her only possessions are a house and 4 acres of land, worth about $500.

On January 26, 1899, Mrs. Bixby made claim under the general law, alleging that
her husband died of asthma and heart disease contracted, as she believes, during his
military service. This claim she can not establish, being unable, after repeated
efforts, to find officers or comrades now living who can give evidence as to soldier's
condition in service. She has, however, supplied evidence of her family physician
and also of several neighbors, showing the continuance of asthma and heart trouble
from the time of soldier's discharge.

Dr. James P. Whittle, of Weare, N. H., testified February 15, 1899, that he was
acquainted with soldier from about 1859 and considered him an able-bodied man at
that time and up to the time of his enlistment; that he was called to see soldier soon
after discharge and found him suffering from asthma and heart disease, and from
his condition judged the diseases were contracted in the Army; that he attended
him in his last sickness, and his death was caused by cardiac asthma.

It seems certain from this evidence that soldier's fatal disease originated while he
was in the Army, notwithstanding the want of technical evidence required by the
Bureau showing his condition in the service. It being shown that he was sound at
enlistment, and that at discharge he was suffering from asthma and heart disease, of
which he died, it is clear that his death is chargeable to his service.

Your committee therefore report the bill back favorably with the recommendation
that it pass.

O

FORTIFICATION APPROPRIATION BILL.

JANUARY 26, 1903.—Committed to the Committee of the Whole House on the state
of the Union and ordered to be printed.

Mr. HEMENWAY, from the Committee on Appropriations, submitted
the following

REPORT.

[To accompany H. R. 17046.]

The Committee on Appropriations, in presenting the accompanying
bill making appropriations for fortifications and other works of defense,
and for the armament thereof, for the procurement of heavy ordnance
for trial and service, and for other purposes, submit the following in
explanation thereof:

The estimates on which the bill is based will be found in the Book
of Estimates for the fiscal year 1904, pages 246–253, and aggregate
$15,004,420, of which sum there is recommended in the accompanying
bill appropriations amounting to $7,093,943, which sum is $205,012
less than was appropriated in the last fortification act.

During the Forty-ninth Congress (fiscal years 1887 and 1888) no
appropriations were made on account of fortifications, their maintenance and armament, and for the twelve fiscal years 1875 to 1886, inclusive, the appropriation by Congress on this account averaged only
$540,750 per annum, and only $463,500 per annum for the fourteen
years including 1887 and 1888, for which latter two fiscal years no
specific appropriations were made, as stated.

The bill reported herewith contains appropriations in continuance
of the policy adopted by the Fiftieth Congress in the passage of the
acts approved September 22, 1888, and March 2, 1889, and by the
Fifty-first, Fifty-second, Fifty-third, Fifty-fourth, Fifty-fifth, Fifty-
sixth, and Fifty-seventh Congresses in acts approved August 18, 1890,
February 24, 1891, July 23, 1892, February 18, 1893, August 1, 1894,
March 2, 1895, June 6, 1896, March 3, 1897, May 7, 1898, March 3,
1899, May 25, 1900, March 1, 1901, and June 6, 1902.

The appropriations by said acts for the fifteen fiscal years 1889–
1903 aggregate $75,718,243.50, or an average of $5,047,882.90 per
annum.

Of the whole sum, $75,718,243.50, appropriated by the fortification acts covering the fifteen fiscal years 1889–1903 the sum of $45,845,391 was appropriated in the seven fortification acts enacted by the present and the last three Congresses.

The fortification appropriation acts enacted during the Fifty-fifth Congress appropriated $14,287,396, in addition to which amount sums aggregating $8,674,898 were provided in deficiency appropriation acts for fortifications and the armament thereof, and the further sum of $12,865,840.60 was allotted for the same objects from the general appropriation of $50,000,000 made for the national defense in the act of March 9, 1898, making in all $35,828,134.60 available for fortifications and the armament thereof under appropriations made during the Fifty-fifth Congress.

The total appropriations made for fortifications and other works of defense since 1888, and since the recommendations of the Endicott board of 1885, including the appropriations made in deficiency acts and allotments made from the national-defense fund, amount to $96,752,982.

The scheme of seacoast fortifications contemplated by the Endicott board, and which has been followed by Congress in the appropriations made since 1888, it is now estimated will cost in the aggregate $99,392,222, of which sum there has been already provided $57,508,983, the Engineer Department having received $25,757,164 and the Ordnance Department $31,608,586.

The difference between the sum, $57,508,983 already provided toward the scheme of the Endicott board and the sum total of appropriations, $96,752,982, for fortifications since 1888 is represented in expenditures for erecting and equipping the gun factory at Watervliet, the gun-carriage factory at Watertown, the Ordnance and Fortification Board, purchase of land for fortification sites, torpedoes for harbor defense, providing ammunition for service and for tests, manufacture of field guns, and for sundry other objects incident to providing and maintaining a system of seacoast defenses.

The following shows the aggregate amount appropriated under each natural subdivision of the accompanying bill, namely:

Gun and mortar batteries	2,236,425
Searchlights for defenses in important harbors	223,500
Sites for fortifications	200,000
Installation of range and position finders	150,000
Preservation and repair of fortifications	300,000
Plans for fortifications	5,000
Tools, etc., for maintaining and operating electric plants	35,000
Sea walls and embankments	89,575
Construction of mining casemates, etc	50,000
Purchase of submarine mines, etc	100,000
Torpedo depot at Fort Totten	3,000
Armament of fortifications	3,480,500
Proving ground, Sandy Hook, N. J	77,943
Frankford Arsenal, Pa	43,000
Ordnance and Fortification Board	100,000
Total	7,093,943

O

MINIMUM PUNISHMENT IN CERTAIN CASES ARISING IN THE INDIAN TERRITORY.

JANUARY 26, 1903.—Referred to the House Calendar and ordered to be printed.

Mr. PARKER, from the Committee on the Judiciary, submitted the following

REPORT.

[To accompany S. 3512.]

The Committee on the Judiciary, having had under consideration the bill (S. 3512) concerning minimum punishment in certain cases arising in the Indian Territory, do report the said bill favorably, and recommend the same do pass with amendment as follows:

Strike out all after the enacting clause, to wit:

That section thirty-three of the act of Congress of May third, eighteen hundred and ninety, entitled "An act * * * to enlarge the jurisdiction of the United States courts in the Indian Territory, and for other purposes," is hereby amended by adding the following proviso:

"*Provided*, That in all cases where punishment prescribed by the laws of Arkansas is adopted by said section, the court shall not be compelled thereby to impose the minimum punishment established therein, but may in its discretion impose a less punishment by way of fine or imprisonment, or both, as justice shall seem to require."

And insert in lieu thereof the following:

That any person, whether an Indian or otherwise, who shall hereafter be convicted in the Indian Territory of stealing any horse, mare, gelding, filly, foal, mule, ass, or jenny, or of stealing, or marking, killing, or wounding with intent to steal, any kind of cattle, pigs, hogs, sheep, or goats, shall be punished by a fine of not more than one thousand dollars, or by imprisonment for not more than fifteen years, or by both such fine and imprisonment, at the discretion of the court.

SEC. 2. That all acts and parts of acts inconsistent with this act are hereby repealed: *Provided, however,* That all such acts and parts of acts shall remain in force for the punishment of all persons who have heretofore been guilty in the Indian Territory of the offense or offenses herein mentioned: *And provided further,* That this act shall not affect or apply to any prosecution now pending or the prosecution of any offense already committed.

Also amend the title so as to read as follows: "An act fixing the punishment for the larceny of horses, cattle, and other live stock in the Indian Territory, and for other purposes."

The present statute in force punishes horse stealing with not less than five years, and false branding with intent to steal any cattle, pigs, sheep, or goats with not less than one year.   Such punishment is often cruelly excessive.

The substitute embodies the language of House bill 13404, which was reported by the Committee on Indian Affairs and passed the House in December and is now pending in the Senate.   Any difference as to the language by which this relief shall be granted can be readily settled in conference.   Both bills abolish all minimum punishment.

We add two letters of the Attorney-General, as follows:

DEPARTMENT OF JUSTICE,
Washington, D. C., December 18, 1902.

SIR: This Department is just advised that Senate bill 3512, amending the law of May 3, 1890, concerning the punishment for larceny of horses, cattle, and other live stock in the Indian Territory, and passed by the Senate on March 3, 1902, has been referred to your committee.

The House of Representatives on the 6th instant passed House bill 13404, having the same purpose as the Senate bill above referred to.

Inasmuch as the act of May 2, 1890 (not May 3, 1890, as set out in the Senate bill) has heretofore been amended, it is believed that the enactment of House bill 13404 instead of Senate bill 3512 is to be preferred.

The wishes of this Department in this matter have been communicated to the chairman of the Committee on Indian Affairs in the Senate, to which committee House bill 13404 has been referred.

Respectfully,   P. C. KNOX,
                                                     Attorney-General.
Hon. JOHN J. JENKINS,
   Chairman Committee on the Judiciary,
      House of Representatives.

DEPARTMENT OF JUSTICE,
Washington, D. C., January 3, 1903.

SIR: Replying to your letter of December 19 concerning Senate bill 3512 and House bill 13404, fixing the penalty for larceny of horses and cattle in the Indian Territory, in which you suggest that the House amend Senate bill 3512 by striking out all after the enacting clause and substitute as the first section a paragraph inclosed in your letter and the second section of House bill 13404, I have to say that this course would be entirely satisfactory to this Department, if it seems necessary to substitute the section as drawn by you for the first section of the House bill.   It appears, however, that the first section of the House bill covers any violations of the law which are sought to be defined and punished.

The first section of the said House bill may be divided into two clauses: First, "that any person * * * who shall hereafter be convicted in the Indian Territory of stealing any horse, mare, gelding, filly, foal, mule, ass, or jenny," and second, "of stealing or marking, killing or wounding with intent to steal any kind of cattle, pigs, hogs, sheep, or goats" shall be punished, etc.

This first section is based upon sections 1629 and 1628 of the laws of Arkansas, which are now in effect in the Indian Territory, and are as follows:

"SEC. 1629. Whoever shall be convicted of stealing any horse, mare, gelding, filly, foal, mule, ass, or jenny shall be imprisoned in the penitentiary not less than five nor more than fifteen years."

"SEC. 1628. Every person who shall mark, steal, or kill, or wound with intent to steal, any kind of cattle, pigs, hogs, sheep, or goats shall be guilty of a felony, and, upon conviction thereof, be imprisoned at hard labor in the penitentiary for any time not less than one year nor more than five years."

In the substitute proposed by you it is provided, first, that any person who shall be convicted of stealing any cattle, or other animals specifically named, and second, that any person who shall mark, kill, or wound, with intent to steal, the same animals named in the first half of the clause shall be punished, etc.

It appears to me that the only difference between this section and section 1 of House bill 13404 is a fuller and more specific enumeration of the animals and (1) a provision punishing the stealing of any of these animals, and (2) the provision punishing the marking, killing, or wounding, with intent to steal, any of these animals.

The first section of House bill 13404 provides for the punishment of all offenses which are actually committed; for although the offense of marking, killing, and wounding cattle, pigs, hogs, sheep, and goats, with intent to steal them, is committed, animals of the horse kind are not marked, wounded, or killed with intent to steal.

As heretofore stated, the substitute proposed by you is entirely satisfactory to this Department, and I have gone into the matter thus fully in order to show why House bill 13404, as it now stands, appears to this Department to be also satisfactory, and because if you concur in this view it would seem simpler to secure the enactment by the Senate of the House bill than the amendment by the House of Senate bill 3512, and the subsequent resubmission of it to the Senate.

Respectfully,   .   P. C. KNOX,
Attorney-General.

Hon. JOHN J. JENKINS,
    Chairman Committee on the Judiciary, House of Representatives.

Mr. Jenkins's proposed substitute for section 2 referred to in foregoing letter:

That any person, whether an Indian or otherwise, who shall hereafter be convicted in the Indian Territory of stealing any cattle, live animal, bull, cow, ox, steer, bullock, heifer, calf, sheep, lamb, hog, pig, goat, horse, mare, gelding, filly, foal, mule, ass, or jenny, or of marking, killing, or wounding with intent to steal, any cattle, live animal, bull, cow, ox, steer, bullock, heifer, calf, sheep, lamb, hog, pig, goat, horse, mare, gelding, filly, foal, mule, ass, or jenny shall be punished by a fine of not more than one thousand dollars or by imprisonment for not more than fifteen years, or by both such fine and imprisonment at the discretion of the court.

O

DITTMAR POWDER COMPANY.

JANUARY 26, 1903.—Committed to the Committee of the Whole House and ordered
to be printed.

Mr. NEVIN, from the Committee on Claims, submitted the following

REPORT.

[To accompany H. R. 9995.]

On July 21, 1898, the Ordnance Department of the U. S. Army, through D. W. Flagler, brigadier-general, Chief of Ordnance, requested the Dittmar Powder Company to submit a proposition to the Government for furnishing that Department with 150,000 pounds of compressed gun cotton for filling shell to conform to specifications inclosed therewith. Considerable correspondence ensued, all of which, together with the contract and all papers connected with this subject-matter, we publish in full in connection with this report.

On the 8th day of December, 1898, articles of agreement between the Dittmar Powder Works, of New York, etc., of the first part, and Brig. Gen. D. W. Flagler, Chief of Ordnance of U. S. Army, acting under direction and by authority of the Secretary of War, of the second part, were entered into, by which the said powder company agreed to deliver to the Government, at the times and in the manner in said agreement set forth, "100,000 pounds of compressed gun cotton for filling shells, in accordance with the specifications hereto attached and forming part of this contract," copy of which agreement in full is printed and attached hereto.

A bond signed by a number of sureties was given to the Government in the penal sum of $7,000 for the carrying out on the part of the Dittmar Powder Company of its part of said agreement.

The Dittmar Powder Company went forward and prepared for the manufacture of the gun cotton, purchasing hydraulic presses and necessary pumps, buying material, and getting ready for the fulfillment of the contract upon its part.

On March 6, 1900, the Department notified the Dittmar Powder Company that they had returned the communication of the powder company of February 21, notifying the Department that the company was ready to go forward and fill its part of the contract, to Capt. O. B. Mitcham, with instructions for him to ascertain what expense the

Dittmar Powder and Chemical Company had incurred in making preparation for the manufacture of this gun cotton, with a view to making satisfactory arrangements for the cancellation of the contract, "as the gun cotton to be furnished under this contract is not required by the Department and it is most desirable that the contract should, if practicable, be canceled." (Signed A. R. Buffington, brigadier-general, Chief of Ordnance.)

Pursuant to that cancellation by the Government, thus arbitrarily made, because it did not need the gun cotton which it had contracted for, negotiations were had between the parties looking to a sum to be paid to the Dittmar Powder and Chemical Company for what it had lost by reason of the Government canceling the contract aforesaid.

After considerable correspondence back and forth, set out in the copies printed herewith, the Dittmar Powder Company said they would accept $10,000, and the Chief of Ordnance finally recommended the payment of a sum not exceeding $7,500.

By a letter of May 17, 1901, the Dittmar Powder and Chemical Company were notified that "it is recognized that the company did go to certain expense in the preparation for this contract, but their claim is not such a one as the law permits the Department to settle," and stating further that the powder and chemical company would either have to go before the Court of Claims and have their matter adjudicated or appeal to Congress for an appropriation to reimburse them, and adds:

This latter course would be the better one for the company, and this office would be inclined to favorably recommend a fair claim in that direction.

The Dittmar Powder Company claims of the Government that it should receive not less than $10,000, but on January 21, 1902, Brig. Gen. William Crozier, Chief of Ordnance, says, in reference to the matter:

This office, in consideration of all the circumstances of the case, will be willing to recommend payment to you of a sum not exceeding $7,500.

This matter has been before the committee, and after looking into it thoroughly the committee believe that the Dittmar Powder Company should be paid the sum of $7,500 in full, if it will accept the same in full of all its claims, rights, and demands of every nature and kind whatsoever by reason of the cancellation by the Government of the contract aforesaid and by reason of all loss it has suffered on account thereof.

OFFICE OF THE CHIEF OF ORDNANCE, U. S. ARMY,
Washington, July 21, 1898.

GENTLEMEN: You are requested to submit a proposal for furnishing this Department with 150,000 pounds of compressed gun cotton for filling shell, to conform to specifications inclosed herewith. State the time when deliveries can commence and the amount that can be turned out per day thereafter. This cotton when complete is to be delivered at the United States Powder Depot, Dover, N. J., and the price named in your proposal should include delivery at that point.

Respectfully,   D. W. FLAGLER,
                              Brigadier-General, Chief of Ordnance.

DITTMAR POWDER COMPANY,
    62 Liberty street, New York City.

WILMINGTON, DEL., *July 29, 1898.*

GENTLEMEN: Referring to letter from the Chief of Ordnance recently forwarded to you asking for bids for furnishing 150,000 pounds of gun cotton for shells, I have been examining more closely into what shapes and sizes the blocks will be required for filling these shells. I write to inform you, in order that you may more intelligently make your bid. The gun cotton is desired for filling siege shells of two kinds; tracings of the cavities of these shells are forwarded to you herewith. It will be observed that there is to be left a cylindrical, or slightly conical, cavity for the fuse.

It is desired that the form of blocks be such as to enable these shells to be expeditiously filled and to allow the use of the largest charge consistent with reasonable expense. The following methods are suggested:

1. Make disks of a diameter about one-sixteenth or one-eighth less than greatest diameter of the cavity and turn some of them off, so as to enable them to be built up into a column fitting the shape of the cavity.

The hole for the fuse may be obtained by boring the blocks or by running a cut in from the side of the blocks with a band saw and cutting out a circular hole. This method would give the greatest practical charge.

2. To avoid the cost of turning the head, the head might be filled with the small blocks of gun cotton described below and the body with the disks as above. Or the portion of the body around the fuse might also be filled with the blocks, using disks for the remainder.

3. The shell may be filled with a combination of small blocks and large blocks of a convenient size for pressing, say 3 inches square and 1 to 2 inches thick, employing the large blocks so far as practicable and filling in around them with the small ones.

4. The whole shell may be filled with small blocks poured in loose and shaken down as much as possible.

After the shell is filled by any of the above methods it is intended to pour a melted mixture of carnauba wax and paraffin into it, completely filling the space and making the charge solid.

The small blocks above referred to are small cubes of about one-half inch on the edge, or cylinders or prisms of about the same volume, which are obtained by sawing up larger blocks. These small blocks would be quite brittle, and would form dust and break up readily. To obviate this difficulty they should be dipped into or sprayed with a solvent that would furnish a thin coating of colloided cotton over the surface to hold them together. While this coating would to a certain extent tend to prevent the escape of water, its main object is to harden the surface of the grains so as to keep them entire.

It is hoped that this explanation will be of assistance to you in formulating your bid on this subject.

Very respectfully,   SIDNEY E. STUART,
                               Captain, Ordnance Department, U. S. Army, Inspector.
The DITTMAR POWDER COMPANY,
            New York, N. Y.
You might make bids for each form, disks, large blocks, and small blocks.

———

OFFICE OF CHIEF OF ORDNANCE, U. S. ARMY,
                               Washington, September 3, 1898.
GENTLEMEN: Referring to your letter of August 16, quoting prices on gun cotton, I have to request that you will quote also prices for pressed gun cotton delivered in the form of cylindrical disks of stated diameter (slightly less than the diameter of the shell cavity), also for conical disks of stated diameters, and also for small prismatic blocks about three-fourths of an inch square and from one-fourth to 1 inch long, coated to prevent their breaking up by handling.

By order of the Chief of Ordnance.
Respectfully,   CHAS. S. SMITH,
                               Major, Ordnance Department, U. S. Army.
The DITTMAR POWDER WORKS,
    62 Liberty Street, New York City.

———

NEW YORK, *September 8, 1898.*
DEAR SIR: Referring to your letter of the 3d instant, we can quote you on compressed gun cotton, delivered in form of cylindrical disks of stated diameter, or of

conical disks of stated diameter, at 64 cents per pound, and in the form of small prismatic blocks about three-fourths of an inch square and from one-fourth to 1 inch long, coated to prevent breakage, at 65 cents per pound, delivered at powder depot station near Dover, N. J.   Weight of gun cotton to be dry weight.

Hoping this may be satisfactory, we are,

Very truly, yours,   DITTMAR POWDER WORKS,
                                                                          G. F. HAMLIN, *General Agent.*

CHIEF OF ORDNANCE, *Washington, D. C.*

NEW YORK, *November 9, 1898.*

DEAR SIR: We inclose proposal in duplicate for compressed gun cotton as directed in yours of the 8th instant.

You will note we made date of delivery sixty days after award of contract and receipt of specifications, giving size of disks required.

We make this date so far ahead because after we are advised by you of size of the disks the necessary dies for the hydraulic press will have to be made, and we are informed that it may take sixty days to make them.   If, however, it is possible for us to obtain them at an earlier date, which we will make an effort to do, we will commence the manufacture of the gun cotton that much earlier.

Hoping this may be satisfactory, we are,

Very truly, yours,   DITTMAR POWDER WORKS,
                                                                          G. F. HAMLIN, *General Agent.*

CHIEF OF ORDNANCE, U. S. ARMY,
         Washington, D. C.

NEW YORK, *November 9, 1898.*

DEAR SIR: Sixty-four cents per pound for compressed gun cotton in the form of cylindrical discs of stated diameter, and in the form of conical discs of stated diameter.

Sixty-five cents per pound for compressed gun cotton in the form of small prismatic blocks about three-fourths of an inch square, and from one-fourth to 1 inch long, coated to prevent their breaking up by handling.

The weight of guncotton to be dry weight.

Deliveries to commerce sixty days after award of contract and receipt of specifications giving size of disc, or earlier if dies required for the discs can be made in less than sixty days.

Six hundred pounds to be delivered daily; but if not sufficient the amount will be increased to 1,200 pounds daily.

CHIEF OF ORDNANCE, *Washington, D. C.*

OFFICE OF THE CHIEF OF ORDNANCE, U. S. ARMY,
                                        Washington, December 8, 1898.

GENTLEMEN: Referring to your proposal of 9th ultimo, under advertisement from this office of 3d ultimo, I inclose a contract in quintuplicate for 100,000 pounds of compressed gun cotton for execution by you and return to this office for completion.

Respectfully,

                                                                          D. W. FLAGLER,
                                                           Brigadier-General, Chief of Ordnance.

DITTMAR POWDER WORKS,
         62 Liberty Street, New York City.

NEW YORK, *December 13, 1898.*

DEAR SIR: In reply to yours of the 12th instant, we have requested Captain Stuart to forward you, direct, specifications for compressed gun cotton covering contract of December 8.   As soon as these are received, or you arrive at a conclusion, please advise us, giving particulars as to press required for the purpose so that we can order same.

Will speak to the One hundred and thirtieth street office about check.

Very truly, yours,

DITTMAR POWDER WORKS,
G. F. HAMLIN, General Agent.

Prof. CHAS. E. MUNROE,
Columbian University, Washington, D. C.

Specifications for compressed gun cotton for shell charges.

[Prescribed by the Ordnance Department, U. S. Army.]

Inspection.—The Chief of Ordnance will designate an officer as inspector. The manufacture of the gun cotton in all its details must be open to inspection by the designated inspector, who will take such samples of the materials at any stage of manufacture as he may desire. The contractor shall deliver such samples at Frankford Arsenal, free of cost to the United States, when so required by the inspector.

Nitration.—The gun cotton must be of the highest practicable nitration, containing always more than 13 per cent of nitrogen, estimated on a dry sample. It must be clean, free from foreign substances, and generally of the best quality.

Stability.—The gun cotton must withstand successfully the following test: Heated to a temperature of 150° to 155° F., it must not produce any discoloration of potassium iodide starch paper partly moistened with dilute glycerin in less than twenty minutes.

Chemical tests made by the Ordnance Department according to its standard methods will be regarded as standard for the purposes of these specifications.

Density.—The gun cotton must be compressed to a density when dry of about 1.1, always exceeding that of water.

Size and shape.—The compressed blocks must be of such practicable size and shape as may be required by the Chief of Ordnance, U. S. Army, to obtain the most suitable loading of the projectile.

Packing.—The gun cotton is to be packed for delivery in zinc-lined boxes sealed with a rubber gasket of such pattern as the Chief of Ordnance may require.

D. W. FLAGLER,
Brigadier-General, Chief of Ordnance.

OFFICE OF THE CHIEF OF ORDNANCE, U. S. ARMY,
War Department, May 24, 1898.

Articles of agreement entered into this eighth day of December, eighteen hundred and ninety-eight, between Dittmar Powder Works, of New York, in the county of New York, State of New York, of the first part, and the United States, by Brig. Gen. D. W. Flagler, Chief of Ordnance, U. S. Army, acting under the direction and by authority of the Secretary of War, for and in their behalf, of the second part.

First. This agreement witnesseth, that the said party of the first part, for themselves and their successors, etc., and the said party of the second part, for and in behalf of the United States of America, have mutually agreed, and by these presents do mutually covenant and agree, to and with each other as follows, viz:

Under advertisement dated November 3, 1898, the said party of the first part does hereby contract and engage with the said United States to manufacture for the Ordnance Department, U. S. Army, and deliver at the United States powder depot, Dover, N. J.; the Sandy Hook Proving Ground, Sandy Hook, N. J., or such other place as may be designated by the Chief of Ordnance, U. S. Army, 100,000 pounds of compressed gun cotton for filling shells, in accordance with the specifications hereto attached and forming part of this contract, viz:

In the form of cylindrical discs of stated diameters, and in the form of conical discs of stated diameters, at sixty-four (64) cents per pound.

In the form of small prismatic blocks about three-fourths of an inch square, and from one-fourth to one inch long, coated to prevent their breaking up by handling, at sixty-five (65) cents per pound.

The weight of gun cotton to be dry weight.

Deliveries to commence within sixty (60) days after date of contract, and to be continued at the rate of six hundred (600) pounds daily, to be increased to twelve hundred (1200) pounds if desired by the Chief of Ordnance, U. S. Army, until the whole amount is delivered.

The gun cotton will be required to pass the usual inspection by the Ordnance Department and will be subject to such modifications as to density, etc., not affecting the cost of production, as the Department may prescribe.

It is further stipulated and agreed that the party of the first part will furnish such additional gun cotton as above, and at the prices and rates of delivery stated, as the party of the second part may desire, under available appropriations.

If any doubts or disputes arise as to the meaning of anything in this or any of the papers hereunto attached and forming this contract the matter shall be at once referred to the Chief of Ordnance, U. S. Army, for determination. If, however, the party of the first part shall feel aggrieved at any decision of the Chief of Ordnance it shall have the right to submit the same to the Secretary of War, and his decision shall be final.

Second. All the gun cotton herein contracted for shall be delivered by the party of the first part as aforementioned.

Third. The said party of the first part shall indemnify the United States and all persons acting under them for all liability on account of any patent rights granted by the United States which may affect the gun cotton herein contracted for.

Fourth. For the gun cotton herein contracted for, which shall be delivered, inspected, and accepted as aforesaid, there shall be paid by the United States to the said party of the first part, on bills in duplicate, made in approved form and duly authenticated by the proper officers of the Ordnance Department, the price aforementioned in the funds furnished for the purpose by the United States.

Fifth. If any default shall be made by the party of the first part in delivering all or any of the gun cotton mentioned in this contract, of the quality and at the times and places herein specified, then, in that case, the said party of the second part may supply the deficiency by purchase in open market or otherwise (the articles so procured to be of the kind herein specified as near as practicable), and the said party of the first part shall be charged with the expense resulting from such failure. Nothing contained in this stipulation shall be construed to prevent the Chief of Ordnance at his option, upon the happening of any such default, from declaring this contract to be thereafter null and void without affecting the right of the United States to recover for defaults which have occurred, but in case of overwhelming and unforeseen accident by fire or otherwise, the circumstances shall be taken into equitable consideration by the United States before claiming forfeiture for nondelivery at the time specified.

Sixth. Neither this contract nor any interest therein shall be transferred by the said party of the first part to any other party, and any such transfer shall cause the annulment of the contract so far as the United States are concerned. All rights of action, however, to recover for any breach of this contract by the said party of the first part are reserved to the United States.

Seventh. No Member of or Delegate to Congress, nor any person belonging to or employed in the military service of the United States, is or shall be admitted to any share or part of this contract, or to any benefit which may arise herefor.

DITTMAR POWDER WORKS,
By MARIA W. DITTMAR, *Owner.*

Witness:
G. F. HAMLIN.

D. W. FLAGLER,
Brigadier-General, Chief of Ordnance.

Know all men by these presents that we, Dittmar Powder Works, by Maria W. Dittmar, owner, of the State of New York, as principal, and Dennis W. Moran, residing at No. 563 Buckhout street, in the city, county, and State of New York, and Michael McGrath, residing at No. 216 East One hundred and fourteenth street, in said city, county, and State, as sureties, are held and firmly bound unto the United States of America in the penal sum of seven thousand dollars, to the payment of which sum, well and truly to be made, we bind ourselves and our successors, jointly and severally, firmly by these presents.

The condition of this obligation is such that whereas the above-bounden Dittmar Powder Works has, on the 8th day of December, 1898, entered into a contract with the United States, represented by Brig. Gen. D. W. Flagler, for gun cotton.

Now, therefore, if the above-bounden Dittmar Powder Works and their successors, etc., shall and will in all respects duly and fully observe and perform all and singular the covenants, conditions, and agreements in and by the said contract agreed and covenanted by said Dittmar Powder Works, to be observed and performed according to the true intent and meaning of the said contract, and as well during any period of extension of said contract that may be granted on the part of the United States as during the original term of the same, then the above obligation shall be void and of no effect; otherwise to remain in full force and virtue.

In witness whereof the parties hereto have executed this instrument this 23d day of January, 1899, their respective names and seals being hereto affixed.

DITTMAR POWDER WORKS,
By MARIA W. DITTMAR, *Owner.*

In presence of—
JAMES KEARNEY.

DENNIS W. MORAN,
By MICHAEL McGRATH.

STATE OF NEW YORK, *City and County of New York, ss:*

Dennis W. Moran and Michael McGrath, being each duly sworn, each for himself, deposes and says that he is a resident of the city of New York and a freeholder within the State of New York, and is worth the sum of fourteen thousand dollars, being double the amount of the foregoing bond, over all his just debts and liabilities and exclusive of property exempt by law from levy and sale under an execution.

DENNIS W. MORAN.
MICHAEL McGRATH.

Subscribed and sworn to before me this 23d day of January, A. D. 1899.

JAS. I. McNEIRNY,
Notary Public, New York County.

STATE OF NEW YORK, *City and County of New York, ss:*

I, the undersigned, a justice of the supreme court of the State of New York, the same being a court of record, having common-law jurisdiction, a clerk, and a seal, do hereby certify that Dennis W. Moran and Michael McGrath, the sureties named in the foregoing bond are known to me and that to the best of my knowledge and belief are pecuniarily worth, over and above all their just debts and liabilities, the sum stated in their affidavit of justification.

Dated New York, January 23, 1899.

H. W. BOOKSTAVER,
Justice of the Supreme Court of the State of New York.

STATE OF NEW YORK, *County of New York, ss:*

I, William Sohmer, clerk of the county of New York, and also clerk of the supreme court for the said county, the same being a court of record, do hereby certify that James L. McNeirny, before whom the annexed deposition was taken, was at the time of taking the same a notary public of New York, dwelling in said county, duly appointed and sworn and authorized to administer oaths to be used in any court in said State and for general purposes; that I am well acquainted with the handwriting of said notary, and that his signature thereto is genuine, as I verily believe.

In testimony whereof I have hereunto set my hand and affixed the seal of the said court and county the 28th day of January, 1899.

WM. SOHMER, *Clerk.*

STATE OF NEW YORK, *County of New York, ss:*

I, William Sohmer, clerk of the county of New York, and also clerk of the supreme court for the said county, do hereby certify that H. W. Bookstaver, before whom the annexed deposition was taken, was at the time of taking the same a justice of the supreme court of the State of New York, duly elected and sworn and authorized to administer oaths to be used in any court in said State and for general purposes; that I am well acquainted with the handwriting of said justice, and that his signature thereto is genuine, as I verily believe.

In testimony whereof I have hereunto set my hand and affixed the seal of the said court and county the 28th day of January, 1899.

WM. SOHMER, *Clerk.*

OFFICE OF INSPECTOR OF POWDER, U. S. ARMY,
Wilmington, Del., February 18, 1899.

GENTLEMEN: I have the honor to inclose herewith duplicate copy of contract, dated December 8, 1898, for 100,000 pounds of compressed gun cotton. I am appointed inspector under this contract, and correspondence relating thereto should, as a matter of convenience and saving time, be conducted with or through this office.

We have not yet determined in what form we shall want this gun cotton. I can not, therefore, at present inform you the size and shape of the disks or whether we shall want any of it in the form of pellets. As soon as the matter is determined I will give you the necessary information so that you can go ahead.

Very respectfully,

SIDNEY E. STUART,
Captain, Ordnance Department, U. S. Army, Inspector.

The DITTMAR POWDER COMPANY, *New York, N. Y.*

————

NEW YORK, *February 20, 1899.*

DEAR SIR: We are in receipt of yours of the 18th instant with inclosure of duplicate copy of contract, December 8, 1898, for 100,000 pounds of compressed gun cotton.

We note that you have not yet determined what form you desire this gun cotton, and we wish you would inform us when we may expect to have the size and shape of the disks, or if you desire any of the cotton in the form of pellets. We were in hopes that we would have received this information some time ago, as it will take quite some time to have the disks, etc., manufactured.

Awaiting your reply, we remain,

Very truly, yours,

DITTMAR POWDER WORKS.
C. H. DITTMAR.

Capt. SYDNEY E. STUART,
Office of Inspector of Powder, U. S. Army, Wilmington, Del.

————

THE COLUMBIAN UNIVERSITY,
Washington, D. C., April 14, 1899.

DEAR SIR: I have seen Major Smith and had an opportunity of getting very detailed information concerning the series of accidents and the trials that it is now proposed to make. It must be considerable time before a definite opinion can be reached on the size, shape, and composition of the powder grains, so that you will now have ample time for the development of the navy powder.

I also brought up the gun cotton matter and urged that a speedy decision be made as to the form in which it is wanted, so that you could begin filling your contract. Tell me how direct and easy railroad connection from Farmingdale to Sandy Hook is, as I have a scheme in my mind that may be of value to you.

Yours, truly,

CHARLES E. MUNROE.

Capt. G. F. HAMLIN,
General Agent Dittmar Powder and Chemical Company,
203 Broadway, New York.

————

ARMY BUILDING, *New York, December 4, 1899.*

DEAR SIRS: On the 18th of November I forwarded to you a letter from the Chief of Ordnance, U. S. Army, requesting to know if you desired to have canceled your contract with the Ordnance Department for 100,000 pounds of gun cotton. No reply has been received to this communication and I write to ask whether you have decided to allow the contract to be canceled as requested.

Very respectfully,   O. B. MITCHAM,
Captain of Ordnance, U. S. Army.

The DITTMAR POWDER AND CHEMICAL COMPANY,
No. 203 Broadway, New York.

NEW YORK, *December 6, 1899.*

DEAR SIR: We beg to acknowledge receipt of yours of the 4th instant, referring to contract for 100,000 pounds of gun cotton.

We beg to advise you that we have no desire to have this contract canceled, and are ready at any time to commence the manufacture of same on receipt of specifications as to what you will require as covered by the terms of the contract.

You will note under the terms of this contract and bid the manufacture was to commence sixty days after receipt of specifications as to form of disks required and method of packing, etc., and when the Department advises us, giving this information, we expect to put our plant in shape and be able to fulfill the terms of the contract.

Hoping this may be satisfactory, we are,

Very truly, yours,

DITTMAR POWDER AND CHEMICAL COMPANY.

Capt. O. B. MITCHAM,

Ordnance Department, U. S. Army, Army Building, New York, Room A.

NEW YORK, *February 21, 1900.*

DEAR SIR: Referring to our contract with the Ordnance Department for 100,000 pounds of compressed gun cotton, in response to your telephone message, we have no desire to cancel contract in question; in fact, are ready to commence to manufacture at any time on receipt of specifications as to form of disks, etc., required by the Department.

We have everything ready to commence the manufacture of gun cotton, and have the hydraulic press and necessary pumps, which will only require to be placed in position, so that as soon as the dies can be made we can commence to manufacture; but of course nothing can be done about the dies until the Department advises us as to the size of the disks required.

Hoping this may be satisfactory, we are,

Very truly, yours,

DITTMAR POWDER AND CHEMICAL COMPANY,

G. F. HAMLIN, *General Manager.*

Capt. O. B. MITCHAM,

Room 4, Army Building, New York.

[Second indorsement.]

OFFICE OF THE CHIEF OF ORDNANCE,

Washington, March 6, 1900.

Respectfully returned to Capt. O. B. Mitcham, Room E-4, Army building, New York City, with instructions to ascertain from the Dittmar Powder and Chemical Company what expense they have incurred in making preparations for the manufacture of this gun cotton, with a view to making satisfactory arrangements for the cancellation of this contract, if possible, by the Department assuming its proportion of the cost of said preparations, as the gun cotton to be furnished under this contract is not required by the Department, and it is most desirable that the contract should, if practicable, be canceled.

A. R. BUFFINGTON,

Brigadier-General, Chief of Ordnance.

Official copy respectfully furnished the Dittmar Powder and Chemical Company for their information in connection with personal conversation with their Mr. G. F. Hamlin, this date.

O. B. MITCHAM,

Captain, Ordnance Department, U. S. Army.

SPRINGFIELD ARMORY,

Springfield, Mass., March 10, 1900.

DEAR SIR: I shall be at my office in the Army building on Monday. Please call to see me as I wish to have an interview with you. Telephone Monday morning so that I shall not be away from the office when you come. I leave the city Monday evening or Tuesday morning.

Very truly,

O. B. MITCHAM, *Ordnance.*

Mr. G. F. HAMLIN,

General Manager Dittmar Powder and Chemical Company,

203 Broadway, New York.

ARMY BUILDING, *New York, April 19, 1900.*
SIRS: I had a conversation with your representative, Mr. Hamlin, on March 12, 1900, with reference to making some arrangements for the cancellation of the gun-cotton contract between the Ordnance Department and your company. Since that time nothing further has been heard from your firm, and I beg to ask what steps you have taken, or propose to take, to lead to the cancellation of this contract, as desired by the Chief of Ordnance.
Very respectfully,   O. B. MITCHAM,
                                        Captain, Ordnance Department, U. S. Army.
The DITTMAR POWDER AND CHEMICAL COMPANY,
                        203 Broadway, New York.

NEW YORK, *May 17, 1900.*
DEAR SIR: In reply to yours of April 19 and conversation on March 12, 1900, we have gone over carefully cost of our plant for making gun cotton, and find we have spent in cash $30,700. This, we think, will cover inquiry of the Chief of Ordnance, second indorsement, Washington, March 6, 1900, and we are ready at any time to consider a proposition referring to our contract for gun cotton to bring about the result desired by the Chief of Ordnance.
Hoping this may be satisfactory, we are,
Very truly, yours,
                                        DITTMAR POWDER AND CHEMICAL COMPANY.
                                        G F. HAMLIN, *General Manager.*
Capt. O. B. MITCHAM,
    Ordnance Department, U. S. Army, Room 4, Army Building, New York City.

ARMY BUILDING, *New York, May 25, 1900.*
DEAR SIRS: Your letter of May 17, 1900, written to me regarding the gun-cotton contract between your firm and the Ordnance Department of the Army, was sent by me to the Chief of Ordnance, U. S. Army. In reply, the latter informs me that the matter is not in a sufficiently advanced state to necessitate a personal interview in Washington with a representative of your company. The Department desires to obtain a full statement of what work has been done in preparing for the contract, in detail if practicable, and what proportion of the cost should, in your opinion, be fairly borne by the Department. This letter should then be submitted through this office to the Chief of Ordnance, U. S. Army, Washington, D. C.
Very respectfully,
                                                     O. B. MITCHAM,
                                        Captain, Ordnance Department, U. S. Army.
The DITTMAR POWDER AND CHEMICAL COMPANY,
                        203 Broadway, New York.

NEW YORK, *February 13, 1901.*
DEAR SIR: We inclose statement of "construction for the purpose of manufacturing gun cotton," addressed to the Chief of Ordnance, U. S. Army, Washington, D. C., duly signed as requested by you.
We regret not being able to obtain this earlier.
Very truly, yours,
                                        DITTMAR POWDER AND CHEMICAL COMPANY,
                                        L. H. ELLINGWOOD, *Treasurer.*
Capt. O. B. MITCHAM,
    Ordnance Department, Army Building, New York.

NEW YORK, *February 7, 1901.*

DEAR SIR: At the request of Capt. O. B. Mitcham, Ordnance Department, we herewith send you statement of construction for the purpose of manufacturing gun cotton under your contract.

Nitrating house complete, with pots, troughs, wringer, engine, etc.:
1 8-inch artesian well, 1,000 feet deep.
1 air compressor and air lift for pumping water.
1 water tank and tower.
1 Horne heating engine and building containing boiling tubs, etc.
1 150-horsepower Babcock & Wilcox pattern boiler.
1 cotton dry house, blower, heater, etc.
1 press, pumps, etc., for compressing gun cotton.
1 pulp house.
1 storehouse, pipe lines for steam, water, and air.
400 feet of railroad track.
Storage tanks for acid.

Making a total expenditure of about $30,700.

It will be impossible for us to give this cost in detail without going over the books for the past two years, but we have already gone over the matter for the purpose of procuring the above information.

Very truly, yours,

DITTMAR POWDER AND CHEMICAL COMPANY,
G. F. HAMLIN, *General Manager.*

CHIEF OF ORDNANCE, U. S. ARMY, *Washington, D. C.*

(Through Capt. O. B. Mitcham, Ordnance Department, U. S. Army, Army Building, New York.)

STATE OF NEW YORK, *County of New York, ss:*

George F. Hamlin, being duly sworn, says that he has read the annexed letter signed by him, and that the statements therein contained are true, to his own knowledge.

G. F. HAMLIN.

Sworn to before me this 7th day of February, 1901.

SAML. RIKER, Jr., *Notary Public.*

STATE OF NEW YORK, *County of New York, ss:*

Marie W. Dittmar, being duly sworn, says that she has read the annexed letter signed by George F. Hamlin, and that the statements therein contained are true to her own knowledge.

MARIE W. DITTMAR.

Sworn to before me this 13th day of February, 1901.

JAS. CARNEY, *Notary Public.*

STATE OF NEW YORK, *County of New York, ss:*

Carl H. Dittmar, being duly sworn, says that he has read the annexed letter signed by George F. Hamlin, and that the statements therein contained are true to his own knowledge.

CARL H. DITTMAR.

Sworn to before me this 13th day of February, 1901.

JAS. CARNEY, *Notary Public.*

NEW YORK, *May 7, 1901.*

SIR: Referring to statement of cost of construction of plant for manufacture of compressed gun cotton for Ordnance Department, under contract made 1898, sent you on February 13, 1901, at your request, through Captain Mitcham, Ordnance Department: This was forwarded at your suggestion to enable you to arrive at some decision as to what would be a fair cash compensation to us to pay in part for our outlay in constructing plant, as the Department did not now desire the explosives contracted for and wished the contract canceled.

We would be glad if you would advise us what disposition has been made of the matter.

Very truly,   DITTMAR POWDER AND CHEMICAL COMPANY.
                                     G. F. HAMLIN, General Manager.

CHIEF OF ORDNANCE U. S. ARMY, Washington, D. C.

(Through Captain Mitcham, Ordnance Department, Army building, New York.)

                                               ARMY BUILDING,
                                          New York, May 17, 1901.

SIRS: Your letter of the 7th instant to the Chief of Ordnance U. S. Army, Washington, D. C., in connection with your claim regarding contract made in 1898 for compressed gun cotton for the Ordnance Department, has been returned to this office with the following indorsement:

[Second indorsement.]

                          "OFFICE OF THE CHIEF OF ORDNANCE,
                                     "Washington, May 15, 1901.

"Respectfully returned to the inspector of powder, U. S. Army, Army building, New York City, referring to the reports previously made by him on this subject. The contract with the Dittmar Powder Works expired by limitation, and not only that, but the appropriation from which the contract was to be paid will lapse on the 30th of June, and even if allowed to go on it is not at all probable that any cotton could be produced.

"It is recognized that the company did go to certain expense in preparation for this contract, but their claim is not such a one as the law permits the Department to settle. It would either have to be adjudicated in the Court of Claims or else appeal to Congress for an appropriation to reimburse them. This latter course would be the better one for the company, and this office would be inclined to favorably recommend a fair claim in that direction."

This indorsement is furnished for your information and guidance.

Very respectfully,

                                               O. B. MITCHAM,
                                     Captain, Ordnance Department, U. S. Army.

DITTMAR POWDER AND CHEMICAL COMPANY,
              203 Broadway, New York.

                                          NEW YORK, December 7, 1901.

DEAR SIR: Referring to yours of May 17, 1901, regarding an appeal to Congress for an appropriation to reimburse us in part for expenses in preparation for contract for 100,000 pounds of compressed gun cotton:

As the Chief of Ordnance states in his indorsement on our letter of May 7 that such an appeal would be favored or approved by the Ordnance Department, on Wednesday last I was in Washington to make an effort to come to an agreement with the Department as to the amount we should ask from Congress.

I saw Major Smith and he advised us to confer with you, as you were familiar with our plant, etc., and better able to judge as to what amount would be a fair compensation for us.

It is our intention to introduce a bill in Congress now in session asking for an appropriation for $10,000, expecting that so small an amount will be acceptable to the Ordnance Department.

If this amount is satisfactory we would be glad to be advised to that effect, so we can have our bill introduced as soon as possible.

Very truly, yours,

                                     DITTMAR POWDER AND CHEMICAL COMPANY.
                                     G. F. HAMLIN, General Manager.

Capt. O. B. MITCHAM,
Inspector of Powder, U. S. Army, Army Building, New York, N. Y.

OFFICE OF THE CHIEF OF ORDNANCE, U. S. ARMY,
Washington, January 21, 1902.

GENTLEMEN: Referring to conversation had with your Mr. Hamlin on this date, I would state that when the bill which you propose to have introduced for reimbursement of expenses in connection with the preparation and manufacture of gun cotton, under contract with this Department, dated December 8, 1898, is referred here for report thereon, this office, in consideration of all the circumstances of the case, will be willing to recommend payment to you of a sum not exceeding $7,500.

Respectfully,

WILLIAM CROZIER,
Brigadier-General, Chief of Ordnance.

DITTMAR POWDER AND CHEMICAL COMPANY,
203 Broadway, New York City.

O

BILL REQUIRING RETURNS FROM CORPORATIONS, PROHIBITING REBATES, ETC.

JANUARY 26, 1903.—Committed to the Committee of the Whole House on the state
of the Union and ordered to be printed.

Mr. LITTLEFIELD, from the Committee on the Judiciary, submitted
the following

REPORT.

[To accompany H. R. 17. A bill requiring corporations engaged in interstate commerce to make returns, prohibiting rebates and discriminations and the use of interstate commerce in attempts to destroy competition, and for other purposes.]

Your committee have carefully considered all of the various bills
introduced in the House and referred to it relative to the question of
trusts and industrial combinations. They have given hearings to all
members introducing such measures and desiring to be heard. They
have also had several conferences with the Department of Justice with
reference to its suggestions in connection with the pending legislation.
The bill prepared by the committee is a substitute for H. R. 17. Its
purpose is to more effectively regulate and control, on conservative
lines, industrial and business combinations which in their operation
prove injurious to the public welfare. It is believed to be a decided
step in the advance of existing legislation. It involves the idea of
publicity, additional legislation to prevent discriminations by rebates
or special privileges, upon the part of railroad companies, and seeks
to prevent the effort to destroy competition in particular localities
by discrimination in prices, and prohibits railroad companies from
transporting goods in violation of the provisions of law, and contains
provisions intended to facilitate the enforcement of this act as well
as existing legislation upon the same lines.
The features of publicity upon the part of corporations engaged in
interstate commerce is contained in the first section of the bill. The
utility and necessity of publicity upon the part of corporations as
bearing upon the question of their relation to the public in the matter
of overcapitalization of great combinations, whose tendency is to
monopolize trade and oppress the public by the imposition of abnormal prices upon the products which are essential to the public convenience as well as necessary for its use, is one that has been widely
discussed. While no one claims that publicity in and of itself will
necessarily prove to be a specific for any of the evils which it is
expected to alleviate, there does, however, seem to be a general con-

sensus of opinion as to its necessity, both as a remedial measure and as one tending to lay the foundation for more intelligent legislative action in the line of direct control of such combinations.

PRESIDENT ROOSEVELT.

In discussing the general question of combinations and their relation to the public and the importance of publicity in connection therewith the idea was well stated by Theodore Roosevelt, in his message to the New York State legislature when governor of that State, on the 23d of January, 1900, as follows:

We do not wish to put any burden on honest corporations. Neither do we wish to put an unnecessary burden of responsibility on enterprising men for acts which are immaterial; they should be relieved from such burdens, but held to a rigid financial accountability for acts that mislead the upright investor or stockholder, or defraud the public.

The first essential is knowledge of the facts—publicity. Much can be done at once by amendment of the corporation laws so as to provide for such publicity as will not work injustice as between business rivals.

The chief abuses alleged to arise from trusts are probably the following: *Misrepresentation or concealment regarding material facts connected with the organization of an enterprise; the evils connected with unscrupulous promotion; overcapitalization;* unfair competition, resulting in the crushing out of competitors who themselves do not act improperly; raising of prices above fair competitive rates; the wielding of increased power over the wage-earners. * * * Some of these evils could be partially remedied by a modification of our corporation laws; here we can safely go along the lines of the more conservative New England States, and probably not a little further. Such laws will themselves provide the needed publicity and the needed circumstantiality of statement. *We should know authoritatively whether stock represents actual value of plants, or whether it represents brands, or good will; or, if not, what it does represent, if anything.* It is desirable to know how much was actually bought, how much was issued free, and to whom, and, if possible, for what reason. In the first place, this would be invaluable in preventing harm being done as among the stock-holders, for many of the grossest wrongs that are perpetrated are those of promoters and organizers at the expense of the general public who are invited to take shares in business organizations. * * * Care should be taken not to stifle enterprise or disclose any facts of a business that are essentially private; but the State for the protection of the public should exercise the right to inspect, to examine thoroughly all the workings of great corporations just as is now done with banks; and wherever the interests of the public demand it, it should publish the results of its examinations. Then, if there are inordinate profits, competition or public sentiment will give the public the benefit in lowered prices; and if not, the power of taxation remains. *It is therefore evident that publicity is the one sure and adequate remedy which we can now invoke.* There may be other remedies, but what these others are we can only find out by publicity, as the result of investigation. *The first requisite is knowledge, full and complete.*

Directly in line and consistent with these recommendations were those made by President Roosevelt in his first message to the first session of the Fifty-seventh Congress. In this message, in discussing this question, he said:

All this is true; and yet it is also true that there are real and grave evils, *one of the chief being overcapitalization because of its many baleful consequences;* and a resolute and practical effort must be made to correct these evils.

There is a widespread conviction in the minds of the American people that the great corporations known as trusts are in certain of their features and tendencies hurtful to the general welfare. This springs from no spirit of envy or uncharitableness, nor lack of pride in the great industrial achievements that have placed this country at the head of the nations struggling for commercial supremacy. It does not rest upon a lack of intelligent appreciation of the necessity of meeting changing and changed conditions of trade with new methods, nor upon ignorance of the fact that combination of capital in the effort to accomplish great things is necessary when the world's progress demands that great things be done. It is based upon sincere conviction that combination and concentration should be, not prohibited, but supervised and within reasonable limits controlled; and in my judgment this conviction is right.

It is no limitation upon property rights or freedom of contract to require that when men receive from Government the privilege of doing business under corporate form, which frees them from individual responsibility, and enables them to call into their enterprises the capital of the public, they shall do so upon absolutely truthful representations as to the value of the property in which the capital is to be invested. Corporations engaged in interstate commerce should be regulated if they are found to exercise a license working to the public injury. It should be as much the aim of those who seek for social betterment to rid the business world of crimes of cunning as to rid the entire body politic of crimes of violence. Great corporations exist only because they are created and safeguarded by our institutions; and it is therefore our right and our duty to see that they work in harmony with these institutions.

The first essential in determining how to deal with the great industrial combinations is knowledge of the facts—publicity. In the interest of the public the Government should have the right to inspect and examine the workings of the great corporations engaged in interstate business. *Publicity is the only sure remedy which we can now invoke.* What further remedies are needed in the way of governmental regulation or taxation can only be determined after publicity has been obtained, by process of law and in the course of administration. *The first requisite is knowledge, full and complete—knowledge which may be made public to the world.*

In his message to the second session of the present Congress upon this subject, he said:

In my message to the present Congress at its first session I discussed at length the question of the regulation of those big corporations commonly doing an interstate business, often with some tendency to monopoly, which are popularly known as trusts. *The experience of the past year has emphasized, in my opinion, the desirability of the steps I then proposed.* * * * A fundamental base of civilization is the inviolability of property; but this is in no wise inconsistent with the right of society to regulate the exercise of the artificial powers which it confers upon the owners of property, under the name of corporate franchises, in such a way as to prevent the misuse of these powers. Corporations, and especially combinations of corporations, should be managed under public regulation. Experience has shown that under our system of government the necessary supervision can not be obtained by State action. It must therefore be achieved by national action. * * * *Publicity can do no harm to the honest corporation, and we need not be over tender about sparing the dishonest corporation.* * * *

I believe that monopolies, unjust discriminations which prevent or cripple competition, fraudulent overcapitalization, and other evils in trust organizations and practices which injuriously affect interstate trade can be prevented under the power of the Congress to "regulate commerce with foreign nations and among the several States" through regulations and requirements operating directly upon such commerce, the instrumentalities thereof, and those engaged therein.

ATTORNEY-GENERAL KNOX.

Attorney-General Knox, a clear-headed and able lawyer and especially familiar with great corporate organizations, in his Pittsburg speech October 14, 1902, advocated publicity as a leading feature in the line of remedies. In discussing this branch of the question, he said:

The conspicuous noxious features of trusts existent and possible are these: *Overcapitalization, lack of publicity of operation,* discrimination in prices to destroy competition, insufficient personal responsibility of officers and directors for corporate management, tendency to monopoly, and lack of appreciation in their management of their relations to the people, for whose benefit they are permitted to exist.

Overcapitalization is the chief of these and the source from which the minor ones flow. It is the possibility of overcapitalization that furnishes the temptations and opportunities for most of the others. Overcapitalization does not mean large capitalization or capitalization adequate for the greatest undertakings. *It is the imposition upon an undertaking of a liability without a corresponding asset to represent it. Therefore overcapitalization is a fraud upon those who contribute the real capital either originally or by purchase, and the efforts to realize dividends thereon from operations is a fraudulent imposition of a burden upon the public.* When a property worth a million dollars upon all the sober tests of value is capitalized at five millions and sold to the public, it is rational to assume that its purchasers will exert every effort to keep its earnings up to the basis of their capitalization.   When the inevitable depression comes, wages must be reduced, prices enhanced, or dividends foregone.   As prices are naturally not increased but lowered in dull periods, it usually resolves itself into a question of wages or dividends.

While this condition may exist under any circumstances, it is exaggerated by over-capitalization in the illustrating case five to one.   *The overcapitalized securities enter into the general budget of the country, are bought and sold, rise and fall, and they fluctuate between wider ranges and are more sensitive in proportion as they are further removed from intrinsic values, and, in short, are liable to be storm centers of financial disturbances of far-reaching consequence.   They also, in the same proportion, increase the temptation to mismanagement and manipulation by corporate administrators.*

In discussing the remedy, he said:

They should be subject to visitorial supervision, and full and accurate information as to their operations should be made regularly at reasonable intervals.   Secrecy in the conduct and results of operation is unfair to the nonmanaging stockholders, and should, as well for reasons of state, be prohibited by law.

INDUSTRIAL COMMISSION.

The Industrial Commission, after a very long and exhaustive investigation and mature consideration of the whole question, made, early in 1900, certain recommendations in accordance with the requirements of the statute under which they were acting, on this point saying:

To prevent the organizers of corporations or industrial combinations from deceiving investors and the public, either through suppression of material facts or by making misleading statements, your Commission recommend—

(a) That the promoters and organizers of corporations or industrial combinations which look to the public to purchase or deal in their stocks or securities should be required to furnish full details regarding the organization, the property or services for which stocks or securities are to be issued, amount and kind of same, and all other material information necessary for safe and intelligent investment.

(b) That any prospectus or announcement of any kind soliciting subscriptions which fails to make full disclosures as aforesaid, or which is false, should be deemed fraudulent, and the promoters with their associates held legally responsible.

(c) That the nature of the business of the corporation or industrial combination, all powers granted to directors and officers thereof, and all limitations upon them or upon the rights or powers of the members should be required to be expressed in the certificate of incorporation, which instrument should be open to inspection by any investor. * * *

The larger corporations—the so-called trusts—should be required to publish annually a properly audited report, showing in reasonable detail their assets and liabilities, with profit or loss, such report and audit under oath to be subject to Government inspection.   The purpose of such publicity is to encourage competition when profits become excessive, thus protecting consumers against too high prices and to guard the interests of employees by a knowledge of the financial condition of the business in which they are employed.

On February 10, 1902, this Commission in its final report, said—

The further consideration given to the subject by the Commission has justified in nearly all particulars our former conclusions and recommendations.

It recommended the establishment of a bureau, the duties of which should be—

To register all State corporations engaged in interstate or foreign commerce; to secure from such corporations all reports needed to enable the Government to levy a franchise tax with certainty and justice and to collect the same; to make such inspection and examination of the business and accounts of such corporations as will guarantee the completeness and accuracy of the information needed to ascertain whether such corporations are observing the conditions prescribed in the act and to enforce penalties against delinquents, and to collate and publish information regarding such combinations and the industries in which they may be engaged, so as to furnish to the Congress proper information for possible future legislation.

The publicity secured by the governmental agency should be such as will prevent the deception of the public through secrecy in the organization and management of industrial combinations or through false information.   Such agency would also have at its command the best sources of information regarding special privileges or discriminations, of whatever nature, by which industrial combinations secure monopoly or become dangers to the public welfare. It is probable that the provisions herein recommended will be sufficient to remove most of the abuses which have arisen in connection with industrial combinations. The remedies suggested may be employed with little or no danger to industrial prosperity and with the certainty of securing information which should enable the Congress to protect the public by further legislation, if necessary.

In conclusion, after having further discussed the whole question, it said:

In the meantime the separate States should amend their corporation laws *so as to require greater publicity*, as outlined in our preliminary report.

thus emphasizing the importance and necessity of publicity.

JOHN D. ROCKEFELLER.

Even Mr. John D. Rockefeller, who is understood to be at the head of one of the largest industrial corporations in existence, in effect advised publicity in his statement before the Industrial Commission. In his answer to the following question, "What legislation, if any, would you suggest regarding industrial combinations?" he said:

First. Federal legislation under which corporations may be created and regulated, if that be possible.
Second. In lieu thereof, State legislation as nearly uniform as possible, encouraging combinations of persons and capital for the purpose of carrying on industries, *but permitting State supervision*, not of a character to hamper industries, *but sufficient to prevent frauds upon the public*.

Publicity, such as is provided for in this bill, would seem to be one of the most feasible methods of preventing frauds upon the public. In the absence of State supervision "as nearly uniform as possible" the only thing that can take its place is Federal legislation operating uniformly upon all State corporations engaged in interstate commerce, which is precisely the idea involved in the legislation recommended.

MR. DILL.

Mr. Dill, who has had very large experience in the organization of corporations, is the author of several works upon corporations, and was the attorney organizing the United States Steel Company, testifying upon the question of overcapitalization before the Industrial Commission, said:

Q. From your experience in the organization of some of the large corporations have you been able to form any judgment on the question of overcapitalization, as to whether or not they are in many cases capitalized for considerably more than the real value of the properties put in?—A. If you will let me answer that question in my own way, I will do so by saying that there are corporations and corporations. There are very many corporations, which we will call combines, which are organized on a basis that presents no dangerous aspects to the public; but there are very many also organized with a good deal of capital that, in my judgment, *if not intended originally for fraudulent purposes, will become the cause of fraudulent action.*
Q. Will you explain that a little more in detail?—A. I assume that there are corporations that are grossly overcapitalized for various reasons and with various purposes. *Any corporation that is grossly overcapitalized is presumably organized in the first instance for the purpose of getting the stock to the public. Now, in order to get such stock to the public, there must be either a misrepresentation of facts, or, what in my judgment is just as bad, a concealment of material facts; and in my judgment in many of the so-called combines there is a concealment of material facts.*

Q. Do you base that opinion on what has come under your own observation?—A. Yes; if you do not take that answer to mean that I am of that opinion with respect to corporations I have organized myself. I have declined many organizations. Now, without calling names at all, a corporation was brought to my attention—I will say two months ago, so as not to bring it too near—concerning which, after a careful examination of the assets, *the conclusion was reached in our office that $500,000 would be a maximum fair valuation. We declined to organize that corporation for $8,000,000 and float it.* I should not want to be brought into any unpleasant position by having you ask the name; but it is advertised before the public to-day at $8,000,000. *Well, I do not know from reading the prospectus that any man could be indicted for making false representations; but I do know it lacks dreadfully in the statement of material facts—facts that the public ought to know.*

Q. Does this overcapitalization and misrepresentation, in your judgment, chiefly affect the buyers of stock, or does it affect the consumers of goods through prices?— A. *It affects industry in general, and I can not agree with very many of my colleagues, who say that the question of the amount of capitalization is simply a matter of adjustment with the public;* because the ordinary company, largely capitalized, does not, as a rule, have the same directors as it has at first. It does not, as a rule, consist of exactly the same men the second year as the first. Now, whoever is in office as a director the first or second year feels it necessary, in order to keep his standing, and especially with concerns that have a Wall street end, either to make a showing of a dividend earned or to declare one that is not earned. In other words, so far as the race with honest competitors is concerned, the fraudulently capitalized company is bound to make an equal showing of honest earnings; *and it results either in a robbing of the capital or in a resorting to artificial means to earn that dividend, which artificial means commonly consist, in addition to putting up the price of material, in putting down the price of labor. So, I say, I can not agree with the statement so frequently made, that the question of capital is merely a matter of adjustment. Inflation always, in my judgment, leads to a material error and possible wrongdoing.*

Mr. Dill's experience with great corporations has led him to the conclusion that publicity in connection therewith is both necessary and proper. In another part of his testimony before the Commission he made the following statement:

The English law, which in my judgment will have to be passed in all States that desire to stand as proper charter-granting States, is about as follows: All stock issued by any company, in whosesoever hands it shall be or shall come, shall be deemed to be held subject to be paid in full in cash, unless before the stock is issued a contract shall have been filed in the office of the company, and *open to the public, which shall show which part of the stock has been issued for cash and which for property, and which* shall disclose the character and value of the property thus taken. The statute then goes on to provide that anybody may have a copy of that contract on payment of a fixed fee. That is publicity.

This statement of his is a fairly good general description of the publicity provided for in this bill, except that it goes further than the provisions of the bill.

CHICAGO TRUST CONFERENCE.

Sometime in 1900 there was held in Chicago what has since been known as a trust conference, in which the question of combinations and business conditions connected therewith was quite fully discussed. Mr. Howe, of New Orleans, a lawyer of ability and experience, was chairman of the conference. At its conclusion he summed up its results by saying:

It seems to me—simply as an individual, of course—that almost every paper or address we have heard has made some admissions or concessions which may form a basis for some conclusions, and if you will allow me I will formulate some of them, as follows:

Upon the question of overcapitalization, he said:

As for issues of stock, they should be safeguarded in every possible way. They should only be allowed either for money or for property actually received by the company, and dollar for dollar. And when the property is so conveyed it should be on an honest appraisement of actual value, so that there may be no watering of stock.

Upon the question of publicity relating to the business condition of corporations, he said, as a final summing up of his conclusions as to what was in substance agreed upon by all of the parties to the conference:

4. *And finally there should be a thorough system of reports and Government inspection, especially as to issues of bonds and stock and the status and value of property.* Yet at the same time, in the matter of trading, business, and industrial companies, there are many legitimate secrets which must be respected by the general public.

In short, we need frankly to recognize the fact that trading and industrial corporations are needed to organize the activities of our country, and they are not to be scolded or be belied, but controlled, as we control steam and electricity, which are also dangerous if not carefully managed, but of wonderful usefulness if rightly harnessed to the car of progress.

What he meant by control is very obvious, as he emphasizes the idea as to what control should be imposed when he says that the "*reports and Government inspection, especially as to issues of bonds and stock and the status and value of property,*" should be thorough.

The only publicity that is now required with reference to corporate organizations is that required by the interstate-commerce law with reference to railroad companies engaged in interstate commerce, by the Statutes of the United States with reference to national banks, and by the various States with reference to banks, building and loan associations, insurance companies, railroad companies, other public-service corporations and business corporations.

The returns required from railroad companies under the interstate-commerce law are as "to issues of bonds and stock and the status and value of property." While these are directed to the business condition of the corporation, they are not as full and complete as the requirements under this bill. These returns are not required by the statute to be made on oath. While the Commission may require an oath thereto and does, it is not a requirement of the law; such an oath, even if false, could not be punished as perjury and adds nothing to the verity of the return. The returns now filed under these conditions with that Commission are practically valueless for the purpose of disclosing the financial condition of the railroad corporation and its capital stock. A statement by the corporation or one of its officers that has not behind it the obligations of a valid oath is of very trifling value for these purposes. The returns made by national banks and the supervisory power exercised over them under the Statutes of the United States are far more drastic and inquisitorial than the provisions of this bill. The returns made by and the examination of insurance companies by the various State authorities are also much more searching than the provisions of this bill. The same is true of building and loan associations and of State banks. All of these various institutions have had appar ently no difficulty in flourishing and prospering, notwithstanding the publicity involved by their returns and examinations. In the case of all meritorious organizations of that character, the returns and examinations have in fact facilitated rather than retarded their growth and success. The greater the publicity the more they have inspired public confidence.

The following abstract of the legislation of the various States will show to what extent publicity is required of the ordinary business corporation:

ALABAMA.

Annual return for taxation.—The president or chief officer of every corporation is required to make an annual return under oath to the assessors of the county where the corporation is located showing the number of shares of the capital stock and par value, names and residences of the stockholders, actual par value and market value of shares, date of the last sale with names of seller and purchaser and price obtained, amount of dividends declared for the last three years, value of shares as shown by the books of such corporation and by the last report of the officers to stockholders, amount of surplus, amount of undivided profits not included in surplus, together with sworn statement of all taxable property, real and personal estate in the State, and the valuation and assessment thereof. (§ 3942, Alabama Code.)

ARKANSAS.

President and secretary are required to make and file with the county clerk on or before February or August 15, annually, certificate showing the condition of the affairs of the corporation on January 1 or July 1, next preceding, containing the following particulars: Amount of capital stock actually paid in, cash value of real estate, cash value of personal estate, cash value of its credits, amount of indebtedness, names of shareholders and number of shares held by each. (Arkansas Statutes (Sanders & Hill, 1894), § 1337.)

Return for taxation.—In addition to the other property required to be listed, every corporation except those specially provided for shall, through the president, secretary, or principal accounting officer annually, during July, deliver to the assessor of the county a sworn statement of capital stock setting forth name and location of corporation, amount of capital stock authorized and number of shares, amount paid up, market value, or, if no market value, then the actual value, total indebtedness except current expenses, excluding from current expenses purchase or improvement of property, and true value of all tangible property belonging to such corporation. (§ 6462, Id.)

CALIFORNIA.

Every corporation shall keep an office in the State and books for the inspection of any person having an interest therein in which shall be recorded the amount of the capital stock subscribed and by whom, names of owners and amount owned by each, respectively, amount paid in and by whom, transfers, amount of assets and liabilities, and names and residences of officers. (Const. Art. 12, § 14.)

COLORADO.

An annual report shall be made within sixty days of January 1, showing amount of capital stock, names of officers, residences, and addresses, amount of capital stock, amount paid in and how paid, amount of indebtedness, whether in active business in the State, other information to show with fullness and reasonable certainty the condition of its real and personal property and financial condition. (Mills Annotated Statutes of Colorado, § 491.)

If stock issued for property at value, the facts to be stated in reports. § 490, id.

Foreign corporations to file copy of charter, etc. § 500, id. See also § 499, id.

Every corporation except those assessed by State assessors to make return, sworn to by president or officer, to assessor of county, containing a sworn statement and schedule showing name and location of corporation, amount of capital stock and number of shares, amount of capital stock paid in and bonds outstanding, market value of stock and bonds or actual value, total indebtedness except for current expenses, excluding purchase or improvement of property, value and location of all property, gross earnings for the year ending April 30 preceding, net earnings for the same period, difference in value between tangible property and capital stock, and the mortgage or bonded indebtedness, name and description of each franchise or privilege owned or enjoyed, and its value.

CONNECTICUT.

The president and secretary of every corporation not required to make a similar report to the general assembly or some officer, on or before the 15th of February or

August, shall file in the offices of the secretary of state and county clerk where located a certificate signed and sworn to by them (does not state where or before whom), showing condition on the 1st of December or January or June or July next preceding, and showing—

Amount of capital stock paid in—amount paid in cash and amount paid in property.
Cash value of real estate.
Name, residence, and number of shares of each stockholder.
Amount of its debts.
Cash value of personal estate.
Cash value of its credits. (General Statutes, § 3344.)

President and treasurer annually, on or before February 15 or August 15, shall file with the secretary of state and town clerk a certificate setting forth as of January 1 or July 1—

Names, residences, and post-office addresses of officers and directors.
Name, residence, and post-office address of each of the shareholders whose stock is not paid in full, with amount due thereon.
Location of the principal office in the State.
Number of shares and amount of other securities issued by other corporations owned by it, with their names and locations. (Id., § 3382.)

Report made by officer to assessors of names of stockholders residing in assessment district, with amount and value of stock held by each.

DELAWARE.

The president and secretary of every corporation shall annually, on December 1, make a return to the assessors under oath, showing the number of shares of capital stock, market value per share, aggregate market or real value of all the shares, with names of owners and number of shares owned by each. (Chap. 381, Laws 1897, as amended by chap. 25, Laws 1898.)

Chapter 15, Laws 1901, section 2 (tax law), contains requirements as to certain corporations. All others shall file a report with the secretary of state January 1, showing location of office in State, names of officers, amount of authorized capital stock, amount paid in, amount invested in real estate, tax annually paid thereon, and amount invested in manufacturing and mining in the State.

President, with the secretary and treasurer, upon payment of each installment of capital stock, shall make and file with the secretary of state a certificate, stating the amount of the installment paid and whether in cash or property, also total amount of capital stock, if any, previously paid and reported. (Chap. 167, Laws 1901, § 23.)

FLORIDA.

Annual return shall be made to controller by the treasurer of every corporation, showing—

Names and residences of stockholders and number of shares owned by each.
Par and cash market value of shares.
Whole amount of capital stock and amount paid in.
Real and personal estate subject to taxation. (R. S., Florida, § 2134.)

GEORGIA.

Whenever corporations are required to make returns of property, etc., for taxation, such returns shall contain an itemized statement of property, each class or species to be separately named and valued or an itemized account of gross receipts, or business, or income, as above defined, or other matters required to be returned; and in case of net income only an itemized account of gross receipts and expenditures to show how the income returned is ascertained, etc. (Code, 1895, § 812.)

IDAHO.

Records and stock book open to directors, stockholders, members, and creditors. (Statutes of Idaho, §§ 2639, 2640.)

ILLINOIS.

A sworn statement shall be made to assessors giving the name and location of the corporation, amount of capital stock and number of shares, amount of capital stock paid up, market value of shares, or, if no market value, the actual value, total indebtedness except for current expenses, excluding from current expenses purchase or improvement of property, assessed valuation of all tangible property.

Certificate of vote filed with secretary of state and recorder of deeds affecting changes as to name, place, enlargement or change of objects, increase or decrease of stock, or in number of directors, etc., or consolidation.   (R. S. 1899, p. 443.)

Corporations annually between February 1 and March 1 to report to secretary of state location, names of officers with residences, and date of expiration of office, whether pursuing active business and kind of business, made under seal, signed, and sworn to by president, secretary, or other officer or assignee or receiver. (Laws 1901, p. 124.)

INDIANA.

Manufacturing and mining corporations shall make annual report within twenty days from January 1, under oath of president and majority of directors and verified by them and the secretary, to be published in some newspaper in the county, showing amount of capital stock, amount of assessments made and actually paid in, amount of existing debts.

The president or other accounting officer of every corporation shall annually between April 1 and June 1 return a sworn statement to the assessor of its capital stock, setting forth particularly the name and location of the corporation, amount of capital stock and number of shares, amount paid up, market value, or if no market value the actual value of shares, total indebtedness, except current expenses, excluding from current expenses purchase and improvement of property, value of tangible property, difference in value between all tangible property and capital stock, name and value of each franchise or privilege owned or enjoyed by such corporation. (Thornton's Indiana Statutes, § 8988, et seq.)   Officers may be examined.

IOWA.

In January annually corporations shall file with the secretary of state a list of officers and directors and any change in location.   (Code of Iowa (1897), § 1612.)

Statement of amount of capital stock subscribed and amount actually paid in and amount of indebtedness in a general way, to be posted in like manner and corrected as often as changes occur. (§ 1625, id.)

Stock book shall be open to general inspection. (§ 1626, id.)

Corporations, on or before January 25, annually, shall furnish to the assessor of the district a verified statement showing specifically, with reference to the year next preceding January 1, total authorized capital stock and number of shares, number of shares issued and par value of each, amount paid into treasury on each share and total capital paid in, description and value of each tract of real estate owned by said corporation, date, rate per cent, and amount of each dividend declared and amount of capital on which declared, gross and net earnings, respectively, during the year and amount of surplus, amount of profit added to sinking fund, highest price of sale of stock between 1st and 10th of January of current year, and highest price of sale during preceding year and average of such sales. (§ 1323, id.)

KANSAS.

The president and secretary of every corporation shall annually as of June 30 make a statement to the secretary of state, showing the amount of authorized capital stock, amount of paid-up capital, par and market value per share, complete and detailed statement of assets and liabilities, a complete and detailed statement of the receipts of the corporation for the year next preceding, complete list of stockholders and post-office address of each, number of shares held and paid for by each, names and post-office addresses of trustees and manager and of directors. (General Statutes, Dassler, 1901, §§ 1283, 1263.) The secretary of state may at any time require a report as above.

KENTUCKY.

Public-service corporations shall annually, between September 15 and October 1, make a statement to the auditor of public accounts, verified by the president or other officer showing name of the corporation and principal place of business, kind of business, amount of capital stock, preferred and common, and number of shares of each, amount of capital stock paid up, par and real value, highest price at which sold within twelve months, amount of surplus and undivided profits and value of other assets, total indebtedness as principal, amount of gross and net earnings or income, amount and kind of tangible property in the State and where situated and the fair cash value thereof, and such other facts as the auditor may require. (Statutes, Carroll, 1899, §§ 4077, 4078.)

LOUISIANA.

President, cashier, secretary, or agent of each corporation on or before March 1, annually, shall make a written statement under oath to the State collector or assessors of the parish or district, specifying the real estate owned by the corporation and where situated in the State, the amount of capital stock paid in and not invested in real estate, the principal place of business or where principal operations are carried on in which the corporation is liable to be taxed. (R. S., § 736.)

Stock book and books containing amount of capital stock subscribed, names of owners of stock and amounts owned by them, respectively, amount of stock paid and by whom, transfers of stock with dates, amount of assets and liabilities, and names and places of residence of officers, to be open to public inspection. (Const., art. 273.)

MAINE.

The cashier, clerk, or treasurer of each corporation shall, between November 1 and December 8, annually make return to the secretary of state of the names of stockholders and residences, amount of stock owned by each, and the whole amount of stock paid in as of November 1. The secretary of state shall lay the same before the legislature within the first thirty days. (R. S. Maine, ch. 46, § 31.)

Cashiers, clerks, or treasurers holding property liable to be taxed shall, by the 8th of April, annually return under oath to assessors of town in which any of stockholders reside names of such holders, amount of stock owned by them on the 1st of April, and amount of stock paid in to such corporation. (§ 30, id.)

MARYLAND.

During the first week in January and July in each year a full and particular statement of affairs of every corporation shall be made, verified by oath of the president and treasurer or chief finance officer, which statement shall consist of a particular account of its assets and liabilities in minute detail to date. Recorded in book kept in principal office in State. (Public General Laws, Art. 23, § 73.)

The president and directors of every corporation shall keep full, fair, and correct accounts of their transactions, which shall be open at all times to the inspection of stockholders or members, and they shall annually prepare a full and true statement of the affairs of the corporation which shall be certified to by the president and secretary and submitted at the annual meeting of the stockholders or members. (§ 5, id.)

MASSACHUSETTS.

Every corporation shall annually, within thirty days of the annual meeting, file with the secretary of state a report sworn to by the president, treasurer, and a majority of the directors, showing the amount of capital stock, amount paid in, names of shareholders and the number of shares of each, assets and liabilities in form and detail as the commissioner of corporations shall require or approve. (Revised Laws of Mass., 1902, ch. 110, § 51.)

If the capital stock is over $100,000, such certificate shall be accompanied by a statement under oath of an auditor to be employed by three stockholders not directors, stating that such certificate represents the true condition as shown by the books. (§ 52, id.)

MICHIGAN.

Every manufacturing and mining corporation shall, in the month of January, annually file in the office of the secretary of state a statement under oath of the president or a director, giving names and number of shares held by each stockholder and places of residence, as of January 1. (Compiled Laws, 1897, § 6975.)

Every manufacturing corporation shall annually, in January or February, file with the secretary of state and county clerk a report, signed by a majority of the directors and verified by the oath of the secretary, showing the amount of the capital stock, the amount paid in, amount invested in real estate and in personal estate, amount of debts and credits, names of stockholders and number of shares of each, and such other information as the secretary of state may require. (§ 7048, id.)

It shall be the duty of the attorney-general, whenever and as often as required by the governor, to examine into the affairs of corporations and report examination in detail, with statement of facts, to the governor, who shall lay the same before the legislature. The attorney-general has power to administer oaths and to examine officers and directors on oath in relation to the affairs and condition of corporations and to examine vaults, books, papers, and documents.

The legislature has authority to make examinations, and may appoint a committee for that purpose which shall have the same powers as above. (§ 8551, id.]

MINNESOTA.

Corporations authorized to acquire private property.—By-laws shall be posted in principal place of business, subject to inspection. (§ 2597, Stats.)

A statement of the amount of capital stock subscribed, paid, and indebtedness in a general way, kept posted in principal place of business and corrected for changes. (§ 2598, id.)

Other corporations for profit.—The attorney-general, when required by the governor, shall examine into the affairs of corporations and report his examination in writing to the governor, with a detailed statement of facts, who shall lay the.same before the legislature. The attorney-general has power to administer oaths to officers and directors and to examine vaults, books, papers, and documents belonging to the corporation or pertaining to its business. The legislature has same powers. (§ 3436, id.)

MISSISSIPPI.

No general requirement for publicity.

MISSOURI.

Foreign corporations shall file a copy of articles of incorporation-in the office of the secretary of state and a certificate accompanying the same showing the location of its principal officer or agent in the State, and a sworn statement of the proportion of its capital stock represented by property and business transacted in Missouri. (Revised Laws, § 1025.)

Corporations shall make annual reports July 1, showing location of its principal business office, the names of the president and secretary, amount of capital stock subscribed and the amount paid up, par value and actual value of shares, cash value of all its personal property and of all its real estate within the State, and the amount of taxes paid for the preceding year. (§ 1013, id.)

Foreign corporations shall make annual report in July to secretary of state, signed and sworn to by principal officer in the State, showing the name of the principal officer in the State, location of principal office in the State, cash value of all real estate and personal property in the State as of June 1, amount of taxes paid in the State for the preceding year. (§ 1014, id.)

MONTANA.

Foreign corporations shall file with the secretary of state and county clerk a copy of charter or articles of incorporation, verified by oath of president and secretary and attested by a majority of the board of directors, showing name, location of principal place of business, out of State and in State, amount of capital stock, amount paid in in money, amount paid in in other ways, and in what amount of assets, and of what they consist and actual value, liabilities, and, if secured, how and on what property, also consent to be sued in State on cause arising in State, and designating person to be served. (Civil Code (1895), § 1030.)

Foreign corporations shall annually give statement containing same information as above. (L. 1901, p. 150.)

Domestic corporations shall make annual reports within twenty days from September 1, showing amount of capital stock and proportion paid in and amount of existing debts. The report shall be signed by president and a majority of directors and verified by the president, vice-president, or secretary, and published in a newspaper of the village or city of principal office and filed in county clerk's office. (Code, § 451.)

NEBRASKA.

By-laws of corporations shall be posted in conspicuous places at place of doing business, subject to public inspection. (Statutes (1899), § 1838.)

Corporations shall give notice annually in some newspaper printed in the county or counties where business transacted or nearest newspaper in State of amount of indebtedness. Signed by president and majority of directors. (§ 1839, id.)

Corporations shall make sworn statement to assessor showing name and location, amount of capital stock and number of shares, amount of stock paid up, market value, and if no market value, then real value of shares, total amount of indebtedness, except current expenses, excluding from expense account amount paid for purchase or improvement of property, assessed valuation of real and personal property, same to be listed. (§ 4313, id.)

NEVADA.

Stock book and all other books of corporations shall be open to stockholders. Creditors and stockholders may have certified copy of any entry or of any paper on file in the office of such corporations and the same shall be presumptive evidence against such corporations. (Compiled Laws, § 881.)

NEW HAMPSHIRE.

All records, accounts, and papers of corporations should be open to the inspection of every member and stockholder and such petitions as relate to overdue and unpaid demand of creditor open to such creditor. (Pub. Stats. (1901), ch. 148, § 12.)
Certified copy furnished on payment of fee. (§ 13, id.)
Until capital stock fully paid and certificate thereof filed and recorded clerk shall annually, in May, file in office of town or city clerk at place of business a list of names and residence stockholders certified under oath. (Ch. 150, § 10, id.)
Directors and treasurer to file certificate when stock fully paid under oath with town or city clerk. (§ 14, id.)
Corporations shall make annual return in May, under oath, of treasurer and majority of directors to secretary of state and town clerk of amount of assessments voted by corporation and actually paid, amount of all debts due to and by corporation and value of all property and assets as of May 1. (§ 16, id.)

NEW JERSEY.

Contracts or agreements for sale, letting, leasing, consolidating, merging, or in any way disposing of or transferring the franchises, privileges, or any part thereof, shall be recorded in office of secretary of state.
Changes in name, amount of capital stock, par value of shares, etc., shall be certified to secretary of state.
List of corporations and names of officers and location of offices published annually by secretary of state (p. 949, § 200).
Corporations shall file list of officers within thirty days of annual meeting, date of election or appointment, term of office and residence of each, and place of business of corporation in State (p. 970, § 293, id.), character of business, and name of agent in charge of office on whom to serve.
Stock books open to stockholders thirty days prior to annual election (p. 914, id.).
Certificate filed when whole capital stock paid (p. 965, § 272, id.).
Every certificate filed must state location of office in State and name of agent in charge thereof on whom process may be served.

NEW YORK.

[Extract from volume entitled "Revised Statutes, Codes, and General Laws of New York," compiled by Clarence F. Birdseye, third edition, 1901, volume 3, page 3414.]

SEC. 30. *Annual report.*—Every domestic stock corporation and every foreign stock corporation doing business within this State, except moneyed and railroad corporations, shall, annually, during the month of January, or, if doing business without the United States, before the 1st day of May, may make a report as to the 1st day of January, which shall state—
1. The amount of its capital stock and the proportion actually issued.
2. The amount of its debts, or an amount which they do not exceed.
3. The amount of its assets, or an amount which its assets at least equal.
Such report shall be made by the president or a vice-president or the treasurer or a secretary of the corporation, and shall be filed in the office of the secretary of state. If such report be not so made and filed, any such officer who shall thereafter neglect or refuse to make and file such report, within ten days after written request so to do shall have been made by a creditor or by a stockholder of the corporation, shall forfeit to the people the sum of $50 for every day he shall so neglect or refuse.
Stock or bonds shall only be issued for money, labor done, or property actually received, and in all statements and reports of the corporation stock issued for property purchased shall be so stated. (Page 3416, id.)
Increases or reductions of capital stock, changes in number of shares, place of business, etc., to be certified.

NORTH CAROLINA.

Property of corporations shall be listed for taxation in a statement .showing the name and location of the corporation, amount of capital stock and number of shares, amount of capital stock paid up, market value of shares, or if no market value, actual value, assessed valuation of real property and of personal property listed and valued by items. (Act March 12, 1895, § 39.)

NORTH DAKOTA.

Such corporations (business) annually within twenty days from January 1 shall make a report and publish the same in a newspaper in the nearest place in the State, showing: Capital stock and amount paid in, amount and nature of indebtedness and amount due corporation, number and amount of dividends and when paid, and net amount of profits. Such report to be signed by president and majority of directors and verified by oath of president or secretary. Filed in office of register of deeds of county. (Revised Code of North Dakota (1895), § 3158, id.)

OHIO.

An annual report of the financial condition setting forth assets and liabilities of corporations shall be made and furnished to each stockholder with a list of the stockholders and residences. (Bates's Annotated Statutes of Ohio (1902), § 3268.)
Property of corporations shall be listed for taxation. (§ 2744, id.)
Books and records of corporations shall be open to stockholders. (§ 3254, id.)

OREGON.

Stock book of corporations open to any person interested therein. (Hill's Annotated Laws, § 3228.)

PENNSYLVANIA.

Certificate of incorporation states, among other things, what property is taken in payment for capital stock, and that such property is necessary for the purposes of the corporation. (Act of April 29, 1874, P. L. 73, as amended.)
Corporations shall make annual report in November by president, chairman, or treasurer, showing "total authorized capital stock, total authorized number of shares, number of shares of stock issued, par value of each share, amount paid into treasury on each share, amount of capital paid in, amount of capital on which dividend was declared, date of each dividend declared during said year ended with the first Monday of November, rate per centum of each dividend declared, amount of each dividend during the year ended with the first Monday of said month, gross earnings during the year, net earnings during the year, amount of surplus, amount of profits added to sinking fund during said year, highest price of sales of stock between the first and fifteenth days of November aforesaid, highest price of sales of stock during the year aforesaid, average price of sales of stock during the year; and in every case any two of the following-named officers, president, chairman, secretary, and treasurer, after being duly sworn or affirmed to do and perform the same with fidelity and according to the best of their knowledge and belief, shall, between the first and fifteenth days of November of each year, estimate and appraise the capital stock of the said company at its actual value in cash, not less, however, than the average price which said stock sold for during said year, and not less than the price or value indicated or measured by net earnings or by the amount of the profit made and either declared in dividends or carried into surplus or sinking fund, and when the same shall have been so truly estimated and appraised they shall forthwith forward to the auditor-general a certificate thereof, accompanied with a copy of their said oath or affirmation, signed by them and attested by a magistrate or other person duly qualified to administer the same: Provided, That if the auditor-general and State treasurer, or either of them, is not satisfied with the appraisement and valuation so made and returned, they are hereby authorized and empowered to make a valuation thereof based upon the facts contained in the report herein required, or upon any information within their possession or that shall come into their possession, and to settle an account on the valuation so made by them for the taxes, penalties, and interests due the Commonwealth thereon," etc. (Act of June 8, 1891, § 4 P. L., amending the act of June 1, 1889, § 20.)

RHODE ISLAND.

Manufacturing corporations shall file in the office of the town clerk annually, on or before February 15, a certificate signed by a majority of directors truly stating the amount of capital stock paid in, the value as last assessed for a town tax of its real estate, the value of its personal assets, and amount of its debts and liabilities on December 31 of the year next preceding. (General Laws, title 19, ch. 180, § 11.)

Corporations shall make returns of stockholders and amount owned by each to assessors of towns where stockholders reside.

SOUTH CAROLINA.

All subscriptions to the capital stock of any corporation shall be payable in money or in labor or in property at its money value, and shall be listed, the labor or the property, and the value thereof to be specified in the list of subscriptions; but no subscription in labor or in property shall be received unless such labor or property and the value thereof, so to be specified as aforesaid, be approved by said board of corporators, etc. (Civil Code (1902), § 1882.)

SOUTH DAKOTA.

The president, secretary, or principal accounting officer shall make and deliver to the assessor a sworn statement of the amount of capital stock, specifically setting forth the name and location of the corporation, amount of capital stock and number of shares, amount paid up, market value, if any, and, if not, the actual value, total indebtedness, except for current expenses, excluding from current expenses purchase and betterment of property, value of real estate and personal property. (Act of March 9, 1891.)

TENNESSEE.

The president of every corporation shall, annually, during the month of January, make and publish in a newspaper printed in the county of its principal place of business a sworn statement showing the amount of its capital stock and existing liabilities and list of names of stockholders. (Code (1884), § 1855.)

TEXAS.

When required by one-third of the stockholders of any corporation, a report shall be made of the situation and amount of business by the directors, and they shall declare and make such dividend as they shall deem expedient or the by-laws require. (Civil Code, art. 663.)

UTAH.

If property taken in payment of stock subscriptions, the same must be described and the value given in the articles of incorporation, and an affidavit filed of three persons that such property is worth the amount at which it is taken. (R. S., § 316.)

VERMONT.

Every corporation shall annually, on or before April 15, make to the clerk of the town in which stockholders reside a return, giving a list of the names of such, number of shares standing in the name of each on April 1, the amount paid on the same, and to the clerk where the principal place of business is located a full list of stockholders with the same information. (Statutes, § 380.)

Before commencement of business, certificate to be filed of amount of capital stock paid in. (§ 3722.)

VIRGINIA.

Manufacturing and mining corporations shall exhibit books and statement of property and condition to such agent as the general assembly may from time to time appoint to examine same. (Code, § 1142.)

WASHINGTON.

The president, secretary, or principal accounting officer of each corporation shall make sworn return or statement to assessor, setting forth the name and location of the corporation, its real estate and where situated, the nature and value of its personal property. (Act March 15, 1897, § 20.)

WEST VIRGINIA.

The board of directors of every corporation shall make a report to stockholders at the annual meeting, showing property and funds and estimated value, debts due it and from it, amount of capital paid in and estimated surplus or deficiency, dividends declared, and losses or profits for year.

Copy report, with list of stockholders, delivered to stockholders. (Code, p. 551.)

Property, books, correspondence, and funds open to inspection by board or committee.

Every corporation to exhibit books and property to such agent or committees as legislature may appoint to examine same and to report when legislature requires full, fair, and detailed statement on oath of president and secretary or principal bookkeeper. (Page 554, id.)

WISCONSIN.

The attorney-general, when required by the governor, shall examine into the affairs of corporations and report his examination in writing to the governor, with a detailed statement of facts, who shall lay the same before the legislature. The attorney-general has power to administer oaths to officers and directors and to examine vaults, books, papers, and documents belonging to corporation or pertaining to business. Legislature has same power. (Statutes, § 1766.)

Books of stock and accounts open to stockholders, and every creditor shall be informed at any time of amount of capital stock subscribed, amount paid in, who are stockholders, number of shares of each, amount unpaid by each, and if any unpaid shares transferred within six months, by whom, and amount unpaid at the time of transfer thereon. (§ 1757, id.)

Foreign corporations shall, within sixty days after request by any resident creditor, and annually thereafter, file with the secretary of state a statement showing the capital stock subscribed, amount paid in, and full names of stockholders, and amount of stock held by each. (§ 1770, id.)

WYOMING.

On request of 15 per cent of the capital stock the treasurer of any corporation shall render a statement of the affairs of the corporation, under oath, embracing a particular account of all assets and liabilities in minute detail within twenty days after such request, and the same shall be kept on file in the office of the corporation for six months, open to the inspection of stockholders, but such statement shall not be required oftener than once in six months. (R. S. (1899), § 3057.)

DISTRICT OF COLUMBIA.

Annual reports.—Every such company (manufacturing, etc.) shall annually, except insurance companies, within twenty days from the 1st day of January, make a report, which shall be published in a newspaper in the District, which shall state the amount of capital and of the proportion actually paid, and the amount of existing debts, which report shall be signed by the president and a majority of the trustees, and shall be verified by the oath of the president or secretary of the company, and filed in the office of the recorder of deeds of the District. (U. S. Stat. L., vol. 31, ch. 854, § 617.)

Many States require returns as a basis of taxation which are not included in the foregoing, the only purpose in this report being to give a general summary as to general publicity, with references to aid in verification.

There is no such thing as a corporate franchise except it be granted by the State. While it confers upon the stockholders the privilege of limiting their personal liability for the undertakings of the corporation, it gives a perpetual or continuing life. Unlike a firm, the death or withdrawal of one of the parties interested therein does not in any way interfere with its operation. It gives unity of control and management through its officers, so that, unlike a partnership, its members can exercise no direction or control over its business except through the power to change its officers. It furnishes the most convenient medium for the aggregating together of large amounts of capital, enabling the investor to distribute his investments between numerous enterprises, and thus minimize the hazards involved in all investments. It furnishes the only practicable medium for combining the large amounts of capital necessary for the prosecution of great enterprises. While the State confers these valuable privileges, it is bound to regulate and control their exercise, so that in other respects they will not have an undue advantage over the individual operator and enjoy artificial facilities for oppressing the public. It is bound to see that the facts essential to the protection of the public in all of its relations thereto are at least made available for public information. Upon this artificial creation is conferred the power to do great good. Its creator is bound to minimize its power for evil.

FUTURE INVESTMENTS AND THEIR RELATION TO OVERCAPITALIZATION.

Investors are by no means confined to speculators on Wall Street. If they were all the persons concerned in corporate bonds and stocks it might well be that we should not need to be especially solicitous on their account. The total wealth of the United States, according to provisional figures of the census of 1900, is $90,000,000,000. The sum total of railroad securities of the United States at par in 1901 was $11,688,147,091. In the Stock Exchange Handbook for 1902 statistics are given of 500 industrial corporations which represent the combination of previously existing independent interests. The securities of these 500 industrial corporations actually issued are:

Bonds...	$1,327,941,111
Preferred stocks..	1,833,899,251
Common stocks..	4,318,616,061
Total...	$7,480,460,423

"These facts," says Mr. Robert L. Raymond, from whose article this statement is taken, "have created the trust problem." The figures given are not understood to include electric light, gas, telegraph, and telephone companies. Here we have an aggregate of $19,168,607,414 in steam railroads and industrial combinations—in round numbers $20,000,000,000, or more than 20 per cent of the total wealth of the country. When the securities of gas, electric light, water, street railways, telegraph, and telephone companies are added to this $20,000,-000,000, it will be seen how vast is the stake of the investing public in the integrity of corporate investments. Such securities are the common medium for investment by banks and trust companies, institutions for saving, life-insurance companies, as well as individual investors. Their investments aggregate billions.

The governor of New Jersey tells us that the stockholders of New Jersey corporations alone run up into hundreds of thousands if not millions. All classes invest; the rich, the well to do, the poor, the widow, and the orphan. In the case of stocks large dividends furnish the inducement to allure the investor. The corporate bond, if based upon a first mortgage of the corporate property, is clearly the safest form of investment. Who is there to-day not intimately connected with the management of the corporation that holds a corporate bond of any kind that knows what value there is behind it? Where can the intending purchaser of such a bond go to ascertain that information? He

H. Rep. 3375——2

can not find it anywhere outside of Massachusetts and Pennsylvania, and possibly one or two other States, where comparatively few corporations are organized, by reason of the greater facilities for concealment offered elsewhere. None of the great combinations of which complaint is made could exist if their bonds could not be floated. It is doubtful if any of the large overcapitalized combinations now in existence could have been financed if the facts as to value involved in their organization had been fully known to the public. In a great many instances the bonds negotiated represent all of the actual investment in the cor-. poration, the stock being largely speculative. It is certainly doubtful if the public would buy a bond when it knew that the only cash capital invested in the enterprise was the proceeds of the bonds in which it was invited to invest. If upon a public statement it appeared that the bondholders were the only parties assuming any real hazard, and that the only hazard undergone by the promoters was the ability to so control and manipulate the market as to be able to declare a dividend on a fictitious capitalization in order to give it simply a market value, and thus unload upon the public, fewer combinations would be floated, or be successful if floated. Where is the individual who, purposing to engage in any enterprise, would have the courage to go into the market and endeavor to borrow, secured by a mortgage on the enterprise, all the capital to be invested therein? If a man contemplated the purchase of a piece of real estate for the sum of $10,000 he would hardly expect to borrow upon the security of the real estate the whole of the purchase price. Yet, he can take with him two other men—dummies—organize as a corporation, make a bond issue to cover the full investment, comply with every provision of the law, and in that respect, in a perfectly legitimate manner, accomplish that result.

A corporate bond seems to impart an air of security not found in a secured promissory note, although the note does have in addition to the security, which is all there is behind the bond so far as individual liability is concerned, the individual responsibility of the promisor. It does not meet the situation to say "let the purchaser take heed." When the purchaser buys an article of food, or clothing, a horse, a dwelling, a farm, or any other tangible property it may well be that he must "take heed," as there he has, or can have, full opportunity to learn of the qualities and attributes of the subject of the purchase. The inspection of a bond, or a stock certificate, or the reading of the ordinary prospectus does not give the slightest idea as to the intrinsic value of the property represented by the bond or stock. The State makes it possible for the corporation to place bonds and stock upon the market and conceal every material fact essential to a determination of its value. In the absence of a knowledge of these facts it is an absolute impossibility for a purchaser to form any idea of the real value of the stock or bond. "Surely in vain," says the sacred writer, "the net is spread in the sight of any bird." When the requisite degree of publicity shall place within the reach of the purchaser the information that will disclose the true value of the stock or bond, then the maxim "caveat emptor" may be properly invoked. To carefully keep from him the necessary information, to enable a corporation to dig a pitfall and then cover it up so as to ensnare the unwary, and then say, "Look out for yourself," is an unjustifiable use of the maxim. There is a simple test that will settle the propriety of these essential disclosures. If an article is intrinsically desirable and valuable the more its special qualities are made known and advertised the quicker it will sell and the better price it will bring.

If a capital stock is all paid in, the corporation doing a large and profitable business, and has accumulated a handsome surplus the greater the publicity that is given to these important facts the more the market value of the stock will be increased. Such a corporation seeks publicity. On the other hand, suppose the stock is only partly paid in, the corporation doing a losing business, and has accumulated a deficit. The more these facts are known the more the market value of the stock becomes a negligible quantity. In other words, if a man has a good bond or stock, the more publicity he gets the better he likes it. If he has a poor bond or stock, the less publicity he receives the better he is satisfied. But why are not the public, the insurance companies, and the saving banks, which are relied upon as the final depositories of these securities, entitled to the same information in each case? A sound corporation will make no objection to such publicity; an unsound one always objects. The States, or some of them, legislate so as to enable the corporation to place the questionable bond and stock upon the market under apparently the same conditions that obtain in case of a first-class security. The information will tend to deter the investment. The States that charter these corporations can not be relied on to give it. The nearest approach to a uniform rule is for the United States to require returns that will give this information from all corporations engaged in interstate commerce. It is the fear that the prospective investor will be deterred that leads the promoters and organizers of great combines to insist upon the maintenance of conditions that will enable them to continue to create fictitious wealth.

THE PUBLIC INTEREST FROM THE BROAD STANDPOINT OF THE CONSUMERS.

It is through the medium of consumers, the purchasers of its products, that the overcapitalized combination finds its most extensive and oppressive contact with the public. Successful overcapitalization involves the necessity of declaring a dividend upon the overcapitalization equal to a dividend upon actual value, thus giving to the stock an earning capacity and creating an artificial market value. If all of the overcapitalization were held by the promoters and organizers, and was not held for the purpose of increasing the return, there would be no object in overcapitalizing. So long as the aliquot interest of the stockholder remained the same his share of the earnings would be the same, whether he held one share of stock or ten. It would be of no consequence to him whether his rate of dividend was 10 or 1 per cent so long as the aggregate of the dividend remained the same. His relative control in the affairs of the corporation would be the same. From this point of view, if no other result was sought or attained, the overcapitalization would be immaterial so far as the public is concerned, it is only from this view that overcapitalization is a matter of no concern to the public. If there is no other purpose, overcapitalization is meaningless and valueless to the stockholder. The real purposes of overcapitalization are believed to be of an entirely different character, and they all have an injurious effect upon the public. The purpose to create for the stock a fictitious value and thus arbitrarily increase the wealth of the persons interested is undoubtedly the main purpose in overcapitalization. In order to accomplish this, in nearly every instance the price to the consumer must either be increased or maintained above its natural normal level. It is no doubt true that by a consolidation of a number of competing firms or corporations business economies may pe produced by having one management instead of a number, by having one instead of a number of sets of traveling men, and by running one instead of a number of lines of advertising, etc. It is also true that an increase in the volume of business done with practically the same cost of operation results in a larger return to the operator, or that a smaller percentage of profit will on the larger volume of business produce the same aggregate return and enable the producer to sell to the consumer at a less price.

This aggregation of large capital, great volume of business on a small margin, giving a fair return to the capital invested, with a reduction in price to the consumer, is what is termed the new phase of modern industrial development; and the corporate form of organization, with its evils of overcapitalization, is the medium through which the development has largely taken place. Theoretically, on paper, this reasons well, looks-well, and works well. The chief ultimate result in which the public has an abiding interest, the reduction of the price to the consumer, is in practice seldom attained. This result is the only fact that can justify this phase of industrial development from the public standpoint. It is not believed that any of these corporations yet organized have ever been dominated by, or organized for, the altruistic purpose of reducing the price to the consumer. The controlling purpose in such organizations is believed to be what it naturally would be—the profit of the parties thereto. If the public receives any benefit, it is incidental. Profit to the persons in control inspires their operation as well as organization.

That overcapitalization, which in every one of its attributes is sought to be made equivalent to actual capital, is an unjust burden upon our industrial and commercial energies seems to us clear. As capital is entitled to a fair return, the public is vitally interested in the amount of capital necessary to carry on a given enterprise. Such fair return is a proper element of the cost of the article, and the public must pay for it, and the other elements of cost involved, when it buys the article. An actual investment of $1,000,000 would require a price for the product that after the payment of operating expenses and fixed charges would yield in profit, say, $60,000. On the other hand, if $10,000,000 actual investment were employed in the same enterprise with the same output, the net earnings would have to be $600,000 in order to give the same fair return on the investment. Assuming, for the purpose of testing this idea, that all the other elements such as cost and output remain the same, clearly in the last instance the public must pay a largely increased price by reason of the large investment. If, for the purpose of the illustration, $9,000,000 of this were overcapitalization or inflation, the public would be clearly paying in price $540,000 more than it ought to pay, or enough more in price to produce nine times the return that ought properly to be received, or more than it naturally would pay independent of a monopoly of the market, and the transaction of the business through the medium of an overcapitalized corporation. Again, as a business proposition, if it is legitimate and proper for one corporation to thus place fictitious stock upon a par with actual value, it is for all, and every corporation should do so for the purpose of placing its stockholders on a par with others as to earning and dividend-paying capacity. In such case the consumers of all articles of commerce would be paying an abnormal price in order to produce a return upon constructive capital employed that would be from five to ten times as large as it ought to be, or, as in the instance cited by Mr. Dill, of capitalizing $500,000 at $8,000,000, sixteen times the return that ought to be made. How long could even our great resources stand that drain?

To what extent we are now paying exorbitant prices to produce such abnormal returns no one can tell, as no reports are now made to any authority, State or national, that give any adequate information on that point. This is one of the things that this bill seeks to accomplish. It is through the facility offered for overcapitalization that the promoters of great combinations, formed from independent corporations and competing business concerns, get their enormous fees. The desire to get these fees in many instances no doubt contributes as largely to the launching of the scheme as does the fact that the constituent companies see an opportunity to double, treble, quadruple—yes, increase ten or sixteen fold, perhaps—their original holdings, and thus by the alchemy of a new corporation lithograph themselves rich. The attempt to monopolize the market is not the principal purpose, but an incident thereto, and follows as a necessary corollary of the condition. In order to perfectly realize the Crœsus-like dream of wealth by arithmetical progression, it becomes necessary to absorb all similar business interests, in order to eliminate competition and enable the resultant corporation to fix the price of the product at will, so as to produce the dividend essential to the creation of apparent market value. The fact that the promoter is able to advertise that his scheme involves the monopoly of the product and will thereby enable the combination to fix at will the price to the consumer is believed to be a potent element in successfully financing it. Unwarranted dividends and not monopoly are the moving cause. Monopoly is invoked to produce that result.

CAPITALIZATION OF EARNING CAPACITY.

One of the elements involved for the purpose of justifying this artificial process of accumulating wealth is what is called the capitalization of earning capacity or profits. While it is undeniable that the dividend paid upon a stock or the interest paid upon a bond largely determines its market value, it by no means follows that capitalization can be based upon earning capacity. As the Attorney-General has very aptly said, by this method shrewd men capitalize for their own benefit the country's prosperity. Profits are greater in times of prosperity. The consumer is then better able to pay larger prices. Capitalization at high-water mark would be grossly unjust when low-water mark was reached.

Again, profits are based upon the selling price. If the price is such as to yield a disproportionately large return upon the capital actually invested, then competition, if unimpeded by unlawful restraints or combinations, will by the operation of natural laws reduce the price so as to bring the return down to the general level enjoyed by capital in like employments.

Then, by the operation of natural laws, the price to the consumer would be lowered, while a fair return upon the actual capital would be assured.

If it is assumed that you can legitimately capitalize the profits or earning capacity, you exclude the operation of this natural law and permanently impose upon the consumer the payment of a price away above the natural level. You insure to the corporation the price in prosperity through the season of adversity. Once capitalized, the price can not be cut down without impairing the capital, and you have no right to impair the capital. By capitalizing the profits you deliver the public bound hand and foot to the capitalist, whom they must continue to serve that he may receive the stipulated reward.

OVERCAPITALIZATION ENABLES CONCEALMENT OF PROFITS.

Overcapitalization furnishes the convenient opportunity for concealing the profitable character of the enterprise. It is said that it was first employed for that purpose. There are instances where corporations have increased their capitalization 100 per cent in order that what was really, say, a 12 per cent dividend would appear to be only a 6 per cent dividend, and thus avoided the danger of making their employees uneasy and restive because they were not receiving in wages a fair proportion of the earnings of the business. Concealment of this character tends to minimize the dangers of successful competition. An annual dividend of $600,000 would be 60 per cent on an actual investment of $1,000,000. If an ordinary business enterprise unprotected by patents or copyrights was known to be paying 60 per cent annually, competition would as surely engage therein as water runs down hill, resulting in a reduction of price to the consumer. This laudable result is rendered improbable in so far as the facts as to the real rate of dividends are more or less successfully concealed.

But where there is no competition, as in the case with many of the large industrial combinations, the public have no means of determining whether the price charged is a reasonable one or not, for the reason that the public have no knowledge whether the combination is overcapitalized or not; nor have they any knowledge as to what proportion of the profits made by the combination go into new construction and are not paid out in dividends upon the overcapitalized stock. Even if we assume that the combination is greatly overcapitalized in the beginning, the profits may be sufficiently large so that after a period of years profits may have been reserved for the improvement and enlargement of the plant, so that the corporation ceases to be overcapitalized; but it is the consumer in that instance who has paid not only dividends, but has contributed to make up the deficiency in the overcapitalization.

Publicity, by creating an intelligent public sentiment, will go far toward ameliorating oppressive conditions. If it is a fact that competitors are ruthlessly destroyed and prices are increased in order that enormous returns may be received upon a relatively insignificant investment, and the searchlight of publicity can be turned thereon, it is doubtful if the persons who are responsible for such a reprehensible condition could long stand the well-directed public indignation that would be thus aroused.

It is not claimed that publicity is a cure-all. It is hoped that by its application the operation of natural laws may in an appreciable degree alleviate existing conditions. The whole subject unhampered by constitutional provisions that circumscribe and limit us is intricate, involved, and extremely difficult of solution. All legislation should be conservative and tentative. Full publicity should add materially to our information upon this abstruse subject, and enable us, in the light of the decisions of the court construing existing and new legislation, to act more intelligently and efficiently in enacting legislation that will more effectively regulate and control these conditions, so far as they are susceptible of legislative regulation and control.

It is idle to wait for the States to pass uniform legislation upon this subject. The financial incentive to furnish an asylum and breeding place for vicious, unrestrained, corporate vagrants is too strong for human nature to withstand. In 1884 the State of New Jersey conceived the laudable idea that it could add materially to its revenue by opening up great possibilities for corporations. Its revenue then was $195,273.15 annually in fees and taxes from corporations. After eighteen years of endeavor in this direction they have increased their revenues from this source, so that they now receive the tidy sum of $3,447,310.11, which it is understood pays the running expenses of the State and leaves a comfortable margin for contingencies. They can hardly be expected to surrender this revenue. Other States are engaging in friendly rivalry with New Jersey for a portion of this sum. They have become envious of the prosperity of New Jersey, and within the past few years have enacted fresh statutes under the provisions of which incorporators residing in any State in the Union may obtain a charter from those States without ever entering the State from which the charter is granted, and not being required to ever hold a stockholders' meeting within the State, or ever doing any business therein, and its officers and stockholders being relieved of all personal liability for whatever acts they may commit in connection with said corporation. It is only by the enactment of a uniform law as to all corporations engaged in interstate commerce as is proposed by this bill that an approximation of the result desired can be reached.

PUBLICITY IN OTHER COUNTRIES.

In the matter of publicity of the facts involved in the organization and the operation of business corporations, our existing legislation and regulations fall very far short of similar legislation in other commercial countries. England is undoubtedly one of the most important industrial and commercial nations, and has very large and widely diffused business interests, many of which are necessarily operated through corporate organizations. Their requirements as to corporations, and the elements of publicity, are applied to the original prospectuses issued as the basis of their organization and for the purpose of inducing investment therein rather than in the line of making a report, but the same principles are involved. The English statutes as to the requirements necessary to be inserted in the prospectus was adopted in 1900, and reads as follows:

SEC. 6. SPECIAL REQUIREMENTS AS TO PARTICULARS OF PROSPECTUS.—Every prospectus issued by or on behalf of a company, or any person engaged or interested in the formation of the company, must state (a) the contents of the memorandum of association, with the names, descriptions, and addresses of the signatories, and the number of shares subscribed for by them, respectively, and the number of founder's or management shares, if any, and the nature and extent of the interest of the holders in the property and profits of the company; and (b) the number of shares, if any, fixed by the articles of association as the qualification of a director, and any provisions in the articles of association as to the remuneration of directors; and (c) the names, descriptions, and addresses of the directors or proposed directors; and (d) the minimum subscription on which the directors may proceed to allotment and the amount payable on application and allotment on each share, and in the case of a second or subsequent offer of shares the amount offered for subscription on each previous allotment and the amount actually allotted, and the amount, if any, actually paid on such shares; and (e) the number and amount of shares and debentures issued, or agreed to be issued, as fully or partly paid up otherwise than in cash, and in the latter case the extent to which they are so paid up, and in either case the consideration for which such shares or debentures have been issued or are proposed or intended to be issued; and (f) the names and addresses of the vendors of any property purchased or acquired by the company, or proposed to be so acquired, which is to be paid for wholly or partly out of the proceeds of the issue offered for subscription by the prospectus, or the purchase or acquisition of which has not been completed at the date of publication of the prospectus, and the amount payable in cash, shares, or debentures to the vendor, and where there is more than one separate vendor, or the company is a subpurchaser, the amount so payable to each vendor; and (g) the amount, if any, paid or payable as purchase money in cash, shares, or debentures of any such property as aforesaid, specifying the amount payable for good will; and (h) the amount paid or payable as commission for subscribing or procuring or agreeing to procure subscriptions for any shares in the company, or the rate of any such commission; and (i) the amount or estimated amount of preliminary expenses; and (j) the amount paid or intended to be paid to any promoter and the consideration for any such payment; and (k) the dates and parties to every material contract, and a reasonable time and place at which any material contract or a copy thereof may be inspected, provided that this requirement shall not apply to a contract entered into in the ordinary course of the business carried on or to any contract entered into more than three years before the date of publication of the prospectus; and (l) the names and addresses of the auditors, if any, of the company; and (m) full particulars of the nature and extent of the interest, if any, of every director in the promotion of or in the property proposed to be acquired by the company, with a statement of all sums paid or agreed to be paid to him in cash or shares by any person either to qualify him as a director or otherwise for services rendered by him in connection with the formation of the company.   In this section the term "vendor" includes lessor, and "purchase money" includes rent.   Any condition requiring or binding any applicant for shares or debentures to waive compliance with any requirement of this section, or purporting to affect him with notice of any contract, document, or matter not specially referred to in the prospectus, shall be void.

The statutes of Victoria, an important colony of Great Britain, which in some respects follows and in other notable respects leads the mother country upon its legislation upon this and similar subjects, reads as follows with reference to the prospectus:

SEC. 10. PROSPECTUS TO GIVE NAMES OF DIRECTORS AND STOCK HELD BY EACH—THE CONTRACTS MADE BY COMPANY OR ITS OFFICERS—MEMORANDUM OF ASSOCIATION—CONSIDERATION GIVEN FOR PROPERTY, BONUS GIVEN FOR OBTAINING SUBSCRIPTIONS, ALLOTMENT, DIRECTORS' STOCK QUALIFICATION SHARES PAID FOR OTHERWISE THAN IN MONEY—THE VENDORS OF PROPERTY TO THE COMPANY—PRELIMINARY EXPENSES—WORKING CAPITAL—AUDITORS—LIABILITY FOR FAULTY PROSPECTUS.—Every prospectus, however published or issued, which is published or issued with a view of obtaining subscriptions for shares in a company, or directly or indirectly inviting persons to subscribe for shares in a company, shall specify (a) the names, addresses, and occupations of the promoters and directors and the number of shares held or agreed to be taken up by them, respectively, and whether wholly paid up or partly paid up, and the consideration, remuneration, or reward (if any) to the directors, promoters, or members of the company; (b) the date of and the names of the parties to any contract directly or indirectly relating to the company, or to the promotion thereof, entered into by the company, or the promotors, directors, or trustees thereof, within two years before the issue of such prospectus; and shall also state a place where such contract, if in writing, may be inspected: Provided, That this subdivision of this section shall not apply to a contract entered into by the company after its incorporation in the ordinary course of the business carried on by the company; (c) the contents of the memorandum of association (if any), with the names and addresses of the signatories and the number of shares subscribed for by them, respectively; (d) the consideration paid or to be paid (and if so, how and when) for any property purchased or acquired or to be purchased or acquired by the company, and from whom and when purchased or acquired, and whether any part (and if so, how much) of such consideration money is for good will; (e) the amount (if any) payable as commission, bonus, or reward for subscribing or agreeing to subscribe, or procuring or agreeing to procure, subscriptions for any shares in the company, or the rate of any such commission; (f) the minimum subscription upon which directors will proceed to allotment; (g) the number of shares (if any) fixed by the articles of association as the qualification of a director; (h) the minimum amount payable on application and allotment on each share; (i) the number and amount of shares issued or agreed to be issued as fully paid or partly paid up otherwise than in money, and in the latter case the extent to which they are so paid up, and in either case the consideration for which and the person or persons to whom such shares have been issued or are proposed or intended to be issued; (j) the names, addresses, and occupations of the venders of any property purchased or acquired by the company, or to be so purchased or acquired, which is to be paid for wholly or partly out of the proceeds of the issue offered for subscription by the prospectus or the purchase or acquisition of which has been contemplated at the date of publication of the prospectus, and where there is more than one vender or the company is a subpurchaser, the amount payable in money or shares to each vender; (k) the amount or estimated amount of preliminary expenses; (l) the amount paid or intended to be paid and the shares allotted or intended to be allotted to or for any promoter and the consideration therefor; (m) the amount intended to be reserved for working capital; (n) the proposed application of the proceeds of the issue of the shares, and (o) the names and addresses of the auditors or intended auditors (if any) of the company. A prospectus which does not comply with the foregoing requirements shall be deemed fraudulent on the part of every promoter or director, and every person having authorized the insertion of his name in the prospectus as a director or as having agreed to become a director, and unless they show the fault was neither willful nor negligent they shall be jointly and severally liable for all damages caused thereby, and any person taking shares on the faith of such prospectus may, besides suing for damages, rescind the contract.

This section became a law in 1896. They have a further section which provides that no applicant for shares can waive any condition, such waiver being expressly declared to be void.

It is fully understood that this bill, upon the question of publicity, is not as far-reaching and does not attempt to produce many of the results that are within the contemplation of many of those who believe in the efficacy of the idea. For that reason it is conceded that the enactment and enforcement of its provisions will not necessarily furnish the final adequate or proper test by which the wisdom or efficacy of the idea of publicity can be determined. It is believed that it is a step in the right direction. If the operation of this bill proves to some extent advantageous and is not attended by any pronounced or serious business disturbance, it may then well be that further legislation on these lines, in order to apply the idea of publicity to its full and complete extent, may be deemed wise and justifiable.

PROVISIONS OF THE SUBSTITUTE BILL.

Section 1.

Section 1 describes in detail the character of the return to be made. These details are expected to disclose with a reasonable degree of accuracy the financial foundation of the corporation and its capitalization, demonstrating approximately the amount of overcapitalization. The information made public is an abstract of this return. In addition to the return the Commission is authorized to make inquiries in writing of the officer having the requisite knowledge of corporations in order to clear up any ambiguity or uncertainty that may result from

the returns filed.   These inquiries are confined to the items specified.
The returns and answers are to be made on oath, and if they are false
in any material particular the persons making the oath shall be deemed
guilty of perjury and punished accordingly.   While it is true that the
act requires many details, as to some of which the information in some
cases may not be obtainable, provision is made for that difficulty by
authorizing the Commission to excuse a corporation in writing wherever
it is impracticable, without fault of the corporation, to furnish any
such items.   After the first return is filed, if there is no change in the
condition of the corporation as to the items involved, the next return
is not required to restate the details, as a simple statement under such
circumstances that it is a duplicate will be sufficient.   If a corporation
fails to file the return, the court may restrain it from engaging in interstate commerce until such return is made.

As to all corporations hereafter organized, returns are absolutely
required to be filed at the time of their engaging in interstate commerce.   It is expected that this requirement will tend to discourage
the promotion and organization of any more overcapitalized industrial
combinations.   As to all existing corporations engaged in interstate
commerce, the returns are to be filed only upon the request of the
Interstate Commerce Commission.   It is no doubt true that the bill
could have required a return from all corporations engaged in interstate commerce.   It is no doubt also true that a very large majority
of the corporations that would thus be required to file returns are such
as are not only legitimately organized, but in their business operation
produce no injurious effect upon the public.   And as to them, they
would be subjected not only to unnecessary inconvenience, but in many
instances, perhaps, to great hardship, and as to such returns there is
not only no necessity but no public demand therefor.

In order to obviate this obvious serious inconvenience of requiring returns from all corporations engaged in interstate commerce,
it has been suggested that the bill could have been limited in its
operation to corporations above a certain amount of capitalization.
To this it was objected that it would be a discrimination against the
corporations as to which returns were required; that the law would
not be uniform in its operation, and for that reason would be unconstitutional.   The constitutionality of such a law would certainly be
open to grave question.   It is believed that this discretion vested in
the Commission will be exercised in such a way as to reach all corporations as to which returns are essential for the purposes above indicated
without subjecting the vast majority of legitimate corporations to
unnecessary inconvenience.   It seems to be clear that this provision
will avoid, so far as it can be avoided, any pronounced business disturbance as the result of this legislation and will for that reason be
generally and properly regarded as conservative and judicious legislation.

Section 2.

Section 2 relates to the oath and provides for punishment in case
the returns are false in any material particular.   It also provides that
whoever knowingly prepares a return that is false in any material
particular shall be guilty of suborration of perjury and punished
accordingly.

Section 3.

Section 3 provides for making public the abstract of the returns. They are to be published in such number for free distribution as the Commission may deem necessary and to be distributed under its direction.

Section 4.

Section 4 gives the Commission the same authority to inquire into the management of affairs of corporations relating to interstate and foreign commerce as is provided in the act to regulate commerce. The particular provisions of that act are found in section 12 of the act approved February 4, 1887, as amended March 2, 1889, and February 10, 1891, and reads as follows:

SEC. 12. That the Commission hereby created shall have authority to inquire into the management of the business of all common carriers subject to the provisions of this act, and shall keep itself informed as to the manner and method in which the same is conducted, and shall have the right to obtain from such common carriers full and complete information necessary to enable the Commission to perform the duties and carry out the objects for which it was created * * * and for the purposes of this act the Commission shall have power to require, by subpœna, the attendance and testimony of witnesses and the production of all books, papers, tariffs, contracts, agreements, and documents relating to any matter under investigation.

Such attendance of witnesses and the production of such documentary evidence may be required from any place in the United States at any designated place of hearing. And in case of disobedience to a subpœna the Commission, or any party to a proceeding before the Commission, may invoke the aid of any court of the United States in requiring the attendance and testimony of witnesses and the production of books, papers, and documents under the provisions of this section.

And any of the circuit courts of the United States within the jurisdiction of which such inquiry is carried on may, in case of contumacy or refusal to obey a subpœna issued to any common carrier subject to the provisions of this act, or other person, issue an order requiring such common carrier or other person to appear before said Commission (and produce books and papers, if so ordered) and give evidence touching the matter in question; and any failure to obey such order of the court may be punished by such court as a contempt thereof. * * *

The testimony of any witness may be taken, at the instance of a party in any proceeding or investigation depending before the Commission, by deposition at any time after a cause or proceeding is at issue on petition and answer. The Commission may also order testimony to be taken by deposition in any proceeding or investigation pending before it at any stage of such proceeding or investigation. Such depositions may be taken before any judge of any court of the United States, or any commissioner of a circuit, or any clerk of a district or circuit court, or any chancellor, justice, or judge of a supreme or superior court, mayor or chief magistrate of a city, judge of a county court, or court of common pleas of any of the United States, or any notary public, not being of counsel or attorney to either of the parties nor interested in the event of the proceeding or investigation. Reasonable notice must first be given in writing by the party or his attorney proposing to take such deposition to the opposite party or his attorney of record, as either may be nearest, which notice shall state the name of the witness and the time and place of the taking of his deposition. Any person may be compelled to appear and depose and to produce documentary evidence in the same manner as witnesses may be compelled to appear and testify and produce documentary evidence before the Commission, as hereinbefore provided.

Every person deposing as herein provided shall be cautioned and sworn (or affirm, if he so requests) to testify the whole truth, and shall be carefully examined. His testimony shall be reduced to writing by the magistrate taking the deposition, or under his direction, and shall, after it has been reduced to writing, be subscribed by the deponent.

If a witness whose testimony may be desired to be taken by deposition be in a foreign country, the deposition may be taken before an officer or person designated by the Commission, or agreed upon by the parties by stipulation in writing to be filed with the Commission. All depositions must be promptly filed with the Commission.

Witnesses whose depositions are taken pursuant to this act, and the magistrate or other officer taking the same, shall severally be entitled to the same fees as are paid for like services in the courts of the United States.

These provisions are applicable so far as they relate to the subject-matter of this bill. This section also provides a penalty for neglecting or refusing to make returns or attend and testify or answer any lawful inquiry or produce books, papers, contracts, or agreements.

Section 5.

Section 5 of this act covers the suggestions of the Attorney-General in his communication of January 3, 1903, to the special subcommittee on trusts of this committee. Upon this point, among other things, he made the following suggestions:

I believe the rebates and kindred advantages granted by carriers to large operators in the leading industries of the country as against their competitors in many years amounted to a sum that would represent fair interest upon the actual money invested in the business of such operators. * * *

My suggestion, therefore, is that as a first step in a policy to be persistently pursued until every industry, large and small, in the country can be assured of equal rights and opportunities, and until the tendency to monopolization of the important industries of the country is checked, that all discriminatory practices affecting interstate trade be made offenses to be enjoined and punished. Such legislation to be directed alike against those who give and those who receive the advantages thereof, and to cover discrimination in prices as against competitors in particular localities resorted to for the purpose of destroying competition in interstate and foreign trade, as well as discrimination by carriers.

Such practices are so obviously unreasonable that to inhibit them would be a measure of regulation of commerce to keep it free and unrestrained and not an attempt to exercise arbitrary power.

Upon the necessity of this legislation he says :

It may be said that under the "Act to regulate commerce" a shipper may be punished for receiving rebates or special rates less than the lawful published rates, and that it is unnecessary to provide additional legislation in this respect to curb trusts, monopolies, and combinations. This, however, is an erroneous statement.

Whatever the Congress may have designed in the act to regulate commerce regarding the punishment of shippers for participation in violation of that act, as construed by the courts, their punishable offenses fall under two heads:

First. Where the shipper has solicited or participated in instances of unjust discrimination, and

Second. In cases of fraud perpetrated by him against the carrier, e. g., by false representation of the contents of a package.

As to the first, the courts have held that to constitute unjust discrimination it is necessary to prove that at the time the lower unlawful rate was being granted to the favored shipper the higher lawful rate was imposed against another shipper on like commodities between the same points.

In many cases of departure by a carrier from its published tariffs the favored shipper has enjoyed his advantage for so long a time that all rivals have disappeared. In such cases, and they are the most numerous, no illegal discrimination exists; consequently the recipient of the unlawful rebates escapes the penalties of the act to regulate commerce.

The act prohibits the carrier from charging anyone a greater or less rate than the rates named in its schedules; but the penalties provided therefor have been held by the courts not to be applicable to any carrier that is an incorporated company.

The officers or agents of such incorporated company, who grant the rebate or make the unlawful concession in rates, are subject to indictment and punishment. That, however, is generally an impracticable remedy, because the agent who makes the concession is usually the only person by whom it can be ascertained that the rebate has been paid, and when he has testified in relation to the matter he has thereby obtained amnesty from prosecution.

Even if the corporation and its officers could be effectively reached by criminal proceedings, the law leaves unrestrained the persons, corporations, and combinations who are beneficiaries of the unlawful rebates.

This *casus omissus* of the act to regulate commerce should be supplied by imposing a penalty upon the incorporated carrier and beneficiary alike, and the right of the courts to restrain such practices at the suit of the United States—a right not settled and now vigorously challenged—should be made certain.

I think the operation of such an act should be limited to the transportation by common carriers subject to the act to regulate commerce. This is necessary for the reason that there is no requirement of law that rates shall be published by common carriers, except by railroad, or railroad and water carriers acting as one line. When the act to regulate commerce was under consideration, it was deemed impracticable, if not unwise, to attempt to regulate the rates of water or other common carriers. It was understood that in the nature of things water rates could not be stable.

In addition to that, it was believed that water competition must be unrestricted. As it is the least expensive means of transportation, it, wherever it could directly or indirectly compete with carriers by rail, would, approximately, furnish a basis for rates by railroad, and measurably keep such rates within the limits of extortion.

So that if provision is made by law to prevent rebates, a standard or established schedule must be referred to; and as the admitted abuse of magnitude has been in the favors granted by railroad companies, their rates, which the law requires shall be made public, should be taken as the rates which must be adhered to and made equal to all the people under similar conditions.

It should therefore be made unlawful to transport traffic by carriers subject to the "Act to regulate commerce" at any rate less than such carriers' published rate, and all who participate in the violation of such law should be punished.

The section herewith reported is substantially the section of the bill drawn by the Department of Justice, the particular distinction being the insertion of the language " or shall receive any advantage by way of facilities or service," the occasion for its insertion being that it was as necessary to prohibit the undue advantage conferred upon the shipper by way of facilities which placed his competitor at a disadvantage as it was to prohibit the shipper from receiving annual rebates and thus making the cost of carriage less for him than his competitor, this branch of the proposition being inadvertently omitted in the draft made by the Department of Justice. With this exception the section is substantially its draft, and it is also in substance the first section of a bill introduced in the Senate by Senator Nelson February 5, 1902 (S. 3575). The necessity for the adoption of this section for the reasons given by the Attorney-General in his suggestions has been urged upon Congress for the past five or six years by the Interstate Commerce Commission. It seems to us there can be no question about its propriety, as all concur as to its necessity.

Section 6.

Section 6 prohibits any corporation engaged in the production, manufacture, or sale of any article of commerce violating the provisions of the bill, in relation to rebates or facilities, or attempting to monopolize or control the production, manufacture, or sale by destroying competition in any particular locality by a discrimination in prices or special privileges from using in aid of that purpose any of the facilities or instrumentalities of interstate commerce. This is in response to the suggestion of the Attorney-General, which reads as follows:

An additional provision should be made to reach corporations, combinations, and associations which produce and manufacture wholly within a State, but whose products or sales enter into interstate commerce. It should relate, first, to such concerns as fatten on rebates in transportation (this has already been provided for in our section 5); and, second, to concerns which sell below the general price of a commodity in particular localities, or otherwise in particular localities wantonly seek to destroy competition. These could be excluded with their commodities, products, or manufactures from crossing State lines.

Section 6 is intended to answer the second suggestion. It will be observed that this section proceeds to a certain extent upon a new idea or perhaps a departure from the existing method of reaching the desired result. The Sherman antitrust law proceeds in effect upon the hypothesis that contracts and agreements are being made that in their operation restrain interstate trade and commerce, and it is directed against such contracts and agreements and such acts upon the part of individuals. This section proceeds upon the theory of the existence of the same conditions and reaches them from another direction. It in effect provides that no corporation manufacturing, producing, or selling an article of commerce and discriminating in prices for the purpose of destroying competition in any particular locality, shall in any way use, directly or indirectly, in aid of accomplishing that purpose, any of the facilities or instrumentalities of interstate commerce. It goes as far as we can go for the purpose of reaching this particular object within constitutional lines.

Instead of undertaking to control the manufacture, production, and sale directly in the State, it attempts to exercise control when the purpose is illegal by depriving the manufacture, production, or sale within a State, of the use of the facilities and instrumentalities of interstate commerce in aid of such illegal purpose. It says, while we can not control your illegal act in the State, you shall not use the instrumentalities of interstate commerce in aid thereof. There is probably no instance where the production, manufacture, and sale is carried on for the purposes indicated in the act where the facilities and instrumentalities of interstate commerce are not absolutely essential to the success of the business.

To meet the suggestion that the provisions of this act could be easily evaded by the principal corporation selling its output in the State where it is produced or manufactured, to other persons or corporations who would necessarily engage in interstate commerce for the purpose of distributing the article of commerce thus produced, manufactured, or sold, and thus enable the principal corporation to carry on its business with the prohibited purpose without being engaged in interstate commerce, we provide that no other person or corporation shall use any of the facilities of interstate commerce in order to enable the first-mentioned corporation to continue its production, manufacture, or sale for the prohibited purpose. While it is not insisted that this statute can not to some extent be evaded it is believed that the last paragraph of this section goes as far as we can go in providing against such contingencies.

THE KNIGHT CASE.

This section is an effort, within constitutional limitations, to enlarge the scope of the Sherman antitrust law to reach the situation indicated by the opinion in the case of E. C. Knight & Co. (156 U. S., 1). It should be said, however, in reference to that case, that its scope is ordinarily somewhat misconceived, and it is supposed to go further in narrowing the scope of the Sherman antitrust law than it really does. That case was an equity suit brought for the purpose of annulling certain agreements under which the unlawful combinations were alleged to have been made, and for preventing and restraining violations of the Sherman antitrust act. The bill was based mainly upon the written contracts, and it appears from the examination of the opinion that the court felt confined to the terms of these contracts in determining the issue raised by the bill. The Government does not seem to have made a case, as it might have done, upon general principles against the defendants, relying upon these contracts as one of the elements making out their case, but by the allegations in the bill appear to have narrowed the contention to the construction of the written contracts themselves. That this was the theory of a majority of the court in reaching its conclusion and pronouncing its opinion is, we think, clear. The court say:

> But the monopoly and restraint denounced by the act are the monopoly and restraint of interstate and international trade or commerce, while the conclusion to to be assumed *on this record* is that the result of the transaction complained of was the creation of a monopoly in the *manufacture* of a necessary of life.

Note the question which the court here assert was the only question raised upon the record, and that was that the contracts resulted in the "creation" of a monopoly in the *manufacture* of a "necessary of life," not a monopoly and restraint of interstate commerce, a very different and very much broader proposition. If the bill and the record had made a case coming within the last alternative above suggested, the result might have been and undoubtedly would have been exactly the reverse. It does not appear that there were any difficulties in the way of laying a foundation in the bill and sustaining it by proper evidence, for such a case as would have shown a contract or agreement in restraint of interstate commerce, which would have been, therefore, restrainable under the act. It is because of this circumscribed foundation made by the bill and disclosed by the record, to which the court were very obviously confined in their conclusion, that led it to make all along through the opinion the very clear and obvious distinction between manufacture and commerce. They say, for instance:

> The fundamental question is whether, conceding that the existence of a monopoly *in manufacture* is established by the evidence, that monopoly can be directly suppressed under the act of Congress in the mode attempted by this bill.

That is to say, a monopoly in manufacture alone can not be shown to have any connection by the record with interstate commerce. Could such a monopoly be suppressed?

Again, "commerce succeeds to manufacture and is not a part of it." The record disclosed simply a contract to manufacture, not a contract to enter in or engage in or regulate or control interstate commerce. Hence the court say:

> The power to regulate commerce is the power to prescribe the rule by which commerce shall be governed, and is a power independent of the power to suppress monopoly. But it may operate in repression of monopoly whenever that comes within the rules by which commerce is governed or whenever the transaction is itself a monopoly of commerce.

But the record did not show that the monopoly in question had anything to do with commerce. The court emphasizes this point throughout the opinion, saying later, with this precise question in mind as to what was disclosed by the record in that case:

> The object was manifestly private gain in the *manufacture* of the commodity, *but not through the control of interstate or foreign commerce.*

That is to say, that object was the only object disclosed by the contract and the record. In order to have been reached under the anti-

trust act, however, the contract should have disclosed that object and
the additional object of controlling interstate or foreign commerce
which neither the contract or the record did show. The fact that there
was an incidental allegation that the product of the refineries was to
be distributed among the several States in the judgment of the court
added nothing to the substance of the case under the bill, as they say:

It is true that the bill alleged that the products of these refineries were sold and
distributed among the several States, and that all the companies were engaged in
trade or commerce with the several States and with foreign nations; but this was no
more than to say that trade and commerce served manufacture to fulfill its function.

Again:

There was nothing in the proofs *to indicate any intention to put a restraint upon trade
or commerce*, and the fact, as we have seen, that trade or commerce might be indirectly affected was not enough to entitle complainants to a decree.

And again:

The subject-matter of the sale was shares of manufacturing stock, and the relief
sought was the surrender of property which had already passed and the suppression
of the *alleged monopoly in manufacture* by the restoration of the status quo before the
transfers; yet the act of Congress only authorized the circuit courts to proceed by
way of preventing and restraining violations of the act in respect of contracts,
combinations, or conspiracies in restraint of interstate or international trade or
commerce.

Note the significance of the language. Here, in summing up the
whole case, the court expressly say that the relief sought was "the
suppression of the alleged monopoly in manufacture," not in alleged
monopoly or restraint of interstate or international trade or commerce.
Very clearly, from the view taken by the court of the allegations in
the bill and the facts disclosed by the record, the whole controversy
was absolutely narrowed and confined to the construction to be placed
upon the written contracts, which by their terms did not either directly
or indirectly relate to or undertake to control interstate trade and
commerce, and it is very clear that under the act, which only prohibited the control of interstate trade and commerce, the court could not
declare a contract void which in terms was confined to manufacture
alone.

Section 7.

Section 7 of the act is in response to another suggestion of the
Attorney-General, which reads as follows:

Such legislation, to certainly reach producers guilty of practices injurious to
national and international commerce, should, in my judgment, take the form of penal-
izing the transportation of the goods produced by the guilty parties, and the Federal courts should be given power to restrain such transportation at the suit of the
Government.

This section prohibits, in effect, transportation companies now subject to the provisions of the act to regulate commerce from knowingly
transporting any property produced, manufactured, or sold in violations of the provisions of this bill and of the act to protect trade and
commerce against unlawful restraints and monopolies. This section is
in substance a bill introduced by Mr. Gillett, of Massachusetts, at the
first session of this Congress, H. R. 3105, which in turn is a bill introduced by him in the Fifty-fourth Congress, H. R. 10249, and favorably reported by the Committee on the Judiciary to the House, House
Report No. 3062. It is also in substance section 10 of a bill reported

by the Judiciary Committee to the House during the Fifty-sixth Congress, H. R. 10539, Report No. 1506.

The propriety and the necessity of a section like this is also suggested by a remark of Judge Harlan in his dissenting opinion in the case of United States against E. C. Knight Co. (156 U. S., p. 40), where he says:

If it be suggested that Congress might have prohibited the *transportation* from the State in which they are manufactured of any articles, by whomsoever at the time owned, that had been manufactured by combinations formed to monopolize some designated part of trade or commerce among the States, my answer is that it is not within the functions of the judiciary to adjudge that Congress shall employ particular means in execution of a given power, simply because such means are, in the judgment of the courts, best conducive to the end sought to be accomplished. Congress, in the exercise of its discretion as to choice of means conducive to an end to which it was competent, determined to reach that end through civil proceedings instituted to prevent or restrain these obnoxious combinations in their attempts to burden interstate commerce by obstructions that interfere in advance of transportation with the free course of trade between the people of the States.

From this quotation it is reasonably to be inferred that during the consultations of the court and as a part of their discussion it was probably assumed that Congress could legally prohibit the transportation from the State in which they are manufactured of any articles by whomsoever at the time owned that had been manufactured by combinations. And it may, perhaps, be further assumed that in the judgment of the court this would have been a measure that could properly have been enacted to accomplish the purposes in view, and to that extent it may be said that the citation is an approval of this section.

Section 8.

Section 8 is a section relating to the testimony of witnesses and deprives them of the privilege of claiming their constitutional exemption from testifying upon the ground of criminating themselves and applies to all prosecutions, hearings, and proceedings under this bill, as well as under the act to protect trade and commerce against unlawful restraints and monopolies. This is in substance the act in relation to testimony before the Interstate Commerce Commission approved February 11, 1893, which has the same purpose in view, this last mentioned act having been sustained by the United States Supreme Court as constitutional. (Brown *v.* Walker, 161 U. S., 591.)

Section 9.

Section 9 vests the circuit courts of the United States with jurisdiction to restrain the violations of any provisions of this act, and with a little condensation is one of the sections drawn by the Department of Justice.

Sections 10 and 11.

Sections 10 and 11 are taken verbatim from the bill drawn by the Department of Justice, and with section 9, are understood to be essential to the efficient administration of the law.

The provision as to threefold damages is the same provision that has been in existence since 1890 as a part of the act to protect trade and commerce against unlawful restraints and monopolies, known as the Sherman anti-trust law.

This section appears to be somewhat drastic in its terms, and may be thought to be open to abuse. It should, however, be borne in mind that the similar section of the Sherman antitrust law has been in force nearly thirteen years, and the committee are not advised of a single instance where it has been improperly used. While the legislation proposed by this bill is along the lines of the Sherman anti-trust law, it is obvious from a comparison between the two that this section is not so comprehensive and far-reaching, and it is therefore fairly to be assumed that no injurious results may be expected from its adoption. It is not believed that any of the provisions of this bill are open to successful criticism from a constitutional standpoint. All of its provisions are along the lines of the legislation which has already been sustained by the Supreme Court as constitutional, and are confined to and depend upon their relation to and connection with interstate commerce.

The committee therefore recommend the adoption of the following amendment by way of substitute for H. R. 17:

Amend H. R. 17 by striking out all after the enacting clause and insert in lieu thereof the following substitute:

That every corporation which may be hereafter organized shall, at the time of engaging in interstate or foreign commerce, file the return hereinafter provided for; and every corporation, whenever organized, and engaged in interstate or foreign commerce shall file a return with the Interstate Commerce Commission for the year ending December thirty-first, whenever, and at such time, as requested by said Commission, stating its name, date of organization, where and when organized, giving statutes under which it is organized, and all amendments thereof; if consolidated, naming constituent companies and where and when organized, with the same information as to such constituent companies, so far as applicable, as is herein required of such corporation; if reorganized, name of original corporation or corporations, with full reference to laws under which all the reorganizations have taken place, with the same information as to all prior companies in the chain of reorganization, so far as applicable, as is herein required of such corporation; amount of bonds issued and outstanding; amount of authorized capital stock, shares into which it is divided, par value, whether common or preferred, and distinction between each; amount issued and outstanding; amount paid in; how much, if any, paid in in cash, and how much, if any, in property; if any part in property, describing in detail the kind, character, and location, with its cash market value at the time it was received in payment, giving the elements upon which said market value is based, and especially whether in whole or in part upon the capitalization of earnings, earning capacity, or economies, with the date and the cash price paid therefor at its last sale; the name and address of each officer, managing agent, and director; a true and correct copy of its articles of incorporation; a full, true, and correct copy of any and all rules, regulations, and by-laws adopted for the management and control of its business and the direction of its officers, managing agents, and directors. Nothing herein contained shall be construed as relieving any corporation from making, in addition to the foregoing, such returns as are now required by the "Act to regulate commerce," approved February fourth, eighteen hundred and eighty-seven, and all amendments thereof; but the provisions of this Act, as to signing and making oath to returns and making answers on oath to written inquiries, shall be applicable to returns and such answers made under said Act and amendments thereof.

So far as any return may be a duplicate of one already filed, that fact may be stated, and the details, which are in such case duplicates, need not be repeated. Upon its being made to appear to the satisfaction of the Commission that without fault on its part it is impracticable for such corporation to furnish any of the items aforesaid, it may, by a written order of said Commission, be excused from furnishing such item or items.

Said Commission shall cause to be prepared a blank return for the use of such corporations, containing the foregoing requirements, and shall make such rules and regulations as may, in its judgment, be necessary to carry out the purposes of this Act. The president, treasurer, and a majority of the directors of such corporation shall make oath in writing on said return that said return is true. The treasurer, or other officer of such corporation, having the requisite knowledge, shall answer on oath all inquiries that may be made in writing on the direction of said Commission in relation to said return. Any corporation failing to make such return, or whose treasurer or other officer shall fail to make the answers aforesaid, may be restrained, on the suit of the United States, from engaging in interstate commerce until such return is made. Suit may be brought in any district of the United States at the election of the Attorney-General.

SEC. 2. That whoever knowingly swears to a return that is false in any material particular, or knowingly swears to an answer to any such inquiry that is false in any material particular, shall be deemed guilty of perjury and punished as provided in section fifty-three hundred and ninety-two of the Revised Statutes of the United States. Whoever shall knowingly prepare, or cause to be prepared, a return or answer that is false as aforesaid shall be deemed guilty of subornation of perjury and punished as aforesaid.

SEC. 3. That it shall be the duty of said Commission to cause to be prepared and published, on or before the first day of June in each year, a list of all corporations making returns, with an abstract of such returns, for free distribution in such number as said Commission may deem necessary to meet any reasonable and proper demand therefor, to be distributed under the direction of the Commission.

SEC. 4. That said Commission shall have the same authority to inquire into the management of the business of said corporations, relating to interstate and foreign commerce, in the same manner and to the same extent, with the same power to compel the attendance of, and the giving of testimony by, witnesses, and the production of books, papers, contracts, and agreements, as is provided in "An Act to regulate commerce," approved February fourth, eighteen hundred and eighty-seven, and all amendments thereof. Said Commission may employ such agents and clerks, as in its judgment may be necessary for properly executing the provisions of this Act, and shall make an annual report to the President, containing, among other things, such specific recommendations for additional legislation as it may deem necessary.

Any person who shall neglect or refuse to make returns, attend and testify or answer any lawful inquiry hereinbefore provided for, or produce books, papers, contracts, agreements, and documents, if in his custody, control, or power to do so, in obedience to the subpoena or lawful requirements of the Commission, shall be deemed guilty of an offense against the United States, and upon conviction thereof by a court of competent jurisdiction shall be punished by a fine of not less than five hundred dollars nor more than five thousand dollars.

SEC. 5. That any person, carrier, lessee, trustee, receiver, officer, agent, or representative of a carrier, subject to the Act to regulate commerce, who, or which, shall offer, grant, give, solicit, accept, or receive any rebate, concession, facilities, or service, in respect to the transportation of any property, in interstate or foreign commerce, by any common carrier subject to said Act, whereby any such property shall, by any device whatever, be transported at a less rate, than that named in the tariffs, published and filed by such carrier, as is required by said Act to regulate commerce, or shall receive any advantage by way of facilities or service, shall be deemed guilty of a misdemeanor, and shall upon conviction thereof be subject to a fine of not less than one thousand dollars.

SEC. 6. That no corporation engaged in the production, manufacture, or sale of any article of commerce, violating any of the provisions of section five of this Act, or attempting to monopolize or control the production, manufacture, or sale thereof, in any particular locality, by discrimination in prices, or by giving special privileges or rebates or otherwise, in order to destroy competition therein, in such locality, shall use, either directly or indirectly, any of the facilities or instrumentalities of interstate commerce, or in any way engage in interstate commerce, for the purpose of aiding or facilitating, either directly or indirectly, such production, manufacture, or sale, with such intent; nor shall any other person or corporation use any of the facilities or instrumentalities of interstate commerce, or in any way engage in interstate commerce, in buying, selling, or disposing of any such article of commerce, for the purpose of enabling such first-mentioned corporation to engage or to continue to engage in such production, manufacture, sale, or control, with such intent. Every corporation or person, violating the provisions of this section, shall be punished, on conviction, by a fine of not less than five hundred and not exceeding five thousand dollars.

SEC. 7. That any common carrier, lessee, trustee, receiver, or transportation company, engaged in interstate commerce, now subject to the provisions of said Act to regulate commerce, knowingly transporting any property produced, manufactured, or sold in violation of the provisions of this Act, or in violation of the provisions of "An Act to protect trade and commerce against unlawful restraints and monopolies," approved July second, eighteen hundred and ninety, in interstate commerce, shall be subject to a penalty of not less than one thousand dollars, to be recovered by the

United States in any court of the United States, having jurisdiction thereof, which suit may be brought in any district in which such common carrier, lessee, trustee, or receiver, or transportation company has an office or conducts business.

Sec. 8. That in all prosecutions, hearings, and proceedings under the provisions of this Act, and under the provisions of "An Act to protect trade and commerce against unlawful restraints and monopolies," approved July second, eighteen hundred and ninety, whether civil or criminal, no person shall be excused from attending and testifying, or from producing books, papers, contracts, agreements, and documents before the courts of the United States, or the commissioners thereof, or the Interstate Commerce Commission, or in obedience to the subpœna of the same, on the ground, or for the reason, that the testimony or evidence, documentary or otherwise, required of him, may tend to criminate him, or subject him, to a penalty or forfeiture; but no person shall be prosecuted or subjected to any penalty or forfeiture for, or on account of, any transaction, matter, or thing concerning which he may testify or produce evidence, documentary or otherwise, before said courts, commissioners, or Commission, or in obedience to the subpœna of either of them, in any such case or proceeding.

Testimony of witnesses under the provisions of the Act to regulate interstate commerce and amendments thereof, and of this Act, before said Commission, or any member thereof, shall be on oath, and either of the members of said Commission may administer oaths and affirmations and sign subpœnas.

Sec. 9. That the several circuit courts of the United States are hereby invested with jurisdiction to prevent and restrain the violation of any of the provisions of this Act. It shall be the duty of the several district attorneys of the United States in their respective districts, under the direction of the Attorney-General, to institute proceedings in equity to prevent and restrain the several acts herein forbidden. Such proceedings may be by way of petition, setting forth the case, and praying that the acts hereby made unlawful, shall be enjoined or otherwise prohibited. When the parties complained of shall be duly notified of such petition, the court shall proceed as soon as may be to the hearing and determination of the case, and upon such petition, and before final decree, the court may at any time make such temporary restraining order or prohibition as shall be deemed just.

Sec. 10. That whenever it shall appear to the court before which any proceedings under this Act shall be pending, that the ends of justice require that other parties shall be brought before the court, the court may cause them to be summoned, whether they reside in the district where the court is held or not, and subpœnas to that end may be served in any district by the marshal thereof.

Sec. 11. That any person or corporation injured in business or property, by any other person or corporation, by reason of anything forbidden or declared to be unlawful by this Act, may sue therefor in any circuit court of the United States in the district in which the defendant or defendants reside or are found, without respect to the amount in controversy, and shall recover threefold the damages sustained and the costs of suit, including a reasonable attorney's fee.

Sec. 12. That this Act shall take effect May first, nineteen hundred and three.

Also amend the title so it will read as follows: "A bill requiring corporations engaged in interstate commerce to make returns, prohibiting rebates and discriminations, and the use of interstate commerce in attempts to destroy competition, and for other purposes."

O

BILL REQUIRING RETURNS FROM CORPORATIONS, PROHIBITING REBATES, ETC.

JANUARY 29, 1903.—Committed to the Committee of the Whole House on the state of the Union and ordered to be printed.

Mr. DEARMOND, from the Committee on the Judiciary, submitted the following

VIEWS OF THE MINORITY.

[To accompany H. R. 17, entitled "A bill requiring all corporations engaged in interstate commerce to file returns with the Secretary of the Treasury, disclosing their true financial condition, and of their capital stock, and imposing a tax upon such as have outstanding capital stock unpaid in whole or in part.]

The undersigned do not oppose the passage of the measure reported by the committee, but urge that it should be amended and perfected, or at least greatly improved.

We realize that there is a strong popular demand, the outgrowth of bitter experience and balked efforts for redress, for legislation, honestly and wisely conceived, for the abatement as speedily as possible of many as possible of the ills which the people suffer from the exactions of the trusts.

Trying to respond to this righteous demand, we wish to impress upon the House the importance of making this bill the best its wisdom can devise.

We believe this great demand for antitrust legislation springs from experience, not anticipation. The people are suffering now from the evil operations of the trusts now in existence. Of course they are warranted in believing and fearing that if they longer tamely submit to trust robbery more robbers will appear and all will become more ruthless.

They understand that the best deterrent they can bring to bear upon the spoiler who may be is that which proves most effective when applied to the spoiler that is.

A large part of the bill is devoted to "publicity." Indeed, publicity is its most prominent feature. Publicity as a panacea for the trust evil is not new.

But of late this remedy has been advertised so extensively that we may not unnaturally be surprised when we find that it is now prescribed mainly for the trusts that may be, while as for the trusts that are—those which have wrought and are still working much of evil, and which threaten to work still more in the future, near and far—the publicity remedy may be administered to some of them, sometime, in broken doses, without being prescribed.

In other words, the bill provides for requiring every corporation hereafter organized to lay bare, at the time of entering interstate commerce, its foundation and superstructure, its strength and its weakness. No matter that it may be organized to compete with some mighty trust, that trust, covered, standing in the shadow, must have the opportunity to gaze upon the nakedness of its fledgeling rival; and thus it is easier to strike the fatal blow.

The bill requires "every corporation which may be hereafter organized," "at the time of engaging in interstate or foreign commerce," to make a full report; a report so full, it is supposed, as to advise dealers and investors in corporation stocks to buy its shares understandingly, or understandingly refrain from investing in them.

It is claimed that there is no hardship in requiring of a new corporation what is not required of an old one, for it is said that those who enter the new corporation are not under compulsion to enter it—they have the option not to call it into being. Of course that is true, but, viewed from the standpoint of the suffering public, what reason is there for exempting existing corporations from the universal, enforced scrutiny to which the new corporations are to be subjected?

Is it because the people are concerned about future corporations, whether good or bad, great or small, but have neither need nor wish to know something of existing corporations, even if they are bad? Surely that can not be the reason for flying from the ills we suffer to those we know not of.

The argument most relied upon for this partiality to corporations now in being, including numerous trusts, is that upon very many existing corporations it would be onerous, and to the public, as to them, profitless, to require the report exacted of new corporations.

A complete answer to this contention is that any publicity worthy of the name, enforced through legislation, must be comparatively valueless in many instances, and the compulsion required to secure it annoying, embarrassing, even prejudicial, in many instances.

If publicity is deemed of enough importance to justify an effort—not to say a pretentious effort—to secure it, then the annoyance, the embarrassment, the injury incidental to its acquisition for the public welfare, must not prove a bar to the enactment of an effective statute for securing publicity. This does not mean that there shall not be recognized the fact that a line may be drawn between the great corporations and the small ones.

Another view: What could tend more surely and effectively to a perpetuation of the great power and baleful influence of a giant trust than this requirement that every newcomer shall be stripped naked before it, while it may remain covered? Suppose a corporation were organized to enter the lists against the sugar trust, or the steel trust, or the Standard oil trust, or the tobacco trust, would enforced publicity, applied to the new corporation, be anything else than its exposure, defenseless, to the mighty forces of the colossal trust now in being?

We propose to amend the bill so as to *require* the great corporations, among them the trusts from which the public suffer *now*, to make public that *information* which is deemed essential to the general welfare. If what it is most important to know can not be given publicity by positive requirement, then is vaunted publicity a pretense, and not a thing of substance and value.

A number of things not specified should be reported, among them the amount of taxes paid for the preceding year, and we offer an amendment to include that additional item. We believe there can be no good objection to this simple amendment, and we hope no bad objection will be interposed, or, if it is, that it may not prevail.

The first section of the substitute, which requires returns to be filed by corporations with a view of securing the advantages of "publicity," shows a most remarkable case of omission. It provides no penalty for noncompliance. Any corporation may with impunity neglect to file its returns. The law may be practically ignored without punishment. Not the slightest harm or inconvenience would follow that policy of inaction until the particular corporation was singled out and proceeded against by the United States in a suit for an injunction to restrain the corporation from shipping its products into another State, and then a filing of the return would end the suit. A prompt filing of returns would confer no advantage. A delayed filing of returns after suit would impose no disadvantage. We suggest an amendment.

A simple amendment, but a valuable one, we think, is suggested as an addition to sections 5, 6, and 7 of the substitute, declaring each day's violation of the respective sections to constitute a distinct offense.

Section 6 of the substitute purports to deny to certain corporations "the facilities and instrumentalities" of interstate commerce. Why not also deny these same facilities and instrumentalities to associations, trustees, and individuals under the like circumstances? We know of no good reason for the omission—we are warranted in denominating it a refusal—to do so. And we propose to enumerate, as embraced within and constituting a part of such "facilities and instrumentalities," the mails, the telegraph, and the telephone.

Why does the committee refuse to do this? Perhaps the answer will be that "facilities and instrumentalities" include the mails, the telegraph, and the telephone. But the gentlemen who answer thus, when pressed, can go no further than to say they *believe* what at first they appear to confidently assert.

If they wish to deny to the offending corporations such facilities and instrumentalities as the mails, the telegraph, and the telephone, how can they so strenuously object to passing from belief to certainty by expressly mentioning them? At most and worst the few words employed in the cautionary specification would be but surplusage. This bill, of many pages and little substance, is proof conclusive that its authors are not niggardly with words.

If section 6 would be valuable in dealing with corporations, the section which we recommend, containing precisely the same provisions applied to natural persons, ought to be unobjectionable.

Criticism has been directed by some against section 7 of the substitute, purporting to provide for punishing the common carrier for transporting trust-made or monopolistic goods, putting the responsibility of deciding the intricate legal question involved, not upon a court, but upon the carrier; that is to say, upon its officers. If the carrier refuses to transport goods which should be carried, it is liable to penalties. If it consents to transport goods which should not be carried, it is also liable to penalties. But how are its officers to decide whether to carry or refuse to carry the freight offered? It has taken the courts days and weeks to decide such an issue, but the officer of the transportation company must decide it *instanter* at his peril.

Besides, by refusing transportation on the plea, whether founded in fact or not, that it is unlawful under this act, the transportation officer of a railroad might bankrupt any shipper, and thus play into the hands of the trusts. To make the provision fair and effective, a system of branding or otherwise marking articles offered for shipment should be established, with suitable penalties for evasion of the requirement and fraud in pretending to comply with it.

The simpler the remedy, if effective, and the larger the number of those who are qualified to administer it whenever interested, the greater the good accomplished. It is not easy to find a sovereign remedy for the trust evil, nor is it wise to depend upon the zeal, industry, and integrity of just a few officials to administer the remedy prescribed. If something at once simple and easily used could be provided, so that any man aggrieved could seek and find a plain, open way to relief and redress of grievances, much good would be accomplished.

May not the bankruptcy law be extended to offending corporations? If so, the way to relief and redress is plain enough, and the multitude may walk safely and confidently therein.

Can it be a stretch of reason or of law to denounce over-capitalization as an act of bankruptcy? The individual who, having $100,000 worth of property, and only that much, floats $200,000 in paper, based upon the $100,000 worth of property, is in a fair way to be adjudged a bankrupt.

Now, why shall not the corporation whose property is worth but $100,000, but which issues $200,000 in stock, be liable to be adjudged a bankrupt by reason of that act—why may not that over-issue of stock, that over-capitalizing, be justly and legally declared to be an act of bankruptcy? In what respect would a law making the over-issue of stock—the stock-watering industry—an act of bankruptcy be lacking in constitutional sanction or in broad public policy? We propose an amendment of this character.

The constitutionality of an enactment providing for the forfeiture and confiscation of articles transported in interstate commerce in violation of a valid law would be questioned by but few. If the same offending were declared by a Federal statute to be an act of bankruptcy, who is authorized to denounce that statute as being unconstitutional?

Simple insolvency, unmixed with anything else, may constitute bankruptcy, but "bankrupt" means more than "insolvent." The main ingredient in a bankruptcy may be wrong-doing. So it is not unreasonable to believe that Congress may constitutionally declare each of the potent evil performances, whereby the trusts violate the law or the fundamental principles of public policy, to the manifest injury of the public, an act of bankruptcy. Accordingly, we submit further amendments to enable anyone interested to seek redress from trust oppression, by resort to proceedings in bankruptcy.

We believe no one who permits himself to do even a little thinking upon the subject will care to question the simplicity or efficacy of a resort to bankruptcy proceeding to break the backbone of a trust; he may raise the question of constitutionality. But what more can he say than that he doubts the constitutionality of the legislation proposed, or that he believes, with varying degrees of intensity, that such legislation would be declared unconstitutional? We trust the courts would uphold it as constitutional.

Why not test the matter? That can be done by passing such a law as we urge, but can not be done otherwise in a thousand years—can never be done. If declared unconstitutional, that part of the enactment would simply be worthless—be nothing—but if adjudged constitutional, how invaluable it might be. If you really wish to do something against the trusts and for the people, try it.

Articles tainted in the clutch of a trust, when carried beyond the border of the State in which they are produced, ought to be subject to seizure and confiscation, and to that end we suggest an amendment, the provisions of which are embodied in H. R. 3105, introduced by Mr. Gillett, of Massachusetts.

So, also, should every corporation engaged ·in interstate commerce be subject to the jurisdiction of the courts of any State in which it shall carry on any business, as completely as citizens and residents of the State are subject to such jurisdiction; and·we recommend that the bill be amended accordingly. With the power of the United States over interstate commerce wisely and honestly exercised, and the corporations engaged in interstate commerce amenable to State laws, in State courts, in each State in which they shall do business, to the same extent as if created in and by that State, many trust abuses will soon be things of the past.

As a speedy, direct, and sure relief from many most grievous monopolies and exactions of the trusts, we earnestly recommend a repeal of so much of the tariff law as imposes high protective tariff duties upon certain articles of prime necessity in the American household and in the development of the material wealth and the extension of the commerce of the nation, and which are well known to be controlled by great trusts, to the serious detriment of both the individual citizen and the commonwealth.

Without going into the tariff question, we submit that upon whatever theory a tariff law may be framed we are unable to conceive upon what theory, tinctured with honesty or justice, any particular item of tariff taxation can be persistently, doggedly, defiantly continued when notoriously a greedy trust is the beneficiary and a suffering public the victims of the legislation, and of the vicious perversity which perpetuates it. We believe a fair revision of the tariff laws would afford the best of remedies for many trust abuses.

In addition to the recommendation of specific amendments of the tariff laws, we further urge that the President be clothed with the power and intrusted with the duty of withdrawing from the trusts the sheltering and fostering care of the tariff, whenever, in his judgment, on facts brought to his attention, the public welfare requires such action by him. In this is nothing of coercion—merely an appeal to the President's patriotism and sense of right, coupled with an extension of the power to act.

It was foreseen when the present tariff law was passed that in it would be found an invitation, and sheltered by it a breeding ground for the trusts, and it was then proposed to give the President the power by proclamation to take off or suspend any item of the tariff taxation, whenever he should be convinced that a trust had taken advantage of it to monopolize and rob.

A number of times since the like proposition has been made and always it was scornfully rejected. Again we bring it forward. Will you again reject it? Have you more confidence in the trusts than you have in the President? We have not. We would far rather look to the President, charged with a solemn duty, for the protection of the people than to the trusts that have been and are despoiling them. The taxing power of the Government has not been invoked in dealing with the trusts. We believe that much revenue may be raised and many trust abuses corrected by a resort to this great power; and so we submit an amendment for its exercise.

An apparent omission may be supplied by the adoption of an amendment which we propose, making the legislation applicable to the Territories and the District of Columbia as well as the States, as to interstate commerce.

We are not opposed to the publicity treatment; we favor it. But we do not regard it as a cure, much less as a substitute for better remedies. If, however, by the potent agency of a majority vote, publicity is to be heralded as the great cure-all, we insist that enough of it shall be administered to test its efficacy. We are opposed to playing with publicity and discarding all else. The case is too serious.

As for the prohibitions and penalties hurled at certain corporations in certain sections of the bill, they bristle somewhat upon paper, but are not likely to accomplish much, if anything, not attainable by a vigorous enforcement of existing laws. Still, if the majority in the House will not permit anything better to pass, we shall vote for the substitute bill, placing, as we believe the country will place, the responsibility for another miscarriage where it belongs.

The amendments which we recommend are appended hereto.

DAVID A. DEARMOND.
D. H. SMITH.
HENRY D. CLAYTON.
R. L. HENRY.

We concur generally in the foregoing without committing ourselves to each specific amendment or to what is said concerning each.

WM. ELLIOTT.
WM. H. FLEMING.

AMENDMENTS TO THE SUBSTITUTE PROPOSED BY THE MINORITY.

Amendment No. 1.

Amend by striking out the following words at the beginning of the substitute, to wit:

"That every corporation which may be hereafter organized shall, at the time of engaging in interstate or foreign commerce, file the return hereinafter provided for, and every corporation whenever organized and engaged in interstate or foreign commerce shall file a return with the Interstate Commerce Commission for the year ending December thirty-first, whenever and at such time as requested by said Commission."

And insert the following in lieu thereof:

"That every corporation, whether now or hereafter organized and engaged or that may engage in interstate or foreign commerce, and having a capital of one hundred thousand dollars or more, shall annually, during the month of January of each year, unless the Interstate Commerce Commission from time to time substitute another date, make and file with said Commission for the preceding year a return and report,"

Amendment No. 2.

Amend by adding at the end of section 6 the following: "The facilities and instrumentalities of interstate commerce," as the terms are employed in this act, shall embrace the mails, the telegraph, and the telephone.

Amendment No. 3.

Amend the first section of the substitute by inserting just after "sale," fifth line, sixth page, the words "the amount of taxes paid for the preceding year."

Amendment No. 4.
Add to section 1 the following:
"Any corporation failing to make such return in the time and manner required by this act shall be subject to a penalty of not less than 1 per cent on its capital stock."

Amendment No. 5.
Amend by adding at the end of sections 5, 6, and 7 the following:
" Each day's violation of this section shall constitute a separate and distinct offense."

Amendment No. 6.
Amend by adding the following:
"SEC. —. That in addition to the grounds of bankruptcy now existing by law, a corporation shall have committed an act of bankruptcy, and shall accordingly be subject to proceedings to adjudge it an involuntary bankrupt and wind up its affairs and distribute its assets, first, whenever it shall have issued stock in excess of the fair, reasonable value of its property; or, second, whenever it shall have given or offered to any person, association, or corporation any privilege, preference, advantage, facilities, discount, or rebate denied to or withheld from any other person, association, or corporation; or, third, whenever directly or indirectly it shall have engaged in any conspiracy or entered into any combination, agreement, or understanding to monopolize or aid in monopolizing any product of general utility, or so much thereof as to affect injuriously the general welfare, or to stifle lawful competition, or to control or affect injuriously the price of or the market for any commodity in general use or demand; or, fourth, whenever it shall have effected or attempted to effect any consolidation, combination, cooperation, undertaking, or agreement with any other corporation, association, or person, contrary to any law of the United States or of any State in which it shall do or offer to do any business."

Amendment No. 7.
Amend by adding the following section:
"SEC. —. Every corporation engaged in interstate commerce, wherever organized, shall be subject to the jurisdiction of the courts of any State in which it shall carry on business as it would be if created by such State, or as citizens thereof are subject to such jurisdiction."

Amendment No. 8.
Amend by adding the following:
"SEC. —. That any property owned or manufactured under any contract or by any trust or combination or pursuant to any conspiracy forbidden by the laws of a State, and being in the course of transportation from such State to another State, the District of Columbia, a Territory, or a foreign country, or to such State from another State, the District of Columbia, a Territory, or a foreign country, shall be forfeited to the United States, and may be seized and condemned by like proceedings as are provided by law for the forfeiture, seizure, and condemnation of property imported into the United States contrary to law; and every person who shall, knowing that any property to be owned or manufactured in any of the ways above described, transport it, or cause or order, or contract for its transportation as above described, shall be deemed guilty of a misdemeanor, and, on conviction, be punished by a fine not exceeding twenty thousand dollars, or by imprisonment not exceeding five years, or by both such fine and imprisonment: *Provided*, That nothing herein contained shall be held to interfere with any proceedings in a State court for the violations of any law thereof."

Amendment No. 9.
Amend the substitute by adding the following:
"SEC. —. That hereafter the following articles may be imported into the United States free of all duty:
"1. Steel rails, structural steel, tin plate, iron pipe, and other metal tubular goods; wire nails, cut nails, horseshoe nails, barb wire, and all other wire; cotton ties, plows, and all other agricultural tools and implements.
"2. Borax, borate of lime, and boracic acid.
"3. Binding twine.
"4. Paris green.
"5. Paper and pulp for the manufacture of paper.
"6. Salt.
"7. Plate glass and window glass."

Amendment No. 10.
Amend the substitute by adding the following:
"SEC. —. The President is hereby authorized, and it shall be his duty, whenever it shall be shown to his satisfaction that by reason, wholly or materially, of the existence of the tariff or customs duty upon any article, such article, or articles of its class

and kind, are monopolized or controlled by any person, organization, or combination to the detriment of the public, by proclamation to remove or suspend such duty, in whole or in part, until the next assembling of Congress, or until the abuse prompting him to such action shall have ceased."

Amendment No. 11.
Amend by adding the following:
"SEC. —. There is hereby levied and shall be assessed and collected annually the following taxes on all corporations, whether domestic or foreign, doing business in the United States for profit or gain, and having a capital stock of two hundred thousand dollars or more, at the rate of ten per centum on its capital stock. The amount of the capital stock of any taxable corporation for the purposes of taxation shall be estimated according to its par value fixed by the charter, or by resolution of its board of stockholders or directors, and shall include all assets owned by such corporation which are reserved or funded or set aside for the benefit of its stockholders.

"SEC. —. Those corporations are exempt from taxation under this act whose income (or profits), after the payment of necessary expenses of operation and administration thereof, is devoted exclusively to purposes of charity or religion or benevolence, or to hospital, medical, surgical, or hygienic purposes; or to education, or the promotion of the useful arts; or to scientific purposes; or to literary or musical purposes; or to public entertainment.

"SEC. —. If any corporation liable to taxation under this act shall establish to the satisfaction of the Commissioner of Internal Revenue, by competent proof, under oath, that it is not engaged or about to be engaged in any way with any other corporation or person in any of the acts or combinations, conspiracies, agreements, or in any act or conduct that is prohibited in the act entitled 'An act to protect trade against unlawful restraints and monopolies,' approved July second, eighteen hundred and ninety, or in the act entitled 'An act to provide revenue for the Government and to encourage the industries of the United States,' approved July 24, 1897, or an act entitled 'An act to regulate commerce,' approved February fourth, eighteen hundred and eighty-seven, or this act, or any amendment of any of said acts, the said taxes of said corporation shall be remitted, except one per centum thereof, which shall be collected and paid into the Treasury of the United States.

"SEC. —. The Commissioner of Internal Revenue, under the direction of the Secretary of the Treasury, is charged with and is empowered to direct and enforce the execution of this act, and the Secretary of the Treasury shall make such regulations as are needful for such purpose. All laws applicable to the collection of internal-revenue taxes by the United States, whether civil or criminal, shall apply to corporations that are taxable under this act and to their officers and directors, and to the enforcing of the provisions hereof."

Amendment No. 12.
Amend by inserting the following just after section 6:
"SEC. 7. That no person engaged in the production, manufacture, or sale of any article of commerce, or violating any of the provisions of section five of this act, or attempting to monopolize or control the production, manufacture, or sale thereof by driving out competition in any particular locality by discrimination in prices or by giving special privileges or rebates or otherwise in order to destroy competition therein in such locality, shall use, either directly or indirectly, any of the facilities or instrumentalities of interstate commerce, or in any way engage in interstate commerce for the purpose of aiding or facilitating, either directly or indirectly, such production, manufacture, or sale with such intent; nor shall any other person or corporation use any of the facilities or instrumentalities of interstate commerce or in any way engage in interstate commerce in buying, selling, or disposing of any such article of commerce for the purpose of enabling such first-mentioned corporation to engage or to continue to engage in such production, manufacture, or sale or control with such intent. Every person violating any of the provisions of this section shall be punished, on conviction, by a fine of not less than five hundred and not exceeding five thousand dollars."

Amendment No. 13.
Amend by adding a new section, as follows:
"SEC. —. The words 'interstate commerce' wherever they occur in this act shall be held to embrace commerce from any State or Territory of the United States or the District of Columbia to any other State or Territory or the District of Columbia."

O

BILL REQUIRING RETURNS FROM CORPORATIONS, PROHIBITING REBATES, ETC.

JANUARY 31, 1903.—Committed to the Committee of the Whole House on the state of the Union and ordered to be printed.

Mr. PARKER, from the Committee on the Judiciary, submitted the following

VIEWS.

[To accompany H. R. 17.]

The report of the committee is unanimous in favor of the bill, each member reserving the right and duty of informing the House where certain sections may and should be bettered.

Sections 1, 2, 3, 4.

Sections 1 to 4 provide for sworn returns that will provide valuable statistics as to corporations engaged in interstate commerce, and will, it is hoped, protect against overcapitalization. It is noted that the scope of the bill applies only to such corporations as are engaged in interstate commerce, and not to local companies having monopolies of the public streets for gas, water, trolleys, telephones, etc. (over which the United States has jurisdiction only in the District of Columbia and the Territories), in which the question of overcapitalization is perhaps of more importance, but must be reserved for further legislation through appropriate committees.

The requirements of these sections as to returns are practically those enforced in each State as to its own corporations, and the massing of the information can not fail to prove of value.

Section 5.

This section deals with what is probably the paramount question, namely, the prevention of rebates, special privileges, and advantages in interstate freight contracts. It is by the aid of such unlawful privileges and advantages that the great monopolies of the land are believed to have been built up and maintained. The interstate-commerce law forbids all such advantages, but its penal provisions have utterly failed to prevent them.

They perhaps usually consist not in rebates of money, but in special privileges as to which it is difficult or impossible to prove criminal intent, so that prosecutions of the carrier under that act have generally failed, and prosecutions of the shipper under section 5 will probably be just as futile.

A remedy is wanted that will put in issue, not the question of the intent with which a special privilege is given, but the question of fact whether it has been actually given.   For this purpose many members of the committee believe that a simple action at law to recover the value of the rebate, special privilege, or advantage will have a much better result.

In such an action the defendant can not plead the purity of his intent or refuse to testify for fear of criminating himself, or do anything except to ask a fair trial of the question whether his contract, privileges, or freight rates are valid under the law of the land.   If he have received unlawful advantages, recovery will be had, not of a mere fine, but of the full value of these advantages.

It is therefore proposed to add to section 5 (or substitute for it) the following:

Any person who shall receive from any common carrier any benefit or advantage, whether by rebate, special privileges, or contract, or otherwise, which benefit or advantage is prohibited by an act to regulate commerce, or by this act, shall be liable to pay to the United States the value of such benefit or advantage, to be recovered with costs in an action of law brought by the United States in any circuit court, which action may be instituted by the Attorney-General.

It is fair to add that some members of the committee favored adding to this the following language:

Such action may be instituted by the Attorney-General, or, by leave of the court, by any other person as informant, after notice to the Attorney-General to bring such suit.   Such informant shall receive half the amount recovered in such suit instituted by him, but shall pay the expenses thereof: *Provided, however,* That such informant shall not dismiss or settle such suit without leave of the court, after notice to the Attorney-General or district attorney of the district wherein such suit is brought, and in case of such notice of application for leave to dismiss, or on notice to such informant by the Attorney-General, or in case such informant unduly delays or fails to prosecute such suit, the Attorney-General may be ordered by the court to assume said suit, and said informant shall lose all interest therein upon proper terms as to costs and expenses already incurred by him, to be settled by the court.

Some also favor allowing recovery of double the value of the rebate when intentional.   But suits by informants or for penalties are so disfavored by courts and juries that, in the complications attending the conditions of trade and the reasons for freight rates, it seems wiser to leave the grosser cases to the penal provisions of the present law, while providing a civil remedy by which anything illegal may be corrected, even if done by mistake or in the utmost good faith. The suit proposed appears adapted to that end.

Section 6.

This section prohibits all interstate commerce to any corporation that attempts to secure local monopoly by discrimination in prices.

The section is a new departure in the law.   Its effect can be best realized by instances.   The corporation may be within or without the State where the local monopoly is attempted.

For example, a corporation carrying on a general or department store in some town of a State may, by lowering prices on one article temporarily, drive out of business all the local dealers in that article, no matter what it be. In this case the section would prohibit the corporation from buying the article from another State. Or the corporation may be a manufacturer or wholesale dealer in that article outside of the State and may temporarily favor prices to one local dealer who does business exclusively with them, so as to drive all other local dealers out of trade. In this case the section prohibits the corporation from sending goods to the State.

It is plain that the injury in each case (if made one by law) is in underselling in the State in question. It is an injury done there and to local dealers of the State. That State may punish, if it be proper to punish. The jurisdiction of the United States is more doubtful. It is true that in the second instance the State can not always exercise jurisdiction, for if the goods are shipped in original package the State can not touch them, and the shipment is part of interstate commerce and part of the transaction.

This matter of a "boycott," and of underselling small dealers by large concerns, has in modern times reached an importance which was unknown before the great concerns had grown so great. The law may have to find a remedy. It is, perhaps, doubtful whether the United States has jurisdiction to make sales illegal within a State which are not prohibited by the law of the State and create only a local monopoly. That State law can create this illegality, and until the State takes action the United States may not have the right to deny to any man, or any corporation, the right to use the facilities of interstate commerce. The courts will construe this section as to its constitutionality and decide whether the whole question of local monopolies and local boycotting of trade must be left to State law.

A United States statute might assist State jurisdiction by providing that any article of commerce shipped from one State or Territory into another to or by any person attempting to monopolize or control the production, manufacture, or sale thereof in any particular locality in the State or Territory by discrimination in prices, or by giving special privileges or rebates, or otherwise, in order to destroy competition therein in such locality, such articles of commerce, from the time of entering or of arriving within the boundaries of such State of delivery, shall become subject to the operation of all the laws of the said last State, preventing or remedying such monopoly or control by the aforesaid means and with the above intent.

Such a provision might be added as a new section. But the whole question is a difficult one.

Section 7.

Section 7 provides that any railroad corporation knowingly transporting any such articles of commerce or any property produced, manufactured, or sold in violation of the Sherman Act shall be subject to $1,000 penalty.

For the railroad company to protect itself its officers must act as judge and jury to determine whether any article is trust-made or not. If it determine that the article is shipped to aid a monopoly, it is to stop all the business of the corporation concerned. The proposition states itself. The law can not properly blacklist goods before trial, and the man who has the property has the right to sell. Any such restraint upon transportation would simply result in shipping by a jobber or exporter instead of by the manufacturer, whereupon the act utterly fails to apply.

Section 8 relieves witnesses from liability to punishment for testimony given and will have a wide and beneficent effect.

Section 9 gives a remedy by injunction, which is wise and far-reaching.

Section 10 allows the bringing in of absent parties.

Section 11 allows a suit for treble damages caused by any acts forbidden, and is properly adopted from existing law.

Liberty is taken to refer the House to Report No. 1506, Part 3, Fifty-sixth Congress, first session, as to an amendment providing for civil suit for the value of rebates therein suggested, as printed on pages 6492 and 6493 of the record.

R. WAYNE PARKER.

O

BILL REQUIRING RETURNS FROM CORPORATIONS, PROHIBITING REBATES, ETC.

JANUARY 31, 1903.—Committed to the Committee of the Whole House on the state of the Union and ordered to be printed.

Mr. NEVIN, from the Committee on the Judicary, submitted the following

VIEWS.

[To accompany H. R. 17.]

I am in favor of this bill in all its details and measures, excepting section 7 thereof. I can not agree to this section unmodified, and think it should be stricken out entirely. There are two valid reasons, at least, why section 7 should not be retained:

First. Because it places upon the common carrier, receiver, transportation company, etc., the burden of determining in advance of any authoritative finding or adjudication what property is "produced, manufactured, or sold in violation of the provisions of this act or in violation of the provisions of 'An act to protect trade and commerce against unlawful restraints and monopolies,' approved July 2, 1890."

Second. Because it places in the hands of such carrier, receiver, transportation company, etc., the power, under color of law and under the claim of carrying out the provisions of this act, to refuse to accept and transport property in its or his judgment "produced, manufactured, or sold in violation of the provisions of this act," etc., and thus places in its or his hands the power to cripple, injure, or ruin certain manufacturing or producing concerns to the benefit and advantage of other manufacturing and producing plants.

FIRST.

Who shall say in advance of some authoritative finding or some adjudication what property is produced, manufactured, or sold in violation of the provisions of this act, or of those of the act approved July 2, 1890? This section says that the common carrier, receiver, transportation company, etc., must determine. Why put on them this great responsibility? Here, for example, is a plant having by virtue of Government patents (and there are many such) not only a virtual, but an actual monopoly. Such companies and corporations not only are "attempting to monopolize or control the production, manufacture, or sale" of their output, but do, by reason of their patents, absolutely monopolize and control them. Other companies and corporations manufacture goods claimed to be in violation of law.

Now, if any of these various corporations or companies take their products to the common carrier, receiver, etc., and it or he refuses to receive and transport them, an action of damages would lie that might result in a judgment against the common carrier or receiver to the amount of thousands or tens of thousands of dollars. Nor does the word "knowingly" in this section affect the argument in the least, as the very question to be determined is whether or not the manufacturing concern does violate the law. The sole question is upon whom shall be placed the burden of determining that the property produced is produced, manufactured, or sold contrary to law. To say that the common carrier or transportation company must act "knowingly" is begging the whole question, because it places upon them the burden of determining whether the property produced, manufactured, or sold is contrary to law or not.

I can see good reason for punishing the corporation violating the provisions of this act by producing, manufacturing, or selling in violation of the same, or of the act approved July 2, 1890, but I can see no good reason why the common carrier, at its own risk, is to determine what property is produced, manufactured, or sold in violation of the provisions of this act, or of the act approved July 2, 1890, under penalty of being mulct in damages at the hands of the company offering its goods for transportation if the same are not in violation of law, and a penalty of not less than $1,000 under this section, if it be finally determined that they are produced, etc., in violation of law.

SECOND.

This section puts an unwarranted and heretofore unheard-of power in the hands of the common carrier. When goods are offered to it for transportation it can refuse to receive and transport them under the claim that they are produced and manufactured in violation of the provisions of this act and law. It is true it is compelled to do so at its peril. But it certainly gives a carrier, under color of complying with this law, the right to refuse and plead this section for its reason of refusal. It thus places in its hands the power to cripple and may be ruin the business of the offering concern, and this without reference to the effect such action might have upon other and like producers.

In a word, if this section is to be enforced it will compel common carriers and transportation companies to elect, at their peril, what goods they will receive for transportation, the Government to bring suit "in any district in which such common carrier, etc., has an office or conducts business," and enforce this penalty if it accepts the property offered, and if it refuses to accept, then the aggrieved company or corporation to bring suit for such refusal and compel the common carrier to pay it damages. This seems to me to be putting the transportation companies of our country between the upper and nether millstones and compel them to bear the burden and pay a penalty that should be placed upon the companies that produce, manufacture, or sell in violation of the provisions of this act, or in violation of law.

R. M. NEVIN.

O

DIVESTING THE UNITED STATES OF ITS TITLE TO CERTAIN PROPERTY IN ALABAMA, ETC.

JANUARY 26, 1903.—Committed to the Committee of the Whole House and ordered to be printed.

Mr. CLAYTON, from the Committee on the Judiciary, submitted the following

REPORT.

[To accompany S. 6333.]

The Committee on the Judiciary, to whom was referred Senate bill 6333, have carefully considered the same and report it back with a favorable recommendation.

House bill No. 15512 is identical with Senate bill No. 6333, which was favorably reported upon by the Judiciary Committee of the Senate and unanimously passed by the Senate, and is now upon the Calendar of the House.

The purpose of the bill is as set out in its title:

A bill to divest out of the United States all its right, title, and interest of, in, and to certain real estate situated at and near the city of Montgomery, State of Alabama, and to vest the same in the Southern Cotton Oil Company, Bessie R. Maultsby, James S. Pinckard, trustee, M. V. B. Chase, and Edwin Ferris.

It appears from the preamble to the bill, and from the records and other facts submitted to your committee, that Eugene Beebe was surety upon the bonds of Charles W. Dustin, a defaulting postmaster at Demopolis, Ala., and Charles H. Davis, a defaulting postmaster at Union Springs, Ala., and that Eugene Beebe and Ferri Henshaw were also sureties upon the bond of Francis Widmer, a defaulting collector of internal revenue for the second district of Alabama; that suits were brought upon which judgments were recovered by the United States against Beebe, and certain real estate mentioned in the bill and alleged to belong to him (the said Beebe) was seized and taken in execution in satisfaction of said judgments and sold to and purchased by the United States at marshal's sale and subsequently conveyed by marshal's deed to the United States.

In addition to the property acquired by the Government from Beebe, the Government also claimed the interest of Henshaw by reason of judgment against him as the surety on the bond of Widmer, and the fact that Henshaw and Beebe were partners.

The litigation resulting from the purchase of this property by the United States, and its efforts to enforce its rights thereto and to enjoy the same, has continued for a period of about fourteen years, most of the interest purchased by the Government being undivided interests in real estate situated at or near the city of Montgomery, Ala.

To end this litigation and to purchase the interest of the Government in the lands thus acquired by it from Beebe, and to settle and end its claim to the interest of Henshaw therein, defendants mentioned in the bill made a proposition of settlement to the Government, offering to pay it for the release, relinquishment, and conveyance of its interest as set forth in the bill the sum of $25,000.

This proposition of settlement, when made to the Secretary of the Treasury, was referred to the district attorney for the United States at Montgomery, Ala., who thereupon reported that Beebe's interest in the property mentioned in the bill was estimated by him to be worth $15,500, which did not include, however, the possible value of the Government's claim to Henshaw's interest, which was not included in that valuation, the Government not yet having established in the pending litigation its claim thereto.

After carefully and at great length reviewing all the facts relating to the suits by the Government, the value of the property involved, the difficulties attending the enforcement of the Government's rights, and all questions relating to the suits, the district attorney reported as follows:

In view of the difficulties which the Government, both as to the question of facts and law, will have to overcome in order to ultimately recover in this case and for the many reasons heretofore given, I would respectfully request that this offer of $20,000 made in this case and set out in your letter to me of the 19th ultimo be accepted.

It will be noted that the original offer made by the proponents and thus recommended for acceptance by the United States district attorney at Montgomery was $20,000. When F. A. Reeve, the Acting Solicitor of the Treasury, upon receiving this report from the United States district attorney under date of June 28, 1902, suggested, for reasons stated by him in his letter of that date, that the offer should be increased to $25,000, it was done.

Thereupon the honorable Acting Solicitor of the Treasury, F. A. Reeve, reported favorably upon the proposition of settlement to the Secretary of the Treasury, and the latter, through the Acting Secretary of the Treasury, Hon. O. L. Spaulding, accepted the proposition of settlement so made by proponents upon condition that they would secure such action by Congress as might enable the Solicitor of the Treasury and the Secretary of the Treasury to carry the same into effect, both of those officers of the Government being of the opinion that the power heretofore conferred upon them by the various acts of Congress was not sufficient to enable them to convey to the defendants, in accordance with the terms of proposition of settlement, the interest in the land owned by the Government, for the reason that the title thereto was already vested in the United States.

Mr. Spaulding, in accepting the proposition of settlement, uses the following language in his letter to the Solicitor of the Treasury of date October 10, 1902:

Upon a careful consideration of the correspondence and the statement of facts accompanying your letters, I agree with you as to the advisability of a settlement as proposed, and the Department will cooperate with the proponents in any appropriate action they may take with a view to securing the requisite Congressional authority for carrying the proposed compromise into effect.

The bill therefore is merely for the purpose of carrying out the settlement approved by the Secretary of the Treasury upon the recommendation of the Solicitor of the Treasury and the district attorney for the United States at Montgomery, Ala.

The bills in question, before they were introduced in Congress, were submitted to the Solicitor of the Treasury, to the district attorney at Montgomery, and to the Secretary of the Treasury, and were by them approved, as will appear by the reports of the Secretary of the Treasury and the Solicitor of the Treasury to the Judiciary Committee of the Senate in response to a request from that committee for a report upon the matter.

Some question was raised before your committee as to the accuracy of the description of one of the properties, to wit, that about to be conveyed by the United States to the Southern Cotton Oil Company, but your committee finds, and so reports, that the description of that property as embodied in the bill is the identical description used by the United States in the bill in equity filed by the United States against defendants in the circuit court of the middle district of Alabama, as appears by the record of the case of United States against Beebe et al., No. 71, October term, 1899, in the Supreme Court of the United States.

After having conferred with the Department of Justice with reference thereto your committee are not satisfied that the question raised has any such substantial foundation as should prevent the passage of legislation necessary to make effective a compromise of long-continued litigation upon terms that are both favorable and satisfactory to the Government.

This bill passed the Senate December 20, 1902. We submit as a part of this report the letter to Hon. George F. Hoar from the Secretary of the Treasury, and accompanying papers, and the letter to Hon. George F. Hoar from the acting Attorney-General, approving this bill.

The United States and all the parties in interest unite in asking for favorable action upon the bill, and your committee recommends that it be passed.

<hr/>

TREASURY DEPARTMENT, OFFICE OF THE SECRETARY,
Washington, December 16, 1902.

SIR: I have the honor to acknowledge the receipt of your letter of the 15th instant, inclosing Senate bill 6333, "To divest out of the United States all right, title, and interest of, in, and to certain real estate situated at and near the city of Montgomery, State of Alabama, and to vest the same in the Southern Cotton Oil Company, Bessie R. Maultsby, James S. Pincard, trustee, M. V. B. Chase, and Edwin Ferris."

You request an opinion and any suggestions regarding the legislation proposed by said bill.

In reply I have the honor to transmit copy of Department letter of October 10, 1902, to the Solicitor of the Treasury, approving the compromise of the litigation growing out of the suretyship of Eugene Beebe et al.

The bill was submitted to the Solicitor of the Treasury, and herewith find copy of his report of this date. It will be seen that he approves the bill, and that it has also been approved by the United States attorney for the middle district of Alabama.

As this Department has approved the compromise, subject to the action of Congress as proposed in the bill, there is no objection to its being enacted into law.

Respectfully,

L. M. SHAW, *Secretary.*

Hon. GEORGE F. HOAR,
Chairman Judiciary Committee, United States Senate.

TREASURY DEPARTMENT, OFFICE OF THE SECRETARY,
Washington, October 10, 1902.

SIR: Your letters of September 10 and October 9, 1902, in relation to the so-called Beebe cases are received. It appears therefrom that on June 16, 1902, an offer was made by Mr. Henry S. Cattell on behalf of certain persons in interest to pay to the United States the sum of $20,000 in compromise and settlement of all litigation growing out of the suretyship of Eugene Beebe and Ferrie Henshaw on certain bonds of Charles H. Davis, Charles W. Dustan, and Francis Widmer, and of all claim of the United States to certain specified real property. The United States attorney for the middle district of Alabama was called upon by you for a report and recommendation on said offer, and that official strongly recommended the acceptance thereof. Later the offer at your instance was increased to $25,000, and said amount has been duly deposited to the credit of the Secretary of the Treasury, special deposit account No. 5. In your letter of September 10, above referred to, you say that in your opinion the offer made is a fair and reasonable one, and you ask the concurrence of the Department in any Congressional action that may be taken by the proponents looking to the settlement of the matter as made, the case, in your opinion, not coming strictly within the purview of section 3469, United States Revised Statutes, or any other existing law, and it being the intention of the proponents, as you are advised, to apply to Congress for authority to effect a settlement on the terms and in the manner indicated.

Upon a careful consideration of the correspondence and the statement of facts accompanying your letters, I agree with you as to the advisability of a settlement as proposed, and the Department will cooperate with the proponents in any appropriate action they may take with a view to securing the requisite Congressional authority for carrying the proposed compromise into effect.

Respectfully,

O. L. SPAULDING,
Acting Secretary.

The SOLICITOR OF THE TREASURY.

———

DEPARTMENT OF JUSTICE, OFFICE OF THE SOLICITOR OF THE TREASURY,
Washington, D. C., December 16, 1902.

SIR: I have examined the bill (S. 6333, Fifty-seventh Congress, second session) referred by you to this office. The bill in its present form was submitted to and approved by me before being introduced in Congress, and it was also submitted to and approved by the United States attorney for the middle district of Alabama, to whom it was sent by me for examination.

The Department having consented to accept the amount named in the bill, as set out therein, no further statement by me in relation to the matter seems to be called for.

I return herewith, as requested, the letter of the chairman of the Committee on the Judiciary, United States Senate.

Very respectfully,

F. A. REEVE,
Acting Solicitor.

The SECRETARY OF THE TREASURY.

———

DEPARTMENT OF JUSTICE,
Washington, D. C., December 17, 1902.

SIR: I beg leave to acknowledge the receipt of your communication of the 2d instant relative to Senate bill 6333, a bill to divest out of the United States all its right, title, and interest of, in, and to certain real estate situated at and near the city of Montgomery, State of Alabama, and to vest the same in certain designated parties, and to furnish you with such information as is in this Department concerning the matters out of which this proposed legislation arises.

One Eugene Beebe, together with others, became surety on two bonds of Charles H. Davis, postmaster at Union Springs, Ala. Default having been made on these bonds, suits were instituted by the United States and judgments entered against the principal and sureties for $1,606.68 and costs and $991 and costs, respectively. Executions were issued on both judgments and levied on the property of Beebe and Candee, sureties on the bonds. On July 2, 1877, the property of Candee was sold for $1,000, which was collected and paid into the Treasury. On the same day executions were levied upon the property of Beebe, which was an undivided interest in the property described in the Senate bill 6333. The property was sold to the United

States for $1,000, and a deed therefor to the United States was executed by the marshal on July 2, 1877, and recorded May 16, 1878. Whatever was the exact interest Beebee had in the property, which more fully appears in the papers accompanying this note, that interest was sold and conveyed to the United States by the marshal's deed.

Subsequently an enforced payment of $229.82 by Candee and a like payment of $750 by Sheets, another surety, were credited upon the judgment. By these several payments and the real property, conveyed for the stated consideration, the judgments were satisfied and satisfaction entered on the record.

The undivided interest of Beebe in these lands was an interest he held as tenant in common with one Ferrie Henshaw, who was his partner in business.

Francis Widmer, as collector of internal revenue, second district of Alabama, executed a bond to the United States on April 26, 1869, with Henry E. Faber, Joshua Morse, Joseph Goetter, Joseph Bihler, and Henry Moore as sureties. On June 2, 1873, Widmer gave a second bond, with Eugene Beebe (the same person hereinbefore mentioned), Ferrie Henshaw, Frederick Wolfe, Patrick Robinson, and Eliphalet Metcalf as sureties.

By a final statement of the First Comptroller on June 2, 1882, it appeared that Widmer was in default to the United States in the sum of $29,658.56. On which bond the default occurred does not appear; but on February 9, 1877, the Secretary of the Treasury accepted $2,000 from Goetter in compromise of his liability on the first bond and on May 9, 1883, the Secretary accepted $1,500 in satisfaction of the claim against Faber, a surety on the first bond, and Wolfe, a surety on the second bond. Previous to this latter compromise, in December, 1899, separate suits were brought by the United States against each of the sureties on the two bonds, except Bihler and Morse on the first bond, who had died insolvent, and Goetter, whose liability had been compromised.

On February 9, 1885, in the United States circuit court at Montgomery, separate judgments were entered for $100 each against Beebe, the administrator of Henshaw, deceased, Wolfe, Robinson, and Metcalf. The judgments against Beebe and Robinson were paid. The other judgments, including that against Henshaw's administrator, have not been paid.

On March 10, 1890, the United States filed a bill in chancery against the aforesaid Beebe and the heirs of Henshaw, praying that these last-named judgments be set aside, because, although the judgment records showed a regular trial before a jury and a verdict in each case, yet in truth there had been no jury, no witnesses, no evidence, and no verdict, and the judgments were simply the result of a compromise of the claim in each suit, as agreed upon by the district attorney on the one side and the defendants upon the other, and that therefore the judgments were void for want of jurisdiction in the court to authorize them. Demurrers were interposed to this bill, and after proceedings in the circuit court and the circuit court of appeals the Supreme Court remanded the cause to the circuit court, directing the summons to be overruled and leave to defendants to answer. (United States v. Beebe, 180 U. S., 343.)

The persons named in Senate bill 6333 who seek to have the right, title, and interest in the named properties divested out of the United States and vested in them, respectively, were made defendants to this bill. The interests which they claim were derived from Beebe or Henshaw, or both of them. As involved in their claims of title, certain conveyances are alleged to have been fraudulently made; and it is alleged in the bill that the claims of these parties are subordinate to the rights of the United States to condemn and subject the lands to the satisfaction of the indebtedness of Beebe and Henshaw as sureties on Widmer's bonds; and it is further alleged that the conveyances made by Beebe or Henshaw, or Henshaw's heirs, were void and ought to be set aside. The prayers for relief are directed to subjecting the lands to this liability.

Beebe and Henshaw are dead, and the estates of both are insolvent.

The claims above mentioned have been for several years before the Department of the Treasury upon applications for compromise under section 3469, Revised Statutes. The last proposition was accompanied by a deposit of $25,000. This compromise has been strongly recommended by the district attorney and the Solicitor of the Treasury; and the Acting Secretary of the Treasury, October 10, 1902, expresses his agreement in the advisability of the settlement. This action seems to fully meet the objects and requirements of the law upon the subject of compromises.

The purpose of the bill is to effectuate this settlement which is offered by the parties in possession of the premises under titles from Beebe and the heirs of Henshaw.

Accompanying this communication are statements of the present condition of the affairs growing out of the defaults of the bonded officers, and the recommendations of the district attorney and the Solicitor of the Treasury, and the action of the Acting Secretary. These papers have been compiled and arranged in the office of the Solicitor of the Treasury.

Very respectfully,

J. K. RICHARDS,
Acting Attorney-General.

Hon. GEORGE F. HOAR,
 Chairman Committee on the Judiciary, United States Senate.

O

LIMITING THE EFFECT OF THE REGULATIONS OF COMMERCE BETWEEN THE SEVERAL STATES, ETC.

JANUARY 26, 1903.—Referred to the House Calendar and ordered to be printed.

Mr. CLAYTON, from the Committee on the Judiciary, submitted the following

REPORT.

[To accompany H. R. 15331.]

The Committee on the Judiciary, to whom was referred the bill (H. R. 15331) to amend an act to limit the effect of the regulations of commerce between the several States and with foreign countries in certain cases, approved August 8, 1890, having considered said bill, submit the following report:

Nearly all of the States have passed laws, as police regulations, differing to some extent in their provisions, for the prohibition, regulation, or control of intoxicating liquors within their respective boundaries.

In the case of Leisy v. Hardin (135 U. S., 100) the Supreme Court held that any citizen of a State had the right under the Constitution of the United States to import any intoxicating liquors into another State, and that in the absence of Congressional permission the State into which such liquors were imported had no power, in the exercise of its authority of police regulations, to enact laws to prohibit or regulate the sale of such liquors while they remained in the original packages.

The effect of this decision of the Supreme Court was to deny to the States all power to control or prohibit the sale of intoxicating liquors transported from one State into another while they remained in the original packages.

To remove the effect of this decision, and to authorize the several States, in the exercise of their police powers, to prohibit or control the sale of intoxicating liquors, the act of August 8, 1890, was passed. That act provided—

that all fermented, distilled, or other intoxicating liquors or liquids transported into any State or Territory or remaining therein for use, consumption, sale, or storage therein, shall upon arrival in such State or Territory be subject to the operation and effect of the laws of such State or Territory enacted in the exercise of its police powers, to the same extent, and in the same manner, as though such liquids or liquors had been produced in such State or Territory, and shall not be exempt therefrom by reason of being introduced therein in original packages or otherwise.

In the case In re Rahrer (140 U. S., 545) the Supreme Court of the United States held that this act was constitutional and valid, and conferred upon the States the powers enumerated therein. But in the case of Rhodes v. Iowa (170 U. S., 415) a question arising under this act again came before the Supreme Court, and, in defining the scope and meaning of the act, the court held that under its provisions liquors transported from one State into another remained under the protection of the interstate-commerce laws until they were delivered to the consignee, and that the State law was inoperative to reach them until they were delivered by the common carrier to the person to whom they were consigned.

The effect of this decision was practically to nullify the act of 1890 so far as the transportation and delivery of intoxicating liquors within the State was concerned. Under the law, as thus construed, dealers in intoxicating liquors located in some of the States sent out their soliciting agents and established agencies in other States, who traveled over and canvassed the country and solicited sales and took orders for intoxicating liquors to be shipped in by the principal, consigned to the subscribers—sometimes to be sent to them direct, and in other cases to be sent to them in care of the soliciting agent.

By this method regular business of dealing in intoxicating liquors by the foreign dealer has been kept up in many of the States with impunity. Under this system the States are entirely powerless either to prohibit such sales or to exercise any control or regulation over them. They can not even impose a license or any restrictions whatever on the business carried on in this manner.

It is the purpose of this bill to correct this evil and to subject intoxicating liquors imported from one State into another to the jurisdiction of the laws of the State into which they are imported on the arrival of such liquors within the boundaries of such State.

Your committee therefore reports the bill back to the House with the following substitute amendment, and recommends that the bill as amended do pass:

That all fermented, distilled, or other intoxicating liquors or liquids transported into any State or Territory or remaining therein for use, consumption, sale, or storage therein, shall, upon arrival within the boundary of such State or Territory, before and after delivery, be subject to the operation and effect of the laws of such State or Territory enacted in the exercise of its police powers to the same extent and in the same manner as though such liquids or liquors had been produced in such State or Territory, and shall not be exempt therefrom by reason of being introduced therein in original packages or otherwise.

SEC. 2. That all corporations and persons engaged in interstate commerce shall, as to any shipment or transportation of fermented, distilled, or other intoxicating liquors or liquids, be subject to all laws and police regulations with reference to such liquors or liquids, or the shipment or the transportation thereof, of the State in which the place of destination is situated, and shall not be exempt therefrom by reason of such liquors or liquids being introduced therein in original packages or otherwise.

Amend the title so as to read: "A bill to limit the effect of the regulations of commerce between the several States and with foreign countries in certain cases."

O

TERMS OF UNITED STATES COURTS IN COLORADO.

JANUARY 26, 1903.—Referred to the House Calendar and ordered to be printed.

Mr. PALMER, from the Committee on the Judiciary, submitted the following

REPORT.

[To accompany H. R. 16334.]

The Committee on the Judiciary, to whom was referred the bill (H. R. 16334) fixing terms of United States courts in Colorado, have had the same under consideration and respectfully submit the following report:

The purpose of the bill is to establish an additional term of the circuit and district courts of the United States at Montrose in the State of Colorado, to be held annually on the first Tuesday in August.

The law now provides for a term at Denver on the first Tuesday of May and November in every year, at Pueblo on the first Tuesday in April annually, at Del Norte on the first Tuesday in August.

It appeared to the committee that the term of the said courts at Del Norte is not productive of sufficient business to justify their continuance and that the public convenience and the interests of the Government will be better served by discontinuing the term of the said courts at Del Norte and establishing a term at Montrose. Upon that subject reference is made to a letter of Hon. Moses Hallett, district judge, a copy of which is appended to the report.

The committee therefore recommend that the said bill be amended as follows:

Strike out in lines 7 and 8 the words " at Del Norte on the first Tuesday in August annually."

Strike out section 2 and insert the following:

SEC. 2. The term of said courts heretofore provided to be held at Del Norte, Colorado, on the first Tuesday in August annually, is hereby discontinued, and all business now pending in said courts, including all records, files, books, or other property of the United States pertaining to said court, shall be transferred to Montrose, Colorado, and all cases pending at Del Norte, Colorado, shall be tried at Montrose, Colorado, the same as if originally begun at the latter place, and all requirements for return of process or persons to said court at Del Norte shall hereafter be made or complied with at said term at Montrose, Colorado.

Add section 3, as follows:

SEC. 3. All acts and parts of acts inconsistent herewith are hereby repealed.

Amend the title so as to read: " A bill fixing terms of United States courts in Colorado, and for other purposes."

DENVER, COLO., *January 20, 1903.*

SIR: Mr. Bell, of Colorado, has called my attention to House bill No. 16334, for establishing courts at Montrose, Colo., in addition to courts held at other places in this State. I am of the opinion that the bill should be changed to transfer the courts now held at Del Norte, Colo., to Montrose, and the courts at Del Norte discontinued. Courts have been held at Del Norte for many years, in fact ever since Colorado became a State. We have never been able to do much business there. Sometimes we try one or two cases in a term, at other times none.

There is not much business in that part of the State which can come into a Federal court and the expense of holding court there is considerable. The courts at Del Norte ought to be abolished. Probably more business can be done on the western slope of the mountains, and Montrose is as convenient for suitors as any other place in that region.

If the courts at Del Norte shall be abolished, the records and files at that place should be transferred to the new place designated for holding the courts. There is also a set of Supreme Court reports and some statutes which should be transferred.

I am, very respectfully,

MOSES HALLETT,
District Judge.

The ATTORNEY-GENERAL, *Washington, D. C.*

O

PHARMACY IN THE INDIAN TERRITORY.

JANUARY 26, 1903.—Referred to the House Calendar and ordered to be printed.

Mr. STEPHENS, from the Committee on Indian Affairs, submitted the following

REPORT.

[To accompany H. R. 16776.]

The Committee on Indian Affairs, to whom was referred the bill (H. R. 16776) in relation to pharmacy in the Indian Territory, beg leave to submit the following report, and recommend that said bill do pass without amendment:

This is a bill enacting that it shall hereafter be unlawful for any person other than a registered pharmacist to retail, compound, or dispense drugs or medicine in the Indian Territory. Persons over 21 years of age having two years' practical experience as a pharmacist shall, on a satisfactory examination (before the board provided for by this bill), be entitled to registration. Graduates from approved schools of pharmacy shall, on payment of a fee of $5, be entitled to registration without examination.

The chief justice of the court of appeals in the Indian Territory appoints a board of pharmacists for said Territory consisting of five members.

No part of the salaries or expenses of this board is paid by the United States Government, but is paid by fees in the manner provided for in the bill.

O

REGULATING THE PRACTICE OF MEDICINE AND SURGERY IN INDIAN TERRITORY.

JANUARY 26, 1903.—Referred to the House Calendar and ordered to be printed.

Mr. STEPHENS, from the Committee on Indian Affairs, submitted the following

REPORT.

[To accompany H. R. 15986.]

The Committee on Indian Affairs, to whom was referred the bill (H. R. 15986) regulating the practice of medicine and surgery in the Indian Territory, beg leave to submit the following report, and recommend that said bill do pass without amendment:

This is a bill enacting that hereafter no person shall practice medicine and surgery, or either, as a profession in the Indian Territory without first being registered as a physician and surgeon, or either, in the office of the clerk in the district in which he or she offers to practice.

The bill provides that the United States judge of each district in that Territory shall appoint in his district a board of medical examiners consisting of three graduates of some reputable medical college recognized by either of the American medical college associations. This board holds office for four years.

They are required to examine and grant certificates of qualification to practice medicine to all persons of good moral character and duly qualified in knowledge and capacity to practice medicine and surgery in the Indian Territory, and no person shall be excluded from registration on account of having studied any particular school of medicine. Every applicant for registration shall pay to the board in advance a fee of $10, which shall be equally divided among the board, and this shall be their only compensation. Each applicant also shall pay $1.50 to the clerk for recording his certificate. This law will not cost the Government anything.

Physicians holding diplomas from reputable medical colleges shall pay a fee of $1 to the board and shall be entitled to a certificate of approval without being required to undergo an examination.

The necessity for this legislation arises from the fact that any person, however ignorant, is now permitted to practice medicine in the Indian Territory, and as a result the Indian Territory is filled with many disreputable and ignorant quack doctors, who prey upon an unprotected people. This bill will, if it becomes a law, furnish the desired legal protection.

O

INDIANOLA, MISS., POST-OFFICE CORRESPONDENCE.

JANUARY 26, 1903.—Ordered to be printed.

Mr. LOUD, from the Committee on the Post-Office and Post-Roads, submitted the following

REPORT.

[To accompany H. Res. No. 398.]

The Committee on the Post-Office and Post-Roads have had under consideration House resolution No. 398, and beg to report the same back to the House with the recommendation that the same pass with the following amendment:

Strike out all after the word "Mississippi," in line 6.

O

NOAH DILLARD.

JANUARY 27, 1903.—Committed to the Committee of the Whole House and ordered
to be printed.

Mr. GRAFF, from the Committee on Claims, submitted the following

REPORT.

[To accompany H. R. 17059.]

The Committee on Claims, to whom was referred the bill (H. R. 17059)
for the relief of Noah Dillard, submit the following report:
The facts in this case are fully set forth in the letter of the auditor
for the District of Columbia, which is appended hereto and made a
part of this report.
Your committee recommend the favorable passage of this bill without amendment.

OFFICE AUDITOR OF THE DISTRICT OF COLUMBIA,
Washington, April 2, 1902.

GENTLEMEN: I have the honor to submit the following report in relation to bill,
Senate 339, Fifty-seventh Congress, first session, "For the relief of Noah Dillard."
It appears from the records of the board of audit that two retents, of $106.14
and $52.05, respectively, amounting in the aggregate to $158.19, remain unpaid and
due to Noah Dillard for work done by him under an extension of contract No. 388,
made by the board of public works with Noah Dillard and Parker Moulton in July,
1872, said extension bearing date of July 22, 1875. This claim, which was once
before the Court of Claims under the act of June 16, 1880, is no longer upon the
docket of that court; but as the amount is shown to be equitably due, I am of opinion that it should be allowed, provided that it be accepted by the claimant, without
interest, as a full acquittance of all and every obligation of whatsoever character of
the District of Columbia on account of contract 388 and any extension of the same.
I would suggest that the bill be amended by inserting, after the word "Dillard," in
line 5, the words "one-half," and after the end of the word "appropriated," in line
6, the words "and one-half out of the revenues of the District of Columbia."
Also that the following proviso be added after the word "eighty-eight," in line 16:
"*Provided,* That the acceptance by the claimant of the amount herein appropriated
shall be taken and considered as a full discharge and acquittance of the District of
Columbia of all and every obligation of whatsoever character under and on account
of contract 388 as aforesaid, and every extension of the same."
With the amendments suggested I have the honor to recommend that the bill be
returned to Congress with a request for favorable consideration by that body.
Very respectfully,

J. T. PETTY,
Auditor District of Columbia.

The COMMISSIONERS OF THE DISTRICT OF COLUMBIA.

O

ORDER REGARDING BILLS PRESENTED BY THE COMMITTEE ON THE JUDICIARY.

JANUARY 27, 1903.—Ordered to be printed.

Mr. GROSVENOR, from the Committee on Rules, submitted the following

REPORT.

[To accompany H. Res. No. 394.]

The Committee on Rules, to whom was referred the resolution of the House (H. Res. No. 394), have had the same under consideration, and report the same herewith with the recommendation that it be agreed to by the House.

O

HEIRS OF JOHN MORGAN.

JANUARY 27, 1903.—Committed to the Committee of the Whole House and ordered
to be printed.

Mr. KYLE, from the Committee on War Claims, submitted the following

REPORT.

[To accompany H. Res. No. 411.]

The Committee on War Claims, to whom was referred the bill (H. R.
8821) for the relief of the heirs of John Morgan, submit the following
report:

This is a claim for stores and supplies alleged to have been taken by
or furnished to the military forces of the United States for their use
during the late war for the suppression of the rebellion. Claim stated
at $7,975.

The evidence offered in support of this claim is in the form of ex
parte affidavits, and your committee have no opportunity of subjecting
the witnesses to a cross-examination, and are therefore of the opinion
that this claim should be referred to the Court of Claims, where
depositions can be taken in the usual manner prescribed by law,
counsel for the Government and for the claimant having the right to
cross-examine the witnesses making such depositions, and when the
facts shall have been determined by the court upon the legal testimony
thus taken and submitted, said facts to be reported to Congress for
its consideration; and report herewith a resolution to that effect and
recommend its adoption.

O

JULIUS C. KLEONNE.

JANUARY 27, 1903.—Committed to the Committee of the Whole House and ordered
to be printed.

Mr. MAHON, from the Committee on War Claims, submitted the
following

REPORT.

[To accompany H. Res. No. 412.]

The Committee on War Claims, to whom was referred the resolution (H. Res. No. 412) for the relief of Julius C. Kleonne, submit the
following report:

This is a claim for services alleged to have been rendered by Julius
C. Kleonne, late captain Company K, Seventeenth Indiana Volunteers,
during the war for the suppression of the rebellion.

The evidence offered in support of this claim is in the form of ex parte
affidavits, and your committee have no opportunity of subjecting the
witnesses to a cross-examination, and are therefore of the opinion that
this claim should be referred to the Court of Claims, where depositions
can be taken in the usual manner prescribed by law, counsel for the
Government and for the claimant having the right to cross-examine
the witnesses making such depositions; and when the facts shall have
been determined by the court upon the legal testimony thus taken and
submitted, said facts to be reported to Congress for its consideration;
and report herewith a resolution to that effect, and recommend its
adoption.

O

HEIRS OF JAMES M. HINTON.

JANUARY 27, 1903.—Committed to the Committee of the Whole House and ordered to be printed.

Mr. SIMS, from the Committee on War Claims, submitted the following

REPORT.

[To accompany H. Res. No. 413.]

The Committee on War Claims, to whom was referred the resolution (H. Res. No. 413) for the relief of the heirs of James M. Hinton, deceased, submit the following report:

This is a claim for supplies furnished 50 military prisoners taken from the county jail at Nashville, Tenn., and used on fortifications around Nashville for seven and one-half months, in the years 1862 and 1863. Claim stated at $2,508.

The evidence offered in support of this claim is in the form of ex parte affidavits, and your committee have no opportunity of subjecting the witnesses to a cross-examination, and are therefore of the opinion that this claim should be referred to the Court of Claims, where depositions can be taken in the usual manner prescribed by law, counsel for the Government and for the claimant having the right to cross-examine the witnesses making such depositions; and when the facts shall have been determined by the court upon the legal testimony thus taken and submitted, said facts to be reported to Congress for its consideration; and report herewith a resolution to that effect, and recommend its adoption.

()

FIRST PRESBYTERIAN CHURCH OF KNOXVILLE, TENN.

JANUARY 27, 1903.—Committed to the Committee of the Whole House and ordered
to be printed.

Mr. GIBSON, from the Committee on War Claims, submitted the
following

REPORT.

[To accompany H. Res. No. 414.]

The Committee on War Claims, to whom was referred the resolution (H. Res. No. 414) for the relief of the First Presbyterian Church of Knoxville, Tenn., submit the following report:.

The evidence offered in support of this claim is in the form of ex parte affidavits, and your committee have no opportunity of subjecting the witnesses to a cross-examination, and are therefore of the opinion that this claim should be referred to the Court of Claims, where depositions can be taken in the usual manner prescribed by law, counsel for the Government and for the claimant having the right to cross-examine the witnesses making such depositions; and when the facts shall have been determined by the court upon the legal testimony thus taken and submitted, said facts to be reported to Congress for its consideration; and report herewith a resolution to that effect, and recommend its adoption.

O

BRIDGE ACROSS MONONGAHELA RIVER, PENNSYLVANIA.

JANUARY 27, 1903.—Referred to the House Calendar and ordered to be printed.

Mr. WANGER, from the Committee on Interstate and Foreign Commerce, submitted the following

REPORT.

[To accompany H. R. 16643.]

The Committee on Interstate and Foreign Commerce, to whom was referred the bill (H. R. 16643) to authorize the Donora Southern Railroad Company, a corporation organized and existing under the laws of the Commonwealth of Pennsylvania, to construct and maintain a bridge across the Monongahela River in the State of Pennsylvania, beg leave to submit the following report, and recommend that said bill do pass without amendment.

The report of the Chief of Engineers of the U. S. Army to the honorable Secretary of War, and transmitted to the committee, is herewith appended as part of this report.

OFFICE OF THE CHIEF OF ENGINEERS, U. S. ARMY,
Washington, January 17, 1903.

SIR: I have the honor to return herewith a letter, dated the 14th instant, from the Committee on Interstate and Foreign Commerce of the House of Representatives, inclosing for the views of the War Department thereon H. R. 16643, Fifty-seventh Congress, second session, "A bill to authorize the Donora Southern Railroad Company, a corporation organized and existing under the laws of the Commonwealth of Pennsylvania, to construct and maintain a bridge across the Monongahela River in the State of Pennsylvania," and, in reply to its reference to this office, I beg to say that the bill appears to make ample provision for the protection of navigation interests, and I know of no objection to its passage by Congress, so far as those interests are concerned.

Very respectfully, your obedient servant,

· G. L. GILLESPIE,
Brigadier-General, Chief of Engineers, U. S. Army.

Hon. ELIHU ROOT,
Secretary of War.

O

MARKING THE GRAVES OF THE SOLDIERS OF THE CONFEDERATE ARMY AND NAVY.

JANUARY 27, 1903.—Committed to the Committee of the Whole House on the state of the Union and ordered to be printed.

Mr. PRINCE, from the Committee on Military Affairs, submitted the following

REPORT.

[To accompany S. 6486.]

The Committee on Military Affairs, to whom was referred the bill (S. 6486) to provide for the appropriate marking of the graves of the soldiers and sailors of the Confederate army and navy and for other purposes, report the same back to the House with the recommendation that it do pass.

This bill passed the Senate, and the report made thereon is hereto annexed and made a part of this report.

[Senate Report No. 2589, Fifty-seventh Congress, second session.]

The Committee on Military Affairs has had under consideration the following bill:

[S. 6486, Fifty-seventh Congress, second session.]

A BILL to provide for the appropriate marking of the graves of the soldiers of the Confederate army and navy, and for other purposes.

Be it enacted by the Senate and House of Representatives of the United States of America in Congress assembled, That the Secretary of War be, and he is hereby, authorized and directed to ascertain the locations and condition of all the graves of the soldiers of the Confederate army and navy in the war between the States, eighteen hundred and sixty-one to eighteen hundred and sixty-five, who died in Federal prisons and military hospitals in the North, and who were buried near their places of confinement; to acquire possession or control over all grounds where said prison dead are buried not now possessed or under the control of the United States Government; to cause to be prepared accurate registers in triplicate, one for the superintendent's office in the cemetery, one for the Quartermaster-General's Office, and one for the War Record's Office, Confederate archives, of the places of burial, the number of the grave, the name, company, regiment, and State, of each Confederate soldier who so died, by verification with the Confederate archives in the War Department at Washington, District of Columbia; to cause to be erected over said graves white marble headstones similar to those recently placed over the graves in the "Confederate section" in the National Cemetery, at Arlington, Virginia, similarly inscribed; to build proper fencing for the preservation of said burial grounds, and to care for said burial grounds in all proper respects not herein specifically mentioned.

That for the carrying out of the objects set forth herein there be appropriated, out of the money in the Treasury of the United States not otherwise appropriated, the sum of one hundred thousand dollars, or so much thereof as may be necessary.

And the Secretary of War is hereby authorized and directed to appoint some competent person as commissioner to ascertain the location of such Confederate graves not heretofore located, and to compare the names of those already marked with the registers in the cemeteries, and correct the same when found necessary, as preliminary to the work of marking the graves with suitable headstones, and to fix the compensation of said commissioner, who shall be allowed necessary traveling expenses

The committee recommend that the bill do pass with the following amendments:

On page 1, line 6, after the word "the," insert the words "late civil."

On page 1, line 6, after the word "war," strike out the words "between the States."

On page 2, line 15, strike out the word "one" and insert in lieu thereof the word "two."

The bill as amended will then read as follows:

A BILL to provide for the appropriate marking of the graves of the soldiers of the Confederate Army and Navy, and for other purposes.

Be it enacted by the Senate and House of Representatives of the United States of America in Congress assembled, That the Secretary of War be, and he is hereby, authorized and directed to ascertain the locations and condition of all the graves of the soldiers of the Confederate Army and Navy in the late civil war, eighteen hundred and sixty-one to eighteen hundred and sixty-five, who died in Federal prisons and military hospitals in the North, and who were buried near their places of confinement; to acquire possession or control over all grounds where said prison dead are buried not now possessed or under the control of the United States Government; to cause to be prepared accurate registers in triplicate, one for the superintendent's office in the cemetery, one for the Quartermaster-General's Office, and one for the War Record's Office, Confederate archives, of the places of burial, the number of the grave, the name, company, regiment, and State, of each Confederate soldier who so died, by verification with the Confederate archives in the War Department at Washington, District of Columbia; to cause to be erected over said graves white marble headstones similar to those recently placed over the graves in the "Confederate section" in the national cemetery at Arlington, Virginia, similarly inscribed; to build proper fencing for the preservation of said burial grounds, and to care for said burial grounds in all proper respects not herein specifically mentioned.

That for the carrying out of the objects set forth herein there be appropriated, out of the money in the Treasury of the United States, not otherwise appropriated, the sum of two hundred thousand dollars, or so much thereof as may be necessary.

And the Secretary of War is hereby authorized and directed to appoint some competent person as commissioner to ascertain the location of such Confederate graves not heretofore located, and to compare the names of those already marked with the registers in the cemeteries, and correct the same when found necessary, as preliminary to the work of marking the graves with suitable headstones, and to fix the compensation of said commissioner, who shall be allowed necessary traveling expenses.

These Confederate prisoners are buried in many different places. Their number is about 30,152. It is estimated that it will cost to carry this legislation into effect in the neighborhood of $200,000.

The necessity for making the provision contemplated by this bill arises from the fact that there is no one in charge of these cemeteries. These, in many cases, are in a state of utter neglect, the inclosures being in a dilapidated condition, and the headboards of the graves having long since rotted away.

All these facts are fully set forth in the exhibits hereto annexed from the War Department, and from data compiled by Dr. S. E. Lewis, late assistant surgeon, C. S. Army, and commander of the Charles Broadway Rouss Camp, No. 1191, United Confederate Veterans.

WAR DEPARTMENT, QUARTERMASTER GENERAL'S OFFICE,
Washington, January 13, 1903.

SIR: I have the honor to return herewith Senate bill 6486, Fifty-seventh Congress, second session, appropriating the sum of $100,000, or so much thereof as may be necessary, "To provide for the appropriate marking of the graves of the soldiers of the Confederate Army and Navy, and for other purposes," referred by direction of the chairman of the Committee on Military Affairs, United States Senate, for any information relative to the measure in possession of the War Department.

In response thereto I respectfully report that according to a report made February 6, 1869, by Bvt. Brig. Gen. Alex. J. Perry, quartermaster, U. S. Army, there were buried, in 89 localities throughout the country, 30,152 Confederate prisoners of war, viz: Officers, 455; enlisted men, 28,490; unknown, 726, and citizens, 481.

Many of these having been buried in trenches (as in the case of the removal of the Confederate remains from Fort Delaware and Pea Patch Island, Pennsylvania, to the Finns Point, New Jersey, National Cemetery), it would be impracticable to identify individual graves, notwithstanding the fact that the names of the persons may be found of record.

Approximately 9,300 Confederates were buried in national cemeteries.

Were it possible to locate all such graves, the amount appropriated by the bill would be totally inadequate for the purposes stated, as at the present contract price for headstones, $2.13 each at the place of manufacture, 30,000 headstones would cost $63,900, to which should be added the cost of transportation, handling, and setting, approximately $1.25 each ($37,500), making a total of $101,400 for headstones, irrespective of the cost of purchase of ground, and for care, maintenance, and fencing the same; and for compensation and traveling expenses of the commissioner provided for in the bill.

From the foregoing it will appear that the sum named is not sufficient to carry out the provisions of this bill; it will probably require about $200,000.

At the close of the civil war the Quartermaster's Department took up the matter of locating the graves of the dead Confederate prisoners of war, since which time some changes have been made by removals of remains to other places, etc. Attention is invited to House Report No. 45, Fortieth Congress, third session, page 775.

Respectfully,

M. I. LUDINGTON,
Quartermaster-General U. S. Army.

The SECRETARY OF WAR.

[Extract from Senate Document No. 93, second session Forty-fifth Congress. Accompanying reports from the Quartermaster-General, Surgeon-General, and Commissary-General of Subsistence, U. S. Army.]

The following is a copy of a report compiled in the office of the Quartermaster-General U. S. Army, by Bvt. Brig. Gen. A. J. Perry and forwarded to this office by the Quartermaster-General:

QUARTERMASTER-GENERAL'S OFFICE,
Washington, D. C., February 6, 1869.

GENERAL: I have the honor to submit, with report, a communication of the honorable Secretary of War of the 5th of January, 1869, requesting information relative to deceased prisoners of war, prisons, etc., for the use of the Congressional Committee on the Treatment of Prisoners of War, etc., and to inclose the following statements, viz:

1. List marked "A," showing the locality of the different Confederate prisons used for the confinement of Union prisoners of war, as required in paragraph 15 of the inclosed letter of the committee; also showing the number of Union prisoners, known and unknown, officers, enlisted men, and citizens who died and were buried at these prisons, as required in paragraphs 9 and 21 of the letter of the committee.

From this list it will appear that the number of deceased Union prisoners of war as reported is 36,401. They were originally buried in the sixty-eight localities mentioned in the list, but many of them have been removed from these places and are now resting in the various national cemeteries throughout the South.

These data are obtained from the rolls of honor published by this office and from the annual reports for the fiscal year ending June 30, 1868, furnished by officers of the Quartermaster's Department. It is believed, however, that the actual number of Union prisoners who suffered martyrdom in the rebel prisons far exceeds the number given above, as the records furnished this office are not complete. It is well known that at many places, as, for instance, at Salisbury, N. C., and at Florence, S. C., etc., the bodies were buried in trenches, often two, three, sometimes even four deep, so that the accurate number of bodies interred at these places can not be determined.

2. List marked "B," showing localities of the different prisons used by the Federal authorities for the confinement of rebel prisoners of war, as required by paragraph 16 of the letter of the committee, with the number of deceased rebel prisoners, known

and unknown, officers, enlisted men, and citizens interred at these localities, as required by paragraph 22 of that letter.

The number of rebel prisoners of war reported to be buried at eighty-nine localities throughout the country is 31,152.

This list has been prepared in part from copies of the mortuary records of prisoners, obained from the late office of the commissary-general of prisoners, and in part from reports received at this office from officers of the Quartermaster's Department. It is therefore not unlikely that there are a good many repetitions.

There being no authority to publish in general orders the names of deceased rebel prisoners of war, the arrangement of the records and comparison of the reports, giving their names, has been postponed until the publication of the names of Union soldiers who died in defense of the country shall have been completed. With the present reduced clerical force in the cemeterial branch of this office, it would take so long a time to make a comparison of the different reports as to make it impracticable to ascertain within any reasonable period of time the desired information relative to the number of known and unknown rebel prisoners who died at the Federal prisons at the North.

I am, General, very respectfully, your obedient servant,

ALEX. J. PERRY,
Brevet Brigadier-General and Quartermaster, U. S. Army.

Brevet Brig. Gen. M. C. MEIGS,
Quartermaster-General U. S. Army, Washington, D. C.

SOME DATA RELATING TO THE LOCATIONS AND CONDITION OF THE GRAVES OF CONFEDERATE SOLDIERS WHO DIED IN FEDERAL PRISONS AND MILITARY HOSPITALS AND WERE BURIED NEAR THEIR PLACES OF CONFINEMENT; ALSO SOME SUGGESTIONS AS TO THE NECESSARY CONGRESSIONAL LEGISLATION TO PROVIDE FOR REMEDIAL MEASURES.

[Prepared by Samuel E. Lewis, M. D., late assistant surgeon, C. S. A., of Washington, D. C., commander of the Charles Broadway Rouss Camp, No. 1191, United Confederate Veterans; first vice-president of the Association of Medical Officers of the Army and Navy of the Confederacy.]

WASHINGTON, D. C., *December 6, 1902.*

DEAR SIR: I beg leave respectfully to transmit herewith for your consideration a paper prepared by me, prompted by the resolution of Gen. Stephen D. Lee, passed by the United Confederate Veterans, in session at Memphis May 28–30, 1901, requesting "that Congress take appropriate action looking to the care and preservation of the graves of the Confederate dead now in the various cemeteries in the Northern States." This paper has been read by General Lee and meets with his full approval, and it is in compliance with his wish that I bring the matter to your attention and request your kind offices in securing the necessary Congressional legislation as suggested by the draft of a bill for enactment embodied in the paper.

Inclosed you will also please find a letter from Gen. Marcus J. Wright, transmitting copy of letter from General Lee bearing upon the subject.

I also hand you copy of letter of the Secretary of War, George W. McCrary, to President of the United States Senate, June 3, 1878, transmitting report of Q. M. Gen. M. C. Meigs relating to purchase of Confederate burial grounds by the Government.

May I say that I have been greatly encouraged to request your aid by your thoughtful action in caring for the graves of Confederate dead at Camp Chase and Johnsons Island when you were the governor of the State of Ohio.

I have the honor to be, your obedient servant,

SAMUEL E. LEWIS, M. D.,
Commander.

Hon. J. B. FORAKER,
United States Senate.

WASHINGTON, D. C., *December 5, 1902.*

MY DEAR SIR: I inclose you a letter from Gen. Stephen D. Lee to accompany the paper prepared by you relating to "the locations and condition of the graves of the Confederate soldiers who died in Federal prisons and military hospitals and were buried near their places of confinement."

I am very glad of this action of the United Confederate Veterans. There is nothing that the surviving Confederate soldiers and their families more desire than the proper care of the graves of those of their comrades who fell in action or died from disease. The graves of those who are buried in the South receive proper attention, but those in the North are neglected. General Lee has expressed the wish that Senator Foraker, of Ohio, who is a broad-minded and liberal man, be asked to take charge of the matter and endeavor to secure the necessary legislation by Congress.

I fully agree with him in this suggestion, and think it would be well for you to call on the Senator and lay the whole matter before him and ask him to take charge of it.

Very truly, yours,   MARCUS J. WRIGHT.
SAMUEL E. LEWIS, M. D.,
        Washington, D. C.

[Headquarters Army of Tennessee Department, United Confederate Veterans. Adjutant-general's office. Stephen D. Lee, lieutenant-general commanding. E. T. Sykes, adjutant-general and chief of staff.]

COLUMBUS, MISS., December 9, 1901.

MY DEAR GENERAL: I had the honor to introduce the resolution at Memphis at our last reunion requesting Congress to take appropriate action looking to the care and preservation of the graves of the Confederate dead, now in the various cemeteries in the Northern States. The resolution was passed without a dissenting vote.

I believe this was done in full appreciation of the noble and humane sentiments expressed by our late lamented President in his speech at Atlanta, Ga., December 14, 1898. There was no object so near his patriotic heart as that to obliterate sectional feeling incident to our unhappy civil strife. He seemed to take advantage of every incident in his administration of public affairs to cause it to bear in the welding together of sections of his country once estranged. Had he lived, he no doubt would have brought about his cherished project, in causing the Government to share in the expense of the care and preservation of the graves of the Confederate dead, whose valor, with that of the Union dead, is now the valor of the American soldier, a sacred heritage of the American people.

I think that Mr. McKinley's speech at Atlanta, Ga., touched the Southern heart more than any other act of any President, and the South mourned his death as sincerely as any part of our great Republic.

I believe Congress could do no wiser act than to carry out the spirit and object of the resolution so unanimously passed by the large assembly of surviving ex-Confederate soldiers at their great gathering in the city of Memphis, Tenn., May 30, 1901.

Yours, truly,
                                                    STEPHEN D. LEE.
Gen. MARCUS J. WRIGHT,
        Washington, D. C.

[Senate Ex. Doc. No. 93. Forty-fifth Congress, second session.]

WAR DEPARTMENT,
Washington City, June 3, 1878.

The Secretary of War has the honor to transmit to the United States Senate, for the information of the Committee on Military Affairs, a communication from the Quartermaster-General, dated the 31st ultimo, submitting estimate of the cost of acquiring title to and inclosing lands in which Confederate prisoners of war are buried and of erecting headstones over their graves.

GEO. W. McCRARY,
                                                    Secretary of War.
The PRESIDENT OF THE UNITED STATES SENATE.

WAR DEPARTMENT,
QUARTERMASTER-GENERAL'S OFFICE,
Washington, D. C., May 31, 1878.

SIR: On the 14th instant I had the honor to report, in reference to the proposed sale to the War Department of a lot of ground near Columbus, Ohio, on which were buried prisoners of war who died at Camp Chase, that the question submitted was one to be decided only by Congress and that the War Department could only execute the laws when enacted.

I have seen the report of the Committee on Military Affairs of the Senate of the United States upon this subject, and I find that the committee is of opinion that the United States, being charged with the sepulture of those who died prisoners in its hands, is required to provide not only suitable place of sepulture, but to protect the title to their graves against all adverse claimants, so that the dead may not be disturbed; that the laws of humanity are not fulfilled by laying them in the earth without securing their resting place from molestation, and that as the matter now stands, the United States being lessee, not owner in fee simple of the land, no such security exists, and that, "should there be other deceased Confederate prisoners of war who died under similar circumstances, lying buried upon private lands, it is the duty of the Government to make reasonable outlay to secure title to the narrow earth in which their remains do rest."

In furtherance of this object, I have the honor to submit a list of places at which, according to information in this office, prisoners of war were buried by the United States authorities during the late struggle. It is extracted from House Document, Fortieth Congress, third session, Report 45, page 768.

The number of prisoners dying in captivity is stated at nearly 27,000, the number of places at 110. On page 771 of same document I find a list of Federal prisons, twenty in number. The greater number of those reported to have died in captivity were buried by the United States near the prisons; those who died in this city were buried at national military cemeteries; others near the place of decease.

The care of prisoners of war was laid upon a special officer of the War Department (the commissary-general of prisoners), and his report will doubtless give fuller information than the records of this office supply.

But as the termination of the session of Congress approaches, it is proper to submit at least an approximate estimate of the quantity of land to be purchased, and the number of graves to be cared for, and of the cost of preserving and inclosing them.

It is not possible at this time to make an exact estimate of the cost of purchasing those prison cemeteries not now owned by the United States, but the estimate below is as nearly correct as can now be made:

For purchase of prison cemeteries used during the late war.............. $10,000
For inclosing the same.. 100,000
For 27,000 stones and blocks to be placed at graves of deceased prisoners.. 94,500

Total 204,500

As no existing law authorizes the War Department to purchase land for this purpose, a special enactment will be necessary, which may probably be made most conveniently by an amendment extending the law of February 22, 1867, relating to national military cemeteries, so as to embrace lands on which prisoners of war are buried.

Very respectfully, your obedient servant,

M. C. MEIGS,
Quartermaster-General, Brevet Major-General, U. S. Army.

The honorable SECRETARY OF WAR.

Detailed statement of the number of Confederate prisoners of war who died in the hands of the United States authorities during the rebellion of 1861-1865, with locality of prison and the number of graves.

Place.	Number of deaths.	Graves.	
		Known.	Unknown.
Alexandria, Va........................	53	45	8
Alton, Ill............................	1,613	850	763
Annapolis, Md.........................	5	3	2
Army corps stations..................	133	118	15
Army of Potomac......................	7	....	7
Atlanta, Ga..........................	5	2	3
Baltimore, Md........................	119	77	42
Batesville, Ark......................	1	1	....
Beaufort, N. C.......................	1	1	....
Beaufort, S. C.......................	4	1	3
Bermuda Hundred, Va..................	4	....	4
Bowling Green, Ky....................	4	....	4
Bridgeport, Ala......................	18	14	4
Camp Butler, Ill....................	816	....	816
Camp Chase, Ohio....................	2,108	1,900	208
Camp Douglas, Ill...................	3,759	2,317	1,442
Camp Morton, Ind....................	1,763	1,556	207
Camp Nelson, Ky.....................	13	13	....
Camp Randall, Wis...................	187	2	185
Chambersburg, Pa.....................	1	1	....
Charleston, S. C.....................	1	....	1
Chattanooga, Tenn...................	74	40	34
Chester, Pa..........................	213	177	36
Cincinnati, Ohio (McLean Barracks)...	6	....	6
City Point, Va.......................	34	21	13
Clarksburg, Va.......................	1	1	....
Cleveland, Ohio......................	2	....	2
Columbus, Ohio.......................	1	....	1
Corinth, Miss........................	13	5	8
Covington, Ky........................	5	2	3
Cumberland, Md.......................	5	1	4
Cumberland Gap, Tenn.................	1	1	....
Davids Island, New York Harbor......	178	177	1

Detailed statement of the number of Confederate prisoners of war who died in the hands of the United States authorities during the rebellion of 1861-1865, etc.—Continued.

Place.	Number of deaths.	Graves.	
		Known.	Unknown.
Elmira, N. Y.	2,980	2,928	52
Fairfax Seminary, Va.	1	1	
Farmington, Miss.	2	1	1
Farmville, Va.	67	65	2
Fort Columbus, New York Harbor.	35	24	11
Fort Delaware, Del.	2,502	1,685	817
Fort Donelson, Tenn.	1		1
Fort La Fayette, New York Harbor.	2		2
Fort Leavenworth, Kans.	5	5	
Fort McHenry, Md.	33	2	31
Fort Mifflin, Pa.	3	1	2
Fort Monroe, Va.	35		35
Fort Pickens, Fla.	1		1
Fort Pulaski, Ga.	11	9	2
Fort Scott, Kans	10	10	
Fort Smith, Ark.	7	4	3
Fort Warren, Boston Harbor.	13	5	8
Fort Wood, New York Harbor	6	1	5
Franklin, Tenn.	2	2	
Frederick, Md.	226	223	3
Gallipolis, Ohio	5		5
Gettysburg, Pa	210	169	41
Goldsborough, N. C.	2		2
Harpers Ferry, Va	2	2	
Harrisburg, Pa.	4		4
Hart Island, New York Harbor	230	176	54
Helena, Ark.	2		2
Hickman Bridge, Ky.	2		2
Hilton Head, S. C.	14	6	8
Jacksonville, Fla.	1		1
Johnsons Island, Ohio.	270	243	27
Jordan Springs, Ky.	5		5
Kansas City, Mo.	12	12	
Keokuk, Iowa.	1		1
Key West, Fla.	2	2	
Knoxville, Tenn.	138	118	20
La Grange, Tenn.	5	3	2
Lexington, Ky.	16	8	8
Little Rock, Ark.	220	215	5
Louisville, Ga.	1		1
Louisville, Ky.	139	110	29
McMinnville, Tenn.	1		1
Martinsburg, Va.	1		1
Memphis, Tenn (post).	109	102	7
Montgomery, Ala.	1		1
Morris Island, S. C.	3	2	1
Mound City, Ill.	3		3
Murfreesborough, Tenn.	16	15	1
Nashville, Tenn.	569	504	65
New Albany, Ind.	2	2	
Newbern, N. C.	112	107	5
New Creek, Va.	7	7	
New Market, Tenn.	4		4
New Orleans, La.	329	314	15
Newport News, Va.	89	70	19
Paducah, Ky.	6		6
Petersburg, Va.	107	94	13
Philadelphia, Pa.	22	13	9
Pittsburg, Pa	13		13
Point Lookout, Md	3,446	2,594	852
Portsmouth, Va.	2		2
Portsmouth Grove, R. I.	1		1
Raleigh, N. C.	9	8	1
Richmond, Va.	178	172	6
Rock Island, Ill.	1,922	1,854	68
St. Louis, Mo.	689	387	302
Savannah, Ga.	40	24	16
Ship Island, Miss	162	151	11
Stevenson, Ala.	6	4	2
Tullahoma, Tenn.	3		3
Unknown places	66	22	44
Vicksburg, Miss	61	2	59
Vinings Station, Ga.	7		7
Washington, D. C.	457	111	346
Wheeling, W. Va (hospital)	3		3
Willets Point, New York Harbor.	3	1	2
York, Pa.	4	4	
Total	26,774	19,920	6,854

List of United States prisons used to confine Confederate prisoners of war.

Alton, Ill.
Camp Butler, Ill.
Camp Chase, Ohio.
Camp Douglas, Ill.
Camp Morton, Ind.
Elmira, N. Y.
Fort Delaware, Del.
Fort McHenry, Md.
Johnsons Island, Ohio.
Louisville, Ky.

Fort La Fayette, New York Harbor.
Hart Island, New York Harbor.
Newport News, Va.
New Orleans, La.
Old Capitol Prison, Washington, D. C.
Point Lookout, Md.
Rock Island, Ill.
St. Louis, Mo.
Ship Island, Miss.
Fort Warren, Boston Harbor, Mass.

THE LOCATIONS AND CONDITION OF THE GRAVES OF THE CONFEDERATE SOLDIERS WHO DIED IN FEDERAL PRISONS AND MILITARY HOSPITALS AND WERE BURIED NEAR THEIR PLACES OF CONFINEMENT.

At the re union of the United Confederate Veterans, Memphis, May 28, 29, 30, 1901, in the session on the 29th there was unanimously adopted with great enthusiasm the following resolution submitted by Gen. Stephen D. Lee:

Resolved, That we respectfully request that Congress take appropriate action looking to the care and preservation of the graves of the Confederate dead now in the various cemeteries in the Northern States. Resolution.

Prompted by the above action, it has been deemed advisable to collect such data as was possible, without official aid, for an intelligent presentation of the facts relating to the location of the graves of the Confederate soldiers who died in Federal prisons and military hospitals, 1861–1865, and their present condition, with the view to obtaining the necessary legislation providing for remedial measures. Prompting to collection of data.

Without commenting upon the causes which led to the lamentable congestion of all military prisons and hospitals during the deplorable war period, it is sufficient to mention here the well-known fact, and that many of these valorous soldiers died and were buried near the places of their confinement. In compliance with a resolution in the House of Representatives, dated July 12, 1866, directing the Secretary of War, Edwin M. Stanton, to report the number of Union and rebel soldiers who died while held as prisoners of war, he reported on July 19, 1866 (see Appendix A), that it appeared by a report of the commissary-general of prisoners that there had been 26,436 deaths of rebel prisoners of war. Causes. Facts. Number of deaths.

The report of Maj. Gen. E. A. Hitchcock, commissary-general of prisoners, made to Secretary of War Edwin M. Stanton, under date of July 18, 1866 (see Appendix B), states that from the records of his office "it appears that 26,436 deaths have been reported among the rebel prisoners of war," and he also states in the same report, "We have accurate reports of the deaths which occurred among rebel prisoners in the North." These reports from those so high in office must be accepted as being as nearly correct as it was possible to make at that date. Deaths.

On October 19, 1866, Maj. Gen. E. A. Hitchcock reported to Bvt. Maj. Gen. E. D. Townshend, assistant adjutant-general, U. S. Army, "a list of stations from which reports Locations.

11

of death and burials of rebel prisoners have been received at this office at periods during the secession rebellion." (See Appendix C.)

National cemeteries. At present there are 83 national cemeteries (see Appendix D), in which are buried 9,300 Confederate soldier prisoners of war.

Gen. M. J. Wright's report. On February 17, 1899, Gen. Marcus J. Wright, of the Records and Pension Office, War Department, reported the places in which Confederate dead are buried, so far as he was able to ascertain. (See Appendix E.)

Condition. It appears that prior to 1874 all graves in the national cemeteries were marked by temporary headboards, in about the same manner as recent interments are marked at **Legislation.** this date. By section 1, act of February 22, 1867 (General Orders, No. 8, Adjutant-General Office, 1867), it is declared that each grave shall be marked with a small headstone, or block, with the number of the grave inscribed thereon, corresponding to the number of the grave in a register. This act was amended June 8, 1872 (General Orders, No. 65, Adjutant-General's Office, 1872), requiring each grave to be marked with a small headstone, with the name of the soldier and the name of his State inscribed thereon, in addition to the number. And on June 10, 1872, an appropriation of $200,000 was made for the erection of headstones upon the graves of soldiers in the national cemeteries (General Orders, No. 52, Adjutant-General's Office, 1872). (See Appendix F.)

By an act approved March 3, 1873 (General Orders, No. 44, Adjutant-General's Office, 1873) the act of February 22, 1867, and the act amendatory thereof, approved June 8, 1872, it is required that said headstones shall be of durable stone, and of such design and weight as shall keep them in place when set; and the sum of $1,000,000 was appropriated for supplying the same. (See Appendix F.)

$1,200,000 appropriated. Thus by the acts of Congress mentioned there were special appropriations for headstones for the Union soldiers of $1,200,000.

Civilians. The legislation noted above entirely related to the headstones of Union soldiers; but it is understood that, at a later date, many of the other graves in the national cemeteries, classed as civilian (of which there were a very large number), such as quartermaster's employees, citizens, State prisoners, Confederate soldiers, and contrabands, were marked, not under special legislation, but out of the annual appropriation for cemeteries, by a thin white marble headstone having inscribed the number of the grave and **Present condition of graves of Confederates.** the name of the occupant, but no mark by which they might be otherwise classified or distinguished. Thus the headstones on such of the graves of the Confederate soldiers in national cemeteries as were marked at all failed to distinguish them as soldiers (nor were they distinguished by location or grouping) or to show from whence they came; and that is their condition at this day, excepting those recently reburied and marked with new headstones in Arlington Cemetery, under the act of Congress approved June 6, 1900.

But the temporary headboards formerly marking the Confederate graves in the national cemeteries long ago rotted away, and though some graves are now marked with the thin marble slabs mentioned, many have to-day no mark whatever, while a few have merely a number referring to a corresponding number in the cemetery register.

Outside the national cemeteries there are probably 20,000 of these dead, uncared for by the Government in any manner; and but a few of them have had any care whatever other than that given by the kind people in the vicinity of a few of the burial grounds. The graves of very many are entirely obliterated, and if their registers be also destroyed, as is sometimes the case, there remains no possible way to locate them; and thus, in a few years, will it be with all the remaining graves uncared for by the Government.

In the growth of large cemeteries it becomes necessary from time to time to make new and larger registers, which is customarily done by transcribing from the older registers. With every transcription clerical errors are likely to be made, and with each additional transcription new errors creep in and the older ones are increased and perpetuated; so that to secure such accuracy as is at all possible it is necessary to resort to the muster rolls of the Confederate archives in the War Department at Washington and any other sources from which it may be possible to obtain information. *Registers—their growing inaccuracy.*

Our lamented President, William McKinley, at Atlanta, Ga., December 14, 1898, delivered a most patriotic address, which met with the heartfelt approval of the people throughout the entire country; and especially did he thereby greatly endear himself to the Southern people. It is fitting, in view of the object of this paper, that his remarks upon this subject should be given here in full: *Address of Mr. McKinley.*

Sectional lines no longer mar the map of the United States. Sectional feeling no longer holds back the love we bear each other. Fraternity is the national anthem, sung by a chorus of forty-five States and our Territories at home and beyond the seas. The Union is once more the common altar of our love and loyalty, our devotion and sacrifice. The old flag again waves over us in peace with new glories, which your sons and ours have this year added to its sacred folds. What cause we have for rejoicing, saddened only by the fact that so many of our brave men fell on field or sickened and died from hardship and exposure, and others, returning, bring wounds and disease from which they will long suffer. The memory of the dead will be a precious legacy, and the disabled will be the nation's care.

A nation which cares for its disabled soldiers, as we have always done, will never lack defenders. The national cemeteries for those who fell in battle all prove that the dead as well as the living have our love. What an array of silent sentinels we have, and with what loving care their graves are kept! Every soldier's grave made during our unfortunate civil war is a tribute to American valor.

And while, when these graves were made, we differed widely about the future of this Government, these differences were long ago settled by the arbitrament of arms * * * *and the time has now come in the evolution of sentiment and feeling under the providence of God, when in the spirit of fraternity we should share with you in care of the graves of the Confederate soldiers.*

The cordial feeling now happily existing between the North and South prompts this gracious act, and if it needed further justification *it is found in the gallant loyalty to the Union and the flag so conspicuously shown in the year just passed by the sons and grandsons of these heroic dead.*

What a glorious future awaits us if unitedly, wisely, and bravely we face the new problems now pressing upon us, determined to solve them for right and humanity.

Having previously investigated the condition of the graves of the Confederate dead at Arlington, Va., and encouraged by President McKinley's address, the Charles Broadway Rouss Camp of United Confederate Veterans, at Washington, D. C., petitioned the President June 5, 1899, setting forth somewhat in detail the condition of the graves of the dead referred to in said cemetery, and requested remedial measures. This petition was received by the President in the most kindly manner, with an earnest expression by him that it was a matter in which he was deeply interested. The result was an enactment by Congress, approved June 6, 1900, above referred to, appropriating $2,500 for the purpose of carrying out the remedial measures which had been requested. The order for the execution of the work was given by the honorable Secretary of War, Mr. Elihu Root, April 25, 1901, and proceedings were immediately initiated in compliance therewith, and the work completely finished about October 1, 1901, in a manner eminently satisfactory and creditable to all concerned. The act of Congress was duly acknowledged by the United Confederate Veterans, at the annual reunion at Memphis, on May 29, 1901, by the passage by the convention of the following resolution, which was adopted unanimously with great enthusiasm:

Resolved, That we hereby extend our thanks to the Congress, and to the President of the United States, for the act of Congress, approved on the 6th day of June, 1900, for the reinterment in Arlington Cemetery of the Confederate dead now in the national cemeteries at Washington, D. C.

In addition to the recognition by the United Confederate Veterans, as shown by their resolution of thanks, there have been enthusiastic praises wherever the facts regarding this reburial have become fully known, and high appreciation by all of this generous tribute to the valor of American soldiers.

But the reburial at Arlington was only an incident in carrying out the noble views of President McKinley; and Gen. Stephen D. Lee in submitting his resolution, heretofore given in full, to the convention at Memphis, felt and thereby showed his appreciation of the sincerity of the President and the comprehensiveness of his conception, the full fruition of which shall not have been accomplished till all that is possible be done in caring for the graves and registers of all the remaining Confederate soldiers who died in Federal prisons and military hospitals and were buried near their places of confinement.

There are a great many national cemeteries and other Government burial grounds from which it has not been possible to obtain information; but it may be said in general that it is not improbable that Confederate prison dead are buried in all national cemeteries unless they have been removed since the end of the war between the States.

Furthermore it is well known that many of the prison dead are scattered throughout the North, not in national cemeteries or receiving the care of the Government, such as those at Madison, Wis.; Terre Haute, Ind.; Alton, Ill.; Camp Chase, Ohio; Camp Douglas, Ill.; Elmira, N. Y.; Fort Warren, Boston, Mass., etc. (See Appendix C.)

There are at this time 83 national cemeteries (see list of national cemeteries, Quartermaster-General's Office, War Department), and October 19, 1866, the commissary-general of prisoners, General Hitchcock, reported "81 stations from which reports of deaths and burials of rebel prisoners have been received at this office at periods during the secession rebellion." Of these 81 stations but 21 are now national cemeteries, leaving 60 other places where Confederate dead are buried. (See Appendix C.)

There are known to be in existing national cemeteries 9,300 Confederate dead, so that more than two-thirds of the Confederate prison dead are buried in places other than national cemeteries, and presumably not under Government control or receiving the care of the Government.

The unfortunate friction which occurred between the Federal and Confederate Governments regarding the carrying out the cartels of exchange during the war unhappily resulted in the accumulation of prisoners on both sides, with consequent congestion, and the enormous number of deaths which occurred in the Federal prisons and hospitals reported by Secretary of War, Edward M. Stanton; and, therefore, it is but right that the United States Government should care for the graves of these Confederate prisoners, not alone those already in the national cemeteries, but also those outside of them wherever they may be found; and their identification should be accomplished if at all possible through the Confederate archives in the War Department, and such other sources of information as may be accessible, and proper records made of the same. *It is but right that the United States Government should care for all Confederate prison dead.*

The reburial at Arlington having been completed, there remains the greater work to be done of giving proper care to the remaining Confederate dead who died in Federal prisons and military hospitals. In the first place it is of the utmost importance that the locations of all be definitely ascertained, and wherever found, if on ground not under the control of the United States Government that proper measures be taken to effect such control. Having ascertained the locations and acquired the necessary control, new registers of all should be prepared and verified by the Confederate archives in the War Department at Washington; and new headstones erected like those recently placed on the graves in the new "Confederate section" at Arlington, inscribed with the number of the grave, the name of the occupant, his company, regiment, and State, and letters "C. S. A.;" and, finally, arrangements should be made for the care of all the burial grounds by necessary fencing, and in all other proper respects. *The greater work to be done.*

Allowing for the unreported deaths, it may well be assumed that the total number of these Confederate prison *28,000 Confederate dead.*

dead is not far from 28,000 (the Part III, Medical and Surgical History of the Rebellion, 1888, reports that according to the monthly reports on file in the Surgeon-General's Office 30,716 rebel soldiers died in Northern prisons, p. 45), and that the present condition of their graves is by no means so good as was that of those at Arlington before the recent reburial must be conceded by all persons.

Estimate as to the cost of the work.   It has been ascertained at the Quartermaster-General's Office (unofficially) that white marble headstones like those recently placed over the graves in the new "Confederate section" at Arlington, similarly inscribed, can be delivered at national cemeteries at $2.50 each, ready for setting—thus making the cost, 28,000 by $2.50 = $70,000. For the preparation of new registers there will be needed a considerable sum for clerical labor and material, etc., which may reasonably be estimated at $10,000; and for the acquisition and care of burial grounds not yet under the control of the Government, the possible advance in the prices of material and labor, etc., a further considerable expense will be necessary. Therefore the total amount needed to satisfactorily accomplish this desirable work may be estimated at $100,000.

The good results.   The good results to accrue from the removal of a fruitful and persistent cause of friction and bitterness, and the honor thus done to valiant American soldiers, whose love of country led to their separation from home, and to death, and the honor the Government would confer on itself in carrying out the comprehensive, noble and patriotic sentiment of President McKinley at Atlanta, Ga., would well repay the trouble and expense.

To this end it is proposed to submit for the consideration of the Congress and the President the following bill for adoption:

Be it enacted by the Senate and House of Representatives of the United States of America in Congress assembled, That the Secretary of War be, and he is hereby, authorized and directed to ascertain the locations and condition of all the graves of the soldiers of the Confederate Army and Navy in the war between the States, eighteen hundred and sixty-one to eighteen hundred and sixty-five, who died in Federal prisons and military hospitals in the North, and were buried near their places of confinement; to acquire possession or control over all grounds where said prison dead are buried not now possessed or under the control of the United States Government; to cause to be prepared accurate registers (in triplicate, one for the superintendent's office in the cemetery, one for the Quartermaster-General's Office, and one for the War Records Office, Confederate archives), of the places of burial, the number of the grave, the name, company, regiment, and State of each Confederate soldier who so died, by verification with the Confederate archives in the War Department at Washington, District of Columbia; to cause to be erected over said graves white marble headstones like unto those recently placed over the graves in the "Confederate section," in the national cemetery at Arlington, Virginia, similarly inscribed; to build proper fencing for the preservation of said burial grounds; and to care for said burial grounds in all proper respects, not herein specifically mentioned.

That for the carrying out of the objects set forth herein there be appropriated, out of the moneys in the Treasury of the United States not otherwise appropriated, the sum of one hundred thousand dollars, or so much thereof as may be necessary. And the Secretary of War is hereby authorized and directed to appoint some competent person as commissioner to ascertain the location of Confederate graves not heretofore located, and to compare the names of those already marked with the registers in the cemeteries, and correct the same when found necessary as preliminary to the work of marking the graves with suitable headstones, and to fix the compensation of said commissioner, who shall be allowed necessary traveling expenses.

Respectfully submitted for the consideration of the Hon. J. B. Foraker, United States Senate.

SAMUEL E. LEWIS, M. D.,
Commander Charles Broadway Rouss Camp, No. 1191,
United Confederate Veterans.

1418 FOURTEENTH STREET NW.,
Washington, D. C., December 6, 1902.

H. Rep. 3389——2

APPENDIX.

A.

WAR DEPARTMENT,
Washington, D. C., July 19, 1866.

SIR: In compliance with a resolution of the House of Representatives dated July 12, directing the Secretary of War to report the number of Union and rebel soldiers who died while held as prisoners of war, I have the honor to state that it appears by a report of the commissary-general of prisoners, first, that 26,436 deaths of rebel prisoners of war are reported; second, that 22,576 Union soldiers are reported as having died in Southern prisons.

The reports also show that 220,000 rebel prisoners were held in the North and about 126,940 Union prisoners in the South.

Your obedient servant,
EDWIN M. STANTON,
Secretary of War.

Hon. SCHUYLER COLFAX,
Speaker of the House of Representatives.

Reference: War of the Rebellion, Official Records of the Union and Confederate Armies, Series II, Volume VIII, Prisoners of War, etc., serial No. 121, page 948.

B.

OFFICE COMMISSARY-GENERAL OF PRISONERS,
Washington, D. C., July 18, 1866.

SIR: In answer to the resolution of the House of Representatives of the 12th instant calling for a report of the number of deaths among Union soldiers while in Southern prisons, and also the deaths among rebel soldiers while held as prisoners of war, I have the honor to state that from the records of this office it appears that 26,436 deaths have been reported among the rebel prisoners of war, and 22,576 Union soldiers are reported as having died in Southern prisons.

    *   *   *   *   *

It should also be noticed that while we have accurate reports of the deaths which occurred among rebel prisoners in the North, the reports from Southern prisons were exceedingly irregular.

E. A. HITCHCOCK,
Major-General, U. S. Volunteers,
Commissary-General of Prisoners.

Reference: War of the Rebellion Official Records of the Union and Confederate Armies, Series II, Volume VIII, Prisoners of War, etc., serial No. 121, page 946.

OFFICE COMMISSARY-GENERAL OF PRISONERS,
Washington, D. C., October 19, 1866.

GENERAL: * * * The following is a list of stations from which reports of deaths and burials of rebel prisoners have been received at this office at periods during the secession rebellion: *Alton* Military Prison, Ill.; Alexandria, Va.; Army Corps—Sixteenth, Seventeenth, and Twentieth; Army of the Potomac: Annapolis, Md.; *Atlanta*, Ga.; *Baltimore*, Md.; Beaufort, S. C.; *Bridgeport*, Ala.; *Bowling Green*, Ky.; *Batesville*, Ark.; Camp *Chase*, Ohio; Camp *Douglas*, Ill.; Camp Butler, Ill.; Camp *Morton*, Ind.; Camp Nelson, Ky.; Camp *Randall*, Wis.; *Chester*, Pa.; *Covington*, Ky.; *Columbus*, Ohio; *Cumberland Gap*, Tenn.; Cleveland, Ohio; City Point, Va.; *Chambersburg*, Pa.; *Clarksburg*, W. Va.; Chattanooga, Tenn.; *Cumberland*, Md.; *Charleston*, S. C.; *Davids Island*, New York Harbor; *Elmira*, N. Y.; Fort *Warren*, Boston Harbor; Fort *Lafayette*, New York Harbor; Fort *Delaware*, Del.; Fort *McHenry*, Md.; Fort *Pulaski*, Ga.; Fort Scott, Kans.; Fort Columbus, New York Harbor; Fort *Leavenworth*, Kans.; Fort *Mifflin*, Pa.; Fort Monroe, Va.; Fort Smith, Ark.; Fort Donelson, Tenn.; Fort *Wood*, New York Harbor; *Franklin*, Tenn.; *Frederick*, Md.; *Farmville*, Va.; Gettysburg, Pa.; *Gallipolis*, Ohio; *Harrisburg*, Pa.; *Hilton Head*, S. C.; *Harts Island*, New York Harbor; *Johnsons Island*, Ohio; Knoxville, Tenn.; *Kansas City*, Mo.; *Key West*, Fla.; *Louisville*, Ky.; Little Rock, Ark.; *Lincoln General Hospital*, District of Columbia; Lexington, Ky.; Memphis, Tenn.; Murfreesboro, Tenn.; *Martinsburg*, W. Va.; *Morehead City*, N. C.; *McLean Barracks*, Ohio; *New Orleans*, La.; Nashville, Tenn.; *Newport News*, Va.; Newbern, N. C.; *New Creek*, W. Va.; *Old Capitol Prison*, District of Columbia; *Paducah*, Ky.; *Pittsburg*, Pa.; Philadelphia, Pa.; *Petersburg*, Va.; Point Lookout, Md.; Raleigh, N. C.; Rock Island, Ill.; *Stevenson*, Ala.; *Ship Island*, Miss.; St. Louis, Mo.; *Savannah*, Ga.; Vicksburg, Miss.; *Wheeling*, W. Va.; Willets Point, N. Y.

*   *   *   *   *   ≈   *   *

Very respectfully, your obedient servant,

E. A. HITCHCOCK,
Major-General, U. S. Volunteers,
Commissary-General of Prisoners

Bvt. Maj. Gen. E. D. TOWNSEND,
Assistant Adjutant-General U. S. Army, Washington, D. C.

Reference: War of the Rebellion Official Records of the Union and Confederate Armies, Series II, Volume VIII, Prisoners of War, etc., serial No. 121, page 970.

NOTE: There appears to be no national cemeteries at the stations italicized. National cemeteries, 21; others than national cemeteries, 60; total, 81.

D.

WAR DEPARTMENT, QUARTERMASTER-GENERAL'S OFFICE,
Washington, D. C., July 1, 1901.

List of national cemeteries, showing the number of interments in each, June 30, 1901.

[Those marked with an asterisk * also contain Confederate dead.]

Name of cemetery.	Interment.		Total.
	Known.	Unknown.	
Alexandria, La.	587	772	1,309
Alexandria, Va.*	3,419	123	3,542
Andersonville, Ga.	12,791	925	13,716
Annapolis, Md.*	2,290	204	2,494
Antietam, Md.	2,876	1,866	4,742
Arlington, Va.	14,046	4,610	18,656
Balls Bluff, Va.	1	24	25
Barrancas, Fla.	877	710	1,587
Baton Rouge, La.	2,534	532	3,066
Battle Ground, D. C.	43	....	43
Beaufort, S. C.*	4,829	4,544	9,373
Beverly, N. J.	171	7	178
Brownsville, Tex.	1,472	1,379	2,851
Camp Butler, Ill.*	1,011	356	1,367
Camp Nelson, Ky.*	1,457	1,189	3,646
Cave Hill Ky.	3,578	582	4,160

List of national cemeteries, showing the number of interments in each, June 30. 1901—
Continued.

Name of cemetery.	Interment.		Total.
	Known.	Unknown.	
Chalmette, La.	7,064	5,745	12,809
Chattanooga, Tenn. *	8,368	4,970	13,338
City Point, Va. *	3,780	1,379	5,159
Cold Harbor, Va.	672	1,290	1,962
Corinth, Miss.	1,791	3,989	5,730
Crown Hill, Ind.	680	32	712
Culpeper, Va.	461	912	1,373
Custer Battlefield, Mont.	978	243	1,221
Cypress Hills, N. Y. *	5,626	378	6,004
Danville, Ky.	349	8	357
Danville, Va.	1,176	153	1,329
Fayetteville, Ark.	456	782	1,238
Finns Point, N. J. *	109	2,539	2,648
Florence, S. C.	213	2,804	3,017
Fort Donelson, Tenn. *	161	511	672
Fort Gibson, Ind. T.	251	2,212	2,463
Fort Harrison, Va.	242	575	817
Fort Leavenworth, Kans. *	1,788	1,445	3,233
Fort McPherson, Nebr.	475	349	824
Fort Scott, Kans. *	565	177	-742
Fort Smith, Ark. *	833	1,485	2,318
Fredericksburg, Va.	2,500	12,801	15,301
Gettysburg, Va. *	2,001	1,632	3,633
Glendale, Va.	238	967	1,205
Grafton, W. Va.	642	620	1,262
Hampton, Va. *	7,938	600	8,538
Jefferson Barracks, Mo. *	8,993	2,906	11,899
Jefferson City, Mo.	388	411	799
Keokuk, Iowa	699	43	742
Knoxville, Tenn. *	2,230	1,067	3,297
Lebanon, Ky.	595	277	872
Lexington, Ky.	840	112	952
Little Rock, Ark. *	3,401	2,373	5,774
Loudon Park, Md	2,629	380	3,009
Marietta, Ga.	7,316	2,967	10,283
Memphis, Tenn. *	5,227	8,822	14,049
Mexico City, Mex.	730	750	1,480
Mill Springs, Ky	352	366	718
Mobile, Ala.	823	229	1,052
Mound City, Ill.	2,593	2,732	5,325
Nashville, Tenn. *	11,937	4,711	16,648
Natchez, Miss	394	2,780	3,174
New Albany, Ind	2,249	676	2,925
Newbern, N. C. *	2,243	1,091	3,334
Philadelphia, Pa. *	2,448	188	2,636
Poplar Grove, Va.	2,200	4,010	6,210
Port Hudson, La	597	3,239	3,836
Quincy, Ill	230	57	287
Raleigh, N. C. *	638	572	1,210
Richmond, Va.	856	5,700	6,556
Rock Island, Ill. *	288	20	308
Salisbury, N. C.	110	12,035	12,145
San Antonio, Tex	1,184	283	1,467
San Francisco, Cal	2,773	432	3,205
Santa Fe, N. Mex	361	421	782
Seven Pines, Va.	157	1,230	1,387
Shiloh, Tenn	1,239	2,372	3,611
Soldiers' Home, D. C.	6,503	291	6,794
Springfield, Mo	979	740	1,719
St. Augustine, Fla.	1,470	....	1,470
Staunton, Va.	236	527	763
Stones River, Tenn.	3,818	2,333	6,151
Vicksburg, Miss. *	4,018	12,760	16,778
Wilmington, N. C.	731	1,577	2,308
Winchester, Va.	2,100	2,387	4,487
Woodlawn, N. Y. *	3,068	7	3,075
Yorktown, Va.	751	1,435	2,186
Total	192,683	151,690	344,363

NOTE.—Of these interments about 9,300 are those of Confederates, being mainly in the national cemeteries at Camp Butler, Cypress Hills, Finns Point, Fort Smith, Hampton, Jefferson Barracks, and Woodlawn.

NOTE.—There are 26 national cemeteries which are known to contain 9,300 Confederate dead.

E.

WAR DEPARTMENT, WAR RECORDS OFFICE,
Washington, February 3, 1899.

DEAR SIR: I have the honor to hand you a tabulated statement of location of Confederate cemeteries or graveyards in which Confederate soldiers are buried, with number of interments in each, as far as has been ascertained.

I beg to say that from the date I received the order to obtain this information I have used all diligence and dispatch, but the report is by no means complete, and it will take several months to make such complete returns as are possible.

I am, sir, very respectfully, your obedient servant,

MARCUS J. WRIGHT,
Agent War Department.

Hon. JOS. G. CANNON,
Chairman of Appropriation Committee, House of Representatives.

[Report of Gen. Marcus J. Wright, War Records Office, February 3, 1899.]

Statement of location of Confederate cemeteries or graveyards in which Confederate soldiers are buried, with number of interments in each, so far as has been ascertained.

	Interments.			Interments.	
	Known.	Un-known.		Known.	Un-known.
ALABAMA.			**GEORGIA.**		
Bridgeport			Atlanta		
Stevenson			Andersonville National Cemetery		
Auburn City Cemetery	98	54	Fort Pulaski		
Gainesville	192		Savannah		
ARKANSAS.			**ILLINOIS.**		
Batesville			Alton	1,576	640
Fort Smith National Cemetery			Camp Butler (Riverton)		
Little Rock			Confederate Cemetery	470	
			Chicago, Oakwood Cemetery		
ARIZONA.			Camp Douglas, prisoners dead.	4,317	
Phoenix Confederate Cemetery	a 10		Government Smallpox Hospital	412	
Army Corps, Sixteenth, Seventeenth, and Twentieth *b*			Interments, estimated from prison register	1,500	
Army of the Potomac *b*			Mound City National Cemetery, military prisoners, interments.	84	
DELAWARE.			Rock Island, in Confederate cemetery at arsenal, interments	1,960	
Pea Patch Island					
Fort Delaware					
DISTRICT OF COLUMBIA.			**INDIANA.**		
Soldiers' Home National Cemetery			Indianapolis, Greenlawn Cemetry Camp Morton	1,484	
Old Capital Prison Cemetery					
Lincoln General Hospital			**KANSAS.**		
FLORIDA.			Fort Scott National Cemetry		
			Bowling Green		
Barrancas (national cemetery)			Fort Leavenworth		
Madison					
Key West			**KENTUCKY.**		
Olustee	160				
Lake City	170		Camp Nelson		
Tallahassee	10		Covington		
Quincy	20		Louisville		
Pensacola	80		Lexington		
Marianna	15		Paducah		
Gainesville	6		Frankfort		
Jacksonville	10		Perryville		
Fernandina	15		Richmond		
St. Augustine	12		Lebanon		
Ocala	15		Green River Bridge		

a All marked.

b These from report of Gen. E. A. Hitchcock, commissary of prisoners, to Gen. E. D. Townsend, October 19, 1866.

Statement of location of Confederate cemeteries or graveyards in which Confederate soldiers are buried, with number of interments in each, etc.—Continued.

	Interments.			Interments.	
	Known.	Un-known.		Known.	Un-known.
KENTUCKY—continued.			**NORTH CAROLINA—continued.**		
Bardstown			Smithfield	20	
Mount Sterling			Kinston		
Nicholasville			Washington City Cemetery	43	
Lawrenceburg			Howard's field, near Trinity		
Cynthiana			Church	2	
			Trinity Churchyard	4	
LOUISIANA.			Methodist Churchyard	7	
			Presbyterian Churchyard	14	
New Orleans			Episcopal Churchyard	17	
			Clinton	32	
MARYLAND.			Statesville Old Presbyterian		
			Church Graveyard	32	
Annapolis					
Cumberland			**OHIO.**		
Fort McHenry					
Frederick			Columbus		
Point Lookout (Camp Delaware)		2,159	In Confederate and city cemeteries	2161	
Baltimore			Johnsons Island (Lake Erie, near Sandusky)		
London Park, in national cemetery			In Confederate cemetery, military prisoners dead	206	
Military prisoners dead (interments unknown)		100	Gallipolis		
			Sandusky		
MASSACHUSETTS.			Cleveland		
			McLean Barracks		
Fort Warren, Boston Harbor					
			PENNSYLVANIA.		
MISSISSIPPI.					
			Mount Moriah Cemetery		
Ship Island			Philadelphia, National Cemetery, prisoners dead removed from Chester rural cemetery to the Odd Fellow Cemetery	224	
Vicksburg			Gettysburg National Cemetery		
MISSOURI.			Fort Mifflin		
			Pittsburg, strangers ground in Allegheny Cemetery, military prisoners dead	15	
St. Louis					
Jefferson Barracks National Cemetery			Chester		
Jefferson City National Cemetery			Chambersburg		
Kansas City			Harrisburg		
NEW YORK.			**SOUTH CAROLINA.**		
Woodlawn National (Elmira) Cemetery			Beaufort		
The military prisoners dead	2,947		Charleston		
Willetts Point			Hilton Head		
Long Island					
In Cypress Hill Cemetery, the military prisoners dead	488		**TENNESSEE.**		
Harts Island			Columbia		
Davids Island, New York Harbor			Cumberland Gap		
Fort Lafayette, New York Harbor			Clarksville		
Fort Columbus, New York Harbor			Chattanooga		
Fort Wood, New York Harbor			Dover (Fort Donelson)		
			Franklin		
NEW JERSEY.			Gallatin		
			Jackson		
Finns Point National Cemetery, in the Confederate cemetery, the Fort Delaware prisoners dead, interments reported	1,434		Knoxville		
			Lewisburg		
			Murfreesboro		
			Memphis		
			Nashville		
			Tullahoma		
NORTH CAROLINA.					
			TEXAS.		
Averasboro, Harnett County			Austin, the State Cemetery	164	
Morehead City			Tyler, Confederate Cemetery	180	
Newbern	70				
Raleigh	674		**VIRGINIA.**		
Kittrell	50		Alexandria		
Goldsboro, Willow Dale Cemetery	800		Arlington National Cemetery	131	10
Bentonville	200		City Point National Cemetery		
			Culpeper Courthouse		
			Charlottsville		

Statement of location of Confederate cemeteries or graveyards in which Confederate soldiers are buried, with number of interments in each, etc.—Continued.

	Interments.			Interments.	
	Known.	Un-known.		Known.	Un-known.
VIRGINIA—continued.			**VIRGINIA—continued,**		
Fort Monroe....................			Winchester.....................		
Farmsville			Woodstock.....................		
Fredericksburg................			Yorktown National Cemetery..		
Louisa Courthouse			Near Appomatox Court House.	19	
Manassas......................					
Meade Station, Ninth Corps			**WISCONSIN.**		
Cemetery, near Petersburg..			Camp Randall.................		
Mount Jackson................			Madison.......................		
Newport News................			Confederate burying plot or		
New Creek			cemetery		
Petersburg			Prisoners dead	137	
Poplar Grove..................			Forrest Hill		
Richmond.....................					
Hollywood Cemetery..........	30,000		**WEST VIRGINIA.**		
Oakwood......................	14,000		Clarksburg		
The Hebrew Cemetery.........			Martinsburg...................		
Staunton......................			New Creek		
Strasburg.....................			Wheeling		
Warrenton					

WAR DEPARTMENT,
  War Records Office, January 17, 1899, and February 3, 1899.

F.

CONGRESSIONAL LEGISLATION RELATING TO HEADSTONES FOR MARKING THE GRAVES OF UNION SOLDIERS.

1867.

Be it enacted, etc., That in the arrangement of the national cemeteries established for the burial of deceased soldiers and sailors, the Secretary of War is hereby directed to have the same inclosed with a good and substantial stone or iron fence; and to cause each grave to be marked with a small headstone, or block, with the number of the grave inscribed thereon, corresponding with the number opposite to the name of the party in a register of burials to be kept at each cemetery and at the office of the Quartermaster-General, which shall set forth the name, rank, company, regiment, and date of death of the officer or soldier; or, if unknown, it shall be so recorded. (Sec. 1, act of February 22, 1867; General Orders, No. 8, Adjutant-General's Office, 1867.)

1872.

Be it enacted, etc.. That section one of an act entitled "An act to establish and to protect national cemeteries," approved February twenty-second, eighteen hundred and sixty-seven, be amended as follows:
"The Secretary of War shall cause each grave to be marked with a small headstone, with the name of the soldier and the name of his State inscribed thereon, when the same are known, in addition to the number required to be inscribed by said section; and he shall, within ninety days from the passage of this act, advertise for sealed proposals of bids for the making and erection of such headstones, which advertisements shall be made for sixty days successively in at least twenty newspapers of general circulation in the United States, and shall call for bids for the doing of said work, in whole or in part; and upon the opening of such bids the Secretary of War shall, without delay, award the contracts for said work to the lowest responsible bidder or bidders, in whole or in part; and said bidders shall give bond to his satisfaction for the faithful completion of the work." (Approved June 8, 1872; General Orders, No. 65, Adjutant-General's Office, 1872.)
Appropriated to provide for the erection of headstones upon the graves of soldiers in the national cemeteries, $200,000. (Act approved June 10, 1872; General Orders, No. 52, Adjutant-General's Office, 1872.)

1875.

Unexpended balance continued and rendered available for its original purposes. (Act approved March 3, 1875; General Orders, No. 24, Adjutant-General's Office, 1875.)

1873.

The headstones required by an act entitled "An act to establish and protect national cemeteries," approved February twenty-second, eighteen hundred and sixty-seven, and the act amendatory thereof, approved June eighth, eighteen hundred and seventy-two, shall be of durable stone, and of such design and weight as shall keep them in place when set; and the contract for supplying the same shall be awarded by the Secretary of War, after sixty days' advertisement in ten newspapers of general circulation, to some responsible person or persons whose samples and bids shall in the greatest measure combine the elements of durability, decency, and cheapness; and the sum of one million dollars is hereby appropriated for said purpose, out of any money in the Treasury not otherwise appropriated; and the Secretary of War shall first determine for the various cemeteries the size and model for such headstones, and the standard of quality and color of the stone to be used, and bids shall be made and decided with reference thereto; and contracts may be made for separate quantities of such headstones; and the contracts made under this act shall provide for furnishing and setting all the said headstones, and shall not in the aggregate exceed the sum hereby appropriated. (Act approved March 3, 1873; General Orders, No. 44, Adjutant-General's Office, 1873.)

G.

[Public—No. 163.   Page 47.]

AN ACT making appropriations for sundry civil expenses of the Government for the fiscal year ending June thirtieth, nineteen hundred and one, and for other purposes.

Be it enacted by the Senate and House of Representatives of the United States of America in Congress assembled, That the following sums are hereby appropriated for the object hereinafter expressed, for the fiscal year ending June thirtieth, nineteen hundred and one, namely:

UNDER THE WAR DEPARTMENT.

NATIONAL CEMETERIES.

To enable the Secretary of War to have reburied in some suitable spot in the national cemetery at Arlington, Virginia, and to place proper headstones at their graves, the bodies of about one hundred and twenty-eight Confederate soldiers now buried in the National Soldiers' Home, near Washington, District of Columbia, and the bodies of about one hundred and thirty-six Confederate soldiers now buried in the national cemetery at Arlington, Virginia, two thousand five hundred dollars, or so much thereof as may be necessary.

H. Rep. 3389——3   O

DEDICATING TO COLUMBUS, OHIO, CERTAIN PROPERTY FOR USES AND PURPOSES OF THE PUBLIC STREETS.

JANUARY 27, 1903.—Committed to the Committee of the Whole House on the state of the Union and ordered to be printed.

Mr. HULL, from the Committee on Military Affairs, submitted the following

REPORT.

[To accompany S. R. 156.]

The Committee on Military Affairs, to whom was referred the joint resolution (S. R. 156) dedicating to the city of Columbus, in the State of Ohio, for uses and purposes of the public streets, part of property conveyed to the United States by Robert Neil by deed dated February 17, 1863, recorded in Deed Book 76, page 572, etc., Franklin County records, report the same back to the House with the recommendation that it do pass.

This act passed the Senate January 24, 1903, and the report made thereon is as follows:

[Senate Report No. 2588, Fifty-seventh Congress, second session.]

The Committee on Military Affairs, having had under consideration the following Senate joint resolution, recommend that the same do pass:

"JOINT RESOLUTION dedicating to the city of Columbus, in the State of Ohio, for uses and purposes of the public streets, part of property conveyed to the United States by Robert Neil by deed dated February seventeenth, eighteen hundred and sixty-three, recorded in deed book seventy-six, page five hundred and seventy-two, and so forth, Franklin County records.

"*Resolved by the Senate and House of Representatives of the United States of America in Congress assembled,* That there be, and hereby is, dedicated to the city of Columbus, Franklin County, Ohio, for the uses and purposes of public streets and highways forever, so much of the property conveyed to the United States by Robert Neil by deed dated February seventeenth, anno Domini eighteen hundred and sixty-three, and recorded in deed book numbered seventy-six, at page numbered five hundred and seventy-two, of said Franklin County's record of deeds, as is described as follows: Being part of the streets bounding the seventy-seven acres three rods and eight poles of land known as the Columbus Barracks, situate in the city of Columbus, Ohio, said dedication being more specifically described as follows: Being the United States's part of Buckingham street, seventy-seven feet wide; Cleveland avenue, sixty-six feet wide; Stanton street, seventy feet wide; and Jefferson avenue, sixty-six feet wide.

"SEC. 2. That the Secretary of War be, and he hereby is, authorized and directed to execute such paper writing as will carry out the purposes of this resolution."

This resolution simply dedicates to the city of Columbus, Franklin County, Ohio, for the uses and purposes of public streets and highways forever, one-half of the streets immediately surrounding the United States barracks, which occupy a tract of ground containing 77 and a fraction acres.

The necessity for the dedication is in the fact that the city of Columbus desires, at its own expense, under the laws of Ohio, to improve these streets, but is without authority to do so, because, under the laws of Ohio, it is prohibited from the improvement of streets that have not been dedicated to the public use.

These two streets have been open and in use by the public as streets for many years.

The commanding officer of the United States barracks at Columbus, Lieut. Col. Charles G. Penny, recommends that the dedication be made, as shown by his letter to the adjutant-general of the Department of the Lakes, Chicago, Ill., dated April 20, 1902, and printed herewith:

COLUMBUS BARRACKS, OHIO, *April 20, 1902.*

SIR: In a separate package I have this day forwarded to you a form of dedication of property appertaining to grounds of this post for street purposes. I have the honor to recommend that this dedication be made. The city government and many citizens express a desire for this dedication in order that the city may improve the streets. It is claimed that statutory provisions of the State of Ohio require this formal "dedication" before the city can expend money on street improvements. As the streets have been opened for many years and are in use as public highways, I can not see any reason why they should not be formally "dedicated," as requested.

I am, sir, very respectfully, your obedient servant,

CHAS. G. PENNY,
Lieutenant-Colonel Twenty-third Infantry, Commanding.

The ADJUTANT-GENERAL DEPARTMENT OF THE LAKES,
Chicago, Ill.

This recommendation is indorsed by Major-General MacArthur, commanding the Department of the Lakes, and by the chief quartermaster.

The necessity for the passage of a joint resolution is due to the fact that the Judge-Advocate-General has held that the property can not be dedicated without action by Congress.

These facts are all shown by the correspondence and indorsements following:

DEPARTMENT OF LAW,
Columbus, Ohio, November 7, 1902.

DEAR SIR: Herewith find correspondence relative to the dedication of streets around the Columbus Barracks and copies of the original communications between the officers of the barracks and the Department of the Lakes; also a blue print and a linen stencil plat, which explain the whole matter.

By virtue of an act of the general assembly of the State of Ohio, passed April 10, 1900 (94 O. L., 543), the city authorities have been improving streets around the barracks, paying one-half the cost out of the general fund of the city of Columbus. Section 1 of that act provides "That cities of the first grade of the second class shall have authority to pay that portion of the costs and expenses of paving and improving any streets, avenues, alleys, or parts thereof of said cities that abut upon lands owned by the Government of the United States of America that would be assessed under the existing laws against such Government land for such improvements."

Section 2 provides for the authority to issue bonds.

While it is true these streets have been used by the public for some time as public highways, yet in order to clear up the legal difficulties which might arise and cause the city trouble at some future time, it is desired that formal dedication be made by the United States of these streets shown on the plat within the red lines thereof. As there seems to be no objection on the part of the military authorities of the Department of the Lakes, we urgently request you to use your influence with Congress looking toward proper action upon the part of Congress to provide for this dedication. We desire to improve Stanton street and to complete Jefferson avenue, and we earnestly request that this matter be given your prompt attention in the next session of Congress. We are ready to furnish at any time any information that may be desired and to assist in any way we can toward the accomplishment of this step, which we deem to be necessary.

Thanking you in advance for anything you may do in the matter, we have the honor to be,

Yours, very truly,

DEPARTMENT OF LAW,
FRANKLIN RUBRECHT,
First Assistant Director of Law.

Hon. EMMETT TOMPKINS, *Columbus, Ohio.*

DEPARTMENT OF PUBLIC IMPROVEMENTS,
Columbus, Ohio, September 12, 1902.

GENTLEMEN: While Colonel Penny was commandant at the barracks the question of securing governmental dedication of the streets around the barracks was taken up and correspondence was had with the various departmental headquarters relative to the same, a copy of which please find herewith; also a blue print showing the barracks property, together with the streets to be dedicated. From the correspondence we learn that it will be necessary to secure the adoption of an enabling act by Congress authorizing the Secretary of War to make this dedication.

Will you kindly prepare a form of bill for this purpose, so that the entire matter may be taken up with Congressman Tompkins at the earliest opportunity in order that action may be taken by Congress at its session this winter?

Yours, respectfully,

JULIAN GRIGGS, *Chief Engineer.*

Messrs. BYRNE, RUBRECHT, and WILDERMUTH,
Department of Law, Columbus, Ohio.

DEPARTMENT OF PUBLIC IMPROVEMENTS,
Columbus, Ohio, March 21, 1902.

DEAR SIR: As per your request, I hand you herewith plat of the dedication to be made by the United States to the city of Columbus, Ohio, of a portion of the tract of ground conveyed to the United States by Robert Neil in 1863 for the purpose of dedicating to the city of Columbus, Ohio, so much of said tract as to make Buckingham street 77 feet wide, Cleveland avenue 66 feet wide, Stanton street 70 feet wide, and Jefferson avenue 66 feet wide.

This is in line with your statement that Colonel Penny, in charge of the Columbus Barracks, will aid in securing the proper dedication from the War Department in order to enable the city of Columbus to improve the streets around the Columbus Barracks under the existing State law for street improvements, and which will in all probability be taken up by the city as soon as the dedication becomes effective.

Buckingham street is contracted for improvement. The proceedings have passed council for paving Cleveland avenue, and Jefferson avenue is already improved from Buckingham street to Leonard avenue, which will leave for further consideration the improvement of Jefferson avenue from Leonard avenue to Stanton street and Stanton street from Jefferson avenue to Cleveland avenue.

Yours, truly,

JULIAN GRIGGS, *Chief Engineer.*

Dr. R. D. CONNELL, *Columbus, Ohio.*

[NOTE.—Letter of Lieutenant-Colonel Penny, which immediately preceded this, will be found elsewhere in this report.]

[Second indorsement.]

HEADQUARTERS DEPARTMENT OF THE LAKES,
CHIEF QUARTERMASTER'S OFFICE,
Chicago, Ill., April 23, 1902.

Respectfully returned to the adjutant-general Department of the Lakes, recommending approval and that the papers be forwarded for consideration of the War Department.

E. P. ATWOOD,
Assistant Quartermaster-General, U. S. Army, Chief Quartermaster.

[Third indorsement.]

HEADQUARTERS DEPARTMENT OF THE LAKES,
Chicago, May 9, 1902.

Respectfully returned to the commanding officer, Columbus Barracks, Ohio.

It is understood from the remarks of the commanding officer that the property proposed to be dedicated has been heretofore surrendered by the Government for street purposes. Information is desired as to the authority under which the former surrender was granted and what conditions, if any, were imposed. The idea of the proposed dedication is approved by the department commander, but before action is

taken full and complete information is desired. It has not been thought necessary to return the drawing, which is retained at these headquarters.
By command of Major-General MacArthur:

P. B. BROWN,
Captain, Fourth Cavalry, Aid-de-Camp, Acting Adjutant-General.

[Fourth indorsement.]

COLUMBUS BARRACKS, OHIO, *May 14, 1902.*

Respectfully returned to the adjutant-general, Department of the Lakes.
Careful and exhaustive search of the records of the county of Franklin and city of Columbus has been made, from which search the following information has been obtained, viz: Cleveland avenue and Jefferson avenue have been public highways (county roads) for more than sixty years. When the United States took over property Stanton street was opened to the public as a highway and has so remained. Buckingham street was originally a public alley, known as "Forest alley."
This street was widened and opened for public use by act of Congress approved July 21, 1892. (See G. O., No. 56, D. A. G. O., August 13, 1892.)

CHAS. G. PENNY,
Lieutenant-Colonel Twenty-third Infantry, Commanding.

[Fifth indorsement.]

HEADQUARTERS DEPARTMENT OF THE LAKES,
Chicago, May 16, 1902.

Respectfully forwarded to the Adjutant-General of the Army.
It appears that the ground proposed to be dedicated has been used for public highways for an indefinite period, and there appears to be no objection to transferring to the city of Columbus the ground included in the proposed plan of dedication.

ARTHUR MACARTHUR,
Major-General, Commanding.

[Sixth indorsement.]

WAR DEPARTMENT, ADJUTANT-GENERAL'S OFFICE,
Washington, May 21, 1902.

Respectfully referred to the Judge-Advocate-General for remark, through the Quartermaster-General, for any additional information his records may afford in this matter.
By order of the Secretary of War:

J. PARKER,
Major of Cavalry, Assistant Adjutant-General.

[Seventh indorsement.]

WAR DEPARTMENT, QUARTERMASTER-GENERAL'S OFFICE,
Washington, D. C., June 14, 1902.

Respectfully transmitted to the Judge-Advocate-General U. S. Army, inclosing blue print showing present reservation as taken from the records of this office.
So far as this office is concerned, there is no objection to the dedication as within referred to. There is, however, no authority known to this office by which the Secretary of War can dedicate this land in the city of Columbus without being authorized so to do by special act of Congress.
Attention is invited to the fourth indorsement of the commanding officer, which shows that these streets are all in public use, and have been for a number of years; so practically there would be no change in the present use of the reservation.

M. I. LUDINGTON,
Quartermaster-General U. S. Army.

[Eighth indorsement.]

WAR DEPARTMENT, JUDGE-ADVOCATE-GENERAL'S OFFICE,
Washington, D. C., June 23, 1902.

Respectfully returned to the Adjutant-General, concurring in the view that Congress alone can authorize the dedication of land belonging to the United States to the city of Columbus, Ohio, for street purposes.
It is, however, noticed that the statement is made in the fourth indorsement that "Cleveland avenue and Jefferson avenue have been public highways (county roads)

for more than sixty years, and when the United States took over the property Stanton street was opened to the public as a highway and has so remained. Buckingham street was originally a public alley known as Forest alley."

If the land which it is now proposed to dedicate to the city was legally dedicated to the public for road purposes when the United States acquired it, the title of the United States to it is subject to that easement; but if the present proposition is to dedicate additional land not subject to such easement, the consent of Congress is necessary.

GEO. B. DAVIS,
Judge-Advocate-General.

[Ninth indorsement.]

WAR DEPARTMENT, ADJUTANT-GENERAL'S OFFICE,
Washington, June 28, 1902.

Respectfully returned to the commanding general Department of the Lakes, Chicago, Ill., with reference to remarks of the Judge-Advocate-General in preceding indorsement.

By order of the Secretary of War:

J. PARKER,
Major of Cavalry, Assistant Adjutant-General.

[Tenth indorsement.]

HEADQUARTERS DEPARTMENT OF THE LAKES,
Chicago, July 2, 1902.

Respectfully returned to the commanding officer Columbus Barracks, Ohio, inviting attention to the seventh and eighth indorsements.

By command of Major-General MacArthur:

F. J. KEMAN,
Captain, Second Infantry, Acting Department Commander,
Acting Adjutant-General.

A similar resolution was introduced in the House of Representatives and referred to the honorable Secretary of War for information and remarks, and was returned with the following remarks:

[Second indorsement.]

WAR DEPARTMENT, January 23, 1903.

Respectfully returned to the chairman Committee on Military Affairs, House of Representatives, inviting attention to the accompanying report of the Quartermaster-General of the Army, dated January 21 instant.

W. SANGER,
Assistant Secretary of War.

WAR DEPARTMENT, QUARTERMASTER-GENERAL'S OFFICE,
Washington, January 21, 1903.

SIR: I have the honor to return herewith House joint resolution 221, "Dedicating to the city of Columbus, in the State of Ohio, for uses and purposes of the public streets, part of property conveyed to the United States by Robert Neill by deed dated February 17, 1863."

The lands described in the within joint resolution, adjacent to the Columbus Barracks Military Reservation, are and have been for many years in use as public streets. No objection to their dedication to the city for street purposes is known to this office. Their transfer, which will involve no change in the present use of the reservation, has heretofore been recommended by the Department and post authorities and by this office.

Respectfully,

M. I. LUDINGTON,
Quartermaster-General U. S. Army.

The SECRETARY OF WAR.

O

ABOLISHING THE CUSTOMS DISTRICT OF TECHE, LA:

JANUARY 27, 1903.—Committed to the Committee of the Whole House on the state of the Union and ordered to be printed.

Mr. ROBERTSON, from the Committee on Ways and Means, submitted the following

REPORT.

[To accompany H. R. 12271.]

The Committee on Ways and Means, to whom was referred the bill (H. R. 12271) to abolish the district of the Teche, in the State of Louisiana, and to attach to and make part of the district of New Orleans the territory now comprising said district, as described in act of February 25, 1873, entitled "An act to define the limits of the collection district of the Teche, in the State of Louisiana, and for other purposes," beg leave to report back favorably the same without amendment, with a recommendation that the same do pass.

It appears from an examination that the amount of business done in the customs district of the Teche is insignificant. The report of the Secretary of the Treasury shows that the customs collected in said district for the fiscal year ending June 30, 1901, was $86.39, while the expenses of collection were $2,943.03. The cost of collecting $1, therefore, of customs revenues in this district was $34.067.

On the 20th of March, 1902, the Secretary of the Treasury directed the following letter to the Hon. Sereno E. Payne, in answer to a communication from him requesting the views of the Department upon House bill 12271:

TREASURY DEPARTMENT, OFFICE OF THE SECRETARY,
Washington, March 20, 1902.

SIR: I have the honor to acknowledge the receipt of your communication of the 18th instant, with which was inclosed for an expression of my views thereon, House bill 12271, providing for the abolishment of the customs collection district of the Teche and to attach the territory now comprising said district to the collection district of New Orleans.

In reply I have to state that in a letter addressed to you on the 27th of January last, in relation to House bill 9500, which bill provided for the extension of the district of the Teche to include Port Arthur, Tex., and make that place the chief port of the proposed district, it was stated that "the alternative of the bill would be the abolishment of the district of the Teche, annexing its territory to the district of New Orleans, and making Port Arthur a subport of entry in the district of Galveston."

House bill 12271 is in line with the letter to you above quoted, and its passage would not be objectionable to this Department.

Respectfully,

O. L. SPAULDING,
Acting Secretary.

Hon. SERENO E. PAYNE,
Chairman Committee on Ways and Means, House of Representatives.

O

ANTHONY R. RAVENSCROFT.

JANUARY 27, 1903.—Committed to the Committee of the Whole House and ordered
to be printed.

Mr. CAPRON, from the Committee on Military Affairs, submitted the
following

REPORT.

[To accompany H. R. 6745.]

The Committee on Military Affairs, to whom was referred the bill
(H. R. 6745) to remove the charge of desertion against Anthony R.
Ravenscroft, report the same back to the House with the recommenda-
tion that it do pass with the following amendment:

Amend the title so as to read: "A bill for the relief of Anthony R.
Ravenscroft."

Also, strike out all after the enacting clause and insert in lieu thereof
the following:

That Anthony R. Ravenscroft shall hereafter be held and considered to have been
honorably discharged from the military service of the United States as a captain of
the Twenty-second Regiment of Indiana Infantry Volunteers, on the twenty-second
day of August, eighteen hundred and sixty-four, by reason of the expiration of his
term of service; and the Secretary of War is hereby authorized and directed to issue
a certificate of honorable discharge for him in accordance with the terms of this act:
Provided, That no pay or other allowances shall be due or payable to any person by
reason of the passage of this act.

It appears from the records that this soldier was mustered into the
United States service August 15, 1861, as a second lieutenant of Company I, Twenty-second Indiana Infantry Volunteers, to serve three
years; that he was promoted to first lieutenant on November 10, 1862,
and to captain on March 19, 1863; that he served faithfully, on
detached duty most of the time, and that he was relieved from duty
in the Ordnance Department and directed to rejoin his regiment on
August 10, 1864, from the Department of the Cumberland.

He did not take the benefits of a veteran furlough, as he did not desire
to reenlist, his term of enlistment naturally expiring on August 15,
1864.

The records show that he served faithfully during the entire term of
his enlistment, and your committee believe that it was simply a matter
of oversight, or technical error, that he did not receive his honorable

discharge, to which he was entitled at the close of his term of enlistment.

The facts in the case are very fully shown in a report from the War Department, as follows:

Case of Anthony R. Ravenscroft, late captain Company I, Twenty-second Indiana Infantry Volunteers.

A report in this case was furnished the Committee on Military Affairs, United States Senate, on Senate bill No. 2969, Fifty-fifth Congress, second session, January 11, 1898.

Following is a copy:

"It is shown by the records that Anthony R. Ravenscroft was mustered into service August 15, 1861, as a second lieutenant with Company I, Twenty-second Indiana Infantry Volunteers, to serve three years. He was mustered into service as first lieutenant, same company and regiment, to date November 10, 1862, and as captain, same company and regiment, to date March 19, 1863. He was detached for duty as military conductor on the Louisville and Nashville Railroad in orders from the headquarters of the Fourteenth Army Corps dated November 26, 1862, and was relieved from that duty and ordered to his regiment in orders dated August 23, 1863, from the Department of the Cumberland. On September 8, 1863, he was detached for duty in the Ordnance Department in orders of that date from the same authority.

"On July 13, 1864, Maj. Thomas Shay, commanding the regiment, in a communication addressed to the assistant adjutant-general of the Department of the Cumberland in relation to the officers and men of the regiment who were entitled to be mustered out of service with it on the following 15th day of August, stated that Capt. Anthony R. Ravenscroft, of Company I, who was then absent on detached service in the ordnance department of the Department of the Cumberland, and who had been promoted since entering the service, but who did not receive the benefit of veteran furlough or express a desire to reenter the service, was among the officers entitled to be mustered out with the nonveteran detachment. Captain Ravenscroft was accordingly relieved from duty in the ordnance department and directed to rejoin his regiment in orders dated August 10, 1864, from the Department of the Cumberland.

"The muster rolls of his company from October 31, 1863, to October 31, 1864, report him absent on detached service in ordnance department; subsequent rolls to February 28, 1865, report him absent without leave.

"On January 23, 1865, Capt. W. H. Snodgrass, then commanding the regiment, addressed a communication to the assistant adjutant-general of the Fourteenth Army Corps, which was forwarded through intermediate headquarters to this Department. A copy thereof, with the indorsements thereon, follows:

"HEADQUARTERS TWENTY-SECOND INDIANA VOLUNTEERS,
"*Toolies Station, Ga., January 23, 1865.*

"COLONEL: I have the honor to report Capt. A. R. Ravenscroft, Company I, Twenty-second Indiana Volunteers, absent without leave since the 22d day of August, 1864. This officer applied for muster out of service as a nonveteran and was refused said muster on account of not having served three years in his present grade. He, however, went home with the nonveterans from Chattanooga and has not reported since. I learn from members of his company that he is now at his home in Bloomington, Monroe County, Ind.

"I most respectfully recommend that said officer be dismissed the service, that his position may be filled by a more worthy officer.

"I am, Colonel, very respectfully, your obedient servant,

W. H. SNODGRASS,
"*Captain, Commanding Twenty-second Indiana Volunteers.*

"HEADQUARTERS THIRD BRIGADE,
"SECOND DIVISION, FOURTEENTH ARMY CORPS,
"*Poolers Station, Ga., January 24, 1865.*

"Respectfully forwarded.   Approved and recommended.

"BEN. D. FERNING,
"*Brevet Brigadier-General Commanding.*

"HEADQUARTERS SECOND DIVISION, FOURTEENTH ARMY CORPS,
"*In the Field, Georgia, January 29, 1865.*
"Respectfully forwarded.
"JAMES D. MORGAN,
"*Brigadier-General.*

"HEADQUARTERS FOURTEENTH ARMY CORPS,
"*Sisters Ferry, January 30, 1865.*
"Respectfully forwarded to the Adjutant-General of the Army with the recommendation that this officer be reduced to the ranks for absence without leave, or dishonorably dismissed the United States service.
"JEF. C. DAVIS,
"*Brevet Major-General Commanding.*

"HEADQUARTERS LEFT WING, ARMY OF GEORGIA,
"*Sisters Ferry, Ga., January 31, 1865.*
"Respectfully forwarded. Approved.
"H. W. SLOCUM,
"*Major-General Commanding.*

"WAR DEPARTMENT, ADJUTANT-GENERAL'S OFFICE,
February 15, 1865.
"Respectfully submitted to Major-General Halleck, chief of staff.
"THOMAS M. VINCENT,
"*Assistant Adjutant-General.*

"Dismissal approved.
"H. W. HALLECK,
"*Major-General, Chief of Staff.*

"WAR DEPARTMENT, ADJUTANT-GENERAL'S OFFICE,
"*Washington, D. C., February 18, 1865.*
"Approved.
"By order of the Secretary of War:
"THOMAS M. VINCENT,
"*Assistant Adjutant-General.*

"Captain Ravenscroft was thereupon, by direction of the President, dishonorably dismissed from the service of the United States for absence without leave, in orders from this Department, dated February 20, 1865.

"On June 20, 1874, an application for revocation of his dismissal and for his honorable discharge was received at this Department. The following is a copy of said application:

"BLOOMINGTON, *June 11.*

"DEAR SIR: You will doubtless remember my speaking to you about having the order dismissing me from the service revoked and obtain an honorable discharge. The facts are as follows:

"There was an order that all officers who had been promoted and who did not accept the veteran furlough (which I did not) should be mustered out at the expiration of their original term, three years. Under this order I was relieved from duty with other officers and men of my regiment and ordered to report to Captain Block, mustering officer, Second Division, Fourteenth Army Corps, and he, with Captain Fulmer, mustering officer of the Fourteenth Army Corps, delivered to me the muster-out rolls and discharges of the nonveterans (I then being the senior officer), and ordered me to proceed with the men to Nashville to have them paid off and finally discharged.

"At Nashville I was ordered to Louisville, and there the men were paid. Captain Fulmer assured me that my discharge should follow by the hands of the other officers, who stayed to have their rolls made out, etc. I waited at Louisville two days for the other officers, but unfortunately the day I left or the day after an order came from the front to Chattanooga ordering all the officers (myself included) back to our regiment, and the other officers went back and were discharged soon after, but that order I never received, or knew of such an order, for some months afterwards. This is why or how I was reported absent without leave and dishonorably dismissed the service, after I had signed the blanks of my muster-out rolls before leaving Chattanooga.

"Now, General, if you will make a statement of these facts to the War Department, or whatever authority is necessary, and obtain for me an honorable discharge, I shall always remember your kindness and try to repay you in some way. I feel amply the injustice of my discharge and am very anxious to have my record clear as a soldier, and I think if anyone can do anything for me you can. The orders referred to I have lost, but my colonel, that is, Colonel Willis, said he would do anything he could to have this matter fixed up for me. If there is any more that I can do, please let me know and you will confer a great favor on your humble servant,

"C. R. RAVENSCROFT.

"Hon. M. C. HUNTER.

"The application above quoted bears an indorsement as follows:

"'I am personally acquainted with the within-named officer. He is a good man, and, my information is, made a good soldier.

"'I hope the records will be so changed that he may stand on them as honorably discharged.

"'Respectfully,   "'MORTON C. HUNTER.'

" Upon this presentation of the case the application for revocation of the order of dismissal and for the honorable discharge of this officer was denied, and now stands denied, on the ground that the order which dismissed him from the service having been carried into execution, it is beyond the power of any executive officer to revoke, modify, or set it aside, however unmerited or injudicious that order may be deemed to have been."

Since the date of the report quoted above the status of the case has not been changed.

Respectfully submitted.

F. C. AINSWORTH,
Chief Record and Pension Office.

RECORD AND PENSION OFFICE,
War Department, June 24, 1902.

The SECRETARY OF WAR.

O

CONSTRUCTION OF BRIDGE ACROSS MONONGAHELA RIVER BY THE EASTERN RAILROAD COMPANY.

JANUARY 27, 1903.—Referred to the House Calendar and ordered to be printed.

Mr. WANGER, from the Committee on Interstate and Foreign Commerce, submitted the following

REPORT.

[To accompany H. R. 16975.]

The Committee on Interstate and Foreign Commerce, to whom was referred the bill (H. R. 16975) to authorize the construction of a bridge across the Monongahela River, in the State of Pennsylvania, by the Eastern Railroad Company, beg leave to submit the following report and recommend that said bill do pass with amendments:

This is a bill enacting that "the Eastern Railroad Company, a corporation created and organized under the laws of the State of Pennsylvania, its successors and assigns, be, and it is hereby, authorized to construct and maintain a bridge and approaches thereto over the Monongahela River, in the State of Pennsylvania, from a point on the north shore between Hazelwood avenue and the Glenwood highway bridge to a point on the south shore in the township of Baldwin or the township of Lower St. Clair, in the county of Allegheny and State of Pennsylvania."

The committee having referred the bill to the Secretary of War and the latter having transmitted, with approval, a letter from the Chief of Engineers, which is hereto appended as part of this report, and your committee deeming the suggestions of the Chief of Engineers respecting amendments are needed to perfect the measure, have adopted the amendments recommended by him, as follows:

At the end of line 11, on page 1, strike out the period and insert a colon and the following:

Provided, That such location is suitable to the interests of navigation.

After the word "purposes," in line 11, on page 2, strike out the period and insert a colon and the following:

Provided, That all railroad companies desiring the use of said bridge shall have and be entitled to equal rights and privileges in the passage of railroad trains over the same and the approaches thereto upon payment of a reasonable compensation for such use; and in case the owner or owners of said bridge and the several railroad companies or any one of them desiring such use shall fail to agree upon the sum or sums to be paid and upon the rules and conditions to which each shall conform in the use of said bridge, all matters at issue between them shall be decided by the Secretary of War upon a hearing of the allegations and proofs of the parties.

With these amendments the rights of the public are fully protected

---

OFFICE OF THE CHIEF OF ENGINEERS,
UNITED STATES ARMY,
Washington, January 24, 1903.

SIR: I have the honor to return herewith a letter, dated the 23d instant, from the Committee on Interstate and Foreign Commerce of the House of Representatives, inclosing for the views of the War Department thereon H. R. 16975, Fifty-seventh Congress, second session, "A bill to authorize the construction of a bridge across the Monongahela River, in the State of Pennsylvania, by the Eastern Railroad Company," and in reply to its reference to this office, I beg to recommend certain amendments to the bill, which are indicated on a copy of the same herewith submitted.

As thus amended, the bill, in my opinion, makes ample provision for the protection of navigation interests, and I know of no objection to its passage by Congress, so far as those interests are concerned.

Very respectfully, your obedient servant,   A. MACKENZIE,
Acting Chief of Engineers.

Hon. ELIHU ROOT,
Secretary of War.

O

LIGHT-HOUSE DEPOT, BOSTON HARBOR, MASSACHUSETTS.

JANUARY 27, 1903.—Committed to the Committee of the Whole House on the state
of the Union and ordered to be printed.

Mr. WANGER, from the Committee on Interstate and Foreign Commerce, submitted the following

REPORT.

[To accompany H. R. 16882.]

The Committee on Interstate and Foreign Commerce, to whom was
referred the bill (H. R. 16882) to establish a light-house depot for the
Second light-house district, Boston Harbor, Massachusetts, beg leave
to submit the following report, and recommend that said bill do pass
with an amendment.

This is a bill enacting that the Secretary of the Treasury be authorized and directed to expend, out of any money in the Treasury not
otherwise appropriated, the sum of $50,000 for the location and estab-
lishment of a light-house depot for the Second light-house district, in
Boston Harbor, Massachusetts.

Section 2 repeals that part of the act making appropriations for
sundry civil expenses of the Government for the fiscal year ending
June 30, 1903, approved June 28, 1902, appropriating the sum of
$25,000 for the establishment of a light-house depot at Castle Island,
Boston Harbor, Massachusetts.

The appended letter of the Secretary of the Treasury shows why
the citizens of Boston do not desire the light-house depot to be erected
on Castle Island, and that it is not the only available site within the
harbor. No reason has been given for increasing the limit of cost
beyond the amount appropriated heretofore.

Accordingly, your committee recommend that all after the word
"to," in line 4 in section 1, be struck out, and that the following be
inserted:

locate and establish a light-house depot for the Second light-house district in Boston
Harbor, Massachusetts, at a cost not to exceed the sum of twenty-five thousand
dollars.

With the bill thus amended and enacted the Secretary of the Treasury can select the most available site for the depot and Congress will
doubtless appropriate the money within the limit of cost specified for
erection and construction, and being so amended the committee
recommend the passage of the bill.

TREASURY DEPARTMENT, OFFICE OF THE SECRETARY,
Washington, January 21, 1903.

SIR: Your letter dated January 17, asking suggestions touching the merits of a bill to appropriate $100,000 to establish a light-house depot for the second light-house district in Boston harbor, is received.

In reply I have the honor to state, by an act approved June 28, 1902, $25,000 were appropriated for the establishment of a light-house depot on Castle Island. Plans have been made for the structure and the Light-House Board is ready to commence work at once. The present bill to appropriate $100,000 has been introduced in the hope of preserving the symmetry and beauty of Castle Island.

I am informed that Castle Island is a part of the park system of Boston; that a bridge has been built to the island at considerable expense. A light-house depot is necessarily unsightly, and its presence, I am advised, would block or at least interfere with the use of the island as a part of the park system. While the location is satisfactory to the Light-House Service, it is not the only available site within the harbor. Thus, while the Department does not ask a modification of the provision already made, it does not object to the pending bill. Its passage will preserve the beauty of the harbor and protect the city from an unsightly structure in a very conspicuous place.

Respectfully,

L. M. SHAW.

The CHAIRMAN COMMITTEE ON INTERSTATE AND FOREIGN COMMERCE.

O

BRIG. GEN. H. C. MERRIAM.

JANUARY 27, 1903.—Committed to the Committee of the Whole House and ordered
to be printed.

Mr. ESCH, from the Committee on Military Affairs, submitted the
following

REPORT.

[To accompany S. 5891.]

The Committee on Military Affairs, to whom was referred the bill
(S. 5891) to authorize the President to appoint Brig. Gen. H. C. Merriam to the grade of major-general in the U. S. Army and place him
on the retired list, report the same back to the House with the recommendation that it do pass.

A bill was reported identical to this one by the Committee on Military Affairs on January 15, 1903, being House bill 14375, report being
Report No. 3154.

It is desired by the committee that this bill be substituted for the
aforesaid House bill, which is now on the Calendar.

O .

MONUMENTS ON THE BATTLEFIELD OF GETTYSBURG, PA., ETC.

JANUARY 27, 1903.—Committed to the Committee of the Whole House on the state of the Union and ordered to be printed.

Mr. ADAMS, from the Committee on Military Affairs, submitted the following

REPORT.

[To accompany H. R. 7.]

The Committee on Military Affairs, to whom was referred the bill (H. R. 7) authorizing the Secretary of War to cause to be erected monuments and markers on the battlefield of Gettysburg, Pa., to commemorate the valorous deeds of certain regiments and batteries of the U. S. Army, report the same back to the House with the recommendation that it do pass with the following amendments:

Strike out all after the enacting clause and insert in lieu thereof:

That the Gettysburg National Park Commission be, and hereby are, authorized and directed, under the supervision of the Secretary of War, to erect such monuments and markers on the battlefield of Gettysburg, in the State of Pennsylvania, as will fittingly designate the positions, indicate the movements, and commemorate the valorous services of the following batteries and regiments of United States Regulars upon the battlefield: Batteries E, G, H, I, and K, First United States Artillery; A, B, D, G, L, and M, Second United States Artillery; C, F, and K, Third United States Artillery; A, B, C, F, G, and K, Fourth United States Artillery; C, D, F, I, and K, Fifth United States Artillery; Second, Third, Fourth, Sixth, Seventh, Eighth, Tenth, Eleventh, Twelfth, Fourteenth, and Seventeenth Regiments of United States Infantry; First, Second, Fifth, and Sixth Regiments of Cavalry, and United States Engineers Detachment.

The Secretary of War shall, so far as practicable, procure the appointment of committees of the survivors of these regiments and batteries, with whom the said Commission shall consult, and, with the approval of the Secretary of War, determine the designs and positions of said monuments and markers and the inscriptions they shall bear, and for the purpose of carrying out the provisions of this Act sixty-one thousand five hundred dollars is hereby appropriated out of any moneys not otherwise appropriated, and the disbursements under this Act shall be made on the approval of the Secretary of War.

This bill was referred to the Secretary of War for information and remarks. He in turn referred it to John P. Nicholson, chairman National Military Park Commission, who suggested the amendments as stated above.

The letters of the Secretary of War and of the park commissioners are hereto attached and made a part of this report.

WAR DEPARTMENT, *March 24, 1902.*

Respectfully returned to the chairman Committee on Military Affairs, House of Representatives, inviting attention to the accompanying report of the chairman of the Gettysburg National Park Commission, dated 5th instant, and inclosures therein referred to.

ELIHU ROOT, *Secretary of War.*

GETTYSBURG NATIONAL PARK COMMISSION,
Gettysburg, Pa., March 5, 1902.

SIR: The Gettysburg National Park Commission respectfully approves of the objects of the bill introduced in the House of Representatives by the Hon T. M. Mahon, of Pennsylvania (H. R. 7), for the following, among other reasons:

There were 42 organizations of United States regulars in the Gettysburg campaign, namely: Twelve light batteries with the several army corps, 9 batteries of horse artillery with the cavalry, 5 light batteries with the reserve artillery, 10 regiments of infantry in the Fifth Army Corps, 1 regiment at headquarters of the Army of the Potomac, 4 regiments of cavalry in the cavalry corps, and United States Engineers detachment. These organizations are not represented by any monuments on the battlefield other than by cast-iron tablets tentatively placed in the positions occupied by them. while all the volunteers of the Army of the Potomac who were at Gettysburg have appropriate artistic monuments erected there by the several States.

The States of New York and Pennsylvania appropriated the sum of $1,500 for a monument to each battery and regiment, and the State of New York appropriated an additional sum of $90,000 for a State monument and an equestrian statue to Maj. Gen. Henry W. Slocum, and the State of Pennsylvania appropriated the sum of $250,000 for a State monument and $100,000 for equestrian statues of Generals Meade, Hancock, and Reynolds.

It would seem eminently proper for the United States to appropriate at least as much for each of its organizations at Gettysburg as the States of New York and Pennsylvania did for each of theirs; such an appropriation for the regulars would amount to $61,500.

The experience of two of the commissioners as State commissioners for the erection of monuments for the States of New York and Pennsylvania induce them to suggest some changes in the language of the bill, which will not affect its main provisions. Their suggestions accompany this paper.

A map showing the locations of the United States troops is also forwarded for your information.

Yours, respectfully,

JOHN P. NICHOLSON,
Chairman.
WM. M. ROBINS,
CHAS. A. RICHARDSON,
Commissioners.

The SECRETARY OF WAR.

O

AKRON, STERLING AND NORTHERN RAILROAD.

JANUARY 28, 1903.—Referred to the House Calendar and ordered to be printed.

Mr. POWERS, of Maine, from the Committee on the Territories, submitted the following

REPORT.

[To accompany S. R. 146.]

The Committee on the Territories, to whom was referred the Senate joint resolution (S. R. 146) to extend the time for construction of the Akron, Sterling and Northern Railroad, in Alaska, having had the same under consideration beg leave to report it back with a recommendation that it do pass.

The committee adopt the Senate report upon the merits of said bill, as follows:

The Committee on Public Lands, to whom was referred the joint resolution (S. R. 146) to extend the time for construction of the Akron, Sterling and Northern Railroad, in Alaska, having had the same under consideration, beg leave to report it back and recommend that it do pass.

Under the act of May 28, 1898, provision was made that if any section of a proposed railroad shall not be completed within one year after the definite location of said section so approved the rights granted by the said act shall be forfeited. In this particular instance the map of definite location of the company's line of road for 20 miles was approved January 28, 1902, so that by the law the right would lapse on January 28, 1903. Owing to the extreme difficulty of obtaining and transshipping supplies for the construction of the road in Alaska and securing laborers in that district, and for other reasons submitted in a communication received from the officials of the road, the committee recommend favorable action on the measure.

The following correspondence on the bill is submitted:

DEPARTMENT OF THE INTERIOR,
Washington, January 13, 1903.

SIR: I have the honor to acknowledge the receipt from your committee, in a letter of the 6th instant, of a copy of S. R. 146, "A joint resolution to extend the time for construction of the Akron, Sterling and Northern Railroad, in Alaska," with the request for information as set forth.

In answer I inclose a copy of the report in the premises by the Commissioner of the General Land Office, under date of the 10th instant, which supplies the desired information.

Very respectfully, E. A. HITCHCOCK, *Secretary.*
The CHAIRMAN OF THE COMMITTEE ON PUBLIC LANDS,
Senate.

DEPARTMENT OF THE INTERIOR, GENERAL LAND OFFICE,
Washington, D. C., January 10, 1903.

SIR: By reference from the Department, for early report in duplicate and return of papers, I have the honor to acknowledge the receipt of a letter from the clerk of the Senate Committee on Public Lands, transmitted under instructions of the committee, inclosing a copy of S. R. 146, "A joint resolution to extend the time for the construction of the Akron, Sterling and Northern Railroad, in Alaska," and asking "for all information as to what this company has done in the way of construction, together with the date of filing of plats, etc., date of expiration of time limit within which construction had to be completed or all rights forfeited."

The records of this office show that on May 1, 1901, there was filed in the Department a map showing the preliminary location of the line of the Akron, Sterling and Northern Railroad Company, under the provisions of the act of Congress approved May 14, 1898 (30 Stat. L., 409), from a point on Valdez Bay, along Lowe River, through the Dutch Valley, and through Thompson Pass, to a point on Ptarmigan Lake, a distance of 32 miles. The said map was noted as satisfactory and accepted by this office as a preliminary survey June 24, 1901. On November 5, 1901, the register and receiver at Sitka, Alaska, forwarded to this office map showing the definite location of the company's line of road practically upon the same line of road as noted on the map of preliminary survey, extending, however, a distance of only 20 miles from Valdez Bay, approved by the Department January 28, 1902.

Section 5 of the act of May 14, 1898, as above, provides that "within twelve months after filing the preliminary map of location the company must file with the register of the land office for the district where such land is located a map and profile of at least a twenty-mile section of its road, or a profile of its entire road of less than twenty miles, as definitely fixed; and shall thereafter each year definitely locate and file a map of such location as aforesaid, of not less than twenty miles additional of its line of road, until the entire road has been thus definitely located. And upon the approval thereof by the Secretary of the Interior the same shall be noted upon the records of said office, and thereafter all such lands over which such rights of way shall pass shall be disposed of subject to such right of way: *Provided,* That if any section of said road shall not be completed within one year after the definite location of said section so approved, or if the map of definite location be not filed within one year as herein required, or if the entire road shall not be completed within four years from the filing of the map of definite location, the rights herein granted shall be forfeited as to any such uncompleted section of said road, and thereupon shall revert to the United States without further action or declaration, the notation of such uncompleted section upon the records of the land office shall be canceled, and the reservations of such lands for the purpose of said right of way, stations, and terminals shall cease and become null and void without further action."

It will thus appear that map of preliminary right of way has been filed for a distance of 32 miles, and that within the time prescribed by the act the map of definite location was filed covering the first 20 miles of said line, and under the rulings the Department the time for construction of that portion of the line of road under the provisions of the act began to run from the date of the approval of said map of definite location by the Secretary of the Interior. Therefore the time for construction of said portion of the road would expire on January 28, 1903. This office has not been advised that any portion of the road has been constructed.

As to the balance of the road, for which preliminary survey has been filed, but for which no map of definite location has been submitted, the rights of the company would expire two years from the date of filing the said map of preliminary survey, namely, May 1, 1903.

The papers referred by the Department, together with a duplicate of this report, are herewith inclosed.

Very respectfully,

BINGER HERMANN,
Commissioner.

The SECRETARY OF THE INTERIOR.

MEMORANDUM SUBMITTED FOR CONSIDERATION OF THE COMMITTEE.

The Akron, Sterling and Northern Railroad Company is a corporation organized and existing under the laws of the State of Colorado, and was incorporated for the purposes, among others, of locating, constructing, and operating a railroad within the district of Alaska, for the purpose primarily of opening up and developing the interior of Alaska and connecting the Yukon River by rail with the ocean.

After spending large sums of money in exploration work it was decided by the stockholders of this corporation to make a survey for this line, beginning at tide water of the port known as Port Valdez, the inlet from Prince William Sound, in the gulf of Alaska, to a point on the Yukon River to or near Eagle City.

This line was surveyed in the summer of 1899, and thereafter maps of preliminary location were prepared, executed, and filed in the local land office at Sitka. These maps were not approved until August, 1900. Subsequently maps of definite alignment were filed and approved by the Secretary of the Interior some time in 1902. It was not, therefore, until the last-named date that this corporation secured any tangible and permanent rights.

Owing to the shortness of the period between the time of the approval of the preliminary maps and the time within which the maps of definite location were required to be filed, affording, because of the shortness of the Alaska season, —— working days, a period entirely inadequate for a careful, reliable survey, a careful examination of the map and field notes, following the approval of the maps of definite location, disclosed the necessity of prosecuting another survey. This survey was completed last fall, and the maps thereof are now being prepared and will be filed with the proper officer within a few days. These surveys have cost the stockholders of this corporation large sums of money.

While the surveys were being accomplished the other business of the corporation was being forwarded with as little delay as possible, which, in the case of a new company promoting a novel, if not uncertain, enterprise, is always vexatious. Arrangements to finance the enterprise have been practically completed. Rails and ties have been ordered and are on the way to Valdez. Portions of the grade have been put into shape to receive the rails.

The stockholders, who are men of large experience in railway matters and men of standing in the neighborhood in which they reside, are absolutely confident of their ability to complete their undertaking within a period of from two to three years.

Should Congress refuse to grant the extension requested, the money already invested, amounting to many thousands of dollars, will be lost to the persons furnishing it, and the enterprise—one of the most important ever conceived for the development of Alaska—itself be destroyed.

It is believed that the framers of the act of Congress granting a right of way to railroads in Alaska did not fully grasp the situation in respect of conditions in that Territory, or they would not have hedged the grant with so many restrictions and limitations, or made it, as they did, less liberal in its provisions than are the provisions of the act of 1875, granting rights of way to railroads over the public lands of the United States.

In the act of 1875 railroad companies are given five years within which to complete a section of the road, while in the acts relating to Alaska they are entitled to but one year. Why this limitation as to Alaska, where, it must be assumed, the difficulties of building a road and interesting capital therein are a thousand times greater than in the United States?

New enterprises of uncertain issue always require time for their development. In this case everything that could have been done to comply with the requirements of the act has been done, and yet the section of the road remains uncompleted. There has been no unnecessary delay on the part of the directors of the corporation.

The extension asked for should be granted for the purpose, if none other, of removing the law's discrimination against Alaska. The directors of the Akron, Sterling and Northern Railroad Company confidently believe that with its proposed road completed the development of Alaska will be given an extraordinary impetus.

Port Valdez has a deep-water harbor, capable of floating the largest vessels at low tide. With this the condition, why should not Valdez become the most important seaport in the southern coast of Alaska? The interior of Alaska teems with mineral wealth. There is need that this mineral be carried to a seaport for transportation to market by sea. The line of this railroad as proposed cuts through this mineralized zone, where already great mines of copper and gold are in operation, and if means for transporting their product be not found, their success will be retarded, if not jeopardized.

The directors of this company feel certain of their ability to complete their railroad within the time limited by the proposed resolution of Congress. They therefore submit that the resolution should pass and be approved as a matter of right.

O

BRIDGE ACROSS RAINY RIVER, MINNESOTA.

JANUARY 28, 1903.—Referred to the House Calendar and ordered to be printed.

Mr. FLETCHER, from the Committee on Interstate and Foreign Commerce, submitted the following

REPORT.

[To accompany S. 6446.]

The Committee on Interstate and Foreign Commerce, to whom was referred the bill (S. 6446) to provide for the construction of a bridge across Rainy River, in Minnesota, having considered the same, report thereon with a recommendation that it pass.

The bill has the approval of the War Department, as will appear by the letter attached and which is made a part of this report.

OFFICE OF THE CHIEF OF ENGINEERS, U. S. ARMY,
Washington, December 27, 1902.

SIR: I have the honor to return herewith a letter, dated the 9th instant, from the Senate Committee on Commerce, inclosing for the views of the War Department thereon S. 6446, Fifty-seventh Congress, second session, "A bill to provide for the construction of a bridge across Rainy River, in Minnesota," and in reply to its reference to this office I beg to recommend certain amendments to the bill which are indicated on a copy of the same herewith.

As thus amended the bill, in my opinion, makes ample provision for the protection of navigation interests on the river, and I know of no objection to its passage by Congress, so far as those interests are concerned.

Very respectfully, your obedient servant,

G. L. GILLESPIE,
Brig. Gen., Chief of Engineers, U. S. Army.

Hon. ELIHU ROOT,
Secretary of War.

O

H R—57—2—Vol 2——48

PAYMENT, ETC., OF PENSION MONEY DUE TO INMATES
OF THE GOVERNMENT HOSPITAL FOR THE INSANE.

JANUARY 28, 1903.—Committed to the Committee of the Whole House on the state
of the Union and ordered to be printed.

Mr. LOUDENSLAGER, from the Committee on Pensions, submitted the
following

REPORT.

[To accompany H. R. 17084.]

The Committee on Pensions, to whom was referred the bill (H. R.
17084) relating to the payment and disposition of pension money due
to inmates of the Government Hospital for the Insane, have considered
the same and respectfully report as follows:

On April 9, 1902, the Secretary of the Interior addressed the following communication to the chairman of the Committee on Pensions,
United States Senate:

DEPARTMENT OF THE INTERIOR,
Washington, April 9, 1902.

SIR: The existing legislation embraced in the acts of August 7, 1882 (22 Stat. L.,
330), and February 26, 1881 (21 Stat. L., 350), relating to the payment and disposition of pension money due to inmates of the Government Hospital for the Insane
and members of the National Home for Disabled Volunteer Soldiers, has been
attended with much difficulty in its administration. The Board of Managers of the
National Home, the superintendent of the Government Hospital, and the Commissioner of Pensions have severally called my attention to the defects in the existing
legislation and have suggested its amendment. As a result of these suggestions, I
have caused to be drafted a provision amending and reenacting the existing legislation along lines which it is believed will free its administration from confusion and
difficulty, will make it operate equitably toward pensioners, their widows, minor
children, and dependent parents, and will make it acceptable to the managing officers of the two institutions concerned.

I inclose herewith the draft of the proposed legislation, and respectfully recommend that, if it meets the approval of your committee, it be inserted in the pending
sundry civil appropriation bill, or be introduced as a separate measure.

Very respectfully,

E. A. HITCHCOCK, Secretary.

The CHAIRMAN OF THE COMMITTEE ON PENSIONS,
United States Senate.

The draft of the proposed legislation referred to by the Secretary in the above communication was practically identical with the bill hereby reported by your committee, with the exception that the bill now reported provides for the disposition of pension money due female pensioners as well as that due male pensioners who are inmates of the hospital or who may die while in the hospital. The Secretary of the Interior reiterated his recommendation for this legislation in his last annual report, to which attention was drawn in the following communication:

DEPARTMENT OF THE INTERIOR,
Washington, January 8, 1903.

SIR: I have the honor to transmit herewith a copy of my annual report to the President of the operations of this Department for the fiscal year ended June 30, 1902, and to commend to your early and favorable consideration the recommendation therein contained, on page 154, in relation to the enactment of necessary legislation governing the payment and disposition of pension moneys due to inmates of the Government Hospital for the Insane. On pages 229 and 230 of the appendix to my report will be found a form of bill which, if enacted into law, will operate equitably toward pensioners, their widows, minor children, and dependent parents.

I would be glad to have the Superintendent of the Government Hospital for the Insane appear before the committee, at such time as may be convenient, to explain the difficulties attendant upon the administration of the existing law regarding pension moneys payable to insane pensioners at that institution.

Very respectfully,

E. A. HITCHCOCK, *Secretary.*

Hon. HENRY C. LOUDENSLAGER,
Chairman Committee on Pensions, House of Representatives.

In support of the proposed legislation and in explanation of the provisions of the same, and the necessity for its enactment, the following statement by Dr. A. B. Richardson, superintendent of the Government Hospital for the Insane, has been submitted to the committee:

GOVERNMENT HOSPITAL FOR THE INSANE,
Washington, D. C., January 21, 1903.

DEAR SIR: Referring to the bill pending in your committee, relating to the disposition of pensions belonging to pensioners who are inmates of this hospital, I beg to ask that the committee report the bill favorably for the following reasons:

An act of Congress passed August 7, 1882, provides that when any pensioner is transferred from the National Homes for Disabled Volunteer Soldiers to this hospital, if he has no dependent relative under the law, his pension and accrued pension shall be made payable to the superintendent and credited to the support account of the hospital.

This includes all cases, without reference to the amount of pension, which ranges from $6 to $72 per month. When the pension is once credited to the support account of the hospital, it can only be expended in the same manner as this fund is expended in general, and can not be applied to the individual use of the pensioner. The charge for board in the case of independent or pay patients while inmates of this hospital is $5 per week. In some instances the pensions thus made payable to the hospital are considerably in excess of the regular charge, yet the surplus must go to the hospital as well.

Where pensioners are admitted to the hospital from other sources, as from the Regular Army and the Navy, the law does not apply. Some of these pensioners have very considerable sums to their credit, and do not pay board.

The purpose of the act is to place all pensioners on the same footing, and to ask that board be paid only in those cases where there is a balance remaining to the credit of the pensioner, after allowing him a sufficient amount for his incidental expenses, and only in such cases as have no dependent relatives under the law; and also to permit the balance to be placed to his credit, to be used by him as he may choose or to go to the dependent relatives, if he has any, and where none exist, in case of the death of the pensioner, to go to the hospital.

It would seem that this would be an equitable distribution, and the present arrangement is very unsatisfactory and very unjust to the pensioner. Quite a number of them receive only $6 to $8 per month, and should have this amount placed to their credit, so they can use it, under the supervision of the hospital authorities, as they choose for little extras which the hospital can not supply.   It will be noted that this distribution is to be made under regulations established by the honorable Secretary of the Interior.

Very respectfully,
A. B. RICHARDSON,
Superintendent.

Hon. HENRY C. LOUDENSLAGER,
Committee on Pensions, House of Representatives,
Washington, D. C.

In the bill submitted by your committee provision is made for the disposition of pension money due female as well as male inmates of the hospital, as it often happens that female pensioners are admitted to the institution from the District of Columbia.   The entire matter of an equitable distribution of such pension money is fully covered by the bill, and these provisions are fully concurred in by the superintendent of the hospital and by the Interior Department as being just and fair to all concerned.

The passage of the bill is therefore recommended with the following amendments:

In line 6, page 2, strike out the word "still."

In line 17, after the word "shall," insert "if a female pensioner, be paid to her minor children, and, in the case of a male pensioner."

In lines 18 and 19, where the word "dependent" occurs, strike out that word and insert "minor."

In line 20, after the word "his," insert "or her."

O

DAM ACROSS THE ST. CROIX RIVER NEAR ST. CROIX FALLS, WIS.

JANUARY 28, 1903.—Referred to the House Calendar and ordered to be printed.

Mr. FLETCHER, from the Committee on Interstate and Foreign Commerce, submitted the following

REPORT.

[To accompany H. R. 16974.]

The Committee on Interstate and Foreign Commerce, to whom was referred the bill (H. R. 16974) permitting the building of a dam across the St. Croix River at or near the village of St. Croix Falls, Polk County, Wis., having considered the same, report it with amendments, and, as amended, recommend its passage.

The bill thus amended has the approval of the War Department, as will appear by the annexed letter, the amendments referred to therein having been incorporated in the bill as reported.

Amend as follows:

In lines 11, 12, and 13, section 1, page 2, strike out all after the word "further" and insert in lieu thereof the following:

That there shall be placed and maintained in connection with said dam a sluice-way so arranged as to permit logs, timber, and lumber to pass around, through, or over said dam, without unreasonable delay or hindrance, and without toll or charges; that the Government of the United States may at any time construct in connection therewith a suitable lock for navigation purposes, may at any time without compensation control the said dam for purposes of navigation, but shall not destroy the water power created by said dam to any greater extent than may be necessary to provide proper facilities for navigation; and that the Secretary of War may at any time require and enforce, at the expense of the owners, such modifications and changes in the construction of said dam, and may make such regulations for the operation of said dam, as he may deem advisable in the interests of navigation.

In line 21, section 3, page 2, after the word "be," add "commenced within two years and."

Amend the title by striking out the word "Saint," in lines 1 and 2, and inserting in lieu thereof the letters "St."

In lines 3, 5, and 9, page 1, and lines 3 and 4 on page 2, strike out the word "Saint" and insert in lieu thereof the letters "St."

OFFICE OF THE CHIEF OF ENGINEERS, U. S. ARMY,
Washington, January 27, 1903.

SIR: I have the honor to return herewith a letter, dated the 23d instant, from the Committee on Interstate and Foreign Commerce of the House of Representatives, inclosing, for the views of the War Department thereon, H. R. 16974, Fifty-seventh Congress, second session, "A bill permitting the building of a dam across the St. Croix River at or near the village of St. Croix Falls, Polk County, Wis."

The object of the bill is to authorize certain private corporations to build a dam and appurtenant works across the St. Croix River for the purpose of developing water power for industrial purposes. Bills of this character should be given very careful consideration and investigation, which has not been possible in this case, owing to the fact that the committee desires a report on the bill by the 27th instant. I have indicated on the bill, however, certain amendments which, if adopted, will, in my opinion, safeguard the interests of navigation.

If amended as suggested by me, I see no objection to favorable consideration of the bill by Congress.

Very respectfully, your obedient servant,

G. L. GILLESPIE,
Brigadier-General, Chief of Engineers, U. S. Army.

Hon. ELIHU ROOT,
Secretary of War.

O

LIGHT-SHIP OFF OUTER BAR OF BRUNSWICK, GA.

JANUARY 28, 1903.—Committed to the Committee of the Whole House on the state of the Union and ordered to be printed.

Mr. ADAMSON, from the Committee on Interstate and Foreign Commerce, submitted the following

REPORT.

[To accompany H. R. 10705.]

The Committee on Interstate and Foreign Commerce, to whom was referred the bill (H. R. 10705) to construct and place a light-ship off the outer bar of Brunswick, Ga., having considered the same report it with amendment and as amended recommend its passage.

The bill thus amended has the approval of the Treasury Department, as will appear by the annexed letter, the amendment referred to therein having been incorporated in the bill as reported.

Amend as follows:

Strike out all of the preamble.

In lines 2, 3, and 4, page 2, section 1, strike out all after the word, "light-ship," and insert in lieu thereof the following: "*Provided*, That the cost shall not exceed one hundred thousand dollars."

TREASURY DEPARTMENT, OFFICE OF THE SECRETARY,
Washington, April 1, 1902.

SIR: This Department has the honor to acknowledge the receipt of a letter from your committee, dated February 8, 1902, inclosing for suggestions a copy of H. R. bill No. 10705, authorizing the construction of a light-vessel to be placed off the outer bar of Brunswick, Ga., and appropriating $100,000 therefor.

The Department in reply begs to state that the Light-House Board, to whom the matter was referred for investigation, after consultation with its local officer, reports that the establishment of a light-vessel off the outer bar of Brunswick, Ga., would be a serviceable aid to navigation, and therefore that the passage of this bill is recommended.

Respectfully,   L. M. SHAW, *Secretary.*

The CHAIRMAN OF THE COMMITTEE ON INTERSTATE AND FOREIGN COMMERCE,
House of Representatives.

TREASURY DEPARTMENT, OFFICE OF THE SECRETARY,
Washington, December 5, 1902.

SIR: The Department has the honor to send you inclosed herewith certain correspondence of the Light-House Board relative to the propriety of passing H. R. bill No. 10705, authorizing the construction of a light-vessel to be placed off the outer bar of Brunswick, Ga., and appropriating $100,000 therefor.

This correspondence is sent you in accordance with your oral request, and at the instance of the Light-House Board, to whom the request was addressed.

Respectfully,

L. M. SHAW, *Secretary.*

Hon. WILLIAM G. BRANTLEY, M. C.,
House of Representatives.

TREASURY DEPARTMENT, OFFICE OF THE SECRETARY,
Washington, April 1, 1902.

SIR: This Department has the honor to acknowledge the receipt of a letter from your committee, dated February 8, 1902, inclosing for suggestions a copy of H. R. bill No. 10705, authorizing the construction of a light-vessel to be placed off the outer bar of Brunswick, Ga., and appropriating $100,000 thereof.

The Department, in reply, begs to state that the Light-House Board, to whom the matter was referred for investigation, after consultation with its local officer, reports that the establishment of a light-vessel off the outer bar of Brunswick, Ga., would be a serviceable aid to navigation, and therefore that the passage of this bill is recommended.

Respectfully,

L. M. SHAW, *Secretary.*

The CHAIRMAN OF THE COMMITTEE ON INTERSTATE AND FOREIGN COMMERCE,
House of Representatives.

TREASURY DEPARTMENT,
OFFICE OF THE LIGHT-HOUSE BOARD,
Washington, February 12, 1902.

SIR: Inclosed the board sends you a copy of a letter of February 8, 1902, from the House of Representatives Committee on Interstate and Foreign Commerce, inclosing for suggestions a copy of H. R. bill No. 10705, appropriating $100,000 to establish a light-vessel off the outer bar of Brunswick, Ga.

The board requests you to make an early examination into the advisability of establishing a light-vessel at the point specified and to submit a report and recommendation thereon.

Respectfully,

W. MAYNARD,
Captain, U. S. Navy, Naval Secretary.

Commander W. L. FIELD, U. S. Navy,
Inspector Sixth Light-House District, Charleston, S. C.

LIGHT-HOUSE ESTABLISHMENT,
OFFICE OF THE LIGHT-HOUSE INSPECTOR, SIXTH DISTRICT,
Charleston, S. C., March 26, 1902.

SIRS: In obedience to your instructions as contained in board's letter of February 12, I have the honor to report:

(1) I was in Brunswick when this communication arrived, and at once put myself in communication with all parties interested in the placing of a light-ship off the entrance to this port.

(2) I inclose such correspondence as I have had with the people of Brunswick, giving the data concerning the amount of commerce, the wrecks on the coast, etc., for your reference in considering the subject.

(3) After visiting the ports of Fernandina and Jacksonville, I find that if bills have not already been placed before Congress for light-vessels for these ports, they probably will be in the near future. Each seems to feel that their port is of sufficient importance to entitle them to this aid to navigation.

(4) By examining the coast chart, it will be found that the coast makes a bight off these ports into which south-bound vessels have to run. The land is low and can not be seen at any great distance in thick weather. From the evidence of the masters of our own buoy tenders and of the coasting vessels, very much thick weather, especially hanging over the low shores, may be expected. Most of this thick weather does not extend very far at sea. The soundings are such as to give very unreliable information. For these reasons, I believe a light-ship so placed as to serve as a point of departure for the general use of the coast would be of great use.

(5) I have examined the coast, talked with all the captains I have been able to see, and have to recommend that a first-class light-ship, with an auxiliary engine and propeller, first-class fog signal, oil lights, because of the difficulty in keeping the vessel supplied with coal if lighted by electricity, be placed in about 9 fathoms of water, in latitude 31°, about 15 miles outside the bar off St. Andrews Sound.

A vessel at this point would make an excellent landfall for anything passing up or down the coast, particularly for anything desiring to enter Doboy Sound, Altamaha Sound, St. Simon Sound, St. Andrews Sound, Cumberland Sound, or the St. Johns River, and might prevent those vessels running to the coast of Mexico, our Gulf ports, or to Cuba from twice crossing the Gulf Stream. Of this, however, I am uncertain, having had no opportunity for consulting with any of the captains running that way.

Respectfully, yours,

W. L. FIELD,
Commander, U. S. Navy; Inspector Sixth Light-House District.

The LIGHT-HOUSE BOARD, *Washington, D. C.*

NEW YORK, *June 11, 1902.*

DEAR SIRS: Having been advised that Captain Field, of the Light Service Department, Washington, has visited Brunswick, Jacksonville, and Fernandina for the purpose of seeing if there was reasonable ground for the request of those in interest that a light-ship be located in that district being granted, we write to say that as we run a line of steamers New York to Brunswick, Ga., we think such a light-ship would be of great value to navigation, and naturally we prefer that said light-ship should be located off Brunswick.

With the hope that the light-ship may be put in position at an early date, we are,
Yours, truly,

C. H. MALLORY & Co.

The UNITED STATES LIGHT-HOUSE BOARD,
Washington, D. C.

TREASURY DEPARTMENT,
OFFICE OF THE LIGHT-HOUSE BOARD,
Washington, June 13, 1902.

SIRS: Referring to your letter of June 11, 1902, the Board states that it has under consideration the subject of placing a light-vessel off the coast of Georgia, probably in about the latitude of Brunswick. As it has no light-vessel at present available for this purpose, an appropriation for the construction of one will have to be asked at the next session of Congress.

Respectfully,

W. MAYNARD,
Captain, U. S. Navy, Naval Secretary.

Messrs. C. H. MALLORY & Co.,
General Agents, 16 Burling Slip, New York, N. Y.

O

BRIDGE ACROSS THE CHOCTAWHATCHEE RIVER, IN GENEVA COUNTY, ALA.

JANUARY 28, 1903.—Referred to the House Calendar and ordered to be printed.

Mr. ADAMSON, from the Committee on Interstate and Foreign Commerce, submitted the following

REPORT.

[To accompany H. R. 16881.]

The Committee on Interstate and Foreign Commerce, to whom was referred the bill (H. R. 16881) to authorize the court of county commissioners of Geneva County, Ala., to construct a bridge across the Choctawhatchee River in Geneva County, Ala., having considered the same, report thereon with a recommendation that it pass.

The bill has the approval of the War Department, as will appear by the letter attached and which is made a part of this report.

OFFICE OF THE CHIEF OF ENGINEERS, U. S. ARMY,
Washington, January 23, 1903.

SIR: I have the honor to return herewith a letter, dated the 20th instant, from the Committee on Interstate and Foreign Commerce of the House of Representatives, inclosing for the views of the War Department thereon H. R. 16881, Fifty-seventh Congress, second session, "A bill to authorize the court of county commissioners of Geneva County, Ala., to construct a bridge across the Choctawhatchee River in Geneva County, Ala.," and, in reply to its reference to this office, I beg to say that the bill appears to make ample provision for the protection of navigation interests, and I know of no objection to its passage by Congress, so far as those interests are concerned.

Very respectfully, your obedient servant,

G. L. GILLESPIE,
Brig. Gen. Chief of Engineers, U. S. Army.

Hon. ELIHU ROOT, Secretary of War.

O

BRIDGE OVER CUMBERLAND RIVER AT OR NEAR CARTHAGE, TENN.

JANUARY 28, 1903.—Referred to the House Calendar and ordered to be printed.

Mr. ADAMSON, from the Committee on Interstate and Foreign Commerce, submitted the following

REPORT.

[To accompany H. R. 16909.]

The Committee on Interstate and Foreign Commerce, to whom was referred the bill (H. R. 16909) to amend an act entitled "An act authorizing the construction of a bridge across the Cumberland River at or near Carthage, Tenn.," approved March 2, 1901, having considered the same, report thereon with a recommendation that it pass.

The bill has the approval of the War Department, as will appear by the letter attached and which is made a part of this report.

OFFICE OF THE CHIEF OF ENGINEERS, U. S. ARMY,
Washington, January 23, 1903.

SIR: I have the honor to return herewith a letter, dated the 20th instant, from the Committee on Interstate and Foreign Commerce of the House of Representatives, inclosing for the views of the War Department thereon H. R. 16909, Fifty-seventh Congress, second session, "A bill to amend an act entitled 'An act authorizing the construction of a bridge across the Cumberland River at or near Carthage, Tennessee,' approved March second, nineteen hundred and one."

The object of the bill is to extend the time for the commencement and completion of a bridge authorized by the act of Congress of March 2, 1901, to be built across the Cumberland River at or near Carthage, Tenn. I know of no objection to favorable action on the bill, so far as the interests of navigation are concerned.

Very respectfully, your obedient servant,

G. L. GILLESPIE,
Brig. Gen., Chief of Engineers, U. S. Army.

Hon. ELIHU ROOT, *Secretary of War.*

O

GRANT OF CERTAIN PUBLIC LANDS TO TOWN OF MONTROSE, COLO.

JANUARY 28, 1903.—Committed to the Committee of the Whole House on the state of the Union and ordered to be printed.

Mr. SHAFROTH, from the Committee on the Public Lands, submitted the following

REPORT.

[To accompany H. R. 16731.]

The Committee on the Public Lands, to whom was referred the bill (H. R. 16731) permitting the town of Montrose, Colo., to enter 160 acres of land for reservoir and water purposes, have examined the same and would recommend that said bill be amended by striking out all after the word "namely," in line 8 on page 1, and inserting the following in lieu thereof:

Beginning at a point one and three-fourths miles north and three miles west of the quarter section corner on the west line of section eighteen, township forty-eight north, range six west, of the New Mexico principal meridian; thence north two thousand six hundred and forty feet; thence west two thousand six hundred and forty feet; thence south two thousand six hundred and forty feet; thence east two thousand six hundred and forty feet to the place of beginning, and containing one hundred and sixty acres of unsurveyed nonmineral mountain land, which should, if the Government survey was extended to said locality, constitute the south half of the northeast quarter and the north half of the southeast quarter of section four, township forty-eight north, range seven west, New Mexico principal meridian, in Montrose County, Colorado,

and upon adding the following proviso, viz:

Provided, That nothing herein contained shall be so construed as to impair any valid existing rights to any portion of said lands,

that the same, as so amended, do pass.

The letters of the Assistant Commissioner of the United States Land Office and one from the Secretary of the Interior recommending the passage of this bill is hereto appended.

DEPARTMENT OF THE INTERIOR,
Washington, January 24, 1903.

The CHAIRMAN OF THE COMMITTEE ON THE PUBLIC LANDS,
House of Representatives.

SIR: I have the honor to acknowledge the receipt of your letter of the 16th instant in which you inclosed a copy of House bill 16731, entitled "A bill permitting the town of Montrose, Colo., to enter 160 acres of land for reservoir and water purposes," and asked for such suggestions or information thereon as I may think proper to offer to aid the committee in its further consideration.

In answer I inclose a copy of the report on the bill by the Assistant Commissioner of the General Land Office, dated the 22d instant.

In the report an amendment of the bill is suggested which will cure an inconsistency in the description of the tract and protect any existing valid adverse rights to any portion thereof.

With this amendment I recommend the passage of the bill.

Very respectfully,

E. A. HITCHCOCK, *Secretary.*

DEPARTMENT OF THE INTERIOR, GENERAL LAND OFFICE,
Washington, D. C., January 22, 1903.

SIR: I am in receipt by reference from the Department of a letter from Hon. John T. Lacey, chairman of Committee on the Public Lands, House of Representatives, inclosing House bill No. 16731, Fifty-seventh Congress, second session, entitled "A bill permitting the town of Montrose, Colo., to enter 160 acres of land for reservoir and water purposes."

Mr. Lacey states that he would be glad to have this Department offer any suggestions or information thereon that the Department may think proper in order to aid the Committee on the Public Lands in its further consideration.

The said bill reads as follows:

Be it enacted by the Senate and House of Representatives of the United States of America in Congress assembled, That the town of Montrose, in the State of Colorado, is hereby authorized to enter and receive patent for the lands hereinafter described, by and in the name of the mayor of said town, and in trust for it, for reservoir and water purposes, upon its paying one dollar and twenty-five cents per acre therefor, namely: Beginning at a point whence the west quarter section, corner of section eighteen, township forty-eight north, range six west, New Mexico principal meridian, bears south fifty-nine degrees thirty minutes east, eighteen thousand four hundred and thirty-nine feet; running thence north two thousand six hundred and forty feet; thence west two thousand six hundred and forty feet; thence south two thousand six hundred and forty feet; thence east two thousand six hundred and forty feet to the place of beginning, and containing one hundred and sixty acres of unsurveyed non-mineral mountain land. The place of beginning is one and three-fourths miles north and three miles west of said corner eighteen, and if the Government survey was extended should constitute the south half of the northeast quarter and the north half of the southeast quarter of section four, township forty-eight north, range seven west, New Mexico principal meridian, in Montrose County, State of Colorado.

I have read said bill and having considered the provisions and wording thereof, would respectfully suggest that the same be amended as follows:

Strike out all after the word "namely," in line 8 on the first page of the bill, and insert the following:

"Beginning at a point one and three-fourths miles north and three miles west of the quarter section corner on the west line of section eighteen, township forty-eight north, range six west, of the New Mexico principal meridian; thence north two thousand six hundred and forty feet; thence west two thousand six hundred and forty feet; thence south two thousand six hundred and forty feet; thence east two thousand six hundred and forty feet to the place of beginning, and containing one hundred and sixty acres of unsurveyed nonmineral mountain land, which should, if the Government survey was extended to said locality, constitute the south half of the northeast quarter and the north half of the southeast quarter of section four, township forty-eight north, range seven west, New Mexico principal meridian, in Montrose County, State of Colorado: *Provided,* That nothing herein contained shall be so construed as to impair any existing valid adverse rights to any portion of said land."

The above change in the description is recommended for the reason that the bearing "south fifty-nine degrees thirty minutes east, eighteen thousand four hundred and thirty-nine feet," is not consistent with the distance north and west of the said quarter corner as stated in the language of the proposed bill.

Mr. Lacey's letter and the inclosed bill are herewith returned.

Very respectfully,

W. A. RICHARDS,
Assistant Commissioner.

The SECRETARY OF THE INTERIOR.

VESSEL OF THE FIRST CLASS FOR THE REVENUE-CUTTER SERVICE,
TO BE STATIONED AT HONOLULU, HAWAII.

JANUARY 28, 1903.—Committed to the Committee of the Whole House on the state
of the Union and ordered to be printed.

Mr. DAVEY, from the Committee on Interstate and Foreign Commerce,
submitted the following

REPORT.

[To accompany S. 6534.]

The Committee on Interstate and Foreign Commerce, to whom was
referred the bill (S. 6534) providing for the construction of a vessel
of the first class for the Revenue-Cutter Service, to be stationed with
headquarters at Honolulu, Hawaii, having considered the same, report
thereon with a recommendation that it pass.

The bill has the approval of the Treasury Department, as will appear
by the letter attached and which is made a part of this report.

TREASURY DEPARTMENT, OFFICE OF THE SECRETARY,
Washington, December 15, 1902.

SIR: I have to acknowledge the receipt of a letter, dated the 12th instant, from the
Committee on Commerce, inclosing Senate bill 6534, "Providing for the construction
of a vessel of the first class for the Revenue-Cutter Service, to be stationed with headquarters at Honolulu, Hawaii," for such suggestions as may be deemed proper touching the merits of the bill and the propriety of its passage.

In reply I have respectfully to state that there is not at this time any vessel of the
Revenue-Cutter Service which can be spared for duty in the waters of Hawaii, and
that the Service should be represented there by an able seagoing vessel does not seem
to be open to question. The maritime laws of the United States, the enforcement of
which comes under the purview of this Department directly and by implication, are
fully applicable to our insular possessions, and for their enforcement the Department
must necessarily be largely dependent upon the Revenue-Cutter Service. Among
these laws may be mentioned:

1. The protection of the customs revenue (secs. 2747, 2760, 2762, 3059, Rev. Stats.).
2. Assistance of vessels in distress (secs. 1536, 2759).
3. Enforcement of the neutrality laws (sec. 5288, Rev. Stats.).
4. The enforcement of the navigation and other laws governing merchant vessels;
suppression of mutinies on board merchant vessels, etc.

A suggestion for the employment of private vessels for the purposes of the Revenue-
Cutter Service should not be entertained. Such a course would result not only in
inefficiency because of the absence of the commissioned ranks of the service from
such vessels, and therefore of indispensable authority for the proper government of

the same, but it would be found exceedingly expensive and in every way unsatisfactory to charter or hire vessels for this purpose.

All considerations in the interest of the Government appear to emphasize the necessity of making provision for a ship for duty in the waters of Hawaii, and I therefore recommend the passage of Senate bill 6534 without amendment.

The bill is herewith returned.

Respectfully,

L. M. SHAW, *Secretary*.

The CHAIRMAN COMMITTEE ON COMMERCE,
United States Senate.

O

BRIDGE ACROSS THE MISSOURI RIVER, ETC.

JANUARY 28, 1903.—Referred to the House Calendar and ordered to be printed.

Mr. SHACKLEFORD, from the Committee on Interstate and Foreign Commerce, submitted the following

REPORT.

[To accompany H. R. 7648.]

The Committee on Interstate and Foreign Commerce, to whom was referred the bill (H. R. 7648) to authorize the construction of a bridge across the Missouri River and to establish it as a post road, having considered the same, report it with amendments, and as amended recommend its passage.

The bill thus amended has the approval of the War Department, as will appear by the annexed letter, the amendments referred to therein having been incorporated in the bill as reported.

Amend as follows:

In line 3, section 2, page 2, after the word "not," insert "unreasonably."

In line 4, section 2, page 2, strike out all after the word "river."

In line 5, section 2, page 2, strike out all up to and including the word "granted."

Strike out all of section 3 and insert the following in lieu thereof:

SEC. 3. That the bridge herein authorized to be constructed may be constructed either as a drawbridge or as a high bridge with unbroken and continuous spans. If constructed of unbroken and continuous spans, that it shall not be of less elevation than fifty-two feet above the high-water grade line for bridges as established by the Missouri River Commission. Nor shall any of the spans of the said bridge over the waterway be less than four hundred feet in the clear between the piers and abutments, and the piers thereof shall be parallel with the current of the river and the bridge itself at right angles thereto as nearly as may be. If said bridge is constructed as a drawbridge, the same shall be constructed as a pivot drawbridge, with a draw over the main channel, with spans of such clear width of opening as the Secretary of War shall prescribe, and the next adjoining spans to the draw shall also be of such length as he shall prescribe, and the said span shall not be less than ten feet above extreme high-water mark measuring from the bottom chord of said bridge; and the piers of said bridge shall be parallel with the current of the river and the bridge itself at right angles thereto as near as may be: *Provided*, That the said corporation, its successors or assignes, shall build and maintain at all times, as accessory works to said bridge, such booms, piers, dikes, guard fences, and similar devices as may be necessary, in the judgment of the Secretary of War, to insure at all times a permanent channel for a sufficient distance above and below the bridge site, and for the

2   BRIDGE ACROSS THE MISSOURI RIVER, ETC.

guiding of rafts, steamboats, and other water craft safely through or under said bridge: *And provided further,* That said draw shall be opened promptly upon proper signal for the passage of boats.

In line 16, section 4, page 3, after the word "telegraph," insert "and telephone."

In line 17, section 4, page 3, after the word "postal-telegraph," insert "and telephone."

In line 2, section 5, page 4, after the word "toll," add:

as may be approved from time to time by the Secretary of War, and in case of any disagreement between the owner or owners of said bridge and those desiring its use, in respect to tolls to be paid and the rules and conditions to be complied with in using said bridge, all matters at issue between them shall be decided by the Secretary of War upon a hearing of the allegations and proofs of the parties.

In line 5, section 6, page 4, after the word "thereof," insert "and a map of the location giving."

In line 3, section 7, page 5, strike out the words "Secretary of War" and insert the words "Light House Board" in lieu thereof.

In line 4, section 7, page 5, strike out the word "may" and insert the word "shall" in lieu thereof.

O

BRIDGE ACROSS ST. FRANCIS RIVER NEAR ST. FRANCIS, ARK.

JANUARY 28, 1903.—Referred to the House Calendar and ordered to be printed.

Mr. SHACKLEFORD, from the Committee on Interstate and Foreign Commerce, submitted the following

REPORT.

[To accompany H. R. 16573.]

The Committee on Interstate and Foreign Commerce, to whom was referred the bill (H. R. 16573) to authorize the construction of a bridge across St. Francis River at or near the town of St. Francis, Ark., having considered the same, report thereon with a recommendation that it pass.

The bill has the approval of the War Department, as will appear by the letter attached and which is made a part of this report.

OFFICE OF THE CHIEF OF ENGINEERS, U. S. ARMY,
Washington, January 14, 1903.

SIR: I have the honor to return herewith a letter, dated the 10th instant, from the Committee on Interstate and Foreign Commerce of the House of Representatives, inclosing for the views of the War Department thereon H. R. 16573, Fifty-seventh Congress, second session, "A bill to authorize the construction of a bridge across St. Francis River at or near the town of St. Francis, Ark.," and, in reply to its reference to this office, I beg to say that the bill, in my opinion, makes ample provision for navigation interests, and I know of no objection to its passage by Congress so far as those interests are concerned.

Very respectfully, your obedient servant,

G. L. GILLESPIE,
Brig. Gen., Chief of Engineers U. S. Army.

Hon. ELIHU ROOT, *Secretary o War.*

O

BRIDGE ACROSS BOGUE CHITTO, LOUISIANA.

JANUARY 28, 1903.—Referred to the House Calendar and ordered to be printed.

Mr. DAVEY, from the Committee on Interstate and Foreign Commerce, submitted the following

REPORT.

[To accompany H. R. 16646.]

The Committee on Interstate and Foreign Commerce, to whom was referred the bill (H. R. 16646) to authorize the construction of a bridge across Bogue Chitto, in the State of Louisiana, having considered the same, report it with amendments and as amended recommend its passage.
. The bill thus amended has the approval of the War Department, as will appear by the annexed letter, the amendment referred to therein having been incorporated in the bill as reported.
Amend as follows:
In line 10, section 3, page 2, after the word "year," insert "and completed within three years."
Add section 4, as follows:

SEC. 4. That the right to alter, amend, or repeal this act is hereby expressly reserved.

OFFICE OF THE CHIEF OF ENGINEERS, U. S. ARMY,
Washington, January 17, 1903.
SIR: I have the honor to return herewith a letter, dated the 14th instant, from the Committee on Interstate and Foreign Commerce of the House of Representatives, inclosing for the views of the War Department thereon H. R. 16646, Fifty-seventh Congress, second session, "A bill to authorize the construction of a bridge across Bogue Chitto, in the State of Louisiana," and, in reply to its reference to this office, I beg to recommend certain amendments to the bill, which are indicated on a copy of the same herewith submitted.
As thus amended, the bill, in my opinion, makes ample provision for the protection of navigation interests, and I know of no objection to its passage by Congress so far as those interests are concerned.
Very respectfully, your obedient servant,
G. L. GILLESPIE,
Brig. Gen., Chief of Engineers, U. S. Army.
Hon. ELIHU ROOT,
Secretary of War.

O

LIFE-SAVING STATION AT MOUTH OF BLACK RIVER, OHIO.

JANUARY 28, 1903.—Referred to the House Calendar and ordered to be printed.

Mr. COOMBS, from the Committee on Interstate and Foreign Commerce, submitted the following

REPORT.

[To accompany H. R. 14384.]

The Committee on Interstate and Foreign Commerce, to whom was referred the bill (H. R. 14384) providing for a life-saving station at the mouth of Black River, at or near the city of Lorain, Lorain County, in the State of Ohio, and for life-saving crew, etc., having considered the same, report it with amendment and, as amended, recommend its passage.

The bill thus amended has the approval of the Treasury Department, as will appear by the annexed letter; the amendment referred to therein having been incorporated in the bill as reported.

Amend the title to read as follows: "To establish a life-saving station at the mouth of Black River, at or near the city of Lorain, in the State of Ohio."

Strike out all after the enacting clause and insert in lieu thereof the following:

That the Secretary of the Treasury be, and he is hereby, authorized to establish a life-saving station at the mouth of Black River, at or near the city of Lorain, Ohio, at such point as the Superintendent of the Life-Saving Service may recommend.

TREASURY DEPARTMENT, OFFICE OF THE SECRETARY,
Washington, January 3, 1903.

SIR: I have the honor to acknowledge the receipt of your letter of May 14, 1902, transmitting bill H. R. 14384, Fifty-seventh Congress, first session, "Providing for a life-saving station at the mouth of Black River, at or near the city of Lorain, Lorain County, in the State of Ohio, and for life-saving crew, and so forth," and asking for suggestions touching the merits of the bill and the propriety of its passage.

The matter was referred to the General Superintendent of the Life-Saving Service for report, which has been received and is herewith transmitted with my concurrence.

Respectfully,

O. L. SPAULDING, Acting Secretary.

The CHAIRMAN COMMITTEE ON INTERSTATE AND FOREIGN COMMERCE,
House of Representatives.

TREASURY DEPARTMENT,
OFFICE GENERAL SUPERINTENDENT OF LIFE-SAVING SERVICE,
Washington, January 3, 1903.

SIR: I have the honor to acknowledge the receipt, for report, of a letter from the Committee on Interstate and Foreign Commerce, dated May 14, 1902, transmitting bill H. R. 14384, Fifty-seventh Congress, first session, "Providing for a life-saving station at the mouth of Black River, at or near the city of Lorain, Lorain County, in the State of Ohio, and for life-saving crew, and so forth," and asking for suggestions touching the merits of the bill and the propriety of its passage.

The city of Lorain, at or near which the bill under consideration proposes to establish a life-saving station, is situated on the southern coast of Lake Erie, about midway between the Cleveland station on the east and Point Marblehead station on the west, about 30 miles from each. The harbor of Lorain is in the mouth of Black River, a small stream, for the improvement of which appropriations have been made from time to time by Congress since 1828, and work of this character is still in progress. The emergency act of June 6, 1900, designated the location of the work as "Lorain Harbor, Ohio," instead of "Black River, Ohio," as theretofore. A 20-foot channel connects the harbor with the lake, and vessels drawing 18½ feet of water use the harbor, though they do not load to the full depth.

The commerce of the harbor of Lorain shows a constant increase for a considerable period. The receipts and shipments for the year 1900 amounted to 1,546,709 tons, an increase over 1899 of 123,552 tons. About 500 vessels entered the harbor in 1900, having a registered tonnage of 773,315 tons. No report of the commerce for 1901 has yet reached this office. I am reliably informed, however, that enterprises of great importance are contemplated in the near future at Lorain, which will greatly enhance the value of a life-saving station at the point contemplated, and in view of the facts that, at present, there is no station along the lake coast in that vicinity for 50 miles, from which aid could be rendered to vessels in distress; that Lorain is about midway of the exposed coast; that the commerce of the harbor is already of considerable importance and rapidly increasing, and that this increase may be expected to continue even at a greater ratio than heretofore, I am of the opinion that the needs of commerce and the demands of humanity render desirable the establishment of a life-saving station as proposed by the bill under consideration.

A recent disaster (November 25, 1902) to the steamer *Quito*, of 1,372 tons burden, strongly tends to justify this conclusion. She was valued at $75,000, and carried a cargo estimated at $40,000, all of which was totally lost. Her crew numbered 18, a portion of whom the local tug *Cascade* rescued with much difficulty and risk, but several remained on board, whom the tug was unable to save and who would have perished but for the arrival of the Cleveland life-saving crew, which hurried to the scene by special train and finally rescued them. There have been several other disasters in recent years to smaller craft, and several accidents involving loss of life by drowning in and near the harbor.

Should the committee decide to report the bill favorably, I beg to suggest that it be so, amended as to conform to the wording of bills usually drawn for a like purpose. It would then read as follows:

"A BILL to establish a life-saving station at the mouth of Black River, at or near the city of Lorain, Ohio.

"*Be it enacted by the Senate and House of Representatives of the United States of America in Congress assembled,* That the Secretary of the Treasury be, and he is hereby, authorized to establish a life-saving station at the mouth of Black River, at or near the city of Lorain, Ohio, at such point as the General Superintendent of the Life-Saving Service may recommend."

Respectfully,

S. I. KIMBALL,
General Superintendent.

The SECRETARY OF THE TREASURY.

O

BRIDGE ACROSS CONECUH RIVER IN ESCAMBIA COUNTY, ALA.

JANUARY 28, 1903.—Referred to the House Calendar and ordered to be printed.

Mr. RICHARDSON, of Alabama, from the Committee on Interstate and Foreign Commerce, submitted the following

REPORT.

[To accompany H. R. 16915.]

The Committee on Interstate and Foreign Commerce, to whom was referred the bill (H. R. 16915) authorizing the commissioners' court of Escambia County, Ala., to construct a bridge across Conecuh River at or near a point known as McGowens Ferry, in said county and State; having considered the same, report it with amendment, and as amended recommend its passage.

The bill thus amended has the approval of the War Department, as will appear by the annexed letter, the amendment referred to therein having been incorporated in the bill as reported.

Amend as follows:

In line 6, section 1, page 1, after the word "at," insert "a point suitable to the interests of navigation, at."

In line 9, section 2, page 2, strike out the word "subjected" and insert "subject" in lieu thereof.

In line 13, section 3, page 2, after the word "same," strike out the period and insert a semicolon in lieu thereof, and insert the following:

and for the safety of vessels passing at night there shall be displayed on said bridge, by the owners thereof at their own expense, such lights or other signals as the Light-House Board may prescribe.

In lines 14 and 15, section 3, page 2, strike out the words "deem necessary to be made, and shall prescribe," and insert in lieu thereof "order in the interest of navigation."

In lines 16 and 17, section 3, page 2, strike out all after the word "made," and insert in lieu thereof "by the owners thereof at their own expense."

In line 2, section 4, page 3, after the word "postal," strike out the word "and," and insert after the word "telephone" the words "and other."

OFFICE OF THE CHIEF OF ENGINEERS, U. S. ARMY,
Washington, January 23, 1903.

SIR: I have the honor to return herewith a letter, dated the 21st instant, from the Committee on Interstate and Foreign Commerce of the House of Representatives, inclosing for the views of the War Department thereon H. R. 16915, Fifty-seventh Congress, second session, "A bill authorizing the commissioners' court of Escambia County, Ala., to construct a bridge across Conecuh River at or near a point known as McGowans Ferry, in said county and State," and in reply to its reference to this office I beg to recommend certain amendments to the bill, which are indicated on a copy of the same herewith submitted.

As thus amended the bill, in my opinion, makes ample provision for the protection of navigation interests, and I know of no objection to its passage by Congress so far as those interests are concerned.

Very respectfully, your obedient servant,

G. L. GILLESPIE,
Brigadier-General, Chief of Engineers, U. S. Army.

Hon. ELIHU ROOT, *Secretary of War.*

O

MUSCLE SHOALS POWER COMPANY.

JANUARY 28, 1903.—Referred to the House Calendar and ordered to be printed.

Mr. RICHARDSON, of Alabama, from the Committee on Interstate and Foreign Commerce, submitted the following

REPORT.

[To accompany H. R. 16602.]

The Committee on Interstate and Foreign Commerce, to whom was referred the bill (H. R. 16602) to extend the time granted to the Muscle Shoals Power Company by an act approved March 3, 1892, within which to commence and complete the work authorized in the said act to be done by said company, and for other purposes, having considered the same, report it with amendment, and as amended recommend its passage.

The bill thus amended has the approval of the War Department, as will appear by the annexed letter, the amendment referred to therein having been incorporated in the bill as reported.

Amend as follows:

In lines 1, 2, 3, and 4, page 2, strike out all after the word "determined" and insert in lieu thereof "and the Secretary of War is authorized, in his discretion, to permit the said company to erect and construct dams which may abut on lands of the United States along the line of the Muscle Shoals Canal, upon such terms and conditions as may be deemed just and equitable to the public interests."

OFFICE OF THE CHIEF OF ENGINEERS, U. S. ARMY,
Washington, January 16, 1903.

SIR: I have the honor to return herewith a letter, dated the 13th instant, from the Committee on Interstate and Foreign Commerce of the House of Representatives, inclosing for the views of the War Department thereon H. R. 16602, Fifty-seventh Congress, second session, "A bill to extend the time granted to the Muscle Shoals Power Company by an act approved March third, eighteen hundred and ninety-nine, within which to commence and complete the work authorized in the said act to be done by said company, and for other purposes."

This bill contains two propositions. The first merely extends the life of a franchise previously granted by Congress, and to this I know of no objection; the second authorizes the company to occupy and use Government property along the line of the Muscle Shoals Canal. The latter is an entirely new proposition, and has hitherto had no consideration by the Department in connection with the project of the Muscle Shoals Power Company. The privilege proposed to be granted is one that may result in embarrassment to the Government, and it may be a valuable one for which the company should be required to pay. As it is necessary that action shall be taken on the bill during the present session of Congress, in order to preserve the life of the franchise, there is not sufficient time to properly and carefully investigate these questions; but I am of the opinion that, if the bill is amended as indicated on a copy of the same herewith submitted, the interests of the Government will be protected, and that there will be no objection to favorable action by Congress thereon.

Very respectfully, your obedient servant,

G. L. GILLESPIE,
Brig. Gen., Chief of Engineers, U. S. Army.

Hon. ELIHU ROOT, *Secretary of War.*

. O

BRIDGE ACROSS PEARL RIVER, MISSISSIPPI.

JANUARY 28, 1903.—Referred to the House Calendar and ordered to be printed.

Mr. RICHARDSON, of Alabama, from the Committee on Interstate and Foreign Commerce, submitted the following

REPORT.

[To accompany H. R. 16509.]

The Committee on Interstate and Foreign Commerce, to whom was referred the bill (H. R. 16509) to authorize the Pearl and Leaf Rivers Railroad Company to bridge Pearl River, in the State of Mississippi, having considered the same, report it with amendment, and as amended recommend its passage.

The bill thus amended has the approval of the War Department, as will appear by the annexed letter, the amendments referred to therein having been incorporated in the bill as reported.

Amend as follows:

At the end of line 13, section 3, page 2, add—

and equal privileges in the use of said bridge shall be granted to all telegraph and telephone companies, and the United States shall have the right of way across said bridge and its approaches for postal telegraph and telephone purposes.

In line 15, section 4, page 2, after the words "a draw," strike out the words "or pivot."

In line 15, section 4, page 2, after the words "the draw," strike out the words "or pivot."

In line 2, section 4, page 3, after the word "draw," strike out the words "or pivot span."

In line 10, section 6, page 4, after the word "built," insert "or commenced."

In line 10, section 6, page 4, after the word "and," strike out all of the balance of the line and all of lines 11, 12, 13, 14, 15, 16, 17, 18, 19, 20, and 21, and insert the following in lieu thereof:

No change shall be made in said bridge during the progress of construction nor after completion, unless approved by the Chief of Engineers and the Secretary of War, and the said company shall, at its own expense, make from time to time such changes in said bridge as the Secretary of War may order in the interest of navigation.

In line 2, section 8, page 5, strike out the word "two" and insert the word "one" in lieu thereof.

In line 2, section 8, page 5, strike out the word "five" and insert the word "three" in lieu thereof.

In line 3, section 8, page 5, strike out the words "its passage" and insert the words "approval hereof."

OFFICE OF THE CHIEF OF ENGINEERS, U. S. ARMY,
Washington, January 13, 1903.

SIR: I have the honor to return herewith a letter, dated the 9th instant, from the Committee on Interstate and Foreign Commerce of the House of Representatives, inclosing for the views of the War Department thereon House bill 16509, Fifty-seventh Congress, second session, "A bill to authorize the Pearl and Leaf Rivers Railroad Company to bridge Pearl River, in the State of Mississippi," and in reply to its reference to this office I beg to recommend certain changes in the bill, which are indicated on a copy of the same herewith submitted.

As thus amended, I know of no objection to the passage of the bill by Congress so far as the interests of navigation are concerned.

Very respectfully, your obedient servant,

G. L. GILLESPIE,
Brigadier-General, Chief of Engineers, U. S. Army.

HON. ELIHU ROOT, *Secretary of War.*

O

SAMUEL LEE.

JANUARY 28, 1903.—Committed to the Committee of the Whole House and ordered to be printed.

Mr. FOSTER, of Vermont, from the Committee on Claims, submitted the following

REPORT.

[To accompany H. R. 14483.]

The Committee on Claims, to whom was referred the bill (H. R. 14483) to pay Samuel Lee for services in the Forty-seventh Congress, beg leave to submit the following report, and recommend that said bill do pass without amendment:

It appears that in the election of a Representative to Congress from the First district of South Carolina in 1882 the face of the returns indicated the election of John S. Richardson, but a contest for the seat was entered by Samuel Lee. The contest was referred to the Committee on Elections in the Forty-seventh Congress, and subsequently, when the case was being considered by the House, the House voted, by a vote of 124 to 114, that Richardson was not elected and entitled to have or hold a seat as Representative from the said district, and that Lee was duly elected and entitled to have and hold said seat.

At this point dilatory tactics were employed by the minority, which were kept up until the expiration of said Congress, which prevented Lee from taking his seat.

The House having by a decisive affirmative vote declared Lee entitled to the seat in question, and he having been prevented purely by dilatory tactics of the minority from taking his seat, we are of the opinion that an injustice was done Lee, and consequently we believe the bill should pass.

The proceedings relative to this contest are to be found in volume 14, part 4, page 3752 et seq., of the Congressional Record, Forty-seventh Congress.

O

CHARLES W. CARR.

JANUARY 29, 1903.—Committed to the Committee of the Whole House and ordered
to be printed.

Mr. GRAFF, from the Committee on Claims, submitted the following

REPORT.

[To accompany H. R. 14164.]

The Committee on Claims, to whom was referred the bill (H. R. 14164) for the relief of Charles W. Carr, submit the following report:

This bill provides that the sum of $83.71 be allowed to Charles W. Carr, former postmaster at Englewood, Ill., being the amount deposited by him to cover a deficiency caused by the payment at said post-office of two forged money orders, and that the amount of this allowance be paid to him out of any money in the Treasury of the United States not otherwise appropriated.

The communication of the Post-Office Department, which is hereto attached, fully sets forth the circumstances and facts surrounding this claim and recommends the passage of the bill with amendments formal in character.

The committee recommend that the bill be amended as follows, viz:

Strike out the word "forty" in line 10 and insert in lieu thereof the word "forty-three."

· Insert the words "issued at Lansing, Mich.," after the word "forty-three" in line 10.

And that when so amended it be passed.

A copy of the communication of the Post-Office Department, with memorandum of the Superintendent of the Money-Order Division, is hereto attached and made a part of this report.

POST-OFFICE DEPARTMENT,
OFFICE OF THE FIRST ASSISTANT POSTMASTER-GENERAL,
Washington, D. C., December 19, 1902.

SIR: In the matter of House bill No. 14164, appropriating the sum of $83.71 for the relief of Charles W. Carr, late postmaster at Englewood, Ill. (which was introduced by Mr. Feely on May 1, 1902), and in response to your request for a statement of facts and opinion relative thereto, your attention is invited to the inclosed memorandum prepared by the Superintendent of the Money-Order System.

In view of all the facts set forth in the memorandum mentioned, this Department would advise that the bill, with the slight amendments thereto suggested in the memorandum, be favorably reported.

Very respectfully, etc.,   R. J. WYNNE,

First Assistant Postmaster-General.

Hon. JOSEPH V. GRAFF,
Chairman of Committee on Claims, House of Representatives.

WASHINGTON, *December 19, 1902.*

Memorandum in regard to H. R. 14164, entitled "A bill for the relief of Charles W. Carr," introduced by Mr. Feely, May 1, 1902, and referred to the Committee on Claims.

The bill provides that the sum of $83.71 be allowed to Charles W. Carr, former postmaster at Englewood, Ill., being the amount deposited by him to cover a deficiency caused by the payment at said post-office of two forged money orders, and that the amount of this allowance be paid to him out of any money in the Treasury of the United States not otherwise appropriated.

The money orders in question are No. 1166 and No. 1543, issued at Lansing, Mich., on April 17, 1894, and May 6, 1894, respectively, for $35 and $48.71, the former to the Michigan Knitting Company, in favor of E. M. Slayton, on Chicago, Ill., and the latter to J. H. Barnett, in favor of the Geneva Optical Company, on Chicago, Ill. Order No. 1166 was paid at Englewood, Ill., on April 20, 1894, and order No. 1543 was paid at the same post-office on May 12, 1894, after having been fraudulently altered both as to name of payee and name of paying office.

Reports made by Post-Office Inspectors Stuart and Mayer giving the result of investigation of the circumstances connected with payment of these two money orders are on file in this Department. It appears that the said money orders and a number of others were stolen from the mails by one William H. Hansen, an employee of the railroad company at the Dearborn street station, Chicago, Ill., whose duty it was to transfer mails at this station and to accompany the wagons carrying mails therefrom to the Illinois Central depot in the same city.

As set forth in the reports mentioned, Hansen manufactured a mail key, opened mail pouches therewith, examined the mail, and abstracted therefrom official letters which contained advices of money orders. Possessed of the information contained in advices, he would further examine the mails in the same pouch for letters addressed to payees named in the advices. Securing these letters, which contained the money orders, he would, after expunging the particulars by the use of chemicals, substitute another name for that of paying office, as well as another name for that of payee, and sometimes raise the amounts, making order and advice as altered agree in all respects. He would then reinclose the advice in the official envelope, which bore the postmark of the issuing office, change the address thereon to that of the office named in the altered advice, and forward the same in a pouch destined for that office. Having in his possession the letter in which the order was mailed, he would by the use of acids obliterate the original address on such envelope and write thereon the name and address given as those of payee in the altered advice. He would then destroy the original letter of the remitter, and write one in its stead to the address substituted in the order and advice, and which he might show to the paying postmaster or clerk, who would perceive that the envelope bore the postmark of the office at which the order and advice were issued. In this way, satisfying the postmaster at Englewood, Charles W. Carr, or his clerk that he was the true payee, he obtained payment of the sum of $83.71 on the two money orders in question at that post-office.

The amount of order No. 1166 was repaid to the remitter at Lansing on a duplicate order on May 30, 1894, while the amount of order No. 1543 was paid to the true payee thereof at Chicago, June 29, 1894, and Charles W. Carr was subsequently required to make good to the Department the sum erroneously paid by him on the original orders to Hansen. For theft and fraudulent alteration of the original orders Hansen was brought to trial and was sentenced to imprisonment for thirteen months in the Joliet penitentiary.

As regards identification of the person claiming payment of a money order, postmasters and paying clerks must rely largely on the protection which the advice affords; it is not always practicable to secure personal identification; and under stress of business, orders are often paid without personal identification, the paying official depending upon the advice and the corroborative statements of the applicant.

In many cases somewhat similar to the one under consideration, the orders having been paid to the wrong person, the Department has been constrained to assume the loss, it appearing that the paying official exercised all the precaution that could reasonably have been expected of him under the circumstances. In the case of these two orders the postmaster at Englewood, or his clerk, apparently had no reason to suspect that they or the advices thereof were not genuine.

In view of all the circumstances set forth in the reports mentioned, I consider this a meritorious case, and in some respects quite like other cases in which the Department has assumed such losses as incidental to the operation of the system. It is suggested that the bill be amended, however, by changing the number of one of the orders therein from 1540 to 1543 and by insertion of the words "issued at Lansing, Michigan," after the word "forty-three" in line 10.

Respectfully submitted.

JAMES T. METCALF,
Superintendent Money-Order System.

O

BISHOP GUTTA-PERCHA COMPANY.

JANUARY 29, 1903.—Committed to the Committee of the Whole House and ordered
to be printed.

Mr. GRAFF, from the Committee on Claims, submitted the following

REPORT.

[To accompany S. 679.]

The Committee on Claims, to whom was referred the bill (S. 679)
directing the issue of a check in lieu of a lost check drawn by Capt.
E. O. Fechet, disbursing officer U. S. Signal Service Corps, in favor
of the Bishop Gutta-Percha Company, submit the following report:

This is a bill asking that Capt. E. O. Fechet, disbursing officer U. S.
Signal Corps, be authorized and directed to issue to the Bishop Gutta-
Percha Company a duplicate of an original check issued by said
E. O. Fechet, September 29, 1900, No. 35821, upon the assistant
treasurer of the United States at New York, in their favor for $2,793,
the check alleged to have been lost in transmission through the clear-
ing house before reaching the said assistant treasurer of the United
States at New York.

The committee, having looked into the matter, unanimously agrees
that a duplicate check be issued under the regulations of the Department of the Treasury, as set forth in detail in the bill.

·Correspondence fully covering the case and setting up the facts is
appended.

The committee recommend that the bill do pass.

STATE OF NEW YORK, *County of New York, ss:*

I, J. Frederick Sweasy, being duly sworn, depose and say:

First. That I am the J. Frederick Sweasy who made an affidavit in this matter
verified on the 23d day of May, 1901.

Second. That since the making of said affidavit verified the 23d day of May, 1901,
search has been made for the check drawn by Capt. E. O. Fechet, dated the 29th
day of September, 1900, to the order of the Bishop Gutta-Percha Company for the
sum of $2,793, and the same has not been found.

FREDERICK SWEASY.

Sworn and subscribed to before me this 2d day of December, 1901.

[SEAL.] A. H. GRAHAM,
Notary Public, New York County.

STATE OF NEW YORK, *County of New York, ss:*

I, J. Frederick Sweasy, being duly sworn, depose and say:

First. That I reside in the city of Newark, in the county of Essex and the State of New Jersey.

Second. That I am an assistant cashier of The National Bank of North America in New York, a corporation organized under the laws of the United States and doing business in the city of New York, in the county and State of New York.

Third. That heretofore and on the 29th day of September, in the year 1900, one Capt. E. O. Fechet, a disbursing officer of the U. S. Signal Service Corps, did make and issue a check upon the assistant treasurer of the United States of America at New York in favor of the Bishop Gutta-Percha Company for the sum of $2,793.

Fourth. That said check was so drawn by Capt. E. O. Fechet in payment of an invoice of merchandise theretofore delivered by the Bishop Gutta-Percha Company to and for the use of the U. S. Signal Service Corps.

Fifth. That said check was No. 35821.

Sixth. That thereafter said check No. 35821 was received by the Bishop Gutta-Percha Company, the payee therein named, and by said company duly indorsed, and, so indorsed, on the 3d day of October, in the year 1900, was, by the said Bishop Gutta-Percha Company, deposited with The National Bank of North America in New York and the amount thereof credited to the account of the Bishop Gutta-Percha Company on the books of said The National Bank of North America in New York.

That thereafter and on the 3d day of October, in the year 1900, the said check, to-wit, $2,793, was listed on the slip of the New York Clearing House to the assistant treasurer of the United States at New York, and, so listed, as deponent verily believes, was placed with other checks in the envelope which was sent through the clearing house to the said assistant treasurer on the morning of October 4th, in the year 1900.

Seventh. That thereafter and after the settlement of the clearing-house balance due to The National Bank of North America in New York, on the 4th day of October, in the year 1900, by the assistant treasurer of the United States at New York, said assistant treasurer of the United States at New York made a demand upon The National Bank of North America in New York for the repayment to him of the sum of $2,793, alleging as a basis for such demand that the said check, No. 35821, drawn by said Capt. E. O. Fechét, disbursing officer of the U. S. Signal Service Corps, to the order of the Bishop Gutta Percha Company on the assistant treasurer of the United States at New York for $2,793, was not received by him, the assistant treasurer of the United States at New York, and was not inclosed in the envelope with the other checks above referred to sent to said the assistant treasurer of the United States at New York through the clearing house at New York.

Eighth. That thereafter said Bank of North America in New York refunded to the assistant treasurer of the United States at New York the said sum of $2,793, and at the same time files with said the assistant treasurer of the United States at New York a formal notice of the loss of said check No. 35821, drawn by said Capt. E. O. Fechét, disbursing officer of the U. S. Signal Service Corps, to the order of the Bishop Gutta Percha Company, for the sum of $2,793, and requested that payment upon said check be refused.

Ninth. That deponent has caused careful search to be made in all and every place where said check was likely to be and same can not be found; wherefore deponent verily believes that said check has been lost.

Wherefore deponent prays in behalf of the said The National Bank of North America in New York that the said Capt. E. O. Fechét, disbursing officer of the U. S. Signal Service Corps, be authorized and instructed to issue a duplicate of said original check to the Bishop Gutta Percha Company, under such regulations in regard to its issue and payment as have or may be prescribed by the Secretary of the Treasury for the issue of duplicate checks under the provisions of section 3646, Revised Statutes of the United States.

                                             FREDERICK SWEASY.

Sworn and subscribed to before me this 23d day of May, A. D. 1901.

[SEAL.]   A. H. GRAHAM,
                                        Notary Public, New York County.

———

STATE OF NEW YORK, *County of New York, ss:*

I, Henry A. Reed, being duly sworn, depose and say:

First. That I reside in the city of Newark and State of New Jersey.   .

Second. That I am the secretary and treasurer of the Bishop Gutta Percha Company.

Third. That the Bishop Gutta Percha Company is a corporation, and I am one of its officers, to wit, secretary and treasurer.

Fourth. That heretofore, on the 29th day of September, in the year 1900, one Capt. E. O. Fechét, a disbursing officer in the U. S. Signal Service Corps, did make and issue a check upon the assistant treasurer of the United States at New York in favor of the Bishop Gutta Percha Company for the sum of $2,793.

Fifth. That said check was so drawn by said Capt. E. O. Fechét in payment of an invoice of merchandise theretofore delivered by the Bishop Gutta Percha Company to and for the use of the U. S. Signal Service Corps of the U. S. Army.

Sixth. That said check so drawn and delivered was No. 35821.

Seventh. That thereafter said check, No. 35821, was received by the Bishop Gutta Percha Company, the payee therein named, and by said company duly indorsed to The National Bank of North America in New York, and so indorsed on the 3d day of October, in the year 1900, was by the said Bishop Gutta Percha Company deposited with The National Bank of North America in New York, and the amount thereof, to wit, $2,793, credited to the account of the Bishop Gutta Percha Company on the books of the said The National Bank of North America in New York.

Eighth. That this deponent is informed and verily believes that said check was lost on or about the 4th day of October, in the year 1900, more than six months last past, and that although due and diligent search has been made therefor said check has not and can not be found.

Ninth. I have read the affidavit of J. Frederick Sweasy, verified the 23d day of May, 1901, relating to the loss of the said check, and I verily believe that the statements made in the said affidavit are true.

HENRY A. REED.

Sworn and subscribed to before me this 24th day of May, A. D. 1901.

[SEAL.]   W. H. WOODHULL,
                                              Notary Public, New York County.

___

UNITED STATES OF AMERICA, *District of Columbia, ss:*

On this 6th day of March, A. D. 1901, personally appeared before me, John B. Randolph, a notary public in and for the District of Columbia, Capt. E. O. Fechét, disbursing officer, U. S. Signal Service Corps, Washington, D. C., who, being duly sworn, deposes and says that on the 29th day of September, 1900, he drew check No. 35821 upon the assistant treasurer of the United States at New York, N. Y., in favor of the Bishop Gutta Percha Company, for the sum of $2,793, in payment for 21 miles of land cable for Alaska, as per invoice dated September 14, 1900, which check was mailed to the firm's address by the deponent on October 1, 1900.

Deponent further says that in the monthly statements furnished to him by the proper officials of the United States Treasury Department the aforesaid check has not been reported on any of said statements as having been presented and paid by the assistant treasurer at New York; and that to the best of the knowledge and belief of the deponent said check still remains as outstanding and unpaid.

EUGENE O. FECHÉT,
Captain and Disbursing Officer, U. S. Signal Service Corps.

Subscribed and sworn to before me this 6th day of March, A. D. 1901.

[SEAL.]   JNO. B. RANDOLPH,
                                                      Notary Public.

O

EASTERN JUDICIAL DISTRICT OF TEXAS, ETC.

JANUARY 30, 1903.—Referred to the House Calendar and ordered to be printed.

Mr. HENRY, of Texas, from the Committee on the Judiciary, submitted
the following

REPORT.

[To accompany H. R. 17088.]

The Committee on the Judiciary have considered the bill (H. R.
17088) to create a new division of the eastern judicial district of Texas,
and to provide for terms of court at Taxarkana, Tex., and for a clerk
for said court, and for other purposes, and respectfully recommend
that the same do pass without amendment.

A Federal court should be established at Texarkana because it is a
city of approximately 15,000 people and is one of the most important
railway centers in the Southwest. It is the point of convergence for
several great trunk lines of railway, namely, the St. Louis, Iron
Mountain and Southern, the Texas and Pacific, with its branch, the
Transcontinental, the St. Louis Southwestern, the Kansas City, Pittsburg and Gulf, the Texarkana, Shreveport and Natchez, and minor
lines. The eastern terminus of the Texas and Pacific and Transcontinental, the northern terminus of the Texarkana, Shreveport and
Natchez, and the southern terminus of the St. Louis, Iron Mountain
and Southern are at Texarkana. It is therefore very accessible from
all parts of the proposed division.

It has electric car lines, lights, sewerage, and all the appurtenances
of a modern city. Being situated on the line dividing Arkansas from
Texas, Texarkana is immediately connected with many States of the
Union. Texarkana is thus the most important gateway to Texas. The
nearest Federal courts in Texas at present are at Paris, 90 miles
west, and at Jefferson, about 60 miles south. On the ground of
diverse citizenship these railways and their opposing litigants have
the right to remove many cases arising in Texarkana and Bowie
County to United States courts. The Texas and Pacific may remove
by law every case so arising. Again, the fact that Texarkana is on
the State line causes a large number of cases to arise between citizens
of different States which are triable in the Federal courts.

Many litigants in Arkansas, Texas, Louisiana, and other States are greatly inconvenienced by the present condition. On this account many people decline to litigate, and the present condition amounts to a practical denial of justice in many instances. Litigation is thus made oppressive and expensive. The proposed term at Texarkana disturbs no existing division, and leaves each court in the First Congressional district, wherein Texarkana is situated, with practically equal territory. The committee therefore recommends that the bill do pass without amendment.

O

RELIEF OF THE STATE OF IOWA.

JANUARY 30, 1903.—Committed to the Committee of the Whole House on the state of the Union and ordered to be printed.

Mr. HAUGEN, from the Committee on War Claims, submitted the following

REPORT.

[To accompany H. R. 16950.]

The Committee on War Claims, to whom was referred the bill (H. R. 16950) for the relief of the State of Iowa, beg leave to submit the following report, and recommend that said bill do pass without amendment:

The committee finds the facts to be as stated in an affidavit of the governor and adjutant-general of the State of Iowa, and letters from the Auditor for the War Department, Secretary of the Treasury, and adjutant-general of the State of Iowa, which affidavits and letters are hereto appended and made a part of the report. In addition it is proper to state that in a report made by the Auditor for the War Department on this bill on January 26, 1903, to the Secretary of the Treasury, he states that—

The amount stated in the bill, namely, $20,445.02, can not be verified by figures from the records on file in this office. In the official report which will be furnished the governor of Iowa within a few days it will be shown that the total disallowance of every nature amounts to $21,293.60.

WASHINGTON, D. C., *January 27, 1903.*

DEAR SIR: In the matter of the claim of the State of Iowa for $20,445.02, disallowed by the Auditor for the War Department, for which I request you to prepare a bill and present to Congress to reimburse the State of Iowa for money expended in aiding the United States in raising, equipping, subsisting, and maintaining the Volunteer Army for the war with Spain, desire to say that the amount herein contained is for money expended and bills paid after the mustering into the United States service of the Iowa Volunteers, was paid by direction of the governor, L. M. Shaw (who is now Secretary of the Treasury of the United States).

I personally had the supervision and paid all claims through my department, and that before any bill was paid they had the approval of Capt. J. A. Olmstead, of the Ninth United States Cavalry, mustering officer, then on duty at Des Moines, Iowa. The great majority of the bills disallowed by the Auditor for the War Department were bills that were paid and contracted after the troops were mustered into the United States service. There were two regiments returned to Iowa for mustering out and were kept at Camp McKinley for thirty to thirty-five days each, and were furloughed under orders from the War Department, but were without means to pay their transportation to their homes.

The State of Iowa furnished these men transportation to their homes and return, realizing that the State was not bound to do so, but as we had a contract with all railroads in the State to transport our soldiers at the rate of one cent per mile, that we did so, thinking that the best under the circumstances, and hoping that the General Government might see fit in its generosity to reimburse the State for the money so paid out.

There was arranged by Captain Omlstead what was known as the Red Cross Hospital at Camp McKinley. These soldiers coming home from Chickamauga and Jacksonville were very sick with fevers, and a hospital had to be provided to care for them; and when this hospital was filled up some of the private hospitals were filled, and all of the expenses were paid by the State of Iowa. After being approved by the mustering officer of the United States, the State of Iowa paid all claims that were contracted within the State, whether by Government officials or by State officials, for these volunteers.

There was also a contract for the fair grounds of the State Agricultural Society, made by myself and Captain Olmsted, of the Regular Army, mustering officers then on duty, for the use of their grounds, at $400 per month. These grounds were continually in use from the 25th day of April, 1898, until the 30th day of November, 1898, and I believe these bills are just and legitimate and should be paid by the General Government through an appropriation by act of Congress.

Very respectfully,

M. H. BYERS, *Adjutant-General Iowa.*

Hon. G. N. HAUGEN,
House of Representatives, Washington, D. C.

———.

TREASURY DEPARTMENT, OFFICE OF THE SECRETARY,
Washington, January 27, 1903.

SIR: Referring to your communication of the 22d instant, addressed to the Auditor for the War Department, inclosing House bill No. 16950, Fifty-seventh Congress, second session, "For the relief of the State of Iowa," for payment to the State, out of any money not otherwise appropriated, the sum of $20,445.02, to reimburse the State for money and supplies furnished Iowa troops after being mustered into the United States service, I have the honor to inclose herewith the report made by the Auditor on the bill on the 26th instant, showing that in the settlement of claims of States against the United States for reimbursement on account of expenditures made in the war with Spain, it has been uniformly held that expenditures for accounts of officers and men after muster into the United States service were not a proper charge, under the act of July 8, 1898, and amendments thereto, and were therefore disallowed.

Respectfully,

O. L. SPAULDING,
Acting Secretary.

Hon. THAD. M. MAHON,
Chairman Committee on War Claims,
House of Representatives.

———

STATE OF IOWA, EXECUTIVE DEPARTMENT,
Des Moines, September 15, 1900.

To the Auditor for the War Department:

We, the undersigned, L. M. Shaw and M. H. Byers, who were the governor and adjutant-general, respectively, of the said State of Iowa during the years 1898–99, and are at the present time governor and adjutant-general of the State of Iowa, and as governor and adjutant-general are responsible for the purchases and expenditures of the mobilization, examination, quartering, subsisting, equipping, and generally maintaining of the volunteers from Iowa under the call of the President of the United States for 125,000 volunteers on April 23, 1898, and subsequent calls, beg leave to state in reply to file No. 55801, dated September 6, 1900, as follows:

In regard to the claim for pay of rejected men or recruits, will say that only the men who were members of the Iowa National Guard at the time of mobilization were paid upon their rejection, and these men presented themselves in good faith for muster into the United States service and were rejected by the medical examining surgeons or by the mustering officer; and further, that none of the men who presented themselves who did not belong to the National Guard prior to April 26, 1898, and were rejected have been paid by the State, nor any claim made by the State for them; and further, all the rejection slips or certificates were taken up by the mustering officer when the bills for pay of rejected men were approved by him prior to their payment by the State, and we presume were forwarded to the War Department with his report.

In the matter of supplies (that in your letter you say seems, from date of original bill, were furnished after muster into United States service) the facts are that the goods had been ordered before muster in and memorandum made out, but some bills were not made out until the 1st of the month following, the bills only being presented for payment once a month. All bills were approved by the United States mustering officer before payment was made by the State, and all payments were made by the State in good faith, supposing that the approval of the United States officers on duty, as mustering officers and quartermaster on part of the United States Government, was sufficient authority for reimbursement by the General Government. You ask for correct transcript of the order book sworn to by one of the firm. This can not be furnished for the reason that you do not specify the firm or the supplies referred to.

In regard to the lumber and hardware bills, these materials were used in building sinks and closets for the use of the volunteers on the grounds at Camp McKinley, Des Moines, Iowa, and in replacing boards on buildings and fences destroyed or burned up by the volunteers. The regimental quartermasters' receipts were not taken for any of these materials, but such materials were ordered by M. H. Byers, adjutant-general, and used by engineer officer and commander of the camp, upon recommendation of medical officers and examining surgeons in the Regular and Volunteer Service of the United States.

All the lumber used for building sinks and closets was used (after the volunteers were ordered to Jacksonville, Chickamauga, and San Francisco) in making repairs of buildings and fences upon the premises used at Camp McKinley, Des Moines, Iowa, by order of Adjutant-General Byers, in accordance with an agreement between himself, representing the State of Iowa, and Capt. J. A. Olmsted, representing the United States Government, with the State Agricultural Society, upon the occupation of the premises as a camp of mobilization, and we were compelled to purchase additional lumber and hardware to complete the work. No part of said supplies were sold, but used up in repairs faithfully performed.

The stoves purchased were secondhand and were bought outright, and were worthless when the camp was broken up and could not be sold for anything. We found that it was cheaper to buy secondhand stoves and throw them away after the camp was done than to rent good stoves.

Considerable property got into the hands of the different regiments of Iowa Volunteers and was taken into the United States service without getting the regimental quartermasters' receipts for the same. Efforts were made to procure receipts, but in some instances we failed.

All the money expended by the State in aid of the United States Government in the mobilization, organization, and supplying the Iowa United States Volunteers was expended in good faith and bears the approval of the mustering officers, either Capt. J. A. Olmsted, Ninth U. S. Cavalry, or Maj. J. B. Guthrie, late Fifteenth U. S. Infantry, and no part of the materials were sold, but actually used up in the service of the United States and camp of mobilization for volunteers for the Spanish-American war at Des Moines, Iowa.

Further, that the adjutant-general, as acting quartermaster-general, had general and special supervision on the part of the State in all purchases, expenditures, and general management of the same for these troops, by the approval of the army officers of the United States on duty at this camp at date of purchase and disposal.

L. M. SHAW, *Governor.*
M. H. BYERS, *Adjutant-General.*

STATE OF IOWA, *Polk County.*

Subscribed and sworn to before me by L. M. Shaw, governor, and M. H. Byers, adjutant-general, of Iowa. this —— day of September, A. D. 1900.

C. T. JONES,
Clerk of the Supreme Court of the State of Iowa.

TREASURY DEPARTMENT,
OFFICE OF AUDITOR FOR THE WAR DEPARTMENT,
Washington, August 23, 1903.

SIR: This office is in receipt of your favor of the 19th instant, in relation to the acceptance of warrant in payment of settlement No. 16265, amounting to $2,271.50, and the effect of such acceptance in precluding the reconsideration of items disallowed in the above settlement.

Under act of Congress approved July 31, 1894, governing settlement of claims and accounts by the accounting officers of the Treasury, it is held that acceptance of payment of the amount allowed precludes revision by the Comptroller of the Treasury and by the Auditor of any item on account of which any allowance has been made.

By an examination of the statement of differences arising in above settlement, transmitted on the 13th instant, you will observe that the item of rent of fair grounds referred to having been allowed in part you are advised that acceptance of the settlement would, under the section of act of July 31, 1894, preclude the State from further prosecution of said item before any of the accounting officers of the Treasury.

Respectfully,

E. P. SEEDS, *Acting Auditor.*

Hon. LESLIE M. SHAW,
Governor of the State of Iowa, Des Moines, Iowa.

O

CONFIRMING CERTAIN FOREST LIEU SELECTIONS.

January 30, 1903.—Committed to the Committee of the Whole House on the state of the Union and ordered to be printed.

Mr. Eddy, from the Committee on the Public Lands, submitted the following

REPORT.

[To accompany H. R. 15985.]

The Committee on the Public Lands, to whom was referred the bill (H. R. 15985) to confirm certain forest lieu selections made under the act approved June 4, 1897 (30 Stats., 36), having had the same under consideration, beg leave to report it back with the recommendation that it do pass.

The circumstances which call for the remedial provisions contained in this bill are briefly these: The lands involved are in that part of the State of Montana, formerly embraced in an Indian reservation, which were opened to entry under the provisions of the act approved May 1, 1888. The act declared the said lands open to the operation of the laws regulating homestead entry, and to entry under the town site, coal land, desert land, and mineral land laws.

The beneficiaries of the pending measure are citizens of the United States, who have selected tracts in the above-described area in exchange for equal quantities of land situated in forest-reserve areas, which have been surrendered by them, as is provided may be done by the act of June 4, 1897 (commonly called the "forest-reserve law"), and its amending act of June 6, 1900. The lands permitted to be taken in exchange under these later acts were (act of 1897) "vacant land open to settlement;" (act of 1900) "vacant surveyed and nonmineral public lands which are subject to homestead entry."

Acting on the view that the lands selected were by the terms of the several pertinent acts subject to the exchange desired, they being lands "open to settlement," and lands "subject to homestead entry," application was made accordingly at the proper local land office, and the register and receiver being of the same opinion the selections were allowed and reported to the General Land Office.

The public records show that the General Land Office was for some time, and down to October 20, 1902, of the same opinion. Upon that date in Ramsey's case it was held to the contrary. Prior to that finding a number of patents had been issued upon selections of the same class of lands, and precisely similar to those which are the subject of this bill, and in August, 1899, a formal decision had been rendered by the Commissioner holding that the lands in this same area were open to other forms of appropriations under later statutes than those forms which the act of May 1, 1888, had provided. Patents were issued on like selections as late as October 16, 1902.

Under these circumstances the claimants rested securely on their titles, and very largely improved their tracts. It is shown to your committee that houses have been erected, fields have been fenced and plowed, and many other improvements of a lasting and expensive character made. Upon one of the exchanged tracts improvements costing $8,000 have been made. One of the exchange selections, consisting of 40 acres, has been subdivided as a village site, and many lots sold and improved with residence and other buildings, including one by a Presbyterian church. These exchange selections were most of them made in 1899, 1900, 1901, and 1902. Owing to the backward state of business in the General Land Office, though more than three years had elapsed in some instances since the date of selection, they had not been reached for final action when the Ramsey case was decided. Under the rules of the Land Department when selection is made a deed absolute of the forest tract offered in exchange must be made to the United States, duly recorded in the proper county, and delivered to the custody of the Department of the Interior.

There is no provision of law by which any officer of the United States is empowered to reconvey that title to the grantor on failure of the lieu selection.

The quantity of land involved in the provisions of this bill, as shown by an official report of the register and receiver, transmitted by the Commissioner of the General Land Office, is 16,408.01 acres.

The number of selections is 137, showing an average of about 120 acres to each. The actual selections are variant in size, being for 40, 80, 120, and 160 acre tracts, and a few for larger quantities. The tracts involved lie within the arid-land belt, are devoid of timber, and are useful for grazing purposes only.

A bill identical in terms (S. 6339) was before the Senate Committee on Public Lands and has been favorably considered. Since the report of that committee (Report No. 2357) contains the report of the Commissioner of the General Land Office and Secretary of the Interior on this bill it is made a part of this report and is as follows:

The Committee on Public Lands, to whom was referred the bill (S. 6339) to confirm certain forest lieu selections made under the act approved June 4, 1897 (30 Stat., 36), having had the same under consideration, beg leave to report it back with the recommendation that it do pass.

The necessity and justice of the proposed legislation are fully set forth in the report made upon this bill by the Secretary of the Interior and the Commissioner of the General Land Office, which is herewith printed.

DEPARTMENT OF THE INTERIOR,
Washington, December 18, 1902.

SIR: I have the honor to acknowledge the receipt, by reference from your committee for views, of a copy of S. 6339, entitled "A bill to confirm certain forest lieu selections made under the act approved June 4, 1897" (30 Stat. L., 36).

In answer, I transmit herewith a copy of the report on the bill by the Commissioner of the General Land Office dated the 13th instant, with inclosures.

For reasons stated, the Commissioner has recommended the passage of the bill, and I concur in the recommendation.

Very respectfully,   E. A. HITCHCOCK,
                                                                        Secretary.

The CHAIRMAN OF THE COMMITTEE ON PUBLIC LANDS, *Senate.*

DEPARTMENT OF THE INTERIOR, GENERAL LAND OFFICE,
Washington, D. C., December 13, 1902.

SIR: I am in receipt by reference, for early report in duplicate, with recommendation and return of paper, of a bill (S. 6339) to confirm certain forest lieu selections made under the act approved June 4, 1897 (30 Stat. L., 36).

The bill proposes to confirm all bona fide selections made under said act prior to the decision of this office "R," of October 20, 1902, in the case of George L. Ramsey, of lands in Montana which lie within the territory opened to entry under the provisions of the act approved May 1, 1888 (25 Stat. L., 113), "to ratify and confirm an agreement with the Gros Ventre, Piegan, Blood, Blackfeet, and River Crow Indians in Montana," where no other valid objection to the selection appears.

By the said decision of this office "R," of October 20, 1902, it was held that lands within the territory opened to entry by said act of May 1, 1888 (supra), were not subject to selection under the acts of June 4, 1897 (supra), and of June 6, 1900 (31 Stat. L., 614).

The act of May 1, 1888 (supra), provides:

"SEC. 3. That lands to which the right of the Indians is extinguished under the foregoing agreement are a part of the public domain of the United States, and are open to the operation of the laws regulating homestead entry, except section twenty-three hundred and one of the Revised Statutes, and to entry under the town-site laws and the laws governing the disposal of coal lands, desert lands, and mineral lands, but are not open to entry under any other laws regulating the sale or disposal of the public domain."

This clearly indicates the manner in which Congress intended the lands to be disposed of to the exclusion of all other forms of disposition.

The later act, of June 4, 1897 (supra), provides that the owner of a tract of land within the limits of a forest reserve may "relinquish the tract to the Government and may select in lieu thereof a tract of vacant land open to settlement not exceeding in area the tract covered by his claim or patent." And by the act of June 6, 1900 (supra), it was provided that selections under the act of June 4, 1897, "shall be confined to vacant surveyed and nonmineral public lands which are subject to homestead entry, not exceeding in area the tract covered by such claim and patent."

The act of May 1, 1888, is local, and limited in its operation to certain specified lands, and the restrictions made are in most positive terms; while the provisions of the acts of June 4, 1897, and June 6, 1900, are general and indicate no purpose to repeal the former act. The specific provisions of earlier acts that are local in their application are not repealed by implication by the general provisions of later acts. (30 L. D., 268, 536; 31 L. D., 243.)

It thus appears that the land within the territory opened to entry by the act of May 1, 1888, was not made subject to selection under the acts of June 4, 1897, and July 6, 1900.

But it is contended by the advocates of the bill, and, as to the facts, the contention appears to be sustained by the records, that by decision of this office "G," of August 2, 1899, the right of the State of Montana to make selections under the act of February 22, 1899 (25 Stat. L., 676), of lands within the limits in question was sustained; that the selections proposed to be confirmed, and other like selections, were allowed by the district land officers without objection, and that, prior to the said decision of October 20, 1902, in Ramsey's case, several such selections had been approved by this office and carried into patent. Such action, it is claimed, justified the selectors in believing the holding of the Department to be that the lands in question were properly subject to such selection. It is further claimed, and nothing appears to the contrary, that the selections sought to be confirmed were made in good faith, and in the belief that the lands were subject to such form of disposal; that the parties now holding under such selections have taken possession, and, in some instances, made considerable expenditures upon the land, and that a rejection of such selections would work considerable hardship.

Such contention is not without weight, and in view of the facts that the proposed confirmation is, by the bill, limited to selections made prior to October 20, 1902, an1 that the selections to be thereby affected are estimated to aggregate in area less than 16,500 acres, I respectfully recommend the passage of the bill.

Said bill (S. 6339) is returned herewith, with the affidavits and brief filed in this office in support thereof.

Very respectfully,

BINGER HERMANN,
Commissioner.

The SECRETARY OF THE INTERIOR.

It thus appears that the selections in question were made in accordance with the law as then construed and administered in the Land Department, that the Government holds the consideration for the lands selected, and unless the selections are saved from rejection the claimants will not only be deprived of the title to their base tracts, which they have conveyed to the Government by formal and duly recorded deeds (there being no existing law providing for the reconveyance thereof by the United States), but also of the tracts selected, and the valuable improvements made thereon in good faith and in the belief, based on the action of the Land Department, that the selections were valid and lawful.

These considerations strongly appeal for the prompt bestowal of the equitable relief provided for in the bill.

The committee recommend the following amendment:

Amend the title so as to read: " A bill to confirm certain forest lieu selections made under the act approved June fourth, eighteen hundred and ninety-seven."

O

ERECTION OF A LIGHT-HOUSE IN BOSTON HARBOR.

JANUARY 30, 1903.—Referred to the House Calendar and ordered to be printed.

Mr. LOVERING, from the Committee on Interstate and Foreign Commerce, submitted the following

REPORT.

[To accompany H. R. 16727.]

The Committee on Interstate and Foreign Commerce, to whom was referred the bill (H. R. 16727) for the erection of a light-house in Boston Harbor, having considered the same, report it with amendment, and as amended recommend its passage.

The bill thus amended has the approval of the Treasury Department, as will appear by the annexed letter, the amendment referred to therein having been incorporated in the bill as reported.

Strike out all after the enacting clause and insert the following:

That the Light-House Board be authorized to change the location of Broad Sound light, at the entrance to Broad Sound channel, in Boston Harbor, to such point or location in the vicinity as in their judgment shall be practicable and safe.

An act was approved June 28, 1902, establishing a light-house on the Northeast Grave, at the entrance to Broad Channel, in Boston Harbor, Massachusetts. On a careful examination it was found that the ledge at this point did not afford a secure foundation for such a structure. This bill authorizes the Light-House Board to change the location of the light to such other point in the vicinity as in its judgment shall be suitable.

The Acting Assistant Secretary of the Treasury has furnished the committee with the following report:

TREASURY DEPARTMENT, OFFICE OF THE SECRETARY,
Washington, January 17, 1903.

SIR: This Department has the honor to acknowledge the receipt of a letter from your committee of January 15, 1903, referring a copy of House bill No. 16727, for the erection of a light-house in Boston Harbor, and asking suggestions touching the merits of the bill and the propriety of its passage.

This Department, at the instance of the Light-House Board, to whom this bill was referred, and on which it has reported, begs leave to state that an appropriation was made by the act approved June 28, 1902, appropriating $75,000, and authorizing the construction, at a cost not exceeding $188,000, of a first-order light and fog signal at The Northeast Graves, on a granite tower, to mark the entrance to the new Broad Sound Channel, in Boston (Mass.) Harbor.

An examination of the ledges called The Graves for a site for the Broad Sound Channel light station, Boston Harbor, Massachusetts, made by the engineer of the Second light-house district on December 12, 1901, was made on the only day in a long period preceding and following that day when a landing could be effected on these ledges.

During the smooth weather of the past summer careful and exhaustive examination and survey were made of the ledge proposed for the site. This examination, made at an extremely low tide, much lower than the tide at the previous examination, shows that the rock on some sides contracts considerably at and below the extreme low stages of the tide. All the ledges of The Graves are more or less seamed and fissured, but the seams and fissures in that particular ledge, together with its contracted area and its shape, still more contracted under water, make it imprudent to build, and, indeed, forbids the building upon it, of a tall and massive tower, severely exposed to the shock of heavy seas.

The ledge known as The Northeast Grave was the most desirable for the site as regards location and because of all the ledges that rise above low water it is the nearest to the entrance to the new Broad Sound Channel.

In the entire group of ledges at The Graves, the ledge best adapted for the site as regards safety of the foundation is situated about 1,300 feet southwesterly from the ledge originally suggested.

The site which is now recommended is ample in area above low water and very extensive in area below it, and is less fissured than many of the other ledges. A good bed for the light-house tower can be formed by cutting the ledge down to about 2 feet below high water.

This Department, at the instance of the Light-House Board, recommends the adoption of this ledge for the site of the tower instead of The Northeast Grave, which is named in the act authorizing the construction of a light station at this point at a cost not exceeding $188,000. This Department, therefore, at the instance of the Light-House Board, recommends that Congressional authority be given to build the light-house tower upon such one of the group of ledges known as The Graves as the Light-House Board may select, inasmuch as that ledge which is selected has no name by which it can be definitely described. To this end the Department suggests that the clause in the sundry civil appropriation act approved June 28, 1902, now standing thus:

"BROAD SOUND CHANNEL, BOSTON HARBOR, MASSACHUSETTS: For constructing a first-order light and fog signal at The Northeast Graves, on a granite tower, to mark the entrance to the new Broad Sound Channel in Boston Harbor, seventy-five thousand dollars; and the Secretary of the Treasury is hereby authorized to enter into a contract for the construction of said light station at a total cost not exceeding one hundred and eighty-eight thousand dollars—"

be reenacted so that it will stand thus:

"BROAD SOUND CHANNEL LIGHT STATION, BOSTON HARBOR, MASSACHUSETTS: For constructing a first-order light and fog signal on one of the ledges known as The Graves, on a granite tower, to mark the entrance to the new Broad Sound Channel in Boston Harbor, seventy-five thousand dollars, and the Secretary of the Treasury is hereby authorized to enter into a contract for the construction of said light station at a total cost not exceeding one hundred and eighty-eight thousand dollars."

So that the Light-House Board may be enabled to establish the light tower on that one of the ledges constituting The Graves which it may deem best adapted for that purpose.

The appropriation, as before stated, of $75,000 was made by the act approved June 28, 1902, and it is found that a like sum will enable the board to do all the work upon this light station that is practicable before the end of the current year.

As House bill No. 16727 authorizes the construction of a first-order light and fog signal at The Graves, and as it appropriates $75,000 for continuing the work, and as it authorizes the making of a contract at a total cost not exceeding $188,000 for the whole work, this Department, at the instance of the Light-House Board, recommends its passage.

Respectfully,

H. A. TAYLOR,
Acting Secretary.

The CHAIRMAN OF THE COMMITTEE ON INTERSTATE
AND FOREIGN COMMERCE, HOUSE OF REPRESENTATIVES.

O

PROMOTION OF EDUCATION IN THE PUBLIC MARINE SCHOOLS.

JANUARY 30, 1903.—Referred to the House Calendar and ordered to be printed.

Mr. LOVERING, from the Committee on Interstate and Foreign Commerce, submitted the following

REPORT.

[To accompany H. R. 16846.]

The Committee on Interstate and Foreign Commerce, to whom was referred the bill (H. R. 16846) to promote education in the public marine schools, having considered the same report thereon with a recommendation that it pass.

This bill authorizes the President to appoint superintendents or instructors to public marine schools from the Revenue-Cutter Service, when in his judgment it can be done without detriment to the service. Heretofore such instructors have been appointed from the Navy, but owing to the fact that there are not sufficient officers in the Navy to make any detail for that service, it becomes necessary to draw upon the Revenue-Cutter Service when practicable.

O

RESERVATION AND SALE OF TOWN SITES ON THE PUBLIC LANDS.

JANUARY 30, 1903.—Committed to the Committee of the Whole House on the state of the Union and ordered to be printed.

Mr. EDDY, from the Committee on the Public Lands, submitted the following

REPORT.

[To accompany S. 6278.]

The Committee on the Public Lands, to whom was referred the bill (S. 6278) to extend the provisions of chapter 8, Title XXXII, of the Revised Statutes, entitled "Reservations and sale of town sites on public lands," to ceded Indian lands in the State of Minnesota, have had the same under consideration and report the bill with the recommendation that the same do pass.

Under the Nelson law (act of January 14, 1889, 25 Stat. L., 24) as amended by the Morris law (act of June 27, 1902) there is only one way by which the ceded lands on the Chippewa Indian reservations in Minnesota can be disposed of, and that is under the homestead law. The general town-site law (chap. 8, Title XXXII, R. S.) does not apply to these lands. The homesteader can not sell any of his land until he has proved up his homestead claim, and he can not prove up, under any circumstances, in less than fourteen months, by commuting his entry, and without commuting it takes five years; and it generally takes from six months to two years after final proof is made before the same can be approved by the General Land Office and patent issue.

This bill extends the provisions of the general town-site law to reservations. Under the provisions of this law the land desired to be used for town a site is platted into lots under the supervision and direction of the Interior Department and sold at public auction at not less than $10 per lot.

Under the original agreement with the Indians, as embraced in the Nelson law, the Indians are entitled to all the proceeds of the sale of the land and timber on these reservations.

This bill will not only be of great benefit to the people who want to start towns and engage in business on said ceded lands by enabling them to immediately get title from the Government of the United

States to the lots upon which they desire to make improvements, but it will also be of great benefit to the Indians, as they will realize more from the land if it is platted into town lots and sold at public auction under the provisions of the general town-site law than they will get under the homestead law, viz, $1.25 per acre.

It is urgently necessary for the development of these ceded reservations that this bill be passed, so that people who desire to start towns and engage in business along the railroads that are built or are under construction through these lands can get a good and valid title to town lots without waiting from two to six years for the homesteader to get title under the homestead law. The general town-site law provides for an equitable disposition of such portions of the public domain as are suitable for town sites, and in the opinion of your committee this bill should pass.

The salient points of the general town-site law are as follows:

1. Parties having founded or who desire to found a city or town on the public lands, under the provisions of sections 2382, 2383, 2384, 2385, and 2386 must file with the recorder of the county in which the land is situate a plat thereof, describing the exterior boundaries of the land according to the lines of public surveys, where such surveys have been made.

2. Such plat must state the name of the city or town, exhibit the streets, squares, blocks, lots, and alleys, and specify the size of the same, with measurements and area of each municipal subdivision, the lots in which shall not exceed 4,200 square feet, with a statement of the extent and general character of the improvements.

3. The plat and statement must be verified by the oath of the party acting for and in behalf of the occupants and inhabitants of the town or city.

4. Within one month after filing the plat with the recorder of the county a verified copy of said plat and statement must be sent to the General Land Office, accompanied by the testimony of two witnesses that such town or city has been established in good faith.

5. Where the city or town is within the limits of an organized land district a similar map and statement must be filed with the register and receiver. The exterior boundary lines of the town, if upon the land over which Government surveys have not been extended, may, when such surveys are so extended, be adjusted according to those lines, where it can be done without impairing vested rights.

6. In case the parties interested shall fail or refuse, within twelve months after founding a city or town, to file in the General Land Office a transcript map, with the statement and testimony called for by section 2382, the Secretary of the Interior may cause a survey and plat to be made of said city or town, and thereafter the lots will be sold at an increase of 50 per cent on the minimum price of $10 per lot.

7. When lots vary in size from the limitation fixed in section 2382 (4,200 square feet) and the lots, buildings, and improvements cover an area greater than 640 acres, such variance as to size of lots or excess in area will prove no bar to entry, but the price of the lots may be increased to such reasonable amount as the Secretary may by rule establish.

O

AMENDING BOUNDARIES OF FEDERAL JUDICIAL DISTRICTS IN ALABAMA.

JANUARY 30, 1903.—Referred to the House Calendar and ordered to be printed.

Mr. CLAYTON, from the Committee on the Judiciary, submitted the following

REPORT.

[To accompany H. R. 14512.]

The Committee on the Judiciary, to whom was referred the bill (H. R. 14512) to amend "An act to add certain counties in Alabama to the northern district therein and to divide the said northern district, after the addition of said counties, into two divisions, and to prescribe the time and places for holding courts therein, and for other purposes," approved May 2, 1884, have carefully considered the same and submit the following report:

This bill merely provides an additional place for holding court in the northern district of Alabama. No new officials are provided for and no additional expense is put upon the United States. The new place for holding the court is at Anniston, which is nearer every county included in the new division than is Birmingham or Huntsville, the other two cities where the United States courts of the district are held. Anniston is more accessible to the people included within the territory of the court for Anniston than either Birmingham or Huntsville. Anniston is a thriving and growing manufacturing city of perhaps 20,000 people and has many large industries, car works, pipe works and the like. The court at Anniston will, it is believed, save expense of mileage of witnesses and marshals in many cases. It will prove of public convenience. The counties composing the new division, namely, Calhoun, Talladega, Clay, Cleburne, Etowah, and Cherokee are growing rapidly in population and industries.

To the amended bill the United States district judges of Alabama make no objection.

The committee therefore recommend the adoption of the following amendment by way of substitute for H. R. 14512 and that the bill as thus amended do pass:

Strike out all after the enacting clause and insert in lieu of the words stricken out the following:

That section two of an act approved May second, eighteen hundred and eighty-four, entitled "An act to add certain counties in Alabama to the northern district therein, and to divide the said northern district, after the addition of said counties, into two divisions, and to prescribe the times and places for holding courts therein, and for other purposes," be amended so as to read as follows:

"Sec. 2. That the said northern district is hereby divided into three divisions, which shall be known as the northern, southern, and eastern divisions of the northern district of Alabama.   The southern division of said northern district shall include the counties of Sumter, Greene, Hale, Pickens, Tuscaloosa, Lamar, Fayette, Walker, Jefferson, Blount, Bibb, Shelby, Saint Clair, and Dekalb, and a term of the circuit court and district court of the United States for said northern district shall be held for said southern division at the city of Birmingham, in the said county of Jefferson, twice in each year at the times provided by law.

"The eastern division of said northern district shall include the counties of Etowah, Calhoun, Cleburne, Clay, Talladega, and Cherokee, and a term of the circuit court and the district court of the United States for said northern district shall be held for said eastern division in the city of Anniston, in the said county of Calhoun, twice in each year, on the first Mondays in May and November.   The remaining counties of of said northern district shall constitute the northern division thereof, and the terms of the circuit and the district courts of the United States for said northern district shall be held therein at the times and places prescribed by law."

Sec. 2. This act shall be in force from its passage, and all other provisions of the act aforesaid, approved May second, eighteen hundred and eighty-four, and all acts amendatory thereof not inconsistent with this act, shall remain in full force and effect and, so far as they are applicable, shall relate to and govern the eastern division of the northern district of Alabama.

Sec. 3. That a place for holding the courts for the eastern division of the northern district of Alabama shall be furnished to the Government free of cost by the county of Calhoun until other provision is made therefor by law.

Sec. 4. That all civil process issued against persons resident in said counties of Etowah, Calhoun, Cleburne, Clay, Talladega, and Cherokee and cognizable before the United States courts shall be made returnable to the courts respectively to be held at the city of Anniston, and all prosecutions for offenses committed in either of said counties shall be tried in the appropriate United States court at the city of Anniston.

Sec. 5. That all cases, civil and criminal, now pending on the dockets of the southern division of the northern district of Alabama, as herein created, shall remain on the docket of the southern division of said district and be tried in Birmingham, Alabama, unless transferred to the dockets of the eastern division of said district by consent of all the parties thereto entered of record, or unless transferred by the order of court for good cause shown.

Sec. 6. That the clerks of the circuit and district courts of the southern division of the northern district of Alabama shall maintain an office, in charge of themselves or a deputy, at said city of Anniston, which shall be kept open at all times for the transaction of the business of said courts.

O

EDWARD MONTGOMERY.

JANUARY 30, 1903.—Ordered to be printed.

Mr. MONDELL, from the Committee on Military Affairs, submitted the
following

ADVERSE REPORT.

[To accompany H. R. 2906.]

The Committee on Military Affairs, to whom was referred the bill
(H. R. 2906) to remove the charge of desertion against Edward Montgomery, as a private of Company K, Twenty-fifth Ohio Volunteer
Infantry, find that this soldier has no charge of desertion standing
against him as a member of that organization.

It is found, however, that Edward Montgomery deserted from Company C, Second Battalion Fifteenth United States Infantry, and no
good reason is given why the record should be changed in that regard,
as it is unquestionably correct. The views of the War Department
with regard to this case are indicated by a letter from the Secretary
of War under date of January 27, as follows:

[Third indorsement.]

WAR DEPARTMENT, January 24, 1903.

Respectfully returned to the chairman Committee on Military Affairs, House of
Representatives, inviting attention to the accompanying reports of the Chief of the
Record and Pension Office and Adjutant-General of the Army, dated December 10
and 15th ultimo, respectively.

The following remarks, transmitted to your committee under date of March 11,
1902, in the case of James Donnallan, are applicable to this case:

"This appears to be an ordinary example of a class of applications to Congress,
which I believe to be much against the public interest. The general statute authorizing the War Department to relieve soldiers from an unjust charge of desertion is
liberal and adequate. This bill proposes to relieve the person named from a just
charge of desertion, and to do it by requiring that the record be falsified; that an
honorable discharge be given to a man who is not entitled to it. The effect of this
class of legislation is to enable deserters to obtain pensions to which they are not
entitled and to degrade the honorable roll of men who fought the battles of the civil
war by placing upon the same list with them the dishonored names of men who ran
away. I earnestly hope the bill will not receive favorable consideration."

E. ROOT, Secretary of War.

If the soldier in question did not receive a local bounty at the time
of his enlistment in Company K, Twenty-fifth Ohio Volunteer Infantry, he is probably pensionable under the provisions of section 2 of the
act "Public—No. 42," approved July 1, 1902.

The committee report the bill back with the recommendation that it
do not pass.

ANTON ERNST.

JANUARY 30, 1903.—Ordered to be printed.

Mr. MONDELL, from the Committee on Military Affairs, submitted the following

ADVERSE REPORT.

[To accompany H. R. 8071.]

The Committee on Military Affairs, to whom was referred the bill (H. R. 8071) to remove the charge of desertion standing against Anton Ernst, as a private of Company K, Second Maryland Infantry Volunteers, report the same back with the recommendation that it do not pass.

A summary of the evidence in this case was made by the Committee on Military Affairs of the Senate in the Fifty-fifth Congress and is as follows:

It appears that Regina Ernst is the widow of Anton Ernst, who, according to the report of the War Department, was enrolled September 5, 1861, as a private in Company K, Second Regiment Maryland Infantry, to serve three years, and appears to have served faithfully until August 31, 1862. The muster roll for September and October, 1862, reports him "deserted from October 15, 1862." He never rejoined his company, although he owed service to September 5, 1864. The medical records furnish no information concerning him. In applying for a removal of the charge of desertion from the records by the War Department, Regina Ernst, on June 22, 1891, testified that in 1862, when she brought her husband home from the Army "under a furlough," he was an invalid, suffering from asthma, heart affection, and the effects of the hardships of the service; that he was never thereafter in a fit condition to return to the Army, and was an invalid on her hands for ten years after she brought him home, she having to support him during that time by her daily toil.

Under date of June 22, 1891, Comrade Boettger testified that he was second lieutenant of Ernst's company; that the said Ernst was a good, brave soldier, and never showed the slightest disposition to shirk his duty, always doing it manfully, and further corroborated so much of the widow's testimony as went to show that the soldier was suffering from a severe illness and was taken home "under a furlough."

On July 7, 1891, Angeline Wennig and Wendelin Kessler testified that they saw the soldier when he was brought home from the Army; that he was in very bad condition and seemed to be suffering from asthma and lung trouble, being hardly able to get his breath at all; that they were his neighbors and saw him frequently, and that he was never able to return to the service, being almost entirely helpless.

Philip Engerd, Daniel Cooper, and John Luber, on July 18, 1890, testified that they were members of the Second Maryland Infantry; that Ernst became very sick in the service, having a bad cough and difficulty in catching his breath—a wheezing way

*

of breathing that was extremely noticeable on account of his unusual height; that
his efforts to breathe caused him to bend over in a peculiar manner, and that he continued in this way "until discharge."

John Gerhard, on September 9, 1890, declared under oath that he served with Ernst,
who, during the latter part of his service, suffered from a severe hacking cough and
cold brought on by exposure in the service.

George Lintenberger, on July 16, 1891, testified that he served with Ernst, and
corroborates the statement of Gerhard.

John Luber, again, on July 17, 1891, corroborates the statements, substantially, of
the witnesses Angeline Wennig and Wendelin Kessler.

On August 29, 1891, Boettger, who also testified on June 22, 1891, stated, in reply
to a letter from the War Department, that after the battle of Antietam, Md.,
September 17, 1862, when the regiment was encamped at Pleasant Valley, Ernst
received a pass from First Lieut. F. W. Heck, then commanding the company, to go
through the lines, he remembering the incident distinctly on account of the soldier's
sickness. He further stated that he was not able to "diagnose fully" the nature of
the soldier's ailment, but was impressed at the time with the fact that he was a very
sick man; that he seemed to be suffering from asthma, lung affection, and general
debility.

In reply to a letter addressed by the War Department to Louis Fleckenstein, late
a lieutenant of Ernst's company, he stated under date of September 5, 1891, that at
and after the time said Ernst is shown by the records to have deserted he was an
able-bodied man, and that he was charged with desertion according to the rules and
discipline of war.

On July 17, 1891, Regina Ernst again testified that her husband was a well man
before his enlistment; that he was taken very ill while in the service and sent for
her; that he was suffering from asthma in a bad form and had treated himself, using
anything that was suggested to him, hoping to obtain relief; that after he went
home he was treated by affiant with "home remedies," as it was thought that a
physician "would not be of much use;" that the spells would come on suddenly and
he would suffer terribly; that he had no intention of deserting, and had he been
able would have returned to the service, but was not fit for any work after he went
home, and that it was impossible for her to furnish medical testimony.

Hannibald Gutman and Henry Freund testified, under date of October 12, 1891,
that this soldier was completely incapacitated from performing the duties of a soldier
from the time he arrived home until the day of his death, in October, 1875, and that
his wife supported him during this time; that Ernst was in good health when he
enlisted, but was in wretched health after his return from the Army.

On October 18, 1893, Regina Ernst, then being 62 years of age, made an affidavit,
which has been presented to your committee, wherein she stated that after the battle
of Sharpsburg, or Antietam, she went to the battlefield to see her husband, who had
been sick, but participated in the engagement, and that he carried the company
colors; that when she got to the camp, about September 20, 1862, she found her husband very poorly, so she went to Captain Seedsburg and got a pass to go home, and
her husband was so much worse next day that Lieutenant Heck went to the captain
and talked with him, and the captain told Heck to give a furlough to her husband
with a pass for eight days, which he did, and then said if he was no better at the end
of eight days tell him to stay till sent for; that she and her husband came to their
home in Baltimore. When his eight days' furlough expired he was no better, nor
did he ever get much better; that his disease soon developed into a severe case of
asthma.

and he never was able to get but a few blocks from their home or do any work, and
for twelve years was an invalid, and died of the disability in 1876; that he never did
desert in any way, but came away with his furlough, accompanied by her, and with
full consent and knowledge of his superior officers, and never was able to go back or
do any duty again during the remainder of his life.

On September 15, 1894, Wanobatl Gutman, John H. Hoeck, and John Luber each
testified of their personal knowledge that Anton Ernst was treated by one Dr. Troutman for several years after said Ernst returned home, in September, 1862, until the
death of Dr. Troutman, and corroborate the statement of the widow as to her husband's ill condition of health until his death, and the witness Gutman also corroborates the widow as to the fact that she supported her husband and family by her
own labors until the time of his death.

The committee is unable to find anything in this evidence to warrant
a favorable report in this case. No hospital record is found to support the claim that the soldier was ill or unfit for duty at the time he

left his command. There is no record to substantiate the statement that he received an eight days' furlough; there is no evidence that he made any special effort to communicate with his command or to inform the military authorities of his condition or of his whereabouts, during the two years during which he owed military service after deserting his command.

The soldier lived in Baltimore, where it would have been very easy, indeed, for him or his relatives or friends to have notified the military authorities of his condition. The only officer of his command who has made any statement in regard to the case is a lieutenant who states that—

At and after the time said Ernst is shown by the record to have deserted he was an able-bodied man; that he was charged with desertion according to the rules and discipline of war.

Although this statement was not made on oath and therefore is not entitled to the weight which would be given to a statement so made, it perhaps explains why none of Ernst's former officers were called upon for testimony in his behalf. The committee has before it many cases where practically the same claims are made and the same argument used for the removal of the charge of desertion. The law is very liberal at this time, and the charge of desertion can be removed where the soldier was prevented by his physical condition from returning to his command during the term for which he owed service.

O

DANIEL F. LEE.

JANUARY 30, 1903.—Committed to the Committee of the Whole House and ordered to be printed.

Mr. MONDELL, from the Committee on Military Affairs, submitted the following

REPORT.

[To accompany H. R. 15461.]

The Committee on Military Affairs, having had under consideration the bill (H. R. 15461) to remove the charge of desertion standing against Daniel F. Lee, late of Company H, Sixth Kansas Cavalry Volunteers, report the same back to the House with the recommendation that it do pass with the following amendment:

Strike out all after the enacting clause and insert in lieu thereof the following:

That Daniel F. Lee shall hereafter be held and considered to have been honorably discharged from the military service of the United States as a private of Company H, Sixth Kansas Cavalry Volunteers, on the first day of August, eighteen hundred and sixty-two, and the Secretary of War is hereby authorized and directed to issue a certificate of honorable discharge for him in accordance with the terms of this act: *Provided*, That no pay or other allowance shall be due or payable to any person by reason of the passage of this act.

It appears from the record in this case that Daniel F. Kee was enrolled November 20, 1861, and mustered into the service March 3, 1862, as a corporal in Company H, Sixth Kansas Cavalry Volunteers; that on April 30, 1862, he is reported as "absent, sick from wounds received in action;" that he rejoined his company prior to May 27, 1862, on which date he was promoted sergeant. The roll of August 31, 1862, shows that he left his command August 7, near Baxter Springs, Mo.; and the evidence filed in this case clearly establishes the following facts: That the soldier was living in Jasper County, Mo., in 1861, being at that time a boy 18 years of age; he was arrested as a Union sympathizer, escaped, went to Fort Scott, Kans., and joined the Sixth Kansas Cavalry.

On March 6, while scouting near Carthage, Mo., he was seriously wounded in the left hip.

After his recovery from his wound he continued to serve with this command, going as far south as Fort Gibson, in Indian Territory, which place was captured by the command, and rendered good service in the numerous engagements in which the command participated. In the latter part of September, 1862, he had a serious misunderstanding with his captain with regard to matters not in any way connected with his military service, with the result that he made repeated efforts to be transferred into another company. His statement is as follows:

The immediate cause of my leaving was a personal difficulty with my captain. At the place above named I was placed under arrest by order of Captain Mefford in a summary way; and no charge being preferred against me, I was released by order of Lieutenant-Colonel Jewel as soon as he found out I was in the guardhouse, and I went about my duties as a soldier. Captain Mefford then ordered that I should be disarmed whilst in camp, and made threats against my life, and told me that he would kill me. I knew the desperate character of the man and I wanted to get away from him. I made repeated efforts to get transferred to another company, but failed to get it.

I believed that if I stayed I would be killed or would have to kill my captain, and all hopes of getting away from the threatened danger without leaving, and acting under the advice of my comrades, I left as above stated. Captain took special delight in giving me the hardest service, and kept me acting as scout at all times, and would allow me no privileges whilst in camp. My health was not good. The wound in my leg was healed but painful, and it hurt me to be constantly in the saddle, and, in addition to the trouble with the wound, I was badly ruptured, which was caused by being thrown on the horn of the saddle whilst on parade at Cato. Captain Mefford knew of my wound and also of the rupture, but he never tried to favor me, but always gave me the worst of it.

Several of the soldier's comrades testified as to the trouble between him and the captain, who, it seems, was a man of rather violent temper. According to the testimony of several comrades, he had threatened to kill him. The soldier's testimony that he was unable to reenter the service is substantiated by the record of the War Department to the effect that when examined in December 16, 1864, in Jersey County, Ill., where he was then living under the name of Daniel Fields, he was exempted from military service on account of his physical condition, as per letter from the Chief of Record and Pension Office of the War Department, as follows:

RECORD AND PENSION OFFICE, WAR DEPARTMENT,
Washington, January 16, 1903.

DEAR SIR: In response to your telephonic request of to-day, relative to the draft of Daniel Fields, of Illinois, in 1864, I have the honor to advise you that the official records show that Daniel Fields was drafted in Illinois Township, Jersey County, Ill., December 16, 1864, but that he was not held to military service, he having been exempted from the operation of the draft by the board of enrollment of the tenth district of Illinois on January 21, 1865, because of scrotal hernia of the right side.

Very respectfully,

F. C. AINSWORTH,
Chief Record and Pension Office.

Hon. M. E. BENTON,
House of Representatives.

O

TO EFFECTUATE THE PROVISIONS OF THE ADDITIONAL ACT OF THE INTERNATIONAL CONVENTION FOR THE PROTECTION OF INDUSTRIAL PROPERTY.

JANUARY 31, 1903.—Referred to the House Calendar and ordered to be printed.

Mr. CURRIER, from the Committee on Patents, submitted the following

REPORT.

[To accompany H. R. 17085.]

The Committee on Patents, to whom was referred the bill (H. R. 17085) to effectuate the provisions of the additional act of the International Convention for the Protection of Industrial Property, having had the same under consideration, beg leave to report it back to the House without amendment and with the recommendation that it do pass.

The purpose of the first section of the bill is to carry into effect the provisions of an additional act concluded at Brussels, December 14, 1900, by the Convention for the International Protection of Industrial Property, which act modified the act of the convention of March 20, 1883.

The United States Government was represented at this convention, and the other Governments participating in the convention were Belgium, Brazil, Denmark, the Dominican Republic, Spain, France, Great Britain, Italy, Japan, Norway, Netherlands, Portugal, Servia, Sweden, Switzerland, and Tunis.

Article 4 of this convention is as follows:

Anyone who shall have regularly deposited an application for a patent of invention, of an industrial model, or design, of a trade or commercial mark, in one of the contracting States, shall enjoy for the purpose of making the deposit in the other States, and under reserve of the rights of third parties, a right of priority during the periods hereinafter mentioned.

In consequence the deposit subsequently made in one of the other States of the Union before the expiration of these periods can not be invalidated by acts performed in the interval, especially by another deposit, by the publication of the invention or its working, by the sale of copies of the design or model, by the employment of the mark.

The periods of priority above mentioned shall be twelve months for patents of invention and four months for designs or industrial models, as well as for trade or commercial marks.

Section 4887 of the Revised Statutes, as amended in 1897, required that an inventor should file his application in this country within seven months from the date of his application for a foreign patent, to avoid the bar which would otherwise be created by the issuance of a patent abroad prior to the issue of his patent in this country. The extension of this period of priority to twelve months instead of the term of seven months, which had been before provided, made it necessary that action should be taken by Congress to amend this section of the Revised Statutes to give effect to the provision of this article 4 of the convention, and section 1 of the present bill amends section 4887 so as to do this. The reciprocity provisions of this section will carry out the language of article 4, hereinbefore mentioned, and provide that the extension of the period of priority from seven months to twelve months is applicable only to citizens of countries which give our citizens a similar privilege.

The following countries have adopted legislation giving full force and effect to the provisions of the additional act, either in the form of a general act approving and giving force to the additional act or by a specific amendment to their laws providing for carrying into force the provisions of the additional act as regards the extension of the "delay and priority" to twelve months: Belgium (December 9, 1901; general act), Denmark (March 29, 1901; specific act), France (December 13, 1901; general act), Great Britain (August 17, 1901; specific act), Italy (December 12, 1901; general act), Japan (February 12, 1901; specific act), Netherlands (July 7, 1902; general act), Norway (March 29, 1902; specific act), Portugal (May 21, 1896; general act), Spain (May 16, 1902; specific act), Sweden (May 9, 1902; specific act), Switzerland (March 27, 1901; general act), and Tunis (December 13, 1901; general act).

Germany has not yet formally adhered to the convention, but your committee is informed that legislation is now pending, and will soon be adopted, giving full force and effect to the convention, including the additional act.

Brazil, Dominican Republic, and Servia were represented at the Brussels conference. None of these countries have as yet adopted legislation giving force and effect to the provisions of the additional act, but it is believed that all of these countries will soon ratify the act.

The last clause of section 1 of the bill, beginning at line 17, page 3, is intended to prevent this amended section 4887 from being construed to extend the period of two years, which is permitted by section 4886 prior to filing the application in this country.

Section 2 of this bill is intended to permit oaths executed in foreign countries, in applications for letters patent to be filed in this country, to be taken before judges or magistrates of those countries who are authorized to administer oaths there. The reason for this is that notaries public are not always authorized to administer oaths, and this extends the power to take the oath before any authorized local officers, proof of their authority being made by certificate of the foreign representatives of this country.

Section 3 of the bill, which amends section 4886 of the Revised Statutes, is intended to permit foreign executors or administrators to apply for patent upon the right of deceased foreign inventors, as at the present time it would be necessary for such officers to take out ancillary letters of administration for this purpose in this country.

Section 4 of this bill amends section 4902 of the Revised Statutes, which authorizes the filing of caveats, so as to extend its privileges to foreigners, as well as to citizens of the United States. This gives to the subject of caveats the same breadth as has been already given by section 4886 to the matter of applications for patents for inventions by foreigners; or, in other words, we no longer discriminate against foreigners in respect to caveats, as we have long since ceased to discriminate against them in respect to applications for letters patent.

O

SUNDRY CIVIL APPROPRIATION BILL.

FEBRUARY 2, 1903.—Committed to the Committee of the Whole House on the state
of the Union and ordered to be printed.

Mr. CANNON, from the Committee on Appropriations, submitted the
following

REPORT.

[To accompany H. R. 17202.]

In presenting the bill making appropriations for sundry civil
expenses of the Government for the fiscal year 1904, the Committee
on Appropriations submit the following in explanation thereof:

The estimates on which the bill is based will be found in the Book
of Estimates submitted to Congress for the fiscal year 1904, amounting
to $80,048,957.52, and in sundry House documents recommending
amounts aggregating $6,845,404, making a total of estimates con-
sidered by the committee in the preparation of the bill amounting to
$86,894,361.52.

The bill appropriates $78,017,929.10, being $8,876,432.42 less than
the regular and supplemental estimates and $17,365,870.97 more than
the appropriations for the current fiscal year.

The apparent excess recommended in the accompanying bill over
the appropriations for the current fiscal year, namely, $17,365,870.97,
is more than accounted for in the increase for river and harbor contract work, $14,464,393.49, and the amount of $3,000,000 which is
recommended to relieve the distress of the people in the Philippine
Islands.

Compared with the appropriations for the current fiscal year, the
amounts recommended in the accompanying bill are as follows: For
public buildings, within their present limit of cost, including quarantine stations, annual repairs, heating apparatus, vaults, safes, and
locks, and plans therefor, $10,429,412.79, an increase of $923,816.56.

For light-houses, beacons, and fog signals, $187,000, a reduction of
$626,300.

For the Light-House Establishment, $3,824,000, an increase of
$118,987.

For the Life-Saving Service, $1,837,110, an increase of $18,170.

For current expenses of the Revenue-Cutter Service, $1,450,000, an increase of $95,000.

For engraving and printing, $2,738,035, an increase of $537,435.

For the Coast and Geodetic Survey, $959,525, an increase of $131,000, which includes $120,000 for a new vessel.

For objects under the Smithsonian Institution, including International Exchanges, American Ethnology, Astrophysical Observatory, National Museum, and National Zoological Park, $423,400, a reduction of $32,000.

For the Fish Commission, $628,240, an increase of $132,100, which sum includes $99,800 for extension and improvement of various fish hatcheries and special repairs to the steamer *Albatross.*

For the Interstate Commerce Commission, $325,000, an increase of $15,000, which sum is given as an increase from $35,000 to $50,000 of the appropriation to enable the Interstate Commerce Commission to keep informed regarding compliance with the act to promote the safety of employees and travelers upon railroads.

For miscellaneous objects under the Treasury Department, $4,128,670, an increase of $705,755. Included under this head are items such as pay of assistant custodians and janitors for public buildings, $1,150,000, an increase of $50,000; furniture for public buildings, $300,000, an increase of $50,000; fuel, lights, and water for public buildings, $925,000, an increase of $35,000, and enforcement of the Chinese-exclusion act, $500,000, an increase of $300,000.

For the quarantine service, $325,240, an increase of $240.

For the prevention of epidemics the unexpended balance is reappropriated, which sum is estimated to be about $569,000.

For repairs of Interior Department buildings, $10,000, the same as appropriated for the current year.

For work at the Capitol and for general and special repairs thereto, $362,950, an increase of $312,950.

For improving the Capitol grounds, $25,000, an increase of $5,000.

For lighting the Capitol and grounds, $42,500, the same as the amount appropriated for the current year.

For expense of collection of revenue from sales of public lands, $1,335,500, an increase of $153,500.

For surveying the public lands, $341,480, a reduction of $2,000.

For the United States Geological Survey, $1,026,570, a reduction of $100,000.

For the Government Hospital for the Insane, $491,720, a reduction of $240,560.

For other miscellaneous objects under the Interior Department, including the Deaf and Dumb Institution, Howard University, national parks, and the introduction of reindeer into Alaska, $183,372, a reduction of $29,209.

For armories and arsenals, $274,500, a reduction of $71,200.

For buildings and grounds in and around Washington, D. C., $79,950, a reduction of $73,500.

For expenses of the Executive Mansion, $80,500, an increase of $40,500.

For lighting the Executive Mansion and public grounds, $20,000, an increase of $7,500.

For the Washington Monument, $11,500, an increase of $500.

For the improvement of rivers and harbors under contract authorizations contained in the river and harbor acts of 1892, 1896, 1899, and 1902, $20,233,150.99, an increase of $14,464,393.49.

For national cemeteries, headstones, etc., $294,380, a reduction of $56,434.

For the relief of distress in the Philippines, the sum of $3,000,000 is recommended as a new item.

For the construction of buildings at and the enlargement of military posts, including the erection of barracks and quarters for the artillery in connection with the adopted policy for seacoast defenses, and for the purchase of suitable sites for the latter, and for certain special objects under this title, $2,765,500, an increase of $705,450.

For enlargement of Governors Island, N. Y., $150,000, a reduction of $50,000.

For maintenance of the sewer and street system of Fort Monroe, Va., $9,437.50, an increase of $757.50.

For improvement of the Yellowstone National Park, $250,000, the same as was appropriated for the current fiscal year.

For national military parks, $170,000, a reduction of $95,000.

For artificial limbs, $152,000, a reduction of $362,000.

For other miscellaneous objects under the War Department, including the survey of Northern and Northwestern lakes, protecting the harbor of New York from injurious deposits, the California Débris Commission, and for Providence and Garfield hospitals, the amounts do not differ from the appropriations for the current fiscal year.

For the National Home for Disabled Volunteer Soldiers, $4,769,808, an increase of $1,025,139. The former sum includes $900,000 for completing the Mountain Branch Home, at Johnson City, Tenn., and $350,000 for completing the Battle Mountain Sanitarium, in South Dakota.

For continuing aid to State and Territorial Homes for the support of disabled volunteer soldiers, $950,000, being the same as the amount appropriated for the current fiscal year.

For payments of amounts certified to be due on account of pay of bounty to volunteer soldiers, including volunteers in the war with Spain, $500,000, being the same as the amount appropriated for the current fiscal year.

For demarcation and mapping of the boundary line between the United States and Canada, the sum of $100,000 is recommended as a new item.

For court-house, Washington, D. C., $5,000, an increase of $3,000.

For continuing construction of the penitentiary at Fort Leavenworth, Kans., $75,000, a reduction of $175,000.

For miscellaneous objects under the Department of Justice, $335,900, an increase of $10,900.

For expenses of United States courts, $5,933,280, an increase of $460,300.

For objects under legislative, $7,500; the same as was appropriated for the current fiscal year.

For Public Printing and Binding, $6,485,137.82, an increase of $968,137.82.

LIMITATIONS.

The following limitations touching certain branches of the public service for which appropriations are recommended and not heretofore imposed are submitted in the bill, namely:

On page 23, the following:

Hereafter, the purchase of specially prepared paper for the duplication of plans, and such other incidental expenses and supplies as the Secretary of the Treasury may deem necessary and specially order for the use of the office of the Supervising Architect, exclusively for the purpose of carrying into effect the various appropriations for public buildings, shall be paid for from and equitably charged against such appropriations, in accordance with existing practice.

On page 59, the following with reference to the lobster hatchery in Maine:

And said lobster hatchery shall be erected, furnished, and equipped in all of its details ready for operation within the limit of cost hereby extended to and fixed at twenty thousand dollars.

On page 71, the following:

The Secretary of the Treasury is authorized to sell such lands as have been or may hereafter be acquired by the United States by devise, upon such terms and after such public notice by advertisement as he may deem best for the public interest.

On page 85, the following:

The Secretary of the Interior may authorize such expenditure as may be necessary, not exceeding one thousand five hundred dollars, for rent of office accommodations in the city of Washington for the reclamation service, established by act approved June seventeenth, nineteen hundred and two, entitled "An act appropriating the receipts from the sale and disposal of public lands in certain States and Territories to the construction of irrigation works for the reclamation of arid lands."

On page 85, the following:

The Secretary of the Interior may authorize the purchase of such law books, books of reference, periodicals, engineering and statistical publications as are needed in carrying out the surveys and examinations authorized by the act of June seventeenth, nineteen hundred and two, entitled "An act appropriating the receipts from the sale and disposal of public lands in certain States and Territories for the construction of irrigation works for the reclamation of arid lands;" and such expenditures shall not exceed the sum of five hundred dollars.

On page 93, the following:

The officer in charge of public buildings and grounds may hereafter authorize the temporary use of a portion of the Monument grounds, or grounds south of the Executive Mansion, or other reservations in the District of Columbia for playgrounds for children and adults, under regulations to be prescribed by him.

On page 115, the following:

Private parties or companies doing business in the Yellowstone National Park under authority from the Government may be permitted, in the discretion of the Secretary of War, to use electricity furnished by the electric lighting and power plant of Fort Yellowstone and Mammoth Hot Springs at actual cost to the Government for operation, maintenance, and depreciation of the plant and ten per centum additional, under such regulations as may be prescribed by the Secretary of War.

On page 131, in connection with the sum recommended for completion of buildings at the new Branch of the Soldiers' Home at Johnson City, Tenn., the following:

The Board of Managers of the National Home for Disabled Volunteer Soldiers shall cause to be procured plans for all of said buildings and other objects mentioned in said act and authorized herein, based upon accurate estimates, and cause the same to be constructed or furnished within said estimates, to the end that said Mountain Branch shall be completed and ready for occupancy and operation in all of its details within the sums herein and heretofore appropriated for the establishment of said Mountain Branch.

On page 132, in connection with the sum recommended, to enable the Board of Managers of the National Home for Disabled Volunteer Soldiers to complete the Battle Mountain Sanitarium, at Hot Springs, S. Dak., the following:

The said board shall cause to be procured plans for all buildings authorized herein and in the act of May twenty-ninth, nineteen hundred and two, establishing said sanitarium, based upon accurate estimates, and cause the same to be constructed within said estimates, and cause to be furnished all other needful objects authorized herein or by said act, to the end that said sanitarium shall be completed and ready for occupancy and operation in all of its details within the sums herein and heretofore appropriated for the establishment of said sanitarium.

On page 150, the following:

The Secretary of War be, and he is, authorized and directed to furnish to each Senator, Representative, and Delegate of the Fifty-seventh Congress one set of the Official Records of the Rebellion, and to furnish two sets of said Records to such permanent libraries and educational institutions as may be designated by each of the said Senators, Representatives, and Delegates, and for this purpose there shall be used any volumes or parts of volumes remaining unsold or unclaimed by beneficiaries heretofore designated to receive them: Provided, That the Secretary of War may call upon the Public Printer to print and bind such additional numbers of the several volumes and maps as may be necessary to complete the sets herein provided for, and that when such additional volumes shall have been printed the plates used in printing the sets now and heretofore authorized shall be destroyed.

COMPARATIVE STATEMENT.

Submitted herewith as a part of this report is a comparative statement exhibiting in detail the appropriations made by the sundry civil act for 1903, the amounts in the regular estimates for 1904, and the amounts recommended for 1904.

Recapitulation of Sundry Civil Bill for 1904.

Object.	Appropriations for 1903.	Estimates for 1904.	Recommended for 1904.	
			Amounts.	Page of bill.
Alaska, reindeer for	$25,000.00	$25,000.00	$25,000.00	87
Seal fisheries	12,950.00	17,950.00	12,950.00	69
Protecting salmon fisheries in	7,000.00	7,000.00	7,000.00	70
Relief of native inhabitants of	15,000.00	15,000.00	15,000.00	70
Traveling and incidental expenses	15,000.00	10,500.00	10,000.00	138
Transportation of destitute citizens from		4,055.10		
Alaska Commercial Company, payment to		5,000.00		
Apache prisoners at Fort Sill, Okla	4,000.00			
Appraisers, local, expenses meetings of	1,200.00	1,200.00	1,200.00	69
Alien contract-labor law, enforcement of	150,000.00	150,000.00	150,000.00	71
Antietam battlefield	3,000.00	4,500.00	4,500.00	110
Maps		5,600.00		
Armories and arsenals	345,700.00	884,436.00	274,500.00	91
Army Medical Museum		13,000.00		
Arrears of pay and allowances, war with Spain	200,000.00	300,000.00	200,000.00	134
Artificial limbs and appliances for soldiers	516,000.00	154,000.00	164,000.00	118
Appropriations, preparing statement of	2,000.00		2,000.00	148
Assistant custodians and janitors, public buildings	1,100,000.00	1,186,531.50	1,150,000.00	65
Astrophysical Observatory	15,000.00	15,000	15,000.00	45
Atlanta, Ga., penitentiary	100,000.00			
Attorney-General, opinions of, publication				135
Attorney-General, traveling and miscellaneous expenses	7,500.00	7,500.00	7,500.00	137
Botanic Garden	5,500.00	5,500.00	5,500.00	149
Buildings and grounds in Washington	153,450.00	81,950.00	79,950.00	93-98
California Débris Commission	15,000.00	15,000.00	15,000.00	119
Canceling United States securities	200.00	200.00	200.00	65
Capitol, building and grounds, lighting	42,500.00	42,500.00	42,500.00	74
Building, repairs, etc	50,000.00	50,000.00	362,950.00	73
Cleaning works of art in	1,500.00			
Flags for	100.00	100.00	100.00	73

Item				
Capitol, repairs of fire-engine house and stables	1,500.00	1,500.00	1,500.00	74
Steel shelving, Senate library	9,750.00			73
Grounds, improvement of	20,000.00			
Capitol police (E. D. Turnure)	900.00			
Census Office		1,178,660.00		115
Chickamauga and Chattanooga Park	50,000.00	40,000.00	40,000.00	70
Chinese-exclusion act, enforcement of	200,000.00	500,000.00	500,000.00	134
Claims, back pay and bounty to soldiers	300,000.00	300,000.00	300,000.00	35–45
Coast and Geodetic Survey	828,525.00	972,325.00	959,525.00	
Commissioner of Railroads, office of	6,220.00			
Court-house, District of Columbia, repairs	2,000.00	5,000.00	5,000.00	135
Crater Lake National Park (for 1903 in general deficiency act)	2,000.00	3,000.00	2,000.00	87
Custody of dies, rolls, and plates	11,000.00	11,000.00	11,000.00	65
Deaf and Dumb Institution	64,791.00	91,501.00	61,500.00	90
Defending suits in claims	50,000.00	50,000.00	50,000.00	136
Defense of suits before Spanish Treaty Claims Commission	112,000.00	112,000.00	112,000.00	136
Defense in Indian depredation claims	52,000.00	52,000.00	52,000.00	138
Denver mint, machinery and furniture			125,000.00	64
Distinctive paper for United States securities	131,000.00	243,076.20	243,000.00	34
Engraving and printing	2,200,600.00	2,738,085.00	2,738,035.00	45
Ethnology, American	50,000.00	60,000.00	40,000.00	47–60
Fish Commission	496,140.00	647,420.00	628,240.00	114
Fort Monroe, Va., sewer system, etc.	8,680.00	9,437.50	9,437.50	
Fort Mott, N. J., road to		10,000.00		
Fuel, lights, and water, public buildings	890,000.00	989,400.00	925,000.00	67
Furniture, public buildings	250,000.00	384,000.00	300,000.00	66
Garfield Hospital	69,000.00		19,000.00	119
General Grant National Park	2,500.00	2,000.00	2,000.00	87
Garrett, Thomas G., payment to	300.00			
Geological Survey (including $60,000 for 1903 in deficiency act)	1,126,570.00	1,176,920.00	1,026,570.00	82–86
Gettysburg Military Park	75,000.00	60,000.00	60,000.00	116
Governors Island, N. Y., buildings and improvements (for 1903 in general deficiency act)				
Grant memorial	200,000.00	400,000.00	150,000.00	114
Howard University	60,000.00			
Hospital for the Insane	42,100.00	38,500.00	39,100.00	90
Home for Disabled Volunteer Soldiers (including $20,000 for 1903 in special act)	732,280.00	458,720.00	491,720.00	88–90
Home for soldiers in States	3,754,669.00	4,089,458.00	4,769,808.00	120–133
Hot Springs Reservation, Ark	950,000.00	950,000.00	950,000.00	133
	47,562.00	30,500.00	30,500.00	86

Recapitulation of Sundry Civil Bill for 1904—Continued.

Object.	Appropriations for 1903.	Estimates for 1904.	Recommended for 1904.	
			Amounts.	Page of bill.
Independent Treasury, contingent expenses	$200,000.00	$220,000.00	$220,000.00	62
Inspector of supplies for public buildings	5,000.00	5,000.00	5,000.00	66
Inspector of furniture, salary and expenses	4,500.00	5,000.00	4,500.00	66
Insular and Territorial expenses, Department of Justice	25,000.00	25,000.00	25,000.00	139
Interior Department and Pension buildings	10,000.00	10,000.00	10,000.00	73
International exchanges, Smithsonian Institution	26,000.00	29,800.00	26,000.00	45
Inter-State Commerce Commission	285,000.00	325,000.00	325,000.00	60
Justice, Department of, rent		20,400.00	20,400.00	139
Justice, Department of, care of rented buildings	8,000.00	8,000.00	8,000.00	139
Lands and other property of the United States	400.00	400.00	400.00	71
Leavenworth, Kans., penitentiary	250,000.00	75,000.00	75,000.00	135
Life-Saving Service	1,818,830.00	1,837,110.00	1,837,110.00	29–32
Light-houses, beacons, and fog-signals (including $25,000 in special act)	813,300.00	187,000.00	187,000.00	24
Light-House Establishment	3,705,013.00	3,112,965.48	3,824,000.00	25–29
Louisiana Purchase Exposition	1,048,000.00	4,324,886.00		
Malloy, William M., payment to	100.00			
Maps for War Department	5,000.00	5,000.00		
Mexican boundary line, inspection and repair of	5,000.00	5,000.00		117
Military posts, enlargement of	2,060,050.00	4,605,300.00	2,765,500.00	112
Mission Indians, California, counsel for	1,000.00	1,000.00	1,000.00	138
Moieties, compensation in lieu of	20,000.00	25,000.00	20,000.00	69
Mount Rainier National Park		3,000.00		
National cemeteries, headstones, etc	257,814.00	280,880.00	244,880.00	108
National currency, expenses of	24,000.00	24,155.80	24,000.00	65
National Museum	284,400.00	289,400.00	252,400.00	46
New York Harbor, preventing deposits in	70,260.00	120,260.00	75,260.00	119
North American Transportation Company, payments to		5,158.00		
Paper and stamps, internal revenue	50,000.00	65,000.00	65,000.00	62
Paris award, enforcing conditions of			100.00	70
Philippine Islands, relief in	100.00	100.00	3,000,000.00	111

Item				Page
Portrait of William McKinley	2,500.00			
Prosecution and collection of claims	500.00	500.00	500.00	
Prosecution of crimes	45,000.00	45,000.00	45,000.00	138
Providence Hospital	69,000.00		19,000.00	137
Public buildings, construction of, including marine hospitals and quarantine sta- [acts)]	9,505,596.23	10,264,183.79	10,429,412.79	118
500	1,182,000.00	1,537,500.00	1,335,500.00	1–24
sales of	343,480.00	341,480.00	341,480.00	74–78
coin	5,517,000.00	6,235,137.82	6,485,137.82	78–82
vate land claims, etc	100,000.00	100,000.00	100,000.00	149–154
e laws	4,000.00	4,000.00	4,000.00	62
violations of intercourse acts and frauds	325,000.00	365,240.00	325,240.00	137
e Service	3,000.00	6,000.00	6,000.00	71
Recoinage of gold coins	2,500.00	2,500.00	2,500.00	63
Repair of water pipes	1,355,000.00	1,450,000.00	1,450,000.00	98
Revenue-Cutter Service	92,500.00			32
Revenue-cutter steamers	5,768,757.50	18,570,339.33	20,233,150.99	99–108
River and harbor contract work authorized by law	30,000.00	1,750.00	1,750.00	64
San Francisco Mint, new machinery	1,000.00			
Sealing and separating United States securities	1,800.00			86
Senate, rent for storage of documents	10,000.00	15,000.00	10,000.00	116
Sequoia National Park	5,500.00			
Sherman statue	40,000.00	20,000.00	20,000.00	64
Shiloh Military Park	5,000.00	9,000.00		117
Shipping service, contingent expenses	1,565.00	1,570.00	1,570.00	87
Spanish Claims Commission	150,000.00	175,000.00	150,000.00	68
Special witness, destruction of United States securities	608.00	2,272.00	2,272.00	98
Survey of Northern and Northwestern lakes	100,000.00	200,000.00	125,000.00	63
Supreme Court reports	1,500.00	1,500.00	1,500.00	110
Suppressing counterfeiting and other crimes	2,700,000.00	15,000.00	15,000.00	111
Telegraph line connecting Capitol and Departments	15,000.00	40,000.00	40,000.00	118
Tobacco, rebate on	80,000.00			63
Transportation of minor coin	10,000.00	5,000.00	5,000.00	
Transportation of soldiers' remains from abroad	100.00	100.00	100.00	
Transportation of remains of civil employees of Army who die abroad and of soldiers who die on transports	100,000.00	125,000.00	100,000.00	
Transportation of reports and maps to foreign countries				
Transportation of silver coin				
Turner, William B., payment to				
United States and Canada, boundary line	77.40		100,000.00	134

Recapitulation of Sundry Civil Bill for 1904—Continued.

Object.	Appropriations for 1903.	Estimates for 1904.	Recommended for 1904. Amounts.	Page of bill.
United States courts, expenses of (including $16,200 for 1903 in general deficiency act)	$5,472,980.00	$5,949,940.00	$5,933,280.00	139-148
Vicksburg Military Park	100,000.00	50,000.00	50,000.00	117
Washington Monument	11,020.00	11,520.00	11,520.00	98
White House, ... of	40,000.00	40,000.00	90,500.00	98
... buil idg ...	65,196.00			
...	475,445.00			
Rent of temporary office	2,000.00			
White House and public grounds, lighting	17,180.00	17,180.00	24,680.00	96
Yellowstone ... ark, ..., etc. (including $15,000 for 1903 in general deficiency act)	22,800.00	30,745.00	5,000.00	86
Improvement	250,000.00	250,000.00	250,000.00	115
... Nati nl Park	6,000.00	12,850.00	6,000.00	86
Zoological Park	100,000.00	160,000.00	90,000.00	47
Total	60,652,059.13	80,048,957.52	78,017,929.10	

O

HANNAH W. MILLARD.

FEBRUARY 2, 1903.—Committed to the Committee of the Whole House and ordered
to be printed.

Mr. GRAFF, from the Committee on Claims, submitted the following

REPORT.

[To accompany H. R. 3527.]

The Committee on Claims, to whom was referred the bill (H. R.
3527) for the relief of Hannah W. Millard, have had the same under
consideration and report the bill back favorably.

The bill provides for the payment by the Secretary of the Treasury
to Hannah W. Millard, widow of the late Capt. M. V. B. Millard, of
Fall River, Mass., the sum of $4,500 in full compensation for the loss of
his voyage as master of the steamer *Belvedere* in the Arctic Ocean during
the season of the year 1897, whereby he was detained on the 21st day
of September of said year in caring for and preserving the lives of the
crews of the steamers *Orca* and *Jessie Freeman*.

Your committee recommends that the bill do pass.

The evidence submitted in this claim shows the following state of
facts. The beneficiary in this bill is the widow of the late Capt. M. V.
B. Millard, who, as a master of the steamer *Belvedere*, was engaged
in the perilous occupation of whaling in the Arctic Ocean during the
season of 1897. In September of that year, while near the steamers
Orca and *Jessie Freeman*, these two vessels were caught and crushed
by the ice which had set in two weeks earlier than usual in those seas.
They set signals of distress, and the *Belvedere*, which was making for
open water with a clear passage ahead, stopped and took on board the
crews of these two vessels, causing a delay of several hours. In the
meantime the ice closed in between the *Belvedere* and open water and
she was held fast in the Arctic Ocean until the next summer, her captain thereby losing the profits of an entire season. It is the purpose
of this bill to reimburse the widow of Captain Millard for the loss so
sustained by him in consequence of stopping to rescue the crews of
the *Orca* and *Jessie Freeman*.

Your committee think that the amount recommended, $4,500, is a moderate estimate of that season's profits of the captain of a whaling ship in those waters, made upon actual catches that season by other ships in those waters, and believe that its allowance in this case would be both an act of justice and a due recognition by Congress of heroism in saving the lives of the crews of the two wrecked vessels at the risk of his own and to his own financial detriment.

Many precedents for such action on the part of Congress will be found in the accompanying letter of the Secretary of the Treasury relative to this case.

Your committee also attach hereto the statement of Captain Millard and the affidavit of Capt. Stephen F. Cottle, second officer of the *Belvedere* at the time referred to; further, correspondence of the State Department touching provisions to be made for the care of the shipwrecked crews, and letters from Capts. Joshua G. Baker and Ezra B. Lapham, of South Dartmouth, Mass., giving estimates of the profits of a captain for that season's catch in the Arctic Ocean.

TREASURY DEPARTMENT, OFFICE OF THE SECRETARY,
Washington, D. C., March 28, 1900.

SIR: I have the honor to acknowledge the receipt of your letter dated the 22d instant, relating to H. R. 7761, for the relief of Hannah W. Millard.

The master of the ship *Belvedere* sets forth the facts substantially as follows:

"This is to certify that on the 21st of September, 1897, the whaling ship *Belvedere*, of which I was captain, was located in the Arctic Ocean, 10 miles north of Point Belcher. We were on our way west to the whaling grounds in company with the steamers *Orca* and *Jessie Freeman*. During my previous experience in arctic whaling the ice had usually set in about the 1st of October. This season was an exception, as it came in about two weeks earlier than usual. On the above date the situation was as follows: The *Orca* was leading through the drift ice, when it closed in and she was crushed. Her crew numbered between the *Belvedere* and *Jessie Freeman*. At this time we were within 3 miles of open water. The ice, however, had closed, rendering it impossible for us to continue in the course we were going.

"We now turned back toward the Sea Horse Islands, intending to make a harbor. On the way to that place an opening was seen from the *Belvedere* between the ice pack and the land leading to open water. The *Belvedere* was so situated that she could have reached open water by this passage. At this time the ice closed in on the *Jessie Freeman*, and she set signals of distress asking us to stay by them. We found she was leaking badly, and took her crew of 45 men on board; also the other half of the *Orca's* crew. This took several hours, and in the meantime the passage to open water had closed, making it impossible for us to escape. Although there was every possibility of getting out with my own ship, I felt it my duty to stand by these men, but by so doing I lost all chances of escape, as the ice had set at this place for the winter, and we were compelled to stay where we were for the following ten months. These men remained on my ship for two weeks, when they were sent to the Cape Smythe whaling and trading station. There had been a Government station at Cape Smythe for the relief of whalemen in an emergency of this nature, but it was given up a few months previous to this disaster. Had it been there I could have escaped with my ship, as it would not have been necessary for me to have stopped to save these men. I have not only been censured by the owners of the vessel, through pursuing the course that I did in this matter, but also lost the season's whaling, they claiming that I was not sent there to save shipwrecked men, as the United States Government provided a vessel for that purpose. At the time of this occurrence the revenue cutter *Bear* was hundreds of miles away and no possibility of any communication with her, so that the folly of any such view is obvious."

Capt. Stephen H. Cottle makes affidavit that he was second officer of the *Belvedere*, and that he believes they would have reached open water but for the fact that they received signals of distress from the steamers *Orca* and *Jessie Freeman* at the time of the disaster on the 21st of September, 1897.

You state that your committee would like to have the "opinion of this Department on the claim," and "also the facts as to the payment of claims similar to this in case this claim should be deemed worthy of favorable consideration."

From the above statement of facts, the case seems to be analogous to that of the vessels *Midas*, *Progress*, *Lagoda*, *Daniel Webster*, and *Europa*, which abandoned their business of whale catching and rescued 900 seamen in the Arctic seas. An appropriation was made in the case by the act of February 21, 1891, chapter 263, 26 Stat. United States. The statute specified the manner in which the amount appropriated should be distributed among the owners, the officers, and crews.

Another case somewhat analogous was that of the steamer *Amsterdam*, in which money was appropriated for the dependent relatives of the officers and crew who lost their lives, as stated by the act, "in a heroic effort to save the master and crew of the shipwrecked American schooner *Maggie E. Wells*," and for the sole survivor of the rescuing party (chapter 182, volume 28, page 992). Still another case is that of the whaling schooner *Franklin*, for whose agent and managing owner, the captain and crew, money was appropriated by the act of February 21, 1891 (chapter 258, 26 Stat. L.), the amount representing the estimated loss in the case of the *Franklin*, by its "rescue of the passengers and crew, 26 persons, after they had abandoned at sea the burning steamer *Lorenzo D. Baker*, of Boston." The voyage of the *Franklin* was broken up. Other cases are those of William Lewis, of New Bedford, owner of the whaling vessel *North Star*, for whom an appropriation was made by the Forty-ninth Congress (volume 22, chapter 143, page 620), the master being specially compensated, and of the crew of the schooner *Era*, of New London, for whom an appropriation was asked.

This Department has reason to believe that some correspondence upon the case is on file in the Department of State.

Assuming the circumstances to be as set forth in the petition, the allowance after due proof as to the facts stated of compensation to the master or his widow would tend to induce the exercise of humanity and to promote endeavor to save life in such cases. The question, however, whether an allowance should be made in the present case, and if so, to what extent, is exclusively for the consideration of Congress.

I return herewith the papers accompanying your communication.

Respectfully,

L. J. GAGE, *Secretary*.

Hon. H. S. BOUTELL,
Chairman Subcommittee on Claims,
House of Representatives, Washington, D. C.

This is to certify that on the 21st of September, 1897, the whaling ship *Belvedere*, of which I was captain, was located in the Arctic Ocean, 10 miles north of Point Belcher.

We were on our way west to the whaling grounds in company with the steamers *Orca* and *Jessie Freeman*.

During my previous experience in Arctic whaling the ice had usually set in about the 1st of October. This season was an exception, as it came in about two weeks earlier than usual.

On the above date the situation was as follows: The *Orca* was leading through the drift ice, when it closed in and she was crushed. Her crew was divided between the *Belvedere* and *Jessie Freeman*. At this time we were within 3 miles of open water. The ice, however, had closed, rendering it impossible for us to continue in the course we were going.

We now turned back toward the Sea-Horse Islands, intending to make a harbor. On the way to that place an opening was seen from the *Belvedere* between the ice pack and the land leading to open water.

The *Belvedere* was so situated that she could have reached open water by this passage. At this time the ice closed in on the *Jessie Freeman*, and she set signals of distress, asking us to stand by them. We found she was leaking badly, and took her crew of 45 men on board; also the other half of the *Orca's* crew. This took several hours, and in the meantime the passage to open water had closed, making it impossible for us to escape.

Although there was every possibility of getting out with my own ship, I felt it my duty to stand by these men, but by so doing I lost all chances of escape, as the ice had set at this place for the winter, and we were compelled to stay where we were for the following ten months. These men remained on my ship for two weeks, when they were sent to the Cape Smythe whaling and trading station.

There had been a Government station at Cape Smythe for the relief of whalemen in an emergency of this nature, but it was given up a few months previous to this disaster. Had it been there I could have escaped with my ship, as it would not have been necessary for me to have stopped to save these men.

I have not only been censured by the owners of the vessel, through pursuing the course that I did in this matter, but also lost the season's whaling, they claiming that I was not sent there to save shipwrecked men, as the United States Government provided a vessel for that purpose.

At the time of this occurrence the revenue cutter *Bear* was hundreds of miles away, and no possibility of any communication with her, so that the folly of any such view is obvious.

A captain's share of an average Arctic whaling season is $8,000. The United States Government having abandoned its station and I having suffered the above-stated loss, I hereby request it to pay me this sum.

As a precedent I cite the burning of the U. S. S. *Rogers* at St. Lawrence Bay in 1882. In this instance the crew was taken off by the *North Star*, a steam whaler, and the owners were paid the sum of $20,000.

I understand that the owners of the *Belvedere* have filed a claim for a sum of money. If the United States Government can allow any money for this loss, I wish my portion to be paid to me individually.

Capt. M. V. B. MILLARD.

This is to certify that I was second officer of the whaling steamer *Belvedere*, of which Capt. M. V. B. Millard was master, during the season of the year 1897.

I hereby state that I believe we should have reached open water but for the fact that we received signals of distress from the steamers *Orca* and *Jessie Freeman* at the time of the disaster, on the 21st day of September.

Capt. STEPHEN F. COTTLE.

Subscribed and sworn to before me this 16th day of February, 1900.

[SEAL.]   O. C. PRATT,
          Notary Public in and for the City and County of San Francisco, Cal.

CITY AND COUNTY OF SAN FRANCISCO, *State of California, ss.:*

On this 16th day of February, in the year 1900, before me, O. C. Pratt, a notary public in and for the city and county of San Francisco, State of California, residing therein, duly commissioned and qualified, personally appeared Capt. Stephen F. Cottle, known to me to be the person whose name is subscribed to the within instrument, and acknowledged to me that he executed the same.

In witness whereof I have hereunto set my hand and affixed my official seal, at my office in the city and county of San Francisco, the day and year in this certificate first above written.

[SEAL.]   O. C. PRATT,
          Notary Public in and for the said City and County of San Francisco, Cal.

No. 50.]   CONSULATE OF THE UNITED STATES,
                                          Victoria, British Columbia, April 4, 1898.

SIR: I have the honor to state that Geo. F. Tilton, third officer United States steam whaler *Belvidere*, wrecked in the ice off Point Barrow, Alaska, arrived at Nanaimo, British Columbia, this morning, on steamer *Albion*, en route for Portland, Oreg., and San Francisco, and made the inclosed statement before the United States consular agent at Nanaimo concerning 305 shipwrecked American seamen, which is herewith inclosed.

I have the honor to be, sir, your obedient servant,

ABRAHAM E. SMITH, Consul.

Hon. A. A. ADEE,
     Assistant Secretary of State, Washington, D. C.

NANAIMO, BRITISH COLUMBIA, *April 4, 1898.*

I, George F. Tilton, third officer of the steam whaler *Belvedere*, volunteered to go south from Point Barrow to report the condition of 305 shipwrecked men and to procure assistance at the earliest possible moment.

I left Point Barrow on the 22d of October, 1897, and traveled south by dog teams, with the assistance of natives, to 50 miles north of St. Michael, where I met Lieutenant Jarvis, of the U. S. revenue cutter *Bear*, on his way to Cape Prince of Wales, to get the reindeer for the relief expedition.

From him I received instructions to proceed south at the expense of the Government to San Francisco, and he wrote a letter to Colonel Randall, at Fort St. Michael, instructing him to put me in the hands of the Government.

I have with me duplicates of all bills contracted on the road, and wish to have instructions as to what I am to do on my arrival at San Francisco.

The following ships are wrecked or in such condition that they would be crushed by the ice within a short time: *Belvedere, Orca, Jesse H. Freeman, Rosera, Fearless, Newport, Jeanie,* and *Wanderer.*

The crews of the above ships number 298 men, and in addition there are 7 men belonging to the *Navarch* who were saved from the wreck after the captain and his wife had been taken out by the *Bear.*

The condition of these men is as follows: They are living at the whaling station owned by Lebius (?) & Co., of San Francisco, and at the refuge station now in charge of Michael Henry, and the only supplies which they have are those turned over to them by Lebius (?) & Co. and what little was saved from the ships. This will give the men two short meals a day until July 1, but they must be short ones to last out that long.

I also have with me the guide, Mr. Poltoff, that Lieutenant Jarvis carried in with him, and he gave him to me to come out with. I also have two natives from Point Hope.

GEO. F. TILTON,
Third Officer of Ship Belvedere.

Signed before me this 4th day of April, 1898.
[SEAL.]

GEO. L. SCHETKY,
United States Consular Agent.

VICTORIA, BRITISH COLUMBIA, *April 5.*

Hon. A. A. ADEE,
Assistant Secretary of State, Washington.

George F. Tilton states he left Point Barrow to secure help October 22 last. Was ordered by Lieutenant Jarvis, of the *Bear*, whom he met near St. Michaels, to go south to San Francisco to secure aid from Government. He says the American whalers *Belvedere, Orca, Jessie H. Freeman, Ronera, Fearless, Newport, Jeanie,* and *Wanderer* were wrecked or so crushed in ice that they would be short time. There are 305 men of these ships' crews hemmed in at Refuge Station. They have barely enough provisions for two meals a day till July 1. Tilton's address at San Francisco is 26 East street. He will be there Thursday and wants instructions. Original full text of Tilton's report mailed to Department last night.

ABRAHAM E. SMITH,
United States Consul.

SOUTH DARTMOUTH, MASS., *May 4, 1900.*

DEAR SIR: Replying to yours of the 16th of April, would say that in my opinion and from my best observation I should think that $5,000 would not be an exorbitant compensation for the captain's season referred to.

For this reason, that the following-named ships, which were in company with Captain Millard, caught 11 whales each, which would net any captain about $5,000:

William Bayliss 11
Alexandria 11
Mary D. Hume 11
Karluk 11
Jeanette 8

Yours, kindly,

EZA B. LAPHAM.

Mr. BOUTELL.

SOUTH DARTMOUTH, MASS., *April 18, 1900.*

DEAR SIR: Your note of the 15th ultimo at hand, and would say: From my thirteen years' experience as master in the Arctic Ocean I think that a fair average profit for a captain would be about $4,500.

Very respectfully, yours,

JOSHUA G. BAKER.

H. S. BOUTELL, Esq.,
Washington, D. C.

O

ANNA C. BINGHAM.

FEBRUARY 2, 1903.—Committed to the Committee of the Whole House and ordered
to be printed.

Mr. SULLOWAY, from the Committee on Invalid Pensions, submitted
the following

REPORT.

[To accompany H. R. 16480.]

The Committee on Invalid Pensions, to whom was referred the bill
(H. R. 16480) granting a pension to Anna C. Bingham, submit the
following report:

This bill proposes to increase the pension of Anna C. Bingham,
widow of Lafayette Bingham, late lieutenant-colonel Ninety-second
New York Infantry, from $8 to $50 per month.

The officer named in this bill served as lieutenant-colonel of the
Ninety-second New York Infantry from December 14, 1861, to March
13, 1862, when honorably discharged on tender of resignation.

In January, 1862, the officer's horse took fright and ran violently
against the side of the house used for the regimental headquarters,
falling on his right side with the officer's right leg under him,
injuring his shoulder, back, knees, and hips.

Upon due proof that he received such injury to the lumbar region
and to the right leg and knee, the officer was pensioned under the general law for said disabilities at $15 per month from discharge, and at
$30 from August 11, 1885.

The health records of the District of Columbia show that the officer
died November 4, 1898, from albuminuria.

The beneficiary named in the bill, now 54 years of age, who married the officer on April 6, 1880, is now pensioned under the act of
June 27, 1890, at $8 per month, upon proof that she had no income
from any source and no means of support and no property except
some unimproved lots, valued at about $2,025 or $2,050, encumbered
by a mortgage of $2,000 which was placed upon these lots in order to
afford her living expenses.

Her claim under the general law was rejected by the Pension Bureau
in January, 1899, upon the ground that her husband's fatal disease
could not be accepted as a result of the injuries for which he had been
pensioned.

In support of that claim the beneficiary filed the affidavit of Dr. C. B. Small, of Saratoga Springs, N. Y., setting forth that he began attending the officer on July 10, 1897, and thence to October, 1897, and again from May to September, 1898; that during these periods he was suffering from chronic irritable spine and marked chronic interstitial nephritis with albuminuria; that he was emaciated in body, could walk but a short distance without experiencing fatigue and shortness of breath, that he suffered constantly from deep-seated and intense pain radiating from the spine into the lower extremities, the chest and the head, and that his mental condition was one of childishness.

The affidavit of Dr. James B. Dexter was also filed by the beneficiary in the Pension Bureau, who testified that if the officer received an injury to the lumbar region and right leg and knee in the service for which he was pensioned, affiant had no difficulty in reaching the conclusion that the venous circulation must have been more or less obstructed by that injury and to have remained obstructed; that there would result venous congestion, and that the kidneys would have remained in a diseased condition from that time until his death; that any cause which arrested the venous circulation of blood through the kidneys would induce albuminuria, etc.

The papers filed in the Pension Bureau show that the beneficiary has been greatly prostrated by years of watching, toil, and suffering in her untiring efforts to relieve and care for her late husband.

Your committee believe that the doubts in this case as to whether the officer's fatal disease was directly due to the injury received by him while in the service should be resolved in favor of the beneficiary and recommend an increase of her pension from $8 to $30 per month, and report the bill back with the recommendation that it pass after the same shall have been amended as follows:

Strike out all after the enacting clause and insert in lieu thereof the following:

That the Secretary of the Interior be, and he is hereby, authorized and directed to place on the pension roll, subject to the provisions and limitations of the pension laws, the name of Anna C. Bingham, widow of Lafayette Bingham, late lieutenant-colonel Ninety-second Regiment, New York Volunteer Infantry, and pay her a pension at the rate of thirty dollars per month in lieu of that she is now receiving.

Amend the title so as to read: "A bill granting an increase of pension to Anna C. Bingham."

O

SARAH E. GIFFORD.

FEBRUARY 2, 1903.—Committed to the Committee of the Whole House and ordered to be printed.

Mr. SULLOWAY, from the Committee on Invalid Pensions, submitted the following

REPORT.

[To accompany H. R. 6442.]

The Committee on Invalid Pensions, to whom was referred the bill (H. R. 6442) granting an increase of pension to Sarah E. Gifford, submit the following report:

This bill proposes to increase the pension of the beneficiary named therein from $8 to $50 per month.

The beneficiary, now 64 years of age, is the widow of Obed H. Gifford, who served as first lieutenant in Companies K and G, Second Rhode Island Infantry, from June 5, 1861, to June 17, 1864, when honorably discharged, and as carpenter's mate in the U. S. Navy from February 28, 1865, to February 27, 1869, when honorably discharged, and she is now pensioned under the act of June 27, 1890, at $8 per month upon proof of her marriage to the soldier on December 12, 1865, his death on October 7, 1877, her legal widowhood, and that she is without any means of support other than her labor.

In an application for increase of pension filed by her in the Pension Bureau on May 5, 1899, she alleged that she was then nearly blind in both eyes.

There has been filed with your committee the statement of the honorable Mr. Bull, the member who introduced the bill, setting forth that the beneficiary, an estimable lady, is totally blind, and that her case was one worthy of consideration.

In view of the age of the beneficiary and her helpless condition from blindness, and the fact that her husband rendered over four years' service during the civil war, an increase of her pension from $8 to $17 per month appears justified, and the bill is therefore reported back with the recommendation that it pass after the same shall have been amended as follows:

In line 7 strike out the word "Company" and insert in lieu thereof the words "Companies K and."

In line 8, after the word "Infantry," insert the words "and carpenter's mate, United States Navy."

In same line strike out the word "fifty" and insert in lieu thereof the word "seventeen."

O

JOHN W. COPLEY.

FEBRUARY 2, 1903.—Committed to the Committee of the Whole House and ordered
to be printed.

Mr. SAMUEL W. SMITH, from the Committee on Invalid Pensions, submitted the following

REPORT.

[To accompany H. R. 11122.]

The Committee on Invalid Pensions, to whom was referred the bill
(H. R. 11122) granting an increase of pension to John W. Copley,
submit the following report:

This bill proposes to increase the pension of the soldier named in
this bill from $12 to $30 per month.

This soldier, now 56 years of age, was a private in Companies H and
C, Fourteenth Kentucky Infantry, from March 19, 1864, to September
15, 1865, when honorably discharged; never applied for pension under
the general law, but is now and has been since August 29, 1890, a pensioner under the act of June 27, 1890, at the maximum rating, namely,
$12 per month, for total inability to earn a support by manual labor,
the result of rheumatism and disease of heart.

The certificate of medical examination in the case made on August
12, 1891, rated him $6 for rheumatism and $4 for disease of heart.

There has been filed with your committee the affidavit of Dr. J. C.
Ranfield to the effect that the beneficiary has anchylosis of the left
ankle joint, that his muscles are in an atrophied state and that he can
get about only by the aid of a cane and that he is permanently disabled.

Other testimony filed with your committee shows that the beneficiary has been in a crippled condition for the last ten years.

The statement of Hon. J. A. Hughes, the member who introduced
this bill, also filed with your committee, sets forth that he had a personal acquaintance with the beneficiary for the past fifteen years; that
his present condition is such that he is wholly incapacitated for any
kind of labor, and that it is only with great difficulty that he gets
around with a cane; that he is a poor man with no property and has a
family dependent upon him for support.

The case of this crippled and destitute soldier falls within numerous
precedents in which Congress and the Senate have increased pensions

from $12 to $24 per month, and a like increase is recommended in this case, and the bill is reported back with the recommendation that it pass after the same shall have been amended as follows:

In line 6 strike out the word "Company" and insert in lieu thereof the word "Companies."

In the same line, before the word "Fourteenth," insert the words "and C."

In line 8 strike out the word "thirty" and insert in lieu thereof the word "twenty-four."

O

JOSEPH H. LUDLUM.

FEBRUARY 2, 1903.—Committed to the Committee of the Whole House and ordered to be printed.

Mr. SAMUEL W. SMITH, from the Committee on Invalid Pensions, submitted the following

REPORT.

[To accompany H. R. 13046.]

The Committee on Invalid Pensions, to whom was referred the bill (H. R. 13046) granting an increase of pension to Joseph H. Ludlum, submit the following report:

This bill proposes to increase the pension of the beneficiary named therein from $12 to $30 per month.

Mr. Ludlum, now 64 years of age, served as a private in Company A, Twelfth Ohio Infantry, from April 20, 1861, to July 11, 1864, when honorably discharged.

The medical records of the War Department furnish no information as to any treatment of the soldier during his term of service.

He has been pensioned since February 8, 1897, at $12 per month under the act of June 27, 1890, for total inability to earn a support by manual labor, the result of paralysis of the left side and injury to left foot.

His claim to pension under the general law, filed on May 24, 1900, and based upon an injury to the brain from heavy cannonading over his head and resulting paralysis in 1897, was rejected in January, 1901, upon the ground that a ratable disability from the alleged disease of brain had not existed since the filing of the claim, and that the paralysis of left side, for which pensioned under the act of June 27, 1890, was not the result of any disease of the brain, but due to an attack of apoplexy in 1897.

The beneficiary filed some testimony of members of his company and regiment tending to show that after the battle of Second Bull Run, and after the regiment had dropped back to Upton Hill, near Washington, and while lying under the guns of one of the forts after cannonading had taken place, the claimant complained of his head hurting him, caused by the heavy firing, and that these severe pains of the head continued to exist since discharge, and medical testimony shows that in February,

1897, he had an apoplectic seizure with complete hemiplegia of the left side.

When last examined, on August 1, 1900, the board of surgeons found him to be suffering from paralysis and heart disease to such a degree as to require the frequent and periodical aid and attendance of another person.

This soldier, who rendered three years' service, is now so helpless from paralysis as to require the aid and attendance of another person, and is therefore entitled to an increase of his pension to $30 per month.

The bill is therefore reported back with the recommendation that it pass.

O

JULIAETTA ROWLING.

FEBRUARY 2, 1903.—Committed to the Committee of the Whole House and ordered
to be printed.

Mr. CROWLEY, from the Committee on Invalid Pensions, submitted the
following

REPORT.

[To accompany H. R. 16427.]

The Committee on Invalid Pensions, to whom was referred the bill
(H. R. 16427) granting an increase of pension to Juliaetta Rowling,
submit the following report:

This bill proposes to increase the pension of the beneficiary named
therein from $8 to $24 per month on account of a helpless imbecile
child, with a proviso that in the event of the death of such child the
pension of the beneficiary shall continue only at $12 per month.

The soldier named in this bill served as a private in Company C,
Thirty-seventh Illinois Infantry, from August 1, 1861, to October 4,
1864, when honorably discharged.

He was pensioned under the general law on account of chronic diarrhea at $4 per month, and under the act of June 27, 1890, at $12 per
month on account of diarrhea, disease of rectum, and lungs.

He died April 6, 1901, from disease of the kidneys.

The beneficiary named in the bill, now 51 years of age, who was
married to the soldier on July 27, 1873, is now drawing a pension
under the act of June 27, 1890, at $8 per month and $2 per month
additional on account of two minor children, the youngest of whom
will become 16 years of age in May, 1907, and this pension was allowed
upon proof that she was not in receipt of an income exceeding $250
per year as provided under the act of May 9, 1900, she having in fact
no means of support and no property except 86 acres of land encumbered by $1,600, which land was rented at $240 per year, and out of
which rental interest on the mortgage and other debts had to be paid.

Her claim under the general law was rejected in January, 1903, upon
the ground that her husband's death from disease of the kidneys was
not a result of the chronic diarrhea for which he had been pensioned.

In support of that claim the beneficiary filed the testimony of Dr.
Shaffer who testified before the special examiner of the Pension Bureau

that he was the soldier's family physician from about 1890 to the time of his death, during which time the soldier suffered from chronic disease of the liver and bowels; that during his last illness his urine was heavily charged with albumin; that in the final stages there was uræmic poisoning; that there was enlargement of the liver, and at times diarrhea; that it was impossible for him, however, to determine to what extent the enlargement of the liver and the chronic diarrhea were factors in the Bright's disease of which he died.

According to the statements of the soldier made on July 4, 1898, the helpless child, George, named in this bill, was born December 9, 1880.

There has been filed with your committee the affidavit of Dr. Palmer, setting forth that he examined George Rowling, the son of the soldier, now 22 years of age, in December, 1902; that his height was 38 inches, his weight 50 pounds, his chest measurement 23 inches, waist measurement 25 inches; that he had a large mouth, and tongue protruding; that he was unable to speak, and never had been able to carry on a conversation, and that physically he never had and never would be able to support himself, and that mentally he was a perfect imbecile and always would remain so.

Congress having repeatedly granted an increase of $12 per month to the widow of a soldier who has a helpless child dependent upon her for support, a like increase is therefore justified in this bill, and the same is reported back with the recommendation that it pass after the same shall have been amended as follows:

In line 6 strike out the words "a private."

In line 7 strike out the word "in" and insert in lieu thereof the words "late of."

In same line, before the word "Illinois," insert the word "Regiment."

In same line, before the word "Infantry," insert the word "Volunteer."

In line 8 strike out the word "four."

In same line after the word "month" insert the words "and two dollars per month additional for each of the minor children of said soldier."

Strike out all of lines 9, 10, 11, 12, and 13, and insert in lieu thereof the following:

of that she is now receiving: *Provided, however,* That in the event of the death of the helpless child, George Rowling, on whose account the pension of Juliaetta Rowling is increased, the pension of said Juliaetta Rowling shall continue only at the rate of $8 per month from and after the date of death of said helpless child.

O

HENRY H. WINDES.

FEBRUARY 2, 1903.—Committed to the Committee of the Whole House and ordered
to be printed.

Mr. MIERS, from the Committee on Invalid Pensions, submitted the
following

REPORT.

[To accompany H. R. 11958.]

The Committee on Invalid Pensions, to whom was referred the bill
(H. R. 11958) granting an increase of pension to Henry H. Windes,
submit the following report:

This bill proposes to pension Henry H. Windes, late of Company
G, Forty-seventh Enrolled Missouri Militia, at $24 per month.

The soldier named in this bill, whose post-office address is Linncreek, Mo., is shown by the records of the adjutant-general of Missouri to have served as a sergeant in Company G, Forty-seventh
Enrolled Missouri Militia, from August 12, 1862, to April 30, 1864,
when relieved.

He filed no claim to pension in the Pension Bureau.

In an affidavit filed with your committee he sets forth that he served
as a sergeant in Company G, Forty-seventh Enrolled Missouri Militia;
that he was also a private in Company H, Ninth Provisional Missouri
Militia; that he was advised, however, that his name did not appear
on the rolls of the last-named regiment; that while a member of the
Ninth Provisional Regiment he performed general and special duty;
that he was specially detailed as scout, guide, and to convey dispatches
from headquarters of the regiment at Linncreek to Jefferson City,
Lebanon, and Springfield, Mo., to the Federal authorities at these
places; that he was especially selected at all times to do all hazardous
work of the company, and in this capacity was often exposed to great
dangers, and at one time was shot in the right thigh; that by reason
of this service his general health was greatly impaired, and that he
also contracted disease of eyes, which had resulted in total loss of
sight of the right eye.

He further stated that he had no means of support for himself and
wife and that advanced age and physical infirmities disabled him from
earning a support.

H R—57-2—Vol 2——54

A comrade who served with the beneficiary in both the Forty-seventh Enrolled and Ninth Provisional Regiments of Missouri Militia, and whom the records of the Auditor for the War Department show to have been a member of the last-named organization, testified that the beneficiary, aside from his active service in the above-named regiments, acted as scout and guide for the Union troops and officers at various points in south central Missouri; that in one of these scouts he was wounded in his right leg, which came near proving fatal, and that comrade Windes was prompt and reliable and ready to go wherever duty called him at any and all times, regardless of danger.

This affiant further testified that the beneficiary is now an old man, blind in one eye and nearly so in the other, and broken down in health generally, and that he is without any means of support.

The testimony of the foregoing witness as to the beneficiary's services as scout, etc., is corroborated by that of another party, who further testified that he was at one time detailed with the beneficiary to carry a dispatch sent to the colonel of their regiment from the commander of the district forces at Springfield, Mo., and that while on another detail the beneficiary was wounded in one of his legs.

From the testimony of Dr. Ford, also filed with your committee, it appears that the beneficiary is now totally blind in the right eye and nearly so in the left; that he also is suffering from rheumatism and disease of the kidneys, and is in fact a physical wreck.

Your committee is satisfied that the beneficiary rendered service as scout and guide for the Union forces as testified to by his witnesses, and that he was wounded while so serving.

Under these circumstances, taking into consideration also that he is now nearly blind, your committee is of the opinion that relief to the extent of granting him a pension of $20 per month is justified, and the bill is therefore reported back with the recommendation that it pass after the same shall have been amended as follows:

In line 6 strike out the words "of Company G, Forty-seventh" and all of line 7, and insert in lieu thereof the words "scout and guide, United States Volunteers and."

In line 8 strike out the word "twenty-four" and insert in lieu thereof the word "twenty."

In line 9 strike out all after the word "month."

Amend the title so as to read: "A bill granting a pension to Henry H. Windes."

O

MABEL A. WOOLSEY.

FEBRUARY 2, 1903.—Committed to the Committee of the Whole House and ordered
to be printed.

Mr. SULLOWAY, from the Committee on Invalid Pensions, submitted
the following

REPORT.

[To accompany H. R. 10505.]

The Committee on Invalid Pensions, to whom was referred the bill
(H. R. 10505) granting a pension to Mabel A. Woolsey, daughter of Harvey Woolsey, submit the following report:

This bill proposes to pension Mabel A. Woolsey, daughter of Harvey Woolsey, late of Company D, Seventh Ohio Infantry, at $12 per
month.

Harvey Woolsey, the soldier named in this bill, served as a private
in Company D, Seventh Ohio Infantry, from June 7, 1861, to July
14, 1862, when he was discharged on surgeon's certificate of disability
by reason of—

pulmonary consumption of eleven months' standing. Disease at present in the third
stage, accompanied by frequent attacks of diarrhea, general debility, and emaciation.

He was a pensioner under the general law ever since his discharge,
and at the time of his death drew a pension of $30 per month on
account of chronic diarrhea and resulting debility, partial paralysis,
and disease of lungs.

He left no widow surviving him.

From proof filed with your committee it appears that the beneficiary,
a daughter of the soldier, who was born on December 25, 1864, about
the time that she became 16 years of age sustained an injury to her
spinal column from a fall upon the ice, which has produced such a condition of helplessness that she has not been able to stand upon her feet
or take a step for years; that she is wholly destitute of means of subsistence and dependent upon those not legally bound for her support.

Under the rules of the committee and the action of the House and
Senate relief to the extent asked for in the bill is warranted, and the

bill is reported back with the recommendation that it pass after the
same shall have been amended as follows:

In line 6, before the word "daughter," insert the words "helpless
and dependent."

In lines 6 and 7 strike out the words "soldier in" and insert in lieu
thereof the word "of."

In line 7, after the word "Seventh," insert the word "Regiment."

In line 8 strike out the word "to."

Amend the title so as to read: "A bill granting a pension to Mabel
A. Woolsey."

O

BENJAMIN F. HUGHES.

FEBRUARY 2, 1903.—Committed to the Committee of the Whole House and ordered
to be printed.

Mr. SULLOWAY, from the Committee on Invalid Pensions, submitted
the following

REPORT.

[To accompany H. R. 16754.]

The Committee on Invalid Pensions, to whom was referred the bill
(H. R. 16754) granting an increase of pension to Benjamin F. Hughes,
submit the following report:

This bill proposes to increase the pension of the soldier named
therein from $12 to $20 per month.

This soldier, now 78 years of age, served as a private in Company
F, Third West Virginia Infantry, from June 25, 1861, to May 29,
1866, when honorably discharged, and again as a private in Company
C, Twenty-second United States Infantry, from October 30, 1869, to
October 30, 1874, when honorably discharged.

He is now a pensioner under the act of June 27, 1890, at the maximum rating, namely, $12 per month, on account of total inability to
earn a support by manual labor, the result of senility, debility, and
disease of kidneys.

When last examined, on June 6, 1884, the board of surgeons stated
that he was physically broken down; that he was suffering from a
double hernia, diabetes insipidus, and fracture of the patella, and the
board of surgeons then stated that the claimant was not able to work at
all, and was in the poorhouse, about 12 miles from Custer City, S. Dak.

There has been filed with your committee the statement of the member who introduced the bill, setting forth that some months ago the
beneficiary had a stroke of paralysis and that he recently had another
stroke which rendered him helpless.

In view of the soldier's helpless condition from paralysis, relief to
the extent of increasing his pension from $12 to $30 per month is
warranted under the action of the House taken on June 16, 1902, and
the bill is therefore reported back with the recommendation that it
pass after the same shall have been amended as follows:

In line 6 strike out the words "a private in" and insert in lieu
thereof the word "of."

In same line strike out the letter "L" and insert in lieu thereof the
letter "F."

In line 8 strike out the word "twenty" and insert in lieu thereof
the word "thirty."

O

MILTON D. WELLS.

FEBRUARY 2, 1903.—Committed to the Committee of the Whole House and ordered to be printed.

Mr. SAMUEL W. SMITH, from the Committee on Invalid Pensions, submitted the following

REPORT.

[To accompany H. R. 15696.]

The Committee on Invalid Pensions, to whom was referred the bill (H. R. 15696) granting an increase of pension to Milton D. Wells, submit the following report:

This bill proposes to increase the pension of the officer named in the bill from $12 to $50 per month.

This officer, now 71 years of age, served as private, quartermaster-sergeant, and second lieutenant of Company H, One hundred and twenty-first Ohio Volunteers, from August 22, 1862, to April 12, 1864, when promoted to first lieutenant and quartermaster of said regiment, and served as such to June 8, 1865, when honorably discharged.

He is now pensioned under the act of June 27, 1890, at $12 per month for total inability to earn a support by manual labor, due to disease of heart, urinary organs, mouth, nasal catarrh, and rheumatism.

When last examined, in April, 1891, the board of surgeons at Mount Gilead, Ohio, described his condition as follows:

Claimant is aged in appearance and is evidently in poor health. Has chronic cystitis.

Rheumatic tenderness of lumbar muscles and impairment of power to raise right arm to level with shoulder. Cardiac dullness extended half an inch to right and downward; irregular in rhythm; second sound prolonged, with diastolic murmur; slight hypertrophy.

Nasal septum is deflected to right side. The same side presents an inflamed and ulcerated condition. Teeth all gone except one, and the gums are very much shrunken, so much so that we believe it would be impossible for him to wear artificial teeth.

General debility quite well marked.

There has been filed with your committee the statement of Hon. J. A. Norton, the member who introduced this bill, setting forth that he had an opportunity to meet Captain Wells very frequently during the past four or five years, he being an inmate of the Soldiers' Home ın Erie County, Ohio, which was in his district; that he is now about the age of 72 or 73 years; that the last time he met him he was upon crutches, scarcely able to walk, pale and cadaverous, respiration rapid, and every evident sign of heart disease present; that he had general rheumatism, caused by uric acid in the blood, and a general inflammation of the internal organs was evident from appearances, and that he believed him to be a sufferer from cystitis; that it was impossible for him to dress himself or to raise his right arm much above the hip; that from observance he would say that he had been at one time afflicted with scurvy, as he had no teeth left, and there was a general shrinkage of the gums, and that in his opinion he would continue to be a physical wreck, anticipating death almost daily.

The case of this officer comes clearly within the action taken by the House on June 16, 1902, increasing from $12 to $30 per month the pension of those who require the aid and attendance of another person.

Like relief is recommended in this officer's case, and the bill is reported back with the recommendation that it pass after the same shall have been amended as follows:

In line 6, after the word "lieutenant," insert the words "and quartermaster."

In line 7, before the word "Ohio," insert the word "Regiment."

In line 8 strike out the word "fifty" and insert in lieu thereof the word "thirty."

O

CATHARINE A. SAWDY.

FEBRUARY 2, 1903.—Committed to the Committee of the Whole House and ordered
to be printed.

Mr. APLIN, from the Committee on Invalid Pensions, submitted the
following

REPORT.

[To accompany H. R. 2913.]

The Committee on Invalid Pensions, to whom was referred the bill
(H. R. 2913) granting a pension to Catherine A. Sawdy, submit the
following report:

This bill proposes to pension Catharine A. Sawdy, dependent mother
of Henry J. Sawdy, late of Company I, First Michigan Light Artillery,
at $17 per month.

Records of the War Department show that Henry J. Sawdy, the
officer named in this bill, served as first sergeant in Company I, First
Michigan Light Artillery, from August 18, 1862 to February 8, 1864,
when he was promoted to first lieutenant of the same company and
regiment, and that his resignation, tendered on account of family
affairs, was accepted, to take effect February 1, 1865.

He was a pensioner under the general law at $4 per month, from
July 2, 1888, on account of varicose veins of left leg, shown to have
been due to his military service, and contracted while holding the rank
of first sergeant.

This rating was increased to $6 per month from March 2, 1895, by
operation of an act of Congress of that date.

The officer was examined by pension examining surgeons in 1888
and 1889, but none of these certificates of examination revealed any
disease of the kidneys.

The officer, however, informed the board of surgeons in October,
1899, that he had been suffering from disease of the urinary organs
for about fifteen years.

Catharine A. Sawdy, the beneficiary named in this bill, and now 93
years of age, applied for pension on February 2, 1900, as the dependent mother of the officer, alleging that he died, leaving no widow or
children, surviving him, on December 27, 1899; that his father died
November 10, 1874; that she was without any means of support other
than her daily labor, and that the officer had been her sole support for
many years past.

In support of that claim the beneficiary filed a certificate of the
board of health of Chicago, Ill., showing that the officer died Decem-

ber 27, 1899, of chronic nephritis; also proof showing that she was the mother of the officer; that the officer supported her, and that she was dependent upon her manual labor and the voluntary contributions of others for her support, and that at her great age (92 years) she was too feeble to do manual labor, and that she was, in fact, destitute.

Other proof filed in the Pension Bureau shows that the officer was divorced from his wife on May 12, 1886.

The claim was rejected by the Pension Bureau upon the ground that the officer's fatal nephritis was not shown to have been due to his military service.

Subsequent to the rejection of the claim the beneficiary filed a claim for pension under the act of June 27, 1890, as the dependent mother of the officer, and the testimony of Dr. McArthur, of Chicago, Ill., setting forth that he had known the officer and attended him at different times for the past twenty-five years, and that he was his attending physician at the time of his death, which occurred December 27, 1899; that the immediate cause of his death was, in affiant's opinion, the result of infection from varicose veins of left leg which so debilitated him that death resulted, and that in affiant's opinion such death was directly traceable to his hardships and exposures during his army service.

There has been filed with your committee a petition signed by a large number of residents of Hudson, Mich., setting forth that the beneficiary is an old resident and estimable citizen of Hudson, who has passed her ninety-second birthday; that she was dependent for her support upon her only son, Henry J. Sawdy, late first lieutenant Battery I, First Michigan Light Artillery; that he was a good soldier and good son; that like others, however, he did not realize that with the close of his active life his old mother might find herself dependent entirely upon the care of others, and thus he made no provision for a pension for her, that would at least have been a small income for her; that they believe the case to be one of unusual worth, and that all can see that whatever is done has to be done now, etc.

Your committee does not believe that this beneficiary at her great age (93 years) should suffer want, her son upon whom she was dependent having given three years' service to his country, and recommend that she be granted a pension of $12 per month in order to make comfortable her few remaining days, etc.

The bill is therefore reported back with the recommendation that it pass after the same shall have been amended as follows:

In line 6 strike out the word "Catherine" and insert in lieu thereof the word "Catharine."

In line 7 strike out the word "of" and insert in lieu thereof the words "first lieutenant."

In same line, after the word "Michigan," insert the word "Volunteer."

In line 8 strike out the word "seventeen" and insert in lieu thereof the word "twelve."

Amend the title so as to read: "A bill granting an increase of pension to Catharine A. Sawdy."

O

MARTHA MADDOX.

FEBRUARY 2, 1903.—Committeed to the Committee of the Whole House and ordered
to be printed.

Mr. KLEBERG, from the Committee on Invalid Pensions, submitted the
following

REPORT.

[To accompany H. R. 17043.]

The Committee on Invalid Pensions, to whom was referred the bill
(H. R. 17043) granting an increase of pension to Martha Maddox, submit the following report:

This bill proposes to pension Martha Maddox, as widow of Samuel
Maddox, late of Company G, One hundred and sixteenth U. S.
Colored Troops, at $30 per month.

Samuel Maddox, the husband of this beneficiary, served in the organization named above from June 27, 1864, to January 17, 1867, when
honorably discharged, and was pensioned under the general law on
account of an injury to hips, knees, and body incurred in the service
and line of duty, and subsequently was pensioned under the act of
June 27, 1890, at $12 per month.

The claim of the beneficiary as the widow of the soldier, which
claim was filed under the act of June 27, 1890, on May 1, 1899, was
rejected by the Pension Bureau in 1900 upon the ground that the slave
marriage entered into between her and the soldier about 1858 was not
ratified according to the laws of the State of Kentucky, where they
resided, agreeable to the act of February 14, 1866, which required the
parties to appear before the clerk of the county court and there to
declare that they had been and desired to continue living together as
husband and wife, etc., and that the ceremonial marriage entered into
by them in 1892 had no effect whatever toward ratifying any former
slave marriage.

It appears that soldier and claimant, both being slaves, were married
in Kentucky about 1858 by a customary ceremony. They lived
together as husband and wife and appeared to have been known and
treated by their friends and acquaintances as such during slavery and
after their emancipation up to November 6, 1892, when they were for-

mally married in Lee County, Ky., and thereafter until the soldier's death, which occurred in that State April 15, 1899.

It appears from the testimony that claimant and soldier, subsequent to their emancipation, understood that a law had been passed requiring all slaves to remarry, and with the idea of ratifying and legalizing their said former slave marriage in conformity with said law, they appeared before a representative of the Bureau of Refugees, Freedmen, and Abandoned Lands, and acknowledged themselves to be husband and wife, etc.   There is a certificate of said declaration filed in evidence which has every appearance of authenticity, dated June 13, 1866, but as no record of such marriage appears upon the records of the above-stated bureau in the War Department, the certificate referred to was not accepted as evidence of a marriage of these parties "under the flag," and the Secretary of the Interior held that this agent of the Government had no power whatever under the law to ratify a slave marriage.

The beneficiary has not remarried since the soldier's death and is shown to be dependent upon her daily labor.

Had the soldier died of disease contracted during his military service, the beneficiary, under section 4705 of the Revised Statutes, would have had title to pension under the general law upon simply proving that she and the soldier habitually recognized each other as man and wife and were so recognized by their neighbors, and lived together as such during slavery up to the soldier's enlistment and after his discharge to the date of his death, and a ratification of their slave marriage was not necessary under the general law.

When that statute was enacted no pension was granted to a widow except her husband died of disease contracted in the service, hence it is clear that it was passed in order to legalize slave marriages, and it should therefore be held to apply not only to the general law, but also to the act of June 27, 1890.

The beneficiary is therefore fully entitled to a pension under the act of June 27, 1890, at the rate provided therein, namely, $8 per month, and the bill is reported back with the recommendation that it pass after the same shall have been amended as follows:

In line 6 strike out the word "corporal."

In line 7, before the words "United States," insert the word "Regiment."

In line 9 strike out the word "thirty" and insert in lieu thereof the word "eight."

Amend the title so as to read: "A bill granting a pension to Martha Maddox."

O

NELLIE A. BATCHELDER.

FEBRUARY 2, 1903.—Committed to the Committee of the Whole House and ordered
to be printed.

Mr. DEEMER, from the Committee on Invalid Pensions, submitted the
following

REPORT.

[To accompany H. R. 1519.]

The Committee on Invalid Pensions, to whom was referred the bill
(H. R. 1519) granting a pension to Nellie A. Batchelder, submit the
following report:

This bill proposes to pension Nellie A. Batchelder, widow of Winfield S. Batchelder, late first lieutenant Company H, One hundred and
eighteenth Pennsylvania Infantry, at $20 per month.

Records of the War Department show that Winfield S. Batchelder,
the officer named in this bill, served as private in Company F, Seventy-
first Pennsylvania Infantry from June 10, 1861, and as first sergeant
and sergeant major to August 19, 1862, when he was discharged by
reason of promotion to first lieutenant of Company H of the One hundred and eighteenth Pennsylvania Volunteers; that he was mustered
into the service as such first lieutenant on August 20, 1862, and honorably discharged on account of physical disability on tender of resignation on November 16, 1863.

The files of the Pension Bureau show that he was pensioned in 1883,
from January 22, 1883, the date of the filing of his declaration, at
$8.50 per month (one-half of total of rank of first lieutenant) on
account of chronic diarrhea contracted by him during his military
service.

The pension which accrued to the officer between his last quarterly
payment and the date of his death on December 25, 1900, from angina
pectoris, was allowed to his widow, Nellie A. Batchelder, the beneficiary named in this bill, upon proof that she was married to him on
March 2, 1865; that he died, as stated above, on December 25, 1900,
and that she was his legal widow at the time of his death.

The beneficiary has never applied for pension as the widow of the
officer in her own right.

It is evidently impossible for the beneficiary to prosecute to a successful completion a claim under the general law in the Pension Bureau and to prove that her husband's death from angina pectoris was the result of the chronic diarrhea for which he had been pensioned.

Your committee believing, however, that the officer's death may have in part been due to his service of over two years, recommend relief to the extent of granting her a pension of $12 per month and report the bill back with the recommendation that it pass after the same shall have been amended as follows:

Strike out all after the enacting clause and insert in lieu thereof the following:

That the Secretary of the Interior be, and he is hereby, authorized and directed to place on the pension roll, subject to the provisions and limitations of the pension laws, the name of Nellie A. Batchelder, widow of Winfield S. Batchelder, late first lieutenant, Company H, One hundred and eighteenth Regiment Pennsylvania Volunteer Infantry, and pay her a pension at the rate of twelve dollars per month.

O

PHILIP KROHN.

FEBRUARY .2, 1903.—Committed to the Committee of the Whole House and ordered
to be printed.

Mr. SULLOWAY, from the Committee on Invalid Pensions, submitted
the following

REPORT.

[To accompany H. R. 4066.]

The Committee on Invalid Pensions, to whom was referred the bill
(H. R. 4066) granting an increase of pension to Philip Krohn, submit
the following report:

This bill proposes to increase the pension of the soldier named
therein from $12 to $50 per month.

Philip Krohn, the officer named in this bill, and now 60 years of
age, is shown by the records of the War Department to have served
as quartermaster-sergeant, second lieutenant, and first lieutenant of
Company G, Fifth New York Cavalry, from August 22, 1861, to May
15, 1865, when honorably discharged, and these records further show
that he was captured at Orange, Va., July 17, 1862, confined at Richmond, and paroled at Aikens Landing, Virginia, August 5, 1862; that
he was again captured, at Ashland, Va., June 1, 1864, and paroled
December 10, 1864.

He is now pensioned under the act of June 27, 1890, at $12 per
month for total inability to earn a support by manual labor, the result
of paralysis of the right side and disease of the digestive organs.

His claim to pension under the general law, filed in August, 1899,
and based upon a shell wound of the head, resulting in paralysis,
chronic diarrhea, piles, and catarrh, was rejected by the Pension Bureau
in January, 1901, upon the ground of no record and claimant's inability to furnish evidence showing the existence of said disabilities in the
service.

Medical testimony filed in the Pension Bureau shows that the beneficiary has suffered from deafness, diarrhea, and piles since about
1890; that about 1896 he had a paralytic stroke, and that on October
25, 1897, he had another stroke.

When last examined, on July 3, 1900, the board of surgeons stated
that the beneficiary was a Congregational minister, and rated him $4

for disease of rectum, $17 for paralysis of the right side, and $22 for
impaired hearing, and the board of surgeons then stated that sensation and motion was much impaired by reason of paralysis; that he
walked with a limp; that loss of motion was more marked in the right
arm and hand, his speech indistinct, and the mental faculties impaired.

Papers filed with your committee show that the beneficiary can not
preach and is a total wreck physically; and a petition signed by a
number of citizens of the town of Candor, N. Y., also filed with your
committee, sets forth that he is in every way unable to perform any
kind of labor to support himself and that his only income was a pension
of $12 per month.

An increase of this soldier's pension, following precedents, is warranted in view of his service of four years and the fact that he is
paralyzed and that his mental faculties are impaired.

The bill is therefore reported back with the recommendation that it
pass after the same shall have been amended as follows:

In line 3 strike out the word "is."

In same line, before the word "hereby," insert the word "is."

In line 6, before the word "Company," strike out the word "of"
and insert in lieu thereof the words "first lieutenant."

In same line, after the word "Fifth," insert the word "Regiment."

In same line, before the word "Cavalry," insert the word "Volunteer."

In line 7 strike out the word "fifty" and insert in lieu thereof the
word "twenty-four."

O

JAMES GARLAND.

FEBRUARY 2, 1903.—Committed to the Committee of the Whole House and ordered
to be printed.

Mr. CROWLEY, from the Committee on Invalid Pensions, submitted the
following

REPORT.

[To accompany H. R. 6065.]

The Committee on Invalid Pensions, to whom was referred the bill
(H. R. 6065) granting an increase of pension to James Garland, submit the following report:

This bill proposes to increase the pension of the beneficiary named
therein from $12 to $25 per month.

Records of the Navy Department show that James Garland, now 67
years of age, served as a seaman on the U. S. S. *Active* from August
14, 1861, to June 17, 1862, when honorably discharged; that he reenlisted June 18, 1862, and served on the U. S. S. *Active* and *Marcy*,
and was honorably discharged April 22, 1863.

He is now pensioned under the act of June 27, 1890, at the maximum
rating, namely, $12 per month, for total inability to earn a support
by manual labor, the result of progressive muscular atrophy.

When last examined, in May, 1899, the board of surgeons stated that
he was entitled to a rating of $24 per month on account of progressive
muscular atrophy, anchylosis of the left index finger, and varicose veins
of both legs, and the board of surgeons then further stated that claimant had a stooping position in standing and walking, that the muscles
of the shoulders, arms, and thighs showed a great amount of atrophy,
that the scapulæ branched out winglike and that the muscles in that
region were wasted and atrophied, that he had a characteristic swing
in walking, and required aid in dressing.

There has been filed with your committee the affidavit of the beneficiary, setting forth that he is totally unable to perform any kind of
labor by reason of degeneration of the lateral columns of the spinal
cord, that he was an inmate of the United States marine hospital at
San Francisco, Cal., and that he had no other means of support except
the pension of $12 per month.

The certificate of the medical officer in command of the marine hospital at the port of San Francisco, Cal., also filed with your committee, shows that the beneficiary had been a patient at that hospital since July 27, 1897, suffering from degeneration of the lateral columns of the spinal cord and probably also of the posterior columns, and that there had been little improvement in his condition since his admission to the hospital, and that while he was able to use his hands, he could walk only with difficulty.

Other testimony filed with your committee shows that the beneficiary is a man of good character, sober and peaceful, etc.

Following precedents, it being shown that the beneficiary suffers from disabilities of an extreme nature (disease of the spinal cord), an increase of his pension from $12 to $24 per month is warranted, and the bill is therefore reported back with the recommendation that it pass after the same shall have been amended as follows:

In line 4 strike out the word "upon" and insert in lieu thereof the word "on."

In line 6, after the word "the," insert the words "United States ships Active and Mercy."

In line 7 strike out the word "twenty-five" and insert in lieu thereof the word "twenty-four."

O

CHARLES M. WALKER.

FEBRUARY 2, 1903.—Committed to the Committee of the Whole House and ordered
to be printed.

Mr. APLIN, from the Committee on Invalid Pensions, submitted the
following

REPORT.

[To accompany H. R. 2911.]

The Committee on Invalid Pensions, to whom was referred the bill
(H. R. 2911) granting a pension to Charles M. Walker, submit the
following report:

This bill proposes to pension the soldier named therein at $12 per
month.

Mr. Walker is now 63 years of age, and served as an unassigned
recruit of the Second Vermont Infantry from March 3, 1862, to May
8, 1862, when he was discharged on surgeon's certificate of disability
by reason of "a strumous diathesis."

His claim to pension under the general law, filed in February, 1873,
and based upon disease of the lungs alleged to have been contracted
from exposure while quartered with a number of recruits in a building at Burlington, lying on a floor wet and damp with snow and water
and without any blankets, and subsequently aggravated by exposure
while ordered out on inspection on the ice of Lake Champlain, was
rejected in May, 1900, upon the ground of no record, no medical
testimony showing treatment for disease of lungs in the service, at
date of discharge, nor at any time since, and the testimony of comrades filed being insufficient, in view of the claimant's brief period of
service, to prove the origin of disease of the lungs in the service.

The certificate of disability upon which the soldier was discharged
is signed by B. W. Carpenter, assistant surgeon of the Second Vermont
Infantry.

In support of this claim the beneficiary filed proof showing that
neither himself nor any of his family before the war suffered from
disease of the lungs or a disability of that nature; also the testimony
of three comrades as to his contracting a bad cold and a severe cough
under the circumstances alleged by him, and that he was finally discharged on account of disease of lungs.

A number of claimant's acquaintances, who had known the soldier ever since his return from the Army and while he was a resident of Vermont and Michigan, testified that upon his return from the Army he was terribly poor, sick with lung trouble, and unable to do anything for two or three years; that he was under the treatment of Drs. Wiley and Robinson, who pronounced him far gone into consumption; that about 1869 he was advised to go to the salt water, from which he received some benefit, but that his cough returned and that he had ever since suffered from lung trouble.

When last examined, on November 17, 1897, the board of surgeons found as follows:

Percussion not normal, vesicular murmur roughened over entire portion of upper lobe of each lung. Rate, $6.

Just to the left of the seventh cervical vertebra is a tumor 3 inches in diameter and projecting one-half inch, evidently containing fluid, and is very tender on touch, and turning his head is painful.

Find all large joints snap and crack on motion; can only raise arms to an angle of 45°; motion of shoulders one-fourth impaired; all muscles and tendons covering all large joints stiffened and tense. Rate, $6.

Heart's action varies from 72 to 86; action irritable and irregular, and there is dyspnoea on exercise. Rate, $6.

Proof filed with your committee shows that the soldier for the last eight or ten years has been suffering, aside from lung trouble, with rheumatism affecting his arms and back; that he has a hard time to get along, and was not possessed of any property, except a house and lot assessed at $400 and mortgaged at $300.

The affidavit of Dr. Kirkpatrick, also filed with your committee, sets forth that he had been the soldier's family physician for fourteen years and knew that he had been afflicted with disease of lungs, rheumatism, and disease of heart; that he also suffers from a hernia, poor eyesight, and a bunch on his spine, etc.

It is a well-known fact that the first few months of a soldier's life were the most trying upon his system.

Your committee do not doubt, in view of the evidence above stated, that the soldier contracted a severe cold while in service and line of duty, and that the disease of the respiratory organs from which he is now suffering is a natural result of the same.

In view of this your committee believe that the relief sought for in the bill is fully warranted, and the bill is reported back with the recommendation that it pass after the same shall have been amended as follows:

In line 6 strike out the words "of Company I" and insert in lieu thereof the word "unassigned."

O

DEBORAH J. FOGLE.

FEBRUARY 2, 1903.—Committed to the Committee of the Whole House and ordered
to be printed.

Mr. SULLOWAY, from the Committee on Invalid Pensions, submitted
the following

REPORT.

[To accompany H. R. 4734.]

The Committee on Invalid Pensions, to whom was referred the bill
(H. R. 4734) granting a pension to Deborah J. Fogle, submit the following report:

This bill proposes to pension the beneficiary as the widow of James
B. Fogle, late first lieutenant Company I, Fourteenth West Virginia
Infantry, at $20 per month.

The husband of this beneficiary served as private, first sergeant, and
first lieutenant of Company I, Fourteenth West Virginia Infantry,
from August 16, 1862, to January 3, 1865, when he was dismissed the
service for drunkenness, disorderly conduct, and utter worthlessness.

The medical records of the War Department show that he was under
treatment in November, 1864, for diarrhea.

He was pensioned under the general law on account of total deafness
of the right ear and slight deafness of the left ear, chronic diarrhea,
and piles, all of which disabilities were contracted by him while holding
the rank of first sergeant.

The two medical examinations in his case, made in July, 1890, and
November, 1891, showed that his liver was engorged and tender, that
he was tender over the stomach and bowels, that his spleen was
enlarged and tender, and that he was somewhat emaciated.

He died August 24, 1894, from stricture of the œsophagus.

The beneficiary named in the bill, now 60 years of age, who was
married to the officer on February 27, 1868, applied for pension under
the general law. Her claim, however, was rejected in November,
1897, upon the ground that her husband's death from stricture of the
œsophagus had no connection with the chronic diarrhea and piles for
which he had been pensioned.

In support of that claim the beneficiary filed the testimony of the
surgeon of her husband's regiment, setting forth that he had treated

the soldier in December, 1864, for a severe cold, which finally developed into catarrh of the stomach; and medical testimony that the soldier for some time prior to his death was suffering from chronic catarrh of the stomach and stricture of the œsophagus, that in the opinion of the physicians the catarrhal condition started in the stomach and culminated in the stricture, and that he practically died of starvation, as nothing could remain on his stomach.

From proof filed in the Pension Bureau it appears that the beneficiary has not remarried since her husband's death; that at the time of his death he left two children under 16 years of age surviving him; and that the beneficiary has no means of support and no property except a house and lot in the town of Terra Alta, W. Va., assessed for taxation purposes at $700 and encumbered by a mortgage of $1,200.

The question in the case is simply as to whether the chronic diarrhea and catarrh of the stomach from which the evidence shows the soldier suffered in the service and since produced the stricture of the œsophagus of which he died.

The Pension Bureau holds that it did not, while the physicians who attended the soldier for years before his death, and who gave a history of the case which is entirely probable, hold that it was due to the stomach trouble.

The question as to whether the beneficiary's husband received an honorable or dishonorable discharge from the service cuts no figure in the case, for the reason that under the general law (acts of July 14, 1862, and March 3, 1873) that question does not enter into the case.

Your committee believe that the doubts in the case should be resolved in favor of the beneficiary, in view of the testimony of the physicians stated above, and therefore recommend that the beneficiary be given relief at the rate of $12 per month, the diarrhea for which the soldier had been pensioned, and which was no doubt a part of the stomach trouble, having been contracted by him while an enlisted man.

The bill is therefore reported back with the recommendation that it pass after the same shall have been amended as follows:

Strike out all after the enacting clause and insert in lieu thereof the following:

That the Secretary of the Interior be, and he is hereby, authorized and directed to place on the pension roll, subject to the provisions and limitations of the pension laws, the name of Deborah J. Fogle, widow of James B. Fogle, late of Company I, Fourteenth Regiment West Virginia Volunteer Infantry, and pay her a pension at the rate of twelve dollars per month.

O

JAMES E. WALLACE.

FEBRUARY 2, 1903.—Committed to the Committee of the Whole House and ordered
to be printed.

Mr. SULLOWAY, from the Committee on Invalid Pensions, submitted
the following

REPORT.

[To accompany H. R. 4740.]

The Committee on Invalid Pensions, to whom was referred the bill
(H. R. 4740) granting an increase of pension to J. E. Wallace, submit
the following report:
This bill proposes to increase the pension of the soldier named
therein from $12 to $24 per month.
James E. Wallace, the soldier named in this bill, and now 58 years
of age, served as a private in Company M, Twelfth Pennsylvania Cavalry, from February 5, 1862, to July 20, 1865, when honorably discharged.
The medical records of the War Department furnish no information
as to any treatment of the soldier while in the service. The military
records, however, show that the regiment was home on veteran furlough from March 18 to April 17, 1864.
The soldier filed a claim to pension under the general law on June
11, 1879, alleging that he accidentally lost his left thumb from a gunshot wound, and that he contracted measles, resulting in disease of
the lungs.
The claim, so far as it related to loss of the left thumb from gunshot wound, was allowed in 1899 at $4 per month from discharge and
at $8 per month from April 3, 1884.
The beneficiary is now and has been since August 15, 1891, a pensioner under the act of June 27, 1890, at $12 per month for total ina-
bility to earn a support by manual labor by reason of the loss of the
left thumb, disease of heart, and disease of the respiratory organs.
The claim on account of disease of lungs (catarrh or asthma) under
the general law was rejected in February, 1899, upon the ground of
no record and no medical or other satisfactory evidence to prove that
said disability originated during the soldier's service and in line of duty.
The soldier alleged that he was given a veteran furlough in March,

1864; that on the way home he took sick, and that about three or four days after arriving home measles broke out and that he had a cough and shortness of breath following the same.

A number of the soldier's comrades testified that they knew that the beneficiary had lost his voice at one time in the service, but they could not tell when this occurred; that he recovered, however; others testified that upon his return from veteran furlough he could only speak in a whisper; that during the winter of 1864–65 he was in that condition and that he coughed a great deal, but none of these witnesses knew of any lung trouble in the service.

Relatives with whom the soldier stopped while on veteran furlough testified that he came home in the spring of 1864; that he had measles while there; that he had a cough thereafter and was very hoarse, and that he was still in that condition when he went back to the regiment; that after his return from the service he had a cough which continued right along and finally turned into a kind of phthisic.

One of his employers after the war testified that upon his return from the service he had a cough and was short of breath, and a fellow-workman testified that he had phthisic and was all stuffed up and had a slight cough; and a physician testified to treatment of the soldier since 1888 for catarrh of stomach, bronchitis, and nasal catarrh; that for a few years prior to July, 1897, he had several attacks of grippe; that he had functional disease of the heart since 1895, and pulmonary trouble since 1897.

When last examined, on December 28, 1898, the board of surgeons rated him $8 for the loss of the thumb of the left hand, and found hypertrophy and dilatation of the right ventricle of the heart, with dyspnœa and cyanosis, with both moist and dry rales over the entire lungs, asthma following measles, voice very hoarse and rasping, due to catarrhal condition of the respiratory organs, and rated him $17 for asthma and $4 for catarrh.

The evidence in the case tends probably to the service origin of the asthma from which the soldier is now suffering; hence your committee is willing to resolve whatever doubts there are in favor of the soldier who rendered over three years' service. The board of examining surgeons having rated him $17 for asthma and $8 for the loss of the left thumb of accepted service origin, an increase of his pension to the amount sought for in the bill is therefore warranted, and the bill is reported back with the recommendation that it pass after the same shall have been amended as follows:

Strike out all after the enacting clause and insert in lieu thereof the following:

That the Secretary of the Interior be, and he is hereby, authorized and directed to place on the pension roll, subject to the provisions and limitations of the pension laws, the name of James E. Wallace, late of Company M, Twelfth Regiment Pennsylvania Volunteer Cavalry, and pay him a pension at the rate of twenty-four dollars per month in lieu of that he is now receiving.

Amend title so as to read: "A bill granting an increase of pension to James E. Wallace."

O

THEODORE BURI.

FEBRUARY 2, 1903.—Committed to the Committee of the Whole House and ordered
to be printed.

Mr. DEEMER, from the Committee on Invalid Pensions, submitted the
following

REPORT.

[To accompany H. R. 13701.]

The Committee on Invalid Pensions, to whom was referred the bill
(H. R. 13701) granting a pension to Theodore Buri, submit the following report:

This bill proposes to pension Theodore Buri, late of Company B
Sixteenth Pennsylvania Infantry, at $24 per month.

Records of the War Department show that the soldier named in this
bill, now 77 years of age, served as a private in Company B, Sixteenth
Pennsylvania Infantry, from May 4, 1861, to July 30, 1861, when
honorably discharged.

He never filed a claim to pension under the general law.

His claim to pension under the act of June 27, 1890, was rejected by
the Pension Bureau in 1892 upon the ground that he did not serve
ninety days during the war of the rebellion.

The beneficiary alleged, and his discharge certificate corroborates his
allegation, that he was enlisted on April 29, 1861, and discharged on
July 29, 1861. The War Deparment, however, when its attention had
been called to the certificate of discharge, stated that no change could
be made in the records to show an earlier date of enlistment of the
soldier.

The only certificate of medical examination of the soldier, made on
February 17, 1892, rated him $4 for chronic rheumatism and $4 for
piles.

Had the War Department recognized a service of ninety days of
this beneficiary instead of eighty-seven days, he would, under the
rules of the Pension Bureau, be entitled, by reason of senility, to the
maximum rating under the act of June 27, 1890, namely, $12 per month.

In view of his great age, your committee are of the opinion that the
requirement as to period of service may well be waived in this case,
the soldier only lacking three days to make up the necessary ninety
days.

The bill is therefore reported back with the recommendation that it
pass after the same shall have been amended as follows:

In line 7, before the word "Infantry," insert the word "Volunteer."

In line 8 strike out the word "twenty-four" and insert in lieu
thereof the word "twelve."

O

JOHN C. SAUTTER.

FEBRUARY 2, 1903.—Committed to the Committee of the Whole House and ordered
to be printed.

Mr. SAMUEL W. SMITH, from the Committee on Invalid Pensions, submitted the following

REPORT.

[To accompany H. R. 16786.]

The Committee on Invalid Pensions, to whom was referred the bill
(H. R. 16786) granting an increase of pension to John C. Sauther,
submit the following report:

This bill proposes to increase the pension of the soldier named
therein from $17 to $30 per month.

John C. Sautter, the soldier named in this bill, and now 63 years of
age, who served as a private in Company K, Fifth Michigan Infantry,
from August 28, 1861, to July 5, 1865, when honorably discharged,
and whom the records of the War Department show to have received
a gunshot wound of the right thumb at the battle of Spottsylvania
Court-House in May, 1864, to have been a prisoner of war from May 3,
1863, to May 14, 1863, and to have been under treatment for the wound,
rheumatism, remittent fever, and debility during his period of service,
is now pensioned under the general law at $17 per month on account
of disability arising from gunshot wound of the right thumb, chronic
diarrhea, and resulting piles and hemorrhages.

A claim on account of a double rupture, alleged to have been incurred
from a fall while on the march to Malvern Hill, was rejected by the
Pension Bureau in June, 1891, upon the ground of no record and
claimant's inability, with the aid of a special examination, to furnish
satisfactory evidence of the origin of the same in the service and line
of duty.

This rejection was affirmed by Assistant Secretary Campbell, under
date of March 25, 1902, and a careful reading of the evidence filed
and that obtained upon special examination shows conclusively that
the action of rejection was proper.

A claim for increase of pension, in which the soldier alleged chronic
catarrh, bronchitis, disease of the kidneys, and spinal rheumatism as
results of the pensioned causes, was rejected in November, 1902, upon

the ground that the disabilities of accepted service origin did not warrant a rating in excess of $17 per month and that the alleged results
could not be accepted as such.

When last examined, on August 13, 1902, the board of surgeons
rated him $4 for the gunshot wound of thumb, $12 for chronic diarrhea and resulting piles, $6 for chronic catarrh, $6 for rheumatism,
$14 for a double rupture, and $6 for disease of heart, and the board
of surgeons then stated that for the combined disabilities he was
entitled to a rating of $24 per month.

An examination of the certificate of the board of examining surgeons shows, in the opinion of your committee, judging by the descrip
tion of the disabilities for which the soldier is now pensioned, that for
the disabilities of accepted service origin the soldier is entitled to a
rating of $24 per month, an increase of his pension of $7 per month;
and the bill is therefore reported back with the recommendation that
it pass after the same shall have been amended as follows:

In line 6 strike out the word "Sauther" and insert in lieu thereof
the word "Sautter."

In line 8 strike out the word "thirty" and insert in lieu thereof the
word "twenty-four."

Amend the title so as to read: "A bill granting an increase of pen
sion to John C. Sautter."

O

FRANK E. HILLS.

FEBRUARY 2, 1903.—Committed to the Committee of the Whole House and ordered
to be printed.

Mr. CROWLEY, from the Committee on Invalid Pensions, submitted the
following

REPORT. ·

[To accompany H. R. 14788.]

The Committee on Invalid Pensions, to whom was referred the bill
(H. R. 14788) granting a pension to Frank E. Hills, submit the
following report:

This bill proposes to increase the pension of the soldier named
therein from $12 to $35 per month.

Frank E. Hills, now 60 years of age, served as a private in Company D, One hundredth Illinois Infantry, from August 18, 1862, to
June 12, 1865, when honorably discharged, and according to the
records of the War Department received a wound of the first finger
of the left hand while in action at Franklin, Tenn.

He is now pensioned under the general law at $12 per month for
nearly total deafness of left ear and rheumatism.

The claim on account of the wound of the finger was rejected by the
Pension Bureau in December, 1890, upon the ground that a disability
from that cause had not existed since the filing of the claim.

It appears from the medical testimony filed in the Pension Bureau
that the beneficiary was suddenly stricken with right hemiplegia on
May 6, 1899, and some of the physicians testified that the cerebral
hemorrhage depended upon arterio-sclerosis and that this sclerosis
was due to rheumatism and endocarditis; another physician testified
that the lesion, in his opinion, was thrombotic and attributed the
same to an injury to the soldier's ear from a bullet wound incurred in
the service.

The Pension Bureau, however, held that while it was shown that the
beneficiary suffered from muscular rheumatism, and that this was contracted in the service, the same was not of a serious character, inasmuch as the board of surgeons that examined him as late as May, 1890,
could find no evidence thereof and then rated him only $2 on his own
statements, and therefore held that the paralysis could not be attrib-

uted to the rheumatism and endocarditis and that the slight wound of the ear due to a spent ball, leaving no scar, but only a rupture of the tympañum resulting, could not be accepted as a cause of the paralysis at this late date.

It appears from papers on file in the Pension Bureau that on July 5, 1899, a guardian was appointed over the soldier by reason of his insanity.

When last examined, on December 6, 1899, the board of surgeons then stated that the beneficiary was suffering from paralysis of the right side; that he could dress and undress himself, however, and attend to calls of nature without assistance, but could not express himself, either by voice or in writing, and that by reason of the paralysis and deafness he was entitled to a pension of $30 per month.

The statement of Drs. Winne and Brown, filed with your committee, sets forth that since the beneficiary was stricken with paralysis he had been entirely disabled from manual labor and also from any work involving mental integrity, and one of these physicians stated that from the anatomical relation of the parts, a middle-ear disease being so contiguous to the location in the brain of the centers that govern the organs of speech, he was fully convinced that the present condition was the result of the injury to ear.

A statement signed by the county judge, county clerk, and other officers of Dekalb County, Ill., also filed with your committee, sets forth that the beneficiary's case is a very unusual one and attracts the attention and sympathy of the whole community; that his affliction deprives him of all means of doing anything toward a livelihood, and that he is worthy and deserving in every respect.

Following the action of the House on June 16, 1902, in Senate bill 4850, relief to the extent of increasing this soldier's pension from $12 to $30 per month, he being shown to be a sufferer from paralysis, etc., is justified, and the bill is therefore reported back with the recommendation that it pass after the same shall have been amended as follows:

In line 8 strike out the word "thirty-five" and insert in lieu thereof the word "thirty."

Amend the title so as to read: "A bill granting an increase of pension to Frank E. Hills."

O

MILTON C. NORTON.

FEBRUARY 2, 1903.—Committed to the Committee of the Whole House and ordered
to be printed.

Mr. CROWLEY, from the Committee on Invalid Pensions, submitted the following

REPORT.

[To accompany H. R. 15403.]

The Committee on Invalid Pensions, to whom was referred the bill (H. R. 15403) granting an increase of pension to Milton C. Norton, submit the following report:

This bill proposes to increase the pension of the soldier named therein from $17 to $30 per month.

This soldier, now 62 years of age, who served as a private in Company A, First Wisconsin Heavy Artillery, from November 16, 1863, to August 18, 1865, when honorably discharged, and who was under treatment during his term of service at various dates for diarrhea, constipation, and intermittent fever, has been pensioned under the general law at $17 per month on account of piles, rheumatism, and resulting disease of heart.

A claim for increase of pension filed November 16, 1901, in which the soldier alleged nervous prostration and loss of sight of the left eye as results of the pensioned causes was rejected by the Pension Bureau in July, 1902, upon the ground that these alleged results had no pathological connection with the disabilities of accepted service origin.

When last examined, on April 2, 1902, the board of surgeons described his disabilities as follows:

There are 4 internal piles from one-eighth to one-half inch in diameter, and 4 internal piles size of a hazel nut, which bleed on examination. Rectum inflamed and tender.

There is crepitation in both shoulders, left elbow, and knee. There is some tenderness, no swelling or œdema, and only slight limitation of motion.

There is decided mitral regurgitant murmur. Apex beat not evident on inspection or palpitation; is behind the sixth rib, one inch to the right of the nipple line. Claimant is poorly nourished, tongue coated, skin sallow, nervous, and very anæmic.

Left eye totally blind, due to large cataract.

Urine straw colored; albumen present, but no sugar.

Rate for piles, $5; heart lesion, $8; rheumatism, $3; nervousness, $2; eye injury, $17.

The petition of the beneficiary filed with your committee sets forth that he has no property of any kind nor income except the pension of $17 per month, and that his disabilities have increased so as to render him very infirm and requiring care and attendance.

A petition signed by a large number of residents of Steel Rock, Iowa, also filed with your committee, sets forth that the beneficiary has no property and has a wife dependent upon him for support, is very infirm, and totally incapacitated from performing any manual labor; that he constantly requires medical attendance, and petitions Congress to grant the beneficiary an increase of his pension in order that himself and wife may be comfortably cared for in their declining years.

The description of the soldier's disabilities in the certificate of examination of April 2, 1902, is such that in the opinion of your committee the soldier by reason of the pensioned causes is disabled to an extent equivalent to the loss of a hand or a foot, and that he is therefore entitled to the rate for that degree of disability, namely, $24 per month, and the bill is therefore reported back with the recommendation that it pass after the same shall have been amended as follows:

In line 8 strike out the word "thirty" and insert in lieu thereof the word "twenty-four."

O

WILLIAM M. HATTERY.

FEBRUARY 2, 1903.—Committed to the Committee of the Whole House and ordered to be printed.

Mr. CROWLEY, from the Committee on Invalid Pensions, submitted the following

REPORT.

[To accompany H. R. 15404.]

The Committee on Invalid Pensions, to whom was referred the bill (H. R. 15404) granting an increase of pension to William M. Hattery, submit the following report:

This bill proposes to pay the soldier named a pension of $12 per month in lieu of that he is now receiving.

William M. Hattery, now 65 years of age, served as a private in Company A, Forty-second Ohio Infantry, from September 20, 1861, to September 30, 1864, when honorably discharged with his company, and is now in receipt of a pension under the act of June 27, 1890, at $12 per month, the maximum rating, for total inability to earn a support by manual labor, the result of left varicocele and paralysis agitans.

When last examined, on July 16, 1902, upon which certificate of examination his pension, under the act of June 27, 1890, was increased from $6 to $12 per month, the board of surgeons stated that his hands and arms were in constant motion; that his fingers were partly closed on the palm and could not be extended, giving the hands a claw-like appearance; that he can feed himself and dress and undress himself excepting in fastening buttons, which was difficult for him; and also found the superficial veins of the scrotum slightly varicosed, and the spermatic veins on both sides varicosed, and the lower side of the scrotum on both sides a mass 2 by 1 inches in size, same on each side.

There has been filed with your committee the statement of the beneficiary setting forth that in October, 1902, he was receiving a pension of $6 per month; that were he getting a pension of $12 per month in his almost helpless condition it could only help him in part.

It being shown that this soldier, who rendered three years of service, is now suffering from paralysis agitans and in a helpless condition, an increase of his pension from $12 to $24 per month is warranted under precedents, and the bill is reported back with the recommendation that it pass after the same shall have been amended as follows:

In line 8 strike out the word "twelve" and insert in lieu thereof the word "twenty-four."

O

FRANK STAFFORD.

FEBRUARY 2, 1903.—Committed to the Committee of the Whole House and ordered to be printed.

Mr. CROWLEY, from the Committee on Invalid Pensions, submitted the following

REPORT.

[To accompany H. R. 15915.]

The Committee on Invalid Pensions, to whom was referred the bill (H. R. 15915) granting an increase of pension to Frank Stoppard, submit the following report:

This bill proposes to increase the pension of the soldier named therein from $12 to $30 per month.

Frank Stafford is now 57 years of age, and served as a private in Company B, Sixteenth Kansas Cavalry, from November 2, 1863, to December 6, 1865, when honorably discharged.

He never applied for pension under the general law, but is now a pensioner under the act of June 27, 1890, at $12 per month for total inability to earn a support by manual labor by reason of rheumatism and disease of the heart.

From proof filed in the Pension Bureau and from the soldier's allegations on file in that Bureau it appears that on May 12, 1902, while present at the tearing down of a house the house collapsed, falling upon him, breaking three ribs and dislocating his right hip joint, since which time he has been able to walk only with the aid of crutches, there being general atrophy of the muscles of the right leg.

An increase of this soldier's pension from $12 to $20 per month appears warranted, it being shown that he is now suffering from disabilities of an extreme nature and able to walk only with the aid of crutches.

The bill is therefore reported back with the recommendation that it pass after the same shall have been amended as follows:

In line 6 strike out the word "Stoppard" and insert in lieu thereof the word "Stafford."

In line 8 strike out the word "thirty" and insert in lieu thereof the word "twenty."

Amend the title so as to read: "A bill granting an increase of pension to Frank Stafford."

O

BYRON C. KNAPP.

FEBRUARY 2, 1903.—Committed to the Committee of the Whole House and ordered to be printed.

Mr. MIERS, from the Committee on Invalid Pensions, submitted the following

REPORT.

[To accompany H. R. 7433.]

The Committee on Invalid Pensions, to whom was referred the bill (H. R. 7433) granting an increase of pension to B. C. Knapp, submit the following report:

This bill proposes to increase the pension of the soldier named therein from $6 to $50 per month.

Byron C. Knapp, the soldier named in this bill, and now 63 years of age, is shown by the records of the War Department to have served in Company K, First Minnesota Volunteers, from May 22, 1861, to February 27, 1862, when discharged on surgeon's certificate of disability by reason of varicocele and hæmoptysis.

The records of the War Department show that he again entered the service as a private in Company B, Second Battalion, Sixteenth U. S. Infantry, on April 23, 1862, and that he was honorably discharged April 23, 1865.

On June 5, 1883, the soldier applied for pension under the general law on account of the varicocele and hæmoptysis for which discharged the service, and which were contracted by him while on the retreat after the first Bull Run fight, and the Pension Bureau in September, 1891, admitted from a legal standpoint that he had contracted a right varicocele in the service, but the claim was rejected by the medical division of the Pension Bureau upon the ground that a disability from such varicocele and from hæmoptysis had not existed since the filing of the claim.

The first medical examination of the soldier, made in July, 1883, found no varicocele nor hernia. The next examination, made in September, 1888, stated that there was no varicocele, but there was marked enlargement of the abdominal rings on the right side, and the next examination, made April 15, 1891, found a small varicocele, for which the board of surgeons rated him $2.

Notwithstanding the fact that in 1891 the Pension Bureau held that there was no disability from the right varicocele, the soldier was pensioned in 1894, under the act of June 27, 1890, at $6 per month for partial inability to earn a support by manual labor by reason of an injury to the right arm and a right varicocele, and the soldier is now in receipt of that pension, a claim for increase of pension, filed in 1898, having been rejected in October, 1899.

The soldier injured his right arm on June 10, 1888, and incurred a contusion of the left ankle in 1896.

When last examined, on September 28, 1898, the board of surgeons found no disease of lungs or heart, but did find a fracture of the right arm, affecting both pronation and suppination, with loss of right ring and middle fingers at middle joints, and rated him $10 for that disability, but could not then find any varicocele or hernia.

There has been filed with your committee the affidavit of Dr. J. B. Murfree, of Murfreesboro, Tenn., setting forth that he carefully examined the soldier on April 3, 1902, and found him in feeble health and disabled from active manual labor on account of a deformity of the right arm, the result of a badly united fracture, the deformity consisting in shortening of the arm, with wasting of the muscles; and also a slight ossific union between the ulna and radius, which prevented rotation of the bones upon each other and interfered with the proper pronation and suppination of the hand.

Your committee are of the opinion that this soldier, who rendered four years of service during the civil war, is totally disabled from earning a support by manual labor, and that consequently he is entitled to the maximum rating under the act of June 27, 1890, namely, $12 per month, and recommend relief to that extent, and report the bill back with the recommendation that it pass after the same shall have been amended as follows:

Strike out all of lines 7, 8, and 9 and insert in lieu thereof the following:

of Byron C. Knapp, late of Company B, Second Battalion, Sixteenth Regiment United States Infantry, and pay him a pension at the rate of twelve dollars per month in lieu of that he is now receiving.

Amend the title so as to read: "A bill granting an increase of pension to Byron C. Knapp."

O

JAMES HARRISON.

FEBRUARY 2, 1903.—Committed to the Committee of the Whole House and ordered to be printed.

Mr. MIERS, from the Committee on Invalid Pensions, submitted the following

REPORT.

[To accompany H. R. 16419.]

The Committee on Invalid Pensions, to whom was referred the bill (H. R. 16419) granting a pension to James Harrison, submit the fol·lowing report:

This bill proposes to increase the pension of the soldier named therein from $12 to $30 per month.

The soldier, now 60 years of age, served as a private in Company C, Forty-third Ohio Volunteers, from October 8, 1862, to August 19, 1863, when honorably discharged, and is pensioned under the act of June 27, 1890, at $12 per month for total inability to earn a support by manual labor by reason of total blindness, incurred in November, 1889, while handling lime in a glass factory.

Papers filed in the Pension Bureau show that the soldier has a wife and four children dependent upon him for support, and that the pension of $12 per month is entirely inadequate to support them.

A medical examination of the soldier on January 21, 1891, showed him totally blind by reason of complete opacity of cornea of both eyes, and requiring the aid and attendance of another person.

The relief sought for in this bill is warranted in view of the action of the House, taken on June 16, 1902, increasing from $12 to $30 per month the pension of those who, by reason of blindness, paralysis, etc., require the aid and attendance of another person, and the bill is reported back with the recommendation that it pass after the same shall have been amended as follows:

In line 6, before the word " Ohio," insert the word "Regiment."

Amend the title so as to read: "A bill granting an increase of pension to James Harrison."

O

OLIVER W. KILE.

FEBRUARY 2, 1903.—Committed to the Committee of the Whole House and ordered
to be printed.

Mr. MIERS, from the Committee on Invalid Pensions, submitted the
following

REPORT.

[To accompany H. R. 16857.]

The Committee on Invalid Pensions, to whom was referred the bill
(H. R. 16857) granting an increase of pension to Oliver H. Kile,
submit the following report:

This bill proposes to increase the pension of the soldier named therein
from $17 to $50 per month.

Oliver W. Kile, the soldier named in this bill and now 63 years of
age, served as private, corporal, and sergeant in Company B, Ninth
Ohio Cavalry, from October 17, 1862, to July 20, 1865, when honorably discharged.

He is now pensioned under the general law at $17 per month on
account of fistula in ano and disease of lungs.

Claims on account of additional disabilities—namely, chronic diarrhea,
disease of the stomach, and rheumatism—were rejected in August, 1902,
upon the ground of no record of treatment for said disabilities in the
service, no medical evidence showing treatment for same while in the
service or at or soon after discharge, and testimony obtained upon
special examination being insufficient to prove the origin of said diseases in the service or their existence at discharge and for several
years thereafter.

The beneficiary, who is now a minister of the gospel, alleged that he
contracted inflammatory rheumatism in February or March, 1864, and
that he incurred diarrhea in July, 1864.

A number of comrades testified before the special examiner that the
soldier, while in the service, had diarrhea or something like dysentery
or flux; that he complained of rheumatism and appeared to be lame
toward the last of his service, and complained of great pain and soreness in his limbs and joints and walked lame and stiff; and a number of
neighbors and acquaintances testified that upon his return from the
service his health was poor; that he walked with a cane; that he complained of rheumatism and was at times hardly able to get around;

that he was confined to his house a good many times by reason of
rheumatism; and another witness testified that he first noticed the
beneficiary walking stiff and stooped over and complaining of. rheumatism about a year after his discharge from the service.

The beneficiary filed medical testimony showing treatment since
1869 for stomach and diarrheal trouble, for stomach, diarrheal, and
tubercular trouble, and for bronchitis, and also for chronic rheumatism
especially affecting the back.

When last examined, on August 8, 1900, the board of surgeons rated
him $12 for the fistula in ano, $6 for disease of lungs, $4 for nervous
prostration, $6 for rheumatism, and $12 for disease of digestive organs
and piles.

The evidence in the case indicates that the disease of the digestive
organs and piles, as well as rheumatism, are traceable to this soldier's
service of nearly three years, and that by reason of these disabilities
and the fistula in ano and disease of lungs of accepted service origin
he is wholly disabled for the performance of any manual labor, and is
entitled, therefore, to an increase of his pension to $30 per month.

In view of this the bill is reported back with the recommendation
that it pass after the same shall have been amended as follows:

In line 6 strike out the letter "H" and insert in lieu thereof the
letter "W."

In line 8 strike out the word "fifty" and insert in lieu thereof the
word "thirty."

Amend the title so as to read: "A bill granting an increase of pension to Oliver W. Kile."

O

MICHAEL HOWE.

FEBRUARY 2, 1903.—Committed to the Committee of the Whole House and ordered
to be printed.

Mr. MIERS, from the Committee on Invalid Pensions, submitted the
following

REPORT.

[To accompany H. R. 16784.]

The Committee on Invalid Pensions, to whom was referred the bill
(H. R. 16784) granting an increase of pension to Michael Howe,
submit the following report:

This bill proposes to increase the pension of the soldier named
therein from $12 to $50 per month.

Michael Howe, now 60 years of age, served as a private in Company
G, Twentieth Wisconsin Volunteer Infantry, from July 30, 1862, to
June 15, 1864, when honorably discharged on surgeon's certificate of
disability by reason of—

chronic diarrhea of ten months' duration, producing much debility and emaciation,
and during this time he has been furloughed with but little improvement. As the
hot weather advances the case becomes more aggravated. He is physically unfit for
the Veteran Reserve Corps.

The medical records of the War Department show that he was
under treatment at various dates from June, 1863, to June, 1864, for
intermittent fever, remittent fever, and chronic diarrhea.

He was pensioned under the general law on account of chronic diarrhea and resulting disease of rectum at $4 per month from discharge,
at $6 from August 21, 1889, and at $8 from September 24, 1890.

A claim for increase of pension under that law, filed December 3,
1900, was rejected October 29, 1901, upon the ground that the disabilities of accepted service origin did not warrant a rating in excess of $8
per month.

He is now a pensioner under the act of June 27, 1890, at $12 per
month, the maximum rating, for total inability to earn a support by
manual labor, the result of disease of rectum and loss of sight of both
eyes.

When last examined, on March 19, 1902, the board of surgeons described his physical condition as follows:

This claimant came before the board, being led by a neighbor, as he could not see. He can not see the sun shining. Can not tell if the window blind is down or up. He says that he lost the sight of his left eye within the eight months before his right eye failed him, which was last fall. It is the opinion of this board that he has amorosis of central origin. He has nasopharyngeal catarrh.

We noticed he could not put on his coat alone on account of pain in his right shoulder joint. Upon examination, however, we find no contracted tendons, no enlarged joints, yet we believe he has rheumatism in this shoulder. His muscles are all soft and flabby, palms of hands soft.

We find that he is suffering from total blindness of both eyes, nasoypharyngeal catarrh, chronic diarrhea and resulting diseases of rectum, functional disease of the heart, and rheumatism of the right shoulder.

Medical and lay testimony filed in the Pension Bureau shows that the beneficiary became totally blind during the year 1901; that he is entirely dependent, having no means of support except the pension which he is now receiving, and of course wholly incapacitated for the performance of any labor.

An increase of this soldier's pension to $30 per month is warranted under precedents, it being shown that he is totally blind, served nearly two years, requires the aid and attendance of another person, and is in destitute circumstances.

The passage of the bill is therefore recommended after the same shall have been amended as follows:

In line 6 strike out the word " private."

In same line, after the word " Twentieth," insert the word " Regiment."

In line 7 strike out the word " Volunteers " and insert in lieu thereof the words " Volunteer Infantry."

In line 8 strike out the word " fifty " and insert in lieu thereof the word " thirty."

O

RICHARD G. HANSCOM.

FEBRUARY 2, 1903.—Committed to the Committee of the Whole House and ordered to be printed.

Mr. APLIN, from the Committee on Invalid Pensions, submitted the following

REPORT.

[To accompany H. R. 16787.]

The Committee on Invalid Pensions, to whom was referred the bill (H. R. 16787) granting an increase of pensiou to R. G. Hanscom, submit the following report:

This bill proposes to increase the pension of the soldier named therein from $12 to $24 per month.

This soldier, now 72 years of age, served as a private in Company I, Second Wisconsin Cavalry, from December 31, 1863, to January 9, 1865, when honorably discharged on surgeon's certificate of disability by reason of "chronic diarrhea of eight months' standing."

The medical records of the War Department show that he was under treatment from July 10 to 28, 1864, for intermittent fever; from August 8 to August 22, 1864, for diarrhea; that he was furloughed from August 24 to September 21, 1864, on a certificate showing him suffering from chronic diarrhea and general debility, and that he again entered hospital on October 19, 1864, with chronic diarrhea, and was discharged as stated above.

He is now pensioned under the act of June 27, 1890, at the maximum rating, namely, $12 per month, for total inability to earn a support by manual labor, the result of chronic diarrhea, hemorrhoids, total deafness of right ear and severe deafness of the left, rheumatism, disease of heart and lungs.

He was formerly pensioned under the general law on account of chronic diarrhea and resulting hemorrhoids at $2 per month from discharge, and at $4 per month from April 2, 1884, and showed himself to be entitled to a rating of $8 per month on account of these disabilities, but a certificate was not issued under the general law for the reason that he was then in receipt of a higher pension under the act of June 27, 1890.

A claim on account of deafness, filed under the general law, was rejected in May, 1897, upon the ground of no record of treatment for said disability in the service and no medical evidence of treatment in service or at discharge, nor any other evidence as to the existence of said disability in the service, and claimant's apparent inability to furnish the necessary proof to connect his deafness with his service.

When last examined, on October 29, 1902, the board of surgeons described his disabilities as follows:

Chronic diarrhea and resulting disease of rectum: Applicant is weak and emaciated, skin dry and harsh, palms soft, teeth all gone but three, tongue tremulous and coated, abdomen tympanitic, rectum relaxed. Rate, $10.

Deafness: Severe deafness in each ear. Could hear loud conversation at 3 feet, but does not at 1 foot. Rate, $22.

Rheumatism: Both shoulders grating, stiff, tender, painful; motion limited one-half in each. Other joints normal. Muscles of back stiff, tender, painful; motion limited one-half. Rate, $10.

Heart: Action weak, intermittent, and so irregular that pulse could not be counted even after many attempts. There is dilitation with hypertrophy. Dyspnœa and cyanosis are constant and œdema is frequent. It is impossible to exercise this applicant on account of the extreme weakness of his heart. This man can not live long and is liable to die at any moment.

This applicant often requires the aid and attendance of another person in dressing and undressing.

This claimant is so disabled from chronic diarrhea, deafness, rheumatism, and disease of heart as to require the frequent and periodical, though not the regular and constant, personal aid and attendance of another person, and is entitled to $50 per month.

It being shown from the certificate of medical examination of October 29, 1902, that this beneficiary, who is now quite aged, requires the periodical aid and attendance of another person, your committee, following precedents, recommend the relief sought for in the bill, and report the bill back with the recommendation that it pass after the same shall have been amended as follows:

In line 6 strike out the letter "R" and insert in lieu thereof the word "Richard."

In line 7, before the word "Cavalry," insert the word "Volunteer."

Amend the title so as to read: "A bill granting an increase of pension to Richard G. Hanscom."

O

KATHINKA SICHEL.

FEBRUARY 2, 1903.—Committed to the Committee of the Whole House and ordered
to be printed.

Mr. KLEBERG, from the Committee on Invalid Pensions, submitted the
following

REPORT.

[To accompany H. R. 17133.]

The Committee on Invalid Pensions, to whom was referred the bill
(H. R. 17133) granting a pension to Kathinka Sichel, submit the following report:

This bill proposes to pension Kathinka Sichel as widow of Maurice
Sichel, late first lieutenant, Fifty-second New York Infantry, at $20
per month.

The records of the War Department show that Maurice Sichel served
as quartermaster of the Fifty-second New York Infantry from August
6, 1861, to October 8, 1864, when honorably discharged, and that he
was under treatment for bronchial catarrh in 1864.

He again entered the service as first lieutenant and quartermaster
of the One hundred and ninetieth New York Volunteers, but was never
recognized by the War Department as having been in that service, his
muster in having been canceled.

The claim of the beneficiary, filed under the act of June 27, 1890,
was rejected by the Pension Bureau in September, 1895, upon the
ground that title under said act could not obtain for the reason that
the officer was dishonorably discharged from his final service.

Your committee can not understand how this action could have been
taken by the Pension Bureau in view of the fact that the War Department canceled his muster in as an officer of the One hundred and
ninetieth New York Volunteers, the Adjutant-General having stated,
under date of February 27, 1865, that if he had been an enlisted man
prior to his muster in as an officer of the One hundred and ninetieth
New York Volunteers he would be held to his enlistment, but not having been an enlisted man in that regiment it canceled his muster in
as an officer.

The beneficiary, who is now 58 years of age, married the officer on
October 15, 1879, and filed proof of her husband's death on October

28, 1892, that she had not remarried since his death and was dependent upon her daily labor for support.

In view of the above your committee is fully satisfied that the beneficiary should have title under the act of June 27, 1890, and the bill is therefore reported back with the recommendation that it pass after the same shall have been amended as follows:

In lines 6 and 7 strike out the words " first lieutenant " and insert in lieu thereof the words " regimental quartermaster."

In line 8 strike out the word " twenty " and insert in lieu thereof the word " eight."

O

JOHN GRAHAM.

FEBRUARY 2, 1903.—Committed to the Committee of the Whole House and ordered
to be printed.

Mr. SAMUEL W. SMITH, from the Committee on Invalid Pensions, submitted the following

REPORT.

[To accompany H. R. 16048.]

The Committee on Invalid Pensions, to whom was referred the bill
(H. R. 16048) granting a pension to John Graham, submit the following
report:

This bill proposes to increase the pension of the soldier named therein
from $10 to $50 per month.

The soldier named in this bill, now 71 years of age, served as a private in Company I, Third Michigan Cavalry, from January 4, 1864,
to February 12, 1866, when honorably discharged.

He is now pensioned under the general law at $10 per month on
account of disease of throat and lumbago (rheumatism).

Claims for increase of pension, in which the soldier alleged disease
of heart, lungs, and spine, partial paralysis, and affection of the limbs,
hips, arms, etc., and whole muscular system, as results of the lumbago,
were rejected upon the ground that the disease of lungs and bronchial
tubes could not be accepted as a result of disease of throat, and that
the other disabilities had no connection with the lumbago, the disease
of heart found being a result of general rheumatism and not of rheumatism of the lumbar muscles.

When last examined, in 1902, the board of surgeons described his
disabilities as follows:

There is nasopharyngeal catarrh, the nasopharynx being red and engorged and
the right eustachian tube obstructed. He hears normally with left ear, but can not
hear ordinary conversation at or beyond 6 feet with the right ear. Rate, $6.

There is marked paralysis agitans of the right hand and impaired sensation over
all of the right limb, supplied by the sciatic nerve and its branches, but not over
that supplied by the interior inferior cerval. Paralysis, $8.

There is no atrophy of muscles, but he complains of lameness of all muscles of the
back, especially the loins.

Pulse sounds intermittent. There is mitral regurgitant murmur, systolic, with the
loudest over the apex and transmitted to the left.

He was assisted upstairs by a nurse and claimed to be unable to take active exercise.
Rate for rheumatism, $8. Rate for hypertrophy of heart, $8.

A previous examination, made March 5, 1902, states that the claimant had a paralytic stroke affecting the right side of body about a year prior to March, 1902; that the use of the right arm and leg was very much impaired; that the arm and hands shake badly; that he walked with difficulty, using a cane, and that his mind was then affected.

Medical testimony filed in the Pension Bureau in September, 1902, shows that the beneficiary was then suffering from sciatic rheumatism, that the right leg was shrunken and wasted to a considerable extent, and that he had palsy of the right arm and hand, with constant trembling of the hand and arm.

An increase of this soldier's pension from $10 to $24 per month is justified under numerous precedents, it being shown that the beneficiary is suffering from paralysis agitans, and, of course, wholly disabled for the performance of any manual labor.

The bill is therefore reported back with the recommendation that it pass after the same shall have been amended as follows:

In line 8 strike out the word "fifty" and insert in lieu thereof the word "twenty-four."

In same line, after the word "month," insert the words "in lieu of that he is now receiving."

Amend the title so as to read: "A bill granting an increase of pension to John Graham."

O

CHARLES STRONG, ALIAS WILLIAM CLARK.

FEBRUARY 2, 1903.—Committed to the Committee of the Whole House and ordered
to be printed.

Mr. SAMUEL W. SMITH, from the Committee on Invalid Pensions, submitted the following

REPORT.

[To accompany H. R. 15619.]

The Committee on Invalid Pensions, to whom was referred the bill
(H. R. 15619) granting an increase of pension to Charles Strong, submit the following report:

This bill proposes to increase the pension of the soldier named
therein from $12 to $24 per month.

Charles Strong, alias William Clark, now 54 years of age, enlisted
in Company I, One hundred and fifteenth New York Infantry, under
the name of William Clark on October 28, 1863, and was discharged
August 30, 1865, as of Company C, Forty-seventh New York Infantry,
to which transferred.

Medical records of the War Department show that he was wounded
at the battle of Olustee, Fla., February 20, 1864; that he was under
treatment in June, 1864, for typhoid fever, pneumonia, and incipient
phthisis, and from June 27 to October 17, 1864, for consumption.

He is now pensioned under the act of June 27, 1890, at $12 per
month for total inability to earn a support by manual labor, the result
of rheumatism and disease of heart, dyspepsia, and dropsy.

When last examined, on September 26, 1900, the board of surgeons
described his physical condition as follows:

Rheumatism: Both hips stiff, tender, painful; motion limited in each one-half.
Muscles of back tender, stiff, and painful; motion limited one-half.

Heart: There is dilatation, with hypertrophy; pulse sitting, 90; standing, 102. It
is impossible to exercise him on account of lameness of left leg.

Dyspepsia: Applicant suffers from indigestion of stomach. His abdomen is
enormously distended and measures 56 inches.

Dropsy: There is dropsy of the entire left leg, the left calf measuring 19½ inches,
the right 17 inches, the left thigh 28 inches and the right 24 inches. The skin is
broken in many places and is blue and rotten throughout.

The testimony of Dr. E. A. Wittwer, of Auburn, N. Y., filed with
your committee, sets forth that the beneficiary is unable to do manual

labor on account of varicose veins of both legs, extending to the groin; that the left leg is swollen and very badly discolored and measures 2½ inches in circumference more than the right leg; that he is confined to his bed very frequently in consequence; that his heart is weak and the circulation poor, and that he is troubled with shortness of breath after the slightest exercise, such as merely walking, his weight being 295 pounds.

Other papers filed with your committee set forth that the beneficiary has no property or other means of support, except the pension of $12 per month.

This soldier is shown to be a physical wreck, as shown by the last certificate of medical examination, is now very often confined to his bed, and is in destitute circumstances.

There are many precedents for increasing the pension of those who suffer from disabilities of an extreme nature as this soldier does; hence the relief sought for in the bill appears to be justified, and the bill is reported back with the recommendation that it pass after the same shall have been amended as follows:

In line 6, after the word "Strong," insert the words "alias William Clark."

Amend the title so as to read: "A bill granting an increase of pension to Charles Strong, alias William Clark."

O

WILLIAM KING.

FEBRUARY 2, 1903.—Committed to the Committee of the Whole House and ordered to be printed.

Mr. SULLOWAY, from the Committee on Invalid Pensions, submitted the following

REPORT.

[To accompany H. R. 12841.]

The Committee on Invalid Pensions, to whom was referred the bill (H. R. 12841) granting a pension to William King, submit the following report:

This bill proposes to increase the pension of William King, late acting third assistant engineer, U. S. Navy, from $12 to $40 per month.

William King, the officer named in this bill, and now 69 years of age, served as acting third assistant engineer, ranking with midshipman in the Navy, on the U. S. S. *Mohawk* from June 2, 1862, to June 21, 1863, when his resignation was accepted.

He incurred an injury to his back while in the service and line of duty, and was pensioned under the general law at $4 per month on account of the same from May 25, 1889, and at $8 per month from March 4, 1890.

He is now pensioned under the act of June 27, 1890, at $12 per month for total inability to earn a support by manual labor, the result of injury to back, indigestion, disease of the bladder, and debility.

When last examined, on March 4, 1890, the board of surgeons described his disabilities as follows:

Some loss of muscular tissue in lumbar region; tenderness on pressure over this region; can not bend over to touch floor to-day; squats to pick up anything; absence of tendon reflex in each patella; is constipated, emaciated, and feeble.

There has been filed with your committee the affidavit of Dr. Eugene B. Sanger, of Bangor, Me., setting forth that the beneficiary is wholly disabled from the performance of any manual labor and that he suffers from chronic gastritis, indigestion, and piles, and is gradually getting worse from week to week.

While it is not shown that all of this officer's disabilities are due to his military service, yet the probabilities are that his service was in a measure responsible for that condition.

Inasmuch as he was shown to be much emaciated and feeble when examined in 1890, and as he is shown by medical testimony filed with your committee to be getting worse every week, an increase of his pension from $12 to $24 per month seems justified; hence the bill is reported back with the recommendation that it pass after the same shall have been amended as follows:

In line 7, after the word "midshipman," insert the words "United States Navy."

In the same line strike out the word "forty" and insert in lieu thereof the word "twenty-four."

In line 8, after the word "month," insert the words "in lieu of that he is now receiving."

Amend the title so as to read: "A bill granting an increase of pension to William King."

O

CAROLINE SCHAEFER.

FEBRUARY 2, 1903.—Committed to the Committee of the Whole House and ordered
to be printed.

Mr. SULLOWAY, from the Committee on Invalid Pensions, submitted
the following

REPORT.

[To accompany H. R. 17093.]

The Committee on Invalid Pensions, to whom was referred the bill
(H. R. 17093) granting a pension to Caroline Schaefer, submit the
following report:
This bill proposes to pension the beneficiary named therein at $12
per month.
Vincent Schaefer, the soldier named in this bill, is shown by the
records of the War Department to have served as a private in Company E, First Arkansas Infantry, from March 1, 1863, to August 10,
1865, when honorably discharged.
The claim of the beneficiary as the widow of the soldier, and filed
under the act of June 27, 1890, was rejected on May 11, 1894, upon
the ground of her inability to furnish evidence showing the death of
her former husband.
The beneficiary testified that her former husband, Calvin Holt, was
taken from his home while hiding from being conscripted in the Confederate service in August or September, 1862, while a resident of
Murray County, Ga., to Calhoun, Ga.; that she saw him at the latter
place on October 8, 1862, for the last time, and that it was thereafter
reported that he was taken to Nashville or Knoxville, Tenn., very
sick with typhoid fever and jaundice, and that after the surrender she
was advised by a man named Daniel Taylor that he was left in the
hospital at Nashville or Knoxville, Tenn., in a dying condition, since
which time she had not heard from him.
The beneficiary filed proof as to her marriage to the soldier Schaefer
on November 26, 1885, and that he died on June 5, 1891, and that she
was dependent upon her daily labor and had not remarried since the
death of the soldier.
The marriage of the beneficiary to the soldier is of record in Sebas-
tian County, Ark.

There has been filed with your committee a petition, signed by a large number of residents of the beneficiary's neighborhood, setting forth that the beneficiary, believing the report to be true that her first husband was in a dying condition in October, 1862, married the soldier and lived with him as his wife until his death, should be recognized by Congress as the legal widow of the soldier, no information as to her former husband having been obtained for forty years.

The beneficiary having married the soldier in good faith, and having been his wife until his death, your committee believe that the continued absence of her first husband for twenty-three years prior to her marriage to the soldier, and for eighteen years after such marriage, should be sufficient to warrant the presumption of his death, and relief should therefore be extended to the beneficiary to the extent of granting her a pension at the rate of $8 per month, to which amount she would have been entitled in the Pension Bureau had she proved the death of her first husband in that Bureau.

The bill is therefore reported back with the recommendation that it pass after the same shall have been amended as follows:

In line 8 strike out the word "twelve" and insert in lieu thereof the word "eight."

O

JOHN KEEN.

FEBRUARY 2, 1903.—Committed to the Committee of the Whole House and ordered to be printed.

Mr. DEEMER, from the Committee on Invalid Pensions, submitted the following

REPORT.

[To accompany H. R. 14929.]

The Committee on Invalid Pensions, to whom was referred the bill (H. R. 14929) granting a pension to John Keen, submit the following report:

This bill proposes to increase the pension of the beneficiary named therein from $12 to $30 per month.

Records of the War Department show that John Keen, the soldier named in this bill and now 63 years of age, served as sergeant in Company K, Seventh Pennsylvania Reserves Infantry, from June 4, 1861, to November 24, 1862, and as second lieutenant of the same company and regiment from November 25, 1862, to March 12, 1865, when honorably discharged, and the records further show that he was captured May 5, 1864, at the battle of the Wilderness, and paroled March 1, 1865.

He is now a pensioner under the act of June 27, 1890, at the maximum rating, namely, $12 per month, for total inability to earn a support by manual labor, the result of impaired vision and disease of rectum and nervous system.

His claim to pension under the general law, filed on September 11, 1888, and based upon chronic diarrhea, injury of stomach, and disease of feet was rejected November 5, 1894, upon the ground that a disability from these causes had not existed since the filing of the claim.

When last examined on February 28, 1900, the board of surgeons rated the beneficiary at $24 per month, and described his physical condition as follows:

Vision of right eye, twenty one-hundred-and-fiftieths; left, twenty one-hundredths, corrected. No improvement with glasses.

Heart apex beat in sixth interspace, neither visible nor palpable. Action frequent and irritable to a marked degree, probably due to atheroma, with cyanosis, dilatation, dyspnœa, and atheroma.

Three-fourths loss of motion of all the fingers of the right hand, most marked in index finger and thumb, due to paralysis, with three-fourths loss of power. One-half loss of power and one-half loss of motion in right wrist joint.

Sphincter relaxed. Hemorrhoidal vessels engorged. Mucus membrane inflamed. Is totally incapacitated for performing any manual labor.

From medical testimony filed in the Pension Bureau in November, 1900, it appears that the beneficiary was then suffering from softening of the brain, with paresis of the right side, vertigo, epileptic attacks, both petit mal and grand mal of frequent occurrence, aphasia and other nervous symptoms; that he was not only totally disabled for the performance of any labor, but required the personal aid and attendance of another person.

From a resolution passed by W. S. Birely Post, No. 511, of Quarryville, Pa., passed November 24, 1900, it appears that this post had to help to defray the expenses of the person who attended the beneficiary, and that he required the attendance of some one day and night.

There has been filed with your committee the affidavit of Dr. C. E. Helm, of Bart, Pa., setting forth that he has attended the beneficiary almost constantly for the last two or three years; that he is now suffering from softening of the brain with the following symptoms: Partial paralysis of the right side, vertigo, attacks of convulsions of an epileptic nature, retention of urine which is relieved only by catheterization, failure of memory, failure of power of concentrating the memory, catarrh of the stomach, and general inactivity of all the organs of the body, due to the condition of the brain; that he was not only incapacitated from the performance of all kinds of labor, but was confined to his room, and for the last two years required the constant and regular personal aid and attendance of another person.

Petitions signed by a large number of citizens of Bart, Pa., and members of John A. Ross and W. S. Birely Posts, Grand Army of the Republic, Department of Pennsylvania, also filed with your committee, set forth that the beneficiary requires the aid and attendance of another person, and that he is in destitute circumstances.

The relief sought for in this bill is justified in view of the action of the House on June 16, 1902, it being shown that the beneficiary, who rendered nearly three years' service, is now so disabled as to require the aid and attendance of another person.

The bill is therefore reported back with the recommendation that it pass after the same shall have been amended as follows:

In line 6, before the word "Company," strike out the word "of" and insert in lieu thereof the words "second lieutenant."

In line 7, before the word "Volunteer," insert the word "Reserve."

In line 8, after the word "month," insert the words "in lieu of that he is now receiving."

Amend the title so as to read: "A bill granting an increase of pension to John Keen."

O

LEROY N. BUELL.

FEBRUARY 2, 1903.—Committed to the Committee of the Whole House and ordered
to be printed.

Mr. CROWLEY, from the Committee on Invalid Pensions, submitted the
following

REPORT.

[To accompany H. R. 16667.]

The Committee on Invalid Pensions, to whom was referred the bill
(H. R. 16667) granting an increase of pension to Leroy N. Buell, submit the following report:

This bill proposes to increase the pension of the soldier named
therein from $14 to $30 per month.

Leroy N. Buell, now 72 years of age, served as a private in Company D, Thirty-ninth Wisconsin Infantry, from May 18 to September
22, 1864, and as first sergeant of Company I, Forty-eighth Wisconsin
Infantry, from February 2 to November 28, 1865, when honorably discharged on surgeon's certificate of disability by reason of general
debility of system from the effects of typhoid-malarial fever contracted
while in the line of duty with the regiment.

He is now pensioned under the general law at $14 per month on
account of erysipelas and resulting disease of the eyes and nervous
debility.

A claim for increase of pension filed October 9, 1899, was rejected
on November 17, 1900, upon the ground that the rating of $14 per
month was fully commensurate with the degree of disability arising
from the pensioned causes.

The beneficiary filed in support of that claim the affidavits of Drs.
McCreary and Boise, of Knoxville, Tenn., setting forth that he examined the beneficiary on December 18, 1900, and found him suffering
from erysipelas and resulting disease of the eyes and nervous debility
to such an extent as to render him unfit for any manual labor, the
nervous condition taking the form of severe clonic spasms occurring
at night after any attempt at manual labor, rendering him sleepless, etc.

When last examined, on November 2, 1900, upon which examination
the rejection of the claim for increase of pension was based, the board
of surgeons stated that vision of the right eye was twenty-seventieths

and not improved with lens; that of the left eye twenty-fiftieths and
not improved with lens; that he was very thin and delicate, and his
skin around the eyes covered with a bran like form of scales like
eczema, which was perhaps like erysipelas; that the skin disease was
the cause of the eye trouble, and that this disease affected the scalp as
well as the face; that his physical condition was not good, although he
could go where he wanted, but the examining surgeons then stated that
he had to be careful of any exposure on account of the skin disease.

A prior examination of the soldier, on March 14, 1900, rated the soldier $6 for erysipelas, $6 for disease of eyes, $5 for nervous debility,
$5 for functional heart trouble, $10 for a hernia, and $6 for hydrocele,
and the board of surgeons then stated that, in their opinion, the hernia
which came on about two years prior thereto without any strain or violence was a result of the weakened and relaxed muscles caused by
malnutrition and want of vital force.

The beneficiary in an affidavit filed with your committee sets forth
that while with the Thirty-ninth Regiment and while detailed as nurse
in the hospital he was kicked by a typhoid-fever patient in the groin
and privates, causing a rupture; that being alone in the hospital when
those injuries were received such proof as the Government would
require would be difficult or impossible to furnish, etc.

Your committee is of the opinion that the heart trouble found upon
examination on March 14, 1900, is a direct result of the nervous debility for which he is pensioned, and that in view of the recommendation
of the board of surgeons on March 14, 1900, an increase of his pension from $14 to $20 per month is therefore warranted.

The bill is therefore reported back with the recommendation that it
pass after the same shall have been amended as follows:

In lines 6 and 7 strike out the words "Company D, Thirty-ninth
Regiment, Wisconsin Volunteer Infantry, and."

In line 9 strike out the word "thirty" and insert in lieu thereof the
word "twenty."

O

JOHN H. AMADON.

FEBRUARY 2, 1903.—Committed to the Committee of the Whole House and ordered
to be printed.

Mr. SULLOWAY, from the Committee on Invalid Pensions, submitted
the following

REPORT. -

[To accompany H. R. 16000.]

The Committee on Invalid Pensions, to whom was referred the bill
(H. R. 16000) granting an increase of pension to John A. Amadon, submit the following report:

This bill proposes to increase the pension of the soldier named therein
from $12 to $30 per month.

John H. Amadon, now 55 years of age, who served as a private in
Companies I and D, First Vermont Heavy Artillery, from November
25, 1863, to August 25, 1865, when honorably discharged, and who
was under treatment during his term of service on various dates on
account of chronic diarrhea and intermittent fever, is now pensioned
under the act of June 27, 1890, at $12 per month for total inability to
earn a support by manual labor by reason of chronic diarrhea and
resulting disease of the rectum, malarial poisoning, loss of left hand,
and of middle finger of the right hand.

He was formerly a pensioner under the general law at $6 per month
on account of chronic diarrhea and resulting disease of rectum and
malarial poisoning.

He lost his left hand and the middle finger of his right hand and the
partial loss of the use of the right hand while firing a cannon in a
sham fight at the reunion at Morrisville, Vt., on July 4, 1891.

When last examined in 1892 the board of surgeons rated him $12
for chronic diarrhea and results, $30 for loss of the left hand just
above the wrist joint, and $2 for loss of the middle finger of the other
hand.

From a statement filed by the member who introduced this bill it
appears that the beneficiary is in destitute circumstances.

Following numerous precedents, it being shown that the beneficiary
suffers from disabilities of an extreme nature, an increase of the soldier's pension from $12 to $24 per month seems justified, hence the bill

is reported back with the recommendation that it pass after the same shall have been amended as follows:

In line 6 strike out the letter "A" and insert in lieu thereof the letter "H."

In same line, after the word "First," insert the word "Regiment."

In line 7 strike out the words "Regiment Volunteers" and insert in lieu thereof the words "Volunteer Heavy Artillery."

In same line, after the word "pension," insert the words "at the rate."

In same line strike out the word "thirty" and insert in lieu thereof the word "twenty-four."

Amend the title so as to read: "A bill granting an increase of pension to John H. Amadon."

O

JOHN FULLERTON.

FEBRUARY 2, 1903.—Committed to the Committee of the Whole House and ordered
to be printed.

Mr. SULLOWAY, from the Committee on Invalid Pensions, submitted
the following

REPORT.

[To accompany H. R. 15440.]

The Committee on Invalid Pensions, to whom was referred the bill
(H. R. 15440) granting an increase of pension to John Fullerton, submit the following report:

This bill proposes to increase the pension of the officer named
therein from $10 to $30 per month.

John Fullerton, now 61 years of age, served as a private in Company K, Fourth New Hampshire Volunteers, from August 22, 1861,
to July 24, 1865, when he was promoted to second lieutenant of Company E, of the same regiment, and served as such second lieutenant
until August 23, 1865, when honorably discharged.

The medical records of the War Department show that he was under
treatment at various dates for remittent fever and debility.

The beneficiary is now pensioned under the general law at $10 per
month on account of malarial poisoning and resulting disability, and
nervous prostration, the result of sunstroke incurred by him while holding the rank of private in Company K, Fourth New Hampshire Volunteers.

A claim for increase of pension, filed in April, 1889, was rejected in
March, 1891, upon the ground that the disability of accepted service
origin did not warrant a rating in excess of $10 per month.

A claim on account of disease of lungs was rejected by the Pension
Bureau in November, 1898, upon the ground that a pensionable disability from that cause had not existed since the filing of the claim.

There has been filed with your committee the affidavit of Dr. W. H.
Pattee, setting forth that he had treated the beneficiary for the last
five years for a nervous condition which incapacitated him from manual
labor; that any undue exercise of said man would bring on an attack
of myoclonus multiplex, which would last from an hour up to several
days and totally disable him; that this trouble had increased during

the past year, the attacks becoming more frequent, so that he was unable to attend to his usual duties.

The affidavit of the beneficiary, also filed with your committee, sets forth that he has frequent and severe spells of sickness from nervous prostration, and on account of this disability was wholly incapacitated for the performance of any manual labor.

In view of the medical testimony filed with your committee, showing the degree of the soldier's disability from nervous prostration, the result of sunstroke of accepted service origin, and his inability to perform labor by reason of the same, your committee believes that an increase of his pension from $10 to $20 per month is justified, hence the bill is reported back with the recommendation that it pass after the same shall have been amended as follows:

In line 6, before the word "Company," strike out the word "of."

In line 8 strike out the word "thirty" and insert in lieu thereof the word "twenty."

O

VISA C. MORRILL.

FEBRUARY 2, 1903.—Committed to the Committee of the Whole House and ordered to be printed.

Mr. CROWLEY, from the Committee on Invalid Pensions, submitted the following

REPORT.

[To accompany H. R. 6969.]

The Committee on Invalid Pensions, to whom was referred the bill (H. R. 6969) for the relief of Visa C. Morrill, submit the following report:

This bill proposes to pension the beneficiary named therein as the widow of Col. John Morrill, of the Sixty-fourth Illinois Infantry, at $50 per month.

John Morrill, the officer named in this bill, is shown by the records of the War Department to have served as captain of Company A, Sixty-fourth Illinois Infantry, and as lieutenant-colonel and colonel of said regiment from September 25, 1861, to July 11, 1865, when honorably discharged, and that while colonel of the regiment, on July 22, 1864, at the battle of Peach Tree Creek, Georgia, he received a gunshot wound of the right shoulder and arm, and that he was a pensioner ever since his discharge on account of said wound at $30 per month, the total of his rank as colonel.

Certificates of medical examination of the officer, made in 1865, 1873, 1875, and 1877, show that as a result of the wound of the shoulder and arm his right arm became paralyzed and atrophied, and that it was hanging helplessly by his side, the ball passing through the right axilla, severing the axillary plexus of the nerves and emerging beneath the inferior angle of the scapula.

Visa C. Morrill, the beneficiary named in this bill, now 61 years of age, who was married to the officer on September 27, 1869, filed a claim to pension under the general law on December 26, 1893. This claim, however, was rejected June 10, 1895, upon the ground that the paralysis of which her husband died was not shown to have been a result of the wound of right shoulder and arm for which he had been pensioned.

This action of the Pension Bureau was based upon proof tending to show that it was generally understood that the officer fell through a chute in his barn and died a few weeks thereafter of paralysis induced by the injuries received in the fall.

Proof obtained upon special examination shows that on July 6, 1893, the officer was found in his barn in an unconscious condition; that he was removed to the house; that the officer himself did not know the cause of the trouble that resulted in this condition; that he denied to the last that he had been up in the loft at all, and that prior to that time he had been subject to dizzy and falling spells due to a temporary congestion of the brain, and the physician who attended him during his last illness testified that in his opinion the officer's death was the result of the gunshot wound, the immediate cause of death being a cerebral hemorrhage superinduced by spinal and cerebral irritation caused by the destruction of the median and other nerves and the consequent disturbance of the nerve centers.

The contention of the beneficiary was that owing to the wound the officer's heart action was irregular and respiration disturbed; that either from nerve tumor at the severed ends or from the shock received at the time of the wound and partly from the condition of an almost lifeless limb, there was produced a pathological change in the spinal-cord substance and also of the brain, which resulted in his fall at the time of his death; that whatever fall there was the same was simply a falling down from an erect position to a recumbent position on the floor, and that even if the officer had become dizzy and fallen from the loft as a result of the condition produced by the gunshot wound such disturbance should be the remote if not the proximate cause of his death.

Your committee is of the opinion that whatever doubts there are as to the officer's death from paralysis being a result of the wound of the shoulder and arm should be resolved in favor of the beneficiary, and that she should be granted the rate provided by the general pension laws for the widow of a colonel, namely, $30 per month.

The bill is therefore reported back with the recommendation that it pass after the same shall have been amended as follows:

Strike out all after the enacting clause and insert in lieu thereof the following:

That the Secretary of the Interior be, and he is hereby, authorized and directed to place on the pension roll, subject to the provisions and limitations of the pension laws, the name of Visa C. Morrill, widow of John Morrill, late colonel Sixty-fourth Regiment Illinois Volunteer Infantry, and pay her a pension at the rate of thirty dollars per month.

Amend the title so as to read: "A bill granting a pension to Visa C. Morrill."

O

JULIA STILWELL.

FEBRUARY 2, 1903.—Committed to the Committee of the Whole House and ordered to be printed.

Mr. MIERS, from the Committee on Invalid Pensions, submitted the following-

REPORT.

[To accompany H. R. 6724.]

The Committee on Invalid Pensions, to whom was referred the bill (H. R. 6724) granting an increase of pension to Julia A. Stilwell, submit the following report:

This bill proposes to increase the pension of the beneficiary named therein from $8 to $24 per month.

Joseph A. Stilwell, the husband of the beneficiary named in the bill, served as assistant surgeon and surgeon of the Twenty-second Indiana Volunteers from August 15, 1861, to July 24, 1865, when honorably discharged.

His claim to pension under the general law, filed on May 26, 1894, and based upon diarrhea, jaundice, and scurvy, the two first-named disabilities having been contracted in the fall of 1861 and the last-named one in November, 1863, and on account of resulting disease of the heart and nervous prostration was allowed, in August, 1890, after his death, at $21 per month on account of diarrhea and scurvy, and pension was made payable to the beneficiary as his widow, to terminate May 30, 1894, the date of his death.

The Pension Bureau then declined to accept disease of heart and nervous prostration as results of the diarrhea and scurvy.

The diarrhea was contracted by the officer while he was an assistant surgeon and the scurvy while he held the rank of surgeon.

Julia Stilwell, the beneficiary named in this bill and now 64 years of age, who married the officer on November 11, 1860, is now and has been since November 18, 1896, a pensioner under the act of June 27, 1890, at $8 per month upon proof of her marriage to the officer, as stated above, that she was his legal widow and was dependent upon her daily labor.

The claim of the beneficiary under the general law was rejected in August, 1896, upon the ground that her husband's death from disease of heart and atheromatous degeneration of the arteries was not the result of the diarrhea and scurvy for which he had been pensioned.

It was subsequently reopened and again rejected on November 7, 1899, upon the ground that it was not shown that the officer incurred rheumatism and disease of heart in the service; that while it was true that attempts had been made to show the existence of these disabilities in the service, yet the officer's own allegations, as well as those of the beneficiary, before a special examiner in 1896 entirely destroyed the value of the evidence tending to show the army origin of the disabilities in question.

Proof, however, was obtained upon the special examination tending to show that the officer complained of rheumatism from the time that he returned from the Army; that sometimes it would affect his fingers, at other times his whole body; that it increased during the last few years of his life, and that heart disease and atheroma finally ensued.

Of course the beneficiary's husband, being a physician, treated himself, but physicians who called him into consultation in their practice testified that they often heard him speak of his rheumatism, which was in the form of sciatica.

Physicians who attended the officer during his last illness testified that he was then suffering from an enlarged liver and jaundice, and gave it as their opinion that the scurvy from which it was claimed he was suffering would have a tendency to give rise to atheromatous and degenerative condition of the arteries.

Dr. Beachly, who served as assistant surgeon in the Twenty-second Indiana Volunteers from March, 1863, to the latter part of June, 1864. however, testified that the beneficiary's husband complained of rheumatism in the service some time in 1863, when he held the rank of surgeon, and that he also complained of his heart being affected from articular rheumatism, and that at times thereafter, while both were members of the regiment, he complained of this rheumatism.

Medical testimony filed with your committee shows that the beneficiary is greatly affected with chronic rheumatism and disease of heart and that at times she has been completely unable to even perform her household work.

A petition of Gordon Tanner Post, No. 159, Grand Army of the Republic, of Indiana, also filed with your committee, asks Congress to come to the relief of this beneficiary by granting her an increase of her pension to $25 per month, as allowed to widows of surgeons.

Your committee believe that the doubts in this case should be resolved in favor of the beneficiary, in view of the testimony filed by her tending to show that her husband's death was the result either of the scurvy or of the rheumatism contracted by him while holding the rank of surgeon.

The bill is therefore reported back with the recommendation that it pass after the same shall have been amended as follows:

In line 8 strike out the word "twenty-four" and insert in lieu thereof the word "twenty-five."

Amend the title so as to read: "A bill granting an increase of pension to Julia Stilwell."

O

OLIVER W. NEWTON.

FEBRUARY 2, 1903.—Committed to the Committee of the Whole House and ordered
to be printed.

Mr. APLIN, from the Committee on Invalid Pensions, submitted the
following

REPORT.

[To accompany H. R. 5586.]

The Committee on Invalid Pensions, to whom was referred the bill
(H. R. 5586) granting a pension to Oliver W. Newton, submit the following report:

This bill proposes to pension Oliver W. Newton, helpless child of
Francis L. Newton, late of Company E, Fiftieth New York Engineers,
at $12 per month.

Francis L. Newton, the soldier named in this bill, served as a private
in Company E, Fiftieth New York Engineers, from August 26, 1861,
to September 20, 1864, when honorably discharged.

No claim for pension was ever filed by the soldier.

On January 2, 1891, the beneficiary named in this bill, and now 47
years of age, applied for pension as the helpless son of the soldier.
Said claim, however, was rejected in August, 1891, upon the ground
that inasmuch as he had been over 16 years of age at the date of the
passage of the act of June 27, 1890, title to pension could not obtain.

Proof filed in that claim shows that the soldier and the mother of
the beneficiary were married in November, 1854; that the soldier died
May 4, 1877, and that his widow remarried on June 25, 1881; that the
beneficiary is a son of the soldier, born June 4, 1856, and that in April,
1891, the beneficiary was suffering from cerebro-spinal sclerosis of a
marked and advanced type.

There has been filed with your committee the statement of the beneficiary setting forth that when a babe about six months old he had
a scrofulous swelling of the neck; that the attending physician instead
of drawing said swelling to a head and thereby discharging the poison
from his system applied remedies which scattered the poison to all
parts of his system, since which time he had been suffering from a permanent physical disability which had rendered him permanently helpless so far as to prevent a support by his own manual labor; that it is

impossible for him to fully dress or undress himself, and that he can only walk around in a feeble way.

Proof filed with your committee shows that the beneficiary, ever since he had been a small child, was suffering from cerebro-spinal sclerosis; that he was permanently crippled; that he can not talk plain; that he walks around with extreme difficulty, and wabbles around worse than a man who is intoxicated, and that he has been unable to do manual labor or to earn a support.

Following precedents, the relief sought for this helpless and dependent son of the soldier named in the bill is fully warranted, and the bill is reported back with the recommendation that it pass after the same shall have been amended as follows:

In line 6, after the word "helpless," insert the words "and dependent son."

In same line strike out the word "child."

In line 7, before the word "New York," insert the word "Regiment."

○

WILLIAM H. TRITES.

FEBRUARY 2, 1903.—Committed to the Committee of the Whole House and ordered to be printed.

Mr. SAMUEL W. SMITH, from the Committee on Invalid Pensions, submitted the following

REPORT.

[To accompany H. R. 16929.]

The Committee on Invalid Pensions, to whom was referred the bill (H. R. 16929) granting an increase of pension to William H. Trites, have considered the same and respectfully report as follows:

William H. Trites, of No. 1076 South Second street, Camden, N. J., enlisted July 1, 1861, as a sergeant in Company C, Twenty-ninth Regiment Pennsylvania Volunteer Infantry, and served until December 8, 1863, when he reenlisted as a veteran volunteer. He was subsequently promoted to sergeant-major, and on November 9, 1864, was made first lieutenant of Company D of said regiment, and served with this rank until mustered in as captain of Company C, to date March 25, 1865; he was finally honorably mustered out with the company July 17, 1865.

In 1887 Captain Trites was granted a pension under the general law at $6 per month on account of varicose veins of left leg. After the passage of the act of June 27, 1890, he made application thereunder, and a medical examination showed that he was in a totally disabled condition, and he was granted the maximum rating of $12 under said act, and this pension he is now drawing.

The last medical examination in this case was held March 7, 1896, before the Camden, N. J., board, and the report of same is as follows:

Claimant is slightly emaciated; muscles soft and flaccid; hands soft; tongue slightly furred; teeth all lost, with the exception of the incisors of the lower jaw; system poorly nourished; * * * the knees are enlarged, both being bent at an angle of 45 degrees, unable to straighten them on account of the deposits; his knees are partially fixed for want of passive motion, having been in one position so long; both ankles are swollen and painful, with a slight increase of temperature and marked dryness upon motion; the toes of the right foot are partially flexed, with the second toe resting upon the first toe, and the little toe resting on its fellow; the proximal joints are dry, but all are movable; the left foot is in the same condition, with dryness and swelling of proximal and distal joint of great toe; the toe nails on the great and second toes of left foot are diseased, also the second toe of the right foot.

The lower extremities are very much emaciated; marked dryness in left wrist and tendinous sheath of left forearm; dryness and enlargement of the second and distal joints of thumb and fingers of left hand; crepitation in right shoulder; dryness in right wrist and tendinous sheath of right forearm; dryness in distal joint of thumb of right hand; enlargements and dryness of the second joints of all fingers of the right hand; there is marked apathy of the lumber structures with painful and restricted up and down movements. * * * Claimant is unable to get out of his bed and on that account he was very difficult to examine, as movements caused him considerable distress and discomfort.   He is totally unable to do any labor; at present not being able to wait upon himself, beyond using his hands and arms in feeding, arranging bed clothing, sitting up in bed and lying down.

Testimony accompanying the bill shows that the condition of general helplessness outlined above still exists, and it is further shown that claimant is utterly without means of support or anyone to depend upon for maintenance, his wife being an invalid and his child, a boy of 14 years, having a hip-joint disease which prevents him from doing any labor.   It further appears that a small business which the claimant formerly conducted has had to be abandoned, and that claimant is now in a helpless and hopeless condition, badly in debt and entirely dependent upon his pension.   He is confined to his bed and has been for years, unable to walk.

This soldier served from the beginning to the ending of the war, and from start to finish his record is clean and honorable.   He was repeatedly promoted and his service throughout was of the highest and best character.   He is now in an exceedingly helpless and needy condition and under the action of the House taken on June 16, 1902, he is entitled to an increase of his pension from $12 to $30 per month.

The bill is therefore reported back with the recommendation that it pass after the same shall have been amended as follows:

In line 6 after the word "late" insert the word "captain."

O

COLLINS W. WIGHT.

FEBRUARY 2, 1903.—Committed to the Committee of the Whole House and ordered
to be printed.

Mr. APLIN, from the Committee on Invalid Pensions, submitted the
following

REPORT.

[To accompany H. R. 16785.]

The Committee on Invalid Pensions, to whom was referred the bill
(H. R. 16785) granting an increase of pension to Collins W. Wright,
submit the following report:

This bill proposes to increase the pension of this soldier from $12 to
$24 per month.

Collins W. Wright, the soldier named in this bill, and now 60 years
of age, is shown by the records of the War Department to have served
as a private in Company B, First New Hampshire Heavy Artillery,
from August 29, 1863, to September 11, 1865, when honorably discharged, and to have been under treatment at various dates in 1865
for fever and ague, and in 1864 for intermittent fever.

He was formerly pensioned under the general law on account of
malarial poisoning at $4 per month from discharge, and at $8 per month
from September 4, 1889, but is now pensioned under the act of June
27, 1890, at $12 per month—the maximum rating—for total inability
to earn a support by manual labor, the result of malarial poisoning,
rheumatism, catarrh, and general debility.

When last examined, on May 26, 1902, the board of surgeons
described his physical condition as follows:

Height, 5 feet 8½ inches; weight, 115 pounds; has chills and fever about every
other day; skin dry, greenish-yellow cast; spleen enlarged to about double its normal size and very tender; the digestive functions are very poorly performed; there
is marked atrophy of the muscles of the legs and arms; not much limitation of
motion; cardiac dullness, normal; there is great feebleness of heart's action; there
are no murmurs except a distinct metallic ring; no dilatation or hypertrophy; some
dyspnœa; his general debility is very marked; it is with the greatest difficulty that
he can stand on his feet; the prostate is large and double its normal size; this came
on about one year ago, and does not know what caused it; bladder is very irritable
and considerably hypertrophied with incontinence due to catarrhal condition.

There is a great quantity of mucus which is very stringy and tenacious. He has been confined to his bed since the first of December, 1901; is not able now to sit up but a few minutes at a time.

This man is totally disabled from any manual labor.

The affidavit of Dr. Stanley N. Insley, of Grayling, Mich., filed with your committee, sets forth that the beneficiary is now confined to his bed on an average of one-half of his time during the year; that he is suffering from an enlarged prostate and cystitis, causing frequent micturition which is very painful; that it is necessary to draw off his water during the severe attacks with a catheter and to wash the bladder frequently; that he is also suffering with chronic catarrh of the lower bowels and stomach, also of bronchial tubes and throat.

The affidavit of the beneficiary, also filed with your committee, sets forth that he is confined to his bed for more than one-half of the time and is obliged to have the attendance of other persons; that he has no property, either real or personal, and no income except the pension of $12 per month, and this statement of the beneficiary as to his physical and financial condition is corroborated by that of two of his neighbors.

It being shown that the soldier is suffering from disabilities of an extreme nature and that he rendered two years' service, the relief sought for in the bill, being an increase of his pension from $12 to $24 per month, is therefore warranted and the bill is reported back with the recommendation that it pass after the same shall have been amended as follows:

In line 6 strike out the word "Wright" and insert in lieu thereof the word "Wight."

In same line, before the words "New Hampshire," insert the words "First Regiment."

In line 7, before the word "Heavy," insert the word "Volunteer."

Amend the title so as to read: "A bill granting an increase of pension to Collins W. Wight."

O

WILLIAM J. CHITWOOD.

FEBRUARY 2, 1903.—Committed to the Committee of the Whole House and ordered to be printed.

Mr. KLEBERG, from the Committee on Invalid Pensions, submitted the following

REPORT.

[To accompany S. 6018.]

The Committee on Invalid Pensions, to whom was referred the bill (S. 6018) granting an increase of pension to William J. Chitwood, have examined the same and adopt the Senate report thereon and recommend that the bill do pass.

[Senate Report No. 2831, Fifty-seventh Congress, second session.]

The Committee on Pensions, to whom was referred the bill (S. 6018) granting an increase of pension to William J. Chitwood, have examined the same and report:

This bill proposes to increase from $12 to $20 per month the pension of William J. Chitwood, late of Company A, Eighty-second Regiment Indiana Volunteer Infantry.

Soldier enlisted August 15, 1862, and was discharged June 9, 1865. During service he bore the rank of private and sergeant. He is now receiving a pension of $12 per month under the act of June 27, 1890, for total disability, due to impaired vision, senile debility, and disease of rectum. March 8, 1888, he made claim under the general law, alleging that he contracted chronic diarrhea, piles, and indigestion during service, which claim was rejected July 24, 1894, on the ground that he was not ratably disabled by causes alleged.

Claimant's post-office address is Kuttawa, Ky. He is past 74 years of age. His last medical examination, made February 19, 1896, rated him $10 for loss of sight of left eye, $6 for cataract of right eye, $6 for senility, and $6 for general debility. The examining surgeons stated that he had senile cataract nearly complete in left eye, and traumatic cataract in right eye, covering one-half of lens, and the other half is cloudy.

From evidence on file it appears that claimant has been nearly blind for the past four or five years, can barely see his way, and is unable to recognize anyone by sight. The sight of both eyes is just about gone, and he is totally incapacitated for any kind of employment or labor. It also appears that he is in destitute circumstances, has no property of any kind, and is absolutely dependent on his pension.

In view of his faithful service of nearly three years, his advanced age, great poverty, and almost total blindness, your committee are of opinion that his case is one in which the bounty of the Government might very properly be bestowed.

The bill is therefore reported back favorably with a recommendation that it pass.

O

ALICE F. SMALLEY.

FEBRUARY 2, 1903.—Committed to the Committee of the Whole House and ordered to be printed.

Mr. GIBSON, from the Committee on Invalid Pensions, submitted the following

REPORT.

[To accompany S. 6370.]

The Committee on Invalid Pensions, to whom was referred the bill (S. 6370) granting a pension to Alice F. Smalley, have examined the same and adopt the Senate report thereon and recommend that the bill do pass after the same shall have been amended as follows:

In line 8 strike out the word "twelve" and insert in lieu thereof the word "eight."

[Senate Report No. 2840, Fifty-seventh Congress, second session.]

The Committee on Pensions, to whom was referred the bill (S. 6370) granting a pension to Alice F. Smalley, have examined the same and report:

Alice F. Smalley, whose post-office address is Hardy, Ark., is the widow of Amos P. Smalley, late of Company G, Second Regiment Missouri State Militia Volunteer Cavalry.

Soldier enlisted February 27, 1862, and was honorably discharged April 1, 1865. During service he bore the rank of sergeant. He died of consumption November 7, 1899. At the time of his death he was receiving a pension under the general law at the rate of $22 per month for severe deafness of both ears contracted during his service.

Alice F. Smalley was married to the soldier February 27, 1893. She has two children by the soldier who are under the age of 16 years. On April 19, 1900, she made claim under the act of June 27, 1890, which was rejected May 9, 1902, for the reason that she was married to the soldier subsequent to the enactment of that law. March 1, 1900, she made claim under the general law, which was rejected October 16, 1902, on the ground that the soldier's fatal disease was not a result of the disability for which he was pensioned and was not shown to have been otherwise due to his military service.

Mrs. Smalley is desperately poor. She has no means, and supports herself and children by hard labor at the washtub. Her knowledge of the soldier is limited to a period commencing a few years prior to her marriage to him, and for this reason she is unable to furnish but little evidence showing that his death was due to his service. One neighbor testified that soldier was always troubled with a cough after his discharge, and a physician testified that for some years back he had the look of a consumptive. It is highly probable that the soldier's fatal disease had its origin during the three years of his active service, and, considering the utter poverty of the widow, your committee are of opinion that she should be allowed a pension.

The bill is therefore reported back favorably with a recommendation that it pass.

O

SARAH C. MERRELL.

FEBRUARY 2, 1903.—Committed to the Committee of the Whole House and ordered
to be printed.

•

Mr. HOLLIDAY, from the Committee on Invalid Pensions, submitted
the following

REPORT.

[To accompany S. 7003.]

The Committee on Invalid Pensions, to whom was referred the bill
(S. 7003) granting an increase of pension to Sarah C. Merrell, have
examined the same and adopt the Senate report thereon and recommend that the bill do pass.

[Senate Report No. 2600, Fifty-seventh Congress, second session.]

The Committee on Pensions, to whom was referred the bill (S. 7003) granting an
increase of pension to Sarah C. Merrell, have examined the same and report:

Sarah C. Merrell, whose post-office address is Santa Monica, Cal., is the widow of
Micah R. Merrell, late first lieutenant Company C, Tenth Regiment Minnesota
Volunteer Infantry.

The military records show that Micah R. Merrell was mustered in August 14, 1862,
and served until August 19, 1865, when he was honorably discharged. He entered
the service as second lieutenant Company I, Tenth Minnesota Infantry, and was
promoted first lieutenant Company C, same regiment, May 12, 1864.

Lieutenant Merrell was pensioned under the general law at $8.50 per month for
disease of eyes contracted while first lieutenant. He died at Milwaukee, Wis., June
25, 1889, the cause of his death being disease of lungs.

Mrs. Merrell is now receiving the pension of $8 per month provided by the act of
June 27, 1890. On January 26, 1898, she made claim under the general law, which
was rejected October 24, 1902, on the ground that her husband's fatal disease was not
due to disease of eyes, for which he was pensioned, and not otherwise shown to have
resulted from his military service.

Mrs. Merrell, who is 62 years of age, was married to the officer November 27, 1873.
She is in very destitute circumstances, her income being limited to her small pension of $8 per month. She has a small shack by the seashore, wherein she lives. It
is a shelter and nothing more. At certain seasons of the year she rents her shack to
aid in her support, and lives in a little tent near by.

There is no evidence showing that the officer's death was the direct result of his
military service. There is medical evidence showing that after his discharge he
suffered from malaria contracted during service, and it is quite probable that this
trouble was connected with his fatal disease. However that may be, his long period
of service and the extreme destitution of his widow seem to warrant favorable action
on the bill, and the passage of the same is recommended.

O

ARRA M. FARNSWORTH.

FEBRUARY 3, 1903.—Committed to the Committee of the Whole House and ordered to be printed.

Mr. HENRY C. SMITH, from the Committee on War Claims, submitted the following

REPORT.

[To accompany H. R. 17164.]

The Committee on War Claims, to whom was referred the bill (H. R. 17164) for the relief of Arra M. Farnsworth, submit the following report:

The sole object and effect of this bill is to relieve the claimant of the bar of the statute of limitations prescribed by the "Act to provide for the adjudication and payment of claims arising from Indian depredations," approved March 3, 1891. The facts as shown to the committee make a prima facie showing of a claim on account of depredations of the Sioux and Cheyennes in the capture of certain wagons and teams owned by the claimant. Through inadvertence of the attorneys for the claimant, his petition failed to be filed in the Court of Claims under the act referred to within the time limited by said act. Claimant is an old man and resides in Michigan. He does not seem to have been guilty of laches on his own part, but employed and relied on attorneys, who failed to give his case due and timely attention. The whole facts seem to entitle him in justice and equity to the privilege of a hearing in court, where the rights of all parties can be heard and adjudicated.

Your committee recommend the passage of the bill.

O

WILLOUGHBY L. WILSON, ADMINISTRATOR.

FEBRUARY 3, 1903.—Committed to the Committee of the Whole House and ordered
to be printed.

Mr. CALDWELL, from the Committee on War Claims, submitted the
following

REPORT.

[To accompany H. Res. No. 424.]

The Committee on War Claims, to whom was referred the bill
(H. R. 14368) for the relief of Willoughby L. Wilson, administrator
of Willoughby Wilson, deceased, submit the following report:

This is a claim for stores and supplies alleged to have been furnished
to the military forces of the United States for their use during the war
for the suppression of the rebellion. Claim stated at $2,125.

The evidence offered in support of this claim is in the form of ex parte
affidavits, and your committee have no opportunity of subjecting the
witnesses to a cross-examination, and are therefore of the opinion that
this claim should be referred to the Court of Claims, where depositions
can be taken in the usual manner prescribed by law, counsel for the
Government and for the claimant having the right to cross-examine
the witnesses making such depositions; and when the facts shall have
been determined by the court upon the legal testimony thus taken and
submitted, said facts to be reported to Congress for its consideration;
and report herewith a resolution to that effect, and recommend its
adoption.

O

SAMPSON KINNA.

FEBRUARY 3, 1903.—Committed to the Committee of the Whole House and ordered
to be printed.

Mr. CALDWELL, from the Committee on War Claims, submitted the
following

REPORT.

[To accompany H. Res. No. 425.]

The Committee on War Claims, to whom was referred the bill (H. R.
16798) for the relief of Sampson Kinna, submit the following report:
This is a claim for stores and supplies alleged to have been furnished
to the military forces of the United States for their use during the
late war for the suppression of the rebellion by Sampson Kinna, of
Frederick County, Md. Claim stated at $850.
The evidence offered in support of this claim is in the form of ex
parte affidavits, and your committee have no opportunity of subjecting the witnesses to a cross-examination, and are therefore of the
opinion that this claim should be referred to the Court of Claims,
where depositions can be taken in the usual manner prescribed by law,
counsel for the Government and for the claimant having the right to
cross-examine the witnesses making such depositions, and when the
facts shall have been determined by the court upon the legal testimony
thus taken and submitted said facts to be reported to Congress for its
consideration, and report herewith a resolution to that effect and
recommend its adoption.

O

HEIRS OF WILEY FRANKS, DECEASED.

FEBRUARY 8, 1903.—Committed to the Committee of the Whole House and ordered to be printed.

Mr. SPIGHT, from the Committee on War Claims, submitted the following

REPORT.

[To accompany H. Res. No. 426.]

The Committee on War Claims, to whom was referred the bill (H. R. 16577) for the relief of Mrs. G. W. Ross, Mrs. H. C. Cary, Mrs. Annie Brooks, L. C. Wilcoxon, et al, heirs of Wiley Franks, deceased, submit the following report:

The evidence offered in support of this claim is in the form of ex parte affidavits, and your committee have no opportunity of subjecting the witnesses to a cross-examination, and are therefore of the opinion that this claim should be referred to the Court of Claims, where depositions can be taken in the usual manner prescribed by law, counsel for the Government and for the claimant having the right to cross-examine the witnesses making such depositions; and when the facts shall have been determined by the court upon the legal testimony thus taken and submitted, said facts to be reported to Congress for its consideration; and report herewith a resolution to that effect, and recommend its adoption.

O

REMOVAL OF PERSONS ACCUSED OF CRIME TO AND FROM THE PHILIPPINE ISLANDS FOR TRIAL.

FEBRUARY 3, 1903.—Referred to the House Calendar and ordered to be printed.

Mr. COOPER, of Wisconsin, from the Committee on Insular Affairs, submitted the following

REPORT.

[To accompany S. 7124.]

The Committee on Insular Affairs, to whom was referred the bill (S. 7124) to provide for the removal of persons accused of crime to and from the Philippine Islands for trial, beg leave to submit the following report and recommend that said bill do pass with an amendment, to wit:

Strike out the words "Guam, Tutuila, or Manua," in line 8, page 1, of the bill, so that said bill when amended shall read as follows:

AN ACT to provide for the removal of persons accused of crime to and from the Philippine Island for trial.

Be it enacted by the Senate and House of Representatives of the United States in Congress assembled, That the provisions of section ten hundred and fourteen of the Revised Statutes, so far as applicable, shall apply throughout the United States for the arrest and removal therefrom to the Philippine Islands of any fugitive from justice charged with the commission of any crime or offense against the United States within the Philippine Islands, and shall apply within the Philippine Islands for the arrest and removal therefrom to the United States of any fugitive from justice charged with the commission of any crime or offense against the United States. Such fugitive may, by any judge or magistrate of the Philippine Islands, and agreeably to the usual mode of process against offenders therein, be arrested and imprisoned, or bailed, as the case may be, pending the issuance of a warrant for his removal to the United States, which warrant it shall be the duty of a judge of the court of first instance seasonably to issue, and of the officer or agent of the United States designated for the purpose to execute. Such officer or agent, when engaged in executing such warrant without the Philippine Islands, shall have all the powers of a marshal of the United States so far as such powers are requisite for the prisoner's safe-keeping and the execution of the warrant.

SEC. 2. That the provisions of sections fifty-two hundred and seventy-eight and fifty-two hundred and seventy-nine of the Revised Statutes, so far as applicable, shall apply to the Philippine Islands, which, for the purposes of said sections, shall be deemed a Territory within the meaning thereof.

The purpose of this bill is simply to extend the extradition laws of the United States to the Philippine Islands, and thus supply a serious omission in existing statutes. It was drawn by the Solicitor-General of the Department of Justice at the request of the Secretary of War.

O

CONSTRUCTION, REPAIR, AND PRESERVATION OF CERTAIN PUBLIC WORKS, ETC.

FEBRUARY 3, 1903.—Referred to the House Calendar and ordered to be printed.

Mr. BURTON, from the Committee on Rivers and Harbors, submitted the following

REPORT.

[To accompany H. R. 17243.]

The Committee on Rivers and Harbors, to whom was referred the bill (H. R. 16339) to amend "An act making appropriations for the construction, repair, and preservation of certain public works on rivers and harbors, and for other purposes," approved June 13, 1902, submit the following report:

The object of this bill is to authorize the expenditure of $125,000, appropriated by the river and harbor act, approved June 13, 1902, for the construction of a channel through Sabine Lake, on the westerly side, so as to connect with Taylors Bayou, or with the Port Arthur Canal. This amount was appropriated by the act named, but contained this provision:

Provided further, That in the discretion of the Secretary of War, he may select a route at or near the west shore of said lake, and said channel may be connected with Port Arthur Canal.

The Port Arthur Canal is a private waterway. At the time of the passage of the bill it was reported to this committee that the corporation controlling the canal would allow such connection to be made, thereby affording a route through a channel already constructed along the lower portion of Sabine Lake. There has been some difficulty in obtaining this permission, and the War Department has interpreted the provision quoted to mean that in case the channel provided for is constructed at or near the west shore of Sabine Lake, it is compulsory that connection shall be made with Port Arthur Canal.

In view of these facts, to render the appropriation made by Congress effective, it is necessary that there be legislation. The members of the committee are of the opinion that this should be done, but that the legislative will can be expressed more clearly by a reenactment or amendment of the provision referred to in the river and harbor act of June 13, 1902. They accordingly recommend the accompanying substitute, and when the bill is amended by the adoption of said substitute they recommend that the bill do pass.

O

EXTENSION OF TIME FOR PRESENTATION OF CLAIMS.

FEBRUARY 3, 1903.—Referred to the House Calendar and ordered to be printed.

Mr. KEHOE, from the Committee on War Claims, submitted the following

REPORT.

[To accompany H. R. 16133.]

The Committee on War Claims, to whom was referred the bill (H. R. 16133) to extend the time for presentation of claims under the act entitled "An act to reimburse the governors of States and Territories for expenses incurred by them in aiding the United States to raise and organize and supply and equip the Volunteer Army of the United States in the existing war with Spain," approved July 8, 1898, and under acts amendatory thereof, have examined same and recommend that the bill do pass.

The passage of this bill is deemed just and proper because of the fact that many of the States still have just claims pending against the United States growing out of expenses incurred by them in aid of the Government during the war with Spain. Under the act of March 3, 1899, it was provided that all such claims should be presented to the Treasury Department "on or before January 1, 1902," and most of the claims were presented before that time, but owing to the fact that many of the States did not succeed in fully ascertaining their claims until after the date provided by the act of March 3, 1899, it is deemed proper to pass this bill that they may be given an opportunity to do so.

In many cases it was impossible for certain States to determine what their claims were until after the Treasury Department had determined what character of claims were contemplated by above-mentioned act, and after said decisions the date fixed by above act had passed.

The passage of this bill does not authorize the filing of any new character of claim, but is simply intended to extend the date for filing of State claims, within the contemplation of the act of March 3, 1899.

O

AMENDMENT TO RIVER AND HARBOR ACT APPROVED JUNE 13, 1902.

FEBRUARY 3, 1903.—Referred to the House Calendar and ordered to be printed.

Mr. BURTON, from the Committee on Rivers and Harbors, submitted the following

REPORT.

[To accompany H. R. 17170.]

The Committee on Rivers and Harbors, to whom was referred the bill (H. R. 17170) to amend an act entitled "An act making appropriations for the construction, repair, and preservation of certain public works on rivers and harbors, and for other purposes," approved June 13, 1902, submit the following report:

The object of this bill is to change the river and harbor act approved June 13, 1902, in that portion relating to the Fox River, Illinois, so that the permission given at that time may not restrict the privilege granted to a specific locality. By the act as it passed on the date mentioned it was provided that the dam, permission to construct which was granted, might be located "about 3,000 feet" below the highway bridge at McHenry, McHenry County, Ill. It has been ascertained that other and more convenient localities can be obtained, and the committee see no objection to the passage of the bill referred to, H. R. 17170, and which this report accompanies. The bill provides that the dam may be constructed at a point "not exceeding 3,000 feet" below the highway bridge at McHenry, McHenry County, Ill., and safeguards all public and private interests in the same manner as in the river and harbor act referred to. Accordingly, the committee recommend that the bill do pass.

O

BRIBERY CHARGES.

FEBRUARY 3, 1903.—Referred to the House Calendar and ordered to be printed.

Mr. TAYLER, of Ohio, from the Committee on Naval Affairs, submitted the following

REPORT.

[In compliance with H. Res. No. 404.]

The Committee on Naval Affairs, in compliance with the following resolution, beg leave to submit the following report:

Whereas information has come to the Committee on Naval Affairs through a member of said committee of an attempt to corruptly influence his action respecting proposed legislation pending before said committee and the House:

Resolved, That the Committee on Naval Affairs, or such subcommittee thereof as said committee may appoint, be, and is hereby, authorized and directed to fully investigate said matter; and for such purpose it is hereby authorized and empowered to send for persons and papers, to compel the attendance of witnesses, and to administer oaths. Said committee shall have authority to report at any time, and the expenses incurred hereunder shall be paid out of the contingent fund of the House on vouchers approved by the chairman.

At a meeting of the Committee on Naval Affairs held January 20, 1903, during the consideration of the naval appropriation bill, Mr. Lessler, a member of the committee, charged that he had been corruptly approached for the purpose of influencing his action respecting proposed legislation providing for the purchase of Holland submarine torpedo boats.

The committee immediately appointed a subcommittee to make a preliminary investigation of Mr. Lessler's charge. The following day Philip Doblin, of New York, appeared before the subcommittee and confessed that he had so approached Mr. Lessler.

The substance of this statement having been reported the following day to the full committee, the chairman was directed to present to the House and procure the adoption of the resolution above set out.

In compliance with the direction and authority of said resolution your committee proceeded at once to take testimony, and examined such witnesses as were believed to have knowledge of the subject of inquiry. That testimony is set out in full in the appendix to this report, and in view of the fact that your committee in this report makes an explicit finding of its conclusions it becomes unnecessary to quote from or to comment upon the evidence.

Mr. Lessler, in his testimony before the committee, stated that Philip Doblin had come to him some weeks ago and had said that Mr. Lemuel E. Quigg had said to him (Doblin) that there was $5,000 in it if Lessler could be brought to support the proposition to buy more Holland boats.

This statement, in substance, Doblin corroborated when he first testified before the full committee, stating that Mr. Quigg had said to him that if Lessler could be brought to vote for more Holland boats "there would be $5,000 in it," and that he (Quigg) added, "I think I can make it a thousand for you."

Subsequently Doblin again went on the stand and retracted this statement, declaring that Mr. Quigg had never suggested money to him, and that he (Doblin) had not told Lessler that Quigg had made such a proposal to him, and that he had made his first statement at the request of Lessler and for his protection.

Section 5450, Revised Statutes of the United States, provides that:

Every person who promises, offers, gives, or causes or procures to be promised, offered, or given, any money or other thing of value, or makes or tenders any contract, undertaking, obligation, gratuity, or security for the payment of money, or for the delivery or conveyance of anything of value, to any member of either House of Congress, either before or after such member has been qualified or has taken his seat, with the intent to influence his vote or decision on any question, matter, cause, or proceeding which may be at any time pending in either House of Congress, or before any committee thereof, shall be fined not more than three times the amount of money or value of the thing so offered, promised, given, made, or tendered, or caused or procured to be so offered, promised, given, made, or tendered, and shall be, moreover, imprisoned not more than three years.

Section 5392 provides that:

Every person who, having taken an oath before a competent tribunal, officer, or person, in any case in which a law of the United States authorizes an oath administered, that he will testify, declare, depose, or certify truly, or that any testimony, declaration, or certificate by him subscribed is true, willfully and contrary to such oath states or subscribes any material matter which he does not believe to be true. is guilty of perjury, and shall be punished by a fine of not more than two thousand dollars, and by imprisonment, at hard labor, not more than five years; and shall, moreover, thereafter be incapable of giving testimony in any court of the United States until such time as the judgment against him is reversed.

A witness, sworn by the chairman, as in this case, who "states any material matter which he does not believe to be true," before a committee of the House conducting an investigation under authority of the House, commits perjury, and is liable to punishment therefor under section 5392.

Your committee has most carefully heard and considered the testimony taken before it, and upon the same has come to the following conclusions:

1. That the charge made by Mr. Lessler that an attempt had been made to corruptly influence his action respecting proposed legislation is sustained by the evidence; such attempt, in the opinion of the committee, having been made by one Philip Doblin, on his own initiative and responsibility, with the idea of making money for himself if he should find Mr. Lessler corruptly approachable.

2. That there is no evidence to sustain the charge of an attempt by Lemuel E. Quigg to corruptly influence a member of the Committee on Naval Affairs respecting proposed legislation pending before said committee and the House.

3. That there is no evidence to sustain the charge of an attempt by the Holland Submarine Boat Company or any of its agents to corruptly influence a member of the Committee on Naval Affairs respecting proposed legislation before said committee and the House.

In view of the foregoing we recommend that the clerk of the committee be directed to certify to the Attorney-General of the United States a copy of the testimony taken at the hearing with a request that he take such action as the law and the facts warrant.

APPENDIX.

HEARING BEFORE COMMITTEE ON NAVAL AFFAIRS, HOUSE OF REPRESENTATIVES, ON A RESOLUTION SUBMITTED BY MR. FOSS (H. RES. NO. 404), JANUARY 22, 1903.

COMMITTEE ON NAVAL AFFAIRS,
HOUSE OF REPRESENTATIVES,
Washington, D. C., January 23, 1903.

The committee met at 10.30 o'clock a. m., Hon. George Edmund Foss in the chair.

The CHAIRMAN. We are met together to-day, gentlemen, in pursuance of a resolution adopted by the House yesterday, which I will read:

Resolved, That the Committee on Naval Affairs, or such subcommittee thereof as said committee may appoint, be, and it is hereby, authorized and directed to fully investigate said matter; and for such purpose it is hereby authorized and empowered to send for persons and papers, to compel the attendance of witnesses, and to administer oaths. Said committee shall have authority to report at any time, and the expenses incurred hereunder shall be paid out of the contingent fund of the House on vouchers approved by the chairman.

That is the resolution in pursuance of which we are met here to-day. The first evidence before the committee will be that of Mr. Lessler, who is the member of the committee referred to in that resolution, and I will ask Mr. Tayler to act for the committee in interrogating Mr. Lessler.

TESTIMONY OF HON. MONTAGUE LESSLER, A REPRESENTATIVE IN CONGRESS FROM THE STATE OF NEW YORK (SWORN).

By Mr. TAYLER:

Q. When were you elected a member of the Fifty-seventh Congress?— A. The 3d of January, 1902.

Q. When did you take your seat?—A. The 15th of January.

Q. You are a member of the Committee on Naval Affairs of the House of Representatives?—A. I am.

Q. When were you made a member of the committee?—A. The 15th of May, 1902.

Q. What has been your attitude respecting the proposition to build more Holland submarine boats?—A. I have been against it—against the proposition.

Q. What is Mr. Doblin's first name?—A. Philip.

Q. Who is Philip Doblin?—A. Philip Doblin is a young man in New York who, for a month or so preceding my election, and part of the time during 1902, looked after political affairs in the district during election and subsequent to it.

Q. That is, in your district?—A. Yes, sir.

Q. Was he about your office, or had he a desk in your office in New York?—A. No, he had no desk, but he was about there every day, or every other day. Of course when I was here I do not know how often. I was in New York Saturdays, was the only time.

3

Q. Were you in the habit of going home each week to New York?—
A. I have been in the habit of going home Friday or Saturday and
coming back Sunday.

Q. And you saw him when you went home?—A. Sometimes.

Q. You had your Congressional secretary here in Washington with
you?—A. Yes, sir.

Q. Had Mr. Doblin, before your election to Congress, been intimately
your friend, or politically—— A. 1 only knew him casually up to about
the time that I was nominated on the 21st of December, 1901.

Q. He was, as you understood it, generally understood to be one of
your closest political friends in your district?—A. He was not in the
district.

Q. I mean respecting matters in your district.—A. He has been aiding my election throughout.

Q. Did you have a talk with him a month or two ago respecting the
subject of Holland submarine boats?—A. Yes.

Q. About when was that?—A. My recollection is that it was between
the election in November and the opening of the session on the first of
December; somewhere within that period—in November.

Q. And where was that conversation?—A. In my office, No. 31 Nassau street, New York City.

Q. Tell us, if you please, how this conversation arose?—A. He came
in one morning and he asked me if the Holland submarine boat proposition was before the House—would come again before the House—and
I said that I supposed so. He said, "Are you still opposed to it?" I
said, "Yes." He then said that he had been sent for by Mr. Quigg,
and that Quigg had said to him that there was $5,000 in it if I could
be brought to the other side. My recollection is that I simply laughed
at it and told him that I did not want to hear anything more about it.
That is all there was said on that proposition.

Q. You think you have told us all he said?—A. I would add this,
that he said that Quigg was a man of power and influence in New
York, and that of course it subsequently I wanted to come back here,
in aiding him I would aid myself in such a proposition in doing him
such a favor.

Q. Did he tell you where he had this conversation with Mr. Quigg?—
A. Yes; 100 Broadway, in Quigg's office. That was all that was said.

Q. Did you later see Mr. Quigg in connection with this Holland boat
business?—A. Mr. Quigg telephoned me one morning later.

Q. When, about?—A. It was my impression that it was prior to the
opening of the session, on the first of December, but it may have been
during the Christmas recess.

Q. Tell us, how did that conversation come about?—A. He asked
me if I could see him, and if he could come over, and I told him to
come right over, and he came over to my office, No. 31 Nassau street,
within an hour, about the middle of the day.

Q. Tell us what occurred there.—A. We passed the amenities, and
I said to him at once that there should be no question of money in this
business; that I——

Q. Had anything been said about Holland submarine boats before
you made that observation?—A. No, no.

Q. Well—— A. (Continuing.) I said at once that there should be no
question of money in this business.

Q. What business?—A. The Holland submarine boat. I knew his
specific errand.

Q. Had there been any conversation over the telephone about the Holland submarine boats?—A. He simply wanted to see me.

Q. You inferred at once that it was about that that he wanted to see you?—A. I had no business, or nothing else, with Mr. Quigg in any way.

Q. Tell us what occurred.—A. I started right in in that way—that there must not be any question of money.

Q. What reply did he make?—A. He stood silent; did not say anything. And I explained to him at quite some length my proposition about these boats, going into the history of the construction, and what they were, and describing the whole business—the technical—so far as I knew it; and he asked questions along the line of what they were for, and how many the Government had, and the purely naval features.

Q. Did he say anything about how his interest of this matter arose?—A. He got up and said, "I see that you are opposed to this proposition, and have evidently looked into it. I have no interest in it;" and my recollection is that he also spoke about Mr. Rice, of the Holland torpedo-boat people—I don't remember; expressed some opposition to him—and said he had absolutely no interest in the boat or the company, but said that a man by the name of Hunter—my recollection is that he had done him some favors—had asked him to see me and look into it. That ended the conversation, and he went out.

Q. Did he further identify Mr. Hunter by stating who he was?—A. My recollection is that he said "Mr. Hunter, of Virginia," but I am not certain about the "Virginia."

Q. Have you told us all now that transpired?—A. Absolutely every word, except the definite conversation, which was perhaps an hour long.

Q. Did you have a conversation with Mr. John McCullagh?—A. Yes, sir; in Washington.

Q. At the last session of Congress?—A. Yes, sir; in Washington.

Q. In Washington?—A. Yes, sir.

Q. Where did that conversation occur?—A. In my room.

Mr. ROBERTS. Is that within the scope of this inquiry?

The WITNESS. Yes.

By Mr. TAYLER:

Q. State what that conversation was.—A. I had received a telegram while I was in Cincinnati that Mr. McCullagh, who was the superintendent of State elections in New York, desired to see me, and that was wired to me by my secretary to Cincinnati, I think, sometime in the latter part of April or the beginning of May. My papers are in New York.

Q. Was that after you became a member of the Naval Affairs Committee?—A. Yes, sir; it was right after.

Q. You succeeded Mr. Cummings as a member of this committee?—A. Yes, sir, I succeeded Mr. Cummings; and I wrote Mr. McCullagh that I would be very glad to see him at my office when I got home Saturday, and I received a note from him stating that the matter which he wanted to see me about had passed.

After we passed the naval bill, and it was pending in the Senate, I went to Atlantic City from Friday to Sunday, and I received a wire saying that John McCullagh wanted to see me. I did not get back until Sunday night on that 8 o'clock train—Monday night, I think, eight something train from Atlantic City, and about 9 o'clock Mr. McCullagh came to my room and said that he was glad to meet me, as we had not met before.

Q. You mean by that that you had had no personal acquaintance with him before that time?—A. I had met him, but he did not know me.

Q. State what his official position then was.—A. He was State superintendent of elections. I said then that I was glad to meet him, and he sat down, and he said that he had come over on the Baltimore and Ohio train; that he was stopping down at the Willard and had waited over for me, and his exact wording of this was that he had been sent by men in New York who could reelect me or beat me, to ask me to vote for the Holland submarine boat. The situation then was, regarding the bill, that it had come out of the Senate, and I think the conversation took place on the Monday night preceding the first meeting of the committee when we considered the Senate bill after it had gone through that; and so he said, "I have been sent by some men in New York who can reelect you or beat you, to ask you to vote for the Holland submarine boat." I said to him, "I will see you in hell first—I will see them in hell first." He then said, "Then do it for me;" but I said, "No, Chief; I can not do it;" and I remember very distinctly the simile that I drew in explaining to him the whole proposition.

I put it this way to him: "Suppose the governor of the State of New York should ask the last subordinate that came into your bureau his opinion of running the bureau. You would think that the governor was foolish. So that my judgment is following simply the men in the Navy who are running the affairs of the Navy." I remember getting down the books that I had on the subject and explaining to him in detail, so far as I could, what I knew about the boat, and he left me about 10 o'clock in the evening. He said to me, "Congressman, I am sorry that I came. I did not understand the situation." That was the end of that whole conversation. I have never spoken to him since on the subject.

Q. At this time, if you are correct as to the time, the House had passed the bill without the provision for the Holland submarine boats, and the Senate had put it in; is that correct?—A. That is correct.

Q. The House was considering whether it would agree to the Senate amendment?—A. No; it was going to consider it in a day or two, and I think we held a meeting the next morning. I think if the clerk will look up the meeting after that bill came back it will fix it absolutely.

Q. Was anything else said in these interviews?—A. No. I have told you all, as I have said, without going absolutely into everything. pro and con.

Q. On the subject of building these boats?—A. Yes. Mr. Quigg and Mr. McCullagh had no statement to make on the subject of the propriety.

Mr. TAYLER. Mr. Chairman, I think that is all.

Mr. RIXEY. Mr. Chairman, I wish to suggest a question for Mr. Tayler to ask.

The CHAIRMAN. Very well. Suggest the question to Mr. Tayler. (Mr. Rixey did so.)

By Mr. TAYLER:

Q. At the time Mr. McCullagh had this conversation with you what position did Mr Doblin hold?—A. None, I think.

Q. That is correct, I believe.—A. He has now—was at the time he made this proposition.

Mr. RIXEY. I say at the time he made the statement with regard to Quigg.

By Mr. TAYLER:

Q. What position does Mr. Doblin hold now?—A. I don't know that he holds any; I don't know that he holds any now.

At the suggestion of Mr. Tate the following question was asked:

By Mr. TAYLER:

Q. Do you know whether Mr. Doblin had any position under John McCullagh at the time when he told you that Quigg had sent him to you?—A. He had a position in that Bureau as an outside man. Chief McCullagh has a number of deputies, and he was one during—preceding election. I do not know whether he was one at that time. They discharge them, you know, after election. I don't know whether he was discharged. I don't know.

Q. Now, Mr. Lessler, I am requested to press you further upon this point.—A. Yes, sir.

Q. (Continuing.) As to how you came to say to Mr. Quigg when he came in that there was no money in this matter, as to whether you merely inferred that that was the subject that he came to talk upon, or whether the subject of the Holland torpedo boats was mentioned by him before you made that remark.—A. I don't remember whether he mentioned the subject. He had nothing else to talk to me about. He had, as Mr. Doblin says, sent Mr. Doblin to sound me. I don't remember just how the conversation was introduced, other than that fact.

Q. But subsequent to that—— —A. (Continuing.) But I want to be very frank with you and say that Mr. Quigg had no other business with me, or any business with me, or any relations with me, that I know of, to induce him to visit my office.

Q. And there was no other subject of conversation actually taken up after you commenced talking, except the Holland submarine boat subject; I mean seriously discussed?—A. No; nothing else.

Mr. RIXEY. Now, I would like to suggest to Mr. Tayler to ask the witness this question: When he stated to Mr. Quigg that he did not want to consider any money proposition, what reply did Mr. Quigg make?

Mr. TAYLER. I asked him that question.

Mr. RIXEY. I didn't remember that you did.

Mr. TAYLER. I asked Mr. Lessler that question, to which he replied that he said nothing.

At the suggestion of Mr. Rixey, Mr. Tayler questioned the witness as follows:

By Mr. TAYLER:

Q. Did Mr. Quigg express surprise that you should make a remark of that sort—that you should meet him in that way?—A. No——

Q. Did he say anything that would indicate that he came on other business?—A. Not at all.

By Mr. ROBERTS:

Q. Does Doblin now get his mail through your business office?—A. I don't know whether he does now; he has.

Q. Was Mr. Doblin getting his mail at or through your office at the time he carried this proposition to you?—A. I don't believe he had very much mail to get, but it is quite possible he got his mail there. During the year when he had no office he came down there frequently to get whatever mail was there. I never saw it. I am unable to say. He had the freedom of the office.

By Mr. TAYLER:

Q. Did he have the use of a desk in your office at any time?—A. He has had no separate desk. He may have written a letter. I never saw him sit at it.

Mr. ROBERTS. He has stated that he was a political friend, and I would like to ask if he was at any time a business friend?

By Mr. TAYLER:

Q. Has he been a personal or business friend of yours?—A. The relation arose just as I told it to you. When I was nominated, on the 21st of December, 1901, he was then connected with the Republican county committee of New York and had been since Mr. Quigg was chairman of it. That is my first recollection of him. He was ardent, faithful, helpful in every way, and I felt under great obligations to him for his assistance to me during the campaign, and where I could would have assisted him at at any time I could have assisted him. He had been at my house—if the purport of the question is that—maybe five or six or seven times. He was on to Washington when I was sworn in here. I think I procured for him some little receiverships in the courts under the bankruptcy law, and now I mention it, I think that was the main business, the letters that came from the referee in bankruptcy, or from the mail of the house for which he was receiver, which were repostmarked and sent to the office. Otherwise, I know of no mail. I have seen some of that mail around.

By Mr. TAYLER:

Q. Have you visited at his house?—A. Never, in any way.

By Mr. ROBERTS:

Q. Was anybody else present in your office when Mr. Doblin made this proposition to you?—A. No.

Mr. RIXEY. I understand you to say that when he came to you with the proposition his opening remark was "Are you still opposed to the Holland submarine boats?" Will Mr. Tayler ask him if that is correct?

By Mr. TAYLER:

Q. When he came to you, are we correct in understanding that his first statement was "I understand you are still opposed to these Holland submarine boats?"—A. No; I have made no statement as outside of—as to the chronology of the remarks, exact statements, back in November. The man's statement was introduced in that way; whether I was opposed to the Holland submarine boat in some way opened the conversation. Whether it opened with that exact phrase I do not remember.

Mr. ROBERTS. Now, I would like to ask if I am correct in my understanding of the testimony, that prior to this day when the alleged bribe was offered there had been no conversation with Mr. Doblin respecting the submarine boat?

By Mr. TAYLER:

Q. Had you had any conversation with Doblin prior to this proposal by him to you respecting it?—A. I may have talked to him, as I have spoken to others, of the general proposition of what the boat is, but I recall no conversation on the proposition.

By Mr. ROBERTS:

Q. Had you ever expressed to him that you were opposed to the boats prior to this?—A. I may have.

At the request of Mr. Roberts the following was asked:

By Mr. TAYLER:

Q. You are not positive about it?—A. I do not remember. I am not positive that I have not expressed my opposition to the Holland boat to this man.

By Mr. ROBERTS:

Q. Did you know anything about Mr. Doblin's reputation, or know of his being employed as a lobbyist at any time?—A. I only know of one incident; that is all I know of.

Q. Do you know whether or not he was charged on the floor of the aldermanic chamber as being a lobbyist and ordered off the floor during a session of the board of aldermen?

Mr. WHEELER. I do not see the relevancy of that.

Mr. ROBERTS. I think it is perfectly fair to show how much Mr. Lessler knew of this man and of his reputation and of those charges.

The WITNESS. I think his question was perfectly fair.

Mr. WHEELER. Wait a moment, Mr. Lessler; you are a witness now.

Mr. DAYTON. I suggest in connection with that that Mr. Roberts is asking him now about individual matters instead of general reputation, which is never allowed.

Further discussion among the members of the committee followed.

Mr. VANDIVER. The question is not whether it is a question of law. I would like to hear all the questions answered. We want to get the truth.

Mr. ROBERTS. I am perfectly satisfied, if it is ruled out on a legal technicality, that it should go out.

The CHAIRMAN. I think that it would come more properly later in the investigation.

Further discussion among the members of the committee followed.

Mr. TATE. Ask him his source of information about that, and we can tell more about it.

The WITNESS. Gentlemen, I prefer to answer that question, if you will allow me to do so.

Mr. TAYLER. Very well; go on and answer the question.

The question was repeated by the stenographer, as follows:

"Q. Do you know whether or not he was charged on the floor of the aldermanic chamber as being a lobbyist, and ordered off the floor during a session of the board of aldermen?"—A. The only thing I know about that is seeing a little squib in the newspaper. It seems that he was in a telephone booth, telephoning to somebody, and some alderman came along and ordered him out of the booth. That is all I heard of it.

By Mr. ROBERTS:

Q. You have no knowledge of the fact that an alderman charged him with being a lobbyist in the employ of certain corporations, and that he was ordered off the floor of the chamber on that ground?

The WITNESS. I have no knowledge of his being a lobbyist at any time, and I do not believe he has been.

The CHAIRMAN. Are there any further questions?

At the suggestion of Mr. Rixey the following questions were asked:

By Mr. TAYLER:

Q. State the political and business relations, so far as you know them, between John McCullagh and Mr. Quigg.—A. Mr. Quigg has been chairman of the county committee of New York, and, as I believe, one of its members, and Mr. McCullagh was the former superintendent of police, and became, when this law went into effect, the State superintendent of elections. I don't know of any political relations any more than in the point of time I think Mr. Quigg was the chairman of the county committee, and a member of the State committee, and probably was one of those who viséed or indorsed the appointment of Mr. McCullagh; and I don't know of any other relations except those.

By Mr. WHEELER:

Q. Is Mr. Quigg an ex-member of Congress?—A. Mr. Quigg is an ex-member of Congress; yes, sir.

By Mr. MUDD:

Q. Will Mr. Tayler please ask him whether anyone was present at the time Mr. Quigg called at his office?
Mr. TAYLER. I was about to ask him that question.
The WITNESS. No one was in the room; no, sir.

By Mr. BUTLER:

Q. Was anyone present in his office at the time Mr. McCullagh called?
The WITNESS. Yes, sir.

By Mr. TAYLER:

Q. Who?—A. My secretary in Washington.

By Mr. BUTLER:

Q. What is the name of that secretary?
The WITNESS. Frank P. Son.
Q. What is his address?—A. I can get him on the telephone in a minute.
Q. What is his address?—A. I don't know. It is somewhere on Twelfth street. I can get him on the telephone.

By Mr. MEYER:

Q. I would like to ask this question: When Mr. Quigg called upon Mr. Lessler at his office, and after Mr. Lessler's statement to him that he did not wish to talk about matters with reference to this matter, did Mr. Quigg continue the conversation in a manner to convince Mr. Lessler that that was the sole object of his visit?
Mr. ROBERTS. Which; the money?
Q. (Continuing.) The question of the Holland torpedo boats and the money. Did he continue the conversation in a natural strain on that subject?—A. My recollection is that there was conversation on natural and political matters in the campaign not affecting this subject at all, and that nothing else was mentioned except the boats.

By Mr. WHEELER:

Q. I desire to propound an inquiry. While we are refreshing your recollection I will ask you if it is not true that at the time of the conversation between you and Doblin, when you say that he told you Mr. Quigg informed him that there was $5,000 in it for you, that he did not say there was $1,000 in it for him?—A. No; I never knew of that. I never heard of that until—my recollection is that I did not know of that until you brought it out in committee from Doblin the other day.

Q. He did not mention in the conversation what he was to receive, in stating the proposition to you?—A. No, sir.

By Mr. RIXEY:

Q. In the conversations that you had with Mr. McCullagh did Mr. McCullagh state that Mr. Rice, the president of the company, was a friend of his?—A. No names were mentioned. I asked him directly if he would tell me who sent him, and he said no; that he would not tell me.

Q. I am asking for information for myself on this line. You said that some one mentioned Mr. Rice, the president of the company?—A. Yes; I said Mr. Quigg had spoken of some controversy with Rice during our conversation, and my recollection is that the inference that I obtained was that he was not personally friendly to Rice.

Mr. TAYLER. That was the way I understood Mr. Lessler to testify originally.

By. Mr. MUDD:

Q. I would like to ask Mr. Lessler, Mr. Tayler, if there was any statement as to how the money was to be paid—by check or otherwise—whether there was any such statement?—A. I have told you all the conversation. It did not take a minute and a half, that conversation.

Mr. MUDD. I would like to ask that question.

By Mr. TAYLER:

Q. Was anything said about a check or money, or how it was to be paid? To that I understand your answer is no.

The WITNESS. No, Mr. Chairman; one of the newspapers publishes the following, which I desire to put in the record and to deny absolutely.

A handsome young woman, to whose charms it was believed Mr. Lessler would fall a victim, was used in an effort to sway his vote in favor of submarine boats. She did not say that she was authorized to make him an offer, but she did urge him to use his best efforts toward purchasing Holland boats.

I want to say that no such statement was ever made by me; no such woman, handsome or otherwise, ever approached me, and I do not remember ever having a conversation with a woman on the subject at any time, place, or in any manner. I want that to go in the record. The story is absolutely untrue, in every shape, way, and form.

By Mr. BUTLER:

Q. In what newspaper did that appear?—A. The New York Evening Sun of January 22, 1903.

By Mr. BUTLER:

Q. Who is the correspondent of the New York Sun here in Washington?

The CHAIRMAN. I submit that this matter does not affect the question under consideration——

Mr. LESSLER. I submit that it is competent.

Mr. ROBERTS. It is a charge made publicly. I have no objection to its going in.

Mr. LESSLER. I want it to go in.

The CHAIRMAN. Denying newspaper reports?

Mr. LESSLER. I insist upon that going in.

Mr. BUTLER. I think that he should have it in, in justice to himself.

Several MEMBERS. Yes, yes.

Mr. ROBERTS. Will Mr. Tayler ask Mr. Lessler if he continued on the same terms of intimacy with Mr. Doblin after he had made the offer of a bribe as he was on before.

By Mr. TAYLER:

Q. Have you been on the same terms of intimacy with Mr. Doblin since this proposition as before?—A. Yes, sir; with the exception that I have not seen him as often as before. I have been away from the city.

By Mr. VANDIVER:

Q. Bearing on that line of inquiry, at whose instance did Mr. Doblin appear here before the committee yesterday or day before; was it at Mr. Lessler's suggestion?—A. The subcommittee went into session and called me before them, and I told them the same story that I have told here, and they asked for the name of the intermediary, as you have called, and asked me if I could get him here, and I wired him that night, and he appeared the next day before the Naval Affairs Committee.

Q. In response to your telegram?—A. In response to my telegram.

Mr. QUIGG. I would like to have the permission of the committee to have Mr. Nicoll, who is here at my request, interrogate Mr. Lessler.

The CHAIRMAN. Is there any objection from the committee?

Mr. WHEELER. He is his attorney?

Mr. QUIGG. Yes, sir.

The CHAIRMAN. Mr. Quigg has asked permission that Mr. Nicoll, who is the attorney for Mr. Quigg, shall interrogate the witness. Is there any objection?

There was no objection.

Mr. NICOLL. I would ask Mr. Lessler a few questions.

By Mr. NICOLL:

Q. Where did you first meet Doblin?—A. That is pretty hard to answer. Doblin was for a number of years around the county committee, and there is where I first met him that I know of.

Q. You have been quite active in Republican politics in New York?—A. A part of the time, only a part of the time. A part of the time I was out of the business of politics.

Q. Do you mean to say that your acquaintance with Doblin has lasted so long that you do not now recall exactly when and where you met him?—A. I was a member of the county committee of the city of New York, I think, during the year 1894, and he was there connected with the committee as a clerk of some kind, or a member from, I think, the then Twenty-eighth assembly district. I do not know.

Q. Until the time you were first nominated for Congress?—A. Yes.

Q. Had you, up to that time, any business or social relations with him?—A. No; none at all.

Q. Not at all. Your acquaintance continued just as a political and friendly acquaintance?—A. I do not think I saw him for a number of years.

Q. Your friendship with him grew, did it not, in that campaign——A. You heard me tell——

Q. By reason of his efforts in your behalf?—A. You heard me say that.

Q. Yes; I just wanted to go over it.—A. Yes; but you must not go over it too much.

Q. Have you any objection to my going over it?—A. If I have, I will tell you.

Q. When did you form this office connection with him?—A. I have had no office connection with him.

Q. Well, his headquarters have been at your office for some time.—A. That is not quite accurately stated.

Q. What is the accurate statement?—A. The accurate statement is that he had the run of the office. He came in and went out, and whatever little mail he had for a time he got there.

Q. Had he any other office but yours, so far as you know?—A. During the time he was with the county committee and during the time that he was at times with the State superintendent of elections, as I have said before.

Q. Yes, I understood you had procured him some employment as referee in bankruptcy, and that that gave him some business that he had to have an office for.—A. That is about the fact.

Q. That is about the fact, is it not?—A. I think that one he received. I do not know of any more. You see, I was here in Washington.

Q. That would necessitate his having an office, his being a receiver in bankruptcy?—A. Yes, that is about right.

Q. Did he come to visit you in Washington during the year?—A. Never.

Q. So that you never saw him except when Congress was in session?—A. As I have already stated.

Q. Take, for instance, this month of November, which was prior to the assembling of Congress?—A. Yes.

Q. You were at your office every day then, were you not?—A. Yes, pretty regularly.

Q. Was Mr. Doblin in every day?—A. No; because—he was not in much during the period from September on until election, because he was employed otherwise.

Q. Yes.—A. he did not take any active part in the campaign, so far as I was concerned, this year, because he was employed otherwise.

Q. After election, down to the time when you came back to Washington, was he there then constantly?—A. Not constantly; he would drop in about 11 o'clock.

Q. It was on one of these occasions, between the 8th of November, or whatever day election day was, and the 1st of December, when you had this conversation with him?—A. That is my recollection, as I have already stated it.

Q. Now, how do you fix the date?—A. How do I fix that date?

Q. Yes.—A. I fix that date because my recollection is that I came to Washington and told some members of the committee a day or two after Congress assembled of this whole business.

Q. That is, of his approach to you?—A. Of the whole business.

Q. You mean this proposition?—A. Yes, sir; this proposition.

Q. This corrupt proposition?—A. Well, yes.

Q. Had he ever made any other proposition of this kind to you?—A. No.

Q. Mr. Doblin?—A. No.

Q. Well, it made quite an impression on your feelings, did it not, Mr. Lessler?—A. Are you asking me for facts now, or are you asking me for impressions?

Q. No; I am asking this pursuant to a suggestion made by one of the committee as to what your feelings were toward this man, who had been your friend.—A. I will tell you what my feelings are toward him—toward Doblin.

Q. Not now; at the time.—A. Yes; at the time; and after that offer from him?

Q. Yes.—A. This man, I believe, would go a good ways to serve me, and, as I think back on it, his idea was that in getting me persona grata to Mr. Quigg, who is or has been in a political position in New York, he was doing me an instrumentality. That is the way I regarded it and still regard it.

Q. That was quite separate and apart from the question of the money?—A. The question of money was dismissed in about half a second or half a minute, Mr. Nicoll.

Q. Would you mind telling me how he opened that conversation to you—A. I think that I have detailed that already.

Q. Do you mind telling that again?—A. Yes; I will if you desire me to.

Q. And if you will kindly be specific about it.—A. As specific as I can be. He came in in considerable excitement that morning, as I remember it. He said, "Is the Holland suomarine boat business coming up in the next Congress?" I said, "I don't know; I guess it is." He said, "Are you still opposed to it?" I said, "Yes." "Well," he said, "I have been down to see Quigg, and had a talk with him about it, and he said that if we could gain your influence in that committee"—I am not giving you the exact words—"there is $5,000 in it."

Q. Did he say for you?—A. There is $5,000 in it.

Q. He did not say there was $5,000 in it for you, did he?—A. Well, I will not be certain about that, for this reason—that the other day my understanding is that Mr. Doblin appeared before the committee and said that he made the remark to me at the time that there was $5,000 in it, without saying it was in it for me.

Q. Yes. Well, those were his words, "There is $5,000 in it?"—A. That is my recollection.

Q. That is all that he said to you on the subject of money, is it not, as nearly as you recall?—A. Well, that is as nearly as I recall it, Mr. Nicoll.

Q. He said nothing about there being a thousand dollars in it for him?—A. No; I don't recollect.

Q. Did he say anything about there being anything in it for him?—A. The conversation stopped there on the money proposition.

Q. Yes. Then he said nothing about there being anything in it for him?—A. I say the conversation stopped there. I have said that twice, now, and I said that in answer to Mr. Tayler.

Q. Yes. Did he use the words "there is $5,000 in it for you," Mr. Lessler?—A. Mr. Nicoll, I have——

Q. Please answer that.—A. I have told you three times what I consider to be—what I remember that he said, and I have answered Mr. Tayler fully as to what I remember he said.

Q. What day of the week was this?—A. I am unable to tell you.

Q. What day of the month?—A. I am unable to tell you.

Q. In the fore part or the latter part of November?—A. I am unable to say, except that it was after election and before Congress opened.

Q. What day did Congress open?—A. On a Monday.

Q. And what day of the month was that?—A. The 1st day of December.

Q. The 1st?—A. Yes, sir.

Q. You came to Washington on a Saturday?—A. No, sir; I did not; I came on Sunday.

Q. From that time back, how far was it?—A. I am unable to tell you more definitely than that.

Q. You have no recollection as to whether it was a week or more?—
A. I have; it was between those dates, so far as my recollection goes.

Q. It was not the day before you came, was it? Mr. Lessler, the reason why I am interrogating you on this point is this—of course, it seems to me, if you will excuse me for saying so——. A. Yes; certainly.

Q. (Continuing.) That you would recollect, pretty certainly, this proposition, because Mr. Doblin never made any other proposition of this kind?—A. No.

Q. No; that is the reason I am interrogating you, and it is important to Mr. Quigg that you should be as accurate as you can.—A. I would like to aid Mr. Quigg.

Q. Yes; it is important on that account.—A. Yes; I am unable to fix it more definitely.

Q. What time in the day was it?—A. I have a recollection that it was somewhere about midday. Of course, I arrived at my office about 10 o'clock, and used to leave about 3 or 4.

Q. Yes.—A. That is about right. Somewhere about the middle of the day, Mr. Nichol.

Q. You saw Mr. Quigg, did you not, in the Christmas holidays, during the recess?—A. I am unable to say whether the conversation I had with Mr. Quigg was before Congress opened or during the Christmas holidays. My impression was that it was before Congress opened, but I am not certain about that.

Q. You mean that it was in November?—A. That was my impression, but I will not be certain about it, Mr. Nichol. Mr. Doblin says that I saw Quigg——

Q. I don't care what Doblin said. We will take care of Doblin. Doblin has enough before him.—A. I know Mr. Quigg in the campaign——

Q. (Continuing.) I want to know from you.

Mr. DAYTON. I want to object, Mr. Chairman, as a member of this committee, to the side remark of counsel as to Mr. Doblin or any other witness.

Mr. BUTLER. Yes; the committee will pass upon Mr. Doblin.

Mr. DAYTON. As to whether he "has enough before him," or anything else.

(Further discussion among the members of the committee followed.)

Mr. DAYTON. I move that counsel be confined strictly to cross-examination on the subject under inquiry.

Mr. NICOLL. I would not intentionally offend; but sometimes, in the heat of cross-examination, we all say things that are not germane. I would be very glad to have the committee limit me in any way when I transgress.

The WITNESS (continuing). The doubt that arose in my mind as to the date arose from the fact that some of the gentlemen of the committee in telling me what Doblin said when he came over the other day—for I was not present when he made his statement—said he thought that it was in Christmas week, Christmas vacation time, that Quigg had come to my office.

By Mr. NICHOLL:

Q. You have no independent recollection of it yourself?—A. No; I have not. I tried to recollect that time.

Q. Did Mr. Quigg call you up on the telephone just prior to his visit to your office?—A. I have already stated that.

Q. Yes. Did he talk over the telephone?—A. He said that he wanted to see me, and I said, "Come right over." He asked me to come to lunch with him, but I said no; that I could not.

Q. When he arrived did you know what he was coming to see you about?—A. I think I did.

Q. You thought that it was the Holland boat, did you?—A. Yes, sir.

Q. Did you believe Mr. Doblin when he said to you that Mr. Quigg had authorized him to make that proposition to you?—A. I certainly did then, and I do now.

Q. You did?—A. Yes, sir.

Q. And you do now believe it?—A. Yes, sir.

Q. What was the first thing Mr. Quigg said to you, if you recollect?—A. I believe he gave a cigar out.

Q. The usual greetings—— A. Yes; amenities.

Q. (Continuing.) Between friends who had not seen each other for some time?—A. Yes, sir.

Q. And then you took up the conversation immediately?—A. Yes, sir.

Q. And you said what? "There is no question of money in it?"—A. "There must not be any question of money in this business." In that order; pretty nearly to that straight effect.

Q. Did you tell him that Doblin had been to you in the month of November and had said to you that there was $5,000 in it if you would support the proposition to build more torpedo boats?—A. I did not; I did not, because I——

Q. Did you—I beg your pardon.—A. (Continuing.) I did not say that to Quigg, because the scale between Doblin and Quigg is a large and a vast one, and I did not want to have to kick an ex-member of Congress out of my office, where I might excuse it in a man like Doblin, whose feeling of helpfulness to me would probably be the guiding motive in his idea.

Q. You had forgiven Doblin at that time? Had you forgiven Doblin?—A. We will not put it in that way, quite.

Q. Yes? Very well.—A. The subject between myself and Doblin was dropped, and not mentioned.

Q. Did you mention Mr. Doblin's name to Mr. Quigg at all?—A. I did not.

Q. Did you ask Mr. Quigg whether he had any relations with the Holland people?—A. Mr. Quigg volunteered the statement that I made to Mr. Tayler. Do you want that again?

Q. No; not if you object to repeating it. Did he say that he had any business connection with them?—A. No. He said absolutely this: That he had no personal interest in the Holland boat or the Holland people; that a friend of his, a Mr. Hunter, as I remember the name, who had done him some favor, and to whom he was obligated, had asked his help with me; that he had no further interest in it; that he felt if I was so strongly disposed on the subject that that was the end of it.

Q. Is it not a fact that you went quite at length with Mr. Quigg in explaining to him all your objections to the Holland boat?—A. You heard me say that to Mr. Tayler.

Q. You explained that to him from a scientific standpoint?—A. I do not believe that I am able to do that.

Q. Well—— A. I went at it. I remember using "hydroplanes" and things of that sort that had puzzled us here a whole lot. You can put it that way if you want to.

Q. Don't you remember Mr. Quigg, after your long talk on the subject, saying that you knew a great deal more about it than he did, and if you felt that way about it—— A. I remember the honor done me.

Q. Yes; and it was probably true, was it not, from your being a member of this committee?—A. Probably so; I think you can safely say that.

Q. Yes; and did he not say that he did not feel like urging you, in view of the fact that you had given so much study to the subject and understood it so well?—A. Have I not already stated that?

Q. Well, do you recall it?—A. I recall it, and that he said so, and I have so stated.

Q. Mr. Quigg asks me to ask you if you are sure that he mentioned any person named to you as the person on whose account he came to you?—A. Yes; he mentioned the name of a Mr. Hunter, as I recall it, and my recollection is that he said Mr. Hunter, of Virginia, and I think he called the first name, too, but I do not remember it.

Q. Was the conversation that you had with Mr. Doblin the first conversation you ever had with him about the Holland boat?—A. I have already answered that.

Q. No; I do not think you have.—A. Yes, sir; I have already said to you that I might have mentioned it casually, because I went down in the boat, and of course it was a very interesting trip. I might have spoken of it, as I would if I had met you, some time, or met another man; that it was an interesting experience for a man to have traveled under the water.

Q. Yes; I didn't know you had done that?—A. (Continuing.) So that I can not say that I have not spoken to him. In all probability I mentioned it that way because I went down in the boat once.

Q. I don't exactly mean that. I want to know whether Mr. Doblin at any prior time had asked you to aid the Holland people in their legislation.—A. No.

Q. Or had expressed any interest in them or the company?—A. No.

Q. He had not?—A. No, sir.

Mr. NICOLL. I am very much obliged to you, gentlemen.

The CHAIRMAN. Not at all.

Mr. VANDIVER. I would like to ask just one question which I would like to have answered, because my recollection may be at fault, though I do not think it is. As I understand Mr. Lessler, now, he does not state that Mr. Quigg made this offer to him himself. But my recollection is that in Mr. Lessler's first statement to this committee he said that he was approached by an intermediary, and afterwards by an ex-member of Congress, who stated to him that if he would vote right on this proposition he would give him a check for $5,000.

The WITNESS. You are entirely mistaken, Mr. Vandiver, and I think every member of the committee, probably, if you ask them, will tell you so.

Mr. VANDIVER. I want to know whether I am mistaken.

The WITNESS. I say that I never made any such statement. You are mistaken, and I would like to have the gentlemen reenforce my recollection that you are mistaken.

The CHAIRMAN. Is there anything further?

Mr. ROBERTS. I would like to have Mr. Tayler ask Mr. Lessler one or two questions which occur to me which were brought out by the questions of Mr. Nicoll. I would like to ask, through Mr. Tayler, if you had indicated in any way to Mr. Doblin, prior to the time that he made you the offer, that you were hostile to any legislation in favor of the Holland torpedo boat.

H. Rep. 3482——2

By Mr. TAYLER:

Q. Answer the question.—A. I will have to answer you the way that I have answered Mr. Tayler and Mr. Nicoll, that I do not remember any specific conversation with Mr. Doblin on the subject of the Holland submarine boat, except as it might have happened from a scientific standpoint, as Mr. Nicoll brought out, or the curious proposition of a man traveling or under water, or something of that sort.

By Mr. ROBERTS:

Q. Then, so far as you knew, Mr. Doblin did not know your peculiar state of mind concerning the Holland torpedo boat?—A I am unable to answer that. He might have known it from my vote.

Q. Another point. It was brought out here that Mr. Lessler, prior to the time he stated to the committee that an attempt had been made to bribe him, had informed other parties that the attempt had been made.—A. I think that you had better ask that through Mr. Tayler, because I will not answer it otherwise.

Mr. ROBERTS. I desire to ask a question, Mr. Tayler, if you will act as interlocutor. I will put the question in a little different way.

By Mr. ROBERTS:

Q. When did you first mention, and to whom did you first mention it, the fact that an attempt had been made to bribe you?

Mr. WHEELER. If the witness does not object ——

Mr. TAYLER. I was going to ask that question.

Mr. QUIGG. The date is important. I do not care what member of this committee he made any statement to, but I hope the gentlemen will bring out the date when he made it.

The WITNESS. There is no good of discussing it. I will tell you anything that you want to know.

Mr. ROBERTS. This is outside the record. If you will interrogate Mr. Lessler, Mr. Tayler, and ask the times and places and persons to whom he made this statement, and every person to whom he made it, prior to this announcement to the committee, I will be satisfied.

By Mr. TAYLER:

Q. That is what I am about to do. You may state to whom, if. anybody, after this proposition was made to you by Mr. Doblin, you communicated the information that it had been made.—A. Well, I do not recollect anybody except some gentlemen of the committee, when the session opened.

Q. To whom did you make these statements, if you can remember?—A. To Mr. Foss and Mr. Dayton.

Q. And how long after the proposition was made to you did you make this revelation to them?—A. I think I talked over this proposition with either Mr. Foss or Mr. Dayton a day or two after Congress opened.

Mr. BUTLER. After the recess?

The WITNESS. No, no; after Congress opened.

By Mr. TAYLER:

Q. At any rate, you disclosed it very soon—a very few days after the proposition had been made to you?—A. I would not put it quite that way, because I am unable to fix the exact date.

Q. I understand that, but—— A. When you say "very soon," I spoke to these gentlemen. My recollection is that in the other room there, a day or two after the 1st of December——

Q. I was not inquiring so much as to the exact time, because that would be a matter of inference more than of direct statement, but as to the lapse of time after the proposition had been made to you, before you made the statement to these gentlemen.—A. Well, if the conversation with Mr. Doblin took place between the election and the 1st of December some time——

Q. Exactly.—A. (Continuing.) And the conversation with Mr. Foss and Mr. Dayton took place a few days after that, the lapse of time is very easy to understand.

Q. Yes, if it was a short time after, of course the lapse would be short.—A. Yes, sir.

Q. If the conversation between you and Mr. Doblin occurred after the opening of the present session of Congress, after the 1st of December, on your return home.—A. Then I spoke to them after the 5th of January when I came back. Then the time would be about the same in either case. What I am trying to fix now, in turning over my recollection in regard to the suggestion of Mr. Quigg, is as to the very day we had the conversation, and that is not clear. Maybe Mr. Quigg can state that.

Q. Now, were you at home between the 1st day of December, the opening of Congress, and the Christmas vacation?—A. Yes, sir; I was.

Q. How many times?—A. I think I was home on each Friday afternoon, or each Saturday.

Q. On each Friday and each Saturday?

Mr. NICOLL. Mr. Quigg says that it was in the holidays.

Mr. LESSLER. I am quite willing to take his word for it.

By Mr. TAYLER:

Q. May it not have been on one of these Fridays or Saturdays, after the 1st of December, that Mr. Doblin made this proposition to you?—A. Quite possible; quite possible.

Mr. ROBERTS. Are you through with that line of examination?

Mr. TAYLER. Yes, sir.

Mr. ROBERTS. I would like to pursue it a little further, Mr. Tayler. Will you please ask Mr. Lessler if he informed Mr. Foss and Mr Dayton of this attempt to bribe him——

The WITNESS. Mr. Wheeler refreshes my recollection. He says that I spoke to him about this, too.

Mr. NICOLL. When?

Mr. WHEELER. Mr. Lessler spoke to me some time since the holidays, and the conversation occurred, as I remember, some time when the torpedo-boat question was being discussed between us, and he told me about this proposition, and, as I remember it, he indicated that he did not intend to mention the fact if he could avoid it. Unless the torpedo-boat question was forced to the front, he did not intend to say anything about it.

By Mr. TAYLER:

Q. Now, if this communication was made to you by Mr. Doblin between the 1st of December and the Christmas holidays, on one of the occasions when you went home on Friday, is it not likely that you made your disclosure to Mr. Foss and Mr. Dayton prior to the Christmas holidays, immediately or shortly after your return from New York after that weekly visit?—A. I do not think I told Mr. Foss and Mr. Dayton anything about it until Mr. Quigg had come to my office.

Mr. TAYLER. Oh; I see.

By Mr. TAYLER:

Q. Do you remember how much time elapsed between Mr. Doblin's visit to you with this proposal and the visit of Mr. Quigg?—A. I should judge about ten days.

Mr. DAYTON. Mr. Chairman, if it is proper to say here, in view of Mr. Wheeler's statement, I want to say that I have a recollection of Mr. Lessler telling me of this matter.

Mr. VANDIVER. At what time?

Mr. DAYTON. That I can not remember, but it is my recollection that it was after we came to Congress, some time, whether before the holidays or not I do not remember.

The CHAIRMAN. I will say that my impression is that Mr. Lessler spoke of this matter to me prior to the holidays. I was busy at the time and did not pay very much attention to it, and I did not understand that it was a matter that he was going to bring up.

By Mr. KITCHIN:

Q. Did you tell any other members of the committee except Mr. Wheeler and Mr. Dayton and Mr. Foss? Can you recollect?—A. I am trying to recollect.

Q. Can you recall whether you told any others except those three?—A. No; I think not. I am pretty certain not, Mr. Kitchin.

Mr. KITCHIN. I would like to know if it was suggested at any of these conversations that you should have an investigation of this matter.

The WITNESS. No; it never struck—I never thought of an investigation in the matter.

Q. There was nothing said about an investigation until you told it in the committee?—A. There was nothing said about an investigation; that is right.

By Mr. TAYLER:

Q. At this time, Mr. Lessler—and I am asking you for information as much for myself as for the committee—at the time that you mentioned this matter to Mr. Foss and Mr. Dayton had the Holland submarine boat proposition come up before the committee in any substantive way?—A. No proposition had come before us until the very day that we were discussing or considering the paragraph under the increase of the Navy, and, as you know, a gentleman offered a resolution.

Q. And the proposition to provide for the Holland submarine boats did not appear in the bill as reported by the subcommittee on Appropriations to the full committee?—A. That is correct.

Q. To the full committee?—A. Yes, sir; that is correct.

Mr. ROBERTS. Will you not ask Mr. Lessler, Mr. Tayler, if it is not a fact that the proposition to purchase submarine torpedo boats was pending in this committee by a motion the day before the bill was reported?

Mr. TAYLER. Yes, I understood him to say that.

Mr. ROBERTS. I did not understand him so. The situation was that there was a motion and two amendments pending, and a motion was made to adjourn immediately after that.

Mr. TAYLER. There was a motion perhaps on one day, and the hearing was continued until the next day.

Mr. ROBERTS. I would like another fact to appear, if you are going into these facts here. There had been one decisive vote on the proposition before the charge of bribery was made.

The WITNESS: That is not correct.

Mr. ROBERTS. We can simply fix that by the record. There had been one substantial vote. There had been that proposition voted on, and there had been two decisive votes, and the record of the committee will show that.

Mr. RIXEY. I would like Mr. Tayler to ask Mr. Lessler the question. Whilst this matter might not have come up for a vote until the time he mentioned, it was generally understood that the proposition to build more Holland submarine boats would be made, and that understanding really had existed since the beginning of the Congress.

The WITNESS. No. My understanding was very, very different on that proposition.

By Mr. TAYLER:

Q. State what your understanding was.—A. My understanding was that the Senate having given them that chance to get the boats, no further attempt would be made. When I say "understanding" it was one of those general things that nobody was responsible for. I did not consider that they would make the attempt seriously in this committee again.

By Mr. ROBERTS:

Q. I would like to know if Mr. Lessler has any general recollection as to the time when what is termed the "Roberts bill" was introduced in this session of Congress.—A. Yes.

Q. Will you state it?—A. Of course, your bill will show it.

Q. I am asking you if you knew.—A. I think the bill was introduced about a week and a half before I introduced the subject.

Q. For the guidance of the committee I will say that the bill was introduced December 13, the first time any proposition came before this committee for Holland submarine boats.—A. Then I will amend it by saying that I did not know of the proposition until a few days before you advocated the proposition in full committee.

By Mr. VANDIVER:

Q. I will just ask this one other question. Mr. Lessler has mentioned talking to two or three members of the committee about this proposition. I would like to ask him in that connection if he had also talked with any member of the committee about bringing this before the committee.—A. You know very well the way the question arose——

Q. This is a very simple matter.—A. (Continuing.) I am going to answer your question. I imagined this committee of 17 members was in session, and I imagined that any statement I made to these 17 would be kept in and among these 17 members. No man likes to be the target of a proposition like this, and I do not, and did not want to be. But it has got beyond my power in the matter, and I simply stand here and tell you what I know. I responded to your suggestion before your committee, and I have responded to every suggestion. I do not have any other feeling than that the subject has come up, and I must stand what comes from it. But my object in telling that that day was to tell it to the members of this committee, and I had no idea that any man on this committee would go and repeat it outside of this room. My faith in this committee was not justified.

Mr. VANDIVER. The gentleman can still be assured that I never mentioned it.

The WITNESS. Oh, well, Mr. Vandiver——

Mr. WHEELER. I submit that this is not examination.

Mr. VANDIVER. He has not answered the question.

(The question was read by the stenographer.)

A. I talked with these members of the committee, because these were the members of the committee who were working on the bill, and I did not see so many of the members who were working on this bill until about that time. All the members did not make this their headquarters, and that is the way I happened to talk with these gentlemen about this. My association in the committee has been more closely with these gentlemen.

By Mr. VANDIVER:

Q. My question did not go to the propriety of your mentioning it, but only as to whether or not you had discussed with these same gentlemen you have mentioned as to your mentioning or bringing it before the committee.—A. No; I did not. They had no hand in my bringing it before the committee. It was brought, just as I told you, to the attention of the committee, thinking that it would remain right in the committee.

Mr. WHIELER. There is a matter suggested to me by Judge Butler which I desire to interrogate the witness upon.

Mr. ROBERTS. Will you pardon me, before you take up an entirely different matter?

Mr. WHEELER. If it bears on this question, certainly.

By Mr. ROBERTS:

Q. I would like to ask Mr. Lessler what his intent was in bringing the matter to the notice of the committee; whether it was his intention and design to injure the Holland Boat Company?

Mr. WHEELER. I object to that question. It is not proper.

The WITNESS. I would like to answer that.

The CHAIRMAN. Go ahead and answer it.

A. It has been common knowledge in Washington, in the vague, rumory way that we call "common knowledge," that all sorts of pressure has been brought, and as you know has been mentioned in this committee, about this submarine proposition; and my intention was to tell the members of my committee just what had happened in the proposition, and I repeat again that I thought I was telling the members of my committee and no one else.

By Mr. ROBERTS:

Q. Your intent, then, was to injure the Holland people?

The WITNESS (to Mr. Tayler). Will you ask that question, if you desire to?

Mr. WHEELER. I submit that is not proper.

(Discussion followed.)

The WITNESS. My purpose in making this statement when it came up was to tell my fellow-committeemen of the whole thing, and I did.

Mr. RIXEY. And to put them in possession of the position?

The WITNESS. That is all, Mr. Rixey.

By Mr. WHEELER:

Q. After this conversation which you had with this man Doblin, is it not true that you subsequently met Mr. Quigg, or Mr. Doblin, and some other gentleman at the Waldorf-Astoria and had a conversation about this proposition?—A. No, sir; that is not so.

Q. Is it not true that some other gentleman mentioned this thing to you? And if so, kindly give his name.—A. No, I never met anyone else.

I understood that Mr. Doblin had met a Mr. Frost at the Waldorf-Astoria, but that is all I know.

Q. Did not some friend of yours, whose name you have not yet disclosed, have a conversation with you on this subject?—A. No, not that I recollect. You have the facts twisted.

Q. No; I have not. I remember very distinctly the conversation I am trying to arrive at.—A. Mr. Doblin told us, I think, that he had had a conversation on the Holland torpedo boat——

Q. No; that is not it.—A. No?

Q. Is it not a fact that some one else had a conversation with you on this subject, whose name you decline to disclose to the subcommittee?

Mr. RIXEY. Is not this about the way you get your impression, Mr. Wheeler; that is, that a friend of yours told Mr. Lessler that he had been approached also by some parties, but he did not want to give the name of his authority? Is not that it?

Mr. WHEELER. I do not remember it that way.

By Mr. WHEELER:

Q. Do you recall that you declined to give us the name of a gentleman who was your friend, who had been approached on this subject?—A. No, sir; I do not.

Mr. WHEELER. Maybe I have got it wrong.

By Mr. WHEELER:

Q. At the time we declined to press you for the name of this friend and you declined to give us the name.

Mr. TATE. Was that in full committee, Mr. Wheeler, or in subcommittee?

Q. (Continuing.) And you said that if you desired an investigation you would give the name?—A. No, sir; I do not recollect that.

Q. My recollection is that Mr. Doblin had told you something about meeting Mr. Frost at the Waldorf.

Mr. RIXEY. He did not say that he had met Mr. Frost at the Waldorf, but there was some statement.

The CHAIRMAN. About Mr. Lessler meeting Mr. Frost?

Mr. RIXEY. No, sir; about his having a conversation with some friend; but we would not press him on it.

Mr. WHEELER. It is possible that I may be in error on it.

Mr. LESSLER. I would be perfectly willing to give it to you.

Mr. WHEELER. Well, I beg your pardon, Mr. Lessler.

Mr. ROBERTS. Just one other question. It is not just clear in my mind, from something Mr. Lessler has just said, whether from something Mr. Doblin told him he declared he had met Mr. Frost at the Waldorf-Astoria.

Mr. TAYLER. That should not go into the record.

By Mr. TAYLER:

Q. Did he, Doblin, tell you that he had met Mr. Frost in the Waldorf-Astoria?—A. Doblin states that.

Mr. WHEELER. I have not heard that from Mr. Lessler at all.

Senator THURSTON. Mr. Chairman, I represent the company that constructs these Holland torpedo boats at the present time, and as nothing has been shown connecting that company with this matter, I do not care to ask any questions.

Mr. WHEELER. I object to this going into the record.

Mr. ROBERTS. It is entitled to go into the record.

Mr. WHEELER. No, not that statement.

Mr. ROBERTS. He is stating his opinion.

Mr. WHEELER. It is not entitled to go in the official record.

Mr. ROBERTS. I think it is.

The CHAIRMAN. It is not important that it should go in or go out.

Mr. WHEELER. I do object to the statement going in there that there is nothing connecting the Holland company with this matter.

Senator THURSTON. I do not care about it going into the record, Mr. Chairman, but as I said, I would like to reserve the right, if at any future time in this investigation the interests of my client seem to require it, to then ask Mr. Lessler some additional questions.

Mr. DAYTON. I want to agree to that, but if Senator Thurston does not object I would like to have him state who all the representatives, attorneys, and agents of this company are, besides himself, so that we may know who are the parties representing this company.

Senator THURSTON. Mr. Chairman, you will have to ask somebody outside of myself that. I have only been employed for the purpose of attending this hearing.

The CHAIRMAN. That is a matter that can be deferred.

If there are no further questions to be asked this witness, Mr. Lessler desires his secretary to be examined.

Mr. LESSLER. I would like to have him in here on that proposition.

TESTIMONY OF HON. EPPA HUNTON (SWORN).

By Mr. TAYLER:

Q. What relation, if any, do you sustain to the Holland Torpedo Boat Company?—A. I have been counsel for the company here.

Q. How long?—A. Probably two years.

Q. Are you acquainted with Mr. Quigg, formerly a member of the House from New York?—A. I am, sir. My acquaintance with him commenced to-day, at 11 o'clock, in the anteroom of this committee.

Q. Had you had any conversation with him respecting the business of the Holland Torpedo Boat Company?—A. Never at all.

Q. If Mr. Quigg had any conversation respecting the business of the Holland Torpedo Boat Company a month or two ago, it was not on your initiative?—A. It was not what?

Q. It was not at your suggestion?—A. I never heard of Mr. Quigg in connection with the company until the last day or two.

Mr. TAYLER. I think that is all.

Mr. DAYTON. Will Mr. Tayler please ask Senator Hunton whether it is a Virginia corporation or whether they have any office or business of any kind in Virginia?

Mr. BUTLER. Ask him what their relations are, and how many counsel they have.

Mr. TAYLER. I think that any gentlemen who are going to ask questions of that kind had better ask them themselves.

Mr. BUTLER. Very well; I have no objection to asking them.

By Mr. BUTLER:

Q. You have been counsel for this company for two years?—A. About that, sir.

Q. Is it your business to try the cases of that company, and to advise the company generally?—A. They have no cases, so far as I know of, here, except before this committee.

Q. This is all?—A. Yes, sir.

Q. Do you know of the company employing any other counsel except yourself?—A. I don't know of it of my own knowledge.

By Mr. DAYTON:

Q. Have you ever appeared before this committee in its matters before it as counsel?—A. Never, sir.

Q. Then you never have had any business for them, in fact, although associated with them?—A. I beg your pardon; I have. I have been in consultation with them about their business very often.

Q. Is this a Virginia corporation?—A. It is not, sir, as I understand it.

Q. Did it ever have any office in Virginia?—A. Not that I am aware of.

Q. Or any business of any kind there?—A. Not that I know of.

Q. Do you know where their office is?—A. I do not.

Q. Or where their business is?—A. Their business is manufacturing these Holland boats; that is all I know, sir.

Q. Do you know where their plant and works are?—A. I did know, but I declare I would not be able to state it. I have heard it frequently.

Q. Your connection with them has been here in the city of Washington, has it not?—A. Yes, sir; entirely.

Q. Alone?—A. Yes, sir.

By Mr. ROBERTS:

Q. General Hunton, I would like to ask, sir, if you conduct a law business on your own account or have you partners?—A. I have no partners

Q. Have you an office in Washington?—A. Sir?

Q. Have you a law office in Washington?—A. I had until probably the 1st of last July, when I gave it up.

Mr. ROBERTS. That is all.

(Witness excused.)

FRANK P. SON, sworn.

By Mr. TAYLER:

Q. You are Mr. Lessler's secretary, are you?—A. Yes, sir.

Q. How long have you been engaged in that capacity?—A. Since April 1.

Q. Were you present when John McCullagh had a conversation with Mr. Lessler respecting the Holland submarine boats?—A. Yes, sir.

Q. About when did that occur?—A. Well, I think it was in June.

Q. Of last year?—A. Of last year—yes, sir.

Q. Now, you may state your recollection of that conversation.—A. Well, I think I had better go back a few days before that.

Q. Tell it in your own way.—A. I think it was one Friday or Saturday that a telegram came for Mr. Lessler from Mr. McCullagh, and I wired back that Mr. Lessler was in the West, and I forwarded the message to Mr. Lessler. Then, a few days after that, or a couple of days, perhaps, Mr. McCullagh came to Washington, and came up to see me, and he asked me if I had heard anything from Mr. Lessler, and I said that I had not. Then he telephoned to me once or twice, and I said that I had not heard that he was coming, but I thought he was going home by way of New York. Then Mr. Lessler came back, I think about Tuesday, and about 8 or 9 o'clock, I should say, I was in his room with him, and Mr. McCullagh came in, and he said that he had a matter that he wanted to talk to him about, but—and he looked at me, and Mr. Lessler said: "Whatever you say to me is all right; this is my secretary." Then he went on, and I don't remember the words, but he said that he was interested in the passage of some amendment to the naval bill, and he told Mr. Lessler that he would like to have him vote for it, and one conversation led to another, and finally he made the statement that he represented men who could beat his nomination or nominate him. I didn't hear him say anything about his election. Then Mr. Lessler told him that he would see him in hell first.

Q. What was it he wanted him to favor an amendment on?—A. On the Holland submarine boat. Then Mr. Lessler went into detail, and told him that he guessed that he did not understand the question, and he explained his position fully in the matter. Then Mr. McCullagh asked him if he would not vote for it for him personally, and he said he would not. And that is really all the conversation I heard. Of course there was a great deal of detail to it, but that was—after a while I went out and went home.

Q. Were you there when the conversation concluded, or did you leave them together?—A. I was not there. I think he went out just after I did, but they were practically finished in their talk, and so I left.

By Mr. ROBERTS:

Q. Where was this?—A. In room 163, in the Normandie.
Q. Mr. Lessler's private apartments?—A. Yes, sir.
Mr. ROBERTS. That is all I care to ask.
Senator THURSTON. I would like to ask him a question, Mr. Chairman.
The CHAIRMAN. Senator Thurston.

By Senator THURSTON:

Q. Did Mr. McCullagh say what people he represented in making this request?—A. No, sir; he did not; not to my knowledge.
Q. Did he use the name of any individual, or of any company?—A. No, sir; I do not remember hearing him.
Q. He appealed to Mr. Lessler on political and personal grounds?—A. I should say that is the way it occurred.
Q. Yes; and so far as you heard, there was no suggestion of any improper interest or inducement held out?—A. Except as I said.
Q. Except as you have stated?—A. In a political way.
Q. Some political people were interested who could do him good or harm?—A. Yes, sir.
Q. But he did not state who those were?—A. No, sir.

By Mr. MEYER:

Q. Did Mr. McCullagh appear satisfied with Mr. Lessler's explanation, and leave?—A. He appeared surprised.
Q. Did he appear much affected by what he said?—A. He did not seem very much affected, but still he seemed to be disappointed, and he seemed very anxious to see him before that.
Mr. ROBERTS. Mr. Tayler, will you ask the witness if the language used by Mr. McCullagh was a threat?
Mr. WHEELER. That is asking for a conclusion.

By Mr. ROBERTS:

Q. In what manner was the language used—in a threatening manner?—A. I could not say that, because he was talking in rather a low tone of voice, but he was using more of persuasive language, as though he was doing him a good turn in assisting him in that way.

Q. Did Mr. McCullagh say that he personally could or would defeat Mr. Lessler's renomination?—A. I did not understand him to mean that.

Q. Your understanding was that Mr. McCullagh stated there were certain parties who were in a position to aid or defeat Mr. Lessler's renomination?—A. Yes, sir.

Q. As a matter of fact, his renomination was not defeated; he was renominated?—A. Yes, sir; he was.

(Witness excused.)

TESTIMONY OF EPPA HUNTON—Recalled.

By Mr. RIXEY:

Q. You did not hear Mr. Lessler's testimony?—A. No, sir; I could not hear it.

Q. He testified in effect that a young man by the name of Doblin came to him with a proposition of an offer of $5,000 to influence his vote and action in the committee, and stated to him that he came from Mr. Quigg. Mr. Lessler then stated that he afterwards had an interview with Mr. Quigg, and Mr. Quigg stated, after some conversation, that he himself had no personal interest in the matter, and that the only interest he felt was for a friend whom he had in Virginia who had served him, and he thought that his name was Hunter. Now, what I want to ask you is, if you know in any way of any attempt, directly or indirectly, by you or through anyone else, to influence any member of this committee?—A. I certainly do not, gentlemen. And I will say further that if such information had come to me I should have withdrawn from the service of the company on the spot. I want to say that I never did know anything about an attempt to bribe a member of Congress from the time I entered Congress in 1873 down to the present time.

Mr. RIXEY. Mr. Lessler wants me to state that he did not suggest your name at all. It is simply from the similarity of the names, and the fact that you are the counsel for the company, I suggested possibly you were the party referred to, instead of a man by the name of Hunter.

Mr. WHEELER. Did I understand him to say that he had never spoken to a member of this committee about these votes?

The WITNESS. No, sir; I never said that. I think I have spoken probably to two. I have spoken to Mr. Rixey, who is my Representative, and my esteemed friend and relative, and I think I spoke to General Meyer once, in passing, but it was a casual talk with Mr. Meyer of a minute or two.

Mr. MEYER. I can state, Mr. Chairman, that the reference Senator Hunton made to me regarding these votes upon one or two occasions was, in my judgment, entirely proper and entirely what was right from an attorney representing the company.

Mr. QUIGG. Gentlemen, this story has gone out to the effect that Mr. Doblin has used my name, and I think the committee should do me the justice to permit me to say what I know about this matter.

Mr. DAYTON. My suggestion was simply in your interest.

Mr. WHEELER. I object to Mr. Quigg being heard at this time, and I want to state my grounds for it. I think it would be highly improper to do Mr. Quigg any injustice, and we ought to give him every opportunity to be heard. But we are not conducting this examination for the purpose of protecting or injuring the reputation of any man, but for the purpose of preserving the integrity of the House of Representatives, and I do not think we ought to break the continuity of our examination.

We are presenting the case here in its proper form, and to break the continuity of the examination would be in violation of legal precedent and certainly detrimental to a thorough investigation of the case. I think it is proper for us to hear the statements of the witnesses we know of, and after an investigation as to the truth of those statements, if Mr. Quigg desires to be heard in order to protect his character from aspersion and his reputation from injury I certainly would be swift to give him every assistance for obtaining full justice at the hands of this committee.

Mr. RIXEY. Mr. Quigg, is it your idea that if the committee permit you to testify now that you will leave before we get through with this investigation?

Mr. QUIGG. It is my idea to stay here before this committee if Mr. Doblin is procured as a witness.

Mr. RIXEY. Have you any doubt as to his being procured?

Mr. QUIGG. I don't know; I don't know where Mr. Doblin is.

Mr. RIXEY. He is in New York, is he not?

Mr. QUIGG. I am sure I don't know.

The CHAIRMAN. I have had a telegram from Mr. Doblin, which has just been handed to me, and is addressed to me saying that he can not come until Monday, and to advise him if that will do, signed Doblin.

Mr. RIXEY. Where is that from?

The CHAIRMAN. It is from New York and it is directed to me. The first telegram which I read to you gentlemen was directed to Mr. Lessler.

Mr. LESSLER. He came voluntarily the other day.

Mr. VANDIVER. Why not proceed with Mr. Quigg's testimony and then we can get Mr. Doblin later?

Mr. RIXEY. Can we not get Doblin here by to-morrow morning?

Mr. WHEELER. Of course we can get him here if we send the Sergeant-at-Arms after him.

Mr. QUIGG. The evidence of Mr. Doblin is known to some of the committee, from their examination of him. I do not know what that evidence is. The manner in which Mr. Doblin associates me with an offer of money to Mr. Lessler is certainly well known and has been given out to the newspapers.

Mr. WHEELER. We are not trying this question by newspapers.

Mr. QUIGG. No; but I am individually sensitive about my own reputation, and I do feel that the very earliest opportunity should be given to me, after such a story has been printed and circulated, to tell what the facts are as I know them, and I hope the committee will give me that opportunity.

Mr. WHEELER. If Mr. Quigg wants me to, I will go into that question, although I do not like to go into that phase of the question in open session.

Mr. RIXEY. Why is it that you made use of an expression suggesting doubt as to whether Mr. Doblin can be gotten here?

Mr. QUIGG. I did not express any doubt about it, especially. I do not know anything about it. I simply know he is not here.

Mr. RIXEY. I thought you expressed some doubt as to whether he was in New York or whether he could be gotten here.

Mr. QUIGG. I do not know anything about it.

Mr. WHEELER. I think we had better go into executive session.

There are some things I would like to suggest to this committee if it is not exactly proper I should say in public.

Mr. ROBERTS. Before we go into that phase of the question I would like to ask if the Major Hunter whose name was mentioned yesterday is present.

The CHAIRMAN. Yes; Major Hunter was here this morning, and I said to him that we would call him up by telephone in his office when we wanted him.

Mr. ROBERTS. Is there any other witness present, other than Mr. Quigg, whom we could examine?

The CHAIRMAN. There is no other witness present that I know of.

Mr. RIXEY. You can have Major Hunter here in five minutes.

The CHAIRMAN. He said he knew nothing about it and did not know how his name was brought into it in any way.

Mr. VANDIVER. I move that we take a recess for thirty minutes for lunch and that we then proceed with the examination of Mr. Quigg.

Mr. RIXEY. Mr. Wheeler's motion takes precedence. He has moved that we go into executive session.

Mr. WHEELER. I have already moved that we exclude these witnesses and the attorneys and settle this question among ourselves in executive session.

The motion was agreed to, and the committee, at 1.30 p. m., went into executive session.

WASHINGTON, D. C., *January 4, 1903.*

The committee met at 10.30 o'clock a. m., Hon. George Edmund Foss in the chair.

TESTIMONY OF PHILIP DOBLIN (SWORN).

By Mr. TAYLER:

Q. Your name is Philip Doblin, is it?—A. Yes, sir.

Q. How old are you?—A. Thirty-eight the 13th of July.

Q. Where do you live?—A. 433 East Eighty-second street, New York City.

Q. How long have you lived there?—A. Twelve years; about twelve years.

Q. Where were you born?—A. I was born on Twenty-ninth street, county of New York.

Q. In New York? That is what I mean; you were born in New York?—A. Yes, sir; in the county.

Q. You have lived in New York all your life?—A. Yes, sir.

Q. What is your employment now?—A. I have none at present.

Q. What have you been doing for the last year or two?—A. I have been variously employed.

Q. State in a general way what you have been doing.—A. How long back?

Q. Well, I want to get back for a year, covering the period of your intimate relations with Mr. Lessler.—A. During the campaign of 1902 I was employed by the Republican county committee, in charge of literature—the distribution of literature. When the campaign was over, and during that campaign also, I was employed as deputy superintendent of elections, and the time that I did not have any employment as a superintendent of elections I was attending to the distribution of literature. When the campaign was over there was a special election.

Q. A special election?—A. A special election to succeed a Congress-man who had resigned from the Seventh district, whose name is Nicholas Muller.

Q. Yes.—A. (Continuing.) And during the preliminaries I attended to whatever there was to be attended to that came my way, and I was going around and trying to aid in bringing about Mr. Lessler's election.

Q. That is, you mean his election a year ago?—A. Yes, sir. That, as I understand. is an answer to your question regarding what I was doing during that period in which I became intimately acquainted with Congressman Lessler, although I had known him. I originally met him in 1894, I think it was, during a political controversy in the county.

Q. You have been interested in politics, have you, for many years in New York?—A. Over twenty years.

Q. By the way, Mr. Doblin, I am reminded to ask you what it was in my mind to do in a preliminary way. How did you come to get here this morning; were you subpœnaed by the Sergeant-at-Arms or did you come on a telegram from the committee?—A. I got a telegram from the chairman to come here yesterday, and I got it at 1 o'clock in the morning, so that I immediately telegraphed that I would be here on Monday, thinking that the gentlemen would take the usual adjournment, and asked whether that would be satisfactory, but when I looked at the papers last night I found the statement there that Chairman Foss had sent for me, and I immediately telephoned home and told them that I would leave for Washington at midnight, which I did.

Q. You did not come, then, on the subpœna?—A. No, sir.

Q. That is, you did not see the Sergeant at-Arms or his representa-tive?—A. No, sir.

Q. Now, Mr. Doblin, you may state descriptively what relations you sustained with Mr. Lessler after his election a year ago. How often did you meet, and what was the occasion of your meeting?—A. Why, whenever he was in town I used to see him pretty near every day. As a matter of fact, during the month of March, I think it was, I was appointed a receiver in bankruptcy by a city court judge, and in my papers I made No. 31 Nassau street my office, having my mail addressed there, and after that I was appointed by the United States circuit court judge, or district judge, receiver in bankruptcy. And of course in my papers there that I filed—the bonds, etc.—I gave the address No. 31 Nassau street.

Q. You had no business relations with Mr. Lessler?—A. Not other than politics, except that I stood willing to serve him in any way that I could. No other business than that which I have just stated.

Q. How often were you at his office?—A. Why, sometimes every day; that is, some weeks every day; other weeks I may only go there—or I had only gone there—once or twice. When I was employed I did not go there only on Saturday; I tried to get in when he was in town.

Q. Do you know Mr. Quigg?—A. Yes, sir.

Q. How long have you known him?—A. I became acquainted with Mr. Quigg when I was the secretary of the Fifteenth Congressional district conference committee, just prior to the time Mr. Quigg was made—or at least elected—chairman of the Republican county commit-tee of New York.

Q. When was that? That is, of course, a matter of national inter-est and importance, but we can not remember it.—A. 1896.

Q. 1896?—A. Yes, sir.

Q. And how often did you see him, and how intimate was your acquaintance with him, from that time?—A. Oh, I used to see Mr. Quigg off and on at conventions, during the regular convention of the State——

Q. Yes.—A (continuing). And occasionally met him at the receptions of clubs in the city.

Q. Were you well acquainted with him?—A. Oh, no; not exactly well acquainted with him, except that I think through the influence of the district leader I received his indorsement for political preferment.

Q. Then you saw him a few times each year; is that about the way you would have us understand it, from 1896?—A. Yes, sir.

Q. Up to the present time?—A. Yes, sir. I may have seen him more than a few times. I met him at the county court-house—no, at the city hall. I may have walked through there and met him somewhere around.

Q. Prior to the convening of the present session of Congress—about the 1st of November—had you heard Mr. Lessler talk about the Holland submarine boat?—A. I heard him say one day that he was on an excursion or a visit to go under with the boat, on one of the boats. He said that it was quite an experience.

Q. Had you had any talk with him about the merits of the proposition to build submarine boats?—A. No, sir.

Q. Or to buy them?—A. No, sir.

Q. Had you any knowledge about his attitude in that respect prior to the convening of this session of Congress from the 1st of December?—A. No, sir.

Q. When did the question as to how Mr. Lessler stood on that proposition come up?—A. You mean with me?

Q. Yes; between you and anybody else. Let me lead right up to what I want without wasting any time. Did you have a talk with Mr. Quigg respecting the subject of the Holland submarine boats?—A. Yes, sir.

Q. Was that the first time you had any discussion with anybody about the matter?—A. Yes, sir.

Q. Now, when was it that you had a talk with Mr. Quigg, approximately?—A. I think it was sometime between the 10th and the 18th of December.

Q. And where?—A. I received a telephone message asking me to come to No. 100 Broadway.

Q. Where were you when you received this message?—A. I think I was in my brother's office on Church street.

Q. Your brother's office on Church street?—A. Yes, sir.

Q. Were you reached on the telephone yourself?—A. Yes, sir.

Q. And who at the other end of the telephone talked to you?—A. Somebody said Mr. Quigg wanted to talk to me.

Q. And did Mr. Quigg talk with you over the telephone?—A. He asked me to come down to see him.

Q. At what time in the day was this?—A. It was about half past 11.

Q. Did you at once go?—A. Yes, sir.

Q. Had you seen Mr. Quigg recently before that time to talk with him about anything?—A. Yes, sir.

Q. Where?—A. I went over, I think I went over, and asked him—I told him that I referred the bond company to him for an indorsement. I had to get certain references, and among the names I gave Mr. Quigg.

Q. Is that the only time you had seen him recently before that?—A. Excepting at the State convention in September.

Q. Yes. Well, about half past 11, you think it was, you went to his office?—A. Yes, sir.

Q. And you saw him there?—A. Yes, sir.

Q. You may state what occurred.—A. Why, we went out to lunch together.

Q. Did he invite you to lunch?—A. Yes, sir.

Q. Where did you go?—A. It was the Mutual Café—a restaurant on Liberty street.

Q. Near by?—A. Yes, sir.

Q. Near by 100?—A. Oh, two blocks away.

Q. Tell us what occurred with respect to this subject of the Holland submarine boat while you were there at lunch together.—A. Mr. Quigg wanted to know how Mr. Lessler and I were. I told him that I thought Mr. Lessler and I were very intimate. He wanted to know whether I heard anything about submarine boats. I said, "Yes, I understand that Mr. Lessler made a trip on the boat, and that he was against the proposition."

Q. Yes.—A. (Continuing.) Of course I had heard Mr. Lessler say that he was against the proposition.

Q. Well, what else?—A. We talked over the Roberts bill. That was, I understand, the name of the submarine boat bill. There was no mention of any other title excepting "Roberts bill," and it provided for 10 submarine boats. Mr. Quigg was anxious to try to get Mr. Lessler's friendly disposition toward the bill, and he said, after a talk on various things, that there was $5,000 in it.

Q. Tell us, as near as you can, what he said.—A. He said that he was not personally interested in this thing. "There is some friend of mine whom I desire to favor if I can. If I can get the aid that I want, why, there will be $5,000 in it." Then he said, "I think I can make it a thousand for you, but," he says, "you telephone me at 3 o'clock and I will let you know about that."

Q. For whom did he say there was $5,000?—A. Why, that man we were talking about. He did not use the name.

Q. That is Mr. Lessler?—A. (Continuing.) But we were talking about Mr. Lessler. We were not talking about anybody else. Indeed, he did not use his name when he specifically said, "I may be able to fix it for a thousand dollars for you, but you telephone me at 3 o'clock and I will let you know about it."

We left one another, and at 3 o'clock I telephoned him.

Q. Well, you went to see Mr. Lessler, did you?—A. Mr. Lessler was not in town. I told him that I would see him in the morning.

Q. You telephoned him at 3 o'clock, did you?—A. I telephoned him at 3 o'clock, and I was told "That will be all right."

Q. Do you know who was on the other end of the telephone?—A. No, sir.

Q. You could not tell by the voice?—A. Well, I——

Q. Tell us what occurred then.—A. I asked for Mr. Quigg, and I presumed I was connected.

Q. Tell us what occurred.—A. The gentleman on the other side said: "That will be all right." I said "This is Doblin," and "That will be all right." That is all there was said.

Q. Did you make any reference to the previous arrangement to call him up at 3 o'clock, or any reference?—A. "This is Doblin," and "Is Quigg in?" And somebody on the other end of the phone says "Yes, hello." Then, "This is Doblin," I said, and I heard "That will be all right."

Q. You said nothing but "This is Doblin?"—A. That is all.

Q. Now, when did you see Mr. Lessler?—A. The following day.

Q. Do you know what day of the week it was?—A. Saturday morning.

Q. What occurred when you found Mr. Lessler?—A. He was sitting at his desk, opening his mail, and I asked him whether the torpedo submarine boat business was going to come up again, and he said it might, and I said "I was sent for yesterday," and he said "By whom?" I said "Quigg." I told him just what I——

Q. What did you tell him? Tell us just what you told him.—A. I told him there would be $5,000 in this "If you can see a way clear to be friendly disposed to it." He kind of huffed and laughed and threw his paper down, and there wasn't any more to it. He said "That drops that," and he said "Quit." I tried to talk, but he said "Quit."

Q. And you quit?—A. Why, I quit; that is all.

Q. Did you communicate this to Mr. Quigg?—A. Yes, sir.

Q. Where did you see him?—A. No. 100 Broadway.

Q. When?—A. I think it was the same afternoon.

Q. What did you say to him?—A. I told him Mr. Lessler would not. "It can not be done." I think that was the language I used—"It can not be done."

Q. What "can not be done?"—A. The mission I was engaged on—trying to get Lessler.

Q. Was anything said about money in that conversation?—A. No, sir.

Q. What did Mr. Quigg say?—A. "All right; I can not help it"—something of that kind. I apologized to Mr. Quigg. I think I said, "I am awful sorry, Mr. Quigg, that Lessler feels that way."

Q. Did you see Mr. Quigg again in connection with this subject?—A. Yes; I think I telephoned. He asked me whether he could see Mr. Lessler, and I told him that I would find out; and I think I telephoned Mr. Quigg and told him that Mr. Lessler would see him any time he felt disposed. If he could call him up on the 'phone, he could talk to Mr. Lessler any time he made it a point.

Q. Is that all with Mr. Quigg in relation to this proposition?—A. In relation to the money proposition?

Q. Yes.—A. Yes, sir.

Q. And in relation to the Holland torpedo-boat proposition, did you see him at any other time?—A. I called at his office.

Q. When?—A. I think a week ago—not a week ago—it may have been the week before that. Last week, I guess—week before last week.

Q. Did you have a talk with him then about it?—A. Yes.

Q. Tell us what this conversation was.—A. I called him up on the telephone before that and told him that I had a friend who was very close to Mr. Lessler, and I thought we might be able to get this thing done without any financial consideration. I felt as though if Mr. Lessler would help this thing along it would do him some good politically, because Mr. Quigg is a political influence in New York, and I know of his power regarding political matters. I know that he has been very friendlily disposed to me, and I was very friendlily disposed to try to bring about an amicable way of assisting one another, and I suggested to Mr. Obermier, who is an attorney, who was coming down here, to have a talk with Mr. Quigg, to see whether Mr. Lessler could not be persuaded to think that the boat proposition was all right, irrespective of any financial proposition.

Q. Well, go on.—A. We went there, and Mr. Obermier said that he

H. Rep. 3482——3

would try and talk with Lessler and see if he could not persuade him to feel friendly toward this proposition.

Q. Did Mr. Quigg go with you to Obermier?—A. No, sir; I went with Obermier to Mr. Quigg.

Q. Oh, I see. Well, what occurred there? What was said?—A. Mr. Quigg said now he was not interested in this matter personally, but there is some friend of his that he would very much like to aid if he could. "He is a gentleman who has influence, and I would like very much to aid him if I could." He said if Mr. Obermier could help the matter he would be very pleased to have it done.

Q. Was that all that occurred at that time?—A. Yes; all that occurred.

Q. That is the last time you saw him in this relation?—A. Yes, sir; until I see Mr. Quigg now, here.

Q. Yes; that is what I say. You do not recollect anything else, Mr. Doblin, that you have had no opportunity to speak of and that you want to mention now?—A. No; not as between Quigg and——

Q. Yes; I mean in relation to this subject. Have you seen anybody else in connection with this torpedo-boat business?—A. Why, I met a gentleman one night at the Waldorf Astoria, who I understood was Mr. Frost. There was nothing said. I was seated at a table, and I don't know how the subject came up, but anyhow it came up, and Mr. Frost said this man Lessler was a kind of a clever fellow and he was kind of sorry that he felt this way toward this proposition. There was nothing said more.

Q. Who introduced you to Mr. Frost?—A. I think it was Mr. Van Wyck.

The CHAIRMAN. Who?

The WITNESS. A man named Van Wyck. He is a button man.

Q. And that is all the conversation that occurred at that time with Mr. Frost?—A. Yes, sir.

Q. How did the subject of Mr. Lessler arise?—A. I think some man I know came along and said that this was Mr. Frost, of the Holland Torpedo Boat Company, and I was introduced as a man who knew Mr. Lessler very well.

Q. Yes.—A. (Continuing.) And that I was associated with him in politics; and one word followed another as to the Holland torpedo-boat proposition, and he said that he was opposed to it; that is, Frost said that he was opposed to it.

Q. Who was opposed to it?—A. Mr. Lessler was opposed to it.

Mr. LESSLER. I would like to ask if Mr. Doblin has appeared before a subcommittee of the Naval Affairs Committee.

By Mr. TAYLER:

Q. You appeared two or three days ago before a subcommittee of the Naval Affairs Committee, voluntarily, or at the request of the Naval Affairs subcommitte?—A. Yes, sir.

Q. And you narrated your account of these transactions, did you?—A. Yes, sir; after I was told by one of the gentlemen of the committee that I must answer in the end; so I might as well answer here and have the thing out. At that time I was assured by the members of the committee that this was all a matter of confidential investigation, and owing to that fact I simply answered as I was directed. As I said to the chairman, I was then under a verbal invitation, or at least a voluntary request, to appear, and I at that time said that I did not like to answer any questions here, because I was in a peculiar position. Some gentleman of the committee, whose name I do not know, told me that I must answer.

Mr. WHEELER. I told you you would have to answer or the House of Representatives would make you answer.

The WITNESS. I said "Gentlemen, under the circumstances, as long as I have got to answer these questions, I am here to answer." But I did not want to talk. I was not given an opportunity to ask advice on this situation, or anything, which was very unfortunate.

By Mr. TAYLER:

Q. You were told, were you not, that you could not be compelled to answer questions before that subcommittee?—A. Yes; but this gentleman [indicating Mr. Wheeler] arose, and he might as well have taken a gun and pointed it at me and said "Give up or I will kill you."

Mr. WHEELER. If you wanted to hire a lawyer you could have had advice.

Mr. BUTLER. I want to make a statement. I think Mr. Doblin should, perhaps, have been warned of the effect of his testimony upon himself. That was not done. I said to him that what he said when he was present before this subcommittee, so far as I was concerned, would be communicated to no one except the full committee; that he would not be called upon to repeat it, so far as I was concerned, unless this investigation was ordered.

Mr. RIXEY. I would like to ask a question through Mr. Tayler.

Mr. TAYLER. Mr. Rixey and Mr. Chairman and gentlemen, it occurs to me that, always doing it in order, of course, and without confusion, it would probably be better if the members of the committee would interrogate the witness in their own language and get their own responses. I know that up to a certain point this method we have been pursuing is very economical and saves a great deal of time, because there is no place where confusion arises so easily as among a committee of seventeen members; but I think if Mr. Rixey, for instance, would arise and ask permission of the chairman to interrogate the witness, and when he has finished interrogating him the next member in order should ask similar permission to be given by the chair, and so on, that we would avoid confusion, and it would be much the better way.

Mr. RIXEY. That is agreeable to me. I only want to ask two or three questions.

Mr. TAYLER. I think, Mr. Rixey, that you are quite as competent as I am, to say the least.

The CHAIRMAN. If there is no objection, that order will be followed. There is no objection, I understand.

By Mr. RIXEY:

Q. I will ask you to refresh your recollection as to your testimony before the subcommittee. Did you not state before that subcommittee that you stated specifically to Mr. Lessler that you were authorized by Mr. Quigg to tell him that if he would support the submarine-boat proposition there was $5,000 in it for him and $1,000 for yourself?—A. I do not know that that was the specific language that I used to Mr. Lessler. I may in the committee have used that language specifically.

Q. Yes; Mr. Tayler has interrogated you as to what positions you held in New York since 1902—the beginning of 1902. Will you state what political positions you held in the city of New York for the past ten years?—A. The Hon. James A. Roberts, when comptroller of the State of New York, appointed me an excise agent during the year 1896.

It may have been earlier than that. The Raines law legislated me out of office. I was appointed to look after steamboats.

Mr. ROBERTS. What?

A. (Continuing.) Steamboats, and the excise law of steamboats. When I was legislated out Mr. Roberts appointed me, or designated me, as an inspector of race tracks, which position I held until a bill was passed legislating me out. I was appointed a corporation examiner. In other words, I was assigned by the Department at Washington to a local bureau—or the department at Albany to a local bureau—in the World Building, looking after delinquent corporations which were about to be examined in practically supplemental proceedings. When Mr. Roberts—Mr. Gorman—became comptroller of the city, I held that position, and when W. B. Atbury was made a deputy tax commissioner, the appropriation providing for my stipend was left out, and I was left out.

In the latter part of 1899 the honorable chief of the census, Mr. Merriam, I think his name is, appointed me a special agent for the department of enumeration for the county and city—for the county of New York. That position I held until the census went out of business. Then I was appointed deputy superintendent of elections, which office I held on and off at various times since that.

By Mr. RIXEY:

Q. Under whom were you deputy superintendent of elections?—A. John McCullagh.

Q. On whose recommendation were you appointed to that position?— A. Originally?

Q. Well, give me the indorsements at different times.—A. My district. John H. Gunner, port warden of the State of New York, was one of them. I think my original indorsement held all the way through.

Q. Are you still deputy superintendent?—A. No, sir.

Q. When were you removed?—A. I was removed by statute on the 1st of January, and I am sworn in as a deputy superintendent for this year, because we are to have a special election this year in New York, and as yet I have not been called on.

Q. You have had quite a race with the legislature?—A. I don't know.

Q. When was the last appointment?—A. The 5th of January.

Q. For how long?—A. Ten days.

Q. You stated, in answer to a question, that after you had had that interview with Mr. Lessler, and reported to Mr. Quigg, at some time subsequent, Mr. Quigg wanted to know when he could see Mr. Lessler, and you stated to him that he could see him at any time?—A. Yes, sir; after I asked Lessler.

Q. Were you authorized by Mr. Lessler to say that he would see Mr. Quigg at any time after that?—A. Yes, sir; I had told him after I had asked Mr. Quigg to talk with him.

Q. Asked whom?—A. Lessler.

Q. How long was it after you had told Mr. Lessler that Quigg had authorized you to offer him this bribe?—A. The beginning of the next year; the beginning of the next week.

Q. The beginning of the next week?—A. Yes, sir.

Q. And you told Mr. Quigg that Mr. Lessler would talk with him at any time. Did you tell Mr. Lessler what Mr. Quigg wanted to talk to him about—A. No, sir; I did not. He did not tell me.

Q. He did not tell you; but had he ever told you of anything else but the submarine boat?—A. No, sir.

Mr. MUDD. I would like to ask Mr. Doblin a question to fix a date.

By Mr. MUDD:

Q. I understood the witness to say that he called to see Mr. Lessler between the 10th and the 18th of December?—A. Somewhere between them.

Q. I think you said that, and I think you said that it was on a Saturday morning?—A. Is that a December calendar which you have in your hand?

Q. Yes; I think you said somewhere between the 10th and the 18th. You said that it was on a Saturday morning.—A. That would make it the 13th.

Q. Do you know how long after that Mr. Quigg saw Mr. Lessler?—A. I said I thought it was the beginning of the next week.

Q. You don't know the date?—A. No, sir.

By Mr. ROBERTS:

Q. I would like to ask a few questions of the witness. You think that you have now fixed December 13 as the date that you saw Mr. Quigg?—A. I think that was the date.

Mr. TAYLER. Don't put it that way. He does not fix the date.

The WITNESS. I think it was.

By Mr. ROBERTS:

Q. This date, the 13th, is the date that you fix as when you saw Quigg?—A. No, sir; no.

Q. Is that the time Quigg made the offer to you to go and see Lessler and offer him the $5,000, when he gave you authority to make that offer?—A. You said the 13th.

Q. Wait a moment.—A. You said the 13th.

Q. No; you fixed this, the 13th, as the date of your interview with Mr. Quigg.—A. That was on Friday, if my impression serves me.

Q. Then you saw Mr. Quigg on Friday?—A. Yes, sir.

Q. That was the 12th?—A. Yes, sir; I think so.

Q. On Friday, the 12th, Mr. Quigg authorized you to make a proposition to Mr. Lessler involving the offer of $5,000?—A. Well, it is just as I said——

Q. I am asking you now.—A. We were talking on submarine boats, and we were talking about Mr. Lessler, and he said there was $5,000 in it, and "I forgot about you. I will be able to fix it for a thousand dollars for you. But you call me up at 3 o'clock and I will be able to let you know about it."

Q. That is the first time that Mr. Quigg ever mentioned money to you in connection with the Holland submarine boats, is it not?—A. Yes, sir.

Q. Now, has Mr. Quigg ever asked you to perform any other service for him at any time?—A. No, sir.

Q. This is the only service that he has ever asked you to perform?—A. Yes, sir.

Q. Now, this Friday, the 12th of December, did Mr. Quigg say to you that the Roberts bill was pending in Congress, calling for ten submarine boats?—A. Yes, sir.

Q. You are positive about that?—A. Yes, sir.

Q. And it was from Mr. Quigg that you learned that a measure was pending, and from him you learned the title of the bill.—A. As to the specific language, I heard of submarine; of course, as I told you, Mr. Lessler said that he had paid a visit to the boat.

Q. I am asking you about this specific measure, for which the bribe was offered, to procure Mr. Lessler's vote. This was on Friday, December 12, then, that Mr. Quigg told you that the Roberts bill was pending, as you have already stated?—A. We had already disposed of that specific language in our conversation.

Q. That is, on this day?—A. Yes, sir.

Q. But what I am getting at is, this is the time that Mr. Quigg told you that a specific proposition, called the Roberts bill, was pending?—A. I think in the early part of the conversation.

Q. And that was the first time that you knew that any specific legislation was pending in this session of Congress?—A. I heard it said that there was a bill in for ten boats when Mr. Lessler and his secretary, I think, were invited to take a trip on the boat.

Q. When?—A. I don't know. That was some time in the last session.

Q. And you heard then that there was a specific bill in the last session for a specific number of boats?—A. Yes, sir.

Q. Now, I am interrogating you as to when you learned that there was a specific proposition pending in this session for a specific number of boats. Am I right in saying that it was on Friday, December 12?—A. That was at the time that Mr. Quigg and I had a conversation.

Q. That was on December 12?—A. I think so.

Q. And that was the first conversation Mr. Quigg had had with you about this alleged bribe?—A. Yes, sir.

Q. Now, when you went to see Mr. Lessler after that did you say anything to Mr. Lessler as to the fact that you were to get any compensation for your services in the matter?—A. At first, no, sir.

Q. Did you at any time inform Mr. Lessler that you were to get any compensation?—A. I think one afternoon we walked up Broadway and I said, "I will be all right when I get my money."

Q. When was that in relation to the time that you brought the offer to him?—A. I think it was some time in Christmas week.

Q. That is a week or more after you had carried the bribe to him from Mr. Quigg?—A. I didn't carry the bribe. I only had a conversation with him.

Q. I am not speaking of the money; but the offer, then, if that suits you.—A. It is not a question of suiting me.

Q. It was a week or more after you carried Mr. Quigg's alleged offer to Mr. Lessler that you told Mr. Lessler that you would be all right?—A. I think it was; yes, sir.

Q. On your end?—A. Yes, sir.

Q. You say that you saw Mr. Quigg the week before the last week. That would be substantially two weeks ago?—A. Yes, sir.

Q. Did Mr. Quigg send for you?—A. No, sir.

Q. Has Mr. Quigg ever sent for you since you had—since you reported to him that Mr. Lessler could not be—that the thing would not work?—A. No, sir.

Q. And any interviews you have had with Mr. Quigg since have been of your own seeking?—A. Yes, sir.

Q. Has anyone else ever offered you any money or consideration for procuring Mr. Lessler's favorable influence?—A. No, sir.

Q. You state that you met Mr. Frost one night in the Waldorf-Astoria?—A. Yes, sir.

Q. Can you fix the date when you met him?—A. Some time after that.

Q. After what?—A. Prior to the 25th of January, or the 25th of December, some time before Christmas, a couple of days.

Q. It was some time before Christmas that you met him?—A. Yes, sir.

Q. You are positive about that?—A. Yes, sir.

Q. What time in the day was it?—A. It was in the evening—11 o'clock.

Q. Eleven o'clock in the evening?—A. Yes, sir.

Q. Did you meet him there by appointment?—A. Well——

Q. Just answer that question, please.—A. No, sir.

Q. Did you go there expecting to meet him?—A. No, sir.

Q. Are you positive as to who was present when you did meet him?—A. No. There was quite a crowd there. I would occasionally meet friends of mine. I had walked from the Fifth Avenue Hotel up to the Waldorf, and as a matter of fact I was going home. It was about half past 10 or 11 o'clock.

Q. Is it not a fact that you and another gentleman were sitting at a table when Mr. Frost came along?—A. It may have been.

Q. And there were only you three present?—A. Yes, sir.

Q. You are sure about that, now that you come to think of it?—A. Yes, sir; there were three of us.

Q. Now, can you not fix the identity of this third person?—A. It may have been George Cromwell. Yes, I guess it was.

Q. Who is George Cromwell?—A. He is president of the Borough of Richmond.

Q. A man of reputation in New York?—A. Yes, sir.

Q. Had you any thought in your mind that Mr. Cromwell had prearranged this interview with Mr. Frost?—A. No, sir.

Q. Now I want to ask just one other question. When you were before the subcommittee were you promised any immunity if you would tell freely what you knew?—A. Why, just as I said. The gentlemen said that I must answer.

Q. But they did not offer to protect you in any way, shape, or manner?—A. I did not hear of it.

Q. You knew that if you testified it would be on your own responsibility, with no hope of protection held out?—A. Yes, sir. What I mean by that is that I understood the committee to say that they were protecting anybody in the matter; that it was just as I said before, it was given me to understand that there was nothing to this; that they just wanted to know where I was standing in it.

Q. Just one or two other questions I would like to ask. Mr. McCullagh's name has been brought into the question.

Mr. VANDIVER. Just before you leave that point, may I ask one question?

Mr. ROBERTS. Certainly.

By Mr. VANDIVER:

Q. You stated a few moments ago, and it was practically the same just now, that you were sure this was just for the committee, and in confidence, when you gave this testimony. Now, I would like to ask you who it was; was it the full subcommittee, or any particular member of it that gave you that assurance?—A. They all talked up. There were six of them present. They all talked up.

Q. I understood that Mr. Butler was speaking only for himself.

Mr. BUTLER. I heard what the others said.

The CHAIRMAN. Let Mr. Tayler make a statement on that.

Mr. TAYLER. Whenever the right time comes I can state just what occurred there. It was on my mind to state it. I can make that statement now.

The statute provides in the first place, as to Congressional investigations, that no person shall be permitted to refuse to answer a question because it may tend to bring him into contempt or infamy, and that, in the second place, no testimony given by any witness before a Congressional committee can be used against him in any criminal prosecution. In these respects the two usual shields thrown about a witness are taken away from him; of course the Constitutional right remains—and the witness, Doblin, appeared before this subcommittee, which was purely informal and whose action was informal.

They had no power to subpœna witnesses and did not supœna any witnesses, and Mr. Lessler said that he would send for Mr. Doblin and that he was sure that he would come. Mr. Doblin did come on receiving a telegram, promptly, and when he appeared before the committee we expressed our gratitude to him for having so promptly come, without any authority of the House to demand his presence. We stated that we had no power whatever to compel him to answer any question, but that if he did not respond to our inquiries, we would feel compelled to go to the House and get authority for the full committee to investigate. And then came the question as to whether he could be compelled to answer. Under the law and the power of the House he would be compelled to answer. And he said that he did not have anything to conceal; that he was perfectly willing to make his disclosure then, in that informal way and before that committee which had no power to compel his attendance. There was no request made by Mr. Doblin to the subcommittee for immunity from prosecution, no intimation of such immunity on the part of the subcommittee, and so far as I know it did not enter into the minds of anybody there. It was never touched upon directly or indirectly, that phase of the subject.

Now, I think that is about what occurred, and the members of the subcommittee will agree with me.

Mr. WHEELER. I think your statement probably does the witness an injustice, unintentionally, because when the chairman stated to him that he was not required to answer—he had no power to compel him to answer—he indicated that he did not want to answer; but I said that if he did not answer the House of Representatives would compel him to do so, and he said then, "Well, if I have got to, I will tell it all."

Mr. LESSLER. I would like to state for the record that when I appeared before the subcommittee it was understood that nothing that went on there before the committee should be given to the public. I should like to add, also, that at the last meeting of the full committee, in executive session, the same resolution was passed—that nothing was to be given out in public.

Mr. WHEELER. Unless a prosecution was ordered by the House of Representatives.

Mr. LESSLER. Yes.

Mr. VANDIVER. You mean an investigation by the House?

Mr. WHEELER. If you prefer that phraseology.

Mr. ROBERTS. I would like to continue my examination of the witness.

By Mr. ROBERTS:

Q. I would like to ask if you have read the testimony given before this committee yesterday, or any part of it?—A. I read a part of it.

Q. When?—A. This morning, in the other room.

Q. Mr. McCullagh's name has been brought into this matter, and it has transpired that you are or have been one of his employees.—A. Yes, sir.

Q. I want to ask if Mr. McCullagh has ever requested you to interview or intercede with Mr. Lessler in behalf of the Holland submarine boat?—A. No, sir.

Q. Has Mr. McCullagh ever had any talk or conversation with you in relation to the Holland submarine boat?—A. No, sir.

Q. He has made absolutely no request of you in connection with that matter?—A. No, sir. I do not think that Mr. McCullagh ever knew that I knew Mr. Lessler politically, except that during that election I was up to his office with a case of arrest in one of the election districts.

Q. Has Mr. McCullagh asked you to see anybody else in regard to this matter?—A. I never spoke to anybody else about it.

Mr. WHEELER. I will ask one question, with permission of the chairman.

The CHAIRMAN. Very well.

By Mr. WHEELER:

Q. I understand, Mr. Doblin, that you did not undertake to fix with absolute certainty the dates upon which you had the conversations with Lessler or Quigg. Am I correct in that?—A. Yes, sir.

Mr. WHEELER. That is all.

By Mr. NICOLL:

Q. Mr. Doblin, in the course of your answers to Mr. Tayler, you stated that Mr. Quigg knew that you were very intimate with Mr. Lessler. Had you—— A. I did not so understand it.

Q. You did not so testify?—A. I say I did not understand that I knew Mr. Quigg knew that I was.

Q. Did you testify that you were never very intimate with him?—A. Politically; yes, sir.

Q. What?—A. Politically. I have done whatever was necessary to aid him in any political matters.

Q. Were you not socially intimate with him also?—A. Yes, sir; I have went to his house.

Q. You mean dined there?—A. Yes, sir.

Q. And been introduced to his family?—A. Yes, sir.

Q. And had other social engagements with him?—A. No, sir.

Q. Just state—— —A. I do not quite understand what you mean by other social engagements.

Q. I mean to go to the theater with him and—— —A. I have been to the theater with him once.

Q. Had you no other business relations with him except in the matter of these receiverships that you speak of?—A. That is all.

Q. Only those two?—A. That is all.

Q. And not interested in any kind of business except those?—A. That is it; yes, sir.

Q. He was not interested in those, was he?—A. No, sir.

Q. I understood Mr. Lessler to say yesterday that those were secured by him for you as an act of friendship.—A. I think that he asked Commissioner Alexander if he could see his way clear to appoint me, and I think he asked Judge McCarty in New York, one of the receiverships I was appointed to in the city. Well, in New York I was not appointed—the bond company was not——

Q. You were never appointed?—A. I was appointed and filed my bond, but I never received anything in the matter.

Q. You never received anything in the matter?—A. That is right.

Q. Did you ask Mr. Lessler for permission to occupy his office in your capacity as receiver?—A. Yes; I asked him one time if I could have a desk there, and he said, " No; you can come in here, but you need not have any desk."

Q. When was that?—A. Last March.

Q. What did he say?—A. " No; you don't need any desk in here."

Q. What permission did he give you to use the office?—A. Oh, I could use his desk.

Q. Use his desk?—A. Yes, sir.

Q. After he gave you that permission did you use his desk?—A. His boy there had a key to the desk, and any time that I went in there and wanted to sit down and read and write I could.

Q. And you did?—A. I think I did; yes.

Q. Yes? Take the period from the time when Congress adjourned last year until December. You were in and out of the office there?—A. Yes, sir.

Q. Almost every day?—A. Pretty near.

Q. Except during the period when you were acting—— A. As superintendent of elections.

Q. Of elections? That kept you busy?—A. Yes, sir.

Q. And did you spend most of the day in the office, except at that time?—A. Not most of the day. I was in and out.

Q. You were in and out?—A. Yes, sir.

Q. You saw Mr. Lessler every day?—A. When he was in town.

Q. I am speaking—— A. When he was in town. During that time he went to Chicago.

Q. Was he in town most of the time between the adjournment and the opening of the next session of Congress?—A. Most of the summer; yes, sir.

Q. Did you talk with him about various subjects that interested you both?—A. Yes; we discussed politics and other things.

Q. Did you not know, from your conversations with Mr. Lessler, about the Holland bill which had been before Congress at its last session?— A. Yes; I heard of him—I heard him say that he was going on a visit to where the submarine boats were.

Q. I didn't mean that. You know, as a matter of fact, do you not, that there was a bill pending before the committee at the last session of Congress?—A. I heard it was.

Q. Did you hear it from Mr. Lessler?—A. No, sir.

Q. Not from him?—A. I might have overheard him say so. I might have.

Q. Yes. Didn't you and he talk about the fact that he had taken an unfavorable view of these submarine boats? Did he not explain that he was against the purchase by the Government of submarine boats?— A. I think he did.

Q. I mean during your talks.—A. I think he did. I think he did. I think I heard him say one day that that bill was killed; it was dead.

Q. When was that?—A. Some time before—during the last session.

Q. Before Congress adjourned last summer?—A. Yes, sir.

Q. Did he not tell you about his talk with Captain McCullagh— Superintendent McCullagh?—A. Yes, sir; he did. He did.

Q. He told you that McCullagh wanted him to vote for the bill?—A. I understood that he called on him in reference to the torpedo-boat bill.

Q. In Washington?—A. In Washington; yes, sir.

Q. And did he not tell you that McCullagh had asked him to vote for it and that he declined to do so?—A. Yes, sir.

Q. Did he undertake to repeat the conversation, as he recollected it that he had had with McCullagh?—A. I think in changing his correspondence from his case that he had, the letter in some way—I see a letter regarding it, or a telegram, or something, asking Lessler if McCullagh could see him.

Q. Yes; but after McCullagh's visit, at their conversation here in Washington, did he tell you in substance what he and McCullagh had talked about?—A. No, sir.

Q. He told you that he could not comply with McCullagh's wishes; was that it?—A. I didn't discuss it with him.

Q. Yes; you knew, did you not, last summer, of his antagonistic attitude toward the Holland boat proposition?—A. Not exactly, no. I didn't know of his opposition.

Q. After all these conversations did you not know that he was against the purchase by the Government of Holland boats?—A. I so understood it; yes, sir.

Q. Why, then, did you say to Mr. Tayler, or in response to his questions, that when you had your first conversation with Quigg you knew nothing of Mr. Lessler's attitude toward the Holland boat proposition?—A. What I meant by that was that I did not know anything from Mr. Quigg regarding Mr. Lessler's attitude.

Q. Mr. Tayler asked you, if I recollect it, whether, when you came to talk with Mr. Quigg, you knew of the hostility of Mr. Lessler toward the proposition to purchase by the Government some of the Holland torpedo boats, and you said that you did not. Do you not so recollect it?—A. I may have said that to Mr. Quigg.

Q. What?—A. I may have said that because of my remarks to Mr. Quigg.

Q. You may have?—A. Yes, sir.

Q. As a matter of fact, you did know of his hostility, did you not?—A. Yes, sir.

Q. Now, Mr. Doblin, what was the earliest date in December that you can recall that you saw Mr. Quigg at his office?—A. It may have been early in December.

Q. Early in December?—A. Yes, sir.

Q. Do you not recollect visiting Mr. Quigg's office early in December and having some conversation with him about your position on the staff of Superintendent McCullagh?—A. Oh, yes.

Q. Yes?—A. Yes, sir.

Q. When was that?—A. At that time; that was in December, right after the election. It may have been in the middle of November.

Q. The middle of November?—A. Yes, sir.

Q. Did you go to his office yourself?—A. Yes, sir.

Q. Yourself?—A. Yes.

Q. Of your own accord?—A. Yes, sir.

Q. And you saw him?—A. Yes, sir.

Q. And spoke to him about the fact that by the 1st of January you went out of office?—A. Yes, sir.

Q. And did you ask him to do what he could with McCullagh to keep you in office?—A. Yes, sir.

Q. As one of his limited staff, after the 1st of January?—A. Yes.

Q. What did he say?—A. He said he would do what he could.

Q. He would do what he could?—A. Yes, sir.

Q. Did he not say to you that he was really out of politics now and that that was a matter that would have to be done by Mr. Morris, who was the chairman of the committee?—A. I don't remember his using that.

Q. Did he not say, as a matter of fact, that he could not interfere in those matters now, because he was really out of politics?—A. He may have said that.

Q. Have you any recollection of it? That is my question.—A. No, sir.

Q. You have no recollection of it?—A. No, sir.

Q. Was that all of the conversation you had with him on this visit in November?—A. I think we talked about—we did not have any conversation outside of myself; that was all.

Q. That was all?—A. In reference to my position. We did not talk about anything else.

Q. Was not this conversation had upon the day that you went in to see him and you and he went out to lunch together?—A. I beg your pardon?

Q. Was not this conversation about keeping you on McCullagh's staff had on the day when you went in to see him and you went out to lunch together?—A. No, sir.

Q. It was not?—A. No, sir.

Q. At what time of the day, when you went to see him and went out to lunch, did you get to his office?—A. About 12 o'clock.

Q. Was he in?—A. Yes, sir.

Q. Did you go into his private room?—A. I think the boy went in, and when he came back he said: "Mr. Quigg will see you in a moment."

Q. Did you go in to see him?—A. Yes, sir.

Q. Had you any conversation with him there?—A. He said: "Have you had your lunch?" I says: "No." He says: "Come along," and we went out.

Q. Didn't you say anything to him on that occasion about liking to stay, or wanting to stay, in McCullagh's employ?—A. No, sir.

Q. Not a word?—A. No, sir.

Q. And did he say anything more to you on that occasion except "Have you had your lunch?" and "Come along?"—A. At No. 100 Broadway?

Q. Yes; this one time.—A. Yes.

Q. Only that?—A. Yes, sir.

Q. Did you go down in the elevator?—A. Yes, sir.

Q. And you went out on what street?—A. Pine street.

Q. How far is it from there to the place you say you went to lunch?—A. About a block and a half—two blocks.

Q. And during that trip, did he talk with you at all about any subject?—A. During the walk?

Q. Yes; while you were walking over?—A. No, sir.

Q. Nothing at all?—A. That is, I do not remember outside of he may have talked about the weather, or it was a cold day.

Q. Just the ordinary talk that people have?—A. Yes, sir.

Q. Then you got to this place and sat down to lunch?—A. Yes, sir.

Q. What was the first thing that he said to you then?—A. "Mr. Doblin, do you know Lessler?" I said, "Pretty well." "What have been your relations with him?" I told him I was——

Mr. BUTLER. Excuse me; did he ask you what your relations with him had been?

A. (Continuing.) Yes, sir; I told him that I had been connected with his campaign, and had aided him the best that I could, and that he had been very friendly, and that he was very friendly disposed to me;

and he said something about the bill that was pending in the last session, and I said, "I understand Mr. Lessler was against it," and he says, "Yes; I know it, but," he said—I think he said "How close are you with Lessler?" "How close are you?" I said that I was pretty intimate with him, and very friendly, and I felt as though I could talk to him on any proposition.

Q. Well, go on; tell us the whole thing now, as you recall it.—A. Well, he said: "Some friends of mine are interested in this torpedo-boat proposition." I am not so positive whether he said "friends." I think he said "A friend of mine is interested in this boat proposition;" and he said in substance "There is $5,000 in it."

Q. Well, did he ask you to go and see Mr. Lessler and ask him to take $5,000?—A. I said that I would have to talk with Lessler about it.

Q. Did he ask you to go and see Lessler?—A. That is what he was talking about.

Q. Did he ask you in so many words to go and see him?—A. I think so.

Q. Do you swear to that?—A. Yes, sir.

Q. He did ask to go and see him?—A. Yes, sir.

Q. I understood you to say that later on you were walking up town with Mr. Lesser, and you said to him, "When I get my money it will be all right." What did you mean by that?

Mr. LESSLER. I ask that the minutes of the stenographer be referred to to show that. He did not say that.

Mr. NICOLL. I have taken it down here. There is no doubt about that. "One afternoon I was walking uptown with Mr. Lessler and I said, 'I will be all right when I get my money.'"

A. Flippantly, I think I said that. I think I was broke at the time, and I guess that I was trying to make a touch.

Q. On whom?—A. To ask Mr. Lessler to lend me some money.

Q. What did you mean when you said, "I will be all right when I get my money?"

Mr. LESSLER. I object. He did not put it that way.

By Mr. NICOLL:

Q. Did you make any reference or have any reference to what you have testified to to day in that conversation?—A. I may have had.

Q. Did you?—A. I may have had.

Q. Well, did you?—A. I don't recall to my mind at that time why I said "it will be all right when I get my money."

Q. As I understand it, you went to see Mr. Lessler at his office the very next day from the time after you had gone to see—after you had had this talk with Mr. Quigg. Is not that a fact?—A. Yes, sir.

Q. What exact words did you say to him?—A. "I have been sent for by Mr. Quigg." At first I asked him as to the Holland proposition; if that is likely to come up again. He said that it might. I said: "I have been sent for by Quigg."

Q. He said what?—A. That it might.

Q. Very well; and what did you say then?—A. I said: "I have got a telephone message from Quigg, and I saw him yesterday."

Q. Yes?—A. (Continuing.) And I told him the conversation I had in reference to——

Q. What did you say—— A. I told him——

Q. What did you say to Mr. Lessler?—A. I told him after I asked him about it whether it is likely to come up again, and I said there would be $5,000 in it.

Q. You said to him: "There will be $5,000 in it?"—A. Yes, sir.

Q. Was that all you said to him?—A. I might have told him that. I don't remember the exact language, but I referred to the money proposition that I had been told of the day before.

Q. I want you to tell us as near as you can, Mr. Doblin, the exact language that you used when you talked with Mr. Lessler.—A. "There is $5,000 in it."

Q. What do you call Mr. Lessler?—A. "Congressman."

Q. "Congressman," you call him?—A. Yes, sir.

Q. Did you say "Congressman?"—A. "Congressman, there will be $5,000 in this, Mr. Quigg told me, if you can see the way clear to help this proposition."

Q. Yes. And that was all you said to him?—A. That is all I remember now.

Q. Did it occur to you, Mr. Doblin, that you were making an improper proposition to Mr. Lessler?—A. Well, I did not—no; it did not occur to me.

Q. It did not?—A. Not at that time, because put in a friendly effort for the purpose of having Mr. Quigg's friendly disposition all around.

Q. Did you think you were doing a lawful and an honorable thing?

Mr. WHEELER. Just a moment. I think I will object to that. I do not think that should be permitted.

A. I am not a lawyer; I am not able to answer that question; I do not know.

Q. What I want to find out from you is this. You have been in public life for ten years, have you not?—A. Yes, sir.

Q. You know, do you not, that it is a felony or a crime for any member of Congress to accept any money to influence his official action? Don't you know that?—A. I never read the law on the subject.

Q. But don't you know it as a matter of common knowledge?—A. No, sir; I do not.

Q. What?—A. No, sir; I do not.

Q. Do you think that members of Congress are exempt and are permitted to receive money for their official actions?—A. They might be.

Q. They might be?

Q. Do you understand that members of the State legislature are authorized to receive money for their official action?—A. I never heard of it.

Q. Never heard of it?—A. No, sir.

Q. Let me get along. When you made this proposition to Mr. Lessler, did you believe that he had a right to accept this money?—A. I did not believe anything about it. I can not answer that question.

Q. Did you not—did you appreciate the fact, Mr. Doblin, that you were inducing, or trying to induce, your friend to commit a crime?—A. No, sir; I did not.

Q. You did not appreciate that?—A. I did not see—I did not appreciate it. I did not think that I was.

Q. You did not think that you were?—A. No, sir.

Q. Why not?—A. Of course I have not looked into the subject at all. It was just a question of one friend asking another friend to come in and help him.

Q. But you, as I understood you to say, knew that he was opposed to this Holland proposition?—A. I heard he said he was.

Q. You heard it? But you were offering him money to change his position on that subject, were you not?—A. I was doing what I was told.

Q. Did you not understand what you were doing?—A. Of course I understood what I was doing; yes, sir.

Q. Yes?—A. Yes, sir.

Q. Didn't you understand that you were trying to induce him to change his opinion on the subject?—A. He might have said——

Q. Did you—or won't you answer that question?—A. I beg your pardon. Let me get that exactly.

(The question was read by the stenographer.)

A. Yes, sir.

Q. And didn't you understand that you were offering him money as an inducement to change his opinion?—A. Yes, sir; that I was told I would get.

Q. What?—A. That I was told I would get.

Q. Get for yourself?—A. I have already answered that.

Q. I don't think so.—A. I beg your pardon. I answered it.

Q. You did not tell Mr. Lessler anything about the thousand dollars that you say you were to get, did you?—A. No, sir.

Q. All you said to him was that there was $5,000 in it?—A. Yes, sir.

Q. Is that it?—A. Yes, sir.

Q. But you meant $5,000 in it for him, didn't you?—A. That is what we were talking about.

Q. Certainly. Didn't it occur to you that you were insulting Mr. Lessler by making this proposition to him?—A. Well, coming from where it did, I did not think. I thought it would do Mr. Lessler some good.

Q. Well, leave out the words "coming from where it did."

Mr. WHEELER. No; leave it in. That is what we want in.

Mr. NICOLL. Well, leaving it out, then putting it in. Take it both ways.

Mr. WHEELER. No; leave it in.

By Mr. NICOLL:

Q. It did not occur to you that you were insulting him?—A. No; not for the minute.

Q. Did it at any time?—A. It does now.

Q. When did it first occur to you that you were insulting him?—A. What I mean by that is, that it coming from where it did, I felt that the relation would be very friendly all along the line, and I presumed that it was all right.

Q. Did that feeling conclude your appreciation of the fact that you were doing a wrong and criminal thing?—A. Not at that time.

Mr. WHEELER. I desire to ask some questions along that line. Are you through?

Mr. NICOLL. No, sir.

Mr. WHEELER. Very well; I prefer that you should get through with him:

By Mr. NICOLL:

Q. What were the exact words that Mr. Lessler said to you when you made this statement?—A. "Oh, pshaw! That—there is nothing to that."

Q. "Oh, pshaw! There is nothing to that!"—A. Yes, sir.

Q. Had you ever had any previous conversation with him about money?—A. No, sir.

Q. To that time?—A. No, sir.

Q. This was the first time in all your acquaintance with him that you had ever talked with him on that subject?—A. Yes, sir.

Q. And all he said—— A. In relation to this particular matter?

Q. Or any other matter.—A. I borrowed money of him already.

Q. I am speaking about the money to affect his position on different public matters?—A. No, sir.

Q. What?—A. No, sir.

Q. Are you indebted to him now?

Q. I understood you to say, Mr. Doblin, that this was the only time you ever had any conversation with Mr. Lessler on the subject of money to be given him to influence his official action as a member of Congress?—A. Yes, sir.

Q. That is so?—A. Yes, sir.

Q. Do I understand you to say that you borrowed money of him?—A. Yes, sir.

Q. Are you now indebted to him?—A. I do not think so.

Q. You have discharged your debt?—A. I think so; I do not think I owe him anything now.

Q. Has he accommodated you at different times?—A. Yes, sir.

Q. Did he say anything else except "Pshaw, there is nothing in it?"—A. I don't remember his saying anything more about it.

Q. Had you any more conversation on that morning with reference to the Holland boat?—A. No, sir.

Q. Not another word?—A. No, sir.

Q. Now, I understand you to say that on the same day you called up Mr. Quigg's office on the telephone, did you not?—A. The same day I talked with Mr. Lessler?

Q. Yes; the very day.—A. No, sir.

Q. What?—A. No, sir.

Q. Did you at any time thereafter call up Mr. Quigg's office on the telephone?—A. Yes, sir.

Q. When?—A. I think it was the next Monday.

Q. Where from?—A. I think it was Mr. Lessler's office; I guess it was.

Q. Was Mr. Lessler there?—A. I am not sure whether he had got over yet or not.

Q. Monday was the day on which he was usually absent, was he not, attending to his Congressional duties?—A. I think the session had adjourned then.

Q. It had adjourned, you mean, for the holidays?—A. Yes, sir; for the recess.

Q. For the holidays?—A. Yes, sir. That was the next Monday following. I think they were in recess then. I do not know whether it was.

Q. Your best recollection, I understood you to say in answer to some gentleman of the committee, was that it was Saturday, the 13th, when you had this conversation with Mr. Lessler.—A. Yes, sir.

Mr. VANDIVER. Friday, the 12th.

Q. On Friday, the 12th, as I understand it, with Mr. Quigg?—A. Yes, sir.

Q. How do you fix the date?—A. The gentleman held the calendar up over there, and I thought it was on a Friday or a Saturday, and I think I had some meat and Mr. Quigg had fish. That is what recalls it to my mind about Friday.

Q. You had fish and he had meat?—A. No, sir. He had fish and I had meat.

Q. Mr. WHEELER. Who ate the fish?

Mr. NICOLL. Mr. Quigg ate the fish.

By Mr. NICOLL:

Q. You called him up the following Monday from Mr. Lessler's office?—A. Yes, sir.

Q. Did you speak to Mr. Quigg on the telephone?—A. I think it was him.

Q. Don't you know his voice pretty well?—A. I could not say as to that.

Q. You have heard it a good many times in the course of your life?—A. Yes, sir.

Q. It is a familiar voice to you?—A. I don't know. There may be others talk the same as he does.

Q. Do you mean to say you were in doubt as to whom you were talking with on the phone on that following Monday?—A. No.

Q. Well, who was it?—A. I called up the office and asked if this was Quigg, and I said I spoke to Lessler, and he said that he would see him any time; that he could telephone when he wanted to.

Q. Was that all you said?—A. Yes, sir.

Q. You said, "I have spoken to Lessler, and he will see you any time you telephone;" when he wanted him?—A. Yes, sir.

Q. And that was all the conversation you had with him over the telephone at that time?—A. Yes, sir.

Q. Had you seen Mr. Quigg at any time between the Saturday morning you had the conversation with Mr. Lessler and this time over the telephone?—A. I may have called him.

Q. Did you see him?—A. I do not think I saw him.

Q. Had you any conversation with him; that is what I mean?—A. No, sir.

Q. Now, when did you see Mr. Quigg again?—A. As I explained, when I called on him with Mr. Obermier.

Q. When Mr. Lessler came back from Washington did you not call Mr. Quigg up from Mr. Lessler's office and say to him that Mr. Lessler was now in his office?—A. I may have done it.

Q. And don't you recollect that?—A. No, sir.

Q. You do not?—A. No, sir. You mean after the first telephoning?

Q. Yes; I mean a week later than the time when you say that you had this conversation with Mr. Lessler.—A. I don't remember calling him.

Q. You don't recollect it?—A. No, sir.

Q. Don't you recollect calling his office up and saying that Mr. Lessler was now in his office and would see Mr. Quigg?—A. I called Mr. Lessler up?

Q. Oh, no; you called up Mr. Quigg's office from Mr. Lessler's office.—A. I don't remember that.

Mr. TATE. I don't think that the witness said that he called up Quigg from Lessler's office.

Mr. NICOLL. No; that is what I am asking him.

By Mr. NICOLL:

Q. I am asking you whether you did not call up Mr. Quigg's office and say that Mr. Lessler was now in his office and would see him, a week later?—A. I do not think it was a week later. I think it was the Monday following.

Q. The Monday following what?—A. The Monday following my conversation with Mr. Lessler.

Q. You have just told us that conversation over the telephone with Mr. Quigg. You have told us about that.—A. Well——

H. Rep. 3482——4

Q. What?—A. What is the——

Q. I am asking you now whether or not a week later than that you did not call up Mr. Quigg's office and say Mr. Lessler was now in his office?—A. I don't remember telephoning him.

Q. Did you never so communicate with Mr. Quigg?—A. As I have already stated——

Q. No; but didn't you tell him later on that Lessler was there and would see him?—A. I don't think so.

Q. Who suggested to you that you should bring Mr. Obermier to Mr. Quigg?—A. Myself; nobody.

Q. Nobody else?—A. No, sir.

Q. You wanted to—— A. By the way, I desire to correct my statement. The way that I happened to get Obermier down there was: I asked Mr. Quigg if I could bring Mr. Obermier down. Mr. Obermier was going on to Washington, and I thought maybe Mr. Obermier would aid him in bringing about——

Q. Why did you think that Mr. Obermier would be of any service in the matter?—A. Because Mr. Obermier was the manager of Mr. Lessler's campaign and he was going down to Washington, and I thought maybe if he would go to Mr. Quigg and they talk it over maybe he could be of assistance in bringing about the result desired.

Q. You expected to get $1,000, did you?—A. Yes, sir.

Q. And was that what you were working for?—A. Yes, sir.

Q. How often did you go to Mr. Quigg's office with Mr. Obermier?—A. I only went there once.

Q. And did you go at any other time except with Obermier—before Obermier went with you?—A. Not other than I have already stated.

Q. When did you first hear that Mr. Lessler had stated to this committee that an attempt had been made to corrupt him or to bribe him?—A. When I read the Washington Post.

Q. What is that?—A. When I read the Washington Post—Wednesday morning.

Q. Did you receive any communication from him that day?—A. You mean on the day that I read this in the Washington Post? No, sir.

Q. Did you the next day?—A. I got a telegram.

Q. When?—A. On Tuesday night, to come to Washington.

Q. That was the day before you read it, was it?—A. Yes, sir.

Q. From whom did you receive the telegram?—A. From Congressman Lessler.

Q. Did he state why he wanted you?—A. No, sir.

Q. Just to come to Washington?—A. Yes, sir.

Q. Did you go at once?—A. Yes, sir; that is, I went on the 12 o'clock train. I attended a meeting first.

Q. At night, you mean?—A. Yes, sir.

Q. And you arrived here the next morning?—A. At 12 o'clock.

Q. Did you see Mr. Lessler the next morning?—A. Yes, sir.

Q. Where?—A. At the Normandie.

Q. Did he tell you then that he had stated to the committee that an attempt had been made to bribe him?—A. He showed me the morning papers.

Q. Did they so state?—A. The Post stated so; the one that I read.

Q. Yes. Did he say that was right—that he had done so?—A. I did not have any conversation with him about it, except that he said, "The committee wants to see you at half past 10."

Q. You mean to say that you had no conversation with him that morning as to what he had stated to the committee?—A. No, sir; it was all in the paper there.

Q. And when you read it—you read it?—A. Yes, sir.

Q. And asked him no questions about it?—A. I only said: "This is terrible; this ought not to be."

Q. "This ought not to be?"—A. Yes, sir.

Q. What did he say?—A. He said: "There is nothing to this; it will be all right. The committee wants to see you."

Q. "There is nothing to this; it will be all right?"

Mr. LESSLER. I will state that I had promised to the committee and said to the committee that I would say absolutely nothing to him.

By Mr. NICOLL:

Q. Yes. Was your name used in this article?—A. No, sir.

Q. Nothing more than the statement of Mr. Lessler that an attempt had been made to bribe him?—A. Yes, sir.

Q. Did you come down with him to the Capitol?—A. No, sir.

Q. You came alone?—A. No. sir.

Q. With whom?—A. With Mr. Son.

Q. He is his secretary?—A. I believe he is.

Q. Did you meet him here?—A. Who?

Q. Mr. Lessler.—A. No, sir; I did not see him from that time until I saw him this morning.

Q. So that all the conversation he ever had with you on the subject was that conversation which you have now narrated about the Normandie?—A. Yes, sir.

Q. Yes. Did you understand what you were coming to the Capitol for that morning, when you came?—A. No, sir.

Q. Had he not intimated to you?—A. No, sir.

Q. Had you any suspicion of what you were coming for?—A. No, sir.

Q. Didn't you understand that you were coming here to corroborate him?—A. No, sir; I did not know a thing about it until I read it in the Post, and at that time, when I was told that I had got to go before the committee; Mr. Son told me that. At a quarter of 11, I guess it was, or somewhere along there, Mr. Son came into the room and said, "The committee is waiting for you and we will go up to the Capitol," and I went along.

Q. A quarter of 11?—A. About a quarter of 11.

Q. He came to the Normandie?—A. Yes, sir.

Q. And Mr. Lessler was there?—A. No, sir.

Q. When had he left you?—A. He left then about a quarter past 10, I think it was; about 10 o'clock, I guess.

Q. When you read this article in the Post, did not Mr. Lessler say to you, "Philip," or "Doblin"—whatever he calls you—"I have made this statement to the gentlemen of the committee, and you must go down and tell them about it?"—A. No, sir.

Q. Or anything to that effect?—A. No, sir.

Q. And he gave you no intimation of what was wanted of you, at all?—A. No, sir. I did not talk to him the whole morning.

Q. Very well. Did you talk to Mr. Son about it?—A. Coming up from the hotel?

Q. Yes.—A. I asked Mr. Son what about it, and he said: "Well, I suppose it has all got to come out, whatever there is."

Q. Did Mr. Son tell you then that Mr. Lessler had made this statement to the committee?—A. No, sir; he did not tell me that, but I was reading the paper——

Q. That you knew from the paper?—A. Yes, sir.

Q. And you never knew it from any other source?—A. Not at that time.

Q. And you did not understand when you went to the Capitol with Mr. Son what you were going for?—A. Except I presumed that it was a question about this investigation. It said in the Post that this was some matter of bribery, as I understood it, with the torpedo boat submarine business.

Q. But you did not know that you were expected to make any statement, did you?—A. No, sir.

Mr. NICOLL. I am through.

By Mr. RIXEY:

Q. Just one question, I want to ask you. Up to the time you appeared before the subcommittee in the adjoining room, had you received any communication from the Committee on Naval Affairs?—A. No, sir.

By Mr. TATE:

Q. In answer to a cross question, a question by counsel for Mr. Quigg, you stated that when you approached Mr. Lessler in respect to this question you used this language: "I was doing what I was told to do." That is your language. Did you mean by this language that when you mentioned this offer of $5,000 to Mr. Lessler you were doing what Mr. Quigg had told you to do?—A. Yes, sir.

By Mr. ROBERTS:

Q. I would like to ask one or two questions. Did you visit Mr. Lessler in Washington at any time prior to the last visit that you have just spoken of?—A. No, sir. I was not here during his whole term in Congress.

Q. Did you ever talk with Mr. Lessler about the Holland submarine boat after you made him the offer that you say Mr. Quigg authorized?—A. No, sir.

Q. The subject never was mentioned between you?—A. No, sir.

Q. You never repeated the money offer?—A. Not after that time.

Q. Nor ever discussed the proposition in any phase whatever?—A. That is, I asked Mr. Obermier to go to Mr. Quigg and see whether he could not find out from Mr. Quigg what he wanted, and to go to Washington and see if he could not change——

Q. I am talking about your conversation with Mr. Lessler and not about your conversation with anybody else.

Mr. BUTLER. Let him finish his answer. See if he could not change who?

A. (Continuing.) Change Mr. Lessler's opinion in regard to the Holland Torpedo Boat Company.

Q. That is, after Lessler told you that he would not accept the bribe you still persisted in your efforts to change his vote?—A. Yes, sir.

Q. At whose instigation did you do that?—A. At my own.

Q. At your own instigation?—A. Yes, sir.

Q. And what was your object in doing that?—A. To get friendly relations between Quigg and Lessler.

Q. You, out of the goodness of your heart and in order to establish a friendly relation between Lessler and Quigg, persisted in your efforts to change Mr. Lessler's attitude on the Holland submarine boat proposition after he had refused the bribe that you offered him?—A. I can not answer that very well.

Q. Why not?—A. You say it was through the goodness of my heart.

It is a business proposition, and in the political exigencies, in my opinion, it would have been wise, in my opinion, to assist in bringing about what Mr. Quigg wanted.

By Mr. BUTLER:

Q. Bringing about what?—A. What Mr. Quigg wanted.

By Mr. ROBERTS:

Q. Wherein was it a business proposition for you?—A. I was promised a thousand dollars if he was friendly disposed.

Q. That is what I wanted. You were working not so much to establish friendly relations between Lessler and Quigg as for the thousand dollars that you would get. Is that about the size of it?—A. You can put it that way if you want to.

Q. I am asking you if that is not the fact?—A. No, sir.

Q. The thousand dollars you were to get had no weight in your desire to establish the friendly relations?—A. No, sir.

Q. How about the business proposition?—A. If I could get it, I would have been very pleased to have it.

Q. Then it was not a business proposition, in your mind, to get them on friendly relations?—A. Not after the money proposition had ceased to exist.

Q. Had it ceased to exist?—A. Yes, sir.

Q. And, as you say, you were trying to get a thousand dollars for yourself?—A. I think if the proposition had gone through I would not have needed any thousand dollars. I would have been taken care of politically.

Q. If it had gone through when?—A. At any time.

Q. Then you had no thought in your mind of the thousand dollars for yourself after Mr. Lessler refused the bribe, and you knew that he could not be secured that way?—A. Yes, sir.

Q. You had no thought—— A. No thought of it.

Q. Then you were looking out for yourself from a political standpoint in your efforts to turn Mr. Lessler in his attitude?—A. I think both.

Q. Both what?—A. Both Mr. Lessler and myself.

Q. You were looking out for his political welfare as well as your own?—A. Yes, sir.

By Mr. WHEELER:

Q. I will ask you a question along the same line in response to that portion of the cross-examination seeking to elicit your motive. Is it not a fact that you regard, and still regard, Mr. Quigg as a very powerful political factor in New York politics?—A. He is the most influential man we have got in New York County.

Q. And you desired to establish a kindly relation between yourself and Mr. Quigg, and thought you were making secure your political future?—A. I did, sir.

Q. And when he transmitted this proposition to buy Mr. Lessler's vote you were influenced not only by the hope of the thousand dollars, but likewise by the hope that you would be cared for politically in the future if you could put Mr. Quigg under obligations to you; is that correct?—A. I would not try to put Mr. Quigg under obligations to me.

Q. I will state it differently; to establish a friendly relation between you and Mr. Quigg?—A. Yes, sir; yes, sir.

Q. Your persistent efforts, after Mr. Lessler had declined to accept the bribe, were dictated by that. All right. You were still hopeful of establishing this friendly relation?—A. Yes, sir.

Q. And it was for that reason that you still persisted in trying to secure a change of Mr. Lessler's attitude?—A. Yes, sir.

By Mr. DAYTON:

Q. I would like to ask the full name of this man Obermier you mentioned, and his residence and address?—A. Leonard J. Obermier, No. 35 Nassau street.

Q. What is his business?—A. Lawyer.

By Mr. NICOLL:

Q. Did he come with you last night?—A. No, sir.

Q. To Washington?—A. No, sir.

Q. Isn't he here with you?—A. No, sir.

By Mr. WHEELER:

Q. Have you ever been employed by Mr. Quigg to do any political work for him?—A. No, sir.

Q. Has he ever requested you to look out for any political matters for him before?—A. No, sir.

Q. Have you ever transmitted any offer from him to anyone else to influence their attitude in any other manner?—A. No, sir; not directly from Mr. Quigg.

Q. Not from Mr. Quigg?—A. No, sir.

Q. What is Mr. Quigg's business?—A. He is an attorney and counselor at law.

Q. What is his actual business, if you know?—A. Formerly he was editor of the New York Press. That was his actual business the last that I knew of it.

Q. Is he not interested in some New York interests before the New York legislature?—A. I do not know.

Q. Is not that his reputed attitude?—A. I don't know from my own personal knowledge.

By Mr. MEYER.

Q. I understood you to fix the date of your interview with Mr. Quigg as the 12th of December.—A. I think that was the date.

Q. And unless I misunderstood you, you also said that the Roberts bill was referred to.—A. Yes, sir.

Q. And a Roberts bill for an appropriation?—A. For ten boats.

Q. For ten torpedo boats?—A. Yes, sir.

Q. Are you aware of the fact that that bill was introduced in the House of Representatives on the 13th of December?—A. No, sir.

Q. Had you heard of a Roberts bill, or a proposed Roberts bill, prior to that time, then?—A. I did not know the title of the old bill.

Q. I have the Roberts bill before me, which is dated the 13th of December. That is the date on which it was introduced in the House of Representatives, the 13th of December.

By Mr. WHEELER:

Q. What is the Roberts bill, do you know; what is the Roberts bill?—A. As I understand, the Roberts bill was in relation to ten torpedo boats.

Q. Ten torpedo boats. You are speaking of Roberts bills and bills in Congress. What is your idea of how these torpedo boats have been ordered heretofore?—A. I do not know; have no idea about it; have never looked it up.

Q. You do not know whether the bill you have been talking of was called the Roberts bill or not?—A. It just comes to my mind that the Roberts bill was mentioned.

Q. Was mentioned? And it was torpedo-boat legislation?—A. On a submarine torpedo boat.

Q. You do not want to be understood by the committee as attempting to fix absolutely the name of any bill that was referred to?—A. No, sir.

By Mr. RIXEY:

Q. Did you tell Mr. Obermier that Mr. Quigg was very much interested in securing Mr. Lessler's support of these boats?—A. Yes, sir.

Q. Did you communicate to Mr. Obermier that Mr. Quigg had authorized you to offer a money consideration to Mr. Lessler?—A. I do not think I did.

By Mr. ROBERTS:

Q. I just want to ask one other question. You did say to me, in answer to my question, that on this Friday, which you said was the 12th day of December, Mr. Quigg did say to you that the Roberts bill was before Congress?—A. Yes, sir; the old Roberts bill.

Q. Now, if it transpires that there is no old Roberts bill, how do you account for his using that language?—A. I don't know.

Q. What I am getting at is this: You are positive in your own mind that on this Friday, the 12th of December, Mr. Quigg did use those words "the Roberts bill?" You have so stated before.—A. I think so.

Q. Are you now of that same mind?—A. That is my impression.

Q. You are sure he used—— A. I will not say whether he used that name or not.

Q. You are not sure, then, that he used that name "the Roberts bill?" You were sure a while ago, but you are not sure now?

Mr. WHEELER. I submit that that is not proper.

Mr. ROBERTS. Just wait a minute——

A. The name "Roberts bill" was used.

Mr. WHEELER. I maintain that that statement is an assumption on the part of the gentleman.

Mr. ROBERTS. The record will bring out the fact.

By Mr. ROBERTS:

Q. I would like to have a specific answer to the question. You were sure a while ago, in answer to my questions, that Mr. Quigg used the words "Roberts bill." Are you sure now that he used those words in the course of the conversation?—A. Roberts's name came up in connection with the torpedo-boat bill.

Q. Roberts's name came up in the course of that conversation in connection with the Holland torpedo-boat bill?—A. I will not say "Holland."

Q. You are not sure now that this conversation related to the Holland torpedo boat?—A. No, sir; the name "Holland" was not mentioned.

Q. The name "Holland" was not mentioned?—A. No, sir.

Q. Let us pursue that a little further. Did Mr. Quigg, in any of his conversations with you, mention the name "Holland torpedo boat?"—A. No, sir.

Q. He never has mentioned to you the name "Holland torpedo boat?"—A. No, sir.

Q. You are positive about that?—A. Yes, sir.

Q. To get back now to Friday, the 12th. Are you sure that he mentioned the words "Roberts bill for submarine torpedo boats?"—A. In the course of the conversation Roberts's name came up.

Q. Now, I want to know in what way that name came up?—A. "The Roberts bill is dead," as I understood it.

Q. Your understanding now is that Mr. Quigg told you on that occasion, which was the 12th of December, that the Roberts bill was dead?—A. Yes, sir; and that "this matter now goes into the naval appropriation bill," as I understood it, for five or ten boats—torpedo boats.

Q. And he did not ask you to make a proposition to Mr. Lessler, as you once stated here, to support the Roberts bill for ten boats for a consideration of $5,000?—A. I never said that.

Q. Didn't you say that was the bill he told you that he wanted Mr. Lessler's support on?—A. No, sir. I don't remember saying it.

Q. Is it a fact that he asked you to get Mr. Lessler's support for the Roberts bill for torpedo boats?—A. I understood that the bill was killed by that time, and was a matter of last session, and had not been introduced at that time.

Q. But he did say there was a Roberts bill in the last session, did he not?—A. I so understood it.

Q. Are you positive about that?—A. Yes, sir.

Q. You will swear that he told you there was a Roberts bill in the last session?—A. I—yes, sir.

Mr. Roberts. That is all.

By Senator THURSTON:

Q. Mr. Doblin, you conversation with Mr. Quigg on this matter took place while you were at lunch?—A. Yes.

Q. That was at the noon hour?—A. Yes, sir; about n .

Q. What lunch room was it in?—A. On Liberty street. I think they call it the Mutual Restaurant.

Q. Is that a general lunch place?—A. Yes, sir.

Q. How large a room?—A. Well, not as big as this.

Q. Did you and Mr. Quigg go into a private apartment to lunch?—A. No, sir.

Q. To take lunch?—A. No, sir.

Q. You took lunch in the general room?—A. Yes, sir.

Q. Were other people eating about you?—A. Yes, sir.

Q. It was pretty full, was it not?—A. No; there were other people there.

Q. And all this conversation took place in this room, at that table?—A. Yes, sir.

Q. Coming back just a moment, when did you first begin to make general use of Mr. Lessler's office?—A. Sometime in February, 1902.

Q. And continuing that same use up to this time?—A. Yes, sir.

Q. Did you carry a key of it?—A. No, sir.

Q. You do not have a key to the office?—A. No, sir.

Q. Do you have a key to the desk?—A. No, sir.

Q. The boy is there attending to the office, and—— A. Yes, sir.

Q. (Continuing.) You go in and use the desk when you wish to, and the office?—A. Yes, sir.

Q. How long was it after you had your conversation with Mr. Quigg that you were walking on the street and spoke to Mr. Lessler and made a remark to Mr. Lessler something to the effect that you would be all right when you got that money?—A. A week or so.

Q. A week or so afterwards?—A. Yes, sir; some time before Christmas.

Q. That was after Mr. Lessler had refused this proposition?—A. Yes, sir.

Q. And you say you made that remark at that time, you rather think, in order to touch him?—A. I think so.

Q. To borrow money of him?—A. Yes, sir.

Q. Did the touch work?—A. I did not ask him for any money.

Q. You did not ask him for the money?—A. I did not ask him for anything.

Q. Then you did not borrow money of him at that time?—A. No, sir.

Q. Have you since that time?—A. No, sir.

Q. You have not borrowed anything of him since that transaction?—A. No, sir.

(Witness excused.)

TESTIMONY OF JOHN McCULLAGH (SWORN).

By Mr. TAYLER:

Q. Where do you live?—A. In New York City.

Q. You have lived there how long?—A. For about thirty-three years.

Q. What is your official position at present?—A. I am State superintendent of elections for the metropolitan election district.

Q. Which includes what?—A. Five counties, New York, Kings, Queens, Westchester, and Richmond.

Q. You have held that position how long?—A. Four years and six months.

Q. Prior to that what official position did you hold in the city of New York?—A. I was then chief of police of the city of New York.

Q. How long have you known Mr. Lessler?—A. The first time I met Mr. Lessler, to know him, was in Washington. I think that was in the month of May—the latter part of May or the 1st of June, 1902.

Q. Of course you had known of him before that time?—A. I never knew of him until he ran for Congress at the special election in January, 1902.

Q. What was the occasion of your visit to him in the latter part of last May or the 1st of June?—A. Now, gentlemen, I am not represented here by counsel, neither do I think it is necessary. I shall have to ask this committee to be patient with me if I make blunders. I do not know that I can confine myself to the rules of evidence, nor do I know that this committee is being governed by such rules in this matter.

The CHAIRMAN. Make your own statement, Mr. McCullagh, as you think best.

A. (Continuing.) I will now submit an affidavit here, which I trust you gentlemen will read aloud and have it placed in evidence. That will explain my visit.

The chairman thereupon read the affidavit of Henry B. Hertz, as follows:

STATE OF NEW YORK,
    City and County of New York, ss:

Henry B. Hertz, being duly sworn, deposes and says: I am 32 years of age and reside at No. 22 West Forty-third street, in the city and county of New York. I am an architect by profession and a member of the architectural firm of Hertz & Tallant, doing business at No. 32 East Twenty-eighth street, in the city and county of New York. I know Isaac L. Rice, president of the Holland Submarine Boat Construction Company and the Electric Boat Company. The said Isaac L. Rice is and was in March last a client of the firm of which I am a member. I am not a member of any political organization, club, or association. Early in

March, 1902, while superintending the construction of the residence which our firm is erecting for Mr. Rice on Riverside drive and Eighty-ninth street, in the city and county of New York, I had a conversation with him in the course of which the subject of the Holland submarine boat came up. He informed me that Congressman Montague Lessler, who was a member of the Naval Committee of the House of Representatives, was opposed to the purchase of the Holland submarine boat for use of the Navy, and stated his regret that he had encountered opposition from Mr. Lessler, who he thought was not fully informed as to the merits of the boat.

In the course of the conversation I suggested to Mr. Rice that it would be proper for some gentleman who knew Mr. Lessler to interview him on the subject. Thereafter I consulted my brother, Mr. A. H. Hertz, a member of the firm of Freedman Bros. & Co., in reference to the matter. He informed me that the only person he knew of who was acquainted with Mr. Lessler was Mr. John McCullagh, the State superintendent of elections, and that he would see Mr. McCullagh, who is a personal friend of his of many years' standing. In company with my brother, I called upon Superintendent McCullagh at his office, No. 585 Broadway, and laid the facts of the matter before him, explaining to him my interest in the matter, which was enterly personal. I impressed upon Superintendent McCullagh the fact that I was a firm believer in the utility and value of the submarine boat from having witnessed demonstrations of its efficiency both in this country and in France, and that I considered the submarine boat one of the most important adjuncts to the national defense that had ever been discovered.

I requested Superintendent McCullagh to go to Washington to see Mr. Lessler. Mr. McCullagh informed me and my brother that he had only a casual acquaintance with Mr. Lessler and did not know what influence, if any, he might have with Mr. Lessler, but that he did not see any impropriety in acceding to my request.

I am not now, nor have I ever been, financially interested, directly or indirectly, in the Holland Submarine Torpedo Boat Company or in the Electric Boat Company.

HENRY B. HERTZ.

Subscribed and sworn to before me this 23d day of January, 1903.

ARTHUR HOFFMAN,
Commissioner of Deeds, New York City, No. 115.

The WITNESS. That is correct, sir.

By Mr. TAYLER.

Q. As far as you know, the statements in that affidavit are correct?—A. Yes, sir.

Q. In consequence of the invitation and suggestion made by the gentleman who made this affidavit, what did you do?—A. I came to Washington. I want to say, further, before we proceed further, that there is Mr. Hertz's brother, a gentleman I have been personally acquainted with for thirty-five years. I was not very well acquainted with Mr. Hertz, the architect, but at the solicitation of his brother I asked him then to come to my office. He came, and it was through his brother here, who will be a witness, with your consent, that he came. A conversation ensued. There is something he says in the affidavit about "March." Mr. Hertz is not sure that it was in March. I do not know anything about what time he had the conversation with Mr. Rice, but it was some time in the latter part of May, I know, that he came to my office, as far I can recollect.

Q. And at that time you said you saw no impropriety in coming to see Mr. Lessler, and agreed to do so?—A. I agreed to do so, which I did.

Q. Now tell us what you did, and what conversation you had with **Mr. Lessler.**—A. Yes, sir. Mr. Lessler was not in Washington when I arrived here, and I called on his secretary, a gentleman by the name, I think, of Mr. Son. He told me that he was out of town, and he expected him, I think, on Monday or Tuesday. I remained over. I think I got in Sunday, and I think it was the following Tuesday I called on Mr. Son again at the hotel. Yes, it was the Normandie. He informed me that he expected him that evening. I went there that evening and was taken up to Mr. Lessler's room.

When I entered the room a gentleman rose whom I did not know, but he introduced himself as Congressman Lessler. He said, "I am very glad to see you, Mr. McCullagh." I thanked him. He said, "I had the pleasure of meeting you before." I said, "I do not remember. Where have you met me?" He said it was at the Fifth Avenue Republican Club. I said that I really did not remember. He said, however, "I owe you an apology." "What for?" I said. He said, "I am greatly indebted to you for my election." "Why," I said, "Mr. Lessler, I don't understand it that way. If I did anything for you, I did it in the performance of my duty as State superintendent of elections." He asked me to take a seat. We sat down and talked for a little while about the interesting things that occurred during the special election, but what they were I can not say. I do not recollect that part of it. So I then said, "Now, Mr. Lessler, I have come here to ask for a favor." I said to him: "A personal friend of mine has requested me to come. He has no interest whatever that I know of, and he has so stated to me, in the Holland submarine boat. Neither have I. It is purely a personal matter with him, so far as I know. Now," I said, "If you can see your way clear to vote for this"—we talked about the merits of the boat, and I said, "I believe it has got some merits. You have been appointed on the committee to act on this appropriation."

He abruptly said to me: "I want to be frank with you, Mr. McCullagh. I won't vote for it." He says: "You don't understand this situation as I do." Then he spoke something about the governor of the State, in a general way, sending down to my office and asking a subordinate in my office his opinion about how to run the office, and how ridiculous it would be. "Now," he said, "I have made a thorough investigation of this thing, and I am perfectly familiar with the details. I want to say to you, Mr. McCullagh, that I am not a damn fool. I was not born yesterday, sir. I have got my suspicions about this thing. There is not a man on that committee with me that I would trust except one man," and he named the man, but I will not. I can not recall the man's name. I believe I can conscientiously state the name, to the best of my information and belief, but it is not necessary, because there is doubt in my mind about it. I will not name him, with your permission. He said: "There is not a man on that committee that I would trust except one man." What brought that about was that I said: "Why, you are the only man, Mr. Lessler, that seems to be standing out on this thing. It seems to me ridiculous. You are a young man just elected to Congress. What is the object of it?"

Then he repeated just what I have said. "Furthermore," he said, "I have weighed the whole thing, and while I can't prove it I believe there is a lobby here and there is boodle. The position of the whole thing down there, from my standpoint, and what I have seen of it, is wine, terrapin, and woman"—and the "woman" was the most vulgar expression I have ever heard a man use. I said: "Now, Mr. Lessler, if that be true I am sorry I came here. I shall certainly go back and tell my friend in New York City." We talked about some other matters in a friendly way. His secretary was sitting there. I got up and he walked with me to the elevator. We shook hands and I bade him good-bye. I never saw him since, until about two months ago, and I think that it was on the day of the registration, or it may have been on election day, at the polls or at my office. He was telling me about some irregularities that were going on in his district, and I told him that I was perfectly familiar with them and they were receiving attention. I did not know the man was nominated for Congress, nor did I know that he was running for Congress, until he happened in my office on that day.

Is there any other question you gentlemen would like to ask me?

The CHAIRMAN. Proceed in your own way.

The WITNESS. I believe he says I mentioned the names of three men when I entered his room.

Mr. MEYER. No; he did not mention their names.

The WITNESS. He did not mention their names, but he said I was sent there by three men.

Mr. ROBERTS. He says, on page 4 of the record, in the second question on the page: "I have been sent by some men in New York, who can reelect you or beat you, to ask you to vote for the Holland submarine boat."

The WITNESS. Yes; "'I have been sent by some men in New York, who can reelect you or beat you, to ask you to vote for the Holland submarine boat.' I said to him: 'I will see you in hell first—I will see them in hell first.'"

Now, gentlemen, is it reasonable to suppose——

Mr. ROBERTS. Do not argue it. Just state the facts.

The WITNESS. That man never made use of any such expression.

Mr. RIXEY. Did you make use of that expression?

The WITNESS. I did not, sir. Which expression do you refer to?

Mr. RIXEY. "I have been sent by some men in New York who can reelect you or beat you."

The WITNESS. I had been sent by a personal friend of mine, to which I have testified, and no other conversation ensued between us.

Mr. MEYER. Did you say, "Then do it for me?"

The WITNESS. No, sir; positively not.

By Mr. KITCHIN:

Q. Did you intimate to him that his action upon that matter would in any way affect his reelection or his renomination?—A. I did not, and if I had said so he would say I was crazy. If I went in to you, as a sane man, an intelligent gentleman, and said such a thing, you would say: "Mr. McCullagh, you require a physician; I am sorry for you."

Q. He says he told you he would see you in hell first.—A. He did not. He never used any such expression.

Q. And you never said anything that referred to his election or renomination?—A. No, sir; and I could not control it, gentlemen. It is impossible.

By Mr. ROBERTS:

Q. You have stated, Mr. McCullagh, that before you held your present position you were chief of police in New York?—A. Yes, sir.

Q. May I ask how long you held that position?—A. Nine months.

Q. Did you have any connection with the police department before that?—A. Yes, sir; for twenty-eight years.

Q. What positions did you hold?—A. I was appointed patrolman, roundsman, sergeant, and captain. I was promoted from captain to the chief of police of the old city, and when the New York charter went into effect I was promoted to chief of police of greater New York, and I reorganized the police force of the greater city—7,500 men.

Mr. BUTLER. Who was mayor at that time?

The WITNESS. Mayor Van Wyck.

Mr. MEYER. I would like to ask if you ever held a position in the police department known as chief of detectives?

The WITNESS. No, sir; never in my life. There is a man named McLaughlin who held that position, and you may have gotten that idea from the similarity of names.

Mr. ROBERTS. Mr. Lessler said—and if I misstate the testimony I hope I will be corrected—that when you came to his room here in Washington at the time you have testified to that you requested Mr. Lessler to dismiss his secretary, so that you two, you and Mr. Lessler, would be alone.

The WITNESS. He said that I looked at his secretary, and so I did. I want to be frank. I looked over to the gentleman, and he said: "Never mind, McCullagh, anything you say in this man's presence is all right. He is my secretary." Then I see in the testimony that I spoke in an undertone. I did not speak as loud as I am speaking here, because there was no necessity for it. The secretary sat about 10 feet away from me, and I paid no more attention to him than I would to any other person that might be sitting around.

By Mr. DAYTON:

Q. Mr. McCullagh, you said you came from New York here to see Mr. Lessler about this matter?—A. Yes, sir.

Q. Did you come on any other business?—A. I did not.

Q. How many days were you here?—A. I came here on Sunday.

Q. You found that Mr. Lessler was not here?—A. I found him not here.

Q. You remained how long?—A. I communicated with his secretary, and he told me that he had returned from the West and was at Atlantic City, and that he expected him on Monday. I waited over on Monday and he did not come, and I then waited until Tuesday.

Q. Then you remained from Saturday until Tuesday?—A. Yes, sir.

Q. Will you kindly tell the committee whether you came without compensation or pay of any kind or character?—A. I paid my way from New York to Washington, and I paid my expenses. My friend wanted to pay my expenses, but I would not accept it, from personal friendship. I never, gentlemen, had a pass on a railroad or to a theater in my life.

Q. This was purely a matter of friendship on your part?—A. Purely a matter of friendship, personal friendship to my friend of twenty-five years' standing.

Q. You understood that his motive was purely out of friendship for Mr. Rice?—A. No, sir; his motive was to help his brother, who was an architect for Mr. Rice, for building a house that is in course of erection on Riverside drive, and the building is there.

By Mr. BUTLER:

Q. You came down to discuss the Holland torpedo boat proposition with Mr. Lessler.—A. That is it exactly.

Q. Did you know anything about the merits or demerits of the Holland torpedo boat?—A. Simply what I read in the newspapers, and what Hertz told me about it; that is all.

Q. You were of the opinion, then, that it was a good weapon for the Government?—A. Yes, sir.

Q. Did you come to that conclusion before you had talked with Mr. Hertz, or after that time?—A. After my conversation with Mr. Hertz. My attention had not been directly drawn to it, and I had not come to any conclusion by what I had read about it. But after my conversation with Mr. Hertz, the brother of the architect, and then my thinking of going to Washington, and the propriety of going there made me think seriously about it, and I at last came to the conclusion that it was a proper thing, and that it was a proper thing for me to do to come down and see Mr. Lessler and discuss the subject with him.

Q. Did you before that time, or have you since that time, interested yourself, directly or indirectly, toward procuring a weapon of any character for the Government to employ?—A. I have not.

Q. Then this is the only one you have ever advocated?—A. It is the only one I have ever advocated.

By Mr. TAYLER:

Q. Had you made any effort, prior to your journey to Washington, to see Mr. Lessler?—A. Yes; I tried to locate him at his office, and they notified me that he was out of town. I wired, I think to Washington, and I received a telegram. I think the telegram was signed by Mrs. Lessler, that he had gone to Cincinnati. I thought that the committee was going to act immediately on the appropriation, and I then wrote him a letter. It seems the letter did not reach him. So then I came to the conclusion that the best thing I could do was to come and see him, which I did.

Q. That was shortly afterwards?—A. Yes, sir.

By Mr. DAYTON.

Q. Was it your purpose to come down here and present to Mr. Lessler the merits of that boat, and convince his reason and judgment that he ought to vote for it?—A. Not particularly that. The main object, gentlemen, of my coming here was an entirely outside thing. There is the gentleman through whose instrumentality I came, because of the interest he had in his brother. He was not particularly interested at all in the Holland submarine boat.

Q. You went to all this expense and trouble, in other words, of making an appeal to Mr. Lessler to vote for this boat, without knowing very much about its merits except what you had casually read in the newspapers and from the conversations you had had with your friends, because of your friendship for your friend, who was connected with the Holland submarine torpedo boat?

Mr. ROBERTS. I object to the last part of the question going into the record. That is a pure inference.

The question was read by the stenographer.

Q. (Continuing.) My question is simply this: You went to all this trouble and expense to see Mr. Lessler and make an appeal to him to vote for this measure, without knowing very much about it, save and except what you had casually read about it in the newspapers and what your friends had told you, solely on account of your friendship for your friend who was connected with the Holland submarine torpedo boat.

Mr. ROBERTS. He has not said that. He has not said his friend was connected with the Holland torpedo boat.

The CHAIRMAN. You can make your explanation.

A. I want to hear the question first.

Mr. TAYLER. It was on account of your friend, who was a brother of Mr. Rice's architect.

By Mr. DAYTON:

Q. Then on account of your friendship for your friend, who was a brother of Mr. Rice's architect?—A. Yes, sir; that is it. If you will refer to that affidavit there you will see that I was very careful not to act on the suggestion of Mr. Hertz, my friend, who was not familiar with the boat; but I sent for his brother. I asked him to bring his brother to the office, which he did. We discussed the matter thoroughly. What he said to me about the boat, and other things that I had read about it in the public press, made the impression on me that it was a good thing, and then, through my personal friendship for my friend, I came here. As I stated, and as Mr. Hertz says in the affidavit, I told him I did not see any impropriety in my coming and discussing the matter with Mr. Lessler.

Q. It did not present itself to your mind that it was proper, if you were so thoroughly convinced of the merits of these boats, to ask for a hearing before this committee of the whole, where you could express your opinion to the committee and present your reason for it, instead of going to an individual member in this way?—A. I did not think it was necessary for me to come before this committee, gentlemen. I had no interest at all in it. If I were financially interested, or took any great interest in it, if I were a member of the firm, I suppose it would be a natural consequence for me to come and ask the privilege of appearing before the committee; but having no other interest, as I said before, gentlemen, why, I simply did it to oblige my friend.

Q. Your patriotic motive did not extend beyond seeing one member of this committee; is that right?—A. I don't know, Mr. Congressman, that you could call it "patriotism" in this matter. I know I would not.

By Mr. TATE:

Q. I believe you said that you did not know Congressman Lessler?—A. I did not know him.

Q. You had never met him, to your knowledge?—A. I had never met him, to my knowledge.

Q. You had no reason to believe, then, that you had any particular personal influence with him, had you?—A. I have so stated, and Mr. Hertz has so stated in that affidavit.

Q. Why was it, Mr. McCullagh, then, that you came here to Washington to see him, and that you were selected as the person to come here and see him, and not some other person, or the attorney of some other person? What reason did these gentlemen urge or state to you that you could offer to this Congressman different from what they could offer? Were you in a position to influence him?—A. No; I have so stated. I had no influence with him.

Q. Why did you come? You say you knew nothing about the boat and did not know the man. If you were not in a position to influence him, why did you come?—A. I came through the solicitation of my personal friend, Mr. Hertz.

Mr. DAYTON. Why did he not come?

The WITNESS. I do not know. He stated to you to-day that his brother, the architect, was ready to come and testify here the reason why he did not come.

By Mr. WHEELER:

Q. Can you tell us why he did not come?— A. I do not know his mind; he came to me and told me that his brother had this contract with Mr. Rice, who was a client of his, and that he would like to retain that clientage, and that his brother was just beginning business, and was a bright young man who had just started a short time ago in business.

Q. Is it not a fact that your understanding was that by virtue of your position in politics in New York these gentlemen came to you because they thought that because of your position you would have influence, and asked you go and see Lessler?—A. Mr. Hearst asked me if I knew him.

Q. I understand that; but answer my question, please. Is it not your understanding now, in perfect frankness, that by virtue of your commanding position in politics in New York these gentlemen approached you because they believed that by virtue of this commanding position your voice would be potential in determining this man Lessler's attitude?—A. I can not tell, gentlemen, what their opinion might be about it; but I know this, that I do not hold any commanding position in politics in New York. I am a State officer, appointed to perform a certain duty. I take no active part in politics at all. I do not go to conventions. I am not elected as a delegate to any convention, and never have been To keep out of politics, I even did not enroll.

Q. Did it not strike you as a little bit singular that a total stranger should be selected by a total stranger to come and see a man and influence his action upon a vote in Congress?—A. No.

Q. Did not that occur to you as a little strange?—A. It did not.

Q. Have you ever been approached by any other friend to go and see a total stranger and to change his attitude upon a matter pending before a legislative body?—A. I can not recall any in my life.

Q. And you state to this committee that at the time of this you attributed no importance to the fact that you, the superintendent of elections, and having general supervision over election returns in this man's district—— A. Yes.

Q. (Continuing.) That you did not connect that in any way with this interview in which these people had asked you to come and see Lessler?—A. He made use of the expression, "Mr. McCullagh, I owe my election to you;" but I did not look at it in that way. I knew that he did not. I never gave it a thought.

By Mr. ROBERTS:

Q. Do you have anything to do with the returns of elections in New York?—A. I do not.

Q. Do they come under your supervision in any way, shape, or manner?—A. They do not. I will explain my position in brief, if you will permit me. I appoint, under the law, 800 men, for the purpose of investigating illegal registration and detecting and arresting any person committing any crime against the elective franchise. I employ these men for forty days. I notify, on or before the 15th day of August of each year, the chairman of each county committee of the two dominant parties—the Democratic and Republican parties—as to the number of men I am going to appoint The chairman of the county committee submits the names to me. The men are recommended to me. These men are supposed to possess the qualifications of inspectors of elections. I examine them, and if they pass, it is mandatory that I must appoint them. They are employed for forty days; and where it is necessary, in some cases, in carrying out the work of the office, their service may be continued.

By Mr. BUTLER:

Q. Do I understand you to say that you do not register as a voter?—A. I said I did not enroll.

Mr. TAYLER. Enrollment means to join a party organization?—A. (Continuing.) No; enrollment means to vote at the primaries to elect delegates.

Q. Then you take no part at the primary elections?—A. I say I do not.

Q. Not even by participating to the extent of casting your vote?—A. No, sir.

By Mr. WHEELER:

Q. Have you got any party affiliations?—A. I have.

Q. What is your party affiliation?—A. Republican.

By Mr. KITCHIN:

Q. When you came to Washington to see Congressman Lessler you were hoping and expecting to have some influence with him?—A. Well, yes; I thought I might.

Q. I ask you if it is not a fact that for that influence you were depending more upon your official and political position than upon the arguments you might put before him?—A. No; I could not say that, because I have already said——

Q. You deny that?—A. I said I would go and discuss it. I did not say I would go to influence him. I said I would go and discuss the matter with him and lay it before him in the most intelligent way I possibly could.

Q. So you deny that you expected, in your official position, to have any more influence with him than the argument that you should make to him would have?—A. Yes; I did not expect it.

Q. What arguments did you make to him in relation to submarine torpedo boats?—A. Simply that I had been requested by a personal friend.

Q. There is no argument in that.—A. There was no argument at all. I just told him my little story and that is all there is of it. Then he told me the history of the whole thing, and I said: "Mr. Lessler, I am sorry I came, and I shall go back to New York and tell my friends exactly what you said." I see by his testimony here that he refers to an expression that came over my face when he referred to the situation, that is the situation he told me existed.

By Mr. ROBERTS:

Q. I should like to ask you a question or two concerning Philip Doblin, who has been a witness here, and who has testified that he was deputy inspector of elections?—A. A deputy State superintendent of elections.

Q. Do you know this person?—A. I know him, but my acquaintance with him is very slight. Mr. Doblin is one of those men who are recommended to me by the chairmen of the county committees. I think—I am not sure—that the first time he came into my office Mr. Quigg was the chairman of the county committee, and he recommended him, which

H. Rep. 3482——5

he had to do, as his name was submitted by some district leader. I think he came from some district up on the east side. Mr. Quigg resigned—I don't know whether he resigned or not, but I know that he is not chairman of the county committee—and another chairman submitted his name. He has been employed in the office there. I employ 800 men for forty days. They are all strangers to me. I divide them into squads and detail them. I do not believe I ever spoke to Mr. Doblin more than three or four times in my life.

Q. He is an annual employee?—A. No, sir: there is no such employee in my office except my secretary and chief clerk and chief deputy.

Q. He was a deputy?—A. Yes, sir; a deputy.

Q. Was he employed in your department from the 1st of last November until the 1st day of January?—A. He was.

Q. The forty days have not expired?—A. Yes; the forty days have expired, but the law says that where necessary services may be continued, and Mr. Doblin's services are continued with those of other men. Cases are to be prosecuted in court. I have subpœnas to issue and investigations to make to carry out the work of the office.

Q. What compensation does Mr. Doblin get?—A. Five dollars a day.

Q. Entirely a per diem?—A. Per diem; yes, sir.

Q. Have you ever talked with Mr. Doblin concerning the Holland torpedo boat?—A. I never talked to a human being in my life about that, with the exception of the gentlemen who have spoken to me about it.

By Mr. RIXEY:

Q. Something has been said here about Mr. Obermier. What position does he hold?—A. I do not know the gentleman.

Q. What is his first name?

A MEMBER. Leonard J. Obermier.

Mr. NICOLL. You never heard of him?

The WITNESS. I don't know.

Mr. NICOLL. You never heard of him; you don't know him?

The WITNESS. I employ 800 men, as I told you.

Mr. ROBERTS. He is a lawyer; he is not one of your men.

The WITNESS. I have got lawyers down there, too, gentlemen.

The CHAIRMAN. Are there any further questions?

The WITNESS. There is one thing more, gentlemen, if you will permit me. I see, through the public press, something about Doblin being employed in my office; and about Mr. Quigg; and if you read it, it looks very peculiar. Mr. Quigg is a gentleman whom I have not seen three times in the past three years, and the last time I saw him was at a public dinner and across the table.

The CHAIRMAN. If there are no further questions, the witness is excused.

The WITNESS. This affidavit that has been offered has not been corroborated. If you will give me the privilege of hearing Mr. Hertz and getting this corroboration I will be very much indebted to you.

By Mr. DAYTON:

Q. Is there any reason that the man who made the affidavit should not come here?—A. If you want him he will come here.

Q. He seems to be the gentleman who induced you to make this visit?—A. This is the party who got me to make the visit. The other man simply explained the situation.

(Witness excused.)

The committee thereupon took a recess until 2 o'clock.

The committee met, pursuant to adjournment, at 2.15 p. m.

TESTIMONY OF HON. LEMUEL E. QUIGG (SWORN).

By Mr. TAYLER:

Q. Mr. Quigg, you live in New York?—A. Yes, sir.

Q. How long have you lived there?—A. I have lived there eighteen or twenty years.

Q. What is your business?—A. I am just now a student of law, very diligently, and hope to be admitted in the course of a few weeks. I have not yet taken my bar examination. My business formerly was that of a newspaper man.

Q. What official positions in the Republican party have you held in New York?—A. I have held in the party organization the office of president of the county committee and a member of the State committee.

Q. How long have you held official positions in the party organization?—A. I am not now——

Q. I understand.

A. (Continuing.) In any other official position than that of a member of the State committee and a member of the county committee.

Q. How long were you president of the county organization?—A. I think for nearly three years.

Q. And when did you become an incumbent of that position?—A. I should say that it was in 1897.

Q. And when did you leave?—A. I should say it was in 1900 or 1901.

Q. Were you succeeded by Mr. Morris immediately afterwards?—A. I was succeeded by General Greene, and General Greene was succeeded by Mr. Morris.

Q. And your profession has been that of a newspaper man?—A. Yes, sir.

Q. You were elected to Congress when?—A. I was elected to the Fifty-third Congress at a special election held in January, 1894.

Q. And served how long?—A. I served in three Congresses.

Q. Through the Fifty-fifth Congress?—A. Through the Fifty-fifth Congress.

Q. You have known Mr. Lessler how long?—A. I should say for eight or ten years, perhaps.

Q. He has been active in politics, has he not?—A. (Continuing) Or perhaps not so long.

Q. He has been active in politics there, has he, somewhat?—A. He has always certainly been interested in politics.

Q. Has your acquaintance with him been intimate or otherwise?—A. It has not been intimate. It has been what I should call cordial.

Q. You know Philip Doblin?—A. I know Doblin.

Q. How long have you known him?—A. I suppose about the same length of time.

Q. How did you come to know him?—A. Really, I don't know.

Q. I don't mean the specific origin of it, but what was the character of the acquaintance, and how did it originate?—A. Doblin is what is more or less accurately described as a district worker.

Q. Yes.—A. And I have known of him as such.

Mr. KITCHIN. A district what?

The WITNESS. Worker.

Mr. KITCHIN. A worker?

The WITNESS. Yes, sir. He is an active little fellow around the polls, and in the organization, and in the district organization, and I have known of him as of thousands of others.

By Mr. TAYLER:

Q. You have had no intimate acquaintance with him?—A. Oh, no.

Q. Now, Mr. Quigg, you have heard the account given by Mr. Doblin?—A. Yes, sir.

Q. Of a transaction which he claims to have had with you respecting Mr. Lessler's vote on the Roberts bill to buy submarine torpedo boats?—A. Yes, sir.

Q. I think it would be fair to you and more satisfactory to the committee if you would proceed in your own way to tell what you have to say of that transaction with Mr. Doblin.—A. I thank you, Mr. Tayler; I should prefer to do it that way.

On, I am pretty sure, the 9th of December last I called at the Waldorf-Astoria Hotel and sent my card to Senator Hanna. The object of my visit was to ask the Senator to be present at a dinner—at a public dinner which was to be held and has since been held. I locate the day—I remember the day—by reason of the circumstance that the Senator was not in. He was in attendance upon the Civic Federation. And I sent a letter to him, asking when I might see him; sent it there, and I have since looked up the date of that letter and find that it was December 9; so that I am pretty sure that it was that morning I called at the hotel. While I was waiting for the return of the card, or at about the time when it returned, I saw—encountered—Dr. Kerr, of Chicago, who was standing or passing. He accosted me. I had known him as a partner of Mr. Milholland in his pneumatic-tube enterprise.

Mr. DAYTON. A partner of whom?

The WITNESS. His name is Kerr.

Mr. TAYLER. A partner of Mr. Milholland.

A. (Continuing.) And when I knew him he was a partner of Mr. Milholland in the pneumatic-tube enterprise. I do not know whether he is now or not. I do not know anything about it.

Dr. Kerr asked me if I knew Congressman Lessler, and I said I did. He said, "I wonder if you would be willing to do a favor for me in speaking with Mr. Lessler." I said, "About what?" He said, "About the Holland torpedo boat." I said, "Are you interested in that?" He said, "Yes; I am." I said, "Well, I don't know anything about the Holland torpedo boat." He said, "Well, you know sufficiently what it is; you know it is a diving boat." I said "Certainly, I know that." He said, "Are you opposed to it in any way?" I said, "Not at all." "Well," he said, "I wish very much you would speak with Mr. Lessler." I said, "What is the matter with Lessler?" "Well," he said, "he is not only opposing it, but he is opposing it in a very personal and bitter and vindictive way. The character of his opposition has been violent and noisy. Now," he says, "I don't suppose that you can do much with him in any way, but if you could cool him off a little"—I remember that expression—"it would be about all that I should suppose you could do." "Well," I said, "if I get a chance to speak with him I will. I do not often run across him." He said, "Will you not take the trouble to see him?" "Well," I said, "Kerr, I might go to see him; yes. It is a good deal of a nuisance to do that sort of thing, and I can not make much of an argument for the Holland torpedo boat, because I do not know much about it." "Well," he said, "I do not expect you to do so, but if you would ask him not to be so violent and pestiferous in his opposition, that is all I want you to do." I said, "All right, if I get a chance to see him, I will do it;" and with that we parted, and of course I forgot it. Not that I intended to. I should have spoken to Lessler agreeably to the promise, if I had run across him, but I forgot it.

It was two or three days later that Dr. Kerr called me on the telephone, and asked me if I had seen Mr. Lessler, and I told him that I had not. He said, "Will you not please try to see him?" He says, "That matter is coming up now, and I wish very much you would ask him not to be bitter and vindictive about it." I said "All right, Kerr; if you want me to do it, I will go and see him;" and I did call Lessler on the telephone, and found that he was not in; and I forgot it again.

I did not feel myself heavily charged with it, to tell the truth. It was as much as a week later than that that Dr. Kerr called me again on the telephone, and I said that I had not seen him; that I supposed that he was down in Congress. "Well," he said, "doesn't he come home the end of the week?" I said I thought likely he did, and I would try to see him this week; and again I had my office call him up. My office connected me with Lessler's office, and somebody told me that Lessler was with Doblin, and that if I could locate Doblin I would find him; that he was not in the office, but that he was with Doblin. So I told my office to call around where they could, and see if they could find Doblin. I don't know what was done; I got no report about it; but the next day, or perhaps the day after, I should say the next day—and now we must come down to about ten or twelve days after I met Kerr—Doblin came into the office, and I should say it was the day after I had made these telephone inquiries for his whereabouts.

By Mr. TAYLER:

Q. Now, if that was on a Saturday, it would be the 20th, would it not; and if on a Friday, it would be the 19th?—A. I should say it was around——

Q. That is, if your first interview with Kerr was on the 9th?—A. Yes, sir.

Q. And this meeting with Doblin was on Friday or Saturday; so that it would be either the 19th or 20th?—A. Yes, sir. Well, I would come very close to taking my oath that it was on the 9th.

Q. That is, the first?—A. I have only been guided by the fact that it may have been on one of those days. But the letter that I wrote Senator Hanna was the 9th.

Q. Yes.—A. (Continuing.) Doblin came into the office and said that he wanted to see me, and said—no, he said I wanted to see him, and said, "You sent for me." To tell you the truth, for the moment it slipped my mind what I wanted to see him about. I had my overcoat on and my hat and was leaving the office, and I said, "Yes." I said, "Come along," and I started out, thinking up what it was I wanted to see him about.

On the way to the elevator he said, "Mr. Quigg, won't you ask Captain McCullagh to keep me in his office?" He said, "He can do that, and I think he would do it if you would ask him." And he said, "I asked you about that some time ago." He mentioned some other occasion on which he had asked me about it. I said, "Doblin, I can not do that sort of thing any longer. My time is out for that kind of work." I said, "Mr. Morris, you know, makes all those designations, and I do not want to interfere with him in any way, and I have no idea that any request that I would address to McCullagh on the subject would amount to anything, and I do not want to make the request, and I would rather you would not bother me with it. You must get somebody else to do it." He said, "I haven't any influence with Morris, and the only man I know is Congressman Lessler who could do it for me, and Lessler's relations with McCullagh are not good." And that brought the whole thing into my mind, and that was the first time that I remembered what I wanted Doblin for. I said, "What is the matter between McCullagh and Lessler?" He said, "It is about the Holland torpedo boat." And I said, "What is that about?" That, of course, interested me as a coincidence. I said, "What is that about?" "Well," he said, "McCullagh went down to Washington and threatened Lessler that he would beat him unless Lessler voted for that." I said, "Oh, nonsense." "Oh, yes: he did," he said.

By that time we had arrived at the place where I usually go to take luncheon, which is a few steps from my office, and we were standing in the door of it, and I said, "Well, tell me about that; tell me all about it." "Well," he said, "McCullagh went down to Washington and insisted that Lessler should vote for the Holland bill, and they got very excited and had a very disagreeable interview, and McCullagh told him that he would beat him." "Well," I said, "I don't believe that of McCullagh. That is not the way McCullagh does." I said, "Have you had luncheon?" He said, "No." I said, "Come in and get a bite with me;" and we went into the restaurant. It is a little restaurant. There are three or four—four or five—two or three rooms, half the size of this. It is cut up a little; some ten or twelve tables in each of them—two, I think—two rooms. And we sat down at one of the tables, and I ordered some single dish; I don't know what it was. He ordered something; I don't recollect that, either. I said, "Now, that is funny, Doblin; it is about the Holland torpedo boat that I wanted to speak with Lessler." And I said, "Is he very positively opposed to it?" "Oh," he said, "he is bitterly opposed to it." He said, "I don't know but what he would support it if you asked him to." "Well," I said, "I really do not want to ask him to support it. I do not know enough about it to ask him to support it. I have promised a man that I will see him about it and ask him to simmer down a little in the violence of his opposition, but I have never studied anything about the Holland torpedo boat, and I do not know as I want to ask him to support it. But my friend has pestered me about it a little, and he is a man I would like to oblige, and I suppose that I must go to see him. So I called him up yesterday, and they said he was with you." "Oh, no," he said, "he was in Washington, and he is in Washington yet, and he will probably be home the end of the week."

Now, it could not have been a Saturday, because his statement was that he would be home probably the end of the week, and he hardly would have used that language on that day.

"Well," I said, "I wish you would let me know when he comes home. Ask him to call me up on the telephone, or you call me." He said, "I will."

I then introduced political subjects, asked him about the little gossip in the district, and the rest of the meal was occupied with that. It was not long; only a few minutes. And at the end of it I said again, "Now, as soon as Lessler comes to town I wish you would call me up and let me know, because I want to keep this agreement to go to see him."

It was all of a week after that before I heard from Doblin. It was not the next day, as he says. I have told you all the conversations, substantially, about the Holland torpedo boat. There was no mention

of money or anything else. I did not ask Lessler to vote for it, or anything of that kind. It was all of a week after that talk with Doblin
that Doblin came into the office and told me that Lessler was in his
office and would see me if I wanted to go over there.

By Mr. TAYLER:

Q. That is, in his, Lessler's, office?—A. In his, Lessler's, office. But
he says, "He is pretty hot about this Holland torpedo boat, and I do
not believe he will support it." I did not pay any attention to that,
because it did not make any difference to me whether he did support
it. I called—I told my people to get Lessler, and they did so, on the
telephone. I wanted to see to it that he had not gone out, and they
got him, and he said yes, that he was there, and would be glad to see
me; and I said, "By the way, what has been done about the post office
at Stapleton?"

Q. You said this to Lessler at his office or at the telephone?—A. No,
sir; over the telephone. I said, "There is a friend of mine who is very
much interested in a Miss McRoberts, a daughter of Hugh McRoberts."
Hugh McRoberts was the old leader of an old district which is in Mr.
Lessler's Congressional district, and he had died, and a Catholic clergy-
man in New York had asked me to speak to Mr. Lessler in the interest
of Miss McRoberts's reappointment. I said, "What have you done
about that?" "Oh," he says, "she is reappointed." And I said, "I am
very glad about that." And I said, "I will be over presently;" and he
said, "All right."

I went over, and as soon as I went in I said, "I am awful glad that
you have seen your way clear to reappoint Miss McRoberts, because
her father was a very dear friend of mine and a good man." He said,
"Yes, he was;" and he said, "That has been all settled." I then said,
"Lessler, I have called here to talk to you about the Holland torpedo
boat." I said, "I do not know much about the Holland torpedo boat,
but a friend of mine, whom I should like to oblige, has told me that
your opposition to it is very ugly and malignant and that you have
said all manner of nasty and disagreeable things about the enterprise
of the people, and he wanted to see if I could not prevail on you not to
be so stiff about the thing." I said, "What is the matter with it?"
Lessler smiled and said that he had been very much opposed to it, and
entered upon a long and detailed description of the Holland torpedo
boat; I mean a description of its mechanism; and he showed why, in
his opinion, it was not a success and why, in his opinion, it would
never be, and gave what seemed to me, if he had the facts, pretty con-
vincing reasons why he was opposed to it and why he should be. I
listened to them.

He talked, I should say, ten or fifteen minutes to explain to me the
merits or the demerits of the boat. Well, I said that was all right, and
that was a good reason for being opposed to the boat; but what was the
use of making so much fuss about it, so much—if it was a fact that he
had been so bitter? "Well," he said, "they are the worst lot down
there." He says, "They are a set of rascals through and through." He
says, "You have got no idea of the abominable methods to which those
people have resorted." He said, "They maintain the most unscrupulous
lobby in Washington, and it is as much as anybody's reputation is
worth to have anything to do with them." Well, I said that I did not
suppose there was much in that; that naturally no individual was going
to buy plunging boats; that it was not an enterprise for a private individual, and that whatever was done to develop that idea of naval

architecture would have to be done by the Government, of course, and that it seemed to me a very legitimate subject of Government investigation and experiment, and that naturally, as the Government was the one customer of the company projecting and developing such a boat, it was not remarkable that they should have agents and that they should seek to interest members in the matter, and that I should not be offended if anybody came and talked to me about the torpedo boat, if I was a member.

I said, "There has not anybody attempted to bribe you, have they?" He said, "No, nobody has attempted to bribe me; but," he says, "they are down there and all around." "Well." I said, "I would not pay much attention to that. It is very natural that they should be down there and all around, and it is very natural that they should come here to you to talk over the thing and very natural that they should send their friends to you, and there is no ground for offense about that." I said, "As for what you have said about the boat, I dare say that that is conclusive. It would be on my mind, if the facts are as you state them; and," I said, "it puts me in the position where I have not got any request to make of you whatever, unless the request that you do not get so excited about it." He said, "Well, of course I shall have to oppose it;" he said, "the Navy Department is opposed to it." I said, "How is Mr. Foss on the subject?" "Well," he said, "he is opposed to it." "Well," I said, "of course, if the Secretary and your chairman are both opposed to it, that is some reason why you, a young man, a young member, just in the House, should look at it pretty seriously;" and I said, "I have not any fault to find with that, but do not get so excited and ill-tempered about it, and do not talk about this lobby business, because it seems to me very silly." Well, he said that he would go on opposing it, and I said that was all right, and I got up and went on out.

It was some while after that—now, how long I do not know, because the matter dropped from my mind at that point, and I had discharged my errand, and the thing was out of my mind—that Doblin came into my office and said he thought that if I would go to see Mr. Lessler again I could get him to vote for that bill. I said "I do not want Lessler to vote for it. I have not any interest in it. I certainly should not go to see him again;" and I said that I had not asked him to vote for it. Mr. Doblin then talked to me—oh, Doblin then said, "A funny thing," he said, "last night"—I am quite sure he said "last night," so that that would locate this conversation—he said, "last night I was in the Waldorf Astoria with George Cromwell, and we met Mr. Frost." I said, "Who is Frost?" He said, "He is the attorney for the Holland torpedo boat." I said, "What have you been doing with Frost?" He said, "Oh, nothing at all. I just saw him there." I know Mr. Cromwell very well. He is a man of the highest character, and I said, "Was Cromwell there with you when you were there with Frost?" He said, "Yes." I said, "All the time?" Says he, "Yes." I said nothing more, because I knew Mr. Cromwell. And then he began to ask me again if I would not see Mr. McCullagh for him, and I said no.

Mr. VANDIVER. Mr. McCullagh?

The WITNESS. Yes, sir; Mr. McCullagh. About keeping him in office.

Mr. VANDIVER. Oh, yes.

A. (Continuing.) I said no, I would not. Some days later than that, I can, or should say about a week or ten days ago, Mr. Obermier, a young attorney in New York, and Doblin, came to the office again. They said—Doblin said—that Obermier was going over to Washington, and that he was a great friend of Lessler's and that he would speak to Lessler about the torpedo boat if I wanted him to, and he believed Obermier could get Lessler to vote for it. I said to Obermier, "Well, Mr. Obermier, I don't know as I want you to do anything about that." I said: "I spoke to Mr. Lessler about it, and he did not want to do it, and I do not ever give a man a chance to deny a request of mine twice." "Well," he said, "Mr. Quigg, I should like very much to oblige you, and if it would be a matter of interest to you I should speak to him about it with great pleasure." "Well," I said, "speak to him. I have already informed the party who spoke to me that Mr. Lessler would oppose the bill, and I was afraid would oppose it just as bitterly as ever, but if you should succeed in making any impression on his mind let me know," and he said that he certainly would.

And that is the last I know or have heard of the Holland torpedo boat until I saw Mr. Lessler's explosion in the newspapers. At first I did not suppose that it related to me. It said something about a bribe having been offered to his secretary or clerk by an ex-Representative, and I read it, but did not think of myself. I did not know Doblin as his secretary, and I paid no attention to it until I saw the next day's paper, when I sent a telegram to Mr. Foss asking him to hear this testimony.

Now, gentlemen, I am at your disposition.

By Mr. TAYLER:

Q. You heard Mr. Lessler's statement as to a remark that he made early in the interview that you had with him?—A. Yes, sir.

Q. Touching money?—A. Yes, sir; he made no such statement early or late, no such statement at all.

Q. There was no reference, direct or indirect, to any money involved in the proposition?—A. No, sir; not the slightest.

Q. To induce his influence for or against this?—A. No, sir; not the slightest, at all. He talked about this lobby influence, you know, and I told him that it was silly—silly talk.

Q. And in your conversations with Doblin there was no mention of money by him or by you?—A. Of course not.

Q. Either one of you?—A. No, sir; nor any request of Doblin whatever except that he should let me know when Lessler came back.

Q. Did you think it strange that Doblin should return to you on his third visit with Mr. Obermier, after you had so distinctly stated that your hands were off of it?—A. I did not; no. Doblin is—I should explain. He wanted me to speak to Mr. McCullagh. I had recommended him in connection with others for appointment, to McCullagh, and he wanted me to do it again. No; the only thing that attracted my attention was his remark about having seen Frost. That did strike me, but his return and coming back a second time did not impress me one way or the other.

Q. Nothing further occurs to you to state in this connection?—A. There is nothing further, so far as I recollect.

Mr. WHEELER. Mr. Chairman, I desire to question Mr. Quigg.

Mr. NICOLL. There are perhaps one or two omissions in looking over this record, which I will wish to supply by questioning him. I am not going to cross-examine him, but I do not wish to interfere with you, Mr. Wheeler.

Mr. WHEELER. You can take those up when I get through.

Mr. NICOLL. All right, Mr. Wheeler.

By Mr. WHEELER:

Q. What business are you engaged in now?—A. I am engaged in preparing myself for the bar, Mr. Wheeler, more than anything else.

Q. How long have you had an office?—A. I have had an office—well, substantially since I withdrew from Congress; that is four years ago; nearly four years ago.

Q. What is that?—A. That is nearly four years ago; and I do work in that office.

Q. What business do you conduct in that office?—A. I do a great deal of law business in that office, a great deal. Mr. McEverly is a practicing attorney.

Q. This young gentleman over here [indicating a gentleman in the committee room]?—A. Yes, sir.

Q. He is in your office?—A. He is in my office; and he and I have the office.

Q. You keep a corps of clerks there, do you?—A. No, sir; I keep a boy.

Q. Keep a boy?—A. A stenographer.

Q. Are you not the legislative agent of some corporation in New York?—A. I am not, sir.

Q. Have you never been?—A. I never have been.

Q. How much of your time have you spent in the last two or three years about the New York general assembly when it was in session, Mr. Quigg?—A. I never have spent any time there.

Q. Never have been in Albany when the general assembly was in session?—A. Oh, yes; when I was the president of the county committee.

Q. Eliminate politics from it.—A. Eliminating politics——

Q. From the equation.—A. Eliminating politics, I never have been there except——

Q. You never represented the New York street railroad corporations before the New York general assembly?—A. Oh, no; oh, no.

Q. Yes.—A. I never have been to Albany in connection with legislation other than political, and never in connection with political since I retired from the presidency of the county committee.

Q. Or before the general council of the city of New York, or whatever you are pleased to term your municipal body there, have you appeared as a legislative agent?—A. No, sir.

Q. For those people there?—A. Certainly not.

Q. Do you state, Mr. Quigg, that you have not—I put it in as rude a form as is possible—— A. Put it as you like, sir.

Q. (Continuing.) That you have not been acting as a lobbyist for New York corporations for the last three or four years?—A. I never did such a thing in my life.

Q. Not now, and never have been?—A. No, sir; not now, and never have been.

Q. Will you please tell us the full name of this Dr. Kerr?—A. I think his name is Dr. William R. Kerr.

Q. And his address is what?—A. He is now stopping at the New Willard.

Q. He is in the city?—A. He is in the city of Washington. I saw him last night.

Q. Do you know how he came to be here at this particular time?—A. No, sir; I do not.

Q. Did he come at your request?—A. No, sir; he did not come at my request.

Q. Did you know that he was coming?—A. No, sir.

Q. Do you know when he got here?—A. No, sir.

Q. Did you know Mr. Frost before Mr. Doblin mentioned his name?—A. No, sir; I never saw Mr. Frost to know him. He has an office in my building, I understand. I will not say that I do not know him, but I never have identified a face with the name of Frost.

Q. Did you know who he was before Mr. Doblin told you?—A. No; I did not.

Q. What excited your suspicions, then, when Mr. Doblin told you that he had been with Mr. Frost?—A. Did I know who Frost was?

Q. Yes.—A. I knew Mr. Frost was an attorney in my building, and I knew that he was identified with the Holland boat.

Q. Before Mr. Doblin spoke to you?—A. Oh, yes.

Q. You knew that he was identified with it. Had anyone ever told you—who told you that?—A. I don't know. The Holland boat is in my building.

Q. What floor; the same floor with you?—A. The same floor with me. No, no; I had an office on one floor; and Mr. Frost and, I think, the Holland boat were on the same floor.

Q. Had you ever been in Mr. Frost's office?—A. I do not think I ever had been there.

Q. How did you know his office was on that floor?—A. Because that is my floor—it was my floor.

Q You had been on the same floor with him?—A. Yes, sir.

Q. What excited your suspicion when Mr. Doblin mentioned the name of Mr. Frost?—A. The fact that I knew Mr Frost was identified with the Holland boat.

Q. Well, what excited your suspicion? You indicated, Mr. Quigg——A. Yes; my suspicions were aroused.

Q. What aroused your suspicions?—A. Simply the circumstance that Mr. Doblin mentioned his having met Mr. Frost, and I could not see why Doblin should have met Frost. It did not strike me that Frost was the kind of a person that Doblin would be likely to meet.

Q. What is wrong with Doblin?—A. The only thing that I know is wrong with Doblin is what he has stated here to day.

Q. Up to that time you regarded him as quite an honorable young fellow, did you not?—A. I knew nothing against him.

Q. You seemed to have—— A. I had no impression against him.

Q. I understand—a very nondescript idea as to his position; but you seemed to indicate that you had some sort of a sinister idea from that impression?—A. I don't want to go as far as that. It just struck my mind, that is all.

Q. There was nothing in his conduct to lead you to believe that there had been any questionable connection between the two?—A. No, no.

Q. Now, you say that the only connection you ever had with the Holland torpedo-boat people grew out of the request preferred by one Kerr to you on the street, when you were returning from a call on Senator Hanna?—A. No; in the hotel.

Q. In the hotel, when you were returning from a call on Senator Hanna?—A. Yes, sir.

Q. How long had you known Dr. Kerr?—A. I have known Kerr, I suppose, five or six years.

Q. How intimately?—A. Not intimately.

Q. You say that you knew him in connection with the pneumatic-tube service?—A. Yes, sir.

Q. You refer to the same pneumatic-tube service that acquired a malodorous notoriety in Congress here two years ago?—A. I shall not adopt your language. I knew him in connection with the pneumatic tube.

Q. That is the same pneumatic tube that the present Secretary of the Navy made some sort of a charge on the floor of the House concerning?—A. It is the pneumatic tube. I do not know that he made a charge.

Q. Made some statement about; well, I will put it that way.—A. Yes, sir.

Q. Did you have any conversation with Dr. Kerr on the subject of the pneumatic-tube business?—A. Never did.

Q. Did you ever confer with him about any legislative matters before this time you refer to?—A. No.

Q. How many times had you seen him prior to that time?—A. Mr. Milholland was a very warm personal friend of mine; we were colleagues together on the New York Tribune, and I interested myself for the pneumatic tube when Mr. Milholland was first pressing it, very warmly, and in that way I saw Dr. Kerr. I never had any conferences with him.

Q. You saw him quite frequently?—A. Although I will not say that he was not present when I talked with Mr. Milholland a great many times, he seemed to be with Mr. Milholland most of the time.

Q. Was your acquaintance with him sufficiently intimate. do you think, to justify him in preferring the request that he did?—A. No; I do not think it was.

Q. You do not think so?—A. No; I do not think it was.

Q. And he called you up once or twice after that, and requested it?—A. Yes; he pestered me about it until I said I would go and see Lessler.

Q. Had you ever called on Lessler to perform any political service for you, or any service of any character?—A. I do not recall that I had.

Q. And you state to the committee that the testimony of this man Doblin, so far as it relates to the offer on your part of a moneyed consideration for the change of Lessler's vote, is an absolute falsehood?—A. An absolute falsehood.

Q. Not a word of truth whatever in it?—A. Not the first scintilla of truth.

Q. And you say the statement of Mr. Lessler, so far as his declaration is concerned that in his conversation with you he greeted you with the expression that money had no attraction to him, is an unfounded statement?—A. Is a lie; yes, sir.

Q. Is a lie?—A. Yes, sir.

Q. And you have narrated the circumstances just as they occurred?—A. Exactly. The first part of the conversation with Lessler was about Miss McRoberts, that postmistress; and it was I who introduced the subject of the Holland boat. It occurred just that way.

Q. You have no interest in this Holland boat?—A. No, sir; not the slightest.

Q. No stock in it?—A. No.

Q. Didn't know any of the attorneys?—A. No, sir. Another thing: I never said anything about Mr. Hunton, and I mentioned no name whatever.

Q. That goes without saying.—A. I do not know General Hunton, and never saw him before.

Q. Nor Major Hunter, here in Washington?—A. I don't know who he is.

By Mr. RIXEY:

Q. You did not say that it was for a friend in Virginia?—A. Not at all. I did not say who it was, except that it was for a person whom I would like to oblige.

Q. I would like to ask you—Mr. Doblin stated that you indicated to him that it was your desire that he should secure Mr. Lessler's advocacy of these boats, and stated that there was $5,000 in it, and something was said as to what he should get, and that you said you would let him know later, and that he called you up about 3 o'clock over the phone?—A. There is absolutely no truth in that.

Q. There is no truth in his statement that he called you up over the phone?—A. Absolutely none. He never called me up on the phone, and never said he did, and never made any such request. And the only thing I ever asked Doblin in connection with the matter was that he would let me know when Mr. Lessler was in town and I would come to see him.

By Mr. ROBERTS:

Q. I would like to ask Mr. Quigg if in any of his conversations with Mr. Doblin he referred to a Roberts bill for the Holland submarine boat which was pending in Congress?—A. Whether I did, or whether he did?

Q. Whether you referred to it?—A. No, sir; I did not know there was a Roberts bill.

Q. Did Doblin use the expression, in your presence, at any time, that there was a Roberts bill pending?—A. I don't know; I don't think so. Mr. Doblin apparently did not know anything more about it than that there was a great deal—that there was Holland torpedo-boat legislation.

Mr. DAYTON. By the by, Mr. Roberts, did you not introduce a bill at the end of the last session?

Mr. ROBERTS. I don't think so; I am sure I did not. The proposition we had last year came from the Senate.

Mr. DAYTON. I thought that you introduced a bill with two or three others.

Mr. ROBERTS. No, sir. Mr. Cummings introduced a bill, but I am sure that I did not.

By Mr. DAYTON:

Q. Mr. Quigg, do you know Mr. Rice, the president of this Holland Torpedo Boat Company?—A. No, sir; I do not.

Q. In your conversation with Mr. Lessler, was Mr. Rice's name mentioned?—A. Yes, sir.

Q. Now, tell us what was said about Mr. Rice.—A. In connection with my statement that I had come to see him in behalf of a friend whom I should like to oblige, I said that he was not Mr. Rice nor Mr. Frost. Now, whether that was drawn out by something that Mr. Lessler said about Frost or Rice, I do not know, but the fact is that I made that statement, that it was neither of them on whose behalf I had come to him.

Q. Did you say anything about your having any difficulty with Mr. Rice?—A. With Mr. Rice? No.

Q. You don't know Mr. Rice?—A. I never met Mr. Rice. I don't know that I ever saw him.

Q. Would you know him to day?—A. No, sir. Of course, Mr. Rice and Mr. Frost have been coming up in the same elevator that I have been on for some time, and I may have seen them, but I never have identified either of them with their names.

Q. In that conversation you did not say anything about having had some difficulty heretofore with Mr. Rice?—A. No, sir.

Q. Had Mr. Rice been in any trouble there in New York City?—A. Not that I know of. I do not know anything about Mr. Rice's affairs.

By Mr. NICOLL:

Q. You never have been introduced to Mr. Rice, have you?—A. No, sir; I never have seen him.

Q. Or to Mr. Frost?—A. No, sir.

Q. Now, I want to ask you whether you have now, or ever have had, directly or indirectly, any interest of a pecuniary nature in the Holland torpedo boat?—A. I never have had, and have not now.

Q. Or in the Holland Torpedo Boat Company, or the Electric Boat Company?—A. Or in anything relating to the subject. It is as remote from me as the North Pole. I do not know anything about it.

Q. Now, had you any talk with your friend, Dr. Kerr, about money in connection with the Holland torpedo boat?—A. Of course not.

Q. Not a word?—A. Not a word.

Q. Did Dr. Kerr explain to you what interest he had in the matter?—A. No, sir; he said that he was interested in it.

Q. Said that he was interested in it?—A. He said he was interested.

Q. But what the nature of his interest was—— A. He did not say.

Q. He did not indicate?—A. He did not state.

Q. Has he since indicated to you what the nature of his interest was?—A. He has told me that it was not a financial interest.

Q. That he had no financial interest in the company?—A. No, sir.

By Mr. DAYTON:

Q. I suggest that that is mere hearsay. We will have the gentleman on the stand if you want to prove that he has no interest.

Mr. NICOLL. I do not want to prove anything.

Mr. DAYTON. I would like to have somebody representing this company explain who their stockholders are and what their interests are in this country.

Mr. ROBERTS. That has no bearing on this investigation.

Mr. NICOLL. I told Mr. McEverly to tell Dr. Kerr that perhaps you might call him. My understanding is that he is a friend of Mr. Frost's and was trying to help him along and that he had no interest whatever. You can get his attendance. He is right here and ready to come any time, so he said.

By Mr. NICOLL:

Q. Now, did you hear the testimony of Mr. Lessler, at page 3 of the record?

Q. Tell us what occurred.—A. I started right in in that way—that there must not be any question of money.

Q. What reply did he make?—A. He stood silent; did not say anything.

A. There was no such statement or situation, or anything that resembled it.

Q. Did you hear the statement this morning of Mr. Doblin, that while sitting at lunch in the restaurant you said to him, "There is $5,000 in it?"—A. I heard the statement.

Q. Did you ever make such a statement to Mr. Doblin?—A. No.

Q. Did you ever make a statement to Mr. Doblin that there was $5,000 in it for Lessler, or for anyone?—A. Oh, no.

Q. Or that there was any money in it?—A. No.

Q. For anyone?—A. No.

Q. Did you hear the statement of Mr. Doblin that after that statement you went on to say, "I have forgotten you, but I will see if I can not make it a thousand for you?"—A. I heard it.

Q. Was that statement true?—A. It was not true.

Q. Did you make that statement to Mr. Doblin?—A. I never made any statement to Mr. Doblin. I never made that statement to Mr. Doblin.

Q. Or a statement that you would try and see that there was something in it for him?—A. No, sir; nothing of that kind.

Q. Or anything of the kind?—A. Oh, no; nothing of the sort.

Q. Did you ever hear the statement of Mr. Doblin that on that afternoon at 3.30 o'clock he called you up on the telephone?—A. I heard the statement.

Q. And that you said to him that that would be all right, meaning the thousand dollars for him?—A. I heard the statement.

Q. Did you ever make any such statement to him?—A. I never made any such statement at all.

Q. Did he call you up on the telephone?—A. He did not call me up on the telephone, nor did I hear from him after the time when I told him that I would like him to locate Mr. Lessler until about a week after.

Q. Did you ever directly or indirectly, either by expressed words or in suggestion, ever authorize Mr. Doblin or suggest to Mr. Doblin that he should make a corrupt proposition to Mr. Lessler to influence his action in regard to the Holland submarine boat?—A. I never did; or any other proposition whatever to Mr. Lessler, corrupt or otherwise.

By Mr. DAYTON:

Q. Do you know Mr. Obermier's city address in New York?—A. I do not, sir.

Mr. KITCHIN. You know his city address, do you not, Mr. Lessler?

Mr. LESSLER. It has been given here.

By Mr. VANDIVER:

Q. Mr. Quigg, you have stated very explicitly that you made no proposition for a specific sum of money to Mr. Doblin or Mr. Lessler. Let me ask you if you in any way suggested to him the idea that there might be an advantage to him in supporting this proposition?—A. I should like to make the most sweeping as well as the most particular denial of that statement, that I ever said anything to Mr. Doblin in Mr. Lessler's interest, or to Mr. Lessler in his own, or in Mr. Doblin's, or to either of them, in respect of any money or other advantage that would come to both or either from doing anything in connection with the matter. And when I saw Mr. Lessler I concluded my conversation by saying to him that I had no request whatever to make of him, as I think he has stated, substantially.

Q. Now, in your conversation with Mr. Lessler, you spoke a while ago of part of the conversation being on politics—the gossip of the district.—A. That was with Doblin.

Q. Your conversation with Doblin, I mean.—A. Yes, sir.

Q. Now, in connection with that part of your conversation, did you in any way intimate to him that the political situation in the district would be influenced by his action in this matter?—A. No, sir; he could not influence the situation in any way.

Q. Please speak louder.—A. No, sir; he could not influence the situation in his district. There was nothing that he could do.

By Mr. RIXEY:

Q. Is it not rather a question of getting others to influence the situation in his district?—A. I see. Your question was: Did I suggest that the political situation would be influenced by his complaisance?

Mr. VANDIVER. Yes, sir.

A. Oh, no.

By Mr. RIXEY:

Q. Did you state that you had quite a lengthy conversation with Mr. Lessler in regard to these boats?—A. Yes, sir.

Q. In that conversation did Mr. Lessler refer to the visit which had been made to him by Mr. McCullagh?—A. No, he did not.

Q. Did you ever have any talk with Mr. Lessler as to Mr. McCullagh's visit to him, and what passed?—A. No, sir; no, sir.

By Mr. VANDIVER:

Q. One other question. You heard the statement of Mr. McCullagh in regard to Mr. Lessler's remarks about the lobby and the surroundings here, and the integrity of the committee. In your conversation with Mr. Lessler you referred also to his remarks along the same line, as to the lobby?—A. Yes, sir.

Q. Did he, in his conversation with you, say anything of the same nature that Mr. McCullagh quoted?—A. Yes. The only thing he said to me was this: That on the subject of the Holland torpedo boat this committee would be divided into honest men and knaves, and that he could not be——

Q. This committee would be divided into honest men and knaves?—A. (Continuing.) Yes; and that he could not be in the wrong crowd. He made that statement. He talked generally and very violently about the lobbying methods to which he said the company was resorting.

Q. There is one other question, also. You referred to the fact that subsequent to that conversation with Mr. Lessler his friend, Mr. Doblin, visited your office again and urged you to see Mr. Lessler again.—A. Yes; to go and see him.

Q. Was it once or twice that he visited you after your conversation with Mr. Lessler?—A. It was once by himself and once with Obermier.

Q. Twice, altogether?—A. Yes, sir.

Q. And in both instances he suggested your seeing Mr. Lessler again?—A. No; in the first instance he suggested my seeing Mr. Lessler, and the second visit was ostensibly, so far as words went, for the purpose of having me say to Mr. Obermier that I would like Mr. Obermier to see Mr. Lessler.

Q. To see Mr. Lessler?—A. Yes, sir.

Q. Let me ask you; I don't know whether it is a legitimate question, strictly speaking, or not. If it is, I would like an answer, but if it is not, you can decline. What was your inference from the fact that Mr. Doblin, being a special friend of Mr. Lessler's, should convey to you the idea of influencing Mr. Lessler?—A. I did not at that time draw any inference from it. I thought simply that Doblin wanted to be serviceable, and may be a little too serviceable.

Q. A little too serviceable?—A. Yes, sir; a little too active. But I thought it was natural that he should interest himself in anything he thought I wanted, so that it did not leave any impression on my mind. The only thing that struck my mind at that time was his remark about seeing Frost, and even as to that, I dismissed it about as it was said.

By Mr. KITCHIN:

Q. Did Mr. Lessler specify to you what members of the committee he would trust? I believe Mr. McCullagh said he said there was only one member of the committee he would trust.—A. No, sir; he did not.

By Mr. VANDIVER:

Q. Did he specify what members of the committee were knaves?—A. No. I can not identify that gentleman. I shall have to leave him in his isolation.

The CHAIRMAN. Are there any further questions?

The WITNESS. Now, Mr. Chairman, I do not know that I see at this time the motive of Doblin for what he has said here. I do not quite make it out. I do not know whether Doblin has seen anybody in connection with this enterprise, or what he has done. I do not understand it. But I deem it proper to say, not of course as a matter of testimony, that I served in three Congresses with many members of this committee, and I can not believe that any member of this committee will believe what has been said here. I can not believe it.

Mr. DAYTON. I do not quite hear what you say.

The WITNESS. (Continuing.) I said that I can not believe, Mr. Dayton, that any member of this committee, or especially any member who served with me in other Congresses and knows that such an imputation could not have lain against me, and who has never seen me down here at Washington lobbying for anything, or ever seen me here except in the most occasional way, and mostly on occasions of a social character, can believe such terrible statements.

Now, I beg you not to grind me between the millstones of an interest for or against this boat. You gentlemen have formed your minds as to whether this boat is a good thing or whether it is not; whether you want to support it or whether you do not; but I want to beg that each one of you will put yourself in my position—will know that a thousand requests are made of you in this way to do this, that, and the other, and how idly they are made sometimes, and sometimes how idly you consent to them; and then when you have consented and have promised, how you feel that you have got to do it, and how any one of you might find yourself in the position that I am in at this minute. I beg that you will remember that and that you think of it. That is all I have to say, and I am very much obliged to you.

Mr. RIXEY. I would like to state that there is another Virginian here who wants to disclaim any connection with this matter. It is Major Hunter. He has been waiting here all day, and he says his home paper has made some statement, and he wishes to disclaim it. It will not take five minutes.

Mr. ROBERTS. Certainly. If his name has been brought into this in any way, let him be heard.

TESTIMONY OF ROBERT W. HUNTER (SWORN).

By Mr. TAYLER:

Q. Major, did you ever hear of the Holland torpedo boat?—A. Oh, yes.

Q. Have you any interest in that proposition?—None whatever.

Q. Have you any employment in respect to it?—None whatever.

Q. Have you ever undertaken to secure legislation in its interest?—A. None whatever; never.

H. Rep. 3482——6

Q. You have not sought to interest anybody, indirectly or directly, in it?—A. Directly or indirectly; no, sir.

Q. In the proposition to secure legislation in its favor?—A. Never in my life.

Q. Are you acquainted with Mr. Quigg, of New York?—A. I never met Mr. Quigg, of New York, until yesterday morning in the reception room of your committee.

Q. I do not want to offend Mr. Quigg, but did you ever hear of him before?—A. I have heard of him. I have seen his name in the papers and heard of him. Not to have heard of Mr. Quigg would make a man out a very unintelligent man, a man not reading the newspapers.

Q. Well, they have located you so indefinitely—"in Virginia"—that I do not suppose you were ever referred to; but I did not know whether you had ever heard of Mr. Quigg.—A. Yes. I just wanted to say to the committee that I find in the New York Herald and the Washington Post statements of this sort: "General Hunton was called, when it was explained to him that he was called because of the similarity between his name and the name 'Hunter' mentioned by Mr. Lessler."

The Herald says, "A friend of his, Mr. Hunter, of Virginia, was interested in it, and Mr. Quigg wanted to do him a favor."

Now, I do not care what the New York Herald and the Washington Post say, but the Alexandria Gazette, which is the organ of my own home, makes this statement:

"We were both silent for a time, and then I explained my opposition to the Holland bill." This is what Mr. Lessler said: "He said that he had no interest in the Holland boat himself, but a man by the name of Hunter, formerly of Virginia"—I just want to state to the committee that until yesterday I had not the honor of any personal acquaintance with Mr. Quigg, and never met Mr. Lessler, and Doblin I never heard of.

Q. Then you are not the Hunter referred to, if that is the name Mr. Quigg used?—A. No, sir; I am not.

By Mr. RIXEY:

Q. Are there any other Hunters in Virginia?—A. Yes; I think there are. I have two sons there. I would not like to say that I am the most prominent Hunter in Virginia.

(Witness excused.)

TESTIMONY OF JOHN M'CULLAGH—Recalled.

The WITNESS. Mr. Chairman, there is one omission I have made in my testimony. It may not be very important, but it seems to me it will require just a few words of explanation. I will be sworn again.

The CHAIRMAN. You have been already sworn once and that is sufficient.

The WITNESS (continuing). When that man there [pointing to Mr. Lessler] made his remarkable statement to me I said to him——

The CHAIRMAN. You are referring to whom.

The WITNESS. I am referring to Mr. Lessler.

Mr. LESSLER. The chairman should caution the gentleman that the amenities must be observed or he must leave the room.

The WITNESS (to Mr. Lessler). What do you mean, sir?

Mr. KITCHIN. I do not think that a witness should refer to Mr. Lessler in that manner—as "that man there."

The WITNESS. I will say "that gentleman."

Mr. RIXEY. Or "Mr. Lessler," if you choose.

The WITNESS. "Mr. Lessler" or "Congressman Lessler." I have got probably rather an impulsive way of expressing myself, but it does not mean anything. I am not at all angry. When he made his remarkable statement to me I said to him, "Congressman, you are a young man; if your statement is true I would not vote for that bill if I was in your place; and you take my advice and do not do it. I would not do it," I said. That is all. We parted on the very best of terms. The gentleman escorted me right to the elevator, and that was all. I simply wanted to say that I have no interest in the matter at all.

(Thereupon the committee went into executive session.)

COMMITTEE ON NAVAL AFFAIRS,
HOUSE OF REPRESENTATIVES,
Washington, D. C., January 26, 1903.

The committee met at 10.30 o'clock a. m., Hon. George Edmund Foss in the chair.

The CHAIRMAN. The first witness is Mr. Obermeier, who desires to take an early train back to New York.

TESTIMONY OF LEONARD J. OBERMEIER (SWORN).

By Mr. TAYLER:

Q. Mr. Obermeier, are you acquainted with Philip Doblin?—A. I am.

Q. How long have you known him?—A. I should say six or seven years.

Q. Did you make a call with him on Mr. Quigg?—A. I did.

Q. When was that?—A. The 8th day of January.

Q. You may state what was the occasion of your calling on him at that time.—A. The way in which I came to call on Mr. Quigg with Mr. Doblin was this: My relations with Mr. Lessler had been very intimate, very friendly. Mr. Doblin, who is also very much interested in Mr. Lessler, and desirous in every way of advancing his interests, suggested to me that it might be possible to gain Mr. Quigg's good will for Mr. Lessler by possibly urging upon Mr. Lessler the advisability or desirability of voting affirmatively in favor of an appropriation for some Holland submarine torpedo boats. It appears, if my memory serves me in good stead, that Mr. Doblin had spoken to Mr. Quigg before this time about this matter, and that nothing had come of it at all; and it occurred to Mr. Doblin that perhaps, in view of my friendship with Lessler, I might be able, perhaps, to urge upon him the advisability of voting for an appropriation for those boats.

I called with Mr. Doblin on Mr. Quigg and explained that I was very anxious, if I possibly could—I was very anxious to do anything that might be of service to Mr. Lessler in the way of furthering his political interests. I told Mr. Quigg, and repeat it now, that I considered his political friendship as something distinctly worth having, and that if I could serve him in any way I should be very pleased so to do. Mr. Quigg answered me, and he has so testified before your committee, because I have seen his testimony, that he had already made a request in connection with this matter upon Mr. Lessler, and had met with a refusal, and that he was not in the habit of repeating his requests after having failed in the first attempt. I told Mr. Quigg that was—Mr. Quigg added that he had no personal interest of any kind in the matter; that he had been asked by some friend to see if perhaps he could get Mr. Lessler to change his position, which he understood was one of fixed opposition to this scheme, and that he did not know that he had anything further to say.

I answered Mr. Quigg and said that I was going to Washington on business, and that while in Washington I should take occasion to talk with Mr. Lessler and possibly urge upon him any argument which occurred to me which might induce him to change his position; that while I did not feel that I should succeed, I should at least make the attempt.

Q. Have you stated all that occurred, that you remember?—A. I have not given the detail of the conversation.

Q. Well, the substance of it?—A. The substance of it, pretty much. I can give some further details of the actual talk. I think, if I remember rightly, that Mr. Quigg added that he was not trying to serve any of the gentlemen who were connected with the Holland Boat Company; that the directors were all very estimable gentlemen, who served their purpose in the directorate admirably, but that he had no connection with any of them and did not represent any of those interests.

Q. Is that the only conversation you had with Mr. Quigg?—A. That is the only conversation I had with Mr. Quigg.

Q. That is all that I desire to ask.

Mr. RIXEY, I would like to ask a question, Mr. Chairman.

The CHAIRMAN. Mr. Rixey.

By Mr. RIXEY:

Q. Did you communicate to Mr. Lessler what Mr. Quigg had said?—A. When I came to Washington, I spoke to Mr. Lessler. It may have been the day after my arrival. I was here all of the week of the 12th of this month. I spoke to him about it—merely mentioned it. I started to advance certain arguments that occurred to me, and he told me to quit—that he had heard enough of the subject. If you care to, I can repeat those arguments now.

Mr. ROBERTS. That is not material.

Q. Did you tell him you came from Mr. Quigg?

A. I told him I had seen Mr. Quigg. I didn't come on that particular business.

Q. Did you tell him you came at the instance and request of Mr. Quigg to see him about those boats?—A. My answer to that might be misleading if I answered the question baldly. I was stopping at the Normandie Hotel, and I saw Mr. Lessler every day of my stay here, and told him I had seen Mr. Quigg in New York City.

Q. Did you tell him Mr. Quigg requested you to see him about those boats?—A. I don't think Mr. Quigg had requested me to see him on this matter. I had been asked to see Mr. Quigg by Doblin, and I had told Mr. Quigg that I would talk to Mr. Lessler. I did not understand Mr. Quigg as having made a positive request on me.

Q. How did Lessler understand, then, that you were talking with him about the Holland boat? Did he bring the subject up to you?—A. No; I brought the subject up to him.

Q. How did he understand you were interested in the subject?—A. Simply because I told him I had seen Mr. Quigg, and I started to tell him I had seen Mr. Quigg, because I believed Mr. Quigg was a man distinctly worth gaining favor with, and Mr. Lessler immediately told me that he didn't care to hear anything on the matter; that he had been approached from various sources, and that he was getting tired of it. I think he added: "I want you to quit now, because somebody will get hurt if this thing don't stop."

Q. That is the point I wanted to ask you about. You said you told him you thought it was distinctly to anyone's interest to have Mr. Quigg's influence, but why should you make that statement unless you stated to him that Mr. Quigg was very much interested in this subject?—A. That is not so.

Q. How is it? Just explain that matter. You stated to him that you had seen Mr. Quigg and that Mr. Quigg's influence was worth having. Why did you make that statement to him unless you stated that Mr. Quigg had requested you to see him? Why should you bring Mr. Quigg's name into it at all?—A. For the simple reason that I had seen Mr. Quigg, and I had seen Mr. Quigg because——

Q. You had seen him on this subject, had you not?—A. Yes.

Q. And that in pursuance of that interview with Mr. Quigg you were then seeing Mr. Lessler?—A. Well, I didn't put it in that form, in the form of any deduction of that sort. I presume it could be interpreted that way.

Q. Then, in your conversation with Mr. Lessler, when he said he wanted you to stop; that somebody might get hurt; did he tell you he had been approached with an offer of a bribe?—A. No; he didn't go any further into details. I knew at the time that Mr. Lessler, by the way, had been approached months before by McCullagh, because I had heard of that at the time. That was months before. I paid no attention to it at the time, because I had no earthly interest in the matter.

Q. Prior to this conversation, did you know that Mr. Lessler had been approached with an offer of a bribe?—A. I had heard so; yes.

Q. From whom did you hear it?—A. Or not with an offer of a bribe; I knew he had been approached. Mr. Quigg himself told me he had seen Mr. Lessler and that he had met with a refusal so far as a change of position on Mr. Lessler's part was concerned.

Q. Did you ever know of the fact, as testified to here by Doblin, that Mr. Lessler had been approached with an offer of a bribe?—A. No; I ascertained that subsequently.

Mr. BUTLER. When?

The WITNESS. From the reading of it.

By Mr. RIXEY. Did you have an intimation of that prior to the interview you had with Lessler?—A. You mean the interview in Washington here with Mr. Lessler?

Q. Yes.—A. I had an intimation of it; yes.

Q. From whom did you have that intimation?—A. I had seen Doblin and heard so from him.

Q. You had heard so from him? Tell us what Doblin told you at that interview, and when it was.

Mr. BUTLER. That is right; when it was.

The WITNESS. Oh, I should say, offhand, it was a few days subsequent to the time I had seen Mr. Quigg.

By Mr. RIXEY:

Q. You saw Quigg on the 9th?—A. I think I said I saw him on the 8th.

Q. I believe you did.

Mr. BUTLER. The 8th of January.

The WITNESS. I should say it was a day or so subsequently. I happen to know the date of that meeting, because I jotted down a memorandum on my daybook of the appointment which Mr. Doblin made for me.

By Mr. RIXEY:

Q. State what occurred at the interview with Doblin on a day or two subsequent to the 9th.—A. If I remember rightly, Doblin said to me that there had been talk—he gave me no particulars—there had been talk of money in connection with this attempt to gain Lessler's vote for this appropriation—to gain Mr. Lessler's vote in the committee for this appropriation. I think his exact words were "There is nothing to it," or something of that sort; that he believed that if the end was to be gained at all it was to be gained on the ground of friendship and on the ground of appeal to him to do this thing as a personal favor.

He came to me—Mr. Doblin it was, who made the appointment for me to see Mr. Quigg—and told me that because of my close relations with Mr. Lessler (I had had charge of his two campaigns and our relations were very intimate; our offices are in adjoining rooms on Nassau street)—he came to see me and said, "I would like you to see Mr. Quigg and talk it over with him." No; he asked me whether I thought Mr. Lessler's position could possibly be changed. I told him I didn't know. He said, "I will see about this and let you know." He came back—no; I am mixing two conversations. That was the conversation in which he made the appointment for me to see Mr. Quigg. That had nothing to do with this talk about this matter. That came out subsequently. It was after I had had this talk with Mr. Quigg, in which Mr. Quigg spoke to me in the manner I have outlined.

Q. I understand. Well, you had the talk with Mr. Quigg?—A. It was after that talk that Doblin told me that there had been talk of money in connection with it.

Q. That is exactly what you stated in the beginning. It was after that?—A. Yes.

Q. Now, I want to know what passed between you and Doblin in that conversation?—A. Doblin urged upon me the desirability or the good that could be gained in case Mr. Lessler changed his vote. Mr. Doblin said, "Mr. Quigg is a man of great influence, and he can be of great assistance in a dozen ways. Now, if Lessler can be gotten to change his vote in this matter, I think Mr. Quigg's good will can be gained, and I think it is something worth having."

Mr. BUTLER. Did you say "something will happen?"

The WITNESS. "Something worth having."

By Mr. RIXEY:

Q. You stated a few moments ago that you had some intimation from Mr. Obermeier—— A. No; that is my name.

Q. I mean from Mr. Doblin—in regard to the fact that Mr. Lessler had been approached by the offer of a bribe. Now, I want you to tell me what passed between you and Doblin in regard to that matter.— A. I have stated it. Mr. Doblin told me there had been such an approach made, and he added, "There is nothing doing," or "Nothing in it." That is all.

Q. Did he mean by "nothing in it" that it was not true he had been approached?—A. No; I understood him to mean that the attempt had been unsuccessful—had been met with a rebuff.

Q. You are a brother-in-law of Mr. Lessler, are you not?—A. No, sir.

Q. I beg your pardon. I was under that impression. You are an intimate friend of Mr. Lessler?—A. Yes, sir: that is all.

Q. As an intimate friend of Mr. Lessler, when he told you there had been an attempt at a bribe, did you follow up the conversation and ask him to give you the particulars.—A. No.

Q. You did not?—A. I did not. I didn't feel the slightest interest in the matter.

Q. Although you are an intimate friend of Mr. Lessler?—A. The mere fact that he had been approached by an offer of a bribe by somebody didn't interest me particularly. I had no desire to follow up that statement.

Q. You did not, when this gentleman told you it was very important to secure Mr. Lessler's vote; that there was nothing in a bribe, at least it could not be secured in that way, and your services as a friend were engaged to secure his influence?—A. My services as a friend might succeed in securing that object.

Q. And you did not make any inquiry as to the details?—A. None whatever.

Q. Passing from that to your conversation with Mr. Lessler here in the city, did Mr. Lessler refer to that fact at all that he had been approached with the offer of a bribe?—A. Mr. Lessler told me that people had been up with him from all quarters. And, he added—I am almost certain that he added—he had been approached with money offers; and he said, "And if this thing don't stop somebody will get hurt."

Q. Did Mr. Lessler tell you who had approached him in that way?—A. He did not. He ordered me himself to quit the talk, so that I didn't follow it up.

Q. Did you ask him?—A. No.

Q. In your conversation with Mr. Doblin did he tell you who had made this offer to Mr. Lessler?—A. He did not.

Q. Did he say anything about it having been made through him?—A. He did not. I was just going to add that. He not only did not say he did not offer it, but he did not tell me who was the intermediary.

By Mr. MUDD:

Q. Did he mention Quigg's name in that connection at all?—A. He did not.

Q. In connection with the money offer?—A. No, sir.

By Mr. ROBERTS:

Q. You have never been present when there has been any conversation about a bribe being offered to Mr. Lessler?—A. I never was present at any such conversation.

Q. And what you say of Doblin's story, that an attempt had been made to use money, is merely hearsay?—A. Merely a statement by Doblin; call it anything you will.

Q. You have no personal knowledge of that?—A. I have no personal knowledge of a conversation when an offer of money was made by anybody through anybody else in connection with this entire matter.

Q. You said something about reading the testimony and gathering from that that Mr. Quigg had no interest in this Holland submarine proposition. Am I correct—am I correct in that?—A. I may state I had seen this testimony. Let me add, by the way, that I saw it in the chairman's room this morning, and that I saw in the paragraph in which my name was mentioned that Mr. Quigg there said he had said to me that he had no interest in the matter except trying to serve his friend; and I say again that is all he said to me.

Q. You state that from your own recollection and not alone from reading the testimony.—My own recollection, positively.

Q. Am I correct in my understanding that at this conference with Mr. Quigg, when Doblin was present, you volunteered to go to Mr. Lessler and urge his support?—A. I distinctly volunteered to go to Mr. Lessler.

Q. And that Mr. Quigg made absolutely no request of you in the premises?—A. None at all. When I outlined my position Mr. Quigg said, "I should be glad if you would talk to Mr. Lessler;" and that was the sum total of the conversation. We then shifted, if I remember rightly.——

Q. He made no request of you in the matter?—A. No, sir.

Q. And I also understand that at the time you were talking to Mr. Quigg you knew through Mr. Doblin that an attempt had been made to bribe Mr. Lessler?—A. I think so. I said it may have been a day or so later. I will not be positive on that point. I think I may have known of it at that time already that somebody had spoken to him.

Q. From whom did you first learn that an attempt had been made to bribe Mr. Lessler?—A. I think from Doblin.

Q. Did Mr. Lessler ever say anything to you about it?—A. I think Mr. Lessler, in his talk to me in Washington week before last, mentioned it to me. I am sure he mentioned it to me when he told me "they have been up against me in various quarters, and there is money in this thing, and I want you to quit, quit. If this thing don't quit, somebody is going to get hurt."

Q. When you were talking with Mr. Lessler here in Washington, the 12th?—A. Yes, sir.

Q. The week of the 12th?—A. Yes, sir.

Q. And you were explaining to him that Mr. Quigg had requested you to talk with him about the Holland boat proposition. You know that he had been approached with a bribe?—A. Yes.

Q. From Mr. Doblin?—A. Yes.

Q. And Mr. Lessler then and there told you also that somebody had approached him with a bribe?—A. I don't remember whether he said he had been approached. He said, "There has been money in this thing and I want to hear no more of it."

Q. Did Mr. Lessler indicate in any way to you who had approached him, or the source from which it had come?—A. I think not. I am sure not. He didn't state it to me.

Q. He did not indicate to you in the conversation in any way the source from which it had come?—A. No, sir.

Q. Did it occur to you when Mr. Lessler absolutely refused to hear you, his friend, in the discussion of this proposition, because improper methods had been resorted to, that an explanation was due from you as to why you came to him?—A. Mr. Lessler asked me how I came to speak of this thing, and I had told him that Doblin had arranged a meeting with Mr. Quigg; and I told him, and I told him I believed, and again I repeated, that I believed Mr. Quigg's friendship a thing distinctly worth having, and I believed Mr. Quigg, like every other man, would be grateful in case this affirmative vote could be secured.

Q. Did Mr. Lessler seem at all surprised when you stated that Doblin had asked you to see Quigg and then see him? Did he express any surprise at all?—A. I don't remember what his comment was at the time.

Q. Did he go on to say anything about Doblin, or drop him right there?—A. He said to me, "So you have seen Quigg, too," or something of that sort.

Q. He did not express any surprise that Doblin should be pursuing you in the matter and trying to get you to interest yourself?—A. No.

Q. Trying to get you to interest yourself?—A. No.

Q. Did Mr. Doblin, in any of his talks with you in this matter, ever say or intimate to you that he was to get any money out of it himself?—A. No; I didn't know that.

Q. He did not say that?—A. I learned of that afterwards.

Q. When?—A. I think it was Mr. Lessler himself who told me that Doblin had stated to him—I am sure that Mr. Lessler stated to me that Doblin had told him—that he would get some money in case this change could be secured.

Q. When did Mr. Lessler tell you this?—A. During—I think it was at the time of our talk on this thing when I stated——

Q. At the time of your talk in Washington?—A. Yes; in Washington. When I had stated I had seen Mr. Quigg through Doblin, he stated, "Why, Doblin told me there is money in this for him," and I think he named a sum, which I have forgotten—$500 or $1,000, or something.

Q. Now, your interest in the whole matter was to further Mr. Lessler's political interests, if I understand you?—A. If you want my very full answer to that, I will give it to you very simply, and I will tell you how——

Q. I am asking you what your statement was.—A. Yes.

Q. If you will pardon me a moment——

Mr. WHEELER. Let him answer.

By Mr. ROBERTS:

Q. He has answered.—A. I will tell you just how those interests could have been subserved, in my opinion.

Q. The witness has made a statement, and I want to inquire in regard to that statement. What political interests did Mr. Lessler have the 1st day of January that could or would be furthered?—A. None.

Q. Mr. Quigg you knew to be out of politics?—A. In so far as any man who is reputed and who is believed, and I think correctly believed, to possess considerable influence, may be called out of politics.

Q. And Mr. Lessler was a defeated man at the polls?—A. Surely. That is a matter of record.

Q. What political interests did he have which you could further in that way? I think you can state there what your interest was.—A. I had hoped to enlist Mr. Quigg's support in securing, when the time came, or when the time shall come, for Mr. Lessler a nomination in a Republican district in New York City.

Q. And you were arranging the wires in advance?—A. It would so appear.

By Mr. BUTLER:

Q. Had you learned at this time that Mr. Quigg had been unable or had declined to indorse Mr. Doblin for a $200 job?—A. No, sir; I had not. I don't know anything about anybody's $200 job.

Q. You may not know anything about anything that is as small as that, but there is a statement here that he had declined to indorse him for a $200 job, and you evidently thought he might be able to secure his nomination for Congress in some other district.—A. What connection has Doblin's $200 job got with anybody's nomination?

Q. I am asking you the question. If he could not get a man a $200 job, what influence could he have to secure his nomination to Congress?—A. That question strikes me as being rather irrelevant.

Q. I am glad you have that opinion. You are about the most versatile witness I have seen.

By Mr. VANDIVER:

Q. I want to ask a question or two bearing on the point he has already brought out. Who was the first person, Mr. Obermeier, who mentioned to you the desirability of bringing Mr. Lessler to Mr. Quigg's way of thinking on this subject?—A. Mr. Doblin.

Q. And in that conversion Mr. Doblin requested you to go with him to see Mr. Quigg?—A. He so did.

Q. Did you know at that time, or had you any intimation in any way to lead you to believe at that time, that Mr. Doblin was expecting to get any money out of the matter?—A. No, sir; I didn't know at that time that Mr. Doblin, either directly or indirectly, was to procure a penny from anybody.

Q. But Mr. Doblin was the man who was instrumental in getting you interested in the matter?—A. Mr. Doblin certainly was. He was the first and only man that spoke to me about the matter and about going to see Mr. Quigg.

Q. Now, one other question. You referred to having read the testimony there. You perhaps read the statement made in Mr. Quigg's testimony that when you and Mr. Doblin approached him on the subject, with the suggestion that you might be able to bring Mr. Lessler over to the other side, that you were coming down to Washington and would see him, and so on. When Mr. Quigg said he had no further request to make of Mr. Lessler and so on, did he say anything further to indicate that he would like to have you try your influence on him?—A. Yes; he said he should be very glad if I would talk to Mr. Lessler and see if I could change his position.

Q. But he made no request that you do so?—A. No positive request; no.

STATEMENT OF MR. GUSTAVUS A. ROGERS.

Mr. ROGERS. If Mr. Nicoll will permit me to interrupt the proceedings for a moment, I want to introduce myself to the committee. I have already introduced myself to the chairman. I am Mr. Rogers, of New York. I appear here with Mr. Philip Doblin to-day as his counsel. Mr. Doblin came to me yesterday, on the advice of his family, as he stated, to seek my advice and have a conference. As a result of that conference Mr. Doblin has made a written statement which I have in my possession now and which he desires——

Mr. TATE. Let us get through with this witness.

Mr. ROGERS. If Mr. Nicoll has no objection——

Mr. NICOLL. I have no objection. I have no questions to ask the witness myself.

Mr. BUTLER. Have you read Mr. Doblin's statement?

Mr. ROGERS. I have read Mr. Doblin's statement generally in the newspapers, and have gotten from him generally what he has testified to.

Mr. BUTLER. Let me ask you, What is your relation with Mr. Doblin?

Mr. ROGERS. I am his counsel.

Mr. BUTLER. Employed to represent him in this matter?

Mr. ROGERS. Yes, sir; and by the courtesy of the committee I would like to represent him here.

Mr. TATE. I do not know of anything that is before this committee about Mr. Doblin. We have disposed of the matter.

Mr. ROGERS. Excepting this, Mr. Chairman——

Mr LOUDENSLAGER. Mr. Chairman, I think we had better finish with this witness before we have anything else interjected into the proceedings.

Mr. ROGERS. I thought Mr. Nicoll had agreed to permit me to interrupt him.

The CHAIRMAN. I think we had better finish with the witness.

By Mr. NICOLL:

Q. There is only one question, Mr. Obermeier. You say that Mr. Lessler told you that Doblin said to him there was money in it for him?—A. Pardon me.

Q. I say you testified that Mr. Lessler had told you that Doblin said there was money in it for him (Doblin).—A. Yes; so Mr. Lessler told me.

Q. What was the date he told you that?—A. Here in Washington.

Q. When?—A. Why, during that week. I can't tell which particular day.

Q. It was after you came here?—A. Oh, yes; after.

Q. On some day within a week from the 8th?—A. Yes.

By Mr. RIXEY:

Q. I would like to ask the witness this question: I understood you to say a few moments ago that you did not know that Doblin claimed there was any money in this for him.—A. No.

Q. What do I understand by "No"?—A. From Doblin. You asked me at the time I saw Mr. Quigg. The question was put to me, did I know there was money in it for Mr. Doblin, and I said, "No."

Q. I am under the impression that you said that Mr. Lessler informed you that he had been approached with an offer of a bribe——

Mr. VANDIVER. Subsequently?

Mr. RIXEY. Subsequently, of course.

A. (Continuing.) Yes.

Q. Did Mr. Lessler, in that conversation, tell you that not only he had been approached by an offer of a bribe, but that Mr. Doblin was also interested in the matter?—A. I think so. I think it was at that time, in the course of that general conversation.

Q. That both had been approached?—A. Yes, sir.

Mr. WHEELER. Mr. Chairman, I would like to ask a question.

The CHAIRMAN. Mr. Wheeler.

By Mr. WHEELER:

Q. If my recollection is at fault, of course you can correct me, Mr. Overmeier. I believe you stated that when you approached Lessler he replied or opened the conversation by saying, "So you have seen Quigg, too?" Is that correct?—A. Those may not be the exact words, but something of that sort.

Q. And in the same conversation he told you that money had been offered to him—in substance, that money had been offered to him?—A. Yes, yes.

Q. And that Doblin was to get money also?—A. I think it was in that same general conversation he made that remark; yes.

By Mr. MUDD:

Q. You say he said, "So you have seen Quigg" before you mentioned that you had seen Quigg?—A. I beg your pardon.

Q. Did he make that remark, "So you have seen Quigg, too," before you had mentioned that you had seen Mr. Quigg?—A. No; after. When I first told him about it, you see, I knew that Mr. Quigg had seen Mr. Lessler, because Mr. Quigg had so stated to me.

Q. He remarked, "So you have seen Quigg, too," after you had told him that?—A. Yes.

The CHAIRMAN. If there are no further questions we will hear Mr. Rogers.

(Witness excused.)

Mr. ROGERS. I was about to say, if I may be permitted, that Mr. Doblin called upon me yesterday, as I have already said, for the purpose of having a conference. He told me he came there on the advice of his family. He said he had given testimony before this committee on Saturday. He said a portion of that testimony he gave was true and a large portion was not true—that it was false.

Mr. WHEELER. I object to hearing anything of that kind. We want Doblin present.

Mr. ROGERS. Mr. Doblin is here.

Mr. WHEELER. Let us have him here.

Mr. ROBERTS. Let him go back on the stand.

Mr. VANDIVER. Please repeat that statement you made just now.

Mr. ROGERS. I said Mr. Doblin stated to me that some of the testimony he gave before this committee was true, that some of it was not true, and was false; and I want to say at this point, gentlemen of the committee, that after I have finished my statement to you Mr. Doblin will be before this committee upon my advice and answer any questions that this committee may desire to put to him now.

Mr. WHEELER. Let us have Mr. Doblin here now before you make his statement.

Mr. KITCHIN. I think it is all right to hear the statement.

Mr. ROGERS. Mr. Chairman and gentlemen, I do not desire to appear to be persistent. Perhaps, after I have finished, this committee may conclude it does not want to hear Mr. Doblin. Perhaps what I have to say may be so irrelevant and foreign and immaterial to the issue here that this committee may not want to hear Mr. Doblin. After I finish, if the committee is of the opinion, as I am, that Mr. Doblin ought to be heard, or examined, or cross-examined, he may appear for that purpose. He is in the room now.

Mr. TATE. If he wants to change his testimony, let him go on the stand and state it.

Mr. WHEELER. We want to observe the ordinary rules of procedure here. If the witness has made a false statement let him correct it, and if he wants to retract what he has said let him retract it; but I do not want any third-party testimony. One of the fundamental rules of law is that that testimony is first admissible which is the best testimony. If Mr. Doblin wants to correct his former testimony, let him take the stand and do so. I do not think it would be right to hear an affidavit on that subject until we hear Mr. Doblin.

Mr. ROBERTS. Just a moment, Mr. Chairman, if Mr. Wheeler is through. I agree in the main with Mr. Wheeler, that this whole hearing and investigation should have been conducted on strictly legal lines. Mr. Wheeler will bear me out that it was my strong effort when we started in to have it carried out on legal and technical lines. It has not been carried out on those lines. All sorts of irrelevant and hearsay testimony has been admitted here without the slightest protest. Now, it seems to me perfectly fair and proper and competent for Mr. Doblin's counsel to make a preliminary statement to this committee, and then the committee, as he has said, can determine for themselves whether they want to put Mr. Doblin under oath again, or whether they are satisfied to brush the whole statement aside, made by counsel, or what course they will pursue in the premises. I move that Mr.— what is your name, sir?

Mr. ROGERS. Gustavus A. Rogers.

Mr. ROBERTS. That Mr. Rogers be allowed to proceed with the statement he has begun and which he desires to make.

Mr. RIXEY. I would suggest that he be allowed to make his statement as counsel, and when he offers this affidavit we can then decide that matter.

Mr. WHEELER. I do not object to that at all.

The CHAIRMAN. I do not understand he is trying to testify for Mr. Doblin.

Mr. RIXEY. But he has an affidavit, and we must pass upon the reading of that when he offers it.

Mr. KITCHIN. It would be very much like the affidavit that Mr. McCullagh was allowed to read here. He was allowed to read it, and it was put in the record.

Mr. ROGERS. Perhaps I can clarify the situation somewhat by saying it never was my intention to offer this affidavit nor to read from it. I think the distinguished Congressman, Mr. Wheeler, is correct when he says the rules of evidence are that I can not give evidence for Mr. Doblin. I do not propose to do so. I simply had this statement in my hand for the purpose of exhibiting it and considering it in my statement generally to the committee. It is a sworn statement, made by Mr. Doblin voluntarily; and what he has said in this written statement he is willing to tell you gentlemen if he is called here to-day.

If anything he should say reflects in any way upon Mr. Lessler I am exceedingly sorry for it. No one regrets it more than I do, because I have always prized Mr. Lessler's friendship very highly. I have known him very well, and nothing said here now is intended to reflect in any way upon Mr. Lessler. I am simply carrying out my duty as the attorney for Mr. Doblin and he is here in the interest of justice, to right a wrong, which he thinks he has committed against Mr. Quigg. And, generally, Mr. Doblin, with the permission of this committee, would like to go back upon the witness stand and say that he never had any——

Mr. MUDD. Do not tell what he is going to say.

Mr. TAYLER. Mr. Chairman, I object. We want the truth, and I, as much as any man on this committee, want the truth. I do not think any question I have asked in this examination has indicated any other desire. Now, let us get the truth; and we can not get the truth from the lips of counsel, because he is not qualified to speak the truth. He can speak as counsel, but he is not here under oath. Nobody can be presumed to speak here as to facts unless he is under oath, and when under oath only as to facts that are relevant and competent. If an injustice has been done let us see that that is wiped out at the first possible moment. If Doblin has said anything that is unfair to Mr. Quigg, let him be swift to take that chair. Do not let us wait for counsel to say something here which is to the last degree a work of supererogation. Let Doblin take the stand.

Mr. BUTLER. Let the Chair rule.

Mr. ROGERS. Mr. Chairman, may I have a word to say?

Mr. KITCHIN. Let us hear the statement of the counsel.

Mr. VANDIVER. I think, Mr. Chairman, as we have had counsel appear here on, you may say, both sides of this matter to state their case, and as Mr. Doblin is certainly very seriously implicated in this matter—it may be a very serious matter to him—we should permit his counsel to speak.

The CHAIRMAN. Let Mr. Doblin take the stand.

Mr. BUTLER. Mr. Nicoll, as counsel for Mr. Quigg, has not made any statement. He simply cross-examined witnesses.

Mr. WHEELER. We do not want counsel to be marking out the line of procedure here for this witness. Let him take the stand and testify himself.

Mr. VANDIVER. Allow me to ask, Mr. Chairman, not professing much knowledge of the law, if it is not customary, even in criminal courts, to allow the counsel to outline to the jury what he is going to prove in his testimony?

Mr. WHEELER. Yes; but after the witness has testified to a lie, and comes back on the stand to say that it was a lie, counsel are not allowed to mark out a line of procedure for the witness to pursue. He makes his statement before the testimony is heard.

Mr. BUTLER. I move that Mr. Doblin be immediately called back to the witness stand.

The motion was agreed to.

Mr. ROGERS. Mr. Chairman, before Mr. Doblin takes the witness stand, I ask of this committee the courtesy and privilege of appearing as Mr. Doblin's counsel before the committee.

The CHAIRMAN. There is no objection, I think, to that.

Mr. BUTLER. Oh, no; there is no objection to that.

The CHAIRMAN. Before we hear Mr. Doblin, Mr. Obermeier wishes to know whether he can be excused.

Mr. OBERMEIER. I would like to know whether either the witness or his attorney want me to stay. I want to take the train back.

Mr. ROBERTS. I move that Mr. Obermeier be excused from further attendance, if you want it formal.

Mr. LESSLER. I desire Mr. Obermeier to stay.

Mr. OBERMEIER. All right.

TESTIMONY OF PHILIP DOBLIN—Recalled and resworn.

(The witness was again sworn by the chairman.)

The CHAIRMAN. Let Mr. Doblin make his own statement.

Mr. WHEELER. I do not know that it cuts any figure, but I wish you would administer the oath, Mr. Chairman, " You solemnly swear that the evidence you are about to give before this committee will be the truth, the whole truth, and nothing but the truth." Of course, that is technical.

Mr. ROBERTS. I do not know what procedure is intended, but if it is necessary, I move that Mr. Rogers, the counsel of Mr. Doblin, be permitted to conduct the examination of him now.

Mr. WHEELER. I object to that.

Mr. RIXEY. Let it be conducted in the way the other was, Mr Chairman.

The CHAIRMAN. I think it is best for Mr. Tayler to interrogate him.

Mr. ROGERS. Before Mr. Doblin is interrogated, may I ask of this committee, as counsel, that the committee extend to Mr. Doblin such immunity as this committee has the power to extend under the section of the Revised Statutes.

Mr. BUTLER. No, sir; no promises will be made.

Mr. TAYLER. The witness can have any immunity which section 859 of the Revised Statutes gives him.

Mr. ROGERS. I have read the section this morning. I know just how far the committee can go.

Mr. TAYLER. But he can not have any immunity from any crime he may have committed last Saturday.

Mr. ROGERS. I appreciate that, Mr. Chairman and gentlemen of the committee, and I simply ask that the committee extend such immunity as it may have under the Revised Statutes, and Mr. Doblin claims that right now.

Mr. TAYLER. Whatever immunity he has by force of the statute he may have. The committee is powerless. It has no greater or less power. It is simply limited, or the public rather is limited, in its powers by force of section 859.

Mr. KITCHIN. Here is a question, may it please the chairman. I want to know whether this witness is to be examined now by the committee in pursuance of that statute. The witness, so far as we understand, wants to take back something or correct something. Of course, it seems to me he ought to have every immunity in this examination that he had in the examination of last Saturday.

The CHAIRMAN. He has it under the law, but we can not modify or change the statute.

Mr. KITCHIN. But here is the only difference. He comes here voluntarily now. I know when you send for a witness and compel him to appear, then he has the immunity; but whether that immunity will appertain to him now, since he comes back voluntarily, is the only question.

Mr. TAYLER. Mr. Chairman, in reply to Mr. Kitchin, I say the committee is powerless to either grant immunity or withhold immunity. It can say to the witness that he is not bound to answer any question that will incriminate himself.

Mr. KITCHIN. Here is the point: This witness comes back here voluntarily. I know if we subpoena him again and bring him back here, then the immunity attaches.

Mr. ROBERTS. There is no difference between his voluntary appearance and his forced appearance, with respect to immunity.

Mr. KITCHIN. Does the statute provide in regard to voluntary or compulsory?

Mr. ROBERTS. It applies to whatever testimony is given.

Mr. KITCHIN. I have not consulted the statute.

Mr. ROGERS. My only purpose was to have the record show that at this time Mr. Doblin claims immunity and the protection of the statute. That was all; and of course I understand, gentlemen, that you can not alter the statute. I simply want the record to show that he claims immunity.

Mr. BUTLER. I move that the examination of the witness proceed.

Mr. MUDD. That statement ought to go in the record.

Mr. LOUDENSLAGER. It is in the record.

The CHAIRMAN. Proceed, Mr. Tayler.

By Mr. TAYLER:

Q. Mr. Doblin, you testified before this committee last Saturday respecting a charge that through you an effort had been made to corruptly influence the action of Mr. Lessler respecting a proposition to provide for the building of more Holland submarine boats in this Congress?—A. Yes, sir.

Q. I understand from your counsel that there is some part of the testimony that you then gave that you desire now to change or correct?—A. Yes, sir.

Q. Will you state to the committee in what respects the testimony that you then gave is not true, if any?—A. It is in relation to my being called to Washington, and in relation to the conversation that I had with Congressman Lessler at the Hotel Normandie on Saturday morning at 8 o'clock, or thereabouts.

Q. Tell us what the fact is in that respect.—A. The fact is that the statements I made regarding Mr. Quigg were not true. I read the article as it was handed to me, and I was told by Lessler "You have got to stand for this story," and I said "Oh, that can't be done." "Well," he says, "Then I am politically dead." Then I said " Well, you will carry me with you." He said, "You will be all right. You just appear before this committee. I will go and see the Speaker and I will fix it up." He goes out of the room and comes back and says he has seen the Speaker, and it will be all right. And he says: "Now, all you have got to do is to go up before the committee and substantiate my story." (To Mr. Rogers:) "Will you let me have those telegrams, please?" When I was called to Washington I got this telegram: "Take midnight train and come to me. Want to see you. Keep this confidential."

Q. What is the date of the telegram?—A. January 20, 1903, addressed to me in New York City.

By Mr. BUTLER:

Q. Signed by whom?—A. "Monte."

Q. Is it signed "Monte?"—A. Signed Monte; knowing that it came from Washington, and signed as some other correspondence I had received, of course I immediately complied.

By Mr. TAYLER:

Q. Let the stenographer identify that telegram. In your association with people, who is "Monte?"—A. "Monte" is Congressman Lessler.

Q. Proceed.

Mr. LOUDENSLAGER. Mr. Tayler, would it be proper for me to ask him if he does not correspond with somebody who signs himself in that way?

By Mr. TAYLER:

Q. I understood you to say you have had correspondence with him?—A. I have had correspondence signed "Monte."

Q. I think he had already said that.—A. While we were at breakfast I was reading the article, familiarizing myself as to the statement he had made, and when we got upstairs he said, "Do as you want about it." "Well," I said, "I never can stand for anything like this." "Oh," he says, "you have got to." He says, "I will be back in a minute." He went out of the room, and he came back and he said, "I will have Son come for you. I will go down and see the committee;" and just before that he said, "Now, you needn't have any fear, there is nothing going to happen to you; you appear before this committee, and they are friends of mine and the members of the committee and all there will be to it, they will report to the whole committee and there won't be anything further to it."

The Congressman left the room. I laid on the sofa, and took the paper again and read it over, and in about half an hour or three-quarters, or maybe a little less, along comes Son, and says, "You come along with me, and we will get into the Capitol all right. Nobody will see you. You will be able to go up through a side elevator which is right close to the Naval Committee door, and you can get in, and I will see that nobody sees you." I came to the door and—that is, I was on the elevator door there, standing at the door—and Son says, "Wait a minute." Son came in this door, and in quite a few minutes after the elevator was about to go down, and Son came out of the door, and I says, "Just a minute, Mr. Elevator Man;" and Son came out, and he took me to the other room and the door opened. I think it was Mr. Foss came to the door, and the other gentlemen were standing about, and Son says, "This is Mr. Doblin," or something to that effect.

I don't know the exact language. The other gentlemen all shook hands with me and had me take a seat. I sat down, and after a little time Mr. Foss handed me a cigar. I took the cigar and smoked it. It made me feel, agreeably to the conversation I had with Lessler, that these were possibly friends of his, and he was inclined to be a good fellow anyhow. He specially was to me from time to time, and I took it for granted that it was all right; and the first thing I knew one of the gentlemen of the committee—I had explained my relations in politics in New York City, and how long I had been in politics—one of the gentlemen said, "Wasn't it Mr. Quigg said to you that there was $5,000 in it for Lessler and $1,000 for you?" And I said, "No, sir; I didn't say that at that time." All the gentlemen around said, "It is all right; you go on." And then there was a discussion in the room as to how I stood. I refused to answer at that time until the gentlemen seemed to all agree "There is nothing to it; you just go on and make your statement." Feeling agreeably at home, I made my statement according to the way I read it in the paper, and Mr. Tayler put in my mouth—I think it was Mr. Tayler—something about the money proposition which I didn't state before, until I realized that I was in the hands of my friends, and "it is all right: I will back up Lessler, and it will be a cinch for Lessler. There won't be anything about it. All there would be to it is the committee will report to the whole committee and Lessler will be vindicated and I will be vindicated and that will be all right."

After I got out of the committee room I went down to the hotel and asked for Lessler. Lessler wasn't there. I telephoned to the House and tried to get him on the telephone and I couldn't get him, and I left the city, thinking it was all right. I came home. There is a telegram at home that I will produce in which the words used, as I remember them, is "Statement all right. Have no fear." I will produce that telegram, but it is a matter of record in one of the telegraph offices here. Well, of course I consequently go on about my business and think no more about it. I had done another fellow a turn, in my way of thinking. I went out, and I got home pretty late that night, and I found this telegram:

I am instructed by Naval Committee to request your appearance for hearing before it to-morrow (Friday) morning at ten thirty.

GEO. EDMUND FOSS, *Chairman.*

That is dated January 22. I replied to that, thinking the committee would adjourn, that I could come on Monday, thinking it was a friendly thing. I didn't notice in the paper that the House had passed a resolution demanding my presence, or to send for any witnesses they desired. I went out, and the first intimation I had about this before I got the telegram was in the papers, and I thought that was a part of Lessler's statement. Well, when I came on here it was a question whether

H. Rep. 3482——7

I was going to substantiate myself before a subcommittee of friends and Lessler, or whether I was there and then going to make Lessler to appear untrue. However, I decided with myself that "I will just make my same statement as to that which I spoke of before this subcommittee." I made it; and I now retract every word in which I said that Mr. Quigg tendered me any bribe in any way. After I got through being examined before this committee, I went down to the station with Mr. Lessler, and he sent this telegram:

Phil examined. Substantiated story in every way. He is all right. Will stay here for a time.

Mr. ROBERTS. Who is that from?
The WITNESS. Signed "Montague Lessler;" to my wife.

BY Mr. TAYLER:
Q. Read the whole telegram.—A.

WASHINGTON, D. C., *January 24. 1903.*
To Mrs. PHILIP DOBLIN, *433 East Eighty-second Street.*
Phil examined. Substantiates story in every way. He is all right. Will stay here for a time.

Afterwards—I beg your pardon—I desire to introduce this telegram also. This is a telegram that I got here on Saturday morning to my wife:

To Mrs. PHILIP DOBLIN, *433 East Eighty-second Street:*
Phil arrived all right and will stay with me in Washington. You need have no fear about him at all. I shall try and see you if possible. He sends love to you and children.
MONTAGUE LESSLER.

I also want to say now that after I got out of the committee we had a talk and he says: "You might as well stay here and stay over. It is all right, and you can occupy my room if you want to." "Oh," I says, "no; I will get a room of my own." I went up to the hotel and I put my name down at the Normandie Hotel. I told him I would be back. The Congressman expected to go away earlier, and he didn't go, and when I went looking for him I went down to the station and expected him to be there at 3 o'clock and he wasn't there. So I telephoned to the House here and he says: "I may not be able to go. I may catch the quarter of 4." Well, of course, I didn't come back until I guess it was quarter past 4 or something like that. I walked down to the depot and then walked up here leisurely, and afterwards I come here and the committee was in executive session. I stayed in the hallway and waited until the committee got through, and he says: "Come on;" and, by the way, he told me to look out for his grip up at the hotel, which I did. When we went down to the depot I says: "What shall I do here over Sunday? I will go home to my folks and I would rather be home than here." In reply to that I says: "We had better send a telegram." "Well," he says, "all right." This is the telegram:

WASHINGTON, D. C., *January 24, 1903.*
Mrs. P. DOBLIN, *433 East Eighty-second street:*
Philip leaves for New York on 5 train. Will be home at 12 o'clock.
LESSLER.

To go back to January 22 a minute, I got a personal telegram from Mr. Lessler, which I found at the same time that Mr. Foss's telegram was at the house, which is dated January 22, 1903, Washington, D. C.:

PHILIP DOBLIN, *433 East Eighty-second street, New York:*
Come on midnight without fail.
——
MONTE.

Q. On page 30 of the printed testimony in this case——
Mr. VANDIVER. Excuse me a minute, Mr. Tayler. I would like to suggest that it would be well to have the witness go on and state——
Mr. TAYLER. I want to ask a question right here; then he can go on. I want to come to the point of this business and then let him make his own statement.
Mr. VANDIVER. Very well.

By Mr. TAYLER:

Q. You testified as follows, in answer to a question, after an interview that you said you had with Mr. Quigg at the Mutual Café:

Mr. Quigg was anxious to try to get Mr. Lessler's friendly disposition toward the bill, and he said, after a talk on various things, that there was $5,000 in it.

Is that statement of yours true or false?
A. It is false.
Q. The question was later asked you on that page:

Q. For whom did he say there was $5,000?—A. Why, that man we were talking about. He didn't use the name.

Is that true or false?
A. That is false.
Q. And you say, generally, that Mr. Quigg made no such proposition, directly or indirectly, involving the use of money to secure Mr. Lessler's support of this bill?—A. He did not.
Q. Now, on page 31, after having testified that you left Mr. Quigg and that you later met Mr. Lessler and that he was sitting at his desk opening his mail, you were asked this question:

What did you tell him? Tell us just what you told him.

To which you replied:

I told him there would be $5,000 in this, if you can see your way clear to be friendly disposed to it.

Is that true or false?
A. False.
Q. You did not say to Mr. Lessler anything about any money that would or might be paid to him if he would change his attitude on this bill?
A. Well, I spoke to him about the question at that time, but I didn't say anything about money.
Q. That is, you spoke to him about the Holland boat?—A. The Holland torpedo-boat proposition at that time.
Q. But you made no improper proposal of any kind to him?—A. I did not.
Q. You did not intimate that anybody, either through you or in any other way, would pay any money for his support of the bill or the proposition?—A. I did have the conversation. I spoke to him about his future, and generally on the subject of submarine torpedo boats, and said nothing about money at any time to the Congressman.
Q. So that——
Mr. MUDD. Let him finish.
A. What I want to do there, if you please, is to say this: The conversation I was talking about at the time was as to Lessler's future. I said, "Now, here, Monte; Mr. Quigg has sent for me—has talked to me about this thing, and this will be for your future." I don't know whether that was the exact terms that I used, but that is as near as I can get it.

Q. So that the statement of Mr. Lessler that you mentioned $5,000 or any other sum in connection with this is absolutely false?—A. Well, as to his impressions I don't know, but as to his statement, it is false.

Q. I do not know that I said anything about his impression.—A. You said his statement, did you not?

Q. I said statement. I did not say impression.—A. I beg your pardon.

Q. Were you present when Mr. Lessler testified before the committee?—A. No.

Q. On page 2 of the printed evidence in this case ——

Mr. RIXEY. Ask him if he has not read the testimony of Mr. Lessler, Mr. Tayler.

By Mr. TAYLER:

Q. That was merely preliminary. Mr. Lessler testifies that you came in one morning and you asked him if the Holland submarine boat proposition was before the House, or would come again before the House, and he said he supposed so. Thereupon Mr. Lessler says you said, "Are you still opposed to it?" to which Mr. Lessler replied, "Yes." Then you said you had been sent for by Mr. Quigg and that Quigg had said to you that there was $5,000 in it if he, Lessler, could be brought to the other side. Is that true?—A. No, sir.

Mr. VANDIVER. Mr. Tayler, will you allow me to make a suggestion? I do not want to interrupt you at all. I think the witness ought to be rigidly cross-questioned; but I would like to know first whether he has completed his direct statement. He stopped at a point after he got home Sunday, I think.

Mr. TAYLER. I do not know that we care so much about that. We want to know just what it is he says is true and what is false.

Mr. VANDIVER. I have no objection to it, but I thought possibly it would be more orderly to have him proceed with the direct statement before the cross-examination.

Mr. KITCHIN. I suggest that you ask him who has seen him, and everything like that. Find out who he has talked with since he arrived here Saturday.

The CHAIRMAN. Let Mr. Tayler proceed, gentlemen. He has a purpose in his mind.

Mr. TAYLER. Of course the witness will say all he wants to say, but we who are seeking facts may want to pursue certain lines.

The CHAIRMAN. Yes.

Mr. TAYLER. I want to say to the committee, since there have been some inquiries and suggestions made as to methods, that so far as my desire goes I have completed the examination of this witness, in so far as I care to go with a view of finding out what it is that is vital in this case that he affirms or denies. I was going to proceed with another line of examination. If some gentleman wants to ask him further what is or is not true in his examination, it had better be asked now.

Mr. RIXEY. You get through with your examination first.

By Mr. TAYLER:

Q. You say that your first information as to the claim of Mr. Lessler that he had been approached corruptly and offered $5,000 to vote for this proposition came to you after you reached Washington last week?—A. Yes, sir.

Q. Had you ever had any intimation from anybody prior to that time that any corrupt proposition had been made as claimed by Mr. Lessler?—A. No, sir.

Q. Or that Mr. Lessler had claimed to have received any such proposition?—A. No, sir.

Q. Did you ever say anything to Mr. Obermeier in that connection?—A. I might have referred to the appropriation.

Q. Did you ever say anything to him about any money——— A. No, sir.

Q (Continuing) being offered to you or to anybody else for support of the Holland submarine boat proposition?—A. No, sir.

Q. Did Mr. Lessler say anything to you as to what you should say before the subcommittee, except what appeared in the newspaper?—A. He simply handed me the newspaper, and said "I blurted that out—oh, do what you want about it."

Q. What newspaper?—A. I think it was the Washington Post, or something like that.

Q. Was it a Washington paper?—A. A·Washington paper; yes.

Q. Did Mr. Lessler name any figures to you as to the amount he had said he had been offered?—A. It was stated in the paper.

Q. Did Mr. Lessler say anything to you about the amount?—A. I don't remember him saying anything about the amount.

Q. How long did Mr. Lessler talk with you?—A. I guess—first his secretary was there a while and he went out, and then we had the room alone a few minutes. He was getting on his clothes, and while he was getting on his clothes he was talking. He took off his night clothes and put on his trousers and went over to the washstand and washed himself and then went downstairs.

Q. Was his clerk, Son, there at that time?—A. I think he was; yes, sir.

Q. Then what did Mr. Lessler say to you?—A. At what time?

Q. All that he said to you after you met him that morning before you came here.—A. "I have got you into trouble." I said, "How is that?" "Well," he says, "there is a subcommittee meeting this morning; I want you to talk to them"—something to that effect. I am not sure what the exact language was, but as I said he was dressing himself, and then he went out of the door and went down stairs and came back with the paper, and while I was reading the paper Son came in.

Q. As to what Lessler claimed to you, what did you learn other than what you saw in the paper? Did Lessler tell you anything about what you should testify to?—A. Why, he said, "read that over; it will be all right," and I read it over.

Q. What else did he say to you?

Mr. NICOLL. Will you not ask him what was in the paper? I do not know what was in it.

By Mr. TAYLER:

Q. I will have the paper. What else did he say to you?—A. He said "The Holland submarine boat business is up."

Q. What else did he say?—A. Well, he didn't say much after that. After he came back with the paper, Son came in and they had some papers they were arranging, and I was sitting looking out of a window or at a desk or table, I don't know which.

Q. Then all you know about the details of what Lessler claimed, you read in the newspaper, did you not?—A. At that time.

Q. When else did you learn anything?—A. Why, when we went down to breakfast I said "What did you say, Monte?" and he said "Can't you read that?" I looked it over, and he said "I was talking about the $5,000 business."

Q. Who was?—A. He was. He says "I blurted it out." I won't be positive whether he said that at the table or whether he said that in the room. He said "I blurted it out, and you have got to help me out here"—something to that effect. I can't remember the exact language.

Q. Is that all that occurred?—A. Well, he said, "I mentioned your name," and he said, "You have simply got to go up and make your statement." I already stated before what happened regarding the way in which I came up here.

Q. What time did you get to the hotel?—A. I guess a little after 8 o'clock. It might have been 8 o'clock.

Q. You came up before the subcommittee?—A. Yes, sir.

Q. And you were asked by the subcommittee to tell us all that you knew about those charges that had been made by Lessler?—A. Yes, sir.

Q. Was there any reference made to the newspaper account in the matter?—A. At what time?

Q. When you were before the subcommittee.—A. I don't remember hearing it.

Q. Do you mean to say you got your information from the subcommittee as to what Mr. Lessler had claimed?—A. No, sir.

Q. Do you mean to say that the subcommittee told you what to tell them?—A. No, sir.

Q. Do you mean to say that I put words into your mouth, and that because I put them into your mouth you then proceeded to accord with what I had said?—A. No, sir.

Q. Apart from the description that you gave of that interview the other day, you told your story freely did you not, voluntarily?—A. Yes, sir; after a talk with the gentlemen of the committee.

Q. And without any suggestions from us as to what you should say?—A. Without any suggestion?

Q. Yes.—A. Yes, sir.

Q. There was no suggestion on the part of any member of that subcommittee as to what you should say?—A. No, sir.

Q. You told to us in the subcommittee practically the same thing that you told the full committee last Saturday?—A. Yes, sir.

Q. There was no variation in any material respect, was there?—A. I didn't hear it.

Q. Between the two stories?—A. I don't remember.

Q. I do not mean as to what you read, but your recollection of what you told us on last Saturday?—A. I don't remember there was any difference.

Q. Now, you appeared before the committee last Saturday and testified and went home, did you?—A. Yes, sir.

Q. With whom did you talk after you left?—A. With whom?

Q. Yes.—A. I didn't talk with anybody except Lessler, riding home.

Q. After you got home, with whom did you talk?—A. I talked with my wife and children. My father came in; my brother came in; my other brother came in. We had a general discussion. My father wanted to know what it was—all about it. He don't talk very much, but he just evidently had the paper with my picture in it, and I said, "I don't want to talk about this thing now. I think it is all right;" and about 11 o'clock I dressed myself and took a walk, my brother and I, and my brother suggested I had better go and consult somebody about this situation, and I went and consulted Mr. Rogers.

Q. Mr. Rogers?—A. Who lives at 162 East Seventy-eighth street, right close to me.

Q. And Mr. Rogers told you you had made yourself subject to criminal prosecution, did he not?—A. After consultation; yes, sir.

Q. How long were you in consultation with him?—A. We stayed there about three-quarters of an hour.

Q. And upon his advice you came here to tell us this story this morning?—A. I made a statement to him which he wrote out and I signed.

Q. I think I do not want to ask any more questions.

Mr. KITCHIN. I should think he ought to identify that piece he read in the paper. He said he thought it was a Washington paper, and if you have got the piece, suppose you show it to him and ask him if that is the article he read.

Mr. ROBERTS. And I ask that it be identified.

Mr. TAYLER. I will just read this and the stenographer will take it down, or he can copy it. I do not want to mutilate the clerk's files.

Mr. KITCHIN. Had you not better let him look at it and see whether that is the article he read?

By Mr. TAYLER:

Q. Please look at the article in Wednesday's Post and tell me if that is the article you read before you testified before the subcommittee?—A. (After reading the article). I wouldn't be positive that that is the paper, but that was the substance of the article I read.

Q. What was the day you reached here; Wednesday of last week?—A. Wednesday morning.

Q. And it was in Wednesday morning's paper that you saw the article referred to?—A. Some one of the Wednesday morning Washington papers.

Q. I believe I have identified last Wednesday's Post and the article headed "Tells of bribe offer," which appears to be the only article in that paper respecting this subject. If so, that is the only article you read that morning?

Mr. RIXEY. It is the only morning paper, too, Mr. Tayler.

The WITNESS. All right, sir.

. Mr RIXEY. Mr. Tayler, I would like to ask a question if you are through.

Mr. TAYLER. Yes.

By Mr. RIXEY:

Q. Mr. Doblin, I understand you now to state explicitly that in no conversation with Mr. Lessler did you mention the subject of money?—A. I won't say as to that.

Q. I want to know as to that.—A. Well, sir, the subjects that I talked with Mr. Lessler from time to time—and I want to say right here I did have other conversations with Mr. Lessler about this matter, but I made it just as brief as I could before, in order to try to substantiate the inference that I got from the reading of that paper that morning——

Q. Now, I want you to answer my question—— A. Yes, sir; if you please.

Q. (Continuing.) Whether, in any conversation with Mr. Lessler on the subject of the submarine torpedo boats, you mentioned the subject of money.—A. Yes, sir.

Q. Now state when it was and what it was.—A. I said one time to Mr. Lessler, "There seems to be a large appropriation here wanted"——

Mr. NICOLL. Will you not ask when this was? "One time," he says.

By Mr. RIXEY:

Q. Let him go ahead. We can interrogate him as to particulars later.—A. (Continuing.) And he said, "Yes; those boats cost $70,000 or $170,000 apiece, and this appropriation will call for, if the ten-bill proposition comes through, $1,700,000."

Q. Was that the only way in which money was mentioned?—A. That is the only way, sir.

Q. Did you in any of the conversations with Mr. Lessler indicate that there would be money in it if his influence could be secured?—A. No, sir.

Q. In no conversation with him?—A. No, sir.

Q. Why is it that you remember now the amount of money that he referred to as being in it; and why was that stated?—A. Because the evening that I was at the Waldorf Mr. Frost was asked—I asked Mr. Frost, I think it was, "How much are these boats worth," and he said, "They are bought for $170,000;" that is, "they are sold for $170,000."

Q. Why did that conversation make an impression on your mind as to the exact amount that the boats were to cost to the Government?—A. Not particularly, except that the discussion came up from time to time afterwards when I met Mr. Lessler at the office.

Q. Why should the discussion come up from time to time if it is as stated by you?—A. Because some time last summer, when the last session was in meeting here, Lessler had told me that McCullagh had come to him, to Washington, and had asked him for his support for this bill, and that he was appealing for some friend of his, and then he also said—I don't know whether it was last summer during the meeting of Congress, or after that, or during recess—that somebody else come to him about it. At one time Mr. Rice's name was mentioned, and in connection with that Mr. Quigg's name was brought up. Mr. Lessler told me that Mr. Rice and Mr. Quigg were not on friendly terms for some reason or other, and, of course, talking about the conversation, I think at that time again the amount of the appropriation came up.

Q. Mr. Doblin, is not this the truth of this matter, that you had been informed that these boats would cost a large amount of money and that there was considerable profit in it to the company, and that you thought it was a proposition where you could make some money?—A. No, sir; I was working on and off during that time.

Q. You may have been working on and off, but did you not have some idea that you could make some money if you could negotiate this matter?—A. No, sir.

Q. You did not expect any pecuniary benefit?—A. No, sir.

Q. You did not have any idea you could make any?—A. No, sir; the only thing I had in mind was Lessler's future.

Mr. ROBERTS. I would like to ask a question or two, Mr. Chairman.

By Mr. ROBERTS:

Q. In any of the conversations you have ever had with Mr. Quigg did he at any time offer or make any suggestions to you that you personally could get a thousand dollars or any sum of money for your good offices?—A. No, sir.

Q. Then your prior statement in that respect is false?—A. Yes, sir.

Q. Now, a little further. In any of your conversations with Mr. Quigg did he say to you that the Roberts bill was pending in Congress, calling for ten submarine boats, and that was the measure he wanted you to secure Lessler's support for?—A. I think that was the name.

Q. Are you certain he used that name?—A. I think so.

Q. That Mr. Quigg—— A. Had used the name of the Roberts bill.

Q. You are sure on that point?—A. Yes, sir; I am sure.

Q. There is no question in your mind on that?—A. There is no question because——

Q. Whatever you said before, this is the absolute truth?—A. This is absolutely so.

Q. You stated a few moment ago, if I understood you, in answer to Mr. Rixey's question, that you had had other talks with Mr. Lessler about this bribe matter, in order that you might better substantiate your story?—A. When?

Q. I am asking you if I understand you correctly to say that?—A. I didn't get that question.

The question was repeated by the stenographer.

A. Not about the bribe matter, at that time.

Q. Let us get down to this. Have you had any other talks with Mr. Lessler, or with anybody representing him, as to what sort of a story you should tell before this committee?—A. No, sir.

Q. You have testified here to all the conversations you ever had with Mr. Lessler on that point?—A. Pretty much so.

Q. Now, what is "pretty much so?" What is excepted?—A. There may be a time that I have left out, when the subject came up, that I spoke to him. .

Q. What subject?—A. The subject of submarine boats.

Q. No; you are off the point. I mean at this time when you say you had a talk with Mr. Lessler, and it was fixed up between you what your statement should be.—A. I was handed a paper.

Q. Now, keep that right in mind. You and Mr. Lessler had a conference, in which it was fixed up what you would testify to?—A. We didn't have any particular conference. I came there that morning.

Q. You were together then?—A. Yes, sir.

Q. And it was then fixed up what you would testify to?—A. I don't know that it was fixed up.

Q. Was there any other time you had any talk with Mr. Lessler as to what you should say, how far you should substantiate the story he had told?—A. I don't recall any.

Q. That was the only time, and you have given us all the conversations? No other details of the story you were to tell were gone into between you and Mr. Lessler or anybody representing him?—A. No, sir.

Q. At that or any other time?—A. Not that I can recall.

Mr. WHEELER. Mr. Chairman, I would like to ask a few questions if the gentleman is through.

The CHAIRMAN. Mr. Wheeler.

By Mr. WHEELER:

Q. Mr. Doblin, you wish the committee to understand now that your purpose in making this statement to the subcommittee and to the committee was to serve the political ends of Mr. Lessler; is that it?—A. Yes, sir.

Q. Do you wish the committee to understand that you came before them deliberately and swore to a lie for the purpose of serving Lessler's political ends? Is that right?—A. I can't answer that.

Q. I think you can answer it.

The WITNESS. Will you kindly read that question?

(The question was read by the stenographer.)

A. Yes, sir.

Q. When did you make up your mind to perjure yourself in order to aid Lessler?—A. I didn't make up my mind about it at all. I simply come in and made my statement, as requested by Mr. Lessler. "It will be all right; there will not be anything to it. They will report to the full committee and that is all there will be to it."

Q. Mr. Lessler, have you ever sworn to a falsehood before?—A. I beg your pardon.

Q. Have you ever perjured yourself before?

Mr. ROGERS. One moment, Mr. Wheeler. I think I have been accorded the privilege here of acting as counsel for Mr. Doblin, and I respectfully suggest to the chair and to the committee that the question is not a proper one. That question, even in a court of law, would not be admissible, and I understand this committee desires to confine itself strictly to the rules of evidence. The question whether Mr. Doblin ever swore falsely before this occasion is not material to the issue. I have no objection to the question being asked of Mr. Doblin, and I think it would be permissible that he should be asked if he was ever convicted of perjury, but I hardly think it is fair to ask a witness before this committee whether he ever swore falsely or perjured himself before. I think Mr. Wheeler will withdraw the question.

Mr. WHEELER. His infamy is already established, and it is simply a question of the degree of it, now. It is more for my own satisfaction than anything else that I ask the question.

Mr. ROGERS. I ask the protection of the committee for the witness. I do not think it is a competent question.

Mr. WHEELER. I see nothing improper in the question.

Mr. ROGERS. I appeal to the committee and ask for a ruling on the objection.

Mr. WHEELER. What difference does it make? He has already admitted his perjury.

Mr. ROBERTS. It might be a question as to whether he is a professional perjurer.

Mr. WHEELER. Yes; I want to find out that fact.

Mr. RIXEY. I do not think you have the right to ask the witness specific questions in regard to his reputation.

Mr. WHEELER. I am not going to withdraw it.

Mr. TATE. Let him go on, Mr. Chairman. He can answer it or refuse to answer it.

By Mr. WHEELER:

Q. You can answer it or refuse, as you see proper. Have you ever sworn falsely before?

Mr. ROGERS. One moment. I object, Mr. Chairman.

The WITNESS. If you will permit me, Mr. Rogers——

Mr. ROGERS. No; I will not permit you. I am your counsel.

Mr. WHEELER. I suppose I have some rights in the matter. The witness may decline to answer if he wishes to do so.

Mr. ROGERS. I understand the Chair to rule that it is not a proper question.

The CHAIRMAN. The Chair only states the opinion of the committee on a vote.

Mr. WHEELER. He is at liberty to answer it if he wants to, or not.

The WITNESS. If I understand that question, it was asked of Mr. Lessler.

Mr. ROGERS. One moment.

The CHAIRMAN. I will take the sense of the committee.

Mr. BUTLER. I move that Mr. Wheeler be allowed to ask the question.

Mr. TATE. I second the motion.

(The question was put. Mr. Rixey voted no.)

Mr. RIXEY. I do not think it is a proper question. This witness is in a position here where he may be called upon to answer for everything that is said here by him.

Mr. BUTLER. We have not observed all the legal technicalities heretofore.

Mr. RIXEY. But he has counsel present, and his counsel raises the question for him.

Mr. WHEELER. He has attempted to impugn the reputation of a man, and we have a right to know the depth of his infamy.

Mr. TATE. Unless the witness himself objects to answering the question, if he is willing to answer it, he should be allowed to do so.

Mr. ROGERS. My objection is his objection.

Mr. WHEELER. Counsel's objection does not have weight with this committee, unless the committee say so.

Mr. ROBERTS. Mr. Rogers has been allowed to appear as counsel for the witness.

Mr. MUDD. The witness can be given to understand that he can answer the question yes or no, as he wishes.

Mr. WHEELER. I have already told him that.

Mr. ROGERS. Do I understand the committee has ruled?

The CHAIRMAN. The witness is at liberty to answer if he chooses to do so.

Mr. ROGERS. May I not have a ruling by the committee?

Mr. RIXEY. You can not keep him from answering it unless he wishes not to do so. You can warn the witness not to answer, but if he persists he has the right to answer.

Mr. ROGERS. I understood, when I was permitted to appear as his counsel, that anything I did was his act.

Mr. RIXEY. You are mistaken about that.

Mr. MUDD. Does the witness object to answering?

The WITNESS. I think that question was asked in the name of Lessler.

Mr. WHEELER. No; it was asked of you.

The WITNESS. No; I beg your pardon It was asked of "Mr. Lessler."

Mr. BUTLER. Yes; you made a mistake, Mr. Wheeler, in addressing the witness. You addressed him as Mr. Lessler.

The question was read by the stenographer, as follows:

Mr. Lessler, have you ever sworn to a falsehood before?
Mr. DOBLIN. I beg your pardon.
Mr. WHEELER. Have you ever perjured yourself before?

Mr. WHEELER. Change that to "Doblin."

Mr. ROGERS. Now, Mr. Chairman and gentlemen of the committee, I make the same objection. I instruct the witness that the question is improper and not to answer it, and I appeal to the committee.

The WITNESS. I simply have to state, under the advice of my counsel, that I can not answer it.

By Mr. WHEELER:

Q. We will recur, now, since you have declined to answer this question—when did you change your determination to aid Mr. Lessler by false testimony?—A. Why, after I had a talk with my counsel I saw the position I was put in.

Q. Did you not know that you were swearing falsely all along?—A. Yes, sir.

Q. Did you not know it was legally punishable to swear to a lie?—A. I did not look up the law.

Q. I know you did not, but do you not know that as a matter of common reputation that a liar is put in the penitentiary?—A. I do not know anything about that.

Q. Have you not been about the courts of New York a good deal?—A. Yes, sir.

Q. Have you never heard of men being punished for swearing falsely?—A. No, sir.

Q. Do they not punish men in New York for swearing falsely?—A. I don't know about that.

Q. Did you not know it was immoral and wrong to swear to a lie?—A. I may have.

Q. You did not regard it as morally reprehensible to give false testimony before a committee of Congress?—A. At that time I never gave it a thought.

Q. Did you believe it was all right for you to come in here and swear that this man Quigg, a citizen of New York, had offered you a bribe?—A. No, sir.

Q. When he had not done it?—A. No, sir.

Q. You did not think that was wrong?—A. No, sir; because I was led to believe by what Mr. Lessler had intimated in the paper and the talk at the hotel that there was nothing to it. I was simply trying to substantiate his story.

Q. But did you not know it was wrong when you did that?—A. I didn't give it a thought. I simply done as I was told.

Q. Do you mean this committee to understand that you thought it was a matter of so small consequence that you swore to a lie without even thinking about it?—A. I can't answer that very well because, as I say, I didn't think about it at that time.

Q. When did you think about it?—A. When my counsel told me what I had done.

Q. How did you come to go to counsel if you never thought of it one way or the other that it was wrong?—A. I had a talk with my brother and he said: "It looks very funny there; what are doing?" And Mr. Rogers being a friend of mine——

Q. Did you tell your brother you had sworn falsely?—A. I didn't say anything to him at all.

Q. Did you not tell anyone at all that you had sworn falsely until you had consulted this lawyer?—A. No, sir.

Q. Is he the first person you told you had sworn falsely?—A. Yes, sir.

Q. Then what did he do?—A. He simply took my statement.

Q. Did he not advise you how to proceed in the premises?—A. Yes, sir.

Q. Did he not tell you it would subject you to a criminal prosecution to come here and say that you had sworn to a lie?—A. No, sir.

Q. Did he tell you it would if you did not say so?—A. Yes, sir.

Q. He told you if you did come and tell that you had sworn falsely it would not subject you to a criminal prosecution?—A. Yes, sir.

Q. But he did not tell you that if you did come and admit it that that would render your conviction a question beyond doubt? Did he not tell you that?—A. Why, we discussed the question and he said "The best thing you can do in the premises," after I explained to him the situation, "is to refute it, because you can't stand for such a statement as that."

Q. What does Mr. Rogers do in New York?—A. Attorney and counsellor at law.

Q. Has he ever represented you before in any transaction?—A. I was associated with him.

Q. How were you associated with him?—A. He was the counsel for the Quick Collection Mercantile Agency, of which I was manager, at 61 Park Row.

Q. The Quick Collection Agency?—A. The Quick Collection Agency.

Q. What are his professional connections in New York now? Who does he represent over there now?—A. I don't know.

Q. When had you seen him before you went to see him on Sunday last?—A. Oh, four or five weeks ago.

Q. And this statement that he wrote out—did you swear to it?—A. Yes, sir.

Q. Before whom?—A. Before a notary public.

Q. When did you swear to it?—A. Last evening.

Q. Where did you swear to it?—A. At Mr. Rogers's house.

Q. Who was the notary public?—A. I don't know the gentleman—somebody associated with Mr. Rogers.

Q. Who was present at the time, besides the notary public, Rogers, and yourself?—A. Nobody.

Q. Who was in Rogers's office when you went there?—A. We were not in the office.

Q. Where were you?—A. At his house.

Q. Who went there with you?—A. My brother.

Q. Who else?—A. Nobody.

Q. Did Rogers send for you?—A. No, sir.

Q. Did you have an appointment with him before you went to his house?—A. No, sir.

Q. Did you telephone around to his house before you went?—A. No, sir.

Q. How did you know he was home?—A. I didn't know it. I asked at the door whether he was in when the girl, or the lady, or whoever it was came to the door.

Q. What is the name of that notary public?—A. I don't even know the name. It is on that document.

Mr. ROGERS. Do you wish the name?

By Mr. WHEELER:

Q. Was there a notary public at Rogers's house when you went there?—A. No, sir.

Q. Who went after him?—A. I don't know.

Q. How did he happen to come in?—A. I think Mr. Rogers had some business with him.

Q. He just happened in there?—A. No, sir.

Q. Was he there when you got there?—A. When I got in in the evening Mr. Rogers was telling him something about some procedure in court to-morrow, to explain to Judge O'Dwyer——

Q. I understood you to state a moment ago he was not there when you reached Rogers's house.—A. Who was not there?

Q. I understood you to say so.—A. I said the first time he was not there.

Q. You were at Rogers's house twice then?—A. Yes, sir.

Q. When did you go the first time?—A. Between 11 and 12 o'clock.

Q. And the second time?—A. I think I went there about half past 2.

Q. And the statement was written out when?—A. I don't think the statement was through until 7 or 8 o'clock—something like that.

Q. And the notary public remained all this time, did he?—A. No; I was downstairs when the notary public came in.

Q. Where was Rogers?—A. He was downstairs attending to some business with clients. Mrs. Rogers was there.

Q. When you went up the notary public was there?—A. Yes, sir.

Q. And Rogers was talking with him on business?—A. I don't know anything about what he was talking to him about.

Q. You just said he was telling him something about some judge.—A. Oh, when I came in; yes.

Q. Came in where?—A. To the room.

Q. From where?—A. From the basement.

Q. And you say you were associated with this quick-collection agency over there in New York?—A. Yes, sir.

Q. Did you have some suits?—A. No, sir.

Q. You never had any suits?—A. No, sir; we just collected bills. I don't know but what there were suits we had emanating out of our business.

Q. Did you ever take any part in those suits?—A. No, sir.

Q. Did you get any witnesses for them?—A. No, sir.

Q. Were you ever a witness in court?—A. No, sir.

Q. Were you ever sworn before you came before this committee?—A. I may have been.

Q. Were you?—A. I don't remember.

Q. Did you never take an oath before?—A. I think I have, as election district polling clerk.

Q. What are your religious proclivities?—A. I beg your pardon?

Q. What are your religious inclinations?—A. Hebrew.

Q. Do you believe in the existence of a God?—A. I do, sir.

Q. And you state to the committee that you did not know it was morally wrong to swear falsely before this committee?—A. I didn't think about it at the time.

Q. Did you subsequently think about it?—A. Yes, sir; after I had a talk with Mr. Rogers.

Q. After you had a talk with Mr. Rogers?—A. Well, I was talking with him, of course.

Q. Did you come to the conclusion it was wrong?—A. Yes, sir.

Q. When did you come to that conclusion?—A. About a quarter of 12, it may have been. It may have been 12 o'clock, Sunday.

Q. Before or after you had seen Rogers?—A. While I was talking with him.

Q. What did you go to see him for, if your conscience was not pricking you on the subject?—A. To see what to do in the situation.

Q. What are you concerned about it for, if it never occurred to you before that nothing was wrong about it?—A. I was simply trying to right the wrong I had done.

Q. You had concluded it was wrong before you saw Rogers, did you?—A. Practically.

Q. Had you ever heard it was legally wrong?—A. No, sir.

Q. My suggestion here is the first time it ever occurred to you that it was legally wrong?—A. Excepting by Mr. Rogers.

Q. Then it was the advice of a lawyer that convinced you of your moral turpitude, was it?—A. No; not exactly.

Q. When you said Rogers read this statement over, and you told him you could not stand for that—you said you could not stand for it?

Mr. LOUDENSLAGER. Do you mean Mr. Rogers now?

By Mr. WHEELER:

Q. When he told you you could not stand for that, what did he mean by that?—A. I don't remember saying that.

Mr. ROGERS. He did not say that. He said Mr. Lessler said that.

By Mr. WHEELER:

Q. I understand. Did Rogers tell you you must not stand for that—that you could not stand for that?—A. No, sir.

By Mr. VANDIVER:

Q. You say you went home from here Saturday night?—A. Yes, sir.

Q. What time did you reach home?—A. You mean at my house or in New York City?

Q. In New York City.—A. I think it was about 11 o'clock—between 11 and 12.

Q. Did you go straight home?—A. I did; yes, sir.

Q. Did you talk with any members of your family about this?—A. No, sir. My folks were asleep when I got in, and I went right to bed; excepting that my wife said "This is annoying;" but I says "It will be all right." I said "Just be peaceful and we will get out of it all right."

Q. Yesterday morning you got up in the usual way and had break-fast at the usual time, did you?—A. Yes, sir; well, Sunday morning time.

Q. Did you talk with anybody else before you went to see Mr. Rogers?—A. No, sir; outside of my brother on the way over.

Q. You talked with your brother?—A. Yes, sir.

Q. Did he advise you to go to see the lawyer?—A. He said I ought to go see somebody about it. He said it looked very funny. "Well," I says, "it will come out all right."

Q. Did you or not talk with any other person who advised you to this course?—A. No, sir.

Q. Or to any other person who had anything to say to you about the advisability of this course?—A. No, sir.

Q. You did not talk with any other person on this subject at all?—A. No.

By Mr. KITCHIN:

Q. Mr. Doblin, when you went to see Mr. Rogers on Sunday did you first tell him what you had stated before this committee and then tell him that that was not true?—A. Yes, sir.

Q. Then he told you that if that was not true you ought not to let it stand?—A. Yes, sir.

Q. That it was after telling him that your story here was not true that you decided you wanted to come back down here and correct it?—A. Yes, sir.

By Mr. VANDIVER:

Q. When did you get back down here?—A. Here?

Q. Yes.—A. This morning.

Q. What time this morning?—A. We got in here, I think, at 7.20.

Q. Did you talk with anyone else about the matter before you came up to the committee room?—A. No, sir.

Q. Where did you stop here—at what hotel?—A. I didn't stop at any hotel. I went up to the Arlington and had something to eat with Mr. Rogers.

Q. Then you came from there up here to the committee room?—A. Yes, sir.

Q. Did you talk with anybody on the subject except counsel before you made your statement here in the committee?—A. Yes, sir.

Q. Who?—A. A porter.

Q. What porter?—A. In the hotel. I asked him to lock the door of room 76.

Q. Why did you want him to lock the door?—A. Because we were going downstairs. I was going to get shaved, and I don't know what Mr. Rogers was going to do.

Q. What did you talk to the porter about this matter for?—A. To tell him to go up and close the door. I didn't have the key. I was standing down in the hall when I told him.

Q. Was that talking about this matter?—A. I didn't understand your question, whether I was talking about any matter. I understood your question, whether I had spoke to anybody.

Q. About this matter.—A. I didn't so understand it.

By Mr. RIXEY:

Q. Did you talk with Mr. Lessler after you reached the city this morning?—A. No, sir.

Q. If you were going to make this statement here absolutely refuting your former testimony, as you were a friend of Mr. Lessler's, do you not think it was fair to him to go to him and tell him you were going now to tell the truth about this statement?—A. I don't know anything about that.

Q. You did not go to his hotel, and you did not seek Mr. Lessler?—A. No, sir.

By Mr. WHEELER:

Q. Have you seen him since you arrived here last Saturday?—A. Congressman Lessler? ·

Q. Yes.—A. No, sir.

By Mr. BUTLER:

Q. Mr. Doblin, you stated in the conversation you had with some member of your family, who doubted the propriety of your conduct, that it would come out all right. What did you refer to as coming out all right?—A. We were discussing the newspaper.

Q. You thought the newspaper would come out all right?—A. No, sir.

Q. What did you mean when you said it would come out all right?—A. I didn't mean anything particular.

Q. Then why did you use the expression "it will come out all right?"—A. Nothing particular.

Q. You meant something in reply to some member of your family when you said it would come out all right, did you not?—A. I presume so.

Q. Then, having presumed that you did, what did you understand?—A. Why the general proposition; that is all.

Q. That the general proposition would come out all right?—A. Yes, sir.

Q. When you referred to the general proposition, what did you mean?—A. I was talking about the general matter of the testimony here at Washington.

Q. What part of the proposition would come out all right?—A. The general proposition.

Q. That the general proposition would come out all right.—A. Yes.

Q. What, in your judgment, would be a proper conclusion of the general proposition?—A. To come here and admit the truth.

Q. Then, before you went to see this lawyer, you had concluded to retract what you had said. Is that so?—A. It was so.

Q. Did you not say to Mr. Wheeler that the change of opinion came over you when you saw the lawyer?—A. Why, on the way to the lawyer's.

Q. Then you think that this is coming out all right for you to come here and retract, do you?—A. No.

Q. Then what did you mean when you said it would come out all right?—A. Nothing particular.

Q. You meant something?—A. I don't remember what I was talking about at the time except that we were discussing the case.

Q. What had your people said to you about it before you made the statement that it would come out all right?—A. They discussed it very fully.

Q. What had they said to you before they made the remark that it would come out all right?—A. Nothing, as I remember.

Q. Therefore, they having said nothing to you, you made the remark that it would come out all right, did you?—A. To my brother, on the way to the lawyer's.

Q. You did not make the remark, then, before you went to the lawyer with your brother?—A. Not that I remember.

Q. I understood you to say that this change in your conscience had come about before you went to the lawyer.—A. I was on my way; yes, sir.

Q. Therefore it was on your way, between your home and the lawyer's?—A. Yes, sir.

Q. That this change came over you?—A. About that, I think.

Q. What had your brother said to you that suggested that remark?—A. Nothing at all.

Q. Therefore, your brother having said nothing to you, you made that remark?—A. We were talking about the proposition.

Q. Talking about changing your testimony?—A. No, sir.

Q. Then you did not talk to any person about changing your testimony until you saw the lawyer?—A. Why, on the way over I was discussing it with my brother.

Q. Did you not mean it would come out all right that Mr. Quigg would be condemned?—A. I didn't think anything about that.

Q. You did not think anything about it?—A. Not at that time.

Q. Then you made the remark without thinking?—A. I might have.

Q. You made the first statement because you were told to make it, did you not?—A. I don't know what statement you refer to.

Q. You made your first statement to the subcommittee in there because you were told to make it?—A. I received the inference by the paper.

Q. Do you mean to say you found an inference in the newspaper that you were to make such a statement as you made before the subcommittee?—A. Well, I got a telegram, and thinking it was all confidential, and Mr. Lessler assuring me there was nothing to it——

Q. Then you made this first statement upon the assurance of Mr. Lessler, did you?—A. I won't say as to that.

Q. Upon whose authority and by whose direction did you make the second statement, the testimony you gave here the other day?—A. My own.

Q. That was voluntary?—A. No, sir; by notice to appear.

Q. You appeared under direction of the chairman of the committee?—A. Yes, sir.

Q. And were sworn as a witness?—A. Yes, sir.

Q. But without having had it suggested to you what you should say,

H. Rep. 3482——8

you made that statement to this committee?—A. To carry out the statement I made before

Q. Following up what you had said the day before—— A. Before the subcommittee.

Q. You knew when you appeared before this subcommittee that you were not qualified as a witness and required to tell the truth in the estimation of some people—— A. I don't know.

Q. Who think that way upon such subjects?—A. I don't know.

Q. You knew the second day when you appeared that you were sworn as a witness?—A. I was sworn.

Q. Did you ever hear of an offense called perjury?—A. I have heard of it.

Q. Where did you ever hear it?—A. I have heard it around court.

Q. You did know, then, when you testified last week that you were committing perjury?—A. I didn't think about it then.

Q. But did you know it?—A. I didn't think about it then.

Q. If you did not think about it, of course you did not know it.—A. I didn't think about it then.

Q. Did you think of the effect of your testimony upon Mr. Quigg?—A No, sir.

Q. At the time?—A. No, sir.

Q You were absolutely lost to all sense of propriety and decency, were you?—A. I was told——

Q. Who told you?—A. I was told by Mr. Lessler there would be nothing to it; it would be all right.

Q. Did Mr. Lessler tell you there would be nothing to the offense you would commit if you should commit perjury?—A. I have a telegram there that says everything was all right.

Q. Did you mean by that that it was all right to commit perjury?—A. I didn't understand that.

By Mr. TATE:

Q. Who suggested to you first that you see a lawyer?—A. Myself.

Q. You were the first one to suggest it?—A. Yes, sir.

Q. Then, it is not true that the members of your family suggested it to you?—A. I did not say that.

Q. I say that it is not true, in point of fact, that the members of your family suggested that you see a lawyer?—A. I was walking——

Q. No; I did not ask you that. No one suggested that you should see a lawyer; you just got the idea of seeing a lawyer, then, yourself?—A. Yes, sir.

Q. You did not see a lawyer by reason of any family conference or the suggestion of any member of your family?—A. No, sir.

Q. You did it upon your own motion?—A. Yes, sir.

Q. How far does this lawyer live from where you live?—A. Seventy-eighth street; about three or four blocks.

Q. You went to his place, and you showed him this article in the paper with your picture?—A. No, sir.

Q. You said something to him about it, did you, or did he mention it to you?—A. No, sir.

Q. What did you say?—A. I said to him that I came here to retract this statement I made.

Q. To retract the statement?—A. Yes, sir.

Q. He said that he knew of it, did he?—A. He said that he read something about it.

Q. He knew something about it, and he told you that you could not stand for a statement like that?—A. No, sir.

Q. He did not tell you any such thing in your conversation?—A. No, sir; I don't remember it.

Q. Then when you told him that he began preparing this paper of yours that you swore to?—A. Not at that time.

Q. When did he prepare that paper?—A. I don't know when he commenced it. It was done some time in the evening. I was downstairs with Mrs. Rogers in the basement, reading the paper.

Q. Did you remain there until he prepared that paper?—A. No, sir.

Q. Where did you go when you went out after the first visit?—A. I went out to dinner.

Q. Where did you go then?—A. I went down to our club on East Eighty-first street.

Q. Whom did you see there?—A. A couple of the boys there. I didn't say anything about it.

Q. Where did you go then?—A. I went down to Mr. Rogers's house.

Q. And he told you that he would prepare this statement, and for you to come back?—A. No, sir.

Q. Did he have it ready?—A. No, sir.

Q. He prepared it then?—A. Yes, sir.

Q. Did he prepare it before you got there, or after?—A. Yes, sir.

Q. He prepared it after you got back there?—A. He prepared it in my presence.

Q. He prepared it in your presence. What did he tell you the particular purpose of preparing that proposed statement was?—A. He did not state the particular purpose. I told him I wanted to make a statement retracting what I had said here.

Q. He then wrote out a statement?—A. No, sir; I told him what was the statement I wanted to retract.

Q. You told him and he wrote it out?—A. Yes, sir.

Q. What did he tell you was the particular purpose of that?—A. He said he would present it to the committee if they would receive it; and if not, he would ask them to put me on the stand.

By Mr. WHEELER:

Q. In perfect frankness, is not this a fact: That you had been induced to make this statement, and that the parties who got you to make it were taking no chances on it and were making you swear to it when you agreed to?—A. No, sir.

Q. Is not that a fact?—A. No, sir.

By Mr. NICHOLL:

Q. Mr. Doblin, do you recollect my examining you the other day?—A. Yes, sir.

Q. In the course of my examination you testified that when you went out with Mr. Quigg to lunch he said to you, in substance, speaking of the Holland boat proposition, "There is $5,000 in it." That, I understand you to say, is not true; that is not true?—A. No, sir.

Q. You also stated that later on Quigg said something to the effect that he would try to see if he could get you a thousand dollars. That is not true, is it?—A. No, sir.

Q. You also stated in your testimony that he told you to call him up on the telephone at half past 3 in the afternoon, at his office, when he would tell you whether or not he could get you this extra thousand dollars. Is that true?—A. No, sir.

Q. You also testified that he called you up over the telephone and that he said over the telephone, when you were speaking of this matter, "That is all right," referring to the thousand dollars. Is that true?—A. I had a talk over the telephone——

Q. No, no. Is it true that he said over the telephone, referring to the thousand dollars, "That is all right?"—A. No, sir.

Q. You also stated in your testimony that thereafter you went and saw Mr. Lessler, the next day, I think, and told him that you had had a talk with Mr. Quigg, and that there was $5,000 in it. That is not true, is it?—A. No, sir.

Q. And then on the same day you reported to Mr. Quigg that Mr. Lessler would not take this money. That is not true?—A. I did not have any talk with him about money.

Q. You did not have any talk with him about money; you had a talk with him?—A. I had a talk with him.

Q. And you said to him—— A. That Mr. Lessler was not inclined to be friendly to the proposition.

Q. You said nothing about money to him in that conversation?— A. No, sir.

Q. Now, I examined you at some length about your coming down to Washington to see Mr. Quigg—to see Mr. Lessler. You told me that you came to Washington on the 12 o'clock train, and got to the Normandie at 10 o'clock in the morning—— A. Somewhere about that.

Q. Seven o'clock in the morning. It was at the arrival of the midnight train from New York?—A. Yes, sir.

Q. Did you go straight to the Normandie?—A. Yes, sir.

Q. Was the train on time?—A. I don't know, sir. It may have been a little late. I didn't pay any attention.

Q. Did you take any such notice of time as that you are able to say when you got to the Normandie on that morning?—A. I think the train is due here at 7.20.

Q. You have already introduced in evidence a telegram dated January 20, signed "Monte," which reads: "Take midnight train, and come to me. Want to see you. Keep this confidential." Did that telegram convey to your mind any idea of why Mr. Lessler wanted to see you?— A. No, sir.

Q. Or why you were to keep it confidential?—A. No, sir.

Q. Did you know at that time that Mr. Lessler had made a statement before his colleagues of the Naval Committee that he had been tempted with a bribe?—A. No, sir.

Q. And that he had virtuously rejected it?—A. No, sir.

Q. Did you know that?—A. No, sir.

Q. Did you know any reason why you should keep the fact confidential that you were coming to Washington to see him?—A. No, sir.

Q. Did you keep it confidential?—A. Yes, sir.

Q. Did you tell anybody about it?—A. No, sir; oh, yes, sir.

Q. You did?—A. I had to get some money, and I said to a particular friend of mine named Mann, Joseph Mann, who is the treasurer of the Republican Union, to lend me some money; "I am going out of town to-night," and "keep this confidential;" and of course it did not go any further.

Q. Of course not. But did you say that Lessler had sent you a telegram from Washington?—A. No, sir.

Q. Summoning you, at midnight?—A. No, sir.

Q. And telling you to keep it confidential?—A. No, sir.

Q. You did not say that?—A. No, sir.

Q. In fact, you did not tell Mr. Joseph Mann that you were going to see Mr. Lessler at all?—A. No, sir.

Q. You said that you were going out of town?—A. No, sir; I might have said that I was going to Washington. I don't remember the exact language.

Q. Now, is it a fact that the first you knew of the circumstance that Mr. Lessler had made a statement concerning the offer of a bribe to him to support the Holland boat proposition was when you got to Washington?—A. Yes, sir.

Mr. WHEELER. Let me suggest something to you. Do you not think that we have had enough of this, Mr. Chairman?

Mr. NICHOLL. You want to cut me off?

Mr. WHEELER. Yes, sir; I want to cut you off. I want to stop this.

The CHAIRMAN. Oh no, no.

Mr. NICHOLL. If you want to cut me off, cut me off.

Mr. TATE. The committee will decide whether you are cut off or not.

Mr. NICHOLL. Cut me off if you want to.

Mr. WHEELER. I just simply suggest it. There is no use of your being so angry.

Mr. NICHOLL. I just desire to examine the witness a very little further. I have not been three minutes yet.

Mr. WHEELER. The witness has taken such an attitude that it is useless to take up the time of the committee to consider any statement that he might make.

Mr. NICHOLL. I beg your pardon, Mr. Wheeler, I take a different view of it. I consider that the wickedest and foulest plot against my client, an ex-member of the House, has been revealed here to-day, and I want to probe it here to-day. It entails consequences which every one of us must see must happen. I want to probe it to the bottom.

Mr. WHEELER. I would certainly be very glad to, but the difficulty is we are looking at only one end of the string.

Mr. NICHOLL. I have no interest in the Holland boat proposition or anything concerning it.

Mr. BUTLER. We all understand that, Mr. Nicholl.

Mr. NICHOLL. It is perfectly obvious that at some time, if this committee does not take it up, there will be some investigation of this matter. Are we not saving time in doing it now? We are all here and are all anxious to get at the truth.

The CHAIRMAN. Go ahead, Mr. Nicholl.

(The last question and answer were read by the stenographer.)

By Mr. NICHOLL.

Q. Now, when you got into the room with Mr. Lessler, as I understand it, on that morning, he did not have this paper, did he [indicating newspaper]?—A. No, sir.

Q. So that at your first session with him, while he was dressing, you did not know of this article in the paper, did you?—A. No, sir.

Q. You have read this article, have you not?—A. Not very carefully—just now. I have read it.

Q. Have you looked it over since the committee was here?—A. You mean the article in the Post?

Q. In the Post.—A. Of Wednesday morning?

Q. Wednesday morning.—A. Yes, sir.

Q. This article reads as follows, the headlines:

"Tells of bribe offer. Mr. Lessler says attempt was made to buy support. Alleged proffer of $5,000. Object sought, he declares, was appropriation of additional submarine torpedo boats. Subcommittee of House Naval Affairs Committee is investigating New York member's charge."

Now, before you ever read the article, did you not learn from Mr. Lessler that he had blurted—made this statement?—A. Yes, sir.

Q. Of an offer to a bribe to him?—A. Yes, sir. Well, he was getting out of bed and putting on his trousers.

Q. Exactly. What did he say then, as nearly as you recollect it?— A. I knocked on the door, and he said "Come in," and I think the door was open, or he may have got up and opened the door, and he was there in his night clothes; and he said, "I got you in trouble."

Q. Tell us just as near as you can recollect the details. That is exactly what I want.—A. He said, "I got you in trouble." "How is that?" I said.

Q. Did you understand what he meant?—A. No, sir.

Q. When he said "I got you in trouble?"—A. No, sir.

Q. That did not convey anything to your mind?—A. No, sir.

Q. Very well; then what did you say?—A. I said, "How do you mean—what do you mean?" "Why," he said, "I blurted it out to the committee yesterday in the Committee of the Whole and they appointed a subcommittee, and," he said, "you got to appear before the subcommittee;" and then, "You appear before the subcommittee and it will be all right," and "Wait a minute." I think it was about that juncture when he went downstairs and got the paper and came back, and I said, "What do you mean?"

Q. Wait a moment; you are going too fast for me. All this time, I understand you, he was putting on his clothes, and taking off—— A. He had already gotten his clothes on when he went down for the paper.

Q. In the meantime your conversation lasted during the period when he was taking off his nightclothes and washing and putting on his day clothes, did it not?—A. Yes, sir.

Q. How long a period did that take?—A. I guess twenty minutes.

Q. Twenty minutes?—A. Yes, sir; fully.

Q. Have you told us all the conversation that occurred within that twenty minutes?—A. No, sir. He said, "I simply blurted it out." I said, "Blurted what out?"

Q. That is right. Go on and tell it.—A. (Continuing.) "Why," he said, "I told the committee yesterday that I had been approached by a bribe, and I told them that you had had a talk with Quigg about this subject."

Q. Yes; that is on the subject of the Holland boat?—A. Yes, of the Holland boat. And he said that he had "blurted out this whole business." I said, "What whole business?" "Your conversation with Quigg." I said, "What conversation with Quigg?" He says, "Wait a minute," and went down and got the paper and brought it back, and I looked at it.

Q. Wait a moment. Until that time you did not understand that he was referring to the conversation with Quigg in which he had been offered $5,000, did you? I want to know that.—A. At that time?

Q. Yes.—A. Why, he was speaking about the proposal.

Q. About—— A. He was getting dressed when he was speaking about the propostiion.

Q. What proposition?—A. About this bribe charge that he had blurted out.

Q. Now, you knew perfectly well, if your story is true here to-day, as you say it is, that you had not had any talk with Mr. Quigg about money, did you not?—A. That is right.

Q. Yes. And that he had not offered you any $5,000 or $1,000?—A. That is right.

Q. Yes. What did you say to Mr. Lessler?—A. I said, "Why, I can not stand for this."

Q. You "can not stand for it?"—A. No, "I can not stand for it." He said, "It's all right. You must go before the subcommittee, and they will report it to the full committee, and that will be all there is to it." I had the paper in my hand.

Q. If I understand, he came back and showed you this paper?—A. At the time I had——

Q. There is nothing said about Quigg in that paper, is there? |Handing witness paper.]—A. He told me that he had said "Quigg."

Q. He told you that Quigg was the man?—A. Yes, sir.

Q. You came and told the subcommittee, in my presence, that you were to get a thousand dollars in addition out of it?—A. Yes, sir.

Q. There is nothing stated about that in the Post. How did that come in?—A. Well, I supposed that Lessler had said something about a thousand dollars and some member of the subcommittee said, when I was talking about the thousand-dollar proposition, or at least before I had made any mention, after the committee had said it was all right, he said—some member of the committee, I do not know who it was— "There was $5,000 in it for you and Lessler and $1,000 extra," and I thought that maybe Lessler had said something to the subcommittee about an extra thousand dollars and I was trying to substantiate it.

Q. Now, Mr. Doblin, did Mr. Lessler say anything to you as to the fact as to whether he had gotten himself into difficulty or in a hole on this subject?—A. Yes, sir.

Q. What did he say on that subject?—A. I can not say exactly that he used—the whole language that he used, because there was twenty minutes' talk, and a lot of talk in that time; but the substance of it was, "I am in a hole here, and you have got to just carry it out."

Q. That was the substance of it?—A. Yes.

Q. Well, were you not brought face to face then with the proposition as to whether or not you would go so far in helping out a friend as to make a false statement concerning another man?—A. I never thought anything about it. When Mr. Lessler told me it was all right I simply carried out his instructions.

Q. That is, did you believe, or did what he told you lead you to believe, that you would make an informal statement to a subcommittee; is that it?—A. He absolutely stated that there would be nothing to it. "Just go up there"—after I had talked to him a few minutes—" go up there and make your statement, and there will be nothing further to it."

Q. "There will be nothing further to it?"—A. "They will report to the"——

Q. To the full committee?—A. (Continuing.) "The full committee," and "that that will be all there will be to it. I will go and see the Speaker." Then he came back, and Son was there, and Son went away, and when Lessler left he told me that he would have Son come for me.

Q. Of course, you must have been conscious that you were doing a great wrong to Mr. Quigg to make statements of that sort if they were not true?—A. Well, I thought Mr. Lessler knew what he wanted.

Q. Did you feel yourself under such deep obligations to Mr. Lessler that you were willing to go there and do that for him?—A. Yes, sir.

Q. And did you think you had rendered him a useful and substantial service when you made these statements to the subcommittee?—A. Yes, sir.

Q. And did you go back to New York satisfied that you had so rendered him a substantial service?—A. He so told me on the way back.

Q. What did he say?—A. He said, "You are all right—it is all right."

Q. He said that it was all right?—A. He was reading some book, and then he didn't want to discuss the subject any more.

Q. Is that all he said to you?—A. Oh, we went to—before I had decided to go to New York he sent this telegram.

Q. He sent the telegram to your wife?—A. Yes, sir.

Q. Which you have already put in evidence here?—A. Yes, sir.

Q. You got back to New York on the night of the 21st, did you not? You went right back, was it—you went back to New York what night? Look at the calendar there [indicating calendar on wall].—A. Wednesday night.

Q. That is the 21st, isn't it?—A. Yes, sir.

Q. And you didn't come back to Washington until the night of the 23d; is that it? You came back to Washington on the night of the 23d?—A. Midnight of the 23d; yes, sir.

Q. You then knew, did you not, that you were wanted by the whole committee?—A. Yes, sir.

Q. When you got to Washington that morning, where did you go?—A. To the Normandie.

Q. Did you see Mr. Lessler?—A. Yes, sir.

Q. Did you go to his room?—A. Yes, sir.

Q. Did you ring the bell or knock at the door?—A. Why, he met me at the train that morning and we walked up.

Q. He met you at the train last Saturday morning?—A. Yes, sir; we walked up and got in a bus, and rode in the bus to the Normandie.

Q. And when you got to the Normandie where did you go?—A. We had breakfast served in the room.

Q. In the room?—A. He did.

Q. What—where?—A. He did. He had breakfast served in his room.

Q. Did you know then that you had been requested by the full committee, through its chairman, to appear before them?—A. Yes, sir.

Q. Did you know then that you would come before the committee and be sworn?—A. Yes, sir.

Q. And repeat this testimony?—A. Yes, sir.

Q. What, if anything, did Mr. Lessler say to this?—A. While we were sitting at breakfast Mr. Lessler said: "I don't remember anything about the thousand-dollar business; where did you get that?" "Well," I said, "at the subcommittee some member of the committee referred to the $5,000 and the thousand dollars, and I supposed that you had said something about a thousand dollars, and it was well to take it up."

Q. You knew, did you not, that you were coming down here that morning?—A. Yes, sir.

Q. Last Saturday morning?—A. Yes, sir.

Q. To be sworn and examined before the subcommittee?—A. Yes, sir. And at that time I was still assured there would not be anything to it.

Q. Who said that to you?—A. Mr. Lessler.

Q. Where did he say it to you?—A. At the Normandie, while we were eating.

Q. What did he say to you?—A. He said, "There will not be anything to this. You just go there and corroborate your statement to the subcommittee, and there will not be anything to it."

Q. Did you appreciate at that time that you were accusing Mr. Quigg of a crime?—A. No, sir.

Q. You did not so understand it, did you?—A. No, sir. Mr. Lessler assured me that it was all right, and I took his word.

Q. You had such supreme confidence in him that you relied on his word?—A. Absolutely.

Q. Ahead of your own experience?—A. Yes, sir.

By Mr. RIXEY:

Q. I want to ask one question. My recollection of the testimony of Mr. Lessler before the subcommittee was that he made no mention of the fact that you were to get a thousand dollars at all. His statement was that he was to get—that your proposition to him was that you were to get $5,000.—A. I would get that; yes, sir.

Q. Now, you say that some member of the subcommittee mentioned the thousand dollars before you said anything about it. Are you positive about that?—A. Yes, sir.

Q. Are you positive of that?—A. At the time some member of the committee, whoever it was, mentioned the $5,000, and the $1,000 extra.

Q. They mentioned that Lessler's statement was that he was to get $5,000, and you were to get $1,000 extra?—A. No, sir; the way the conversation came was, as I remember now, "Didn't Quigg say to you that there was $5,000 in it, and that there was $1,000 in it for you?" And I turned around at the time and I said, "I didn't say anything about Quigg."

Q. Do you mean to say now—I am not talking about Quigg, but about the thousand-dollar proposition—that some member of the subcommittee propounded that question to you?—A. That is the way I heard it. They did not propound any question.

Q. They asked you that question, you said?—A. They simply said: "You remember talking to Lessler about"——

Q. I understand; but you stated a moment or two ago that you never thought of the thousand-dollar statement until some member of the subcommittee suggested it to you. Now, is that true?—A. That is where I got the impression from.

Q. From some member of the subcommittee?—A. In the talk.

Q. It was asked you in your examination before the subcommittee, you said, if you were to get a thousand dollars?—A. Yes sir; that is my recollection.

Q. Before you ever thought of it; and you say that the question suggested to you your answer?—A. Yes, sir.

Q. Now, I don't know how the other committeemen remember it——

By Mr. TAYLER:

Q. Did you not say to the subcommittee, when you opened this matter of the amount that was involved, that the figure named by Quigg was $6,000?—A. I might.

Q. And we asked you what disposition was to be made of that, and you said, why, $5,000 of this was for the other fellow, whoever he might be, and $1,000 for you?—A. I might have.

Q. Was not that the way the matter arose?—A. It might have.

Q. Another matter. You remember going to Mr. Quigg's office with Mr. Obermeier?—A. Yes, sir.

Q. What did you say to Mr. Obermeier about money having been offered for help in this Holland boat business?—A. I don't remember saying anything to him about money.

Q. Didn't you have some talk with him, saying that there had been some suggestion of money respecting Quigg before you had seen Quigg, and that was out of it, and now you wanted to get it without that?

Mr. DAYTON. You mean Lessler?

Mr. TAYLER. I mean Lessler; yes. If I said Quigg I meant Lessler. Just change that question to Lessler. Strike out that question and I will ask it again.

By Mr. TAYLER:

Q. Didn't you say to Mr. Obermeier that there had been some question of securing influence by money, but now you were going to try to get Lessler without the use of money?—A. I don't remember.

Q. Did you?—A. I don't remember.

Q. Did you say that you did not?—A. I might have.

Q. You might have. If you said it, how did you come to say it?—A. I don't remember.

Q. You don't remember. Had there been any talk about money prior to that time?—A. No, sir.

Q. None at all?—A. No, sir.

By Mr. DAYTON:

Q. Just one question I want to ask. Did you ever tell Mr. Obermeier, in any conversation, that there was no money in it, or the money proposition had been made by Quigg, or anyone else, to Lessler?—A. I don't remember.

Q. You don't remember of ever telling him anything to that effect?—A. No, sir.

Q. Can you remember your conversations with Mr. Obermeier? How many did you have?—A. One that I remember.

Q. Did you inform him in that conversation that you were authorized, or that Quigg was authorized, or words to that effect, to offer money to Lessler?—A. I think not.

Q. Did you ever tell anybody——— A. No, sir.

Mr. ROGERS. Mr. Obermeier, in his testimony before the committee, distinctly stated that in the conversation which you had with him you talked of Lessler's anticipated support of the Holland boat proposition, and then you said to Obermeier that there was nothing in it. Now, what did you mean by that expression that there was "nothing in it," if you said that to Obermeier?

The WITNESS. I don't remember that I said anything like that.

Mr. OBERMEIER. I beg pardon. I have been misquoted. I can quote it.

Mr. ROGERS. I would like to have the stenographer read it.

Mr. TAYLER. It will be easier for Mr. Obermeier to state it again than for the stenographer to find it, and I would rather have him state it again.

Mr. OBERMEIER. I said that to the best of my recollection Mr. Doblin had said to me, and I thought the statement had been made after I had seen Quigg, in a general way, that there had been money considerations discussed, but there was nothing in it. And I qualified it by saying that I supposed it meant, and I assumed it meant, that that sort of thing did not go, and he now wanted it discussed from the point of view of doing a personal favor.

Mr. ROGERS Mr. Obermeier says he said there was nothing in it.

Mr. TAYLER. That is not what he said. He said that there had been money in it.

Mr. ROGERS. Mr. Obermeier now states that he said there had been money in it, but that "there was nothing in it."

By Mr. ROGERS:

Q. Mr. Obermeier has stated that you had said that there had been money in it, or a money proposition in it, but there was nothing in it. Will you kindly tell this committee what you meant by saying that "there was nothing in it," if you said so.—A. I asked Mr. Obermeier to go and see Mr. Quigg for the purpose when he went down to Washington, to see if he could not get a friendly disposition toward this, because it would be a good political move. And I said nothing, that I recollect, regarding money, excepting I might have talked about the amount of the appropriation, in a general way, talking about the Holland torpedo boat.

Q. But you did not state, directly or indirectly, that a money proposition had been made to Mr. Lessler?—A. No, sir; not that I remember.

Q. Or that he had rejected it, and that there was nothing in it, so far as Mr. Lessler was concerned?—A. Not that I remember.

Q. Now, when you came and saw Mr. Rogers yesterday at No. 162 East Seventy-eighth street did anybody send you there?—A. No, sir.

Q. Did you come there entirely of your own will?—A. Yes, sir.

Q. You came to employ Mr. Rogers as your counsel?—A. Yes, sir.

Q. How long had you known Mr. Rogers prior to yesterday?—A. I don't know; a long time.

Q. You knew that Mr. Rogers was practicing law in New York City?—A. Yes, sir.

Q. Now, before you saw Mr. Rogers, and on your way back from Washington, whom did you see?—A. Mr. Rogers.

Q. On the way back—— A. Oh; Mr. Lessler.

Q. Was anything said at that time about looking up the law?—A. Yes, sir.

Q. Who said anything about looking up the law?—A. Mr. Lessler said that he would look up the law to-morrow.

Q. For what purpose?—A. He didn't state.

Q. Was it in response to any question you put to him, or any question put to you, that he said he was going to look up the law?—A. We discussed it a little and then we tried to sleep, and then we tried to read the papers.

Q. Was there anything said about looking up a proposition of law?—A. Yes, sir; absolutely.

Q. Referring to this thing?—A. Yes, sir.

Q. And the testimony that you had given?—A. Yes, sir.

Q. Was not that one of the things that prompted you to go and consult counsel?—A. Yes, sir.

Q. You knew that Mr. Lessler had a peculiar interest of his own here, did you not?—A. I did not consider that so much at that time.

Q. Was not that one of the reasons why you did not want to go and see Mr. Lessler about it, that you knew that he was an interested party?—A. Oh, certainly.

Q. Now, Mr. Doblin, you called at No. 162 East Seventy-eighth street, in the morning, the first time?—A. Yes, sir.

Q. Did you remain some time?—A. Yes, sir.

Q. Accompanied by your brother, but he did not take any part in the conference?—A. No, sir. He went in the front room, and the door was closed.

Q. And then you left Mr. Rogers's?—A. Yes, sir.

Q. And returned again?—A. Yes, sir.

Q. And after you had come there, how long was it before the gentleman who took your affidavit came in?—A. Well, we had talked a little while together.

Q. Yes, but how many minutes, or hours, after you came back in the afternoon, after half past 2, before this gentleman came?—A. It was probably 7 or 8 o'clock.

Q. Then two hours had intervened?—A. Yes, sir.

Q. And this gentleman was introduced to you by Mr. Rogers as being an associate of his?—A. Yes, sir.

Q. In his business?—A. Yes, sir.

Q. And when you came into the room they were discussing some other business than yours?—A. Yes, sir. And said, "You wait a moment."

Q. And then your statement was taken down in the presence of Mr. Rogers and this other gentleman, Mr. Horkimer?—A. Yes, sir.

Q. And he was the gentleman who swore you to this affidavit at the time?—A. Yes, sir.

Q. And he assisted in the preparation of that?—A. Yes, sir.

Q. Now, had you seen anybody except Mr. Rogers from the time that you came in his house yesterday until you came here to testify to-day?—A. No, sir.

Q. Did anybody suggest to you from any source, either by writing or by communication of any sort to you, that you should come here and change your testimony?—A. No, sir.

Q. And is it not a fact that you came here to change your testimony only from the fact that you know it is untrue, and that you wanted to come here and correct it?—A. Yes, sir.

Q. Now, something was said about the legal consequences of your acts. You are not in the habit of testifying before legislative committees?—A. Never did.

Q. Did you ever look up the law with regard to the powers and nature of legislative committees, or the effect of testifying before one of them?—A. No, sir.

Q. Do you know whether a legislative committee has the same power as a court does?—A. I do not know.

Q. Did anyone ever tell you before to-day whether a legislative committee was the same as a court of law?—A. No, sir.

Q. Or that the testimony given here was the same as that given upon the stand in a court of justice?—A. No, sir.

Q. Something was said about perjury here to-day. Did you discuss the question of perjury with Mr. Rogers, and have some reference with him to the statute?—A. Yes, sir.

Q. And Mr. Rogers advised you that it was a probability that your testimony might be regarded, as given here the other day, as perjured, and that a criminal prosecution might follow?—A. Yes, sir.

Q. And Mr. Rogers advised you fully as to the legal consequences of your act?—A. Yes, sir.

Q. In coming here and testifying the other day?—A. Yes, sir.

Q. And of coming here and correcting your testimony?—A. Yes, sir.

Q. In what capacity did you consult Mr. Rogers, as a friend or as a lawyer?—A. As a lawyer.

Q. On both occasions that you came to Washington from New York you came in response to telegrams from Mr. Lessler, and you went to see him at his hotel?—A. Yes, sir.

Q. Arriving both times at about the same hour?—A. Yes, sir.

Q. What time was that?—A. Between 7 and 8 o'clock.

Q. And you had breakfast with Mr. Lessler on both occasions?—A. Yes, sir.

Q. And you remained with him until you came to the committee room?—A. Yes, sir.

Q. Now, Mr. Doblin, is it not a fact that you came to this committee, this subcommittee of this committee of the whole, and told this story, because you thought you were doing an act of friendship and evincing your friendship toward Mr. Lessler?—A. Absolutely.

Q. You were all this time friends with Mr. Lessler?—A. Yes, sir; and I am now.

Q. And you had some slight connection with him in his office?—A. Yes, sir.

Q. And visited him there?—A. Yes, sir.

Q. You visited him almost daily?—A. When he was in town.

Q. Did you have a desk there?—A. No, sir.

Q. But you used his desk?—A. Any time I wanted to I had permission to do so.

Q. Now, you knew Mr. Lessler's political progress and reward would be a benefit to you, did you not, Mr. Doblin?—A. I always regarded it very highly.

Q. And you knew that if Mr. Lessler got in the possession of affluence and influence he could assist you to get along in this world yourself?—A. Yes, sir.

Q. And that was one of the reasons you came here to help Mr. Lessler since this question came up in the House?—A. Yes, sir.

Q. Now, I have one other question. Do you want this committee to understand now that you have told them the truth and nothing but the truth?—A. On this testimony?

Q. Yes.—A. Yes, sir.

Q. Is there anything now that you desire to correct?—A. No, sir.

Q. And are you positive now that this is a voluntary statement made by you without any promise of reward?—A. Yes, sir.

Q. Have you been promised any reward for coming here to day?—A. No, sir.

Q. Or anything whatever?—A. No, sir.

By Mr. TAYLER:

Q. Did you try to get immunity from Mr. Nicholl or Mr. Quigg?—A. No, sir.

Q. Did your counsel?—A. I don't know anything about what he did.

Q. Did he?—A. I don't know.

Q. Did he tell you that he did?—A. I don't know.

Q. Did he tell that he was going to try to?—A. No sir.

By Mr. MEYER:

Q. You stated, as I understand, that your sense of obligation to Mr. Lessler was so great that it inspired you to come before this committee and make a false statement, under the belief that it would assist and aid him; is that correct?—A. Yes, sir; at that time.

Q. What is the nature of that obligation to Mr. Lessler? What has he done for you that would inspire you to go to such extremes?—A. He has indorsed me for positions in Mr. McCullagh's office. He has been friendly to me and aided me whenever I needed money; whenever I wanted to borrow a dollar I could go to him.

Q. Have you ever borrowed any considerable sums from him?—A. Large amounts?

Q. Large amounts?—A. A hundred dollars at one time.

Q. A hundred dollars. That is about the extent?—A. I never

needed any more. I never asked him for anything. He always told me anytime I wanted anything I could have it.

Q. Is that all he has done for you, lent you money in sums sometimes equal to $100, and at other times recommended you for political appointments?—A. He did, as I said the other day, recommend me for two or three positions.

Q. But that is about the extent of the obligation under which you are placed?—A. As I say, I was very friendly, and visited his house, and he was very nice to my children, and everything like that.

By Mr. KITCHIN:

Q. Is it true, as you stated the other day, that he had secured some receiverships for you?—A. Yes, sir.

By Mr. ROGERS:

Q. Congressmen Tayler and Wheeler have put some questions to you as to what took place in this subcommittee. Now, you do not want to be understood as saying that Mr. Tayler and Mr. Wheeler put any words in your mouth?—A. No, no, sir.

Q. Tell us, when you first came into the subcommittee room did you volunteer a statement or was the question put to you?—A. The question was put to me before I volunteered any statement.

Q. And tell us generally, as near as you can tell us, not the exact words, but the substance of the question that was put to you?—A. "Did not Quigg tell you that there was $5,000 in it, and $1,000 extra if you got it through?"

Q. Now, are you sure that that was the question, or was not this the question; was not something said in that subcommittee room to this effect: "Mr. Doblin, is it not a fact that Mr. Quigg said something about $6,000 being in it for Lessler and you, or $6,000 for Lessler?"—A. Yes, sir. I heard Congressman Tayler say that a little while ago.

Q. Now, was the question divided up into the $5,000 and $1,000 or was it in the bulk?—A. Six thousand dollars. I don't remember. It might have been stated—I did not get the exact terms in which it was stated. It was $6,000 in it.

Q. You will not be positive as to the language, whether it was $5,000 and $1,000 or whether it was bulked as $6,000?—A. I don't remember the language.

Q. But when that question was put you remembered that you had read in the Washington Post that the bribe was $5,000?—A. Yes, sir.

Q. Or the proffered bribe?—A. Yes, sir.

Q. That is all upon that point, and I have one other question to put. Mr. Doblin, you know that Mr. Rogers is your attorney and is acting in the same good faith that you are?—A. Yes.

Q. And you know that he is politically opposed to you?—A. Yes.

Q. That he is a Democrat in politics?—A. Yes, sir.

Q. I believe you have already stated that you are a Republican?—A. I presumed I was.

By Mr. TAYLER:

Q. I understood you to reply to your counsel, who is of the opposing political party, fortunately, that you were not the first one to mention $6,000 before the subcommittee?—A. Yes, sir.

Q. That is right, is it?—A. Yes, sir.

Q. It was mentioned to you by some member of the subcommittee, was it?—A. As I say, some member of the subcommittee said something about $5,000 or $6,000 that was either divided or together. I don't know.

Q. Were you not the person that said $6,000?—A. I might.

Q. You might have?—A. Yes, sir: I might have done it.

Q. And it was you who named the division of $6,000 into five and one, was it not?—A. I might have.

Q. You might have? Is not that a fact?—A. I don't remember exactly.

Q. You were not very regardful in that interview of the truth, anyhow, were you?—A. I was trying to substantiate the story.

Q. It did not make any difference how you did it, so as you did it? (Question not answered.)

By Mr. WHEELER:

Q. Is not this a fact: In response to a question by Mr. Tayler when he asked you this question, "Did Quigg ever tell you to see Lessler and offer him $5,000?" did you not say, "I have not said that?" And it was then the discussion arose as to whether you were required to answer?—A. It was about that time.

Q. And after some parley, did you not say that Mr. Quigg told you that there was $6,000 in it if you could get Mr. Lessler to vote for these boats, and did you not say that you made the division and offered Mr. Lessler $5,000, and were to take a thousand dollars for yourself?—A. I might have.

Q. Is not that a fact?—A. I might have.

Q. You might not, too?—A. Yes; I might not have.

Q. Have you any recollection on that subject?—A. Excepting that it was discussed at that time.

Q. What is your recollection? Am I speaking truthfully or not?—A. I believe you are.

By Mr. ROGERS:

Q. I would like to ask one or two other questions on something that Mr. Wheeler brought out. When you came in the subcommittee room you had not been sworn?—A. No, sir.

Q. And was not there some discussion there as to whether or not you ought to answer questions?—A. Yes, sir.

Q. And was there not something said there about recourse being had to the House to require you to answer?—A. Yes, sir.

Q. And it was after that talk was had that you made this statement?—A. Yes, sir.

Q. And is it not a fact that you stated to that committee that you did not want to answer any questions unless you had to?—A. Yes, sir.

By Mr. BUTLER:

Q. You came there to sustain Mr. Lessler?—A. Yes, sir.

Q. Then, why could you have any objection to speaking? You came there not to question, but to defend Mr. Lessler?—A. Yes, sir; he told me to.

Q. To sustain Mr. Lessler?—A. Yes, sir.

Q. Then, why did you not speak voluntarily when you came?—A. Because it did not occur to me. I only asked the question whether I had to answer it.

Q. If you came there to sustain Mr. Lessler why did you ask that question?—A. I don't know.

Q. Then, if we had stated to you you need not answer, or that we would not compel you to answer, you would not have said anything, would you?—A. No, sir.

Q. Then, you did not come there to sustain Mr. Lessler?—A. Yes, sir.

Q. How can you reconcile your two statements?—A. I beg your pardon.

Q. How can you reconcile your two statements, that you came there to sustain Lessler—you came there to sustain Lessler?—A. Yes, sir.

Q. And yet you say you declined to answer until we made it plain to you that we would compel you by some process?—A. Mr. Lessler said that it was all right, and I only asked the question.

Q. Do you think that is an answer to the question that I have asked you?—A. Yes, sir.

Q. Well, it may satisfy you—well, I am not going to have anything more to do with it.

(Witness excused.)

Thereupon, at 1.50 p. m , the committee took a recess for one hour, at the conclusion of which the committee went into executive session, and at 3.30 p. m. adjourned until to morrow, Tuesday, January 27, 1903, at 10.30 o'clock a. m.

HOUSE OF REPRESENTATIVES,
Washington, D. C., January 27, 1903.

The committee met at 10.30 o'clock a. m., Hon. George Edmund Foss in the chair.

The CHAIRMAN. Mr. Lessler asks for an executive session of the committee this morning.

Mr. LESSLER. Mr. Chairman, I would like to be recalled first. Mr. Wheeler suggests that before we go into executive session I be recalled.

The CHAIRMAN. Very well.

ADDITIONAL TESTIMONY OF HON. MONTAGUE LESSLER.

By the CHAIRMAN:

Q. Mr. Lessler, do you desire to make a statement?—A. Yes. Mr. Chairman, I desire to deny absolutely and unequivocally as false the statement made by the witness Doblin here yesterday as to any collusive scheme or any of the substantial details sworn to by him here, and I desire to reiterate that the facts as originally told by me are true.

I desire to call attention to the following facts: That as to the telegram referred to on page 94, "Take midnight train and come to me. Want to see you. Keep this confidential," the members of the subcommittee will remember that the statement I made to them was on Tuesday afternoon; that at that time everything before us was in camera, and that I said I would produce the witness Doblin in the morning, but I did not desire his name to appear in any way. The result was that that telegram was sent by me here from this committee room. Mr. Doblin came into my room a few minutes after 8 o'clock. I had left the door unlocked and he knocked at the door, waking me up. I asked "Who is there?" He said, "Phil," or "Doblin," I have forgotten which. I said, "Come in." He came into the room with his overcoat on, and I said, "Phil, I have gotten you into trouble." He said, "How is that?" "Well," I said, "I have told in committee the whole story of the submarine proposition." He said, "Oh, that is terrible; that is terrible." "Well, now," I said, "keep up your nerve; all you have to do is to tell the truth here, and nothing but the truth."

I meanwhile got up and was dressing. I went to the bathroom to attend to the toilet and came back. He was walking up and down. I said to him, "Now, I said to the committee yesterday that when you came over I would say nothing to you as to the testimony or the story, and I don't want it discussed between us." I was then fully dressed. We walked out to the elevator and went down to breakfast, and I did as I do every morning, I picked up the paper, the Washington Post, the only paper that arrives at that time, and bought one. We went into breakfast. I got my mail at the office first, and then we went in together. When we sat down I read the story, and I desire to have in full in the evidence the article in the Post of Wednesday, January 21, which was shown me yesterday.

Mr. LOUDENSLAGER. That is already in, is it not?

The CHAIRMAN. That is already in evidence, is it not, Mr. Lessler?

Mr. LESSLER. No; not in extenso.

The CHAIRMAN. Do you desire to have that made part of the record?

The article referred to is here inserted in the record, as follows:

TELLS OF BRIBE OFFER—MR. LESSLER SAYS ATTEMPT WAS MADE TO BUY SUPPORT—ALLEGED PROFFER OF $5,000—OBJECT SOUGHT, HE DECLARES, WAS APPROPRIATION OF ADDITIONAL SUBMARINE TORPEDO BOATS—SUBCOMMITTEE OF HOUSE NAVAL AFFAIRS COMMITTEE IS INVESTIGATING NEW YORK MEMBER'S CHARGE.

A subcommittee of the House Committee on Naval Affairs is investigating the charge that Representative Lessler, of New York, one of the members of the Naval Committee, has been approached with a bribe of $5,000 for his support of a proposition looking to an appropriation for additional submarine torpedo boats, with a view to ascertaining whether there is sufficient warrant for the committee to ask the House to order a regular investigation of the matter.

The sensational charge was made by Mr. Lessler himself at a meeting of the Naval Affairs Committee yesterday afternoon. The question of the Holland torpedo boats was up, and Mr. Lessler, who was opposing the authorization of additional boats, told the committee that he had been approached with a bribe. His statement startled the committee, and several members, among them Mr. Butler, of Pennsylvania, and Mr. Roberts, of Massachusetts, immediately suggested that so serious a charge should be investigated immediately.

COMMITTEE TO INVESTIGATE.

After some discussion Mr. Wheeler, of Kentucky, offered a resolution, which was adopted, to appoint a subcommittee to investigate at once and to report to the full committee.

The following subcommittee was appointed: Mr. Foss (Rep.), of Illinois, chairman of the Naval Committee; Mr. Butler (Rep.), of Pennsylvania; Mr. Tayler (Rep.), of Ohio; Mr. Wheeler (Dem.), of Kentucky, and Mr. Rixey (Dem.), of Virginia. The subcommittee forthwith entered upon its work, and during the afternoon heard Mr. Lessler's complete story. The subcommittee will summon other witnesses to-day. Their proceedings are secret, and members of both the full and subcommittees have bound themselves not to speak of the matter pending the report of the subcommittee. How definite and specific Mr. Lessler's charge is, therefore, is not known.

Mr. LESSLER. Yes, sir; I desire to have that article in the Post made part of the record. We went upstairs, and the talk that went on was absolutely nothing as to his testimony here. The whole talk was as to his position in New York and what might occur to him; how he was politically ruined in New York. I was very much impressed, of course, by the fact that he was in a serious situation, and I did walk in to the Speaker, and I told the Speaker that the proposition was undergoing examination here and that if it were possible to stop a public investigation—of course no man likes the notoriety of it. He said to me, "It has to go on, and we will see later on." We then came back. I put on my hat and coat and came up and spoke to the gentlemen of the committee. We had a talk, during which it was under-

H. Rep. 3482——9

stood that his name should not be mentioned for the public prints. I
then telephoned my secretary to go over to my hotel, to the Normandie
Hotel——

Mr. VANDIVER. You say " his name." Whose name do you refer to?

Mr. LESSLER. Doblin's name.   I then telephoned my secretary to go
to the Normandie Hotel and bring Mr. Doblin here to the committee.
I was not present.   I don't know what happened, from personal knowledge, of course, before that committee.   Mr. Doblin left the committee
room and I never saw him again until his reappearance in Washington
in answer to the other telegram, after the committee had decided to
ask the House for a resolution of investigation.   Then my testimony
was heard on the 25th.

After the testimony was in a question was asked as to Doblin's
appearance.   I said to the committee that I had no doubt about it that
he would come without having a subpœna served by the processes of
this House.   I then telegraphed him to come and he did come, and I
dictated some of these telegrams to my secretary to send to his wife,
who, of course, as he told me, was very much upset about it.

His testimony was heard here.   He left and went with me to the
train, and a few minutes before train time—he had arranged to stay
here—I said he had better stay; I believe he said to some member of
the committee while we were in the room, had he better stay or not.
At the last minute he said he thought he would be better off if he went
home over Sunday.   I said "Very well," and I telephoned some member of the committee asking him if there was any objection to his going
home.   We went home on the train.   There was very little spoken of
on the train going home.   He recalls the circumstance regarding my
saying I would examine the law as to his immunity from punishment
or not.   The way that arose was that he asked me the substance of
what Mr. Tayler stated was the law on that proposition, and I said I
would look it up.   He left me—the train was a little late—about 11.30
of Saturday night, promising to rejoin me, to come back, as I had promised the committee he would come back on Sunday night, and I never
saw him from that time until he appeared in the committee room, and
had no idea as to what he was doing or what he did.

I would like, in addition, to deny the statement of the witness
McCullagh as to my saying there was but one member of the committee who was absolutely honest, or whatever he testified in that
regard.   I want to point out the fact that while testifying the question
was asked me if anyone was present at the time Mr. McCullagh called.
That is on page 8:

The WITNESS. Yes, sir.

By Mr. TAYLER:

Q. Who?—A. My secretary in Washington.

By Mr. BUTLER:

Q. What is the name of that secretary?
The WITNESS. Frank P. Son.
Q. What is his address?—A. I can get him on the telephone in a minute.
Q. What is his address?—A. I don't know.   It is somewhere on Twelfth street.   I
can get him on the telephone.

I desired to go away on the 3 o'clock train that afternoon to New
York, and I had my bag, and as usual my secretary was to bring my
mail here, and the first intimation the young man had that he was to
testify here was while sitting in this very chair.   The door was open,
and he was sitting in the window seat, and I beckoned him to come in,

and he came right in and sat down in the chair here without any previous word as to his coming as a witness before this committee.

I should like further to deny the statement of the witness Quigg
that I said to the effect that the members of the committee who voted
for the Holland torpedo boat were knaves and that the others who did
not were honest men, or words that effect.

I don't think of anything else.

Mr. BUTLER. Mr. Chairman, may I ask the witness two or three
questions?

The CHAIRMAN. Certainly.

By Mr. BUTLER:

Q. I do not think it is important, what you said to other members of
the committee, but I would like to ask you three or four questions as
to what occurred when Doblin first came to your room Wednesday
morning there. Was it on Wednesday morning?—A. Yes; I have
stated that, and I will state it again.

Q. You had not yet risen from your bed?—A. No.

Q. Mr. Doblin came in alone?—A. Yes, sir.

Q. Was anyone in the room at the time Doblin came in?—A. No
one except myself.

Q. No third person was there?—A. No third person; no, sir.

Q. How soon after Doblin came did your secretary arrive?—A. We
were down eating breakfast, and he came in from the street to the
breakfast table.

Q. And sat down with you?—A. He sat down a minute, and took
my mail after I had opened it. I open it at the breakfast table and he
com s in; and he came in and took my mail and went upstairs, and
then afterwards we went upstairs together.

Q. As soon as you could finish your breakfast you went to your
room?—A. Yes.

Q. You found your secretary, Mr. Son, there?—A. Yes, sir; I think I
went to my room then and Doblin joined me. I think he went down
to get a shave.

Q. Was your secretary then in the room until you departed for the
Capitol?—A. Until I departed for the Capitol.

Q. And you left Mr. Doblin where?—A. In the room.

Q. With the secretary?—A. No; one minute. The secretary left first,
because I sent him with a note, I think, to the Shoreham. No; Mr. Son
left, then I left, and he remained in my room alone. That is the exact
order.

Q. How much of this conversation between you and Mr. Doblin
which occurred that morning did Son hear?—A. Well, Mr. Son was
there. I was dictating mail. I didn't do any talking at all to Mr.
Doblin. I was simply dictating my mail.

Q. Then such conversation as you may have had with Doblin concerning this controversy here occurred with him alone?—A. Well, I
wouldn't like to put it that way, because I had no conversation with
him concerning the controversy here, because, as I have repeated
several times, Mr. Butler, I had told the members of the committee
that I should not talk with him, and I didn't talk with him about the
immediate controversy.

Q. Let me put it this way, Mr. Lessler. Whatever was said to Mr.
Doblin upon this subject which we are investigating was said to him
not in the presence of anyone?—A. That is right.

Q. When he came back to appear before this committee as a witness, after the authority was given the committee to make the investigation, you saw him?—A. I went for him. His train was an hour late and I met him at 8.30 at the Baltimore and Ohio depot.

Q. Where did you go?—A. From there we took a cab and drove down to my hotel, the Normandie.

Q. And you were alone with him in the cab?—A. In the cab; yes. He brought over the evening papers and I read the papers.

By Mr. MUDD:

Q. They contained a statement of what had taken place here, including your testimony and all that?—A. They contained the confidential statement given to the committee.

Q. But what I am getting at is this: You, as I understand, testified here one day and he the next?—A. I testified on Tuesday afternoon before the subcommittee, and he came Wednesday morning before the subcommittee and went home.

Q. Before the subcommittee?—A. Then I testified in public, I think, on Friday.

Q. Thursday, was it not?—A. Friday, the 23d of January.

Q. And Doblin on Saturday?—A. Doblin came over on Saturday. We had wired him, you remember, to come.

Q. You do not know whether in the meantime he had read your statement?—A. No.

Mr. VANDIVER. It was Friday, was it not, instead of Saturday?

The WITNESS. On Friday, the 23d, I testified and I telegraphed and received a telegram from him, "Can not come until Monday." Then I said I thought he would come, and I telephoned to somebody in New York to go out and find him and he came Saturday morning.

By Mr. MUDD:

Q. Did you see him between the time of your testimony before the committee and his testimony before the committee?—A. No, sir; he left the committee room and went out.

Q. I mean the full committee. Between the time you testified before the full committee, under oath, and the time he testified that way, did you see him?—A. Just as I have stated.

Q. In the meantime it had all come out in the paper?—A. Yes, sir; I think some of the New York papers.

Q. I want to ask one question to see if I understand you aright. I do not know that it is very material, but you stated you dictated some of those telegrams?—A. I think so.

Q. Is there any dispute of your having sent any of the telegrams?—A. Oh, no; not a word. I don't know which ones he dictated part of.

Q. You said he dictated some of them. I did not know whether you meant to exclude them all.—A. I mean that I wrote some of them. The next to the last telegram in the depot, he seemed a little nervous——

Q. There is no dispute as to the sending?—A. Oh, no; not at all.

By Mr. RIXEY:

Q. Mr. Lessler, you stated in your former examinations that your relations with Mr. Doblin had been quite intimate for a number of years.—A. No; I did not.

Q. I thought you did.—A. I stated specifically I knew of him since about 1894, and I was nominated for Congress on the 21st of December, 1901; that he was then employed in the county committee in New York, and that he took a very active and strong interest in the campaign. I think you will find that at page——

Q. I understand that. I recollect the substance of your testimony, too, that your relations had been such that you thought you knew him very well, and you thought he was a very warm personal friend of yours, who would do anything he could to advance your interests?—A. Yes, sir; that is true, and I testified to it.

Q. What I wanted to ask you was if anything had occurred, if you had any intimation from any source that he was the character of man he has been proven before this committee to be by his own confession?—A. Absolutely none, Mr. Rixey.

Q. You had no reason to disbelieve the statement he came to you with?—A. No reason in the world to disbelieve it.

Q. So far as you know, up to the beginning of this investigation, Doblin is a man who has enjoyed a good reputation in the city of New York?—A. I never knew of any wrongdoing of Doblin in any form, shape, or manner before. I never knew of his word being doubted at all. I know that he has been in political relations with various presidents of the county committee, and employed there at or around a place where a great many things, confidential and otherwise, are given to members, and I never knew of him being doubted in the slightest. I am totally at a loss to understand the proposition as it now is.

Q. You know of no reason, with your knowledge of all the circumstances out of which this investigation has grown, which accounts for this change of testimony on the part of Doblin?—A. I know of no reason, Mr. Rixey.

By Mr. KITCHIN:

Q. Mr. Lessler, I am not sure that I understood you correctly, but I did understand you to say that the subcommittee told you that if Doblin came down and testified his statement would not be given to the press, and that then you telephoned to your secretary to that effect.—A. Yes, sir; not that effect. I telephoned to bring Doblin.

Q. Before Doblin appeared before that committee, was he not informed, through you or by your secretary, that his name would not be given to the press?—A. No, sir; I 'phoned from the other room in the full presence of six members of the committee. I think six—yes; I am sure, six.

Q. Why were you interested as to whether his name should be given to the press or not, then, if you were not going to communicate it to him?—A. Why I was interested in not communicating his name to the press?

Q. Yes.—A. Because I felt it would put him in the position of a scapegoat and that he would be hounded in New York by the very men with whom for years he had had political relations.

Q. So your real reason for asking that his name be not given to the press was because you did not want to hurt him in New York among his political friends there?—A. The real reason, Mr. Kitchin, was that it was understood in the committee that until such time as the full committee ordered an investigation, or asked the House to order an investigation, no name should be given to the press, and that no man, at least on the subcommittee, should speak on the subject outside of the committee room.

Q. If it had been known to you and Doblin both that his name would be at once given to the press, would that have affected his examina-

tion, in your judgment? Would he still have been examined?—A. I
think he would still have been examined. I simply came up and spoke
to the committee about the whole proposition.

Q. Of course, if you have any objections, I do not want to ask it, but
I would like to know, myself, why you wrote that first telegram and
asked him to keep it confidential. I understand why it was written,
but why was it kept confidential?—A. I wanted his journey here kept
confidential, because the whole matter was confidential before our subcommittee, Mr. Kitchin.

Q. So you thought the whole matter was confidential?—A. It certainly was before our subcommittee.

Q. Now, just one other question I wish to ask. You have stated to
us you told some of the members of this committee about this thing
some time ago. I would like to know whether you told them about the
McCullagh transaction and this charge of bribery, or both—to other
members of the committee?—A. I think I mentioned the McCullagh
transaction to some of the members of the committee.

Q. Did you mention the other to them? Did you mention the bribery
to them?—A. No; I think the main point in my mind is that I spoke
of the so called Quigg-Doblin episode.

Q. But you had not mentioned any bribery to any of these other
members, Mr. Foss, Mr. Dayton, or Mr. Wheeler?—A. Why, I told you
just now, and I told you the other day, that I did mention that very
thing.

Q. What? At first?—A. Yes.

Q. But you say now the main thing you had in mind was the McCullagh—— A. No; you are entirely mistaken.

Q. I want to get that straight.—A. I want to give it to you straight.

Q. I was not before the subcommittee, and I do not know what you
told.—A. Oh, no; this is before there was any committee, we are talking about now, that some time after the session opened I told one or
two or three of these gentlemen this business we are now investigating.

Q. You did tell them a bribe had been offered you of $5,000?—A.
Yes.

Q. Did you give the names of Doblin and Quigg in it?—A. I don't
think I did, sir.

Q. You just simply told them you had an opportunity of selling your
vote for $5,000, or words to that effect?—A. No; not words to that effect.
I just gave the main outline of the episode.

Q. I mean you did tell them enough to let them know the proposition
had been made at a price of $5,000 for your vote?—A. Yes; I think I
did that.

Q. Did you tell each one of these gentlemen that?—A. My recollection is that Mr. Foss and Mr. Dayton were together when I spoke of it,
but I won't be certain of that.

Q. I believe you stated to day that you did think that was before
Christmas?—A. Yes.

Q. In your recollection?—A. But the point of time——

Q. You say you are not certain about that?—A. The point of time is
now so fixed by various things that it must have been after the 1st of
January.

Q. At that time you thought some of this proposition might have
been made prior to the meeting of Congress, some time in the last of
December?— A. I was not certain as to the time.

Q. I mean the last of November.—A. Yes; I was not certain about
the time, but these gentlemen, various of them, fix the dates now, so
that the whole matter must have occurred in the month of December.

Q. Toward the latter part of December, probably.—A. Well, somewhere between the 12th and the 1st of January.

By Mr. RIXEY:

Q. Just one question right there. When did you make up your mind, Mr. Lessler, to inform the Naval Committee of the facts which you finally informed them of on Tuesday, I believe—Tuesday the 20th?—A. I don't think I made up my mind on the proposition, Mr. Rixey. I think, to be frank with you, during the discussion it came right out. That is the whole proposition.

Q. It was not premeditated or intentional on your part?—A. No; it was not.

Mr. MOYER. Mr. Chairman, I would like to ask one question.

The CHAIRMAN. General Meyer.

By Mr. MEYER:

Q. Mr. Doblin stated in his testimony that he made false statements to the committee because of his deep sense of obligation to you. I should like to ask, if you feel disposed to answer, what was the nature of the obligation that he was under to you?—A. Doblin, General, has been in political life, as he told you, about twenty years. He has been a very useful man to a great number of men. My judgment is that most of them have simply used him, and when the use has been through, have thrown him away like a dish rag. The result is he has nothing and remains nobody. He came to me at a time and during a time where his political knowledge, his getting about ability and hustling, as we call it, was of great use to me, and when the opportunity came I simply showed that I was grateful to him, and did not do the way I think others have done—throw him by the board. When he needed something, and I could give it, I gave it. I simply put it that way. He was under no obligations to me.

The exact record of what I have done for him is plain. I never recommended him to McCullagh, as he stated. I never spoke to McCullagh or to any man about him for him to get that position. I never saw McCullagh but once in his office, a few days before election, to tell him of some of the things that had come to me in election connected with his work, and his work only. I had asked that these small receiverships, out of which maybe $10 or $20 are made, be given him, and they were. Otherwise I know of nothing. He did not have a right to sit at my desk in my office, for instance, and when I came home one day I found that he had gone to my desk, and the boy in my office had allowed him to, and I scolded and directed that he must not be allowed to open my desk during my absence and sit there, and I told him that he must not. I think that completely answers your question, General. There is no obligation that would, in my judgment, permit a man to do what he says he had to do.

By Mr. ROBERTS:

Q. It was not just clear in my mind, Mr. Lessler, what you said about not going to the depot with Mr. Doblin after he had testified. Did you deny going down with him after he testified?—A. When, when?

Q. After he had testified?—A. He came on Wednesday, and during that time I had some business on the floor and I went to the floor. When I came back to the full committee Mr. Doblin had already gone. When on Saturday he testified he met me right outside the door and we walked down to the depot, and there I telegraphed his wife—this telegram:

"January 24," I think. "Phil examined. Substantiates story in every way. He is all right. Will stay here for a time." And thereupon he said, " What will I do here over Sunday alone ? I think I had better go home." And I telephoned to the committee and said, Was there any objection to Mr. Doblin's going home ? The answer came that they didn't see any, and I bought his ticket, paid for his seat in the drawing-room and his dinner, and as he, I believe, stated, there was not much talk, because I was reading during the trip and left him at South Ferry at about 11.20 odd, and didn't see him again.

Q. Then it is true you went down to the depot, just as he testified ?—A. Certainly, Mr. Roberts.

Q. You do not deny, as I understood you—— A. Mr. Roberts, I just told you I was. Why should I deny it ?

Q. I was not there, and my understanding was not correct. I under-stood you to say you denied going to the depot.—A. Then your understanding was wrong.

Mr. TATE. You have the statement and the evidence confused.

Mr. LOUDENSLAGER. He has the dates confused, I think, rather.

By Mr. ROBERTS:

Q. That is just what I am driving at. Where and when did Mr. Doblin ever testify that you went to the station with him after he appeared before the subcommittee ?—A. No one ever said so, Mr. Roberts, and I have not said so.

Q. I just want it cleared up.—A. I haven't said so, and no one else said so except yourself.

Q. I have not said so.—A. You just said it, Mr. Roberts.

Q. I had an understanding of what you said, and I wanted to see if it was right.—A. You had it wrong.

Q. That is what I want to get at. You just referred to the McCullagh episode, and if I am wrong, correct me. You said you told one, two, or three members of this committee about the McCullagh episode at the time you told them of the bribe.—A. No; you are again wrong.

Q. You did not so state ?—A. I say you are again wrong.

Q. You did not so state ?—A. I now state to you that I said, in answer to Mr. Kitchin, that I may have told them also about the McCullagh episode, but I am not certain about that.

Q. You are not certain that you said it ?—A. No; I am not certain.

Q. Have you ever said anything to any member of the committee about the McCullagh episode ?—A. I don't think I can put it any more strongly than I have. I have answered that two or three times now.

Q. Answer this question now.—A. Yes.

Q. Did you not state in this committee when we were in session last year, discussing the Holland submarine boat as it came before us under an amendment, that Mr. McCullagh had come to you and attempted to influence you ?—A. I ask you, did I ?

Q. I am asking you.—A. I am asking you, and if you say I did, I am quite willing to take your word for it.

Q. Then you will say, will you, that you did say that in committee ?—A. I say I don't remember it, but if you remember it, then it probably must have been said, because I never told you outside or ever mentioned it to you at all.

Q. Just a moment. Will you take my memory of that transaction as yours ?—A. I will take your memory of the fact of having stated that matter, but you can come on the stand and swear to it, Mr. Roberts.

Q. I am asking if you will take my memory of it as yours and agree that that is correct ?—A. No; I won't take your memory altogether as mine. I will say to you that if you remember that I stated it before this committee you remember something that I am in doubt about.

Q. Then you do not know whether you stated it before this committee in the meeting?—A. I will have to say again that I do not remember.

Mr. DAYTON. Mr. Chairman, with all due respect to my colleague, Mr. Roberts, it does seem to me that this examination is an improper one and one that he ought not to inflict on this committee—that style of examination.

Mr. ROBERTS. Why not?

Mr. DAYTON. A question as to whether a man will take your memory or anybody's memory for his own is not a fact that we are interested in.

Mr. ROBERTS. He said he would take my memory.

The WITNESS. No; I did not.

Mr. TATE. This testimony, I think, is for the committee, anyway, and not for Mr. Lessler and Mr. Roberts.

Mr. MUDD. This is not a place for a trade. They have got to swap outside.

By Mr. ROBERTS:

Q. When you mentioned this offer of the bribe to certain members of the committee, did they ask you any of the details?—A. No; I think not. I say no.

Q. And you did not give them to them?—A. No.

By Mr. VANDIVER:

Q. I desire to ask a few questions. You spoke a while ago of Doblin's character not being revealed to you prior to this episode of yesterday. Let me ask what impression you got of the man from his making you such a proposition as he did?—A. I must answer you again as I answered you before, Mr. Vandiver. The money part of it had no impression for me. The school in which he is brought up does not concern itself with high minded morals, and my idea of it was that this man mentioned that as lightly as he would mention any other thing light, and the point with him was unquestionably, I believed at the time, and believe now, that it was an intense desire to serve me and let me become persona grata to Mr. Quigg, who he believes, or did believe, or does believe to be one of the influential men of New York City.

Q. But you regarded him, then, merely as an intermediary, bringing to you a proposition from Mr. Quigg?—A. I did not regard it at all. He states it exactly as it occurred. I was standing or sitting at my desk opening the mail and he came in just as he describes it, and I said, "Quit, quit," or "Nothing to it, nothing to it;" and that ended that episode with him.

Q. But now you have based your charge of an attempt at bribery upon that very incident?—A. Yes, sir.

Q. An incident which you now say was so quickly disposed of and so lightly considered you made use of to base a serious charge of bribery against a prominent citizen?—A. Yes.

Q. Now, I ask you what impression that gave you as to the character of the man who made the offer of a bribe?—A. I have given you——

Q. Whether you regard Mr. Quigg or Mr. Doblin as the author of the proposition—you certainly must regard one of them as the author of it?—A. I say frankly that I would have regarded Mr. Quigg more at fault in a proposition of that kind than Mr. Doblin, as being a man of different caliber and differently positioned in the world.

Q. Not caring to press that further, I want to ask one or two other questions. You spoke a while ago of seeing Mr. Doblin when he came here at your request, and of his embarrassing position, and not want ing to testify. You went to see the Speaker, as I understood it, with a view to seeing if the investigation could not be kept within limits and not made public. Is that it?—A. Within our own ranks, as I had supposed at first, Mr. Vandiver, I was talking among ourselves.

Q. Was that before the House had passed this resolution authorizing the investigation?—A. As I stated before, it was the morning of Wednesday, January 21, when Doblin came over at my request to make his statement to the subcommittee.

Q. After the Speaker informed you that it must go forward, that there could be no secrecy about it, you went to the subcommittee, you stated, and consulted with them about it and received from them some kind of assurance that his name would not be given out—— A. I received no assurance.

Q. Well, an understanding.—A. Will you let me make a statement, Mr. Vandiver, to clear up that subcommittee business, if I can?

Q. Just wait until I get through, Mr. Lessler. Perhaps I did not state it exactly.—A. You did not state it exactly right.

Q. Instead of saying an assurance, I think your word was you had an understanding with the subcommittee?—A. I had an understanding with the full committee once, if you remember. We all had an understanding with each other that whatever we said here was in executive session and should not be spoken of outside. That was the only thing—that the whole matter should not be given publicity until such time as the House took the matter up.

Q. Mr. Lessler, you have referred again, as you have several times before, to this understanding in the full committee, that we were in executive session. Therefore I must ask you another question right on that point.—A. Yes.

Q. When you first made your statement to the full committee, did you not preface it by saying, "I shall put no ban of secrecy upon the committee?"—A. I don't think I did.

Q. Did you not say you were going to state things which you were intending to state on the floor of the House?—A. Well, I was pretty excited, Mr. Vandiver, and I don't remember making such a statement as that.

Q. I shall not ask other members of the committee to say anything about that, but it seems to me that was the recollection of all the members of the committee that you put it that way. Then, one more question on that point—I only press it a little further because you have several times referred to it yourself. Did you think that a charge of that nature could be made in the presence of seventeen members of this committee, and three clerks, and one or two others standing around, and no investigation follow?—A. I didn't think of the subject of investigation at all, Mr. Vandiver.

Q. Coming back to the point from which this was a digression, this understanding you say you had with the subcommittee that Doblin's name was not to be given out was had before you sent down for him to come up and testify?—A. My understanding—I had no understanding with the subcommittee. My understanding of the position of the sub committee was that nothing that went on, either as coming from me or coming from Doblin or anybody else that they would summon, or ask, or request to testify, would be given out and made public.

Q. You have denied, as I understand, specifically two statements made by two witnesses here in regard to passing judgment on members of the committee?—A. Yes, sir; that is right.

Q. Your denial, of course, is general and also specific as to that incident referred to?—A. I should make the denial as specific as it is possible to make it, and in any form that you would desire to have it made.

Q. I am not trying to press the gentleman—— A. You may press.

Q. Further on that specific charge, but if he does not desire to answer the question I am going to ask now, of course I shall not urge him to do so.—A. Why preface it in that way? I have not refrained from answering anything. Why make a preface like that?

Q. Was anything said in that conversation on that subject?—A. With whom?

Q. With either one of these witnesses whose testimony you desired?—A. The committee was never mentioned by either of us in either conversation or interview with either Mr. Quigg in my office or Mr. McCullagh in my hotel room.

Q. After you had seen the Speaker and then had gone to the subcommittee was anything said in the subcommittee about closing this investigation and not pressing it further?—A. No; the subcommittee said that they would discuss the matter, and when I was present instructed Mr. Tayler to bring the report that you heard to the full committee. The best evidence of what was said in the subcommittee was the report——

Q. Well, that was the conclusion.—A. One minute, Mr. Vandiver. Was the report given to this committee by Mr. Tayler, which you heard, which all of us heard?

Q. Well, I would just like a little more explicit information on that point, as to whether you at any time, either in full committee or in conversation with any member of the committee, spoke of dropping this matter and letting it stop at that, without investigation?—A. Yes; I think I did. I think I spoke to the committee, feeling, of course, that I was the center of a proposition that was more than unpleasant and of which I must, of course, carry the brunt. We discussed it, and whatever was said resulted in the report made by Mr. Tayler to the full committee.

Q. Of course, you must have considered before you made such a charge as this what the serious nature of it was and what it would naturally lead to?—A. I think I have answered you before, or I answered Mr. Rixey, that my my statement here was absolutely unpremeditated.

Q. But you did consider the question of dropping the investigation at that point?—A. I think we all considered it, Mr. Vandiver, right in this committee.

Q. Well, to be just a little more explicit, Mr. Lessler, did you not express a willingness to drop the matter or practically abandon the charge?—A. I wouldn't quite put it that way.

Q. I am willing for you to put it any way you please so as to get the facts.—A. I say I would not put it quite in that way. I certainly expressed a feeling and a desire that I would like to have the matter dropped, but not that I would abandon the charge.

By Mr. BUTLER:

Q. Mr. Lessler, let us begin at the time that Mr. Doblin made this corrupt proposition to you, assuming that he did make it. That proposition, then, was known by you and by him only, leaving Mr. Quigg out of the investigation at this time?—A. Yes; at that date. If the date is fixed, it was somewhere around the 12th.

Q. For the purpose of my inquiry it is not important to know the date.—A. Yes, sir.

Q. That was a close secret between you and him, between Mr. Doblin and Mr. Lessler?—A. If you mean by "understanding" between us, no.

Q. Who knew it besides you?—A. I say if you mean by "understanding" between us, I know nobody else.

Q. You did not at that time know of any person who knew of it?—A. No; I did not.

Q. You heard of Mr. Obermeier having been taken to Mr. Quigg?—A. I did not know of that except, as Obermeier testified, until he came here in January and we were walking up Fifteenth street and he mentioned that he had gone to Quigg, and I told him, "Quit, quit!" The interview as he tells it is correct.

Q. Then Mr. Obermeier knew, up to that time, including you and Mr. Doblin—for, as I understood, you also spoke to Mr. Obermeier about this corrupt proposition generally?—A. Your first question, Mr. Butler, was as to the specific day when Doblin came to me. Now, my answer to you was that I talked about Obermeier's visit to Quigg when Obermeier was in Washington some time in January. Now you will have to repeat that question so I will get it clearly.

Q. Yes. First you and Doblin knew of this proposition.—A. Yes.

Q. You then mentioned it to Mr. Obermeier, did you?—A. I am not certain, Mr. Butler, that I mentioned it to——

Q. Very well. I remember your testimony as you have given it, Mr. Lessler. The next time you spoke of it you spoke to three members of this committee.—A. That is right.

Q. Then we have Mr. Doblin, yourself, and three members of the committee as possessing this information so far as you knew?—A. Yes.

Q. You next spoke of it here in a full committee?—A. That is right.

Q. Up to that time we have yourself, Mr. Doblin, the three members of the committee, and the full committee, as possessing this information?—A. Yes.

Q. The next time that this information was imparted, so far as you know, was to this subcommittee?—A. Yes.

Q. Do you know whether Doblin ever told anybody?—A. Yes; I know that Doblin has told somebody.

Q. Do you object to mentioning the name?—A. That was the matter that I was going to speak of in executive session, when we get through.

Q. You have never mentioned it to anyone except to the people you have mentioned in this investigation?—A. I don't remember speaking of it to anyone.

Q. You do not know that Doblin had told it to anyone?

Mr. WHEELER. Yes; he said he does.

By Mr. BUTLER:

Q. Except the person you speak of? I beg your pardon.—A. Yes, sir.

Q. Will you please explain to me what you meant in this part of your telegram of January 24, addressed to Mrs. Philip Doblin: "Phil examined. Substantiates story in every way?"—A. That telegram was dictated by Doblin over in the station. I wrote it for him. He started writing the telegram, and he trembled so that I wrote the telegram at his dictation for Mrs. Doblin. I absolutely wrote the telegram at his dictation at the station of the Baltimore and Ohio.

Q. Did it excite any suspicion in your mind or make any impression on you that it was rather singular that he should make a statement of that kind to Mrs. Doblin when Mrs. Doblin did not presumably know anything about it?—A. Certainly, she knew all about it, Mr. Butler.

Q. She did?—A. You must remember he had been here on Wednesday. The paper was full of the thing on Thursday. Friday morning's testimony comes out in New York. Saturday morning he comes here to testify. I thought no more of that than I thought of the proposition looking to his registering at my hotel. He went down from here after he testified and registered there, a thing I never knew, never looked for, until he testified here.

Mr. NICOLL. May I ask a question, Mr. Chairman?

By Mr. TATE:

Q. Before you do I would like to know why these telegrams were sent in your name to Mrs. Doblin?—A. Simply because I had a frank.

Q. It was to save him the expense?—A. That is all.

Q. Another question: Is the other telegram to Doblin the same telegram you exhibited here to the committee about getting him here?—A. What is that?

Q. You exhibited certain telegrams to the committee in reference to Doblin's coming here. Are those the same telegrams put in here?—A. Why, certainly. I think I showed the first telegram I sent to somebody in the committee.

Mr. KITCHIN. There was a telegram read here in the committee from Doblin to you.

By Mr. RIXEY:

Q. I just want to ask one more question, Mr. Nicoll, before you take the witness. Mr. Lessler, you stated the other day as to what occurred between you and Mr. McCullagh and what influence he said the people had he was representing here on that occasion.—A. I gave you literally what the man said.

Q. I want to know have you any reason to believe that he or they contributed to your defeat?—A. Oh, no; absolutely. I had no more chance of being elected than if I had—I had no chance of being reelected.

Mr. VANDIVER. Did they take any interest in your nomination, for or against?

The WITNESS. Not that I know of, in any way. The situation changed very considerably down in my district as to any question involving my chance for reelection. I had no chance against the man who was successful in that election.

Mr. RIXEY. Is it or not the fact that Mr. McCullagh, by virtue of his position, could exert a very large influence in determining the election?

The WITNESS. Why, he has control of the election machinery.

By Mr. VANDIVER:

Q. For influencing voters or for counting the results? Which do you mean?—A. Well, he has this influence—he has this in charge—he has charge of the 800 or 900 deputies that oversee elections being fairly performed. For instance, a certain number of men are registered in a district. He goes out and finds out if they are bona fide residents of the district. He is a man that investigates attempts at fraud on electorates or during the electorate. I don't believe he had any influence in the nominating convention at all. I know that he has no influence.

Q. You have just stated also that he had nothing to do with the result of the election. That is the reason why I asked the question.—A. Oh; he had nothing to do with the result of that election at all—absolutely.

By Mr. ROBERTS:

Q. Just on the point of McCullagh's relations to the elections in New York. Under the New York law, can any one of his deputies go in behind the rail, as we term it?—A. Oh, yes.

Q. He cuts the ballots?—A. Oh, no.

Q. Do any of his deputies have any duties in connection with the making up or signing returns, counting ballots?—A. No; they sign a return, Mr. Roberts, but they have nothing to do with the counting.

Q. They do not count or handle the returns or anything of that sort?—A. Not at all.

Q· So they can not influence an election from that end?—A. Not at all—not the slightest.

By Mr. RIXEY:

Q. It is your idea that by virtue of his position and the power he exercises at these elections he has the power to contribute to the defeat or success of a candidate very largely?—A. I will answer you exactly and specifically on that. There are certain portions of our city where it is alleged there are a great number of fraudulent voters. An efficient superintendent of elections will, for instance, in the lodging-house districts, where a great number of men come into the city for purposes of election, ferret these men out and prevent them from voting. That is the only way he can contribute or fail to contribute to the success or support of an election.

By Mr. MUDD:

Q. Is your district one of these?—A. Yes; my district is, more than anything, the whole thing in that line.

By Mr. RIXEY:

Q. It depends entirely on how he exercises his power whether he contributes to the defeat or the success of a candidate, then?—A. Yes. I would illustrate it this way: That when I was first elected, in January, a year ago, to a great extent, having only this one district under his surveillance, his energy, his faithfulness contributed materially to my election. He caught a great number—he caught some men in the act of repeating. I knew of that.

By Mr. VANDIVER:

Q. I understand you to mean by that that he contributed to it by preventing fraudulent votes?—A. That is right.

By Mr. RIXEY:

Q. In a district where they have a great many people who are not acquainted with our election laws and who are perhaps ignorant, that very power, the fear of being arrested and charged with illegal voting, might keep a great many honest people from the polls, might it not?—A. There is a matter for opinion, and you and I have simply individual opinions about.

By Mr. MUDD:

Q. I just want to ask one more question: Is there any suggestion that Mr. McCullagh did not do his full duty the time you last ran?—A. No; not a suggestion.

Q. The idea had been thrown out that he did not prosecute frauds.—A. Oh, no; he was more than efficient in the last election. We were landslided without redemption.

Q. You do not think he could have saved you the last time?—A. There is not a suggestion, Mr. Mudd, that Mr. McCullagh did not do his full duty at the last election.

Q. I am sure you did not mean to make that inference.

By Mr. NICHOLL:

Q. I would like to ask you a few questions. Of course you understand there are so many questions asked you around here that I do not know whether I am repeating a question or not, always?—A. That is all right.

Q. But you will know that I do not do it for the sake of vain repetition.—A. Certainly not. Go ahead.

Q. If my comprehension is correct, you did not mention, at this statement to the full committee on Tuesday a week ago, the names of anybody connected with this transaction?—A. Not a word.

Q. That is correct?—A. You mean on the Tuesday, I believe?

Q. It was Tuesday, I think.—A. Yes. Not a word.

Q. I mean you did not mention Mr. Doblin's name or Mr. Quigg's name?—A. Not a word.

Q. All you stated was that there had been an approach made to you?—A. Yes, sir.

Q. Was a subcommittee immediately appointed at that time?—A. Yes, sir. The minutes will show that.

Q. Yes. I have not seen the minutes or I would not ask you. What time in the afternoon was it that you went before the subcommittee; about, so far as you recollect?—A. I think somewhere about 1 or 2 o'clock. I am not certain.

Q. In the early afternoon of Tuesday?—A. Yes, sir.

Q. Did you then, for the first time, mention to the subcommittee the names of Doblin and Quigg?—A. I told the story as I have told it here, Mr. Nicoll; absolutely without any deviation, as I have stated it here.

Q. Just as you told it here on your first day's examination?—A. Yes, sir; that is right.

Q. Yes. And were you then asked by the subcommittee to send for Doblin?—A. Yes, sir. I was asked if I would send for Doblin.

Q. That is right. And you did?—A. I did; yes, sir.

Q. Now, during that period, it was your belief, was it not, that there was not going to be any public disclosure of this entire matter?—A. Yes; that is right, Mr. Nicholl.

Q. That was right?—A. Yes, sir.

Q. Then you did not think, when you made the statement to the full committee or to the subcommittee, there was going to be any public disclosure of the whole matter, did you?—A. When I made the statement to the full committee I certainly did not think so.

Q. Did you after you made the statement to the full committee?—A. When I thought there was to be a public disclosure—when I made the statement to the subcommittee I did not know. I knew that was a matter more fully in the hands of the entire committee then.

Q. What I want to know is your state of mind and belief on last Tuesday afternoon, after you had made this statement to the subcommittee, as to whether or not you thought that you were then embarked on a public investigation, or whether you thought then that the matter was going to be confined to the subcommittee and the full committee?—A. At the time I made the statement?

Q. Yes.—A. Yes, sir. I remember I thought that evening, or better, after Doblin had testified, that the committee would simply look into this matter, and that there would not be a public investigation.

Q. And that was on Wednesday afternoon?—A. That is right.

Q. That is Wednesday afternoon?—A. Yes, sir.

Q. Now, what engendered that belief in your mind?—A. Well, I had talked over with several members of the committee this business, and told them that I would like to have it stopped right there and then.

Q. That was on Wednesday afternoon?—A. Either Wednesday or Thursday—Thursday morning.

Q. Either Wednesday afternoon or Thursday morning?—A. Both times.

Q. Both times?—A. I had met various members of the committee, Mr. Nicoll, who wanted to talk over things about this.

Q. And you stated to them that you would like to have it stopped right then and there?—A. That is right; so far as my personal inclinations went, that is so.

Q. Now, is it not a fact that when Mr. Doblin arrived here on Wednesday morning you entertained the belief that there would not be any public investigation of this matter?—A. No; I did not, when Mr. Doblin arrived.

Q. Not when he arrived?—A. You heard——

Q. Yes.—A. (Continuing.) Mr. Nicoll, I have just stated to you that when Mr. Doblin arrived I did not have any belief on that subject.

Q. So that up to 11 o'clock that day you did not know what was going to happen?—A. I did not know what was going to happen.

Q. But later in the day, and after Mr. Doblin arrived, you did entertain the belief that the thing would be then confined?—A. I said not that I entertained the belief, but I expressed the desire.

Q. You expressed the desire?—A. Oh, yes; I expressed that desire.

Q. Now, I understood you to say that during this conversation with Mr. Doblin—— A. When?

Q. (Continuing.) While you were dressing you said to Mr. Doblin something to the effect that you were going to see the Speaker.—A. That is right, and I did, Mr. Nicoll.

Q. He testifies here on his examination of yesterday that you got up and went out and said you were going to see the Speaker.—A. The Speaker was not up yet, Mr. Nicoll. The Speaker did not get up until late that morning. I am on the same floor with him.

Q. At the Normandie?—A. Yes, sir. And he was not in his office then, and we went to breakfast, and we were talking——

Q. What were you going to see the Speaker for?—A. Just as I have told you.

Q. Tell me again.—A. Just to tell him about the proposition, the way it had gone, and that I would like it not to go any further, if possible.

Q. Did you not go to see the Speaker because Mr. Doblin had said to you that this was a terrible situation in which to place him?—A. Yes.

Q. Yes?—A. That was one of the causes. I think that would be the main cause.

Q. You did not see the Speaker at all at that time?—A. You did not hear my testimony. I did see the Speaker.

Q. At that time?—A. No, sir. I will give you the order of events.

Q. No. Doblin testified here that you came back and stated that you had seen the Speaker.—A. Then Doblin did not tell the truth.

Q. That is not true?—A. No, sir.

Q. Now, you testified in your—while I was cross-examining Mr. Doblin the other day—you recall when I was cross-examining Mr. Doblin the other day?—A. What page is that on?

Q. Page 49. You interrupted me and said: "I will state that I had promised the committee and said to the committee that I would say absolutely nothing to him."—A. That is right, Mr. Nicholl, and I kept my promise.

Q. You did say a great deal to him.—A. That is a matter of your opinion.

Q. Have you not already testified that you did?—A. I told you just what I said to him. If you desire that explained further, I will say this to you, that I said to the committee that I would not attempt to speak to him as to any story that he was to tell to that committee, so that he should come into that room and they could speak with him on this subject.

Q. Did you not state that you would say absolutely nothing to this man?—A. Yes.

Q. But that you would bring him to the committee fresh, and free from any impressions made by any communications made by you?—A. Yes; I think I did.

Q. Do you think you did that?—A. Mr. Nicholl, I have said that once.

Q. In view of what you told the committee this morning?—A. Yes, sir.

Q. Of your conversation at the hotel?—A. Yes. I made no attempt to influence him in any way. I told him the errand that I had asked him to come on, and that is how I told him. I told him that I said to the committee that I would not discuss this subject with him, and I did not.

Mr. VANDIVER. Excuse me just a moment. There is one point as to which I am not sure as to whether it has been brought out or not

Mr. NICHOLL. Certainly, Mr. Vandiver.

By Mr. VANDIVER:

Q. Did you or not dispute the testimony of Doblin as to whether you showed him that morning's newspaper or not? I don't remember whether you did or not.—A. Yes, sir; I think I read the paper at the table and handed the paper over to him, and you can see by the article that all there is in there is to the effect that I had said to the committee about the $5,000 and the bribe in the morning's paper, which is now a part of the record.

By Mr. NICHOLL:

Q. Mr. Lessler, when you met Mr. Doblin in your room that morning before you were dressed, did he ask you what you had sent him the telegram to come at midnight for?—A. No.

Q. What?—A. No.

Q. You observe that in this telegram you did not ask him to come and see the committee. You say in your examination of him—in your testimony you say—"Take the midnight train and come to me. Want to see you."—A. Mr. Nicholl, that telegram was written right here.

Q. I don't care where it was written.—A. One minute, Mr. Nicholl. That telegram was written right in this room, and, if my memory serves me, it was shown to some one right here.

Q. To whom was it shown?—A. I don't remember to what gentleman it was shown. I think it was written right at the head of the table there.

Q. To whom was it shown?—A. I don't remember to whom it was shown.

Q. Do you mean to say that you showed the gentlemen this telegram

H. Rep. 3482——10

after your statement to them that you would say nothing to Doblin before the committee itself had a chance to examine him?—A. I showed the telegram—wrote the telegram in this room, Mr. Nicholl. I don't know whether it was after the statement to the gentlemen or before, but I made that statement to the gentlemen and I wrote that telegram.

Q. Mr. Lessler, why, if you wanted to carry out your promise to the committee to say absolutely nothing to Doblin, did you send him a telegram saying, "Take the midnight train. Come to me. Want to see you"?—A. There was no particular motive in anything there—in sending that telegram.

Q. Yes?

Mr. TATE. Would it interrupt you for me to ask the witness a question right there, Mr. Nicholl?

Mr. NICHOLL. No, sir.

By Mr. TATE:

Q. That is the telegram that you sent at the request of the committee?—A. Yes, sir.

By Mr. NICHOLL:

Q. You did not see Mr. Doblin, as I understand it, that day after he made his statement?—A. You are correct.

Q. I am correct about that?—A. Yes, sir; absolutely correct.

Q. Did you not send a telegram to him that night?—A. I sent whatever telegrams are there. They are there; you have them there.

Q. No; I have not. Mr. Doblin testified that there is a telegram which he has at home in which you used the words, "The statement is all right. Have no fear."—A. I did not send a telegram that night, because I did not see Mr. Doblin again, and I certainly sent no telegram. The chronological order of events was that Doblin came down on Wednesday and was heard by the subcommittee, went to the station and went home, and I never saw him again until he came down on Saturday morning.

Q. And you sent him no telegram that afternoon or night, to his house in New York, in which, speaking of the statement he had made before the subcommittee, you said: "Statement all right; have no fear," or words to that effect?—A. I don't remember any other telegram, Mr. Nicholl.

Q. When did you learn of his statement that day to the subcommittee?—A. Right after the committee got through with him, five or ten minutes afterwards.

Q. Yes?—A. (Continuing.) A gentleman called me in, and I think Mr. Wheeler spoke to me first, and we then talked of the whole subject.

Q. Yes. Then the statement in his testimony to the effect that you did send him a telegram that afternoon or night, in which you said that his statement to the subcommittee was all right, and "have no fear," is not correct, is it?—A. On what page is that?

Q. Page 95, about two-thirds of the way down?—A. (After examining record.) I do not remember sending him another telegram than those which are here. I do not remember sending him another telegram. I certainly would tell you of it if I did.

Q. Are you unable to answer that question, as to whether that is a correct statement on his part?—A. I don't know whether I sent him a telegram, Mr. Nicholl. The committee spoke to me about him and what he had said. I do not remember a telegram.

Q. Yes. Now, it was on Wednesday afternoon—a week ago to-morrow—that you entertained the belief, after talking with the members of the general committee, that there would not be any further investigation of the subject, was it not?—A. Yes, sir.

Q. What?—A. Yes, sir.

Q. And when you had arrived at that state of mind, did you not then send him the telegram, believing that there would be no further investigation of the subject, "Statement all right; have no fear?"—A. I don't remember the telegram—I don't remember a telegram other than the telegrams he has shown here.

Q. Mr. Lessler, on that afternoon did you not offer to withdraw these charges?—A. I did not.

Q. You did not say to the committee that you were perfectly willing to withdraw the charges if—— A. I said to Mr. Roberts, of this committee, in statuary hall——

Q. To. Mr Roberts?—A. Yes, sir.

Q. To anyone else?—A. And I said to the subcommittee that I would, if they desired——

Q. Yes.—A. (Continuing.) Sign a statement that I had no direct connection at any time with the Holland Torpedo Boat Company. That was the extent of anything I ever said I would ever sign, Mr. Nicholl. That I said to Mr. Roberts.

Q. Didn't you say to the subcommittee this, that you were anxious to withdraw the whole matter, and would withdraw it if the committee would not go on with it any further?—A. I think I have stated to you absolutely——

Q. Did'nt you say that?—A. One minute, Mr. Nicholl? I think I have absolutely stated what in substance I said to the subcommittee. I said to the subcommittee, and I repeat it to you again, that I met Mr. Roberts in Statuary Hall, and I said to him, as he was the one most interested among us in the proposition affected here, that I would sign a statement; and Mr. Roberts the next morning brought a letter to me addressed to the Holland Torpedo Boat Company.

Mr. WHEELER. Who wrote that letter?

The WITNESS. I do not know.

Mr. DAYTON. Mr. Roberts brought that to you?

The WITNESS. Yes, sir.

Mr. DAYTON. A member of this committee?

The WITNESS. Yes, sir.

Mr. WHEELER. Have you got it?

The WITNESS. No, sir. I gave it right back and said that I would not sign any such letter.

Q. You handed it back and said that you would not sign any such letter. Was it written on the Holland Torpedo Boat Company paper or on Congressional paper?—A. No, sir. It was written on a plain sheet of paper. I did not read the letter.

Q. Did he propose to take that to the Holland Torpedo Boat Company?—A. I said to him in Statuary Hall that I would not have anything to do with the Holland Torpedo Boat Company in any form or shape, and when he brought me the letter I declined to sign it when I saw "Holland Torpedo Boat" on it, and that is all there was to it.

Q. Did you read it?—A. No, sir. I just saw the words "Holland Torpedo Boat Company" and "Gentlemen," and I did not even read it.

By Mr. RIXEY:

Q. How do you say it was addressed?—A. "Holland Torpedo Boat Company. Gentlemen."

By Mr. NICHOLL:

Q. Was that statement to Mr. Roberts, of this committee, voluntary on your part?—A. Yes, sir.

Q. Entirely voluntary?—A. Yes, sir.

Q. You met him in Statuary Hall and offered to make that statement, did you?—A. Yes, sir.

Q. And was it before or after that that you saw the Speaker?—A. Mr. Nicholl, I have told you exactly when I saw the Speaker, on Wednesday morning, and this occurred afterwards. All these things were subsequent to Wednesday morning.

Q. What was the date of the time when you said to Mr. Roberts that you would sign such a statement? What was the date; was it Wednesday?—A. A little later than that, on Wednesday.

Q. Do you mean to say Wednesday at noon, or Wednesday at midday?—A. Yes, sir; somewhere around there.

(It was moved and seconded that the committee should go into executive session.)

Mr. VANDIVER. Mr. Chairman, it occurred to me——

Mr. KITCHIN. Have you any other witnesses?

Mr. LESSLER. No, sir; I have no other witnesses.

Mr. VANDIVER. It occurs to me that we ought to go into one or two other questions publicly. We have gotten into considerable trouble about business which occurred several times before because we have had no stenographer, and I for one have been in favor of concluding this investigation publicly. I think the end to be accomplished, and the nature of the charges made here, require public information and public comment, and I am prepared to say what I have to say publicly.

Mr. WHEELER. The question is on the vote.

The CHAIRMAN. Yes, on the vote that we go into executive session.

(The motion was carried, and the committee went into executive session.)

After an interval, the committee went again into open session, and the stenographer was recalled.

The CHAIRMAN. Mr. Roberts.

Mr. ROBERTS. Mr. Lessler, in his testimony just given, referred to an interview or a meeting held with me. The interview was of his own seeking. He gave a portion of the conversation that took place, and I think many members of the committee drew the wrong inference from the actual condition of affairs that existed.

Now, I want to say that I have no wish to make any statement voluntarily that will reflect on any member of the committee in any way, shape, or manner in these proceedings here, but if any member of this committee thinks there was anything improper on my part during the course of that interview, or anything that followed it, I am perfectly willing to answer any or all questions that he wishes to ask.

The CHAIRMAN. Are there any questions, gentlemen?

Mr. WHEELER. I move that we go into executive session.

Mr. VANDIVER. I would like to ask a question, Mr. Chairman. I do not desire to force the inquiry——

The CHAIRMAN. Mr. Wheeler moves that we go into executive session. Are you ready for the question?

Mr. RIXEY. I do not think it is proper to cut me off in that way.

Mr. WHEELER. If he wants to ask further questions, let him do so.

Mr. VANDIVER. I was going to ask him further as to how that interview came about, and what led to it. I do not desire to press the question if it is not desired by the members of the committee.

Mr. WHEELER. I think we ought not to go into that matter.

Mr. BUTLER. If you desire, ask the question.

Mr. VANDIVER. I will withdraw the question if it is desired.

The CHAIRMAN. Mr. Wheeler moves that we go into executive session. All those——

Mr. VANDIVER. I want to say again on that question that I do not see any necessity for confining this whole business within the committee. It is a matter of public record that serious charges have been made here, and that we are investigating them. I never have believed in star-chamber business. I believe in open investigation, in open court. I do not see any reason why we can not settle this whole business, vote on it, call the roll, and put every member on record.

Mr. WHEELER. Did you ever hear of a judge thinking aloud when he is making up his opinion?

(Informal discussion followed.)

Mr. BUTLER. May I be recognized for a minute, Mr. Chairman?

The CHAIRMAN. Yes; certainly.

Mr. BUTLER. Now, if there is any member of this committee, or anyone else present, desiring to make a statement bearing on this accusation made, let him make it and make it publicly.

Mr. VANDIVER. I wish to say right here and now that I am ready to make a statement, and desire to make it.

The CHAIRMAN. Let us go into executive session.

Mr. VANDIVER. Am I to understand that we are to go on with the consideration of this matter?

Mr. ROBERTS. It seems to me that if we are to close the hearing we had better close it.

(Further informal discussion followed, at the conclusion of which the committee went into executive session.)

At the conclusion of the executive session the committee again went into open session, and the stenographer was recalled.

TESTIMONY OF HARRY SCHREIER (SWORN).

The CHAIRMAN. As this witness was presented here by Mr. Lessler, is there any objection to Mr. Lessler examining him?

Mr. KITCHIN. No, this witness is brought here by the committee.

Mr. ROBERTS. The Chairman has the power to say who shall examine him.

Mr. MUDD. Did you subpœna him?

The CHAIRMAN. No, we did not.

Mr. MUDD. He is a voluntary witness?

The CHAIRMAN. Mr. Lessler brought him here, but of course he is here subject to the committee, now that he is here.

Mr. MUDD. He is subject to the committee and should be interrogated by the chairman of the committee.

By the CHAIRMAN:

Q. State your name.—A. Harry Schreier.

Q. Where do you live?—A. New York City.

Q. How long have you been a resident of New York City?—A. About forty years.

Q. You are acquainted with Mr. Lessler?—A. Yes, sir.

Q. How long have you known him?—A. Ever since he was born.

Q. Are you any relation of his?—A. I am his uncle.

Q. Do you know anything about the matter of this investigation?—
A. I do.

Q. Well, state in your own way.—A. It was between Christmas and New Year's holidays that Mr. Lessler called at my office and took lunch with me.

Q. Where is your office?—A. At 503 Broadway, New York.

Q. What is your business, may I ask?—A. I am credit man in a large importing house.

Q. Well, proceed.—A. During the time that Mr. Lessler waited for me Mr. Doblin came in and I invited him to go along with us to lunch.

Mr. ROBERTS. You mean Philip Doblin?

The WITNESS. Philip Doblin.

A. (Continuing.) We went to lunch, and after we got through and were smoking a cigar, Mr. Lessler turned around to Doblin and said: "Now see here, Doblin, this is my uncle, from whom I do not have any secrets, and I want you to repeat the conversation that you related to me, which you had had with Mr. Quigg." Thereupon Doblin said, "I went down to the office of Quigg to see whether I could not get my appointment as a McCullagh deputy prolonged or continued, and while I was there Mr. Quigg said to me, 'By the way, you know Lessler, don't you?'" Doblin said "Yes." He said, "Do you know him very well?" Doblin said, "I know him as good as anybody does." "Well," he says Mr. Quigg asked him, "how close are you to him?" "Well," he says, "I am right next to him." That was the very expression he used.

So then Mr. Quigg said to him, "Now I understand Mr. Lessler is opposed to, and has expressed his opposition to, a certain measure that is before the House, known as the Holland submarine torpedo boat," or something of that kind, and he says to him "Now, I have got some friends who are interested in that boat, and I wish you could help me to get Lessler's vote in support of that measure. I want you to see him, and there is $5,000 in it for him provided we can get his vote."

Well, my nephew turned around to me—Mr. Lessler turned around to me and he says "What do you think of that, uncle?" I said, "I think it is an outrageous proposition, and if you will take my advice you will have nothing to do with this man Quigg; and, above all things, don't have any interviews with him." That was all I know.

By the CHAIRMAN:

Q. This was the conversation that Doblin had with you, as I understand it?—A. That is right; at the dinner table.

Q. Was there anybody else present?—A. Lessler, Doblin, and myself.

Q. That is all?—A. That is all.

By Mr. VANDIVER:

Q. At what time was that conversation?—A. Well, it was the end of December, between Christmas and New Year.

Q. Where was this luncheon taken?—A. At the corner of Broadway and Houghton streets, in a place called Hulse's restaurant.

Q. A large restaurant?—A. Pretty large.

Q. What time was it?—A. Around near 1 o'clock.

Q. Were there many in there?—A. Not very many.

Q. There were people around at all the tables, were there not?—A No, sir; not at the time the conversation took place. At that time it had begun to thin out. I get my dinner late.

Q. Do you call that late?—A. I said between 1 and 2.

Q. Is not that the general lunching hour in New York?—A. No.

Q. It is not?—A. It is not, particularly.

Q. Is this a prominent place?—A. It is quite a well-known place.

Q. There were about as many in there that day as usual?—A. I could not say. Probably.

Q. And this was a discussion right at a dining table in a public restaurant?—A. Yes, sir; it was.

The CHAIRMAN. Are there any further questions, gentlemen?

By Mr. ROBERTS:

Q. Can you fix any more definitely the day when this took place?—A. I think it was either the Friday or the Saturday right after Christmas—either Friday or Saturday.

Q. It was not before Christmas?—A. No, sir.

Q. Do you remember the day of the week?—A. Either Friday or Saturday, between Christmas and New Years.

Q. Now, did Mr. Lessler say anything to you at that time about his already having seen Mr. Quigg?—A. No.

Q. He did not indicate——

Mr. VANDIVER. I can not quite hear.

By Mr. ROBERTS:

Q. I asked if Mr. Lessler said anything to you at that time about his having seen Mr. Quigg.—A. He had not seen him.

Q. He told you that he had not seen Mr. Quigg?—A. Yes, sir.

By Mr. NICOLL:

Q. When did you arrive?—A. I arrived this morning.

Q. Did you go to see Mr. Lessler when you arrived?—A. I did.

Q. Where?—A. At the Normandie Hotel.

Q. Well, did you have a talk with him about what you had come for?—A. Certainly.

Q. Did you talk the matter over with him?—A. Not in regard to the evidence; only in a general way.

Q. You said nothing as to your testimony here to-day?—A. No, sir.

Q. Not a word?—A. Nothing about what I was to testify to.

Q. Did he not tell you that you had come here to state that Doblin had made a statement of this sort to you?—A. No, sir; he asked me if I remembered the conversation, and I told him yes, and he said: "Now, that is all I want to know."

Q. How long have you known Doblin?—A. I have known Doblin about a year.

Q. Who introduced him to you?—A. Mr. Lessler.

Q. Have you ever had any business with him?—A. None.

Q. None at all?—A. None.

Q. Have you any interest in any matter with him at all?—A. None.

Q. What?—A. No, sir.

Q. Have you any interest in a substance called Guttanova?—A. What is that?

Q. Guttanova.—A. I don't hear your question.

Q. Have you any interest in a substance called Guttanova?—A. No, sir; I have heard of it.

Q. You never heard of it at all?—A. I have heard of the substance.

Q. Have you any knowledge concerning or interest in it?—A. None whatever.

Q. You are not interested in it?—A. Not at all.

Q. What is the substance?—A. I believe it is an electric compound for insulating electric wires.

Q. As a matter of fact, do you not know that Mr. Doblin was employed by your friends to present that matter to the fire department of New York as a new material for insulating wires?—A. He was at one time.

Q. He was?—A. Yes, sir.

Q. How do you know that?—A. Because he told me so.

Q. He told you?—A. Yes, sir.

Q. Was not this meeting that you had here on this particular day——

Mr. BACON. Pardon me, but has that anything to do with this matter? I can not understand the connection.

Mr. NICHOLL. It is leading up to it.

Mr. DAYTON. Go on if there is any connection.

By Mr. NICHOLL:

Q. Was not this meeting that you had there this day for the purpose of talking over this subject?—A. No, sir.

Q. It had nothing to do with it?—A. Nothing, sir.

Q. What was Mr. Doblin doing up there at 503 Broadway?—A. Mr. Doblin can answer that; I can not. He may have come to see me.

Q. He did come to see you?—A. Yes, sir.

Q. Did he come to your office?—A. Yes, sir.

Q. Alone?—A. Yes, sir.

Q. Did you know what he had come for?—A. No, sir.

Q. Had he come before?—A. Yes, sir.

Q. He had no business with you?—A. No, sir.

Q. And he came to your office without having any business with you?—A. Yes, sir.

Q. He had come before?—A. Yes, sir.

Q. How many times?—A. Two or three times.

Q. And called on you?—A. Yes, sir.

Q. In your office?—A. In my office.

Q. Did he come just in a social way?—A. A social call.

Q. That is it?—A. Yes, sir.

Q. He came in that day for a social call?—A. I could not say the object of his visit.

Q. Did he come in before Mr. Lessler did?—A. He came in afterwards.

Q. And then you all went to Hulse's together?—A. We went to Hulse's; yes, sir.

Q. Where did you sit in Hulse's?—A. We sat at a table two or three rows from the front of the place.

Q. You mean Hulse's on Broadway?—A. On Broadway; yes, sir.

Q. Between what streets?—A. At the corner of Houghton and Broadway.

Q. You sat three rows back from the Broadway entrance?—A. Yes, sir; from the front entrance.

Q. Now, is it not a matter of fact that whatever conversation you had with Lessler on that day about this matter you had when Doblin had left the table?—A. Doblin had not left the table; he was there at the table continually with us and had not left or did not leave until we all left.

Q. And I understand you to say you advised your nephew under no circumstances to see Quigg. Is that so?—A. That is right.

Q. Did you also advise him under no circumstances to have anything more to do with Doblin?—A. No, sir.

Q. You did not?—A. No

Q. He gave you no advice on that point?—A. No, sir. He knew him longer and better than I did, I supposed.

Q. Was anything said about $50,000 on that day?—A. No, sir.

Q. Not a word on that subject?—A. No, sir.

Mr. NICHOLL. No. That is all.

The CHAIRMAN. Are there any further questions?

Mr. KITCHIN. I want to ask this witness one question.

By Mr. KITCHIN:

Q. Did you say Mr. Lessler joined in this conversation at the table?—A. He did not.

Q. But he was present all the time?—A. All the time.

Q. And heard it, did he?—A. Yes, sir; and heard it all.

Q. Did you not say that you requested Doblin to repeat the story?—A. He requested him to detail the story.

Q. And he did repeat the story to you?—A. Yes, sir.

Q. Did he say anything to Lessler about it?—A. Only what I have said.

Q. Did you not say that Mr. Lessler asked him "What would you do about that, Uncle?"—A. No, sir; "What do you think of it?"

Q. "What do you think of it, Uncle?"—A. Yes, sir.

Q. And then he did join in it?—A. Not until it was ended.

Q. That is, he did not pretend to tell Doblin what to say?—A. No, sir.

Q. But you did talk over it afterwards?—A. Just those few words.

Q. Then if there has been any statement that Mr. Lessler did not talk about it to any others than the members of this committee that would not be correct, would it, because he did talk about it to you?—A. Just those words.

Q. Yes; that is all.

(Witness excused.)

Mr. QUIGG. I should like to have the telegram I sent to the chairman of the committee. As soon as I saw anything in the newspapers relating to this matter I sent a telegram to the chairman of the committee, and I should like to put that in evidence. In that telegram I requested to have a public hearing.

The CHAIRMAN. It is understood that the telegram which Mr. Quigg sent to me requesting a public inquiry shall go into the evidence.

There was no objection, and the telegram referred to is here inserted in the record, as follows:

NEW YORK, *January 22, 1903.*

Hon. GEO. E. FOSS,
 Chairman Naval Affairs Committee, Washington, D. C.:

It is published here that Representative Montague Lessler has in some way connected my name with the alleged attempt to bribe him. If this is not true, please give out official denial. If Lessler says anything of the kind, I respectfully request public inquiry; of course, there is no truth whatever in such a suggestion.

LEMUEL E. QUIGG.

It was moved and seconded that the committee should adjourn for one hour and then go into executive session.

Thereupon, at 1.50 o'clock p. m., the committee adjourned for one hour.

AFTER RECESS.

The committee met pursuant to adjournment.

After informal discussion for some time the stenographer was recalled, when the following took place:

Mr. ROBERTS. Mr. Chairman, I have learned during the intermission

that a wrong impression has gone out, arising from the incident alluded
to by Mr. Lessler in his examination, of the meeting he held with me.
I desire now to state fully my recollection of the entire transaction, not
with any intent or purpose of injuring Mr. Lessler, or of prejudicing him
in the minds of the committee, but merely that it shall be in this record,
and shall go out to the country, just what took place.

It was the forenoon of January 21, which was last Wednesday, that
the meeting mentioned by Mr. Lessler took place. I was coming
through Statuary Hall, on my way to my committee room, and I met
Mr. Lessler coming from the opposite direction. Mr. Lessler spoke to
me, and said, "Can we not stop this thing? My God, I can not stand
it; it is killing me." I said to him——

Mr. VANDIVER. Please speak louder.

Mr. ROBERTS (continuing). The thing he referred to was the proposed investigation which we had authorized to be made by the subcommittee. I said to him that the investigation was nothing of my
seeking; that I had no benefit to gain from pressing it as far as I was
personally concerned. I did not care whether it went on or stopped;
but there were other parties besides myself in this matter.

The statement had gone out to the country in the press that the
Holland Submarine Boat Company had attempted to influence his
action by an offer of money, and I did not know whether the Holland
people would be willing to have the thing smothered; that that phase
of the question would have to be considered. Mr. Lessler thereupon
volunteered—the suggestion came from him—that he would make any
statement regarding the matter that was thought to be fair and reasonable. He said when he made his first statement in the committee he
did not intend to injure the Holland people; and I remarked to him
that if that was his intention—I remarked to him that if he did not
intend to injure the Holland people, the only thing that he could do, as
an honest and upright gentleman, was to make such a statement; and
he said if I would have one prepared he would sign it. I then said to
him—and he said further that he would not sign such a statement to
be published. I said to him that I did not suppose the Holland people
would care to publish any such statement, that I did not think they
would make any use of it whatever unless their interests were to be
jeopardized by the use of his original statement, and then in self-
defense they would be obliged to publish any statement that he would
make.

Then upon that understanding he authorized me to make the statement. Then I said to him: "I think there is another phase of the
situation which I do not think you have considered. When your statement was made to the full committee certain members of the committee
who had been opposed to the submarine legislation seized upon the
statement, and insisted on an investigation," and I said, "I do not
believe those gentlemen will stop." Mr. Lessler said to me, "I think
that I can fix them, and I think I can arrange that all right." He then
went on to make still another statement to me as to what he would do
personally when the Holland submarine proposition came to a vote in
committee. I then left him. He went his way and I went mine. I
had prepared a statement for him to sign.

I did not see Mr. Lessler again that day until shortly after the House
came in session. I was standing on the floor of the House, on the back
of the rail, talking to another member of Congress, when Mr. Lessler
came along with his overcoat on and his hat in his hand, and said to me,
"That thing I told you could be arranged has been fixed." This was

on Wednesday, when the subcommittee, I suppose, were investigating the matter with an idea of on the following day presenting some report to the full committee. The statement that I had prepared for him I submitted to Mr. Lessler in this committee room the next morning. That was the morning when the subcommittee were to report to the full committee, and I handed it to Lessler, which I had in my hand just a moment or two before the committee came in session, saying to him, "Here is the statement that you asked me to have prepared." I will now read that statement:

JANUARY 21, 1903.

HOLLAND TORPEDO BOAT COMPANY,
Corcoran Building, Washington, D. C.

DEAR SIRS: In reference to the statement made by me before the Naval Committee of the House on January 20, in which, by inference, your company was connected with a promise of money for my vote on the proposition of the submarine boat, I desire to say it was never my intention in any manner to create the inference that your company, or any of its officers or stockholders, were connected in the remotest degree, either directly or indirectly, with that offer. That offer, I am now satisfied, was made without your knowledge by an irresponsible party. I sincerely trust that you will not be injured by the publicity given to my statement.

Very truly, yours.

I handed the paper to him. He glanced at it, and did not read it, and said, "That is directed to the Holland Torpedo Boat Company, and I will not sign it, or any other statement."

That ended the incident.

By Mr. WHEELER:

Q. I want to ask you some questions, if it is agreeable, since you have gone into that, and if you are through with your statement.
Mr. ROBERTS. Yes.
Q. When Mr. Lessler first approached you out in Statuary Hall, did you report what he had said to you to any of the agents or officers of the Holland Torpedo Boat Company?—A. Did I report to them?
Q. Yes; make a statement to them.—A. Yes, sir.
Q. To whom?—A. To Mr. Frost.
Q. Where did you see Mr. Frost?—A. I did not see him.
Q. You did not see him?—A. No, sir.
Q. How did you communicate with him; by writing?—A. No, sir.
Q. How did you communicate with him?—A. I telephoned him.
Q. Where did you telephone him?—A. I got him at the office of the Holland Torpedo Boat Company in Washington.
Q. Did you subsequently see him?—A. I saw him, I think, that evening.
Q. Where did you see him?—A. Let me see. I think I saw him at their office.
Q. Did you go there?—A. Yes; I did. Yes; I went there.
Q. Did you go of your own volition or at their invitation?—A. Yes, sir; at my own volition.
Q. Is that the first time you have gone there?—A. No, sir.
Q. You have gone there before?—A. Yes, sir.
Q. How many times have you been there?—A. I could not tell you.
Q. How many times have you been there since this investigation has been pending?—A. Possibly two or three times.
Q. Did you go every time on your own volition, or by invitation?—A. Always of my own volition.
Q. When you got to the office of this company did you talk over with Mr. Frost this incident?—A. I did.

Q. Who was present at the time that you had the conversation?—A. With Mr. Frost?

Q. Yes.—A. Nobody.

Q. Who is Mr. Frost?—A. I don't know, except that he is the counsel of the Holland Torpedo Boat Company, in some capacity.

Q. You do not know what capacity?—A. No, sir; I do not.

Q. Is he not one of the governing officers?—A. I think so.

Q. Now, did you prepare that statement in Mr. Frost's office?—A. No, sir.

Q. Did you prepare it at all?—A. No, sir.

Q. Who did prepare it?—A. I don't know.

Q. How did you get hold of it?—A. It was sent up to me at my request.

Q. Whom did you request to send it?—A. Mr. Frost.

Q. When did you get it?—A. I got it late that afternoon.

Q. Did you and Mr. Frost talk over the purport of the statement that you have got there—what it would embrace?—A. No, sir; not at all.

Q. You did not discuss the preparation of that statement?—A. Not at all. Pardon me just a moment. When Mr. Lessler—I know what you are getting at, and I will tell you to save this long series of questions. When Mr. Lessler told me that he was willing to make a statement of retraction, it was no statement that he could make to me.

Q. How is that?—A. It was no statement that he could make to me, personally.

Q. Yes—A. (Continuing.) Because I had no interest in having a retraction from him. It was a statement that should bemade to the Holland Torpedo Boat Company. They were the partie affected by his statement. I telephoned to Mr. Frost that I had met Lessler, and he had expressed a willingness to make a statement.

Q. Yes, and—— A. Now, do not interrupt me. I prefer to finish my statement.

Q. I know, but I want you to answer my question. You are not the one to say as to that.—A. I am not a witness.

Q. Yes, you are.—A. I am not.

Mr. WHEELER. Mr. Roberts says that he is not a witness. Then I ask that he be sworn.

Mr. ROBERTS. I have no objection to being sworn.

The CHAIRMAN. He is making his own statement.

Mr. ROBERTS. I am making a personal statement, and I have simply consented to answer your questions.

Mr. WHEELER. I beg your pardon.

Mr. ROBERTS. Now, if you will permit me, I will continue my statement.

Mr. WHEELER. Certainly.

Mr. ROBERTS. When Mr. Lessler made that statement it was a matter that concerned the Holland Torpedo Boat Company and not myself. I telephoned to Mr. Frost that I had met Lessler, and he had distinctly stated to me that he would sign a paper. I said, "Mr. Frost, this thing affects the Holland Submarine Boat Company, and I want you to prepare a statement that will be satisfactory to your people, and when it is prepared send it to me." I may say further—no, I will not.

Mr. WHEELER. I want the privilege of examining him as a witness.

Mr. ROBERTS. Now, I want to say this, Mr. Wheeler: I have arisen voluntarily to make this statement.

Mr. WHEELER. Yes, sir.

Mr. ROBERTS. And if you want to call me as a witness——

Mr. WHEELER. I do want to call you as a witness.

Mr. ROBERTS. I have no objection; but if you do not, I object to your cross examining me.

Mr. WHEELER. If you do not give me the right to cross-examine you, I propose to have you sworn.

Mr. ROBERTS. I have made my statement, and I will answer your questions.

Mr. WHEELER. Then I will continue my cross-examination.

Mr. ROBERTS. I deny your right to cross-examine me.

Mr. WHEELER. Then I want him as a witness.

Mr. ROBERTS. Do you want to call me as a witness? That is your privilege.

Mr. WHEELER. Well, I want you as a witness. I want to cross-examine you.

Mr. VANDIVER. I suggest that this is not in the line of procedure of the committee.

Mr. WHEELER. Oh, yes; it is.

Mr. ROBERTS. If Mr. Lessler has any statement which he wishes to make it will be competent for him to make his statement.

Mr. WHEELER. I presume that I have the right to have all the testimony on the subject from any source, and unless I have the unquestionable and indisputable right to make this cross examination of a member of this committee, then I want the gentleman put under oath. I do not care anything about the oath.

Mr. ROBERTS. I do not concede that you have any right to cross-examine me.

Mr. WHEELER. Then I claim the right for his testimony to go into the record just as the rest of the testimony has gone. I want to examine him.

Mr. VANDIVER. I shall object to the witness being cross-examined—to members of the committee being cross examined here as witnesses—unless we are going fully into this subject and put everybody on the stand and make a witness of everybody here.

Mr. WHEELER. I am perfectly willing that any gentleman here shall cross-examine me before this gentleman goes on here, and it is with great pleasure that I concede the right to you to cross-examine me. I did have my regrets at the outset as to this procedure, but I do not regret it now. This whole matter will go before the House of Representatives, and a part of this testimony will be argued and criticised on the floor, and there are some things that I want to know about this matter.

Mr. VANDIVER. I suggest that if we are going into a further investigation and examine other witnesses, there may be a good deal yet to be brought out.

Mr. TATE. If there is, let us have it.

Mr. VANDIVER. I object to this irregular sort of proceeding.

Mr. WHEELER I certainly think that I ought to have the right to cross-examine him. I do not want to be impertinent. I do not want to ask a man questions unless I have a right to do so.

Mr. RIXEY. I am going to submit a motion, under the circumstances, that Mr. Wheeler be permitted to examine the member, and for this reason: Mr. Roberts came in before recess and made his statement as a member of the committee. Now, when he comes back afterwards and undertakes to give the details of a conversation with Mr. Lessler, and about which Mr. Lessler has testified as a witness, he ought to be sworn and cross-examined. I think that he ought to have been sworn before he began to give this testimony.

Mr. WHEELER. So do I. He is making a statement as to what Lessler said, and to some extent it may vary the effect of Mr. Lessler's testimony. Now, it seems to me proper, if any member of the committee—so far as I am concerned I do not desire to ask Mr. Roberts any questions—but it is perfectly plain to me that if any member of the committee desires to cross-examine him he has a right to do so, and I think we would be put in a bad light before the House if we refused it.

The CHAIRMAN. If I understand it, Mr. Roberts desired to make a personal statement.

Mr. ROBERTS. Several similar personal statements appear in the record, and no question has been made here before about a member making a personal statement.

Mr. VANDIVER. I would like to ask Mr. Wheeler——

The CHAIRMAN. Have you any objection to being sworn?

Mr. ROBERTS. Not at all; but, as I told you, my objection—and that is not to being sworn—is not to telling everything or anything that transpired between Mr. Lessler and myself, but I shall certainly object to Mr. Wheeler or any other member of this committee interrogating me on any subject that is directly related to the conversation between Mr. Lessler and myself.

Mr. WHEELER. That is exactly why I want him sworn. I do not want him to have a right to claim immunity from any question that I desire to ask him that can shed light on this investigation.

Mr. VANDIVER. I desire to know whether or not Mr. Lessler desires to make any further statement in reference to that matter. If he desires it, I think he ought to have the privilege of doing it.

Mr. WHEELER. I have the floor. I care nothing about Mr. Lessler. This is a matter that affects this committee and the House of Representatives. I care nothing about the individual members of this committee, and whether Mr. Lessler goes down or up under this investigation. We are here to discharge a public duty, as I understand it, I will say to the gentleman from Missouri, regardless of whom it affects.

Mr. VANDIVER. I agree to that.

Mr. WHEELER. I want the gentleman from Massachusetts to go on, and I want to examine him.

Mr. ROBERTS. Do you want me as a witness?

Mr. WHEELER. Yes, sir; I want you as a witness, and I want the oath administered to him.

TESTIMONY OF HON. ERNEST W. ROBERTS (SWORN).

By Mr. WHEELER:

Q. Now, Mr. Roberts, when you communicated with Mr. Frost by telephone was that the first time you communicated with him after you had heard the disclosure made in here by Mr. Lessler?—A. No; it was not.

Q. When did you communicate that to him before that time?—A. The day before.

Q. Immediately after the adjournment of this committee?—A. No, I think not.

Q. How long after the adjournment before you communicated with Mr. Frost?—A. I can not tell you.

Q. Give your best judgment about it?—A. It was on my way home.

Q. How did you do it, by telephone or personal call?—A. No; I called at his office.

Q. You called at his office?—A. Yes, sir.

Q. Did you tell him what Mr. Lessler had said?—A. I did.

Q. Was anybody present at that conversation?—A. No, sir.

Q. Now, Mr. Roberts, after this statement was prepared you say it was brought to you?—A. Yes, sir.

Q. Who brought it?—A. I don't know, sir.

Q. Did you see the man who brought it?—A. No, sir.

Q. Where did he deliver it to you?—A. My recollection is that I found it in my committee room just before—when I went down there just before I went home.

Q. What day was that?—A. The 21st of January, the day the statement was drawn up.

Q. What did you do with that when you got it?—A. I put it in my pocket.

Q. How long before you saw Mr. Lessler?—A. The next morning.

Q. After you saw Mr. Frost—did you see Mr. Frost or any other officer of the Holland Submarine Boat Company before you saw Mr. Lessler?—A. No, sir.

Q. Mr. Lessler declined to sign it?— A. Yes, sir.

Q. Did you communicate with Mr. Frost or any other attorney or agent of the company?—A. Yes, sir.

Q. Whom?—A. Mr. Frost.

Q. When?—A. Some time that day.

Q. During the session of the House, before, or afterwards?—A. I think it was during the session. I think I telephoned down that Mr. Lessler had declined to sign the statement.

Q. What did he say?—A. He laughed.

Q. He laughed?—A. Yes, sir.

Q. What did you say to him? Did you just tell him that Mr. Lessler had declined to sign it?—A. Yes—no, sir; I did not tell him in just those words. I said, "It has turned out just as I said it would." I had told him when I telephoned him just to prepare such a statement as would satisfy his company, and I would present it to Mr. Lessler, but I did not believe that he would ever sign it.

Q. Did you tell any member of this committee of the conversation that you had with Mr. Lessler?—A. Oh, yes; I think I have.

Q. Who was it?—A. I do not think that I can specify about that.

Q. You can not indicate now any member of the committee that you communicated that to?—A. I think I communicated it to Mr. Rixey.

Q. Before you did to Mr. Frost?—A. I can not state that. I do not know.

Q. Is it not a fact that you communicated with Mr. Frost at once when Mr. Lessler made this statement to you?—A. I think it is.

Q. And before you had communicated with any member of the committee?—A. I was on my way to my committee room when I met Mr. Lessler. I continued on to my committee room and telephoned to Mr. Frost. This was a new phase and turn in the affair.

Q. And Mr. Lessler said to you that he would be willing to sign any sort of statement—— A. No, no.

Q. (Continuing.) That was honorable and fair and that would stop this matter?—A. Yes, sir.

Q. Now, is it not a fact that immediately upon the exposure by Mr. Lessler of this corrupt effort there was a perfect howl went up from the press of this country, and Mr. Lessler was referring in his conversation to you to the fact that he wanted to escape the public con-

demnation and opprobrium that was hurled at him on account of this
matter?—A. I do not know what Mr. Lessler thought——

Q. Is not that the impression that it made?—A. No, sir. It made a
distinctly different impression on my mind.

Q. What kind of an impression?—A. It was a distinctly different
impression.

Q. I beg your pardon; I do not get that.—A. I had a distinctly different impression made on my mind by Mr. Lessler's anxiety to stop
the investigation.

Q. Have you any objection to stating what that impression was?—
A. No, sir; if you want me to.

Q. I would like to have you do so.—A. My idea was that Mr. Lessler
had made a statement to the committee that he knew he could not substantiate.

Q. He was lying, to put it baldly?—A. You can put any words——

Q. He was lying, you mean?—A. You can put any words in the record that you want to.

Q. That is it.   He was not making a truthful statement?—A. You
asked my impression.   I do not assume to pass upon the truth or honesty of this statement.

Q. No, no——

Mr. MUDD. I do not think that one member's impression of another
is competent.   I do not think that he ought to be allowed to state that.

Mr. WHEELER. I will withdraw that question.

By Mr. WHEELER:

Q. I will ask you this question: Is it not a fact that you never have
believed anything that Mr. Lessler has said?

Several MEMBERS. Oh, no, no; that will not do.

Mr. MUDD. That is doing Mr. Lessler an injustice.

The WITNESS. You might as well ask me to give my opinion of all the
members of the committee.

Mr. WHEELER. Let him go ahead and do so.

The WITNESS. Do you really want me to begin with the chairman
and go down through all the members of the committee and give my
impressions about all of them?

By Mr. WHEELER:

Q. I will ask another question—if you have not been a very ardent,
avowed, and aggressive advocate of the Holland torpedo boat proposition?—A. Yes, sir; I have.

Mr. KITCHIN. I object to that.

Mr. WHEELER. He has answered it.

Mr. KITCHIN. I object to it.

A. (Continuing.) Just as you have been always opposed to it.

Mr. WHEELER. Yes, I am; I have been, unquestionably, and I do not
hesitate to avow it.

Mr. KITCHIN. I object to this.   Under this mode of procedure every
member of this committee might have to state his position for or against
this proposition, and it might disqualify him from acting in this matter
afterwards.

Mr. WHEELER. I submit that it is entirely proper.   My object in
asking Mr. Roberts's opinion was something entirely aside from and
not at all affecting the integrity of this committee.

Mr. KITCHIN. The purpose of your examination is to impeach the
witness.

Mr. WHEELER. No, sir; it is to show that his interest in this matter
is as great as that of Mr. Lessler.

Mr. KITCHIN. It has not shown that he had any corrupt interest in it so far.

Mr. WHEELER. I am not trying to show any corrupt interest. The gentleman is doing him an injustice.

Mr. KITCHIN. I can not understand what the object of it is unless it is to impugn the honesty and integrity of the witness.

Mr. WHEELER. Can not you understand how a man can be very ardently interested in a matter, to such an extent that his judgment is colored and warped, without there being any question of corrupt motives?

Mr. KITCHIN. I can not see the purpose of cross-examining him further.

Mr. WHEELER. I am not responsible for your general infirmities.

Mr. KITCHIN. I am glad that the gentleman is not responsible for me.

By Mr. WHEELER:

Q. You say that you have been a champion of this measure here?—A. Yes, sir.

Q. And you believed sincerely that it was a just and desirable project?—A. Yes, sir; I do, decidedly.

Q. Now, do you think you can state with absolute clearness and certainty an interview, with this interest that you say you feel and have felt, and now feel, and give a perfectly impartial and detailed repetition of conversations between you and this man Lessler?—A. Absolutely. The very interest that I have taken in this proposition has fixed the statements in my mind so that I will not forget them.

Q. I will put it on a different line——

Mr. VANDIVER. I submit the best way to test that question as to the correctness of Mr. Roberts's statements, and all that took place in this conversation, is to call Mr. Lessler himself, and see whether there is any contradiction between them.

Mr. WHEELER. I think I have a right to get through with this witness.

By Mr. WHEELER:

Q. Do you know any of the officers and governing agents or attorneys of this concern?—A. I think the president.

Q. What is his name?—A. Mr. Rice.

Q. How long have you known him?—A. I met him first some time last spring.

Q. Now eliminate—— A. Let me finish my answer.

Q. I beg your pardon.—A. (Continuing.) Sometime last spring when this committee, I understood, had been invited to go to Annapolis and witness the trials of the Holland torpedo boat, and I went down with a party—I think there were, in fact I know there were, other members of this committee and other members of Congress in the party—Mr. Rice was in the party and I was introduced to him. It was the first time I had ever seen him or heard of him, and I never have seen Mr. Rice from that day until Mr. Lessler's charge was exploded in the committee here, and this investigation was commenced.

Q. How long have you known Mr. Frost, Mr. Roberts?—A. Two or three years.

Q. What has been the degree of intimacy between you and him?—A. I shall decline to state that.

Q. You decline to answer that?—A. I decline to state the degree of intimacy. I have known him two or three years.

H. Rep. 3482——11

Q. Well, I do not understand why you decline to state. Are you friends?—A. Yes, sir.

Q. Are you very friendly with him?—A. No, sir; not very.

Q. Are you related to him by blood, by consanguinity?—A. No, sir.

Q. Eliminating the question of the Holland torpedo boat proposition entirely from your answer, and understanding that I am not speaking of that at all now, have you ever had any business relations with Mr. Frost?—A. Not with Mr. Frost direct.

Q. Well, jointly with him and others?—A. I have this business relation with Mr. Frost and his partner, Mr. Johnson, to-day. I had a claim sent me from Africa, against——

Q. I do not want to go into details, unless you want to do it.—A. Let me answer the question that you put to me.

Q. Why, certainly. Certainly you can.—A. (Continuing). I had a claim sent me from Africa against a resident of New York City. Knowing no attorneys with whom I had any relations or connections in New York, I wrote on to his firm—I think the firm is Frost & Johnson, attorneys—and sent them all the correspondence in the case, the claim, which was in the form of a draft, and asked him, or them, if they would undertake the collection of it, and they are now working on it.

Q. Are you through with that?—A. Yes, sir.

Q. Is that the only—— A. That is all the business relation of any sort, name, or nature that I have ever had with Frost or his partner, or anybody connected with the Holland Submarine Boat Company.

Q. Well, I wanted to understand. I did not want the details of your business.—A. That is the extent of it. He was to get the fee out of collecting this thing, if there was any in it.

Mr. WHEELER. That is all.

(Witness excused.)

The CHAIRMAN. Mr. Lessler, do you want to say anything?

ADDITIONAL TESTIMONY OF HON. MONTAGUE LESSLER—(Recalled.)

The WITNESS. I simply make the statement that what Mr. Roberts stated was substantially true. I do not remember all the details. I did not read the letter, as I stated; I did not state the matter here except as an answer to a question of Mr. Nicholls, who seemed to know all about the episode with Mr. Roberts. I did meet him in Statuary Hall, but whether I said "Oh, my God" and all the rest of it, I do not remember. I did say to Mr. Roberts that I would like to have the thing stopped, and, just as he states, I volunteered the proposition that if, in his judgment, as the advocate here of the Holland torpedo boat—that I would sign a statement showing that I had made no direct accusation of anything between them and me personally in the charge that was leveled in the committee. I was standing right at the mantelpiece when he brought me the letter.

Mr. ROBERTS. You were standing there [indicating].

The WITNESS (Continuing.) By that mantelpiece there, and I was standing at the mantelpiece when he handed me that letter, and I saw that it was addressed to "The Holland Torpedo Boat Company," and I said, "I will not sign that statement."

By Mr. ROBERTS:

Q. You did not read the statement?—A. I did not read the statement.

By Mr. VANDIVER:

Q. I would like to ask a question.

Mr. LOUDENSLAGER. They agree with each other. What is the use of asking questions?

Mr. VANDIVER. Right on that point I desire to ask a question.

By Mr. VANDIVER:

Q. You had stated to him the day before that you would sign a statement of that nature—something of that kind. Why was it that you objected to signing it without reading—without knowing what was really in it?—A. Because it was addressed to the Holland Torpedo Boat Company.

Q. Let me ask you, is it not true that in the meantime you had seen some members of the subcommittee and had learned that the investigation was to go forward, and you could not stop it?—A. No; that is not true, for the reason that nothing was decided about the investigation going forward until we got in full committee and the report of Mr. Tayler was made, discussion was had, and then Mr. Tayler drew from his pocket a resolution. That was the first time that I knew of the full investigation.

(Thereupon the committee went into executive session, at the conclusion of which it adjourned.)

O

BRIBERY CHARGES.

FEBRUARY 3, 1903.—Referred to the House Calendar and ordered to be printed.

Mr. WILLIAM W. KITCHIN, from the Committee on Naval Affairs, submitted the following as the

VIEWS OF THE MINORITY.

[In compliance with H. Res. No. 404.]

Being unable, from the evidence, to agree with all the conclusions of the majority of the Committee on Naval Affairs touching the matters investigated by that committee under House resolution 404, and having considered all the testimony taken and printed, we are of the opinion that the following views should be adopted, and therefore propose them as a substitute for the report offered by the majority of the committee, to wit:

On the 20th day of January, 1903, Hon. Montague Lessler stated to the Committee on Naval Affairs, while that committee was considering a proposition to secure more Holland submarine boats for the Navy, that these people (meaning the Holland Submarine Boat Company) had, through an ex-Congressman, who used an intermediary, offered him, said Lessler, $5,000 for his support of such a proposition. Thereafter to a subcommittee he gave the name of Lemuel E. Quigg as the ex-Congressman and Philip Doblin as the intermediary referred to by him.

As a result of such statement and an investigation by said subcommittee, the Committee on Naval Affairs directed its chairman to report to the House the following preamble and resolution, to wit:

Whereas information has come to the Committee on Naval Affairs, through a member of said committee, of an attempt to corruptly influence his action respecting proposed legislation pending before said committee and the House:

Resolved, That the Committee on Naval Affairs, or such subcommittee thereof as said committee may appoint, be, and it is hereby, authorized and directed to fully investigate said matter; and for such purpose it is hereby authorized and empowered to send for persons and papers, to compel the attendance of witnesses, and to administer oaths. Said committee shall have authority to report at any time, and the expenses incurred hereunder shall be paid out of the contingent fund of the House on vouchers approved by the chairman.

Which resolution was unanimously adopted by the House on January 22, 1903.

Under said resolution the Committee on Naval Affairs has investigated the matter aforesaid by examining a number of witnesses, the testimony being taken by an official stenographer and printed, and upon due consideration thereof we find:

First. That the charge that an attempt was made to corruptly influence a member of the Committee on Naval Affairs respecting proposed legislation pending before the committee and the House is not sustained.

Second. That there is no evidence to sustain the charge of an attempt by Lemuel E. Quigg to corruptly influence a member of the Committee on Naval Affairs respecting proposed legislation pending before said committee and the House.

Third. That there is no evidence to sustain the charge of an attempt by the Holland Submarine Boat Company, or any of its agents, to corruptly influence a member of the Committee on Naval Affairs respecting proposed legislation pending before the committee and the House.

In view of the foregoing, we recommend that the clerk of the committee be directed to certify to the Attorney-General of the United States a copy of the testimony taken at the hearing, with a request that he take such action as the law and the facts warrant.

W. W. KITCHIN.
W. D. VANDIVER.
ERNEST W. ROBERTS.

O

ALEXANDER G. PENDLETON, JR.

FEBRUARY 3, 1903.—Committed to the Committee of the Whold House and ordered
to be printed.

Mr. PARKER, from the Committee on Military Affairs, submitted the
following

REPORT.

[To accompany H. R. 16105.]

The Committee on Military Affairs, to whom was referred the bill
(H. R. 16105) authorizing the President to reinstate Alexander G.
Pendleton, jr., as a cadet in the U. S. Military Academy, report the
same back to the House with the recommendation that it do pass without amendment.

This is a bill enacting that—

The President is hereby authorized to reinstate former cadet Alexander G. Pendleton, junior, to the United States Military Academy at West Point.

This cadet entered the Academy in 1899 and was dismissed August
9, 1902, when a first classman. The Secretary of War indorses the
bill as follows:

Cadet Pendleton having been found guilty of hazing in a mild form was dismissed
from the Academy. I think the punishment was excessive, but it was required by
the act of Congress of March 2, 1901. He appears to have been a good student, of
general good character and conduct, and he has been already very severely punished.
I think the bill a just one.

The committee concur, except that on the evidence they do not think
that the offense was hazing. It appears that on July 10 as a corporal
he had been put in charge of new cadets in Company D to see that
they cleaned their guns and equipments properly. That for this purpose shortly after supper he went round his company to see if the
cadets were working, and went after Cadet Crafton, who was in Cadet
Davenport's tent. He says he entered the tent to speak to him and
told Cadet Crafton to go back to his tent and get to work on his gun;
that on entering the tent he required the fourth classmen to stand at
attention and, as Cadet Crafton left the tent—

Cadet Davenport passed a remark that made me angry and I said the quotations in
the specifications. I think that is about all that took place. I went back to my tent
right away.

It appears Davenport was of another company and did not know him, and when Crafton was ordered out said: "So long, Crafton, I will see you some more," and Pendleton lost his temper and said:

What do you mean by speaking to another cadet when I am speaking to him; you will get your face smashed if you don't look out.

This was all. By advice of counsel he pleaded guilty, and as the offense charged was of hazing the court were not only forced to find him guilty but the President was bound to dismiss and could not mitigate the sentence. After the plea careful evidence was taken by the court-martial.

It is proved that he went to the tent as an officer on military duty. His loss of temper and violent language under any provocation were a breach of his duty as an officer and of proper military discipline. But they are hardly hazing.

Our conclusions are as follows:

It appears beyond question that as a noncommissioned officer he was detailed to see that the new cadets performed their work and had their guns and equipments in order. His orders to Cadet Crafton to go and clean his gun was within his duties. Cadet Davenport's speaking to Cadet Crafton while under such orders was technically a breach of discipline.

The order to Davenport to stand at attention in the presence of a cadet officer was usual and not improper as a matter of military etiquette. A reasonable and proper reproof to Davenport would have been entirely justified. It was not justifiable for him to lose his temper or to threaten the new cadet, because he was not quick in obeying orders. It was a breach of military courtesy which an officer always owes to the soldier. But it was not, in our opinion, hazing, and the plea of guilty was, in our judgment, improperly interposed. What is more, there was no brutality of action, no injury done, no personal violence, no continuance of harassing. It was a sudden altercation, over in a moment, and if technically within the rules against hazing it would be one of those cases which appears to have been sufficiently punished. The cadet has lost nearly a full year, and will have to graduate a year later with that loss of time upon the rolls.

We recommend passage of the bill.

We append the report of the Judge-Advocate-General, and also the full evidence taken on the court-martial, as well as the recommendations of the Adjutant-General and Secretary of War.

WAR DEPARTMENT, ADJUTANT-GENERAL'S OFFICE,
December 17, 1902.

Respectfully returned to the Secretary of War.

Alexander G. Pendleton, jr., was admitted into the U. S. Military Academy August 30, 1899, as cadet from the Territory of Arizona, and dismissed August 9, 1902, by sentence of general court-martial promulgated in General Orders, No. 90, Headquarters of the Army, Adjutant-General's Office, August 6, 1902, copy herewith.

Attention is invited to the memorandum of the Secretary of War, dated the 11th instant, and its accompanying papers, also herewith.

W. P. HALL,
Acting Adjutant-General.

[Second indorsement.]

WAR DEPARTMENT, *December 19, 1902.*

Respectfully returned to the chairman of the Committee on Military Affairs, House of Representatives, inviting attention to the preceding indorsement of the Acting Adjutant-General and to the papers therein referred to.

Cadet Pendleton, having been found guilty of hazing in a mild form, was dismissed from the Academy. I think the punishment was excessive, but it was required by the act of Congress of March 2, 1901. He appears to have been a good student, of general good character and conduct, and he has already been very severely punished. I think the bill is just one.

ELIHU ROOT, Secretary of War.

WAR DEPARTMENT,
OFFICE OF THE JUDGE-ADVOCATE-GENERAL,
Washington, July 26, 1902.

SIR: I beg leave to submit the following report in the case of Acting Cadet Sergt. Alexander G. Pendleton, jr., first class, U. S. Military Academy.

Cadet Pendleton was tried upon the following charges and specifications.

"CHARGE: Conduct to the prejudice of good order and military discipline, in violation of the sixty-second article of war, and in disregard of the provisions of paragraph 140, Regulations U. S. Military Academy.

"*Specification I.*—In that he, Cadet Acting Sergt. Alexander G. Pendleton, jr., first class, U. S. Military Academy, did visit the tent of new Cadet Calvert L. Davenport, fourth class, U. S. Military Academy, and did haze said cadet by requiring him to assume a constrained position.

"This at Camp Churchman, West Point, N. Y., on or about July 10, 1902.

"*Specification II.*—In that he, Cadet Acting Sergt. Alexander G. Pendleton, jr., first class, U. S. Military Academy, did haze new Cadet Calvert L. Davenport, fourth class, U. S. Military Academy, by requiring him to assume a constrained position and draw in his chin, and did say: 'Draw it in further,' and 'if you don't I will punch it in,' or words to that effect.

"This at Camp Churchman, West Point, N.Y., on or about July 10, 1902.

"*Specification III.*—In that he, Cadet Acting Sergt. Alexander G. Pendleton, jr., first class, U. S. Military Academy, did haze new Cadet Calvert L. Davenport, fourth class, U. S. Military Academy, by treating said new cadet in a harassing, tyrannical, insulting, humiliating, and threatening manner, saying: 'What do you mean by speaking to another cadet when I am speaking to him; you will get your face smashed if you don't look out,' or words to that effect.

"This at Camp Churchman, West Point, N. Y., on or about July 10, 1902."

The accused pleaded "guilty" to both charges and specifications, whereupon the court proceeded to the trial of the case.

As a consequence of the efforts which have been recently put forth with a view to eradicate the practice of hazing at the Military Academy, the various acts which are deemed to constitute the offense of hazing have been made the subject of official definition, and the definition so prepared has been embodied in the following paragraphs of the academic regulations:

"1. Any cadet who shall strike, lay hands upon, treat with violence, disturb in his room or tent, or offer bodily harm to a new cadet or candidate, with intent to punish, injure, annoy, molest, or harass the same; or who shall, with the same intent, invite, order, compel, or permit a new cadet or candidate to sweep his room or tent, make his bed, bring water, clean his arms, equipments, or accouterments, or perform any other menial service for him, or to assume any constrained position, or to engage in any form of physical exercise; or who shall, with the same intent, invite, order, or compel any new cadet or candidate to eat or drink any article of food, or to take into his mouth any article whatever, or to do for him anything incompatible with the position of a cadet and gentleman; or any cadet whose duty it is to enforce camp, barrack, or mess regulations who shall permit any new cadet or candidate to eat or drink any article of food, or to take into his mouth any article whatever, in violation of said regulations, shall be summarily dismissed from the Military Academy.

"2. Any cadet found guilty of participating in or encouraging or countenancing hazing shall be summarily expelled from the Academy and shall not thereafter be reappointed to the corps of cadets or be eligible for appointment as a commissioned officer in the Army or Navy or Marine Corps until two years after the graduation of the class of which he was a member. (Act of Congress approved March 2, 1901.)

"3. Hazing, under the provision of section 2 of this paragraph, is defined to be any of the acts enumerated in section 1 of this paragraph, or any other treatment accorded a candidate or a cadet who has been connected with the Military Academy less than one year, of a harassing, tyrannical, abusive, shameful, insulting, or humiliating nature, or that may endanger the physical well-being of such candidate or cadet. (General Orders, No. 17, headquarters U. S. Military Academy, 1901.)"

It will be observed that the second paragraph of the regulation above cited contains the requirements of the act of March 3, 1901 (31 Stat. L., 911), which was enacted by Congress at the conclusion of the investigation into the practice of hazing, which was conducted by a committee of the House of Representatives during the months of January and February, 1901. The case under consideration is therefore the first which has arisen under the act of March 3, 1901, and the regulations adopted in furtherance thereof.

Lieutenant-Colonel Treat, commandant of cadets, testifying for the prosecution, submitted to the court the orders which had been issued in the matter of hazing at the beginning of the present encampment. Those orders, which are appended to the record (Appendix marked "B" and "C"), were presumably read to the cadets by Colonel Treat, and his testimony is that—

" * * * every cadet in the corps knows of them and understands the desire of the authorities to thoroughly carry out regulations in regard to new cadets."

Cadet Davenport, fourth class, testified for the prosecution that an upper classman came to his tent during the evening of July 10. Upon being asked what occurred, he replied:

"Mr. Crafton had dropped in my tent, sir, and Mr. Crafton, Mr. Layfield, and myself were sitting there talking and somebody passed and saw Mr. Crafton in there. He asked Mr. Crafton what he was doing. Mr. Crafton said that he had dropped in on a visit, or something to that effect. He told him to get up and get out and to get to work on his gun. Mr. Crafton got up, and as he was going out the door I got up and said as near as I can recall, "So long, Crafton; I will see you some more;" and this party, whoever he was, sprang up ont he floor and said something in regard to my speaking to another cadet when he had been spoken to by an upper classman, and said he had a good mind or he would punch my face. Whatever happened after that I don't remember, only he left."

Cadets Crafton and Davenport were unable to testify positively that the accused was the upper classman who made use of the language and gave the orders alleged in the specifications, but this fact was established by the testimony of Acting Cadet First Sergeant Milton, whose testimony was as follows:

"The first thing I heard was, 'What are you doing in this tent with your clothes on,' and the cadet replied he was visiting. Mr. Pendleton said, 'Go to your tent and get to work on your gun.' Then he told Mr. Davenport to stand up and brace, and then, after Mr. Davenport made remark just given, he said, 'What do you mean by speaking to another cadet when I am talking to him? I'll punch your face,' or words to that effect. That is all I remember."

Cadet First Sergeant Milton also testified that Cadet Pendleton had been placed in charge of new cadets that afternoon with orders to see that they worked on their guns and equipments. Cadet Captain Tyler corroborated the statement that the accused was regularly detailed for that purpose by the authority of Lieutenant Summerlin, Fourth Cavalry, the tactical officer in command of the company.

The accused, testifying in his own behalf, gave the following account of the occurrence:

"Shortly after supper, about time for fourth classmen to get back from the sink, I went around to see if all fourth classmen were working. I found they all were with the exception of two who just came off guard, and Cadet Crafton, who was visiting Cadet Davenport's tent. I noticed this cadet in the tent as I went by. I entered the tent to speak to him. While in there I told Cadet Crafton to go back to his tent and get to work on his gun. On entering the tent I required the fourth classmen to stand attention, and as Cadet Crafton left the tent Cadet Davenport passed a remark that made me angry for the moment and I said the quotations in the specifications. I think that is about all that took place. I went back to my tent right away."

The statement of the accused, which was read to the court by his counsel, is appended to the record and marked "D."

The court reached a finding of "guilty" as to the charge and specifications, and sentenced the accused "to be dismissed the service of the United States."

The case is submitted by the reviewing authority with the following remarks:

"HEADQUARTERS, U. S. MILITARY ACADEMY,
West Point, N. Y., July 24, 1902.

"The proceedings, findings, and sentence in the foregoing case of Cadet Acting Sergeant Alexander G. Pendleton, first class, U. S. Military Academy, are approved and forwarded for the action of the War Department.

"I regret I can find no circumstances in this case sufficient to justify on my part a recommendation for a mitigation of the penalty which Congress has prescribed shall be awarded cadets found guilty of hazing. No proper efforts are spared to impress upon cadets their obligations to loyally obey the regulations governing the treatment to be accorded new cadets. Insistence on a reasonable regard for these regulations, in my opinion, is vital to proper training at the Military Academy."

The accused was assisted by counsel in the preparation and presentation of his defense, the case was fully and fairly tried, the charge and specification were fully supported by the testimony, and the sentence imposed was that required by the act of March 3, 1901. It was within the power of the Superintendent, having satisfied himself of the guilt of the accused, to have summarily expelled the accused from the Academy, but he seems to have pursued a more conservative course in referring the case to a general court-martial for trial.

It will be observed that the relations of the accused to the new cadets in the company to which he belonged was to some extent regulated by the orders detailing him to supervise their work in keeping their arms and accouterments in order, but he nowhere contends that the acts which were made the subject of charges were done in execution of such orders, or in the performance of the military duty thereby imposed, his defense being that the acts were done "under the impulse of anger and without deliberate intent to violate the regulations." He further says in his defense, which is appended to the record:

"The accused was guilty of conduct to the prejudice of good order and military discipline in attempting to discipline a cadet, who to him seem disrespectful, by threatening personal violence to the said cadet. In this the accused allowed the impulse of anger to supersede the qualities of dignity and good judgment absolutely essential to a noncommissioned officer."

The Superintendent recommends that the sentence be executed, and the record discloses no reason why that recommendation should not be carried into effect.

Very respectfully,

Geo. G. Davis,
Judge-Advocate-General.

The Acting Secretary of War.

Proceedings of a general court-martial which convened at West Point, N. Y., pursuant to the following order:

Special Orders,
No. 137. } Headquarters U. S. Military Academy,
West Point, N. Y., July 21, 1902.

*   *   *   *   *   *

West Point, N. Y., *July 22, 1902.*
The court met pursuant to the foregoing order at 2 o'clock p. m.

*   *   *   *   *   *   *

The court then proceeded to the trial of Cadet Acting Sergt. Alexander G. Pendleton, jr., first class, U. S. Military Academy.

*   *   *   *   *

To which the accused pleaded as follows:
To the first specification: "Guilty."
To the second specification: "Guilty."
To the third specification: "Guilty."
To the charge: "Guilty."

Lieut. Col. Charles G. Treat, commandant of cadets, a witness for the prosecution, was duly sworn, and testified as follows:

Direct examination by the Judge-Advocate:

Q. Do you know the accused? If so, state who he is.—A. I do; Cadet Acting Sergt. Alexander G. Pendleton, jr., first class, U. S. Military Academy.

Q. Do you recognize this extract (hereto appended, marked "A") as containing paragraph 140, Regulations U. S. Military Academy?—A. I do.

(Paragraph 140, Regulations U. S. Military Academy, was here read to the court by the judge-advocate.)

Q. What orders have you given from time to time with a view to obtaining a cooperation of cadets in carrying out the foregoing regulations?

(Certified copies of orders issued by the commandant, hereto appended, marked "B" and "C," were offered as testimony and read to the court by the judge-advocate.)

Q. Are cadets generally familiar with these orders?—A. The orders were published (No. 32) by myself in person, and both afterwards posted on the bulletin board, where they have remained for two or three weeks. I believe without exception every cadet in the corps knows of them and understands the desire of the authorities to thoroughly carry out regulations in regard to new cadets.

Q. Is paragraph 125, Regulations U. S. Military Academy, which provides that the Superintendent shall have power to investigate violations of regulations and all neglects, disorders, and breaches of discipline by cadets, carried out?—A. Yes.

Q. Has such an investigation been made recently?—A. The last was held about July 13.

Q. Was it through this that the facts were discovered which led to charges being preferred against Cadet Acting Sergeant Pendleton?—A. It was through this that I reported Cadet Pendleton.

(The accused declined to cross-examine the witness.)

Cadet Private DENHAM B. CRAFTON, fourth class, U. S. Military Academy, a witness for the prosecution, was duly sworn, and testified as follows:

Direct examination by the JUDGE-ADVOCATE:

Q. Do you know the accused? If so, state who he is.—A. Yes, sir; Cadet Pendleton.

Q. Were you at or near Cadet Davenport's tent on or about the evening of July 10?—A. Yes, sir.

Q. Did any upper-class man visit this tent while you were there?—A. Yes, sir.

Q. State what occurred.—A. The upper-class man that visited the tent asked me what I was doing. I told him I just came in to see Mr. Davenport. He told me to leave the tent and get to work. I left the tent and proceeded to my own tent. The last thing I heard Mr. Davenport said, "So long, Crafton." That is all I know, sir.

Q. Did you hear the upper-class man say anything to Cadet Davenport as you left?—A. No, sir.

Q. Did you know who the upper-class man was?—A. No, sir.

(The accused declined to cross-examine the witness.)

Examination by the COURT:

Q. Would you recognize the upper-class man to whom you have referred in previous testimony?—A. No, sir.

Cadet Private CALVERT L. DAVENPORT, fourth class, U. S. Military Academy, a witness for the prosecution, was duly sworn, and testified as follows:

Direct examination by the JUDGE-ADVOCATE:

Q. Do you know the accused? If so, state who he is.—A. Yes, sir; Mr. Pendleton, sir.

Q. Were you in your tent on or about the evening of July 10?—A. Yes, sir.

Q. Did any upper-class man visit your tent on that evening?—A. Yes, sir.

Q. State what occurred?—A. Mr. Crafton had dropped in my tent, sir, and Mr. Crafton, Mr. Layfield, and myself were sitting there talking and somebody passed and saw Mr. Crafton in there. He asked Mr. Crafton what he was doing. Mr. Crafton said that he had dropped in on a visit, or something to that effect. He told him to get up and get out and get to work on his gun. Mr. Crafton got up, and as he was going out the door I got up and said, as near as I can recall, "So long, Crafton; I will see you some more." And this party, whoever he was, sprang up on the floor and said something in regard to my speaking to another cadet when he had been spoken to by an upper-class man, and said he had a good mind or he would punch my face. Whatever happened after that I don't remember, only he left.

Q. Were you required to stand in a constrained position?—A. My mind wasn't set on that part and I didn't remember afterwards.

Q. Was anything said to you about drawing in your chin?—A. I don't remember, sir.

Q. Do you know who this man was?—A. No, sir.

Q. Did you know how many upper classmen at that time?—A. I knew those who were over us in barracks and a few after we got to camp, sir.

(The accused declined to cross-examine the witness.)

Examination by the COURT:

Q. Do you recognize the accused as the cadet who visited your tent on July 10?—A. No, sir; I couldn't recognize any of them, sir.

Cadet Private ERNEST L. LAYFIELD, fourth class, U. S. Military Academy, a witness for the prosecution, was duly sworn and testified as follows:

Direct examination by JUDGE-ADVOCATE:

Q. Do you recognize the accused? If so, state who he is.—A. Yes, sir; Sergeant Pendleton, sir.

Q. Are you Cadet Davenport's tent mate?—A. Yes, sir.
Q. Were you in the tent on the evening of July 10?—A. Yes, sir.
Q. Did any upper classmen visit that tent at that time?—A. Yes, sir.
Q. Was anything said to Cadet Davenport?—A. Yes, sir. He was told to stand at "attention" and not to be speaking to anyone else when he was spoken to, sir, and that he was liable to get his face smashed.
Q. Was he required to stand in a constrained position?—A. I don't know whether it was constrained or not; he was required to stand at "attention," sir. [Witness here showed court how Cadet Davenport appeared to be standing.]
Q. Was anything said to him about drawing in his chin?—A. I do not remember, sir.
Q. Do you know what cadets visited your tent?—A. I do not, sir.
Q. Have you since recognized them?—A. I didn't see them that night. I didn,t look up at all.

Cross-examination by the ACCUSED:

Q. Did the accused direct all three of the cadets in your tent to stand at "attention" when he entered the tent?—A. No, sir.
Q. Whom did he direct?—A. Mr. Davenport, sir.

Examination by the COURT:

Q. Were there more than one upper-class man?—A. I am under the impression that there were.
Q. Who required Cadet Davenport to stand at "attention," and, as stated by you, threatened to smash his face?—A. I do not know, sir; I had my back turned toward the street and did not look up at all, sir.
Q. How do you know, then, that the accused ordered Cadet Davenport to stand at "attention?"—A. I do not know, sir.

Cadet Acting First Sergeant ALEXANDER M. MILTON, first class, U. S. Military Academy, was a witness for the prosecution, was duly sworn and testified as follows:

Q. Do you recognize the accused? If so, state who he is.—A. I do; Cadet Pendleton, sir.
Q. Were you anywhere near Cadet Davenport's tent on the evening of July 10, at the time Cadet Crafton was visiting Cadet Davenport?—A. Yes, sir.
Q. Who was with you?—A. Cadet Pendleton, sir.
Q. Which of you spoke to the cadets in the tent?—A. Cadet Pendleton, sir.
Q. What did he say?—A. He asked Cadet Crafton what he was doing in the tent.
Q. What did he say to Cadet Davenport?—A. He told him to stand up and brace, I think, sir.
Q. Did you hear him say anything about smashing Cadet Davenport's face?—A. Yes, sir.

Cross examination by the ACCUSED:

Q. Do you know whether or not the accused was going up the company street on any duty?—A. As I remember, he told me he was placed in charge of new cadets that afternoon to see that they worked on gun and equipments.
Q. Did the accused require all three fourth-class men to stand attention?—A. No, sir; I don't think he did; I am sure he did not require one of them.
Q. What did Cadet Davenport say to Cadet Crafton as the latter left the tent?—A. "So long, Crafton." He also stopped bracing at this time.

Examination by the COURT:

Q. Did Cadet Pendleton say anything to you before going to this tent? If so, what did he say?—A. He did not.
Q. When he, the accused, told Cadet Davenport to brace, as stated by you, did he, the accused, threaten Cadet Davenport or not if he did not comply?—A. He did not.
Q. Did you hear the accused say to Cadet Davenport, "Draw in your chin further; if you don't I will punch it in," or words to that effect?—A. No, sir; I remember no such words.
Q. State exactly and fully what you heard the accused say?—A. The first thing I heard was: "What are you doing in this tent with your clothes on?" and the cadet replied he was visiting. Mr. Pendleton said: "Go to your tent and get to work on your gun." Then he told Mr. Davenport to stand up and "brace," and then after Mr. Davenport made remark just given he said: "What do you mean by speaking to another cadet when I am talking to him? I'll punch your face " or words to that effect. That is all I remember.
(The judge-advocate announced that the prosecution here rested.)

Cadet Capt. M. C. TYLER, first class U. S. Military Academy, a witness for the defense, was duly sworn, and testified as follows:

Direct examination, by the JUDGE-ADVOCATE:

Q. Do you know the accused? If so, state who he is.—A. I do: Cadet Pendleton, sir.

Questions by the accused:

Q. Since the present new cadets have been in camp has it been customary to detail a noncommissioned officer daily to see that they cleaned their guns and equipments properly?—A. It was in Company D when the new cadets first came to camp.

Q. Was Cadet Pendleton so detailed on July 10?—A. Yes, sir.

Q. What has been your observation as cadet captain of the conduct of Cadet Davenport, of the fourth class, as a soldier?—A. I should say that his manner in and out of ranks was indifferent and that his conduct showed that he took the whole matter as funny and not serious, and that he was very provoking to anyone having any dealings with him.

(The judge-advocate declined to cross-examine the witness.)

Examination by the COURT:

Q. By whose orders were these noncommissioned officers detailed over new cadets?—A. When the new cadets first came to camp, Lieutenant Summerlin directed me to hold the noncommissioned officers responsible that new cadets had their guns cleaned and equipments and tents in order and got to formations on time.

Q. By whose authority did you detail Cadet Sergeant Pendleton in charge of new cadets on July 10?—A. By authority from Lieutenant Summerlin.

The accused, at his own request, was duly sworn as a witness, and testified as follows:

Q. Have you always made a conscientious effort to comply with the requirements of the regulations in regard to hazing?—A. Yes, sir.

Q. Previous to the date of these charges or since, have you violated the above regulation?—A. No, sir.

Q. For what purpose did you enter the tent of Cadet Davenport on July 10?—A. To see why Cadet Crafton was not working.

Q. State briefly what you did and the cause or causes that led to your doing it.—A. Shortly after supper, about time for fourth-class men to get back from the sink, I went around to see if all fourth-class men were working. I found they all were, with the exception of two, who just came off guard, and Cadet Crafton, who was visiting in Cadet Davenport's tent. I noticed this cadet in the tent as I went by. I entered the tent to speak to him. While in there I told Cadet Crafton to go back to his tent and get to work on his gun. On entering the tent I required the fourth-class men to stand attention, and as Cadet Crafton left the tent Cadet Davenport passed a remark that made me angry for the moment, and I said the quotations in the specifications. I think that is about all that took place. I went back to my tent right away.

Q. What did you say to the two cadets who told you that they had just come off guard?—A. I told them they could go to bed.

Q. Do the fourth-class men in your company stand attention when a cadet officer or noncommissioned officer enters the tent officially?—A. We have given them orders to do so.

The judge-advocate declined to cross-examine the witness.

The accused having no further testimony to offer, submitted a written statement in his defense, which was read to the court and is hereto appended, marked "D."

The accused and judge-advocate then withdrew and the court was closed, and after mature deliberation upon all the evidence, finds the accused, Cadet Acting Sergt. Alexander G. Pendleton, jr., first class, U. S. Military Academy:

Of the first specification: "Guilty."
Of the second specification: "Guilty."
Of the third specification: "Guilty."
Of the charge: "Guilty."

The judge-advocate and accused were then recalled and the court opened, and the judge-advocate stated that he had no evidence of previous convictions to submit.

The accused and judge-advocate then withdrew, and the court was closed and sentences him, Cadet Acting Sergt. Alexander G. Pendleton, jr., first class, U. S. Military Academy:

To be dismissed the service of the United States.

The judge-advocate was then recalled, and the court at 5.30 p. m. adjourned to meet at the call of the president.

THOS. G. HANSON,
Captain, Nineteenth Infantry, President.
JOHN E. STEPHENS,
Captain, Artillery Corps, Judge-Advocate.

HEADQUARTERS U. S. MILITARY ACADEMY,
West Point, N. Y., July 24, 1902.

The proceedings, findings, and sentence in the foregoing case of Cadet Acting Sergt. Alexander G. Pendleton, first class, U. S. Military Academy, are approved and forwarded for the action of the War Department.

I regret I can find no circumstances in this case sufficient to justify on my part a recommendation for a mitigation of the penalty which Congress has prescribed shall be awarded cadets found guilty of hazing. No proper efforts are spared to impress upon cadets their obligations to loyally obey the regulations governing the treatment to be accorded new cadets. Insistence on a reasonable regard for these regulations, in my opinion, is vital to proper training at the Military Academy.

A. L. MILLS,
Colonel, U. S. Army, Superintendent.

———

A.

[From Regulations U. S. Military Academy, Fred W. Sladen, captain, Fourteenth Infantry, acting adjutant.]

125. The Superintendent shall have power to investigate violations of regulations and all neglects, disorders, and breaches of discipline committed by cadets. These investigations shall be conducted, habitually, by the commandant of cadets, but may, in the discretion of the Superintendent, be carried on by boards of officers appointed for that purpose by the Superintendent. In any investigation, made under the authority conferred by this paragraph, the commandant of cadets, or the board of officers charged with the conduct of the same, has power to administer oaths to attending witnesses to testify or depose in the course of the investigation, and shall have the right to require any cadet to answer questions as to facts material to the inquiry which fall within his knowledge.

A refusal to answer shall be reported to the Superintendent, who may proceed against the offender as in the case of disobedience of orders. If the refusal is on the ground that the answer will tend to criminate the witness, the proposed question, together with the objection of the witness, shall be submitted to the Superintendent in writing, and his decision thereon shall be final.

Under the provisions of this paragraph the Superintendent shall cause immediate investigation to be made of any act or occurrence which leads him to believe that the regulations in regard to hazing are not strictly observed by cadets, and he shall at other times cause like investigations to be made for the purpose of effectually preventing the practice of hazing in the corps of cadets.

140. SECTION I. Any cadet who shall strike, lay hands upon, treat with violence, disturb in his room or tent, or offer bodily harm to a new cadet or candidate, with intent to punish, injure, annoy, molest, or harass the same; or who shall, with the same intent, invite, order, compel, or permit a new cadet or candidate to sweep his room or tent, make his bed, bring water, clean his arms, equipments or accouterments, or perform any other menial service for him, or to assume any constrained position, or to engage in any form of physical exercise; or who shall, with the same intent, invite, order, or compel any new cadet or candidate to eat or drink any article of food, or to take into his mouth any article whatever, or to do for him anything incompatible with the position of a cadet and gentleman; or any cadet whose duty it is to enforce camp, barrack, or mess regulations who shall permit any new cadet or candidate to eat or drink any article of food, or to take into his mouth any article whatever, in violation of said regulations, shall be summarily dismissed from the Military Academy.

SEC. II. Any cadet found guilty of participating in or encouraging or countenancing the practice of hazing shall be summarily expelled from the Academy and shall not thereafter be reappointed to the corps of cadets, or be eligible for appointment as a commissioned officer in the Army or Navy or Marine Corps, until two years after the graduation of the class of which he was a member. (Act of Congress, approved March 2, 1901.)

SEC. III. Hazing under the provision of Section II of this paragraph is defined to be any of the acts enumerated in Section I of this paragraph, or any other treatment accorded a candidate or a cadet who has been connected with the Military Academy less than one year of a harassing, tyrannical, abusive, shameful, insulting, or humiliating nature, or that may endanger the physical well-being of such candidate or cadet. (General Orders, No. 17, Headquarters, U. S. Military Academy, 1901.)

B.

ORDERS, }
No. 32. }

HEADQUARTERS U. S. CORPS OF CADETS,
West Point, N. Y., June 16, 1902.
[Extract.]

VI. Orders in regard to the treatment of new cadets are very explicit and known to all.

It is the duty and should be the pleasure of cadets as well as officers to carry them out in word and spirit.

Those who have no official relations will refrain from any interference with them.

Cadet officers and those on duty and in authority will be firm, gentlemanly, and exacting. Never show temper and report any violation of orders on the part of older cadets or lack of proper obedience, indifference, or intractable conduct on the part of a new cadet.

Remember it is never within the province of a subordinate to punish or ascribe a penalty of any kind. His duty is to faithfully and thoroughly, with energy and dignity, give his instructions and carry out his orders; and if the new cadet fails to respond or shows lack of discipline, he will be immediately reported to the commandant or his representative, the officer in charge of new cadets, who is responsible and who will take steps to correct the conduct and inflict punishment and enforce discipline.

Before any complication has arisen I wish to say that I expect the personal cooperation of every cadet in loyally carrying out orders governing the treatment of new cadets, and while the requirements will be most rigid and discipline enforced with consistency and due severity, there must be an absence of nagging, harassing, or hazing of any description.

Let no cadet be guilty of ungentlemanly conduct or make use of methods, words, or slang expressions that injure the feelings or awaken a spirit of resentment. In acting as drillmasters and instructors of new cadets demonstrate what is demanded by performing the thing required in person. Wordy descriptions convey little to a recruit.

All must be aggressive in carrying out orders and assisting the authorities and show a total lack of defensive spirit against those in authority.

I trust that none will commit himself and violate the spirit of these orders, in defiance of authority or to appear smart or in a spirit of bravado, for the penalty will be swift and sure, and the sacrifice of a career here is too large a stake to risk for a little amusement.

By order of Lieutenant-Colonel Treat:

_____ _____,
Cadet Lieutenant and Adjutant.

A true copy.

CHAS. G. TREAT,
Lieutenant-Colonel, U. S. Army, Commandant of Cadets.

(Published in person by the commandant and posted on bulletin board.)

C.

ORDERS }
No. 39. }

HEADQUARTERS U. S. CORPS OF CADETS,
West Point, N. Y., July 4, 1902.
[Extract.]

*   *   *   *   *   *   *

III. No limits or restrictions are prescribed to guard against improper interference of upper classmen with new cadets. No orders or interference by those not in authority or in the proper discharge of their duties will be tolerated. Any cadet not responding promptly to proper orders and instructions given by another cadet in the proper execution of his office will be immediately reported to the commandant of cadets, or in his absence to the officer in charge, for the action of the commandant of cadets.

Orders pertaining to the treatment of new cadets are explicit, and the penalty for violation of them mandatory, and these orders will be carried out loyally and in spirit by all officers and cadets.

   *   *   *   *   *

By order of Lieutenant-Colonel Treat:

                                            ——— ———.

A true copy.

                                                    CHAS. G. TREAT,
Lieutenant-Colonel, U. S. Army, Commandant of Cadets.

                               · **D.**

STATEMENT OF THE ACCUSED.

The accused realizes that he has been guilty of conduct to the prejudice of good order and military discipline, but begs to state to the court that his acts were without any intent to disregard the provisions of paragraph 140, Regulations of the U. S. Military Academy.

The fact that the accused has not heretofore in a single instance violated the provisions of the said paragraph, and the circumstances of the case in hand, as shown by the testimony, would tend to show that the acts herein charged were done not in disregard of the aforesaid regulations, but under the impulse of anger and without deliberate intent to violate the regulations.

The accused was guilty of conduct to the prejudice of good order and military discipline in attempting to discipline a cadet, who to him seemed disrespectful, by threatening personal violence to the said cadet. In this the accused allowed the impulse of anger to supersede the qualities of dignity and good judgment absolutely essential to a noncommissioned officer.

The accused entered the tent, as shown by the testimony, to carry out the instructions of his proper superior and not to harass in any way the occupants of the tent. While in the tent a circumstance arose which to his mind showed disrespect on the part of a subordinate, and he now realizes that he took an unauthorized and unbecoming means to discipline this subordinate.

                                                A. G. PENDLETON, Jr.,
Cadet Acting Sergeant, Company D, First Class.

                                    WHITE HOUSE, *August 1, 1902.*

The sentence in the case of Acting Cadet Sergt. Alexander G. Pendleton, jr., first class, U. S. Military Academy, is confirmed.

                                              THEODORE ROOSEVELT.

                                    U. S. MILITARY ACADEMY,
                                    West Point, N. Y., August 16, 1902.

DEAR SIR: I am very sorry that I have been the cause of your trouble. When you came in my tent I thought that you were some upper classman who merely came in to worry me. After having learned that you were detailed to see that we fourth classmen worked on our guns, my views have changed. I appreciate now your position, that, as you thought I knew you were so detailed and attending to your duty, my remark and action did savor somewhat of contempt for you and your authority.

Since learning the circumstances, I can not much blame you for losing your temper. I think if our places had been interchanged I myself would have been offended. I no longer feel hurt at your remarks. I felt somewhat hurt that you should send Mr. Crafton out of my tent, thinking you had no authority to do so. Had I known you were so detailed I would not have felt hurt or said anything; would have acted toward you as though you were Lieutenant Summerlin when you came to my tent.

I bear you no ill-will and sincerely wish you every success in future life. Hoping that you will not hold this up against me, I am,

    Yours, truly,

                                                C. L. DAVENPORT.

Mr. A. G. PENDLETON, Jr.

GEORGE F. HOWE, ALIAS HARRINGTON.

FEBRUARY 4, 1903.—Committed to the Committee of the Whole House and ordered
to be printed.

Mr. SULLOWAY, from the Committee on Invalid Pensions, submitted
the following

REPORT.

[To accompany S. 14.]

The Committee on Invalid Pensions, to whom was referred the bill
(S. 14) granting an increase of pension to George F. Howe, alias Harrington, have examined the same and adopt the Senate report thereon
and recommend that the bill do pass.

[Senate Report No. 2457, Fifty-seventh Congress, second session.]

The Committee on Pensions, to whom was referred the bill (S. 14) granting a pension to George F. Howe, have examined the same and report:

This bill proposes to increase from $12 to $20 per month the pension of George F.
Howe, of Togus, Me., who served under the name of George Harrington in Company L, Second Regiment Massachusetts Cavalry, from February 5, 1863, to July 20,
1865, when he was honorably discharged.

Claimant is now receiving a pension of $12 per month under the act of June 27,
1890, for disease of spine. On March 5, 1886, he made claim under the general law,
alleging that he contracted rheumatism, paralysis, and disease of spine during his
service. He was unable, however, to furnish any proof of service origin of these
disabilities, for which reason his claim was rejected February 6, 1888.

Claimant is now 68 years of age. His last medical examination was made over
eleven years ago, at which time he was rated $12 for disease of spine. His present
condition is shown by the following certificate of Dr. Albert Wood, of Worcester,
Mass.:

WORCESTER, MASS., June 19, 1902.

I hereby certify that I have this day examined George F. Howe, late Company L,
Second Massachusetts Cavalry, an inmate of the Soldiers' Home, Togus, Me., and
now on a visit to his friends in Worcester, Mass.

His general appearance is that of a man much broken in health. He carries himself bent forward and can not stand erect.

On stripping off his clothes I find that he has a large right lateral curvature of the
spinal column involving several of the middle vertebræ. Over this region it is quite
tender to the touch. He is decidedly one-sided. From this condition there is resulting marked deformity of the hips, which causes him to walk lame. He has marked

arterio-sclerosis, as shown by thickened radial arteries and tortuous and prominent temporal arteries, increased cardiac impulse, and marked accentuation of aortic and pulmonary sounds.

In my judgment he is so disabled as to be unfitted for any manual labor.

I have no interest in this claim, and, in fact, have never seen him before to-day.

ALBERT WOOD, M. D.,
Ex-Member Worcester Board of Examining Surgeons for Pension.

Other evidence on file shows that claimant has lost his health and is completely broken down. He has no property and no means of support except his pension. His active service covered a period of upward of two years, and it is very probable that his health suffered in consequence.

In view of his good military record, his total disability, and great poverty, your committee report the bill back favorably, with a recommendation that it pass.

O

MERRITT YOUNG.

FEBRUARY 4, 1903.—Committed to the Committee of the Whole House and ordered
to be printed.

Mr. KLEBERG, from the Committee on Invalid Pensions, submitted the
following

REPORT.

[To accompany S. 532.]

The Committee on Invalid Pensions, to whom was referred the bill
(S. 532) granting an increase of pension to Merritt Young, have examined the same and adopt the Senate report thereon and recommend
that the bill do pass.

[Senate Report No. 2194, Fifty-seventh Congress, second session.]

The Committee on Pensions, to whom was referred the bill (S. 532) granting an
increase of pension to Merritt Young, have examined the same and report:

This bill proposes to increase from $17 to $24 per month the pension of Merritt
Young, late of Company C, Thirteenth Regiment Tennessee Volunteer Cavalry.

Soldier enlisted September 24, 1863, and was discharged September 5, 1865. During service he bore the rank of private and sergeant. He was pensioned under the
general law April 18, 1885, for disease of heart, at $4 from discharge and $6 from
March 10, 1885, which was increased to $8 April 14, 1886; to $10 January 25, 1888;
to $14 June 17, 1896, and to $17 January 4, 1899.

On March 5, 1886, he made claim under the general law for additional disability—
rheumatism—and the same was legally approved in the Bureau as to service origin
and continuance, but was medically rejected July 15, 1896, on the ground that a
ratable disability from that cause was not shown to exist. On March 26, 1894, he
made claim for partial deafness, alleging incurrence from cold and exposure in January, 1865, but the same was rejected July 16, 1896, on the ground of no record and
no satisfactory evidence of service origin.

Some of claimant's comrades and neighbors testified that he contracted deafness in
the service and that the same has existed since discharge, but their evidence in
important particulars is contradictory of claimant's own statement, made years ago
to a special examiner of the Bureau, that his deafness is of more recent origin, and
can hardly be accepted as sufficient to show that that trouble is due to his service.

Claimant is upward of 72 years of age. A medical examination, made June 17,
1896, reported him to be nearly totally deaf in both ears and totally incapacitated
for manual labor by reason of heart disease. His last medical examination, made
January 4, 1899, is as follows:

"Cardiac dullness diminished, apex beat plainly evident to inspection and palpation, though not displaced, second sound lost with a slight aortic regurgitant mur-

mur, heard loudest at base of heart; pulse quick and irregular; dyspnœa and cyanosis and great tremulousness. Claimant can not hear ordinary conversation, even on contact with either ear, the opposite ear being plugged, and can only hear the loudest conversation, even hallooing, almost on contact. External and middle ears very dry and anemic; throat highly inflamed; tongue furred. Muscles, tendons, joints, urine, and urinary organs apparently normal. The claimant the secretary of this board has been particularly noticing as to deafness for quite a while, and finds that at all times and under all circumstances claimant is about totally deaf. He is a good citizen and of good habits. Pulse on exertion, 136, and thready; circulation in extremities quite feeble; hands cold.''

It appears from evidence on file in the Bureau that claimant and his family are mainly dependent on his pension for means of support. It may be that his deafness is due to his service, though he is unable to prove it. Apart from this, however, he is old and almost totally disabled by his serious heart trouble, and much in need of relief. He served faithfully for two years, and your committee are of opinion that the small increase proposed in the bill can very properly be allowed.

The bill is therefore reported back favorably with a recommendation that it pass.

O

LYMAN MATTHEWS.

FEBRUARY 4, 1903.—Committed to the Committee of the Whole House and ordered to be printed.

Mr. SULLOWAY, from the Committee on Invalid Pensions, submitted the following

REPORT.

[To accompany S. 1128.]

The Committee on Invalid Pensions, to whom was referred the bill (S. 1128) granting an increase of pension to Lyman Matthews, have examined the same and adopt the Senate report thereon and recommend that the bill do pass.

[Senate Report No. 2494, Fifty-seventh Congress, second session.]

The Committee on Pensions, to whom was referred the bill (S. 1128) granting an increase of pension to Lyman Matthews, have examined the same and report:

This bill proposes to increase from $12 to $20 per month the pension of Lyman Matthews, of Columbia Falls, Mont., late of Company E, Ninth Regiment Minnesota Volunteer Infantry.

Soldier enlisted August 19, 1862, and was honorably discharged August 15, 1865. He was taken prisoner at the battle of Guntown, Miss., June 10, 1864, confined at Andersonville and Millen, Ga., and paroled at Vicksburg, Miss., April 18, 1865, having been in prison over ten months.

Soldier was pensioned under the general law February 14, 1882, for incised wound of right hand, and scurvy and resulting debility, at $6.66⅔ per month from discharge and $7 per month from September 1, 1880, which was increased to $10 per month May 28, 1884, and to $12 per month October 8, 1890. He made claim for increase September 28, 1896, on account of pensioned disabilities, but his claim was rejected April 4, 1901, on the ground that his present rate was proper for the degree of disability from those causes.

On September 28, 1896, claimant made claim for additional disabilities, disease of heart, varicose veins of both legs, dropsy, and severe cramping of lower limbs, which he alleged he incurred while a prisoner of war at Andersonville, Ga. He was unable, however, to find any of his comrades or fellow-prisoners who could testify to service origin of these disabilities, and because of his failure to furnish any evidence on this point his claim was rejected. He was one of over two hundred of his regiment captured at Guntown, Miss., June 10, 1864, and confined in prison, and of this number less than fifty returned, and very few of them are now living, the greater portion having succumbed to the hardships and exposure then endured.

Claimant's last medical examination, made September 12, 1900, shows that he is generally debilitated and broken down, his muscles soft and flabby, and his hands showing no signs of manual labor. He was then rated $8 for amputated fingers of right hand, $2 for stiffness of ring and little fingers of same hand, $6 for scurvy and resulting debility, $4 for varicose veins of both legs, and $6 for disease of rectum.

Evidence filed with the bill shows that claimant is without resources or means of support except his pension. He is unable to perform manual labor whereby he might support himself, and it is altogether probable that his generally broken-down condition is due to his many months of prison life at Andersonville. The results of the hardships he then underwent become more patent as his years increase. He was a good soldier and served faithfully for three years, and your committee consider his case a proper one for Congressional action.

The bill is therefore reported back favorably with a recommendation that it pass.

O

THOMAS DOYLE.

FEBRUARY 4, 1903.—Committed to the Committee of the Whole House and ordered
to be printed.

Mr. DEEMER, from the Committee on Invalid Pensions, submitted the
following

REPORT.

[To accompany S. 1738.]

The Committee on Invalid Pensions, to whom was referred the bill
(S. 1738) granting an increase of pension to Thomas Doyle, have examined the same and adopt the Senate report thereon and recommend
that the bill do pass.

[Senate Report No. 2196, Fifty-seventh Congress, second session.]

The Committee on Pensions, to whom was referred the bill (S. 1738) granting a
pension to Thomas Doyle, have examined the same and report.

This bill proposes to increase from $17 to $24 per month the pension of Thomas
Doyle, late first lieutenant and adjutant, First Regiment Missouri State Militia Volunteer Cavalry.

The military records show that Thomas Doyle rendered service to the United
States for upward of eight years. He first enlisted December 22, 1857, as a private
in Company D, First, now Fourth, United States Cavalry, and served in this command, participating in several engagements with hostile Indians, until April 12,
1862, when he was discharged to enable him to accept promotion in the Missouri
State Militia Cavalry. He was mustered in April 9, 1862, as first lieutenant and
adjutant, First Missouri State Militia Volunteer Cavalry, and was transferred in
November or December, 1864, to Company K, Thirteenth Missouri Cavalry. He
was promoted captain January 6, 1866, and honorably discharged January 11, 1866.

Captain Doyle, who is now 63 years of age, was first pensioned by certificate issued
February 2, 1881, on account of fracture of left clavicle and injury to left shoulder,
incurred in May, 1862, by being thrown from his horse while on a scout. The rate
was then fixed at $12.75 per month, or three-fourths of total for his rank as first
lieutenant. The rate was subsequently increased to total for his rank, $17 per month,
from June 18, 1884.

On December 8, 1885, claimant filed a claim for additional disability, alleging that
in the spring of 1863 he had again been thrown from his horse, receiving at that
time a fracture of his right clavicle and injury of right shoulder. After a special
examination, this claim was also allowed as to injury to right shoulder, but the medical referee of the Bureau, whose province it is to determine the rate which should be
granted, indorsed his action on the brief face as follows:

"Approved for fracture of left clavicle and injury to left shoulder, seventeen-eight-

eenths; no increase. Injury to right shoulder, five-eighteenths; combined disabilities, not to exceed seventeen-eighteenths (total of rank)."

While, therefore, it is admitted that claimant incurred injury of right shoulder
in service and line of duty, and that of itself it constituted a disabling cause which
entitled him to $5 per month, yet no increase of pension was allowed on this adjudi-
cation for the reason that he was already receiving the "total of rank," $17 per
month, and in the opinion of the medical referee his combined disabilities did not
entitle him to the next higher rate known to the law, which is $24 per month. As
a matter of fact, then, claimant is receiving no pension for injury of right shoulder
incurred in the service.

The action of the Pension Bureau in denying claimant a higher rate of pension was
affirmed on appeal by Assistant Secretary Cyrus Bussey, under date of June 10, 1892.

Claimant was last medically examined July 2, 1890, and the report thereof is as
follows:

"Evidence of fracture of both clavicles; displacement of the right, slight; of the left,
the inner fragment overrides about the thickness of the bone; both deltoids atrophied
about one-third. Marked droop to shoulders, sufficient to prevent retaining sus-
penders. Well nourished and good muscular development. Circumference over
acromion, right, three-fourths inch larger; at axilla, 1 inch larger; other measurements equal. Skin florid and moist; nothing abnormal about fasciæ; large eschar 1
foot long, 3 inches wide, extending from 3 inches below the ensiform cartilage upward.
Dilatation of heart 20 per cent, displaced to left 1 inch, apex beat diffused, ringing
sound. Nasopharyngeal catarrh. Unable to extend right humerus more than one-
third of normal and unable to extend left laterally from the body; motion perfect in
other joints. Eyes: Vision, right, twenty one-hundredths; left, twenty two-hundredths; believe to be incipient cataract in both eyes."

Accompanying the bill is the claimant's petition, in which he declares that he is
wholly disabled for earning a support by manual labor; that his property, all told, is
worth but $500, and that his only income is his pension. There is also filed the affi-
davit of Dr. F. A. Clement, of Greenfield, Ill., who states that claimant is totally
disabled for manual labor by reason of injury to both shoulders, and that he also
suffers from frequent attacks of rheumatism and neuralgia, which can only be temporarily relieved.

It is undoubtedly true that the action of the Bureau in this case was correct and in
accord with the general law. The soldier's honorable military record, his many
years of faithful service, marked by promotions for zeal and efficiency, would seem,
however, to merit for his case exceptional consideration. As the bill proposes
increase to the next higher rate of $24 per month only, your committee report it back
favorably with a recommendation that it pass.

O

ELBERT CHITTUM.

FEBRUARY 4, 1903.—Committed to the Committee of the Whole House and ordered
to be printed.

Mr. SAMUEL W. SMITH, from the Committee on Invalid Pensions, submitted the following

REPORT.

[To accompany S. 1914.]

The Committee on Invalid Pensions, to whom was referred the bill
(S. 1914) granting an increase of pension to Elbert Chittum, have
examined the same and adopt the Senate report thereon and recommend that the bill do pass.

[Senate Report No. 2253, Fifty-seventh Congress, second session.]

The Committee on Pensions, to whom was referred the bill (S. 1914) granting an
increase of pension to Elbert Chittum, have examined the same and report:

This bill proposes to increase from $12 to $17 per month the pension of Elbert
Chittum, late of Company F, Ninetieth Regiment Ohio Volunteer Infantry, who
served from July 30, 1862, to June 13, 1865, when he was honorably discharged.

Soldier is now pensioned under the act of June 27, 1890, at the rate of $12 per
month for disease of eyes and right hip. He was formerly pensioned under the general law for disease of eyes, of service origin, at the rate of $4 per month, and his
claim for increase on account of this disability was rejected December 18, 1900.

Claimant is seriously disabled by disease of right hip, so much so that he is wholly
incapacitated for manual labor and requires assistance in dressing and undressing.
His right leg is considerably atrophied and is so weak that he can walk but little.
He claimed that this disability was incurred in the Army, but after special examination his claim was rejected on the ground of his inability to furnish evidence of service origin and of existence at discharge.

There is some evidence on file indicating that claimant walked lame while in the
service, and also that this lameness continued after discharge. This evidence is
somewhat vague and general, and there is no definite showing of his hip disease
until some years after discharge. He suffered from scurvy while in the service,
and it may be that his hip trouble is due to this cause.

Claimant's last medical examination, made April 20, 1898, rated him $4 for disease
of eyes, $24 for disease of right hip, and $3 for results of scurvy. The examining surgeons reported that claimant was so disabled by disease of eyes, disease of right hip,
and scurvy as to require the frequent and periodical aid and attendance of another
person.

Evidence filed with the bill shows that claimant's financial condition is one of
great need and destitution, without any means of support except his pension. It
seems highly probable that all of his disabilities are the result of his army service,
and, in view of his good record, his total disability and great poverty, your committee report the bill back favorably with a recommendation that it pass.

O

JOHN M. DRAKE.

FEBRUARY 4, 1903.—Committed to the Committee of the Whole House and ordered to be printed.

Mr. APLIN, from the Committee on Invalid Pensions, submitted the following

REPORT.

[To accompany S. 1939.]

The Committee on Invalid Pensions, to whom was referred the bill (S. 1939) granting an increase of pension to John M. Drake, have examined the same and adopt the Senate report thereon and recommend that the bill do pass.

[Senate Report No. 2504, Fifty-seventh Congress, second session.]

The Committee on Pensions, to whom was referred the bill (S. 1939) granting an increase of pension to John M. Drake, have examined the same and report:

This bill proposes to increase from $12 to $30 per month the pension of John M. Drake, late captain Company D, First Regiment Oregon Volunteer Cavalry, and lieutenant-colonel First Regiment Oregon Volunteer Infantry.

John M. Drake entered the service November 29, 1861, as first lieutenant Company D, First Oregon Cavalry. He was promoted captain April 16, 1863; major, First Oregon Infantry, March 30, 1865, and lieutenant-colonel July 7, 1865. He was discharged December 2, 1865.

Colonel Drake is 71 years of age. He has never made claim under the general law. He is now receiving a pension of $12 per month under the act of June 27, 1890, for total disability from rheumatism, senile debility, and impaired vision. His last medical examination, made July 2, 1902, shows that he is wholly incapacitated for manual labor by reason of rheumatism, senile and general debility, nervous prostration, dyspepsia, neuralgia, and defective sight.

It is stated by Senator Simon, who introduced the bill in claimant's behalf, that he is destitute and without means of support. He rendered over four years of faithful service, and it is quite probable that his health suffered in consequence. However that may be, he is aged, poor, and totally disabled, and your committee are of opinion that he should have an increase of pension.

The bill is reported back favorably with a recommendation that it pass.

O

MARY A. EVERTS.

FEBRUARY 4, 1903.—Committed to the Committee of the Whole House and ordered
to be printed.

Mr. DEEMER, from the Committee on Invalid Pensions, submitted the
following

REPORT.

[To accompany S. 2007.]

The Committee on Invalid Pensions, to whom was referred the bill
(S. 2007) granting a pension to Mary A. Everts, have examined the
same and adopt the Senate report thereon and recommend that the
bill do pass.

[Senate Report No. 2152, Fifty-seventh Congress, second session.]

The Committee on Pensions, to whom was referred the bill (S. 2007) granting a
pension to Mary A. Everts, have examined the same and report:

Mary A. Everts is the widow of George Everts, who served in Company A, Fifteenth
Regiment Iowa Volunteer Infantry.

Soldier enlisted December 16, 1863, and was discharged June 30, 1865. He died
of paralysis September 17, 1893, being a pensioner at the time of his death at the
rate of $17 per month for disease of heart, disease of spine, and rheumatism.

Mary A. Everts, the claimant under this bill, is 71 years of age, and was married
to the soldier April 15, 1891. She has no title to pension under the act of June 27,
1890, her marriage to the soldier occurring subsequent to the enactment of that law.
On June 16, 1898, she made claim under the general law, which claim was rejected
June 19, 1889, on the ground that there is no record or medical evidence tending to
show that the fatal disease was the result of soldier's military service, and this
rejection was affirmed on appeal by Assistant Secretary F. L. Campbell.

The soldier was pensioned by special act of Congress for the reason that he was
unable to furnish evidence sufficient to show that his disabilities were due to his
military service.

Appended hereto is a copy of the report made in his case. His death from paralysis it appears was the result of the disabilities for which he was pensioned.

Mrs. Everts is well advanced in years, and as she was married to the soldier but a
short while subsequent to the passage of the act of June 27, 1890, your committee
are of opinion that she should have a pension under that law.

The bill is therefore reported back favorably with a recommendation that it pass.

2   MARY A. EVERTS.

[House Report No. 1824, Fifty-first Congress, first session.]

The Committee on Invalid Pensions, to whom was referred the bill (H. R. 8124) to pension George Everts, submit the following report:

George Everts, Company A, Fifteenth Iowa Infantry Volunteers, filed his claim, No. 606803, for an invalid pension.   House bill 8124 is supported by a petition signed by a very large number of his neighbors in which the merit of his claim and his necessity for a pension are vouched for.   The petition states his inability to furnish the proof required by the rules of the Pension Bureau as to the origin of his disability.

C. H. T. St. Clair has filed an affidavit with the committee in which he states that the claimant is old and broken down in health and suffering from heart disease, disease of the spine, and rheumatism; that he is confined to his bed a part of the time each day.   The claimant states that his diseases were contracted from hard marching and exposure on march at Black River, Mississippi, in the spring of 1864.

The surgeon's certificate of the board of examiners at Fairfield, Iowa, states that the disability of the soldier is total.

Rufus A. Eno testifies to his acquaintance with the soldier since 1881, and describes his disability substantially the same as said St. Clair.

E. F. Williams, another neighbor who has known the claimant from 1876 and had opportunities to know him, states the disability to have been continuous.

Dr. J. C. Millikin also testifies as to the disability in 1882.

The records of the War Department show the sickness of the soldier in Marietta, Ga., in July, 1864, and to February, 1865; and absent, sick, in February, 1865; sick in May, 1864; had diarrhea in July, 1864.

Charles Baily testifies that he knew the soldier in 1873, when he was suffering from disease, but does not clearly state the nature of the disease.

A further record of the War Department on file shows that the soldier suffered from remittent fever, chronic diarrhea, and acute diarrhea in 1864, and in 1865 chronic hepatitis.

His continuous sickness during the last two years of his service, and his subsequent illness, as shown by the affidavits on file, clearly indicate that his army service has produced his present condition of health in whole or in part.

The soldier is greatly disabled and his case is an extreme one, so that the liberal provisions of the disability act are inadequate, as his disability was evidently contracted in the service, although the proof is not clear enough to entitle him to pension under the old law.

Owing to the extent of his disability, we deem the new law inadequate, and recommend the passage of this bill.

O

WILLIAM KEPLER.

FEBRUARY 4, 1903.—Committed to the Committee of the Whole House and ordered
to be printed.

Mr. SAMUEL W. SMITH, from the Committee on Invalid Pensions, submitted the following

REPORT.

[To accompany S. 2111.]

The Committee on Invalid Pensions, to whom was referred the bill
(S. 2111) granting an increase of pension to William Kepler, have
examined the same and adopt the Senate report thereon and recommend
that the bill do pass.

[Senate Report No. 2252, Fifty-seventh Congress, second session.]

The Committee on Pensions, to whom was referred the bill (S. 2111) granting an
increase of pension to William Kepler, have examined the same and report:

This bill proposes to increase from $12 to $24 per month the pension of William
Kepler, of Huntington, Ohio, who served in Company C, Fourth Regiment Ohio
Volunteer Infantry, from April 21, 1861, to June 21, 1864.

Soldier is now receiving a pension of $12 per month under the act of June 27,
1890, for disease of heart, nervous system, and rectum, and shell wound of back.
He was formerly pensioned under the general law for shell wound of back at $2 per
month, and his claim for increase on account of this wound was rejected November
9, 1899.

Claimant is a minister of the gospel, and he is reported by a special examiner of
the Bureau to be a physical wreck and unable to attend to the duties of his calling.
His last medical examination shows him to be suffering from injury of left shoulder
or back, disease of nervous system, disease of eyes, and disease of rectum.

Claimant declares that his broken-down condition is the result of his military service,
and he made claim to that effect at the Bureau, but the same was rejected
October 28, 1899, after special examination, on the ground that he could not furnish
satisfactory evidence showing the service origin of any of his disabilities except shell
wound of the back. He also claimed pension for chronic diarrhea, the service origin
of which was established, but the same was rejected on the ground of no present
existing disability from that cause.

The evidence on file in the Bureau is quite voluminous, and it is unnecessary to
quote it here in detail. It indicates very strongly that claimant's disabilities are all
resultant from his service. A special examiner of the Bureau submitted the claim
for allowance, stating that he believed the nervous debility, diarrhea, piles, and disease
of eyes were incurred in the service, and that the nervous trouble may arise
rom injury to spine from the shell wound and concussion.

Claimant was rated on his last medical examination $4 for injury of left shoulder or back, $14 for disease of nervous system, $8 for disease of eyes, and $4 for piles, a total of $30. The examining surgeons stated that his movements are feeble and he is easily fatigued; that coordination of movement in walking is somewhat impaired, and that he has marked muscular tremor.

The evidence on file shows that claimant is without means of support except his small pension and what little he can earn by preaching.

In view of his faithful service of over three years, his poverty, and the great probability that his disabilities all resulted from his army life, your committee report the bill back favorably with a recommendation that it pass.

O

MARGARET A. MUNSON.

FEBRUARY 4, 1903.—Committed to the Committee of the Whole House and ordered
to be printed.

Mr. SULLOWAY, from the Committee on Invalid Pensions, submitted
the following

REPORT.

[To accompany S. 2130.]

The Committee on Invalid Pensions, to whom was referred the bill
(S. 2130) granting a pension to Margaret A. Munson, have examined
the same and adopt the Senate report thereon and recommend that
the bill do pass.

[Senate Report No. 2456, Fifty-seventh Congress, second session.]

The Committee on Pensions, to whom was referred the bill (S. 2130) granting a
pension to Margaret A. Munson, have examined the same and report:

Margaret A. Munson is the widow of John A. Munson, who served in Company D,
Twenty-seventh Regiment Connecticut Volunteer Infantry.

Soldier enlisted September 9, 1862, and was discharged July 27, 1863. During
service he bore the rank of sergeant. He was severely wounded in left thigh in
battle at Fredericksburg, Va., December 13, 1862, and was treated in hospital until
the date of his discharge. He was pensioned under the general law for gunshot
wound of left thigh, and at the time of his death, which occurred May 16, 1898, he
was receiving a rate of $17 per month.

Margaret A. Munson, the claimant under this bill, is 63 years of age. On June 13,
1898, she made claim under the general law, and the same was rejected August
18, 1900, on the ground that the soldier's death from an unknown cause was not a
result of the gunshot wound of left thigh for which he was pensioned, and was not
shown to have been otherwise due to his service. Subsequently additional evidence
was filed, with a view to the reopening of the claim, but after due consideration the
same was held to be not sufficient to warrant such action.

This case develops the fact that there is a great conflict between the soldier's
attending physician and the surgeons of the Pension Bureau. The latter contend
that the cause of death and its connection with the service are not definitely
shown. The former maintains that death was due to neuritis and blood poisoning,
originating in the gunshot wound of thigh for which he was pensioned. The attending physician, who stands high in his profession, states that soldier's last illness
commenced with intense pain in his left leg in the vicinity of his gunshot wound, and
that he died in a state of collapse; that the cause of the pain he considered to be
some local irritation in the gunshot wound, producing acute neuritis which extended

and resulted fatally. He also ascribes soldier's death to blood poisoning from the gunshot wound of left thigh.

A certified copy of the public records shows that the cause of the soldier's death was, "primary, gunshot wound; secondary, blood poison." The burden of proof indicates very strongly that the serious gunshot wound which the soldier received in battle was a dominant factor in the cause of death.

Claimant was married to the soldier April 29, 1874. It appears from papers on file that she is in needy circumstances and is physically incapable of earning a support. Your committee are of opinion that her claim is fairly well established, and therefore report the bill back favorable with a recommendation that it pass.

O

ANDREW J. PENNEL.

FEBRUARY 4, 1903.—Committed to the Committee of the Whole House and ordered
to be printed.

Mr. DEEMER, from the Committee on Invalid Pensions, submitted
the following

REPORT.

[To accompany S. 2256.]

The Committee on Invalid Pensions, to whom was referred the bill
(S. 2256) granting an increase of pension to Andrew J. Pennel, have
examined the same and adopt the Senate report thereon and recommend that the bill do pass.

[Senate Report No. 2515, Fifty-seventh Congress, second session.]

The Committee on Pensions, to whom was referred the bill (S. 2256) granting an
increase of pension to Andrew J. Pennel, have examined the same and report:

This bill proposes to increase from $16 to $24 per month the pension of Andrew J.
Pennel, late of Company F, Ninety-first Regiment Pennsylvania Volunteer Infantry.

Andrew J. Pennel enlisted September 21, 1864, as private in Company F, Ninety-first Pennsylvania Infantry, and was discharged June 7, 1865, for partial anchylosis
of right shoulder joint from gunshot wound. He was wounded by a minie ball
entering the chest while engaged with the enemy at Stony Creek, Virginia, October
27, 1864, and for such wound he was pensioned February 23, 1866, at $8 per month.
His pension was reduced to $3 per month, and later his name was dropped from the
pension roll, June 4, 1873, on the ground that the disability from his wound had
ceased to exist.

On April 7, 1881, claimant's pension for wound of chest was restored to him by
special act of Congress approved March 3, 1881, at the rate of $8 per month from date
of dropping—June 4, 1873. His pension was increased to $12 per month December
9, 1885, and to $16 per month June 15, 1887, for wound of left chest and resulting
atrophy of muscles of left shoulder and arm and irritable heart. Several subsequent
claims for increase were rejected on the ground that his rate was proper for his pensioned disabilities.

Claimant made his last claim for increase October 20, 1896, alleging pensioned disabilities and resulting nervous shock and constipation. Said claim was rejected
February 1, 1900, on the ground that the pension of $16 per month was commensurate with the degree of disability from pensioned causes and that nervous shock
and constipation could not be accepted as results.

In support of his last claim for increase claimant filed the evidence of physicians
and neighbors to the effect that he is totally incapacitated for manual labor by reason
of the disabilities for which he is pensioned.

Claimant is 62 years of age. A medical examination made August 7, 1895, rated him $16 for gunshot wound and results and $8 for hemorrhoids. Another medical examination made November 11, 1896, rated him $24 for the disability caused by gunshot wound of left breast and disease of heart. His last medical examination, made March 22, 1899, is as follows:

"A scar 1½ inches by one-half inch at junction of inner and middle third of left clavicle, well healed, not adherent, but is tender; clavicle broken, considerable callus at seat of fracture. The scar claimed to be the point of entrance of bullet which has not been extracted. One-half inch atrophy of arm and 1 inch of forearm; deltoid slightly flattened; grasp weakened one-fourth; ten-eighteenths. No increase in area of cardiac dullness, but has a systolic bruit at apex; pulse regular, but excited, standing 132; after slight exercise, 140. No cyanosis, dyspnœa, or œdema; twelve-eighteenths. Stands with eyes closed and feet together without swaying, reflexes normal, pupils of equal size, and respond to light and shade; no tremor; no evidence of shock of nervous system; no eighteenths. No abdominal tympanitis, no evidence of fæcal tumors, but has two piles size of filbert each, congested, and one ulcerated and showing evidence of recent bleeding; four-eighteenths. No disease of lungs and no other disability."

Accompanying the bill is the evidence of Dr. J. F. Graham, who testifies that claimant is wholly incapacitated for hard manual labor by reason of gunshot wound of left chest and disease of heart and disease of digestive organs and rectum.

The evidence and medical examinations appear to show that claimant is disabled by pensioned causes in a degree equivalent to the loss of a hand or foot for purposes of manual labor, and your committee are of opinion that he is entitled to the rate which the general law provides for that degree of disability.

The bill is reported back favorably with a recommendation that it pass.

O

SARAH J. SNOOK.

FEBRUARY 4, 1903.—Committed to the Committee of the Whole House and ordered
to be printed.

Mr. DEEMER, from the Committee on Invalid Pensions, submitted the
following

REPORT.

[To accompany S. 2259.]

The Committee on Invalid Pensions, to whom was referred the bill
(S. 2259) granting a pension to Sarah J. Snook, have examined the
same and adopt the Senate report thereon and recommend that the
bill do pass.

[Senate Report No. 2601, Fifty-seventh Congress, second session.]

The Committee on Pensions, to whom was referred the bill (S. 2259) granting a
pension to Sarah J. Snook, have examined the same and report:

Sarah J. Snook is the widow of John Snook, who served from February 28, 1865,
to May 27, 1865, as private in Company H, Seventy-eighth Regiment Pennsylvania
Volunteer Infantry. She made claim at the Bureau under the act of June 27, 1890,
and the same was rejected on the ground that the soldier did not serve ninety days.
She also made claim under the general law, which was rejected on the ground that
the soldier's death was not shown to have resulted from his military service.

Soldier died July 20, 1871. Claimant was married to him September 8, 1860. She
is 67 years of age, and it is shown by evidence on file in the Bureau that she has no
property and is dependent on her daily labor for a support.

Soldier served eighty-nine days, just one day short of the statutory period required
to give his widow title to pension under the act of June 27, 1890. In other respects
the limitations of that law have been fully satisfied, and your committee are of
opinion that the service of the soldier should be accepted as sufficient to give claimant
a dependent widow's pension.

The bill is therefore reported back favorably with a recommendation that it pass.

O

ROSE O. CRUMMETT.

FEBRUARY 4, 1903.—Committed to the Committee of the Whole House and ordered
to be printed.

Mr. APLIN, from the Committee on Invalid Pensions, submitted the
following

REPORT.

[To accompany S. 2302.]

The Committee on Invalid Pensions, to whom was referred the bill
(S. 2302) granting a pension to Rose O. Crummett, have examined the
same and adopt the Senate report thereon and recommend that the
bill do pass.

[Senate Report No. 2480, Fifty-seventh Congress, second session.]

The Committee on Pensions, to whom was referred the bill (S. 2302) granting a
pension to Rose Crummett, have examined the same and report:

Rose O. Crummett, whose post-office address is No. 225 Michigan boulevard, Chicago, Ill., is the widow of George E. Crummett, who served as private, Company D,
Sixteenth New Hampshire Infantry, from October 13, 1862, to August 20, 1863, and
as private and second lieutenant Company L, First New Hampshire Heavy Artillery,
from September 23, 1864, to June 15, 1865.

On June 30, 1898, Mrs. Crummett made claim under the act of June 27, 1890,
which claim was rejected January 2, 1901, on the ground that she was not the legal
widow of the soldier. She has never made claim under the general law.

It appears in evidence that claimant and soldier were ceremonially married in New
York June 12, 1875, and thereafter sustained the marital relation in good faith until
his death in Illinois June 21, 1898, a period of twenty-three years. During this
period they recognized each other as husband and wife and were so recognized in
the community in which they lived. At the date of the marriage of claimant and
soldier he had a former wife living who was subsequently divorced from him October
11, 1875, by decree of the supreme court of the State of New Hampshire.

The soldier told claimant that his former wife was dead, and believing him to be
honorable and truthful she married him in good faith and did not learn of the
impediment existing to a valid marriage until some time subsequent to the soldier's
death when seeking to obtain a pension from the Bureau. It was then she learned
that the soldier's former wife was not dead, but, on the contrary, had been divorced
from him in October, 1875, a few months after the claimant's marriage to him.

At the time of the marriage of claimant and soldier he had shown her what pur-
ported to be a newspaper clipping in regard to the death of his former wife, but
which claimant now thinks really related to the death of his sister, whose name was
the same as that of his former wife.

Mrs. Crummett is 51 years of age. She is in dependent circumstances, having no property and no means of support except what she earns by her own daily labor. She is reputed to be a very estimable woman, and for some years supported and took care of the soldier when he was physically unable to support himself.

The claimant was in fact the wife of the soldier for twenty-three years, and conducted herself as such and ministered to him as such in the days of his sickness and death. The common-law rule is that a marriage entered into in good faith under similar circumstances becomes valid upon removal of the impediment thereto. Your committee are of opinion that this rule is properly applicable in this case, and therefore report the bill back favorably with a recommendation that it pass.

O

JAMES A. CAPEN.

FEBRUARY 4, 1903.—Committed to the Committee of the Whole House and ordered to be printed.

Mr. DEEMER, from the Committee on Invalid Pensions, submitted the following

REPORT.

[To accompany S. 2363.]

The Committee on Invalid Pensions, to whom was referred the bill (S. 2363) granting an increase of pension to James A. Capen, have examined the same and adopt the Senate report thereon and recommend that the bill do pass.

[Senate Report No. 2245, Fifty-seventh Congress, second session.]

The Committee on Pensions, to whom was referred the bill (S. 2363) granting an increase of pension to James A. Capen, have examined the same and report:

This bill proposes to increase from $20 to $30 per month the pension of James A. Capen, late of Company B, Seventh Regiment Kansas Volunteer Cavalry.

Soldier enlisted September 24, 1861, and was discharged September 29, 1865. He was pensioned May 9, 1884, under the general law, for total deafness of right ear, at $1 per month from discharge and $2 per month from April 3, 1884. His pension was increased to $4 per month November 15, 1887; to $10 per month August 27, 1888, and to $20 per month November 12, 1890, for nasopharyngeal catarrh, resulting in total deafness of right ear and slight deafness of left ear.

On October 21, 1898, claimant made claim for increase and also for additional pension on account of rheumatism which he alleged he contracted in the service. The claim for increase was rejected June 16, 1899, on the ground that his rate was commensurate with the degree of disability from pensioned cause. The claim for rheumatism was rejected November 20, 1899, on the ground of no record, and the best obtainable evidence fails to satisfactorily establish origin; and if legally established the next higher rate would not be warranted. This action was affirmed on appeal August 6, 1900, by Assistant Secretary F. L. Campbell.

In support of his claim for rheumatism claimant filed evidence of his officers, comrades, and neighbors. His captain, William S. Morehouse, who is now auditor of Burleigh County, N. Dak., testified that in the fall of 1863 claimant became considerably disabled from rheumatism, and he was appointed company clerk about that time to lighten his work and help him along. His first lieutenant and adjutant, S. M. Fox, now adjutant-general of Kansas, testified that in the early summer of 1865 claimant had lost his hearing in one ear and was not otherwise strong, being troubled with rheumatism.

Two comrades, men of high standing, also testified to rheumatism in service, and there is considerable evidence from neighbors on file to show continuance of that disability.

A medical examination made November 12, 1890, reported that claimant was totally deaf in right ear and severely deaf in left ear, and rated him $25 for that disability. His last medical examination, made March 8, 1899, rated him $4 for catarrh, $8 for loss of teeth, $8 for rheumatism, and $25 for total deafness of right ear and severe deafness of left ear. The examining surgeons stated that claimant could not hear the loudest tone of voice at 1 foot with right ear and that with left ear he could hear loud conversation at 1 foot, but could not hear at 2 feet.

Claimant is 62 years of age. It is shown by evidence that he is in dependent circumstances, without property or income except his pension, and that he is unable to earn a support by manual labor by reason of his afflictions. He is so deaf that no one will employ him, and he is also greatly crippled with rheumatism.

The schedule rating at the Bureau for total deafness of one ear and severe of the other is $25 per month, and it would appear from the claimant's medical examinations that his deafness exists in that degree. In addition to this he is suffering from catarrh, for which he is pensioned, and also from rheumatism, which seems to be fairly well established as of service origin.

Your committee are of opinion that claimant has maintained his right to an increase of pension, and therefore report the bill back favorably with a recommendation that it pass.

O

RICHARD A. LARIMER.

FEBRUARY 4, 1903.—Committed to the Committee of the Whole House and ordered to be printed.

Mr. SAMUEL W. SMITH, from the Committee on Invalid Pensions, submitted the following

REPORT.

[To accompany S. 2439.]

The Committee on Invalid Pensions, to whom was referred the bill (S. 2439) granting an increase of pension to Richard A. Larimer, have examined the same and adopt the Senate report thereon and recommend that the bill do pass.

[Senate Report No. 2359, Fifty-seventh Congress, second session.]

The Committee on Pensions, to whom was referred the bill (S. 2439) granting an increase of pension to Richard A. Larimer, have examined the same and report:

This bill proposes to increase from $12 to $30 per month the pension of Richard A. Larimer, of Ashley, N. Dak., late of Company C, Twenty-fourth Regiment Ohio Volunteer Infantry, who served from June 13, 1861, to June 22, 1864, when he was honorably discharged.

Claimant is now receiving a pension of $12 per month under the act of June 27, 1890, for total inability to earn a support by manual labor, due to sciatica, disease of lungs and heart, and rheumatism. March 24, 1884, he made claim under the general law, alleging that he contracted rheumatism in November or December, 1863. This claim was rejected April 2, 1886, on the ground that a ratable disability from cause alleged did not exist, although subsequently claimant was pensioned for rheumatism under the act of June 27, 1890.

Claimant is 63 years of age. His last medical examination, dated April 14, 1902, shows him to be very feeble and totally disabled by reason of chronic rheumatism and resulting heart disease and bronchitis, of probable service origin. This examination was made at his home, his physical condition being such as to render him unable to report to the surgeons for examination.

Claimant has always depended on his labor for support, and he is now unable to earn anything. His only income is his pension of $12 per month. He has a little property, worth about $500, which is encumbered for $200 and yields no income.

In view of his faithful service for three years, his total disability, and great poverty, your committee report the bill back favorably, with a recommendation that it pass.

GEORGE W. McCOMB.

FEBRUARY 4, 1903.—Committed to the Committee of the Whole House and ordered
to be printed.

Mr. HOLLIDAY, from the Committee on Invalid Pensions, submitted
the following

REPORT.

[To accompany S. 2591.]

The Committee on Invalid Pensions, to whom was referred the bill
(S. 2591) granting an increase of pension to George W. McComb,
have examined the same and adopt the Senate report thereon and
recommend that the bill do pass.

[Senate Report No. 2422, Fifty-seventh Congress, second session.]

The Committee on Pensions, to whom was referred the bill (S. 2591) granting an
increase of pension to George W. McComb, have examined the same and report:

George W. McComb is now receiving a pension of $12 per month under the act of
June 27, 1890, for total inability to earn a support by manual labor, due to injury of
left leg, right inguinal hernia, rheumatism and resulting disease of the heart, and
disease of spine. He enlisted May 2, 1863, in Company I, Eighth Michigan Cavalry;
was transferred to Company K, Eighth Veteran Reserve Corps, November 23, 1864,
and was discharged August 4, 1865. The hospital records show that he was treated
during the service for catarrh and general debility.

Claimant is 56 years of age, and resides at 2118 Central avenue, Indianapolis, Ind.
He declares that his hernia and injury to left leg were incurred during military service. The hernia, he says, was incurred at Cleveland, Tenn., about August, 1863, by
his horse being shot and falling on him. The injury to left leg was due to erysipelas,
contracted about July, 1863, settling in his leg. He has never made claim under
the general law because of his not being able to find any of his comrades by whose
evidence he might establish such a claim.

When claimant was last examined, August 6, 1902, he was found to be a total
physical wreck, altogether unable to do manual labor, and unable to dress and
undress himself without help. He was suffering from paralysis, injury to left leg,
hernia, rheumatism, disease of heart, and disease of spine.

It is also shown by evidence on file in the Pension Bureau that claimant is a poor
man, without property or means of support except his pension. He served for over
two years, and it is probable that some of his disabilities are due to his service.
However that may be, he is poor and totally disabled, and your committee are of
opinion that an increase of pension is warranted.

The bill is therefore reported back favorably with a recommendation that it pass.

O

ISRAEL F. BARNES.

FEBRUARY 4, 1903.—Committed to the Committee of the Whole House and ordered
to be printed.

Mr. SULLOWAY, from the Committee on Invalid Pensions, submitted
the following

REPORT.

[To accompany S. 2596.]

The Committee on Invalid Pensions, to whom was referred the bill
(S. 2596) granting an increase of pension to Israel F. Barnes, have
examined the same and adopt the Senate report thereon and recommend that the bill do pass.

[Senate Report No. 2448, Fifty-seventh Congress, second session]

The Committee on Pensions, to whom was referred the bill (S. 2596) granting an
increase of pension to Israel F. Barnes, have examined the same and report:

This bill proposes to increase from $12 to $24 per month the pension of Israel F.
Barnes, of Everett, Mass., late of Company D, Twenty-sixth Regiment Massachusetts
Volunteer Infantry.

Soldier enlisted September 4, 1861, and was discharged April 12, 1862. During
service he bore the rank of private. He was pensioned under the general law February 14, 1871, for right scrotal hernia at $4 per month from discharge, which was
increased to $6 per month January 17, 1877, and to $8 per month February 5, 1879.
March 29, 1882, his pension was reissued at $6 per month from discharge, $10 per
month from January 17, 1877, and $12 per month from February 5, 1879, for right
scrotal hernia and chronic diarrhea. His last claim for increase for pensioned
causes, filed September 19, 1895, was rejected June 1, 1897, on the ground that his
present rate was adequate for those troubles.

On September 19, 1895, claimant made claim for additional pension based on disease of eyes alleged to be a result of sunstroke incurred in line of duty during his
military service. Said claim was rejected June 1, 1897, on the ground that disease
of eyes was not a result of sunstroke, and this action was affirmed on appeal May 31,
1899, by Assistant Secretary Webster Davis.

Claimant declares that he incurred sunstroke at Ship Island, Miss., which produced disease of eyes and consequent loss of sight. Evidence has been filed tending
to establish the incurrence of something in the nature of a sunstroke, or at least that
he was overcome by heat on one occasion during his service, and that thereafter his
eyes were somewhat affected. Three comrades testified to these facts.

One neighbor testified to continuance of disease of eyes from 1862 to 1868, and Dr.
George C. Osgood, of Lowell, Mass., testified that he treated claimant in 1868 for
ulcers on the cornea of both eyes, the left eye much the worse; that he treated him
for the same troubles at various times since, and that now he has entire loss of vision

in left eye, caused by central opacities in cornea, and some opacity of cornea in right eye, and that he is unable to perform any manual labor whatever. Dr. Osgood gives it as his opinion that the eye trouble was started by sunstroke and kept up by ulcers on the corneas. Two other physicians testified that claimant's eye trouble was due to central opacities of corneas, but express no opinion as to origin.

A medical examination dated December 11, 1895, rated claimant $10 for hernia, $6 for chronic diarrhea, and $6 for disease of eyes. His last examination by an oculist, October 28, 1897, reported vision in right eye twenty two-hundredths, and vision in left eye three two-hundredths.

It appears from other evidence on file that claimant is wholly incapacitated for earning a livelihood by reason of impaired sight, and that as a fact he has not earned a cent for seven years; that he is in needy circumstances and has been compelled to receive aid from a beneficial society of which he is a member.

While it may be technically true that claimant's eye trouble is not a result of sunstroke, yet the evidence tends very strongly to show that it is due to his military service, whether caused by sunstroke or not. Upon the broad ground that the eye trouble was most probably induced by army life, your committee are of opinion that claimant has fairly established his claim and is entitled to an increase of his pension.

The bill is therefore reported back favorably with a recommendation that it pass.

O

ARDENIA DILLON.

FEBRUARY 4, 1903.—Committed to the Committee of the Whole House and ordered
to be printed.

Mr. HOLLIDAY, from the Committee on Invalid Pensions, submitted
the following

REPORT.

[To accompany S. 2626.]

The Committee on Invalid Pensions, to whom was referred the bill
(S. 2626) granting an increase of pension to Ardenia Dillon, have
examined the same and adopt the Senate report thereon and recommend that the bill do pass.

[Senate Report No. 2428, Fifty-seventh Congress, second session.]

The Committee on Pensions, to whom was referred the bill (S. 2626) granting an
increase of pension to Ardenia Dillon, have examined the same and report:
Ardenia Dillon, whose post-office address is 131 North Davidson street, Indian-
apolis, Ind., is the widow of William P. Dillon, who served as captain Company D,
Sixth Indiana Volunteer Infantry, and Company D, One hundred and forty-sixth
Indiana Volunteer Infantry.
The military records show that William P. Dillon served as private, Company A,
Sixth Indiana Volunteer Infantry, from April 19, 1861, to August 2, 1861, when he
was honorably discharged. He next enlisted August 10, 1861, as sergeant, Company
D, Sixth Indiana Volunteer Infantry; was promoted second lieutenant May 30, 1862;
first lieutenant, September 24, 1863; captain, May 28, 1864, and was discharged September 22, 1864. He was mustered in as captain Company D, One hundred and
forty-sixth Indiana Volunteer Infantry, February 28, 1865, and was discharged
August 31, 1865.
Captain Dillon died May 20, 1885, never having made claim for pension. The
cause of his death, as shown by the public records, was apoplexy. Ardenia Dillon,
the claimant under this bill, was married to the soldier August 23, 1870. She is now
receiving the pension of $8 per month provided by the act of June 27, 1890. On
December 1, 1888, she made claim under the general law, which was rejected June
16, 1898, on the ground that her husband's death from apoplexy was not shown to
have resulted from his military service.
Mrs. Dillon is 55 years of age. She is in destitute circumstances, having no means
of support aside from her small pension of $8 per month. It appears in evidence
that she is in very poor health and is almost blind, being scarcely able to get about
unaided.

Upon examination of the evidence on file no reason is found for any exception to the action of the Bureau in rejecting the claimant's general-law claim; it is not proved that soldier's death was due to his military service. However this may be, the claimant is in a deplorable condition—almost blind, and destitute. Her husband enlisted at the first call for troops and served faithfully and honorably for four years, rising from private, through successive promotions, to the rank of captain. A grateful country should not permit the widow of so good a soldier to exist in want, and your committee are of opinion that an increase of her pension is eminently just and proper.

The bill is therefore reported back favorably with a recommendation that it pass.

O

ISRAEL V. HOAG.

FEBRUARY 4, 1903.—Committed to the Committee of the Whole House and ordered to be printed.

Mr. DEEMER, from the Committee on Invalid Pensions, submitted the following

REPORT.

[To accompany S. 2799.]

The Committee on Invalid Pensions, to whom was referred the bill (S. 2799) granting an increase of pension to Israel V. Hoag, have examined the same and adopt the Senate report thereon and recommend that the bill do pass.

[Senate Report No. 2602, Fifty-seventh Congress, second session.]

The Committee on Pensions, to whom was referred the bill (S. 2799) granting an increase of pension to Israel V. Hoag, have examined the same and report:

This bill proposes to increase from $10 to $24 per month the pension of Israel V. Hoag, late of Captain Palmer's independent company, Pennsylvania Volunteer Cavalry.

According to the military records, Israel V. Hoag served in Captain Palmer's company of Pennsylvania Cavalry from November 4, 1861, to March 26, 1863. He was a prisoner of war at Jackson, Miss., from June 19, 1862, to September 7, 1862.

Claimant is suffering from paralysis, affecting his entire left side and totally incapacitating him from all business. When last examined, July 3, 1901, he was found to be wholly disabled by reason of partial paralysis due to cerebral hemorrhage. He is able to dress and undress himself and to attend to his ordinary daily wants, but is not able to perform any effective manual labor.

Claimant is receiving a pension of $10 per month. In his disabled condition he finds this small pension wholly inadequate to supply him even the necessaries of life, and your committee are of opinion that the circumstances of his case will warrant an increase of his pension.

The bill is therefore reported back favorably with a recommendation that it pass.

O

BERTHOLD FERNOW.

FEBRUARY 4, 1903.—Committed to the Committee of the Whole House and ordered to be printed.

Mr. SAMUEL W. SMITH, from the Committee on Invalid Pensions, submitted the following

REPORT.

[To accompany S. 2936.]

The Committee on Invalid Pensions, to whom was referred the bill (S. 2936) granting an increase of pension to Berthold Fernow, have examined the same and adopt the Senate report thereon and recommend that the bill do pass.

[Senate Report No. 832, Fifty-seventh Congress, first session.]

The Committee on Pensions, to whom was referred the bill (S. 2936) granting an increase of pension to Berthold Fernow, have examined the same and report:

This bill proposes to increase from $12 to $30 per month the pension of Berthold Fernow, of Trenton, N. J., late second lieutenant Company I, Third Regiment United States Colored Volunteer Infantry.

Mr. Fernow was born in Prussian Poland in 1837 and came to the United States in 1862. He enlisted as a private in Company M, Fourth Missouri Cavalry, August 12, 1863, and served as such until October 24, 1864, when he was honorably discharged to enable him to accept a commission in the colored troops. He was appointed second lieutenant Company I, Third Regiment United States Colored Troops, November 28, 1864, and was honorably discharged October 31, 1865.

Mr. Fernow is now receiving a pension of $12 per month, under the act of June 27, 1890, for total inability to earn a support by manual labor, caused by locomotor ataxia. He made claim under the general law August 11, 1886, alleging the service origin of bayonet wound of left shoulder and injury to head over right eye, and that the same had resulted in paralysis of left leg. This claim was rejected August 1, 1898, on the ground that no ratable degree of disability from bayonet wound of left shoulder and injury to head over right eye was shown to exist, and paralysis was not accepted as a result.

It is fairly well established that Mr. Fernow, while quelling a mutiny at Jacksonville, Fla., in October, 1865, received the injuries he alleges, but it does not appear that any permanent or serious disability resulted, or that they caused him any trouble after his service. About 1885 he first noticed the symptoms of paralysis, and this trouble has since progressed until now he is totally disabled. His last medical examination, at Troy, N. Y., November 11, 1896, showed that he was then so disabled by paralysis of left leg as to be incapacitated for performing any manual labor, and was rated at $30 per month.

Medical evidence filed with the bill shows that Mr. Fernow is suffering from loco-motor ataxia, the left leg being entirely beyond voluntary control and the right leg nearly so, and that locomotion is very difficult and slow and uncertain, with constant danger of falling.

Mr. Fernow is in very straitened circumstances. He has no real estate and no per-sonal property, except his clothing and a few books. He is temporarily employed in some literary work at a small salary, and this will cease on the 1st of June next, when he will be without any income whatever except his pension.

In view of his long and faithful service, his poverty, and almost helpless condition, your committee are of opinion that an increase of his pension would be both just and proper.

The bill is reported back favorably with a recommendation that it pass.

O

SAMUEL J. BOYER.

FEBRUARY 4, 1903.—Committed to the Committee of the Whole House and ordered
to be printed.

Mr. HOLLIDAY, from the Committee on Invalid Pensions, submitted
the following

REPORT.

[To accompany S. 2974.]

The Committee on Invalid Pensions, to whom was referred the bill
(S. 2974) granting an increase of pension to Samuel J. Boyer, have
examined the same and adopt the Senate report thereon and recommend that the bill do pass.

[Senate Report No. 2520, Fifty-seventh Congress, second session.]

The Committee on Pensions, to whom was referred the bill (S. 2974) granting an
increase of pension to Samuel J. Boyer, have examined the same and report:

This bill proposes to increase from $17 to $40 the pension of Samuel J. Boyer, of
Eldorado Springs, Mo., late of Company G, Nineteenth Regiment United States
Infantry.

The military records show that Samuel J. Boyer enlisted February 7, 1862, and
was discharged February 10, 1865. The medical records show that at Fredericksburg,
Va., December 13, 1862, he received a gunshot wound of back, for which wound he
was under treatment in hospital until March 20, 1863.

On April 18, 1874, claimant made claim under the general law, alleging that while
in battle at Fredericksburg, Va., December 13, 1862, he received a gunshot wound
through the chest, the ball entering on the right side and coming out on the left side,
injuring him severely. He was pensioned September 19, 1874, for gunshot wound of
both lungs, at $6 per month from discharge, which was increased to $8 per month
March 9, 1881; to $12 per month November 27, 1889, and to $17 per month November
26, 1890, for gunshot wound of both lungs, and resulting injury of spine.

Claimant subsequently made several claims for increase, all of which were rejected
on the ground that his pension was adequate for the degree of disability from the
pensioned cause. His last rejection was dated August 1, 1900. In several claims he
alleged nervous debility, partial paralysis, and blindness as due to his gunshot
wound and resulting injury of spine, but these disabilities were not accepted as
results of the pensioned cause.

Claimant is 59 years of age. A medical examination made April 28, 1897, reports
him as so disabled as to require the frequent and periodical aid and attendance of
another person and entitled to $50 per month for gunshot wound, blindness, and
nervous debility. His last medical examination, made February 7, 1900, shows him
to be suffering from gunshot wound, blindness, and general debility. The examining surgeons say he is totally disabled and has to be led from place to place.

Dr. I. N. Haynes and Dr. Kimball Hill testified September 17, 1897, in joint affidavit as follows:

"We have examined S. J. Boyer and find the scars evidence of gunshot wound in the back, the ball having entered on the right side, 5 inches from the spinal column, between the eighth and ninth ribs, which, in our opinion, penetrated the right lung and was taken out, says the pensioner, 3 inches to left of spine below the twelfth rib, a scar showing this point of removal.

"We think the ball must have injured the vetebral column and spinal cord, from which injury may result his present condition of nervous debility and prostration, rendering him unable to perform manual labor.

"In our opinion the condition of applicant's eyes may be due to great nervous debility and prostration resulting from injuries of spinal cord as produced by gunshot wound."

Dr. W. E. Dawson testified April 12, 1902, as follows:

"This certifies that I have been acquainted with Samuel Boyer for the last twelve years, and have been his physician during that time; that he has been suffering from the effects of gunshot wound in the back, and as results of said wound has been partially paralyzed and blind; that for the last twelve months he has been and is now entirely blind, said blindness being the result of paralysis of optic nerve. He is partially paralyzed, has loss of memory, and is blind, and is requires attendance constantly."

There is much other medical evidence to the effect that claimant's disabilities are all due to the severe gunshot wound received in battle.

Claimant is a poor man, his yearly income aside from his pension being less than $50. He has a good military record of three years' service, and it would seem probable that his present deplorable condition is due to his wound. Under the circumstances, your committee are of opinion that his case is a proper one for relief, and therefore report the bill back favorably with a recommendation that it pass when amended as follows:

In line 8 strike out the word "fifty" and insert in lieu thereof the word "forty."

O

LEONARD A. NORTON.

FEBRUARY 4, 1903.—Committed to the Committee of the Whole House and ordered to be printed.

Mr. KLEBERG, from the Committee on Invalid Pensions, submitted the following

REPORT.

[To accompany S. 3081.]

The Committee on Invalid Pensions, to whom was referred the bill (S. 3081) granting an increase of pension to Leonard A. Norton, have examined the same and adopt the Senate report thereon and recommend that the bill do pass.

[Senate Report No. 2197, Fifty-seventh Congress, second session.]

The Committee on Pensions, to whom was referred the bill (S. 3081) granting an increase of pension to Leonard A. Norton, have examined the same and report:

This bill proposes to increase from $12 to $30 per month the pension of Leonard A. Norton, late of Company L, First Regiment Maryland Volunteer Cavalry.

The following is the soldier's petition, which states all the facts in his case:

To the Senate and House of Representatives of the United States in Congress assembled:

The petition of Leonard A. Norton, formerly a resident of Montgomery County, in the State of Maryland, but at present residing at 1017 Delaware avenue NE. in the city of Washington, D. C., respectfully represents as follows:

That he is a native of Montgomery County, Md., and resided there until recent years, and that while residing there he enlisted, September 30, 1862, in Company L, First Maryland Veteran Volunteer Cavalry, and was discharged therefrom May 19, 1865; that he is 58 years of age; that at the battle of Petersburg, on or about August, 1864, he received a gunshot wound of the left lung, for which he is pensioned under the general laws at the rate of $12 per month; that about three years ago he became afflicted with blindness and is unable to distinguish any object and can only tell the difference between light and darkness.

He can, of course, perform no labor or earn any money. He has an invalid sister who is dependent upon him for support; but his pension is insufficient to support even himself, for, besides the cost of his board, clothing, and lodging, he is obliged to have some one to lead him when he goes out of doors, and to do many other things required by one in his condition.

He believes his present blindness to be the result of blows received in the eyes from branches of trees when he was riding in the woods at night during his term of service, for his eyes began to trouble him while he was in the Army and have troubled him ever since. But he can furnish no proof of service origin, and for that reason he has never applied to the Pension Bureau for a pension on account of blindness.

He respectfully prays that a special bill for his relief may be passed by Congress, granting him a pension of $50 per month in lieu of his present pension, in order that he may pass his few remaining years in such comfort as is possible to one who is blind.

LEONARD (his x mark) A. NORTON.

Witnesses—
   BESSIE BALDWIN.
   JOHN G. PARKER.

DISTRICT OF COLUMBIA, ss:

Subscribed and sworn to before me this 18th day of December, 1901.

[SEAL.]   T. BLAIR SHOEMAKER,
                                       Notary Public.

The military records show that soldier enlisted September 30, 1862, and was discharged May 19, 1865, and that he received a gunshot wound of left lung before Petersburg, Va., September 27, 1864, for which wound he is now pensioned at $12 per month. His last medical examination, dated January 14, 1901, shows the following condition of his eyes.

"Right: Complete cataract of right eye; choroiditis of left eye with floating opacities in vitreous; can read Snellen D 60 at 1 foot, left eye; pupils sluggish; accompanied by attendant."

In view of claimant's faithful service of nearly three years, his wound received in battle, and his almost total blindness and great poverty, your committee are of opinion that an increase of his pension would be both just and proper.

The bill is therefore reported back favorably, with a recommendation that it pass.

O

CHARLES W. SCHERZER.

FEBRUARY 4, 1903.—Committed to the Committee of the Whole House and ordered to be printed.

Mr. SULLOWAY, from the Committee on Invalid Pensions, submitted the following

REPORT.

[To accompany S. 324?]

The Committee on Invalid Pensions, to whom was referred the bill (S. 3249) granting an increase of pension to Charles W. Scherzer, have examined the same and adopt the Senate report thereon and recommend that the bill do pass.

[Senate Report No. 2585, Fifty-seventh Congress, second session.]

The Committee on Pensions, to whom was referred the bill (S. 3249) granting an increase of pension to Charles W. Scherzer, have examined the same and report:

This bill proposes to increase from $12 to $30 per month the pension of Charles W. Scherzer, late of Company F, Fourteenth Regiment U. S. Infantry, and Company M, Twenty-first Regiment Pennsylvania Volunteer Cavalry.

The military records show that Charles W. Scherzer was enlisted September 16, 1861, and was a private in Company F, Fourteenth U. S. Infantry, until January 13, 1863, when he was discharged for scabies of an aggravated character of two months' duration. He was next enlisted July 1, 1863, in Company D, Twentieth Pennsylvania Cavalry, and was discharged January 6, 1864. He again enlisted February 17, 1864, and served in Company M, Twenty-first Pennsylvania Cavalry, until July 8, 1865, when he was discharged. The records of this company show that he was wounded in the hand on June 19, 1864, and was sent to hospital.

Claimant is now receiving a pension of $12 per month under the act of June 27, 1890, for paralysis, rheumatism, sciatica, and gunshot wound of left hand. On March 25, 1880, he made claim under the general law, alleging that he was disabled by sciatica contracted from exposure at Fredericksburg, Va., in November, 1862. This claim was rejected July 25, 1885, on the ground of no record or other evidence of service origin or of existence at discharge.

It appears from the evidence on file that claimant is almost helpless from paralysis. His last medical examination, made April 20, 1891, is as follows:

"I find on examination that this man is completely paralyzed on right side, with a general atrophy of arm and leg. He has rheumatic attacks frequently in all of the body, but is confined principally to the sciatic. He has lost the use of his speech, and all he can utter is yes or no, and make signs. He has also received a gunshot wound in middle finger of left hand, deforming it and making it useless.   It is with difficulty he walks with a cane."

The examining surgeon also says that this is a deserving case and commands sympathy.

Claimant's paralysis occurred in 1878, and he avers it is due to sciatica, which he claims he incurred in the service.   Of this, however, there is no proof.   His post-office address is Sharpedale, Colo.   He is 53 years of age, and evidence on file shows that he is very poor and without means of support aside from his pension.   He enlisted when he was very young, and in view of his faithful service of over three years, his total disability and destitution, your committee report the bill back favorably with a recommendation that it pass.

O

WILLIAM H. H. BOUSLOUGII.

FEBRUARY 4, 1903.—Committed to the Committee of the Whole House and ordered
to be printed.

Mr. SAMUEL W. SMITH, from the Committee on Invalid Pensions, submitted the following

REPORT.

[To accompany S. 3405.]

The Committee on Invalid Pensions, to whom was referred the bill
(S. 3405) granting an increase of pension to William H. H. Bouslough,
have examined the same and adopt the Senate report thereon and
recommend that the bill do pass.

[Senate Report No. 2259, Fifty-seventh Congress, second session.]

The Committee on Pensions, to whom was referred the bill (S. 3405) granting an
increase of pension to W. H. H. Bouslough, have examined the same and report:

This bill proposes to increase from $12 to $30 per month the pension of William
H. H. Bouslough, late of Company D, Thirty-eighth Regiment Pennsylvania Volunteer Infantry, and Company F, One hundred and sixty-ninth Regiment Pennsylvania Volunteer Infantry.

Soldier served in Company D, Thirty-eighth Pennsylvania Infantry, from May 3,
1861, to August 10, 1862, and in Company F, One hundred and sixty-ninth Pennsylvania Infantry, from October 16, 1862, to July 25, 1863. He is now receiving a
pension of $12 per month. He made claim under the general law May 6, 1889, alleg-
ing disease of the back incurred in the service, which claim was rejected April 9,
1898, because of his inability to furnish satisfactory evidence showing service origin
and continuance of that trouble.

Claimant is 63 years of age. His last medical examination, dated September 19,
1894, is as follows:

"General appearance only fairly good; is pale and anæmic; has the look of an
invalid. Muscles are small and flabby, and skin relaxed and white. General nutri-
tion below par. Tongue red in center and fissured, fauces red, abdomen distended,
tenderness over region of stomach, liver much enlarged, spleen normal, rectum
healthy. Has but three teeth in lower jaw, only one of which antagonizes with
those of upper maxilla—all of which are in very bad condition from natural decay.
Muscles in lumbar region rigid and show a degree of lumbago.

"Heart's action rapid and irritable—90-100-120; pulse rather small, sounds nearly
normal, the second a little faint. Apex beat not apparent, but in about the usual
position. No increase in area of cardiac dullness; some epigastric pulsation; capillary vessels of the body dilated, with some degree of cyanosis. Heart weak, without
hypertrophy or dilatation. No œdema, but slight dyspnœa. Hands show that he

does no manual labor. We find his disabilities are not the result of vicious habits, and in our opinion they disqualify him for manual labor.

Accompanying the bill is the following petition from the claimant:

MEADVILLE, PA., *January 27, 1902.*

To the Congress of the United States:

My name, William H. H. Bonslough, 575 Washington street,· Meadville, Pa. Will be 63 years of age the 2d day of March, 1902. Was member of Company D, Thirty-eighth, and Company F, One hundred and sixty-ninth, Pennsylvania Regiments, war of rebellion. Applied to the Bureau of Pensions for pension under general or existing laws in 1889. In May, 1898, was notified that claim was rejected "on the ground of no hospital record in the War Department." The disabilities with which I am affected are spinal rheumatism, chronic diarrhea, heart failure, dyspepsia, and loss of teeth. I am now drawing pension on dyspepsia and loss of teeth.

These disabilities were contracted while in the service, caused by cold and exposure to severe weather. While not at that time suffering to such an extent as to compel me to take hospital treatment, I nevertheless suffered and have continually from that time to this, and the older I get the more I suffer. None of these disabilities are due to vicious habits, and disable me from the performance of any manual labor. I do not own a dollar's worth of real estate, and my household goods are the extent of my personal property. I have no annual income except my pension of $12 per month.

Will you please propose and present a bill that will give me the relief asked for? Broken health, energies impaired, and a hopeless future in the ranks of happy success were the burdens thousands bore and are still bearing after their war service as a sacrifice nobly endured for the integrity of the Union.

The sentiment of patriotic duty, leading to suffering of mind and body, can only find its worthy and satisfying compensation in a full sentiment of appreciation for the services rendered in the nation's behalf. Sentiment carries no aid and comfort for satisfying the daily needs of the aged veteran, but the granting of a pension, his due by reason of his service and his needs under laws passed for his relief and happiness, goes to the hearts of himself and family like a sweet song. My claim is just. I ask nothing more. Selfishness may weaken and ambition deaden the old fires of grateful patriotism in some hearts, but the eternal ways of God to men are some assurance that full justice will be done in the end.

Respectfully submitted.

WILLIAM H. H. BOUSLOUGH,
575 Washington Street, Meadville, Pa.

Hon. BOISE PENROSE,
United States Senator from Pennsylvania.

Sworn to and subscribed before me this 27th day of January, 1902.

[SEAL.]   CURTIS S. CLARK, *Clerk of Court.*

In view of the soldier's faithful service of two years, his total disability, and great poverty, your committee report the bill back favorably with a recommendation that it pass.

O

WILLIAM H. SHAW.

FEBRUARY 4, 1903.—Committed to the Committee of the Whole House and ordered
to be printed.

Mr. DEEMER, from the Committee on Invalid Pensions, submitted the
following

REPORT.

[To accompany S. 3542.]

The Committee on Invalid Pensions, to whom was referred the bill
(S. 3542) granting an increase of pension to William H. Shaw, have
examined the same and adopt the Senate report thereon and recommend that the bill do pass.

[Senate Report No. 2516, Fifty-seventh Congress, first session.]

The Committee on Pensions, to whom was referred the bill (S. 3542) granting an
increase of pension to William H. Shaw, have examined the same and report:

This bill proposes to increase from $12 to $24 per month the pension of William H.
Shaw, late of Company H, One hundred and forty-second Regiment Pennsylvania
Volunteer Infantry.

The military records show that William H. Shaw enlisted August 11, 1862, in
Company H, One hundred and forty-second Pennsylvania Infantry, and served until
June 26, 1865, when he was discharged from Company F, Ninth Veteran Reserve
Corps, to which he was transferred in September or October, 1863, by reason of a
severe gunshot wound of left shoulder, received in battle at Fredericksburg, Va.,
December 13, 1862. The hospital records show that he was treated for gunshot
wound of left shoulder and also for bronchitis and diarrhea.

Claimant is now pensioned at $12 per month under the act of June 27, 1890, for
total disability due to wound of left shoulder and disease of nervous system. He
was formerly pensioned under the general law for gunshot wound of left shoulder at
$6 per month.

May 8, 1900, claimant made claim for increase, alleging gunshot wound of left
shoulder and resulting disease of spine and also alleging additional disabilities,
chronic diarrhea and resulting disease of stomach and rectum. This claim was
rejected March 19, 1902, on the ground of no increase in disability from gunshot
wound of left shoulder, disease of spine not being accepted as a result, and on the
ground of no ratable disability from chronic diarrhea and disease of stomach and
rectum.

When last examined, November 27, 1901, claimant was found to be suffering from gunshot wound of left shoulder, disease of nervous system, rheumatism, and disease of bowels and digestive organs. He had paralysis agitans affecting right hand and arm, the use of which was reduced one-half; rheumatism in left hip and knee, with impaired use of same, sciatica, and lumbago, and he was almost totally disabled for manual labor.

Claimant served for nearly three years, and it is probable that all of his disabilities are due to his service. However that may be, he is poor and almost totally disabled, and your committee are of opinion that an increase of his pension is warranted.

The bill is reported back favorably with a recommendation that it pass.

O

JOHN P. TRAVIS.

FEBRUARY 4, 1903.—Committed to the Committee of the Whole House and ordered
to be printed.

Mr. GIBSON, from the Committee on Invalid Pensions, submitted the
following

REPORT.

[To accompany S. 3568.]

The Committee on Invalid Pensions, to whom was referred the bill
(S. 3568) granting an increase of pension to John P. Travis, have
examined the same and adopt the Senate report thereon and recommend that the bill do pass.

[Senate Report No. 2846, Fifty-seventh Congress, second session.]

The Committee on Pensions, to whom was referred the bill (S. 3568) granting an
increase of pension to John P. Travis, have examined the same and report:

The bill as amended proposes to increase from $12 to $24 per month the pension of
John P. Travis, of Ponca, Nebr., late of Company D, Fourteenth Regiment Wisconsin Volunteer Infantry.

The military records show that John P. Travis enlisted February 22, 1864, in Company D, Fourteenth Wisconsin Infantry, and was discharged June 9, 1865. The
hospital records show that he was treated for chronic diarrhea.

Claimant was pensioned February 25, 1887, under the general law, for chronic
diarrhea at $2 per month from discharge and $4 per month from October 18, 1881,
which was increased to $12 per month May 17, 1890, for chronic diarrhea and result-
ing piles. August 20, 1898, he made claim for increase, which was rejected February 10, 1900, on the ground that his pension was proper for the disability resulting
from pensioned causes.

On August 27, 1889, claimant suffered amputation of the right leg between hip
and knee-joint. This was made necessary by dry gangrene, produced by a blood
clot in the femoral artery, caused by enlargement of the heart. It is contended by
claimant that his heart trouble was caused by great debility, produced by the
chronic diarrhea contracted in service and for which he was pensioned, and there is
considerable evidence from his physicians sustaining this view.

Dr. E. F. Rucker, of Ponca, Nebr., one of the surgeons making the amputation,
stated as follows:

"To my mind this blood clot was caused by enlargement of the heart, and I am
satisfied the enlargement was caused by general debility, and the general debility was
caused evidently from the chronic diarrhea; at any rate, I have not discovered any
other cause for his general debility at that time, since. When I was called to see
him his heart was badly enlarged, the beats being about 120 to the minute, and my
opinion is that this enlargement was caused by chronic diarrhea.

The Pension Bureau, however, refused to accept heart disease and loss of right leg as results of chronic diarrhea.

Claimant, who is 57 years of age, was last medically examined February 15, 1899, at which time he was rated $4 for chronic diarrhea, $4 for heart trouble, $2 for rheumatism, and $36 for loss of right leg.

Evidence filed with the bill shows that claimant is entirely dependent, and that he has no property except a small home worth about $200 in which he lives.

In the light of the medical evidence on file it would seem reasonable to conclude that the loss of right leg is probably due to the disability which claimant contracted in service. It would be arbitrary to say that it is not, and under the circumstances your committee are of opinion that claimant is entitled to a reasonable increase of his pension.

The bill is therefore reported back favorably with a recommendation that it pass.

O

JOHN P. POST.

FEBRUARY 4, 1903.—Committed to the Committee of the Whole House and ordered to be printed.

Mr. DEEMER, from the Committee on Invalid Pensions, submitted the following

REPORT.

[To accompany S. 3573.]

The Committee on Invalid Pensions, to whom was referred the bill (S. 3573) granting an increase of pension to John P. Post, have examined the same and adopt the Senate report thereon and recommend that the bill do pass.

[Senate Report No. 2173, Fifty-seventh Congress, second session.]

The Committee on Pensions, to whom was referred the bill (S. 3573) granting an increase of pension to John C. Post, have examined the same and report:

This bill proposes to increase from $12 to $24 per month the pension of John P. Post, of Georgetown, Colo., late second lieutenant Company C, Fourth Regiment Illinois Volunteers, war with Mexico, and colonel Eighth Regiment Illinois Volunteer Infantry.

The military records show that John P. Post served in the Mexican war as second lieutenant Company C, Fourth Illinois Volunteers, from June 13, 1846, to May 25, 1847. He was commissioned major, Eighth Illinois Infantry, July 25, 1861; promoted lieutenant-colonel May 16, 1862, and colonel October 8, 1862, and was honorably discharged September 28, 1863. He also served as regimental quartermaster One hundred and fifty-fourth Illinois Infantry from February 22, 1865, to September 18, 1865. He was captured at Fort Donelson, Tenn., February 15, 1862, and held as prisoner of war until October 12, 1862, when paroled.

Colonel Post is now receiving a pension of $12 per month under the act of June 27, 1890, for rheumatism, disease of heart, and senile debility. He was formerly pensioned at $8 per month under the Mexican war service act of January 29, 1887. On May 26, 1893, he made claim under the general law for rheumatism and enlarged prostate gland, but is not able to furnish any testimony whatever showing that these troubles were incurred while he was in the military service.

Colonel Post is 83 years of age and is totally incapacitated for any kind of labor. His last medical examination, dated April 19, 1899, rated him $10 for rheumatism; $10 for enlarged prostate gland; $10 for right inguinal hernia, and $30 for total disability from senile debility. It is shown in evidence that he is wholly without property or means of support except his pension of $12 a month.

In view of his faithful and highly honorable service in two wars, his advanced age, and total disability and destitution, your committee report the bill back favorably with a recommendation that it pass.

O

HENRY R. BENNETT.

FEBRUARY 4, 1903.—Committed to the Committee of the Whole House and ordered to be printed.

Mr. DEEMER, from the Committee on Invalid Pensions, submitted the following

REPORT.

[To accompany S. 3574.]

The Committee on Invalid Pensions, to whom was referred the bill (S. 3574) granting an increase of pension to Henry R. Bennett, have examined the same and adopt the Senate report thereon and recommend that the bill do pass.

[Senate Report No. 2174, Fifty-seventh Congress, second session.]

The Committee on Pensions, to whom was referred the bill (S. 3574) granting an increase of pension to Henry R. Bennett, have examined the same and report:

This bill proposes to increase from $12 to $20 per month the pension of Henry R. Bennett, late of Company B, Twenty-second Regiment Ohio Volunteer Infantry.

Soldier enlisted September 2, 1861, and was discharged November 18, 1864. He is now receiving a pension of $12 per month under the act of June 27, 1890, for total disability due to varicose veins of both legs, right inguinal hernia, and disease of heart. On January 21, 1884, he made claim under the general law, alleging that he contracted sciatic rheumatism in the service about June, 1863. Said claim was rejected January 13, 1888, because of his failure to furnish the necessary evidence to establish it.

Claimant is 63 years of age. His post-office address is 1423 Market street, Denver, Colo. His medical examination, made June 24, 1897, shows that he is suffering from disease of heart and arterio-sclerosis, varicose veins, œdema of legs, right inguinal hernia, and mutilated left hand, and is totally disabled for manual labor. Other evidence on file shows that he is totally disabled.

It appears that claimant possesses no property, real or personal, and is wholly dependent upon his pension. He served faithfully for over three years, and it is very probable that his health suffered in consequence. Considering his good military record, his total disability, and great poverty, your committee are of opinion that he is worthy of an increase of his pension, and therefore report the bill back favorably with a recommendation that it pass.

O

ALPHONSO T. GOULD.

FEBRUARY 4, 1903.—Committed to the Committee of the Whole House and ordered
to be printed.

Mr. GIBSON, from the Committee on Invalid Pensions, submitted the
following

REPORT.

[To accompany S. 3608.]

The Committee on Invalid Pensions, to whom was referred the bill
(S. 3608) granting an increase of pension to Alphonso T. Gould, have
examined the same and adopt the Senate report thereon and recommend that the bill do pass.

[Senate Report No. 2313, Fifty-seventh Congress, second session.]

The Committee on Pensions, to whom was referred the bill (S. 3608) granting an
increase of pension to Alphonso T. Gould, have examined the same and report:
This bill proposes to increase from $12 to $24 per month the pension of Alphonso
T. Gould, of Aberdeen, S. Dak., late of Company D, Forty-fifth Regiment Illinois
Volunteer Infantry.
Soldier enlisted December 7, 1861, and was discharged July 12, 1865. During
service he bore the rank of sergeant. He was pensioned under the general law
April 5, 1887, for disease of eyes and chronic diarrhea, at $8 per month from June 4,
1881, which was increased to $12 per month June 24, 1891. He made claim for
increase February 25, 1898, which was rejected May 23, 1901, on the ground that
his present rate was adequate for his pensioned disabilities.
Claimant is 61 years of age. He was last medically examined October 3, 1900, and
the report thereof is as follows:
"This man is an old man in every way; he is bent and wrinkled, lame, and nearly
blind, and his halting steps and uncertain movements give a perfect picture of the
last stage of life. Auscultation and percussion show that both lungs are filled with
rales and the bronchial tubes are clogged with mucus. The heart is very uncertain
in its action, it is irregular, and intermits at every third beat; the apex beat is normally located, and the area of cardiac dullness is normal in extent, but there is
marked cyanosis of lips and finger nails. Examination shows liver to be very much
enlarged and the stomach and bowels are very painful on palpitation. The mucous
membrane of the rectum is congested and inflamed and is very painful. Examination
shows acuity of vision in right eye to be four-twentieths; in left, six-twentieths;

both eyes very much congested and inflamed. We find that he is permanently disabled from manual labor and general debility and eye disease."

Claimant's petition is as follows:

"*To the Congress of the United States:*

"Your petitioner would respectfully represent that he is a resident of Aberdeen, S. Dak., and that is his post-office address; that he is 60 years old; that he was sergeant in Company D, Forty-fifth Illinois Infantry; that he served in said company from the 1st day of December, 1861, to the 12th day of July, 1865; that he now draws a pension of $12 per month under the laws passed prior to 1890; that he made application for increase, and that the same was rejected; that his pension was for chronic diarrhea and disease of the eyes; that these diseases have so increased that he is absolutely unable to perform manual labor; that he is so affected in his sight that he can not see to work; that he has no property or income except his pension; that the diseases above described were caused by service while in the Army, while in the line of duty; that at the battle of Fort Donelson he had an attack of measles, and in the exposure at that time, during a snowstorm, he took cold, and the disease settled in his eyes, and never since that time has he recovered the full use of his eyes; that he was in every battle in which his regiment was engaged, the number being 27.

Wherefore he asks that his pension be increased by special act of Congress.

Dated January 31, 1902.

                                                    ALPHONSO T. GOULD.

STATE OF SOUTH DAKOTA, *County of Brown, ss:*

Alphonso T. Gould, being duly sworn, says that he is the above-named petitioner and has heard read the foregoing petition and knows the contents thereof, and that the same is true of his own knowledge.

                                                    ALPHONSO T. GOULD.

Subscribed and sworn to before me, and I certify that I am well acquainted with said Alphonso T. Gould and that he is a credible witness, and that I have no interest in this case.

[SEAL.]   J. H. HAUSER,
                                          Notary Public, Brown County, S. Dak.

If the claimant's totally disabled condition were shown to be wholly due to his military service, he would be entitled to a general-law pension of $30 per month. The proof, however, only shows that chronic diarrhea and disease of eyes are of service origin. His eye trouble is a very serious one and of itself greatly impairs his ability to labor. He rendered faithful service for over three and one-half years, and in view of his poverty and total disability your committee are of opinion that he is in every way worthy of relief.

The bill is therefore reported back favorably with a recommendation that it pass.

O

Lightning Source UK Ltd.
Milton Keynes UK
UKHW040923031218
333381UK00016B/2324/P